DK WORLD FOOTBALL YEARBOOK 2002-3 DAVID GOLDBLATT

THE COMPLETE GUIDE TO THE GAME

LONDON, NEW YORK, MUNICH, MELBOURNE, DELHI

Dorling Kindersley

Project Designer Purple Carol

Project Editors Sam Atkinson, Margaret Hynes

Digital Cartography and Graphics
Peter Winfield

Editorial and Design Assistance
Victoria Clark, Michelle Crane, Wim Jenkins,
Simon Mumford, Julie Turner

Systems Co-ordinator Philip Rowles

Production Louise Daly

Jacket Designer Nicola Powling

Jacket Copywriter Beth Apple

Project Manager David Roberts

Senior Managing Art Editor Philip Lord

Editorial Director Andrew Heritage

Art Director Bryn Walls

Produced for Dorling Kindersley by designsection

Caxton Road, Frome, Somerset, BA11 1DY

Project Editors Julian Flanders
Louise Cassell

Senior Designers Kathie Wilson
Craig Stevens

Editorial and Design Assistance
Sandra Morgan, Samantha Savage, Carole McDonald,
Tim Taylor, Tracey Woodward, Rhiannon Sully

www.designsection.com

Digital Cartography and Graphics
Encompass Graphics Limited
Tom Coulson, Martin Darlison
www.encompass-graphics.co.uk

First published in Great Britain in 2002 by
Dorling Kindersley Ltd
80 Strand, London WC2R 0RL

A Penguin Company

2 4 6 8 10 9 7 5 3 1

A CIP catalogue record for this book is available from the British Library.

ISBN: 0-7513-388-42

Printed and bound in the UK by Butler & Tanner Limited, Frome and London

See our complete catalogue at
www.dk.com

Contents

Foreword

IS THERE ANY CULTURAL PRACTICE MORE WIDESPREAD than football? No world religion can match its extent. The use of the English and the vocabulary of mathematics must run it close, but they remain the lingua francas of the world's elites and not of its masses. Is there any singular event more global than the World Cup? In the sporting world clearly not – even the Olympics pales into insignificance compared to the ratings, money, politics and passion that the World Cup generates. More countries are members of FIFA than of any other international body. In a world order increasingly dominated by the United States, no other global event gives such precedence to the developing world, or comes closer to reflecting the population rather than the power of the world's nations.

Yet despite the cosmopolitanism of the game, its deepest passions are insistently local and national. Clubs, their fans and their hinterlands harbour the deepest passions of all. Support for national teams was once restricted by the absence of television coverage of matches at tournaments that most fans could not contemplate attending. But as the international circuit has been steadily commercialized, travel has become cheaper and broadcasting has been transformed, national teams have acquired more significance and cultural baggage than ever before.

Global and local, cosmopolitan and parochial, the history of football has long demanded to be mapped, and even if you put geography aside, football demands a kind of reference book that is more than the usual rosters of glory and disaster, central as they are to the game's history and meaning. Bill Shankly said, 'Some people believe football is a matter of life and death; I am very disappointed with that attitude. I can assure you it is much, much more important than that.' And, of course, it is. The extraordinary global drama that is football is also about love and money, and if anything trumps life and death, they do.

Football is about drama, because it tells its stories in so many ways and genres: comedy, tragedy, soap opera and epic, each with its equally eclectic cast of characters. Football is about love, because it has become entwined with every conceivable social tension and division. It has served as the focus of identity for German Brazilians of Grêmio and the Turkish Germans of Turkiyemspor Berlin. It has underwritten the solidarity of Catalan nationalism, of Calcutta's Muslims, Vienna's Jews and Australia's Croats. It has served the greater glory of armies and air forces, the secret police, media empires and nation states. But most significantly these days, football is about money, because love demands the best. In the never-ending arms race of competitive sporting glory, even the chance of success must be paid for. From the Lancashire industrialist paying out for the works' team's boots to Nike's virtual ownership of the Brazilian national squad, victory has been pursued with the relentless expenditure of hard cash; so much cash, in fact, that nobody really knows just how much money is whirling through the maw of the global football industry.

The *World Football Yearbook* is an attempt to do some justice to this record. To chart the historical and contemporary drama of global football, and the entwining of sporting drama and athletic brilliance and artistry with the relentless social forces of money, power and identity. This book has been compiled from hundreds of sources and thousands of telephone calls, conversations and clippings. I have no doubt and considerable fears that I have got it wrong sometimes: stadiums on the wrong street, inaccurate scores, repetition of unsubstantiated myths. I welcome correspondence, complaints and corrections with the promise that in future editions it will all be put right.

David Goldblatt

Introduction

'There can be no doubt that we will win the Cup. I believe the whole team are feeling a great strength, which is being passed around. After all the bad times I have a feeling that I can find strength I have never had before.'
Ronaldo in a pre-World Cup interview

AND SO IT CAME TO PASS, on 30 June 2002 in Yokohama International Stadium. The Final of the 17th World Cup, the first between Brazil and Germany, the 67th minute, still goalless. Rivaldo fires the ball straight at German goalkeeper Oliver Kahn, the rock of Germany's almost impregnable defence. He catches but scatters the ball and there, racing 20 metres into the box, is Ronaldo who opens the scoring. Twelve minutes later a speeding Kleberson crosses the ball in from the right to the edge of the penalty area. Rivaldo, flying, steps over it and for a heart-stopping moment the German defence is shredded. The ball is at Ronaldo's feet. A tiny touch controls it and the space between Kahn and his left-hand post appears suddenly enormous and again it is Ronaldo, mercurial but unhurried, shooting the ball into the very corner of the net.

History rewritten

In those two moments history was not erased but rewritten. The piteous shadow of Ronaldo, that had wandered around the pitch in a trance as part of the Brazilian team of players that had capitulated against the hosts at the Stade de France in the 1998 World Cup Final, was not forgotten or eradicated, but put in its proper place as the very lowest point of Ronaldo and Brazilian football's ascent to a unique fifth World Cup Final. And it was a Final won with unquestionably the freest, most skillful and bedazzling football of the tournament.

In the four years since that day in Paris, Ronaldo had suffered two coruscating knee injuries that kept him out of the game for over two years. Brazil had its worst qualifying tournament in memory, using three coaches and over 70 players, suffering unheard-of defeats to the minnows of Ecuador and Paraguay, and even living with the possibility that the team might not qualify at all. Even when Brazil did qualify, it arrived in Japan as merely third favourites behind champions France and the Argentinians, who had so imperiously swept them and the rest of Latin America aside in the qualifiers.

Germany's Asamoah arrives too late to stop Ronaldo's precise shot for his second goal. Although probably still not fully fit during the entire tournament, Ronaldo's capacity to find space and to look unhurried under the closest marking and despite the relentless pace of the games was breathtaking. It's little wonder that his teammates call him the 'Phenomenon'.

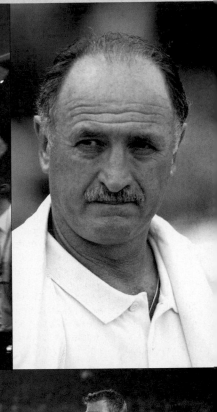

Above left: The 40 days in the wilderness are over: 'God has reserved this for us'.

Left: Cafu lifts Brazil's fifth World Cup with an ecstatic Pele at his feet. In an extraordinary hybrid of political and religious iconography, during the celebrations at the end of the game the Brazilian players were draped in national flags and revealed undershirts with evangelical messages such as 'Jesus loves you' on them.

Above right: Of course he's worried. Big Phil awaits vindication after 18 months of relentless pressure and criticism. 'Remember these winning scenes,' he said to his players after the game.

'The affection, love and friendship there is between the group. This is the path Brazil needs. I'm not political and I don't like politics but this is how we can take Brazil forward.' If so, was it wise for him to announce moments later that he would like a job in Italy's Serie A?

Above: Oliver Kahn, easily the best goalkeeper and perhaps the best player of the tournament, chews on a rather bitter pill. 'Words of consolation have no effect,' he said. But there was a bright side; reflecting after the tournament he remarked, 'There were no squabbles in the camp and we put German football back where it belonged.'

INTRODUCTION

Above left: *Two of the biggest disappointments of the World Cup: Luis Figo of Portugal and Juan Sebastian Veron of Argentina, whose teams were both unexpectedly knocked out at the group stage.*

Above: *The old order crumbles as Bouba Diop scores the only goal of the match for Senegal against France in the tournament's opening game.*

Heroes and villains

But reputations were to count for nothing at Japan/Korea 2002. In an act of revolution, the opening game between France and Senegal saw the West Africans sweep a tired and ageing France aside in its very first World Cup game. And though a patched-up Zidane took the field in the team's final game, the Danes administered the final blow to the *ancien régime*. Argentina, full of guile and disdain, managed to beat an inconsistent Nigeria, but fell to England. Michael Owen won a penalty with all the professional cunning Argentina themselves usually display, and David Beckham, undergoing his own minor redemption for French misdemeanours, duly put the ball away.

Portugal fielded its 'golden generation' at, it appeared, the peak of their professional careers, combining zest and maturity. But against the USA and South Korea, teams that already displayed a boundless energy, a tenacious pressing game and disciplined teamwork, the Portuguese were found wanting. Italy came perilously close to following them out of the first round; defeated by Croatia late in a game the team should have won easily but preferred to try and kill, and was saved only by a late Del Piero equalizer against a talented, entertaining Mexican side.

In the knockout stages the semi-finalists arrived by very different routes. Germany inched past Paraguay and the USA, inspired and protected by the amazing performance of the goalkeeper and captain Oliver Kahn. South Korea in unparalleled displays of fitness and commitment dispatched the Italians and the Spanish to reach the semi-finals. Turkey showed technical skill and muscular composure to defeat Sweden and Senegal. But Brazil alone had looked inspired.

The Brazilians had shown composure in defence, tenacity in central midfield, (combined with formidable width from the running and crossing of Cafu and Roberto Carlos), feeding a front three, Ronaldinho, Rivaldo and Ronaldo, of trickery, guile and power. Forced to defend against Belgium in the second round, Rivaldo's swivelling volley lifted them above the ordinary. In the quarter-finals Ronaldinho's swerving run (for Rivaldo's

goal) and his looping free kick undid England. In the semi-finals, Ronaldo's blistering pace through the Turkish defence and pinpoint toe-poke ended the fabulous Turkish run. In the end he scored eight, took the golden boot, equalled Pele's record of goals in World Cup finals and won the Final for Brazil. And though the Germans had shown enormous appetite and hunger, organization and spirit, the team's possession and pressing – enough to hold and defeat an exhausted South Korea in the semi-finals – came to nothing against the Brazilians.

The moment of redemption was palpable as the entire Brazilian squad and support team gathered in a circle of kneeling prayer at the centre of the pitch before Cafu, atop the FIFA podium, raised the World Cup in supplication. For a moment the sheer artistry, verve and inspiration of the Brazilian team and the Brazilian football culture from which they have sprung

Rio Ferdinand's performance at centre back for England was cultured and composed: as a result his asking price has doubled to around £35 million.

Above left: *Today the semi-finals, tomorrow the Korean presidency: Chung Mong Joon is Chair of the Korean World Cup committee and head of the Korean FA.*

Left: *Unofficially crowned the world's leading referee, Pierluigi Collina smoothed troubled waters during the Argentina v England game and refereed the Final.*

Above: *The heart of the football family: Sepp Blatter (President) and Michel Zen-Ruffinen (ex-General Secretary) beg to differ over the huge hole in FIFA's accounts.*

was redeemed, renewed and celebrated. But beneath the surface the gnawing forces of money and power, the other old order in global football, had left their mark on the tournament. Indeed the tournament had opened with the final showdown in the struggle for football's very biggest prize: the FIFA presidency.

The incumbent, Swiss ex-lawyer Sepp Blatter, had been rocked by a series of financial disasters and accusations of impropriety. ISL, FIFA's main marketing partner, had gone spectacularly bankrupt in 2001, leaving a large hole in the organization's finances. A hole that some, including his own general secretary Michel Zen-Ruffinen, thought much larger than Blatter was prepared to accept. Kirch TV, a German media giant and owner of the World Cup TV rights, had collapsed under a mountain of debt, leaving FIFA's economics even more perilous. Kirch's demise was paralleled by the collapse of pay-per-view football broadcaster ITV digital in the UK and narrowly avoided by a spate of mergers and consolidation in Spain and Italy. In the spring, Issa Hayatou, President of CAF, announced he would challenge Blatter for the FIFA presidency.

But Blatter is a master of football's geopolitical game. Under his charge FIFA has spent heavily on promoting football in the developing world and his networks of allies and supporters in football's regional and national organizations is unmatched. In North and Central America, FIFA development money for tiny football organizations proved a terrific investment. The head of the US football association described Blatter as an 'icon of humanitarianism'. Blatter served his apprenticeship as general secretary of FIFA to the master – Brazilian President of FIFA João Havelange – for nearly 20 years. Once Hayatou threatened to reduce their representation at the World Cup, Latin American support for Blatter was never in doubt.

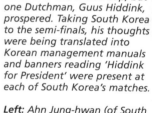

Above: Holland may not have made it to the World Cup, but one Dutchman, Guus Hiddink, prospered. Taking South Korea to the semi-finals, his thoughts were being translated into Korean management manuals and banners reading 'Hiddink for President' were present at each of South Korea's matches.

Left: Ahn Jung-hwan (of South Korea) passes Paolo Maldini (of Italy). For his temerity in scoring a golden goal to put the Italians out of the tournament, the president of his Italian club, Perugia, announced, 'I have no intention of paying a salary to someone who has ruined Italian football'.

Left: One of the surprises of the tournament, Turkish midfielder Hasan Sas had the beating of Brazil's Cafu in both their encounters.

Below: Travelling contingents of supporting fans were small at Korea/Japan 2002, so both hosts arranged for dedicated local sections to cheer on the foreign teams. One of the best-supported teams was England.

Right: Up to 7 million South Koreans took to the streets to watch their team on big screens. Middle-aged Korean men remain wedded to baseball, but young men and women of all ages appear to have found their game.

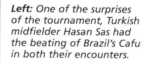

Africa should have been Hayatou's stronghold, especially after South Africa lost its bid to host the 2006 World Cup. But Blatter drew support from small nations, and English- and Portuguese-speaking states. Despite Lennart Johansson's backing for Hayatou, Blatter had strong support from France (who hosted the 1998 World Cup), Germany (who will host the 2006 World Cup) and Spain, who will host FIFA's museum. On 29 May, in South Korea, just before the World Cup kicked off, Sepp Blatter was re-elected as President of FIFA for another four years, beating his challenger, Issa Hayatou, by 139 votes to 56.

The real world of football

For a month the harsh realpolitik, unstable, gyrating economics that shape global football and politics alike were held in abeyance. Senegal held a national holiday after beating France. Turkey followed suit when they made it to the semi-finals. South Korea saw nearly 20 per cent of the population on the streets to watch games on giant screens. Record TV ratings, even with huge and inconvenient time differences, saw Buenos Aires, Dublin, London and Paris grind to a halt for a few hours. Nigerian utility companies begged forgiveness in advance should power supplies fail during games. Political summit meetings had their agendas rescheduled to allow for kick-off

times. The Argentinians and Brazilians put their crippling economic crises and sliding currencies on ice.

Korea/Japan 2002 suffered from a number of great players playing very poorly after increasingly gruelling seasons for the fixture-hungry leading clubs in domestic and continental competitions. Great teams capable of great football played cynically, within and below themselves. The claims of the co-hosts that the tournament would advance the process of reconciliation between Korea and Japan and between North and South Korea were remarkably hollow. Neither the opening nor closing ceremonies contained even the slightest reference or acknowledgement of the other host's presence. As for North/South reconciliation, the day prior to the final witnessed a 20-minute gun battle between the two states' ships, with estimates suggesting up to 30 dead and 70 injured. The claims that the unprecedented investment in infrastructure will drag South Korea's and Japan's wilting economies out of their lethargy or that the fantastic stadiums will be regularly full for domestic football seem hopelessly optimistic. But in Ronaldo's triumph and Brazil's invention and courage, there was enough dramatic and spiritual succour not only to redeem Brazil's own game but to arm us against another few seasons of global football's irreversible enmeshment with the harsh and corrosive forces of the real world.

The Origins of Football

THE ORIGINS OF FOOTBALL

THE IRRESISTIBLE URGE of children to kick things, and the general availability of round objects in the world, suggest that people have been playing some version of football since the beginning of history. Chinese archeologists have found stone balls from the Neolithic era (around 10,000 BC), and have claimed China to be the home of the global game. Reports from South America suggest that access to rubber in the Amazonian rainforest gave the region its head start in ball skills and control. Certainly there is evidence of various ball and kicking games among the indigenous Indian civilizations of Patagonia and the Andes.

Stronger records exist for a game called Tsu Chu played under the Han Empire of China (206 BC–221 AD), which spread into Japan and Korea with local variations and names. A stuffed animal-skin ball was kicked between large bamboo posts; some accounts suggest that it formed part of festivities, others that it was an element of military training. Frescoes from the era clearly indicate women playing the game.

Li Yu, a Chinese writer (c. 50–130 AD), wrote a eulogy to the game, which was intended to be hung on the goalposts:

> *A round ball and a square goal*
> *Suggest the shape of the Yin and the Yang.*
> *The ball is like the full moon,*
> *And the two teams stand opposed:*
> *Captains are appointed and take their place.*
> *In the game make no allowance for relationship*
> *And let there be no partiality.*
> *Determination and coolness are essential*
> *And there must not be the slightest irritation for failure.*
> *Such is the game. Let its principles apply to life.*

Folk football in Europe

Evidence of folk football in Europe dates from around the beginning of the second millennium. A variety of ball games were played by the Celtic periphery of Europe, such as Knappan in Wales and the game of Ba' in the Orkney Islands. First-hand reports from the 11th and 12th centuries mention a game called *La Soule*, popular among the peasantry of medieval Brittany and northern France, while a distinctive rule-bound game called *Calcio* was played by the ruling elites of Florence from the 16th century. But it is in England that the most regular and systematic reports of football come in the medieval period. William Fitzstephen, living in London between 1170 and 1183, wrote:

'After dinner all the youth of the city goes out into the fields for the very popular game of ball. The elders, the fathers and the men of wealth come on horseback to view the contests of their juniors.'

What the game of 'ball' seems to have consisted of was a very tough, often violent, unstructured brawling game in which two ill-defined and often ill-matched mobs moved a ball

This ring is found on the wall of the Ball Court at the Mayan temple at Chichen-Itza in Mexico. Pok-ta-pok was just one of many games played by American Indians before the European conquest, along with Pilimatum in Chile and Tchoekah in Patagonia.

Calcio, or Giuoco del calcio Fiorentino, was played in Florence and other parts of Northern Italy from the 16th century. This fresco by Giovanni Stradano, painted in 1555, shows a game in progress in the city's Piazza Santa Maria Novella.

The Origins of Football

ENGLAND
Mob or folk football (1100)

Location
Early form of football
Approximate date

WALES
Knappan (1000)

ORKNEY ISLANDS
Ba' (1000)

ENGLAND
Mob or folk football (1100)

FRANCE (Brittany)
Soule (1100)

ITALY
Giuoco del calcio Fiorentino (1500)
Harpastum (200 BC)

GREECE
Episkyros (200 BC)

NORTH AMERICA
Passuckquakkohowog (17th century)

MEXICO
Pok-ta-pok (800 BC)

Passuckquakkohowog. This Native American word literally translates as 'those who gather to play football'. The earliest written reports of the game in North America come from 17th century English pilgrims.

CHILE
Pilimatum (1500 BC)

PATAGONIA
Tchoekah

Although a rudimentary form of football called Episkyros could be found in Classical Greece, it was of low status – the domain of women and children. No ball game was allowed into the prestigious ancient Olympic Games.

Though no indigenous forms of African football have been recorded, the game spread like wildfire during the colonization of the continent in the late 19th and early 20th centuries. This batik shows a game in contemporary Uganda.

to some specified location by almost any means, and any limb, available. Reports abound of serious injuries and accidental stabbings, even deaths, during these games. More worrying for local elites, these games often led to, or turned into, acts of major social disturbance and riot. Not surprisingly, Edward II, King of England, issued a proclamation in 1314 banning the game, claiming that there was 'great uproar in the city through certain tumults arising from great footballs in the fields of the public, from which many evils may arise'. The ban was repeated in 1331 and 1365 in the hope of encouraging more archery, but without success.

Derby day

Shrove Tuesday was a particularly popular day for rural football matches – the game played in Derby between the parishes of St. Peter and All Saints was notorious for its unrestrained ferocity, and gave birth to the term for fiercely fought local contests – derbies. In the cities, football often accompanied rites of passage for journeymen and apprentices. An observer in 18th-century London wrote:

> I spy the furies of the football war
> The Prentice quits his shop,
> To join the crew,
> Increasing crowds the flying
> Game pursue...

A 19th-century engraving of mob or folk football, England.

These Chinese characters mean 'to kick with the foot' and 'a ball made of leather ... to allow it to be kicked around for recreation'.

JAPAN
Kemari
(400)

CHINA
Cuju or Tsu Chu
(200 BC)

Kemari, a Japanese variant of a Chinese ball game, was played from around the 5th century AD.

A fierce game called La Soule was popular in Normandy and Brittany in France during the 11th and 12th centuries.

Yet despite ruling class disapproval of folk football, it had begun to find a home in the schools and universities of England. Reports of football at Oxford and Cambridge date from the 16th century.

By the beginning of the 19th century, team sports had been enthusiastically adopted by England's elite public schools as an essential element of the practical and moral education of the ruling class. Football in a variety of forms and with a variety of rules was the predominant sport. Simultaneously, folk and mob football were in decline as the congested spaces and stricter policing of modern industrial cities made the game increasingly difficult to play. It would eventually disappear altogether, to be replaced by a game with fixed rules derived from the public school game (see pages 14–15).

The Global Game

CODIFICATION AND SPREAD

IN 19TH-CENTURY ENGLAND, there was no shortage of rules for the game of football. The elite public schools had embraced team sports as an essential component of ruling-class character formation, and each had created rules that suited their environment. Harrow's heavy ball favoured dribbling, while Winchester's narrow pitch suited kick and rush, and Westminster's cloisters the short pass. These rules collided when old boys played each other at university, so common football rules were drafted in 1846 at Cambridge University. A revised version of these rules formed the basis of the rules drawn up in 1863 by the newly created Football Association and representatives of 12 London clubs. The only dissenters from the rules were Blackheath, who opted to retain handling and hacking; they went on to play the newly codified game of rugby union in 1871.

In the English-speaking world local variations produced codified rules for American, Australian, Canadian and Gaelic football. Armed with the FA rules, an empire and the world's biggest trading network, Britons of every social class carried the game to Europe and the Americas. Sailors played in the ports of Chile and Germany, textile workers in the Netherlands, public schoolboy merchants in Rio and Barcelona. In Britain's formal Empire, in Asia and Africa, the colonial power was more reticent to spread the game, fearing the anti-colonial social organization that might emerge from football.

Caged into the tighter spaces of an urban environment, rural folk football acquired the rudiments of organized play, such as goals and duration, but violence and injury remained regular features of the game.

The Evolution of Football

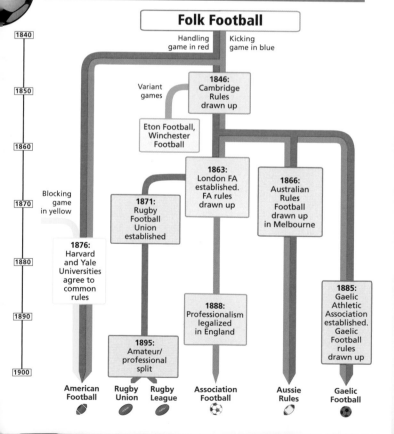

Folk Football

Handling game in red
Kicking game in blue

Variant games

1846: Cambridge Rules drawn up

Eton Football, Winchester Football

1863: London FA established. FA rules drawn up

1866: Australian Rules Football drawn up in Melbourne

Blocking game in yellow

1871: Rugby Football Union established

1876: Harvard and Yale Universities agree to common rules

1888: Professionalism legalized in England

1885: Gaelic Athletic Association established. Gaelic Football rules drawn up

1895: Amateur/professional split

1840
1850
1860
1870
1880
1890
1900

American Football
Rugby Union
Rugby League
Association Football
Aussie Rules
Gaelic Football

The global spread of football 1850–1930

Significant migrant communities playing football

- British
- Armenian
- French
- Spanish
- Greek
- Jewish

Date of formation of national Football Association

- By 1899
- 1900–39
- 1940–79
- After 1980

Reason for spread
(British, unless noted)

- Banking
- Cricket clubs
- Education
- Gymnastics
- Industrialists and workers
- Military
- Mining
- Railways
- Shipping
- Trading

Competing sports

- Football a minor sport
- American sports
- Australian Rules
- Cricket
- Gaelic football
- Ice hockey
- Rugby
- Tennis

CANADA

USA

MEXICO

PERU

CHILE

Codification of the Rules

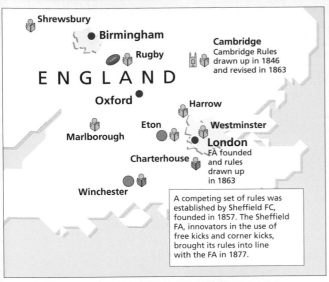

Shrewsbury

Birmingham

Rugby

Cambridge
Cambridge Rules
drawn up in 1846
and revised in 1863

E N G L A N D

Oxford

Harrow

Eton

Westminster

Marlborough

London
FA founded
and rules
drawn up
in 1863

Charterhouse

Winchester

A competing set of rules was
established by Sheffield FC,
founded in 1857. The Sheffield
FA, innovators in the use of
free kicks and corner kicks,
brought its rules into line
with the FA in 1877.

Key

Cambridge University

Public school represented
at the rewriting of the
Cambridge Rules in 1863

Other public school

School with own rules

Rugby rules

Clubs involved in the formation of FA in 1863

Barnes
Blackheath (later withdrew)
Blackheath School
Charterhouse
Crusaders
Crystal Palace
Forest
Kensington School
No Names of Kilburn
Percival House
Surbiton
The War Office

*Harrow School Football XI 1867.
Harrow's poorly drained fields
required a heavy leather ball and
encouraged dribbling rather than
hoofing the ball up the pitch.*

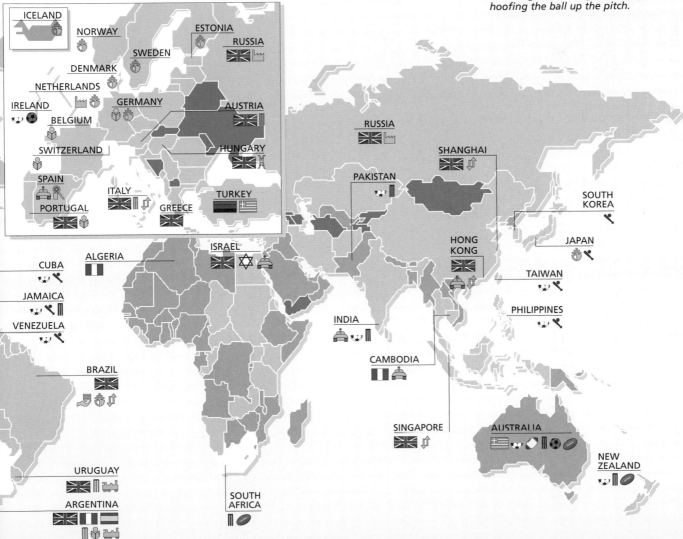

ICELAND

NORWAY

ESTONIA

RUSSIA

SWEDEN

DENMARK

NETHERLANDS

GERMANY

AUSTRIA

IRELAND

BELGIUM

HUNGARY

SWITZERLAND

SPAIN

ITALY

TURKEY

PORTUGAL

GREECE

RUSSIA

SHANGHAI

PAKISTAN

SOUTH
KOREA

HONG
KONG

JAPAN

TAIWAN

CUBA

ALGERIA

ISRAEL

PHILIPPINES

JAMAICA

VENEZUELA

INDIA

BRAZIL

CAMBODIA

SINGAPORE

AUSTRALIA

NEW
ZEALAND

URUGUAY

SOUTH
AFRICA

ARGENTINA

The Laws of the Game

LAW I: FIELD OF PLAY

The field of play must be a rectangle of specific size (see diagram for length). The field must have clear lines marked on it: touchlines, goal lines, halfway line, centre circle, goal area, goal area lines, goals, penalty area, penalty spot, corner arcs and flagposts.

LAW II: BALL

The ball must be made of an approved material. At the start of the match the ball must be 68–70 cm in diameter, 410–450 grams in weight, and have an internal pressure of 0.6–1.1 atmospheres at sea level. It can only be changed by the referee. If the ball bursts during a game, play stops and restarts with a drop ball.

LAW III: PLAYERS

A match consists of two teams of not more than 11 players each including a goalkeeper. Any outfield player may change places with the goalkeeper during a stoppage. Teams need at least seven players to begin a game.

LAW V: REFEREE

The referee is the final arbiter on the interpretation and enforcement of the laws. They decide whether a game can be played and the duration of play. They can suspend and abandon a match, stop play to allow treatment of injured players, caution players (yellow card) for a range of misconduct and fouls or send off a player (red card) for serious foul play, violent conduct, offensive language and for two cautions. Referees make sure all equipment meets the relevant specifications and keeps a record of the match. They have a duty to allow play to flow and refrain from punishing insignificant or non-deliberate infringements.

LAW VI: ASSISTANT REFEREES

Formerly called the linesmen, the assistant referees help the referee primarily by signalling corner kicks, goal kicks, throw-ins and offsides. However, the referee's word is final.

LAW VIII: START & RESTART OF PLAY

Before the start of play a coin is tossed. The winning team chooses ends for the first half and the losing team takes the kick-off. This is reversed in the second half. Play begins after the referee has signalled. The kick-off is taken from the centre spot and must move into the opposition's half of the field. All players must be in their half of the field and opposition players must be at least ten yards from the ball. The ball must be touched by another player before the kicker can touch it again.

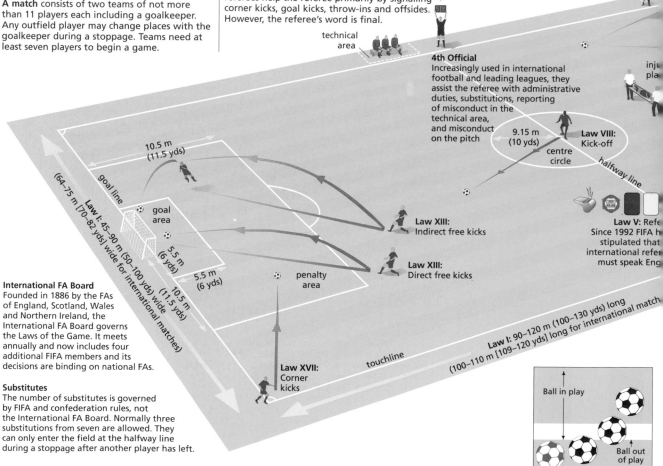

Law VI: Assistant referees

technical area

4th Official
Increasingly used in international football and leading leagues, they assist the referee with administrative duties, substitutions, reporting of misconduct in the technical area, and misconduct on the pitch

9.15 m (10 yds)

Law VIII: Kick-off

centre circle

halfway line

inju pla

10.5 m (11.5 yds)

goal line

Law I: 45–90 m (50–100 yds) wide (64–75 m [70–82 yds] wide for international matches)

goal area

5.5 m (6 yds)

10.5 m (11.5 yds)

5.5 m (6 yds)

penalty area

Law XIII: Indirect free kicks

Law XIII: Direct free kicks

Law V: Refe Since 1992 FIFA h stipulated that international refer must speak Eng

Law XVII: Corner kicks

touchline

Law I: 90–120 m (100–130 yds) long (100–110 m [109–120 yds] long for international match

International FA Board
Founded in 1886 by the FAs of England, Scotland, Wales and Northern Ireland, the International FA Board governs the Laws of the Game. It meets annually and now includes four additional FIFA members and its decisions are binding on national FAs.

Substitutes
The number of substitutes is governed by FIFA and confederation rules, not the International FA Board. Normally three substitutions from seven are allowed. They can only enter the field at the halfway line during a stoppage after another player has left.

Ball in play

Ball out of play

LAW IV: PLAYERS' EQUIPMENT

Compulsory equipment for players are a shirt, shorts, socks, shin-guards and football boots. Goalkeepers must wear kit that distinguishes them from outfield players and officials.

LAW VII: DURATION OF PLAY

There are two equal periods of 45 minutes. Additional time may be added at the discretion of the referee for injuries, time-wasting and substitutions. Time can also be added to allow a penalty to be taken after the end of normal play.

LAW IX: IN & OUT OF PLAY

The game is in play when the ball is inside the field of play and the referee has not stopped play. The ball is out of play when the whole ball, whether in the air or on the ground, has crossed either touchlines or goal lines.

LAW X: SCORING

A goal has been scored when the whole of the ball has crossed the goal line between the goalposts and under the crossbar, provided no other infringements have taken place. The team with the most goals wins.

LAW XI: OFFSIDE

Offside is an illegal playing position taken up by a player relative to the ball, the field of play and opposition players at the moment when the ball is played by an attacking teammate. A player is offside when **a)** they are in the opposition's half of the field, **b)** they are closer to the opponent's goal line than the ball and **c)** there are fewer than two defenders, including the goalkeeper, who are closer to the goal line than the attacking player. A player will be penalized for being offside if they are interfering with play or with an opponent and they can gain some advantage from being in that position.

The Offside Rule

Onside: Attacking player is level with defending players

Onside: Attacking player is further from the opposition's goal line than defending players

Offside: Attacking player is closer to the opposition's goal line than defending players

Extra Time
Determined by the rules of the competition, but usually two periods of 15 minutes play after normal time where the scores are level. If the score remains level this often extends to a penalty shootout. In some competitions the 'golden goal' rule is applied to extra time. This means that during the period of extra time, the team which scores the first goal is declared the winner.

Law XVI: Goal kicks

Law XIV: Penalty kicks First introduced in 1891

penalty area

goalpost 2.44 m (2.67 yds)

penalty spot

Crossbar 7.32 m (8 yds) A cross tape was originally introduced between the posts by the FA in 1886.

corner arc — **corner flag**

Law VI: Assistant referees First introduced as linesmen in 1891

Law XV: Throw-ins

LAW XV: THROW-INS

A throw-in is awarded to a team when the ball has crossed the touchline and an opposition player was the last to touch it. The throw-in is taken from the point where the ball crossed the touchline. The taker must have both feet on the ground, use two hands, throw the ball from behind and over the head and be facing the field of play.

LAW XVI: GOAL KICKS

A goal kick is awarded to the defending team when the ball crosses its goal line, a goal has not been scored, and the last player to touch the ball was from the attacking team. Any player may take the goal kick by placing it within the team's own penalty area. The kick must go outside the penalty area or be retaken. The taker must not touch the ball again until another player has touched it. Opposition players must remain outside the penalty area while the kick is taken. A goal may be scored directly from a goal kick.

LAW XVII: CORNER KICKS

A corner kick is awarded to the attacking team when the ball was last touched by a member of the defending team and crosses its goal line without a goal being scored. A corner kick is also awarded if the ball enters the goal from a throw-in or an indirect free kick. The attacking team restarts the game with the ball placed in the corner arc nearest to where the ball crossed the goal line. Defending players must be at least 10 yards from the ball when it is kicked. The corner taker may not touch the ball after the corner kick until another player has touched it.

LAW XIII: FREE KICKS

Free kicks restart play after the game has been stopped for a foul or another act of misconduct. The referee will award the team which did not commit the offence with a direct free kick (from which a goal can be scored) or an indirect free kick (where the ball must touch another player before a goal can be scored). A free kick is usually taken from the point at which the offence was committed.

LAW XIV: PENALTY KICKS

A penalty is awarded for a foul by a defending player inside their own penalty area. A penalty kick is taken from the penalty spot. All other players, apart from the goalkeeper and penalty taker, must be at least ten yards from the spot and on the field of play. The ball is in play as soon as it is kicked. The penalty taker may touch the ball if it rebounds from the goalkeeper but not if it rebounds from the post or crossbar. Other players may touch the ball in that situation. The goalkeeper must face the penalty taker and stand on the goal line.

LAW XII: FOULS AND MISCONDUCT

A foul is committed if a player **(1)** trips, kicks, pushes, recklessly charges or uses excessive force against another player; **(2)** strikes, attempts to strike, or spits at an opponent; **(3)** makes a tackle but connects with their opponent before the ball; **(4)** deliberately handles the ball (except for goalkeepers inside their penalty area); **(5, 6)** obstructs an opponent or prevents the goalkeeper from releasing the ball. Goalkeepers commit a foul if they: fail to release the ball within six seconds of picking it up; release the ball into play and then handle it; handle a backpass or a throw-in from a teammate; or are guilty of time-wasting. An indirect free kick is awarded for the above.

FIFA and the Confederations

FIFA AND THE CONFEDERATIONS

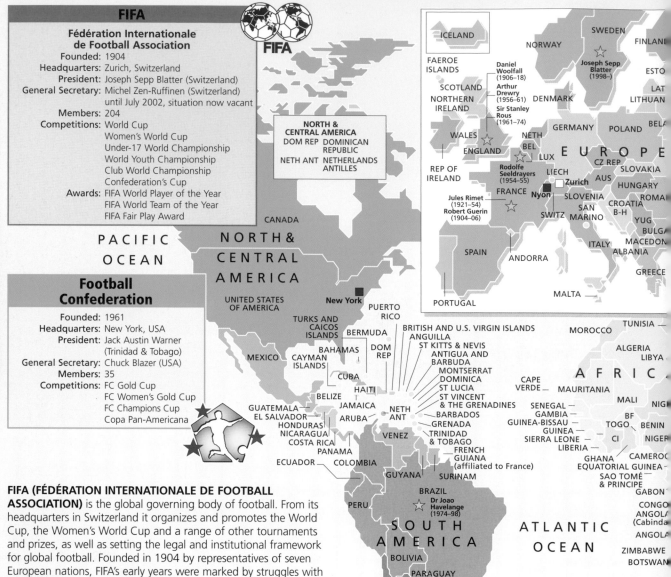

FIFA

**Fédération Internationale
de Football Association**
Founded: 1904
Headquarters: Zurich, Switzerland
President: Joseph Sepp Blatter (Switzerland)
General Secretary: Michel Zen-Ruffinen (Switzerland)
until July 2002, situation now vacant
Members: 204
Competitions: World Cup
Women's World Cup
Under-17 World Championship
World Youth Championship
Club World Championship
Confederation's Cup
Awards: FIFA World Player of the Year
FIFA World Team of the Year
FIFA Fair Play Award

**NORTH &
CENTRAL AMERICA**
DOM REP DOMINICAN
REPUBLIC
NETH ANT NETHERLANDS
ANTILLES

Football Confederation

Founded: 1961
Headquarters: New York, USA
President: Jack Austin Warner
(Trinidad & Tobago)
General Secretary: Chuck Blazer (USA)
Members: 35
Competitions: FC Gold Cup
FC Women's Gold Cup
FC Champions Cup
Copa Pan-Americana

SOUTH AMERICA
VENEZ VENEZUELA

CONMEBOL

**Confederación
Sudamericana de Fútbol**
Founded: 1916
Headquarters: Asunción, Paraguay
President: Dr Nicolas Leóz
(Paraguay)
General Secretary: Eduardo Deluca
(Argentina)
Members: 10
Competitions: Copa América
Copa Libertadores
Copa Pan-Americana

FIFA (FÉDÉRATION INTERNATIONALE DE FOOTBALL ASSOCIATION) is the global governing body of football. From its headquarters in Switzerland it organizes and promotes the World Cup, the Women's World Cup and a range of other tournaments and prizes, as well as setting the legal and institutional framework for global football. Founded in 1904 by representatives of seven European nations, FIFA's early years were marked by struggles with both the British footballing associations and other competing international football groupings. The British nations in particular were slow to join, reflecting both insecurity and indifference. They were also quick to leave after the First World War when the admission of Germany to FIFA was agreed. Similarly, the British Home Countries remained individually represented on the international rule-making Association Football Board, while FIFA represented the rest of the world. Once the British had left and the French visionary Jules Rimet had assumed the presidency, FIFA's growth began. With the successful creation of the World Cup in 1930, FIFA's control of the global game was secured.

The confederations that make up FIFA vary widely: from the fearsomely powerful UEFA to the marginal OFC (Oceanic Football Confederation). All nations get a single vote at FIFA's biennial conferences, but as usual, in the real corridors of power, money and contacts talk.

UEFA
Union of European Football Associations
Founded: 1954
Headquarters: Nyon, Switzerland
President: Lennart Johansson (Sweden)
General Secretary: Gerhard Aigner (Germany)
Members: 51
Competitions: European Championships
European Champions League
UEFA Cup
Intertoto Cup
European Super Cup
European Women's Championships

EUROPE
ARM ARMENIA
AUS AUSTRIA
AZER AZERBAIJAN
BEL BELGIUM
B-H BOSNIA-HERZEGOVINA
CZ REP CZECH REPUBLIC
ISR ISRAEL
LIECH LIECHTENSTEIN
LUX LUXEMBOURG
NETH NETHERLANDS
REP OF IRELAND REPUBLIC OF IRELAND
SWITZ SWITZERLAND
YUG YUGOSLAVIA

FIFA and the Confederations

☆ FIFA presidents
☐ FIFA headquarters
■ Confederation headquarters
Ⓞ Associate members
Ⓞ Non-members

Date of joining FIFA

	UEFA	CONMEBOL	CAF	AFC	OFC	FOOTBALL CONFEDERATION
1900–20	Ⓞ	Ⓞ	Ⓞ	Ⓞ	Ⓞ	Ⓞ
1921–40	Ⓞ	Ⓞ	Ⓞ	Ⓞ	Ⓞ	Ⓞ
1941–60	Ⓞ	Ⓞ	Ⓞ	Ⓞ	Ⓞ	Ⓞ
1961–80	Ⓞ	Ⓞ	Ⓞ	Ⓞ	Ⓞ	Ⓞ
1981–present						

AFC
Asian Football Confederation
Founded: 1954
Headquarters: Kuala Lumpur, Malaysia
President: HRH Sultan Ahmad Shah (Malaysia)
General Secretary: Dato' Peter Velappan (Malaysia)
Members: 45
Competitions: Asian Cup
Asian Games
Asian Super League
Asian Women's Championship

ASIA
AFGHAN AFGHANISTAN
JOR JORDAN
LEB LEBANON
PAL PALESTINE
TAJ TAJIKISTAN
TURK TURKMENISTAN
UZBEK UZBEKISTAN

AFRICA
BF BURKINA FASO
CI CÔTE D'IVOIRE

CAF
Confédération Africaine de Football
Founded: 1957
Headquarters: Cairo, Eygpt
President: Issa Hayatou (Cameroon)
General Secretary: Mustapha Fahmy (Egypt)
Members: 52
Associate Members: 1
Competitions: African Cup of Nations
CAF Cup
African Champions League
African Cup-Winners' Cup
CAF Super Cup

OFC
Oceania Football Confederation
Founded: 1966
Headquarters: Auckland, New Zealand
President: Basil Scarsella (Australia)
General Secretary: Josephine King (New Zealand)
Members: 11
Associate Members: 1 (+1 Provisional)
Competitions: Oceania Nations Cup
OFC Club Championship
Oceania Women's Tournament

Seats on FIFA Executive

FIFA 2
AFC 4
CONMEBOL 3
FOOTBALL CONFEDERATION 3
CAF 4
OFC 1
UEFA 8

Map labels:
RUSSIA, UKRAINE, MOLDOVA, TURKEY, LEB, CYPRUS, ISR, Montenegro, EGYPT, CHAD, SUDAN, CENTRAL AFRICAN REPUBLIC, ETHIOPIA, UGANDA, KENYA, RWANDA, BURUNDI, TANZANIA, MALAWI, ZAMBIA, MOZAMBIQUE, MADAGASCAR, MAURITIUS, RÉUNION (Associate), SEYCHELLES, SWAZILAND, LESOTHO, SOUTH AFRICA, SOMALIA, DEMOCRATIC REPUBLIC OF CONGO (Zaïre), GEORGIA, AZER, ARM, TURK, UZBEK, TAJ, AFGHAN, SYRIA, IRAQ, IRAN, PAL, JOR, KUWAIT, BAHRAIN, QATAR, SAUDI ARABIA, UAE, OMAN, YEMEN, DJIBOUTI, ERITREA, KAZAKHSTAN, KYRGYZSTAN, MONGOLIA, ASIA, CHINA, PAKISTAN, NEPAL, BHUTAN, BANGLADESH, INDIA, BURMA, LAOS, VIETNAM, CAMBODIA, THAILAND, SRI LANKA, MALDIVES, NORTH KOREA, SOUTH KOREA, JAPAN, HONG KONG, TAIWAN, MACAO, GUAM, PHILIPPINES, Kuala Lumpur, BRUNEI, MALAYSIA, SINGAPORE, INDONESIA, PAPUA NEW GUINEA, PACIFIC OCEAN, INDIAN OCEAN, NORTHERN MARIANA ISLANDS, SOLOMON ISLANDS, VANUATU, WESTERN SAMOA, AMERICAN SAMOA, TAHITI, FIJI, OCEANIA, AUSTRALIA, NEW CALEDONIA (Provisional Associate), TONGA, COOK ISLANDS, NEW ZEALAND, Auckland

19

The World Cup

TOURNAMENT OVERVIEW

ALTHOUGH FIFA had given itself the right to organize a global football competition when created in 1904, it did not do so for some 25 years. Prior to this the tournament at the Olympics had functioned as the *de facto* world championships. However, as professionalism took hold in major footballing nations, the amateur ethos of the Olympic Games became a block on the appearance of the world's best players and teams. At the FIFA conference in Barcelona in 1929, Jules Rimet, the French general secretary of FIFA, proposed that an international championship be held within the next 12 months. Almost unanimous agreement saw the tournament established and destined for Uruguay, where on 13 July 1930, the very first World Cup fixture was played between France and Mexico.

The development of the competition parallels the global development of football. From only 13 entrants in 1930, all from Latin America or Europe, it now has over 200 from every corner of the globe in its qualifying stages. Since 1998, the finals have expanded to include 32 participants in a month-long event. The early domination of Europe and Latin America culminated in 1966 when FIFA allocated one place to Africa, Asia and Central America combined, prompting a widespread boycott. In the 2002 qualifiers, there were five places for the CAF, three for the Football Confederation and two for the AFC (plus one further play-off place against a UEFA team). However, South Africa's failure to win the bid to host the 2006 tournament has led many to question FIFA's universality. Most importantly, the finals are now one of the most significant televisual and media events in the calendar, as evidenced by the huge increase in the cost of acquiring TV broadcast rights and the astronomical viewing figures it achieves.

World Cup Finals (1930–98)

YEAR	WINNERS	SCORE	RUNNERS-UP
1930	Uruguay	4-2	Argentina
1934	Italy	2-1 (aet)	Czechoslovakia
1938	Italy	4-2	Hungary
1950	Uruguay	2-1	Brazil
1954	West Germany	3-2	Hungary
1958	Brazil	5-2	Sweden
1962	Brazil	3-1	Czechoslovakia
1966	England	4-2 (aet)	West Germany
1970	Brazil	4-1	Italy
1974	West Germany	2-1	Netherlands
1978	Argentina	3-1 (aet)	Netherlands
1982	Italy	3-1	West Germany
1986	Argentina	3-2	West Germany
1990	West Germany	1-0	Argentina
1994	Brazil	0-0 (3-2 pens)	Italy
1998	France	3-0	Brazil

World Cup Football

Number of appearances at tournament 1930–98	
▣	12+ times
▣	8–11 times
▣	5–7 times
▣	2–4 times
▣	1 time
▢	0 times

World Cup

👕 Winners

🏆 **1954,** *66* Winners in bold / Runners-up in italic

1999 Host country and year

● Rome Location of Final

CANADA

UNITED STATES OF AMERICA — 1994

Pasadena ●

MEXICO — 1970, 86

Mexico City ●

EL SALVADOR
HONDURAS
COSTA RICA

HAITI
CUBA
JAMAICA

COLOMBIA

R
IRELA
WALE
PORTU

PERU

BOLIVIA

PARAGUAY

CHILE — 1962

Montevid
Buenos Aires
Santiago

ARGENTINA — 1978

👕 *1930, 78,* 86, 90

The World Cup Top Goalscorers (1930–98)

YEAR	SCORER	NATIONALITY	GOALS
1930	Stabile	Argentina	8
1934	Nejedly	Czechoslovakia	5
1938	Leonidas	Brazil	8
1950	Ademir	Brazil	9
1954	Kocsis	Hungary	8
1958	Fontaine	France	13
1962	Ivanov	Soviet Union	4
	Sancjez	Chile	
	Garrincha	Brazil	
	Vava	Brazil	
	Albert	Hungary	
	Jerkovic	Yugoslavia	
1966	Eusebio	Portugal	9
1970	Müller	W. Germany	10
1974	Lato	Poland	7
1978	Kempes	Argentina	6
1982	Rossi	Italy	6
1986	Lineker	England	6
1990	Schillachi	Italy	6
1994	Salenko	Russia	6
	Stoichkov	Bulgaria	
1998	Suker	Croatia	6

World Cup Finals: number and origins of participants

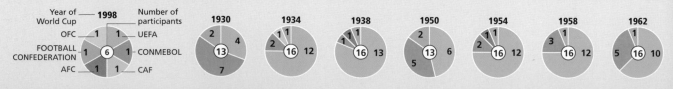

Year of World Cup — **1998** — Number of participants
OFC — 1 / 1 — UEFA
FOOTBALL CONFEDERATION — 1 / (6) / 1 — CONMEBOL
AFC — 1 / 1 — CAF

1930 — 2 / 4 / (13) / 7
1934 — 2 / 1 / 1 / (16) / 12
1938 — 1 / 1 / 1 / (16) / 13
1950 — 2 / (13) / 6 / 5
1954 — 1 / 1 / 2 / (16) / 12
1958 — 3 / 1 / (16) / 12
1962 — 1 / 1 / 5 / (16) / 10

THE WORLD CUP

NORWAY

SWEDEN
1958
1958

NORTHERN
IRELAND

SCOTLAND

IRELAND

DENMARK

Stockholm

RUSSIA

1966

GERMANY
1974
1974, 78
1954, 66, 74, 82, 86, 90

NETH

POLAND

1966

BELGIUM
Munich

CZECH REP
1934, 62

FRANCE
Paris
London

Bern

AUSTRIA

HUNGARY
1938, 54

1938, 98

CROATIA

ROMANIA

YUGOSLAVIA

Rome

BULGARIA

1998

SWITZ
1954

GREECE

TURKEY

RUSSIA

Madrid

ITALY
1934, 90

1982

SPAIN

1934, 38, 70, 82, 94

ISRAEL

TUNISIA

IRAQ

IRAN

KUWAIT

MOROCCO

ALGERIA

EGYPT

SAUDI
ARABIA

UAE

NIGERIA

CAMEROON

DEMOCRATIC
REPUBLIC
OF CONGO
(Zaïre)

NORTH
KOREA

SOUTH
KOREA

JAPAN

INDONESIA

BRAZIL
1950
1950, 58, 62, 70, 94, 98

Rio de
Janiero

AUSTRALIA

URUGUAY
1930
1930, 50

SOUTH
AFRICA

NEW
ZEALAND

World Cup TV Viewing Figures

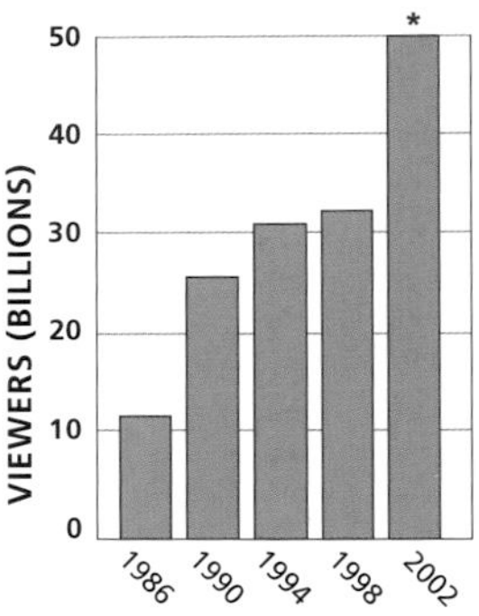

VIEWERS (BILLIONS)

50
40
30
20
10
0

1986 1990 1994 1998 2002 *

*Estimated figures

TV Rights Revenues

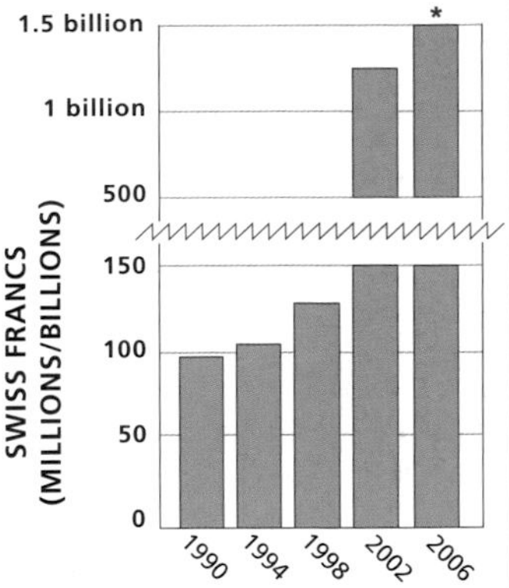

SWISS FRANCS (MILLIONS/BILLIONS)

1.5 billion
1 billion
500
150
100
50
0

1990 1994 1998 2002 2006 *

*Potential payments

The Coupe Jules Rimet *was made by French sculptor Abel Lafleur and presented to Brazil on its third World Cup victory in 1970. It was stolen and recovered in England in 1966 and stolen again in Rio in 1983. It is believed to have been melted down.*

The second *World Cup trophy was made by Italian sculptor Silvio Gazzangia and is solid gold on a base of malachite. Copies are given to the victors but FIFA keeps the real thing.*

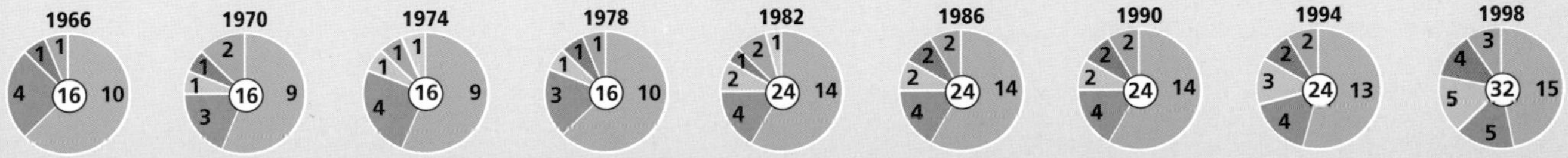

THE WORLD CUP

1966
1
1
4 (16) 10

1970
2
1
1
3 (16) 9

1974
1 1
1
4 (16) 9

1978
1 1
1
3 (16) 10

1982
2 1
1
2
4 (24) 14

1986
2
2
2
4 (24) 14

1990
2
2
2
4 (24) 14

1994
2 2
3
4 (24) 13

1998
3
2
4
5 (32) 15
5

WORLD CUP FINALS (1930–98)

The World Cup has invariably laid bare the distribution of power in world football. Only seven nations have won the tournament, three from Latin America (Argentina, Brazil and Uruguay) and four from Europe (England, France, Germany and Italy), and only four others have appeared in a Final, again all from Europe (Czechoslovakia, Hungary, Sweden, the Netherlands). Only the USA in 1930 has broken the presence of Latin Americans and Europeans in the semi-finals. Similarly, prior to 2002 no country outside of Europe and Latin America has hosted the games. Home advantage has often proved decisive. Only Brazil have won a World Cup on a continent not their own (Sweden 1958) while home victories have been scored by Uruguay (1930), Italy (1934), England (1966), West Germany (1974), Argentina (1978) and France (1998).

A few World Cup Finals have ultimately disappointed. The fantastic play at Italia '90 was crowned with a bad-tempered and rather ugly game between West Germany and Argentina (including two sending-offs for the Argentines). A tense, goalless 120 minutes between Brazil and Italy in the 1994 Final in Los Angeles was ultimately decided by the cruel lottery of a penalty shootout. On the other hand, most Finals have been exhilarating displays of football. The World Cup has delivered the pulsating 1986 Final between Argentina and West Germany in Mexico City, the drama of England's two extra-time goals in the 1966 Final, and the sublime majesty of Brazil's 1970 triumph against Italy, again in Mexico City.

1930: Pedro Cea of Uruguay makes it 2-2 in the 57th minute of the first-ever World Cup Final. The Uruguayans scored twice more to take the trophy.

1934: Italy's squad give the Fascist salute to Il Duce in the VIP box at the Flaminio Stadium, Rome. Italy went on to beat the Czechs 2-1 in extra time.

1938: Italy celebrates its second World Cup title after beating Hungary 4-2. Azzurri coach, Vittorio Pozzo (suited on the left), embraces his players.

1950: The Uruguayans pose before the final pool match against Brazil. In front of nearly 200,000 Brazilian fans, the Uruguayans found the strength to beat their hosts 2-1.

1954: Hidejkuti of Hungary shoots, watched by West Germany's Horst Eckel. The Germans won 3-2 in the Final, the only match the Magical Magyars lost between 1950 and 56.

1958: Just Fontaine celebrates 13 goals in the World Cup, a record that still stands. But France were decisively beaten in the semi-final against Brazil by 5-2.

1962: The battle of Santiago. The first round match between Italy and Chile descended into foul play and violence. The Italian David argues before being sent off.

1966: Wolfgang Weber equalizes for Germany in the dying seconds of normal time in the Final against England. Gordon Banks stretches to no avail.

1970: Pele's World Cup. In the 18th minute of the Final, Pele opens the scoring against Italy. He made two more goals as the Brazilians won 4-1.

THE WORLD CUP

1974: Captain Franz Beckenbauer (left) and manager Helmut Schön (right) exchange an embrace as West Germany go on to win its second World Cup title.

1978: Daniel Pasarella, Argentina's captain and defensive lynchpin, grasps the World Cup. Argentina beat the Netherlands 3-1 after extra time.

1982: Paulo Rossi opens the scoring for Italy in the 56th minute of the Final against West Germany. Harold Schumacher, the German goalkeeper, watches the ball in.

1986: Diego Maradona sets off on the electrifying run through the England midfield and defence for his second goal in Argentina's 2-1 victory in the quarter-finals.

1990: Roger Milla celebrates another Cameroonian goal at Italia '90. In 1994, he became the oldest player to play and score at a World Cup Final tournament.

1994: Roberto Baggio (Italy) contemplates his missed penalty in the final shootout. The Brazilians celebrate their fourth World Cup victory.

THE WORLD CUP

1998: French captain Zinedine Zidane rises above the Brazilian defence to head the opening goal in the Final. France won 3-0 against a team fatally weakened by a clearly under par Ronaldo. The Brazilian centre-forward had been withdrawn from the team sheet after he was taken ill at the team's hotel; a mixture of stress, stomach upset and allergy. But he arrived in the dressing room at the Stade de France and was reinstated minutes before the kick-off.

Korea/Japan 2002

TOURNAMENT REVIEW

THE 17th WORLD CUP FINALS, the first to be played outside of Europe and the Americas, were bound to herald some change in the balance of global football power. Korea/Japan 2002 will be remembered for the giant-killing of the early rounds, the colourful runs of Senegal, Turkey and South Korea and the reassertion of the old order in the Final.

The tournament opened with the sensational defeat of reigning champions France by Senegal in the country's first World Cup finals game. France looked tired, and without Zidane lacked the zest to compete with a skillful and committed Senegalese side. South Korea and the USA meted out a similar fate to the Portuguese. England and Sweden saw off the mighty Argentinians and Nigeria in the Group of Death. South Korea would do the same to Italy and Spain in the following rounds.

But in a tournament where teamwork, fitness and pressure seemed to have the upper hand, Brazil progressed imperiously to the Final where its unparalleled talent in attack was too much for a German defence that had conceded only a single goal on the way to Yokohama.

THE GROUP STAGES

The *ancien régime* appears to crumble as France, Argentina, Portugal, Russia and Cameroon all go out and Italy almost join them. Brazil look in a different league to everyone else. Sweden, Senegal, the USA, England, Ireland, Japan and South Korea all play above expectations. Only Saudi Arabia and China look out of their depth.

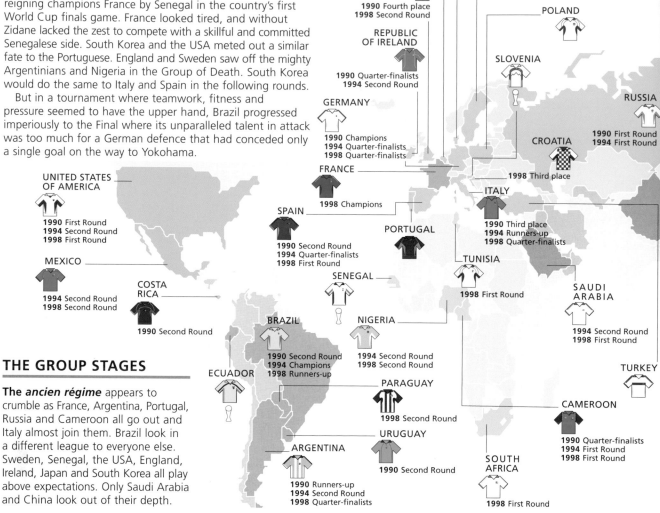

BELGIUM
1990 Second Round
1994 Second Round
1998 First Round

DENMARK
1998 Quarter-finalists

SWEDEN
1990 First Round
1994 Third place

ENGLAND
1990 Fourth place
1998 Second Round

POLAND

REPUBLIC OF IRELAND
1990 Quarter-finalists
1994 Second Round

SLOVENIA

RUSSIA
1990 First Round
1994 First Round

GERMANY
1990 Champions
1994 Quarter-finalists
1998 Quarter-finalists

CROATIA
1998 Third place

FRANCE
1998 Champions

ITALY
1990 Third place
1994 Runners-up
1998 Quarter-finalists

SPAIN
1990 Second Round
1994 Quarter-finalists
1998 First Round

PORTUGAL

TUNISIA
1998 First Round

SAUDI ARABIA
1994 Second Round
1998 First Round

UNITED STATES OF AMERICA
1990 First Round
1994 Second Round
1998 First Round

SENEGAL

MEXICO
1994 Second Round
1998 Second Round

NIGERIA
1994 Second Round
1998 Second Round

TURKEY

COSTA RICA
1990 Second Round

BRAZIL
1990 Second Round
1994 Champions
1998 Runners-up

CAMEROON
1990 Quarter-finalists
1994 First Round
1998 First Round

ECUADOR

PARAGUAY
1998 Second Round

URUGUAY
1990 Second Round

ARGENTINA
1990 Runners-up
1994 Second Round
1998 Quarter-finalists

SOUTH AFRICA
1998 First Round

GROUP A						
Senegal **1-0** France						
Denmark **2-1** Uruguay						
Denmark **1-1** Senegal						
France **0-0** Uruguay						
Denmark **2-0** France						
Senegal **3-3** Uruguay						
	P	W	D	L	F	A	Pts
Denmark	3	2	1	0	5	2	7
Senegal	3	1	2	0	5	4	5
Uruguay	3	0	2	1	4	5	2
France	3	0	1	2	0	3	1

GROUP B						
Paraguay **2-2** South Africa						
Spain **3-1** Slovenia						
Spain **3-1** Paraguay						
South Africa **1-0** Slovenia						
Spain **3-2** South Africa						
Paraguay **3-1** Slovenia						
	P	W	D	L	F	A	Pts
Spain	3	3	0	0	9	4	9
Paraguay	3	1	1	1	6	6	4
South Africa	3	1	1	1	5	5	4
Slovenia	3	0	0	3	2	7	0

GROUP C						
Brazil **2-1** Turkey						
Costa Rica **2-0** China						
Brazil **4-0** China						
Costa Rica **1-1** Turkey						
Brazil **5-2** Costa Rica						
Turkey **3-0** China						
	P	W	D	L	F	A	Pts
Brazil	3	3	0	0	11	3	9
Turkey	3	1	1	1	5	3	4
Costa Rica	3	1	1	1	5	6	4
China	3	0	0	3	0	9	0

GROUP D						
South Korea **2-0** Poland						
USA **3-2** Portugal						
South Korea **1-1** USA						
Portugal **4-0** Poland						
South Korea **1-0** Portugal						
Poland **3-1** USA						
	P	W	D	L	F	A	Pts
South Korea	3	2	1	0	4	1	7
USA	3	1	1	1	5	6	4
Portugal	3	1	0	2	6	4	3
Poland	3	1	0	2	3	7	3

THE WORLD CUP

Korea/Japan 2002 Qualification

FRANCE — Team name

Team shirt

1998 Champions — Performance in last 3 World Cups

First-time qualifiers

- Hosts
- Reigning champions
- Final Round Non-qualifiers

Qualified teams	Qualification Final Round
UEFA	
CONMEBOL	
CAF	
AFC	
OFC	
FOOTBALL CONFEDERATION	

JAPAN

1998 First Round

SOUTH KOREA

1990 First Round
1994 First Round
1998 First Round

CHINA

World Cup 2002: The Venues

43,138 SUWON WORLD CUP STADIUM

49,000 — Tournament stadium with capacity and name
MIYAGI STADIUM

● **Miyagi** — Location of stadium

SAPPORO DOME
42,585 — ● Sapporo

50,256 INCHEON MUNHAK STADIUM

64,640 SEOUL WORLD CUP STADIUM

70,140 DAEGU WORLD CUP STADIUM

ULSAN MUNSU FOOTBALL STADIUM
43,512

49,133 MIYAGI STADIUM

DAEJEON WORLD CUP STADIUM
41,024

NIIGATA STADIUM BIG SWAN
42,300

IBARAKI PREFECTURAL KASHIMA SOCCER STADIUM

● **Seoul**
● Incheon
● Suwon
● **Daegu**

KOBE WING STADIUM
42,000

● **Niigata**

● **Miyagi**
41,800

JEONJU WORLD CUP STADIUM
42,477

● **Daejeon**
● **Jeonju**
SOUTH KOREA
● **Ulsan**
● Gwangju
● Busan

J A P A N
● **Yokohama**
● **Ibaraki**
● **Saitama**
● Shizuoka

SAITAMA STADIUM 2002
63,700

GWANGJU WORLD CUP STADIUM
42,900

● **Seogwipo**

● **Kobe**
● **Osaka**

INTERNATIONAL STADIUM YOKOHAMA
72,370

● **Oita**

OITA STADIUM BIG EYE
43,000

JEJU WORLD CUP STADIUM
42,526

BUSAN STADIUM
55,000

NAGAI STADIUM
50,000

SHIZUOKA STADIUM ECOPA
51,349

Qualification by Confederation

Year of World Cup **2002**

FOOTBALL CONFEDERATION — **3**
AFC — **4**
CAF — **5**
CONMEBOL — **5**
UEFA — **15**

Number of participants

32

AFC includes two co-hosts; UEFA includes last tournament's winners

Football is politics. Japan qualify for the Second Round. The country's leading newspaper writes, 'Finally we understand how important the initiatives and imagination of the individual are to the group.'

GROUP E

Rep. of Ireland **1-1** Cameroon
Germany **8-0** Saudi Arabia
Germany **1-1** Rep. of Ireland
Cameroon **1-0** Saudi Arabia
Germany **2-0** Cameroon
Rep. of Ireland **3-0** Saudi Arabia

	P	W	D	L	F	A	Pts
Germany	3	2	1	0	11	1	7
Ireland	3	1	2	0	5	2	5
Cameroon	3	1	1	1	2	3	4
Saudi Arabia	3	0	0	3	0	10	0

GROUP F

Argentina **1-0** Nigeria
England **1-1** Sweden
Sweden **2-1** Nigeria
England **1-0** Argentina
Sweden **1-1** Argentina
Nigeria **0-0** England

	P	W	D	L	F	A	Pts
Sweden	3	1	2	0	4	3	5
England	3	1	2	0	2	1	5
Argentina	3	1	1	1	2	2	4
Nigeria	3	0	1	2	1	3	1

GROUP G

Mexico **1-0** Croatia
Italy **2-0** Ecuador
Croatia **2-1** Italy
Mexico **2-1** Ecuador
Mexico **1-1** Italy
Ecuador **1-0** Croatia

	P	W	D	L	F	A	Pts
Mexico	3	2	1	0	4	2	7
Italy	3	1	1	1	4	3	4
Croatia	3	1	0	2	2	3	3
Ecuador	3	1	0	2	2	4	3

GROUP H

Japan **2-2** Belgium
Russia **2-0** Tunisia
Japan **1-0** Russia
Tunisia **1-1** Belgium
Japan **2-0** Tunisia
Belgium **3-2** Russia

	P	W	D	L	F	A	Pts
Japan	3	2	1	0	5	2	7
Belgium	3	1	2	0	6	5	5
Russia	3	1	0	2	4	4	3
Tunisia	3	0	1	2	1	5	1

THE SECOND ROUND

More favourites fall, as South Korea beat Italy with a golden goal that provokes the biggest outburst of sour grapes in the tournament's history. Ireland ran Spain to penalties in the round's best match. The USA beat Mexico in a bad-tempered game. Brazil was held for 70 minutes by the Belgians before scoring twice and Germany scraped past Paraguay. It was goodbye to Sweden, Denmark and Japan as Senegal, England and Turkey went through.

June 15 – Seogwipo
Attendance 25,176
1-0
h/t: 0-0
GERMANY — **PARAGUAY**

June 15 – Niigata
Attendance 40,582
0-3
h/t: 0-3
DENMARK — **ENGLAND**

June 16 – Oita
Attendance 39,747
1-2
(Senegal won on golden goal)
h/t: 1-1, f/t: 1-1
SWEDEN — **SENEGAL**

June 16 – Suwon
Attendance 38,926
1-1
(Spain won 3-2 on pens)
h/t: 1-0
SPAIN — **IRELAND**

June 17 – Jeonju
Attendance 36,380
0-2
h/t: 0-1
MEXICO — **USA**

June 17 – Kobe
Attendance 40,440
2-0
h/t: 0-0
BRAZIL — **BELGIUM**

June 18 – Miyagi
Attendance 45,666
0-1
h/t: 0-1
JAPAN — **TURKEY**

June 18 – Daejeon
Attendance 38,588
2-1
(South Korea won on golden goal)
h/t: 0-1, f/t: 1-1
SOUTH KOREA — **ITALY**

THE QUARTER-FINALS

Brazil showed grit as well as flair to come back from one down and kill the game with England when down to ten men. Germany rode its luck against a rampant American team and survived a handball on the line. Turkey and Senegal played end-to-end football separated only by a single strike. South Korea took another Mediterranean scalp, after even more controversial refereeing, beating Spain on penalties.

June 21 – Shizuoka
Attendance 47,436
1-2
h/t: 1-1
ENGLAND — **BRAZIL**

June 21 – Ulsan
Attendance 37,337
1-0
h/t: 1-0
GERMANY — **USA**

June 22 – Gwangju
Attendance 42,114
0-0
(South Korea won 5-3 on pens)
h/t: 0-0, f/t: 0-0
SPAIN — **SOUTH KOREA**

June 22 – Osaka
Attendance 44,233
0-1
(Turkey won on golden goal)
h/t: 0-0, f/t: 0-0
SENEGAL — **TURKEY**

THE SEMI-FINALS

In the end the old order held with Brazil and Germany seeing off the outsiders. A moment of genius from the outside of Ronaldo's boot was enough to take Brazil past a tenacious and technically superb Turkish team. South Korea ran and ran, but Michael Ballack, booked and out of the Final, found the composure to collect a rebound and slot in Germany's winner.

June 25 – Seoul
Attendance 65,625
1-0
h/t: 0-0
GERMANY — **SOUTH KOREA**

June 26 – Saitama
Attendance 61,058
1-0
h/t: 0-0
BRAZIL — **TURKEY**

THE THIRD PLACE PLAY-OFF

Hakan Sukur, Turkey's captain, finally found his form, scoring the World Cup's fastest-ever goal in the first minute. Korea equalized from a free kick, but two more goals for Turkey in the next half an hour left them chasing the game. Even the super-fit Koreans didn't quite have enough after that despite a late strike.

June 29 – Daegu
Attendance 64,483
2-3
h/t: 1-3
SOUTH KOREA — **TURKEY**

THE FINAL

Although they had won seven World Cups between them, Brazil and Germany had never met in a World Cup Final. Germany's pressing game gave them the best of possession and the marking closed down Brazil's flanks, but it was Ronaldo's moment of redemption for France 98, and three chances in the first half became two goals in the second.

Brazil's first goal was Ronaldo's seventh of the tournament. It meant that he equalled his compatriot Jairzinho's record of scoring in every round of the World Cup finals on the way to victory, a record set in Mexico in 1970.

Ronaldo's second goal

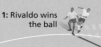

1: Rivaldo wins the ball

The Starting Line-Up

June 30 – Yokohama
Attendance 69,029

BRAZIL	Referee	GERMANY
Formation: 3-5-2	● Pierluigi Collina (Italy)	Formation: 3-5-2
Manager		**Manager**
Luiz Felipe Scolari		Rudi Völler
Substitutes		**Substitutes**
Juninho (19)		(20) Bierhoff
Denilson (17)		(21) Asamoah
		(6) Ziege

Highlights of the Game

KEY

Player booked ☐ ↩ Substitution

Goal ⚽

BRAZIL ▼ KICK OFF 0 mins **GERMANY**

6 min: Roque Junior after clash with Neuville

9 min: Klose for an elbow on Edmilson

14 min: German pressure ends when Bode fails to reach Metzelder's pass

18 min: First clear chance, Ronaldo pokes the ball past Kahn's left post

28 min: Bode fails to reach Schneider's pass

44 min: Kleberson's shot beats Kahn but rockets off the crossbar

41 min: Jeremies shoots over the bar

45 min: Ronaldo shoots from 6 metres but Kahn's legs are in the way

45 mins

HALF-TIME: **0-0**

49 min: Germany's best chance: Neuville's 35-metre free kick is tipped round the right post by Marcos

67 min: Kahn spills Rivaldo's shot and Ronaldo pounces on the ball to score

79 min: Kleberson crosses into the box, Rivaldo steps over, Ronaldo curls the ball past Kahn

73 min: Bierhoff for Klose

78 min: Asamoah for Jeremies

85 min: Juninho for Ronaldinho

83 min: Bierhoff swivels and shoots in the box but Marcos saves at the post

90 min: Denilson for Ronaldo

84 min: Ziege for Linke

90 mins

+ 3 mins injury time

FULL-TIME: **2-0**

4: Ronaldo takes one touch to control and then fires low past Kahn

3: Rivaldo steps over Kleberson's pass

2: Kleberson runs then plays a square pass

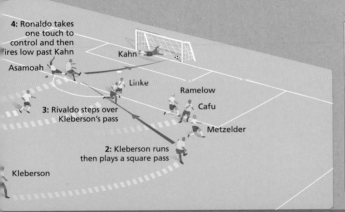

BRAZIL 2-0 GERMANY

	Team			Match Statistics		Team	
	First Half	Second Half	Full Time		First Half	Second Half	Full Time
	45	48	46.5	Possession	55	52	53.5
	–	–	9(7)	Attempts (on target)	–	–	12(4)
	–	–	9	Successful tackles	–	–	12
	–	–	7	Fouls conceded	–	–	4
	2	1	3	Corners won	8	5	13
	0	0	0	Offside	1	0	1

THE WORLD CUP

The World Cup

THE IDEA OF THE WORLD CUP began with the establishment of FIFA in 1904, but for the first three decades of the century the football tournament at the Olympic Games served as the *de facto* football world championships. With the advent of professionalism in many European countries in the 1920s (and the resultant limit to participation in the amateur Olympic football tournament) the World Cup came into being.

The first tournament was held in Uruguay in 1930 as the Uruguayans were the current Olympic champions and promised to pay everybody's expenses. Despite this, only three European countries made the trip to a tournament dominated by South Americans. In 1934, the early group rounds were dispensed with and the tournament became a knockout competition from the beginning. This format was tough on the Americans, Brazilians and Argentinians who often crossed an ocean for a single game.

After the Second World War, the World Cup settled into a 16-team final tournament, with a group phase followed by knockout stages. There were two exceptions: the 1950 tournament in Brazil had a league format for the final placing, and the 1954 competition in Switzerland saw 16 teams divided into four groups, with two teams in each group seeded. The two seeded teams didn't play each other in the group rounds.

The increasing financial attraction of the World Cup, and the increasing strength and numbers of footballing nations outside of Europe and Latin America, has led to a steady expansion of the tournament. There were 24 teams in 1982 (with four second round mini-leagues producing four semi-finalists); and 32 teams in 1998 and 2002 (reverting to opening groups and then knockout stages for the last 16).

1930 URUGUAY

POOL 1

France **4-1** Mexico
Argentina **1-0** France
Chile **3-0** Mexico
Chile **1-0** France
Argentina **6-3** Mexico
Argentina **3-1** Chile

	P	W	D	L	F	A	Pts
Argentina	3	3	0	0	10	4	6
Chile	3	2	0	1	5	3	4
France	3	1	0	2	4	3	2
Mexico	3	0	0	3	4	13	0

POOL 2

Yugoslavia **2-1** Brazil
Yugoslavia **4-0** Bolivia
Brazil **4-0** Bolivia

	P	W	D	L	F	A	Pts
Yugoslavia	2	2	0	0	6	1	4
Brazil	2	1	0	1	5	2	2
Bolivia	2	0	0	2	0	8	0

POOL 3

Romania **3-1** Peru
Uruguay **1-0** Peru
Uruguay **4-0** Romania

	P	W	D	L	F	A	Pts
Uruguay	2	2	0	0	5	0	4
Romania	2	1	0	1	3	5	2
Peru	2	0	0	2	1	4	0

POOL 4

USA **3-0** Belgium
USA **3-0** Paraguay
Paraguay **1-0** Belgium

	P	W	D	L	F	A	Pts
USA	2	2	0	0	6	0	4
Paraguay	2	1	0	1	1	3	2
Belgium	2	0	0	2	0	4	0

SEMI-FINALS

Argentina **6-1** USA
(Monti 20,   (Brown 88)
Scopello 56,
Stabile 69, 87,
Peucelle 80, 85)

Uruguay **6-1** Yugoslavia
(Cea 18, 67, 72,   (Sekulic 4)
Anselmo 20, 31,
Iriarte 60)

THIRD PLACE PLAY-OFF

not held

FINAL

July 30 – Centenario, Montevideo
Uruguay **4-2** Argentina
(Dorado 12,   (Peucelle 20,
Cea 58,   Stabile 37)
Iriarte 68,
Castro 89)
h/t: 1-2 **Att:** 93,000
Ref: Langenus (Belgium)

1934 ITALY

FIRST ROUND

Italy **7-1** USA
Czechoslovakia **2-1** Romania
Germany **5-2** Belgium
Austria **3-2** France
(after extra time)
Spain **3-1** Brazil
Switzerland **3-2** Netherlands
Sweden **3-2** Argentina
Hungary **4-2** Egypt

SECOND ROUND

Germany **2-1** Sweden
Austria **2-1** Hungary
Italy **1-1** Spain
(after extra time)
Replay
Italy **1-0** Spain
Czechoslovakia **3-2** Switzerland

SEMI-FINALS

Czechoslovakia **3-1** Germany
(Nejedly 19, 81,   (Noack 62)
Krcil 71)

Italy **1-0** Austria
(Guaita 19)

THIRD PLACE PLAY-OFF

Germany **3-2** Austria
(Lehner 1, 42,   (Horvath 28,
Conen 27)   Sesta 54)

FINAL

June 10 – Flaminio, Rome
Italy **2-1** Czechoslovakia
(Orsi 81,   (Puc 71)
Schiavio 95)
(after extra time)
h/t: 0-0 **90 mins:** 1-1
Att: 55,000 **Ref:** Eklind (Sweden)

1938 FRANCE

FIRST ROUND

Switzerland **1-1** Germany
(after extra time)
Replay
Switzerland **4-2** Germany
Cuba **3-3** Romania
(after extra time)
Replay
Cuba **2-1** Romania
Hungary **6-0** Dutch East
    Industries
Sweden **w/o** Austria
France **3-1** Belgium
Czechoslovakia **3-0** Netherlands
(after extra time)
Brazil **6-5** Poland
(after extra time)
Italy **2-1** Norway
(after extra time)

w/o denotes walk over

QUARTER-FINALS

Sweden **8-0** Cuba
Hungary **2-0** Switzerland
Italy **3-1** France
Brazil **1-1** Czechoslovakia
(after extra time)
Replay
Brazil **2-1** Czechoslovakia

SEMI-FINALS

Italy **2-1** Brazil
(Colaussi 55,   (Romeo 87)
Meazza 60)

Hungary **5-1** Sweden
(Zsengeller   (Nyberg 1)
18, 38, 86,
Titkos 26,
Sarosi 61)

THIRD PLACE PLAY-OFF

Brazil **4-2** Sweden
(Romeo 43,   (Jonasson 18,
Leonidas 63, 73,   Nyberg 38)
Peracio 80)

FINAL

June 19 – Stade Colombes, Paris
Italy **4-2** Hungary
(Colaussi 5, 35,   (Titkos 7,
Piola 16, 82)   Sarosi 70)
h/t: 3-1 **Att:** 55,000
Ref: Capdeville (France)

1950 BRAZIL

POOL 1

Brazil **4-0** Mexico
Yugoslavia **3-0** Switzerland
Yugoslavia **4-1** Mexico
Brazil **2-2** Switzerland
Brazil **2-0** Yugoslavia
Switzerland **2-1** Mexico

	P	W	D	L	F	A	Pts
Brazil	3	2	1	0	8	2	5
Yugoslavia	3	2	0	1	7	3	4
Switzerland	3	1	1	1	4	6	3
Mexico	3	0	0	3	2	10	0

POOL 2

Spain **3-1** USA
England **2-0** Chile
USA **1-0** England
Spain **2-0** Chile
Spain **1-0** England
Chile **5-2** USA

	P	W	D	L	F	A	Pts
Spain	3	3	0	0	6	1	6
England	3	1	0	2	2	2	2
Chile	3	1	0	2	5	6	2
USA	3	1	0	2	4	8	2

POOL 3

Sweden **3-2** Italy
Sweden **2-2** Paraguay
Italy **2-0** Paraguay

	P	W	D	L	F	A	Pts
Sweden	2	1	1	0	5	4	3
Italy	2	1	0	1	4	3	2
Paraguay	2	0	1	1	2	4	1

POOL 4

Uruguay **8-0** Bolivia

	P	W	D	L	F	A	Pts
Uruguay	1	1	0	0	8	0	2
Bolivia	1	0	0	1	0	8	0

FINAL POOL

Uruguay **2-2** Spain
Brazil **7-1** Sweden
Uruguay **3-2** Sweden

World Cup Winners

Uruguay
1930, 50

Italy
1934, 38, 82

West Germany
1954, 74, 90

Brazil
1958, 62, 70, 94, 2002

England
1966

Argentina
1978, 86

France
1998

THE WORLD CUP

Brazil **6-1** Spain
Sweden **3-1** Spain
Uruguay **2-1** Brazil

	P	W	D	L	F	A	Pts
Uruguay	3	2	1	0	7	5	5
Brazil	3	2	0	1	14	4	4
Sweden	3	1	0	2	6	11	2
Spain	3	0	1	2	4	11	1

THIRD PLACE
Sweden

FINAL
July 16 – Maracana, Rio de Janeiro
Uruguay 2-1 Brazil
(Schiaffino 66,   (Friaca 48)
Ghiggia 79)
h/t: 0-0 **Att:** 199,854
Ref: Reader (England)

1954 SWITZERLAND

POOL 1
Yugoslavia **1-0** France
Brazil **5-0** Mexico
France **3-2** Mexico
Brazil **1-1** Yugoslavia

	P	W	D	L	F	A	Pts
Brazil	2	1	1	0	6	1	3
Yugoslavia	2	1	1	0	2	1	3
France	2	1	0	1	3	3	2
Mexico	2	0	0	2	2	8	0

POOL 2
Hungary **9-0** South Korea
West Germany **4-1** Turkey
Hungary **8-3** West Germany
Turkey **7-0** South Korea

	P	W	D	L	F	A	Pts
Hungary	2	2	0	0	17	3	4
West Germany	2	1	0	1	7	9	2
Turkey	2	1	0	1	8	4	2
South Korea	2	0	0	2	0	16	0

PLAY-OFF
West Germany **7-2** Turkey

POOL 3
Austria **1-0** Scotland
Uruguay **2-0** Czechoslovakia
Austria **5-0** Czechoslovakia
Uruguay **7-0** Scotland

	P	W	D	L	F	A	Pts
Uruguay	2	2	0	0	9	0	4
Austria	2	2	0	0	6	0	4
Czechoslovakia	2	0	0	2	0	7	0
Scotland	2	0	0	2	0	8	0

POOL 4
England **4-4** Belgium
England **2-0** Switzerland
Switzerland **2-1** Italy
Italy **4-1** Belgium

	P	W	D	L	F	A	Pts
England	2	1	1	0	6	4	3
Italy	2	1	0	1	5	3	2
Switzerland	2	1	0	1	2	3	2
Belgium	2	0	1	1	5	8	1

PLAY-OFF
Switzerland **4-1** Italy

QUARTER-FINALS
West Germany **2-0** Yugoslavia
Hungary **4-2** Brazil
Austria **7-5** Switzerland
Uruguay **4-2** England

SEMI-FINALS
West Germany **6-1** Austria
(Schäfer 30,   (Probst 51)
Morlock 49,
F. Walter 54, 65,
O. Walter 60, 89)

Hungary **4-2** Uruguay
(Czibor 13,   (Hohberg 75, 86)
Hidegkuti 47,
Kocsis 111, 116)
(after extra time)

THIRD PLACE PLAY-OFF
Austria **3-1** Uruguay
(Stojaspal 16,   (Hohberg 21)
Cruz o.g. 59,
Ocwirk 79)

FINAL
July 4 – Wankdorf, Berne
West Germany **3-2** Hungary
(Morlock 11,   (Puskas 6,
Rahn 16, 83)   Czibor 8)
h/t: 2-2 **Att:** 60,000
Ref: Ling (England)

1958 SWEDEN

POOL 1
West Germany **3-1** Argentina
N. Ireland **1-0** Czechoslovakia
West Germany **2-2** Czechoslovakia
Argentina **3-1** N. Ireland
West Germany **2-2** N. Ireland
Czechoslovakia **6-1** Argentina

	P	W	D	L	F	A	Pts
West Germany	3	1	2	0	7	5	4
Czechoslovakia	3	1	1	1	8	4	3
N. Ireland	3	1	1	1	4	5	3
Argentina	3	1	0	2	5	10	2

PLAY-OFF
N. Ireland **2-1** Czechoslovakia

POOL 2
France **7-3** Paraguay
Yugoslavia **1-1** Scotland
Yugoslavia **3-2** France
Paraguay **3-2** Scotland
France **2-1** Scotland
Yugoslavia **3-3** Paraguay

	P	W	D	L	F	A	Pts
France	3	2	0	1	11	7	4
Yugoslavia	3	1	2	0	7	6	4
Paraguay	3	1	1	1	9	12	3
Scotland	3	0	1	2	4	6	1

POOL 3
Sweden **3-0** Mexico
Hungary **1-1** Wales
Wales **1-1** Mexico
Sweden **2-1** Hungary
Sweden **0-0** Wales
Hungary **4-0** Mexico

	P	W	D	L	F	A	Pts
Sweden	3	2	1	0	5	1	5
Hungary	3	1	1	1	6	3	3
Wales	3	0	3	0	2	2	3
Mexico	3	0	1	2	1	8	1

PLAY-OFF
Wales **2-1** Hungary

POOL 4
England **2-2** Soviet Union
Brazil **3-0** Austria
England **0-0** Brazil
Soviet Union **2-0** Austria
Brazil **2-0** Soviet Union
England **2-2** Austria

	P	W	D	L	F	A	Pts
Brazil	3	2	1	0	5	0	5
England	3	0	3	0	4	4	3
Soviet Union	3	1	1	1	4	4	3
Austria	3	0	1	2	2	7	1

PLAY-OFF
Soviet Union **1-0** England

QUARTER-FINALS
France **4-0** N. Ireland
West Germany **1-0** Yugoslavia
Sweden **2-0** Soviet Union
Brazil **1-0** Wales

SEMI-FINALS
Brazil **5-2** France
(Vava 2,   (Fontaine 8,
Didi 38,   Piantoni 83)
Pele 53, 64, 76)

Sweden **3-1** West Germany
(Skoglund 30,   (Schäfer 21)
Gren 81,
Hamrin 88)

THIRD PLACE PLAY-OFF
France **6-3** West Germany
(Fontaine   (Cieslarczyk 18,
16, 36, 78, 89,   Rahn 52,
Kopa 27,   Schäfer 83)
Douis 50)

FINAL
June 29 – Rasunda, Stockholm
Brazil 5-2 Sweden
(Vava 9, 32,   (Liedholm 4,
Pele 55, 89,   Simonsson 80)
Zagallo 68)
h/t: 2-1 **Att:** 49,737
Ref: Guigue (France)

1962 CHILE

GROUP 1
Uruguay **2-1** Colombia
Soviet Union **2-0** Yugoslavia
Yugoslavia **3-1** Uruguay
Soviet Union **4-4** Colombia
Soviet Union **2-1** Uruguay
Yugoslavia **5-0** Colombia

	P	W	D	L	F	A	Pts
Soviet Union	3	2	1	0	8	5	5
Yugoslavia	3	2	0	1	8	3	4
Uruguay	3	1	0	2	4	6	2
Colombia	3	0	1	2	5	11	1

GROUP 2
Chile **3-1** Switzerland
West Germany **0-0** Italy
Chile **2-0** Italy
West Germany **2-1** Switzerland
West Germany **2-0** Chile
Italy **3-0** Switzerland

	P	W	D	L	F	A	Pts
West Germany	3	2	1	0	4	1	5
Chile	3	2	0	1	5	3	4
Italy	3	1	1	1	3	2	3
Switzerland	3	0	0	3	2	8	0

GROUP 3
Brazil **2-0** Mexico
Czechoslovakia **1-0** Spain
Brazil **0-0** Czechoslovakia
Spain **1-0** Mexico
Brazil **2-1** Spain
Mexico **3-1** Czechoslovakia

	P	W	D	L	F	A	Pts
Brazil	3	2	1	0	4	1	5
Czechoslovakia	3	1	1	1	2	3	3
Mexico	3	1	0	2	3	4	2
Spain	3	1	0	2	2	3	2

GROUP 4
Argentina **1-0** Bulgaria
Hungary **2-1** England
England **3-1** Argentina
Hungary **6-1** Bulgaria
Argentina **0-0** Hungary
England **0-0** Bulgaria

	P	W	D	L	F	A	Pts
Hungary	3	2	1	0	8	2	5
England	3	1	1	1	4	3	3
Argentina	3	1	1	1	2	3	3
Bulgaria	3	0	1	2	1	7	1

QUARTER-FINALS
Yugoslavia **1-0** West Germany
Brazil **3-1** England
Chile **2-1** Soviet Union
Czechoslovakia **1-0** Hungary

SEMI-FINALS
Brazil **4-2** Chile
(Garrincha 9, 31,   (Toro 41,
Vava 49, 77)   L. Sanchez 61)

Czechoslovakia **3-1** Yugoslavia
(Kadraba 49,   (Jerkovic 69)
Scherer 80, 86)

THIRD PLACE PLAY-OFF
Chile **1-0** Yugoslavia
(Rojas 89)

FINAL
June 17 – Nacional, Santiago
Brazil 3-1 Czechoslovakia
(Amarildo 18,   (Masopust 16)
Zito 69,
Vava 77)
h/t: 1-1 **Att:** 68,679
Ref: Latishev (Soviet Union)

THE WORLD CUP

1966 ENGLAND

GROUP 1

England 0-0 Uruguay
France 1-1 Mexico
Uruguay 2-1 France
England 2-0 Mexico
Uruguay 0-0 Mexico
England 2-0 France

	P	W	D	L	F	A	Pts
England	3	2	1	0	4	0	5
Uruguay	3	1	2	0	2	1	4
Mexico	3	0	2	1	1	3	2
France	3	0	1	2	2	5	1

GROUP 2

West Germany 5-0 Switzerland
Argentina 2-1 Spain
Spain 2-1 Switzerland
Argentina 0-0 West Germany
Argentina 2-0 Switzerland
West Germany 2-1 Spain

	P	W	D	L	F	A	Pts
West Germany	3	2	1	0	7	1	5
Argentina	3	2	1	0	4	1	5
Spain	3	1	0	2	4	5	2
Switzerland	3	0	0	3	1	9	0

GROUP 3

Brazil 2-0 Bulgaria
Portugal 3-1 Hungary
Hungary 3-1 Brazil
Portugal 3-0 Bulgaria
Portugal 3-1 Brazil
Hungary 3-1 Bulgaria

	P	W	D	L	F	A	Pts
Portugal	3	3	0	0	9	2	6
Hungary	3	2	0	1	7	5	4
Brazil	3	1	0	2	4	6	2
Bulgaria	3	0	0	3	1	8	0

GROUP 4

Soviet Union 3-0 North Korea
Italy 2-0 Chile
Chile 1-1 North Korea
Soviet Union 1-0 Italy
North Korea 1-0 Italy
Soviet Union 2-1 Chile

	P	W	D	L	F	A	Pts
Soviet Union	3	3	0	0	6	1	6
North Korea	3	1	1	1	2	4	3
Italy	3	1	0	2	2	2	2
Chile	3	0	1	2	2	5	1

QUARTER-FINALS

England 1-0 Argentina
West Germany 4-0 Uruguay
Portugal 5-3 North Korea
Soviet Union 2-1 Hungary

SEMI-FINALS

West Germany 2-1 Soviet Union
(Haller 44,   (Porkujan 88)
Beckenbauer 68)

England 2-1 Portugal
(R. Charlton   (Eusebio 82)
30, 79)

THIRD PLACE PLAY-OFF

Portugal 2-1 Soviet Union
(Eusebio 12,   (Metreveli 43)
Torres 88)

FINAL

July 30 – Wembley Stadium, London
England 4-2 West Germany
(Hurst   (Haller 13,
19, 100, 119,   Weber 89)
Peters 77)

(after extra time)
h/t: 1-1 **90 mins:** 2-2
Att: 96,924 **Ref:** Dienst (Switzerland)

1970 MEXICO

GROUP 1

Mexico 0-0 Soviet Union
Belgium 3-0 El Salvador
Soviet Union 4-1 Belgium
Mexico 4-0 El Salvador
Soviet Union 2-0 El Salvador
Mexico 1-0 Belgium

	P	W	D	L	F	A	Pts
Soviet Union	3	2	1	0	6	1	5
Mexico	3	2	1	0	5	0	5
Belgium	3	1	0	2	4	5	2
El Salvador	3	0	0	3	0	9	0

GROUP 2

Uruguay 2-0 Israel
Italy 1-0 Sweden
Uruguay 0-0 Italy
Sweden 1-1 Israel
Sweden 1-0 Uruguay
Italy 0-0 Israel

	P	W	D	L	F	A	Pts
Italy	3	1	2	0	1	0	4
Uruguay	3	1	1	1	2	1	3
Sweden	3	1	1	1	2	2	3
Israel	3	0	2	1	1	3	2

GROUP 3

England 1-0 Romania
Brazil 4-1 Czechoslovakia
Romania 2-1 Czechoslovakia
Brazil 1-0 England
Brazil 3-2 Romania
England 1-0 Czechoslovakia

	P	W	D	L	F	A	Pts
Brazil	3	3	0	0	8	3	6
England	3	2	0	1	2	1	4
Romania	3	1	0	2	4	5	2
Czechoslovakia	3	0	0	3	2	7	0

GROUP 4

Peru 3-2 Bulgaria
West Germany 2-1 Morocco
Peru 3-0 Morocco
West Germany 5-2 Bulgaria
West Germany 3-1 Peru
Morocco 1-1 Bulgaria

	P	W	D	L	F	A	Pts
West Germany	3	3	0	0	10	4	6
Peru	3	2	0	1	7	5	4
Bulgaria	3	0	1	2	5	9	1
Morocco	3	0	1	2	2	6	1

QUARTER-FINALS

West Germany 3-2 England
(after extra time)
Brazil 4-2 Peru
Italy 4-1 Mexico
Uruguay 1-0 Soviet Union

SEMI-FINALS

Italy 4-3 West Germany
(Boninsegna 7,   (Schellinger 90,
Burgnich 99,   G. Müller 95, 110)
Riva 104,
Rivera 111)

(after extra time)

Brazil 3-1 Uruguay
(Clodoaldo 45,   (Cubilla 19)
Jairzinho 76,
Rivelino 88)

THIRD PLACE PLAY-OFF

West Germany 1-0 Uruguay
(Overath 26)

FINAL

June 21 – Azteca, Mexico City
Brazil 4-1 Italy
(Pele 18,   (Boninsegna 37)
Gerson 66,
Jairzinho 71,
Carlos Alberto 86)

h/t: 1-1 **Att:** 107,000
Ref: Glockner (East Germany)

1974 WEST GERMANY

GROUP 1

West Germany 1-0 Chile
East Germany 2-0 Australia
West Germany 3-0 Australia
East Germany 1-1 Chile
Australia 0-0 Chile
East Germany 1-0 West Germany

	P	W	D	L	F	A	Pts
East Germany	3	2	1	0	4	1	5
West Germany	3	2	0	1	4	1	4
Chile	3	0	2	1	1	2	2
Australia	3	0	1	2	0	5	1

GROUP 2

Brazil 0-0 Yugoslavia
Scotland 2-0 Zaïre
Brazil 0-0 Scotland
Yugoslavia 9-0 Zaïre
Yugoslavia 1-1 Scotland
Brazil 3-0 Zaïre

	P	W	D	L	F	A	Pts
Yugoslavia	3	1	2	0	10	1	4
Brazil	3	1	2	0	3	0	4
Scotland	3	1	2	0	3	1	4
Zaïre	3	0	0	3	0	14	0

GROUP 3

Netherlands 2-0 Uruguay
Bulgaria 0-0 Sweden
Netherlands 0-0 Sweden
Bulgaria 1-1 Uruguay
Netherlands 4-1 Bulgaria
Sweden 3-0 Uruguay

	P	W	D	L	F	A	Pts
Netherlands	3	2	1	0	6	1	5
Sweden	3	1	2	0	3	0	4
Bulgaria	3	0	2	1	2	5	2
Uruguay	3	0	1	2	1	6	1

GROUP 4

Italy 3-1 Haiti
Poland 3-2 Argentina
Argentina 1-1 Italy
Poland 7-0 Haiti
Argentina 4-1 Haiti
Poland 2-1 Italy

	P	W	D	L	F	A	Pts
Poland	3	3	0	0	12	3	6
Argentina	3	1	1	1	7	5	3
Italy	3	1	1	1	5	4	3
Haiti	3	0	0	3	2	14	0

SECOND ROUND - GROUP A

Brazil 1-0 East Germany
Netherlands 4-0 Argentina
Netherlands 2-0 East Germany
Brazil 2-1 Argentina
East Germany 1-1 Argentina
Netherlands 2-0 Brazil

	P	W	D	L	F	A	Pts
Netherlands	3	3	0	0	8	0	6
Brazil	3	2	0	1	3	3	4
East Germany	3	0	1	2	1	4	1
Argentina	3	0	1	2	2	7	1

SECOND ROUND - GROUP B

Poland 1-0 Sweden
West Germany 2-0 Yugoslavia
Poland 2-1 Yugoslavia
West Germany 4-2 Sweden
Sweden 2-1 Yugoslavia
West Germany 1-0 Poland

	P	W	D	L	F	A	Pts
West Germany	3	3	0	0	7	2	6
Poland	3	2	0	1	3	2	4
Sweden	3	1	0	2	4	6	2
Yugoslavia	3	0	0	3	2	6	0

THIRD PLACE PLAY-OFF

Poland 1-0 Brazil
(Lato 76)

FINAL

July 7 – Olympiastadion, Munich
West Germany 2-1 Netherlands
(Breitner 25 pen,   (Neeskens 2 pen)
G. Müller 43)

h/t: 2-1 **Att:** 77,833
Ref: Taylor (England)

1978 ARGENTINA

GROUP 1

Argentina 2-1 Hungary
Italy 2-1 France
Argentina 2-1 France
Italy 3-1 Hungary
Italy 1-0 Argentina
France 3-1 Hungary

	P	W	D	L	F	A	Pts
Italy	3	3	0	0	6	2	6
Argentina	3	2	0	1	4	3	4
France	3	1	0	2	5	5	2
Hungary	3	0	0	3	3	8	0

GROUP 2

West Germany 0-0 Poland
Tunisia 3-1 Mexico
Poland 1-0 Tunisia
West Germany 6-0 Mexico
Poland 3-1 Mexico
West Germany 0-0 Tunisia

	P	W	D	L	F	A	Pts
Poland	3	2	1	0	4	1	5
West Germany	3	1	2	0	6	0	4
Tunisia	3	1	1	1	3	2	3
Mexico	3	0	0	3	2	12	0

GROUP 3

Austria **2-1** Spain
Sweden **1-1** Brazil
Austria **1-0** Sweden
Brazil **0-0** Spain
Spain **1-0** Sweden
Brazil **1-0** Austria

	P	W	D	L	F	A	Pts
Austria	3	2	0	1	3	2	4
Brazil	3	1	2	0	2	1	4
Spain	3	1	1	1	2	2	3
Sweden	3	0	1	2	1	3	1

GROUP 4

Peru **3-1** Scotland
Netherlands **3-0** Iran
Scotland **1-1** Iran
Netherlands **0-0** Peru
Peru **4-1** Iran
Scotland **3-2** Netherlands

	P	W	D	L	F	A	Pts
Peru	3	2	1	0	7	2	5
Netherlands	3	1	1	1	5	3	3
Scotland	3	1	1	1	5	6	3
Iran	3	0	1	2	2	8	1

SECOND ROUND - GROUP A

Italy **0-0** West Germany
Netherlands **5-1** Austria
Italy **1-0** Austria
Austria **3-2** West Germany
Netherlands **2-1** Italy
Netherlands **2-2** West Germany

	P	W	D	L	F	A	Pts
Netherlands	3	2	1	0	9	4	5
Italy	3	1	1	1	2	2	3
West Germany	3	0	2	1	4	5	2
Austria	3	1	0	2	4	8	2

SECOND ROUND - GROUP B

Argentina **2-0** Poland
Brazil **3-0** Peru
Argentina **0-0** Brazil
Poland **1-0** Peru
Brazil **3-1** Poland
Argentina **6-0** Peru

	P	W	D	L	F	A	Pts
Argentina	3	2	1	0	8	0	5
Brazil	3	2	1	0	6	1	5
Poland	3	1	0	2	2	5	2
Peru	3	0	0	3	0	10	0

THIRD PLACE PLAY-OFF

Brazil **2-1** Italy
(Nelinho 64,   (Causio 38)
Dirceu 71)

FINAL

June 25 – Monumental, Buenos Aires
Argentina **3-1** Netherlands
(Kempes 37, 104,   (Nanninga 81)
Bertoni 114)
(after extra time)
h/t: 1-0 **90 mins:** 1-1 **Att:** 77,260
Ref: Gonella (Italy)

1982 SPAIN

GROUP 1

Italy **0-0** Poland
Peru **0-0** Cameroon
Italy **1-1** Peru
Poland **0-0** Cameroon
Poland **5-1** Peru
Italy **1-1** Cameroon

	P	W	D	L	F	A	Pts
Poland	3	1	2	0	5	1	4
Italy	3	0	3	0	2	2	3
Cameroon	3	0	3	0	1	1	3
Peru	3	0	2	1	2	6	2

GROUP 2

Algeria **2-1** West Germany
Austria **1-0** Chile
West Germany **4-1** Chile
Austria **2-0** Algeria
Algeria **3-2** Chile
West Germany **1-0** Austria

	P	W	D	L	F	A	Pts
West Germany	3	2	0	1	6	3	4
Austria	3	2	0	1	3	1	4
Algeria	3	2	0	1	5	5	4
Chile	3	0	0	3	3	8	0

GROUP 3

Belgium **1-0** Argentina
Hungary **10-1** El Salvador
Argentina **4-1** Hungary
Belgium **1-0** El Salvador
Belgium **1-1** Hungary
Argentina **2-0** El Salvador

	P	W	D	L	F	A	Pts
Belgium	3	2	1	0	3	1	5
Argentina	3	2	0	1	6	2	4
Hungary	3	1	1	1	12	6	3
El Salvador	3	0	0	3	1	13	0

GROUP 4

England **3-1** France
Czechoslovakia **1-1** Kuwait
England **2-0** Czechoslovakia
France **4-1** Kuwait
France **1-1** Czechoslovakia
England **1-0** Kuwait

	P	W	D	L	F	A	Pts
England	3	3	0	0	6	1	6
France	3	1	1	1	6	5	3
Czechoslovakia	3	0	2	1	2	4	2
Kuwait	3	0	1	2	2	6	1

GROUP 5

Spain **1-1** Honduras
N. Ireland **0-0** Yugoslavia
Spain **2-1** Yugoslavia
N. Ireland **1-1** Honduras
Yugoslavia **1-0** Honduras
N. Ireland **1-0** Spain

	P	W	D	L	F	A	Pts
N. Ireland	3	1	2	0	2	1	4
Spain	3	1	1	1	3	3	3
Yugoslavia	3	1	1	1	2	2	3
Honduras	3	0	2	1	2	3	2

GROUP 6

Brazil **2-1** Soviet Union
Scotland **5-2** New Zealand
Brazil **4-1** Scotland
Soviet Union **3-0** New Zealand
Scotland **2-2** Soviet Union
Brazil **4-0** New Zealand

	P	W	D	L	F	A	Pts
Brazil	3	3	0	0	10	2	6
Soviet Union	3	1	1	1	6	4	3
Scotland	3	1	1	1	8	8	3
New Zealand	3	0	0	3	2	12	0

SECOND ROUND - GROUP A

Poland **3-0** Belgium
Soviet Union **1-0** Belgium
Soviet Union **0-0** Poland

	P	W	D	L	F	A	Pts
Poland	2	1	1	0	3	0	3
Soviet Union	2	1	1	0	1	0	3
Belgium	2	0	0	2	0	4	0

SECOND ROUND - GROUP B

West Germany **0-0** England
West Germany **2-1** Spain
England **0-0** Spain

	P	W	D	L	F	A	Pts
West Germany	2	1	1	0	2	1	3
England	2	0	2	0	0	0	2
Spain	2	0	1	1	1	2	1

SECOND ROUND - GROUP C

Italy **2-1** Argentina
Brazil **3-1** Argentina
Italy **3-2** Brazil

	P	W	D	L	F	A	Pts
Italy	2	2	0	0	5	3	4
Brazil	2	1	0	1	5	4	2
Argentina	2	0	0	2	2	5	0

SECOND ROUND - GROUP D

France **1-0** Austria
N. Ireland **2-2** Austria
France **4-1** N. Ireland

	P	W	D	L	F	A	Pts
France	2	2	0	0	5	1	4
Austria	2	0	1	1	2	3	1
N. Ireland	2	0	1	1	3	6	1

SEMI-FINALS

Italy **2-0** Poland
(Rossi 22, 73)
West Germany **3-3** France
(Littbarski 18,   (Platini 27,
Rummenigge 102,   Tresor 93,
Fischer 107)   Giresse 97)
(after extra time)
West Germany won 5-4 on pens

THIRD PLACE PLAY-OFF

Poland **3-2** France
(Szarmach 41,   (Girard 14,
Majewski 44,   Couriol 75)
Kupcewicz 47)

FINAL

July 11 – Estadio Santiago Bernabeu, Madrid
Italy **3-1** West Germany
(Rossi 56,   (Breitner 82)
Tardelli 69,
Altobelli 80)
h/t: 0-0 **Att:** 90,080
Ref: Coelho (Brazil)

1986 MEXICO

GROUP A

Bulgaria **1-1** Italy
Argentina **3-1** South Korea
Italy **1-1** Argentina
Bulgaria **1-1** South Korea
Argentina **2-0** Bulgaria
Italy **3-2** South Korea

	P	W	D	L	F	A	Pts
Argentina	3	2	1	0	6	2	5
Italy	3	1	2	0	5	4	4
Bulgaria	3	0	2	1	2	4	2
South Korea	3	0	1	2	4	7	1

GROUP B

Mexico **2-1** Belgium
Paraguay **1-0** Iraq
Mexico **1-1** Paraguay
Belgium **2-1** Iraq
Paraguay **2-2** Belgium
Mexico **1-0** Iraq

	P	W	D	L	F	A	Pts
Mexico	3	2	1	0	4	2	5
Paraguay	3	1	2	0	4	3	4
Belgium	3	1	1	1	5	5	4
Iraq	3	0	0	3	1	4	0

GROUP C

Soviet Union **6-0** Hungary
France **1-0** Canada
Soviet Union **1-1** France
Hungary **2-0** Canada
France **3-0** Hungary
Soviet Union **2-0** Canada

	P	W	D	L	F	A	Pts
Soviet Union	3	2	1	0	9	1	5
France	3	2	1	0	5	1	5
Hungary	3	1	0	2	2	9	2
Canada	3	0	0	3	0	5	0

GROUP D

Brazil **1-0** Spain
N. Ireland **1-1** Algeria
Spain **2-1** N. Ireland
Brazil **1-0** Algeria
Spain **3-0** Algeria
Brazil **3-0** N. Ireland

	P	W	D	L	F	A	Pts
Brazil	3	3	0	0	5	0	6
Spain	3	2	0	1	5	2	4
N. Ireland	3	0	1	2	2	6	1
Algeria	3	0	1	2	1	5	1

GROUP E

West Germany **1-1** Uruguay
Denmark **1-0** Scotland
Denmark **6-1** Uruguay
West Germany **2-1** Scotland
Scotland **0-0** West Germany
Denmark **2-0** West Germany

	P	W	D	L	F	A	Pts
Denmark	3	3	0	0	9	1	6
West Germany	3	1	1	1	3	4	3
Uruguay	3	0	2	1	2	7	2
Scotland	3	0	1	2	1	3	1

GROUP F

Morocco **0-0** Poland
Portugal **1-0** England
England **0-0** Morocco
Poland **1-0** Portugal
England **3-0** Poland
Morocco **3-1** Portugal

	P	W	D	L	F	A	Pts
Morocco	3	1	2	0	3	1	4
England	3	1	1	1	3	1	3
Poland	3	1	1	1	1	3	3
Portugal	3	1	0	2	2	4	2

SECOND ROUND

Mexico **2-0** Bulgaria
Belgium **4-3** Soviet Union
(after extra time)
Brazil **4-0** Poland
Argentina **1-0** Uruguay
France **2-0** Italy
West Germany **1-0** Morocco
England **3-0** Paraguay
Spain **5-1** Denmark

THE WORLD CUP

QUARTER-FINALS

France **1-1** Brazil
(after extra time)
France won 4-3 on pens
West Germany **0-0** Mexico
(after extra time)
West Germany won 4-1 on pens
Argentina **2-1** England
Belgium **1-1** Spain
(after extra time)
Belgium won 5-4 on pens

SEMI-FINALS

Argentina **2-0** Belgium
(Maradona 51, 62)
West Germany **2-0** France
(Brehme 9, Völler 90)

THIRD PLACE PLAY-OFF

France **4-2** Belgium
(Ferreri 27,   *(Ceulemans 10,*
Papin 42,   *Claesen 73)*
Genghini 103,
Amoros 108)

FINAL

June 29 – Azteca, Mexico City
Argentina **3-2** West Germany
(Brown 22,   *(Rummenigge 73,*
Valdano 56,   *Völler 82)*
Burruchaga 84)
h/t: 1-0 **Att:** 114,590
Ref: Filho (Brazil)

1990 ITALY

GROUP A

Italy **1-0** Austria
Czechoslovakia **5-1** USA
Italy **1-0** USA
Czechoslovakia **1-0** Austria
Italy **2-0** Czechoslovakia
Austria **2-1** USA

	P	W	D	L	F	A	Pts
Italy	3	3	0	0	4	0	6
Czechoslovakia	3	2	0	1	6	3	4
Austria	3	1	0	2	2	3	2
USA	3	0	0	3	2	8	0

GROUP B

Cameroon **1-0** Argentina
Romania **2-0** Soviet Union
Argentina **2-0** Soviet Union
Cameroon **2-1** Romania
Argentina **1-1** Romania
Soviet Union **4-0** Cameroon

	P	W	D	L	F	A	Pts
Cameroon	3	2	0	1	3	5	4
Romania	3	1	1	1	4	3	3
Argentina	3	1	1	1	3	2	3
Soviet Union	3	1	0	2	4	4	2

GROUP C

Brazil **2-1** Sweden
Costa Rica **1-0** Scotland
Brazil **1-0** Costa Rica
Scotland **2-1** Sweden
Brazil **1-0** Scotland
Costa Rica **2-1** Sweden

	P	W	D	L	F	A	Pts
Brazil	3	3	0	0	4	1	6
Costa Rica	3	2	0	1	3	2	4
Scotland	3	1	0	2	2	3	2
Sweden	3	0	0	3	3	6	0

GROUP D

Colombia **2-0** UAE
West Germany **4-1** Yugoslavia
Yugoslavia **1-0** Colombia
West Germany **5-1** UAE
West Germany **1-1** Colombia
Yugoslavia **4-1** UAE

	P	W	D	L	F	A	Pts
West Germany	3	2	1	0	10	3	5
Yugoslavia	3	2	0	1	6	5	4
Colombia	3	1	1	1	3	2	3
UAE	3	0	0	3	2	11	0

GROUP E

Belgium **2-0** South Korea
Uruguay **0-0** Spain
Belgium **3-1** Uruguay
Spain **3-1** South Korea
Spain **2-1** Belgium
Uruguay **1-0** South Korea

	P	W	D	L	F	A	Pts
Spain	3	2	1	0	5	2	5
Belgium	3	2	0	1	6	3	4
Uruguay	3	1	1	1	2	3	3
South Korea	3	0	0	3	1	6	0

GROUP F

England **1-1** Rep. of Ireland
Netherlands **1-1** Egypt
England **0-0** Netherlands
Egypt **0-0** Rep. of Ireland
England **1-0** Egypt
Netherlands **1-1** Rep. of Ireland

	P	W	D	L	F	A	Pts
England	3	1	2	0	2	1	4
Netherlands	3	0	3	0	2	2	3
Rep. of Ireland	3	0	3	0	2	2	3
Egypt	3	0	2	1	1	2	2

SECOND ROUND

Cameroon **2-1** Colombia
(after extra time)
Czechoslovakia **4-1** Costa Rica
Argentina **1-0** Brazil
West Germany **2-1** Netherlands
Rep. of Ireland **0-0** Romania
(after extra time)
Rep. of Ireland won 5-4 on pens
Italy **2-0** Uruguay
Yugoslavia **2-1** Spain
(after extra time)
England **1-0** Belgium
(after extra time)

QUARTER-FINALS

Argentina **0-0** Yugoslavia
(after extra time)
Argentina won 3-2 on pens
Italy **1-0** Rep. of Ireland
West Germany **1-0** Czechoslovakia
England **3-2** Cameroon
(after extra time)

SEMI-FINALS

Argentina **1-1** Italy
(Caniggia 67)   *(Schillaci 17)*
(after extra time)
Argentina won 4-3 on pens
West Germany **1-1** England
(Brehme 59)   *(Lineker 80)*
(after extra time)
West Germany won 4-3 on pens

THIRD PLACE PLAY-OFF

Italy **2-1** England
(R. Baggio 71,   *(Platt 80)*
Schillaci 84)

FINAL

July 8 – Olimpico, Rome
West Germany **1-0** Argentina
(Brehme 84 pen)
h/t: 0-0 **Att:** 73,603
Ref: Codesal (Mexico)

1994 UNITED STATES

GROUP A

USA **1-1** Switzerland
Romania **3-1** Colombia
USA **2-1** Colombia
Switzerland **4-1** Romania
Romania **1-0** USA
Colombia **2-0** Switzerland

	P	W	D	L	F	A	Pts
Romania	3	2	0	1	5	5	6
Switzerland	3	1	1	1	5	4	4
USA	3	1	1	1	3	3	4
Colombia	3	1	0	2	4	5	3

GROUP B

Cameroon **2-2** Sweden
Brazil **2-0** Russia
Brazil **3-0** Cameroon
Sweden **3-1** Russia
Russia **6-1** Cameroon
Brazil **1-1** Sweden

	P	W	D	L	F	A	Pts
Brazil	3	2	1	0	6	1	7
Sweden	3	1	2	0	6	4	5
Russia	3	1	0	2	7	6	3
Cameroon	3	0	1	2	3	11	1

GROUP C

Germany **1-0** Bolivia
Spain **2-2** South Korea
Germany **1-1** Spain
South Korea **0-0** Bolivia
Spain **3-1** Bolivia
Germany **3-2** South Korea

	P	W	D	L	F	A	Pts
Germany	3	2	1	0	5	3	7
Spain	3	1	2	0	6	4	5
South Korea	3	0	2	1	4	5	2
Bolivia	3	0	1	2	1	4	1

GROUP D

Argentina **4-0** Greece
Nigeria **3-0** Bulgaria
Argentina **2-1** Nigeria
Bulgaria **4-0** Greece
Nigeria **2-0** Greece
Bulgaria **2-0** Argentina

	P	W	D	L	F	A	Pts
Nigeria	3	2	0	1	6	2	6
Bulgaria	3	2	0	1	6	3	6
Argentina	3	2	0	1	6	3	6
Greece	3	0	0	3	0	10	0

GROUP E

Rep. of Ireland **1-0** Italy
Norway **1-0** Mexico
Italy **1-0** Norway
Mexico **2-1** Rep. of Ireland
Rep. of Ireland **0-0** Norway
Italy **1-1** Mexico

	P	W	D	L	F	A	Pts
Mexico	3	1	1	1	3	3	4
Rep. of Ireland	3	1	1	1	2	2	4
Italy	3	1	1	1	2	2	4
Norway	3	1	1	1	1	1	4

GROUP F

Belgium **1-0** Morocco
Netherlands **2-1** Saudi Arabia
Belgium **1-0** Netherlands
Saudi Arabia **2-1** Morocco
Netherlands **2-1** Morocco
Saudi Arabia **1-0** Belgium

	P	W	D	L	F	A	Pts
Netherlands	3	2	0	1	4	3	6
Saudi Arabia	3	2	0	1	4	3	6
Belgium	3	2	0	1	2	1	6
Morocco	3	0	0	3	2	5	0

SECOND ROUND

Germany **3-2** Belgium
Spain **3-0** Switzerland
Sweden **3-1** Saudi Arabia
Romania **3-2** Argentina
Netherlands **2-0** Rep. of Ireland
Brazil **1-0** USA
Italy **2-1** Nigeria
(after extra time)
Bulgaria **1-1** Mexico
(after extra time)
Bulgaria won 3-1 on pens

QUARTER-FINALS

Italy **2-1** Spain
Brazil **3-2** Netherlands
Bulgaria **2-1** Germany
Sweden **2-2** Romania
(after extra time)
Sweden won 5-4 on pens

SEMI-FINALS

Brazil **1-0** Sweden
(Romario 80)
Italy **2-1** Bulgaria
(R. Baggio 21, 26)   *(Stoichkov 44 pen)*

THIRD PLACE PLAY-OFF

Sweden **4-0** Bulgaria
(Brolin 8,
Mild 30,
H. Larsson 37,
K. Andersson 39)

FINAL

July 17 – Rose Bowl, Pasadena
Brazil **0-0** Italy
(after extra time)
Brazil won 3-2 on pens
h/t: 0-0 **90 mins:** 0-0 **Att:** 94,000
Ref: Puhl (Hungary)

1998 FRANCE

GROUP A

Brazil **2-1** Scotland
Morocco **2-2** Norway
Brazil **3-0** Morocco
Scotland **1-1** Norway
Norway **2-1** Brazil
Morocco **3-0** Scotland

	P	W	D	L	F	A	Pts
Brazil	3	2	0	1	6	3	6
Norway	3	1	2	0	5	4	5
Morocco	3	1	1	1	5	5	4
Scotland	3	0	1	2	2	6	1

GROUP B

Italy **2-2** Chile
Austria **1-1** Cameroon
Chile **1-1** Austria
Italy **3-0** Cameroon
Chile **1-1** Cameroon
Italy **2-1** Austria

	P	W	D	L	F	A	Pts
Italy	3	2	1	0	7	3	7
Chile	3	0	3	0	4	4	3
Austria	3	0	2	1	3	4	2
Cameroon	3	0	2	1	2	5	2

GROUP C

Denmark **1-0** Saudi Arabia
France **3-0** South Africa
France **4-0** Saudi Arabia
South Africa **1-1** Denmark
France **2-1** Denmark
South Africa **2-2** Saudi Arabia

	P	W	D	L	F	A	Pts
France	3	3	0	0	9	1	9
Denmark	3	1	1	1	3	3	4
South Africa	3	0	2	1	3	6	2
Saudi Arabia	3	0	1	2	2	7	1

GROUP D

Paraguay **0-0** Bulgaria
Nigeria **3-2** Spain
Nigeria **1-0** Bulgaria
Spain **0-0** Paraguay
Paraguay **3-1** Nigeria
Spain **6-1** Bulgaria

	P	W	D	L	F	A	Pts
Nigeria	3	2	0	1	5	5	6
Paraguay	3	1	2	0	3	1	5
Spain	3	1	1	1	8	4	4
Bulgaria	3	0	1	2	1	7	1

GROUP E

Mexico **3-1** South Korea
Netherlands **0-0** Belgium
Belgium **2-2** Mexico
Netherlands **5-0** South Korea
Belgium **1-1** South Korea
Netherlands **2-2** Mexico

	P	W	D	L	F	A	Pts
Netherlands	3	1	2	0	7	2	5
Mexico	3	1	2	0	7	5	5
Belgium	3	0	3	0	3	3	3
South Korea	3	0	1	2	2	9	1

GROUP F

Germany **2-0** USA
Yugoslavia **1-0** Iran
Germany **2-2** Yugoslavia
Iran **2-1** USA
Germany **2-0** Iran
Yugoslavia **1-0** USA

	P	W	D	L	F	A	Pts
Germany	3	2	1	0	6	2	7
Yugoslavia	3	2	1	0	4	2	7
Iran	3	1	0	2	2	4	3
USA	3	0	0	3	1	5	0

GROUP G

England **2-0** Tunisia
Romania **1-0** Colombia
Colombia **1-0** Tunisia
Romania **2-1** England
Romania **1-1** Tunisia
England **2-0** Colombia

	P	W	D	L	F	∧	Pts
Romania	3	2	1	0	4	2	7
England	3	2	0	1	5	2	6
Colombia	3	1	0	2	1	3	3
Tunisia	3	0	1	2	1	4	1

GROUP H

Argentina **1-0** Japan
Croatia **3-1** Jamaica
Croatia **1-0** Japan
Argentina **5-0** Jamaica
Argentina **1-0** Croatia
Jamaica **2-1** Japan

	P	W	D	L	F	A	Pts
Argentina	3	3	0	0	7	0	9
Croatia	3	2	0	1	4	2	6
Jamaica	3	1	0	2	3	9	3
Japan	3	0	0	3	1	4	0

SECOND ROUND

Italy **1-0** Norway
Brazil **4-1** Chile
France **1-0** Paraguay
(after extra time)
Denmark **4-1** Nigeria
Germany **2-1** Mexico
Netherlands **2-1** Yugoslavia
Croatia **1-0** Romania
Argentina **2-2** England
(after extra time)
Argentina won 4-3 on pens

QUARTER-FINALS

France **0-0** Italy
(after extra time)
France won 4-3 on pens
Brazil **3-2** Denmark
Netherlands **2-1** Argentina
Croatia **3-0** Germany

SEMI-FINALS

Brazil **1-1** Netherlands
(Ronaldo 46)   *(Kluivert 87)*
(after extra time)
Brazil won 4-2 on pens
France **2-1** Croatia
(Thuram 47, 70)   *(Suker 46)*

THIRD PLACE PLAY-OFF

Croatia **2-1** Netherlands
(Prosinecki 13,   *(Zenden 21)*
Suker 36)

FINAL

July 12 – Stade St Denis, Paris
France 3-0 Brazil
(Zidane 27, 45,
Petit 90)
h/t: 2-0 **Att:** 75,000
Ref: Belqola (Morocco)

2002 JAPAN/KOREA

GROUP A

Senegal **1-0** France
Denmark **2-1** Uruguay
Denmark **1-1** Senegal
France **0-0** Uruguay
Denmark **2-0** France
Senegal **3-3** Uruguay

	P	W	D	L	F	A	Pts
Denmark	3	2	1	0	5	2	7
Senegal	3	1	2	0	5	4	5
Uruguay	3	0	2	1	4	5	2
France	3	0	1	2	0	3	1

GROUP B

Paraguay **2-2** South Africa
Spain **3-1** Slovenia
Spain **3-1** Paraguay
South Africa **1-0** Slovenia
Spain **3-2** South Africa
Paraguay **3-1** Slovenia

	P	W	D	L	F	A	Pts
Spain	3	3	0	0	9	4	9
Paraguay	3	1	1	1	6	6	4
South Africa	3	1	1	1	5	5	4
Slovenia	3	0	0	3	2	7	0

GROUP C

Brazil **2-1** Turkey
Costa Rica **2-0** China
Brazil **4-0** China
Costa Rica **1-1** Turkey
Brazil **5-2** Costa Rica
Turkey **3-0** China

	P	W	D	L	F	A	Pts
Brazil	3	3	0	0	11	3	9
Turkey	3	1	1	1	5	3	4
Costa Rica	3	1	1	1	5	6	4
China	3	0	0	3	0	9	0

GROUP D

South Korea **2-0** Poland
USA **3-2** Portugal
South Korea **1-1** USA
Portugal **4-0** Poland
South Korea **1-0** Portugal
Poland **3-1** USA

	P	W	D	L	F	A	Pts
South Korea	3	2	1	0	4	1	7
USA	3	1	1	1	5	6	4
Portugal	3	1	0	2	6	4	3
Poland	3	1	0	2	3	7	3

GROUP E

Rep. of Ireland **1-1** Cameroon
Germany **8-0** Saudi Arabia
Germany **1-1** Rep. of Ireland
Cameroon **1-0** Saudi Arabia
Germany **2-0** Cameroon
Rep. of Ireland **3-0** Saudi Arabia

	P	W	D	L	F	A	Pts
Germany	3	2	1	0	11	1	7
Rep. of Ireland	3	1	2	0	5	2	5
Cameroon	3	1	1	1	2	3	4
Saudi Arabia	3	0	0	3	0	12	0

GROUP F

England **1-1** Sweden
Argentina **1-0** Nigeria
Sweden **2-1** Nigeria
England **1-0** Argentina
Sweden **1-1** Argentina
England **0-0** Nigeria

	P	W	D	L	F	A	Pts
Sweden	3	1	2	0	4	3	5
England	3	1	2	0	2	1	5
Argentina	3	1	1	1	2	2	4
Nigeria	3	0	1	2	1	3	1

GROUP G

Mexico **1-0** Croatia
Italy **2-0** Ecuador
Croatia **2-1** Italy
Mexico **2-1** Ecuador
Italy **1-1** Mexico
Ecuador **1-0** Croatia

	P	W	D	L	F	A	Pts
Mexico	3	2	1	0	4	2	7
Italy	3	1	1	1	4	3	4
Croatia	3	1	0	2	2	3	3
Ecuador	3	1	0	2	2	4	3

GROUP H

Japan **2-2** Belgium
Russia **2-0** Tunisia
Japan **1-0** Russia
Tunisia **1-1** Belgium
Japan **2-0** Tunisia
Belgium **3-2** Russia

	P	W	D	L	F	A	Pts
Japan	3	2	1	0	5	2	7
Belgium	3	1	2	0	6	5	5
Russsia	3	1	0	2	4	4	3
Tunisia	3	0	1	2	1	5	1

SECOND ROUND

Germany **1-0** Paraguay
England **3-0** Denmark
Senegal **2-1** Sweden
(golden goal in extra time)
Spain **1-1** Rep. of Ireland
(after extra time)
Spain won 3-2 on pens
USA **2-0** Mexico
Brazil **2-0** Belgium
Turkey **1-0** Japan
South Korea **2-1** Italy
(golden goal in extra time)

QUARTER-FINALS

Brazil **2-1** England
Germany **1-0** USA
Spain **0-0** South Korea
(extra time)
South Korea won 5-3 on pens
Turkey **1-0** Senegal
(golden goal in extra time)

SEMI-FINALS

Germany **1-0** South Korea
(Ballack 78)
Brazil **1-0** Turkey
(Ronaldo 49)

THIRD PLACE PLAY-OFF

Turkey **3-2** South Korea
(Sukur 1,   *(Lee Eul-yong 9,*
Mansiz 13, 32)   *Song Chong-guk 93)*

FINAL

June 30 – Yokohama, Japan
Brazil 2-0 Germany
(Ronaldo 67, 79)
h/t: 0-0 **Att:** 70,000
Ref: Collina (Italy)

THE WORLD CUP

***The French team celebrates** its 3-0 victory over favourites Brazil in the 1998 Final.*

The Olympic Games

TOURNAMENT OVERVIEW

THE FOOTBALL TOURNAMENT at the Olympic Games has changed its status as a global tournament four or five times over its existence. As with all Olympic events, it began as a competition for national teams of amateurs only. As football became a professional sport all over the world, it inevitably collided with the Olympic amateur ethos. As football has acquired its own ruling body – FIFA – and its own global tournament – the World Cup – its relationship with the Olympics has become more complex.

At the earliest Olympics football was played as an exhibition sport. At the first modern Olympics in Athens in 1896, a tournament was played between a Danish XI, an Athenian XI and an Izmir XI (then a Greek area of Asian Turkey), but the records have been lost. In Paris in 1900 Upton Park FC (of east London) took on a French XI, while 1906 saw a rematch of the 1900 Games with the addition of a Thessaloniki XI (whose fixture with Athens descended into violence).

Football becomes official
Football became an official Olympic sport at the 1908 Games in London; it was in effect the first world football championship. With the exception of Egypt, who played at the 1920 games, this was an exclusively European affair until 1924. England and Denmark set the early pace contesting two Finals (1908 and 1912). The 1924 games in Paris saw the arrival of South American teams for the first time and a new global football power was revealed. The dazzling Uruguayans took the title with ease, while 1928 saw them triumph again, beating an equally fearsome Argentinian team in a replayed Final.

The 1932 Olympics in Los Angeles showed that the global spread of football had stopped at Ellis Island; there was no football tournament. By the time football returned to the Olympics in Berlin in 1936, professionalism had been legalized in most of the key footballing nations (England, Scotland, France, Uruguay, Argentina, Brazil, Italy and Spain) and two World Cups had been held; the status of Olympic football plummeted. For the next 30 years the tournament was effectively contested by the enduring amateur teams of Scandinavia and the state-sponsored amateurs of Eastern Europe; teams from these regions contested every Final from 1948 to 1980. This pattern was broken by FIFA's ban on players who had taken part in World Cup qualifiers from appearing at the Olympics – though this, of course, excluded some genuine amateurs.

The Africans are coming
The low to which the tournament had sunk has been redeemed by three changes. First, football's developing nations in Asia and Africa have taken an increasing interest and pride in Olympic performances and the global coverage it provides. Crowds for Olympic football at Seoul and Los Angeles were enormous and FIFA finally squared the amateurism circle by making the Olympic tournament an under-23 competition open to all players. Gold medals for Nigeria (1996) and Cameroon (2000) have kept global interest in the tournament alive.

In 1928 in Amsterdam the Uruguayans returned to the Olympics as holders. They were triumphant once again, beating the Netherlands 2-0, Germany 4-1 (pictured here, Uruguay in white), and Italy 3-2 on the way to the Final. There the team met its fellow South Americans from Argentina and triumphed 2-1 in a replay. This signalled a shift in the balance of power in world football from Europe to Latin America.

The Olympic Games Football Tournament

Number of appearances at Olympic Games

	10+ times
	7–9 times
	4–6 times
	1–3 times
	none

Olympic medals and date

- Gold
- Silver
- Bronze

VI*
1916* Games cancelled

XIX Host city and Olympiad number

● **Sydney** 2000 Location and year of Games

Montreal 1976 **XXI**

XXVI

Los Angeles 1932, 84 **X, XXIII**

Atlanta 1996

Mexico City 1968 **XIX**

GHANA 1992

BRAZIL 1984, 88 1996

CHILE 2000

URUGUAY 1924, 28

ARGENTINA 1928, 96

THE OLYMPIC GAMES

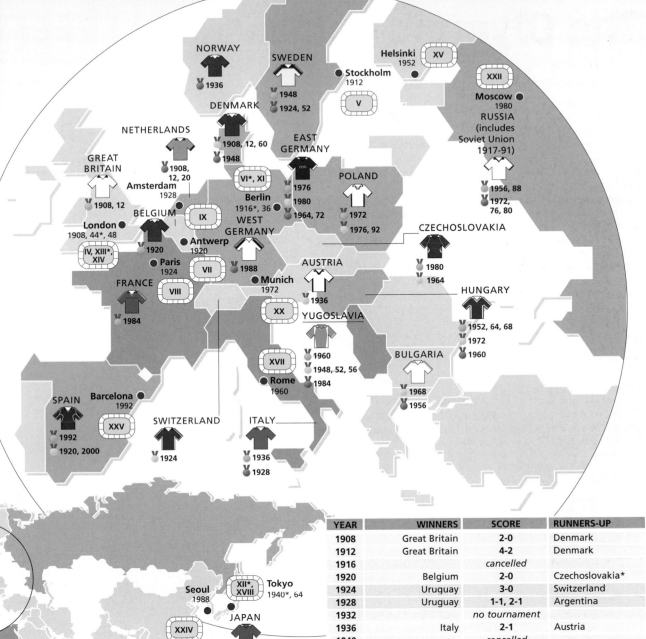

NORWAY
1936

SWEDEN
1948
1924, 52

Helsinki
1952

XV

Stockholm
1912

V

XXII

Moscow
1980
RUSSIA
(includes
Soviet Union
1917-91)

DENMARK
1908, 12, 60
1948

NETHERLANDS
1908,
12, 20

EAST
GERMANY
1976
1980
1964, 72

POLAND
1972
1976, 92

1956, 88
1972,
76, 80

GREAT
BRITAIN
1908, 12

Amsterdam
1928

VI*, XI

Berlin
1916*, 36

WEST
GERMANY

CZECHOSLOVAKIA
1980
1964

London
1908, 44*, 48

IV, XIII*
XIV

BELGIUM
1920

IX

Antwerp
1920

VII

AUSTRIA
1936

HUNGARY
1952, 64, 68
1972
1960

Paris
1924

1988

France
1984

VIII

Munich
1972

XX

YUGOSLAVIA
1960
1948, 52, 56
1984

BULGARIA
1968
1956

XVII

Rome
1960

SPAIN
1992
1920, 2000

Barcelona
1992

XXV

SWITZERLAND
1924

ITALY
1936
1928

Seoul
1988

XII*,
XVIII

Tokyo
1940*, 64

XXIV

JAPAN
1968

CAMEROON
2000

NIGERIA
1996

Melbourne
1956

Sydney
2000

XVI

XXVII

YEAR	WINNERS	SCORE	RUNNERS-UP
1908	Great Britain	2-0	Denmark
1912	Great Britain	4-2	Denmark
1916		cancelled	
1920	Belgium	2-0	Czechoslovakia*
1924	Uruguay	3-0	Switzerland
1928	Uruguay	1-1, 2-1	Argentina
1932		no tournament	
1936	Italy	2-1	Austria
1940		cancelled	
1944		cancelled	
1948	Sweden	3-1	Yugoslavia
1952	Hungary	2-0	Yugoslavia
1956	Soviet Union	1-0	Yugoslavia
1960	Yugoslavia	3-1	Denmark
1964	Hungary	2-1	Czechoslovakia
1968	Hungary	4-1	Bulgaria
1972	Poland	2-1	Hungary
1976	East Germany	3-1	Poland
1980	Czechoslovakia	1-0	East Germany
1984	France	2-0	Brazil
1988	Soviet Union	2-1	Brazil
1992	Spain	3-2	Poland
1996	Nigeria	3-2	Argentina
2000	Cameroon	2-2 (5-3 pens)	Spain

* In 1920 the silver medal was awarded to Spain after Czechoslovakia
was disqualified. Please see over for further details.

The Olympic Games

THE OLMYPIC GAMES

AT THE FIRST THREE OLYMPIADS, between 1896 and 1904, the format for the football tournament was eclectic to say the least, and included exhibition games and mini-leagues with selected XIs and local clubs. For example, at the 1900 Games in France, Club Français of Paris represented the hosts against Upton Park FC from Great Britain and a Belgian Student XI, and at St. Louis in 1904 two local teams, St. Rose Kickers FC and Christian Brothers College, lost to the Canadian side Galt FC. A more formal knockout competition was played between eight teams at the 1908 games, though only after the rest of the Olympics had finished.

In 1912 a consolation tournament for first round losers was also played so that teams that crossed the world would get more than a single game. Sixteen teams, including Egypt – the first team to represent Africa in the Olympic football tournament – played in 1920 at Antwerp. This format was maintained, with the addition of various preliminary rounds to even out the numbers, until the 1956 Melbourne games in Australia.

The Melbourne Olympic tournament was preceded by a qualifying tournament, and this was formalized for the 1960 Olympics with places being allocated to each FIFA football confederation. However, the greater willingness of developing nations to compete at the Olympics saw Africa and Asia gain more places than they did in the World Cup.

Under FIFA regulations the tournament has become an Under-23's World competition since 1992, though a number of over-age players may be included in squads.

1908 LONDON
SEMI-FINALS
Great Britain **4-0** Netherlands
Denmark **17-1** France A
THIRD PLACE PLAY-OFF
Netherlands **2-0** Sweden
France A refused to play
FINAL
October 24 – White City
Great Britain **2-0** Denmark
(Chapman 20,
Woodward 46)
h/t: 1-0 **Att:** 15,000
Ref: Lewis (Great Britain)

1912 STOCKHOLM
SEMI-FINALS
Great Britain **4-0** Finland
Denmark **4-1** Netherlands
THIRD PLACE PLAY-OFF
Netherlands **9-0** Finland
FINAL
July 4 – Olympic Stadium
Great Britain **4-2** Denmark
(Walden 10,   (Olsen 27, 81)
Hoare 22, 41,
Berry 43)
h/t: 4-1 **Att:** 25,000
Ref: Groothoof (Netherlands)

1920 ANTWERP
SEMI-FINALS
Belgium **3-0** Netherlands
Czechoslovakia **4-1** France
SECOND PLACE PLAY-OFF*
Spain **3-1** Netherlands
FINAL
September 5 – Olympisch
Belgium **2-0** Czechoslovakia**
(Coppee 6 pen,
Larnoe 30)
h/t: n/a **Att:** 35,000
Ref: Lewis (Great Britain)

* Spain won the silver medal after a special mini tournament.
** Match abandoned after 39 minutes. Czechoslovakia left the pitch complaining of biased refereeing and were disqualified.

1924 PARIS
SEMI-FINALS
Uruguay **2-1** Netherlands
Switzerland **2-1** Sweden
THIRD PLACE PLAY-OFF
Sweden **3-1** Netherlands
FINAL
June 9 – Colombes
Uruguay **3-0** Switzerland
(Petrone 27,
Cea 63,
Romano 81)
h/t: 1-0 **Att:** 41,000
Ref: Slawick (France)

1928 AMSTERDAM
SEMI-FINALS
Uruguay **3-2** Italy
Argentina **6-0** Egypt
THIRD PLACE PLAY-OFF
Italy **11-3** Egypt
FINAL
June 10 – Olympic Stadium
Uruguay **1-1** Argentina
(Ferreira)   (Petrone)
(after extra time)
h/t: n/a **Att:** n/a
Ref: Lewis (Great Britain)
REPLAY
June 13 – Olympic Stadium
Uruguay **2-1** Argentina
(Figueroa,   (Monti)
H. Scarone)
h/t: n/a **Att:** n/a
Ref: Mutter (Netherlands)

1932 LOS ANGELES
no football tournament

1936 BERLIN
SEMI-FINALS
Italy **2-1** Norway
Austria **3-1** Poland
THIRD PLACE PLAY-OFF
Norway **3-2** Poland
FINAL
August 16 – Olympia Stadion
Italy **2-1** Austria
(Frossi 70, 92)   (Kainberger 80)
(after extra time)
h/t: 0-0 **90 mins:** 1-1 **Att:** 90,000
Ref: Bauwens (Germany)

1948 LONDON
SEMI-FINALS
Sweden **4-2** Denmark
Yugoslavia **3-1** Great Britain
THIRD PLACE PLAY-OFF
Denmark **5-3** Great Britain
FINAL
August 13 – Wembley Stadium
Sweden **3-1** Yugoslavia
(Gren 24, 67)   (Bobek 42)
G. Nordahl 48)
h/t: 1-1 **Att:** 60,000
Ref: Ling (Great Britain)

1952 HELSINKI
SEMI-FINALS
Hungary **6-0** Sweden
Yugoslavia **3-1** West Germany
THIRD PLACE PLAY-OFF
Sweden **2-0** West Germany
FINAL
August 2 – Olympiastadion
Hungary **2-0** Yugoslavia
(Puskas 25,
Czibor 88)
h/t: 1-0 **Att:** 60,000
Ref: Ellis (Great Britain)

1956 MELBOURNE
SEMI-FINALS
Yugoslavia **4-1** India
Soviet Union **2-1** Bulgaria
THIRD PLACE PLAY-OFF
Bulgaria **3-0** India
FINAL
August 12 – Olympic Park
Soviet Union **1-0** Yugoslavia
(Ilyin 48)
h/t: 0-0 **Att:** 120,000
Ref: Wright (Australia)

1960 ROME
SEMI-FINALS
Yugoslavia **1-1** Italy
Yugoslavia won by drawing lots
Denmark **2-0** Hungary
THIRD PLACE PLAY-OFF
Hungary **2-1** Italy
FINAL
September 10 – Flaminio Stadium
Yugoslavia **3-1** Denmark
(Galic,   (F. Nielsen)
Matous,
Kostic)
h/t: n/a **Att:** 40,000
Ref: Lo Bello (Italy)

1964 TOKYO
SEMI-FINALS
Czechoslovakia **2-1** East Germany
Hungary **6-0** United Arab Republic
THIRD PLACE PLAY-OFF
East Germany **3-1** United Arab Republic
FINAL
October 23 – National Stadium
Hungary **2-1** Czechoslovakia
(Weiss o.g. 47,   (Brumousky 80)
Bene 59)
h/t: 1-0 **Att:** 75,000
Ref: Ashkenazi (Israel)

1968 MEXICO CITY
SEMI-FINALS
Hungary **5-0** Japan
Bulgaria **3-2** Mexico
THIRD PLACE PLAY-OFF
Japan **2-0** Mexico
FINAL
October 26 – Azteca Stadium
Hungary **4-1** Bulgaria
(Dimitrov 22,   (Menczel 40)
A. Dunai 41, 49,
Juhasz 62)
h/t: 2-1 **Att:** 75,000
Ref: Le de Diego (Mexico)

Olympic Games Winners

 England 1908, 12

 Belgium 1920

 Uruguay 1924, 28

 Italy 1936

 Sweden 1948

 Hungary 1952, 64, 68

 Soviet Union 1956, 88

 Yugoslavia 1960

 Poland 1972

 East Germany 1976

 Czechoslovakia 1980

 France 1984

 Spain 1992

Nigeria 1996

Cameroon 2000

1972 MUNICH

SECOND ROUND – GROUP A

Poland **2-1** Soviet Union
Poland **1-1** Denmark
Poland **5-0** Morocco
Soviet Union **4-0** Denmark
Soviet Union **3-0** Morocco
Denmark **3-1** Morocco

SECOND ROUND – GROUP B

Hungary **2-0** East Germany
Hungary **4-1** West Germany
Hungary **2-0** Mexico
East Germany **3-2** West Germany
East Germany **7-0** Mexico
West Germany **1-1** Mexico

THIRD PLACE PLAY-OFF

Soviet Union **2-2** East Germany
Bronze medal was shared

FINAL

September 10 – Olympic Stadium
Poland **2-1** Hungary
(Deyna 47, 68)   (Varadi 42)
h/t: 0-1 **Att:** 50,000
Ref: Tschenscher (West Germany)

1976 MONTREAL

SEMI-FINALS

East Germany **2-1** Soviet Union
Poland **2-0** Brazil A

THIRD PLACE PLAY-OFF

Soviet Union **2-0** Brazil A

FINAL

July 31 – Olympic Stadium
East Germany **3-1** Poland
(Schade 7,   (Lato 59)
Hoffmann 14,
Hofner 79)
h/t: 2-0 **Att:** 71,000
Ref: Barreto (Uruguay)

1980 MOSCOW

SEMI-FINALS

East Germany **1-0** Soviet Union
Czechoslovakia **2-0** Yugoslavia

THIRD PLACE PLAY-OFF

Soviet Union **2-0** Yugoslavia

FINAL

August 2 – Luzhniki Stadium
Czechoslovakia **1-0** East Germany
(Svoboda 77)
h/t: 0-0 **Att:** 70,000
Ref: Zade (Soviet Union)

1984 LOS ANGELES

SEMI-FINALS

France **4-2** Yugoslavia
Brazil **2-1** Italy

THIRD PLACE PLAY-OFF

Yugoslavia **2-1** Italy

FINAL

August 11 – Rose Bowl, Pasadena
France **2-0** Brazil
(Brisson 55,
Xuereb 62)
h/t: 0-0 **Att:** 101,000
Ref: Keizer (Netherlands)

1988 SEOUL

SEMI-FINALS

Soviet Union **3-2** Italy
Brazil **1-1** West Germany
Brazil won 3-2 on pens

THIRD PLACE PLAY-OFF

West Germany **3-0** Italy

FINAL

October 1 – Olympic Stadium
Soviet Union **2-1** Brazil
(Dobrovolski 61,   (Romario 30)
Savichev 103)
(after extra time)
h/t: 0-1 **90 mins:** 1-1 **Att:** 73,000
Ref: Bignet (France)

1992 BARCELONA

SEMI-FINALS

Poland **6-1** Australia
Spain **2-0** Ghana

THIRD PLACE PLAY-OFF

Ghana **1-0** Australia

FINAL

August 8 – Nou Camp
Spain **3-2** Poland
(Abelardo 65,   (Kowalczyk 44,
Quico 72, 90)   Staniek 76)
h/t: 0-1 **Att:** 95,000
Ref: Torres (Colombia)

1996 ATLANTA

SEMI-FINALS

Argentina **2-0** Portugal
Nigeria **4-3** Brazil

THIRD PLACE PLAY-OFF

Brazil **5-0** Portugal

FINAL

August 3 – Sanford Stadium
Nigeria **3-2** Argentina
(Babayaro 27,   (C. Lopez 3,
Amokachi 74,   Crespo pen 50)
Amunike 89)
h/t: 1-1 **Att:** 86,000
Ref: Collina (Italy)

2000 SYDNEY

SEMI-FINALS

Spain **3-1** USA
Cameroon **2-1** Chile

THIRD PLACE PLAY-OFF

Chile **2-0** USA

FINAL

September 30 – Olympic Stadium
Cameroon **2-2** Spain
(Amaya o.g. 53,   (Xavi 2,
Eto'o 58)   Gabri 45)
h-t: 0-2 **Att:** n/a
Ref: Rizo (Mexico)
Cameroon won 5-3 on pens

The victorious Nigerian team proudly shows off its gold medals after winning the Olympic football tournament at the 1996 Games in Atlanta in the United States. It beat a powerful Argentinian team 3-2 in the Final having already beaten Brazil 4-3 in the semi-final.

FIFA Club World Championship

TOURNAMENT OVERVIEW

THE FIRST FIFA Club World Championship was held in Brazil in January 2000. However, FIFA's attempt to create a truly global club tournament was plagued by problems and controversy from the start. Its place in an already congested football calendar saw Manchester United given permission to drop out of the English FA Cup and led to the adoption of a compressed schedule that made for slow play from tired players. Selection criteria for the teams in the tournament were also controversial. Outside of South America, teams came as continental champions. By contrast, neither South American team were continental champions: although Palmeiras of São Paulo were the champions in 2000, Corinthians of São Paulo came as Brazilian champions, while Vasco da Gama of Rio took the second spot as continental champions of 1999. The demands of television were equally problematic with European TV schedules requiring afternoon kick-offs, in immensely hot conditions, played in front of tiny crowds.

Creditable performances

More positively, the teams from Africa, Asia and Oceania all performed more than creditably, with none of the predicted walkover matches taking place. In Group A, Raja Casablanca of Morocco played above its usual standards and was desperately unlucky in its match against Corinthians to have Luciano's 68th-minute shot judged to have crossed the line. Replays show it clearly didn't. Raja Casablanca also scored twice against Real Madrid, before losing the match 3-2. Corinthians edged the group on goal difference. In Group B, Vasco just kept on winning while Manchester United (down to just 10 men after the dismissal of David Beckham) and Necaxa of Mexico scrapped it out for a 1-1 draw.

The Final between the two Brazilian sides was unfortunately and predictably a goalless and soulless affair, decided on penalties when Vasco's Edmundo shot wide.

2000 BRAZIL

GROUP A
All matches played in São Paulo

Real Madrid **3-1** Al Nassr

Corinthians **2-0** Raja Casablanca

Al Nassr **4-3** Raja Casablanca

Corinthians **2-2** Real Madrid

Real Madrid **3-2** Raja Casablanca

Corinthians **2-0** Al Nassr

	P	W	D	L	F	A	Pts
Corinthians	3	2	1	0	6	2	7
Real Madrid	3	2	1	0	8	5	7
Al Nassr	3	1	0	2	5	8	3
Raja Casablanca	3	0	0	3	5	9	0

GROUP B
All matches played in Rio de Janeiro

Necaxa **1-1** Manchester United

Vasco da Gama **2-0** South Melbourne

Necaxa **3-1** South Melbourne

Vasco da Gama **3-1** Manchester United

Manchester United **2-0** South Melbourne

Vasco da Gama **2-1** Necaxa

	P	W	D	L	F	A	Pts
Vasco da Gama	3	3	0	0	7	2	9
Necaxa	3	1	1	1	5	4	4
Manchester United	3	1	1	1	4	4	4
South Melbourne	3	0	0	3	1	7	0

THIRD PLACE PLAY-OFF
January 14 – Rio de Janeiro
Necaxa **1-1** Real Madrid
(Delgado 58)   (Raúl 15)
(after extra time)
Necaxa won 4-3 on pens

FINAL
January 14 – Rio de Janeiro
Corinthians **0-0** Vasco da Gama
(after extra time)
Corinthians won 4-3 on pens

h/t: 0-0
Ref: Dick Jol (Netherlands)

After a disastrous PR campaign in Brazil, which saw Manchester United roundly criticized in the press for training behind closed doors, David Beckham finally met some young Brazilian fans.

FIFA Club World Championship Competitors 2000

ENGLAND
SPAIN
MOROCCO
SAUDI ARABIA
MEXICO
BRAZIL
AUSTRALIA

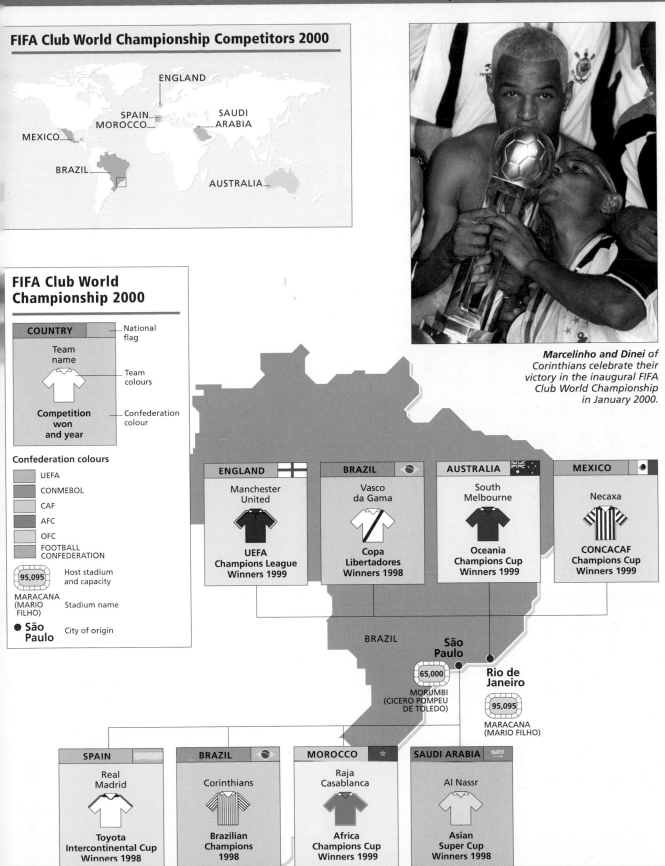

Marcelinho and Dinei of Corinthians celebrate their victory in the inaugural FIFA Club World Championship in January 2000.

FIFA CLUB WORLD CHAMPIONSHIP

FIFA Club World Championship 2000

COUNTRY	— National flag
Team name	— Team colours
Competition won and year	— Confederation colour

Confederation colours

- UEFA
- CONMEBOL
- CAF
- AFC
- OFC
- FOOTBALL CONFEDERATION

95,095 Host stadium and capacity

MARACANA (MARIO FILHO) — Stadium name

● **São Paulo** — City of origin

ENGLAND	BRAZIL	AUSTRALIA	MEXICO
Manchester United	Vasco da Gama	South Melbourne	Necaxa
UEFA Champions League Winners 1999	**Copa Libertadores Winners 1998**	**Oceania Champions Cup Winners 1999**	**CONCACAF Champions Cup Winners 1999**

BRAZIL

São Paulo

65,000

MORUMBI (CICERO POMPEU DE TOLEDO)

Rio de Janeiro

95,095

MARACANA (MARIO FILHO)

SPAIN	BRAZIL	MOROCCO	SAUDI ARABIA
Real Madrid	Corinthians	Raja Casablanca	Al Nassr
Toyota Intercontinental Cup Winners 1998	**Brazilian Champions 1998**	**Africa Champions Cup Winners 1999**	**Asian Super Cup Winners 1998**

The World Club Cup

TOURNAMENT OVERVIEW

THE WORLD CLUB CUP was originally known as the Copa Internacional in Latin America and the Intercontinental Cup in Europe. Henri Delaunay, the then general secretary of UEFA, originally proposed it in 1958 as an annual contest between the champions of the two major footballing continents. With the advent of the Copa Libertadores in Latin America in 1960, following the creation of the European Cup in 1956, an intercontinental championship was finally possible, and the first contest, between Real Madrid and Peñarol, was held in 1960 over two legs, Real winning 5-1 in Madrid after a 0-0 draw in Uruguay.

In the late 1960s and early 1970s, the World Club Cup began to acquire a reputation for on-field violence, particularly matches featuring the Argentinian team Estudiantes. As a

consequence a number of European champions refused to take their place, which was then taken up by the European Cup runners-up – this included Panathinaikos instead of Ajax in 1971, Juventus over Ajax in 72, Atlético Madrid over Bayern München in 74, Borussia Mönchengladbach over Liverpool in 77 and Malmö rather than Nottingham Forest in 1979.

The potential demise of the fixture was halted by transforming the contest into a single match, with extra time and penalties, played in the national stadium in Tokyo and the acquisition of Toyota as sponsors. However, with the creation in 2000 of FIFA's Club World Championship, which is played on a biennial basis, it is not clear whether the World Club Cup can survive in an already congested calendar for the top clubs.

The World Club Cup

CONMEBOL	UEFA	
		Winners
		Runners-up
		Members
		Non-members

Team details

ARGENTINA — Country
● **Buenos Aires** — City of origin
River Plate — Team name

— Team colours

1986, — Winners in bold
96 — Runners-up in italics

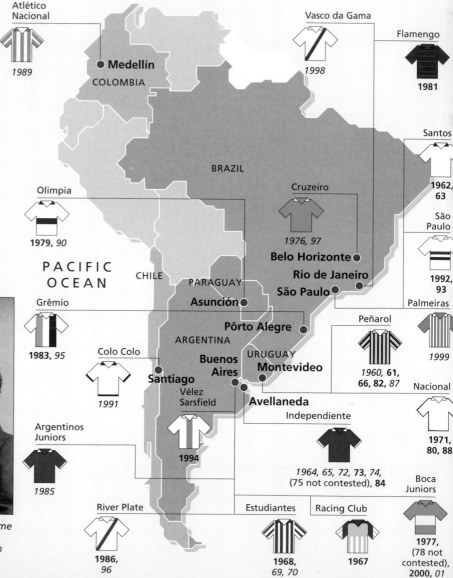

Atlético Nacional — ● **Medellín** — COLOMBIA — *1989*

Vasco da Gama — *1998*

Flamengo — **1981**

Santos — **1962, 63**

BRAZIL

Cruzeiro — *1976, 97*

São Paulo — **1992, 93**

Olimpia — **1979,** *90*

Belo Horizonte
Rio de Janeiro
São Paulo

Palmeiras — *1999*

PACIFIC OCEAN

CHILE

PARAGUAY

Grêmio — **1983,** *95*

Asunción

Peñarol — *1960,* **61,** *66, 82,* **87**

Pôrto Alegre

ARGENTINA

Colo Colo — *1991*

Buenos Aires

URUGUAY
Montevideo

Nacional — **1971, 80, 88**

Santiago

Vélez Sarsfield — **1994**

Avellaneda
Independiente — *1964,* **65, 72,** *73, 74,* (75 not contested), **84**

Argentinos Juniors — *1985*

River Plate — **1986,** *96*

Estudiantes — **1968,** *69, 70*

Racing Club — **1967**

Boca Juniors — *1977,* (78 not contested), **2000,** *01*

Members of the victorious Milan team, some showing signs of battle, on their return to Italy after their Final against Estudiantes in 1969, a match famous for its violence.

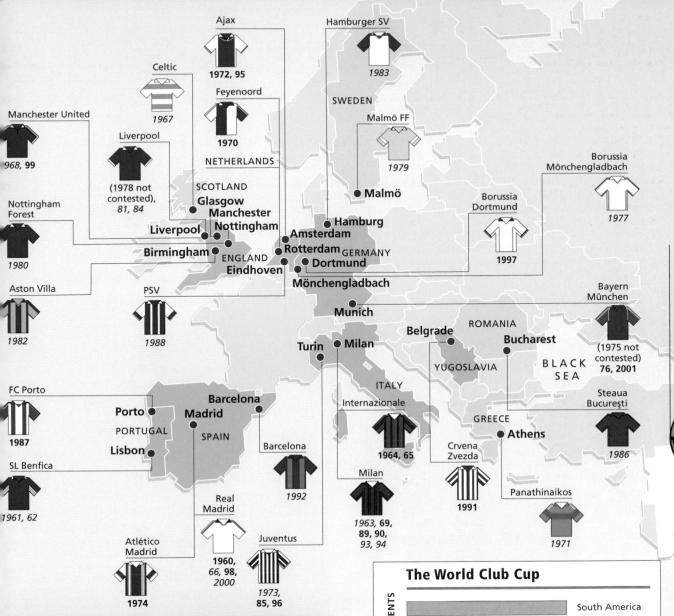

Ajax
1972, 95

Hamburger SV
1983

Celtic
1967

Feyenoord
1970

NETHERLANDS

Malmö FF
1979

SWEDEN

Borussia
Mönchengladbach
1977

Manchester United
968, 99

Liverpool
(1978 not
contested),
81, 84

SCOTLAND
Glasgow
Manchester
Liverpool   Nottingham
Birmingham
ENGLAND
Eindhoven

Hamburg
Amsterdam
Rotterdam GERMANY
Dortmund
Mönchengladbach

Malmö

Borussia
Dortmund
1997

Nottingham
Forest
1980

Aston Villa
1982

PSV
1988

Munich

Belgrade

ROMANIA
Bucharest

Turin **Milan**

YUGOSLAVIA

B L A C K
S E A

Bayern
München
(1975 not
contested)
76, 2001

FC Porto
1987

Barcelona
Porto   Madrid
PORTUGAL
Lisbon
SPAIN

ITALY
Internazionale
1964, 65

GREECE
Athens

Crvena
Zvezda
1991

Steaua
Bucureşti
1986

SL Benfica
1961, 62

Barcelona
1992

Milan
1963, 69,
89, 90,
93, 94

Panathinaikos
1971

Atlético
Madrid
1974

Real
Madrid
1960,
66, 98,
2000

Juventus
1973,
85, 96

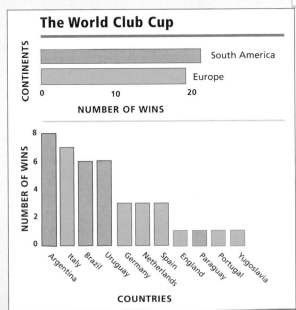

The World Club Cup

CONTINENTS

South America

Europe

0   10   20

NUMBER OF WINS

NUMBER OF WINS

8
6
4
2
0

Argentina Italy Brazil Uruguay Germany Netherlands Spain England Paraguay Portugal Yugoslavia

COUNTRIES

*Clarence Seedorf of Real Madrid in action against Vasco da Gama
of Brazil in the 1998 Final which Real won 2-1. Despite the high
profile of its contestants, the World Club Cup is in danger of
being sidelined in an already crowded football calendar.*

The World Club Cup

AN ANNUAL PLAY-OFF BETWEEN the winners of the European Champions League (formerly the European Cup) and the Copa Libertadores, the format of the World Club Cup and its earlier incarnation, the Intercontinental Cup, has been changed on a number of occasions since its inception in 1960, though extra time and then penalties have always decided matches ending in a draw. The Cup began as a two-leg affair at the two finalists' home grounds. If both sides had won one match, irrespective of aggregate scores over the two games, then a replay was deemed necessary to decide the winners (see 1961, 63, 64 and 67). The fixture acquired a well-deserved reputation for aggressive, even violent play, beginning with the Milan v Santos games in 1963 and peaking in the finals contested by Estudiantes of Argentina between 1968 and 1970.

Between 1969 and 1979 the two-leg format was retained, but aggregate scores determined the winner. However, this change of format couldn't help an ailing fixture that European champions refused to contest.

In 1980, with a new Japanese sponsor, the format shifted to a single match played at the national stadium in Tokyo. With the creation of the more global Club World Championship, the future of this cup competition is increasingly uncertain.

1960 FINAL (2 legs)

July 3 – Centenario, Montevideo
Peñarol 0-0 Real Madrid
(Uruguay)   (Spain)

September 4 – Santiago Bernabeu, Madrid
Real Madrid 5-1 Peñarol
(Puskas 3, 9,   (Borges 69)
di Stefano 4,
Herrera 44,
Gento 54)

Real Madrid won 5-1 on aggregate

1961 FINAL (2 legs)

September 17 – Estadio da Luz, Lisbon
SL Benfica 1-0 Peñarol
(Portugal)   (Uruguay)
(Coluna 60)

September 17 – Centenario, Montevideo
Peñarol 5-0 SL Benfica
(Sasia 10,
Joya 18, 28,
Spencer 42, 60)

PLAY-OFF

September 19 – Centenario, Montevideo
Peñarol 2-1 SL Benfica
(Sasia 6, 41)   (Eusebio 35)

1962 FINAL (2 legs)

September 19 – Maracana, Rio de Janeiro
Santos 3-2 SL Benfica
(Brazil)   (Portugal)
(Pele 31, 86,   (Santana 58, 87)
Coutinho 64)

October 11 – Estadio da Luz, Lisbon
SL Benfica 2-5 Santos
(Eusebio 87,   (Pele 17, 28, 64,
Santana 89)   Coutinho 49,
                        Pepe 77)

Santos won 8-4 on aggregate

1963 FINAL (2 legs)

October 16 – San Siro, Milan
Milan 4-2 Santos
(Italy)   (Brazil)
(Trappattoni 4,   (Pele 59, 87)
Amarildo 15, 65,
Mora 80)

November 14 – Maracana, Rio de Janeiro
Santos 4-2 Milan
(Pepe 50, 67,   (Altafini 12,
Almir 63,   Mora 17)
Lima 63)

PLAY-OFF

November 16 – Maracana, Rio de Janeiro
Santos 1-0 Milan
(Dalmo 26)

1964 FINAL (2 legs)

September 9 – Cordero, Avellaneda
Independiente 1-0 Internazionale
(Argentina)   (Italy)
(Rodriguez 60)

September 23 – San Siro, Milan
Internazionale 2-0 Independiente
(Mazzola 8,
Corso 39)

PLAY-OFF

September 26 – Santiago Bernabeu, Madrid
Internazionale 1-0 Independiente
(Corso 120)
(after extra time)

1965 FINAL (2 legs)

September 8 – San Siro, Milan
Internazionale 3-0 Independiente
(Italy)   (Argentina)
(Peiro 3,
Mazzola 23, 61)

September 15 – Cordero, Avellaneda
Independiente 0-0 Internazionale

Internazionale won 3-0 on aggregate

1966 FINAL (2 legs)

October 12 – Centenario, Montevideo
Peñarol 2-0 Real Madrid
(Uruguay)   (Spain)
(Spencer 39, 82)

October 26 – Santiago Bernabeu, Madrid
Real Madrid 0-2 Peñarol
(Rocha 28,
Spencer 37)

Peñarol won 4-0 on aggregate

1967 FINAL (2 legs)

October 18 – Hampden Park, Glasgow
Celtic 1-0 Racing Club
(Scotland)   (Argentina)
(McNeill 67)

November 1 – Mozart y Cuyo, Avellaneda
Racing Club 2-1 Celtic
(Raffo 32,   (Gemmell 20)
Cardenas 65)

PLAY-OFF

November 4 – Centenario, Montevideo
Racing Club 1-0 Celtic
(Cardenas 55)

1968 FINAL (2 legs)

September 25 –
Bombonera, Buenos Aires
**Estudiantes 1-0 Manchester
de la Plata   United**
(Argentina)   (England)
(Conigliaro 28)

October 16 – Old Trafford, Manchester
**Manchester 1-1 Estudiantes
United   de la Plata**
(Morgan 8)   (Veron 5)

Estudiantes de la Plata won 2-1
on aggregate

1969 FINAL (2 legs)

October 8 – San Siro, Milan
Milan 3-0 Estudiantes
(Italy)   de la Plata
(Sormani 8, 73,   (Argentina)
Combin 44)

October 22 – Bombonera, Buenos Aires
**Estudiantes 2-1 Milan
de la Plata   (Rivera 30)**
(Conigliaro 43,
Aguirre
Suarez 44)

Milan won 4-2 on aggregate

1970 FINAL (2 legs)

August 26 – Bombonera, Buenos Aires
**Estudiantes 2-2 Feyenoord
de la Plata   (Netherlands)**
(Argentina)   (Kindvall 21,
(Echecopar 6,   Van Hanegem 65)
Veron 10)

September 9 –
Feyenoord Stadium, Rotterdam
Feyenoord 1-0 Estudiantes
(Van Daele 65)   de la Plata

Feyenoord won 3-2 on aggregate

1971 FINAL (2 legs)

December 15 – OAKA 'Spiros Louis', Athens
Panathinaikos 1-1 Nacional
(Greece)   Montevideo
(Filakouris 48)   (Uruguay)
                        (Artime 50)

December 29 – Centenario, Montevideo
**Nacional 2-1 Panathinaikos
Montevideo   (Filakouris 89)**
(Artime 34, 75)

Nacional Montevideo won 3-2
on aggregate

1972 FINAL (2 legs)

September 6 – Mozart y Cuyo, Avellaneda
Independiente 1-1 Ajax
(Argentina)   (Netherlands)
(Sa 82)   (Cruyff 6)

September 28 –
Olympish Stadion, Amsterdam
Ajax 3-0 Independiente
(Neeskens 12,
Rep 16, 78)

Ajax won 4-1 on aggregate

1973 FINAL

November 28 – Stadio Olimpico, Rome
Independiente 1-0 Juventus
(Argentina)   (Italy)
(Bochini 40)

1974 FINAL (2 legs)

March 12 – Mozart y Cuyo, Avellaneda
Independiente 1-0 Atlético
(Argentina)   Madrid
(Balbuena 33)   (Spain)

April 10 – Vicente Calderon, Madrid
**Atlético 2-0 Independiente
Madrid**
(Irureta 21,
Ayala 86)

Atlético Madrid won 2-1 on aggregate

1975 FINAL

**Bayern   v   Independiente
München   (Argentina)**
(West Germany)
not contested

1976 FINAL (2 legs)

November 23 – Olympiastadion, Munich
**Bayern 2-0 Cruzeiro
München   (Brazil)**
(West Germany)
(Müller 80,
Kappellmann 83)

December 21 – Mineirao, Belo Horizonte
**Cruzeiro 0-0 Bayern
München**

Bayern München won 2-0 on aggregate

1977 FINAL (2 legs)

March 22 – Bombonera, Buenos Aires
**Boca Juniors 2-2 Borussia
(Argentina)   Mönchen-
(Mastrangelo 16,   gladbach
Ribolzi 51)   (West Germany)
                        (Hannes 24,
                        Bonhof 29)**

THE WORLD CLUB CUP

March 26 – Wildpark Stadion, Karlsruhe
Borussia **0-3** Boca
Mönchen-   Juniors
gladbach   *(Zanabria 2,*
                Mastrangelo 33,
                Salinas 35)

Boca Juniors won 5-2 on aggregate

1978 FINAL

Liverpool v Boca Juniors
(England)   (Argentina)
not contested

1979 FINAL (2 legs)

November 18 – Malmö Stadion, Malmö
Malmö FF **0-1** Olimpia
(Sweden)   (Paraguay)
                (Isasi 41)

March 3 – Manuel Ferreira, Asunción
Olimpia **2-1** Malmö FF
(Solalinde 40 pen,   *(Earlandsson 48)*
Michelagnoli 71)

Olimpia won 3-1 on aggregate

1980 FINAL

February 11 – National Stadium, Tokyo
Nacional **1-0** Nottingham
(Uruguay)   Forest
(Victorino 10) (England)

1981 FINAL

December 13 – National Stadium, Tokyo
Flamengo **3-0** Liverpool
(Brazil)   (England)
(Nunes 13, 41,
Adilio 34)

1982 FINAL

December 12 – National Stadium, Tokyo
Peñarol **2-0** Aston Villa
(Uruguay)   (England)
(Jair 27,
Charrua 68)

1983 FINAL

December 11 – National Stadium, Tokyo
Grêmio **2-1** Hamburger SV
(Brazil)   (West Germany)
(Renato 37, 93)   *(Schröder 85)*

1984 FINAL

December 9 – National Stadium, Tokyo
Independiente **1-0** Liverpool
(Argentina)   (England)
(Percudiani 6)

1985 FINAL

December 8 – National Stadium, Tokyo
Juventus **2-2** Argentinos
(Italy)   Juniors
(Platini 63,   (Argentina)
M. Laudrup 82) *(Ereros 55,*
                  Castro 75)

Juventus won 4-2 on pens

1986 FINAL

December 14 – National Stadium, Tokyo
River Plate **1-0** Steaua
(Argentina)   Bucureşti
(Alzamendi 28) (Romania)

1987 FINAL

December 13 – National Stadium, Tokyo
FC Porto **2-1** Peñarol
(Portugal)   (Uruguay)
(Gomes 41,   *(Viera 80)*
Madjer 108)

(after extra time)

1988 FINAL

December 11 – National Stadium, Tokyo
Nacional **2-2** PSV
(Uruguay)   (Netherlands)
(Ostolaza 7, 119) *(Romario 75,*
                     R. Koeman 109)

(after extra time)

Nacional won 7-6 on pens

1989 FINAL

December 17 – National Stadium, Tokyo
Milan **1-0** Atlético
(Italy)   Nacional
(Evani 118) (Colombia)

1990 FINAL

December 9 – National Stadium, Tokyo
Milan **3-0** Olimpia
(Italy)   (Paraguay)
(Rijkaard 43, 65,
Stroppa 62)

1991 FINAL

December 8 – National Stadium, Tokyo
Crvena Zvezda **3-0** Colo Colo
(Yugoslavia)   (Chile)
(Jugovic 19, 58,
Pancev 72)

1992 FINAL

December 13 – National Stadium, Tokyo
São Paulo **2-1** Barcelona
(Brazil)   (Spain)
(Rai 26, 79)   *(Stoichkov 13)*

1993 FINAL

December 12 – National Stadium, Tokyo
São Paulo **3-2** Milan
(Brazil)   (Italy)
(Palinha 20,   *(Massaro 48,*
Cerezo 59,   *Papin 82)*
Müller 86)

1994 FINAL

December 1 – National Stadium, Tokyo
Vélez Sarsfield **2-0** Milan
(Argentina)   (Italy)
(Trotta 50 pen,
Asad 57)

1995 FINAL

November 28 – National Stadium, Tokyo
Ajax **0-0** Grêmio
(Netherlands)   (Brazil)
(after extra time)

Ajax won 4-3 on pens

1996 FINAL

November 26 – National Stadium, Tokyo
Juventus **1-0** River Plate
(Italy)   (Argentina)
(Del Piero 82)

1997 FINAL

December 2 – National Stadium, Tokyo
Borussia **2-0** Cruzeiro
Dortmund   (Brazil)
(Germany)
(Zorc 34,
Herrlich 85)

1998 FINAL

December 1 – National Stadium, Tokyo
Real Madrid **2-1** Vasco da Gama
(Spain)   (Brazil)
(Nasa o.g. 26, *(Juninho 56)*
Raúl 82)

1999 FINAL

November 30 – National Stadium, Tokyo
Manchester **1-0** Palmeiras
United   (Brazil)
(England)
(Keane 35)

2000 FINAL

November 28 – National Stadium, Tokyo
Boca Juniors **2-1** Real Madrid
(Argentina)   (Spain)
(Palermo 2, 5)   *(Roberto Carlos 11)*

2001 FINAL

November 27 – National Stadium, Tokyo
Bayern **1-0** Boca Juniors
München   (Argentina)
(Germany)
(Kuffour 109)

(after extra time)

Real Madrid's Roberto Carlos (left, white shirt) shoots past Oscar Cordoba, the Boca Juniors goalkeeper, in the 11th minute of the 2000 World Club Cup Final. However, Boca, for whom Martin Palermo scored twice in the first five minutes, held on to win 2-1.

THE WORLD CLUB CUP

43

Women's Football

WORLD CUP AND OLYMPIC FOOTBALL

PICTURES FROM CHINA during the Han Dynasty (206 BC–221 AD) clearly show women playing rudimentary forms of football, but other evidence of early participation in the game is rare. The male predominance at English public schools gave the boys 30 years head start when the new codified rules were drawn up in 1863. The catch up began with the first recorded women's football match under FA rules played on 23 March 1895, at Crouch End in North London, when South of England beat North of England 7-1. However, the backlash soon arrived in the shape of systematic opposition to women's football from the male football establishment all over Europe.

In 1896, the Dutch football authority, KNVB, banned a women's match between a Sparta Rotterdam XI and an England XI and followed this up with a ban on women's games at any stadium of a club affiliated to it. Similar policies of exclusion were pursued by the English FA and by the German FA, the DFB, who banned women from affiliated stadiums in the 1950s. Medical, social and footballing commentators claimed that football was detrimental to the moral and physical health of women.

Despite all this, women's football grew in popularity and with the massive flow of European women into industrial employment during the First World War, players and teams multiplied. In fact, so great was the growth of women's football that the English FA moved to a stadium ban for women's teams in 1920, and women's football was forced into the world of exhibition matches and charity events. Dick Kerr's Ladies, a Preston-based factory team, played to large audiences in the 1920s, while Manchester Corinthians was the leading women's club in England in the 1940s and 50s.

The tide turns

Independent attempts to organize international women's football began with the creation of the International Ladies Football Association in 1957 and a Women's European Championship won by Manchester Corinthians. The Italian-based CIEFF was formed in 1969 and held informal women's world cups, the Mundialato, in Italy in 1970 and Mexico in 1971. Driven by fear of losing control and by some dim recognition that women's football was a significant sporting force, FIFA and UEFA acted. UEFA called for all member nation's FAs to incorporate women's football into the mainstream of the game (though in England this took until 1993).

In terms of participation and sporting success women's football has three strongholds: North America, China and Northern Europe. In America and China, the relative weakness of men's football has created the space in which women's football could grow. In northern Europe, the egalitarianism and social engineering of social democratic governments has helped promote women's football. Not surprisingly then these regions have hosted the official FIFA Women's World Cup and contested its Finals (as well as the Olympic Finals). As the women's game grows, professional leagues are beginning to emerge. The first, in Japan in 1993, has been joined by leagues in the USA, England and other countries.

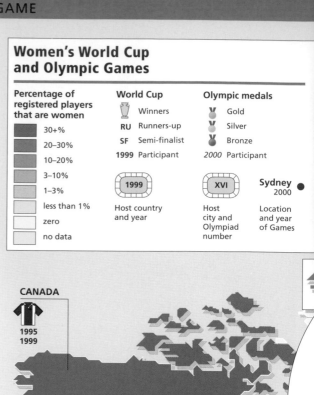

Women's World Cup and Olympic Games

Percentage of registered players that are women			
30+%			
20–30%			
10–20%			
3–10%			
1–3%			
less than 1%			
zero			
no data			

World Cup
- Winners
- RU Runners-up
- SF Semi-finalist
- 1999 Participant

Olympic medals
- Gold
- Silver
- Bronze
- 2000 Participant

1999 — Host country and year

XVI — Host city and Olympiad number

Sydney 2000 — Location and year of Games

CANADA — 1995 1999

USA — 1991, 1995 SF, 1996, 1999, 2000 — 1999

MEXICO — 1999

XXVI — Atlanta 1996

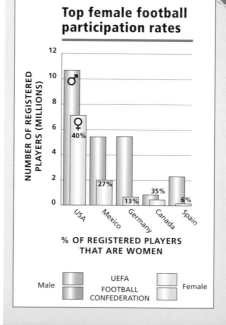

Top female football participation rates

NUMBER OF REGISTERED PLAYERS (MILLIONS)

♂ ♀ 40%

USA — 40%
Mexico — 27%
Germany — 13%
Canada — 35%
Spain — 6%

% OF REGISTERED PLAYERS THAT ARE WOMEN

Male — UEFA FOOTBALL CONFEDERATION — Female

WOMEN'S FOOTBALL

The Preston Ladies football team prepares for a European tour at Bedford in 1939. Though women's football was confined to exhibition matches and charity events during the 1930s and 40s, it remained hugely popular with players and spectators, and tours such as this were regular events.

With players like Sun Wen, recently voted FIFA's Woman Player of the Century, China is one of the leading forces in women's football, along with the other strongholds in the USA and Northern Europe.

WOMEN'S FOOTBALL

NORWAY
1991 RU
1995
1996
1999 SF
2000

SWEDEN
1991 SF
1995
1996
1999
2000

1995

GERMANY
1991 SF
1995 RU
1996
1999
2000

DENMARK
1991
1995
1996
1999

RUSSIA
1999

NORTH KOREA
1999

JAPAN
1991
1995
1996
1999

ENGLAND
1995

ITALY
1991
1996

TAIWAN
1991

GHANA
1999

CHINA
1991
1995 SF
1996
1999 RU
2000

1991

BRAZIL
1991
1995
1996
1999 SF
2000

NIGERIA
1991
1995
1999
2000

AUSTRALIA
1995
1999
2000

Sydney
2000
XXVII

NEW ZEALAND
1991

Women's World Cup Finals (1991–99)

YEAR	WINNERS	SCORE	RUNNERS-UP
1991	USA	2-1	Norway
1995	Norway	5-2	Germany
1999	USA	0-0 (5-4 pens)	China

Women's Olympic Finals (1996–2000)

YEAR	WINNERS	SCORE	RUNNERS-UP
1996	USA	2-1	China
2000	Norway	3-2	USA

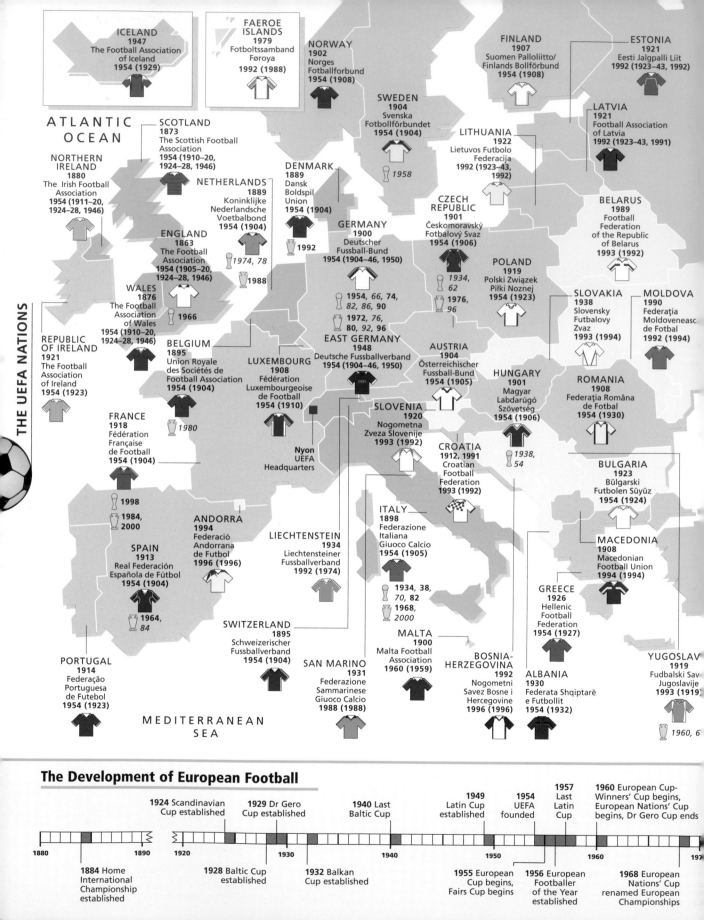

ICELAND
1947
The Football Association of Iceland
1954 (1929)

FAEROE ISLANDS
1979
Fotboltssamband Føroya
1992 (1988)

NORWAY
1902
Norges Fotballforbund
1954 (1908)

FINLAND
1907
Suomen Palloliitto/ Finlands Bollförbund
1954 (1908)

ESTONIA
1921
Eesti Jalgpalli Liit
1992 (1923–43, 1992)

ATLANTIC OCEAN

SCOTLAND
1873
The Scottish Football Association
1954 (1910–20, 1924–28, 1946)

SWEDEN
1904
Svenska Fotbollförbundet
1954 (1904)

1958

LATVIA
1921
Football Association of Latvia
1992 (1923–43, 1991)

LITHUANIA
1922
Lietuvos Futbolo Federacija
1992 (1923–43, 1992)

NORTHERN IRELAND
1880
The Irish Football Association
1954 (1911–20, 1924–28, 1946)

NETHERLANDS
1889
Koninklijke Nederlandsche Voetbalbond
1954 (1904)

DENMARK
1889
Dansk Boldspil Union
1954 (1904)

CZECH REPUBLIC
1901
Českomoravský Fotbalový Svaz
1954 (1906)

BELARUS
1989
Football Federation of the Republic of Belarus
1993 (1992)

1992

ENGLAND
1863
The Football Association
1954 (1905–20, 1924–28, 1946)

1974, 78

1988

GERMANY
1900
Deutscher Fussball-Bund
1954 (1904–46, 1950)

1954, *66*, **74**, *82*, **86**, **90**

1972, *76*, **80**, *92*, **96**

1934, 62

1976, *96*

POLAND
1919
Polski Związek Piłki Nożnej
1954 (1923)

SLOVAKIA
1938
Slovensky Futbalovy Zvaz
1993 (1994)

MOLDOVA
1990
Federaţia Moldovenească de Fotbal
1992 (1994)

WALES
1876
The Football Association of Wales
1954 (1910–20, 1924–28, 1946)

1966

BELGIUM
1895
Union Royale des Sociétés de Football Association
1954 (1904)

LUXEMBOURG
1908
Fédération Luxembourgeoise de Football
1954 (1910)

EAST GERMANY
1948
Deutsche Fussballverband
1954 (1904–46, 1950)

AUSTRIA
1904
Österreichischer Fussball-Bund
1954 (1905)

HUNGARY
1901
Magyar Labdarúgó Szövetség
1954 (1906)

1938, 54

ROMANIA
1908
Federaţia Română de Fotbal
1954 (1930)

REPUBLIC OF IRELAND
1921
The Football Association of Ireland
1954 (1923)

FRANCE
1918
Fédération Française de Football
1954 (1904)

1980

SLOVENIA
1920
Nogometna Zveza Slovenije
1993 (1992)

Nyon
UEFA Headquarters

CROATIA
1912, 1991
Croatian Football Federation
1993 (1992)

BULGARIA
1923
Bŭlgarski Futbolen Sŭyŭz
1954 (1924)

1998

1984, 2000

SPAIN
1913
Real Federación Española de Fútbol
1954 (1904)

1964, *84*

ANDORRA
1994
Federació Andorrana de Futbol
1996 (1996)

LIECHTENSTEIN
1934
Liechtensteiner Fussballverband
1992 (1974)

ITALY
1898
Federazione Italiana Giuoco Calcio
1954 (1905)

1934, **38**, *70*, **82**

1968, *2000*

MACEDONIA
1908
Macedonian Football Union
1994 (1994)

GREECE
1926
Hellenic Football Federation
1954 (1927)

PORTUGAL
1914
Federação Portuguesa de Futebol
1954 (1923)

SWITZERLAND
1895
Schweizerischer Fussballverband
1954 (1904)

SAN MARINO
1931
Federazione Sammarinese Giuoco Calcio
1988 (1988)

MALTA
1900
Malta Football Association
1960 (1959)

BOSNIA-HERZEGOVINA
1992
Nogometni Savez Bosne i Hercegovine
1996 (1996)

ALBANIA
1930
Federata Shqiptarë e Futbollit
1954 (1932)

YUGOSLAV
1919
Fudbalski Sav Jugoslavije
1993 (1919)

1960, 6

MEDITERRANEAN SEA

The Development of European Football

1924 Scandinavian Cup established

1929 Dr Gero Cup established

1940 Last Baltic Cup

1949 Latin Cup established

1954 UEFA founded

1957 Last Latin Cup

1960 European Cup-Winners' Cup begins, European Nations' Cup begins, Dr Gero Cup ends

1880   1890   1920   1930   1940   1950   1960   197

1884 Home International Championship established

1928 Baltic Cup established

1932 Balkan Cup established

1955 European Cup begins, Fairs Cup begins

1956 European Footballer of the Year established

1968 European Nations' Cup renamed European Championships

The UEFA Nations

The UEFA Nations

Date of formation of the national Football Association

■	Before 1899
▨	1900–39
▧	1940–79
□	After 1980

Formation of national FA — **COUNTRY**
1916
Name of Football Association
Date of affiliation to UEFA — **1916 (1912)** — Date of affiliation to FIFA

Team colours

World Cup — 🏆 **1990** — Winners in bold
European Championship — 🏆 *1990* — Runners-up in italic

UEFA

European Tournaments and Cup Competitions:
European Championships
European Champions League
UEFA Cup
Intertoto Cup
European Super Cup
European Women's Championships

UKRAINE
1991
Football Federation of Ukraine
1992 (1992)

RUSSIA
1912, 1991
Rossiyskiy Futbol'nyy Soyuz
1954 (1912, 1992)
🏆 **1960**, *64, 72, 88*

BLACK SEA

CASPIAN SEA

GEORGIA
1990
Georgian Football Federation
1992 (1992)

TURKEY
1923
Türkiye Futbol Federasyonu
1962 (1923)

AZERBAIJAN
1992
Association of Football Federations of Azerbaijan
1994 (1994)

CYPRUS
1934
Kipriaki Omospondia Podosferu
1962 (1948)

ARMENIA
1992
Football Federation of Armenia
1993 (1992)

ISRAEL
1928
Israel Football Association
1992 (1929)

1978 European Under-21 Championships established

1984 Last Home International Championship

1991 Last Baltic Cup

1999 Last European Cup-Winners' Cup

1980 — 1990 — 2000

1972 UEFA establishes Women's Football Committee

1982 First European Championship for Women

1992 European Cup becomes European Champions League

The UEFA Nations

IN 1954, ALMOST 50 YEARS after the foundation of FIFA, and 38 years after the formation of CONMEBOL in South America, Europe acquired its own football federation in the form of UEFA: the Union of European Football Associations, based in Nyon, Switzerland. Football may have spread to every corner of the continent, but it took two world wars to overcome the Continent's divisions in order to reach agreement on the organization of football. UEFA had 35 founding members, and with the break-up of the Soviet Union and Yugoslavia it has grown to 51. Israel has transferred in from the Asian and Oceanic confederations as UEFA's contribution to global peacekeeping.

With the arrival of UEFA, the older international competitions, like the Scandinavian Cup organized by national FAs and ad hoc committees, were replaced by the European Nations' Championship. UEFA also spurred the development of European club competition in the 1950s and early 1960s, replacing the Latin Cup and Mittel Europa Cup with the European Cup. In the 1990s, UEFA had to fight to retain its political weight within world football, as FIFA, the European Community and the biggest European clubs have challenged its authority. At the turn of the century, its place was no more secure.

***Lennart Johannsson**, the Swedish-born President of UEFA, was re-elected to the post in January 2002 as the sole nominee and will serve a further four years in the hot seat.*

Calendar of Events

Club Tournaments	European Champions League 2002–03 UEFA Cup 2002–03 Intertoto Cup 2003 European Super Cup 2003
International Tournaments	European Championships 2004, Qualifying Tournament

Scandinavia

THE SEASONS IN REVIEW 2001, 2001–02

A HUNDRED YEARS OF WAITING was finally over. With no single major trophy to show since its foundation in 1897, southern Stockholm's favourite team Hammarby took its first-ever league title. Chased all season by Djurgårdens, IFK Göteborg and the improving AIK, the title race went right down to the wire; with a past history of last-minute disasters hanging gloomily over the club, Hammarby faced Ögryte at home in its penultimate game, needing three points for the championship. Hammarby went 3-1 up, but with Ögryte scoring a second goal and pressing hard, it was a nail-biting climax. The victory was followed by a most un-Swedish, delirious pitch invasion. Amazingly, the Hammarby board announced two-thirds of the way through the season that, irrespective of results, coach Soren Cratz would be retiring. Major protests by fans at the club's offices followed, though it was only after the title had been won that the board finally relented.

In Norway, Rosenborg of Trondhiem took its tenth consecutive title, but it was the tightest and toughest fight yet. In fact, the side looked lost in mid-season, but the accumulation of Champions League cash over a decade has given the side strength in depth, in particular with the arrival of midfielder Odd Inge Olsen from Molde (a move so unpopular with Molde fans that at the first match after he had left there was a coordinated mass departure from the ground on the referee's starting whistle). Lillestrøm was the strongest challenger, but needing to beat Brann in Bergen on the last day of the season it blew its chance in a devastating 6-2 defeat. In Finland, the long time leader of the league, HJK Helsinki, was finally caught by Tampere United, who won its first national championship.

Denmark's season was a two-horse race between Brøndby and FC København, with Brøndby just taking it on the final day. FC København's misery intensified as it was beaten in the Cup Final by rank outsiders OB. Money overshadowed football as it became more apparent all season that the league cannot sustain all its professional teams. Lyngby was declared bankrupt in mid-season and could not field professional footballers; its youth team, called in to fulfill the first-team's fixtures, promptly lost 7-0 to AGF in Aarhus (itself only recently saved from bankruptcy by a rich patron) and its season was effectively nullified. Its misery was compounded by the fact that the team has been automatically relegated to the third division.

Above: Tampere United celebrates its first Finnish League title.

Left: Eric Mykland (white shirt) provides the heart of FC København's midfield.

Below: The Norwegian Cup Final. Viking's Hannu Tihinen celebrates his goal against Bryne FK.

Below right: Lyngby's Morten Juhl Hansen (right) and goalkeeper Soeren Bysko enter the stadium as two of the amateur players fielded in a league game against Aarhus.

Soren Cratz takes the fans' plaudits after guiding Swedish club Hammarby to a first league title.

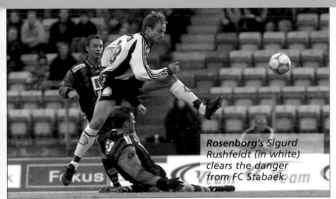

Rosenborg's Sigurd Rushfeldt (in white) clears the danger from FC Stabaek.

Top Goalscorers 2001, 2001–02

PLAYER	CLUB	NATIONALITY	GOALS
*Kaspar Dalgas	OB Odense	Danish	20
Paulus Roiha	HJK Helsinki	Finnish	22
Thorstein Helstad	SK Brann	Norwegian	17
Frode Johnsen	Rosenborg BK	Norwegian	17
Clayton Zane	Lillestrøm SK	Norwegian	17
Stefan Selakovic	Halmstads BK	Swedish	15

* Denotes 2001–02 season.

International Club Performances 2001–02

CLUB	COMPETITION	PROGRESS
FC København (Den)	Champions League	3rd Qualifying Phase
	UEFA Cup	3rd Round
Haka Valkeakoski (Fin)	Champions League	3rd Qualifying Phase
	UEFA Cup	1st Round
Halmstads BK (Swe)	Champions League	3rd Qualifying Phase
	UEFA Cup	2nd Round
Rosenborg BK (Nor)	Champions League	1st Group Phase
SK Brann (Nor)	Champions League	2nd Qualifying Phase
Brøndby IF (Den)	UEFA Cup	3rd Round
IF Elfsborg (Swe)	UEFA Cup	1st Round
Helsingborgs IF (Swe)	UEFA Cup	2nd Round
HJK Helsinki (Fin)	UEFA Cup	1st Round
FC Jokerit (Fin)	UEFA Cup	Qualifying Round
FC Midtjylland (Den)	UEFA Cup	1st Round
MyPa Anjalankoski (Fin)	UEFA Cup	Qualifying Round
Odd Grenland (Nor)	UEFA Cup	1st Round
Silkeborg IF (Den)	UEFA Cup	1st Round
Viking FK (Nor)	UEFA Cup	2nd Round

National Cup Finals 2001, 2001–02

COUNTRY	WINNERS	SCORE	RUNNERS-UP
*Denmark	OB Odense	2-1	FC København
Finland	Atlantis Helsinki	1-0	Tampere United
Norway	Viking FK	3-0	Bryne FK
Sweden	IF Elfsborg	1-1 (9-8 pens)	AIK

* Denotes 2001–02 season.

Danish League Table 2001–02

CLUB	P	W	D	L	F	A	Pts	
Brøndby IF	33	20	9	4	74	28	69	Champions League
FC København	33	20	9	4	62	25	69	UEFA Cup
FC Midtjylland	33	16	9	8	47	27	57	UEFA Cup
AaB Aalborg	33	16	6	11	52	45	54	
AB	33	13	11	9	48	38	50	
OB Odense	33	13	10	10	56	51	49	UEFA Cup (cup winners)
Esbjerg fB	33	13	6	14	42	44	45	
Viborg FF	33	10	11	12	46	45	43	
Silkeborg IF	33	8	8	17	41	50	32	
AGF Aarhus	33	7	10	16	42	56	31	
Vejle BK	33	6	10	17	38	72	28	Relegated
Lyngby FC	33	2	9	22	25	92	15	Relegated

Promoted clubs: Farum, Køge BK

Finnish League Table 2001

CLUB	P	W	D	L	F	A	Pts	
Tampere United	33	21	5	7	47	31	68	Champions League
HJK Helsinki	33	19	10	4	64	19	67	UEFA Cup
MyPa Anjalankoski	33	17	11	5	45	23	62	
Haka Valkeakoski	33	14	10	9	44	29	52	
FC Inter	33	15	4	14	46	47	49	
VPS Vaasa	33	14	3	16	50	51	45	
Atlantis Helsinki	33	12	9	12	45	47	45	UEFA Cup (cup winners)
KuPS Kuopio	33	9	10	14	37	48	37	
FC Lahti	33	9	9	15	38	49	36	
FC Jazz	33	7	11	15	35	52	32	
FC Jokerit	33	7	7	19	32	56	28	Relegated
RoPS Rovaniemi	33	5	9	19	25	56	24	Relegated

Promoted clubs: FC Hämeenlinna, Jaro Pietarsaari

Norwegian League Table 2001

CLUB	P	W	D	L	F	A	Pts	
Rosenborg BK	26	17	6	3	71	30	57	Champions League
Lillestrøm SK	26	17	5	4	64	33	56	UEFA Cup
Viking FK	26	14	7	5	43	29	49	UEFA Cup (cup winners)
Stabaek IF	26	14	3	9	45	39	45	UEFA Cup
Molde FK	26	13	5	8	54	41	44	
Odd Grenland	26	12	6	8	50	40	42	
SK Brann	26	12	5	9	63	48	41	UEFA Cup (Fair play)
Sogndal	26	9	5	12	45	61	32	
FK Bodø/Glimt	26	7	8	11	45	47	29	
Moss FK	26	9	2	15	35	48	29	
Lyn	26	6	8	12	40	49	26	
Bryne FK	26	6	4	16	33	61	22	
IF Strømgodset	26	3	10	13	40	73	19	Relegated
Tromsø IL	26	4	4	18	23	52	16	Relegated

Promoted clubs: Start, Vålerenga

Swedish League Table 2001

CLUB	P	W	D	L	F	A	Pts	
Hammarby IF	26	14	6	6	45	28	48	Champions League
Djurgårdens IF	26	13	8	5	36	24	47	UEFA Cup
AIK	26	12	9	5	45	29	45	
IFK Göteborg	26	12	8	6	41	31	44	
Helsingborgs IF	26	11	9	6	47	29	42	
Örgryte IS	26	10	9	7	36	33	39	
Halmstads BK	26	10	8	8	50	31	38	
Örebro SK	26	8	9	9	48	44	33	
Malmö FF	26	9	5	12	39	46	32	
IF Elfsborg	26	9	3	14	31	51	30	UEFA Cup (cup winners)
GIF Sundsvall	26	7	8	11	28	37	29	
IFK Norrköping	26	7	8	11	29	40	29	
BK Häcken	26	5	9	12	35	50	24	Relegated
Trelleborgs FF	26	3	5	18	25	62	14	Relegated

Promoted clubs: Kalmar FF, Landskrona BoIS

SCANDINAVIA

SWEDEN

Association Football in Sweden

1870s: Football introduced to Sweden by British workers and diplomats — 1870

1875

1880

1887: Ögryte IS, Sweden's oldest club formed — 1885

1895: Swedish Sports and Athletics Association formed, football's first governing body — 1890

1896: Gothenburg League begins — 1895

1900: Stockholm clubs allowed into Gothenburg League — 1900

1905

⚽ **1904:** Formation of FA: Svenska Fotbollförbundet. Affiliation to FIFA — 1910

🇩🇰 **1908:** First international, v Norway, won 11-3, venue: Gothenburg — 1915

1920

1925: League format replaces play-offs for championship — 1925

1930

1935

1941: First Swedish Cup Final — 1940

1945

1950

⚽ **1954:** Affiliation to UEFA — 1955

1960

1965

⚥🇩🇰 **1973:** First women's international, v Finland, drawn 0-0 — 1970

1975

⚥ **1978:** National FA incorporates women's football — 1980

1982: League decided by final play-off — 1985

1990: League reverts to simple format — 1990

1995

2000

2005

Gunnar Nordahl moved from IFK Norrköping to Milan in 1949 to become part of an all-Swedish forward line with Gunnar Gren and Nils Liedholm.

Key

🇩🇰 International football

⚽ Affiliation to FIFA

⚽ Affiliation to UEFA

⚥ Women's football

■ World Cup host

▲ World Cup runner-up

▣ European Championships host

○ Competition winner

△ Competition runner-up

IFK – IFK Göteborg
Mal – Malmö FF

International Competitions

1958: ▲ ■

	European Cup	UEFA Cup	European Cup-Winners' Cup
1979:	△ Mal		
1982:		○ IFK	
1987:		○ IFK	
1992:	▪		

Sweden: The main clubs

IFK Elfsborg 1905 — Team name with year of formation

● Club formed before 1912

● Club formed 1912–25

● Club formed 1925–50

○ Club formed after 1950

★ Founder members of League (1925)

👕 Pre-1925 champions

👕 Champions (1925–55)

👕● Colours and date unknown

★ **Örgryte IS** 1887

★ **IFK Göteborg** 1904

Gunnilse

Västra Frölunda 1930

★ **GAIS** 1894

Göteborg IF

BK Häcken 1940

Fässbergs IF 1916

★ **Helsingborgs IF** 1907

Råå IF Helsingborg 1921

★ **Landskrona** 1915

★ **IFK Malmö** 1899

Malmö FF 1887

Sweden

ORIGINS AND GROWTH OF FOOTBALL

FOOTBALL ARRIVED IN SWEDEN IN THE 1870s by a variety of routes: Scottish riveters and English sailors in Gothenburg, British engineers and railway workers, as well as British embassy staff in the parks of Stockholm. Swedish football's centre of gravity was quickly established in Gothenburg with the formation of Ögryte (1887) and GAIS Gothenburg (1894). In 1895 a Gothenburg-based tournament was set up. Stockholm clubs joined in 1900 and a national league was created in 1925. Sweden absorbed footballing influences from Britain and Continental Europe, both providing coaches and managers to leading club sides and the national teams prior to the Second World War.

Swedes in Milan
The development of Swedish football has obvious parallels with wider Swedish society, most clearly an active international presence out of all proportion with the strength of its domestic football. Sweden was a founder member of FIFA, won the gold medal at the 1948 Olympics, has been third or fourth at three World Cups (1938, 1950, 1994) and was runner-up and host at the 1958 World Cup. Domestically, the persistence of amateurism saw the best players migrate south, most famously the forward line of Gren, Nordahl and Liedholm to Milan in 1949. This move was met by the exclusion of professionals from the national team until 1958. The limited economic resources of Swedish clubs combined with a continuing exodus of talent left Swedish clubs weak in postwar European competitions until the de facto arrival of professionalism at the bigger clubs and the UEFA Cup triumphs of IFK Gothenburg in the 1980s.

Women on top
The egalitarian and anti-commercial ethos of much of Swedish society may have been barriers to the success of Swedish men's football but it has certainly encouraged the relatively early adoption and active promotion of women's football in Sweden. The Swedish women's team won the inaugural Women's European Championships in 1984 and was runner-up in the first Women's World Cup in 1988.

SWEDEN

S W E D E N

Arctic Circle

Gefle **1882**

Brynäs **1912**

★ AIK **1891**

Umeå FC
1987

Assyriska **1971**

Djurgårdens IF **1891**

Sundsvall
GIF Sundsvall
1903

★ Hammarby IF **1897**

Café Opera Djursholm **1991**

★ IFK Norrköping **1897**

Gävle

★ Vasterås SK/FK **1904**

★ IK Sleipner **1903**

Borlänge
Brage
1925

Sandvikens IFK
1918

Ik Sylvia **1922**

Degerfors IF
1907

Örebro SK
1908

Enköping
1914 Solna

★ IFK Eskilstuna **1897**

Stockholm

Åtvidabergs FF **1907**

Norrköping

Jönköpings Södra IF

ungskile
anos Ljungskile
26

Åtvidaberg

IFK Elfsborg **1904**

Jönköping

Borås

Halmstads BK **1914**

Gothenburg

Växjö
Kalmar FF
1910

Östers IFK Växjö **1930**

Sölvesborg
Mjällby
1934

lelsingborg

Landskrona

Trelleborgs FF **1926**

Malmö Trelleborg

The Swedish Women's team won the first-ever Women's European Championships in 1984 beating England in the Final.

Sweden

Svenska Fotbollförbundet
Founded: 1904
Joined FIFA: 1904
Joined UEFA: 1954

THE FIRST SWEDISH league championship was played in 1896 and was restricted to clubs from Gothenburg. In 1900, the league was expanded to include teams from Stockholm and the final rounds were played as a knockout competition until 1925, when a normal league format was adopted (this accounts for the two championships awarded that year).

The Swedish Cup was established in 1941, and ran fitfully over the next couple of decades until European qualification for the winners made it a more pressing engagement. Despite this, Finals have attracted crowds of less than 2,000.

Swedish League Record 1896–2001

SEASON	CHAMPIONS	RUNNERS-UP
1896	Örgryte IS	IV Göteborg
1897	Örgryte IS	Örgryte II
1898	Örgryte IS	AIK
1899	Örgryte IS	Göteborg FF
1900	AIK	Örgryte IS
1901	AIK	Örgryte II
1902	Örgryte IS	Jönköpings AIF
1903	Göteborg IF	Göteborg FF
1904	Örgryte IS	Djurgårdens IF
1905	Örgryte IS	IFK Stockholm
1906	Örgryte IS	Djurgårdens IF
1907	Örgryte IS	IFK Uppsala
1908	IFK Göteborg	IFK Uppsala
1909	Örgryte IS	Djurgårdens IF
1910	IFK Göteborg	Djurgårdens IF
1911	AIK	IFK Uppsala
1912	Djurgårdens IF	Örgryte IS
1913	Örgryte IS	Djurgårdens IF
1914	AIK	Helsingborgs IF
1915	Djurgårdens IF	AIK
1916	AIK	Djurgårdens IF
1917	Djurgårdens IF	AIK
1918	IFK Göteborg	Helsingborgs IF
1919	GAIS	Djurgårdens IF
1920	Djurgårdens IF	IK Sleipner
1921	IFK Eskilstuna	IK Sleipner
1922	GAIS	Hammarby IF
1923	AIK	IFK Eskilstuna
1924	Fassbergs IF	Sirius Uppsala
1925	Brynas IF Gävle	Derby BK Linköping
1925	GAIS	IFK Göteborg
1926	Örgryte IS	GAIS
1927	GAIS	IFK Göteborg
1928	Örgryte IS	Helsingborgs IF
1929	Helsingborgs IF	Örgryte IS
1930	Helsingborgs IF	IFK Göteborg
1931	GAIS	AIK
1932	AIK	Örgryte IS
1933	Helsingborgs IF	GAIS
1934	Helsingborgs IF	GAIS
1935	IFK Göteborg	AIK
1936	IF Elfsborg	AIK
1937	AIK	IK Sleipner
1938	IK Sleipner	Helsingborgs IF
1939	IF Elfsborg	AIK
1940	IF Elfsborg	IFK Göteborg
1941	Helsingborgs IF	Degerfors IF
1942	IFK Göteborg	GAIS
1943	IFK Norrköping	IF Elfsborg

Swedish League Record (*continued*)

SEASON	CHAMPIONS	RUNNERS-UP
1944	Malmö FF	IF Elfsborg
1945	IFK Norrköping	IF Elfsborg
1946	IFK Norrköping	Malmö FF
1947	IFK Norrköping	AIK
1948	IFK Norrköping	Malmö FF
1949	Malmö FF	Helsingborgs IF
1950	Malmö FF	Jonköpings Södra
1951	Malmö FF	Råå IF Helsingborg
1952	IFK Norrköping	Malmö FF
1953	Malmö FF	IFK Norrköping
1954	GAIS	Helsingborgs IF
1955	Djurgårdens IF	Halmstads BK
1956	IFK Norrköping	Malmö FF
1957	IFK Norrköping	Malmö FF
1958	IFK Göteborg	IFK Norrköping
1959	Djurgårdens IF	IFK Norrköping
1960	IFK Norrköping	IFK Malmö
1961	IF Elfsborg	IFK Norrköping
1962	IFK Norrköping	Djurgårdens IF
1963	IFK Norrköping	Degerfors IF
1964	Djurgårdens IF	Malmö FF
1965	Malmö FF	IF Elfsborg
1966	Djurgårdens IF	IFK Norrköping
1967	Malmö FF	Djurgårdens IF
1968	Östers IF Växjö	Malmö FF
1969	IFK Göteborg	Malmö FF
1970	Malmö FF	Åtvidabergs FF
1971	Malmö FF	Åtvidabergs FF
1972	Åtvidabergs FF	AIK
1973	Åtvidabergs FF	Östers IF Växjö
1974	Malmö FF	AIK
1975	Malmö FF	Östers IF Växjö
1976	Halmstads BK	Malmö FF
1977	Malmö FF	IF Elfsborg
1978	Östers IF Växjö	Malmö FF
1979	Halmstads BK	Malmö FF
1980	Östers IF Växjö	Malmö FF
1981	Östers IF Växjö	IFK Göteborg
1982	IFK Göteborg	Hammarby IF
1983	IFK Göteborg	Östers IF Växjö
1984	IFK Göteborg	IFK Norrköping
1985	Örgryte IS	IFK Göteborg
1986	Malmö FF	AIK
1987	IFK Göteborg	Malmö FF
1988	Malmö FF	Djurgårdens IF
1989	IFK Norrköping	Malmö FF
1990	IFK Göteborg	IFK Norrköping
1991	IFK Göteborg	IFK Norrköping
1992	AIK	IFK Norrköping
1993	IFK Göteborg	IFK Norrköping
1994	IFK Göteborg	Örebro SK
1995	IFK Göteborg	Helsingborgs IF
1996	IFK Göteborg	Malmö FF
1997	Halmstads BK	IFK Göteborg
1998	AIK	Helsingborgs IF
1999	Helsingborgs IF	AIK
2000	Halmstads BK	Helsingborgs IF
2001	Hammarby IF	Djurgårdens IF

Swedish League Summary

TEAM	TOTALS	CHAMPIONS & RUNNERS-UP (BOLD) (ITALICS)
IFK Göteborg	17, 7	**1908, 10, 18,** *25, 27, 30,* **35,** *40,* **42, 58, 69,** *81,* **82–84,** *85,* **87, 90, 91, 93–96,** *97*
Malmö FF	14, 15	*1944, 46, 48,* **49–51,** *52,* **53,** *56, 57,* **64, 65, 67, 68, 69, 70, 71, 74, 75, 76, 77,** *78–80,* **86,** *87,* **88,** *89,* **96**
Örgryte IS	14, 4	**1896–99, 1900,** *02,* **04–07,** *09,* **12, 13,** *26,* **28,** *29, 32,* **85**
IFK Norrköping	12, 10	**1943, 45–48,** *52,* **53, 56, 57, 58, 59, 60,** *61,* **62, 63,** *66,* **84, 89,** *90–93*
AIK	10, 12	*1898,* **1900, 01, 11, 14,** *15, 16, 17,* **23,** *31,* **32,** *35, 36, 37, 39, 47,* **72,** *74,* **86,** *92, 98, 99*
Djurgårdens IF	8, 11	*1904, 06, 09, 10,* **12, 13,** *15, 16,* **17,** *19,* **20,** *55,* **59,** *62,* **64,** *66,* **67,** *88,* **2001**
Helsingborgs IF	6, 9	*1914, 18,* **28, 29, 30, 33, 34,** *38, 41,* **49,** *54,* **95,** *98,* **99,** *2000*
GAIS	6, 4	**1919, 22, 25,** *26,* **27, 31,** *33, 34,* **42,** *54*
IF Elfsborg	4, 5	**1936, 39, 40,** *43–45,* **61,** *65, 77*
Östers IF Växjö	4, 3	**1968,** *73,* **75, 78, 80, 81,** *83*
Halmstads BK	4, 1	**1955,** *76,* **79, 97, 2000**
Åtvidabergs FF	2, 2	**1970, 71,** *72, 73*
IK Sleipner	1, 3	*1920, 21, 37,* **38**
Hammarby IF	1, 2	*1922, 82,* **2001**
IFK Eskilstuna	1, 1	**1921,** *23*
Brynas IF Gävle	1, 0	**1925**
Fassbergs IF	1, 0	**1924**
Göteborg IF	1, 0	**1903**
IFK Uppsala	0, 3	*1907, 08, 11*
Degerfors	0, 2	*1941, 63*
Göteborg FF	0, 2	*1899, 1903*
Örgryte II	0, 2	*1897, 1901*
Derby BK Linköping	0, 1	*1925*
IFK Malmö	0, 1	*1960*
IFK Stockholm	0, 1	*1905*
IV Göteborg	0, 1	*1896*
Jönköpings Södra	0, 1	*1950*
Jönköpings AIF	0, 1	*1902*
Örebro SK	0, 1	*1994*
Råå IF Helsingborg	0, 1	*1951*
Sirius Uppsala	0, 1	*1924*

Swedish Cup Record 1941–2001

YEAR	WINNERS	SCORE	RUNNERS-UP
1941	Helsingborgs IF	3-1	IK Sleipner
1942	GAIS	2-1	IK Elfsborg
1943	IFK Norrköping	0-0, (replay) 5-2	AIK
1944	Malmö FF	4-3 (aet)	IFK Norrköping
1945	IFK Norrköping	4-1	Malmö FF
1946	Malmö FF	3-0	Åtvidabergs FF
1947	Malmö FF	3-2	AIK
1948	Råå IF Helsingborg	6-0	BK Kenty Linköping
1949	AIK	1-0	Landskrona BoIS
1950	AIK	3-2	Helsingborgs IF
1951	Malmö FF	2-1	Djurgårdens IF
1952	no competition		
1953	Malmö FF	3-2	IFK Norrköping
1954–66	no competition		
1967	Malmö FF	2-0	IFK Norrköping
1968	no competition		
1969	IFK Norrköping	1-0	AIK
1970	Åtvidabergs FF	2-0	Sandvikens IF
1971	Åtvidabergs FF	3-2	Malmö FF
1972	Landskrona BoIS	0-0, (replay) 3-2 (aet)	IFK Norrköping
1973	Malmö FF	7-0	Åtvidabergs FF

Swedish Cup Record (continued)

YEAR	WINNERS	SCORE	RUNNERS-UP
1974	Malmö FF	2-0	Östers IF Växjö
1975	Malmö FF	1-0	Djurgårdens IF
1976	AIK	1-1, (replay) 3-0	Landskrona BoIS
1977	Östers IF Växjö	1-0	Hammarby IF
1978	Malmö FF	2-0 (aet)	Kalmar FF
1979	IFK Göteborg	6-1	Åtvidabergs FF
1980	Malmö FF	3-3 (aet)(4-3 pens)	IK Brage
1981	Kalmar FF	4-0	IF Elfsborg
1982	IFK Göteborg	3-2	Östers IF Växjö
1983	IFK Göteborg	1-0 (aet)	Hammarby IF
1984	Malmö FF	1-0	Landskrona BoIS
1985	AIK	1-1 (aet)(3-2 pens)	Östers IF Växjö
1986	Malmö FF	2-1	IFK Göteborg
1987	Kalmar FF	2-0	GAIS
1988	IFK Norrköping	3-1	Örebro SK
1989	Malmö FF	3-0	Djurgårdens IF
1990	Djurgårdens IF	2-0	Hacken BK Göteborg
1991	IFK Norrköping	4-1	Östers IF Växjö
1992	IFK Göteborg	3-2 (aet)	AIK
1993	Degerfors IF	3-0	Landskrona BoIS
1994	IFK Norrköping	4-3 (gg)	Helsingborgs IF
1995	Halmstads BK	3-1	AIK
1996	AIK	1-0 (gg)	Malmö FF
1997	AIK	2-1	IF Elfsborg
1998	Helsingborgs IF	1-1, 1-1 (aet) (3-0 pens)(2 legs)	Örgryte IS
1999	AIK	1-0, 0-0 (2 legs)	IFK Göteborg
2000	Örgryte IS	2-0, 0-1 (2 legs)	AIK
2001	IF Elfsborg	1-1 (aet)(9-8 pens)	AIK

(gg) denotes victory on golden goal

Swedish Cup Summary

TEAM	TOTALS	WINNERS & RUNNERS-UP (BOLD) (ITALICS)
Malmö FF	14, 3	**1944,** *45,* **46, 47,** *51,* **53, 67,** *71,* **73–75, 78, 80, 84, 86, 89,** *96*
AIK	7, 7	*1943, 47,* **49, 50,** *69,* **76,** *85,* **92,** *95, 96, 97,* **99,** *2000,* **01**
IFK Norrköping	6, 4	**1943,** *44,* **45,** *53, 57,* **69,** *72,* **88,** *91,* **94**
IFK Göteborg	4, 2	**1979, 82, 83,** *86,* **92,** *99*
Åtvidabergs FF	2, 3	*1946,* **70, 71,** *73, 79*
Helsingborgs IF	2, 2	**1941,** *50, 94,* **98**
Kalmar FF	2, 1	*1978,* **81, 87**
Landskrona BoIS	1, 4	*1949,* **72,** *76, 84, 93*
Östers IF Växjö	1, 4	*1974,* **77,** *82, 85, 91*
Djurgårdens IF	1, 3	*1951, 75, 89,* **90**
IF Elfsborg	1, 2	*1981, 97,* **2001**
GAIS	1, 1	**1942,** *87*
Örgryte IS	1, 1	*1998,* **2000**
Degerfors IF	1, 0	**1993**
Halmstads BK	1, 0	**1995**
Råå IF Helsingborg	1, 0	**1948**
Hammarby IF	0, 2	*1977, 83*
BK Kenty Linköping	0, 1	*1948*
Hacken BK Göteborg	0, 1	*1990*
IK Brage	0, 1	*1980*
IK Elfsborg	0, 1	*1942*
IK Sleipner	0, 1	*1941*
Örebro SK	0, 1	*1988*
Sandvikens IF	0, 1	*1970*

DENMARK

Association Football in Denmark

1876: Continental Europe's oldest club, København Boldklub, established

1889: Formation of FA: Dansk Boldspil Union

1904: Affiliation to FIFA

1908: First international, v France, won 9-0, venue: London. Runners-up in Olympic tournament

1912: Runners-up in Olympic tournament

1913: National League established

1915: League abandoned during war

1954: Affiliation to UEFA

1955: First Danish Cup Final

1972: Women's committee established by Danish FA

1973: Women's National League established

1974: First women's international, v Sweden

1976: Law banning Danes who played overseas from the national side ended

1978: Professionalism introduced

1991: Professional Premier League, the Superliga, formed

1992: Victory over Germany made Denmark European Champions

1995: Superliga expanded to 12 clubs

1875 1880 1885 1890 1895 1900 1905 1910 1915 1920 1925 1930 1935 1940 1945 1950 1955 1960 1965 1970 1975 1980 1985 1990 1995 2000 2005

Nils Bohr, the only Dane ever to win the Nobel Prize for Physics, was also a member of the Danish Olympic football squad, which won silver medals at both the 1908 and 1912 Games.

Jan Molby was transferred from Molding to Liverpool in 1984. His success in England paved the way for a generation of other Danish exports.

Key

	International football
	Affiliation to FIFA
	Affiliation to UEFA
	Women's football
	European Championships winner
	War

International Competitions	European Cup	UEFA Cup	European Cup-Winners' Cup
1992:			

Denmark: The main clubs

Skive 1901	Team name with year of formation
●	Club formed before 1912
●	Club formed 1912–25
●	Club formed 1925–50
○	Club formed after 1950
★	Founder members of League (1927)
☆	Founder members of Superliga (1991)
	Champions (1913–45)
	Champions (1946–91)

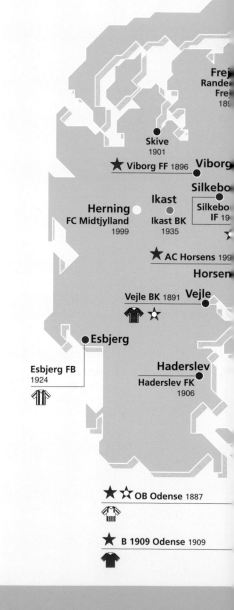

Frej
Rande
Fre
189

Skive 1901

★ **Viborg FF** 1896 **Viborg**

Silkebo

Herning FC Midtjylland 1999

Ikast Ikast BK 1935

Silkebo IF 19

★ **AC Horsens** 199

Horsen

Vejle BK 1891 **Vejle**
☆

● **Esbjerg**

Esbjerg FB 1924

Haderslev Haderslev FK 1906

★ ☆ **OB Odense** 1887

★ **B 1909 Odense** 1909

☆ Lyngby BFC 1921

★ AB (Akademisk Boldklub) 1889
Moved to Gladsaxe (1965)

★ Skovshoved IF 1909

★ ☆ B 1903 København 1903–92

Merged into FC København

FC København 1992
Merger of B 1903 København
and KB København

Brønshøj 1919

B
5

Aalborg

★ ☆ Frem
København 1886

Hvidovre BK 1925

FC Aarhus 1918

☆ ★ AGF 1880

arhus

DENMARK

Odense

Naestved
Næstved IF
1939

BAGASVAERD/
COPENHAGEN

★ B 93 København 1893

★ KB København 1876–1992

Merged into FC København

★ Fremad Amager 1910

☆ Brøndby IF 1964

BAGASVAERD/
COPENHAGEN
(see inset)

Køge BK 1927

Herfølge
1921

★ B 1913 Odense 1913

Denmark

ORIGINS AND GROWTH OF FOOTBALL

PERHAPS IT WAS JUST PROXIMITY and the regular flow of British sailors and ships through Danish ports that explains Denmark's early enthusiasm for football. The dockside games recorded in the 1860s were soon followed by the foundation of Europe's oldest continental football club, København Boldklub, in 1876. KB was soon joined by Copenhagen teams Akademisk, Frem and B93, who played together as Staevnet against touring top British club sides. A national FA was formed in 1889 and four clubs were founded in provincial cities: AGF Aarhus in 1880, AAB in Aalborg in 1885, OB Odense in 1887 and Viborg FF in 1896. Denmark was also a founder member of FIFA in 1904.

Early enthusiasm and organization brought international success as Denmark took the silver medal at the Olympic tournaments in 1908 and 1912 (losing both Finals to England, 2-0 and 4-2). Despite this the game remained unequivocally amateur in Denmark. Both Olympic squads included the Bohr brothers, professors at Copenhagen University. Nils Bohr went on to be a Nobel Prize winner. In the wake of this success a league was established in 1913 which has run ever since, but for a single season in 1915.

Ups and downs

However, it was not a professional league and the standard of Danish football steadily fell relative to the rest of Europe and Latin America. Each crop of promising players (including the Olympic squads of 1948 and 1960) were spirited away to foreign clubs as the Danish FA insisted on banning foreign-based professionals from the national side. Change came in the 1970s as a new generation of Danes, like Allan Simonsen at Barcelona and Jan Molby at Liverpool, played at the highest level in Europe. The national team ban was lifted and Denmark qualified for its first World Cup in 1986. In 1992, as late entrants to the European Championships, it took the title, beating Germany in the Final.

This success helped encourage a transformation of the domestic scene, and in 1991, a professional Premier League was finally established. Since then, a wave of mergers and club reorganizations have ensured that Danish football has been drawn into the modern age.

John Jensen is buried underneath a pile of his teammates after giving Denmark the lead in the 1992 European Championships Final against Germany in Gothenburg. Denmark won the match 2-0.

DENMARK

Denmark

Dansk Boldspil Union
Founded: 1889
Joined FIFA: 1904
Joined UEFA: 1954

FOOTBALL ARRIVED EARLY IN DENMARK, making its way into Scandinavia through the ports. KB København, the first Danish club, was founded in 1876, considerably in advance of most English and Scottish clubs. Despite this early enthusiasm, the formation of a national football association in 1889, and becoming a founder member of FIFA, organized domestic competition lagged behind. Nonetheless, Denmark made it to the Finals of the first two Olympic Games with a football competition (1908 and 1912). Future international successes were limited by the DBU's fierce amateurism, as Danes playing professionally overseas were excluded from the national team. In 1913 a national league was established and it has run uninterrupted since 1916. The championship was won by Copenhagen clubs until the 1950s, when Køge, Aarhus and Vejle broke the capital's stronghold.

A Danish Cup competition was created in 1955 and professionalism arrived in 1978. In 1976 the DBU allowed players playing outside Denmark to play for the national teams for the first time which, combined with the advent of professionalism, led to the beginnings of an exodus of Danish talent. In response to this, and the uneven quality of Danish football clubs, the Danish league was reorganized in 1991 with the creation of an eight-team, wholly professional, Superliga, with clubs playing each other four times a year. In 1992, these changes seemed to have borne fruit, as Denmark were crowned unexpected winners of the European Championship. In 1995 the Superliga was expanded to 12 teams playing each other three times a season. There is a standard two-up/two-down promotion/relegation system between the Superliga and the second division.

Danish League Record 1913–2002

SEASON	CHAMPIONS	RUNNERS-UP
1913	KB København	B93 København
1914	KB København	B93 København
1915	*no championship*	
1916	B93 København	KB København
1917	KB København	Akademisk
1918	KB København	Frem København
1919	Akademisk	B93 København
1920	B1903 København	KB København
1921	Akademisk	B1903 København
1922	KB København	Frem København
1923	Frem København	B93 København
1924	B1903 København	KB København
1925	KB København	Akademisk
1926	B1903 København	B93 København
1927	B93 København	B1903 København
1928	B93 København	Frem København
1929	B93 København	KB København
1930	B93 København	Frem København
1931	Frem København	KB København
1932	KB København	Akademisk
1933	Frem København	B1903 København
1934	B93 København	B1903 København
1935	B93 København	Frem København
1936	Frem København	Akademisk
1937	Akademisk	Frem København
1938	B1903 København	Frem København

Danish League Record (*continued*)

SEASON	CHAMPIONS	RUNNERS-UP
1939	B93 København	KB København
1940	KB København	Fremad Amager
1941	Frem København	Fremad Amager
1942	B93 København	Akademisk
1943	Akademisk	KB København
1944	Frem København	Akademisk
1945	Akademisk	AGF Aarhus
1946	B93 København	KB København
1947	Akademisk	KB København
1948	KB København	Frem København
1949	KB København	Akademisk
1950	KB København	Akademisk
1951	Akademisk	OB Odense
1952	Akademisk	Køge BK
1953	KB København	Skovshoved IF
1954	Køge BK	KB København
1955	AGF Aarhus	Akademisk
1956	AGF Aarhus	Esbjerg FB
1957	AGF Aarhus	Akademisk
1958	Vejle BK	Frem København
1959	B1909 Odense	KB København
1960	AGF Aarhus	KB København
1961	Esbjerg FB	KB København
1962	Esbjerg FB	B1913 Odense
1963	Esbjerg FB	B1913 Odense
1964	B1909 Odense	AGF Aarhus
1965	Esbjerg FB	Vejle BK
1966	Hvidovre BK	Frem København
1967	Akademisk	Frem København
1968	KB København	Esbjerg FB
1969	B1903 København	KB København
1970	B1903 København	Akademisk
1971	Vejle BK	Hvidovre BK
1972	Vejle BK	B1903 København
1973	Hvidovre BK	Randers Freja
1974	KB København	Vejle BK
1975	Køge BK	Holbaek BK
1976	B1903 København	Frem København
1977	OB Odense	B1903 København
1978	Vejle BK	Esbjerg FB
1979	Esbjerg FB	KB København
1980	KB København	Naestved IF
1981	Hvidovre BK	Lyngby FC
1982	OB Odense	AGF Aarhus
1983	Lyngby FC	OB Odense
1984	Vejle BK	AGF Aarhus
1985	Brøndby IF	Lyngby FC
1986	AGF Aarhus	Brøndby IF
1987	Brøndby IF	Ikast BK
1988	Brøndby IF	Naestved IF
1989	OB Odense	Brøndby IF
1990	Brøndby IF	B1903 København
1991	Brøndby IF	Lyngby FC
1992	Lyngby FC	B1903 København
1993	FC København	OB Odense
1994	Silkeborg IF	FC København
1995	AaB Aalborg	Brøndby IF
1996	Brøndby IF	AGF Aarhus
1997	Brøndby IF	Vejle BK
1998	Brøndby IF	Silkeborg IF
1999	AaB Aalborg	Brøndby IF
2000	Herfølge	Brøndby IF

Danish League Record (*continued*)

SEASON	CHAMPIONS	RUNNERS-UP
2001	FC København	Brøndby IF
2002	Brøndby IF	FC København

Danish League Summary

TEAM	TOTALS	CHAMPIONS & RUNNERS-UP (BOLD) (*ITALICS*)
KB København	15, 15	**1913, 14,** *16, 17, 18, 20,* **22,** *24,* **25,** *29, 31,* **32, 39, 40,** *43,* **46, 47, 48–50,** *53, 54,* **59–61, 68, 69, 74,** *79,* **80**
B93 København	10, 5	*1913, 14,* **16,** *19, 23, 26,* **27–30, 34,** *35,* **39, 42, 46**
Akademisk	9, 11	*1917,* **19, 21,** *25,* **32,** *36,* **37,** *42,* **43, 44, 45, 47, 49, 50, 51, 52,** *55,* **57, 67,** *70*
Brøndby IF	9, 6	**1985,** *86,* **87, 88, 89, 90, 91,** *95,* **96–98,** *1999–2001,* **02**
B1903 København	7, 8	**1920,** *21,* **24,** *26, 27,* **33, 34, 38,** *69,* **70,** *72,* **76,** *77,* **90,** *92*
Frem København	6, 12	*1918, 22,* **23,** *28, 30,* **31,** *33, 35, 36, 37, 38,* **41,** *44,* **48,** *58, 66, 67, 76*
AGF Aarhus	5, 5	*1945,* **55–57,** *60,* **64,** *82,* **84,** *86,* **96**
Esbjerg FB	5, 3	*1956,* **61–63,** *65,* **68,** *78, 79*
Vejle BK	5, 3	**1958,** *65,* **71,** *72,* **74,** *78,* **84,** *97*
OB Odense	3, 3	*1951,* **77,** *82,* **83, 89,** *93*
Hvidovre BK	3, 1	**1966,** *71,* **73, 81**
Lyngby FC	2, 3	*1981,* **83,** *85,* **91,** *92*
FC København*	2, 2	**1993,** *94,* **2001,** *02*
Køge BK	2, 1	*1952,* **54, 75**
AaB Aalborg	2, 0	**1995, 99**
B1909 Odense	2, 0	**1959, 64**
Silkeborg IF	1, 1	**1994,** *98*
Herfølge	1, 0	**2000**
B1913 Odense	0, 2	*1962, 63*
Naestved IF	0, 2	*1980, 88*
Fremad Amager	0, 2	*1940, 41*
Randers Freja	0, 1	*1973*
Ikast BK	0, 1	*1987*
Holbaek BK	0, 1	*1975*
Shovshoved IF	0, 1	*1953*

* Formed in 1993 after a merger of KB København and B1903 København.

Danish Cup Record 1955–2002

YEAR	WINNERS	SCORE	RUNNERS-UP
1955	AGF Aarhus	4-0	Aalborg Chang
1956	Frem København	1-0	Akademisk
1957	AGF Aarhus	2-0	Esbjerg FB
1958	Vejle BK	3-2	AGF Aarhus
1959	Vejle BK	1-1 (aet), (replay) 2-0	AGF Aarhus
1960	AGF Aarhus	2-0	Frem Sakskøbing
1961	AGF Aarhus	2-0	KB København
1962	B1909 Odense	1-0	Esbjerg FB
1963	B1913 Odense	2-1	Køge BK
1964	Esbjerg FB	2-1	Odense KFUM
1965	AGF Aarhus	1-0	KB København
1966	AaB Aalborg	3-1 (aet)	KB København
1967	Randers Freja	1-0	AaB Aalborg
1968	Randers Freja	3-1	Vejle BK
1969	KB København	3-0	Frem København
1970	AaB Aalborg	2-1	Lyngby FC
1971	B1909 Odense	1-0	Frem København
1972	Vejle BK	2-0	Fremad Amager
1973	Randers Freja	2-0	B1901 Nykøbing
1974	Vanlose BK	5-2	OB Odense
1975	Vejle BK	1-0	Holbaek BK

Danish Cup Record (*continued*)

YEAR	WINNERS	SCORE	RUNNERS-UP
1976	Esbjerg FB	2-1	Holbaek BK
1977	Vejle BK	2-1	B1909 Odense
1978	Frem København	1-1 (aet), (replay) 1-1 (aet) (6-5 pens)	Esbjerg FB
1979	B1903 København	1-0	Køge BK
1980	Hvidovre BK	5-3	Lyngby FC
1981	Vejle BK	2-1	Frem København
1982	B93 København	3-3 (aet), (replay) 1-0	B1903 København
1983	OB Odense	3-0	B1901 Nykøbing
1984	Lyngby FC	2-1	KB København
1985	Lyngby FC	3-2	Esbjerg FB
1986	B1903 København	2-1	Ikast BK
1987	AGF Aarhus	3-0	AaB Aalborg
1988	AGF Aarhus	2-1 (aet)	Brøndby IF
1989	Brøndby IF	6-3 (aet)	Ikast BK
1990	Lyngby FC	0-0 (aet), (replay) 6-1	AGF Aarhus
1991	OB Odense	0-0 (aet), (replay) 0-0 (aet) (4-3 pens)	AaB Aalborg
1992	AGF Aarhus	3-0	B1903 København
1993	OB Odense	2-0	AaB Aalborg
1994	Brøndby IF	0-0 (aet) (4-3 pens)	Naestved IF
1995	FC København	5-0	Akademisk
1996	AGF Aarhus	2-0	Brøndby IF
1997	FC København	2-0	Ikast BK
1998	Brøndby IF	4-1	FC København
1999	Akademisk	2-1	AaB Aalborg
2000	Viborg FF	1-0	AaB Aalborg
2001	Silkeborg IF	4-1	Akademisk
2002	OB Odense	2-1	FC København

Danish Cup Summary

TEAM	TOTALS	WINNERS & RUNNERS-UP (BOLD) (*ITALICS*)
AGF Aarhus	9, 3	**1955,** *57,* **58, 59,** *60,* **61, 65, 87,** *88,* **90, 92, 96**
Vejle BK	6, 1	**1958,** *59,* **68, 72, 75, 77, 81**
OB Odense	4, 1	*1974,* **83, 91, 93, 2002**
Brøndby IF	3, 2	**1988,** *89,* **94,** *96,* **98**
Lyngby FC	3, 2	*1970,* **80,** *84,* **85, 90**
Randers Freja	3, 0	**1967, 68, 73**
AaB Aalborg	2, 6	**1966,** *67,* **70,** *87, 91, 93, 99, 2000*
Esbjerg FB	2, 4	*1957, 62,* **64,** *76, 78,* **85**
Frem København	2, 3	**1956,** *69, 71, 78,* **81**
B1903 København	2, 2	*1979, 82,* **86, 92**
FC København	2, 2	**1995,** *98,* **97,** *2002*
B1909 Odense	2, 1	**1962, 71,** *77*
KB København	1, 4	*1961, 65, 66,* **69,** *84*
Akademisk	1, 3	*1956, 95,* **99,** *2001*
B1913 Odense	1, 0	**1963**
Vanlose BK	1, 0	**1974**
Viborg FF	1, 0	**2000**
Hvidovre BK	1, 0	**1980**
Silkeborg IF	1, 0	**2001**
Ikast BK	0, 3	*1986, 89, 97*
B1901 Nykøbing	0, 2	*1973, 83*
Holbaek BK	0, 2	*1975, 76*
Køge BK	0, 2	*1963, 79*
Aalborg Chang	0, 1	*1955*
Frem Sakskøbing	0, 1	*1960*
Fremad Amager	0, 1	*1972*
Naestved IF	0, 1	*1994*
Odense KFUM	0, 1	*1964*

DENMARK

Association Football in Norway

1890

1892: Kongsvinger IL formed, Norway's oldest club

1895

1902: Formation of FA: Norges Fotballforbund. First Norwegian Cup Final

1900

1905: Independence from Sweden

1905

⚽ 🇳🇴 **1908:** Affiliation to FIFA. First international, v Sweden, lost 11-3, venue: Gothenburg

1910

1915

1920

1925

1930

1935

1938: First national championship

1940

⚜ **1941–47:** League abandoned during war, Cup abandoned 1941–44

1945

1950

⚽ **1954:** Affiliation to UEFA

1955

1960

1962: National championship reorganized as full league

1965

1970

⚽♀ **1975:** National FA incorporates women's football

1975

⚽♀ 🇳🇴 **1978:** First women's international, v Sweden

1980

1985

⚽♀ **1991:** Women's World Cup runners-up. Premier League formed

1990

⚽♀ **1995:** Women's World Cup winners

1995

⚽♀ **2000:** Women's team win Olympic gold medal

2000

2005

NORWAY

Key

 International football

⚽ Affiliation to FIFA

⚽ Affiliation to UEFA

⚽ Women's football

⚜ War

Extreme weather *presents a considerable problem for regular football in Norway. Alfheim Stadium (above), home of Tromsø IL, is above the Arctic Circle.*

Since the advent of *the Premier League in 1991, teams like Rosenborg BK from Trondheim (in white, playing against Feyenoord from the Netherlands) have appeared regularly in the Champions League.*

Norway: The main clubs

Moss FK
1906   Team name with year of formation

● Club formed before 1912

● Club formed 1912–25

● Club formed 1925–50

○ Club formed after 1950

★ Founder members of Premier League (1991)

 Leading clubs in 1938 national championship

Colours unknown

Steinkjer IFK 1919

Rosenborg BK 1917

Fyllingen 1946

SK Brann Bergen 1908

Steinkjer

Trondheim

Molde

Molde FK 1911

★ **Gjøvik Lyn** 1902

Sogndal IL 1926

Bergen

Drammen
IF Strømsgodset 1907

Kongsvinger

Lillestrør

FK Haugesund 1993

Stavanger

Horten
Skien

Moss

Larvik

★ **Viking FK**
Stavanger 1899

Kristiansand

★ **IK Start** 1892

★ **Odd Grenland** 1894
Formerly Odd SK Skien

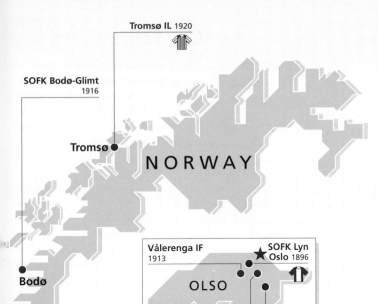

Tromsø IL 1920

SOFK Bodø-Glimt 1916

Tromsø

N O R W A Y

Bodø

ctic Circle

Vålerenga IF 1913

SOFK Lyn Oslo 1896

OLSO

FK Skeid Oslo 1915

Stabaek 1912

Frigg SK Oslo 1904

Sarpsborg

FK Sarpsborg 1903

Fredrikstad

Fredrikstad FK 1903

FREDRIKSTAD AND SARPSBORG

Kongsvinger IL 1892

Lillestrøm SK 1917

OSLO (see inset)

Moss FK 1906

FREDRIKSTAD AND SARPSBORG (see inset)

Mjøndalen IF 1910

Orn FK Horten 1904

IF Fram 1894

Larvik Turn IF 1906

The Norwegian national women's team is one of the strongest in the world. It is shown here sporting its Olympic gold medals from Sydney 2000. The team beat the USA 3-2 in a memorable Final.

Norway

ORIGINS AND GROWTH OF FOOTBALL

LIKE ITS SCANDINAVIAN NEIGHBOURS Norway was exposed to football in the late 19th century, and proved an early and enthusiastic adopter of the game. Clubs emerged all over the country in the years up to and including the First World War, some of the earliest being Kongsvinger IL (1892), Odd SK Skien (1894), SOFK Lyn Oslo (1896) and Viking FK Stavanger (1899).

The cost of amateurism

A national FA was set up in 1902, joining FIFA in 1908. A national cup competition was also early, beginning in 1902. However, the development of the sport was always constrained by weather and sentiment. The extremes of cold and snow present a considerable problem for regular football, and make the competing attractions of winter sports and games compelling. This aside, the prevailing amateurism of Norwegian football has ensured that little money or development could take place in the game relative to the international competition. A national league was not actually created until 1937 and it was decided by play-offs until 1961 when a more conventional league was created. Despite all of this, Oslo, the capital city, has yet to produce a consistently powerful team and leading clubs and players continue to come from small towns and rural Norway.

Powerful women

In the 1990s Norwegian football began to change with the arrival of significant government support for elite sports, the installation of the tough-minded Egil Olsen as national team manager and an increasing place for full-time and professional footballers – in the leading clubs at least. A national premier league has been created, and at European level Rosenborg and SK Brann have performed creditably. By contrast to the men's game, Norwegian women's football is a strong force on the global stage, with the national team winning the inaugural FIFA Women's World Cup in China in 1988 and the Olympic gold in Sydney 2000.

Egil Olsen *(professor of Economics and national team manager 1990–98) brought a new tactical awareness.*

NORWAY

Norway

Norges Fotballforbund
Founded: 1902
Joined FIFA: 1908
Joined UEFA: 1954

NORWAY

NORWEGIAN DOMESTIC FOOTBALL began with the establishment of the Norges Fotballforbund in 1902 when a national cup competition was set up; this has run every year since, only stopping between 1941 and 1944 in the midst of the Second World War. However, antiquity does not guarantee popularity, and attendances at some Finals have dipped below the 2,000 mark. A national league arrived later, and the first championships took place in 1938. Until 1961, the title was decided by a knockout phase, but since 1962 it has kept a simplified league format.

Norwegian League Record 1938–2001

SEASON	CHAMPIONS	RUNNERS-UP
1938	Fredrikstad FK	SOFK Lyn Oslo
1939	Fredrikstad FK	FK Skeid Oslo
1940–47	no championship	
1948	Freidig SK	Sparta Sarpsborg
1949	Fredrikstad FK	Vålerenga IF
1950	Fram Larvik	Fredrikstad FK
1951	Fredrikstad FK	Odd SK Skien
1952	Fredrikstad FK	SK Brann Bergen
1953	Larvik Turn IF	FK Skeid Oslo
1954	Fredrikstad FK	FK Skeid Oslo
1955	Larvik Turn IF	Fredrikstad FK
1956	Larvik Turn IF	Fredrikstad FK
1957	Fredrikstad FK	Odd SK Skien
1958	Viking FK Stavanger	FK Skeid Oslo
1959	Lillestrøm SK	Fredrikstad FK
1960	Fredrikstad FK	Lillestrøm SK
1961	Fredrikstad FK	IF Eik
1962	SK Brann Bergen	Steinkjer IFK
1963	SK Brann Bergen	SOFK Lyn Oslo
1964	SOFK Lyn Oslo	Fredrikstad FK
1965	Vålerenga IF	SOFK Lyn Oslo
1966	FK Skeid Oslo	Fredrikstad FK
1967	Rosenborg BK	FK Skeid Oslo
1968	SOFK Lyn Oslo	Rosenborg BK
1969	Rosenborg BK	Fredrikstad FK
1970	IF Strømgodset	Rosenborg BK
1971	Rosenborg BK	SOFK Lyn Oslo
1972	Viking FK Stavanger	Fredrikstad FK
1973	Viking FK Stavanger	Rosenborg BK
1974	Viking FK Stavanger	Molde FK
1975	Viking FK Stavanger	SK Brann Bergen
1976	Lillestrøm SK	Mjøndalen IF
1977	Lillestrøm SK	SOFK Bodø-Glimt
1978	Start Kristiansand	Lillestrøm SK
1979	Viking FK Stavanger	Moss FK
1980	Start Kristiansand	Bryne FK
1981	Vålerenga IF	Viking FK Stavanger
1982	Viking FK Stavanger	Bryne FK
1983	Vålerenga IF	Lillestrøm SK
1984	Vålerenga IF	Viking FK Stavanger
1985	Rosenborg BK	Lillestrøm SK
1986	Lillestrøm SK	Mjøndalen IF
1987	Moss FK	Molde FK
1988	Rosenborg BK	Lillestrøm SK
1989	Lillestrøm SK	Rosenborg BK
1990	Rosenborg BK	Tromsø IL
1991	Viking FK Stavanger	Rosenborg BK
1992	Rosenborg BK	Viking FK Stavanger
1993	Rosenborg BK	SOFK Bodø-Glimt

Norwegian League Record (*continued*)

SEASON	CHAMPIONS	RUNNERS-UP
1994	Rosenborg BK	Lillestrøm SK
1995	Rosenborg BK	Molde FK
1996	Rosenborg BK	Lillestrøm SK
1997	Rosenborg BK	SK Brann Bergen
1998	Rosenborg BK	Molde FK
1999	Rosenborg BK	Molde FK
2000	Rosenborg BK	SK Brann Bergen
2001	Rosenborg BK	Lillestrøm SK

Norwegian League Summary

TEAM	TOTALS	CHAMPIONS & RUNNERS-UP (BOLD) (*ITALICS*)
Rosenborg BK	16, 5	**1967**, *68*, **69**, **70**, **71**, *73*, **85**, **88**, **89**, **90**, **91**, **1992–2001**
Fredrikstad FK	9, 8	**1938**, *39*, **49**, **50**, *51*, **52**, **54**, *55*, *56*, *57*, *59*, **60**, **61**, *64*, *66*, *69*, *72*
Viking FK Stavanger	8, 3	**1958**, **72–75**, *79*, **81**, **82**, **84**, **91**, *92*
Lillestrøm SK	5, 8	*59*, **60**, **76**, **77**, *78*, *83*, *85*, **86**, *88*, **89**, *94*, *96*, **2001**
Vålerenga IF	4, 1	*1949*, **65**, **81**, **83**, **84**
Larvik Turn IF	3, 0	**1953**, **55**, **56**
SK Brann Bergen	2, 4	*1952*, **62**, **63**, *75*, *97*, *2000*
SOFK Lyn Oslo	2, 4	*1938*, *63*, **64**, *65*, **68**, *71*
Start Kristiansand	2, 0	**1978**, **80**
FK Skeid Oslo	1, 5	*1939*, *53*, *54*, *58*, **66**, *67*
Moss FK	1, 1	*1979*, **87**
Fram Larvik	1, 0	**1950**
Freidig SK	1, 0	**1948**
IF Strømgodset	1, 0	**1970**
Molde FK	0, 5	*1974, 87, 95, 98, 99*
Bryne FK	0, 2	*1980, 82*
Mjøndalen IF	0, 2	*1976, 86*
Odd Grenland (includes Odd Sk Skien)	0, 2	*1951, 57*
SOFK Bodø-Glimt	0, 2	*1977, 93*
IF Eik	0, 1	*1961*
Sparta Sarpsborg	0, 1	*1948*
Steinkjer IFK	0, 1	*1962*
Tromsø IL	0, 1	*1990*

Norwegian Cup Record 1902–2001

YEAR	WINNERS	SCORE	RUNNERS-UP
1902	Grand Nordstrand	2-0	Odd SK Skien
1903	Odd SK Skien	1-0	Grand Nordstrand
1904	Odd SK Skien	4-0	IF Uraed
1905	Odd SK Skien	2-1	Akademisk FK Oslo
1906	Odd SK Skien	1-0	FK Sarpsborg
1907	Mercantile	3-0	FK Sarpsborg
1908	SOFK Lyn Oslo	3-2	Odd SK Skien
1909	SOFK Lyn Oslo	4-3	Odd SK Skien
1910	SOFK Lyn Oslo	4-2	Odd SK Skien
1911	SOFK Lyn Oslo	5-2	IF Uraed

Norwegian Cup Record (*continued*)

YEAR	WINNERS	SCORE	RUNNERS-UP
1912	Mercantile	6-0	Fram Larvik
1913	Odd SK Skien	2-1	Mercantile
1914	Frigg SK Oslo	4-0	Gjøvik Lyn
1915	Odd SK Skien	2-1	Kvik Halden
1916	Frigg SK Oslo	2-0	Orn FK Horten
1917	FK Sarpsborg	4-1	SK Brann Bergen
1918	Kvik Halden	4-0	SK Brann Bergen
1919	Odd SK Skien	1-0	Frigg SK Oslo
1920	Orn FK Horten	1-0	Frigg SK Oslo
1921	Frigg SK Oslo	2-0	Odd SK Skien
1922	Odd SK Skien	5-1	Kvik Halden
1923	SK Brann Bergen	2-1	SOFK Lyn Oslo
1924	Odd SK Skien	3-0	Mjøndalen IF
1925	SK Brann Bergen	3-0	FK Sarpsborg
1926	Odd SK Skien	3-0	Orn FK Horten
1927	Orn FK Horten	4-0	Drafn SK
1928	Orn FK Horten	2-1	SOFK Lyn Oslo
1929	FK Sarpsborg	2-1	Orn FK Horten
1930	Orn FK Horten	4-2	Drammens BK
1931	Odd SK Skien	3-1	Mjøndalen IF
1932	Fredrikstad FK	6-1	Orn FK Horten
1933	Mjøndalen IF	3-1	Viking FK Stavanger
1934	Mjøndalen IF	2-1	FK Sarpsborg
1935	Fredrikstad FK	4-0	FK Sarpsborg
1936	Fredrikstad FK	2-0	Mjøndalen IF
1937	Mjøndalen IF	4-2	Odd SK Skien
1938	Fredrikstad FK	3-2	Mjøndalen IF
1939	FK Sarpsborg	2-1	FK Skeid Oslo
1940	Fredrikstad FK	3-0	FK Skeid Oslo
1941–44	*no competition*		
1945	SOFK Lyn Oslo	1-1, (replay) 1-1, (replay) 4-0	Fredrikstad FK
1946	SOFK Lyn Oslo	3-2	Fredrikstad FK
1947	FK Skeid Oslo	2-0	Viking FK Stavanger
1948	FK Sarpsborg	1-0	Fredrikstad FK
1949	FK Sarpsborg	3-1	FK Skeid Oslo
1950	Fredrikstad FK	3-0	SK Brann Bergen
1951	FK Sarpsborg	3-2	Asker
1952	Sparta Sarpsborg	3-2	Solberg
1953	Viking FK Stavanger	2-1	Lillestrøm SK
1954	FK Skeid Oslo	3-0	Fredrikstad FK
1955	FK Skeid Oslo	5-0	Lillestrøm SK
1956	FK Skeid Oslo	2-1	Larvik Turn IF
1957	Fredrikstad FK	4-0	Sandefjord BK
1958	FK Skeid Oslo	1-0	Lillestrøm SK
1959	Viking FK Stavanger	2-1	Sandefjord BK
1960	Rosenborg BK	3-3, (replay) 3-2	Odd SK Skien
1961	Fredrikstad FK	7-0	SK Hauger
1962	Gjøvik Lyn	2-0	SK Vard Haugesund
1963	FK Skeid Oslo	2-1	Fredrikstad FK
1964	Rosenborg BK	2-1	FK Sarpsborg
1965	FK Skeid Oslo	2-2, (replay) 1-1, (replay) 2-1	Frigg SK Oslo
1966	Fredrikstad FK	3-2	SOFK Lyn Oslo
1967	SOFK Lyn Oslo	4-1	Rosenborg BK
1968	SOFK Lyn Oslo	3-0	Mjøndalen IF
1969	IF Strømgodset	2-2, (replay) 5-3	Fredrikstad FK
1970	IF Strømgodset	4-2	SOFK Lyn Oslo
1971	Rosenborg BK	4-1	Fredrikstad FK
1972	SK Brann Bergen	1-0	Rosenborg BK
1973	IF Strømgodset	1-0	Rosenborg BK
1974	FK Skeid Oslo	3-1	Viking FK Stavanger
1975	SOFK Bodø-Glimt	2-0	SK Vard Haugesund
1976	SK Brann Bergen	2-1	Sogndal IL
1977	Lillestrøm SK	1-0	SOFK Bodø-Glimt
1978	Lillestrøm SK	2-1	SK Brann Bergen
1979	Viking FK Stavanger	2-1	SK Hauger
1980	Vålerenga IF	4-1	Lillestrøm SK
1981	Lillestrøm SK	3-1	Moss FK
1982	SK Brann Bergen	3-2	Molde FK
1983	Moss FK	2-0	Vålerenga IF
1984	Fredrikstad FK	3-3, (replay) 3-2	Viking FK Stavanger
1985	Lillestrøm SK	4-1	Vålerenga IF

Norwegian Cup Record (*continued*)

YEAR	WINNERS	SCORE	RUNNERS-UP
1986	Tromsø IL	4-1	Lillestrøm SK
1987	Bryne FK	1-0	SK Brann Bergen
1988	Rosenborg BK	2-2, (replay) 2-0	SK Brann Bergen
1989	Viking FK Stavanger	2-2, (replay) 2-1	Molde FK
1990	Rosenborg BK	5-1	Fyllingen
1991	IF Strømgodset	3-2	Rosenborg BK
1992	Rosenborg BK	3-2	Lillestrøm SK
1993	SOFK Bodø-Glimt	2-0	IF Strømgodset
1994	Molde FK	3-2	Lyn
1995	Rosenborg BK	1-1, (replay) 3-1	SK Brann Bergen
1996	Tromsø IL	2-1	SOFK Bodø-Glimt
1997	Vålerenga IF	4-2	IF Strømgodset
1998	Stabaek	3-1	Rosenborg BK
1999	Rosenborg BK	2-0	SK Brann Bergen
2000	Odd Grenland	2-1	Viking FK Stavanger
2001	Viking FK Stavanger	3-0	Bryne FK

Norwegian Cup Summary

TEAM	TOTALS	WINNERS & RUNNERS-UP (BOLD) (*ITALICS*)
Odd Grenland (includes Odd Sk Skien)	12, 7	*1902*, **03–06**, *08–10*, **13**, **15**, **19**, *21*, **22**, **24**, **26**, **31**, *37*, *60*, **2000**
Fredrikstad FK	10, 7	**1932**, *35*, **36**, *38*, **40**, *45*, *46*, **48**, **50**, *54*, **57**, *61*, *63*, **66**, *69*, *71*, **84**
Rosenborg BK	8, 5	**1960**, **64**, *67*, **71**, *72*, *73*, **88**, **90**, *91*, **92**, **95**, *98*, **99**
SOFK Lyn Oslo	8, 4	**1908–11**, *23*, *28*, **45**, **46**, *66*, **67**, **68**, *70*
FK Skeid Oslo	8, 3	*1939*, *40*, **47**, *49*, **54–56**, **58**, **63**, **65**, **74**
FK Sarpsborg	6, 6	*1906*, *07*, **17**, *18*, **23**, **25**, *29*, *34*, *35*, **39**, **48**, **49**, *51*, *64*
SK Brann Bergen	5, 8	*1917*, *18*, **23**, **25**, *50*, *72*, **76**, *78*, *82*, *87*, *88*, *95*, *99*
Viking FK Stavanger	5, 5	*1933*, *47*, **53**, **59**, *74*, **79**, *84*, **89**, *2000*, **01**
Lillestrøm SK	4, 6	*1953*, *55*, *58*, **77**, *78*, **80**, **81**, *85*, *86*, **92**
Orn FK Horten	4, 4	*1916*, **20**, *26*, **27**, *28*, **29**, **30**, *32*
IF Strømgodset	4, 2	**1969**, **70**, *73*, **91**, *93*, *97*
Mjøndalen IF	3, 5	*1924*, *31*, **33**, **34**, *36*, **37**, *38*, *68*
Frigg SK Oslo	3, 3	**1914**, **16**, *19*, *20*, **21**, *65*
SOFK Bodø-Glimt	2, 2	**1975**, *77*, **93**, *96*
Vålerenga IF	2, 2	**1980**, *83*, *85*, **97**
Mercantile	2, 1	**1907**, **12**, *13*
Tromsø IL	2, 0	**1986**, **96**
Kvik Halden	1, 2	*1915*, **18**, *22*
Molde FK	1, 2	*1982*, *89*, **94**
Bryne FK	1, 1	**1987**, *2001*
Gjøvik Lyn	1, 1	*1914*, **62**
Grand Nordstrand	1, 1	**1902**, *03*
Moss FK	1, 1	*1981*, **83**
Sparta Sarpsborg	1, 0	**1952**
Stabaek	1, 0	**1998**
IF Uraed	0, 2	*1904*, *11*
Sandefjord	0, 2	*1957*, *59*
SK Hauger	0, 2	*1961*, *79*
SK Vard Haugesund	0, 2	*1962*, *75*
Akademisk FK Oslo	0, 1	*1905*
Asker	0, 1	*1951*
Drafn SK	0, 1	*1927*
Drammens BK	0, 1	*1930*
Fram Larvik	0, 1	*1912*
Fyllingen	0, 1	*1990*
Larvik Turn IF	0, 1	*1956*
Lyn	0, 1	*1994*
Sogndal IL	0, 1	*1976*
Solberg	0, 1	*1952*

Finland

Suomen Palloliitto/Finlands Bollförbund
Founded: 1907
Joined FIFA: 1908
Joined UEFA: 1954

FINLAND'S OLDEST CLUB – Reipas Lahti – was founded in 1891, and its association was founded in 1907. A regular league, based in Helsinki, started almost immediately, and gradually spread to include the rest of the country. Until 1929, the title was decided via a play-off, after which a league format was adopted. A national cup competition was established in 1955.

Finnish League Record 1908–2001

SEASON	CHAMPIONS	RUNNERS-UP
1908	Unitas Helsinki	PUS Helsinki
1909	PUS Helsinki	HIFK Helsinki
1910	ÅIFK Turku	Reipas Viipuri
1911	HJK Helsinki	HIFK Helsinki
1912	HJK Helsinki	HIFK Helsinki
1913	KIF Helsinki	ÅIFK Helsinki
1914	no championship	
1915	KIF Helsinki	ÅIFK Turku
1916	KIF Helsinki	ÅIFK Turku
1917	HJK Helsinki	ÅIFK Turku
1918	HJK Helsinki	Reipas Viipuri
1919	HJK Helsinki	Reipas Viipuri
1920	ÅIFK Turku	HPS Helsinki
1921	HPS Helsinki	HJK Helsinki
1922	HPS Helsinki	Reipas Viipuri
1923	HJK Helsinki	TPS Turku
1924	ÅIFK Turku	HPS Helsinki
1925	HJK Helsinki	TPS Turku
1926	HPS Helsinki	TPS Turku
1927	HPS Helsinki	Reipas Viipuri
1928	TPS Turku	HIFK Helsinki
1929	HPS Helsinki	HIFK Helsinki
1930	HIFK Helsinki	TPS Turku
1931	HIFK Helsinki	HPS Helsinki
1932	HPS Helsinki	VPS Vaasa
1933	HIFK Helsinki	HJK Helsinki
1934	HPS Helsinki	HIFK Helsinki
1935	HPS Helsinki	HIFK Helsinki
1936	HJK Helsinki	HPS Helsinki
1937	HIFK Helsinki	HJK Helsinki
1938	HJK Helsinki	TPS Turku
1939	TPS Turku	HJK Helsinki
1940	Sudet Viipuri	TPS Turku
1941	TPS Turku	VPS Vaasa
1942	HT Helsinki	Sudet Viipuri
1943	no championship	
1944	VIFK Vaasa	TPS Turku
1945	VPS Vaasa	HPS Helsinki
1946	VIFK Vaasa	TPV Tampere
1947	HIFK Helsinki	TuTo Turku
1948	VPS Vaasa	TPS Turku
1949	TPS Turku	VPS Vaasa
1950	Ikissat Tampere	KuPS Kuopio
1951	KTP Kotka	VIFK Vaasa
1952	KTP Kotka	VIFK Vaasa
1953	VIFK Vaasa	Jäntevä Kotka
1954	Pyrkivä Turku	KuPS Kuopio
1955	KIF Helsinki	Haka Valkeakoski
1956	KuPS Kuopio	HJK Helsinki
1957	HPS Helsinki	Haka Valkeakoski
1958	KuPS Kuopio	HPS Helsinki
1959	HIFK Helsinki	RU-38 Pori
1960	Haka Valkeakoski	TPS Turku
1961	HIFK Helsinki	KIF Helsinki

Finnish League Record (*continued*)

SEASON	CHAMPIONS	RUNNERS-UP
1962	Haka Valkeakoski	Reipas Lahti
1963	Reipas Lahti	Haka Valkeakoski
1964	HJK Helsinki	KuPS Kuopio
1965	Haka Valkeakoski	KuPS Kuopio
1966	KuPS Kuopio	HJK Helsinki
1967	Reipas Lahti	KuPS Kuopio
1968	TPS Turku	Reipas Lahti
1969	KPV Kokkola	KuPS Kuopio
1970	Reipas Lahti	MP Mikkeli
1971	TPS Turku	HIFK Helsinki
1972	TPS Turku	MP Mikkeli
1973	HJK Helsinki	KPV Kokkola
1974	KuPS Kuopio	Reipas Lahti
1975	TPS Turku	KuPS Kuopio
1976	KuPS Kuopio	Haka Valkeakoski
1977	Haka Valkeakoski	KuPS Kuopio
1978	HJK Helsinki	KPT Kuopio
1979	OPS Oulu	KuPS Kuopio
1980	OPS Oulu	Haka Valkeakoski
1981	HJK Helsinki	KPT Kuopio
1982	Kuusysi Lahti	HJK Helsinki
1983	Ilves Tampere	HJK Helsinki
1984	Kuusysi Lahti	TPS Turku
1985	HJK Helsinki	Ilves Tampere
1986	Kuusysi Lahti	TPS Turku
1987	HJK Helsinki	Kuusysi Lahti
1988	HJK Helsinki	Kuusysi Lahti
1989	Kuusysi Lahti	TPS Turku
1990	HJK Helsinki	Kuusysi Lahti
1991	Kuusysi Lahti	MP Mikkeli
1992	HJK Helsinki	Kuusysi Lahti
1993	Jazz Pori	MyPa Anjalankoski
1994	TPV Tampere	MyPa Anjalankoski
1995	Haka Valkeakoski	MyPa Anjalankoski
1996	Jazz Pori	MyPa Anjalankoski
1997	HJK Helsinki	VPS Vaasa
1998	Haka Valkeakoski	VPS Vaasa
1999	Haka Valkeakoski	HJK Helsinki
2000	Haka Valkeakoski	Jokerit Helsinki
2001	Tampere United	HJK Helsinki

Finnish League Summary

TEAM	TOTALS	CHAMPIONS & RUNNERS-UP (BOLD) (*ITALICS*)
HJK Helsinki	**19**, *10*	**1911, 12, 17–19, 21, 23, 25, 33, 36,** *37,* **38,** *39, 56,* **64,** *66,* **73,** *78,* **81, 82, 83,** *85,* **87, 88,** *90,* **92,** *97,* **99, 2001**
HPS Helsinki	**9**, *6*	**1920,** *21,* **22,** *24,* **26, 27, 29, 31, 32, 34, 35,** *36, 45, 57, 58*
TPS Turku	**8**, *12*	*1923, 25, 26,* **28,** *30, 38, 39, 40,* **41,** *44, 48, 49, 60, 68,* **71,** *72, 75,* **84,** *86, 89*
Haka Valkeakoski	**8**, *5*	*1955, 57,* **60,** *62, 63,* **65,** *76,* **77,** *80,* **95,** *98,* **99, 2000**
HIFK Helsinki	**7**, *8*	*1909, 11, 12, 28, 29,* **30, 31,** *33, 34, 35,* **37, 47,** *59,* **61,** *71*
KuPS Kuopio	**5**, *9*	*1950, 54,* **56,** *58,* **64,** *65, 66, 67, 69, 74,* **75,** *76, 77, 79*
Kuusysi Lahti	**5**, *4*	**1982, 84, 86,** *87, 88,* **89,** *90,* **91,** *92*
KIF Helsinki	**4**, *1*	**1913, 15, 16, 55,** *61*
ÅIFK Turku	**3**, *3*	**1910,** *15, 16, 17,* **20, 24**
Reipas Lahti	**3**, *3*	*1962,* **63,** *67, 68,* **70,** *74*
VIFK Vaasa	**3**, *2*	**1944,** *46,* **51, 52, 53**
VPS Vaasa	**2**, *5*	*1932, 41,* **45, 48,** *49, 97, 98*

Finnish League Summary (*continued*)

TEAM	TOTALS	CHAMPIONS & RUNNERS-UP (BOLD) (*ITALICS*)
Tampere United (includes Ikissat Tampere, Ilves Tampere)	3, 1	**1950, 83,** *85,* **2001**
Jazz Pori	2, 0	**1993, 96**
KTP Kotka	2, 0	**1951, 52**
OPS Oulu	2, 0	**1979, 80**
KPV Kokkola	1, 1	**1969,** *73*
PUS Helsinki	1, 1	**1908,** *09*
Sudet Viipuri	1, 1	**1940,** *42*
TPV Tampere	1, 1	*1946,* **94**
HT Helsinki	1, 0	**1942**
Pyrkivä Turku	1, 0	*1954*
Unitas Helsinki	1, 0	**1908**

This summary only features clubs that have won the Finnish League. For a full list of league champions and runners-up please see the League Record opposite.

Finnish Cup Record 1955–2001

YEAR	WINNERS	SCORE	RUNNERS-UP
1955	Haka Valkeakoski	5-1	HPS Helsinki
1956	PPojat Helsinki	2-1	TKT Tampere
1957	Drott Pietarsaari	2-1 (aet)	KPT Kuopio
1958	KTP Kotka	4-1	KIF Helsinki
1959	Haka Valkeakoski	2-1	HIFK Helsinki
1960	Haka Valkeakoski	3-1 (aet)	RU-38 Pori
1961	KTP Kotka	5-2	PPojat Helsinki
1962	HPS Helsinki	5-0	RoPS Rovaniemi
1963	Haka Valkeakoski	1-0	Reipas Lahti
1964	Reipas Lahti	1-0	LaPa Lappeenranta
1965	ÅIFK Turku	1-0	TPS Turku
1966	HJK Helsinki	6-1	KTP Kotka
1967	KTP Kotka	2-0	Reipas Lahti
1968	KuPS Kuopio	2-1	KTP Kotka
1969	Haka Valkeakoski	2-0	Honka Espoo
1970	MP Mikkeli	4-1 (aet)	Reipas Lahti
1971	MP Mikkeli	4-1	Sport Vaasa
1972	Reipas Lahti	2-0	VPS Vaasa
1973	Reipas Lahti	1-0	SePS Seinäjoki
1974	Reipas Lahti	1-0	OTP Oulu
1975	Reipas Lahti	6-2 (aet)	HJK Helsinki
1976	Reipas Lahti	2-0	Ilves Tampere
1977	Haka Valkeakoski	3-1	SePS Seinäjoki
1978	Reipas Lahti	3-1, 1-1 (2 legs)	KPT Kuopio
1979	Ilves Tampere	2-0	TPS Turku
1980	KTP Kotka	3-2	Haka Valkeakoski
1981	HJK Helsinki	4-0	Kuusysi Lahti
1982	Haka Valkeakoski	3-2	KPV Kokkola
1983	Kuusysi Lahti	2-0	Haka Valkeakoski
1984	HJK Helsinki	2-1	Kuusysi Lahti
1985	Haka Valkeakoski	2-2 (aet)(2-1 pens)	HJK Helsinki
1986	RoPS Rovaniemi	2-0	KePS Kemi
1987	Kuusysi Lahti	5-4	OTP Oulu
1988	Haka Valkeakoski	1-0	OTP Oulu
1989	KuPS Kuopio	3-2	Haka Valkeakoski
1990	Ilves Tampere	2-1	HJK Helsinki
1991	TPS Turku	0-0 (aet)(5-3 pens)	Kuusysi Lahti
1992	MyPa Anjalankoski	2-0	Jaro Pietarsaari
1993	HJK Helsinki	2-0	RoPS Rovaniemi
1994	TPS Turku	2-1	HJK Helsinki
1995	MyPa Anjalankoski	1-0	Jazz Pori
1996	HJK Helsinki	0-0 (aet)(4-3 pens)	TPS Turku
1997	Haka Valkeakoski	2-1 (aet)	TPS Turku
1998	HJK Helsinki	3-2	PK-35 Helsinki
1999	Jokerit Helsinki	2-1	Jaro Pietarsaari
2000	HJK Helsinki	1-0	KTP Kotka
2001	Atlantis Helsinki	1-0	Tampere United

Finnish Cup Summary

TEAM	TOTALS	WINNERS & RUNNERS-UP (BOLD) (*ITALICS*)
Haka Valkeakoski	10, 3	**1955, 59, 60, 63, 69, 77,** *80,* **82, 83, 85, 88,** *89,* **97**
HJK Helsinki	7, 4	**1966,** *75,* **81, 84,** *85,* **90, 93,** *94,* **96, 98, 2000**
Reipas Lahti	7, 3	*1963,* **64,** *67,* **70,** *72–76,* **78**
KTP Kotka	4, 3	**1958, 61,** *66,* **67,** *68,* **80,** *2000*
TPS Turku	2, 4	*1965,* **79,** *91,* **94,** *96, 97*
Kuusysi Lahti	2, 3	**1981,** *83,* **84,** *87,* **91**
Tampere United (includes Ilves Tampere)	2, 2	*1976,* **79,** *90,* **2001**
KuPS Kuopio	2, 0	**1968, 89**
MP Mikkeli	2, 0	**1970, 71**
MyPa Anjalankoski	2, 0	**1992, 95**
Jaro Pietarsaari (includes Drott Pietarsaari)	1, 2	**1957,** *92, 99*
RoPS Rovaniemi	1, 2	*1962,* **86,** *93*
FC Jokerit (includes PK-35 Helsinki and Jokerit Helsinki)	1, 1	*1998,* **99**
HPS Helsinki	1, 1	*1955,* **62**
PPojat Helsinki	1, 1	**1956,** *61*
ÅIFK Turku	1, 0	**1965**
Atlantis Helsinki	1, 0	**2001**

This summary only features clubs that have won the Finnish Cup. For a full list of cup winners and runners-up please see the Cup Record left.

Faeroe Islands

Fotboltssamband Føroya
Founded: 1979
Joined FIFA: 1988
Joined UEFA: 1992

The tiny Faeroe Islands have played regular league football since 1942. The national team played their first competitive international in 1990, beating a lacklustre and complacent Austrian side.

SEASON	LEAGUE CHAMPIONS
1997	B36
1998	HB
1999	KÍ
2000	VB
2001	GÍ

YEAR	CUP WINNERS
1997	GÍ
1998	HB
1999	KÍ
2000	GÍ
2001	B36

Iceland

The Football Association of Iceland
Founded: 1947
Joined FIFA: 1929
Joined UEFA: 1954

The first Icelandic football club, KR of Reykjavík, was set up in 1899. Football formalized in Iceland in 1912 with the creation of a Reykjavik league, though the national football association was not formed until 1947. A cup was established in 1960, ensuring a berth in the Cup-Winners' Cup for the victors.

SEASON	LEAGUE CHAMPIONS
1997	ÍBV
1998	ÍBV
1999	KR
2000	KR
2001	ÍA

YEAR	CUP WINNERS
1997	Keflavík
1998	ÍBV
1999	KR
2000	ÍA
2001	Fylkir

England

THE SEASON IN REVIEW 2001–02

AT OLD TRAFFORD on 8 May 2002, in the heart of enemy territory, Arsenal manager Arsène Wenger announced a 'shift in power' in English football. After three seasons of Manchester United title triumphs, Arsenal went to Manchester and won 1-0 on a night when the Londoners never looked less than in control. In every way Arsenal's league season was a great one. The team never lost away from home, it scored in every single game and the team put together an unbroken run of 13 games at the end of the season. Composed, consistent, aggressive and inventive, Arsenal showed style and character throughout the campaign. Thierry Henry's balletic performances were complemented by the surging presence of Freddie Ljungberg, whose late-season form carried the champions. Dennis Bergkamp reminded everyone of his talents, Patrick Viera gave the midfield solidity, presence and an unquenchable spirit, and Robert Pires gave it grace and style.

United's poor run

With the Premier League clubs fortified by the announcement of their biggest TV rights deal ever – making it the richest in the world – the season began with a flurry of transfers and reinforcements. At United, Sir Alex Ferguson announced his end-of-season retirement and his European ambitions by spending over £40 million on Ruud van Nistelrooy and Juan Sebastian Veron. Arsenal brought in Sol Campbell on a free transfer from rivals Tottenham, while Chelsea continued to spend freely. In the run up to Christmas, Manchester United showed its poorest run of domestic form for many years. The uncertainty surrounding Ferguson's retirement, and the seeming inability of the team to adapt to or incorporate Veron, saw United slipping off the lead. Most importantly, the shock sale of Jaap Stam to Lazio and his

English Premier League Table 2001–02

CLUB	P	W	D	L	F	A	Pts	
Arsenal	38	26	9	3	79	36	**87**	Champions League
Liverpool	38	24	8	6	67	30	**80**	Champions League
Manchester United	38	24	5	9	87	45	**77**	Champions League
Newcastle United	38	21	8	9	74	52	**71**	Champions League
Leeds United	38	18	12	8	53	37	**66**	UEFA Cup
Chelsea	38	17	13	8	66	38	**64**	UEFA Cup
West Ham United	38	15	8	15	48	57	**53**	
Aston Villa	38	12	14	12	46	47	**50**	
Tottenham Hotspur	38	14	8	16	49	53	**50**	
Blackburn Rovers	38	12	10	16	55	50	**46**	UEFA Cup
Southampton	38	12	9	17	46	54	**45**	
Middlesbrough	38	12	9	17	35	47	**45**	
Fulham	38	10	14	14	36	44	**44**	
Charlton	38	10	14	14	38	49	**44**	
Everton	38	11	10	17	45	57	**43**	
Bolton	38	9	13	16	44	62	**40**	
Sunderland	38	10	10	18	29	51	**40**	
Ipswich Town	38	9	9	20	41	64	**36**	Relegated / UEFA Cup (Fair play)
Derby County	38	8	6	24	33	63	**30**	Relegated
Leicester City	38	5	13	20	30	64	**28**	Relegated

Promoted clubs: Birmingham City, Manchester City, West Bromwich Albion.

Top: £19 million brought Ruud van Nistelrooy from PSV to Manchester United – 23 league goals in his first season looks like a good return on the investment.

Above: Lee Bowyer's explosive midfield form took Leeds to the top of the league before Christmas. But in the aftermath of his trials and O'Leary's autobiography both his and the club's form dipped, and player-club relations are now at an all-time low.

Right: Leicester manager Peter Taylor was one of the season's first managerial casualties. But his successor Dave Bassett couldn't keep the team in contention. There were also mid-season changes at Everton and Derby.

Kevin Lisbie scores against Tottenham as Charlton grinds out another London derby success.

Tension on the Liverpool bench: Gérard Houllier's heart condition kept him away for most of the season while deputy Phil Thompson steered the ship with the able assistance of Sammy Lee.

Alan Shearer scores for Newcastle against Everton. Shearer's early retirement from international football has left him free to concentrate on club duties and he was joint top scorer with 24 goals this season. Newcastle's best performance for five years sees the team back in the Champions League. Everton spent the season keeping just out of the relegation zone.

ENGLAND

replacement by the ageing Lauren Blanc made for a leaky defence. Leeds, Newcastle, Arsenal and Liverpool made the running, and together with United, they bunched at the top of the table.

In the spring Leeds steadily declined. The long-running criminal trial of two of the club's top players (Jonathan Woodgate and Lee Bowyer) disrupted the team, and the publication of an overtly candid autobiography by manager David O'Leary sowed further disquiet in the squad. Bobby Robson's rejuvenated Newcastle couldn't quite stand the pace, and Liverpool seemed stretched by its first season in the Champions League and the mid-season loss of manager Gérard Houllier to a heart condition.

Gunners firing

Sir Alex Ferguson then decided not to retire and United's form picked up; but it was too late. In the final run in, neither United nor Liverpool quite had it in them to pressure Arsenal, and the Gunners never let the lead go. Not did the team allow the pressure to affect its FA Cup run. The Final was held at the Millennium Stadium, Cardiff (and, until the disorganization and hubris that surrounds the redevelopment of Wembley is finally cleared up, it will continue to do so). Arsenal faced Chelsea and took the first half of its double. Again, composure, precision and character saw the Gunners snuff out Chelsea to take the cup 2-0.

The relegation battle took on even greater significance with the collapse of ITV Digital, a pay-TV company and paymasters of the lower divisions. After promising an astronomical £315 million to the league over the next three years, the company was put into administration well short of its subscriber targets. With many clubs spending on the basis of future income, the lower divisions face a rash of bankruptcies, mass player sales and redundancies. The inevitable steadily dawned on Leicester, Derby and finally Ipswich, who all face the financial hell of relegation next season. By contrast, David Beckham finished his season by signing a deal with Manchester United for over £4 million a year – enough to finance a small First Division club all by himself.

Will he, won't he? The postponement of Alex Ferguson's retirement gives him more time to sort out United's leaky defence.

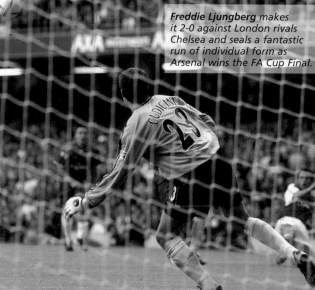

Freddie Ljungberg makes it 2-0 against London rivals Chelsea and seals a fantastic run of individual form as Arsenal wins the FA Cup Final.

League Cup

2001–02 FINAL

February 24 – Millennium Stadium, Cardiff
**Blackburn 2-1 Tottenham
Rovers   Hotspur**
(Jansen 25,   (Ziege 33)
Cole 69)
h/t: 1-1   **Att:** 72,500
Ref: G. Poll

FA Cup

2001–02 FINAL

May 4 – Millennium Stadium, Cardiff
Arsenal 2-0 Chelsea
*(Parlour 70,
Ljungberg 80)*
h/t: 0-0   **Att:** 73,963
Ref: M. Riley

International Club Performances 2001–02

CLUB	COMPETITION	PROGRESS
Arsenal	Champions League	2nd Group Phase
Liverpool	Champions League	Quarter-finals
Manchester United	Champions League	Semi-finals
Aston Villa	UEFA Cup	1st Round
Chelsea	UEFA Cup	2nd Round
Ipswich Town	UEFA Cup	3rd Round
Leeds United	UEFA Cup	4th Round

Top Goalscorers 2001–02

PLAYER	CLUB	NATIONALITY	GOALS
Thierry Henry	Arsenal	French	24
Alan Shearer	Newcastle United	English	24
Jimmy Floyd Hasselbaink	Chelsea	Dutch	23
Ruud van Nistelrooy	Manchester United	Dutch	23
Michael Owen	Liverpool	English	19

Left: *Danny Murphy splits the defence, running through Tottenham's Tarrico and Poyet.*

Below: *Jimmy Floyd Hasselbaink and Eidur Gudjohnsen. The Dutch-Icelandic duo made Chelsea's a freescoring season but woeful inconsistency saw them finish sixth in the league.*

Bottom: *The Professor finally smiles. After three trophyless seasons Arsène Wenger's Arsenal do the double again to unequivocally claim top spot.*

Ray Parlour and Freddie Ljungberg. Arsenal's two goalscorers lift the FA Cup.

The shift of power begins. Arsenal players celebrate the double after beating United at Old Trafford.

ENGLAND

Association Football in England

1846: Cambridge Rules drawn up	1845
	1850
1863: Formation of FA. First game under new rules played 19 December, Richmond v Barnes, drawn 0-0	1855
	1860
1870: First unofficial international, v Scotland, drawn 1-1, venue: London	1865
	1870
1872: First FA Cup Final. First official international, v Scotland, drawn 0-0, venue: Partick	1875
	1880
1885: Professionalism legalized	1885
1888: First league championship	1890
1892: Second Division established	1895
	1900
1905: Affiliation to FIFA	1905
	1910
	1915
1916–19: Seasons cancelled for war	
	1920
1920: Resigned from FIFA. Third Division established	
1924: Reaffiliation to FIFA	1925
1928: Resigned from FIFA	
1921: English Ladies' FA founded. FA bans women's teams from FA member grounds. Fourth Division added, bottom division renamed Third Division North and South	1930
	1935
	1940
1940–46: Seasons cancelled for war	
1946: Reaffiliation to FIFA	1945
1953: England beaten 6-3 at Wembley by Hungary	1950
1954: Affiliation to UEFA	1955
1958: Third Division North and South became Third and Fourth Divisions	
1961: League Cup first played	1960
1966: England host and win World Cup	1965
1969: Women's Football Association formed	
1972: First women's international, v Scotland, won 3-2, venue: Greenock	1970
1970: FA ban on women's teams lifted	
	1975
1983: WFA affiliated to FA	
1989: Hillsborough disaster, 95 killed by crushing. Taylor report calls for all-seater stadiums	1980
1985: Bradford fire, 56 killed. Heysel disaster, 39 killed after crowd disturbances, Liverpool v Juventus, European Cup Final. Beginning of five-year ban on English clubs in European football	1985
1991: Ban on English clubs in Europe lifted	1990
1992: Premier League breaks away from FA	1995
1993: WFA dissolved. Women's football incorporated into FA	2000
	2005

English football's finest hour – Bobby Moore holds up the 1966 World Cup.

Key
- 🏳 International football
- ⚽ Affiliation to FIFA
- ⚽ Affiliation to UEFA
- ⚽ Women's football
- War
- Disaster

England: The main clubs

Arsenal 1886 Team name with year of formation
- ● Club formed before 1912
- ★ Founder members of League (1888)
- Champions (1888–1915)
- Champions (1920–39)
- Originated from a military institution
- Originated from a cricket club
- Originated from a school or college
- Teachers' Association
- Originated from a hockey club
- Singers Cycle factory
- Railway workers
- Salter's Spring Works
- Thames Ironworks
- Originated from a church
- Originated from a rugby club

★ **Blackburn Rovers 1875**

★ **Bolton Wanderers 1874**
Christ Church (1874–77)

★ **Preston North End 1881**

Blackpool 1881
Formed after the break-up of Blackpool St. John's club. Combined with South Shore (1899)

Liverpool 1892

★ **Everton 1878**
St Domingo (1878–79)

Tranmere Rovers 1884
Belmont AFC (1884–85)

Manchester City 1887
Ardwick FC (1887–94) Amalgamation of West Gorton and Gorton Athletic

Manchester United 1878
Newton Heath LYR (1878–80), Newton Heath (1880–1902)

Stockport County 1883
Heaton Norris Rovers (1883–88), Heaton Norris (1888–90)

★ **Stoke City 1863**
Stoke Ramblers (1868–70), Stoke (1870–1925)

★ **Derby County 1884**

★ **Wolverhampton Wanderers 1879**
Merger of St Lukes (1877) and Wanderers Cricket Club

★ **West Bromwich Albion 1879**
West Bromwich Strollers (1878–81)

Blackpool · **Liverpool** · **Crewe Alexa** · **ENGLAND**

England

ORIGINS AND GROWTH OF FOOTBALL

ENGLISH FOOTBALL EMERGED from the coincidence of a rural folk football tradition and the sporting enthusiasm of England's upper-class public schools. Team games became a central part of the culture of these schools and football was the favourite sport. The wide variety of rules of the game at the time were settled with the formation of the world's first FA (1863). While many of the earliest clubs grew out of these schools, they were soon joined by clubs founded by works' teams, churches and boys' clubs from the industrial cities of the West Midlands and Lancashire. The amateur traditions of the south were surpassed in the 1880s by the alliance of working-class fans and players and middle-class directors leading to the creation of the world's first professional league in 1888.

Before the First World War all of today's leading clubs were in existence. However, the security of a hugely popular domestic game left England uninterested in international football. England had reluctantly joined FIFA in 1905 but withdrew in 1920 and again in 1928. The illusion of English dominance was crushed by failure at the 1950 World Cup and a 6-3 thrashing by Hungary at Wembley in 1953.

Pride was partly restored by World Cup victory in 1966 and a good record in Europe for English clubs in the 1970s and early 1980s. But the process of catch up seems to continue unabated.

ENGLAND

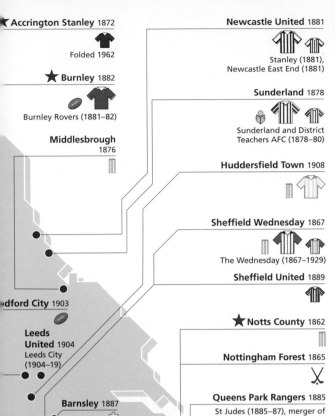

Accrington Stanley 1872
Folded 1962

Burnley 1882
Burnley Rovers (1881–82)

Middlesbrough 1876

Leeds United 1904
Leeds City (1904–19)

...dford City 1903

...chester

Barnsley 1887
Barnsley St Peters (1887–97)

Grimsby Town 1878
Grimsby Pelham (1878–79)

...rt Vale 1876
...urselm Port Vale (1876–1909)

Nottingham

Walsall 1888
Merger Walsall Swifts (1877) and Walsall Town (1879), Walsall Town Swifts (1888–95)

Leicester City 1884
Leicester Fosse (1884–1919)

Birmingham

Coventry City 1883

Aston Villa 1874
Singers FC (1883–98)

Birmingham City 1875
Small Heath Alliance (1875), Small Heath (1888), Birmingham (1905–45)

...ndon Town 1881
Watford 1881
Watford Rovers (1881–93), West Herts (1893–98), 1898 absorbed Watford St Mary's

...uthampton 1885
...uthampton Mary's 85–97)

Portsmouth 1898

London

West Ham United 1895
Thames Ironworks (1895–1900)

Newcastle United 1881
Stanley (1881), Newcastle East End (1881)

Sunderland 1878
Sunderland and District Teachers AFC (1878–80)

Huddersfield Town 1908

Sheffield Wednesday 1867
The Wednesday (1867–1929)

Sheffield United 1889

Notts County 1862

Nottingham Forest 1865

Queens Park Rangers 1885
St Judes (1885–87), merger of Christchurch Rangers and St Jude's Institute

Fulham 1879
Fulham St Andrews (1879–88)

Norwich City 1902

Ipswich Town 1878

Tottenham Hotspur 1882
Hotspurs FC (1882–84)

Arsenal 1886
Dial Square (1886), Royal Arsenal (1886–91), Woolwich Arsenal (1891–1914)

Wimbledon 1889
Wimbledon Old Centrals (1899–1905)

Crystal Palace 1905

Charlton Athletic 1905

Chelsea 1905

Key

- ■ World Cup host
- ● World Cup winner
- ◼ European Championships host
- ○ Competition winner
- △ Competition runner-up

Villa	– Aston Villa
B'ham	– Birmingham City
Ipswich	– Ipswich Town
Leeds	– Leeds United
Lon XI	– London Select XI
L'pool	– Liverpool
Man C	– Manchester City
Man U	– Manchester United
N'castle	– Newcastle United
Notts F	– Nottingham Forest
Spurs	– Tottenham Hotspur
West H	– West Ham United
Wolves	– Wolverhampton Wanderers

International Competitions

	European Cup	UEFA Cup	European Cup-Winners' Cup
1958:			△ Lon XI
1960:			△ B'ham
1961:			△ B'ham
1963:			○ Spurs
1965:			○ West H
1966: ● ◼			△ L'pool
1967:		△ Leeds	
1968:	○ Man U	○ Leeds	
1969:		○ N'castle	○ Man C
1970:		○ Arsenal	○ Chelsea
1971:		○ Leeds	
1972:		○ Spurs ○ Wolves	△ Leeds
1973:		△ Spurs	
1974:			
1975:	△ Leeds	○ L'pool	△ West H
1976:			
1977:	○ L'pool		
1978:	○ L'pool		
1979:	○ Notts F		△ Arsenal
1980:	○ Notts F		
1981:	○ L'pool	○ Ipswich	
1982:	○ Villa		
1984:	○ L'pool	○ Spurs	
1985:	△ L'pool		○ Everton
1991:			○ Man U
1994:			○ Arsenal
1995:			△ Arsenal
1996: ◼			
1998:			○ Chelsea
1999:	○ Man U		
2000:		△ Arsenal	
2001:		○ L'pool	

ENGLAND

Port Vale
(1950–)
VALE PARK

22,546

A53

HANLEY
Birthplace of
Stanley Matthews
VICTORIA GROUND

STOKE-ON-TRENT

RECREATION
GROUND

BRITANNIA
STADIUM

Stoke City
(1878–1997)

Port Vale
(1913–1950)

24,050

Stoke City
(1997–)

A50

A34

The Midlands

22,350	Capacity of stadium
	Stadium no longer in use for top-flight football
	Cricket ground
	Team colours
M8	Motorway
A82	Major road
1900	Champions
2000	Runners-up

Sir Stanley Matthews was born in Hanley, Stoke-on-Trent on 1 February 1915. He retired 50 years later. He is rightly regarded as the first great footballer of the modern era.

A518

DERBY COUNTY 1884

League	*1896, 1930, 36,* **72, 75**
FA Cup	*1898, 99, 1903,* **46**

A38

DERBY

THE BASEBALL
GROUND

PRIDE PARK

33,597

Derby County
(1895–1997)

Derby County

STOKE CITY 1863

League Cup	*1964,* **72**

M6

ASTON VILLA 1874

League	**1889, 94, 96, 97, 99, 1900, 03, 08, 10,** *11, 13, 14, 31, 33,* **81,** *90, 93*
FA Cup	**1887,** *92,* **95, 97,** *1905, 13, 20, 24,* **57, 2000**
League Cup	**1961,** *63,* **71,** *75,* **77,** *94,* **96**
European Cup	**1982**
World Club Cup	*1982*

A51

WOLVERHAMPTON WANDERERS 1879

League	*1938, 39,* **50,** *54, 55,* **58, 59, 60**
FA Cup	**1889,** *93,* **96,** *1908,* **21,** *39,* **49,** *60*
League Cup	**1974,** *80*
UEFA Cup	*1972*

A5

Wolverhampton Wanderers

M54

MOLINEUX

28,525

WOLVERHAMPTON

A458

DUDLEY

M5

Walsall
M6
BESCOT
STADIUM
9,400
WALSALL

Aston Villa
VILLA PARK
39,217

M6

VILLA PARK

39,217	**Club:** Aston Villa
	Built: 1897
	Rebuilt: 1971, 1994
Record Attendance:	76,588 Aston Villa v Derby County, FA Cup Sixth Round, 2 Feb 1946
Significant Matches:	1966 World Cup: two matches; 1996 European Championships: three matches; European Cup-Winners' Cup Final: 1999

BIRMINGHAM CITY 1875

FA Cup	*1931, 56*
League Cup	**1963,** *2001*
Fairs Cup	*1960, 61*

WEST BROMWICH

SALTER'S SPRING WORKS
West Bromwich Albion started as the works' team here. Originally called West Bromwich Strollers

THE HAWTHORNS
25,400

West Bromwich Albion

BIRMINGHAM
ST. ANDREWS
30,200

Birmingham City

SOLIHULL

M42

A452

Coventry City
SINGER'S BICYCLE FACTORY
Coventry City was founded as a works team here called Singers FC

HIGHFIELD ROAD
23,611

M6

COVENTRY

WEST BROMWICH ALBION 1879

League	**1920,** *25,* **54**
FA Cup	*1886, 87,* **88,** *92, 95, 1912,* **31,** *35,* **54, 68**
League Cup	**1966,** *67, 70*

COVENTRY CITY 1883

FA Cup	**1987**

The Midlands

FOOTBALL CITIES

NOTTS COUNTY 1862

FA Cup	1891, **94**

NOTTINGHAM FOREST 1865

League	1967, **78, 79**
FA Cup	**1898,** 1959, **91**
League Cup	**1978, 79, 80, 89, 90, 92**
European Cup	**1979, 80**
World Club Cup	1980

Notts County

MEADOW LANE

21,300
TRENT BRIDGE

NOTTINGHAM
CITY GROUND

30,602

Notts County (1883–1910)

Nottingham Forest

A60

Brian Clough (left) and Peter Taylor steered Nottingham Forest to back-to-back European Cup victories in 1979 and 1980.

LOUGHBOROUGH

Loughborough Athletic (1898–1900)

The record-winning score in a football league match was Arsenal's 12-0 win over Loughborough 12 March 1900. Arsenal's biggest defeat was against Loughborough when it lost 8-0 12 December 1896

LEICESTER CITY 1884

League	1929
FA Cup	1949, 61, 63, 69
League Cup	**1964,** 65, **97,** 99, **2000**

M1 **LEICESTER**
FILBERT STREET

WALKERS BOWL

Leicester City (1891–2002)

32,000

M69

Leicester City (2002–)

West Bromwich Albion began life as West Bromwich Strollers – the works' team of Salter's Spring Works in the Smethwick area of the city.

M1

THE CLUSTER OF CITIES that make up the English Midlands are home to some of the oldest professional clubs in England; six were founder members of the Football League in 1888 (Stoke City, West Bromwich Albion, Aston Villa, Notts County, Derby County and Wolverhampton Wanderers). By the turn of the century, Leicester Fosse (later Leicester City), Nottingham Forest, Small Heath (later Birmingham City) and Loughborough had joined them. Although Loughborough was unable to cut it in the professional leagues, and became defunct in 1900, Coventry's entry into the Second Division in 1919 kept the Midlands' numbers up. The industrial economy of the region provided both works' teams and a large number of spectators. Coventry City was founded as a works' team at the Singer's bicycle factory, West Bromwich at a spring factory in Smethwick, while Birmingham, Aston Villa, Wolves and Derby emerged out of cricket clubs.

Villa dominant

Across the last 120 years Aston Villa has been the dominant team in the region. In the first 12 years of English professional football, Villa won five league championships and three FA Cups, including the double in 1897. Villa remained a force in the First Division for three decades before its first relegation in 1936, after which followed a spiral of decline, culminating in relegation to the Third Division in 1970. But revival came in the shape of manager Ron Saunders who led the team to the title in 1981 and the European Cup in 1982. Wolves (in the 1950s), Derby and Nottingham Forest in the 1970s have all risen to the top of the English game, and under the unique direction of Brian Clough, Forest took the European Cup back-to-back in 1979 and 1980. But the 1990s and beyond have been harder times for the region's clubs. Under the Doug Ellis regime of recent years, Villa has remained on the fringe of the title race despite considerable spending, but it remains the only Midlands' club whose place in the Premiership looks at all secure.

ENGLAND

London

FOOTBALL CITY

ENGLAND

AS FOOTBALL EMERGED out of the public school and university system in England in the 1850s, old boy and graduate networks created teams all over Victorian London, where their players were busy staffing the hub of the British Empire. When the FA was founded in 1863 in Central London, the representatives of the clubs all came from the city. Replays aside, London has hosted all but seven of the FA Cup Finals since the first was played at Kennington Oval in 1872. For a moment in the late 19th century it looked as if London might be displaced as the football capital of the country. The newly professional Football League was a distinctly northern institution, with its headquarters in Lancashire, and not a single London team appeared in the First Division until Woolwich Arsenal in 1904. However, the size, wealth and power of London has steadily brought more clubs into contention: Chelsea made its debut in 1907, Tottenham in 1909, West Ham in 1922. London's place was sealed with the opening of the national stadium – Wembley – in 1923 (see Wembley box overleaf). More recently, the breakaway Premier League has based itself in London alongside the other key institutions in modern English football – the stock market in the City of London and the headquarters of the major television stations.

Despite great strength in depth (with half a dozen London teams in the Premiership at any one time) London's footballing strength has been concentrated for most of the 20th century in the north London rivals Arsenal and Tottenham (see North London box overleaf). Beyond this, constant success has been thin on the ground. South of the river, economic survival and even migration are the preoccupations of groundless Wimbledon and financially crippled Crystal Palace. In the east, West Ham has ridden the modern wave of football money well, but has yet to replicate its cup successes of the mid-1960s. In the west, Chelsea, buoyed up on the combined fortunes and machinations of Ken Bates and Matthew Harding, has turned on the style to take domestic and European cups in the 1990s, but has yet to mount a serious challenge for the league. Its neighbour Fulham is on the rise, care of Mohamed Al Fayed, while QPR remains mired in lower division debt.

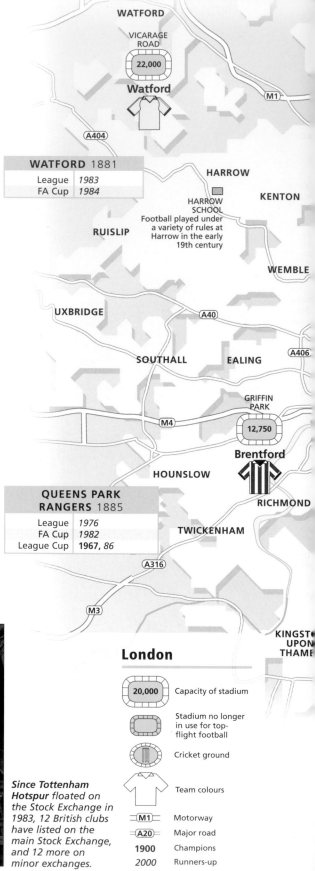

WATFORD 1881	
League	*1983*
FA Cup	*1984*

HARROW SCHOOL
Football played under a variety of rules at Harrow in the early 19th century

QUEENS PARK RANGERS 1885	
League	*1976*
FA Cup	*1982*
League Cup	**1967**, *86*

London

20,000	Capacity of stadium
	Stadium no longer in use for top-flight football
	Cricket ground
	Team colours
M1	Motorway
A20	Major road
1900	Champions
2000	Runners-up

Since Tottenham Hotspur floated on the Stock Exchange in 1983, 12 British clubs have listed on the main Stock Exchange, and 12 more on minor exchanges.

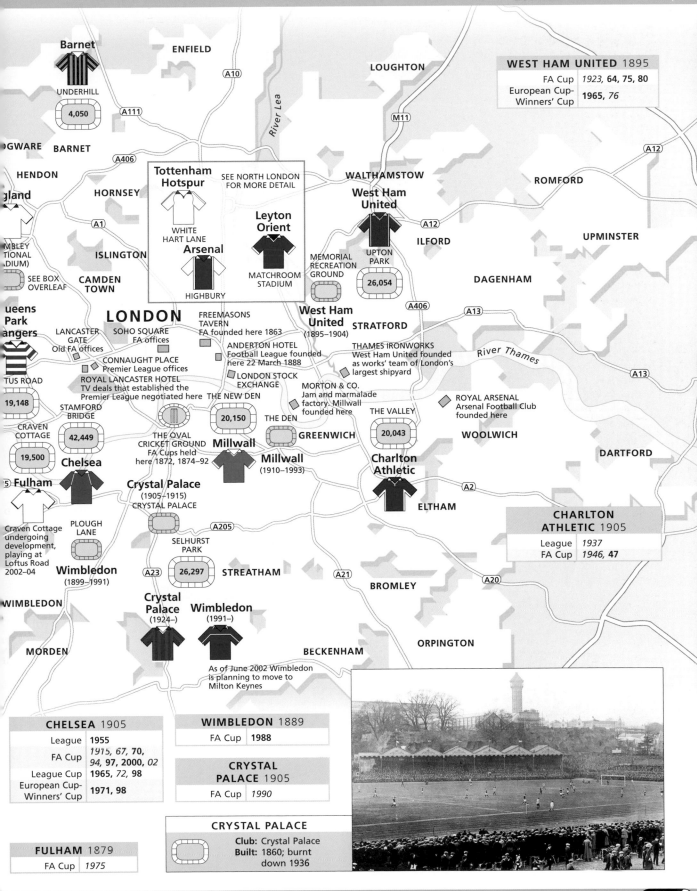

Barnet

ENFIELD

UNDERHILL
4,050

DGWARE

BARNET

A10

A111

A406

WEST HAM UNITED 1895

FA Cup	*1923*, **64, 75, 80**
European Cup-Winners' Cup	**1965**, *76*

LOUGHTON

M11

A12

HENDON

HORNSEY

gland

ROMFORD

WALTHAMSTOW

Tottenham Hotspur

SEE NORTH LONDON FOR MORE DETAIL

West Ham United

UPMINSTER

MBLEY
TIONAL
DIUM)

A1

ISLINGTON

WHITE HART LANE

Leyton Orient

ILFORD

SEE BOX OVERLEAF

CAMDEN TOWN

Arsenal

MATCHROOM STADIUM

DAGENHAM

HIGHBURY

ueens Park angers

LONDON

FREEMASONS TAVERN
FA founded here 1863

MEMORIAL RECREATION GROUND

UPTON PARK
26,054

LANCASTER GATE
Old FA offices

SOHO SQUARE
FA offices

ANDERTON HOTEL
Football League founded here 22 March 1888

West Ham United
(1895–1904)

STRATFORD

A406

A13

River Thames

CONNAUGHT PLACE
Premier League offices

THAMES IRONWORKS
West Ham United founded as works' team of London's largest shipyard

TUS ROAD
19,148

ROYAL LANCASTER HOTEL
TV deals that established the Premier League negotiated here

LONDON STOCK EXCHANGE

THE NEW DEN

MORTON & CO.
Jam and marmalade factory. Millwall founded here

A13

STAMFORD BRIDGE
42,449

20,150

THE DEN

THE VALLEY
20,043

ROYAL ARSENAL
Arsenal Football Club founded here

WOOLWICH

CRAVEN COTTAGE
19,500

Chelsea

THE OVAL CRICKET GROUND
FA Cups held here 1872, 1874–92

Millwall

Millwall
(1910–1993)

GREENWICH

Charlton Athletic

DARTFORD

5 **Fulham**

Crystal Palace
(1905–1915)
CRYSTAL PALACE

A2

ELTHAM

Craven Cottage undergoing development, playing at Loftus Road 2002–04

PLOUGH LANE

A205

CHARLTON ATHLETIC 1905

League	*1937*
FA Cup	*1946, 47*

Wimbledon
(1899–1991)

SELHURST PARK
26,297

STREATHAM

A23

A21

BROMLEY

A20

WIMBLEDON

Crystal Palace
(1924–)

Wimbledon
(1991–)

BECKENHAM

ORPINGTON

MORDEN

As of June 2002 Wimbledon is planning to move to Milton Keynes

CHELSEA 1905

League	**1955**
FA Cup	*1915*, *67*, *70*, *94*, **97, 2000**, *02*
League Cup	**1965**, *72*, **98**
European Cup-Winners' Cup	**1971, 98**

WIMBLEDON 1889

FA Cup	**1988**

CRYSTAL PALACE 1905

FA Cup	*1990*

CRYSTAL PALACE

Club: Crystal Palace	
Built:	1860; burnt down 1936

FULHAM 1879

FA Cup	*1975*

NORTH LONDON

London's footballing power has been gathered in north London for almost a century. To the east of both clubs are the great stretches of Hackney Marshes where amateur football flourishes on a Sunday, but on Saturdays attention turns west. Local schoolboys founded Tottenham Hotspur in 1882. The club first played at Northumberland Park, close to the ancestral home of Henry Percy (nicknamed Harry Hotspur by Shakespeare) before settling at White Hart Lane in 1899. Arsenal began life south of the river in 1886 as Dial Square FC, a works' team from the Royal Arsenal in Woolwich. The team soon turned professional, changing its name to Royal Arsenal in 1891 before migrating north to settle at Highbury in 1913. Tottenham was the first to win a major trophy, but it was Arsenal in the early 1930s under Herbert Chapman that first won the league and, for a time, dominated English football. Tottenham has regularly achieved cup success at home and abroad, as well as winning the first double of the 20th century in 1961, but it is Arsenal that has pulled ahead in its consistent capacity to challenge for the title (winning the double in 1971, 98 and 2002). Tottenham is often cast as London's Jewish team, and the area is certainly one of the strongholds of English Jewry, but in reality Arsenal's fans and board of directors seem to draw on London's Jews in equal number.

ENGLAND

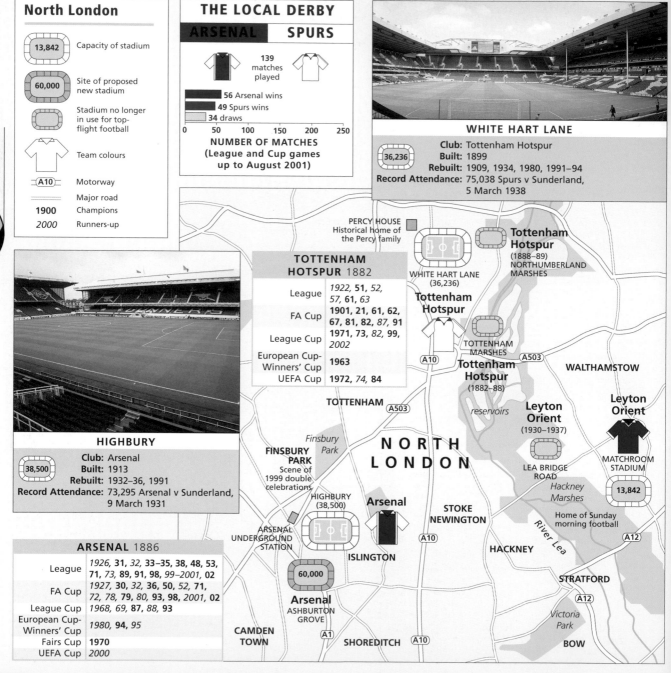

North London

13,842	Capacity of stadium
60,000	Site of proposed new stadium
	Stadium no longer in use for top-flight football
	Team colours
A10	Motorway
	Major road
1900	Champions
2000	Runners-up

THE LOCAL DERBY

ARSENAL	SPURS

139 matches played

56 Arsenal wins
49 Spurs wins
34 draws

0   50   100   150   200   250

NUMBER OF MATCHES
(League and Cup games
up to August 2001)

WHITE HART LANE

Club: Tottenham Hotspur
Built: 1899
Rebuilt: 1909, 1934, 1980, 1991–94
Record Attendance: 75,038 Spurs v Sunderland, 5 March 1938

36,236

HIGHBURY

Club: Arsenal
Built: 1913
Rebuilt: 1932–36, 1991
Record Attendance: 73,295 Arsenal v Sunderland, 9 March 1931

38,500

TOTTENHAM HOTSPUR 1882

League	*1922,* **51, 52,** *57,* **61,** *63*
FA Cup	**1901, 21, 61, 62, 67, 81, 82,** *87,* **91**
League Cup	**1971, 73,** *82,* **99,** *2002*
European Cup-Winners' Cup	**1963**
UEFA Cup	**1972,** *74,* **84**

ARSENAL 1886

League	*1926,* **31, 32,** *33–35,* **38, 48, 53, 71,** *73,* **89, 91, 98,** *99–2001,* **02**
FA Cup	*1927,* **30,** *32,* **36, 50,** *52,* **71, 72,** *78,* **79,** *80,* **93, 98, 2001,** *02*
League Cup	**1968,** *69,* **87,** *88,* **93**
European Cup-Winners' Cup	**1980,** *94,* **95**
Fairs Cup	**1970**
UEFA Cup	*2000*

PERCY HOUSE
Historical home of the Percy family

WHITE HART LANE
(36,236)

Tottenham Hotspur
(1888–89)
NORTHUMBERLAND MARSHES

Tottenham Hotspur

TOTTENHAM MARSHES

Tottenham Hotspur
(1882–88)

WALTHAMSTOW

A10

A503

TOTTENHAM

A503

Leyton Orient
(1930–1937)

LEA BRIDGE ROAD

Leyton Orient

MATCHROOM STADIUM

13,842

Finsbury Park

N O R T H   L O N D O N

FINSBURY PARK
Scene of 1999 double celebrations

reservoirs

Hackney Marshes

Home of Sunday morning football

HIGHBURY
(38,500)

Arsenal

STOKE NEWINGTON

A10

River Lea

A12

ARSENAL UNDERGROUND STATION

ISLINGTON

HACKNEY

STRATFORD

60,000

A12

Arsenal
ASHBURTON GROVE

Victoria Park

CAMDEN TOWN

A1

SHOREDITCH

A10

BOW

WEMBLEY

Closed	**Club:**	None; national stadium
	Built:	1923
	Original Capacity:	100,000 approx
	Rebuilt:	1948, 1963, 1990
Record Attendance:		Approx 200,000, Bolton v West Ham, FA Cup Final, 1923
Significant Matches:		1966 World Cup: nine matches including semi-final, 3rd place play-off, Final; 1996 European Championships: six matches, including semi-final, Final; European Cup Final: 1963, 68, 71, 78, 92; European Cup-Winners' Cup Final: 1965, 93

PC Scorey and his legendary horse Billy organize the huge crowd at Wembley in April 1923. The first-ever FA Cup Final at the new stadium, between West Ham and Bolton, attracted some 250,000 spectators – and only the self-discipline of the fans and the police, led by the white horse, averted a possible disaster.

WEMBLEY STADIUM

Designed by Sir John Simpson and Maxwell Ayrton, Wembley, opened in 1923, was originally the centrepiece of the British Empire Exhibition. It took a mere 300 days to build, cost £750,000 and staged its first football match – the 'White Horse' FA Cup – in April that year. But internationals and the FA Cup Final were not enough to sustain the vast stadium, and it was only saved by the investment of Arthur Elvin, who brought greyhound racing and speedway to Wembley. In its lifetime, Wembley also hosted the 1948 Olympic Games, and sports such as boxing, American football, and rugby league, as well as music concerts.

But it is for football that Wembley is best known: 77 FA Cup Finals, innumerable internationals, as well as the finals of the 1966 World Cup, the 1996 European Championships and numerous European Cup Finals. Nostalgia aside, the stadium's facilities, sightlines and atmosphere have been in steady decline, and the decision to rebuild Wembley with a mixture of government, lottery and private money saw it stage its last match in 2000. However, the enormous cost of the proposed rebuild, including the demolition of the iconic twin towers, has completely foundered in cost overruns and hubris. At the time of writing, the fate of Wembley and any future English national stadium remains hopelessly unresolved. The redevelopment plan has only been saved by the intervention of a German bank.

Chelsea won the last-ever FA Cup Final at Wembley in May 2000, beating Aston Villa 1-0 in a poor game. The venue for the match was changed to the Millennium Stadium in Cardiff on a temporary basis, but its future remains uncertain.

Merseyside

FOOTBALL CITY

AT THE CENTRE of the Merseyside region is the city of Liverpool, and close to its heart is Stanley Park, site of the stadiums of the city's eternal rivals, Everton and Liverpool. In their great shadow, smaller teams (like Bootle and South Liverpool) have withered, and only Tranmere Rovers on the Wirral peninsula across the Mersey has survived. In the city's hinterland, football has been abandoned and rugby league has grown up in the available sporting spaces. Everton was founded in 1878 out of a church team playing as St. Domingo's. Immediate popularity made the club a founder member of the Football League in 1888. In 1892 the club split, with John Houlding, owner of the Anfield ground at which they played, forming Liverpool, while the rest of the club headed to the other side of the park to play at Goodison Park.

Fierce and bitter rivalry

Both teams have garnered fanatical support across the city, and although Houlding was an active member of the Protestant Orange order, no sectarian (Catholic-Protestant) division between the clubs has ever emerged. Nonetheless, rivalry is fierce and bitter. Everton was the stronger side for the first half of the 20th century, its peak coming when it won the 1928 league title courtesy of a record-breaking 60 goals from its centre-forward Dixie Dean. But in the modern era, it is Liverpool that has been dominant. With Bill Shankly's arrival in 1959, successive dynasties of players and managers were created, and style and success were intertwined at Anfield. As the city declined through grim years of de-industrialization and unemployment, the team surged, winning ten league titles and four European Cups between 1976 and 1990. But the Heysel and Hillsborough disasters seemed to bring an end to that glorious era. Over a decade on from Hillsborough, Liverpool (triple cup winners in 2001) has risen again, and both clubs are looking to build new expanded stadiums in the city centre.

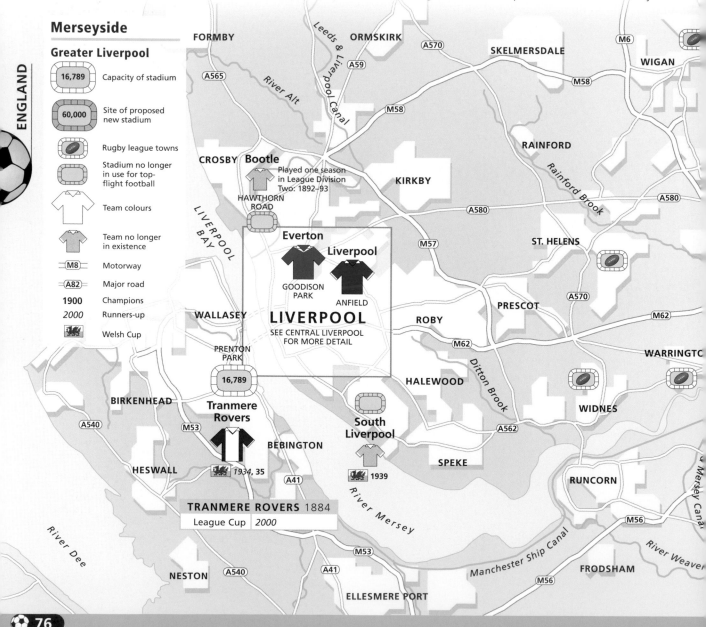

ENGLAND

Merseyside

Greater Liverpool

16,789	Capacity of stadium
60,000	Site of proposed new stadium
	Rugby league towns
	Stadium no longer in use for top-flight football
	Team colours
	Team no longer in existence
M8	Motorway
A82	Major road
1900	Champions
2000	Runners-up
	Welsh Cup

Bootle — Played one season in League Division Two: 1892–93
HAWTHORN ROAD

Everton — GOODISON PARK
Liverpool — ANFIELD

LIVERPOOL SEE CENTRAL LIVERPOOL FOR MORE DETAIL

PRENTON PARK — 16,789

Tranmere Rovers — 1934, 35

South Liverpool — 1939

TRANMERE ROVERS 1884

League Cup	*2000*

FORMBY · ORMSKIRK · SKELMERSDALE · WIGAN · Leeds & Liverpool Canal · A570 · A59 · M6 · River Alt · A565 · M58 · M58 · RAINFORD · Rainford Brook · CROSBY · KIRKBY · A580 · A580 · WALLASEY · M57 · ST. HELENS · ROBY · PRESCOT · A570 · M62 · LIVERPOOL BAY · BIRKENHEAD · A540 · M53 · BEBINGTON · A41 · HESWALL · NESTON · A540 · A41 · M53 · HALEWOOD · Ditton Brook · A562 · SPEKE · WIDNES · RUNCORN · FRODSHAM · M56 · M56 · Manchester Ship Canal · River Weaver · Mersey Canal · WARRINGTON · River Mersey · River Dee · ELLESMERE PORT

GOODISON PARK

40,260

Club: Everton
Built: 1892
Original Capacity: 11,000
Rebuilt: 1906–9, 1926, 1938, 1994
Record Attendance: 78,299 Everton v Liverpool, 18 Sept 1948. Record for women's match: 53,000 for Dick Kerr's Ladies v St Helens, 26 Dec 1920
Significant Matches: 1966 World Cup: three matches including semi-final

Policemen help a fan out of the Anfield Kop before a league match in 1966 – when full during those years, the Kop had a capacity of 28,000 people, all standing.

ANFIELD

45,362

Club: Liverpool
Built: 1884
Original Capacity: Approximately 10,000
Rebuilt: 1906 (the Kop), 1963, 1990–98
Record Attendance: 61,905 Liverpool v Wolverhampton Wanderers, FA Cup 4th Round, 2 Feb 1952
Significant Matches: 1996 European Championships: three matches

EVERTON 1878

League	*1890,* **91,** *95, 1902, 05, 09, 12,* **15, 28, 32, 39,** *63,* **70, 85,** *86,* **87**
FA Cup	*1893, 97,* **1906,** *07,* **33,** *66,* **68,** *84, 85,* **86,** *89,* **95**
League Cup	*1977, 84*
European Cup-Winners' Cup	**1985**

LITTLEWOODS POOLS
Owned by the Moores family, major shareholders at Liverpool, Littlewoods have made a fortune from the Pools, a football betting system

BOOTLE

WALTON (A580)

Everton

GOODISON PARK (40,260)

KIRKDALE

Liverpool
NEW ANFIELD
60,000

(A5058)

NORRIS GREEN

In a post-Hillsborough display of solidarity, a chain of football scarves was hung between the two stadiums

Stanley Park

MELWOOD
Liverpool training ground

ST. DOMINGO'S METHODIST HALL
Everton began life here as St. Domingo's

ANFIELD (45,362)
Everton at Anfield 1884–92

Liverpool

CENTRAL LIVERPOOL

BELLEFIELD
Everton training ground

EVERTON

EVERTON BROW
The tower on Everton's badge is based on the single tower prison built on Everton Brow in 1787

STONEYCROFT

Town Hall and St George's Hall are both sites of the clubs' victory celebrations

(A57)

THE LOCAL DERBY

EVERTON LIVERPOOL

166 matches played

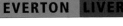
▬	55 Everton wins
▬	60 Liverpool wins
▬	51 draws

0   50   100   150   200   250
NUMBER OF MATCHES
(League only up to August 2001)

TOWN HALL

ST. GEORGE'S HALL

METROPOLITAN CATHEDRAL (Catholic)

Memorial plaques to the Hillsborough victims were laid in both cathedrals

River Mersey

55,000

LIVERPOOL CATHEDRAL (Anglican) (A562)

Everton
KING'S DOCK

TOXTETH

LIVERPOOL 1892

League	*1899,* **1901,** *06,* **10,** *22, 23,* **47, 64,** *66,* **69, 73, 74, 75, 76, 77, 78, 79, 80, 82–84,** *85,* **86, 87, 88,** *89,* **90,** *91, 2002*
FA Cup	*1914, 50,* **65,** *71,* **74,** *77, 86, 88, 89,* **92,** *96,* **2001**
League Cup	*1978,* **81–84,** *87,* **95, 2001**
European Cup	**1977, 78, 81,** *84, 85*
European Cup-Winners' Cup	*1966*
UEFA Cup	**1973, 76, 2001**
World Club Cup	*1981, 84*

BIRKENHEAD

Manchester

FOOTBALL CITY

ALTHOUGH FOOTBALL WAS FIRST DEVELOPED and codified in the public schools and universities of southern England, its transformation into a professional mass-spectator sport was centred on Lancashire – and on the periphery of Manchester and a little further north are many of the country's first professional teams. Some of the key meetings that preceded the Football League's creation took place in Manchester, as did the formation of the Professional Footballers' Association.

The heart and soul of the city
Within Manchester itself, the game took longer to mature. Manchester United began life as a railway works' team in Newton Heath to the north-east of the city centre, while Manchester City was formed from the merger of small teams in the Ardwick area

to the south-east. The rivalry between the two has taken on a religious dimension, with United inclined towards the Catholic community and regularly fielding Scottish and Irish players and City towards the Protestant community. But those sectarian undertones have been lost in what has become a conflict for the soul of the city. United, the richest and most famous club in the world, garners support from every continent, its stands filled with out-of-towners. City, Manchester's own authentic, local team, has stands filled by the Moss Side faithful, where resilience in the face of disaster on and off the pitch is worn as a badge of honour.

Although City has had moments of ascendancy – between the wars, and in the early 1970s when it sent United down with a Denis Law backheel – United has cast an awesome shadow over its rival, with two league titles before the First World War, three in the 1950s before the Munich air disaster, two in the 60s, Sir Matt Busby's European Cup triumph in 1968, and, under Alex Ferguson, seven league titles and the European Cup as one third of a treble in 1999. Nonetheless, City appears to be on its way back, with more stable finances, a new stadium due to open in 2003 and an unflinching fan base.

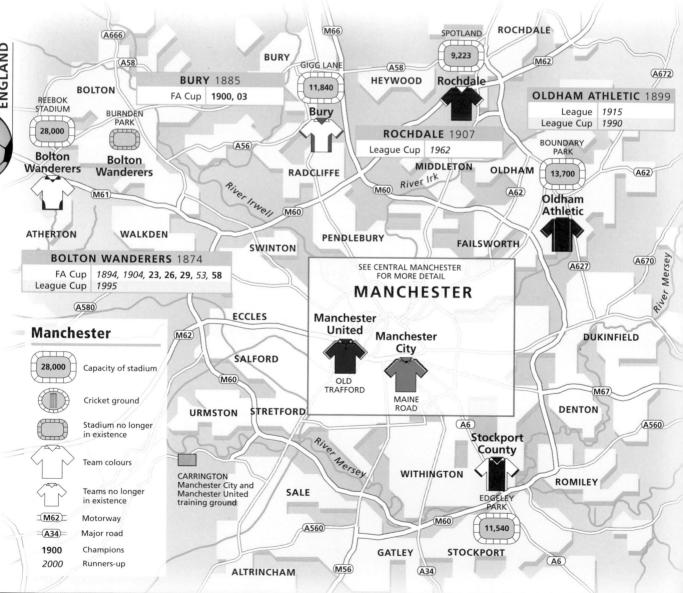

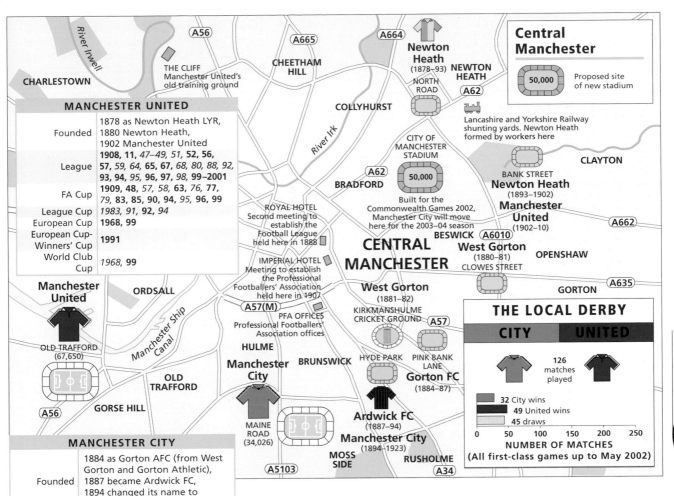

CHARLESTOWN

THE CLIFF
Manchester United's
old training ground

CHEETHAM HILL

COLLYHURST

NEWTON HEATH
North Road
(1878–93)

Central Manchester

50,000 — Proposed site of new stadium

Lancashire and Yorkshire Railway shunting yards. Newton Heath formed by workers here

CLAYTON

BANK STREET
Newton Heath
(1893–1902)
Manchester United
(1902–10)

CITY OF MANCHESTER STADIUM

50,000

Built for the Commonwealth Games 2002, Manchester City will move here for the 2003–04 season

BRADFORD

BESWICK

West Gorton
(1880–81)
CLOWES STREET

OPENSHAW

GORTON

MANCHESTER UNITED

Founded	1878 as Newton Heath LYR, 1880 Newton Heath, 1902 Manchester United
League	**1908, 11,** *47–49, 51,* **52, 56, 57, 59, 64, 65, 67, 68, 80, 88, 92, 93, 94, 95, 96, 97, 98,** *99–2001*
FA Cup	**1909, 48,** *57, 58,* **63,** *76,* **77,** *79,* **83, 85, 90, 94, 95, 96, 99**
League Cup	*1983, 91,* **92,** *94*
European Cup	**1968, 99**
European Cup-Winners' Cup	**1991**
World Club Cup	*1968,* **99**

ROYAL HOTEL
Second meeting to establish the Football League held here in 1888

IMPERIAL HOTEL
Meeting to establish the Professional Footballers' Association held here in 1907

ORDSALL

Manchester United

OLD TRAFFORD
(67,650)

Manchester Ship Canal

A57(M)

PFA OFFICES
Professional Footballers' Association offices

HULME

OLD TRAFFORD

A56

GORSE HILL

West Gorton
(1881–82)

KIRKMANSHULME CRICKET GROUND

A57

BRUNSWICK

HYDE PARK

PINK BANK LANE
Gorton FC
(1884–87)

Manchester City

MAINE ROAD
(34,026)

Ardwick FC
(1887–94)
Manchester City
(1894–1923)

MOSS SIDE

RUSHOLME

A5103

A34

MANCHESTER CITY

Founded	1884 as Gorton AFC (from West Gorton and Gorton Athletic), 1887 became Ardwick FC, 1894 changed its name to Manchester City
League	*1904, 21,* **37, 68,** *77*
FA Cup	**1904,** *26, 33,* **34,** *55,* **56, 69,** *81*
League Cup	**1970,** *74,* **76**
European Cup-Winners' Cup	**1970**

THE LOCAL DERBY

CITY	UNITED

126 matches played

32 City wins
49 United wins
45 draws

0   50   100   150   200   250
NUMBER OF MATCHES
(All first-class games up to May 2002)

MAINE ROAD

34,026

Club: Manchester City
Built: 1923
Original Capacity: 80–90,000 estimate
Record Attendance: 84,569 Manchester City v Stoke City, FA Cup Sixth Round, 3 February 1934
Significant Matches: England internationals: 1946, 48, 49; League Cup Final replay: 1984

On 11 March 1941 Old Trafford was badly damaged by German bombs. United played home games at Maine Road until repairs were complete.

OLD TRAFFORD

67,650

Club: Manchester United
Built: 1910
Original Capacity: 80,000
Rebuilt: Bombed 1940–41, rebuilt 1948–49; rebuilt with Europe's first executive boxes, mid-1966; fully covered 1973; 1992–2000 constant rebuilding
Record Attendance: 76,962 Wolves v Grimsby FA Cup semi-final, 25 Mar 1939
Significant Matches: FA Cup Final: 1915; FA Cup Final replays: 1911, 1970; 1966 World Cup: three group matches; 1996 European Championships: three group matches, quarter-final and semi-final; England internationals: 1926, 97, 2001

England

FANS AND OWNERS

SINCE THE FORMATION of the Premiership, patterns of club ownership in English football have changed. A core of top clubs continue to be owned privately by rich individuals, either directly (the Moores at Liverpool) or indirectly through trusts and offshore arrangements (Ken Bates at Chelsea, Al Fayed at Fulham). Others have floated as public companies on one of the British stock exchanges. Finance companies and media companies (Granada, BSkyB and NTL) have taken the lead in buying stakes in clubs. In a few cases, fans have bought significant blocks of shares in the lower divisions (Ipswich), which has been key to the survival of several small clubs.

Numbers up, volume down

Whoever the fans are, there are more of them. Gates in all divisions, but especially the Premiership, have steadily risen since the lows of the early 1980s. Since then, all-seater stadiums have become compulsory, private boxes and corporate hospitality have become integral features of club incomes, and crowd trouble has all but been eliminated within the grounds (although it has been partially displaced to outside the ground, to the lower division clubs and to the national team's following). The concern remains that these changes have come at a price, as the noise and passion of the crowd has been sanitized.

Old fans, new fans

Inside the stands, the traditional long-term football fans remain but they have been joined by a wave of new fans. These are, on average, wealthier than the older fans and include significantly more women. The enormous number of domestic and foreign black players is not, however, mirrored on the terraces. Unsurprisingly, fans from the north of England tend to be lower earners than fans from the south, and are much more likely to have been born locally to the club. Manchester United is the exception, drawing significant support country-wide.

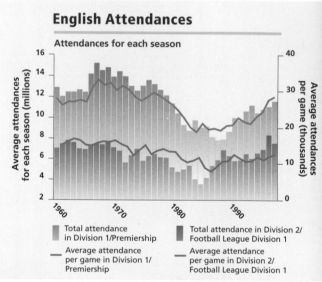

The Future. Fourteen per cent of Premiership season ticket holders are women. At some clubs that means over a third of their new fans are women.

Fans Income

% of season ticket holders earning over £30,000 PA

Fans Origins

% of season ticket holders who were born locally

TEAMS
Arsenal
Aston Villa
Blackburn Rovers
Charlton Athletic
Chelsea
Coventry City
Derby County
Everton
Leeds United
Leicester City
Liverpool
Manchester United
Middlesbrough
Newcastle United
Nottingham Forest
Sheffield Wednesday
Southampton
Tottenham Hotspur
West Ham United
Wimbledon

Details from season 1997–98

ENGLAND

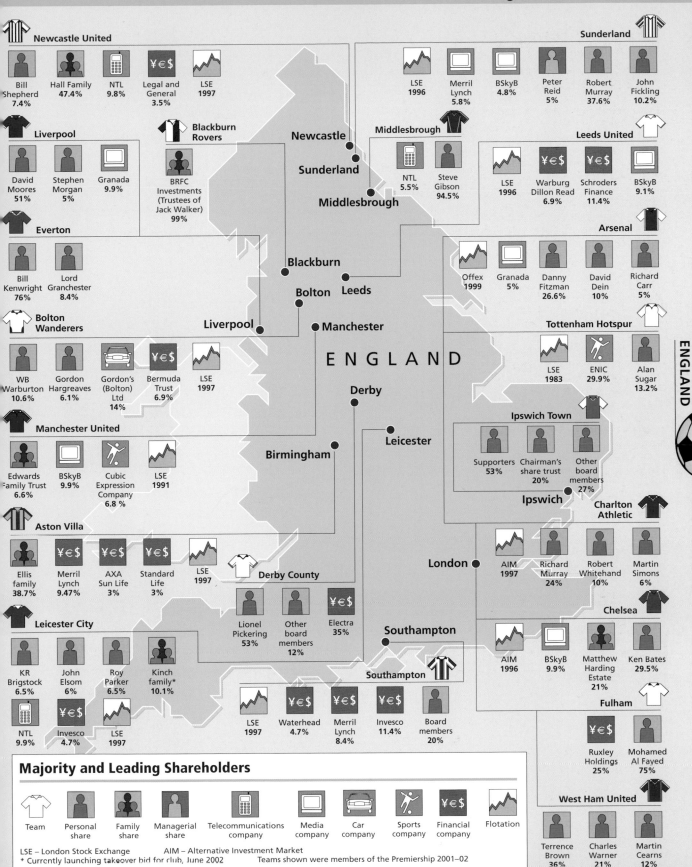

Newcastle United

| Bill Shepherd 7.4% | Hall Family 47.4% | NTL 9.8% | Legal and General 3.5% | LSE 1997 |

Sunderland

| LSE 1996 | Merril Lynch 5.8% | BSkyB 4.8% | Peter Reid 5% | Robert Murray 37.6% | John Fickling 10.2% |

Liverpool

| David Moores 51% | Stephen Morgan 5% | Granada 9.9% |

Blackburn Rovers

| BRFC Investments (Trustees of Jack Walker) 99% |

Middlesbrough

| NTL 5.5% | Steve Gibson 94.5% |

Leeds United

| LSE 1996 | Warburg Dillon Read 6.9% | Schroders Finance 11.4% | BSkyB 9.1% |

Everton

| Bill Kenwright 76% | Lord Granchester 8.4% |

Arsenal

| Offex 1999 | Granada 5% | Danny Fitzman 26.6% | David Dein 10% | Richard Carr 5% |

Bolton Wanderers

| WB Warburton 10.6% | Gordon Hargreaves 6.1% | Gordon's (Bolton) Ltd 14% | Bermuda Trust 6.9% | LSE 1997 |

Tottenham Hotspur

| LSE 1983 | ENIC 29.9% | Alan Sugar 13.2% |

Manchester United

| Edwards Family Trust 6.6% | BSkyB 9.9% | Cubic Expression Company 6.8 % | LSE 1991 |

Ipswich Town

| Supporters 53% | Chairman's share trust 20% | Other board members 27% |

Charlton Athletic

| AIM 1997 | Richard Murray 24% | Robert Whitehand 10% | Martin Simons 6% |

Aston Villa

| Ellis family 38.7% | Merril Lynch 9.47% | AXA Sun Life 3% | Standard Life 3% | LSE 1997 |

Chelsea

| AIM 1996 | BSkyB 9.9% | Matthew Harding Estate 21% | Ken Bates 29.5% |

Derby County

| Lionel Pickering 53% | Other board members 12% | Electra 35% |

Leicester City

| KR Brigstock 6.5% | John Elsom 6% | Roy Parker 6.5% | Kinch family* 10.1% |
| NTL 9.9% | Invesco 4.7% | LSE 1997 |

Fulham

| Ruxley Holdings 25% | Mohamed Al Fayed 75% |

Southampton

| LSE 1997 | Waterhead 4.7% | Merril Lynch 8.4% | Invesco 11.4% | Board members 20% |

West Ham United

| Terrence Brown 36% | Charles Warner 21% | Martin Cearns 12% |

Majority and Leading Shareholders

| Team | Personal share | Family share | Managerial share | Telecommunications company | Media company | Car company | Sports company | Financial company | Flotation |

LSE – London Stock Exchange   AIM – Alternative Investment Market
* Currently launching takeover bid for club, June 2002   Teams shown were members of the Premiership 2001–02

ENGLAND

England

PLAYERS AND MANAGERS

THE CULTURE OF ENGLISH PROFESSIONAL football has changed over the last hundred years, particularly since professionalism was legalized. Before that it had been solidly working class, simultaneously tough and impassioned on the pitch and apparently deferential to authority off it. It was only in the 1960s that money began to move into the game, the maximum wage for players was abolished and contractual freedom was obtained. In the shape of Bobby Moore, Geoff Hurst and Bobby Charlton, a new generation of talent emerged.

But, to the surprise and horror of many of the foreign players that arrived in England in the early 1990s, little else has changed. Heart and lungs are still often valued over technique and training. Scientific analysis, nutritional care and tactical preparation have been disdained in favour of rough and ready measures, fried breakfasts and just getting 'stuck into them'. Above all, the drinking and nightlife culture of professional footballers has not gone away; if anything, the riches of the Premiership have intensified it. For every clean-cut dedicated Michael Owen there seems to be an unruly Stan Collymore, the wasted talent of Paul Gascoigne or the headlining antics of Jonathan Woodgate.

Motivation over technique

The limit of the motivation over technique school of English management was reached with the demise of Kevin Keegan as England manager and his replacement with the national team's first foreign manager, Sven-Göran Eriksson. Although Glenn Hoddle and Bobby Robson continue to thrive as leading managers, the bulk of the Premiership's top teams are coached by Scots (Alex Ferguson at Manchester United), Frenchmen (Gérard Houllier at Liverpool, Arsène Wenger at Arsenal) or Italians (Claudio Ranieri at Chelsea).

With 49 goals in 106 appearances, Bobby Charlton (right) is one of England's greatest players. His brother Jack (left) also played 35 times for England, and both were members of the 1966 World Cup-winning team.

Top 20 International Caps

PLAYER	CAPS	GOALS	FIRST MATCH	LAST MATCH
Peter Shilton	125	0	1970	1990
Bobby Moore	108	2	1962	1973
Bobby Charlton	106	49	1958	1970
Billy Wright	105	3	1946	1959
Bryan Robson	90	26	1980	1991
Kenny Sansom	86	1	1979	1988
Ray Wilkins	84	3	1976	1986
Gary Lineker	80	48	1984	1992
John Barnes	79	11	1983	1995
Stuart Pearce*	78	5	1987	1999
Terry Butcher	77	3	1980	1990
Tom Finney	76	30	1946	1958
Alan Ball	72	8	1965	1975
Gordon Banks	72	0	1963	1972
Martin Peters	67	20	1966	1974
Tony Adams*	66	5	1987	2000
David Seaman*	65	0	1988	2001
Dave Watson	65	4	1974	1982
Kevin Keegan	63	21	1972	1982
Alan Shearer*	63	30	1991	2000

Top 15 International Goalscorers

PLAYER	GOALS	CAPS	FIRST MATCH	LAST MATCH
Bobby Charlton	49	106	1958	1970
Gary Lineker	48	80	1984	1992
Jimmy Greaves	43	57	1959	1967
Nat Lofthouse	30	33	1950	1958
Alan Shearer*	30	63	1991	2000
Tom Finney	30	76	1946	1958
Vivian Woodward	29	23	1903	1911
Stephen Bloomer	28	23	1895	1907
David Platt	27	62	1989	1996
Bryan Robson	26	90	1980	1991
Geoff Hurst	24	49	1966	1972
Stan Mortensen	23	25	1947	1953
Tommy Lawton	22	23	1938	1948
Mick Channon	21	46	1972	1977
Kevin Keegan	21	63	1972	1982

* Indicates players still playing at least at club level.

English International Managers

DATES	NAME	GAMES	WON	DRAWN	LOST
1946–62	Walter Winterbottom	139	78	33	28
1963–74	Alf Ramsey	113	69	27	17
1974	Joe Mercer	7	3	3	1
1974–77	Don Revie	29	14	8	7
1977–82	Ron Greenwood	55	33	12	10
1982–90	Bobby Robson	95	47	30	18
1990–93	Graham Taylor	38	18	13	7
1994–96	Terry Venables	23	11	11	1
1996–99	Glenn Hoddle	28	17	6	5
1999	Howard Wilkinson	2	0	1	1
1999–2000	Kevin Keegan	18	7	7	4
2000	Peter Taylor	1	0	0	1
2000–	Sven Goran Eriksson	11	7	3	1

All figures correct as of 14 February 2002.

Player of the Year

YEAR	PLAYER	CLUB
1948	Matthews	Blackpool
1949	Carey	Manchester United
1950	Mercer	Arsenal
1951	Johnston	Blackpool
1952	Wright	Wolverhampton W
1953	Lofthouse	Bolton Wanderers
1954	Finney	Preston North End
1955	Revie	Manchester City
1956	Trautmann	Manchester City
1957	Finney	Preston North End
1958	Blanchflower	Tottenham Hotspur
1959	Owen	Luton Town
1960	Slater	Wolverhampton W
1961	Blanchflower	Tottenham Hotspur
1962	Adamson	Burnley
1963	Matthews	Stoke City
1964	Moore	West Ham United
1965	Collins	Leeds United
1966	R. Charlton	Manchester United
1967	J. Charlton	Leeds United
1968	Best	Manchester United
1969	Mackay	Derby County
1969	Book	Manchester City
1970	Bremner	Leeds United
1971	McLintock	Arsenal
1972	Banks	Stoke City
1973	Jennings	Tottenham Hotspur
1974	Callaghan	Liverpool
1975	Mullery	Fulham
1976	Keegan	Liverpool

Player of the Year (continued)

YEAR	PLAYER	CLUB
1977	Hughes	Liverpool
1978	Burns	Nottingham Forest
1979	Dalglish	Liverpool
1980	McDermott	Liverpool
1981	Thijssen	Ipswich Town
1982	Perryman	Tottenham Hotspur
1983	Dalglish	Liverpool
1984	Rush	Liverpool
1985	Southall	Everton
1986	Lineker	Everton
1987	Allen	Tottenham Hotspur
1988	Barnes	Liverpool
1989	Nicol	Liverpool
1990	Barnes	Liverpool
1991	Strachan	Leeds United
1992	Lineker	Tottenham Hotspur
1993	Waddle	Sheffield Wednesday
1994	Shearer	Blackburn Rovers
1995	Klinsmann	Tottenham Hotspur
1996	Cantona	Manchester United
1997	Zola	Chelsea
1998	Bergkamp	Arsenal
1999	Ginola	Tottenham Hotspur
2000	Keane	Manchester United
2001	Owen	Liverpool
2002	Pires	Arsenal

Awarded by the English Football Writers' Association.

The legendary Dixie Dean presents the Player of the Year trophy to Liverpool's Kevin Keegan in 1976.

The late Walter Winterbottom, England's first international manager, remained in charge of the team from 1946 to 1962.

ENGLAND

Top Goalscorers by Season 1947–2002

SEASON	PLAYER	CLUB	GOALS
1947–48	Rooke	Arsenal	33
1948–49	Moir	Bolton W	25
1949–50	Davies	Sunderland	25
1950–51	Mortensen	Blackpool	30
1951–52	Robledo	Newcastle Utd	33
1952–53	Wayman	Preston NE	24
1953–54	Glazzard	Huddersfield T	29
1954–55	Allen	WBA	27
1955–56	Lofthouse	Bolton W	33
1956–57	Charles	Leeds United	38
1957–58	Smith	Spurs	36
1958–59	Greaves	Chelsea	33
1959–60	Viollet	Manchester U	32
1960–61	Greaves	Chelsea	41
1961–62	Crawford	Ipswich Town	33
1961–62	Kevan	WBA	33
1962–63	Greaves	Spurs	37
1963–64	Greaves	Spurs	35
1964–65	Greaves	Spurs	29
1964–65	McEvoy	Blackburn R	29
1965–66	Irvine	Burnley	29
1966–67	Davies	Southampton	37
1967–68	Best	Manchester U	28
1967–68	Davies	Southampton	28

SEASON	PLAYER	CLUB	GOALS
1968–69	Greaves	Spurs	27
1969–70	Astle	WBA	25
1970–71	Brown	WBA	28
1971–72	Lee	Manchester C	33
1972–73	Robson	West Ham U	28
1973–74	Channon	Southampton	21
1974–75	McDonald	Newcastle Utd	21
1975–76	MacDougall	Norwich City	23
1976–77	McDonald	Newcastle Utd	25
1976–77	Gray	Aston Villa	25
1977–78	Latchford	Everton	30
1978–79	Worthington	Bolton W	24
1979–80	Boyer	Southampton	23
1980–81	Withe	Aston Villa	20
1980–81	Archibald	Spurs	20
1981–82	Keegan	Southampton	26
1982–83	Blisset	Watford	27
1983–84	Rush	Liverpool	32
1984–85	Dixon	Chelsea	24
1984–85	Lineker	Leicester City	24
1985–86	Lineker	Everton	30
1986–87	Allen	Spurs	33
1987–88	Aldridge	Liverpool	26
1988–89	Smith	Arsenal	23

SEASON	PLAYER	CLUB	GOALS
1989–90	Lineker	Spurs	24
1990–91	Chapman	Leeds United	31
1991–92	Wright	Crystal Palace/ Arsenal	29
1992–93	Sheringham	Nottingham F/ Spurs	22
1993–94	Cole	Newcastle Utd	34
1994–95	Shearer	Blackburn R	35
1995–96	Shearer	Blackburn R	31
1996–97	Shearer	Newcastle Utd	25
1997–98	Owen	Liverpool	18
1997–98	Sutton	Blackburn R	18
1997–98	Dublin	Coventry City	18
1998–99	Yorke	Manchester U	18
1998–99	Owen	Liverpool	18
1998–99	Hasselbaink	Leeds United	18
1999–2000	Phillips	Sunderland	30
2000–01	Hasselbaink	Chelsea	23
2001–02	Henry	Arsenal	24
2001–02	Shearer	Newcastle	24

Foreign Players in England (in top division squads)

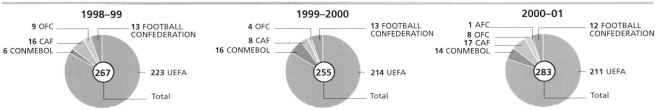

1998–99
9 OFC
16 CAF
6 CONMEBOL
13 FOOTBALL CONFEDERATION
223 UEFA
267 Total

1999–2000
4 OFC
8 CAF
16 CONMEBOL
13 FOOTBALL CONFEDERATION
214 UEFA
255 Total

2000–01
1 AFC
8 OFC
17 CAF
14 CONMEBOL
12 FOOTBALL CONFEDERATION
211 UEFA
283 Total

England

THE PREMIERSHIP 1992–2001

IN 1992, THE ENGLISH PREMIER LEAGUE was established by the country's 22 leading clubs, breaking away from the control of the English FA and the Football League. Correctly anticipating an enormous increase in TV income for football, the Premier League was primarily a device for keeping that income at the top and excluding both non-league and lower division football from the goldrush; to that extent it has succeeded. The most recent TV deal (2001–2004) has brought in nearly £1.6 billion over three years. Combined with rising gate income, sponsorship deals and intensive merchandising, the English Premier League is the richest in global football.

Where does the money go?

Yet as fast as the money comes in, it goes out, drained by the explosive rise in player's wages and the increasingly large transfer budgets of Premiership clubs. Most of the latter have been spent overseas. Clubs have brought players from all over Europe, as well as South America, the Caribbean and Africa. The increasing financial muscle of the Premiership can be seen in the gradual acquisition of players from the strongest European leagues (Italy, Germany and the Netherlands) – and not just players coming to the end of their career (Klinsmann, Gullit, Vialli) but players in their prime (van Nistelrooy, Veron, Viera).

Below the Premiership, the English lower divisions have seen transfer income steadily diminish while wage bills rise, a situation exacerbated by the ITV Digital disaster, which may well see clubs close down. The enormous foreign presence in the Premiership (both among players and, increasingly, managers as well) has raised the technical and tactical sophistication of the game immeasurably, but it remains to be seen what the consequence of this will be for the development of indigenous English talent.

Unite and rule

Financial and sporting success has become increasingly concentrated at the top end of the Premiership. In nine seasons, Alex Ferguson's Manchester United has taken seven championships; in 2000–01 it won at a canter. Ferguson has built a series of teams at United based on an attacking and aggressive 4-4-2 play. Passing, moving and possessed of an unquenchable confidence, his team persistently dominated the weaker teams when its challengers have shown inconsistency. United has shown the capacity to come back from behind, raise its game at the crucial moments of the season and score more goals than anyone else. Only Blackburn Rovers, fuelled by Jack Walker's personal fortune (1995) and Alan Shearer's best year, and Arsenal, under the cerebral Arsène Wenger (1998), have broken the Mancunian monopoly. In both seasons, United still came in a close second. Challenges from Leeds, Liverpool, Chelsea and Kevin Keegan's Newcastle were all seen off.

Life at the bottom

Financial imbalances have created a whole category of clubs that are too strong for Division One but too weak to sustain their place in the Premiership. Manchester City, Bolton, Crystal Palace and others have been condemned to a cycle of relegation and promotion. Excluded from significant TV income while in the First Division, a single year in the Premiership does not deliver enough money to sufficiently strengthen the team. Outspending resources in a gamble to stay up can see clubs left deep in debt. Others constantly teeter on the edge of the relegation precipice, like Everton, Southampton and, in the case of Coventry, eventually fall over it. Even clubs with bigger resources, such as Sunderland, Tottenham and Aston Villa, have been reduced to mid-table scrapping and the fight for a place in the UEFA Cup.

Above: Arsène Wenger and Tony Adams celebrate Arsenal's League and FA Cup double in 1998 at Islington Town Hall, London.

Above right: New money, new talent, new team. Mohamed Al Fayed intends Fulham, under the brilliant French midfielder and now coach Jean Tigana, to be the Manchester United of the south. Stage one was its return to the top flight in 2001.

Player Salaries 1995–2000

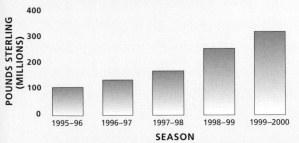

POUNDS STERLING (MILLIONS)

400				
300				
200				
100				
0				
1995–96	1996–97	1997–98	1998–99	1999–2000

SEASON

Total wage bill of Premiership clubs

Annual TV Rights Income

POUNDS STERLING (MILLIONS)

YEAR	0	50	100	150	200	250	300	350	400
1983	(2.6 BBC/ITV)								
1984	(2.6 BBC/ITV)								
1985	(1.3 BBC/ITV)								
1986	(3.1 BBC/ITV)								
1987	(3.1 BBC/ITV)								
1988	(11 ITV)								
1989	(11 ITV)								
1990	(11 ITV)								
1991	(11 ITV)								
1992	(38.3 BskyB)								
1993	(38.3 BskyB)								
1994	(38.3 BskyB)								
1995	(38.3 BskyB)								
1996	(38.3 BskyB)								
1997	(168 BskyB)								
1998	(168 BskyB)								
1999	(168 BskyB)								
2000	(168 BskyB)								
2001	(367 BskyB)								
2002	(367 BskyB)								
2003	(367 BskyB)								

Financial and sporting success has become increasingly concentrated at the top end of the Premiership. In nine seasons, Alex Ferguson's Manchester United (below) took seven championships.

ENGLAND

The new look Liverpool under Gérard Houllier has crept back into contention for the Premiership title since the beginning of the millennium but, like fellow challenger Chelsea, it has yet to deliver the prize.

Key to League Positions Table

- League champions
- Season of promotion to league
- Season of relegation from league
- Other teams playing in league
- 5   Final position in league

English League Positions 1992–2001

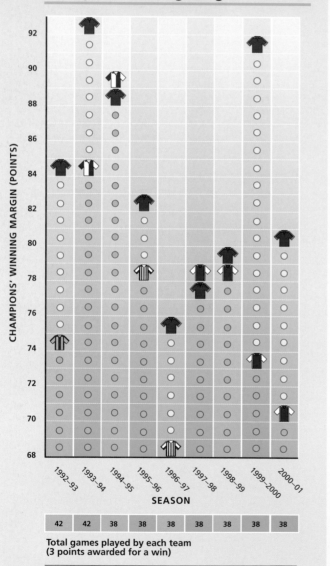

Champions' Winning Margin 1992–2001

CHAMPIONS' WINNING MARGIN (POINTS)

SEASON

	1992-93	1993-94	1994-95	1995-96	1996-97	1997-98	1998-99	1999-2000	2000-01
Total games	42	42	38	38	38	38	38	38	38

Total games played by each team (3 points awarded for a win)

Legend: Arsenal · Aston Villa · Blackburn Rovers · Manchester United · Newcastle United

English League Positions 1992–2001

	SEASON								
TEAM	1992-93	1993-94	1994-95	1995-96	1996-97	1997-98	1998-99	1999-2000	2000-2001
Arsenal	10	4	12	5	3	1	2	2	2
Aston Villa	2	10	18	4	5	7	6	6	8
Barnsley						19			
Blackburn Rovers	4	2	1	7	13	6	19		
Bolton Wanderers			20		18				
Bradford City								17	20
Charlton Athletic							18		9
Chelsea	11	14	11	11	6	4	3	5	6
Coventry City	15	11	16	16	17	11	15	14	19
Crystal Palace	20		19		20				
Derby County				12	9	8	16	17	
Everton	13	17	15	6	15	17	14	13	16
Fulham									
Ipswich Town	16	19	22						5
Leeds United	17	5	5	13	11	5	4	3	4
Leicester City			21		9	10	10	8	13
Liverpool	6	8	4	3	4	3	7	4	3
Manchester City	9	16	17	18					18
Manchester United	1	1	2	1	1	2	1	1	1
Middlesbrough	21		12	19		9	12	14	
Newcastle United		3	6	2	2	13	13	11	11
Norwich City	3	12	20						
Nottingham Forest	22		3	9	20		20		
Oldham Athletic	19	21							
Queens Park Rangers	5	9	8	19					
Sheffield United	14	20							
Sheffield Wednesday	7	7	13	15	7	16	12	19	
Southampton	18	18	10	17	16	12	17	15	10
Sunderland					18			7	7
Swindon Town		22							
Tottenham Hotspur	8	15	7	8	10	14	11	10	12
Watford								20	
West Ham United		13	14	10	14	8	5	9	15
Wimbledon	12	6	9	14	8	15	16	18	

The Premiership

Arsenal — Team name

League champions/
runners-up

1998,
99 — Champions in bold
Runners-up in italics

Other teams in
the Premiership

● **London** City of origin

Newcastle United
*1996,
97*

Blackburn Rovers
*1994,
95*

Manchester
United
**1993, 94,
95, 96, 97,
98,** *99–2001*

Manchester
City

Liverpool

Everton

Derby County

Aston Villa
1993

Sunderland

Middlesbrough

Oldham
Athletic

Bradford
City

Bolton
Wanderers

● **Newcastle**
● **Sunderland**
● **Middlesbrough**

Leeds
United

Sheffield
United

● **Leeds**
● **Bradford**
● **Barnsley**
● **Blackburn**
● **Bolton**
● **Oldham**
● **Manchester**
Barnsley

Sheffield Wednesday

● **Liverpool**
● **Sheffield**

Nottingham Forest
● **Nottingham**
● **Derby**

Norwich City

● **Norwich**

Leicester City
● **Leicester**
Ipswich
Town

● **Birmingham**
● **Coventry**
● **Ipswich**

Watford

Swindon
● **Swindon**
Swindon Town

● **Watford**
● **London**

Arsenal
1998,
99–2001

Fulham

Coventry City

● **Southampton**
Southampton

Charlton Athletic

Chelsea

Tottenham
Hotspur

Crystal Palace

West Ham United

Wimbledon

Queens Park Rangers

ENGLAND

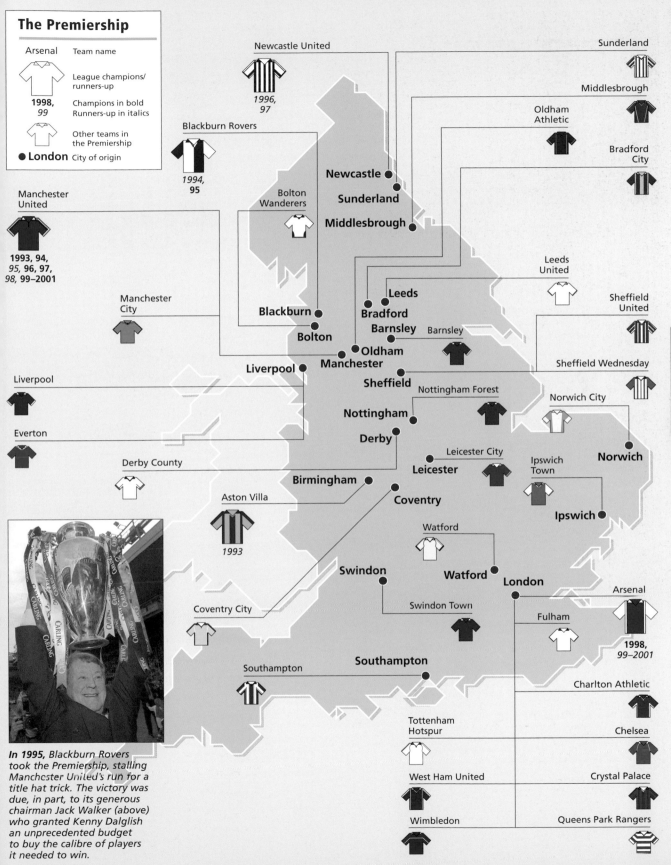

*In 1995, Blackburn Rovers
took the Premiership, stalling
Manchester United's run for a
title hat trick. The victory was
due, in part, to its generous
chairman Jack Walker (above)
who granted Kenny Dalglish
an unprecedented budget
to buy the calibre of players
it needed to win.*

England

The Football Association
Founded: 1863
Joined FIFA: 1905–20, 1924–28, 1946
Joined UEFA: 1954

ENGLAND

IN ENGLAND, UNLIKE MOST NATIONS, national football competitions began with the cup rather than the league. The Football Association Challenge Cup, or FA Cup as it is usually known, began in 1872, and is the oldest formal footballing tournament in the world. It was open to amateur clubs and, after legalization in 1885, to professional teams as well. The Final found a permanent home at Wembley in 1923, but moved to the Millennium Stadium in Cardiff in 2001. Currently, over 500 non-league teams compete in preliminary rounds before the bottom two league divisions join in the first round, and the First Division and Premiership teams join in the third round. Each year the competition takes ten months to complete.

A separate League Cup, not open to amateur teams, was created in 1961. For the first six years, the Final was decided over two legs, home and away, before finding a new home at Wembley in 1967. Despite rather low attendances, often gruelling two-leg rounds, and endless changes of name and sponsor, the lure of a UEFA Cup place for the winners has retained interest in the competition.

The Football League was established in 1888 by a core of 12 professional clubs from the Midlands and the north of England. A second division was added in 1892, a third in 1920 and a fourth in 1921, when the lower division was divided into Third Division North and South. These were amalgamated to create a Third and Fourth Division in 1950. The national leagues were replaced by regional competitions for most of the First and Second World Wars. The FA Cup competition was suspended between 1916 and 1919, and again between 1940 and 1945, though a War Cup, with a Final at Wembley, was hastily organized in 1941 and contested for the next few years.

In 1992, the top 22 clubs broke away from the FA's control to create an independently administered Premiership. Three teams are relegated from the now 20-team league, and three come up from Division One (two automatically and one by play-off).

English League Record 1889–2002

SEASON	CHAMPIONS	RUNNERS-UP
1889	Preston North End	Aston Villa
1890	Preston North End	Everton
1891	Everton	Preston North End
1892	Sunderland	Preston North End
1893	Sunderland	Preston North End
1894	Aston Villa	Sunderland
1895	Sunderland	Everton
1896	Aston Villa	Derby County
1897	Aston Villa	Sheffield United
1898	Sheffield United	Sunderland
1899	Aston Villa	Liverpool
1900	Aston Villa	Sheffield United
1901	Liverpool	Sunderland
1902	Sunderland	Everton
1903	Sheffield Wednesday	Aston Villa
1904	Sheffield Wednesday	Manchester City
1905	Newcastle United	Everton
1906	Liverpool	Preston North End
1907	Newcastle United	Bristol City

English League Record (*continued*)

SEASON	CHAMPIONS	RUNNERS-UP
1908	Manchester United	Aston Villa
1909	Newcastle United	Everton
1910	Aston Villa	Liverpool
1911	Manchester United	Aston Villa
1912	Blackburn Rovers	Everton
1913	Sunderland	Aston Villa
1914	Blackburn Rovers	Aston Villa
1915	Everton	Oldham Athletic
1916–19	*no championship*	
1920	West Bromwich Albion	Burnley
1921	Burnley	Manchester City
1922	Liverpool	Tottenham Hotspur
1923	Liverpool	Sunderland
1924	Huddersfield Town	Cardiff City
1925	Huddersfield Town	West Bromwich Albion
1926	Huddersfield Town	Arsenal
1927	Newcastle United	Huddersfield Town
1928	Everton	Huddersfield Town
1929	Sheffield Wednesday	Leicester City
1930	Sheffield Wednesday	Derby County
1931	Arsenal	Aston Villa
1932	Everton	Arsenal
1933	Arsenal	Aston Villa
1934	Arsenal	Huddersfield Town
1935	Arsenal	Sunderland
1936	Sunderland	Derby County
1937	Manchester City	Charlton Athletic
1938	Arsenal	Wolverhampton Wanderers
1939	Everton	Wolverhampton Wanderers
1940–46	*no championship*	
1947	Liverpool	Manchester United
1948	Arsenal	Manchester United
1949	Portsmouth	Manchester United
1950	Portsmouth	Wolverhampton Wanderers
1951	Tottenham Hotspur	Manchester United
1952	Manchester United	Tottenham Hotspur
1953	Arsenal	Preston North End
1954	Wolverhampton Wanderers	West Bromwich Albion
1955	Chelsea	Wolverhampton Wanderers
1956	Manchester United	Blackpool
1957	Manchester United	Tottenham Hotspur
1958	Wolverhampton Wanderers	Preston North End
1959	Wolverhampton Wanderers	Manchester United
1960	Burnley	Wolverhampton Wanderers
1961	Tottenham Hotspur	Sheffield Wednesday
1962	Ipswich Town	Burnley
1963	Everton	Tottenham Hotspur
1964	Liverpool	Manchester United
1965	Manchester United	Leeds United
1966	Liverpool	Leeds United
1967	Manchester United	Nottingham Forest
1968	Manchester City	Manchester United
1969	Leeds United	Liverpool
1970	Everton	Leeds United
1971	Arsenal	Leeds United
1972	Derby County	Leeds United
1973	Liverpool	Arsenal
1974	Leeds United	Liverpool
1975	Derby County	Liverpool
1976	Liverpool	Queens Park Rangers
1977	Liverpool	Manchester City
1978	Nottingham Forest	Liverpool

English League Record (*continued*)

SEASON	CHAMPIONS	RUNNERS-UP
1979	Liverpool	Nottingham Forest
1980	Liverpool	Manchester United
1981	Aston Villa	Ipswich Town
1982	Liverpool	Ipswich Town
1983	Liverpool	Watford
1984	Liverpool	Southampton
1985	Everton	Liverpool
1986	Liverpool	Everton
1987	Everton	Liverpool
1988	Liverpool	Manchester United
1989	Arsenal	Liverpool
1990	Liverpool	Aston Villa
1991	Arsenal	Liverpool
1992	Leeds United	Manchester United
1993	Manchester United	Aston Villa
1994	Manchester United	Blackburn Rovers
1995	Blackburn Rovers	Manchester United
1996	Manchester United	Newcastle United
1997	Manchester United	Newcastle United
1998	Arsenal	Manchester United
1999	Manchester United	Arsenal
2000	Manchester United	Arsenal
2001	Manchester United	Arsenal
2002	Arsenal	Liverpool

English League Summary

TEAM	TOTALS	CHAMPIONS & RUNNERS-UP (BOLD) (*ITALICS*)
Liverpool	18, 11	*1899*, **1901, 06, 10, 22, 23, 47,** *64, 66, 69,* **73,** *74, 75,* **76, 77,** *78,* **79, 80,** *82–84,* **85,** *86,* **87,** *88,* **89, 90,** *91,* **2002**
Manchester United	14, 12	**1908,** *11,* **47–49,** *51,* **52, 56, 57,** *59,* **64,** *65,* **67,** *68,* **80,** *88,* **92, 93,** *94, 95,* **96, 97,** *98,* **99–2001**
Arsenal	12, 6	**1926,** *31,* **32,** *33–35,* **38, 48, 53,** *71, 73,* **89, 91, 98,** *99–2001,* **02**
Everton	9, 7	*1890,* **91,** *95,* **1902,** *05,* **09,** *12,* **15,** *28,* **32, 39,** *63,* **70,** *85, 86,* **87**
Aston Villa	7, 10	**1889,** *94,* **96,** *97,* **99, 1900,** *03, 08, 10, 11, 13, 14, 31, 33,* **81,** *90, 93*
Sunderland	6, 5	**1892, 93,** *94,* **95, 98,** *1901,* **02,** *13, 23, 35, 36*
Newcastle United	4, 2	**1905, 07, 09, 27,** *96, 97*
Sheffield Wednesday	4, 1	**1903, 04, 29, 30,** *61*
Leeds United	3, 5	*1965, 66,* **69,** *70–72,* **74,** *92*
Wolverhampton Wanderers	3, 5	*1938, 39, 50,* **54, 55,** *58,* **59,** *60*
Huddersfield Town	3, 3	**1924–26,** *27, 28, 34*
Blackburn Rovers	3, 1	**1912, 14,** *94,* **95**
Preston North End	2, 6	**1889, 90,** *91–93,* **1906,** *53, 58*
Tottenham Hotspur	2, 4	*1922,* **51,** *52, 57,* **61,** *63*
Derby County	2, 3	*1896,* **1930,** *36,* **72,** *75*
Manchester City	2, 3	*1904, 21,* **37, 68,** *77*
Burnley	2, 2	*1920,* **21,** *60,* **62**
Portsmouth	2, 0	**1949, 50**
Ipswich Town	1, 2	**1962,** *81, 82*
Nottingham Forest	1, 2	*1967,* **78,** *79*
Sheffield United	1, 2	*1897,* **98,** *1900*
West Bromwich Albion	1, 2	**1920,** *25, 54*
Chelsea	1, 0	**1955**
Blackpool	0, 1	*1956*
Bristol City	0, 1	*1907*
Cardiff City	0, 1	*1924*
Charlton Athletic	0, 1	*1937*
Leicester City	0, 1	*1929*

English League Summary (*continued*)

TEAM	TOTALS	CHAMPIONS & RUNNERS-UP (BOLD) (*ITALICS*)
Oldham Athletic	0, 1	*1915*
Queens Park Rangers	0, 1	*1976*
Southampton	0, 1	*1984*
Watford	0, 1	*1983*

English FA Cup Record 1872–2002

YEAR	WINNERS	SCORE	RUNNERS-UP
1872	Wanderers	1-0	Royal Engineers
1873	Wanderers	2-0	Oxford University
1874	Oxford University	2-0	Royal Engineers
1875	Royal Engineers	1-1 (aet), (replay) 2-0	Old Etonians
1876	Wanderers	1-1 (aet), (replay) 3-0	Old Etonians
1877	Wanderers	2-1 (aet)	Oxford University
1878	Wanderers	3-1	Royal Engineers
1879	Old Etonians	1-0	Clapham Rovers
1880	Clapham Rovers	1-0	Oxford University
1881	Old Carthusians	3-0	Old Etonians
1882	Old Etonians	1-0	Blackburn Rovers
1883	Blackburn Olympic	2-1 (aet)	Old Etonians
1884	Blackburn Rovers	2-1	Queen's Park
1885	Blackburn Rovers	2-0	Queen's Park
1886	Blackburn Rovers	0-0, (replay) 2-0	West Bromwich Albion
1887	Aston Villa	2-0	West Bromwich Albion
1888	West Bromwich Albion	2-1	Preston North End
1889	Preston North End	3-0	Wolverhampton Wanderers
1890	Blackburn Rovers	6-1	Sheffield Wednesday
1891	Blackburn Rovers	3-1	Notts County
1892	West Bromwich Albion	3-0	Aston Villa
1893	Wolverhampton Wanderers	1-0	Everton
1894	Notts County	4-1	Bolton Wanderers
1895	Aston Villa	1-0	West Bromwich Albion
1896	Sheffield Wednesday	2-1	Wolverhampton Wanderers
1897	Aston Villa	3-2	Everton
1898	Nottingham Forest	3-1	Derby County
1899	Sheffield United	4-1	Derby County
1900	Bury	4-0	Southampton
1901	Tottenham Hotspur	2-2, (replay) 3-1	Sheffield United
1902	Sheffield United	1-1, (replay) 2-1	Southampton
1903	Bury	6-0	Derby County
1904	Manchester City	1-0	Bolton Wanderers
1905	Aston Villa	2-0	Newcastle United
1906	Everton	1-0	Newcastle United
1907	Sheffield Wednesday	2-1	Everton
1908	Wolverhampton Wanderers	3-1	Newcastle United
1909	Manchester United	1-0	Bristol City
1910	Newcastle United	1-1, (replay) 2-0	Barnsley
1911	Bradford City	0-0, (replay) 1-0	Newcastle United
1912	Barnsley	0-0, (replay) 1-0 (aet)	West Bromwich Albion
1913	Aston Villa	1-0	Sunderland
1914	Burnley	1-0	Liverpool
1915	Sheffield United	3-0	Chelsea
1916–19	*no competition*		

ENGLAND

English FA Cup Record (*continued*)

YEAR	WINNERS	SCORE	RUNNERS-UP
1920	Aston Villa	1-0 (aet)	Huddersfield Town
1921	Tottenham Hotspur	1-0	Wolverhampton Wanderers
1922	Huddersfield Town	1-0	Preston North End
1923	Bolton Wanderers	2-0	West Ham United
1924	Newcastle United	2-0	Aston Villa
1925	Sheffield United	1-0	Cardiff City
1926	Bolton Wanderers	1-0	Manchester City
1927	Cardiff City	1-0	Arsenal
1928	Blackburn Rovers	3-1	Huddersfield Town
1929	Bolton Wanderers	2-0	Portsmouth
1930	Arsenal	2-0	Huddersfield Town
1931	West Bromwich Albion	2-1	Birmingham City
1932	Newcastle United	2-1	Arsenal
1933	Everton	3-0	Manchester City
1934	Manchester City	2-1	Portsmouth
1935	Sheffield Wednesday	4-2	West Bromwich Albion
1936	Arsenal	1-0	Sheffield United
1937	Sunderland	3-1	Preston North End
1938	Preston North End	1-0 (aet)	Huddersfield Town
1939	Portsmouth	4-1	Wolverhampton Wanderers
1940–45		*no competition*	
1946	Derby County	4-1 (aet)	Charlton Athletic
1947	Charlton Athletic	1-0 (aet)	Burnley
1948	Manchester United	4-2	Blackpool
1949	Wolverhampton Wanderers	3-1	Leicester City
1950	Arsenal	2-0	Liverpool
1951	Newcastle United	2-0	Blackpool
1952	Newcastle United	1-0	Arsenal
1953	Blackpool	4-3	Bolton Wanderers
1954	West Bromwich Albion	3-2	Preston North End
1955	Newcastle United	3-1	Manchester City
1956	Manchester City	3-1	Birmingham City
1957	Aston Villa	2-1	Manchester United
1958	Bolton Wanderers	2-0	Manchester United
1959	Nottingham Forest	2-1	Luton Town
1960	Wolverhampton Wanderers	3-0	Blackburn Rovers
1961	Tottenham Hotspur	2-0	Leicester City
1962	Tottenham Hotspur	3-1	Burnley
1963	Manchester United	3-1	Leicester City
1964	West Ham United	3-2	Preston North End
1965	Liverpool	2-1 (aet)	Leeds United
1966	Everton	3-2	Sheffield Wednesday
1967	Tottenham Hotspur	2-1	Chelsea
1968	West Bromwich Albion	1-0 (aet)	Everton
1969	Manchester City	1-0	Leicester City
1970	Chelsea	2-2 (aet), (replay) 2-1 (aet)	Leeds United
1971	Arsenal	2-1 (aet)	Liverpool
1972	Leeds United	1-0	Arsenal
1973	Sunderland	1-0	Leeds United
1974	Liverpool	3-0	Newcastle United
1975	West Ham United	2-0	Fulham
1976	Southampton	1-0	Manchester United
1977	Manchester United	2-1	Liverpool
1978	Ipswich Town	1-0	Arsenal
1979	Arsenal	3-2	Manchester United

English FA Cup Record (*continued*)

YEAR	WINNERS	SCORE	RUNNERS-UP
1980	West Ham United	1-0	Arsenal
1981	Tottenham Hotspur	1-1 (aet), (replay) 3-2	Manchester City
1982	Tottenham Hotspur	1-1 (aet), (replay) 1-0	Queens Park Rangers
1983	Manchester United	2-2 (aet), (replay) 4-0	Brighton & Hove Albion
1984	Everton	2-0	Watford
1985	Manchester United	1-0 (aet)	Everton
1986	Liverpool	3-1	Everton
1987	Coventry City	3-2 (aet)	Tottenham Hotspur
1988	Wimbledon	1-0	Liverpool
1989	Liverpool	3-2 (aet)	Everton
1990	Manchester United	3-3 (aet), (replay) 1-0	Crystal Palace
1991	Tottenham Hotspur	2-1 (aet)	Nottingham Forest
1992	Liverpool	2-0	Sunderland
1993	Arsenal	1-1 (aet), (replay) 2-1 (aet)	Sheffield Wednesday
1994	Manchester United	4-0	Chelsea
1995	Everton	1-0	Manchester United
1996	Manchester United	1-0	Liverpool
1997	Chelsea	2-0	Middlesbrough
1998	Arsenal	2-0	Newcastle United
1999	Manchester United	2-0	Newcastle United
2000	Chelsea	1-0	Aston Villa
2001	Liverpool	2-1	Arsenal
2002	Arsenal	2-0	Chelsea

English FA Cup Summary

TEAM	TOTALS	WINNERS & RUNNERS-UP (BOLD) (*ITALICS*)
Manchester United	**10**, *5*	**1909, 48**, *57, 58*, **63**, *76*, **77**, *79*, **83, 85, 90, 94**, *95*, **96, 99**
Arsenal	**8**, *7*	*1927*, **30**, *32*, **36**, *50, 52*, **71**, *72, 78, 79, 80*, **93**, *98*, **2001**, *02*
Tottenham Hotspur	**8**, *1*	**1901, 21, 61, 62, 67, 81, 82**, *87*, **91**
Aston Villa	**7**, *3*	**1887**, *92*, **95, 97, 1905, 13, 20, 24**, *57*, **2000**
Newcastle United	**6**, *7*	**1905**, *06, 08*, **10**, *11*, **24**, *32*, **51, 52**, *55*, **74**, *96, 99*
Liverpool	**6**, *6*	*1914, 50*, **65**, *71, 74, 77*, **86, 88, 89, 92**, *96*, **2001**
Blackburn Rovers	**6**, *2*	**1882**, *84–86*, **90, 91, 1928**, *60*
Everton	**5**, *7*	**1893**, *97*, **1906**, *07*, **33**, *66, 68*, **84**, *85, 86, 89, 95*
West Bromwich Albion	**5**, *5*	**1886**, *87, 88*, **92**, *95*, **1912, 31**, *35*, **54**, *68*
Wanderers	**5**, *0*	**1872, 73, 76–78**
Manchester City	**4**, *4*	**1904**, *26, 33, 34*, **55, 56**, *69*, **81**
Wolverhampton Wanderers	**4**, *4*	*1889*, **93**, *96*, **1908**, *21*, **39, 49**, *60*
Bolton Wanderers	**4**, *3*	*1894, 1904*, **23, 26, 29**, *53*, **58**
Sheffield United	**4**, *2*	**1899**, *1901*, **02**, *15*, **25**, *36*
Chelsea	**3**, *4*	*1915, 67*, **70**, *94*, **97, 2000**, *02*
Sheffield Wednesday	**3**, *3*	*1890*, **96**, *1907*, **35**, *66, 93*
West Ham United	**3**, *1*	*1923*, **64, 75**, *80*
Preston North End	**2**, *5*	*1888*, **89**, *22, 37, 38*, **54**, *64*
Old Etonians	**2**, *4*	*1875*, **76**, *79, 81*, **82**, *83*
Sunderland	**2**, *2*	*1913*, **37**, *73*, **92**
Nottingham Forest	**2**, *1*	**1898, 1959**, *91*

English FA Cup Summary (*continued*)

TEAM	TOTALS	WINNERS & RUNNERS-UP (BOLD) (*ITALICS*)
Bury	2, 0	**1900, 03**
Huddersfield Town	1, 4	1920, **22**, 28, 30, 38
Derby County	1, 3	1898, 99, 1903, **46**
Leeds United	1, 3	1965, 70, **72**, 73
Oxford University	1, 3	**1873**, 74, 77, 80
Royal Engineers	1, 3	1872, 74, **75**, 78
Blackpool	1, 2	1948, 51, **53**
Burnley	1, 2	**1914**, 47, 62
Portsmouth	1, 2	1929, 34, **39**
Southampton	1, 2	1900, 02, **76**
Barnsley	1, 1	1910, **12**
Cardiff City	1, 1	1925, **27**
Charlton Athletic	1, 1	1946, **47**
Clapham Rovers	1, 1	1879, **80**
Notts County	1, 1	1891, **94**
Blackburn Olympic	1, 0	**1883**
Bradford City	1, 0	**1911**
Coventry City	1, 0	**1987**
Ipswich Town	1, 0	**1978**
Old Carthusians	1, 0	**1881**
Wimbledon	1, 0	**1988**
Leicester City	0, 4	1949, 61, 63, 69
Birmingham City	0, 2	1931, 56
Queen's Park	0, 2	1884, 85
Brighton & Hove Albion	0, 1	1983
Bristol City	0, 1	1909
Crystal Palace	0, 1	1990
Fulham	0, 1	1975
Luton Town	0, 1	1959
Middlesbrough	0, 1	1997
Queens Park Rangers	0, 1	1982
Watford	0, 1	1984

English League Cup Record 1961–2002

YEAR	WINNERS	SCORE	RUNNERS-UP
1961	Aston Villa	0-2, 3-0 (aet) (2 legs)	Rotherham United
1962	Norwich City	3-0, 1-0 (2 legs)	Rochdale
1963	Birmingham City	3-1, 0-0 (2 legs)	Aston Villa
1964	Leicester City	1-1, 3-2 (2 legs)	Stoke City
1965	Chelsea	3-2, 0-0 (2 legs)	Leicester City
1966	West Bromwich Albion	1-2, 4-1 (2 legs)	West Ham United
1967	Queens Park Rangers	3-2	West Bromwich Albion
1968	Leeds United	1-0	Arsenal
1969	Swindon Town	3-1 (aet)	Arsenal
1970	Manchester City	2-1 (aet)	West Bromwich Albion
1971	Tottenham Hotspur	2-0	Aston Villa
1972	Stoke City	2-1	Chelsea
1973	Tottenham Hotspur	1-0	Norwich City
1974	Wolverhampton Wanderers	2-1	Manchester City
1975	Aston Villa	1-0	Norwich City
1976	Manchester City	2-1	Newcastle United
1977	Aston Villa	0-0, (replay) 1-1 (aet), (replay) 3-2 (aet)	Everton
1978	Nottingham Forest	0-0 (aet), (replay) 1-0	Liverpool
1979	Nottingham Forest	3-2	Southampton
1980	Wolverhampton Wanderers	1-0	Nottingham Forest
1981	Liverpool	1-1 (aet), (replay) 2-1	West Ham United

English League Cup Record (*continued*)

YEAR	WINNERS	SCORE	RUNNERS-UP
1982	Liverpool	3-1 (aet)	Tottenham Hotspur
1983	Liverpool	2-1 (aet)	Manchester United
1984	Liverpool	0-0 (aet), (replay) 1-0	Everton
1985	Norwich City	1-0	Sunderland
1986	Oxford United	3-0	Queens Park Rangers
1987	Arsenal	2-1	Liverpool
1988	Luton Town	3-2	Arsenal
1989	Nottingham Forest	3-1	Luton Town
1990	Nottingham Forest	1-0	Oldham Athletic
1991	Sheffield Wednesday	1-0	Manchester United
1992	Manchester United	1-0	Nottingham Forest
1993	Arsenal	2-1	Sheffield Wednesday
1994	Aston Villa	3-1	Manchester United
1995	Liverpool	2-1	Bolton Wanderers
1996	Aston Villa	3-0	Leeds United
1997	Leicester City	1-1 (aet), (replay) 1-0 (aet)	Middlesbrough
1998	Chelsea	2-0 (aet)	Middlesbrough
1999	Tottenham Hotspur	1-0	Leicester City
2000	Leicester City	2-1	Tranmere Rovers
2001	Liverpool	1-1 (aet)(5-4 pens)	Birmingham City
2002	Blackburn Rovers	2-1	Tottenham Hotspur

English League Cup Summary

TEAM	TOTALS	WINNERS & RUNNERS-UP (BOLD) (*ITALICS*)
Liverpool	6, 2	*1978*, **81–84**, **87**, **95**, 2001
Aston Villa	5, 2	**1961**, *63*, **71**, **75**, 77, **94**, 96
Nottingham Forest	4, 2	**1978**, 79, **80**, **89**, **90**, 92
Leicester City	3, 2	**1964**, 65, **97**, 99, **2000**
Tottenham Hotspur	3, 2	**1971**, 73, 82, **99**, 2002
Arsenal	2, 3	1968, 69, **87**, 88, **93**
Norwich City	2, 2	**1962**, 73, 75, **85**
Chelsea	2, 1	**1965**, 72, **98**
Manchester City	2, 1	**1970**, **74**, 76
Wolverhampton Wanderers	2, 0	**1974**, **80**
Manchester United	1, 3	1983, 91, **92**, 94
West Bromwich Albion	1, 2	**1966**, 67, 70
Birmingham City	1, 1	**1963**, *2001*
Leeds United	1, 1	**1968**, 96
Luton Town	1, 1	**1988**, 89
Queens Park Rangers	1, 1	**1967**, 86
Sheffield Wednesday	1, 1	**1991**, 93
Stoke City	1, 1	**1964**, 72
Blackburn Rovers	1, 0	**2002**
Oxford United	1, 0	**1986**
Everton	0, 2	1977, 84
Middlesbrough	0, 2	1997, 98
Bolton Wanderers	0, 1	1995
Newcastle United	0, 1	1976
Oldham Athletic	0, 1	1990
Rochdale	0, 1	1962
Rotherham United	0, 1	1961
Southampton	0, 1	1979
Sunderland	0, 1	1985
Tranmere Rovers	0, 1	2000

ENGLAND

91

Scotland

THE SEASON IN REVIEW 2001–02

DURING 2002, THE FUNDAMENTAL divide in Scottish football finally erupted into open warfare. Not the enmity of the Glasgow Old Firm (Celtic and Rangers), however, but rather the massive inequalities of wealth, power and talent between the Old Firm and the rest. In the league, Martin O'Neill's triple-winning Celtic picked up where it left off. A creditable run in the Champions League, including a famous victory over Juventus, was eclipsed by a hurricane force of form domestically. The year began with Celtic way out in front. Only one loss (to Aberdeen) and one draw in 22 games gave the team 61 points and a 13-point lead over its nearest rival. It never lost another game. More tellingly, Rangers only lost one game outside of Old Firm matches all season, and still finished way behind the old enemy.

At Rangers, Dick Advocaat began the season with a clearout as van Bronckhorst, Jorge Albertz and Rod Wallace moved on. But, unable to match Celtic's early season form, he was replaced by Alex McLeish. Under McLeish, Rangers has reorganized and found its form. While Advocaat had lost five Old Firm derbies in a row, McLeish's Rangers is now unbeaten in four, took the Scottish League Cup in the spring and ended the season with a triumphant 3-2 defeat over Celtic in the Scottish FA Cup Final.

In another world

With Hampden Park bedecked on the day of the Cup Final with Irish Tricolors at one end and Northern Ireland flags at the other, it is clear that Celtic and Rangers are in another world, symbolically and sportingly, from the rest of the country. Economically, however, they struggle to compete with the biggest clubs in Europe. This year, rumours and claims abound that they might take part in the English League Cup or join the English First Division on their way to the Premiership, and it may happen yet. In heated and acrimonious negotiations over TV rights, the other members of the Scottish Premier League announced that they would be leaving in 2004 and establishing their own league. The Old Firm, who are insistent in their demands for a bigger share of the TV pie, will have to join on the other Premier League teams' terms or not at all. Simultaneously, the collapse of the ITV Digital deal in England has persuaded many clubs that a massive injection of fans and cash from Glasgow would support their own flagging finances. The Old Firm have been in a league of their own for some time; it seems that unless some tough decisions are taken soon, they may well find that it is a league of only two teams.

Scottish Premier League Table 2001–02

CLUB	P	W	D	L	F	A	Pts	
Celtic	38	33	4	1	94	18	103	Champions League
Rangers	38	25	10	3	82	27	85	UEFA Cup
Livingston	38	16	10	12	49	47	58	UEFA Cup
Aberdeen	38	16	7	15	50	49	55	UEFA Cup
Hearts	38	14	6	18	52	57	48	
Dunfermline	38	12	9	17	41	64	45	
Kilmarnock	38	13	10	15	44	53	49	
Dundee United	38	12	10	16	38	58	46	
Dundee	38	12	8	18	41	55	44	
Hibernian	38	10	11	17	50	56	41	
Motherwell	38	11	7	20	49	68	40	
St. Johnstone	38	5	6	27	24	62	21	Relegated

Promoted club: Partick Thistle.

Scottish FA Cup

2002 FINAL

May 4 – Hampden Park, Glasgow
Rangers 3-2 Celtic
(Lovenkrands   (Hartson 19,
21, 90,   Balde 50)
Ferguson 69)
h/t: 1-1   **Att:** 51,138
Ref: Hugh Dallas

Top: Barry Ferguson beats the Celtic wall to equalize for Rangers in the Scottish Cup Final. Rangers went on to win it in the last minute of the game.

Above: Ayr United lines up for the losers' medals after the Scottish League Cup Final.

Top Goalscorers 2001–02

PLAYER	CLUB	NATIONALITY	GOALS
Henrik Larsson	Celtic	Swedish	29
John Hartson	Celtic	Welsh	19
Tore Andre Flo	Rangers	Norwegian	18

International Club Performances 2001–02

CLUB	COMPETITION	PROGRESS
Celtic	Champions League	1st Group Stage
	UEFA Cup	3rd Round
Rangers	Champions League	3rd Qualifying Round
	UEFA Cup	4th Round
Hibernian	UEFA Cup	1st Round
Kilmarnock	UEFA Cup	1st Round

SCOTLAND

Rangers' new manager Alex McLeish lifts the Tennents Scottish Cup.

Top: *Motherwell manager Eric Black contemplates the financial black hole at the club: by the end of the season the entire Motherwell squad was up for sale.*

Above: *Celtic's Moravcik beats the Motherwell wall. Note how small the main stand is for a Premiership ground.*

Left: *Claudio Caniggia (Rangers) is smothered by Livingstone's Stuart Lovell and Oscar Rubio. Newly promoted Livingstone, from a central belt New Town, showed extraordinary heart on a shoestring to claim third spot.*

Centre left: *The locks have gone but the scoring continues. Celtic's Swedish Henrik Larsson was Scotland's top scorer again this season.*

Left: *St. Johnstone's Tommy Lovenkrands tries to find a way through the Kilmarnock defence. But with only five wins and 24 goals in 38 games, St. Johnstone was unceremoniously relegated.*

SCOTLAND

Association Football in Scotland

1867: Queen's Park FC, Scotland's oldest club founded — 1865

1872: First official international, v England, drawn 0-0, venue: Glasgow — 1870

1873: Formation of Scottish FA — 1875

1874: First Scottish Cup Final — 1880

1891: First league championship — 1890

1893: Professionalism adopted, Scottish Second Division created — 1895

1902: Ibrox disaster. Stand collapses at Scotland v England match, 29 killed, 500 injured — 1900

1910: Affiliation to FIFA — 1910

1915

1920: Withdrew from FIFA — 1920

1924: Reaffiliated to FIFA — 1925

1928: Withdrew from FIFA — 1930

1935

1940–46: League abandoned during war — 1940

1946: Reaffiliated to FIFA — 1945

1947: First Scottish League Cup Final — 1950

1954: Affiliation to UEFA — 1955

1968: First women's league formed — 1960

1971: Ibrox disaster. Crush during Rangers v Celtic match, 66 killed — 1965

1972: Scottish Women's Football Association founded. First international, v England, lost 2-3, venue: Greenock — 1970

1975: Scottish league reorganization, creating ten-team Premier League, First and Second Divisions — 1975, 1980

1994: Two lower leagues turned into three with addition of two new clubs from the Highlands — 1985, 1990

1997: Scottish Premier League separates from Scottish FA — 1995

1999: Scottish Women's FA affiliates to SFA — 2000

2005

In March 1878, the annual Scotland v England match ended in a convincing 7-2 victory for the Scots at Queen's Park, Glasgow.

Key

⚔	International football	○	Competition winner
⚽	Affiliation to FIFA	△	Competition runner-up
⚽	Affiliation to UEFA		
♀	Women's football	Dons	– Aberdeen
🌿	Disaster	Dun U	– Dundee United
🚗	War	Gers	– Rangers

International Competitions

	European Cup	UEFA Cup	European Cup-Winners' Cup
1961:			△ Gers
1967:	○ Celtic		△ Gers
1970:	△ Celtic		
1972:			○ Gers
1983:			○ Dons
1987:		△ Dun U	

Scotland: The main clubs

Clyde 1878 — Team name with year of formation

● Club formed before 1912

● Club formed 1912–25

● Club formed 1925–50

○ Club formed after 1950

★ Founder members of league (1890)

👕 Pre-1914 champions

🏴󠁧󠁢󠁥󠁮󠁧󠁿 English origins

🏛 Originated from a military institution

🏏 Originated from a cricket club

🎖 Originated from a school or college

🎗 Mining origins

✝ Catholic allegiances

✝ Protestant allegiances

▼ YMCA

★ **Third Lanark** 1872
🏛 Founded by members of Third Lanark Rifle Volunteers, changed name to Third Lanark (1878). Dissolved 1966

Renton 1872
Left league 1898

Hamilton Academical 1874
🎖

★ **Cambuslang** 1875
Left league 1892

★ **Cowlairs** 1876
Left league 1891

Queen's Park 1867
▼

Clydebank 1965
Played one year (1964–65) as ES Clydebank, merger with East Stirlingshire

Partick Thistle 1876

★ **Rangers** 1873
👕 ✝

★ **Celtic** 1888
👕 ✝

★ **Clydebank** 1914
Dissolved 1931

★ **Abercorn** 1870s
Left league 1915

★ **St. Mirren** 1877

Founded in 1867, Queen's Park is Scotland's oldest club. The team is shown here in action during a friendly match with the English club Corinthians in 1901.

Scotland

ORIGINS AND GROWTH OF FOOTBALL

SCOTTISH FOOTBALL FOLLOWED RAPIDLY on the heels of its English counterpart. Its first club, Queen's Park, was formed in Glasgow in 1867 by members of the YMCA and went on to compete in the English FA Cups of the era. Along with the other home countries Scotland is a political region that has nation status in international football, and in 1872 the first-ever international, against England, was played in Glasgow. The following year saw the establishment of the Scottish FA in Glasgow and the first Scottish Cup competition. In the following decade football swept through the working-class communities of Scotland's central belt. Clubs and followings were often established around Protestant and Irish immigrant/Catholic neighbourhoods and identities, especially in the cities of Glasgow, Edinburgh and Dundee.

The price of success

The world's second oldest national league began in 1890 and professionalism arrived in 1893. But more significant was the fact that Scottish football provided much of the manpower for the early English professional league, also exporting players, missionaries and coaches of the game to Europe and Latin America. They pioneered the passing game – a style at odds with the dreary solo dribbling and long balls of the emerging English game – where players moved the ball on the ground in structured passing and running moves.

But the explosive growth of Scottish football came at a cost. In 1902, 29 people died and over 500 were injured when a new stand at Rangers' Ibrox stadium collapsed during a Scotland v England international match. In 1909, a Celtic v Rangers fixture at Hampden Park descended into football's first full-scale stadium riot.

The economics of failure

Like England, Scotland's international performance during the early World Cups was limited by the SFA's disinterest or active opposition to FIFA. It has yet to recover. In the postwar era, the economic and footballing dominance of Celtic and Rangers has increased, their domestic strength bringing European success in the late 1960s and early 1970s. However, the economics of football in a small country since then has meant that both clubs have failed to repeat those successes.

SCOTLAND

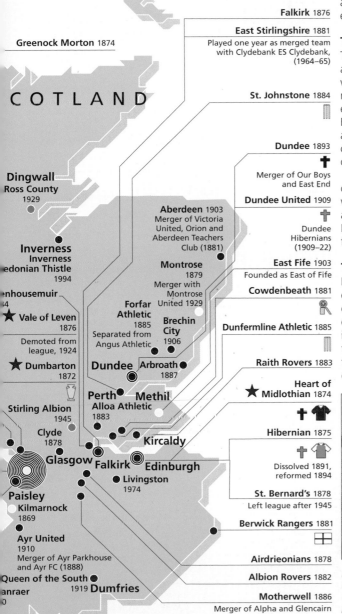

In 1902, at a friendly match between Scotland and England at Ibrox Park, seven rows of wooden planking on the newly-built eastern terrace collapsed under the weight of spectators. Hundreds plunged 40 feet to the ground below, resulting in 29 deaths.

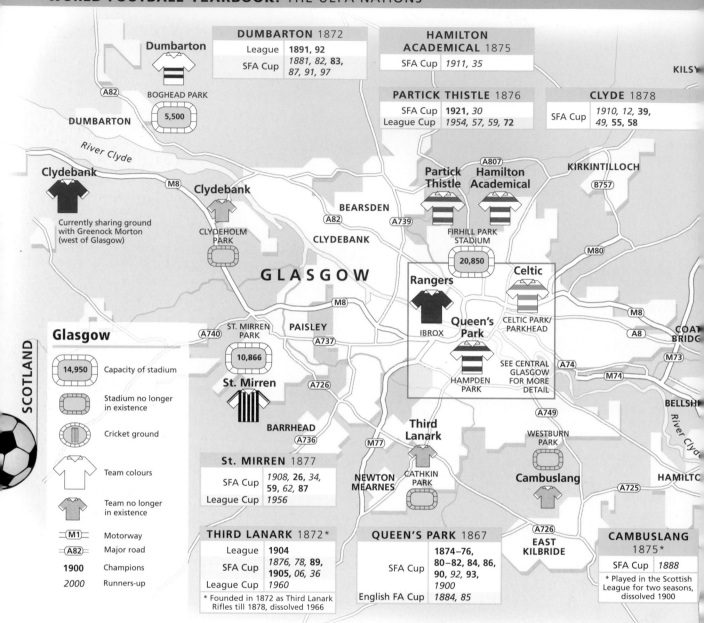

DUMBARTON 1872

League	**1891, 92**
SFA Cup	*1881, 82, 83, 87, 91, 97*

HAMILTON ACADEMICAL 1875

SFA Cup	*1911, 35*

PARTICK THISTLE 1876

SFA Cup	**1921,** *30*
League Cup	*1954, 57, 59, 72*

CLYDE 1878

SFA Cup	*1910, 12, 39, 49, 55, 58*

Dumbarton — BOGHEAD PARK — 5,500

Clydebank — Currently sharing ground with Greenock Morton (west of Glasgow)

Clydebank — CLYDEHOLM PARK

River Clyde

DUMBARTON

BEARSDEN

CLYDEBANK

GLASGOW

Partick Thistle / Hamilton Academical — FIRHILL PARK STADIUM — 20,850

KIRKINTILLOCH

Rangers — IBROX

Celtic — CELTIC PARK/ PARKHEAD

Queen's Park

SEE CENTRAL GLASGOW FOR MORE DETAIL

PAISLEY

ST. MIRREN PARK — 10,866

St. Mirren

BARRHEAD

NEWTON MEARNES

Third Lanark — CATHKIN PARK

HAMPDEN PARK

WESTBURN PARK

Cambuslang

EAST KILBRIDE

River Clyde

Glasgow

14,950	Capacity of stadium
	Stadium no longer in existence
	Cricket ground
	Team colours
	Team no longer in existence
M1	Motorway
A82	Major road
1900	Champions
2000	Runners-up

SCOTLAND

St. MIRREN 1877

SFA Cup	*1908, 26, 34, 59, 62, 87*
League Cup	*1956*

THIRD LANARK 1872*

League	**1904**
SFA Cup	*1876, 78,* **89,** **1905,** *06, 36*
League Cup	*1960*

* Founded in 1872 as Third Lanark Rifles till 1878, dissolved 1966

QUEEN'S PARK 1867

SFA Cup	*1874–76, 80–82, 84, 86, 90, 92, 93, 1900*
English FA Cup	*1884, 85*

CAMBUSLANG 1875*

SFA Cup	*1888*

* Played in the Scottish League for two seasons, dissolved 1900

Glasgow

FOOTBALL CITY

GLASGOW MAY NOT BE the political capital of Scotland, but there was no question that the Scottish FA would be located anywhere but in the country's footballing capital. Scotland's first club, Queen's Park, was founded in the south of the city in 1867. Glasgow saw the world's first international, played in Partick in 1872, the world's first penalty in 1891; the world's first stadium collapse in 1902; and the first stadium riot in 1909.

In the late 19th century, Glasgow's booming heavy industries drew heavily on rural Scottish Protestant and Irish Catholic immigrants. In the following two decades, football clubs sprang up all over greater Glasgow as this divided working class embraced Scottish football. However, the centre of the city was dominated by the rivalry between Celtic and Rangers – the 'Old Firm'.

The origins of the Old Firm

Celtic was founded in 1888 by Brother Walfrid of the Marist Order as both a football club and a social service for Catholic boys. The club's affiliations have remained clear: a shamrock emblem and the flying of the Irish tricolor at the stadium. Rangers was formed over a decade earlier out of a rowing club north of the River Clyde, but soon settled among the docks and Protestant dockworkers of the Govan area. Rangers' affiliation to Unionism and Protestantism, always present, grew with the emergence of Celtic as sporting and cultural rivals. By 1910, Rangers would no longer sign Catholic players, and its strip, predominantly blue, had acquired red and white trimmings. Persistent conflict on and off the pitch has been tempered in recent years by the geographical dispersal of the old religious ghettoes and concerted official efforts to challenge sectarianism, including Rangers' signing of the Catholic Mo Johnston in 1989. But, like the issue of sectarianism in wider Scottish society, it remains largely unexamined and intact.

SCOTLAND

IBROX STADIUM (previously Ibrox Park)

50,467	**Club:** Rangers **Built:** 1899 **Rebuilt:** 1971–81, 94 **Record Attendance:** 118,567 Rangers v Celtic, 2 January 1939

RANGERS 1873

League	1891, *93, 96, 98, 99*–1902, *05, 11*–13, **14**, *16,* **18,** *19,* **20, 21, 22, 23**–25, *27*–31, *32,* **33**–35, *36,* **37,** *39,* **47,** *48,* **49, 50,** *51, 52,* **53, 56, 57,** *58, 59,* **61,** *62, 63,* **64,** *66*–70, **73,** *75,* **76, 77,** *78, 79,* **87,** *89*–97, **98,** *99,* **2000,** *01,* **02**
SFA Cup	*1877, 79,* **94, 97,** *98,* **99,** *1903, 04, 05, 21, 22,* **28,** *29,* **30, 32,** *34*–36, **48**–50, *53,* **60,** *62*–64, *66,* **69,** *71,* **73, 76, 77, 78,** *79, 80,* **81,** *82, 83,* **89,** *92,* **93, 94, 96,** *98,* **99,** *2000,* **02**
League Cup	*1947, 49, 52, 58,* **61,** *62,* **64, 65,** *66,* **67,** *71,* **76, 78, 79,** *82, 83,* **84, 85,** *87*–89, *90,* **91,** *93, 94,* **97,** *99,* **2002**
European Cup- Winners' Cup	*1961, 67,* **72**

CELTIC 1888

League	*1892, 93, 94, 95,* **96,** *98,* **1900**–02, *05*–10, *12,* **13,** *14*–17, *18,* **19,** *20, 21,* **22, 26, 28, 29, 31, 35, 36, 38, 39,** *54, 55,* **66**–74, *76,* **77,** *79,* **80, 81,** *82, 83*–85, *86, 87,* **88,** *96,* **97, 98,** *99,* **2000,** *01,* **02**
SFA Cup	*1889,* **92, 93, 94, 99, 1900,** *01, 02,* **04,** *07,* **08,** *11, 12,* **14,** *23,* **25, 26, 27, 28, 31, 33, 37,** *51,* **54, 55, 56,** *61,* **63, 65, 66, 67, 69, 70, 71,** *72,* **73, 74, 75, 77,** *80,* **84, 85,** *88,* **89, 90,** *95, 99,* **2001,** *02*
League Cup	**1957,** *58,* **65,** *66*–70, *71*–74, **75,** *76*–78, *83,* **84,** *87,* **91, 95, 98, 2000,** *01*
European Cup	**1967,** *70*
World Club Cup	*1967*

CELTIC PARK/PARKHEAD

60,506	**Club:** Celtic **Built:** 1892 **Rebuilt:** 1995 **Record Attendance:** 92,000 Celtic v Rangers, 1 January 1938

Airdrieonians was put into administration in 2002 and its future now as a league team is seriously in doubt

Clyde   Airdrieonians

ROADWOOD STADIUM   **CUMBERNAULD**

8,200	

AIRDRIEONIANS 1878

League	1923–26
SFA Cup	**1924,** *75,* **92, 95**

(A73)

Albion Rovers

LIFTON HILL STADIUM

2,500	**AIRDRIE**

MOTHERWELL 1886

League	1927, 30, **32,** *33, 34,* **95**
SFA Cup	1931, 33, 39, 51, **52, 91**
League Cup	**1951,** *55*

(A721)

MOTHERWELL

FIR PARK STADIUM

(M74)

13,742	

Motherwell

LARKHALL

HAMPDEN PARK

50,670	**Clubs:** Scotland, Queen's Park **Built:** 1903 **Rebuilt:** 1992, 94, 96–98 **Record Attendance:** 149,415 Scotland v England, 24 April 1937

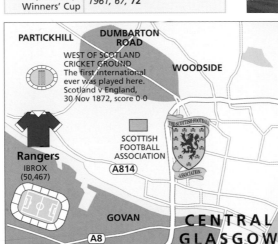

PARTICKHILL

DUMBARTON ROAD

WEST OF SCOTLAND CRICKET GROUND
The first international ever was played here. Scotland v England, 30 Nov 1872, score 0-0

WOODSIDE

Rangers
IBROX
(50,467)

SCOTTISH FOOTBALL ASSOCIATION

THE SCOTTISH FOOTBALL ASSOCIATION

(A814)

GOVAN

(A8)

(A761)

(M8)

CENTRAL GLASGOW

Area of Catholic support at the turn of the 20th century

CARLTON

BRIGTON

(A74)

CELTIC PARK/ PARKHEAD
(60,506)

(M77)

POLLOCKSHIELDS
Area of Protestant support at the turn of the 20th century

(A77)

GORBALS

River Clyde

PARKHEAD

(A749)

Celtic

Scotland   Queen's Park
HAMPDEN PARK
(50,670)

(A728)

(A730)

RUTHERGLEN

At the 1980 Scottish FA Cup Final between Celtic and Rangers, a lap of victory by the Celtic team triggered a pitch invasion and a full-scale riot between fans and police. The incident led to the banning of alcohol from Scottish grounds

THE LOCAL DERBY

CELTIC	**RANGERS**

556 matches played

183 Celtic wins
238 Rangers wins
135 draws

0   100   200   300   400   500

NUMBER OF MATCHES
(All first-class games up to July 2001)

Scotland

PLAYERS AND MANAGERS

ALMOST INEVITABLY SCOTTISH football has been a great exporter of talent. Among the earliest players of the game and the earliest professionals, Scottish players and managers have constantly found themselves outgrowing their small and economically limited leagues. In the late 19th century, Scots were central to the spread of the game in Latin America and continental Europe, while Scottish teams pioneered the short passing game as it was known, displacing the kick and rush that was dominant south of the border. Scots took their talents and their style to Germany, Central Europe and, above all, to England, for it is the old enemy that has most consistently provided the better wages and the bigger stage that Scottish football talent has demanded. It is the same logic that has seen a steady influx of foreign talent not only to the big two Glasgow teams, but also to the smallest Premier Division sides.

Working-class politics

The great Scottish managers of the modern era – Sir Matt Busby, Sir Alex Ferguson and Bill Shankly – have all really made their mark south of the border, not only winning trophies but building teams and clubs that lasted. Only Jock Stein (a disastrous month at Leeds United aside) built his career in Scotland at Celtic and as national team manager. The working-class and often political roots of these men has provided a context in which their special kind of leadership and management talent could be awakened. Similarly, among the greatest players of the modern era it has often been an English club that has provided the home in which their talent could fully mature: Denis Law at Manchester United, and Kenny Dalglish, Alan Hansen and Graeme Souness at Liverpool.

Top 15 International Caps

PLAYER	CAPS	GOALS	FIRST MATCH	LAST MATCH
Kenny Dalglish	102	30	1972	1987
Jim Leighton	91	0	1983	1999
Alex McLeish	77	1	1980	1993
Paul McStay	76	9	1984	1997
Tommy Boyd*	73	1	1991	2001
Willie Miller	65	1	1975	1990
Danny McGrain	62	0	1973	1982
Richard Gough	61	6	1983	1993
Ally McCoist	61	19	1986	1998
John Collins*	58	12	1988	2000
Roy Aitken	57	1	1980	1992
Gary McAllister*	57	5	1990	1999
Dennis Law	55	30	1959	1974
Maurice Malpas	55	0	1984	1993
Billy Bremner	54	3	1965	1976
Graeme Souness	54	4	1975	1986

Top 10 International Goalscorers

PLAYER	GOALS	CAPS	FIRST MATCH	LAST MATCH
Denis Law	30	55	1959	1974
Kenny Dalglish	30	102	1972	1987
Hugh Gallacher	23	53	1924	1935
Lawrie Reilly	22	38	1949	1957
Ally McCoist	19	61	1986	1998
Robert Cumming Hamilton	14	11	1899	1911
Mo Johnston	14	38	1984	1992
John Smith	13	10	1877	1884
Andrew Nesbit Wilson	13	12	1920	1923
Robert Smyth McColl	13	13	1896	1908

* Indicates players still playing at least at club level.

Scottish International Managers

DATES	NAME	GAMES	WON	DRAWN	LOST
1954	Andy Beattie	6	2	1	3
1958	Matt Busby	2	1	1	0
1959–60	Andy Beattie	12	3	3	6
1960–65	Ian McColl	28	17	3	8
1965	Jock Stein	7	3	1	3
1966	John Prentice	4	0	1	3
1966	Malcolm McDonald	2	1	1	0
1967–71	Bobby Brown	28	9	8	11
1971–72	Tommy Docherty	12	7	2	3
1973–77	Willie Ormond	38	18	8	12
1977–78	Ally McLeod	17	7	5	5
1978–85	Jock Stein	61	26	12	23
1985–86	Alex Ferguson	10	3	4	3
1986–93	Andy Roxburgh	61	23	19	19
1993–2001	Craig Brown	70	32	18	20
2002–	Berti Vogts	0	0	0	0

All figures correct as of spring 2002.

Celtic's Billy McNeill is held up by his teammates after their victory in the 1965 Scottish Cup Final against Dunfermline. McNeill's efforts that season earned him the Scottish Player of the Year award.

SCOTLAND

Player of the Year

YEAR	PLAYER	CLUB
1965	McNeill	Celtic
1966	Greig	Rangers
1967	Simpson	Celtic
1968	Wallace	Raith Rovers
1969	Murdoch	Celtic
1970	Stanton	Hibernian
1971	Buchan	Aberdeen
1972	Smith	Rangers
1973	Connelly	Celtic
1974	Scotland World Cup Squad	
1975	Jardine	Rangers
1976	Greig	Rangers
1977	McGrain	Celtic
1978	Johnstone	Rangers
1979	Ritchie	Morton
1980	Strachan	Aberdeen
1981	Rough	Partick Thistle
1982	Sturrock	Dundee United
1983	Nicholas	Celtic
1984	Miller	Aberdeen
1985	McAlpine	Dundee United

Player of the Year (continued)

YEAR	PLAYER	CLUB
1986	Jardine	Heart of Midlothian
1987	McClair	Celtic
1988	McStay	Celtic
1989	Gough	Rangers
1990	McLeish	Aberdeen
1991	Malpas	Dundee United
1992	McCoist	Rangers
1993	Goram	Rangers
1994	Hateley	Rangers
1995	Laudrup	Rangers
1996	Gascoigne	Rangers
1997	Laudrup	Rangers
1998	Burley	Celtic
1999	Larsson	Celtic
2000	B. Ferguson	Rangers
2001	Larsson	Celtic

Awarded by the Scottish Football Writers' Association.

Manager of the Year

YEAR	MANAGER	CLUB
1987	Jim McLean	Dundee United
1988	Billy McNeill	Celtic
1989	Graeme Souness	Rangers
1990	Andy Roxburgh	Scotland
1991	Alex Totten	St. Johnstone
1992	Walter Smith	Rangers
1993	Walter Smith	Rangers
1994	Walter Smith	Rangers
1995	Jimmy Nichol	Raith Rovers
1996	Walter Smith	Rangers
1997	Walter Smith	Rangers
1998	Wim Jansen	Celtic
1999	Dick Advocaat	Rangers
2000	Dick Advocaat	Rangers
2001	Martin O'Neill	Celtic

Awarded by Tennents.

SCOTLAND

Top Goalscorers by Season 1965–2002

SEASON	PLAYER	CLUB	GOALS
1965–66	McBride	Celtic	31
1965–66	A. Ferguson	Dunfermline Athletic	31
1966–67	Chalmers	Celtic	21
1967–68	Lennox	Celtic	32
1968–69	Cameron	Dundee United	26
1969–70	Stein	Rangers	24
1970–71	Hood	Celtic	22
1971–72	Harper	Aberdeen	33
1972–73	Gordon	Hibernian	27
1973–74	Deans	Celtic	26
1974–75	Gray	Dundee United	20
1974–75	Pettigrew	Motherwell	20
1975–76	Dalglish	Celtic	24
1976–77	Pettigrew	Motherwell	21
1977–78	Johnstone	Rangers	25
1978–79	Ritchie	Morton	22
1979–80	Somner	St. Mirren	25
1980–81	McGarvey	Celtic	23
1981–82	McCluskey	Celtic	21
1982–83	Nicholas	Celtic	29
1983–84	McClair	Celtic	23
1984–85	McDougall	Dundee	22
1985–86	McCoist	Rangers	24
1986–87	McClair	Celtic	35
1987–88	Coyne	Dundee	33
1988–89	McGhee	Celtic	16
1988–89	Nicholas	Aberdeen	16
1989–90	Robertson	Heart of Midlothian	17

SEASON	PLAYER	CLUB	GOALS
1990–91	Coyne	Celtic	18
1991–92	McCoist	Rangers	34
1992–93	McCoist	Rangers	34
1993–94	Hateley	Rangers	22
1994–95	Coyne	Motherwell	16
1995–96	Hooijdonk	Celtic	26
1996–97	Cadete	Celtic	25
1997–98	Negri	Rangers	32
1998–99	Larsson	Celtic	29
1999–2000	Viduka	Celtic	25
2000–01	Larsson	Celtic	35
2001–02	Larsson	Celtic	29

Despite limited resources, Craig Brown presided over one of the most successful periods of Scottish footballing history between 1993 and 2001: with a record of 32 wins, 18 draws and 20 defeats in 70 matches he is also Scotland's longest-serving manager.

Foreign Players in Scotland (in top division squads)

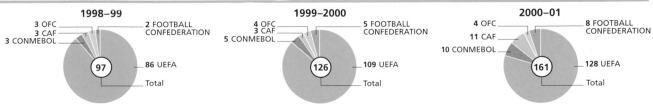

1998–99
3 OFC
3 CAF
3 CONMEBOL
2 FOOTBALL CONFEDERATION
86 UEFA
97 Total

1999–2000
4 OFC
3 CAF
5 CONMEBOL
5 FOOTBALL CONFEDERATION
109 UEFA
126 Total

2000–01
4 OFC
11 CAF
10 CONMEBOL
8 FOOTBALL CONFEDERATION
128 UEFA
161 Total

Scotland

SCOTTISH PREMIER LEAGUE 1975–2001

IN THE LAST 25 YEARS the Scottish League has been through three reorganizations (two under the auspices of the Scottish FA in 1975 and 1994, and then again in 1997 with the establishment of the Scottish Premier League). Each time the issue has been the same – how to create a competitive, financially viable league when two clubs are so much bigger than the others. In spring 2002, a fourth shift looks likely, as all the other Premier League teams have resigned, leaving Celtic and Rangers and their ever-greater demands for TV income out in the cold.

Rangers revolution, Celtic dominance

The era began with the usual Glasgow monopoly on the title, including Jock Stein's last championship with Celtic. Post-Stein, Billy McNeill's team continued to win, but Rangers went into a decade of decline. Into the vacuum stepped Alex Ferguson's Aberdeen and, for a glorious season in 1983, Dundee United. But with the arrival of businessman David Murray at Rangers, the vacuum was filled again. Money was spent on the squad, first in England and then in Europe and, shortly after the appointment of Graeme Souness as manager, the sectarian ban on signing Catholic players was ended.

Under Souness, Walter Smith and Dick Advocaat, Rangers then won 11 out of 12 titles (1989–2000) – a sequence broken by a revived Celtic under Wim Jansen and then by Martin O'Neill's team in 2000, Celtic's best squad for two decades. Beyond these two, only Hearts and Motherwell have been regular members of the Premier League but neither has mounted a sustained challenge to the Old Firm's dominance on the field. It may require the entire league to do so off the field.

SCOTLAND

Scottish League Positions 1975–2001

TEAM	75-76	76-77	77-78	78-79	79-80	80-81	81-82	82-83	83-84	84-85	85-86	86-87	87-88	88-89	89-90	90-91	91-92	92-93	93-94	94-95	95-96	96-97	97-98	98-99	99-00	00-01
Aberdeen	7	3	2	4	1	2	2	3	1	1	4	4	4	2	2	2	6	2	2	9	3	6	6	8	10	7
Airdrieonians						7	10										7	12								
Ayr United	6	8	9																							
Celtic	2	1	5	1	2	1	1	2	2	2	1	2	1	3	5	3	3	3	4	4	2	2	1	2	2	1
Clydebank		10									10	11														
Dumbarton									9																	
Dundee	9					8	6	8	6	6	6	7	8	10			10	12						5	7	6
Dundee United	8	4	3	3	4	5	4	1	3	3	3	3	5	4	4	4	4	6	10			3	7	9	8	11
Dunfermline Athletic													11		8	8	12					5	8	10		9
Falkirk											10	10				9	11		5	10						
Hamilton Academical												12		10												
Heart of Midlothian	5	9		9		10			5	7		5	2	6	3	5	2	5	7	6	4	4	3	6	3	5
Hibernian	3	6	4	5	10		6	7	7	8	8	9	6	5	7	9	5	7	5	3	5	9	10		6	3
Kilmarnock		10		8	9		10												8	7	7	7	4	4	9	4
Livingston																										
Morton					7	6	8	7	9		10		12													
Motherwell	4	7	6	10				8	10		9	8	8	9	6	6	10	9	3	2	8	8	9	7	4	8
Partick Thistle		5	7	8	7	6	9										8	9	8	9						
Raith Rovers																			11		6	10				
Rangers	1	2	1	2	5	3	3	4	4	4	5	1	3	1	1	1	1	1	1	1	1	1	1	2	1	2
St. Johnstone	10				9			9										7	8	6	10		5	3	5	10
St. Mirren			8	6	3	4	5	5	6	5	7	7	9	7	9	10	11									12

Rangers turns the screw in 1990: another goal, another Old Firm derby, another Rangers championship. Mo Johnston, Ally McCoist and Ian Ferguson celebrate.

Manager Alex Ferguson and trainer Archie Knox celebrate as Aberdeen win the 1983 European Cup-Winners' Cup. The two moved on to fame and fortune at Manchester United.

SCOTLAND

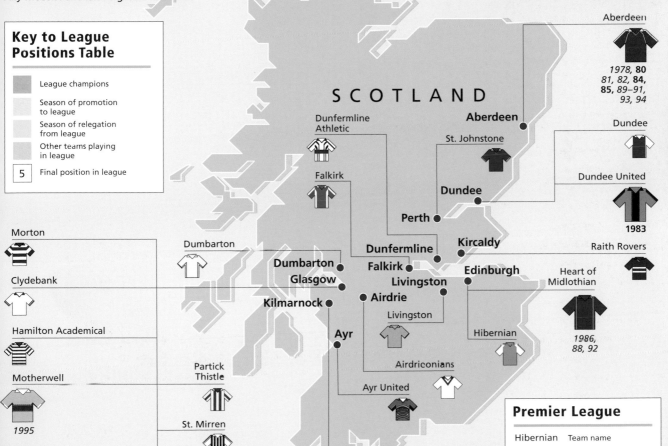

Key to League Positions Table

- League champions
- Season of promotion to league
- Season of relegation from league
- Other teams playing in league
- 5 — Final position in league

SCOTLAND

Aberdeen
1978, **80**
81, 82, 84,
85, 89–91,
93, 94

Dundee

Dundee United
1983

Raith Rovers

Heart of Midlothian
1986,
88, 92

Aberdeen

Dunfermline Athletic

St. Johnstone

Falkirk

Dundee

Perth

Kircaldy

Dunfermline

Falkirk

Livingston

Edinburgh

Dumbarton

Glasgow

Airdrie

Kilmarnock

Livingston

Ayr

Airdriconians

Hibernian

Ayr United

Kilmarnock

Morton

Clydebank

Hamilton Academical

Motherwell
1995

Rangers
1976,
77, **78,**
79, **87,**
89–97,
98, 99,
2000, 01

Dumbarton

Partick Thistle

St. Mirren

Celtic
1976, 77,
79, **80, 81,**
82, *83–85,*
86, *87,* **88,**
96, 97, 98,
99, **2000, 01**

Premier League

Hibernian	Team name
(shirt)	League champions/ runners-up
1982, *83*	Champions in bold Runners-up in italics
(shirt)	Other teams in the Premier League
● Perth	City of origin

Scotland

The Scottish Football Association
Founded: 1873
Joined FIFA: 1910–20, 1924–28, 1946
Joined UEFA: 1954

SCOTLAND'S FOOTBALL INSTITUTIONS are the second oldest in the world. Even before the establishment of the Scottish FA in 1873, Glasgow club Queen's Park was competing in the English FA Cup. With the creation of the SFA came the Scottish Cup, first played in 1874. A national league was created in 1890, rapidly followed by the arrival of professionalism in 1893 and the creation of a second division for the 1893–94 season.

Both these tournaments and the Scottish League Cup, first played in 1947, have been dominated by the Glasgow 'Old Firm' – Celtic and Rangers. There has been an occasional look in for Aberdeen, the two Dundee sides and the two Edinburgh teams – Hibernian and Heart of Midlothian.

During the Second World War, national championships were abandoned and teams played in smaller regional leagues. The continued dominance of the Old Firm led to a reorganization of the league structure for the 1975–76 season. A ten-team Premiership was created, with the big teams playing each other four times a year. Two lower divisions of 14 teams were also created. In 1994–95 the lower divisions were reorganized again, the two being expanded into three, with the addition of two teams from the Highland League. In 1997 the Scottish top flight followed the lead of the English first division, creating a separate and independent Premiership.

However, none of these structural changes can mask the basic problem that the two big Glasgow teams are economically and sportingly in a different class from the rest of the country. The Scottish Premiership continues, but the Old Firm has explored the possibility of forming an Atlantic league with other small European nations (an idea which has been blocked by UEFA) and has continued to pursue the preferred option of joining the English Premiership.

The Old Firm derby between Celtic and Rangers is one of the most keenly contested fixtures in the world.

Scottish League Record 1891–2002

SEASON	CHAMPIONS	RUNNERS-UP
1891	Dumbarton/Rangers*	
1892	Dumbarton	Celtic
1893	Celtic	Rangers
1894	Celtic	Heart of Midlothian
1895	Heart of Midlothian	Celtic
1896	Celtic	Rangers
1897	Heart of Midlothian	Hibernian
1898	Celtic	Rangers
1899	Rangers	Heart of Midlothian
1900	Rangers	Celtic
1901	Rangers	Celtic
1902	Rangers	Celtic
1903	Hibernian	Dundee
1904	Third Lanark	Heart of Midlothian
1905	Celtic	Rangers
1906	Celtic	Heart of Midlothian
1907	Celtic	Dundee
1908	Celtic	Falkirk
1909	Celtic	Dundee
1910	Celtic	Falkirk
1911	Rangers	Aberdeen
1912	Rangers	Celtic
1913	Rangers	Celtic
1914	Celtic	Rangers
1915	Celtic	Heart of Midlothian
1916	Celtic	Rangers
1917	Celtic	Morton
1918	Rangers	Celtic
1919	Celtic	Rangers
1920	Rangers	Celtic
1921	Rangers	Celtic
1922	Celtic	Rangers
1923	Rangers	Airdrieonians
1924	Rangers	Airdrieonians
1925	Rangers	Airdrieonians
1926	Celtic	Airdrieonians
1927	Rangers	Motherwell
1928	Rangers	Celtic
1929	Rangers	Celtic
1930	Rangers	Motherwell
1931	Rangers	Celtic
1932	Motherwell	Rangers
1933	Rangers	Motherwell
1934	Rangers	Motherwell
1935	Rangers	Celtic
1936	Celtic	Rangers
1937	Rangers	Aberdeen
1938	Celtic	Heart of Midlothian
1939	Rangers	Celtic
1940–46	*no championship*	
1947	Rangers	Hibernian
1948	Hibernian	Rangers
1949	Rangers	Dundee
1950	Rangers	Hibernian
1951	Hibernian	Rangers
1952	Hibernian	Rangers
1953	Rangers	Hibernian
1954	Celtic	Heart of Midlothian
1955	Aberdeen	Celtic
1956	Rangers	Aberdeen
1957	Rangers	Heart of Midlothian
1958	Heart of Midlothian	Rangers

Scottish League Record (*continued*)

SEASON	CHAMPIONS	RUNNERS-UP
1959	Rangers	Heart of Midlothian
1960	Heart of Midlothian	Kilmarnock
1961	Rangers	Kilmarnock
1962	Dundee	Rangers
1963	Rangers	Kilmarnock
1964	Rangers	Kilmarnock
1965	Kilmarnock	Heart of Midlothian
1966	Celtic	Rangers
1967	Celtic	Rangers
1968	Celtic	Rangers
1969	Celtic	Rangers
1970	Celtic	Rangers
1971	Celtic	Aberdeen
1972	Celtic	Aberdeen
1973	Celtic	Rangers
1974	Celtic	Hibernian
1975	Rangers	Hibernian
1976	Rangers	Celtic
1977	Celtic	Rangers
1978	Rangers	Aberdeen
1979	Celtic	Rangers
1980	Aberdeen	Celtic
1981	Celtic	Aberdeen
1982	Celtic	Aberdeen
1983	Dundee United	Celtic
1984	Aberdeen	Celtic
1985	Aberdeen	Celtic
1986	Celtic	Heart of Midlothian
1987	Rangers	Celtic
1988	Celtic	Heart of Midlothian
1989	Rangers	Aberdeen
1990	Rangers	Aberdeen
1991	Rangers	Aberdeen
1992	Rangers	Heart of Midlothian
1993	Rangers	Aberdeen
1994	Rangers	Aberdeen
1995	Rangers	Motherwell
1996	Rangers	Celtic
1997	Rangers	Celtic
1998	Celtic	Rangers
1999	Rangers	Celtic
2000	Rangers	Celtic
2001	Celtic	Rangers
2002	Celtic	Rangers

* Both teams had equal points, and the title was held jointly.

Scottish League Summary

TEAM	TOTALS	CHAMPIONS & RUNNERS-UP (BOLD) (*ITALICS*)
Rangers	49, 26	**1891**, *93, 96, 98,* **1899–1902, 05,** *11–13,* **14,** *16,* **18, 19,** *20,* **21, 22,** *23–25,* **27–31,** *32,* **33–35,** *36,* **37, 39, 47, 48, 49, 50,** *51, 52,* **53,** *56, 57,* **58,** *59,* **61,** *62,* **63, 64,** *66–70,* **73,** *75,* **76, 77, 78,** *79,* **87,** *89–97,* **98,** *99,* **2000,** *01,* **02**
Celtic	38, 26	*1892,* **93, 94,** *95,* **96,** *98,* **1900–02,** *05–10,* **12, 13,** *14–17,* **18,** *19,* **20, 21, 22,** *26,* **28, 29,** *31,* **35, 36, 38, 39, 54,** *55,* **66–74,** *76,* **77,** *79,* **80, 81, 82,** *83–85,* **86,** *87,* **88,** *96, 97,* **98,** *99,* **2000,** *01,* **02**
Aberdeen	4, 13	*1911, 37,* **55,** *56, 71, 72, 78,* **80, 81, 82,** *84, 85, 89–91, 93, 94*
Heart of Midlothian	4, 13	*1894,* **95,** *97, 99,* **1904,** *06, 15, 38, 54, 57,* **58,** *59,* **60,** *65, 86, 88, 92*
Hibernian	4, 6	*1897,* **1903,** *47,* **48, 50, 51, 52,** *53, 74, 75*
Dumbarton	2, 0	**1891, 92**
Motherwell	1, 5	*1927, 30,* **32,** *33, 34, 95*
Dundee	1, 4	*1903, 07, 09, 49,* **62**

Scottish League Summary (*continued*)

TEAM	TOTALS	CHAMPIONS & RUNNERS-UP (BOLD) (*ITALICS*)
Kilmarnock	1, 4	*1960, 61, 63, 64,* **65**
Dundee United	1, 0	**1983**
Third Lanark	1, 0	**1904**
Airdrieonians	0, 4	*1923–26*
Falkirk	0, 2	*1908, 10*
Morton	0, 1	*1917*

Scottish Cup Record 1874–2002

YEAR	WINNERS	SCORE	RUNNERS-UP
1874	Queen's Park	**2-0**	Clydesdale
1875	Queen's Park	**3-0**	Renton
1876	Queen's Park	1-1, (replay) **2-0**	Third Lanark
1877	Vale of Leven	0-0, (replay) 1-1, (replay) **3-2**	Rangers
1878	Vale of Leven	**1-0**	Third Lanark
1879	Vale of Leven	1-1, (replay) **w/o**	Rangers
1880	Queen's Park	**3-0**	Thornley Bank
1881	Queen's Park	**3-1***	Dumbarton
1882	Queen's Park	2-2, (replay) **4-1**	Dumbarton
1883	Dumbarton	2-2, (replay) **2-1**	Vale of Leven
1884	Queen's Park	**w/o**	Vale of Leven
1885	Renton	0-0, (replay) **3-1**	Vale of Leven
1886	Queen's Park	**3-1**	Renton
1887	Hibernian	**2-1**	Dumbarton
1888	Renton	**6-1**	Cambuslang
1889	Third Lanark	**2-1****	Celtic
1890	Queen's Park	1-1, (replay) **2-2**	Vale of Levan
1891	Heart of Midlothian	**1-0**	Dumbarton
1892	Celtic	**5-1**	Queen's Park
1893	Queen's Park	**2-1**	Celtic
1894	Rangers	**3-1**	Celtic
1895	St. Bernard's	**2-1**	Renton
1896	Heart of Midlothian	**3-1**	Hibernian
1897	Rangers	**5-1**	Dumbarton
1898	Rangers	**2-0**	Kilmarnock
1899	Celtic	**2-0**	Rangers
1900	Celtic	**4-3**	Queen's Park
1901	Heart of Midlothian	**4-3**	Celtic
1902	Hibernian	**1-0**	Celtic
1903	Rangers	1-1, (replay) 0-0, (replay) **2-0**	Heart of Midlothian
1904	Celtic	**3-2**	Rangers
1905	Third Lanark	0-0, (replay) **3-1**	Rangers
1906	Heart of Midlothian	**1-0**	Third Lanark
1907	Celtic	**3-0**	Heart of Midlothian
1908	Celtic	**5-1**	St. Mirren
1909	*cup withheld* †	2-2, (replay) 1-1	Celtic v Rangers
1910	Dundee	0-0, (replay) 2-2, (replay) **2-1**	Clyde
1911	Celtic	0-0, (replay) **2-0**	Hamilton Academicals
1912	Celtic	**2-0**	Clyde
1913	Falkirk	**2-0**	Raith Rovers
1914	Celtic	0-0, (replay) **4-1**	Hibernian
1915–19	*no competition*		
1920	Kilmarnock	**3-2**	Albion Rovers
1921	Partick Thistle	**1-0**	Rangers
1922	Morton	**1-0**	Rangers
1923	Celtic	**1-0**	Hibernian
1924	Airdrieonians	**2-0**	Hibernian
1925	Celtic	**2-1**	Dundee
1926	St. Mirren	**2-0**	Celtic
1927	Celtic	**3-1**	East Fife
1928	Rangers	**4-0**	Celtic
1929	Kilmarnock	**2-0**	Rangers
1930	Rangers	0-0, (replay) **2-1**	Partick Thistle
1931	Celtic	2-2, (replay) **4-2**	Motherwell

Scottish Cup Record (*continued*)

YEAR	WINNERS	SCORE	RUNNERS-UP
1932	Rangers	1-1, (replay) 3-0	Kilmarnock
1933	Celtic	1-0	Motherwell
1934	Rangers	5-0	St. Mirren
1935	Rangers	2-1	Hamilton Academical
1936	Rangers	1-0	Third Lanark
1937	Celtic	2-1	Aberdeen
1938	East Fife	1-1, (replay) 4-2 (aet)	Kilmarnock
1939	Clyde	4-0	Motherwell
1940–46		*no competition*	
1947	Aberdeen	2-1	Hibernian
1948	Rangers	1-1, (replay) 1-0 (aet)	Morton
1949	Rangers	4-1	Clyde
1950	Rangers	3-0	East Fife
1951	Celtic	1-0	Motherwell
1952	Motherwell	4-0	Dundee
1953	Rangers	1-1, (replay) 1-0	Aberdeen
1954	Celtic	2-1	Aberdeen
1955	Clyde	1-1, (replay) 1-0	Celtic
1956	Heart of Midlothian	3-1	Celtic
1957	Falkirk	1-1, (replay) 2-1 (aet)	Kilmarnock
1958	Clyde	1-0	Hibernian
1959	St. Mirren	3-1	Aberdeen
1960	Rangers	2-0	Kilmarnock
1961	Dunfermline Athletic	0-0, (replay) 2-0	Celtic
1962	Rangers	2-0	St. Mirren
1963	Rangers	1-1, (replay) 3-0	Celtic
1964	Rangers	3-1	Dundee
1965	Celtic	3-2	Dunfermline Athletic
1966	Rangers	0-0, (replay) 1-0	Celtic
1967	Celtic	2-0	Aberdeen
1968	Dunfermline Athletic	3-1	Heart of Midlothian
1969	Celtic	4-0	Rangers
1970	Aberdeen	3-1	Celtic
1971	Celtic	1-1, (replay) 2-1	Rangers
1972	Celtic	6-1	Hibernian
1973	Rangers	3-2	Celtic
1974	Celtic	3-0	Dundee United
1975	Celtic	3-1	Airdrieonians
1976	Rangers	3-1	Heart of Midlothian
1977	Celtic	1-0	Rangers
1978	Rangers	2-1	Aberdeen
1979	Rangers	0-0, (replay) 0-0, (replay) 3-2 (aet)	Hibernian
1980	Celtic	1-0 (aet)	Rangers

Scottish Cup Record (*continued*)

YEAR	WINNERS	SCORE	RUNNERS-UP
1981	Rangers	0-0, (replay) 4-1	Dundee United
1982	Aberdeen	4-1 (aet)	Rangers
1983	Aberdeen	1-0 (aet)	Rangers
1984	Aberdeen	2-1	Celtic
1985	Celtic	2-1 (aet)	Dundee United
1986	Aberdeen	3-0	Heart of Midlothian
1987	St. Mirren	1-0 (aet)	Dundee United
1988	Celtic	2-1	Dundee United
1989	Celtic	1-0	Rangers
1990	Aberdeen	0-0 (9-8 pens)	Celtic
1991	Motherwell	4-3 (aet)	Dundee United
1992	Rangers	2-1	Airdrieonians
1993	Rangers	2-1	Aberdeen
1994	Dundee United	1-0	Rangers
1995	Celtic	1-0	Airdrieonians
1996	Rangers	5-1	Heart of Midlothian
1997	Kilmarnock	1-0	Falkirk
1998	Heart of Midlothian	2-1	Rangers
1999	Rangers	1-0	Celtic
2000	Rangers	4-0	Aberdeen
2001	Celtic	3-0	Hibernian
2002	Rangers	3-2	Celtic

w/o denotes walk over

* Dumbarton protested result of first game.

** SFA ordered replay due to playing conditions.

† Cup withheld due to riots.

Scottish Cup Summary

TEAM	TOTALS	WINNERS & RUNNERS-UP (BOLD) (*ITALICS*)
Celtic	31, 18	*1889*, **92, 93, 94, 99, 1900**, *01, 02,* **04, 07, 08, 11, 12, 14, 23, 25, 26, 27, 28, 31, 33, 37, 51, 54,** *55, 56,* **61,** *63,* **65,** *66,* **67, 69, 70, 71, 72,** *73, 74,* **75,** *77,* **80,** *84,* **85, 88, 89, 90, 95,** *99,* **2001,** *02*
Rangers	30, 17	*1877, 79,* **94, 97, 98,** *99,* **1903,** *04, 05, 21, 22,* **28,** *29, 30, 32,* **34–36,** *48–50,* **53,** *60,* **62–64,** *66,* **69,** *71,* **73,** *76,* **77,** *78,* **79,** *80,* **81,** *82, 83,* **89,** *92, 93,* **94, 96, 98, 99, 2000, 02**
Queen's Park	10, 2	**1874–76,** *80–82,* **84,** *86,* **90,** *92,* **93,** *1900*
Aberdeen	7, 8	*1937,* **47,** *53, 54, 59, 67,* **70,** *78, 82–84,* **86, 90,** *93,* **2000**
Heart of Midlothian	6, 6	**1891, 96, 1901,** *03, 06, 07,* **56,** *68,* **76,** *86, 96,* **98**
Kilmarnock	3, 5	*1898,* **1920, 29,** *32, 38, 57, 60,* **97**
Vale of Leven	3, 4	**1877–79,** *83–85,* **90**
Clyde	3, 3	**1910, 12, 39,** *49,* **55,** *58*
St. Mirren	3, 3	**1908,** *26,* **34,** *59, 62,* **87**
Hibernian	2, 9	**1887,** *96,* **1902,** *14, 23, 24, 47, 58, 72, 79, 2001*
Motherwell	2, 4	*1931, 33, 39, 51,* **52, 91**
Third Lanark	2, 4	**1876, 78,** *89,* **1905,** *06, 36*
Renton	2, 3	**1875,** *85,* **86,** *88, 95*
Dunfermline Athletic	2, 1	**1961,** *65,* **68**
Falkirk	2, 1	**1913, 57,** *97*
Dundee United	1, 6	*1974, 81, 85, 87, 88, 91,* **94**
Dumbarton	1, 5	*1881, 82,* **83,** *87, 91, 97*
Airdrieonians	1, 3	**1924,** *75, 92, 95*
Dundee	1, 3	**1910,** *25, 52, 64*
East Fife	1, 2	**1927,** *38, 50*
Morton	1, 1	**1922,** *48*
Partick Thistle	1, 1	**1921,** *30*
St. Bernard's	1, 0	**1895**
Hamilton Academical	0, 2	*1911, 35*

Though both Celtic and Rangers *attract crowds of over 50,000 every week, Scottish football also incorporates smaller clubs, like Falkirk, whose Brockville Park home regularly hosts crowds in the hundreds.*

SCOTLAND

Scottish Cup Summary (*continued*)

TEAM	TOTALS	WINNERS & RUNNERS-UP	
		(BOLD)	(*ITALICS*)
Albion Rovers	**0**, *1*		*1920*
Cambuslang	**0**, *1*		*1888*
Clydesdale	**0**, *1*		*1874*
Raith Rovers	**0**, *1*		*1913*
Thornley Bank	**0**, *1*		*1880*

Scottish League Cup Record 1947–2002

YEAR	WINNERS	SCORE	RUNNERS-UP
1947	Rangers	4-0	Aberdeen
1948	East Fife	0-0, (replay) 4-1	Falkirk
1949	Rangers	2-0	Raith Rovers
1950	East Fife	3-0	Dunfermline Athletic
1951	Motherwell	3-0	Hibernian
1952	Dundee	3-2	Rangers
1953	Dundee	2-0	Kilmarnock
1954	East Fife	3-2	Partick Thistle
1955	Heart of Midlothian	4-2	Motherwell
1956	Aberdeen	2-1	St. Mirren
1957	Celtic	3-0	Partick Thistle
1958	Celtic	7-1	Rangers
1959	Heart of Midlothian	5-1	Partick Thistle
1960	Heart of Midlothian	2-1	Third Lanark
1961	Rangers	2-0	Kilmarnock
1962	Rangers	1-1, (replay) 3-1	Heart of Midlothian
1963	Heart of Midlothian	1-0	Kilmarnock
1964	Rangers	5-0	Morton
1965	Rangers	2-1	Celtic
1966	Celtic	2-1	Rangers
1967	Celtic	1-0	Rangers
1968	Celtic	5-3	Dundee
1969	Celtic	6-2	Hibernian
1970	Celtic	1-0	St. Johnstone
1971	Rangers	1-0	Celtic
1972	Partick Thistle	4-1	Celtic
1973	Hibernian	2-1	Celtic
1974	Dundee	1-0	Celtic
1975	Celtic	6-3	Hibernian
1976	Rangers	1-0	Celtic
1977	Aberdeen	2-1 (aet)	Celtic
1978	Rangers	2-1 (aet)	Celtic
1979	Rangers	2-1	Aberdeen
1980	Dundee United	0-0, (replay) 3-0	Aberdeen
1981	Dundee United	3-0	Dundee
1982	Rangers	2-1	Dundee United
1983	Celtic	2-1	Rangers
1984	Rangers	3-2 (aet)	Celtic
1985	Rangers	1-0	Dundee United
1986	Aberdeen	3-0	Hibernian
1987	Rangers	2-1	Celtic
1988	Rangers	3-3 (aet)(5-3 pens)	Aberdeen
1989	Rangers	3-2	Aberdeen
1990	Aberdeen	2-1 (aet)	Rangers
1991	Rangers	2-1 (aet)	Celtic
1992	Hibernian	2-0	Dunfermline Athletic
1993	Rangers	2-1	Aberdeen
1994	Rangers	2-1	Hibernian
1995	Raith Rovers	2-2 (aet)(6-5 pens)	Celtic
1996	Aberdeen	2-0	Dundee
1997	Rangers	4-3	Heart of Midlothian
1998	Celtic	3-0	Dundee United
1999	Rangers	2-1	St. Johnstone
2000	Celtic	2-0	Aberdeen
2001	Celtic	3-0	Kilmarnock
2002	Rangers	4-0	Ayr United

Scottish League Cup Summary

TEAM	TOTALS	WINNERS & RUNNERS-UP	
		(BOLD)	(*ITALICS*)
Rangers	**22**, *6*	**1947, 49,** *52, 58,* **61, 62, 64, 65,** *66,* *67,* **71, 76, 78, 79, 82,** *83,* **84, 85,** **87–89, 90, 91, 93, 94, 97, 99, 2002**	
Celtic	**11**, *12*	*1957, 58,* **65,** *66–70,* **71–74,** *75,* **76–78,** *83, 84,* **87,** *91,* **95,** *98,* **2000, 01**	
Aberdeen	**5**, *7*	*1947,* **56,** *77, 79, 80,* **86,** *88, 89, 90,* *93,* **96,** *2000*	
Heart of Midlothian	**4**, *2*	**1955, 59, 60,** *62,* **63,** *97*	
Dundee	**3**, *3*	**1952, 53,** *68,* **74,** *81, 96*	
East Fife	**3**, *0*	**1948, 50, 54**	
Hibernian	**2**, *5*	*1951, 69, 73, 75, 86,* **92,** *94*	
Dundee United	**2**, *3*	**1980, 81,** *82, 85,* **98**	
Partick Thistle	**1**, *3*	*1954, 57, 59,* **72**	
Motherwell	**1**, *1*	**1951,** *55*	
Raith Rovers	**1**, *1*	*1949,* **95**	
Kilmarnock	**0**, *4*	*1953, 61, 63, 2001*	
Dunfermline Athletic	**0**, *2*	*1950, 92*	
St. Johnstone	**0**, *2*	*1970, 99*	
Ayr United	**0**, *1*	*2002*	
Falkirk	**0**, *1*	*1948*	
Morton	**0**, *1*	*1964*	
St. Mirren	**0**, *1*	*1956*	
Third Lanark	**0**, *1*	*1960*	

It's not often that a major Scottish trophy is won by anyone outside the 'Old Firm'. When it is, it's a major cause for celebration, as Aberdeen's Stewart McKimmie shows as he lifts the Scottish League Cup after the team's victory over Dundee in 1996.

Ireland
(Republic of)

The Football Association of Ireland
Founded: 1921
Joined FIFA: 1923
Joined UEFA: 1954

PRIOR TO PARTITION AND INDEPENDENCE in 1921, few clubs from the south of Ireland had made much impression in national competitions. With independence and the creation of a separate league and cup competition in 1922, domestic football improved, but Ireland has never been able to sustain a professional league as money, fans and players cross the Irish Sea to England and Scotland.

Ireland League Record 1922–2002

SEASON	CHAMPIONS	SEASON	CHAMPIONS
1922	St. James' Gate	1964	Shamrock Rovers
1923	Shamrock Rovers	1965	Drumcondra
1924	Bohemians	1966	Waterford
1925	Shamrock Rovers	1967	Dundalk
1926	Shelbourne	1968	Waterford
1927	Shamrock Rovers	1969	Waterford
1928	Bohemians	1970	Waterford
1929	Shelbourne	1971	Cork Hibernians
1930	Bohemians	1972	Waterford
1931	Shelbourne	1973	Waterford
1932	Shamrock Rovers	1974	Cork Celtic
1933	Dundalk	1975	Bohemians
1934	Bohemians	1976	Dundalk
1935	Dolphin	1977	Sligo Rovers
1936	Bohemians	1978	Bohemians
1937	Sligo Rovers	1979	Dundalk
1938	Shamrock Rovers	1980	Limerick United
1939	Shamrock Rovers	1981	Athlone Town
1940	St. James' Gate	1982	Dundalk
1941	Cork United	1983	Athlone Town
1942	Cork United	1984	Shamrock Rovers
1943	Cork United	1985	Shamrock Rovers
1944	Shelbourne	1986	Shamrock Rovers
1945	Cork United	1987	Shamrock Rovers
1946	Cork United	1988	Dundalk
1947	Shelbourne	1989	Derry City
1948	Drumcondra	1990	St. Patrick's Athletic
1949	Drumcondra	1991	Dundalk
1950	Cork Athletic	1992	Shelbourne
1951	Cork Athletic	1993	Cork City
1952	St. Patrick's Athletic	1994	Shamrock Rovers
1953	Shelbourne	1995	Dundalk
1954	Shamrock Rovers	1996	St. Patrick's Athletic
1955	St. Patrick's Athletic	1997	Derry City
1956	St. Patrick's Athletic	1998	St. Patrick's Athletic
1957	Shamrock Rovers	1999	St. Patrick's Athletic
1958	Drumcondra	2000	Shelbourne
1959	Shamrock Rovers	2001	Bohemians
1960	Limerick	2002	Shelbourne
1961	Drumcondra		
1962	Shelbourne		
1963	Dundalk		

Ireland Cup Record 1922–2002

YEAR	WINNERS	YEAR	WINNERS
1922	St. James' Gate	1926	Fordsons
1923	Alton United	1927	Drumcondra
1924	Athlone Town	1928	Bohemians
1925	Shamrock Rovers	1929	Shamrock Rovers

Ireland Cup Record (*continued*)

YEAR	WINNERS	YEAR	WINNERS
1930	Shamrock Rovers	1968	Shamrock Rovers
1931	Shamrock Rovers	1969	Shamrock Rovers
1932	Shamrock Rovers	1970	Bohemians
1933	Shamrock Rovers	1971	Limerick
1934	Cork	1972	Cork Hibernians
1935	Bohemians	1973	Cork Hibernians
1936	Shamrock Rovers	1974	Finn Harps
1937	Waterford	1975	Home Farm
1938	St. James' Gate	1976	Bohemians
1939	Shelbourne	1977	Dundalk
1940	Shamrock Rovers	1978	Shamrock Rovers
1941	Cork United	1979	Dundalk
1942	Dundalk	1980	Waterford
1943	Drumcondra	1981	Dundalk
1944	Shamrock Rovers	1982	Limerick United
1945	Shamrock Rovers	1983	Sligo Rovers
1946	Drumcondra	1984	UCD
1947	Cork United	1985	Shamrock Rovers
1948	Shamrock Rovers	1986	Shamrock Rovers
1949	Dundalk	1987	Shamrock Rovers
1950	Transport	1988	Dundalk
1951	Cork Athletic	1989	Derry City
1952	Dundalk	1990	Bray Wanderers
1953	Cork Athletic	1991	Galway United
1954	Drumcondra	1992	Bohemians
1955	Shamrock Rovers	1993	Shelbourne
1956	Shamrock Rovers	1994	Sligo Rovers
1957	Drumcondra	1995	Derry City
1958	Dundalk	1996	Shelbourne
1959	St. Patrick's Athletic	1997	Shelbourne
1960	Shelbourne	1998	Cork City
1961	St. Patrick's Athletic	1999	Bray Wanderers
1962	Shamrock Rovers	2000	Shelbourne
1963	Shelbourne	2001	Bohemians
1964	Shamrock Rovers	2002	Dundalk
1965	Shamrock Rovers		
1966	Shamrock Rovers		
1967	Shamrock Rovers		

Northern Ireland

The Irish Football Association
Founded: 1880
Joined FIFA: 1911–20, 1924–28, 1946
Joined UEFA: 1954

NORTHERN IRELAND'S league and cup competitions are the third oldest in the world. The cup dates from 1881 and the league from 1890. These all-Ireland competitions organized from Belfast became purely Northern Irish in 1921 after the partition of the island. Derry City, a team based in Catholic Londonderry, withdrew from both competitions in 1972 and joined the FA south of the border.

Northern Ireland League Record 1891–2002

SEASON	CHAMPIONS	SEASON	CHAMPIONS
1891	Linfield	1898	Linfield
1892	Linfield	1899	Distillery
1893	Linfield	1900	Celtic
1894	Glentoran	1901	Distillery
1895	Linfield	1902	Linfield
1896	Distillery	1903	Distillery
1897	Glentoran	1904	Linfield

Northern Ireland League Record (*continued*)

SEASON	CHAMPIONS	SEASON	CHAMPIONS
1905	Glentoran	1960	Glenavon
1906	Cliftonville	1961	Linfield
1907	Linfield	1962	Linfield
1908	Linfield	1963	Distillery
1909	Linfield	1964	Glentoran
1910	Cliftonville	1965	Derry City
1911	Linfield	1966	Linfield
1912	Glentoran	1967	Glentoran
1913	Glentoran	1968	Glentoran
1914	Linfield	1969	Linfield
1915	Celtic	1970	Glentoran
1916–19	*no championship*	1971	Linfield
1920	Celtic	1972	Glentoran
1921	Glentoran	1973	Crusaders
1922	Linfield	1974	Coleraine
1923	Linfield	1975	Linfield
1924	Queen's Island	1976	Crusaders
1925	Glentoran	1977	Glentoran
1926	Celtic	1978	Linfield
1927	Celtic	1979	Linfield
1928	Celtic	1980	Linfield
1929	Celtic	1981	Glentoran
1930	Linfield	1982	Linfield
1931	Glentoran	1983	Linfield
1932	Linfield	1984	Linfield
1933	Celtic	1985	Linfield
1934	Linfield	1986	Linfield
1935	Linfield	1987	Linfield
1936	Celtic	1988	Glentoran
1937	Celtic	1989	Linfield
1938	Celtic	1990	Portadown
1939	Celtic	1991	Portadown
1940	Celtic	1992	Glentoran
1941–47	*no championship*	1993	Linfield
1948	Celtic	1994	Linfield
1949	Linfield	1995	Crusaders
1950	Linfield	1996	Portadown
1951	Glentoran	1997	Crusaders
1952	Glentoran	1998	Cliftonville
1953	Glentoran	1999	Glentoran FC
1954	Linfield	2000	Linfield FC
1955	Linfield	2001	Linfield FC
1956	Linfield	2002	Portadown
1957	Glenavon		
1958	Ards		
1959	Linfield		

Northern Ireland Cup Record 1881–2002

YEAR	WINNERS	YEAR	WINNERS
1881	Moyola Park	1903	Distillery
1882	Queen's Island	1904	Linfield
1883	Cliftonville	1905	Distillery
1884	Distillery	1906	Shelbourne
1885	Distillery	1907	Cliftonville
1886	Distillery	1908	Bohemians
1887	Ulster	1909	Cliftonville
1888	Cliftonville	1910	Distillery
1889	Distillery	1911	Shelbourne
1890	Gordon Highlanders	1912	Linfield
1891	Linfield	1913	Linfield
1892	Linfield	1914	Glentoran
1893	Linfield	1915	Linfield
1894	Distillery	1916	Linfield
1895	Linfield	1917	Glentoran
1896	Distillery	1918	Celtic
1897	Cliftonville	1919	Linfield
1898	Linfield	1920	Shelbourne
1899	Linfield	1921	Glentoran
1900	Cliftonville	1922	Linfield
1901	Cliftonville	1923	Linfield
1902	Linfield	1924	Queen's Island

Northern Ireland Cup Record (*continued*)

YEAR	WINNERS	YEAR	WINNERS
1925	Distillery	1966	Glentoran
1926	Celtic	1967	Crusaders
1927	Ards	1968	Crusaders
1928	Willowfield	1969	Ards
1929	Ballymena United	1970	Linfield
1930	Linfield	1971	Distillery
1931	Linfield	1972	Coleraine
1932	Glentoran	1973	Glentoran
1933	Glentoran	1974	Ards
1934	Linfield	1975	Coleraine
1935	Glentoran	1976	Carrick Rangers
1936	Linfield	1977	Coleraine
1937	Celtic	1978	Linfield
1938	Celtic	1979	Cliftonville
1939	Linfield	1980	Linfield
1940	Ballymena United	1981	Ballymena United
1941	Celtic	1982	Linfield
1942	Linfield	1983	Glentoran
1943	Celtic	1984	Ballymena United
1944	Celtic	1985	Glentoran
1945	Linfield	1986	Glentoran
1946	Linfield	1987	Glentoran
1947	Celtic	1988	Glentoran
1948	Linfield	1989	Ballymena United
1949	Derry City	1990	Glentoran
1950	Linfield	1991	Portadown
1951	Glentoran	1992	Glenavon
1952	Ards	1993	Bangor
1953	Linfield	1994	Linfield
1954	Derry City	1995	Linfield
1955	Dundela	1996	Glentoran
1956	Distillery	1997	Glenavon
1957	Glenavon	1998	Glentoran
1958	Ballymena United	1999	Portadown
1959	Glenavon	2000	Glentoran
1960	Linfield	2001	Glentoran
1961	Glenavon	2002	Linfield
1962	Linfield		
1963	Linfield		
1964	Derry City		
1965	Coleraine		

Wales

The Football Association of Wales
Founded: 1876
Joined FIFA: 1910–20, 1924–28, 1946
Joined UEFA: 1954

In Wales, the strength of rugby and the allure of the English game have seen a weak and often fragmented football culture. The largest clubs (Swansea, Cardiff and Wrexham) play their league football in England, though the Welsh Cup has provided a convenient route for the holders into European football via the Cup-Winners' Cup and now the UEFA Cup. In 1992 a unified semi-professional league was established.

SEASON	LEAGUE CHAMPIONS
1998	Bangor Town
1999	Bangor Town
2000	Total Network Solutions
2001	Barry Town
2002	Barry Town

YEAR	CUP WINNERS
1998	Bangor City
1999	ICT Cardiff
2000	Bangor City
2001	Barry Town
2002	Barry Town

YEAR	LEAGUE CUP WINNERS
1998	Bangor Town
1999	ICT Cardiff
2000	Bangor City
2001	Caersws
2002	Caersws

LOW COUNTRIES

Association Football in the Netherlands

1860s: English textile workers introduce football to Netherlands

1879: Haarlemese FC, oldest Dutch club founded

1889: Formation of FA: KNVB (Koninklijke Nederlandsche Voetbalbond)

1896: KNVB prevents first women's international match, Sparta Rotterdam v England XI

1898: National championship established

1899: First Dutch Cup Final

1904: Affiliation to FIFA

1905: First international, v Belgium, won 4-1, venue: Antwerp

1945: No national championship at the end of the war

1954: Affiliation to UEFA

1955: KNVB bans women's matches from grounds affiliated to the organization

1956: First women's international, v West Germany, lost 1-2, venue: Essen. Professional league, Eredivisie, founded. Dutch women's soccer association formed and league created

1971: Women's football incorporated into KNVB

1996: Introduction of compulsory club membership schemes

1998: All-seater stadiums compulsory in top division

Association Football in Belgium

1880: First club, Royal Antwerp, founded

1895: Foundation of national FA: Union Royale des Sociétés de Football Association

1896: First national championship

1904: Affiliation to FIFA. First international, v France, drawn 3-3, venue: Brussels

1912: First Belgian Cup Final

1915–19: National championship suspended

1915–26: No cup competition

1927: Cup reactivated for one year

1940–41: National League suspended

1945: National League suspended

1954: Affiliation to UEFA

1954–56: Belgian Cup reactivated

1964: Belgian Cup reactivated

1972: League becomes fully professional

1985: Heysel stadium disaster, 29 May, Liverpool v Juventus European Cup Final, 39 killed, over 400 injured

Timeline: 1860, 1870, 1880, 1890, 1900, 1910, 1920, 1930, 1940, 1950, 1960, 1970, 1980, 1990, 2000, 2010

Low Countries: The main clubs

Ajax 1900 Team name with year of formation
● Club formed before 1912
● Club formed 1912–25
● Club formed 1925–50
Club formed after 1950

Winners of Amateur Championship
Runners-up in Amateur Championship
Colours and formation date unknown

Dordrecht 90 1904
DFC Dordrecht (1904–74). Merged with SVV Schiedamse Voetbal Vvereniging (1904) in 1991

Club Brugge KV 1899

Cercle Brugge 1899

Royal Antwerp FC 1880

Beerschot VAV 1899–1999

Germinal Beerschot Antwerpen 1999

FC Germinal Ekiren 1942–99

Berchem Sport 1906

KSV Waregem 1946
Merger of Red Star Waregem and Sportif

R Excelsior Mouscron 1964
Merger of ARA Mouscronnois and R. Stade Mouscron

RC Jet Wavre 1970
Merger of Racing Stade de Bruxelles and RC Jette. Racing Jet de Bruxelles (1970–88)

RSC Anderlecht 1908
Merged with Brussels D' 71 in 1994

RWD Molenbeek 1973
Merger of Racing White Brussels (1963) and Daring CB (1895)

KV Oostende 1981
Merger of AS Oostende and KVG Oostende

KV Kortrijk 1971
Merger of Kortrijk Sport (1901) and Stade Kortrijk

Union FC d'Ixelles 1896
(Folded)

White Star FC 1910–63

Leopold Club de Bruxelles 1893–1990

Union St Gilloise 1899

HBS Den Haag 1893

HVV Den Haag 1885

Quick Den Haag 1896

ADO Den Haag 1971
Merger of ADO Den Hagg (1905) and Holland Sport (1954) in 1971 as FC Den Haag new name 1996

Sparta Rotterdam 1888

Excelsior 1902

Feyenoord 1908

Ajax 1900

De Volewijckers 1

Merged with DWS and Blauwit in 1972 to form FC Amsterdam, demed in 1983

RAP Amsterdam 1887
(Folded)

BVC Amsterdam 1954
(Folded)

Haarlem 1889

Telstar Ijmuid

Haarle

Haarlemese FC 1879

RCH Haarlem

The Hag

Rotterdam

NAC Breda 1912

K Lierse SK 1908

Bred

RBS Roosendaa 191.

KRC Harlebeke 1930

SK Beveren 1935

K. ST Niklase SK 1920

AA Gent 1896

Antwer

Lie

Mechele

Aalst

KSC Eendracht Aalst 1919
Merger of Amical and Standard

KSC Lokeren 1970
Merger of Racing Lokeren and Standard Lokeren

Brussels

Royal Charleroi FC 1904

Charleroi

Daring Club Brussels 1895–1973

Racing Club Brussels 1891–1963

Map labels: Bruges, Ostend, Waregem, Kortrijk, Mouscron

Low Countries

ORIGINS AND GROWTH OF FOOTBALL

THE TRAJECTORIES OF football in Belgium and the Netherlands have clear parallels – early arrival through British influences, the establishment of national FAs and leagues before the end of the 19th century, followed by decades of weak domestic football due to the persistence of amateurism. In Belgium, English colleges in Brussels and Bruges and English workers in Antwerp were the main points of arrival. In the Netherlands, English textile workers in Enschede were playing football in the late 1860s. Pim Mulier, an English-educated journalist, established the country's first club, Haarlemese FC, in 1879.

Professionalism came to the Netherlands in 1956, while in Belgium semi-professionalism began in the late 1950s and full professionalism in 1972. In both countries there has been a massive concentration of football strength into a few big clubs, followed by waves of small club mergers in an attempt to keep up. In Belgium the balance of power has shifted to Brussels, Anderlecht and French-speaking Belgium and away from Flemish-speaking areas in the North. In the Netherlands the big three, Ajax, Feyenoord and PSV, have been dominant.

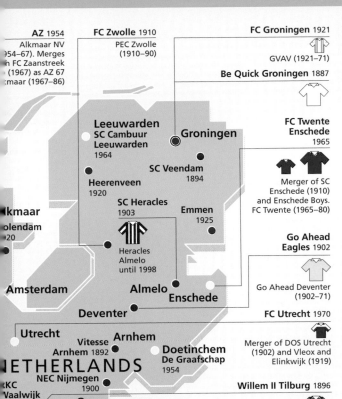

Key

▭ International football (Netherlands)	● European Championships winner
▮ International football (Belgium)	▲ European Championships runner-up
⚽ Affiliation to FIFA	○ Netherlands competition winner
⚽ Affiliation to UEFA	△ Netherlands competition runner-up
⚥ Women's football	◉ Belgian competition winner
War	▲ Belgian competition runner-up
Disaster	
▲ World Cup runner-up	Alk – AZ Alkmaar
▪ European Championships host	And – Anderlecht

Ant – Royal Antwerp FC
Brug – Club Brugge
Feyn – Feyenoord
Liege – Standard Liège
Mech – KV Mechelen
Twen – FC Twente

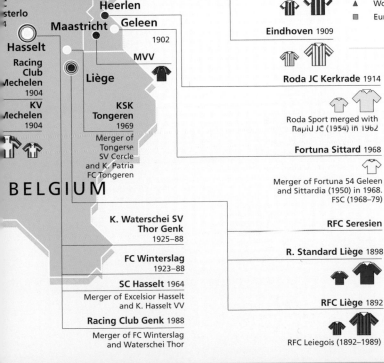

Belgium

THE SEASON IN REVIEW 2001–02

MONEY, OR THE LACK OF IT, overshadowed Belgian football in the 2001–02 season. Anderlecht, the previous year's champions, saw a mass exodus of key players to richer foreign clubs. Both the previous season's top scorers in the Belgian league had moved on: Tomasz Radzinski to Everton and Jan Koller to Borussia Dortmund. Second-placed Club Brugge, under Norwegian coach Trond Sollied, was unable to significantly reinforce its squad, and while both Standard Liège and Genk brought in new coaches (Michel Preud'homme and Dutchman Sef Vergoossen), star players were less in evidence. The relative weakness of Belgium's top clubs was exposed by their early exits from European competition.

At the bottom end of the Jupiler league, life was even harder. After an examination of their debt-ridden accounts by the Belgian FA, both Eendracht Aalst and RWD Molenbeek were refused playing licenses for next season. Both clubs have regularly failed to pay their squads, bounced cheques and faced player strikes. RWD were sufficiently desperate to hand the running of the club to the infamous Patrick de Cock. Past owner of bankrupt Belgian basketball teams, de Cock was sentenced to one year's imprisonment for fraud last year. Second Division champions KV Mechelen were only allowed back into the top flight after biscuit millionaire Willy van den Wijngaert agreed to invest over £5 million in the club.

Financial limitations kept the competition within the league close and at Christmas only two points separated the top five: Brugge and Standard Liège on 37, Genk and Gent a point behind on 36 and Anderlecht on 35. Through the spring, Anderlecht, Gent and Liège all proved inconsistent and fell away, leaving Genk and Brugge fighting for the title. It was decided on the penultimate weekend, not with a bang but a whimper. Leading by three points, Genk could only manage a goalless draw at Westerlo; but Brugge blew it, losing 5-3 to St. Truidense, leaving them four points adrift with a game to go and runners-up for the fourth time in a row. However, some consolation came for Brugge as three goals from striker Andres Mendoza saw the team win the Belgian Cup Final with a 3-1 victory over Excelsior Mouscron.

Above: Wesley Sonck of Genk – the league's top scorer – lets fly past Lokeren's Suvad Katana.

Opposite page, top: While Genk fans (centre) celebrated only the second league title in its history, Eendracht Aalst (left) and RWD Molenbeek fans (right) faced the misery of relegation for unsustainable financial debts.

Right: In compensation for missing out on the league again, Club Brugge KV won the Belgian Cup with a 3-1 victory over Excelsior Mouscron. Brugge's goals all came from 24-year-old striker Andres Mendoza.

Jupiler League Table 2001–02

CLUB	P	W	D	L	F	A	Pts	
KRC Genk	34	20	12	2	85	43	72	Champions League
Club Brugge KV	34	22	4	8	74	41	70	UEFA Cup
RSC Anderlecht	34	18	12	4	71	37	66	UEFA Cup
KAA Gent	34	16	10	8	61	51	58	
Standard Liège	34	15	12	7	57	38	57	
R Excelsior Mouscron	34	17	5	12	68	40	56	UEFA Cup (cup runners-up)
KSC Lokeren	34	15	10	9	43	33	55	
St. Truidense	34	16	5	13	52	47	53	
G Beerschot Antwerpen	34	11	16	7	68	51	49	
RWD Molenbeek	34	13	5	16	50	58	44	Relegated*
La Louviere	34	12	8	14	41	52	44	
KFC Lommelse	34	10	9	15	54	66	39	
RSC Charleroi	34	11	6	17	40	63	39	
KVC Westerlo	34	9	9	16	49	61	36	
K Lierse SK	34	9	8	17	55	65	35	
Royal Antwerp	34	7	10	17	47	67	31	
Eendracht Aalst	34	4	9	21	32	73	21	Relegated**
KSK Beveren	34	2	8	24	30	91	14	†

Promoted clubs: KSV Ingelmunster, KV Mechelen.

* Refused professional license for 2002–03 and relegated to third division.

** Went into liquidation.

† Survived in Jupiler League due to fate of Aalst and Molenbeek.

Belgian Cup

2002 FINAL
May 9 – King Badouin, Brussels
Club 3-1 R Excelsior Brugge KV Mouscron
(Mendoza 22, 74, 81)   *(Blondel 59)*
h/t: 1-0 Att: 30,500
Ref: M Quaranta

Top Goalscorers 2001–02

PLAYER	CLUB	NATIONALITY	GOALS
Wesley Sonck	KRC Genk	Belgian	30
Paul Kpaka	G Beerschot Antwerpen	Sierra Leonean	25
Moumouni Dagano	KRC Genk	Burkinabe	20
Rune Lange	Club Brugge KV	Norwegian	20

International Club Performances 2001–02

CLUB	COMPETITION	PROGRESS
Anderlecht	Champions League	1st Group Phase
Club Brugge	UEFA Cup	Third Round
Standard Liège	UEFA Cup	Second Round
KVC Westerlo	UEFA Cup	First Round

BELGIUM

SUPPORTER << >> SUPPORTER <
EENDRACHT AALST

GENK
2002

RWD We will NEVER die!
Brussels Boys

Sef Vergoossen, Genk's Dutch coach, celebrates winning the league title with his squad.

Club Brugge's Rune Lange tussles with Excelsior's Steve Dugardein during an exciting Cup Final.

Belgium

THE JUPILER LEAGUE 1981–2001

THE LAST 20 YEARS of Belgian football have been dominated by three teams: Standard Liège, who opened the 1980s with a couple of titles; Club Brugge KV, who has consistently challenged for the title and took a string of them in the late 1980s under former player Jan Ceulemans; and the biggest club of all, Anderlecht. Beyond these teams only three minnows have taken the title: Lierse, Beveren and Mechelen.

Anderlecht has risen to the top under the control of Constant Vanden Stock. Previously a player with the club and national team manager, he made an enormous fortune in the brewing industry. Under his control the club won three titles in a row in the mid-1980s, built the first executive boxes in a

European stadium and brought the leading Belgian player of the era – Enzo Schifo – to the club. In the mid-1990s, the championship-winning team was built around Luc Nilis and Marc Degryse.

Competition has consistently come from the likes of Gent, Antwerpen and Charleroi, but most clubs are struggling to survive, and the league has seen a wave of mergers forced on the smaller sides, while older established clubs, like Cercle Brugge, have disappeared from view. In 2002, two top-flight clubs are to be relegated on financial rather than sporting grounds as Eendracht Aalst failed to pay its players and RWD Molenbeek collapsed under its debts.

BELGIUM

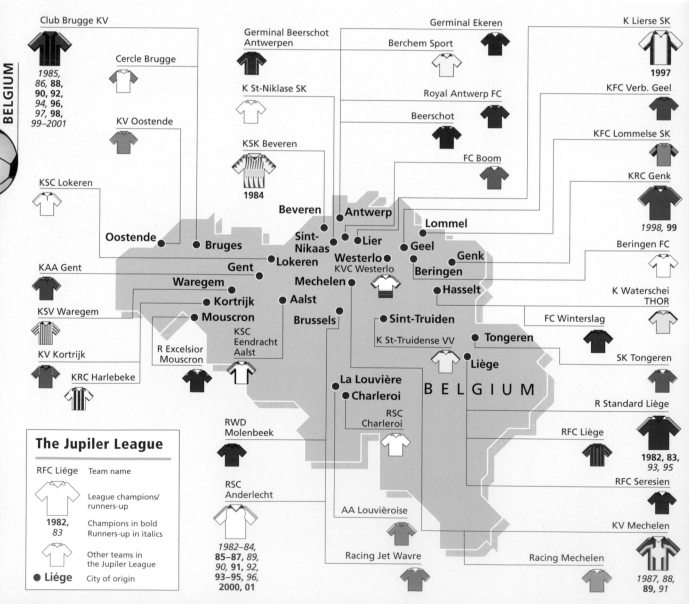

The Jupiler League

RFC Liége — Team name

League champions/runners-up

1982, 83 — Champions in bold
Runners-up in italics

Other teams in the Jupiler League

● **Liége** — City of origin

Key to League Positions Table

- ◼ League champions
- ◼ Other team playing in league
- ◼ Season promoted to league
- ◼ Season of relegation from league
- [5] Final position in league
- ◼ Merger between teams

FC Winterslag and K Waterschei THOR merged to form KRC Genk for the 1988–99 season

R Standard Liège and RFC Seresien merged to form R Standard Liège for the 1996–97 season

Germinal Ekeren and Beerschot merged to form Germinal Beerschot Antwerpen for the 1999–2000 season

Former RSC Anderlecht president Constant Vanden Stock looks benignly down on his son and current supremo, Roger.

Enzo Scifo, the most gifted Belgian player ever and an inspiration for RSC Anderlecht.

Belgian League Positions 1981–2001

TEAM	1981-82	1982-83	1983-84	1984-85	1985-86	1986-87	1987-88	1988-89	1989-90	1990-91	1991-92	1992-93	1993-94	1994-95	1995-96	1996-97	1997-98	1998-99	1999-2000	2000-01
KSC Eendracht Aalst										18				4	10	15	15	13	12	16
RSC Anderlecht	2	2	2	1	1	1	4	2	2	1	2	1	1	1	2	4	4	3	1	1
Royal Antwerp FC	5	3	8	7	9	14	3	5	4	7	5	5	5	16	13	6	18			12
Germinal Beerschot Antwerpen																			7	6
Beerschot		15	16	16	7	9	13	16	8	18										
Berchem Sport						18														
Beringen FC	17		18																	
KSK Beveren	7	6	1	5	5	5	14	12	17		12	8	9	10	17		16	15	15	14
FC Boom											18									
Cercle Brugge	15	12	11	11	10	11	7	15	9	16	9	13	12	15	8	18				
Club Brugge KV	14	5	3	2	2	3	1	4	1	4	1	6	2	3	1	2	1	2	2	2
RSC Charleroi					12	7	8	11	14	8	13	7	4	13	7	13	13	14	16	9
Germinal Ekeren									13	5	8	14	10	6	3	10	3	10		
KRC Genk									18		14	16	15	18		8	2	1	8	11
KFC Verb. Geel																			17	
KAA Gent	3	4	15	6	4	16	17		6	3	6	9	15	14	14	14	8	8	3	5
KRC Harlebeke															12	9	5	11	14	17
KV Kortrijk	6	11	12	13	15	15	9	8	7	15	17						17			
RFC Liège	16	9	13	3	6	6	5	3	12	10	15	12	13	18						
R Standard Liège	1	1	4	8	3	10	10	6	5	6	3	2	6	2	6	7	9	6	5	3
K Lierse SK	8	14	14	15	18			10	10	11	7	10	14	5	1	7	7	7	9	10
KSC Lokeren	4	8	10	10	14	4	16	14	11	9	14	17				12	6	5	10	4
KFC Lommelse SK													16	11	7	9	5	11	16	18
AA Louvièroise																				15
KV Mechelen	18		6	12	11	2	2	1	3	2	4	3	8	11	11	17			11	18
Racing Mechelen									13	18										
RWD Molenbeek	11	10	17		13	13	12		12	11	11	16	12	4	16	17				
R Excelsior Mouscron																3	10	4	4	7
KV Oostende											7	17					18			
K St-Niklase SK				17																
K St-Truidense VV									11	7	15	17		8	15	11	14	9	13	13
RFC Seresien		13	5	14	16	17							3	9	16					
SK Tongeren	10	17																		
KSV Waregem	12	16	7	4	8	8	6	9	16	13	10	4	17			18				
K Waterschei THOR	9	7	9	9	17															
Racing Jet Wavre								18		12	18									
KVC Westerlo																	12	12	6	8
FC Winterslag	13	18					15													

Belgium

Union Royale des Sociétés de Football Association
Founded: 1895
Joined FIFA: 1904
Joined UEFA: 1954

BELGIUM SHARES WITH Sweden the honour of having Europe's oldest football league outside the British Isles. Established in 1895 across both French- and Flemish-speaking Belgium, the league has run for over 100 years, breaking only for the First World War and the beginning and the end of the Second World War. Power in the league has shifted from the early dominance of Brussels-based teams such as Union St. Gilloise and Racing CB, to include the clubs of Antwerp, Anderlecht, Bruges and Liège. By contrast, the Belgian Cup has been a sporadic and low-key affair and was played only once between 1915 and 1954. Interest has risen since the early 1960s when the winners were awarded a place in European competitions. The current league has 18 teams with two relegated each year and two promoted from the lower league in a complex series of play-offs.

Belgian League Record 1896–2002

SEASON	CHAMPIONS	RUNNERS-UP
1896	RFC Liège	Royal Antwerp FC
1897	Racing CB	RFC Liège
1898	RFC Liège	Racing CB
1899	RFC Liège	Racing CB
1900	Racing CB	Royal Antwerp FC
1901	Racing CB	Beerschot
1902	Racing CB	Leopold CB
1903	Racing CB	Union St. Gilloise
1904	Union St. Gilloise	Racing CB
1905	Union St. Gilloise	Racing CB
1906	Union St. Gilloise	Club Brugge KV
1907	Union St. Gilloise	Racing CB
1908	Racing CB	Union St. Gilloise
1909	Union St. Gilloise	Daring CB
1910	Union St. Gilloise	Club Brugge KV
1911	Cercle Brugge	Club Brugge KV
1912	Daring CB	Union St. Gilloise
1913	Union St. Gilloise	Daring CB
1914	Daring CB	Union St. Gilloise
1915–19	no championship	
1920	Club Brugge KV	Union St. Gilloise
1921	Daring CB	Union St. Gilloise
1922	Beerschot	Union St. Gilloise
1923	Union St. Gilloise	Beerschot
1924	Beerschot	Union St. Gilloise
1925	Beerschot	Royal Antwerp FC
1926	Beerschot	R Standard Liège
1927	Cercle Brugge	Beerschot
1928	Beerschot	R Standard Liège
1929	Royal Antwerp FC	Beerschot
1930	Cercle Brugge	Royal Antwerp FC
1931	Royal Antwerp FC	KV Mechelen
1932	K Lierse SK	Royal Antwerp FC
1933	Union St. Gilloise	Royal Antwerp FC
1934	Union St. Gilloise	Daring CB
1935	Union St. Gilloise	K Lierse SK
1936	Daring CB	R Standard Liège
1937	Daring CB	Beerschot
1938	Beerschot	Daring CB
1939	Beerschot	K Lierse SK
1940–41	no championship	
1942	K Lierse SK	Beerschot
1943	KV Mechelen	Beerschot

Belgian League Record (*continued*)

SEASON	CHAMPIONS	RUNNERS-UP
1944	Royal Antwerp FC	RSC Anderlecht
1945	no championship	
1946	KV Mechelen	Royal Antwerp FC
1947	RSC Anderlecht	Olympic Charleroi
1948	KV Mechelen	RSC Anderlecht
1949	RSC Anderlecht	Berchem Sport
1950	RSC Anderlecht	Berchem Sport
1951	RSC Anderlecht	Berchem Sport
1952	RFC Liège	Racing Mechelen
1953	RFC Liège	RSC Anderlecht
1954	RSC Anderlecht	KV Mechelen
1955	RSC Anderlecht	AA Gent
1956	RSC Anderlecht	Royal Antwerp FC
1957	Royal Antwerp FC	RSC Anderlecht
1958	R Standard Liège	Royal Antwerp FC
1959	RSC Anderlecht	RFC Liège
1960	K Lierse SK	RSC Anderlecht
1961	R Standard Liège	RFC Liège
1962	RSC Anderlecht	R Standard Liège
1963	R Standard Liège	Royal Antwerp FC
1964	RSC Anderlecht	FC Beringen
1965	RSC Anderlecht	R Standard Liège
1966	RSC Anderlecht	St. Truidense
1967	RSC Anderlecht	Club Brugge KV
1968	RSC Anderlecht	Club Brugge KV
1969	R Standard Liège	RSC Charleroi
1970	R Standard Liège	Club Brugge KV
1971	R Standard Liège	Club Brugge KV
1972	RSC Anderlecht	Club Brugge KV
1973	Club Brugge KV	R Standard Liège
1974	RSC Anderlecht	Royal Antwerp FC
1975	RWD Molenbeek	Royal Antwerp FC
1976	Club Brugge KV	RSC Anderlecht
1977	Club Brugge KV	RSC Anderlecht
1978	Club Brugge KV	RSC Anderlecht
1979	KSK Beveren	RSC Anderlecht
1980	Club Brugge KV	R Standard Liège
1981	RSC Anderlecht	KSC Lokeren
1982	R Standard Liège	RSC Anderlecht
1983	R Standard Liège	RSC Anderlecht
1984	KSK Beveren	RSC Anderlecht
1985	RSC Anderlecht	Club Brugge KV
1986	RSC Anderlecht	Club Brugge KV
1987	RSC Anderlecht	KV Mechelen
1988	Club Brugge KV	KV Mechelen
1989	KV Mechelen	RSC Anderlecht
1990	Club Brugge KV	RSC Anderlecht
1991	RSC Anderlecht	KV Mechelen
1992	Club Brugge KV	RSC Anderlecht
1993	RSC Anderlecht	Standard Liège
1994	RSC Anderlecht	Club Brugge KV
1995	RSC Anderlecht	Standard Liège
1996	Club Brugge KV	RSC Anderlecht
1997	K Lierse SK	Club Brugge KV
1998	Club Brugge KV	KRC Genk
1999	KRC Genk	Club Brugge KV
2000	RSC Anderlecht	Club Brugge KV
2001	RSC Anderlecht	Club Brugge KV
2002	KRC Genk	Club Brugge KV

BELGIUM

Belgian League Summary

TEAM	TOTALS	CHAMPIONS & RUNNERS-UP (BOLD) (ITALICS)
RSC Anderlecht	26, 16	*1944,* **47, 48, 49–51,** *53,* **54–56,** *57,* *59,* **60, 62, 64–68, 72, 74,** *76–79,* **81,** *82–84,* **85–87,** *89,* **90,** *91,* *92,* **93–95,** *96,* **2000,** *01*
Club Brugge KV	11, 16	*1906, 10, 11,* **20,** *67, 68, 70–72,* **73,** *76–78,* **80,** *85, 86,* **88,** *90,* **92,** *94, 96, 97,* **98,** *99–2002*
Union St. Gilloise	11, 8	*1903,* **04–07,** *08,* **09,** *10,* **12,** *13,* **14,** *20–22,* **23,** *24,* **33–35**
R Standard Liège	8, 9	*1926, 28, 36,* **58,** *61,* **62, 63,** *65,* **69–71,** *73,* **80, 82, 83,** *93, 95*
Beerschot	7, 7	*1901,* **22, 23,** *24–26,* **27,** *28,* **29,** *37, 38, 39,* **42,** *43*
Racing CB	6, 5	**1897, 98, 99, 1900–03,** *04, 05,* **07,** *08*
Daring CB	5, 4	*1909,* **12, 13,** *14,* **21,** *34,* **36, 37, 38**
RFC Liège	5, 3	**1896,** *97,* **98, 99,** *1952,* **53,** *59,* **61**
Royal Antwerp FC	4, 12	*1896, 1900,* **25,** *29,* **30,** *31, 32, 33,* **44,** *46, 56,* **57,** *58, 63, 74, 75*
KV Mechelen	4, 5	*1931,* **43,** *46, 48,* **54,** *87, 88,* **89,** *91*
K Lierse SK	4, 2	**1932,** *35,* **39, 42,** *60,* **97**
Cercle Brugge	3, 0	**1911, 27, 30**
KRC Genk	2, 1	**1998,** *99,* **2002**
KSK Beveren	2, 0	**1979, 84**
RWD Molenbeek	1, 0	**1975**

This summary only features clubs that have won the Belgian League. For a full list of league champions and runners-up please see the League Record opposite.

Belgian Cup Record 1912–2002

YEAR	WINNERS	SCORE	RUNNERS-UP
1912	Racing CB	1-0	Racing Gent
1913	Union St. Gilloise	3-2	Cercle Brugge
1914	Union St. Gilloise	4-1	Club Brugge KV
1915–26		*no competition*	
1927	Cercle Brugge	2-1	Tubantia Borgerhout
1928–53		*no competition*	
1954	R Standard Liège	3-1	Racing Mechelen
1955	Royal Antwerp FC	4-0	Waterschei THOR
1956	Racing Tournai	2-1	CS Verviers
1957–63		*no competition*	
1964	KAA Gent	4-2	FC Diest
1965	RSC Anderlecht	3-2 (aet)	R Standard Liège
1966	R Standard Liège	1-0	RSC Anderlecht
1967	R Standard Liège	3-1 (aet)	KV Mechelen
1968	Club Brugge KV	1-1, (replay) 4-4 (4-2 pens)	Beerschot
1969	K Lierse SK	2-0	Racing White
1970	Club Brugge KV	6-1	Daring CB
1971	Beerschot	2-1	St. Truidense W
1972	RSC Anderlecht	1-0	R Standard Liège
1973	RSC Anderlecht	2-1	R Standard Liège
1974	KSV Waregem	4-1	SK Tongeren
1975	RSC Anderlecht	1-0	Royal Antwerp FC
1976	RSC Anderlecht	4-0	K Lierse SK
1977	Club Brugge KV	4-3	RSC Anderlecht
1978	KSK Beveren	2-0	RSC Charleroi
1979	Beerschot	1-0	Club Brugge KV
1980	Waterschei THOR	2-1	KSK Beveren
1981	R Standard Liège	4-0	KSC Lokeren
1982	Waterschei THOR	2-0	KSV Wagemer
1983	KSK Beveren	3-1	Club Brugge KV
1984	KAA Gent	2-0	R Standard Liège
1985	Cercle Brugge	1-1 (aet)(5-4 pens)	KSK Beveren
1986	Club Brugge KV	3-0	Cercle Brugge
1987	KV Mechelen	1-0	RFC Liège
1988	RSC Anderlecht	2-0	R Standard Liège
1989	RSC Anderlecht	2-0	R Standard Liège
1990	RFC Liège	2-1	Germinal Ekeren

Belgian Cup Record (*continued*)

YEAR	WINNERS	SCORE	RUNNERS-UP
1991	Club Brugge KV	3-1	KV Mechelen
1992	Royal Antwerp FC	2-2 (aet)(9-8 pens)	KV Mechelen
1993	R Standard Liège	2-0	RSC Charleroi
1994	RSC Anderlecht	2-0	Club Brugge KV
1995	Club Brugge KV	3-1	Germinal Ekeren
1996	Club Brugge KV	2-1	Cercle Brugge
1997	Germinal Ekeren	4-2 (aet)	RSC Anderlecht
1998	Racing Genk	4-0	Club Brugge KV
1999	K Lierse SK	3-1	R Standard Liège
2000	Racing Genk	4-1	R Standard Liège
2001	KVC Westerlo	1-0	Lommel
2002	Club Brugge KV	3-1	Excelsior Mouscron

Belgian Cup Summary

TEAM	TOTALS	WINNERS & RUNNERS-UP (BOLD) (ITALICS)
Club Brugge KV	8, 5	*1914,* **68, 70, 77,** *79,* **83, 86, 91, 94, 95, 96,** *98,* **2002**
RSC Anderlecht	8, 3	**1965,** *66,* **72, 73, 75, 76,** *77,* **88, 89, 94,** *97*
R Standard Liège	5, 8	**1954,** *65,* **66, 67,** *72,* **73, 81,** *84, 88, 89, 93, 99, 2000*
Cercle Brugge	2, 3	*1913,* **27,** *85,* **86,** *96*
KSK Beveren	2, 2	**1978,** *80,* **83,** *85*
Beerschot	2, 1	*1968,* **71, 79**
K Lierse SK	2, 1	**1969,** *76,* **99**
Racing Genk	2, 1	*1912,* **98, 2000**
Royal Antwerp FC	2, 1	**1955,** *75,* **92**
Waterschei THOR	2, 1	*1955,* **80, 82**
KAA Gent	2, 0	**1964, 84**
Union St. Gilloise	2, 0	**1913, 14**
KV Mechelen	1, 3	*1967,* **87,** *91, 92*
Germinal Ekeren	1, 2	*1990, 95,* **97**
KSV Waregem	1, 1	**1974,** *82*
RFC Liège	1, 1	*1987,* **90**
KVC Westerlo	1, 0	**2001**
Racing CB	1, 0	**1912**
Racing Tournai	1, 0	**1956**

This summary only features clubs that have won the Belgian Cup. For a full list of cup winners and runners-up please see the Cup Record left.

Luxembourg

Fédération Luxembourgeoise de Football
Founded: 1908
Joined FIFA: 1910
Joined UEFA: 1954

SEASON	LEAGUE CHAMPIONS
1998	Jeunesse Esch
1999	Jeunesse Esch
2000	F91 Dudelange
2001	F91 Dudelange
2002	F91 Dudelange

YEAR	CUP WINNERS
1998	CS Grevenmacher
1999	Jeunesse Esch
2000	Jeunesse Esch
2001	Etzella Ettelbruck
2002	Avenir Beggen

Football in Luxembourg is almost as old as in Belgium, with a league established in 1910 and a cup in 1922.

A new system of play-offs for the top four teams was introduced in 1999–2000 to decide the championship with the remaining teams involved in relegation play-offs.

Netherlands

THE SEASON IN REVIEW 2001–02

THE USUAL SUSPECTS LINED UP as contenders for the Dutch title this season as lesser lights Vitesse Arnhem and Heerenveen looked too financially strapped to make a sustained challenge. Ajax, under Co Adriaanse, began the season under a cloud of dissent as the coach tried to trim an enormous (57-player) squad, dropping and then transferring old favourites like Aron Winter and Richard Witschge. Feyenoord brought in Pierre van Hooijdonk from Benfica, lost Jerzy Dudek to Liverpool and found Shinji Ono, a Japanese midfielder. Originally scorned for just being another shirt-selling device for the Far East market, Ono proved a revelation. Playing with an uncannily Dutch sense of space and geometry, his passing and running were a keystone of Feyenoord's season. PSV coach Eric Gerets managed to hold on to Mark van Bommel, Player of the Year in 2001, but he made a few transfer dealings and rumours were rife of dissent in the dressing room.

Natural rhythm

PSV and Ajax made poor starts to the season, but the natural rhythm of Dutch league football soon asserted itself. At Christmas, four points separated the top six: Ajax led by a point from Feyenoord, two ahead of PSV and NAC Breda, with Heerenveen and Utrecht only four off the pace. In the new year, Ajax ceased to be troubled by European concerns after the team's exit from the UEFA Cup at the hands of FC København. But PSV and Feyenoord proved to be tough, seasoned competitors, dispensing with Leeds United and Rangers respectively on the way to their quarter-final clash. The tie between them went to penalties, and Feyenoord took it after PSV's Gakhokidze missed his kick. Feyenoord went on to seal a famous victory over Internazionale in the semi-final and eventually took the cup, beating Borussia Dortmund in the Final in front of its own fans at De Kuip.

The constant rumours about the tenure of Co Adriaanse at Ajax eventually proved true as he was dismissed mid-season and replaced by ex-player Ronald Koeman. The club gave no explanation and fired him after an amazing 3-2 victory against FC Twente, when Ajax was 2-0 down and playing with only ten men. However, European failures, a seven-game losing streak and unpopularity with fans did him no favours. Koeman brought a defensive solidity to the side that shored up the exuberance of a very young squad and steadily took the team back to the top of the league.

Eredivisie Table 2001–02

CLUB	P	W	D	L	F	A	Pts	
Ajax	34	22	7	5	73	34	73	Champions League
PSV	34	20	8	6	77	32	68	Champions League
Feyenoord	34	19	7	8	68	29	64	Champions League
Heerenveen	34	17	9	8	57	27	60	UEFA Cup
Vitesse Arnhem	34	16	12	6	45	34	60	UEFA Cup
NAC Breda	34	15	9	10	55	52	54	
FC Utrecht	34	14	9	11	60	51	51	UEFA Cup (cup runners-up)
RKC Waalwijk	34	14	6	14	49	43	48	
NEC	34	13	6	15	38	59	45	
AZ Alkmaar	34	12	7	15	42	45	43	
Willem II	34	10	13	11	54	61	43	
FC Twente	34	10	12	12	41	41	42	
Roda JC	34	11	8	15	33	45	41	
De Graafschap	34	10	7	17	43	55	37	
Groningen	34	10	7	17	40	59	37	
FC Den Bosch	34	8	9	17	40	55	33	
Sparta Rotterdam	34	4	12	18	26	75	24	Relegated
Fortuna Sittard	34	3	8	23	27	71	17	Relegated

Promoted clubs: RBC Roosendaal, Excelsior.

Dutch Cup

2002 FINAL

May 12 – De Kuip, Rotterdam
Ajax 3-2 FC Utrecht
(Hossam 21,   (Gluscevic 56,
Wamberto 93,   76 pen)
Ibrahimovic 95)
After sudden death extra-time
h/t: 1-0   **90 mins:** 2-2
Att: 37,000   **Ref:** R Temmink

Right: Co Adriaanse, Ajax coach, reflects on his side's inconsistent early performances and his own departure from the club.

Below left: Trouble breaks out between the police and Utrecht fans.

A tense moment for Ajax Reserves in the penalty shootout at the end of the semi-final clash with Utrecht in the Dutch Cup.

Nikos Machlas, the Ajax striker, heads over the FC Den Bosch defence.

Balletic, powerful and capable of defence-splitting passes, Japanese midfielder Shinji Ono had an influential season for Feyenoord.

NETHERLANDS

The season was marred by periodic outbreaks of violence, both inside and outside football grounds. NAC Breda's game against Willem II was abandoned after only 20 minutes when a hail of coins, golf balls and mobile phones came raining down on the head of Willem goalkeeper, Geert de Vileger. Persistent small-scale trouble and scuffling at Ajax forced the club to threaten to ban fans for fear of further violence, while Utrecht fans were sent home from their match at the Ajax Arena after anti-Semitic chanting in the ground. Worst of all, in early April, at the league match between Feyenoord and NAC Breda, a linesman was shot by a pellet gun from the crowd. Although the violence has yet to hit attendances, there are pressing financial problems in Dutch football already. In April 2002, the Dutch FA announced that the cumulative debts of the Eredivisie were £36 million.

Ajax wins the double

On the penultimate weekend, Ajax beat Den Bosch 2-0 at home to go three points clear of PSV, who won 3-0 against Sparta. Feyenoord guaranteed third place by beating Heerenveen. On the final day of the season Ajax beat NEC 2-0, while PSV was only able to draw 2-2 after trailing De Graafschap 2-0 after 30 minutes. Ajax was looking to make it a double by taking the Dutch Cup a week later. It could have sewn up the double earlier had Ajax Reserves managed to beat Utrecht in one of the semi-finals, but Utrecht took it on penalties. The Ajax first team had already secured its spot in the Final, beating PSV 3-0. In the event, Ajax did achieve the double by winning an exciting Final 3-2 with a golden goal three minutes into extra time.

Above: The Ajax players celebrate with the league championship trophy after beating NEC on the final day of the season.

Above left: Feyenoord's Pierre van Hooijdonk was the leading scorer in the Dutch league.

Right: Ronald Koeman made a mid-season switch from Vitesse Arnhem to Ajax and took the club from a mid-season wobble to a league and cup double.

Opposite page: Christian Chivu and Fred Grim of Ajax celebrate Ajax's cup victory against Utrecht which completed the Amsterdam side's double.

International Club Performances 2001–02

CLUB	COMPETITION	PROGRESS
Ajax	Champions League UEFA Cup	3rd Qualifying Round 2nd Round
Feyenoord	Champions League UEFA Cup	1st Group Phase Winners
PSV	Champions League UEFA Cup	1st Group Phase Quarter-finals
Roda JC	UEFA Cup	4th Round
FC Twente	UEFA Cup	2nd Round
FC Utrecht	UEFA Cup	2nd Round

Top Goalscorers 2001–02

PLAYER	CLUB	NATIONALITY	GOALS
Pierre van Hooijdonk	Feyenoord	Dutch	24
Jan Vennegoor of Hesselink	PSV	Dutch	21
Jon-Dahl Tomasson	Feyenoord	Danish	17

Above: *Now why did I take this job? Frank Rijkaard looks rueful as his side, Sparta Rotterdam, slides steadily towards relegation.*

Below: *It was another solid season for PSV's skipper Mark van Bommel, but the team finished empty-handed and he may well be on his way out of Dutch football.*

Amsterdam

FOOTBALL CITY

NETHERLANDS

FOR THE MOST PART, Amsterdam is a city of footballing ghosts. RAP Amsterdam won the city's first league title in 1898 and the double a year later, but has left no mark. In 1972, a new professional club was formed – FC Amsterdam (from the fusion of three amateur clubs: Blauwit, De Volewijckers and DWS) – only to return to obscurity in 1982. The Olympic Stadium that housed the team sits empty. De Meer, the site of Ajax's greatest years, has gone. The old Jewish areas which provided a significant share of Ajax's support and players have shrunk. Jordaan, home to Surinamese immigrants and their families (including Ruud Gullit), has been gentrified.

Only on the south-eastern edge of the city at the Amsterdam Arena does football have its single, gigantic material expression. And even here Ajax must share it with a weekly roster of concerts and commercial events. Formed in 1900, Ajax has gradually migrated from its first playing field in Amsterdam Noord, down to the south-eastern edge of the city, settling at De Meer in the 1930s. A rash of league titles followed, but the club remained small and intensely local in its connections; a relationship so close that a special area has been set aside in the Westtergaarde Cemetery and laid with De Meer turf, where ashes can continue to be scattered long after the pitch has gone.

The total football revolution

What transformed Amsterdam and Ajax were the 1960s, Johan Cruyff and Rinus Michels. An outburst of political situationism and light anarchic protest erupted in the mid-1960s, bringing first inept police violence and then the elite acceptance that made Amsterdam a bohemian paradise. Out of this peculiar Dutch brew of playful anti-authoritarianism and liberation, Cruyff on the field and Michels off it added technical virtuosity and iron discipline to create the unstable but unstoppable 'total football'. In less than a decade, Ajax had gone from near relegation to triple European champions. Cruyff left in 1972 and the club eventually imploded, though its awesome youth training system (now a global phenomenon) created the team under Louis van Gaal who won the 1995 European Cup. However, the iron laws of post-Bosman economics saw the squad scattered to the richest clubs in Europe.

The sight of thousands of orange-clad Dutch fans is common at the Netherlands' international matches around Europe.

SPIERINGHORN

DWS

OLYMPISCH STADIUM

22,500		
	Club:	Previously Ajax, FC Amsterdam
	Built:	1928
	Original Capacity:	24,700
	Rebuilt:	2000
	Significant Matches:	1928 Amsterdam Olympics; Ajax European matches

OSDORP

WESTTERGAARDE CEMETERY

Ringvaart

A9

BADHOEVEDO

A4

The old Jewish areas of Amsterdam have shrunk, but many Ajax supporters identify themselves and the club with Amsterdam's Jewish legacy, and have taken the Star of David as their symbol.

AMSTERDAM ARENA

51,324		
	Club:	Ajax
	Built:	1996
	Significant Matches:	2000 European Championships: four matches including quarter-final and semi-final; European Cup Final: 1998

Haarlemmermeer

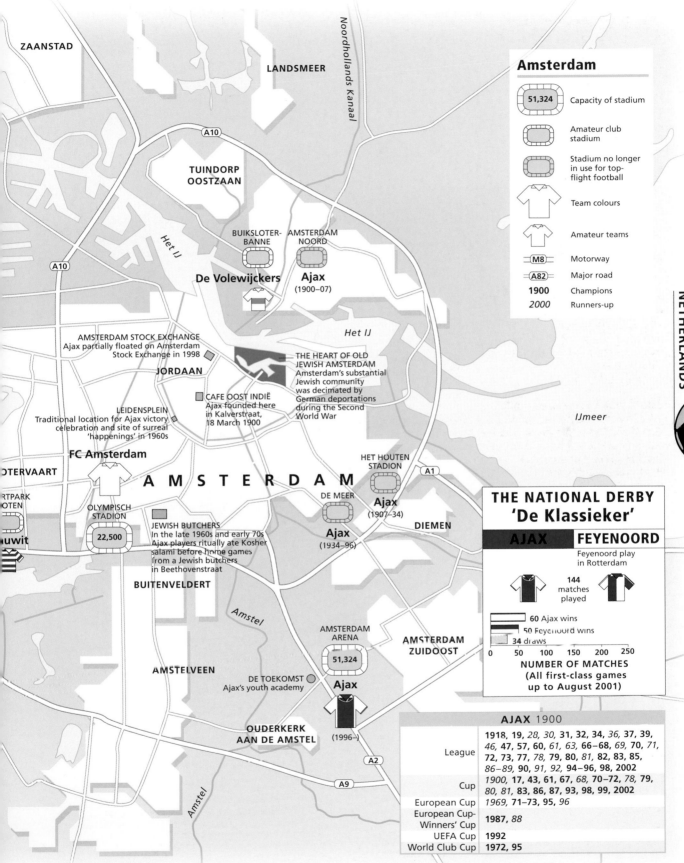

ZAANSTAD

LANDSMEER

Noordhollands Kanaal

Amsterdam

51,324	Capacity of stadium
	Amateur club stadium
	Stadium no longer in use for top-flight football
	Team colours
	Amateur teams
M8	Motorway
A82	Major road
1900	Champions
2000	Runners-up

A10

TUINDORP OOSTZAAN

BUIKSLOTER-BANNE

AMSTERDAM NOORD

Het IJ

A10

De Volewijckers

Ajax
(1900–07)

Het IJ

AMSTERDAM STOCK EXCHANGE
Ajax partially floated on Amsterdam
Stock Exchange in 1998

JORDAAN

THE HEART OF OLD
JEWISH AMSTERDAM
Amsterdam's substantial
Jewish community
was decimated by
German deportations
during the Second
World War

IJmeer

LEIDENSPLEIN
Traditional location for Ajax victory
celebration and site of surreal
'happenings' in 1960s

CAFE OOST INDIË
Ajax founded here
in Kalverstraat,
18 March 1900

NETHERLANDS

...TERVAART

FC Amsterdam

A M S T E R D A M

HET HOUTEN
STADION

A1

...RTPARK
...OTEN

OLYMPISCH
STADION

JEWISH BUTCHERS
In the late 1960s and early 70s
Ajax players ritually ate Kosher
salami before home games
from a Jewish butchers
in Beethovenstraat

DE MEER

Ajax
(1907–34)

DIEMEN

...uwit

22,500

Ajax
(1934–96)

AMSTERDAM

BUITENVELDERT

THE NATIONAL DERBY
'De Klassieker'

AJAX	FEYENOORD

Feyenoord play
in Rotterdam

Amstel

AMSTELVEEN

AMSTERDAM
ARENA

AMSTERDAM
ZUIDOOST

144
matches
played

60 Ajax wins
50 Feyenoord wins
34 draws

| 0 | 50 | 100 | 150 | 200 | 250 |

NUMBER OF MATCHES
(All first-class games
up to August 2001)

51,324

DE TOEKOMST
Ajax's youth academy

Ajax
(1996–)

OUDERKERK
AAN DE AMSTEL

A2

Amstel

A9

AJAX 1900	
League	**1918, 19,** *28, 30,* **31, 32, 34,** *36,* **37, 39,** *46,* **47, 57, 60,** *61,* **63,** *66–68,* **69,** *70,* **71,** *72,* **73, 77,** *78,* **79, 80,** *81,* **82, 83, 85,** *86–89,* **90,** *91, 92,* **94–96,** *98,* **2002**
Cup	*1900,* **17, 43,** *61,* **67,** *68,* **70–72,** *78,* **79,** *80, 81,* **83,** *86,* **87, 93, 98, 99, 2002**
European Cup	*1969,* **71–73,** *95,* **96**
European Cup-Winners' Cup	**1987,** *88*
UEFA Cup	**1992**
World Club Cup	**1972,** *95*

NETHERLANDS

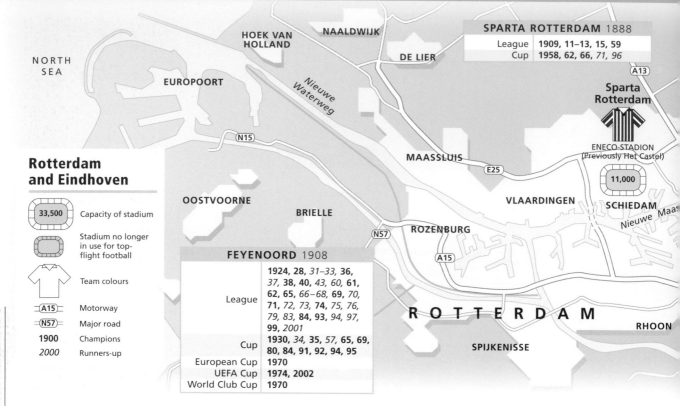

Rotterdam and Eindhoven

Capacity of stadium: 33,500

33,500	Capacity of stadium
	Stadium no longer in use for top-flight football
	Team colours
A15	Motorway
N57	Major road
1900	Champions
2000	Runners-up

SPARTA ROTTERDAM 1888

League	**1909, 11–13, 15, 59**
Cup	**1958, 62, 66,** *71, 96*

Sparta Rotterdam
ENECO-STADION
(Previously Het Castel)
11,000

FEYENOORD 1908

League	**1924,** *28, 31–33,* **36,** **37, 38, 40,** *43,* **60, 61,** **62, 65,** *66–68,* **69, 70,** **71, 72, 73, 74, 75, 76,** *79, 83,* **84, 93, 94, 97,** **99,** *2001*
Cup	**1930,** *34,* **35,** *57,* **65, 69,** **80, 84, 91, 92, 94, 95**
European Cup	**1970**
UEFA Cup	**1974, 2002**
World Club Cup	**1970**

Rotterdam and Eindhoven

FOOTBALL CITIES

IF THE DUTCH are the Brazilians of European football, then Rotterdam is São Paulo – hard working, industrial, no-nonsense, perpetually comparing itself to bohemian glamorous Amsterdam. In footballing terms, the same comparison is made between Feyenoord and Ajax, a fact well demonstrated by the bitterness of their derby matches. Although Feyenoord can claim championships in every decade since the 1960s, and a European Cup in 1970, the team has always remained in Ajax's shadow.

Feyenoord was founded in 1908 in the heart of the old docks area, and there the club remains. Its stadium, De Kuip, was opened in 1937, surviving the carpet bombing of the docks during the Second World War only to disintegrate through neglect before renovation turned it into a venue for the 2000 European Championships.

Bitterness erupts

Feyenoord fans don't all come from Rotterdam, but from right across the Brabant and Zeeland regions as well. In the 1990s a hooligan element emerged; Ajax v Feyenoord matches were often seen as an excuse for organized violence, and fans fought street battles with the police after the Rotterdam club's 1999 championship victory.

The city's second club, Sparta, has scraped along in the top division for most of the century, apart from two golden eras of success in the years before the First World War and in the late 1950s. The city's third team, Excelsior, is as much Feyenoord's nursery club as anything else.

West of Rotterdam, Eindhoven is a prosperous company town. The electronics giant Philips is headquartered there, employing 20 per cent of the population; it founded PSV in 1913 after a company sports event held to celebrate Holland's independence. Considerable sponsorship has seen PSV rise to the top of Dutch football. Across town, tiny Eindhoven ekes out an existence in the lower divisions.

Feyenoord was founded in 1908 in the old docks area of Rotterdam close to where its stadium, De Kuip, stands today.

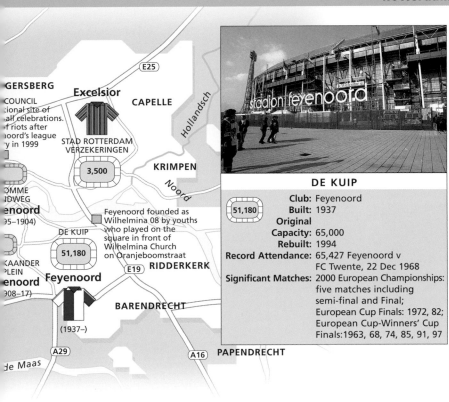

GERSBERG

COUNCIL
tional site of
all celebrations.
f riots after
oord's league
y in 1999

Excelsior

CAPELLE

STAD ROTTERDAM
VERZEKERINGEN

3,500

KRIMPEN

Noord

OMME
DWEG

enoord
95–1904)

DE KUIP

51,180

KAANDER
PLEIN

enoord
908–17)

Feyenoord

(1937–)

Feyenoord founded as
Wilhelmina 08 by youths
who played on the
square in front of
Wilhelmina Church
on Oranjeboomstraat

E19   RIDDERKERK

BARENDRECHT

A29   A16   PAPENDRECHT

de Maas

Hollandsch

E25

DE KUIP

51,180

Club:	Feyenoord
Built:	1937
Original Capacity:	65,000
Rebuilt:	1994
Record Attendance:	65,427 Feyenoord v FC Twente, 22 Dec 1968
Significant Matches:	2000 European Championships: five matches including semi-final and Final; European Cup Finals: 1972, 82; European Cup-Winners' Cup Finals:1963, 68, 74, 85, 91, 97

Heavy policing has been frequent at
De Kuip stadium since the rise of hooligan
activity among Feyenoord fans in the 1990s.

NETHERLANDS

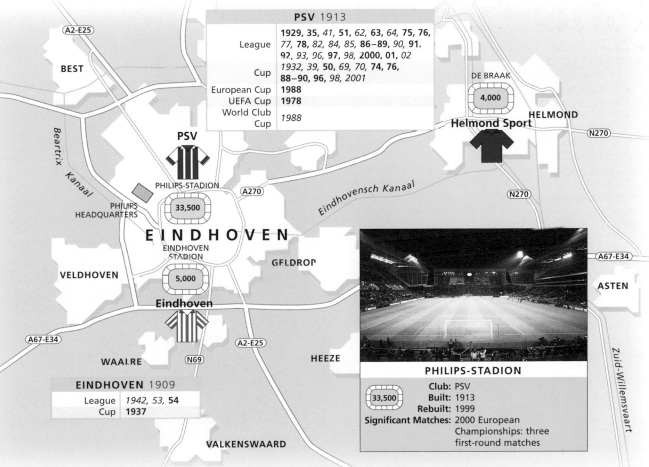

PSV 1913		
League	1929, 35, *41*, **51**, *62*, **63**, **64**, **75**, **76**, *77*, **78**, *82*, *84*, *85*, **86–89**, **90**, **91**, **92**, **93**, *96*, **97**, *98*, **2000**, **01**, *02*	
Cup	*1932, 39,* **50,** *69, 70,* **74, 76,** **88–90, 96,** *98, 2001*	
European Cup	**1988**	
UEFA Cup	**1978**	
World Club Cup	*1988*	

A2-E25

BEST

Beartrix Kanaal

PSV

PHILIPS-STADION

PHILIPS HEADQUARTERS

33,500

EINDHOVEN

EINDHOVEN STADION

5,000

VELDHOVEN

Eindhoven

A67-E34   N69   A2-E25

WAALRE

A270

GELDROP

Eindhovensch Kanaal

HEEZE

DE BRAAK

4,000

Helmond Sport

HELMOND

N270

N270

A67-E34

ASTEN

Zuid-Willemsvaart

VALKENSWAARD

EINDHOVEN 1909

League	*1942, 53,* **54**
Cup	**1937**

PHILIPS-STADION

33,500

Club:	PSV
Built:	1913
Rebuilt:	1999
Significant Matches:	2000 European Championships: three first-round matches

Netherlands

FANS AND OWNERS

PROFESSIONALISM AND COMMERCIALISM arrived late in Dutch football (1956 was the first professional season) and the ownership of Dutch clubs still reflects the amateur and social club character of the past. While many clubs continue as small membership associations, private investors have begun to take more significant shares in some clubs, such as Feyenoord and Vitesse. PSV remains the property of the electronics giant Philips. Only Ajax has so far explored a further option – partial flotation. In 1997, Ajax was allowed to separate out its membership association and commercial activities. The club retained 70 per cent of the Ajax NV and the rest was sold on the stock market. These four clubs are in a different league of income and attendances from the rest of the league, though they remain small by European standards. Dutch TV income is particularly small compared to the big leagues. As a consequence, both Ajax and Feyenoord have bought into foreign clubs to find players that they could otherwise ill afford (see pages 462-463).

The not-so-jolly orange ranks

Dutch fan culture has many sides: from the newly-fashionable executive boxes of the Ajax Arena to the tiny, windswept stands of the small provincial clubs; from the absurdly jolly, mass-orange ranks that follow the national team; to the organized and violent *ultras* of Feyenoord and Ajax. Violence in Dutch football first appeared in the 1970s, when Tottenham fans started fighting at a UEFA Cup tie with Feyenoord. Since then, violence has been concentrated among Ajax, Feyenoord and Den Haag supporters. The peak of trouble was the mid-1980s, and led to intensive and complex policing measures and hefty bans from the courts. The problem has continued to simmer. In March 1997, Feyenoord and Ajax fans fought on an area of wasteland, resulting in one death. In 1999, Feyenoord fans celebrating the club's victory in the league began rioting and fighting with the police in the city streets. Euro 2000 saw a further development of Dutch policing methods, including highly visible preventative work, which was rewarded with the absence of trouble during the tournament.

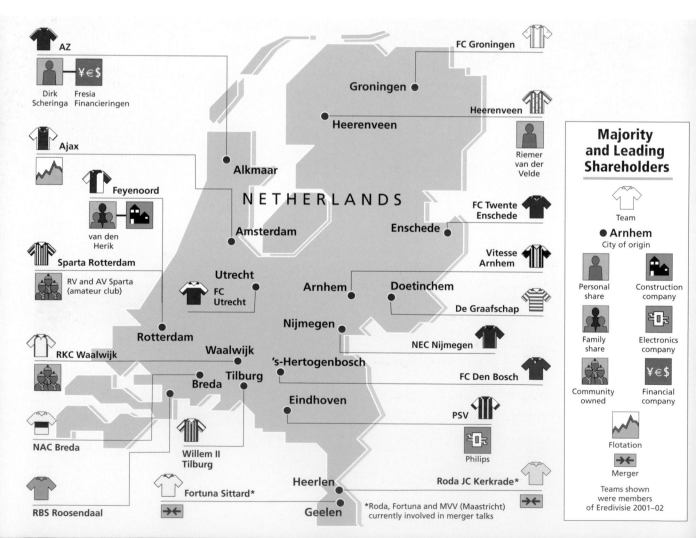

AZ — Dirk Scheringa — Fresia Financieringen

Ajax

Feyenoord — van den Herik

Sparta Rotterdam — RV and AV Sparta (amateur club)

FC Groningen

Groningen

Heerenveen — Riemer van der Velde

Alkmaar

NETHERLANDS

Amsterdam

FC Twente Enschede

Enschede

Vitesse Arnhem

Utrecht — FC Utrecht

Arnhem

Doetinchem

De Graafschap

Nijmegen

Rotterdam

RKC Waalwijk

Waalwijk

NEC Nijmegen

's-Hertogenbosch

FC Den Bosch

Breda

Tilburg

Eindhoven

PSV

NAC Breda

Willem II Tilburg

Philips

Heerlen

Roda JC Kerkrade*

Fortuna Sittard*

RBS Roosendaal

Geleen

*Roda, Fortuna and MVV (Maastricht) currently involved in merger talks

Majority and Leading Shareholders

- Team
- ● Arnhem — City of origin
- Personal share
- Construction company
- Family share
- Electronics company
- Community owned
- Financial company
- Flotation
- Merger

Teams shown were members of Eredivisie 2001–02

Club Budgets 1999–2000, 2000–01

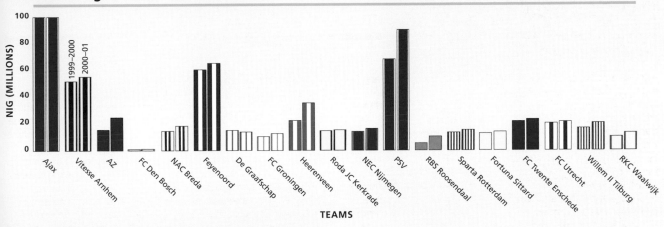

NIG (MILLIONS)

100 / 80 / 60 / 40 / 20 / 0

1999–2000
2000–01

TEAMS

Ajax / Vitesse Arnhem / AZ / FC Den Bosch / NAC Breda / Feyenoord / De Graafschap / FC Groningen / Heerenveen / Roda JC Kerkrade / NEC Nijmegen / PSV / RBS Roosendaal / Sparta Rotterdam / Fortuna Sittard / FC Twente Enschede / FC Utrecht / Willem II Tilburg / RKC Waalwijk

Rotterdam police arrest a fan after trouble at Feyenoord. In 2002 there has been a resurgence of trouble at Ajax as well, with the club threatening to lock fans out of the Amsterdam Arena.

Dutch Attendances

Attendances for each season

Total attendances for each season (millions)

6 / 4 / 2 / 0

Average attendance per game (thousands)

16 / 12 / 8 / 4 / 0

1994 / 1996 / 1998 / 2000

NETHERLANDS

■ Total attendance in Division 1

— Average attendance per game in Division 1

Average Attendance

Average attendance for season 2000–01 (thousands)

40 / 35 / 30 / 25 / 20 / 15 / 10 / 5 / 0

Capacity

Attendance as a percentage of capacity for season 2000–01 (capacity in brackets)

40% / 50% / 60% / 70% / 80% / 90% / 100%

TEAMS	Capacity
Ajax	(51,324)
Vitesse Arnhem	(29,000)
AZ	(8,320)
FC Den Bosch	(6,000)
NAC Breda	(16,400)
Feyenoord	(51,180)
De Graafschap	(11,000)
FC Groningen	(13,000)
Heerenveen	(14,300)
Roda JC Kerkrade	(19,500)
NEC Nijmegen	(12,500)
PSV	(33,500)
Sparta Rotterdam	(11,000)
Fortuna Sittard	(12,500)
FC Twente Enschede	(13,350)
FC Utrecht	(14,220)
Willem II Tilburg	(14,700)
RKC Waalwijk	(7,500)

Riemer van der Velde, president of Heerenveen, has seen attractive small-town football pull almost sell-out crowds at home.

Netherlands

PLAYERS AND MANAGERS

ALTHOUGH FOOTBALL ARRIVED EARLY in the Netherlands, the game did not go professional until 1956, and the only truly great players of this long era were the suitably named Kick Smit and the Italian-suited Faas Wilkes, the dribble-king, whose departure to Valencia triggered the start of professionalism. In their wake, Dutch football was transformed by the social and sporting innovations of the 1960s. From the Ajax crucible of total football and the anti-authoritarian politics of the time a new kind of Dutch footballer was born. Exemplified by Johan Cruyff, Dutch footballers have come to prize technique and tactics above all else. Individual artistry, speed of thought, movement and accurate perception of space have become the hallmark of two generations of Dutch players since the amateur era. Along with Cruyff in the first wave of total footballers were Ruud Krol, Johan Neeskens and Johnny Rep. But self-possession, self-belief and ardent individualism among Dutch players has also been nurtured, and this has made for loose and fragmented teams.

More players overseas

In the 1980s, players of Surinamese origin, like Ruud Gullit and Frank Rijkaard, began to take their place in the Dutch team, and in the 1990s the ethnic divisions within the Dutch national squad boiled over into open conflict. With the advent of Cruyff, Dutch players started playing abroad in significant numbers and today their leading players are more likely to play overseas than those of any other leading European football nation: Edgar Davids, Dennis Bergkamp, Patrick Kluivert, Marc Overmars and the de Boer brothers have all played the bulk of their careers in Spain, Italy and Britain. Ruud van Nistelrooy, now of Manchester United, is just the latest in a long line of homegrown players whose exceptional performances in the Netherlands have seen them transfer overseas. Sadly for a country whose players possess so much talent, the Dutch national team has become the biggest underachiever in Europe.

Top 15 International Caps

PLAYER	CAPS	GOALS	FIRST MATCH	LAST MATCH
Frank de Boer*	91	11	1990	2002
Aron Winter*	84	6	1987	2000
Ruud Krol	83	4	1969	1983
Dennis Bergkamp*	79	37	1990	2000
Ronald Koeman	78	14	1983	1994
Hans van Breukelen	73	0	1980	1992
Frank Rijkaard	73	10	1981	1994
Marc Overmars*	70	15	1993	2002
Jan Wouters	70	4	1982	1994
Ruud Gullit	66	17	1981	1994
Wim Jansen	65	1	1967	1980
Ronald de Boer*	64	13	1993	2002
Edwin van de Saar*	64	0	1995	2002
Puck van Heel	64	0	1925	1938
Willy van der Kerkhof	63	5	1974	1985

Top 15 International Goalscorers

PLAYER	GOALS	CAPS	FIRST MATCH	LAST MATCH
Dennis Bergkamp*	37	79	1990	2000
Faas Wilkes	35	38	1946	1961
Johan Cruyff	33	47	1966	1977
Abe Lenstra	33	48	1940	1959
Patrick Kluivert*	33	58	1994	2002
Bep Bakhuys	28	23	1928	1937
Kick Smit	26	29	1934	1946
Marco van Basten	24	58	1983	1992
Leen Vente	19	21	1933	1940
Mannus Franken	17	22	1906	1914
Tommy van der Linden	17	24	1957	1963
John Bosman	17	30	1986	1997
Wim Tap	17	33	1925	1931
Johan Neeskens	17	49	1970	1981
Ruud Gullit	17	66	1981	1994

* Indicates players still playing at least at club level.

Dutch International Managers

DATES	NAME	GAMES	WON	DRAWN	LOST
1973	Frantisek Fadrhonc	5	3	2	0
1974	Rinus Michels	10	6	3	1
1974–76	Georg Knobel	15	9	1	5
1976–77	Jan Zwartkruis	5	4	1	0
1977–78	Ernst Happel and Jan Zwartkruis	13	8	3	2
1978–81	Jan Zwartkruis	22	8	6	8
1981	Rob Baan	3	3	0	0
1981–84	Kees Rijvers	19	9	3	7
1984–85	Rinus Michels	34	19	8	7
1985–86	Leo Beenhakker	7	4	1	2
1986–88	Rinus Michels	20	12	5	3
1988–90	Thijs Lijbregts	13	6	4	3
1990	Leo Beenhakker	6	1	3	2
1990–92	Rinus Michels	19	11	4	4
1992–95	Dick Advocaat	26	15	5	6
1995–98	Guus Hiddink	37	22	7	8
1998–2000	Frank Rijkaard	22	11	8	3
2000–02	Louis van Gaal	14	8	4	2
2002–	Dick Advocaat	0	0	0	0

All figures correct as of 14 February 2002.

The Dutch national team has had little success during the last 30 years despite the amount of talent available. The most successful team was this one that won the European Championships in 1988 and which included (back row, left to right) van Basten, R. Koeman, Rijkaard, E. Koeman, Gullit, van Breukelen; (front row) van Tiggelen, Muhren, van Aerle, Wouters, Vanenburg.

Player of the Year

YEAR	PLAYER	CLUB
1984	Gullit	Feyenoord
1985	van Basten	Ajax
1986	Gullit	PSV
1987	R. Koeman	PSV
1988	R. Koeman	PSV
1989	Romario	PSV
1990	Wouters	Ajax
1991	Bergkamp	Ajax
1992	Bergkamp	Ajax
1993	Litmanen	Ajax
1994	R. de Boer	Ajax
1995	Nilis	PSV
1996	R. de Boer	Ajax
1997	Stam	PSV
1998–99	van Nistelrooy	PSV
1999–2000	van Nistelrooy	PSV
2000–01	van Bommel	PSV

Manager of the Year

YEAR	MANAGER	CLUB
1996	Louis van Gaal	Ajax
1997	Foppe de Haan	Heerenveen
1998–99	Leo Beenhakker	Feyenoord
1999–2000	Foppe de Haan	Heerenveen
2000–01	Martin Jol	RKC Wallwijk

Awarded by the Dutch Professional
Footballers' Association.

*Johnny Rep,
a mercurial striker
for both Ajax and
the national team
during the golden
age of Dutch
football in the
1970s, followed in
the footsteps of
Faas Wilkes when he
left Holland to join
Valencia in 1976.*

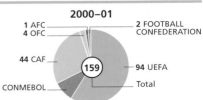

NETHERLANDS

Top Goalscorers by Season 1956–2002

SEASON	PLAYER	CLUB	GOALS
1956–57	Dillen	PSV	43
1957–58	Canjels	NAC Breda	32
1958–59	Canjels	NAC Breda	34
1959–60	Henk Groot	Ajax	38
1960–61	Henk Groot	Ajax	41
1961–62	Tol	Volendam	27
1962–63	Kerkhoffs	PSV	22
1963–64	Guertsen	DWS	28
1964–65	Guertsen	DWS	23
1965–66	van der Kuijlen	PSV	23
1965–66	Kruiver	Feyenoord	23
1966–67	Cruyff	Ajax	33
1967–68	Kindvall	Feyenoord	28
1968–69	van Dijk	FC Twente	30
1969–70	van der Kuijlen	PSV	26
1970–71	Kindvall	Feyenoord	24
1971–72	Cruyff	Ajax	25

SEASON	PLAYER	CLUB	GOALS
1972–73	Janssens	NEC	18
1972–73	Brokamp	MVV	18
1973–74	van der Kuijlen	PSV	27
1974–75	Geels	Ajax	30
1975–76	Geels	Ajax	29
1976–77	Geels	Ajax	34
1977–78	Geels	Ajax	30
1978–79	Kist	AZ 67 Alkmaar	34
1979–80	Kist	AZ 67 Alkmaar	27
1980–81	Geels	Sparta R	22
1981–82	Kieft	Ajax	32
1982–83	Houtman	Feyenoord	30
1983–84	van Basten	Ajax	28
1984–85	van Basten	Ajax	22
1985–86	van Basten	Ajax	37
1986–87	van Basten	Ajax	31
1987–88	Kieft	PSV	29
1988–89	Romario	PSV	19

SEASON	PLAYER	CLUB	GOALS
1989–90	Romario	PSV	23
1990–91	Romario	PSV	25
1991–92	Bergkamp	Ajax	24
1992–93	Bergkamp	Ajax	26
1993–94	Litmanen	Ajax	26
1994–95	Ronaldo	PSV	30
1995–96	Nilis	PSV	21
1996–97	Nilis	PSV	21
1997–98	Machlas	Vitesse Arnhem	34
1998–99	van Nistelrooy	PSV	31
1999–2000	van Nistelrooy	PSV	29
2000–01	Kezman	PSV	24
2001–02	van Hooijdonk	Feyenoord	24

Foreign Players in the Netherlands (in top division squads)

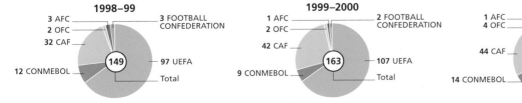

1998–99
3 AFC
2 OFC
32 CAF
12 CONMEBOL
149
3 FOOTBALL CONFEDERATION
97 UEFA
Total

1999–2000
1 AFC
2 OFC
42 CAF
9 CONMEBOL
163
2 FOOTBALL CONFEDERATION
107 UEFA
Total

2000–01
1 AFC
4 OFC
44 CAF
14 CONMEBOL
159
2 FOOTBALL CONFEDERATION
94 UEFA
Total

Netherlands

EREDIVISIE 1981–2001

IN 1981, THE SMALL PROVINCIAL CLUB AZ Alkmaar finally broke the stranglehold of the big three – Ajax, Feyenoord and PSV – by taking the Dutch league title. It was not to last, however, and the next 20 seasons have all gone to one of the big three. Ajax was the first to revive when Johan Cruyff came home from his foreign travels and took the club to two consecutive titles, including a league and cup double in 1983. Alongside Cruyff, the next generation of Dutch internationals was maturing, including the gangly 17-year-old Marco van Basten, Frank Rijkaard, Dennis Bergkamp and Aron Winter. Cruyff left Ajax in 1984, to manage its old rival Feyenoord. There he joined the young Ruud Gullit in a magical display of intelligent and zestful football. But financial decline and poor attendances followed, and the club was close to bankruptcy before being rejuvenated in the early 1990s by the money of building magnate Jorein van den Herik.

The rise of PSV

A further title for Ajax in 1985 was a prelude to the dominance of PSV. A top three spot for the team in the previous five seasons was finally converted into a title in 1986. PSV would go on to win another five titles in six years; only Ajax in 1990 under Leo Beenhakker could stop them. PSV was initially led by Hans Kraay, who systematically bought the leading players of

the other top clubs in the country: Ruud Gullit came in from Feyenoord, Ronald Koeman from Ajax; two titles and a European Cup in 1987 followed. New manager Guus Hiddink added the goalscoring Wim Kieft and Dutch international goalkeeper Hans van Breukelen, and the titles kept coming. Gullit was eventually sold to Milan and with the proceeds PSV bought Brazilian striker Romario. He delivered over 100 goals in five seasons before leaving for Barcelona.

Ajax before Bosman

The rejuvenated Feyenoord under manager Wim Jansen took a surprise title in 1993. Then the new Ajax of Louis van Gaal, previously the club's youth coach, burst on the scene. Drawing on the legendary youth scouting and coaching system at the club, van Gaal nurtured and drilled a new generation of young Dutch internationals: Davids, Seedorf, Overmars, Bogarde, the De Boer brothers and Patrick Kluivert. Fast passing, awesome team play and deadly striking brought three titles and a European Cup. But with the Bosman ruling on transfers coming into force and the perennial pressures of money on the club, the squad was quickly scattered across Europe's biggest clubs. In the late 1990s, with no single dominant club, titles were split between PSV, Ajax and Feyenoord. The lack of competition

In 1984 the Feyenoord team featured Johan Cruyff, in his final playing year, and the rising star Ruud Gullit. The team took an unexpected and unforgettable title. This picture shows Ruud Gullit in action for Feyenoord against Fortuna Sittard.

NETHERLANDS

NETHERLANDS

lower down the league, and the meagre income from gates and television compared to the bigger European leagues, has left the big three looking for an alternative league to play in: Ajax and PSV have been leading forces in campaigning for the creation of either an Atlantic League (with the biggest clubs from western Europe's smaller nations) or a joint league with Belgium.

Ruud's roots

Among the challengers, the tiny SC Heerenveen has been the most surprising. Under a new president and coach in the early 1990s, Riemer van der Velde and Foppe de Haan respectively, the club has seen regular European competition. Clever buys from smaller footballing nations like Denmark, Finland and Romania were combined with nurturing and selling its own talent: Ruud van Nistlerooy being the greatest success. Vitesse Arnhem, under chairman Karel Aalbers, avoided bankruptcy in 1991, built the new Gelredrome stadium, but has yet to do better than third. Regular Eredivisie members include the solidly supported but limited charms of FC Twente Enschede, Roda JC Kerkrade, AZ from Alkmaar and FC Utrecht. While down at the bottom, a range of clubs come up and down the divisions and contemplate mergers and reorganizations in an effort to stay afloat.

Ruud van Nistelrooy's career typifies the dilemmas of Dutch football. A ruthless striker, he has migrated from tiny SC Heerenveen to PSV and on to Manchester United. He is one of many great players lost by a Dutch domestic game which cannot currently pay them enough.

Key to Champions' Winning Margin

Ajax   Feyenoord   SC Heerenveen
PSV   Roda JC   Willem II

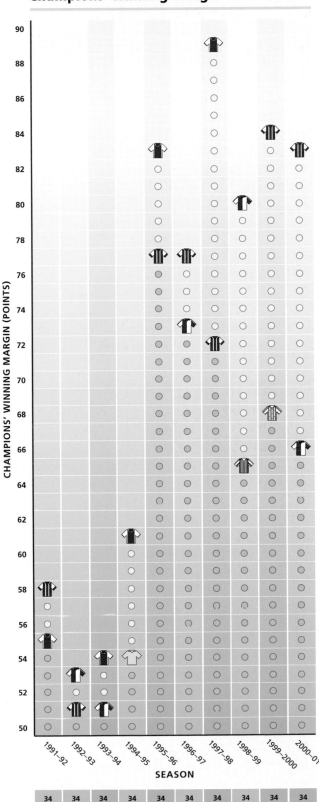

Champions' Winning Margin 1991–2001

CHAMPIONS' WINNING MARGIN (POINTS)

SEASON

1991–92	1992–93	1993–94	1994–95	1995–96	1996–97	1997–98	1998–99	1999–2000	2000–01
34	34	34	34	34	34	34	34	34	34

Total games played by each team
(2 points awarded for a win until 1996, when 3 points awarded)

NETHERLANDS

The strongest side in the Netherlands in the late 1990s, PSV is the model of a medium-sized modern club: it has corporate backing; it is careful in its transfer dealings; it has had huge domestic success, but has a poor record in Europe.

Louis van Gaal, whose great young Ajax squads of the mid-1990s climbed the peaks of Dutch and European football, only to be dismembered in the transfer market, with van Gaal himself moving to Barcelona.

The languid but deadly Patrick Kluivert, discovered and nurtured by the Ajax youth system.

Key to League Positions Table

- League champions
- Season of promotion to league
- Season of relegation from league
- Other teams playing in league
- 5 Final position in league

Dutch League Positions 1981–2001

TEAM	1981-82	1982-83	1983-84	1984-85	1985-86	1986-87	1987-88	1988-89	1989-90	1990-91	1991-92	1992-93	1993-94	1994-95	1995-96	1996-97	1997-98	1998-99	1999-2000	2000-01
Ajax	1	1	3	1	2	2	2	2	1	2	2	3	1	1	1	4	1	6	5	3
Vitesse Arnhem									4	5	4	4	6	5	5	3	4	4	6	
AZ	3	11	5	13	9	15	16									18		9	7	13
FC Den Bosch		10	6	6	10	7	7	17			17							18		
NAC Breda	11	17		17									7	10	8	9	12	18		9
Dordrecht '90									16	15	18		18							
DS '79			18					18												
Excelsior		9	13	12	15	18														
Feyenoord	6	2	1	3	3	3	6	4	11	8	3	1	2	4	3	2	4	1	3	2
Go Ahead Eagles	10	12	12	15	10	16							15	12	17	18				
De Graafschap	18										17				14	8	11	13	14	15
FC Groningen	7	5	7	5	4	13	11	6	9	3	5	12	15	13	9	10	17			14
ADO Den Haag	17						14	17		10	14	16								
Haarlem	4	7	4	9	11	12	9	10	18											
SC Heerenveen										17			13	7	7	6	7	6	2	10
Helmond Sport		15	16																	
SC Heracles								18												
Roda JC Kerkrade	8	6	9	11	5	4	15	5	10	9	11	6	2	4	6	14	5	8	4	
SC Cambuur Leeuwarden														14	18			15	17	
MVV	16		14	16			14	15	7	7	10	16					15	14	16	
NEC	13	18			17				16	18				15	17	17	8	11	15	12
PSV	2	3	2	2	1	1	1	1	2	1	1	2	3	3	2	1	2	3	1	1
RBS Roosendaal																				18
Sparta Rotterdam	9	4	6	4	7	8	12	12	12	13	8	13	9	14	6	13	13	17	13	17
Fortuna Sittard		8	11	7	8	9	8	8	7	12	14	16			13	11	7	10	12	16
FC Twente Enschede	12	16	8	14	7	3	3	3	6	6	5	5	5	10	3	9	8	6	11	
FC Utrecht	5	10	8	10	12	6	10	13	14	4	11	8	14	12	15	12	10	12	10	5
BV Veendam							17	18												
VVV Venlo				13	5	5	17			18		17								
FC Volendam		15	16				14	9	6	9	13	6	11	11	16	14	18			
RKC Waalwijk							11	8	7	10	9	16	8	11	16	16	16	11	7	
Willem II	14	14	17				4	15	13	11	12	10	8	7	12	15	5	2	9	8
FC Zwolle	15	13	14	18		11	13	16												

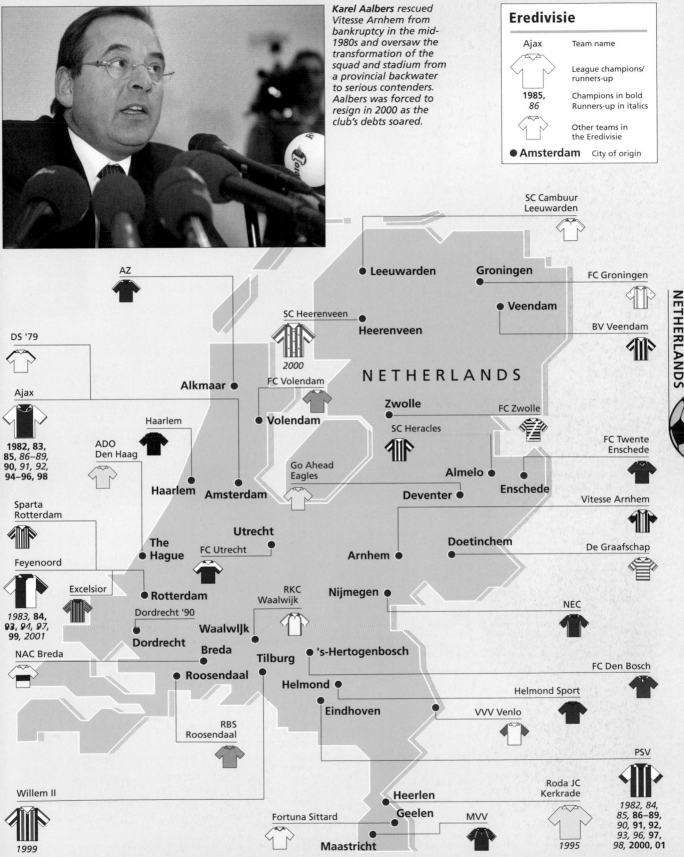

Karel Aalbers rescued Vitesse Arnhem from bankruptcy in the mid-1980s and oversaw the transformation of the squad and stadium from a provincial backwater to serious contenders. Aalbers was forced to resign in 2000 as the club's debts soared.

Eredivisie

Ajax	Team name
	League champions/ runners-up
1985, *86*	Champions in bold Runners-up in italics
	Other teams in the Eredivisie
● **Amsterdam**	City of origin

NETHERLANDS

N E T H E R L A N D S

SC Cambuur Leeuwarden

● Leeuwarden

● Groningen   FC Groningen

● Veendam   BV Veendam

AZ

SC Heerenveen

● Heerenveen

2000

DS '79

Ajax

1982, 83, 85, *86–89,* **90, 91, 92,** *94–96,* **98**

ADO Den Haag

Haarlem

● **Alkmaar**   FC Volendam

● **Volendam**

Zwolle   FC Zwolle

SC Heracles

● **Almelo**   FC Twente Enschede

● **Enschede**

Go Ahead Eagles

● **Deventer**   Vitesse Arnhem

● **Haarlem**   ● **Amsterdam**

Sparta Rotterdam

Utrecht

FC Utrecht

The Hague

● **Arnhem**   ● **Doetinchem**   De Graafschap

Feyenoord

1983, 84, *93,* **94,** *97,* **99, 2001**

Excelsior

● **Rotterdam**

Dordrecht '90

RKC Waalwijk

● Nijmegen   NEC

NAC Breda

● **Dordrecht**   **Breda**

Waalwijk

● **Roosendaal**   **Tilburg**   ● **'s-Hertogenbosch**   FC Den Bosch

Helmond   Helmond Sport

RBS Roosendaal

● **Eindhoven**   VVV Venlo

PSV

Willem II

● **Heerlen**   Roda JC Kerkrade

● **Geelen**   MVV

1999   Fortuna Sittard   **Maastricht**   *1995*

1982, 84, 85, *86–89,* **90, 91, 92, 93, 96, 97, 98, 2000, 01**

Netherlands

Koninklijke Nederlandsche Voetbalbond
Founded: 1889
Joined FIFA: 1904
Joined UEFA: 1954

KNVB

FOOTBALL ARRIVED EARLY in the Netherlands with the first clubs being set up in the late 1870s. But somehow it took until 1956 for a fully-fledged national league to develop. The amateur era in Dutch football ran from the first national competition in 1898 until the legalization of professionalism in 1956.

It is truly extraordinary that despite being enveloped by two world wars the Netherlands has only lost one league season (1945) to social and political chaos.

Dutch Amateur League Record 1898–1956

SEASON	CHAMPIONS	RUNNERS-UP
1898	RAP Amsterdam	Vitesse Arnhem
1899	RAP Amsterdam	PW Enschede
1900	HVV Den Haag	Victoria Wageningen
1901	HVV Den Haag	Victoria Wageningen
1902	HVV Den Haag	Victoria Wageningen
1903	HVV Den Haag	Vitesse Arnhem
1904	HBS Den Haag	Velocitas Breda
1905	HVV Den Haag	PW Enschede
1906	HBS Den Haag	PW Enschede
1907	HVV Den Haag	PW Enschede
1908	Quick Den Haag	UD
1909	Sparta Rotterdam	Wilhelmina
1910	HVV Den Haag	Quick Nijmegen
1911	Sparta Rotterdam	GVC
1912	Sparta Rotterdam	GVC
1913	Sparta Rotterdam	Vitesse Arnhem
1914	HVV Den Haag	Vitesse Arnhem
1915	Sparta Rotterdam	Vitesse Arnhem
1916	Willem II	Go Ahead Deventer
1917	Go Ahead Deventer	UVV
1918	Ajax	Go Ahead Deventer
1919	Ajax	Go Ahead Deventer
1920	Be Quick Groningen	VOC Rotterdam
1921	NAC Breda	Be Quick Groningen
1922	Go Ahead Deventer	Blauw-Wit Amsterdam
1923	RCH Haarlem	Be Quick Groningen
1924	Feyenoord	Stormvogels Velsen
1925	HBS Den Haag	NAC Breda
1926	SC Enschede	MVV Maastricht
1927	Heracles Almelo	NAC Breda
1928	Feyenoord	Ajax
1929	PSV	Go Ahead Deventer
1930	Go Ahead Deventer	Ajax
1931	Ajax	Feyenoord
1932	Ajax	Feyenoord
1933	Go Ahead Deventer	Feyenoord
1934	Ajax	KFC Alkmaar
1935	PSV	Go Ahead Deventer
1936	Feyenoord	Ajax
1937	Ajax	Feyenoord
1938	Feyenoord	Heracles Almelo
1939	Ajax	DWS Amsterdam
1940	Feyenoord	Blauw-Wit Amsterdam
1941	Heracles Almelo	PSV
1942	ADO Den Haag	Eindhoven
1943	ADO Den Haag	Feyenoord
1944	De Volewijckers	VUC Den Haag
1945	*no championship*	
1946	Haarlem	Ajax
1947	Ajax	SC Heerenveen
1948	BVV Hertogenbosch	SC Heerenveen

Dutch Amateur League Record (*continued*)

SEASON	CHAMPIONS	RUNNERS-UP
1949	SVV Schiedam	BVV Hertogenbosch
1950	Limburg Brunssue	Blauw-Wit Amsterdam
1951	PSV	DWS Amsterdam
1952	Willem II	Hermes Schiedam
1953	RCH Haarlem	Eindhoven
1954	Eindhoven	DOS Utrecht
1955	Willem II	NAC Breda
1956	Rapid JC Heerlen	NAC Breda

Dutch Professional League Record 1957–2002

SEASON	CHAMPIONS	RUNNERS-UP
1957	Ajax	Fortuna '54 Geleen
1958	DOS Utrecht	SC Enschede
1959	Sparta Rotterdam	Rapid JC Heerlen
1960	Ajax	Feyenoord
1961	Feyenoord	Ajax
1962	Feyenoord	PSV
1963	PSV	Ajax
1964	DWS Amsterdam	PSV
1965	Feyenoord	DWS Amsterdam
1966	Ajax	Feyenoord
1967	Ajax	Feyenoord
1968	Ajax	Feyenoord
1969	Feyenoord	Ajax
1970	Ajax	Feyenoord
1971	Feyenoord	Ajax
1972	Ajax	Feyenoord
1973	Ajax	Feyenoord
1974	Feyenoord	FC Twente
1975	PSV	Feyenoord
1976	PSV	Feyenoord
1977	Ajax	PSV
1978	PSV	Ajax
1979	Ajax	Feyenoord
1980	Ajax	AZ 67 Alkmaar
1981	AZ 67 Alkmaar	Ajax
1982	Ajax	PSV
1983	Ajax	Feyenoord
1984	Feyenoord	PSV
1985	Ajax	PSV
1986	PSV	Ajax
1987	PSV	Ajax
1988	PSV	Ajax
1989	PSV	Ajax
1990	Ajax	PSV
1991	PSV	Ajax
1992	PSV	Ajax
1993	Feyenoord	PSV
1994	Ajax	Feyenoord
1995	Ajax	Roda JC
1996	Ajax	PSV
1997	PSV	Feyenoord
1998	Ajax	PSV
1999	Feyenoord	Willem II
2000	PSV	SC Heerenveen
2001	PSV	Feyenoord
2002	Ajax	PSV

NETHERLANDS

Dutch League Summary

	TEAM	TOTALS	CHAMPIONS & RUNNERS-UP (BOLD) (ITALICS)
	Ajax	28, 16	**1918, 19,** *28, 30,* **31, 32, 34,** *36,* **37, 39,** *46,* **47, 57, 60, 61,** *63,* **66–68, 69, 70,** *71,* **72, 73, 77,** *78,* **79, 80, 81, 82, 83,** *85,* **86–89, 90, 91, 92, 94–96, 98, 2002**
	PSV	16, 12	*1929, 35, 41, 51,* **62, 63, 64,** *75,* **76, 77,** *78,* **82, 84, 85, 86–89, 90, 91, 92,** *93,* **96, 97, 98, 2000,** *01,* **02**
	Feyenoord	14, 19	*1924, 28, 31–33,* **36, 37, 38,** *40,* **43,** *60,* **61, 62, 65,** *66–68,* **69, 70, 71,** *72, 73, 74, 75, 76, 79,* **83,** *84,* **93, 94,** *97, 99, 2001*
	HVV Den Haag	8, 0	**1900–03, 05, 07, 10, 14**
	Sparta Rotterdam	6, 0	**1909, 11–13, 15, 59**
	Go Ahead Deventer	4, 5	*1916,* **17, 18, 19,** *22,* **29, 30,** *33,* **35**
	Willem II	3, 1	**1916,** *52,* **55,** *99*
	HBS Den Haag	3, 0	**1904, 06, 25**

This summary only features clubs that have won the Dutch League three times or more. For a full list of league champions and runners-up please see the League Records opposite.

Dutch Cup Record 1899–2002

YEAR	WINNERS	SCORE	RUNNERS-UP
1899	RAP Amsterdam	1-0 (aet)	HVV Den Haag
1900	Velocitas Breda	3-1	Ajax
1901	HBS Den Haag	4-3	RAP Amsterdam
1902	Haarlem	2-1	HBS Den Haag
1903	HVV Den Haag	6-1	HBS Den Haag
1904	HFC Haarlem	3-1	HVV Den Haag
1905	VOC Rotterdam	3-0	HBS Den Haag
1906	Concordia	3-2	Volharding
1907	VOC Rotterdam	4-3 (aet)	Voolwaarts
1908	HBS Den Haag	3-1	VOC Rotterdam
1909	Quick Den Haag	2-0	VOC Rotterdam
1910	Quick Den Haag	2-0	HVV Den Haag
1911	Quick Den Haag	1-0	Haarlem
1912	Haarlem	2-0	Vitesse Arnhem
1913	HFC Haarlem	4-1	DFC Dordrecht
1914	DFC Dordrecht	3-2	Haarlem
1915	HFC Haarlem	1-0	HBS Den Haag
1916	Quick Den Haag	2-1 (aet)	HBS Den Haag
1917	Ajax	5-0	VSV Velsen
1918	RCH Haarlem	2-1	VVA
1919		no competition	
1920	CVV	2-1	VUC Den Haag
1921	Schoten	2-1	RFC
1922–24		no competition	
1925	ZFC	5-1	Xerxes
1926	LONGA Lichtenvoorde	5-2	De Spartan
1927	VUC Den Haag	3-1	Vitesse Arnhem
1928	RCH Haarlem	2-0	PEC Zwolle
1929		no competition	
1930	Feyenoord	1-0	Excelsior
1931		no competition	
1932	DFC Dordrecht	5-4 (aet)	PSV
1933		no competition	
1934	Velocitas Groningen	3-2 (aet)	Feyenoord
1935	Feyenoord	5-2	Helmondia
1936	Roermond	4-2	KFC Alkmaar
1937	Eindhoven	1-0	De Spartan
1938	VSV Velsen	4-1	AGOVV
1939	Wageningen	2-1 (aet)	PSV
1940–42		no competition	
1943	Ajax	3-2	DFC Dordrecht
1944	Willem II	9-2	Groene Star
1945–47		no competition	
1948	Wageningen	0-0 (aet)(2-1 pens)	DWV
1949	Quick Nijmegen	1-1 (aet)(2-1 pens)	Helmondia
1950	PSV	4-3	Haarlem
1951–56		no competition	

Dutch Cup Record (continued)

YEAR	WINNERS	SCORE	RUNNERS-UP
1957	Fortuna '54 Geelen	4-2	Feyenoord
1958	Sparta Rotterdam	4-3	Volendam
1959	VVV Venlo	4-1	ADO Den Haag
1960		no competition	
1961	Ajax	3-0	NAC Breda
1962	Sparta Rotterdam	1-0 (aet)	DHC
1963	Willem II	3-0	ADO Den Haag
1964	Fortuna '54 Geelen	0-0 (aet)(4-3 pens)	ADO Den Haag
1965	Feyenoord	1-0	Go Ahead Deventer
1966	Sparta Rotterdam	1-0	ADO Den Haag
1967	Ajax	2-1 (aet)	NAC Breda
1968	ADO Den Haag	2-1	Ajax
1969	Feyenoord	1-1 (aet), (replay) 2-0	PSV
1970	Ajax	2-0	PSV
1971	Ajax	2-2 (aet), (replay) 2-1	Sparta Rotterdam
1972	Ajax	3-2	FC Den Haag
1973	NAC Breda	2-0	NEC Nijmegen
1974	PSV	6-0	NAC Breda
1975	FC Den Haag	1-0	FC Twente
1976	PSV	1-0 (aet)	Roda JC Kerkrade
1977	FC Twente	3-0 (aet)	PEC Zwolle
1978	AZ 67 Alkmaar	1-0	Ajax
1979	Ajax	1-1 (aet), (replay) 3-0	FC Twente
1980	Feyenoord	3-1	Ajax
1981	AZ 67 Alkmaar	3-1	Ajax
1982	AZ 67 Alkmaar	5-1, 0-1 (2 legs)	FC Utrecht
1983	Ajax	3-1, 3-1 (2 legs)	NEC Nijmegen
1984	Feyenoord	1-0	Fortuna Sittard
1985	FC Utrecht	1-0	Helmond Sport
1986	Ajax	3-0	RBC Roosendaal
1987	Ajax	4-2	FC Den Haag
1988	PSV	3-2	Roda JC Kerkrade
1989	PSV	4-1	FC Groningen
1990	PSV	1-0	Vitesse Arnhem
1991	Feyenoord	1-0	BVV Den Bosch
1992	Feyenoord	3-0	Roda JC Kerkrade
1993	Ajax	6-2	SC Heerenveen
1994	Feyenoord	2-1	NEC Nijmegen
1995	Feyenoord	2-1	Volendam
1996	PSV	5-2	Sparta Rotterdam
1997	Roda JC Kerkrade	4-2	SC Heerenveen
1998	Ajax	5-0	PSV
1999	Ajax	2-0	Fortuna Sittard
2000	Roda JC Kerkrade	2-0	NEC Nijmegen
2001	FC Twente	0-0 (aet)(4-3 pens)	PSV
2002	Ajax	3-2 (aet)	FC Utrecht

Dutch Cup Summary

	TEAM	TOTALS	WINNERS & RUNNERS-UP (BOLD) (ITALICS)
	Ajax	15, 5	*1900,* **17, 43, 61, 67,** *68,* **70–72,** *78, 79,* **80,** *81,* **83, 86, 87, 93, 98, 99, 2002**
	Feyenoord	10, 2	**1930,** *34,* **35,** *57,* **65, 69, 80, 84, 91, 92, 94, 95**
	PSV	7, 6	*1932, 39,* **50,** *69, 70,* **74,** *76,* **88-90,** *96, 98,* **2001**
	Quick Den Haag	4, 0	**1909–11, 16**
	Sparta Rotterdam	3, 2	**1958, 62, 66,** *71, 96*
	AZ 67 Alkmaar	3, 0	**1978, 81, 82**
	HFC Haarlem	3, 0	**1904, 13, 15**

This summary only features clubs that have won the Dutch Cup three times or more. For a full list of cup winners and runners-up please see the Cup Record above.

Germany

THE SEASON IN REVIEW 2001–02

WITH THE HOSTING OF THE 2006 WORLD CUP in the bag and a World Cup Finals place for 2002 secured after a play-off victory against Ukraine, German football appeared to be flourishing in autumn 2001. In the event, the Bundesliga campaign was close-fought, well-attended and engaging. In European competition, Bayern München was unable to repeat its sensational form in the previous year's Champions League, but Bayer Leverkusen and Borussia Dortmund went all the way in the Champions League and UEFA Cup, though both were to be disappointed in the end. However, the collapse of the Kirch media empire in spring 2002 may spoil the party yet. Kirch, owners of the Bundesliga and World Cup TV rights, disappeared under the weight of nearly £6 billion debts including £600 million to the Bundesliga. The entire second division and over half the first are consequently threatened with imminent bankruptcy. German political parties have offered a loan rescue package for the hardest hit clubs, but clearly a steep decline in players' wages and transfer fees is on the way.

Among the elite of German football, the pain will be easier to bear. A number of clubs have spun off their commercial arms this year and are attracting outside investment (like the £60 million Adidas spent for a 10 per cent stake in Bayern München). Still flush from its partial stock market flotation, Borussia Dortmund gave Matthias Sammer over £30 million to play with; in came Brazilian Amoroso from Parma and Jan Koller

Right: With little to celebrate Wolfsburg players enjoy their win over Kaiserslautern.

Below centre: Marc Wilmots of Schalke passes through Hertha Berlin's defence of Andreas Schmidt and Rob Maas.

Bottom: Borussia Dortmund's Jan Koller tangles with FC Nürnberg's Tomasz Kos.

Bundesliga Table 2001–02

CLUB	P	W	D	L	F	A	Pts	
Borussia Dortmund	34	21	7	6	62	33	70	Champions League
Bayer Leverkusen	34	21	6	7	77	38	69	Champions League
Bayern München	34	20	8	6	65	25	68	Champions League
Hertha BSC Berlin	34	18	7	9	61	38	61	UEFA Cup
FC Schalke 04	34	18	7	9	52	36	61	UEFA Cup (cup winners)
Werder Bremen	34	17	5	12	54	43	56	UEFA Cup
Kaiserslautern	34	17	5	12	62	53	56	
Vfb Stuttgart	34	13	11	10	47	43	50	
TSV 1860 München	34	15	5	14	59	59	50	
Vfl Wolfsburg	34	12	7	14	57	49	46	
Hamburger SV	34	10	10	14	51	57	40	
Borussia Mönchengladbach	34	9	12	13	41	53	39	
Energie Cottbus	34	9	8	17	36	60	35	
Hansa Rostock	34	9	7	18	35	54	34	
FC Nürnberg	34	10	4	20	34	57	34	
SC Freiburg	34	7	9	18	37	64	30	Relegated
1. FC Köln	34	7	8	19	26	61	29	Relegated
St. Pauli	34	4	10	20	37	70	22	Relegated

Promoted clubs: Hannover 96, Armenia Biefeld, Vfl Bochum.

Bundesliga Top Goalscorers 2001–02

PLAYER	CLUB	NATIONALITY	GOALS
Marcio Amoroso	Borussia Dortmund	Brazilian	18
Martin Max	TSV 1860 München	German	18
Michael Ballack	Bayer Leverkusen	German	17
Giovane Elber	Bayern München	Brazilian	17
Goncalves Ailton	Werder Bremen	Brazilian	16

GERMANY

Bayern München's Roque Santa Cruz holds off Viktor Skripnik of Werder Bremen.

WORLD FOOTBALL YEARBOOK: THE UEFA NATIONS

GERMANY

from Anderlecht, adding to the tight defence he created last season. At Bayern, an injection of Champions League cash allowed Ottmar Hitzfeld to bring in Peruvian Claudio Pizarro and Roque Santa Cruz from Paraguay. Bayer Leverkusen spent less but, after three coaches in a year last season, acquired managerial stability when Klaus Toppmöller was put in charge.

The early pacesetters in the Bundesliga were Kaiserslautern, who had started well in 2001 only to disintegrate towards the end of the season. This year the end came even sooner than that. After winning its first seven games it lost its eighth to bottom-of-the-table Wolfsburg, and never looked in contention again. By Christmas, Bayer Leverkusen and Borussia Dortmund were tied at the top, with Werder Bremen, Kaiserslautern and, astonishingly, Bayern München in the chasing pack, five points off the lead.

Dortmund's title

In the spring as Kaiserslautern fell away, Bremen's challenge also proved insufficient, and Hertha Berlin and Schalke 04 improved to challenge for the UEFA Cup spots. The relegation battle was between Köln, Energie Cottbus, Freiburg, Nürnberg and St. Pauli. At the top, the title race lay between Leverkusen, who held its lead through the spring, Dortmund and Bayern. For Leverkusen, playmaker Michael Ballack and Turkish striker Yildiray Basturk made them dangerous and free scoring. But on the penultimate weekend, returning from a gruelling draw at Old Trafford in the Champions League semi-final, Bayer Leverkusen lost 1-0 to struggling Nürnberg. As a result, Nürnburg secured its top-flight status while Freiburg went down with Köln and St. Pauli. Dortmund took its chance and beat Hamburg 4-3 to go top, while Bayern München stayed in touch beating Wolfsburg.

For the third year in a row, the title race went to the last day. Bayern's Hitzfeld crowed 'We've shown we can stand the pressure, while Leverkusen has already lost its nerve'. But for Bayern bragging was not enough and, despite beating Hansa Rostock on the final day, it had to settle for third. Leverkusen beat Hertha, and for a while looked like it might redeem themselves, but Dortmund showed class and character to come from behind against Bremen, winning 2-1 and taking the title.

Agony for Leverkusen

More disappointment followed for Leverkusen in the Cup Final against Schalke. Despite taking a first-half lead, the teams went in level at the break. During the second half, Schalke scored three more goals and Leverkusen's last minute strike was no consolation and it lost 4-2. Its disappointment continued when it lost the Champions League Final 2-1 to Real Madrid in Glasgow. However, there is no doubting the achievements of Klaus Toppmöller's team, who deserved better than to come so close in three competitions only to finish with no trophy at all.

Above: The Borussia Dortmund team celebrates with the trophy after winning the league championship.

Right: Hertha Berlin's Michael Hartmann rises above Yasser Radwa of Hansa Rostock, in a year when Hertha's late form began to deliver on the cost and promise of the squad.

International Club Performances 2001–02

CLUB	COMPETITION	PROGRESS
Borussia Dortmund	Champions League	1st Group Phase
	UEFA Cup	Runners-up
Bayer Leverkusen	Champions League	Runners-up
Bayern München	Champions League	Quarter-finals
FC Schalke 04	Champions League	1st Group Phase
Hertha BSC Berlin	UEFA Cup	3rd Round
SC Freiburg	UEFA Cup	3rd Round
1. FC Union	UEFA Cup	2nd Round

German Cup

2002 FINAL

May 11 – Olympiastadion, Berlin
FC Schalke 04 **4-2** Bayer
(Böhme 45,   Leverkusen
Agali 68,   (Berbatov 27,
Möller 71,   Kirsten 89)
Sand 84)

h/t: 1-1 Att: 70,000
Ref: Wack

Top: *Marcio Amoroso's goals helped Borussia Dortmund to the Bundesliga title and to the UEFA Cup Final. He finished as joint top scorer in the Bundesliga with 18 goals.*

Above: *Mr Football, Klaus Toppmöller, Bayer Leverkusen coach. Despite being runners-up in three major competitions this season, his enthusiasm and spirit remains undiminished. He said, 'Some people have red and white blood cells in them. I have little red and white footballs.'*

Left: *Yildiray Basturk, Bayer Leverkusen's Turkish midfielder was a major source of inspiration and running in Leverkusen's season.*

GERMANY

Association Football in Germany

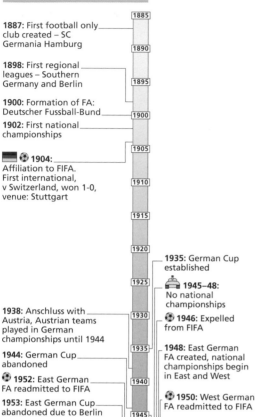

1887: First football only club created – SC Germania Hamburg

1898: First regional leagues – Southern Germany and Berlin

1900: Formation of FA: Deutscher Fussball-Bund

1902: First national championships

1904: Affiliation to FIFA. First international, v Switzerland, won 1-0, venue: Stuttgart

1935: German Cup established

1938: Anschluss with Austria, Austrian teams played in German championships until 1944

1944: German Cup abandoned

1945–48: No national championships

1946: Expelled from FIFA

1948: East German FA created, national championships begin in East and West

1950: West German FA readmitted to FIFA

1952: East German FA readmitted to FIFA

1953: East German Cup abandoned due to Berlin uprising. West German Cup re-established

1954: East and West German affiliation to UEFA

1955: DFB bans affiliated clubs from letting women use their grounds. West German Women's Football Association founded in Essen

1956: First women's international, v Netherlands, won 2-1, venue: Essen

1961: East German Cup and League abandoned. Berlin wall erected

1963: West German Bundesliga established

1970: DFB ban on women at affiliated clubs lifted

1990: East German FA dissolved into all German FA, two Bundesliga places only for eastern teams

Timeline years: 1885, 1890, 1895, 1900, 1905, 1910, 1915, 1920, 1925, 1930, 1935, 1940, 1945, 1950, 1955, 1960, 1965, 1970, 1975, 1980, 1985, 1990, 1995, 2000, 2005

Key

- International football
- Affiliation to FIFA
- Affiliation to UEFA
- Women's football
- War
- ■ World Cup host
- ● World Cup winner
- ▲ World Cup runner-up
- ▣ European Championships host
- ◉ European Championships winner
- ◬ European Championships runner-up
- ○ Competition winner
- △ Competition runner-up

BayL – Bayer Leverkusen
BayM – Bayern München
BorD – Borussia Dortmund
BorM – Borussia Mönchengladbach
Carl – Carl Zeiss Jena
Ein – Eintracht Frankfurt
For – Fortuna Düsseldorf
Ham – Hamburger SV
Köln – 1.FC Köln
Loko – Lokomotive Leipzig
Mag – FC Magdeburg
Schl – FC Schalke 04
TSV – TSV 1860 München
Vfb – Vfb Stuttgart
Wer – Werder Bremen

International Competitions

Year	International	European Cup	UEFA Cup	European Cup-Winners' Cup
1954:	●			
1960:		△ Ein		
1965:	▲			
1966:				○ BorD
1967:				○ BayM
1968:				△ Ham
1972:	◉			
1973:			△ BorM	
1974:	● ■	○ BayM		○ Mag
1975:		○ BayM	○ BorM	
1976:	▲	○ BayM		
1977:		△ BorM		○ Ham
1979:			○ BorM	△ For
1980:	◉	△ Ham	○ Ein	△ BorM
1981:				△ Carl
1982:	▲	△ BayM	△ Ham	
1983:		○ Ham		
1986:	▲		△ Köln	
1987:		△ BayM		△ Loko
1988:	▣		○ BayL	
1989:			△ Vfb	
1990:	●			
1992:	◬			○ Wer
1993:			△ BorD	
1996:	◉		○ BayM	
1997:		○ BorD	○ Schl	
1998:				△ Vfb
1999:		△ BayM		
2001:		○ BayM		
2002:		△ BayL	○ BorD	

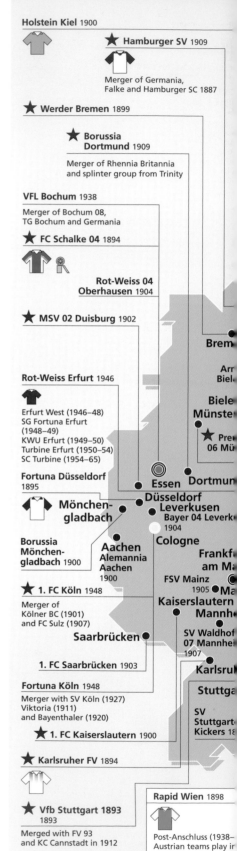

Holstein Kiel 1900

Hamburger SV 1909
Merger of Germania, Falke and Hamburger SC 1887

Werder Bremen 1899

Borussia Dortmund 1909
Merger of Rhennia Britannia and splinter group from Trinity

VFL Bochum 1938
Merger of Bochum 08, TG Bochum and Germania

FC Schalke 04 1894

Rot-Weiss 04 Oberhausen 1904

MSV 02 Duisburg 1902

Rot-Weiss Erfurt 1946
Erfurt West (1946–48)
SG Fortuna Erfurt (1948–49)
KWU Erfurt (1949–50)
Turbine Erfurt (1950–54)
SC Turbine (1954–65)

Fortuna Düsseldorf 1895

Mönchengladbach

Borussia Mönchengladbach 1900

1. FC Köln 1948
Merger of Kölner BC (1901) and FC Sulz (1907)

1. FC Saarbrücken 1903

Fortuna Köln 1948
Merger with SV Köln (1927) Viktoria (1911) and Bayenthaler (1920)

1. FC Kaiserslautern 1900

Karlsruher FV 1894

Vfb Stuttgart 1893 1893
Merged with FV 93 and KC Cannstadt in 1912

Saarbrücken

Essen Dortmun...

Düsseldorf
Aachen Leverkusen
Bayer 04 Leverk...
1904

Aachen Alemannia Aachen 1900

Cologne

Frankf... am Ma...

FSV Mainz 1905 Ma...

Kaiserslautern

Mannhe...

SV Waldhof 07 Mannhe... 1907

Karlsru...

Stuttga...

SV Stuttgart Kickers 18...

Brem...

Arr... Biel...

Biele... Münster

Prem... 06 Mü...

Rapid Wien 1898
Post-Anschluss (1938–...
Austrian teams play in... German championship...

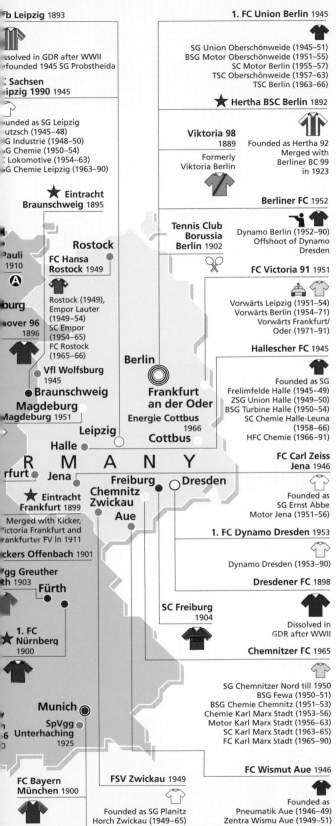

b Leipzig 1893

ssolved in GDR after WWII
founded 1945 SG Probstheida

Sachsen
eipzig 1990 1945

unded as SG Leipzig
utzsch (1945–48)
G Industrie (1948–50)
Chemie (1950–54)
Lokomotive (1954–63)
Chemie Leipzig (1963–90)

★ Eintracht
Braunschweig 1895

Pauli
1910
Ⓐ

urg

over 96
1896

Vfl Wolfsburg
1945

● Braunschweig
Magdeburg
Magdeburg 1951

Leipzig

Halle

R M A N Y

rfurt Jena

Freiburg
Chemnitz
Zwickau
Aue

★ Eintracht
Frankfurt 1899

Merged with Kicker,
ictoria Frankfurt and
rankfurter FV In 1911

ckers Offenbach 1901

gg Greuther
th 1903
Fürth

1. FC
★ Nürnberg
1900

Munich ◎

SpVgg
Unterhaching
1925

FC Bayern
München 1900

★ TSV 1860
München 1900

Rostock
FC Hansa
Rostock 1949

Rostock (1949),
Empor Lauter
(1949–54)
SC Empor
(1954–65)
FC Rostock
(1965–66)

Berlin

Frankfurt
an der Oder

Energie Cottbus
1966
Cottbus

Dresden
●

1. FC Union Berlin 1945

SG Union Oberschönweide (1945–51)
BSG Motor Oberschönweide (1951–55)
SC Motor Berlin (1955–57)
TSC Oberschönweide (1957–63)
TSC Berlin (1963–66)

★ Hertha BSC Berlin 1892

Viktoria 98
1889

Formerly
Viktoria Berlin

Founded as Hertha 92
Merged with
Berliner BC 99
in 1923

Berliner FC 1952

Tennis Club
Borussia
Berlin 1902

Dynamo Berlin (1952–90)
Offshoot of Dynamo
Dresden

FC Victoria 91 1951

Vorwärts Leipzig (1951–54)
Vorwärts Berlin (1954–71)
Vorwärts Frankfurt/
Oder (1971–91)

Hallescher FC 1945

Founded as SG
Frelimfelde Halle (1945–49)
ZSG Union Halle (1949–50)
BSG Turbine Halle (1950–54)
SC Chemie Halle-Leuna
(1958–66)
HFC Chemie (1966–91)

FC Carl Zeiss
Jena 1946

Founded as
SG Ernst Abbe
Motor Jena (1951–56)

1. FC Dynamo Dresden 1953

Dynamo Dresden (1953–90)

Dresdener FC 1898

SC Freiburg
1904

Dissolved in
GDR after WWII

Chemnitzer FC 1965

SG Chemnitzer Nord till 1950
BSG Fewa (1950–51)
BSG Chemie Chemnitz (1951–53)
Chemie Karl Marx Stadt (1953–56)
Motor Karl Marx Stadt (1956–63)
SC Karl Marx Stadt (1963–65)
FC Karl Marx Stadt (1965–90)

FC Wismut Aue 1946

Founded as
Pneumatik Aue (1946–49)
Zentra Wismu Aue (1949–51)
Wismut Aue (1951–54)
Wismut Karl Marx Stadt (1954–63)
BSG Wismut Aue (1963–90)

FSV Zwickau 1949

Founded as SG Planitz
Horch Zwickau (1949–65)
Motor Zwickau (1950–67)
BSG Sachenring
Zwickau (1967–90)

Germany

ORIGINS AND GROWTH OF FOOTBALL

DESPITE AN EARLY START, football was a late developer in Germany. In the early 1870s, English students and traders played the game in Berlin and the northern ports. Oxford University toured in 1875 and the country's first club, SC Germania Hamburg, was founded in 1887. However, football faced considerable athletic and political opposition. It was viewed by German nationalists as a foreign import and a threat to *Turnen*, the Prussian tradition of individual athleticism. It was excluded from Prussian schools and the armed forces and was socially frowned upon by both Protestant and Catholic church leaders.

White-collar success

Despite the foundation of a national FA in 1900, football remained a predominantly lower middle-class amateur game. However, the game found favour with the white-collar population of Germany's new cities. For them it was a perfect vehicle for social mixing, and they adopted the game with enthusiasm. By 1911, the army lifted its ban on the game and it became a huge element of life in the armed forces during the First World War. In the postwar era crowds and players became progressively more working class. This phenomenon culminated in 1934, when a miners' team from the Rühr – Schalke 04 – won the championship.

The Nazi takeover saw the collapse of semi-professionalism and a dismal performance on the international stage. After the war, in 1946, Germany was excluded from FIFA. Partition followed and both West and East Germany rejoined FIFA separately in 1950 and 1952. In East Germany, football remained a relatively minor sport carved up among state agencies, but West German football bloomed. An extraordinary victory in the 1954 World Cup against the unbeatable Hungarians encouraged the gradual introduction of professionalism and the eventual establishment of a national league – the Bundesliga – in 1963.

The world stage

Since then, Germany at all levels has remained a major player on the world football scene, with regular victories at both club and international level. Reunification in 1991 saw a merger of East and West German football, but East German teams were only given two places in the top division.

Germany: The main clubs

St Pauli 1910	Team name with year of formation	Pre-war champions
●	Club formed before 1912	East German champions
●	Club formed 1912–25	
●	Club formed 1925–50	Originated from East German army
	Club formed after 1950	
	Former East Germany	Ⓐ Associated with anarchists
	Former West Germany	Associated with the Stasi
★	Founder members of Bundesliga (1963)	Mining origins
		Originated from a tennis club

GERMANY

The Ruhr

FOOTBALL CITIES

GERMANY

GERMAN INDUSTRIALIZATION and German football were both late developers which rose to world-class status towards the end of the 20th century. The heartland of both is the Ruhr valley in the north-west of the country. The connections are intimate: FC Schalke grew out of a mining community with Polish immigrant roots; Borussia Dortmund remains actively involved in the struggles of the region's steelworkers; Bayer Leverkusen has been owned and run by the chemical giant Bayer since its foundation in 1904. A hundred years later, the post-industrial economy of the Ruhr is churning out vast new stadiums and arenas all over the area.

Changing balance of power

The region's earliest footballing power lay in the north: in Essen, Bochum, Duisburg and Dortmund. Strong traditions were given a practical boost with the fusion in 1924 of two small teams, FC Westfalia 04 and TV 1877 Schalke, to create FC Schalke 04. The footballing authority's strict insistence on amateur regulations were used to exclude Schalke and its squad (made up of miners) from competition, but the team forced its way into the national championships, winning six titles in the 1930s and 40s. The postwar era was altogether harder for the club, and it was only in the 1990s that Schalke started to fill the Parkstadion and challenge for the country's major honours.

Borussia Dortmund was formed from the fusion in 1909 of three clubs: Trinity, Rhenania and Britannia. The club remained in the shadow of Schalke until its first national championship triumph in 1956. However, no dynasty was established, and only the shock of a play-off for relegation in 1986 raised the club from its torpor. A decade of canny commercialism and long-term growth peaked in 1997 when Ottmar Hitzfeld's team took the European Cup. A public flotation soon followed.

To the south of the region, Mönchengladbach, a small industrial town, produced the surprise package of the 1970s, when Borussia became a force both at home and in Europe. Cologne's teams were born from the bombed-out wreckage of the city in the 1940s, when small teams were amalgamated to create two sustainable clubs: 1. FC Köln was formed from KBC and Sülz 07, while its poorer neighbour Fortuna Köln was raised from the ashes of Bayernthaler and SV Köln.

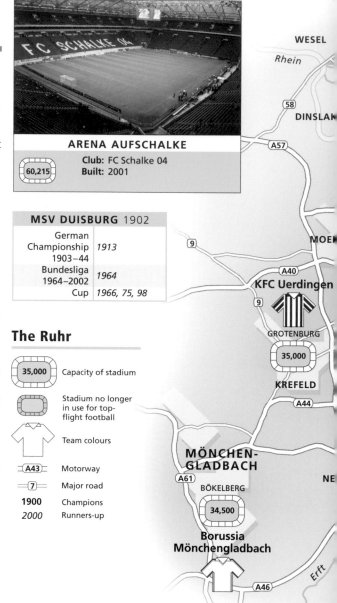

ARENA AUFSCHALKE

60,215 | **Club:** FC Schalke 04
Built: 2001

MSV DUISBURG 1902	
German Championship 1903–44	1913
Bundesliga 1964–2002	1964
Cup	1966, 75, 98

The Ruhr

35,000	Capacity of stadium
	Stadium no longer in use for top-flight football
	Team colours
A43	Motorway
7	Major road
1900	Champions
2000	Runners-up

WESEL
Rhein
58
DINSLAK
A57
9
MOE
A40
KFC Uerdingen
9
GROTENBURG
35,000
KREFELD
A44
MÖNCHEN-GLADBACH
A61
NE
BÖKELBERG
34,500
Borussia Mönchengladbach
Erft
A46

BORUSSIA MÖNCHENGLADBACH 1900	
Bundesliga 1964–2002	**1970, 71,** *74,* **75–77,** *78*
Cup	**1960, 73,** *84, 92,* **95**
European Cup	*1977*
UEFA Cup	*1973,* **75, 79,** *80*
World Club Cup	*1977*

FORTUNA KÖLN 1948	
Cup	*1983*

The Bayer Chemical Works: the German Parliament passed a special law, the 'Lex Leverkusen', allowing Bayer to retain 100 per cent ownership of Bayer Leverkusen.

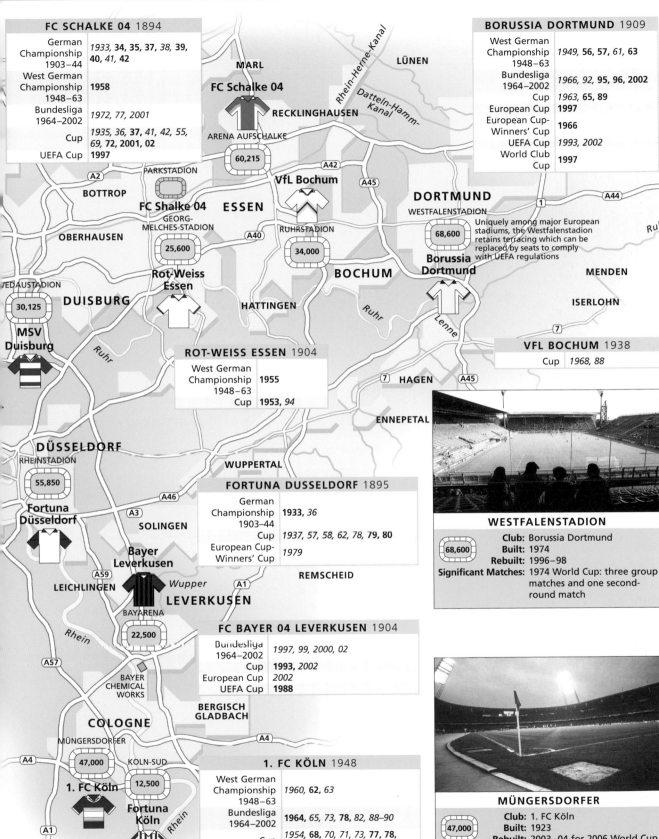

FC SCHALKE 04 1894

German Championship 1903–44	*1933*, **34, 35, 37, 38,** *39,* **40, 41, 42**
West German Championship 1948–63	**1958**
Bundesliga 1964–2002	*1972, 77, 2001*
Cup	*1935, 36,* **37,** *41, 42, 55,* **69, 72, 2001, 02**
UEFA Cup	**1997**

BORUSSIA DORTMUND 1909

West German Championship 1948–63	*1949,* **56, 57,** *61,* **63**
Bundesliga 1964–2002	*1966,* **92, 95, 96, 2002**
Cup	*1963,* **65, 89**
European Cup	**1997**
European Cup-Winners' Cup	**1966**
UEFA Cup	*1993, 2002*
World Club Cup	**1997**

MARL

LÜNEN

RECKLINGHAUSEN

FC Schalke 04

ARENA AUFSCHALKE

60,215

Rhein-Herne-Kanal

Datteln-Hamm-Kanal

A42

A45

A2

PARKSTADION

BOTTROP

FC Shalke 04

GEORG-MELCHES-STADION

25,600

ESSEN

VfL Bochum

RUHRSTADION

34,000

DORTMUND

WESTFALENSTADION

68,600

Borussia Dortmund

Uniquely among major European stadiums, the Westfalenstadion retains terracing which can be replaced by seats to comply with UEFA regulations

A44

Ruhr

A40

OBERHAUSEN

Rot-Weiss Essen

BOCHUM

MENDEN

ISERLOHN

...DAUSTADION

30,125

DUISBURG

MSV Duisburg

HATTINGEN

Ruhr

Ruhr

Lenne

7

ROT-WEISS ESSEN 1904

| West German Championship 1948–63 | **1955** |
| Cup | **1953,** *94* |

7 HAGEN

A45

ENNEPETAL

VFL BOCHUM 1938

| Cup | *1968, 88* |

WESTFALENSTADION

68,600

Club: Borussia Dortmund
Built: 1974
Rebuilt: 1996–98
Significant Matches: 1974 World Cup: three group matches and one second-round match

DÜSSELDORF

RHEINSTADION

55,850

Fortuna Düsseldorf

WUPPERTAL

A46

FORTUNA DUSSELDORF 1895

German Championship 1903–44	**1933,** *36*
Cup	*1937, 57, 58, 62, 78,* **79, 80**
European Cup-Winners' Cup	*1979*

A3 SOLINGEN

Bayer Leverkusen

A59

LEICHLINGEN

Wupper

A1

LEVERKUSEN

REMSCHEID

BAYARENA

22,500

FC BAYER 04 LEVERKUSEN 1904

Bundesliga 1964–2002	*1997, 99, 2000, 02*
Cup	**1993,** *2002*
European Cup	*2002*
UEFA Cup	**1988**

Rhein

A57

BAYER CHEMICAL WORKS

BERGISCH GLADBACH

COLOGNE

MÜNGERSDORFER

A4

47,000

KOLN-SUD

12,500

1. FC Köln

Fortuna Köln

A1

Rhein

1. FC KÖLN 1948

West German Championship 1948–63	*1960,* **62,** *63*
Bundesliga 1964–2002	**1964,** *65, 73,* **78,** *82,* **88–90**
Cup	*1954,* **68,** *70, 71, 73,* **77, 78,** *80,* **83,** *91*
UEFA Cup	*1986*

MÜNGERSDORFER

47,000

Club: 1. FC Köln
Built: 1923
Rebuilt: 2003–04 for 2006 World Cup (capacity 50,000)

GERMANY

Munich

FOOTBALL CITY

IN THE EARLY 20TH CENTURY, Bavaria was a German byword for inept conservatism and peasant values, and Munich was its antiquated capital. In the 21st century, the city has become the new hub of German industrial and commercial success, and in Bayern München, it has the team that has dominated German football for a quarter of a century. Bayern was born in the working-class Schwabing district of the city in 1900, and was bold enough to win a national championship title in 1932. But its provincial obscurity was such that when the professional Bundesliga was formed in 1963, the club chosen to represent Munich was its rival TSV 1860 München. TSV was founded in the south of the city as a gymnastics club that later took up football. Its early inclusion in professional football seemed justified when it won the cup in 1964 and then the league two years later, but a steady decline saw the team lose its licence in 1981 and it only returned to the top flight a decade later. Even further down the footballing ladder is SpVgg Unterhaching on the southern edge of the city – this relative newcomer made it to the Bundesliga in 1999.

Bayern rise to the top

Despite the snub from the Bundesliga, Bayern went professional anyway and gained quick promotion, successive cup victories and then the 1967 European Cup-Winners' Cup. The team now emerging around Sepp Maier, Franz Beckenbauer and Gerd Müller would eventually win three European Cups and sustain a decade of unbroken dominance in German football. In the 1990s, under Beckenbauer, Trapattoni and Hitzfeld, Bayern has returned to the very top of European football. In 1972 Bayern moved to the Olympiastadion and TSV joined the team, having abandoned its old Grunwalderstrasse stadium on its return to the top flight. While Bayern fills the stadium with fans from all across Germany, TSV's defiantly local supporters leave it almost two-thirds empty. Both are due to move to the new Allianz Arena in the city's northern suburbs, which will open in time to host the World Cup Finals tournament in 2006.

GERMANY

OLIMPIASTADION

69,000

Clubs: Bayern München, TSV 1860 München
Built: 1972
Significant Matches: 1974 World Cup: five matches including 3rd place play-off, Final; 1972 Munich Olympics: Final; 1988 European Championships: Final; European Cup Final: 1979, 93

Munich

69,000	Capacity of stadium
	Stadium no longer in use for top-flight football
	Team colours
	Amateur teams
M54	Motorway
8	Major road
1900	Champions
2000	Runners-up

Traditionally the home of such events as the world-famous beer festival, recent years have seen Munich rise in prosperity and wealth. This is mirrored by the rise to prominence of the city's major football team, Bayern München.

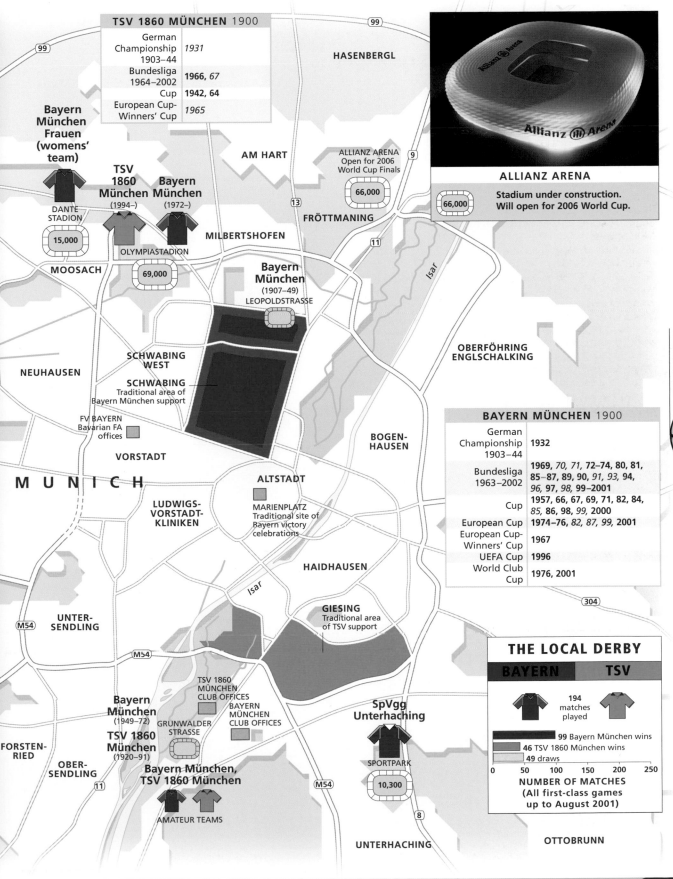

GERMANY

TSV 1860 MÜNCHEN 1900

German Championship 1903–44	*1931*
Bundesliga 1964–2002	**1966**, *67*
Cup	**1942, 64**
European Cup-Winners' Cup	*1965*

Bayern München Frauen (womens' team)
DANTE STADION
15,000

TSV 1860 München (1994–)

Bayern München (1972–)
OLYMPIASTADION
69,000

MOOSACH

HASENBERGL

AM HART

MILBERTSHOFEN

ALLIANZ ARENA Open for 2006 World Cup Finals
66,000

FRÖTTMANING

ALLIANZ ARENA
66,000
Stadium under construction. Will open for 2006 World Cup.

Bayern München (1907–49) LEOPOLDSTRASSE

NEUHAUSEN

SCHWABING WEST

SCHWABING Traditional area of Bayern München support

OBERFÖHRING ENGLSCHALKING

FV BAYERN Bavarian FA offices

VORSTADT

BOGEN-HAUSEN

M U N I C H

LUDWIGS-VORSTADT-KLINIKEN

ALTSTADT

MARIENPLATZ Traditional site of Bayern victory celebrations

BAYERN MÜNCHEN 1900

German Championship 1903–44	**1932**
Bundesliga 1963–2002	**1969**, *70, 71,* **72–74, 80, 81, 85–87, 89, 90,** *91,* **93,** *94, 96,* **97,** *98,* **99–2001**
Cup	**1957, 66, 67, 69, 71, 82, 84, 85,** *86,* **98,** *99,* **2000**
European Cup	**1974–76,** *82, 87, 99,* **2001**
European Cup-Winners' Cup	**1967**
UEFA Cup	**1996**
World Club Cup	**1976, 2001**

HAIDHAUSEN

M54

UNTER-SENDLING

M54

GIESING Traditional area of TSV support

304

THE LOCAL DERBY

BAYERN	TSV

194 matches played

99 Bayern München wins
46 TSV 1860 München wins
49 draws

0   50   100   150   200   250

NUMBER OF MATCHES (All first-class games up to August 2001)

Bayern München (1949–72) GRUNWALDER STRASSE

TSV 1860 München (1920–91)

TSV 1860 MÜNCHEN CLUB OFFICES

BAYERN MÜNCHEN CLUB OFFICES

SpVgg Unterhaching
SPORTPARK
10,300

FORSTEN-RIED

OBER-SENDLING

11

Bayern München, TSV 1860 München
AMATEUR TEAMS

M54

8

UNTERHACHING

OTTOBRUNN

99

99

13

11

Isar

Isar

Berlin

FOOTBALL CITY

BERLIN TOOK TO FOOTBALL more quickly than much of Germany, and produced early national champions like Viktoria Berlin (which still survives as amateur outfit Viktoria 98). But the city did not create a team of sufficient size and working-class popularity until Hertha 92 and Berliner BC 99 combined in 1923 to create Hertha Berlin. Runners-up for four consecutive years in the national championships, Hertha finally took the prize in 1930 and 31. But the winning streak was soon over and the club languished throughout the Nazi era and in the divided, isolated West Berlin of the postwar era. With the erection of the Berlin Wall in 1961, the club was severed from its supporters in the East and the move to the Olympiastadion saw its old fans in Wedding drift away. Berlin's post-unification boom has seen money and sponsors flow in, but fans and trophies are thinner on the ground. West Berlin's other teams to have made the Bundesliga have all fared poorly, though the city's new immigrant communities are making their mark in the lower leagues with clubs like Croatia Berlin and Türkiyemspor Berlin.

Decline in the East

In the East, Vorwärts Berlin, the East German army club, moved into the city from Leipzig, where the immediate postwar team had played. But in the internal struggles of the East German state, Vorwärts and the army lost out. The team was expelled to Frankfurt-an-der-Oder in 1971, where it has declined and now plays in amateur leagues. In its place, and in its now empty stadium, rose Dynamo Berlin, a team staffed, supported and funded by the *Stasi* – the East German secret police. Two decades of bizarre and biased decisions and questionable triumphs followed. As for the rest of the East Berlin teams, 1. FC Union was the people's team of choice and its loyal fan base has seen it survive the post-unification collapse of East German institutions, especially in a glorious Cup run in 2000. Dynamo by contrast has, like its masters, changed its name to Berliner FC, and sunk into grim suburban, lower-league obscurity at the bleak Sportpark Forum.

OLYMPIASTADION

76,243

Clubs: Blau-Weiss 90, Hertha BSC Berlin, Tasmania Berlin
Built: 1936
Rebuilt: 1974
Record Attendance: 88,075 Hertha BSC Berlin v 1. FC Köln, Bundesliga, 26 Sep 1969
Significant Matches: 1936 Berlin Olympics; 1974 World Cup: three group matches; German Cup Final 1992–2001

FALKENSEE

Blau-Weiss 90

Hertha BSC Berlin (1971–)

Tasmania Berlin

5   SPANDAU   OLYMPIASTADION   76,243

HERTHA BSC BERLIN 1892

German Championship 1903–44	*1926–29, 30, 31*
Bundesliga 1964–2002	*1975*
Cup	*1977, 79, 93*

HENNIGSDOR

Havel

Tegel See

KLADOW   Havel   A115

ZEHLENDORF

TELTOW

POTSDAM   A115

Nuthe

The building of the Berlin Wall in 1961 separated Hertha Berlin from many of its fans. Legend has it that many of them assembled by the wall on match days to hear the roar of the crowd.

GERMANY

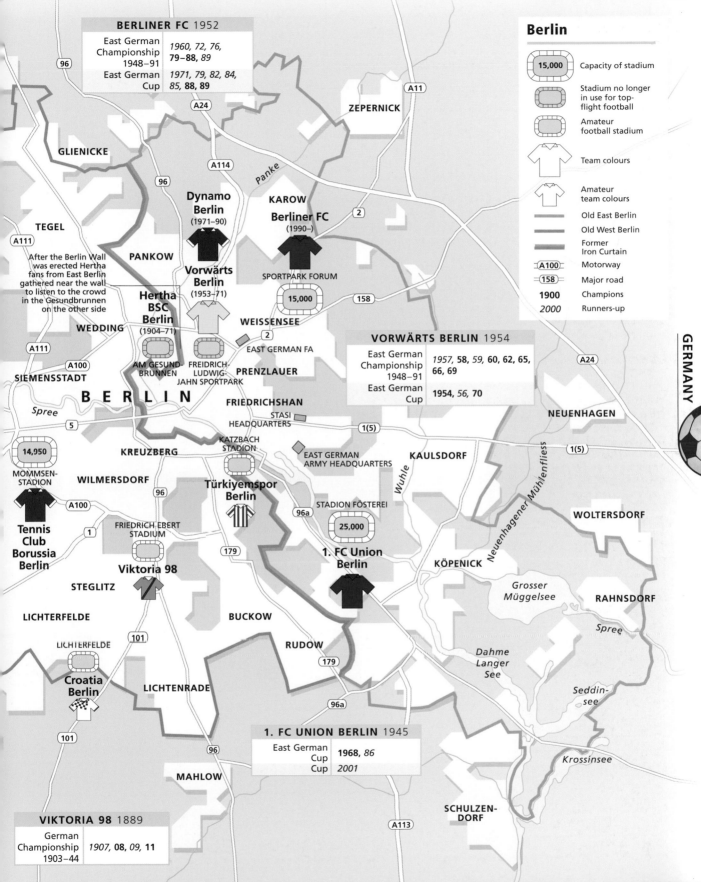

BERLINER FC 1952

East German Championship 1948–91	*1960, 72, 76,* **79–88,** *89*
East German Cup	*1971, 79, 82, 84, 85,* **88,** *89*

Berlin

15,000	Capacity of stadium
	Stadium no longer in use for top-flight football
	Amateur football stadium
	Team colours
	Amateur team colours
	Old East Berlin
	Old West Berlin
	Former Iron Curtain
A100	Motorway
158	Major road
1900	Champions
2000	Runners-up

96

A11

ZEPERNICK

A24

A114

GLIENICKE

Panke

96

KAROW

Dynamo Berlin
(1971–90)

Berliner FC
(1990–)

2

TEGEL

A111

PANKOW

After the Berlin Wall was erected Hertha fans from East Berlin gathered near the wall to listen to the crowd in the Gesundbrunnen on the other side

Vorwärts Berlin
(1953–71)

SPORTPARK FORUM

Hertha BSC Berlin
(1904–71)

WEDDING

AM GESUND-BRUNNEN

FRIEDRICH-LUDWIG-JAHN SPORTPARK

15,000

158

WEISSENSEE

2

EAST GERMAN FA

A111

A100

SIEMENSSTADT

B E R L I N

PRENZLAUER

VORWÄRTS BERLIN 1954

East German Championship 1948–91	*1957,* **58,** *59,* **60,** *62,* **65, 66,** *69*
East German Cup	**1954,** *56,* **70**

A24

Spree

5

FRIEDRICHSHAN

STASI HEADQUARTERS

1(5)

NEUENHAGEN

14,950

MOMMSEN-STADION

KREUZBERG

KATZBACH STADION

EAST GERMAN ARMY HEADQUARTERS

KAULSDORF

1(5)

Neuenhagener Mühlenfliess

WILMERSDORF

Türkiyemspor Berlin

Wuhle

96

A100

96a

STADION FÖSTEREI

WOLTERSDORF

Tennis Club Borussia Berlin

1

FRIEDRICH EBERT STADIUM

25,000

KÖPENICK

RAHNSDORF

STEGLITZ

Viktoria 98

179

1. FC Union Berlin

Grosser Müggelsee

Spree

LICHTERFELDE

BUCKOW

Dahme Langer See

LICHTERFELDE

101

RUDOW

179

Seddin-see

Croatia Berlin

LICHTENRADE

96a

Krossinsee

101

96

MAHLOW

1. FC UNION BERLIN 1945

East German Cup	**1968,** *86*
Cup	*2001*

SCHULZEN-DORF

A113

VIKTORIA 98 1889

German Championship 1903–44	*1907,* **08,** *09,* **11**

GERMANY

Germany

FANS AND OWNERS

GERMANY

THE LEGAL STRUCTURE OF GERMAN CLUBS has been very tightly regulated, leaving control with the elected boards of sports and social clubs. Although German sides have appeared to prosper on smaller turnovers than the giants of Italy, Spain and England, the economic limits of this kind of structure have seen the government allow clubs to either float on the stock exchange or to spin off their professional football activities into a separate public company. That is, as long as the social club continues to holds 51 per cent of the equity. Borussia Dortmund was the first to convert, partially floating the club. Bayer 04 Leverkusen became a plc in 1999, but under a special regulation, the 'Lex Leverkusen', the club is 100 per cent owned by Bayer AG, the chemical company that has run the club for nearly 100 years. Borussia Mönchenglabdach, FC Schalke 04 and Hertha BSC Berlin have all considered floating but have so far declined. More likely, they will follow the path of 1. FC Köln, TSV 1860 München and FC Bayern München, which have opted to take Aktien Gesellschaft status, in which the commercial and amateur sporting components of the club are separated, the latter holding a majority stake in the former, but with the option of external private investment taking the rest. In Bayern's case, Adidas took a 10 per cent stake in 2001, valuing the club at the time at £475 million.

Alternative fans

There are recognizable tribes of German fans. The mainstream combines an older and younger generation, boisterous and noisy but very peaceful. A handful of clubs can claim a following beyond their immediate locality: Bayern München, Dortmund, Schalke and FC Hansa Rostock in particular. Many of the smaller teams, like Berlin's smaller clubs and St. Pauli in Hamburg, attract the alternative scene in Germany: punks, anarchists, Greens and hippies. In the east, skinhead gangs have clustered around some old East German clubs, and have

made a speciality of following the national team, causing extensive trouble at France 98, where a policeman was seriously injured in an encounter with German fans. In response, policing has been tightened and, with a characteristic German mixture of incorporation and social reasonability, clubs have set up *fanprojekts*. These bring autonomous supporters' groups, local authority youth projects and the clubs together in a range of activities, including a chance for fans to meet and quiz clubs' directors.

St. Pauli may rarely trouble *the top of the Bundesliga but it can boast one of the most active and organized fan cultures in the country. Supporters pressed for a ban on racist abuse at their ground before any other club and have been in the vanguard of official and unofficial campaigns against fascist groups in football.*

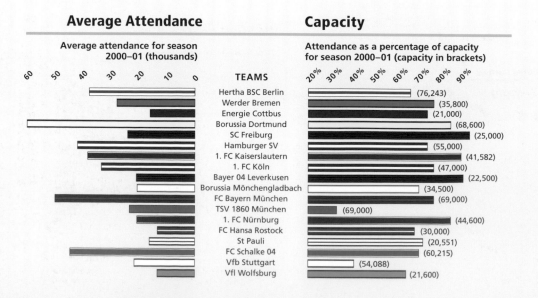

Average Attendance

Average attendance for season 2000–01 (thousands)

TEAMS
Hertha BSC Berlin
Werder Bremen
Energie Cottbus
Borussia Dortmund
SC Freiburg
Hamburger SV
1. FC Kaiserslautern
1. FC Köln
Bayer 04 Leverkusen
Borussia Mönchengladbach
FC Bayern München
TSV 1860 München
1. FC Nürnburg
FC Hansa Rostock
St Pauli
FC Schalke 04
Vfb Stuttgart
Vfl Wolfsburg

Capacity

Attendance as a percentage of capacity for season 2000–01 (capacity in brackets)

TEAMS	Capacity
Hertha BSC Berlin	(76,243)
Werder Bremen	(35,800)
Energie Cottbus	(21,000)
Borussia Dortmund	(68,600)
SC Freiburg	(25,000)
Hamburger SV	(55,000)
1. FC Kaiserslautern	(41,582)
1. FC Köln	(47,000)
Bayer 04 Leverkusen	(22,500)
Borussia Mönchengladbach	(34,500)
FC Bayern München	(69,000)
TSV 1860 München	(69,000)
1. FC Nürnburg	(44,600)
FC Hansa Rostock	(30,000)
St Pauli	(20,551)
FC Schalke 04	(60,215)
Vfb Stuttgart	(54,088)
Vfl Wolfsburg	(21,600)

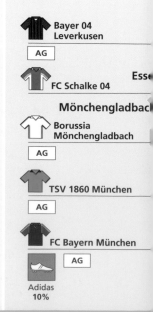

Bayer 04 Leverkusen — AG

FC Schalke 04 — Esse

Mönchengladbac

Borussia Mönchengladbach — AG

TSV 1860 München — AG

FC Bayern München — AG

Adidas 10%

Club Budgets 2000–01, 2001–02

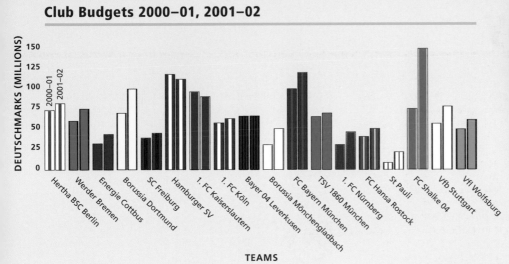

DEUTSCHMARKS (MILLIONS)

150, 125, 100, 75, 50, 25, 0

- 2000–01
- 2001–02

Teams:
Hertha BSC Berlin, Werder Bremen, Energie Cottbus, Borussia Dortmund, SC Freiburg, Hamburger SV, 1. FC Kaiserslautern, 1. FC Köln, Bayer 04 Leverkusen, Borussia Mönchengladbach, FC Bayern München, TSV 1860 München, 1. FC Nürnberg, FC Hansa Rostock, St Pauli, FC Schalke 04, Vfb Stuttgart, Vfl Wolfsburg

TEAMS

Leo Kirch created a media empire that paid enormous sums for the Bundesliga's TV rights. The collapse of the Kirch group in 2002 with debts of £10 billion is likely to see budgets in the Bundesliga slashed.

Majority and Leading Shareholders

- Team
- ● Berlin — City of origin
- Sportswear company
- AG — Aktien Gesellschaft
- Partial flotation

Teams shown were members of Bundesliga 2001–02

Borussia Dortmund, FC Hansa Rostock, Hamburg, Rostock, St Pauli, Bremen, Hamburger SV, Werder Bremen, Hertha BSC Berlin, Vfl Wolfsburg, Wolfsburg, Dortmund, Berlin, Cottbus, Energie Cottbus, Freiburg, Leverkusen, GERMANY, SC Freiburg, Cologne, 1. FC Köln, Nürnberg, 1. FC Nürnburg, Kaiserslautern, 1. FC Kaiserslautern, AG, Stuttgart, Vfb Stuttgart, Munich

Income from Sponsorship

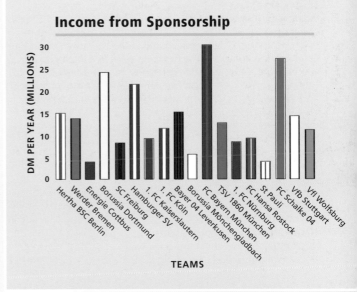

DM PER YEAR (MILLIONS)

30, 25, 20, 15, 10, 5, 0

Teams:
Hertha BSC Berlin, Werder Bremen, Energie Cottbus, Borussia Dortmund, SC Freiburg, Hamburger SV, 1. FC Kaiserslautern, 1. FC Köln, Bayer 04 Leverkusen, Borussia Mönchengladbach, FC Bayern München, TSV 1860 München, 1. FC Nürnberg, FC Hansa Rostock, St Pauli, FC Schalke 04, Vfb Stuttgart, Vfl Wolfsburg

TEAMS

German Attendances

Attendances for each season

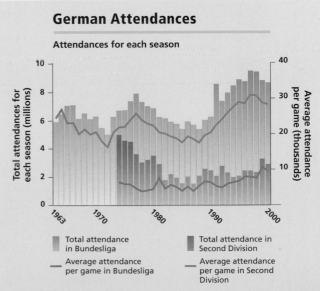

Total attendances for each season (millions): 10, 8, 6, 4, 2, 0

Average attendance per game (thousands): 40, 30, 20, 10

1963, 1970, 1980, 1990, 2000

- Total attendance in Bundesliga
- Total attendance in Second Division
- Average attendance per game in Bundesliga
- Average attendance per game in Second Division

Germany

PLAYERS AND MANAGERS

GERMAN FOOTBALL BEGAN LATER than in many European countries, and remained an amateur and regional affair for longer than in any other leading footballing nation. Originally a middle-class sport, it took two generations to reach the huge German urban working-class and to begin to significantly draw on its pool of talent. From the pre-Second World War generation two names stand out: Fritz Walter and Uwe Seeler. Walter captained the 1954 World Cup-winning side; Seeler the side that lost in 1966. Both played for a single club their whole career: Kaiserslautern and Hamburger SV respectively.

Arrival of the Bundesliga

But Germany's greatest players emerged from the new national professional league – the Bundesliga – formed in 1963. These players would win the 1974 World Cup, and those at Bayern München would come to dominate the national and European game in the mid-1970s: Gerd Müller, whose goalscoring record is almost unsurpassable; Paul Brietner, Bayern's midfield intellectual and bearded radical; and the Kaiser himself, Franz Beckenbauer, Germany's greatest player, manager and football politician.

In the 1990s, German players spread their wings and began to play abroad; Kohler, Klinsmann and Matthäus – the spine of the 1990 World Cup side – have all played in Italy, and displayed consistency, quiet intelligence and longevity. Matthias Sammer, one of the few East Germans to make it to the highest level after unification, picked up Beckenbauer's mantle as sweeper. Simultaneously, the growing wealth of the Bundesliga has seen a steady expansion in its overseas players, with strong African and Eastern European contingents.

Top 20 International Caps

PLAYER	CAPS	GOALS	FIRST MATCH	LAST MATCH
Lothar Matthäus	150	23	1980	2000
Jürgen Klinsmann	108	47	1987	1998
Jürgen Kohler*	105	2	1986	1998
Franz Beckenbauer	103	14	1965	1977
Thomas Hässler*	101	11	1988	2000
Hans-Hubert Vogts	96	1	1967	1978
Sepp Maier	95	0	1966	1979
Karl-Heinz Rummenigge	95	45	1976	1986
Rudi Völler	90	47	1982	1994
Andreas Brehme	86	8	1984	1994
Andreas Möller*	85	30	1988	1999
Karl Heinz Forster	81	2	1978	1986
Wolfgang Overath	81	17	1963	1974
Guido Buchwald	76	4	1984	1994
Harald Schumacher	76	0	1979	1986
Pierre Littbarski	73	18	1981	1990
Hans Peter Briegel	72	4	1979	1986
Uwe Seeler	72	43	1954	1970
Paul Janes	71	7	1932	1942
Manfred Kaltz	69	8	1975	1983

Top 10 International Goalscorers

PLAYER	GOALS	CAPS	FIRST MATCH	LAST MATCH
Gerd Müller	68	62	1966	1974
Rudi Völler	47	90	1982	1994
Jürgen Klinsmann	47	108	1987	1998
Karl-Heinz Rummenigge	45	95	1976	1986
Uwe Seeler	43	72	1954	1970
Fritz Walter	33	61	1940	1958
Klaus Fischer	32	45	1977	1982
Oliver Bierhoff*	32	60	1996	2002
Ernst Lehner	30	65	1933	1942
Andreas Möller*	30	85	1988	1999

* Indicates players still playing at least at club level.

German International Managers

DATES	NAME	GAMES	WON	DRAWN	LOST
1926–36	Otto Nerz	70	42	10	18
1936–63	Sepp Herberger	162	92	26	44
1963–78	Helmut Schön	139	87	30	22
1978–84	Jupp Derwall	67	45	11	11
1984–90	Franz Beckenbauer	66	36	17	13
1990–98	Berti Vogts	102	67	23	12
1998–2000	Erich Ribbeck	24	10	6	8
2000–	Rudi Völler	16	10	3	3

All figures correct as of 14 February 2002.

Places in the Top 20 International Caps and Top 10 International Goalscorers tables above make Rudi Völler the perfect choice as manager of the German national team.

GERMANY

Player of the Year

YEAR	PLAYER	CLUB
1963	Schäfer	1. FC Köln
1964	Seeler	Hamburger SV
1965	Tilkowski	Borussia Dortmund
1966	Beckenbauer	Bayern München
1967	G. Müller	Bayern München
1968	Beckenbauer	Bayern München
1969	G. Müller	Bayern München
1970	Seeler	Hamburger SV
1971	Vogts	Borussia Mönchengladbach
1972	Netzer	Borussia Mönchengladbach
1973	Netzer	Borussia Mönchengladbach
1974	Beckenbauer	Bayern München
1975	Maier	Bayern München
1976	Beckenbauer	Bayern München

YEAR	PLAYER	CLUB
1977	Maier	Bayern München
1978	Maier	Bayern München
1979	Vogts	Borussia Mönchengladbach
1980	Rummenigge	Bayern München
1981	Breitner	Bayern München
1982	Förster	VfB Stuttgart
1983	Völler	Werder Bremen
1984	Schumacher	1. FC Köln
1985	Briegel	Hellas Verona [Ita]
1986	Schumacher	1. FC Köln
1987	Rahn	Borussia Mönchengladbach
1988	Klinsmann	VfB Stuttgart
1989	Hässler	1. FC Köln
1990	Matthäus	Internazionale [Ita]
1991	Kuntz	1. FC Kaiserslautern

YEAR	PLAYER	CLUB
1992	Hässler	Roma [Ita]
1993	Köpke	1. FC Nürnberg
1994	Klinsmann	Tottenham Hotspur [Eng]
1995	Sammer	Borussia Dortmund
1996	Sammer	Borussia Dortmund
1997	Kohler	Borussia Dortmund
1998	Bierhoff	Udinese/Milan [Ita]
1999	Matthäus	Bayern München
2000	Khan	Bayern München
2001	Khan	Bayern München

Awarded by *Kicker* magazine.

Top Goalscorers by Season 1963–2002

SEASON	PLAYER	CLUB	GOALS
1963–64	Seeler	Hamburger SV	30
1964–65	Brunnenmeier	TSV 1860 München	24
1965–66	Emmerich	Borussia Dortmund	31
1966–67	G. Müller	Bayern München	28
1966–67	Emmerich	Borussia Dortmund	28
1967–68	Lohr	1. FC Köln	27
1968–69	G. Müller	Bayern München	30
1969–70	G. Müller	Bayern München	38
1970–71	Kobluhn	Rot-Weiss Oberhausen	24
1971–72	G. Müller	Bayern München	40
1972–73	G. Müller	Bayern München	36
1973–74	G. Müller	Bayern München	30
1973–74	Heynckes	Borussia M'gladbach	30
1974–75	Heynckes	Borussia M'gladbach	29
1975–76	Fischer	FC Schalke 04	29
1976–77	D. Müller	1. FC Köln	34
1977–78	D. Müller	1. FC Köln	24
1977–78	G. Müller	Bayern München	24
1978–79	K. Allofs	Fortuna Dusseldorf	22
1979–80	Rummenigge	Bayern München	26
1980–81	Rummenigge	Bayern München	29
1981–82	Hrubesch	Hamburger SV	27
1982–83	Völler	Werder Bremen	23
1983–84	Rummenigge	Bayern München	26
1984–85	K. Allofs	1. FC Köln	26
1985–86	Kuntz	Vfl Bochum	22
1986–87	Rahn	Borussia M'gladbach	24

SEASON	PLAYER	CLUB	GOALS
1987–88	Klinsmann	VfB Stuttgart	18
1988–89	T. Allofs	1. FC Köln	17
1988–89	Wohlfahrth	Bayern München	17
1989–90	Andersen	Eintracht Frankfurt	18
1990–91	Wohlfahrth	Bayern München	21
1991–92	Walter	VfB Stuttgart	22
1992–93	Kirsten	Bayer Leverkusen	20
1992–93	Yeboah	Eintracht Frankfurt	20
1993–94	Kuntz	1. FC Kaiserslautern	18
1993–94	Yeboah	Eintracht Frankfurt	18
1994–95	Bassler	Werder Bremen	20
1994–95	Herrlich	Borussia M'gladbach	20
1995–96	Bobic	VfB Stuttgart	17
1996–97	Kirsten	Bayer Leverkusen	22
1997–98	Kirsten	Bayer Leverkusen	22
1998–99	Preetz	Hertha Berlin	23
1999–2000	Max	TSV 1860 München	19
2000–01	Barbarez	Hamburger SV	22
2000–01	Sand	FC Schalke 04	22
2001–02	Amoroso	Borrussia Dortmund	18
2001–02	Max	TSV 1860 München	18

One of Germany's first exports was naturally one of its finest players. Jürgen Klinsmann left VfB Stuttgart to join Italian giants Internazionale in 1989. He had three successful years in Milan before moving to AS Monaco of France in 1992.

Foreign Players in Germany (in top division squads)

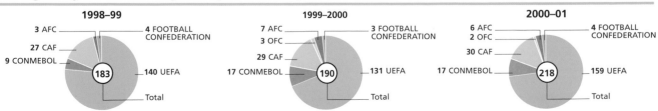

1998–99
3 AFC — 4 FOOTBALL CONFEDERATION
27 CAF
9 CONMEBOL
183 Total
140 UEFA

1999–2000
7 AFC — 3 FOOTBALL CONFEDERATION
3 OFC
29 CAF
17 CONMEBOL — 190 — 131 UEFA
Total

2000–01
6 AFC — 4 FOOTBALL CONFEDERATION
2 OFC
30 CAF
17 CONMEBOL — 218 — 159 UEFA
Total

Germany

BUNDESLIGA 1981–2001

IN THE 1970s, GERMAN FOOTBALL was dominated by Bayern München and an unlikely small-town team from the Ruhr called Borussia Mönchengladbach. However, by the beginning of the 1980s, Hamburger SV was the power in the land. Even without the departed Kevin Keegan (European Footballer of the Year in 1978 and 79) the team from Hamburg was formidable: the side was managed by Austrian warhorse Ernst Happel, Horst Hrubesch led the line and sweeper Manni Kaltz kept it tidy at the back. Hamburger took back-to-back titles (1982 and 83) and was pipped for a third by a revived Stuttgart in 1984.

The rest of the decade saw a reversion to old form as a newly constructed Bayern München, under manager Otto Latek and captain Lothar Mätthaus, took five of the next six championships. The only constant challenge came from Werder Bremen under Otto Rehhagel (who stayed a record 14 years at the club). With very little income Werder fielded a compact, clever and hardworking team, and nurtured future German internationals like Rudi Völler and Karlheinz Riedle. The team became famed for its *Wesermiracles*, as it consistently demonstrated its ability to come back from behind at its home, Weserstadion. Together, the mix allowed Bremen to take two championships (1988 and 93), as well as finding European success.

Formation of the modern Bundesliga

As the Berlin Wall was dismantled in 1991, and East Germany was effectively liquidated by the Federal Republic, the Bundesliga of the newly unified Germany dutifully offered two places to the top East German league sides, Hansa Rostock and Dynamo Dresden. Leipzig came up a year later only to go straight back down, and Dresden lasted only four seasons before relegation. Hansa was immediately relegated only to return in the mid-1990s. With a couple of sixth place finishes, Hansa Rostock is easily the most successful team from the East. Geographically Eastern, but politically and economically from West Berlin, Hertha BSC has made a comeback in the last five years. Buoyed by the money flooding into the new Berlin, it has made the top six regularly. Similarly strong challenges have come from two teams from the Ruhr with substantial crowds and financial support: FC Schalke and Bayer Leverkusen.

Bayern went off the boil in the years immediately after reunification and the title was more evenly spread with Borussia Dortmund, Kaiserslautern, Stuttgart and Bremen all winning the top prize. Dortmund, under inspirational president Gerd Niebaum and manager Ottmar Hitzfeld, was the most consistent team. With a massive programme of redevelopment and commercialization (culminating in partial flotation on the German stock exchange), Hitzfeld brought in the Brazilian César from under the noses of Bayern, and a number of German internationals who had been playing abroad, like Andy Möller and Jurgen Kohler; together they won two Bundesliga titles and the European Cup. But with Hitzfeld moving upstairs the side began to creak and break up. Kaiserslautern, under Otto

Rehhagel, won the title on the last day of the 1998 season by beating Borussia Mönchengladbach 3-2.

Despite fearsome competition and perennial feuding between its leading players, Bayern still managed two titles in the mid-1990s. In 1998, Beckenbauer, now president of the club, recalled manager Trapattoni for his second spell in charge, and the first of three titles duly came back to the Olympiastadion. Two more followed with Ottmar Hitzfeld at the helm. Hitzfeld's Bayern has included leading German internationals (like Steffan Effenberg, Oliver Khan, Jens Jeremies and Mehmet Schol) as well as clever buys in the foreign transfer market (the Brazilian Giovane Elber and French defender Bixente Lizarazu) and one of the strictest wage policies in European football.

The collapse of Kirch

While sponsorship and attendance money has been rising in the Bundesliga, the strict controls on the commercialization of German clubs have left them heavily dependent on TV income. TV money has poured into the Bundesliga in the last decade, but a reality check may be in store. The Kirch group – holder of the Bundesliga TV rights – went spectacularly bankrupt in 2002. With some clubs at the bottom end of the table dependent for 60 per cent of their income on this money, their prospects look bleak; so bleak that the German government has been considering a very expensive safety net for the clubs and their players.

Out with the old, in with the new. Giovanni Trapattoni (left) of Bayern München and Ottmar Hitzfeld of Borussia Dortmund in 1997. A year later, Hitzfeld replaced Trapattoni at the helm of Germany's most famous club.

GERMANY

Karlheinz Riedle (on ground) scores for Werder Bremen, performing one of its Wesermiracles, at home to Hamburger SV in 1988.

TV Rights Income

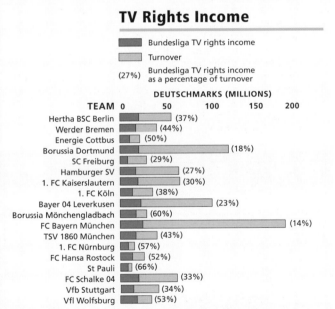

■ Bundesliga TV rights income
□ Turnover
(27%) Bundesliga TV rights income as a percentage of turnover

DEUTSCHMARKS (MILLIONS)

TEAM	
Hertha BSC Berlin	(37%)
Werder Bremen	(44%)
Energie Cottbus	(50%)
Borussia Dortmund	(18%)
SC Freiburg	(29%)
Hamburger SV	(27%)
1. FC Kaiserslautern	(30%)
1. FC Köln	(38%)
Bayer 04 Leverkusen	(23%)
Borussia Mönchengladbach	(60%)
FC Bayern München	(14%)
TSV 1860 München	(43%)
1. FC Nürnburg	(57%)
FC Hansa Rostock	(52%)
St Pauli	(66%)
FC Schalke 04	(33%)
Vfb Stuttgart	(34%)
Vfl Wolfsburg	(53%)

Players' Salaries 1990–2001

Total wage bill of Bundesliga clubs

Champions' Winning Margin 1991–2001

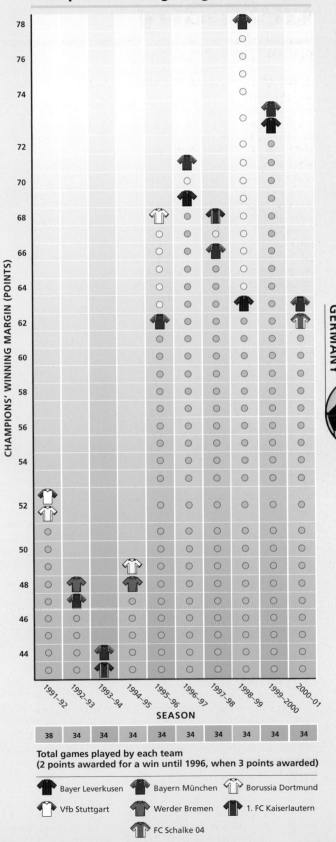

CHAMPIONS' WINNING MARGIN (POINTS)

SEASON

| 38 | 34 | 34 | 34 | 34 | 34 | 34 | 34 | 34 | 34 |

Total games played by each team
(2 points awarded for a win until 1996, when 3 points awarded)

Bayer Leverkusen   Bayern München   Borussia Dortmund
Vfb Stuttgart   Werder Bremen   1. FC Kaiserslautern
FC Schalke 04

GERMANY

151

Key to League Positions Table

- ▉ League champions
- ▉ Season of promotion to league
- ▉ Season of relegation from league
- ▉ Other teams playing in league
- 5 Final position in league

German League Positions 1981–2001

TEAM	1981-82	1982-83	1983-84	1984-85	1985-86	1986-87	1987-88	1988-89	1989-90	1990-91	1991-92	1992-93	1993-94	1994-95	1995-96	1996-97	1997-98	1998-99	1999-2000	2000-01
Blau-Weiss 90 Berlin						18														
Hertha BSC Berlin		18							18								11	3	6	5
Arminia Bielefeld	12	8	8	16												15	18		17	
Vfl Bochum	10	13	15	8	9	12	12	15	16	14	15	16		16		5	12	17		18
Eintracht Braunschweig	11	15	9	18																
Werder Bremen	5	2	5	2	2	4	1	3	7	3	9	1	9	2	9	8	7	14	9	7
Energie Cottbus																				14
Darmstadt 98	17																			
Borussia Dortmund	6	7	13	14	16	5	14	7	4	10	2	4	3	1	1	3	10	4	11	3
1. FC Dynamo Dresden											14	15	12	18						
MSV Duisburg	18										19	8	17		9	8	8	18		
Fortuna Düsseldorf	15	9	14	15	14	17			9	12	20			13	16					
Eintracht Frankfurt	8	10	16	12	15	15	10	16	3	5	3	3	5	9	17			15	14	17
SC Freiburg													15	3	11	17		11	12	6
Hamburger SV	1	1	2	5	7	2	6	4	11	4	12	11	13	13	5	13	9	7	3	13
Hannover 96						18		11	18											
FC Homburg						16	17		18											
1. FC Kaiserslautern	4	6	12	11	11	7	15	9	13	1	5	8	2	4	16		1	5	5	8
Karlsruher SC	14	17		17			13	11	10	13	8	6	6	8	7	6	16			
1. FC Köln	2	5	6	3	13	10	3	2	2	7	4	12	11	10	12	10	17			10
Vfb Leipzig													18							
Bayer 04 Leverkusen	16	11	7	13	6	6	8	8	5	8	6	5	4	7	15	2	3	2	2	4
SV Waldhof Mannheim			11	6	8	14	16	12	17											
Borussia Mönchengladbach	7	12	3	4	3	4	7	3	6	15	9	13	9	10	6	4	11	15	18	
Bayern München	3	4	4	1	1	1	2	1	1	2	10	2	1	5	2	1	2	1	1	1
TSV 1860 München														14	8	7	13	10	4	11
1. FC Nürnberg	13	14	18		12	9	5	14	8	15	7	14	16				16			
Kickers Offenbach		17																		
FC Hansa Rostock											18				6	14	6	13	15	12
1. FC Saarbrücken					17							18								
St Pauli								10	12	16						14	18			
FC Schalke 04		16		9	10	13	18				11	10	14	11	3	12	5	9	13	2
Vfb Stuttgart	9	3	1	10	5	11	4	5	6	6	1	7	7	12	10	4	4	12	8	15
Stuttgarter Kickers								17			17									
KFC Uerdingen		10	7	3	8	9	13	14	17		17			15	18					
SV Ulm																			16	
SpVgg Unterhaching																			10	16
Wattenscheid 09										11	16	13	17							
Vfl Wolfsburg																	14	6	7	9

GERMANY

Since retiring from playing, Franz Beckenbauer has coached both the national team and Bayern München, and become president of both Bayern and Germany's World Cup bidding committees.

Michael Ballack took Bayer Leverkusen to three runners-up spots in the Bundesliga and earned a move to Bayern München in 2002.

Coach Otto Rehhagel celebrates as newly-promoted club 1. FC Kaiserslautern wins the Bundesliga in 1998. It was the first and only time a newly-promoted side had won the championship.

Otmar Hitzfeld claims Bayern München's third consecutive Bundesliga title in 2001. Victory in the European Cup Final followed soon afterwards.

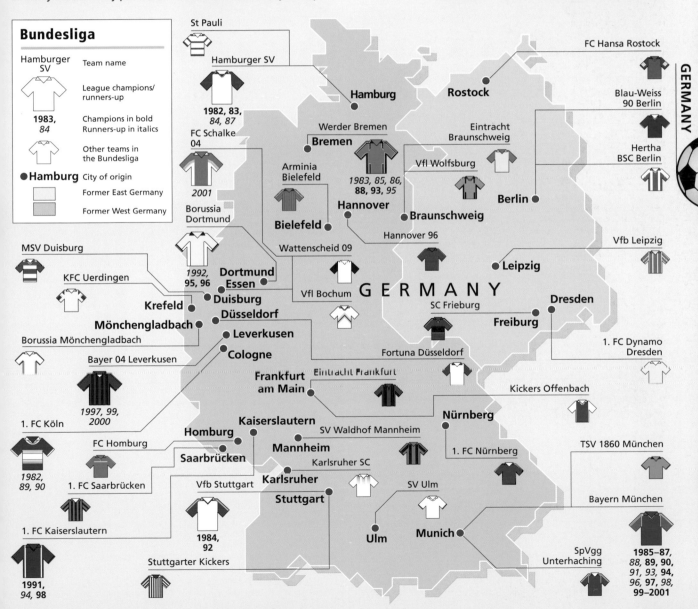

Bundesliga

Hamburger SV — Team name

League champions/ runners-up

1983, *84* — Champions in bold / Runners-up in italics

Other teams in the Bundesliga

● Hamburg — City of origin

Former East Germany

Former West Germany

St Pauli

Hamburger SV

1982, 83, 84, 87

FC Schalke 04

2001

Borussia Dortmund

1992, 95, 96

MSV Duisburg

KFC Uerdingen

Borussia Mönchengladbach

Bayer 04 Leverkusen

1997, 99, 2000

1. FC Köln

1982, *89, 90*

FC Homburg

1. FC Saarbrücken

1. FC Kaiserslautern

1991, *94, 98*

Vfb Stuttgart

1984, 92

Stuttgarter Kickers

Hamburg ●

Werder Bremen

Bremen ●

1983, 85, 86, 88, 93, 95

Arminia Bielefeld

Bielefeld ●

Wattenscheid 09

Dortmund ● / **Essen** ●

Vfl Bochum

Duisburg ● / **Düsseldorf** ●

Krefeld ●

Mönchengladbach ●

Leverkusen ●

Cologne ●

Fortuna Düsseldorf

Eintracht Frankfurt

Frankfurt am Main ●

Kaiserslautern ● / SV Waldhof Mannheim

Homburg ●

Mannheim ●

Saarbrücken ● / Karlsruher SC

Karlsruher ●

Stuttgart ●

Rostock ●

Eintracht Braunschweig

Vfl Wolfsburg

Hannover 96

Hannover ●

Braunschweig ●

SC Frieburg

Freiburg ●

SV Ulm

Nürnberg ●

1. FC Nürnberg

Ulm ● / **Munich** ●

SpVgg Unterhaching

G E R M A N Y

FC Hansa Rostock

Blau-Weiss 90 Berlin

Hertha BSC Berlin

Berlin ●

Vfb Leipzig

Leipzig ●

Dresden ●

1. FC Dynamo Dresden

Kickers Offenbach

TSV 1860 München

Bayern München

1985–87, 88, 89, 90, 91, 93, 94, 96, 97, 98, 99–2001

GERMANY

Germany (including former East and West Germany)

Deutscher Fussball-Bund
Founded: 1900
Joined FIFA: 1904–46, 1950
Joined UEFA: 1954

LOCAL, CITY AND INTER-CITY LEAGUE matches were being played all across Germany in the late 19th century. In 1898 the first national championship was awarded after a play-off between the winners of the two strongest regional leagues: Southern Germany and Berlin. With the formation of the Deutscher Fussball-Bund in 1900 a more systematic play-off system was introduced between the winners of all the regional leagues in 1902. The format remained the same while the German state grew and shrank. Between 1938 and 1944 Austrian teams were included, and after 1948, when the format was recreated, East Germany and its teams had been separated off.

East Germany retained the format until 1949, before moving to a conventional national league format. In 1963–64 the old championship was abandoned and a national professional league – the Bundesliga – was established. Its format has remained broadly the same since, with two teams from the former East Germany being awarded a place after German unification in 1991. There are now two national leagues of 18 teams, with a standard three up, three down promotion system.

The German Cup was set up in 1935 and it too has seen Austrians join and East Germans depart and return.

German National Championship Record 1903–44

SEASON	CHAMPIONS	SEASON	CHAMPIONS
1903	Vfb Leipzig	1926	SpVgg Furth
1904	*	1927	1. FC Nürnberg
1905	Union 92 Berlin	1928	Hamburger SV
1906	Vfb Leipzig	1929	SpVgg Furth
1907	SC Freiburg	1930	Hertha BSC Berlin
1908	Viktoria Berlin	1931	Hertha BSC Berlin
1909	Phoenix Karlsruhe	1932	Bayern München
1910	Karlsruher FV	1933	Fortuna Düsseldorf
1911	Viktoria Berlin	1934	FC Schalke 04
1912	Holstein Keil	1935	FC Schalke 04
1913	Vfb Leipzig	1936	1. FC Nürnberg
1914	SpVgg Furth	1937	FC Schalke 04
1915–19	no championship	1938	Hannover 96
1920	1. FC Nürnberg	1939	FC Schalke 04
1921	1. FC Nürnberg	1940	FC Schalke 04
1922	**	1941	Rapid Wien
1923	Hamburger SV	1942	FC Schalke 04
1924	1. FC Nürnberg	1943	Dresdener FC
1925	1. FC Nürnberg	1944	Dresdener FC

* Final not played after a dispute over semi-final venues.
** Hamburger SV awarded championship but declined it following an appeal by FC Nürnberg.

West German League Record 1948–63

SEASON	CHAMPIONS	SEASON	CHAMPIONS
1948	1. FC Nürnberg	1956	Borussia Dortmund
1949	Vfr Mannheim	1957	Borussia Dortmund
1950	Vfb Stuttgart	1958	FC Schalke 04
1951	1. FC Kaiserslautern	1959	Eintracht Frankfurt
1952	Vfb Stuttgart	1960	Hamburger SV
1953	1. FC Kaiserslautern	1961	1. FC Nürnberg
1954	Hannover 96	1962	1. FC Köln
1955	Rot-Weiss Essen	1963	Borussia Dortmund

East German League Record 1948–91

SEASON	CHAMPIONS	SEASON	CHAMPIONS
1948	SG Planitz	1970	Carl-Zeiss Jena
1949	ZGS Halle	1971	Dynamo Dresden
1950	Horch Zwickau	1972	1. FC Magdeberg
1951	Chemie Leipzig	1973	Dynamo Dresden
1952	Turbine Halle	1974	1. FC Magdeberg
1953	Dynamo Dresden	1975	1. FC Magdeberg
1954	Turbine Erfurt	1976	Dynamo Dresden
1955	Turbine Erfurt	1977	Dynamo Dresden
1956	Wismut KMS	1978	Dynamo Dresden
1957	Wismut KMS	1979	Dynamo Berlin
1958	Vorwärts Berlin	1980	Dynamo Berlin
1959	Wismut KMS	1981	Dynamo Berlin
1960	Vorwärts Berlin	1982	Dynamo Berlin
1961	no championship	1983	Dynamo Berlin
1962	Vorwärts Berlin	1984	Dynamo Berlin
1963	Motor Jena	1985	Dynamo Berlin
1964	Chemie Leipzig	1986	Dynamo Berlin
1965	Vorwärts Berlin	1987	Dynamo Berlin
1966	Vorwärts Berlin	1988	Dynamo Berlin
1967	FC Karl-Marx-Stadt	1989	Dynamo Dresden
1968	Carl-Zeiss Jena	1990	Dynamo Dresden
1969	Vorwärts Berlin	1991	Hansa Rostock

East German Cup Record 1949–91

YEAR	WINNERS	YEAR	WINNERS
1949	BSG Waggonbau Dessau	1971	SG Dynamo Dresden
1950	BSG EHW Thale	1972	FC Carl-Zeiss Jena
1951	no competition	1973	1. FC Magdeburg
1952	SG Volkspolizei Dresden	1974	FC Carl-Zeiss Jena
1953	no competition	1975	BSG Sachsenring Zwickau
1954	Vorwärts Berlin	1976	1. FC Lokomotive Leipzig
1955	no competition	1977	SG Dynamo Dresden
1956	SC Chemie Halle	1978	1. FC Magdeburg
1957	SC Lokomotive Leipzig	1979	1. FC Magdeburg
1958	SC Einheit Dresden	1980	FC Carl-Zeiss Jena
1959	SC Dynamo Berlin	1981	1. FC Lokomotive Leipzig
1960	SC Motor Jena	1982	SG Dynamo Dresden
1961	no competition	1983	1. FC Magdeburg
1962	SC Chemie Halle	1984	SG Dynamo Dresden
1963	BSC Motor Zwickau	1985	SG Dynamo Dresden
1964	SC Aufbau Magdeburg	1986	1. FC Lokomotive Leipzig
1965	SC Aufbau Magdeburg	1987	1. FC Lokomotive Leipzig
1966	BSG Motor Leipzig	1988	Berliner FC Dynamo
1967	BSC Motor Zwickau	1989	Berliner FC Dynamo
1968	1. FC Union Berlin	1990	SG Dynamo Dresden
1969	1. FC Magdeburg	1991	FC Hansa Rostock
1970	Vorwärts Berlin		

Bundesliga Record 1964–2002

SEASON	CHAMPIONS	RUNNERS-UP
1964	1. FC Köln	MSV Duisburg
1965	Werder Bremen	1. FC Köln
1966	TSV 1860 München	Borussia Dortmund
1967	Eintracht Braunschweig	TSV 1860 München
1968	1. FC Nürnberg	Werder Bremen
1969	Bayern München	Alemania Aachen
1970	Borussia Mönchengladbach	Bayern München
1971	Borussia Mönchengladbach	Bayern München
1972	Bayern München	FC Schalke 04
1973	Bayern München	1. FC Köln
1974	Bayern München	Borussia Mönchengladbach
1975	Borussia Mönchengladbach	Hertha BSC Berlin
1976	Borussia Mönchengladbach	Hamburger SV
1977	Borussia Mönchengladbach	FC Schalke 04

GERMANY

Bundesliga Record (*continued*)

SEASON	CHAMPIONS	RUNNERS-UP
1978	1. FC Köln	Borussia Mönchengladbach
1979	Hamburger SV	Vfb Stuttgart
1980	Bayern München	Hamburger SV
1981	Bayern München	Hamburger SV
1982	Hamburger SV	1. FC Köln
1983	Hamburger SV	Werder Bremen
1984	Vfb Stuttgart	Hamburger SV
1985	Bayern München	Werder Bremen
1986	Bayern München	Werder Bremen
1987	Bayern München	Hamburger SV
1988	Werder Bremen	Bayern München
1989	Bayern München	1. FC Köln
1990	Bayern München	1. FC Köln
1991	1. FC Kaiserslautern	Bayern München
1992	Vfb Stuttgart	Borussia Dortmund
1993	Werder Bremen	Bayern München
1994	Bayern München	1. FC Kaiserslautern
1995	Borussia Dortmund	Werder Bremen
1996	Borussia Dortmund	Bayern München
1997	Bayern München	Bayer Leverkusen
1998	1. FC Kaiserslautern	Bayern München
1999	Bayern München	Bayer Leverkusen
2000	Bayern München	Bayer Leverkusen
2001	Bayern München	FC Schalke 04
2002	Borussia Dortmund	Bayer Leverkusen

Bundesliga Summary

TEAM	TOTALS	CHAMPIONS & RUNNERS-UP (BOLD) (ITALICS)
Bayern München	**16**, *6*	**1969**, *70, 71, 72–74*, **80, 81, 85–87, 89, 90,** *91*, **93, 94,** *96*, **97,** *98, 99–2001*
Borussia Mönchengladbach	**5**, *2*	**1970, 71, 74, 75–77,** *78*
Hamburger SV	**3**, *5*	*1976, 79, 80, 81,* **82, 83,** *84, 87*
Werder Bremen	**3**, *5*	**1965,** *68, 83, 85, 86,* **88, 93,** *95*
Borussia Dortmund	**3**, *2*	*1966, 92,* **95, 96, 2002**
1. FC Köln	**2**, *6*	**1964,** *65, 73, 78, 82, 88–90*
1. FC Kaiserslautern	**2**, *1*	**1991,** *94,* **98**
Vfb Stuttgart	**2**, *1*	*1979,* **84,** *92*
TSV 1860 München	**1**, *1*	**1966,** *67*
1. FC Nürnberg	**1**, *0*	**1968**
Eintracht Braunschweig	**1**, *0*	**1967**
Bayer Leverkusen	**0**, *4*	*1997, 99, 2000, 02*
FC Schalke 04	**0**, *3*	*1972, 77, 2001*
Alemania Aachen	**0**, *1*	*1969*
Hertha BSC Berlin	**0**, *1*	*1975*
MSV Duisberg	**0**, *1*	*1964*

German Cup Record 1935–2002

YEAR	WINNERS	SCORE	RUNNERS-UP
1935	1. FC Nürnberg	2-0	FC Schalke 04
1936	Vfb Leipzig	2-1	FC Schalke 04
1937	FC Schalke 04	2-1	Fortuna Düsseldorf
1938	SK Rapid Wien	3-1	FSV Frankfurt
1939	1. FC Nürnberg	2-0	SV Waldhof Mannheim
1940	Dresdener SC	2-1 (aet)	1. FC Nürnberg
1941	Dresdener SC	2-1	FC Schalke 04
1942	TSV 1860 München	2-0	FC Schalke 04
1943	First Vienna FC	3-2 (aet)	Hamburger SV
1944–52	*no competition*		
1953	Rot-Weiss Essen	2-1	Alemania Aachen
1954	Vfb Stuttgart	1-0 (aet)	1. FC Köln
1955	Karlsruher SC	3-2	FC Schalke 04

German Cup Record (*continued*)

YEAR	WINNERS	SCORE	RUNNERS-UP
1956	Karlsruher SC	3-1	Hamburger SV
1957	Bayern München	1-0	Fortuna Düsseldorf
1958	Vfb Stuttgart	4-3	Fortuna Düsseldorf
1959	Schwarz Weiss Essen	5-2	Borussia Neunkirchen
1960	Borussia Mönchengladbach	3-2	Karlsruher FC
1961	Werder Bremen	2-0	1. FC Kaiserslautern
1962	1. FC Nurnberg	2-1 (aet)	Fortuna Düsseldorf
1963	Hamburger SV	3-0	Borussia Dortmund
1964	TSV 1860 München	2-0	Eintracht Frankfurt
1965	Borussia Dortmund	2-0	Alemania Aachen
1966	Bayern München	4-2	MSV Duisburg
1967	Bayern München	4-0	Hamburger SV
1968	1. FC Köln	4-1	Vfl Bochum
1969	Bayern München	2-1	FC Schalke 04
1970	Kickers Offenbach	2-1	1. FC Köln
1971	Bayern München	2-1 (aet)	1. FC Köln
1972	FC Schlake 04	5-0	1. FC Kaiserslautern
1973	Borussia Mönchengladbach	2-1 (aet)	1. FC Köln
1974	Eintracht Frankfurt	3-1 (aet)	Hamburger SV
1975	Eintracht Frankfurt	1-0	MSV Duisburg
1976	Hamburger SV	2-0	1. FC Kaiserslautern
1977	1. FC Köln	1-1 (aet), (replay) 1-0	Hertha BSC Berlin
1978	1. FC Köln	2-0	Fortuna Düsseldorf
1979	Fortuna Düsseldorf	1-0 (aet)	Hertha BSC Berlin
1980	Fortuna Düsseldorf	2-1	1. FC Köln
1981	Eintracht Frankfurt	3-1	1. FC Kaiserslautern
1982	Bayern München	4-2	1. FC Nürnberg
1983	1. FC Köln	1-0	Fortuna Köln
1984	Bayern München	1-1 (aet)(7-6 pens)	Borussia Mönchengladbach
1985	Bayer Uerdingen	2-1	Bayern München
1986	Bayern München	5-2	Vfb Stuttgart
1987	Hamburger SV	3-1	Stuttgarter Kickers
1988	Eintracht Frankfurt	1-0	Vfl Bochum
1989	Borussia Dortmund	4-1	Werder Bremen
1990	1. FC Kaiserslautern	3-2	Werder Bremen
1991	Werder Bremen	1-1 (aet)(4-3 pens)	1. FC Köln
1992	Hannover 96	0-0 (aet)(4-3 pens)	Borussia Mönchengladbach
1993	Bayer 04 Leverkusen	1-0	Hertha BSC Berlin
1994	Werder Bremen	3-1	Rot-Weiss Essen
1995	Borussia Mönchengladbach	3-0	Wolfsburg
1996	1. FC Kaiserslautern	1-0	Karlsruher FC
1997	Vfb Stuttgart	2-0	Energie Cottbus
1998	Bayern München	2-1	MSV Duisburg
1999	Werder Bremen	1-1 (aet)(5-4 pens)	Bayern München
2000	Bayern München	3-0	Werder Bremen
2001	FC Schalke 04	2-0	1. FC Union Berlin
2002	FC Schalke 04	4-2	Bayer Leverkusen

German Cup Summary

TEAM	TOTAL	WINNERS & RUNNERS-UP (BOLD) (ITALICS)
Bayern München	**10**, *2*	**1957, 66, 67, 69, 71, 82, 84,** *85,* **86, 98,** *99,* **2000**
1. FC Köln	**4**, *6*	*1954,* **68,** *70, 71, 73,* **77, 78,** *80, 83, 91*
FC Schalke 04	**4**, *6*	*1935, 36,* **37,** *41, 42, 55, 69, 72,* **2001, 02**
Werder Bremen	**4**, *3*	**1961,** *89, 90,* **91, 94, 99,** *2000*
Eintracht Frankfurt	**4**, *1*	*1964,* **74, 75, 81, 88**

This summary only features clubs that have won the German Cup four times or more. For a full list of cup winners and runners-up please see the Cup Record above.

GERMANY

155

France

FRANCE

THE SEASON IN REVIEW 2001–02

AMONG THE MAIN CONTENDERS for the French title the season started badly, with managerial change, discord and the loss of key players to bigger, richer leagues and clubs. The previous season's champions, Nantes, began with reported friction between coach Reynald Denoueix and his squad. Lyon, under Jacques Santini, held on to stars Sidney Govou and Sonny Anderson, but lost Marlet and Malbranque to Fulham. Lens, who last season came close to relegation, brought in Senegalese playmaker El Hadji Diouf and a job lot of players from relegated St-Etienne. At PSG, coach Luis Fernandez began the season with an unsettled squad: strikers Robert and Anelka were both looking for new clubs (Robert moved to Newcastle and Anelka went on loan to Liverpool). At Auxerre, Guy Roux had finally retired after over three decades in coaching, handing over to his anointed successor Daniel Rolland. However, as Auxerre's form dropped and the team fell to 13th place, Roux returned to rally the squad. Marseille was facing relegation once again for debts of nearly £25 million, until president Robert Louis Dreyfuss once again put up the cash to keep them in the first division.

Lens set the pace

Nantes, who played well in the Champions League, started the domestic league season disastrously at home and looked to be under threat of relegation until pulling out of its nosedive in the second half of the season. Marseille, Monaco and Bordeaux never looked consistent or threatening to the top of the table. Lille and Auxerre kept in touch, but it was Lens that took the initiative, going top in October and maintaining its lead for the next six months, just ahead of Lyon. Although French football has not received the financial shock applied to the leading leagues in the rest of Europe,

Le Championnat League Table 2001–02

CLUB	P	W	D	L	F	A	Pts	
Olympique Lyonnais	34	20	6	8	62	32	66	Champions League
RC Lens	34	18	10	6	55	30	64	Champions League
AJ Auxerre	34	16	11	7	48	38	59	Champions League
Paris SG	34	15	13	6	43	24	58	UEFA Cup
Lille OSC	34	15	11	8	39	32	56	
Bordeaux	34	14	8	12	34	31	50	UEFA Cup (League Cup winners)
A Troyes AC	34	13	8	13	40	35	47	
FC Sochaux	34	12	10	12	41	40	46	
Olympique Marseille	34	11	11	12	34	39	44	
FC Nantes	34	12	7	15	35	41	43	
SC Bastia	34	12	5	17	38	44	41	
Stade Rennais	34	11	8	15	40	51	41	
Montpellier HSC	34	9	13	12	28	31	40	
CS Sedan	34	8	15	11	35	39	39	
AS Monaco	34	9	12	13	36	41	39	
Guingamp	34	9	8	17	34	56	35	
FC Metz	34	9	6	19	31	47	33	Relegated
FC Lorient	34	7	10	17	42	64	31	Relegated, UEFA Cup (cup winners)

Promoted clubs: AC Ajaccio, Nice, Le Havre.

Djibril Cisse of Auxerre finished the season as joint top scorer with Pauleta of Bordeaux.

Nicolas Gillet of Nantes (in yellow) and Pauleta of Bordeaux challenge for the ball. Pauleta was joint top scorer in the league, but Bordeaux could manage no better than sixth.

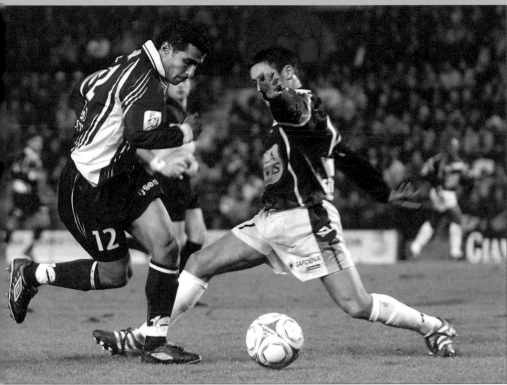

Left: *Saleheddine Bassir of Lille tries to find a way through the Troyes defence. Lille's early form couldn't last, but the tiny team from northern France has shown that it is more than a one-season wonder in the top flight, finishing a creditable fifth.*

Centre left: *Luis Fernandez, PSG's coach, feels the frustration of the big spender's perennial underperformance, while Raynald Denoueix (right) implores his championship-holding Nantes side to show some form in the league.*

Below: *Bordeaux's Ulrich Rame clears his lines against Monaco. Bordeaux's season was rescued with a League Cup victory but Monaco fared badly and only just avoided relegation.*

FRANCE

with TV deals holding firm, the LNF did announce in mid-season that the levels of cumulative debt (55 million Euros) and annual losses among the first division were becoming increasingly unsustainable.

Through the late spring, Lens frittered away its lead, taking only five points from a disastrous five-game stretch. With two games to go they stood three points above chasing Lyon and made no mistakes in a comprehensive defeat of Guingamp. First-half goals from El Hadji Diouf and Adama Coulibaly put the pressure on Lyon at Bordeaux. With both sides reduced to ten men after half an hour, it was Lyon that found the energy and the inspiration to break the deadlock with a Sonny Anderson winner to take three points and prolong the title race to the last day of the season.

Last match drama

For the first time ever, the French league title was decided by the final game between the two top teams, Lens and Lyon. Unbeaten at home all season, Lyon looked to have the edge and within ten minutes had put away two goals. The explosive pace of Sidney Govou took him into the Lens box to open the scoring, while Phillipe Violeau prodded home a cross at the near post. Lens rallied and Bak scored from a rebounding free kick. Lens applied sustained pressure until early in the second half when, against the run of play, Laigle made it three for Lyon. There was no way back for Lens, and Lyon celebrated a first-ever league title in a delirious Stade Garland.

Incredible scenes took place before the Cup Final between Corsican club Bastia and already relegated Lorient. Prime Minister Jacques Chirac stopped proceedings after hearing the Bastia fans booing the *Marseillaise*. He ordered Bastia officials to speak to the team's fans, apologise to the 80,000 strong crowd at the Stade de France in Paris and then held his own press conference about the state of French politics before allowing the game to go ahead. In the event, Lorient took the cup, winning 1-0 with a goal from Jean-Claude Darcheville.

French Cup

2002 FINAL

May 11 – Stade de France, St-Dennis
FC Lorient 1-0 SC Bastia
(Darcheville 41)
h/t: 1-0 **Att:** 79,450
Ref: Eric Poulat

Top Goalscorers 2001–02

PLAYER	CLUB	NATIONALITY	GOALS
Djibril Cisse	AJ Auxerre	French	22
Pedro Miguel Pauleta	Bordeaux	Portuguese	22
Jean-Claude Darcheville	FC Lorient	French	19
Nicolas Gousse	A Troyes AC	French	15

International Club Performances 2001–02

CLUB	COMPETITION	PROGRESS
Lille OSC	Champions League UEFA Cup	1st Group Phase 4th Round
Olympique Lyonnais	Champions League UEFA Cup	1st Group Phase 4th Round
FC Nantes	Champions League	2nd Group Phase
Bordeaux	UEFA Cup	3rd Round
PSG	UEFA Cup	3rd Round
CS Sedan	UEFA Cup	1st Round
RC Strasbourg	UEFA Cup	1st Round
A Troyes AC	UEFA Cup	2nd Round

Right: Jacques Santini looks quizzical as he leads Olympique Lyonnais to its first-ever league title but loses his job in the process.

Below: Olympique Lyonnais players celebrate their title triumph with their fans.

Bottom: French President Jacques Chirac shows his barely concealed displeasure as the Marseillaise is disrupted at the French Cup Final.

Jean-Claude Darcheville (in orange) skips past Bastia's Christophe Deguerville to score the winning goal in the French Cup Final.

Above: *Sonny Anderson, Olympique Lyonnais' Brazilian talisman, splits the Lens line of Fredrick Colly (left) and Jean Guy Wallemme as Lyon steals the title from under Lens' nose on the final day of the season.*

Below: *Lorient players celebrate with the French Cup after their Final triumph.*

Association Football in France

FRANCE

1870

1872: Le Havre Athletic Club formed (although first footballing section not formed until 1892)

1880

1881: Girondins de Bordeaux formed; oldest independent French club

1890

1900

1904: Affiliation to FIFA. First international, v Belgium, drawn 3-3, venue: Brussels

1910

1918: Formation of FA: Fédération Française de Football, (FFF). First French Cup Final

1920

1922: First women's informal international v Dick Kerr's Ladies (England), drawn 1-1, venue: Paris

1930

1932: National league established; professionalism legalized

1940

1940–45: During war league championship played as play-offs between regions, cup continued

1950

1954: Affiliation to UEFA

1960

1970

1980

1992: Cup abandoned after Bastia disaster, a temporary stand collapsed in Cup semi-final, Bastia v Olympique Marseille, over 1,500 injured

1990

1993: Olympique Marseille stripped of European Cup and French League title for match-fixing

2000

2010

Jules Rimet (left) – lawyer, first President of FIFA and pioneer of the World Cup – hands its first-ever trophy to Dr Paul Jude, President of the Uruguayan FA. Uruguay beat Argentina 4-2 in the Final in Montevideo on 30 July 1930.

Key

🏳 International football	◾ European Championships host
⚽ Affiliation to FIFA	● European Championships winner
⚽ Affiliation to UEFA	○ Competition winner
♀ Women's football	△ Competition runner-up
War	Bas – Bastia
Disaster	Bor – Bordeaux
◾ World Cup host	Mon – Monaco
● World Cup winner	OM – Olympique Marseille
	PSG – Paris Saint-Germain
	St-E – St-Etienne
	St R – Stade de Reims

International Competitions

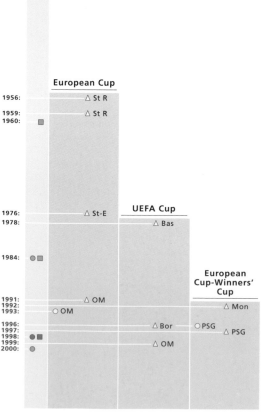

1938: ◾

European Cup

1956: △ St R
1959: △ St R
1960: ◾

1976: △ St-E

UEFA Cup

1978: △ Bas

1984: ● ◾

European Cup-Winners' Cup

1991: △ OM
1992: ○ OM
1993: △ Mon

1996: △ Bor   ○ PSG
1997: ● ◾
1998:   △ PSG
1999: △ OM
2000: ●

Stade Français 1883
Stade Red Star (1948–50). Dissolved 1985

★ **CA Charenton** 1891

★ **Club Français Paris** 1892

★ **Red Star 93** 1897

Merged with Olympique de Paris to form Red Star Olympique, (1926–46)
Merged with Stade Français to form Stade Red Star, (1948–50)
Red Star Olympique Audonien, (1950–67)
Merged with Tolouse to form Red Star Tolouse, (1967–70)
Red Star 93, (1970–present)

Paris Saint-Germain FC 1970

Merger of Paris FC and St-Germain En Laye

★ **Racing Club de Paris** 1932

(Folded 1965)

CAS Généraux

Caen
SM Caen 1913

Le Havre
Le Havre A...
1872

Guingamp ● En Avant Guingamp 1912

Rennes
Stade Rennais FC 1901

Brest
Brest-Armorique FC 1912

Laval
Stade Lavallois MFC 1902

Lorient
FC Lorient 1926

Le M...
Le M...
UC 7...

Angers
SCO Angers 1919

Tours
FC Tours 1951

Nantes

FC Nantes Atlantique 1943

Niort ● Chamois Niortais FC 1925

Angoulême ● AS Angoulême 1925

FC Girondins de Bordeaux 1881

● **Bordeaux**
F   R

★ **Nîmes OSC** 1901
SC Nîmes (1901–1937)

Toulouse
Toulouse FC 1970

★ **FC Sète** 1914

★ **Montpellier HSC** 1919/1974

Founded as Sports Olympique Montpellier, dissolved 1969

FC Martigues 1921

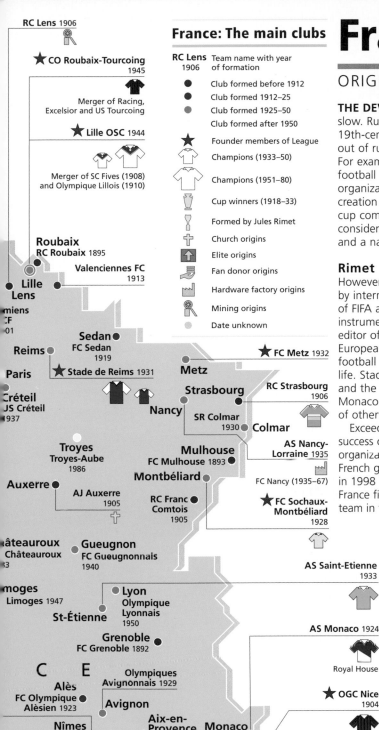

France: The main clubs

RC Lens 1906	Team name with year of formation
●	Club formed before 1912
●	Club formed 1912–25
●	Club formed 1925–50
●	Club formed after 1950
★	Founder members of League
	Champions (1933–50)
	Champions (1951–80)
	Cup winners (1918–33)
	Formed by Jules Rimet
†	Church origins
	Elite origins
	Fan donor origins
	Hardware factory origins
	Mining origins
	Date unknown

RC Lens 1906

CO Roubaix-Tourcoing 1945
Merger of Racing, Excelsior and US Tourcoing

Lille OSC 1944
Merger of SC Fives (1908) and Olympique Lillois (1910)

Roubaix RC Roubaix 1895

Valenciennes FC 1913

Lille
Lens
miens CF -01

Sedan FC Sedan 1919
Reims
Paris
Stade de Reims 1931
Créteil US Créteil 1937

Metz FC Metz 1932
Strasbourg RC Strasbourg 1906
Nancy SR Colmar 1930
Colmar
AS Nancy-Lorraine 1935

Troyes Troyes-Aube 1986
Mulhouse FC Mulhouse 1893
Montbéliard
FC Nancy (1935–67)

Auxerre AJ Auxerre 1905
RC Franc Comtois 1905
FC Sochaux-Montbéliard 1928

âteaurouxChâteauroux 3
Gueugnon FC Gueugnonnais 1940

AS Saint-Etienne 1933

moges Limoges 1947
Lyon Olympique Lyonnais 1950
St-Étienne
Grenoble FC Grenoble 1892

AS Monaco 1924
Royal House

C E
Alès FC Olympique Alèsien 1923
Olympiques Avignonnais 1929
Avignon
Nîmes
Montpellier
Béziers 1913
Sète
Martigues
Toulon
Aix-en-Provence AS Aixoise 1941
Cannes
Monaco
Nice
OGC Nice 1904

Marseille SC Toulon-Var 1945
Hyères AS Cannes 1902
Olympique Marseille 1899
Hyères FC 1912

Bastia SC Bastia 1905
Ajaccio AC Ajaccien 1910
CORSICA

France

ORIGINS AND GROWTH OF FOOTBALL

THE DEVELOPMENT OF French domestic football was slow. Rugby was significantly more popular than football in 19th-century France, and early football clubs often grew up out of rugby clubs or other sport and athletic associations. For example, Le Havre was founded in 1872, but did not play football until 1892. Prior to the First World War, five different organizations claimed the mantle of the national FA before the creation of single institution, the FFF, in 1918. Though a national cup competition began almost immediately, it was only after considerable resistance that professionalism was accepted and a national league was not contested until 1932.

Rimet and Hunot

However, domestic disorganization and weakness was paralleled by international inventiveness. France was a founder member of FIFA and supplied its first president, Jules Rimet. Rimet was instrumental in establishing the World Cup, and Gabriel Hunot, editor of sports paper *L'Équipe*, was the inspiration behind the European Cup. However, it is only since the 1950s that French football has seen signs of sporting rather than organizational life. Stade de Reims' European adventures in the 1950s, Platini and the national team in the 1980s, Olympique Marseille and Monaco in the 1990s have been the high points in an era of otherwise mediocre performances and small crowds.

Exceeding all of these, however, is the extraordinary recent success of the national team and the massive financial and organizational investment in football's infrastructure by the French government. So far, this has delivered the World Cup in 1998 and the European Championships in 2000. In 2001, France finally displaced Brazil as the world's number one team in the FIFA rankings.

Emmanuel Petit is congratulated by teammates (from left) Djorkaeff, Carembeu and Zidane after scoring France's third goal against Brazil in the last minute of the 1998 World Cup Final.

France

FOOTBALL CITIES

THE GEOGRAPHY OF FRANCE'S football teams reflects the peculiar geography of French urbanization: late to develop, slow in coming and massively concentrated on Paris. No French city outside of Paris has been able to sustain two top-flight clubs for very long and even in Paris, where this has happened for a short period, no sustainable derby of the intensity of the Italian or English cities has been created. Paris produced two major clubs in the amateur era: Red Star 93, founded in 1897 by Jules Rimet and based in the Bauer district of the city, and Racing Club, which occupied the exclusive and stylish Colombes ground in the north-west of the city.

The professional era has been unkind to both, and Red Star has been forced to leave its Bauer heartland for the peripheral wastelands of Marville, while the Colombes ground may have hosted the 1938 World Cup but cannot currently sustain even Second Division football. This vacuum in Parisian football was finally filled by the creation of Paris Saint-Germain from FC Paris and Saint-Germain-en-Laye in the early 70s. Basing itself in Racing's old ground, the newly renovated Parc des Princes, PSG has climbed into the upper echelon of French football without ever dominating it.

One city, one team

Outside of Paris, it is one city, one team – Saint-Etienne, Stade Rennais, Girondins de Bordeaux, Olympique Marseille, Nice, Lyon, Nantes, Lens and Auxerre, although in the case of Monaco, it is one principality, one team. That said, in all of these cities, the connection with the football club is intimate: in Marseille, different districts of the town have their own *ultra* (fan group), each with its own space in the Stade Vélodrome, while in Bordeaux the city and regional government have taken special care of their football club.

PARIS SAINT-GERMAIN 1970	
League	1986, *89, 93, 94, 96, 97,* 2000
Cup	1982, *83, 85, 93, 95, 98*
European Cup-Winners' Cup	1996, *97*

RACING CLUB PARIS 1932	
League	1936, *61, 62*
Cup	1936, *39, 40, 45, 49, 50, 90*

RED STAR 93 1897	
Cup	1921–23, *28, 42, 46*

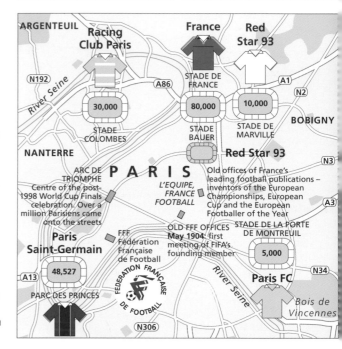

PARC DES PRINCES

48,527

Club: Paris Saint-Germain
Built: 1897
Original Capacity: 50,000
Rebuilt: 1932, 1972
Significant Matches: 1938 World Cup: three matches; 1998 World Cup: six matches; 1984 European Championships: Final; European Cup Finals: 1956, 75, 81; European Cup-Winners' Cup Final: 1978, 95; UEFA Cup Final: 1998; French Cup Final: 1919, 38, 43, 44, 65–97

STADE DE FRANCE

80,000

Club: National team
Built: 1998
Significant Matches: 1998 World Cup: nine matches including quarter-final, semi-final and Final; French Cup Final 1998–present

STADE COLOMBES
(Yves de Manoir)

30,000

Club: Racing Club Paris
Built: 1907
Original Capacity: 45,000
Rebuilt:
Record Attendance: 62,145 France v Soviet Union, 21 Oct 1965
Significant Matches: 1924 Paris Olympics; 1983 World Cup: three matches including quarter-final and Final; French Cup Final: 1925–39, 42–64

STADE RENNAIS 1901

Cup	*1922, 35,* **65, 71**

FC NANTES 1943

League	**1965,** *66, 67,* **73,** *74,* **77,** *78, 79,* **80, 81, 83, 85, 86, 95, 2001**
Cup	**1966,** *70,* **73, 79,** *83,* **93,** *99,* **2000**

GIRONDINS DE BORDEAUX 1881

League	**1950,** *52,* **65,** *66, 69, 83,* **84, 85, 87, 88, 90, 99**
Cup	**1941,** *43,* **52,** *55, 64,* **68, 69, 86, 87**
League Cup	*1997, 98,* **2002**
UEFA Cup	*1996*

RC LENS 1906

League	*1956, 57, 77,* **98,** *2002*
Cup	*1948, 75,* **98**
League Cup	**1999**

AJ AUXERRE 1905

League	**1996**
Cup	*1979, 94,* **96**

LILLE OSC 1944

League	**1946,** *48–51,* **54**
Cup	*1945,* **46–48,** *49* *53,* **55**

STADE DE REIMS 1931

League	**1947,** *49,* **53, 54, 55, 58,** *60,* **62,** *63*
Cup	**1950, 58,** *77*
European Cup	*1956, 59*

AS SAINT-ETIENNE 1933

League	*1946, 57,* **64,** *67–70,* **71,** *74–76,* **81, 82**
Cup	*1960, 62,* **68,** *70,* **74, 75, 77,** *81, 82*
European Cup	*1976*

FÉLIX-BOLLAERT **41,649** — Lens

GRIMONPREZ-JOORIS **21,000** — Lille OSC

STADE DE REIMS CHAMPAGNE **18,000** — Stade de Reims

ABBÉ-DES-CHAMPS **21,000** — AJ Auxerre

LA BEAUJOIRE-LOUIS-FONTENEAU **38,373** — FC Nantes

ROUTE DE LORIENT **23,625** — Stade Rennais

GERLAND **42,000** — Olympique Lyonnais

LOUIS II **20,000** — AS Monaco

PARC LESCURE **34,088** — Girondins de Bordeaux

GEOFFROY-GUICHARD **35,600** — AS Saint-Etienne

MUNICIPAL DU RAY **15,750** — OGC Nice

VÉLODROME **60,000** — Olympique Marseille

F R A N C E

FRANCE

France

 **34,088**	Capacity of stadium
	Stadium no longer in use for top-flight football
	Team colours
M6	Motorway
1900	Champions
2000	Runners-up

France's greatest footballing moment came when Les Bleus beat Brazil in the World Cup Final in Paris in 1998. Captain Zinedine Zidane scored two goals and fittingly won both European and World Footballer of the Year awards that year.

OLYMPIQUE MARSEILLE 1899

League	**1937,** *38, 39,* **48,** *70,* **71, 72,** *75,* **87,** *89–92,* **94,** *99*
Cup	**1924, 26, 27,** *34,* **35,** *38,* **40, 43,** *54,* **69,** *72, 76,* **86, 87,** *89,* **91**
European Cup	*1991,* **93**
UEFA Cup	*1999*

OGC NICE 1904

League	**1951, 52, 56, 59,** *68, 73, 76*
Cup	**1952, 54,** *78,* **97**

OLYMPIQUE LYONNAIS 1950

League	*1995, 2001,* **02**
Cup	*1963,* **64,** *67,* **71,** *73,* **76**
League Cup	*1996,* **2001**

AS MONACO 1924

League	**1961, 63,** *64,* **78,** *82,* **84, 88,** *91,* **92,** *97,* **2000**
Cup	*1960,* **63,** *74,* **80,** *84, 85,* **89,** *91*
League Cup	*2001*
European Cup-Winners' Cup	*1992*

France

FANS AND OWNERS

DESPITE HAVING BEEN World and European champions, France is less financially strong than the other big nations in Europe in terms of domestic football. Attendances and TV revenues have been lower, and the game is generally less commercialized. French clubs also face much larger tax bills, and the big clubs continue to subsidize smaller and amateur clubs. Little wonder that almost the entire French national squad plays overseas, and France's challenge at club level in Europe has been so limited in the last decade.

Rising income, rising debts

French club owners have been lobbying for some time to be allowed to raise more money. The FFF and the government have refused to allow them to float on the stock market but have introduced two categories of ownership: SAOS (*Société Anonyme à Objet Sportif*) and SASP (*Société Anonyme Sportive Professionelle*). The SAOS model is the status quo, leaving the clubs in the hands of private investors and the supporters' association. The SASP allows the clubs to distribute dividends to shareholders, pay salaries to elected officials and reduce the supporters' association share of the club below one-third. This second option is being pursued by the bigger clubs and big companies are beginning to take stakes in some of them. However, despite rising income of all kinds, it is still risky; the clubs in the top division in 2002 are collectively in debt to the tune of £82.2 million

Although France has little of the *ultra* culture of Italy or Spain, in Marseille, Lens, Bastia and Metz the marginal status of the cities, geographically and socially, gives support a peculiar intensity. Marseille's many *ultra* groups, who come from different parts of the city, have their places in the stands clearly marked. There is very little violence in French football, but OM's fans can and do get pretty terse with their club. At the other end of the scale, the executive boxes built during the stadium refurbishment programme for the 1998 World Cup seem full as football acquires an elite glamour it has lacked in France for a long time.

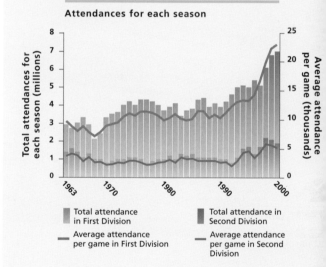

Club Budgets 2001–02

French Attendances

Attendances for each season

Total attendance in First Division

Total attendance in Second Division

Average attendance per game in First Division

Average attendance per game in Second Division

Prince Rainier of Monaco's money took the club to the first division in 1953. Since then the Grimaldi family's subventions have been augmented by a FF50 million subsidy from Monaco's national council.

Average Attendance

Average attendance for season 2000–01 (thousands)

Capacity

Attendance as a percentage of capacity for season 2000–01 (capacity in brackets)

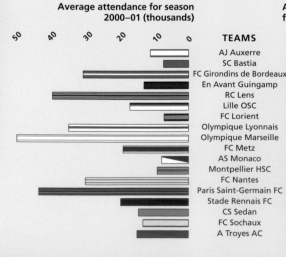
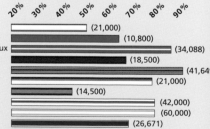
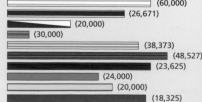

TEAMS	Capacity
AJ Auxerre	(21,000)
SC Bastia	(10,800)
FC Girondins de Bordeaux	(34,088)
En Avant Guingamp	(18,500)
RC Lens	(41,649)
Lille OSC	(21,000)
FC Lorient	(14,500)
Olympique Lyonnais	(42,000)
Olympique Marseille	(60,000)
FC Metz	(26,671)
AS Monaco	(20,000)
Montpellier HSC	(30,000)
FC Nantes	(38,373)
Paris Saint-Germain FC	(48,527)
Stade Rennais FC	(23,625)
CS Sedan	(24,000)
FC Sochaux	(20,000)
A Troyes AC	(18,325)

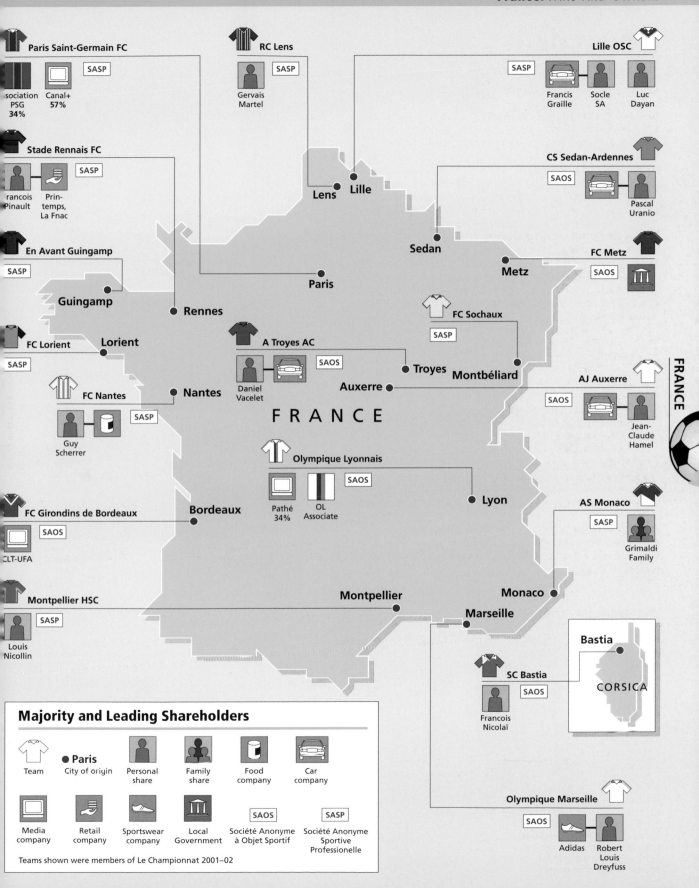

Paris Saint-Germain FC

sociation
PSG
34%

Canal+
57%

SASP

Stade Rennais FC

rancois
Pinault

Prin-
temps,
La Fnac

SASP

En Avant Guingamp

SASP

Guingamp

FC Lorient

SASP

Lorient

FC Nantes

Guy
Scherrer

SASP

Nantes

FC Girondins de Bordeaux

SAOS

CLT-UFA

Bordeaux

Montpellier HSC

SASP

Louis
Nicollin

RC Lens

Gervais
Martel

SASP

Lens   Lille

Paris

FC Sochaux

SASP

Sedan

Metz

A Troyes AC

Daniel
Vacelet

SAOS

Troyes   Montbéliard

Auxerre

F R A N C E

Olympique Lyonnais

Pathé
34%

OL
Associate

SAOS

Lyon

Montpellier

Marseille

Lille OSC

SASP

Francis
Graille

Socle
SA

Luc
Dayan

CS Sedan-Ardennes

SAOS

Pascal
Uranio

FC Metz

SAOS

AJ Auxerre

SAOS

Jean-
Claude
Hamel

FRANCE

AS Monaco

SASP

Grimaldi
Family

Monaco

SC Bastia

Francois
Nicolaï

SAOS

Bastia

CORSICA

Olympique Marseille

SAOS

Adidas   Robert
Louis
Dreyfuss

Majority and Leading Shareholders

Team

● **Paris**
City of origin

Personal
share

Family
share

Food
company

Car
company

Media
company

Retail
company

Sportswear
company

Local
Government

SAOS
Société Anonyme
à Objet Sportif

SASP
Société Anonyme
Sportive
Professionelle

Teams shown were members of Le Championnat 2001–02

France

PLAYERS AND MANAGERS

FRENCH FOOTBALL WENT PROFESSIONAL in the 1930s, but it was not until the postwar era that the first generation of international stars began to emerge. Just Fontaine (who holds the record for the most goals at a single World Cup Finals tournament) was among the first and like many to follow was born in French colonial North Africa – Morocco in his case. Playing alongside Fontaine at Reims was Raymond Kopa. Born of a Polish immigrant family, Raymond Kopaszeweski was the leading centre-forward of the era. France's next wave of great players emerged in the 1980s, built around the prodigious talent of Michel Platini, France's greatest-ever player. Platini's midfield colleagues Alain Giresse and Jean Tigana also stand out from this era and both have gone on to successful managerial careers. This era also saw the beginning of a transformation in the organization of training, management and scouting in France, with massive investment from government and clubs in talent and education.

Fantastic success

The leading players of the early 21st century are a product of this earlier era and again they reflect France's internal diversity and the continuing waves of African and Arabic immigration: Zidane, the outstanding player of his generation, was born of Algerian parents; Patrick Viera transferred from Senegalese to French citizenship. The fantastic success of the French team in recent years has seen the leading players head for Italy, Spain and, increasingly, England. French managers have followed them, with Arsène Wenger, Jean Tigana and Gérard Houllier all employed in the English Premiership. Simultaneously, there has been a huge influx of Africans in particular to the leading French clubs.

Never a favourite of the French national team manager, Eric Cantona raised the profile of French football when he left France for England in 1992. Hugely successful, both at Leeds and Manchester United, Cantona remains one of the finest players of the 1990s.

Top 20 International Caps

PLAYER	CAPS	GOALS	FIRST MATCH	LAST MATCH
Didier Deschamps*	103	4	1989	2000
Laurent Blanc*	97	16	1989	2000
Manuel Amoros	82	1	1982	1992
Marcel Desailly*	80	3	1993	2002
Maxime Bossis	76	1	1976	1986
Michel Platini	72	41	1976	1987
Lilian Thuram*	71	2	1994	2002
Zinedine Zidane*	71	18	1994	2002
Youri Djorkaeff*	69	26	1993	2000
Marius Trésor	65	4	1971	1983
Roger Marche	63	1	1947	1959
Bixente Lizarazu*	61	2	1992	2000
Luis Fernandez	60	6	1982	1992
Robert Jonquet	58	0	1948	1960
Henri Michel	58	4	1967	1980
Patrick Battiston	56	3	1977	1989
Jean-Pierre Papin	54	30	1986	1995
Emmanuel Petit*	54	6	1991	2002
Didier Six	52	13	1976	1984
Jean Tigana	52	1	1980	1988

Top 10 International Goalscorers

PLAYER	GOALS	CAPS	FIRST MATCH	LAST MATCH
Michel Platini	41	72	1976	1987
Just Fontaine	30	21	1953	1960
Jean-Pierre Papin	30	54	1986	1995
Youri Djorkaeff*	26	69	1993	2000
Jean Vincent	22	46	1953	1961
Jean Nicolas	21	25	1933	1938
Paul Nicolas	20	35	1920	1931
Eric Cantona	20	45	1987	1995
Jean Baratte	19	32	1944	1952
Raymond Kopa	18	45	1952	1962
Zinedine Zidane*	18	71	1994	2002

* Indicates players still playing at least at club level.

French International Managers

DATES	NAME	GAMES	WON	DRAWN	LOST
1960–64	Georges Verniet, Henri Guerin	24	4	6	14
1964–65	Henri Guerin	15	5	4	6
1966	Jean Snella, Jose Arribas	4	2	0	2
1967	Just Fontaine	9	2	3	4
1967–68	Louis Dugauquez	31	15	5	11
1969–73	Georges Boulogne	15	6	4	5
1973–75	Stefan Kovacs	15	6	4	5
1976–84	Michel Hidalgo	75	41	16	18
1984–88	Henri Michel	36	16	12	8
1988–92	Michel Platini	29	16	8	5
1992–93	Gérard Houllier	12	7	1	4
1994–98	Aime Jacquet	53	34	16	3
1998–	Roger Lemerre	43	30	8	5

All figures correct as of 14 February 2002.

Player of the Year

YEAR	PLAYER	CLUB
1963	Douis	AS Monaco
1964	Artelesa	AS Monaco
1965	Gondet	FC Nantes
1966	Gondet	FC Nantes
1967	Bosquier	AS Saint-Etienne
1968	Bosquier	AS Saint-Etienne
1969	Revelli	AS Saint-Etienne
1970	Carnus	AS Saint-Etienne
1971	Carnus	AS Saint-Etienne/Olympique Marseille
1972	Trésor	Ajaccio/Olympique Marseille
1973	Bereta	AS Saint-Etienne
1974	Bereta	AS Saint-Etienne
1975	Guillou	Angers/OGC Nice
1976	Platini	FC Nancy
1977	Platini	FC Nancy
1978	Petit	AS Monaco
1979	Bossis	FC Nantes
1980	Larios	AS Saint-Etienne
1981	Bossis	FC Nantes
1982	Giresse	Girondins de Bordeaux
1983	Giresse	Girondins de Bordeaux
1984	Tigana	Girondins de Bordeaux
1985	Fernandez	Paris Saint-Germain
1986	Amoros	AS Monaco
1987	Giresse	Olympique Marseille
1988	Paille	FC Sochaux
1989	Papin	Marseille
1990	Blanc	Montpellier
1991	Papin	Olympique Marseille

Player of the Year (continued)

YEAR	PLAYER	CLUB
1992	Roche	Paris Saint-Germain
1993	Ginola	Paris Saint-Germain
1994	Lama	Paris Saint-Germain
1995	Guérin	Paris Saint-Germain
1996	Deschamps	Juventus [Ita]
1997	Thuram	Parma [Ita]
1998	Zidane	Juventus [Ita]
1999	Wiltord	Girondins de Bordeaux
2000	Henry	Arsenal [Eng]
2001	Viera	Arsenal [Eng]

Manager of the Year

YEAR	MANAGER	CLUB
1970	Batteux	AS Saint-Etienne
1970	Zatelli	O Marseille
1971	Firoud	Nîmes Olympique
1971	Prouff	Stade Rennais
1972	Snella	OGC Nice
1973	Herbin	AS Saint-Etienne
1974	Cahuzac	SC Bastia
1975	Huart	FC Metz
1976	Herbin	AS Saint-Etienne
1977	Cahuzac	SC Bastia
1978	Gress	RC Strasbourg
1979	Le Milinaire	Laval
1980	Hauss	FC Sochaux
1980	Vincent	FC Nantes
1981	Jacquet	Girondins de Bordeaux

Manager of the Year (continued)

YEAR	MANAGER	CLUB
1982	Hidalgo	France
1983	Le Milinaire	Laval
1984	Jacquet	Girondins de Bordeaux
1985	Suaudeau	FC Nantes
1986	Roux	AJ Auxerre
1987	Fernandez	AS Cannes
1988	Roux	AJ Auxerre
1989	Gili	O Marseille
1990	Kasperczak	SCP Montpelier
1991	Jeandupeux	Caen
1992	Suaudeau	FC Nantes
1993	Fernandez	AS Cannes
1994	Suaudeau	FC Nantes
1995	Smerecki	Guingamp
1996	Roux	AJ Auxerre
1997	Tigana	AS Monaco
1998	Jacquet	France
1999	Baup	Girondins de Bordeaux
2000	Dupont	FC Sedan
2001	Halilhodzic	Lille OSC

Elected by *France Football* magazine.

Jean Tigana was an integral part of the legendary French midfield of the 1980s along with Michel Platini and Alain Giresse.

FRANCE

Top Goalscorers by Season 1963–2002

SEASON	PLAYER	CLUB	GOALS
1962–63	Masnaghetti	Valenciennes	35
1963–64	Oudjani	RC Lens	30
1964–65	Simon	FC Nantes	24
1965–66	Gondet	FC Nantes	36
1966–67	Revelli	Saint-Etienne	31
1967–68	Sansonetti	Ajaccio	26
1968–69	Guy	FC Lyon	25
1969–70	Revelli	Saint-Etienne	28
1970–71	Skoblar	O Marseille	44
1971–72	Skoblar	O Marseille	30
1972–73	Skoblar	O Marseille	20
1973–74	Bianchi	Stade Reims	30
1974–75	Onnis	AS Monaco	30
1975–76	Bianchi	Stade Reims	34
1976–77	Bianchi	Stade Reims	28
1977–78	Bianchi	Paris SG	37

SEASON	PLAYER	CLUB	GOALS
1978–79	Bianchi	Paris SG	27
1979–80	Onnis	AS Monaco	21
1979–80	Kostedde	Laval	21
1980–81	Onnis	Tours	24
1981–82	Onnis	Tours	29
1982–83	Halilhodzic	FC Nantes	27
1983–84	Garande	AJ Auxerre	21
1983–84	Onnis	Toulon	21
1984–85	Halilhodzic	FC Nantes	28
1985–86	Bocandé	FC Metz	23
1986–87	Zénier	FC Metz	18
1987–88	Papin	O Marseille	19
1988–89	Papin	O Marseille	22
1989–90	Papin	O Marseille	30
1990–91	Papin	O Marseille	23
1991–92	Papin	O Marseille	27

SEASON	PLAYER	CLUB	GOALS
1992–93	Boksic	O Marseille	22
1993–94	Djorkaeff	AS Monaco	20
1993–94	Boli	RC Lens	20
1993–94	Ouédec	FC Nantes	20
1994–95	Loko	FC Nantes	22
1995–96	Anderson	AS Monaco	21
1996–97	Guivarc'h	Stade Rennais	22
1997–98	Guivarc'h	AJ Auxerre	21
1998–99	Wiltord	Girondins de Bordeaux	22
1999–2000	Anderson	AS Monaco	23
2000–01	Anderson	Lyon	22
2001–02	Cisse	AJ Auxerre	22
2001–02	Pauleta	Bordeaux	22

Foreign Players in France (in top division squads)

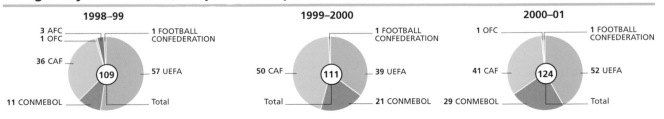

1998–99: 3 AFC, 1 OFC, 36 CAF, 11 CONMEBOL, 1 FOOTBALL CONFEDERATION, 57 UEFA, Total 109

1999–2000: 1 FOOTBALL CONFEDERATION, 50 CAF, 39 UEFA, 21 CONMEBOL, Total 111

2000–01: 1 OFC, 1 FOOTBALL CONFEDERATION, 41 CAF, 52 UEFA, 29 CONMEBOL, Total 124

France

LE CHAMPIONNAT 1981–2001

FRANCE

AT THE BEGINNING OF THE 1980s, the French championship was evenly distributed between clubs built with old money and clubs built with new money. The new money came in the shape of Claude Bez, Girondins de Bordeaux's ambitious president. Without a title since 1950 and with its Lescure stadium devoted mainly to rugby and cycling, Bordeaux was transformed by Bez's injection of money and energy. In the early 1980s a new stadium and training centre were constructed, a considerable deal done with the newly emergent cable TV company Canal Plus, and a stylish team assembled under future national team coach Aimé Jacquet, including Jean Tigana and Alain Giresse. Those years belonged to Bordeaux with three league titles and a top four place for seven seasons. But Bez was accused and convicted of fraud and mismanagement, and Bordeaux was relegated by the league in 1991. The new money at Paris Saint-Germain brought in Luis Fernandez and Osvaldo Ardiles and saw the team finally take its first title in 1986. The old money and old form came in the shape of titles for Monaco, under Arsène Wenger, and for Nantes.

Further south, Olympique Marseille began the decade bankrupt and in the second division. But the potential of the biggest and most fiercely supported club in the country was in no doubt. Enter Bernard Tapie, then boss of Adidas, who bought the club in 1985. Tapie brought money, energy and connections as well as players of the calibre of Jean-Pierre Papin, Chris Waddle, Didier Deschamps and Abedi Pele. Elected as a socialist MP, Tapie was described as the 'Red Berlusconi', and he drove the right-wingers mad as five league titles and three tilts at the European Cup followed. Finally, in 1993, Tapie's Marseille beat Berlusconi's Milan 1-0 to take Europe's top club prize. The day afterwards it was revealed in the French press that there was serious evidence of match-fixing in Marseille's league game against US Valenciennes

that season. The floodgates opened, accusations turned to convictions for match-fixing and illegal payments in the transfer market. Tapie was imprisoned, the club relegated and eventually made insolvent. Since then, despite considerable investment from Adidas's new boss Robert Louis Dreyfuss, the team has yet to show the form of the Tapie years.

TV and its money

In the mid-1990s money began to pour into French football from new TV deals, and salaries and transfers began to rise. But given France's high employment taxes and the relatively lower percentage incomes from sponsorship and TV available to French clubs (in comparison with Spain, Italy and England), the leading French players of the era, including nearly all of the 1998 World Cup-winning squad, played outside France. In their wake, French clubs have drawn extensively on African and Eastern European players, and none have been able to establish any kind of dominance.

In the late 1990s there have been titles for PSG, AJ Auxerre, RC Lens, Monaco and Nantes. At Auxerre, long-standing coach Guy Roux finally hit the jackpot with the club's youth academy. Nantes rose on money from Guy Scherrer, a millionaire in the food industry. Monaco took the 2000 title by a length with an attacking side including David Trezeguet and Marco Simeone. But European success has eluded French clubs, and the struggle to survive at the rarefied level of European competition has left them seriously in debt. Their competitors at the bottom of the league are equally troubled. The only serious new challenger to have emerged from the era of TV money has been Olympique Lyonnais, while for many of the old guard times have been even harder; Saint-Etienne, Stade de Reims, Racing Club Paris, SM Caen and OGC Nice have all found themselves slipping out of the top flight.

FC Nantes may come from a small provincial city, but the team's impressive youth academy and Guy Scherrer's biscuit company millions have kept the club at the top of the French game since the mid-1990s. This is the team that won the 1994–95 championship.

With roots in the mines of north-eastern France, Lens has become a title contender in recent years.

The irrepressible Bernard Tapie and friends celebrate. Despite his downfall in 1993, Tapie has clawed his way back into French football with a short spell behind the scenes at Marseille in 2002.

French League Income (in million francs)

SEASON	1995–96	1996–97	1997–98	1998–99	1999–2000	2000–01
Income	1.81	1.92	2.12	2.58	3.98	3.99
Costs	1.78	1.97	2.42	3.04	3.74	4.24
Gross profit	0.03	-0.05	-0.3	-0.46	0.24	-0.25
Net profit	0.12	0.16	0.34	0.43	0.53	-0.13

Total for all top division clubs

Sources of Income 2000

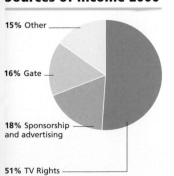

15% Other
16% Gate
18% Sponsorship and advertising
51% TV Rights

Income of French first division clubs in season 1999–2000

Player Salaries 1996–2001

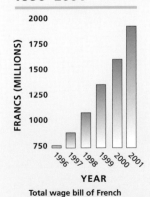

FRANCS (MILLIONS)
YEAR

Total wage bill of French first division clubs

Champions' Winning Margin 1991–2001

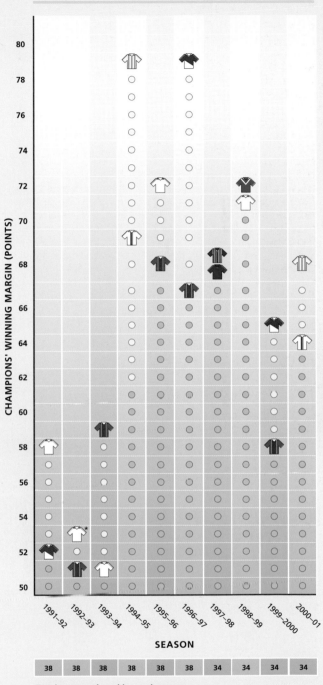

CHAMPIONS' WINNING MARGIN (POINTS)

SEASON

38	38	38	38	38	38	34	34	34	34

**Total games played by each team
(2 points awarded for a win until 1995, when 3 points awarded)**

* Olympique Marseille finished with 53 points but were stripped of the title, which was not awarded

AJ Auxerre
Girondins de Bordeaux
RC Lens
Olympique Lyonnais
Olympique Marseille
FC Metz
AS Monaco
FC Nantes
Paris Saint-Germain

FRANCE

Key to League Positions Table

- ◼ League champions
- ◻ Season of promotion to league
- ◻ Season of relegation from league
- ◻ Other teams playing in league
- | 5 | Final position in league

FRANCE

A young Thierry Henry provided the firepower to take Jean Tigana's AS Monaco to the French championship in 1997.

Guy Roux has been at Auxerre for almost four decades, nurturing talents like Eric Cantona. The club's scouting and youth network is second to none.

French League Positions 1981–2001

TEAM	1981-82	1982-83	1983-84	1984-85	1985-86	1986-87	1987-88	1988-89	1989-90	1990-91	1991-92	1992-93	1993-94	1994-95	1995-96	1996-97	1997-98	1998-99	1999-2000	2000-01
SCO Angers													20							
AJ Auxerre	15	8	3	4	7	4	9	5	6	3	4	6	3	4	1	6	7	14	8	13
SC Bastia	12	17	11	14	20									15	15	7	9	13	10	8
Berrichonne Chat																	17			
Girondins de Bordeaux	4	2	1	1	3	1	2	13	2	10†		4	4	7	16	4	5	1	4	4
Brest-Armorique FC	9	10	17	9	14	8	19		10	11†										
SM Caen								16	16	8	5	11	16	19		17				
AS Cannes							12	12	11	4	19		6	9	14	15	18			
FC Gueugnonnais																18				
En Avant Guingamp														10	12	16				10
Le Havre AC			17	17	20						7	15	17	12	13	14	10	15	17	
Stade Lavallois MFC	5	5	10	10	11	9	14	19												
RC Lens	13	4	13	7	5	10	17	20			8	9	10	5	5	13	1	6	5	14
Lille OSC	14	13	9	15	10	14	11	8	17	6	13	17	15	14	17	19				3
FC Lorient																		16		
Olympique Marseille				17	12	2	6	1	1	1	1	1*	2**			11	4	2	15	15
FC Martigues													18	11	20					
FC Metz	17	9	12	5	6	6	8	15	14	12	12	12	12	8	4	5	2	10	11	12
AS Monaco	1	6	2	3	9	5	1	3	3	2	2	3	9	6	3	1	3	4	1	11
Montpellier HSC	20						3	9	13	7	6	10	7	17	6	10	12	8	18	
FC Mulhouse		20							20											
AS Nancy-Lorraine	8	7	15	12	18	19			17	20						18		11	16	
Olympique Lyonnais	16	19							8	5	16	14	8	2	11	8	6	3	3	2
FC Nantes	6	1	6	2	2	12	10	7	7	15	9	5	5	1	7	3	11	7	12	1
OGC Nice	19						8	11	16	6	18	14†				16	12	20		
Nîmes Olympique		19									15	20								
Chamois Niortais FC					18															
Paris Saint-Germain	7	3	4	13	1	7	15	2	5	9	3	2	1	3	2	2	8	9	2	9
Racing Club de Paris			20			13	7	17	19											
AS Saint-Etienne	2	14	18		16	4	14	15	13	10	7	11	18	19					6	17
CS Sedan Ardennes																			7	5
Stade Rennais FC		20		13	20			20	18					13	8	16	14	5	13	6
FC Rouen		16	14	18																
FC Sochaux	3	12	7	8	15	18		4	4	18	17	16	14	20				17		
RC Strasbourg	10	15	8	16	19		18					8	13	10	9	9	13	12	9	18
SC Toulon-Var			16	6	16	15	5	11	12	16	14	19								
Toulouse FC		11	5	11	4	3	13	10	9	19	11	13	19				15	18		16
FC Tours	11	18	19																	
A Troyes AC																			14	7
US Valenciennes	18										18									

Le Championnat

FC Nantes Atlantique	Team name
(shirt)	League champions/ runners-up
1983, 85	Champions in bold Runners-up in italics
(shirt)	Other teams in Le Championnat
● Nantes	City of origin

The mercurial Jay Jay Okocha (in blue) has shown the same mixed form as Paris Saint-Germain in the last few years; occasionally spellbinding, but fatefully inconsistent in the league. Despite being one of France's richest clubs, PSG's last championship win was in 1994.

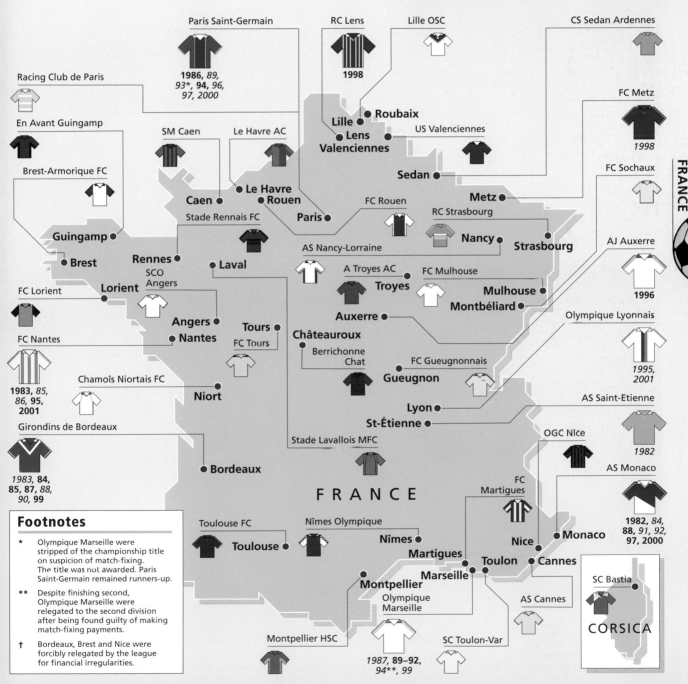

FRANCE

Paris Saint-Germain
1986, 89, 93*, **94**, **96**, **97**, **2000**

RC Lens
1998

Lille OSC

CS Sedan Ardennes

Racing Club de Paris

FC Metz
1998

En Avant Guingamp

SM Caen

Le Havre AC

US Valenciennes

FC Sochaux

Brest-Armorique FC

Stade Rennais FC

FC Rouen

RC Strasbourg

AJ Auxerre
1996

FC Lorient

SCO Angers

A Troyes AC

FC Mulhouse

Olympique Lyonnais
1995, **2001**

FC Nantes
1983, 85, **86**, 95, **2001**

Chamoîs Niortais FC

Berrichonne Chat

FC Gueugnonnais

AS Saint-Etienne

Girondins de Bordeaux
1983, **84**, **85**, **87**, 88, **90**, 99

Stade Lavallois MFC

OGC Nice
1982

AS Monaco
1982, 84, **88**, 91, **92**, **97**, 2000

FC Martigues

Toulouse FC

Nîmes Olympique

AS Cannes

SC Bastia

Montpellier HSC

Olympique Marseille
1987, **89–92**, 94**, 99

SC Toulon-Var

F R A N C E

CORSICA

Cities
Lille ● Roubaix
Lens ●
Valenciennes
Sedan ●
Metz ●
Nancy
Strasbourg
Mulhouse
Montbéliard
Guingamp ●
Brest ●
Rennes ●
Caen ●
Le Havre ●
Rouen ●
Paris ●
Laval ●
Troyes
Auxerre ●
Lorient ●
Angers ●
Nantes ●
Tours ●
Châteauroux ●
Gueugnon
Lyon ●
St-Étienne ●
Niort ●
Bordeaux ●
Nice ●
Monaco ●
Toulouse ●
Nîmes ●
Montpellier ●
Martigues ●
Marseille ●
Toulon ●
Cannes ●

Footnotes

* Olympique Marseille were stripped of the championship title on suspicion of match-fixing. The title was not awarded. Paris Saint-Germain remained runners-up.

** Despite finishing second, Olympique Marseille were relegated to the second division after being found guilty of making match-fixing payments.

† Bordeaux, Brest and Nice were forcibly relegated by the league for financial irregularities.

France

Fédération Française de Football
Founded: 1918
Joined FIFA: 1904
Joined UEFA: 1954

DESPITE BEING AT THE FOREFRONT of the global organization of football, French domestic football began in a chaotic manner. In the early part of the 20th century five different football federations vied to organize the national game and each established a separate national league.

With the creation of the Fédération Française de Football in 1918, the first national cup competition was established. The French Cup has been played for every year since, except for 1992, when tragic events overshadowed the French game. In a semi-final match between the Corsican club SC Bastia and Olympique Marseille, a temporary stand collapsed, leaving 15 dead and over 1,500 injured. The tournament was abandoned. In 2000, Calais, an amateur team from the fourth division, reached the Cup Final, only to lose 2-1 to FC Nantes, who scored the winner in the 90th minute.

A national league was formed in 1926, and was solidified by the advent of professionalism in 1932. The national championships acquired a different format during the Second World War with the champions of different zones (North [Occupied], South and Central) playing off against each other. In 1993 Olympique Marseille won the league, but was stripped of its title for alleged match fixing.

French League Record 1933–2002

SEASON	CHAMPIONS	RUNNERS-UP
1933	Olympique Lille	AS Cannes
1934	FC Sète	SC Fives
1935	FC Sochaux	RC Strasbourg
1936	Racing Club Paris	Olympique Lille
1937	Olympique Marseille	FC Sochaux
1938	FC Sochaux	Olympique Marseille
1939	FC Sète	Olympique Marseille
1940–45	*no championship*	
1946	Lille OSC	AS Saint-Etienne
1947	CO Roubaix	Stade de Reims
1948	Olympique Marseille	Lille OSC
1949	Stade de Reims	Lille OSC
1950	Girondins de Bordeaux	Lille OSC
1951	OGC Nice	Lille OSC
1952	OGC Nice	Girondins de Bordeaux
1953	Stade de Reims	FC Sochaux
1954	Lille OSC	Stade de Reims
1955	Stade de Reims	FC Toulouse
1956	OGC Nice	RC Lens
1957	AS Saint-Etienne	RC Lens
1958	Stade de Reims	Nîmes Olympique
1959	OGC Nice	Nîmes Olympique
1960	Stade de Reims	Nîmes Olympique
1961	AS Monaco	Racing Club Paris

One of France's greatest footballers was Michel Platini. His career started with Nancy, but he joined AS Saint-Etienne in 1979. Almost at the end of its golden era, having won the league title seven times in the previous ten years, Saint-Etienne's fortunes were reignited by Platini. The team won the title again in 1981, and finished second in 1982, before Platini moved to Juventus in Italy.

FRANCE

The legendary Raymond Kopa. He was born to a Polish immigrant family in inter-war France – similar origins to many French players of the era. His goals made Stade de Reims one of the most successful teams in France during the late 1950s. He moved to Real Madrid in 1956, but returned to Reims as European Footballer of the Year two years later.

French League Summary

TEAM	TOTALS	CHAMPIONS & RUNNERS-UP (BOLD) (ITALICS)
AS Saint-Etienne	10, 3	*1946*, **57**, **64**, **67–70**, *71*, **74–76**, **81**, *82*
FC Nantes	8, 7	**1965**, **66**, **67**, **73**, **74**, **77**, **78**, **79**, **80**, **81**, **83**, **85**, **86**, **95**, **2001**
Olympique Marseille	8, 7	**1937**, **38**, **39**, **48**, **70**, *71*, *72*, *75*, **87**, **89–92**, *94*, *99*
AS Monaco	7, 4	**1961**, **63**, *64*, **78**, **82**, *84*, **88**, *91*, *92*, **97**, **2000**
Stade de Reims	6, 3	**1947**, **49**, **53**, *54*, **55**, **58**, **60**, **62**, *63*
Girondins de Bordeaux	5, 7	*1950*, *52*, **65**, *66*, *69*, **83**, **84**, **85**, **87**, *88*, *90*, *99*
OGC Nice	4, 3	**1951**, *52*, **56**, **59**, *68*, *73*, *76*
Paris Saint-Germain	2, 5	**1986**, *89*, *93*, **94**, *96*, *97*, *2000*
Lille OSC	2, 4	**1946**, *48–51*, **54**
FC Sochaux	2, 3	**1935**, *37*, *38*, *53*, *80*
FC Sète	2, 0	**1934**, **39**
RC Lens	1, 4	*1956*, *57*, *77*, *98*, **2002**
Olympique Lyonnais	1, 2	*1995*, **2001**, *02*
Racing Club Paris	1, 2	**1936**, *61*, *62*
Olympique Lille	1, 1	**1933**, *36*
RC Strasbourg	1, 1	**1935**, *79*
AJ Auxerre	1, 0	**1996**
CO Roubaix	1, 0	**1947**
Nîmes Olympique	0, 4	*1958–60*, *72*
AS Cannes	0, 1	*1933*
FC Metz	0, 1	*1998*
FC Toulouse	0, 1	*1955*
SC Fives	0, 1	*1934*

French League Record (*continued*)

SEASON	CHAMPIONS	RUNNERS-UP
1962	Stade de Reims	Racing Club Paris
1963	AS Monaco	Stade de Reims
1964	AS Saint-Etienne	AS Monaco
1965	FC Nantes	Girondins de Bordeaux
1966	FC Nantes	Girondins de Bordeaux
1967	AS Saint-Etienne	FC Nantes
1968	AS Saint-Etienne	OGC Nice
1969	AS Saint-Etienne	Girondins de Bordeaux
1970	AS Saint-Etienne	Olympique Marseille
1971	Olympique Marseille	AS Saint-Etienne
1972	Olympique Marseille	Nîmes Olympique
1973	FC Nantes	OGC Nice
1974	AS Saint-Etienne	FC Nantes
1975	AS Saint-Etienne	Olympique Marseille
1976	AS Saint-Etienne	OGC Nice
1977	FC Nantes	RC Lens
1978	AS Monaco	FC Nantes
1979	RC Strasbourg	FC Nantes
1980	FC Nantes	FC Sochaux
1981	AS Saint-Etienne	FC Nantes
1982	AS Monaco	AS Saint-Etienne
1983	FC Nantes	Girondins de Bordeaux
1984	Girondins de Bordeaux	AS Monaco
1985	Girondins de Bordeaux	FC Nantes
1986	Paris Saint-Germain	FC Nantes
1987	Girondins de Bordeaux	Olympique Marseille
1988	AS Monaco	Girondins de Bordeaux
1989	Olympique Marseille	Paris Saint-Germain
1990	Olympique Marseille	Girondins de Bordeaux
1991	Olympique Marseille	AS Monaco
1992	Olympique Marseille	AS Monaco
1993	Olympique Marseille*	Paris Saint-Germain
1994	Paris Saint-Germain	Olympique Marseille**
1995	FC Nantes	Olympique Lyonnais
1996	AJ Auxerre	Paris Saint-Germain
1997	AS Monaco	Paris Saint-Germain
1998	RC Lens	FC Metz
1999	Girondins de Bordeaux	Olympique Marseille
2000	AS Monaco	Paris Saint-Germain
2001	FC Nantes	Olympique Lyonnais
2002	Olympique Lyonnais	RC Lens

* Title won by Olympique Marseille but taken away from them for alleged match-fixing payments. Title not awarded.

Despite finishing second Olympique Marseille was relegated to the Second Division after being found guilty of match-fixing payments.

Midfielder Salomon Olembe played 30 games during FC Nantes' championship-winning season in 2000–01. The 20-year-old Cameroonian also scored four times during the campaign.

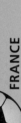

FRANCE

George Weah signed for AS Monaco in 1988, bought from Tonnerre Yaoundé of Cameroon by manager Arsène Wenger. He went on to become one of the finest players in the world, also appearing for PSG, Milan, Chelsea, Manchester City and Olympique Marseille.

French Cup Record 1918–2002

YEAR	WINNERS	SCORE	RUNNERS-UP
1918	Olympique de Pantin	3-0	FC Lyon
1919	CAS Généraux	3-2 (aet)	Olympique Paris
1920	CA Paris	2-1	Le Havre AC
1921	Red Star Paris	2-1	Olympique Paris
1922	Red Star Paris	2-0	Stade Rennais
1923	Red Star Paris	4-2	FC Sète
1924	Olympique Marseille	3-2	FC Sète
1925	CAS Généraux	1-1 (aet), (replay) 3-2	FC Rouen
1926	Olympique Marseille	4-1	AS Valentigney
1927	Olympique Marseille	3-0	US Quevilly
1928	Red Star Paris	3-1	CA Paris
1929	SO Montpellier	2-0	FC Sète
1930	FC Sète	3-1	Racing Club France
1931	Club Français	3-0	SO Montpellier
1932	AS Cannes	1-0	Racing Club Roubaix
1933	Excelsior Roubaix	3-1	Racing Club Roubaix
1934	FC Sète	2-1	Olympique Marseille
1935	Olympique Marseille	3-0	Stade Rennais
1936	Racing Club Paris	1-0	US Charleville
1937	FC Sochaux	2-1	RC Strasbourg
1938	Olympique Marseille	2-1 (aet)	FC Metz

French Cup Record (*continued*)

YEAR	WINNERS	SCORE	RUNNERS-UP
1939	Racing Club Paris	3-1	Olympique Lille
1940	Racing Club Paris	2-1	Olympique Marseille
1941	Girondins de Bordeaux	2-0	SC Fives
1942	Red Star Paris	2-0	FC Sète
1943	Olympique Marseille	2-2 (aet), (replay) 4-0	Girondins de Bordeaux
1944	Nancy-Lorraine XI	4-0	Reims-Champagne XI
1945	Racing Club Paris	3-0	Lille OSC
1946	Lille OSC	4-2	Red Star Paris
1947	Lille OSC	2-0	RC Strasbourg
1948	Lille OSC	3-2	RC Lens
1949	Racing Club Paris	5-2	Lille OSC
1950	Stade de Reims	2-0	Racing Club Paris
1951	RC Strasbourg	3-0	US Valenciennes
1952	OGC Nice	5-3	Girondins de Bordeaux
1953	Lille OSC	2-1	FC Nancy
1954	OGC Nice	2-1	Olympique Marseille
1955	Lille OSC	5-2	Girondins de Bordeaux
1956	FC Sedan	3-1	FC Troyes-Aube
1957	FC Toulouse	6-3	SC Angers
1958	Stade de Reims	3-1	Nîmes Olympique
1959	Le Havre AC	2-2 (aet), (replay) 3-0	FC Sochaux
1960	AS Monaco	4-2 (aet)	AS Saint-Etienne
1961	FC Sedan	3-1	Nîmes Olympique
1962	AS Saint-Etienne	1-0	FC Nancy
1963	AS Monaco	0-0 (aet), (replay) 2-0	Olympique Lyonnais
1964	Olympique Lyonnais	2-0	Girondins de Bordeaux
1965	Stade Rennais	2-2 (aet), (replay) 3-1	FC Sedan
1966	RC Strasbourg	1-0	FC Nantes
1967	Olympique Lyonnais	3-1	FC Sochaux
1968	AS Saint-Etienne	2-1	Girondins de Bordeaux
1969	Olympique Marseille	2-0	Girondins de Bordeaux
1970	AS Saint-Etienne	5-0	FC Nantes
1971	Stade Rennais	1-0	Olympique Lyonnais
1972	Olympique Marseille	2-1	SC Bastia
1973	Olympique Lyonnais	2-1	FC Nantes
1974	AS Saint-Etienne	2-1	AS Monaco
1975	AS Saint-Etienne	2-0	RC Lens
1976	Olympique Marseille	2-0	Olympique Lyonnais
1977	AS Saint-Etienne	2-1	Stade de Reims
1978	AS Nancy	1-0	OGC Nice
1979	FC Nantes	4-1 (aet)	AJ Auxerre
1980	AS Monaco	3-1	US Orléans
1981	SC Bastia	2-1	AS Saint-Etienne
1982	Paris Saint-Germain	2-2 (aet)(6-5 pens)	AS Saint-Etienne
1983	Paris Saint-Germain	3-2	FC Nantes
1984	FC Metz	2-0 (aet)	AS Monaco
1985	AS Monaco	1-0	Paris Saint-Germain
1986	Girondins de Bordeaux	2-1 (aet)	Olympique Marseille
1987	Girondins de Bordeaux	2-0	Olympique Marseille
1988	FC Metz	1-1 (aet)(5-4 pens)	FC Sochaux
1989	Olympique Marseille	4-3	AS Monaco
1990	SCP Montpellier	2-1 (aet)	Racing Club Paris
1991	AS Monaco	1-0	Olympique Marseille
1992*		*no final*	
1993	Paris Saint-Germain	3-0	FC Nantes
1994	AJ Auxerre	3-0	SCP Montpellier
1995	Paris Saint-Germain	1-0	RC Strasbourg
1996	AJ Auxerre	1-0	Nîmes Olympique
1997	OGC Nice	1-1 (aet)(4-3 pens)	Guingamp
1998	Paris Saint-Germain	2-1	RC Lens
1999	FC Nantes	1-0	FC Sedan
2000	FC Nantes	2-1	Calais
2001	RC Strasbourg	0-0 (aet)(5-4 pens)	Amiens
2002	FC Lorient	1-0	SC Bastia

* No final was held in 1992 following the collapse of a temporary stand a the SC Bastia v Olympique Marseille semi-final.

Victorious FC Nantes players celebrate in front of their fans after overcoming fourth division amateurs Calais 2-1 in the Final of the French Cup in 2000. Nantes won with a last minute goal.

French Cup Summary

TEAM	TOTALS	WINNERS & RUNNERS-UP (BOLD) (ITALICS)
Olympique Marseille	10, 6	**1924, 26, 27,** *34,* **35,** *38,* **40, 43,** *54,* **69,** *72,* **76,** *86, 87,* **89,** *91*
AS Saint-Etienne	6, 3	*1960,* **62, 68, 70, 74, 75, 77,** *81, 82*
AS Monaco	5, 3	*1960,* **63,** *74,* **80,** *84,* **85,** *89, 91*
Lille OSC	5, 2	*1945,* **46–48,** *49,* **53, 55**
Racing Club Paris	5, 2	**1936, 39, 40,** *45,* **49,** *50, 90*
Paris Saint-Germain	5, 1	**1982, 83,** *85,* **93, 95, 98**
Red Star Paris	5, 1	**1921–23, 28, 42,** *46*
Girondins de Bordeaux	3, 6	**1941,** *43, 52, 55, 64, 68, 69,* **86, 87**
FC Nantes	3, 5	*1966, 70,* **73,** *79, 83,* **93,** *99,* **2000**
Olympique Lyonnais	3, 3	*1963,* **64, 67,** *71, 73,* **76**
RC Strasbourg	3, 3	*1937, 47,* **51, 66,** *95,* **2001**
OGC Nice	3, 1	**1952, 54, 78,** *97*
FC Sète	2, 4	*1923, 24, 29,* **1930, 34,** *42*
FC Sedan	2, 2	**1956, 61,** *65, 99*
Stade Rennais	2, 2	*1922, 35,* **65, 71**
AJ Auxerre	2, 1	*1979,* **94, 96**
FC Metz	2, 1	*1938,* **84, 88**
Stade de Reims	2, 1	**1950, 58,** *77*
CAS Généraux	2, 0	**1919, 25**
FC Sochaux	1, 3	**1937,** *59, 67, 88*
SC Bastia	1, 2	*1972,* **81,** *2002*
CA Paris	1, 1	**1920,** *28*
Le Havre AC	1, 1	**1920,** *59*
SCP Montpellier	1, 1	**1990,** *94*
SO Montpellier	1, 1	**1929,** *31*
AS Cannes	1, 0	**1932**
AS Nancy	1, 0	**1978**
Club Français	1, 0	**1931**
Excelsior Roubaix	1, 0	**1933**
FC Lorient	1, 0	**2002**
FC Toulouse	1, 0	**1957**
Nancy-Lorraine XI	1, 0	**1944**
Olympique de Pantin	1, 0	**1918**
Nîmes Olympique	0, 3	*1958, 61, 96*
RC Lens	0, 3	*1948, 75, 98*
FC Nancy	0, 2	*1953, 62*
Olympique Paris	0, 2	*1919, 21*
Racing Club Roubaix	0, 2	*1932, 33*
Amiens	0, 1	*2001*
AS Valentigney	0, 1	*1926*

French Cup Summary (*continued*)

TEAM	TOTALS	WINNERS & RUNNERS-UP (BOLD) (ITALICS)
Calais	0, 1	*2000*
FC Lyon	0, 1	*1918*
FC Rouen	0, 1	*1925*
FC Troyes-Aube	0, 1	*1956*
Guingamp	0, 1	*1997*
Olympique Lille	0, 1	*1939*
Racing Club France	0, 1	*1930*
Reims-Champagne XI	0, 1	*1944*
SC Angers	0, 1	*1957*
SC Fives	0, 1	*1941*
US Charleville	0, 1	*1936*
US Orléans	0, 1	*1980*
US Quevilly	0, 1	*1927*
US Valenciennes	0, 1	*1951*

French League Cup Record 1995–2002

YEAR	WINNERS	SCORE	RUNNERS-UP
1995	Paris Saint-Germain	2-0	SC Bastia
1996	RC Metz	0-0 (aet)(5-4 pens)	Olympique Lyonnais
1997	RC Strasbourg	0-0 (aet)(6-5 pens)	Girondins de Bordeaux
1998	Paris Saint-Germain	2-2 (aet)(4-2 pens)	Girondins de Bordeaux
1999	RC Lens	1-0	FC Metz
2000	Gueugnon	2-0	Paris Saint-Germain
2001	Olympique Lyonnais	2-1 (aet)	AS Monaco
2002	Girondins de Bordeaux	3-0	FC Lorient

French League Cup Summary

TEAM	TOTALS	WINNERS & RUNNERS-UP (BOLD) (ITALICS)
Paris Saint-Germain	2, 1	**1995, 98,** *2000*
Girondins de Bordeaux	1, 2	*1997, 98,* **2002**
RC Metz	1, 1	**1996,** *99*
Olympique Lyonnais	1, 1	*1996,* **2001**
RC Lens	1, 0	**1999**
Strasbourg	1, 0	**1997**
Gueugnon	1, 0	**2000**
AS Monaco	0, 1	*2001*
FC Lorient	0, 1	*2002*
SC Bastia	0, 1	*1995*

Andorra

Federació Andorrana de Futbol
Founded: 1994
Joined FIFA: 1996
Joined UEFA: 1996

Better late than never, tiny Andorra became UEFA's 51st member in 1996, equipped with a fledgling league and a national stadium that holds 1,000 people. Their first victory was 2-0 in a friendly against Belarus in April 2000.

SEASON	LEAGUE CHAMPIONS
1998	CE Principat
1999	CE Principat
2000	Constelació Esportiva
2001	FC Santa Coloma
2002	Encamp Dicoansa

YEAR	CUP WINNERS
1997	CE Principat
1998	CE Principat
1999	CE Principat
2000	Constelació Esportiva
2001	FC Santa Coloma

Portugal

THE SEASON IN REVIEW 2001–02

PORTUGAL

THE TITLE FAVOURITES AND last year's top two in Portugal began the season with change. Boavista saw key players (showcased in last year's championship-winning squad) move on, including the heart of the defence Rui Bento to Sporting, and captain Jamie Pacheco to Malaga. Porto replaced long-serving coach Fernando Santos with Octavio Machad. Both suffered over the season from European commitments, especially Boavista, who creditably made it to the second group phase of the Champions League.

Benfica, who had missed out on European competition for the first time in 2001, signed 14 new players. Its early season form was disjointed to say the least. Sporting also began the season disastrously; after a month it was lying 15th, and the pressure was mounting on Romanian coach Laszlo Boloni. But the cavalry arrived in the shape of itinerant Brazilian striker Mario Jardel. He scored in his first game and never stopped, supplied by Sa Pinto, Pedro Barbosa, João Pinto and new boys Ricardo Quaresma and Hugo Viana. Sporting hit the top in week 14 of the league and never relinquished it.

Crisis at Benfica

Not for the first time, Benfica seemed more concerned with matters off the pitch than on it. The club was internally split over the decision to demolish the Stadium of Light and Lisbon city council's refusal to support the proposal financially. Skirmishes also broke out between members of the official fan club, the Red Devils, and the unofficial *ultras*, No Name Boys. The outrageous stabbing of a Red Devil in late December was followed by a spate of anti-Red Devil graffiti at the ground and a Molotov cocktail attack on the Benfica offices in January. In the courts, meanwhile, the club's ex-chairman João Vale e Azevedo was finally sentenced to four-and-a-half years imprisonment for huge fraud during his time at the club.

Sporting could have won the title with two games to spare as the chasing Boavista slipped up at home to lowly Varzim. But only an injury-time penalty rescued a point at home to Benfica. It was Sporting's 100th goal of the season and the prolific Jardel's 40th, and it gave Sporting a comfortable four-point cushion. The following week, Sporting looked to have made things difficult for itself after drawing 2-2 against Vitória Sétubal. But a revitalized Benfica, chasing a UEFA Cup spot, came from behind to beat Boavista 2-1 and gift the title to its Lisbon rival. Mario Jardel completed a magnificent season for him and for Sporting when his 40th-minute goal won the cup and the double for the Lisbon giants against Leixões from the second division.

1 Divisão League Table 2001–02

CLUB	P	W	D	L	F	A	Pts	
Sporting CP	34	22	9	3	74	25	75	Champions League
Boavista FC	34	21	7	6	52	20	70	Champions League
FC Porto	34	21	5	8	66	34	68	UEFA Cup
SL Benfica	34	17	12	5	66	37	63	
CS Marítimo	34	17	5	12	48	35	56	
União Leiria	34	15	10	9	52	35	55	
CF Os Belenenses	34	16	7	11	53	44	55	
Paços Ferreira	34	12	10	12	41	44	46	
Vitória Guimarães	34	11	9	14	35	41	42	
SC Braga	34	10	12	12	43	43	42	
SC Beira Mar	34	10	9	15	48	56	39	
CD Santa Clara	34	9	11	14	32	45	38	
Gil Vicente FC	34	10	8	16	42	56	38	
Vitória Setúbal	34	9	11	143	40	46	38	
Varzim SC	34	8	8	18	27	55	32	
SC Salgueiros	34	8	6	20	29	71	30	Relegated
SC Farense	34	7	7	20	29	63	28	Relegated
FC Alverca	34	7	6	21	39	66	27	Relegated

Promoted clubs: Académica de Coimbra, Moreirense FC, CD Nacional
Leixões enter UEFA Cup as cup runners-up.

Top Goalscorers 2001–02

PLAYER	CLUB	NATIONALITY	GOALS
Mario Jardel	Sporting CP	Brazilian	42
Vandelei da Silva	União Leiria	Brazilian	21
Fary Faye	SC Beira Mar	Senegalese	18
Hugo Henrique	Vitória Setúbal	Brazilian	16

International Club Performances 2001–02

CLUB	COMPETITION	PROGRESS
Boavista FC	Champions League	2nd Group Stage
FC Porto	Champions League	2nd Group Stage
CS Marítimo	UEFA Cup	1st Round
Sporting CP	UEFA Cup	3rd Round

Portuguese Cup

2002 FINAL

May 12 – National Stadium, Lisbon
Sporting CP **1-0** Leixões
(Jardel 40)
h/t: 1-0 **Att:** 40,000
Ref: Benquerenca

Below left: João Vale e Azevado, ex-president of Benfica, leaving court where he spent most of last season in a long-running case over corruption and embezzlement.

Below: Laszlo Boloni, manager of Sporting CP, guided the club from a disastrous start to a triumphant double.

Benfica's Diabos Vermelhos (Red Devils) fly the flag at home to Boavista.

rlos Barades of Porto *(in blue)* ttles for the ball with Armando tit of Boavista. Boavista won 2-0.

Top left: *Mario Jardel scored for Sporting in his first game against União Leiria and never stopped. He scored an astonishing 42 goals during the season.*

Left: *Benfica's Pedro Mantomas in action against Santa Clara.*

Below: *(left to right) Beto, Pedro Barbosa, Mario Jardel and João Pinto celebrate as Sporting complete the double with victory in the Portuguese Cup Final against second division Leixões. However, Leixões gained a UEFA Cup spot as Sporting went into the Champions League.*

João Pinto scores for Sporting CP away at Varzim. Sporting won 3-1.

Association Football in Portugal

PORTUGAL

1903: Boavista formed, Portugal's oldest existing club

1900

1910

1914: Formation of FA: Federação Portuguesa de Futebol

1920

1921: First international, v Spain, lost 1-3, venue: Madrid

1922: First Portuguese Cup Final

1923: Affiliation to FIFA

1930

1935: National league established

1940

1944: National stadium at Caxias, Lisbon inaugurated

1946: OS Belenenses win the Championship, the first time one of the big three did not win it

1950

1954: Affiliation to UEFA

1960

1961: Eusebio joins Benfica

1965: Eusebio given European Footballer of the Year award

1970

1974–76: Portuguese Revolution took place. Football continued, but stadiums were regularly used for political rallys

1980

1983: 1984:

1986–88: Saltillo affair: Portuguese internationals refused to play in conflict over appearance fees

1990

2000: Boavista win league championship, breaking 54-year domination of Benfica, Sporting and Porto

2000

2004: Portugal hosting European Championships

2010

In 1961, a young player from Mozambique, named Eusebio, joined Benfica and started a golden era in Portuguese football.

Key

 International football

 Affiliation to FIFA

 Affiliation to UEFA

○ Competition winner

△ Competition runner-up

Ben – Benfica
Porto – FC Porto
Sport – Sporting CP

International Competitions

	European Cup	UEFA Cup	European Cup-Winners' Cup
1961:	○ Ben		
1962:	○ Ben		
1963:	△ Ben		
1964:			○ Sport
1965:	△ Ben		
1968:	△ Ben		
1983:		△ Ben	
1984:			△ Porto
1987:	○ Porto		
1988:	△ Ben		
1990:	△ Ben		

Portugal: The main clubs

Chaves
1949 — Team name with year of formation

● Club formed before 1912

● Club formed 1912–25

● Club formed 1925–50

● Club formed after 1950

● Date unknown

★ Founder members of National League 1934–35

Champions (1935–80)

Cup winners (1929–80)

Leça FC 1923

★ **Academico do Porto** 1911

★ **FC Porto** 1893

SC Salgueiros 1911

Boavista FC 1903

Leixões SC 1907

THE AZORES

Ponta Delgada ●
CD Santa Clara 1921

★ **Sporting CP** 1906

★ **CF Os Belenenses** 1919

Amadora

Cascais ●
GD Estoril Praia 1939

Lisbon

★ **Atletico CP** 1942

Merger of Carcavelinhos and União (founded league as União)

MADEIRA

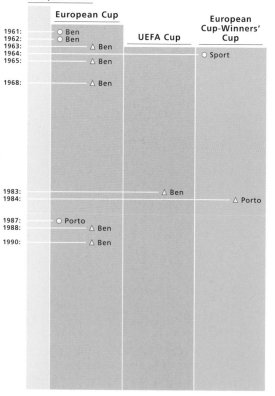

Funchal

CS Marítimo 1910

Barcelos
Gil Vicente FC
1924

SC Braga 1921

Chaves
1949

CD Aves 1930

Desportivo Aves 1930

Vitória
Guimarães
1922

Varzim FC 1915

óvoa
de
rzim

Felgueiras
1934

Rio Ave FC 1939

Aves

Maia
1954

FC Paços Ferreira 1950

Penafiel
1951

SC Freamunde

Porto

São João da Madeira
Espinho
1944

Aviero
SC Beira Mar
1922

Covilhã
SC Covilhã
1923

Coimbra ★ Académica 1876

Figueira
da Foz
Naval 1
de Maio
1893

União Lamas
1932

Leiria
União Leiria
1966

P O R T U G A L

CF Estrela Amadora 1932

FC Marco
1929

FC Alverca
1939

★ SL Benfica 1904

Campo Maior
SC Campomaiorense
1926

Barreiro

FC Barreirense

GD Quimigal

★ Vitória Setúbal 1910

Casa Pia 1920

Amora FC 1921

Oriental Lisboa

FC Seixal

SC Olhānense 1912

Faro
SC Farense
1910

Albufeira
Imortal DC
1920

Olhão

Portugal

ORIGINS AND GROWTH OF FOOTBALL

IN THE LATE 19th century, Portugal was part of an informal British Empire, with extensive British communities trading and sailing from the major cities – Lisbon and Porto. University students were recorded as playing the game as early as 1866, and the first recorded club was Lisbon FC, founded in 1875. By the 1890s Portuguese students returning from England started forming their own teams. The popularity of the sport gathered pace and the country's four biggest clubs were formed in the first decade of the 20th century; in Lisbon, Benfica and Sporting Lisbon in 1904, and in Porto, Boavista in 1903 and Porto in 1906. By 1914, major teams were being established in the provinces and in the smaller cities.

A national FA was set up in 1914 and professional league and cup competitions were running by the 1930s.

The golden era

After the Second World War, the Portuguese game was significantly boosted by the arrival of players from Portugal's African empire – Angola, Mozambique and Guinea-Bissau. Above all, the arrival of Eusebio from Mozambique to play for Benfica heralded a short golden era. Benfica, triumphant at home, also broke Real Madrid's monopoly on the European Cup, winning the tournament in 1961 and 1962. The following year, the Portuguese team made it to the semi-finals of the World Cup only to go out to hosts and eventual winners, England.

Despite the talent at home, this period represents the country's peak international performance, having only qualified for two World Cups since 1934. The rather dormant Portuguese football scene of the 1970s was lifted by Porto's success in the European Cup in 1987, the arrival of many Brazilian players and the recent promise of the national team – semi-finalists at Euro 2000.

PORTUGAL

In recent years the Portuguese national team, with players like Rui Costa (No.10) and Luis Figo (No. 7), has become a real contender for a major footballing prize.

SL BENFICA 1904

League 1935–2002 (including Campionata de Portugal 1922–38)	1930, 31, 35*, 36–38, 38*, 42, 43, 44, 45, 46–49, 50, 52, 53, 55, 56, 57, 59, 60, 61, 63–65, 66, 67–69, 70, 71–73, 74, 75–77, 78, 79, 81, 82, 83, 84, 86, 87, 88, 89, 90, 91, 92, 93, 94, 96, 98
Cup	1939, 40, 43, 44, 49, 51–53, 55, 57, 58, 59, 62, 64, 65, 69, 70, 71, 72, 74, 75, 80, 81, 83, 85–87, 89, 93, 96, 97
European Cup	1961, 62, 63, 65, 68, 88, 90
UEFA Cup	1983
World Club Cup	1961, 62

SPORTING CP 1906

League 1935–2002 (including Campionata de Portugal 1922–38)	1922, 23, 25, 28, 33, 34, 35, 35*, 36*, 37*, 38*, 39, 40, 41, 42, 43, 44, 45, 47–49, 50, 51–54, 58, 60, 61, 62, 66, 68, 70, 71, 74, 77, 80, 82, 85, 95, 97, 2000, 02
Cup	1941, 45, 46, 48, 52, 54, 55, 60, 63, 70, 71, 72, 73, 74, 78, 79, 82, 87, 94, 95, 96, 2000, 02
European Cup-Winners' Cup	1964

ESTADIO DA LUZ

77,844

Club:	SL Benfica
Built:	1954
Original Capacity:	60,000
Rebuilt:	1960 (at 120,000)
Significant Matches:	European Cup Final: 1967; European Cup-Winners' Cup Final: 1992

Lisbon and Porto Socios 2001

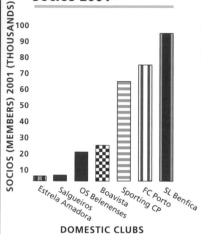

SOCIOS (MEMBERS) 2001 (THOUSANDS)

DOMESTIC CLUBS

CF OS BELENENSES 1919

League 1935–2002 (including Campionata de Portugal 1922–38)	1926, 27, 29, 32, 33, 36*, 37, 46, 55, 73
Cup	1940, 41, 42, 48, 60, 86, 89

Map labels

Estrela Amadora — JOSÉ GOMES — 25,000

PONTINHA

QUINTA DOS LILAZES

JOSÉ ALVALADE — 52,411

SL Benfica — ESTÁDIO DA LUZ — 77,844

Sporting CP — CIDADE UNIVERSITÁRIA

A1

BRANDOA

Casa Pia — ESTASIO PINA MANIQUE

BURACA

BENFICA

Oriental Lisboa — CAMPO CARLOS SELEMA

IC19

IC19

L I S B O N

CAMPOLIDE

ARCO CEGO

ALTO DO PINA

CHELAS

Rio Tejo

Parque

Parque Eduardo VII

SÃO SEBASTIÃO

ESTEFÂNIA

Florestal

EN117

A5

de Monsanto

A5

CAMINHOS DE FERRO

PORTUGUESE STOCK EXCHANGE FC Porto and Sporting CP have both partially floated on the Portuguese Stock Exchange

FEDERACÃO PORTUGUESA DE FUTEBOL HEADQUARTERS

E01

CARAMÃO

TAPADINHA

MADRAGOA

RESTELO — 40,000

SANTO AMARO

Atletico Lisbon

ALCÂNTARA

OS Belenenses — BELÉM

Rio Tejo

E01

Lisbon and Porto

40,000	Capacity of stadium
	Stadium no longer in use for top-flight football
	Team colours
	Semi-professional or amateur team colours
M1	Motorway
A82	Major road
1900	Champions
2000	Runners-up
*	Denotes honours in Campionata de Portugal

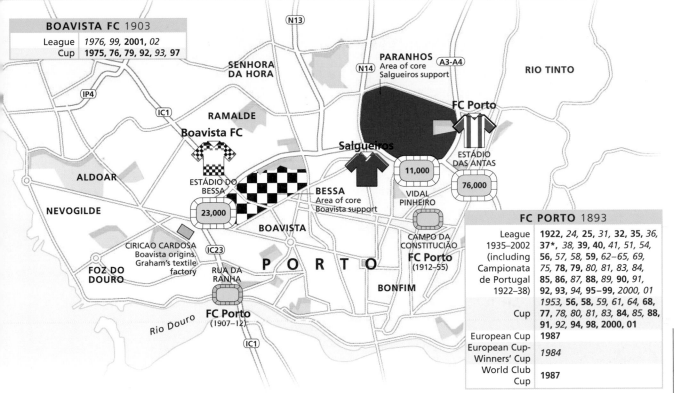

BOAVISTA FC 1903	
League	*1976, 99,* **2001,** *02*
Cup	**1975, 76,** *79,* **92, 93,** *97*

FC PORTO 1893	
League 1935–2002 (including Campionata de Portugal 1922–38)	**1922,** *24, 25,* **31, 32, 35, 36, 37*,** *38,* **39, 40,** *41, 51, 54,* **56, 57, 58, 59,** *62–65,* **69,** *75,* **78, 79, 80, 81, 83, 84, 85, 86, 87, 88, 89, 90, 91, 92, 93, 94,** *95–99, 2000, 01*
Cup	*1953,* **56, 58,** *59, 61,* **64, 68,** *77,* **78,** *80,* **81,** *83,* **84, 85,** *88,* **91,** *92,* **94, 98, 2000, 01**
European Cup	**1987**
European Cup-Winners' Cup	*1984*
World Club Cup	**1987**

PORTUGAL

Lisbon and Porto

FOOTBALL CITIES

PORTUGUESE FOOTBALL IS CONCENTRATED in two cities – Lisbon and Porto – and although both have their local derbies (SL Benfica v Sporting CP and FC Porto v Boavista) neither can match the intensity of the clashes between teams from the two cities. Similar to the contrast between Rio and São Paulo or Amsterdam and Rotterdam, Lisbon is the city of glamour, of bohemian lifestyles and irresponsible hedonism; Porto is the city that gets up and goes to work. Porto makes things and sells them; Lisbon lives off its cut.

Although Lisbon has a scattering of small clubs who have on occasion made it to the top flight, like Casa Pia and Oriental, a medium-sized club in Os Belenenses, who sit in the historic suburb of Bélem to the west of the city, and a penumbra of teams in its distant suburbs, there are only two really big clubs in the city: Benfica and Sporting, who both roamed the city before settling on their current stadiums in the north. Benfica was founded in 1904 in Bélem with a nationalist, Portuguese-only policy – but this policy was bent to allow Portuguese colonial citizens from Africa into the squad. Led by Eusebio and accruing massive support, the team peaked in the 1960s and won two European Cups, famously breaking Real Madrid's stranglehold on the competition. Sporting drew on the land and finances of the Viscount of Alvalade and built the best team in postwar Portugal, though titles have been thinner on the ground in recent years.

Political rally at the Das Antas in 1975. During the Portuguese Revolution (1974–76) football stadiums all over the country hosted enormous political rallies.

The rise of Boavista

Porto's football has for a long time been dominated by FC Porto, who started off at the Campo da Constituciâo before moving to the enormous Estádio das Antas in the 1950s. However, Porto's monopoly on the city's footballing triumphs and affections is being challenged. Boavista, the inner-city team from Bessa, is gaining ground. Founded by the English managers and Portuguese workers of Graham's textile factory, by 1905 the team had acquired a stadium, and in 1909 it changed its name from Boavista Footballers to Boavista Futebol Clube. After many years of obscurity, Boavista finally rose to take a well-deserved championship victory in 2001. The big Porto clubs are joined by tiny Salgueiros from the working-class Paranhos district of the city.

Portugal

1 DIVISÃO 1989–2001

IN 1982, SPORTING CP from Lisbon took the title under the eccentric English manager Malcolm Allison, after which the Portuguese championship was shared between SL Benfica and FC Porto for 19 seasons. Under Sven-Göran Eriksson, Benfica showed something of its old dominance, winning five titles and going to two European Cup Finals. Porto, revived under coach and former player José María Pedroto and striker Fernando Gomes, took three titles in the mid-1980s and two in the early 1990s. Benfica continued to challenge, but was progressively diminished by escalating debts and incredible inconsistency in managers and squads. By contrast, Porto was rock solid, taking a record-breaking five titles in a row in the 1990s, first under Bobby Robson, then Antonio Oliveira, and finally Fernando Santos. The club was unstoppable and in Brazilian Mario Jardel it had one of the greatest goalscorers of the time.

The Boavista surprise

A briefly revived Benfica, under manager Juup Heynckes, looked a threat to the Porto monopoly, but the swirling mists of corruption overtook the club and president João Vale e Azevedo was arrested and later tried and convicted on embezzlement charges. Instead, the challenge has come first from Sporting, who, despite managerial changes and boardroom reshuffles, took the title in 2000 with talismanic Dane Peter Schmeichel in goal. But in 2001, the real surprise package was Porto's Boavista FC. Gradually improving throughout the 1990s, the team took the lead early in the tournament and held it over Porto, showing outstanding discipline and tenacity across the whole season.

Beyond the charmed circle, who have held on to nearly all the money available from European qualification, the composition of the league has been very unstable. The only additional permanent members of the top flight are Vitória SC Guimarães, SC Braga and more recently CS Marítimo, SC Farense and SC Salgueiros. In order to survive, Farense has sold itself to a Spanish businessman, and Braga has floated on the stock exchange. However, the truth is that neither strategy looks likely to upset the *status quo* at the top of the Portuguese football ladder.

Boavista FC celebrates entry to the Champions League after its spectacular league championship in 2001. The club's budget is one-tenth of that available to rivals FC Porto and Sporting CP.

Portuguese League Positions 1989–2001

TEAM	1989–90	1990–91	1991–92	1992–93	1993–94	1994–95	1995–96	1996–97	1997–98	1998–99	1999–2000	2000–01
Academica									15	18		
FC Alverca										15	11	12
CD Aves												17
SC Beira Mar	11	6	8	8	14	17				16		8
CF Os Belenenses	6	19		7	13	12	6	13	18		12	7
SL Benfica	2	1	2	2	1	3	2	3	2	3	3	6
Boavista FC	8	4	3	4	4	9	4	7	6	2	4	1
SC Braga	12	7	11	12	15	10	8	4	10	9	9	4
SC Campomaiorense								17	11	13	13	16
GD Chaves	5	8	9	18		14	15	10	16	17		
Espinho			17					16				
GD Estoril Praia			10	13	18							
CF Estrela Amadora	13	18			9	15	11	9	7	8	8	18
FC Famalicão		14	14	14	17							
SC Farense		11	6	6	8	5	13	11	14	11	14	13
CD Feirense	18											
FC Felgueiras							16					
FC Paços Ferreira			12	10	16							9
Gil Vicente FC		13	13	9	10	13	12	18			5	14
Vitória SC Guimarães	4	9	5	11	7	4	5	5	3	7	7	15
Leça FC						14	14	12				
União Leiria					6	7	17			6	10	5
CD Nacional Madeira	14	20										
CF União Madeira	16	12	18		12	16						
CS Marítimo	10	10	7	5	5	7	9	8	5	10	6	11
FC Penafiel	15	15	17									
Portimonense SC	17											
FC Porto	1	2	1	1	2	1	1	1	1	1	2	2
Rio Ave FC									15	9	14	17
SC Salgueiros		5	15	15	11	11	10	6	8	12	15	10
CD Santa Clara											18	
Vitória Setúbal	7	17			6	18		12	13	5	16	
Sporting CP	3	3	4	3	3	2	3	2	4	4	1	3
FC Tirsense	9	16		16				8	18			
SCU Torreense			16									
Varzim FC											17	

Key to League Positions Table

- █ League champions
- █ Other teams playing in league
- █ Season promoted to league
- █ Season of relegation from league
- 5 Final position in league

SC Braga

GD Chaves

Gil Vicente FC

Barcelos

CD Aves

Vitória SC Guimarães

Guimarães

Varzim FC

Póvoa de Varzim

FC Famalicão

Famalicão

Braga

Chaves

FC Felgueiras

Felgueiras

Aves

Santo Tirso

Ferreira

FC Tirsense

Rio Ave FC

Leça FC

Leça de Palmeira

Porto

Penafiel

FC Penafiel

FC Paços Ferreira

SC Salgueiros

São João da Madeira

FC Porto

1990,
91, 92,
93, 94,
95–99,
2000, 01

Boavista FC

1999,
2001

Aviero

SC Beira Mar

Espinho

Coimbra

Academica

União Leiria

Leiria

PORTUGAL

THE AZORES

Ponta Delgada

CD Santa Clara

CF Estrela Amadora

SC Campomaiorense

FC Alverca

Campo Maior

Alverca

Amadora

Lisbon

Cascais

Setúbal

GD Estoril Praia

Vitória Setúbal

Sporting CP

1995, 97
2000

SL Benfica

1990,
91, 92,
93, 94,
96, 98

CF Os Belenenses

MADEIRA

CS Marítimo

CF União Madeira

Funchal

SC Farense

Faro

PORTUGAL

1 Divisão

Boavista FC	Team name
	League champions/ runners-up
1999, *2001*	Champions in bold Runners-up in italics
	Other teams in the 1 Divisão
● Porto	City of origin

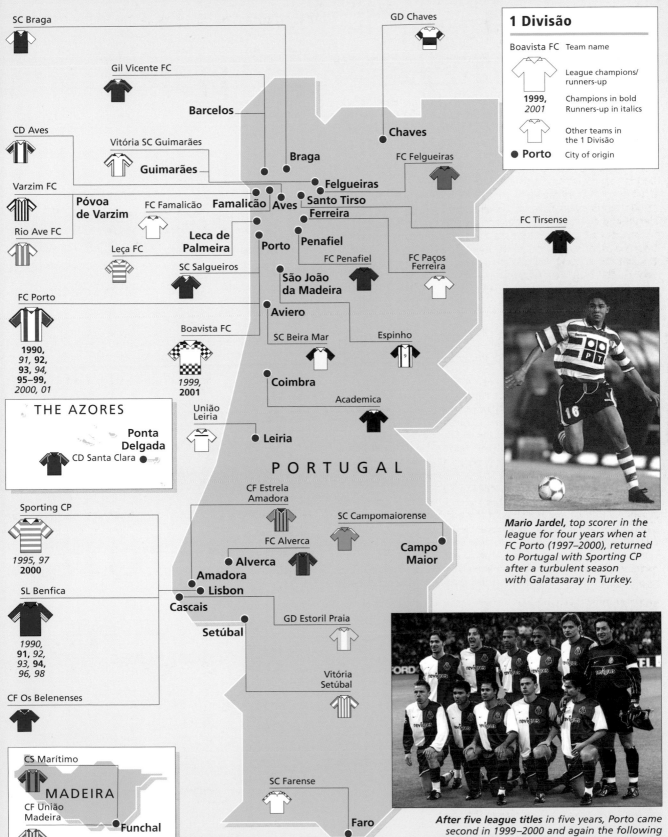

Mario Jardel, top scorer in the league for four years when at FC Porto (1997–2000), returned to Portugal with Sporting CP after a turbulent season with Galatasaray in Turkey.

After five league titles in five years, Porto came second in 1999–2000 and again the following season. New coach José Mourinho hopes for better things from his talented squad.

Portugal

Federação Portuguesa de Futebol
Founded: 1914
Joined FIFA: 1923
Joined UEFA: 1954

PORTUGAL

PORTUGUESE FOOTBALL WAS ESTABLISHED in the early years of the 20th century, but no national league championship was properly organized until 1935. Prior to this, local tournaments centred on Lisbon and Oporto had been played and, in 1922, a national cup competition, the Campionata de Portugal, had been established. The winners of this cup were considered to be national champions.

Since 1935, the league championship has been dominated by three clubs – Benfica, FC Porto and Sporting CP from Lisbon –

with only CF Os Belenenses and Boavista FC occasionally making waves. Unlike most of mainland Europe, Portuguese neutrality ensured that league football continued throughout the Second World War. The league currently consists of 18 teams with a standard three up, three down promotion and relegation system.

The entrance to the Stadium of Light, home to SL Benfica of Lisbon.

Campionata de Portugal 1922–38

YEAR	WINNERS	SCORE	RUNNERS-UP
1922	FC Porto	3-1	Sporting CP
1923	Sporting CP	3-0	Academica
1924	SC Olhãnense	4-2	FC Porto
1925	FC Porto	2-1	Sporting CP
1926	CS Marítimo	2-0	CF Os Belenenses
1927	CF Os Belenenses	3-0	Vitória Setúbal
1928	Carcavelinhos	3-1	Sporting CP
1929	CF Os Belenenses	2-1	União de Lisboa
1930	SL Benfica	3-1	FC Barreirense
1931	SL Benfica	3-0	FC Porto
1932	FC Porto	2-0	CF Os Belenenses
1933	CF Os Belenenses	3-1	Sporting CP
1934	Sporting CP	4-3	FC Barreirense
1935	SL Benfica	2-1	Sporting CP
1936	Sporting CP	3-1	CF Os Belenenses
1937	FC Porto	3-2	Sporting CP
1938	Sporting CP	3-1	SL Benfica

Portuguese League Record 1935–2002

SEASON	CHAMPIONS	RUNNERS-UP
1935	FC Porto	Sporting CP
1936	SL Benfica	FC Porto
1937	SL Benfica	CF Os Belenenses
1938	SL Benfica	FC Porto
1939	FC Porto	Sporting CP
1940	FC Porto	Sporting CP
1941	Sporting CP	FC Porto
1942	SL Benfica	Sporting CP
1943	SL Benfica	Sporting CP

Portuguese League Record (*continued*)

SEASON	CHAMPIONS	RUNNERS-UP
1944	Sporting CP	SL Benfica
1945	SL Benfica	Sporting CP
1946	CF Os Belenenses	SL Benfica
1947	Sporting CP	SL Benfica
1948	Sporting CP	SL Benfica
1949	Sporting CP	SL Benfica
1950	SL Benfica	Sporting CP
1951	Sporting CP	FC Porto
1952	Sporting CP	SL Benfica
1953	Sporting CP	SL Benfica
1954	Sporting CP	FC Porto
1955	SL Benfica	CF Os Belenenses
1956	FC Porto	SL Benfica
1957	SL Benfica	FC Porto
1958	Sporting CP	FC Porto
1959	FC Porto	SL Benfica
1960	SL Benfica	Sporting CP
1961	SL Benfica	Sporting CP
1962	Sporting CP	FC Porto
1963	SL Benfica	FC Porto
1964	SL Benfica	FC Porto
1965	SL Benfica	FC Porto
1966	Sporting CP	SL Benfica
1967	SL Benfica	Academica
1968	SL Benfica	Sporting CP
1969	SL Benfica	FC Porto
1970	Sporting CP	SL Benfica
1971	SL Benfica	Sporting CP
1972	SL Benfica	Vitória Setúbal
1973	SL Benfica	CF Os Belenenses
1974	Sporting CP	SL Benfica
1975	SL Benfica	FC Porto
1976	SL Benfica	Boavista FC
1977	SL Benfica	Sporting CP
1978	FC Porto	SL Benfica
1979	FC Porto	SL Benfica
1980	Sporting CP	FC Porto
1981	SL Benfica	FC Porto
1982	Sporting CP	SL Benfica
1983	SL Benfica	FC Porto
1984	SL Benfica	FC Porto
1985	FC Porto	Sporting CP
1986	FC Porto	SL Benfica
1987	SL Benfica	FC Porto
1988	FC Porto	SL Benfica
1989	SL Benfica	FC Porto
1990	FC Porto	SL Benfica
1991	SL Benfica	FC Porto
1992	FC Porto	SL Benfica
1993	FC Porto	SL Benfica
1994	SL Benfica	FC Porto
1995	FC Porto	Sporting CP
1996	FC Porto	SL Benfica
1997	FC Porto	Sporting CP
1998	FC Porto	SL Benfica
1999	FC Porto	Boavista FC
2000	Sporting CP	FC Porto
2001	Boavista FC	FC Porto
2002	Sporting CP	Boavista FC

Portuguese League Summary

| TEAM | TOTALS | CHAMPIONS & RUNNERS-UP |
		(BOLD) (ITALICS)
SL Benfica	33, 23	**1930, 31, 35*, 36–38, 38*, 42, 43, 44,** 45, 46–49, 50, 52, 53, **55, 56, 57,** 59, **60, 61, 63–65, 66, 67–69, 70, 71–73, 74, 75–77, 78, 79, 81, 82, 83, 84, 86, 87, 88, 89, 90, 91, 92, 93, 94, 96, 98**
FC Porto	22, 25	1922, 24, 25, **31, 32, 35,** 36, **37*,** 38, 39, 40, 41, 51, 54, **56, 57, 58, 59,** 62–65, 69, 75, **78, 79, 80, 81, 83, 84, 85, 86, 87, 88, 89, 90, 91, 92, 93, 94, 95–99, 2000, 01**
Sporting CP	22, 21	1922, 23, 25, 28, 33, **34, 35*,** 35, 36*, 37*, 38*, 39, 40, 41, 42, 43, 44, 45, 47–49, 50, 51–54, 58, 60, 61, 62, 66, 68, 70, 71, 74, 77, 80, 82, 85, 95, 97, **2000, 02**
CF Os Belenenses	4, 6	1926, 27, 29, 32, 33, 36*, 37, 46, 55, 73
Boavista FC	1, 3	1976, 99, **2001,** 02
Carcavelinhos	1, 0	**1928**
CS Marítimo	1, 0	**1926**
SC Olhãnense	1, 0	**1924**
Academica	0, 2	1923, 67
FC Barreirense	0, 2	1930, 34
Vitória Setúbal	0, 2	1927, 72
União de Lisboa	0, 1	1929

* denotes honours in Campionata de Portugal.

Portuguese Cup Record 1939–2002

YEAR	WINNERS	SCORE	RUNNERS-UP
1939	Academica	4-3	SL Benfica
1940	SL Benfica	3-1	CF Os Belenenses
1941	Sporting CP	4-1	CF Os Belenenses
1942	CF Os Belenenses	2-0	Vitória SC Guimarães
1943	SL Benfica	5-1	Vitória Setúbal
1944	SL Benfica	8-0	GD Estoril Praia
1945	Sporting CP	1-0	SC Olhãnense
1946	Sporting CP	4-2	Atletico CP
1947		no competition	
1948	Sporting CP	3-1	CF Os Belenenses
1949	SL Benfica	2-1	Atletico CP
1950		no competition	
1951	SL Benfica	5-1	Academica
1952	SL Benfica	5-4	Sporting CP
1953	SL Benfica	5-0	FC Porto
1954	Sporting CP	3-2	Vitória Setúbal
1955	SL Benfica	2-1	Sporting CP
1956	FC Porto	3-0	SCU Torreense
1957	SL Benfica	3-1	SC Covilhã
1958	FC Porto	1-0	SL Benfica
1959	SL Benfica	1-0	FC Porto
1960	CF Os Belenenses	2-1	Sporting CP
1961	Leixões SC	2-0	FC Porto
1962	SL Benfica	3-0	Vitória Setúbal
1963	Sporting CP	4-0	Vitória SC Guimarães
1964	SL Benfica	6-2	FC Porto
1965	Vitória Setúbal	3-1	SL Benfica
1966	SC Braga	1-0	Vitória Setúbal
1967	Vitória Setúbal	3-2	Academica
1968	FC Porto	2-1	Vitória Setúbal
1969	SL Benfica	2-1	Academica
1970	SL Benfica	3-1	Sporting CP
1971	Sporting CP	4-1	SL Benfica
1972	SL Benfica	3-2	Sporting CP
1973	Sporting CP	3-2	Vitória Setúbal
1974	Sporting CP	2-1	SL Benfica
1975	Boavista FC	2-1	SL Benfica
1976	Boavista FC	2-1	Vitória SC Guimarães
1977	FC Porto	2-1	SC Braga

Portuguese Cup Record (continued)

YEAR	WINNERS	SCORE	RUNNERS-UP
1978	Sporting CP	1-1, (replay) 2-1	FC Porto
1979	Boavista FC	1-1, (replay) 1-0	Sporting CP
1980	SL Benfica	1-0	FC Porto
1981	SL Benfica	3-1	FC Porto
1982	Sporting CP	4-0	SC Braga
1983	SL Benfica	1-0	FC Porto
1984	FC Porto	4-1	Rio Ave FC
1985	SL Benfica	3-1	FC Porto
1986	SL Benfica	2-0	CF Os Belenenses
1987	SL Benfica	2-1	Sporting CP
1988	FC Porto	1-0	Vitória SC Guimarães
1989	CF Os Belenenses	2-1	SL Benfica
1990	CF Estrela Amadora	3-1 (aet)	SC Farense
1991	FC Porto	3-1	SC Beira Mar
1992	Boavista FC	2-1	FC Porto
1993	SL Benfica	5-2	Boavista FC
1994	FC Porto	2-1 (aet)	Sporting CP
1995	Sporting CP	2-0	CS Marítimo
1996	SL Benfica	3-1	Sporting CP
1997	Boavista FC	3-2	SL Benfica
1998	FC Porto	3-1	SC Braga
1999	SC Beira Mar	1-0	SC Campomaiorense
2000	FC Porto	3-1 (aet)	Sporting CP
2001	FC Porto	2-0	CS Marítimo
2002	Sporting CP	1-0	Lexiões SC

Portuguese Cup Summary

| TEAM | TOTALS | WINNERS & RUNNERS-UP |
		(BOLD) (ITALICS)
SL Benfica	23, 8	1939, 40, **43, 44,** 49, **51–53, 55,** 57, 58, **59, 62, 64, 65, 69, 70, 71, 72,** 74, 75, **80, 81, 83, 85–87,** 89, 93, **96,** 97
Sporting CP	13, 10	**1941,** 45, 46, 48, 52, **54,** 55, 60, 63, 70, 71, 72, **73, 74, 78,** 79, **82,** 87, 94, **95,** 96, **2000,** 02
FC Porto	11, 10	1953, **56,** 58, 59, 61, 64, **68,** 77, **78,** 80, 81, 83, **84, 85, 88,** 91, 92, **94,** 98, **2000, 01**
Boavista FC	5, 1	**1975, 76, 79,** 92, **93, 97**
CF Os Belenenses	3, 4	1940, 41, **42, 48,** 60, **86,** 89
Vitória Setúbal	2, 6	1943, 54, 62, **65,** 66, **67,** 68, 73
Academica	1, 3	**1939,** 51, 67, 69
SC Braga	1, 3	**1966,** 77, 82, 98
Leixões SC	1, 1	**1961,** 2002
SC Beira Mar	1, 1	1991, **99**
CF Estrela Amadora	1, 0	**1990**
Vitória SC Guimarães	0, 4	1942, 63, 76, 88
Atletico CP	0, 2	1946, 49
CS Marítimo	0, 2	1995, 2001
GD Estoril Praia	0, 1	1944
Rio Ave FC	0, 1	1984
SC Campomaiorense	0, 1	1999
SC Covilhã	0, 1	1957
SC Farense	0, 1	1990
SC Olhãnense	0, 1	1945
SCU Torreense	0, 1	1956

PORTUGAL

185

Spain

THE SEASON IN REVIEW 2001–02

THE SPANISH LEAGUE MAY not be the richest in Europe, but it is surely the most competitive. In season 2001–02 up to eight sides were seriously vying for Champions League spots and the lowliest teams regularly turned in performances that defeated the very biggest. Real began its centenary year with a clear statement of intent, announcing the much heralded arrival of Zinedine Zidane from Juventus for a record-breaking £47 million. Just as importantly it finally sold its city centre training ground for over £150 million and almost cancelled out the club's unbelievable debts. Barcelona began the season with another new manager, Carles Rexach, previously Johan Cruyff's assistant, making it four managers in five years. New arrivals included the gifted Argentinian teenager Saviola, Patrick Anderson from Bayern München, as well as the Brazilian Giovanni. Valencia, twice defeated in European Champions League Finals, appeared on the point of implosion. It successively lost its coach, Hector Cuper, who took over the reins at Internazionale; its captain and star player, talismanic Gaizka Mendieta, who moved to Lazio; and its president Pedro Cortes, who resigned in despair. Coach Rafa Benitez, who had taken Tenerife up the previous season, was installed at the Mestalla.

Poor form

The season began badly for Real Madrid and Mallorca, both distracted by Champions League engagements, and Valencia, where Benitez's hard-working but apparently unglamorous side was booed by the crowd. Early pace-setters were the newly-promoted Real Betis and Villareal. The new model Barça was top after five games, playing a distinctly more muscular football than usual. But no side could establish a commanding advantage in the first half of the season, and in the New Year only five points separated the top eight clubs: Real Madrid, Deportivo, Valencia, Celta, Athletic Bilbao, Real Betis, Barcelona and Alavés.

Above: Rafa Benitez guided Tenerife to promotion last season and Valencia to the league title this year.

Above: Real Madrid's coach Vicente del Bosque faced a tough task guiding his side through its centenary year.

Below: Fourth place in La Liga and a semi-final in the Champions League were not enough to keep Carles Rexach in his job as coach at Barcelona. A tactically chaotic and inconsistent season saw him replaced by Dutchman Louis van Gaal for his second stretch.

Primera Liga Table 2001–02

CLUB	P	W	D	L	F	A	Pts	
Valencia CF	38	21	12	5	51	27	**75**	Champions League
RC Deportivo	38	20	8	10	65	41	**68**	Champions League
Real Madrid	38	19	9	10	69	44	**66**	Champions League
Barcelona	38	18	10	10	65	37	**64**	Champions League
RC Celta	38	16	12	10	64	46	**60**	UEFA Cup
Real Betis	38	15	14	9	42	34	**59**	UEFA Cup
Dep Alavés	38	17	3	18	41	44	**54**	UEFA Cup
Sevilla FC	38	14	11	13	51	40	**53**	
Málaga CF	38	13	14	11	44	44	**53**	
Athletic Bilbao	38	14	11	13	54	66	**53**	
Rayo Vallecano	38	13	10	15	46	52	**49**	
Real Valladolid	38	13	9	16	45	58	**48**	
Real Sociedad	38	13	8	17	48	54	**47**	
RCD Espanyol	38	13	8	17	47	56	**47**	
Villareal	38	11	10	17	46	55	**43**	
Real Mallorca	38	11	10	17	39	52	**43**	
Osasuna	38	10	12	16	36	48	**42**	
Las Palmas	38	9	13	16	40	50	**40**	Relegated
Tenerife	38	10	8	20	32	58	**38**	Relegated
Real Zaragoza	38	9	10	19	35	54	**37**	Relegated

Promoted clubs: Recreativo Huelva, Atlético Madrid, Racing Santander.

SPAIN

Javier Saviola, Barcelona's Argentinian teenage wonder, celebrates one of his 17 goals. But Barcelona's leaky defence meant a poor season for the Catalans.

Raúl (Real Madrid, left) and Miroslav Djukic (Valencia). Real outscored Valencia, but couldn't match the team's awesome defensive solidity.

Merion (left) in action for Real Betis against Malaga. Newly-promoted Betis was back in the big time and back in Europe.

187

Right: RC Deportivo's captain Fran collects the Copa del Rey, putting paid to Real Madrid's plans for a treble in its centenary year.

Below right: Luis Figo (Real Madrid, left) and Mauro Silva (RC Deportivo) chase the ball during the Copa del Rey Final. Figo's season was a shadow of the previous year's.

Spanish Cup

2002 FINAL

March 6 – Bernabeu Stadium, Madrid
RC Deportivo 2-1 Real Madrid
(Sergio 6, (Raúl 58)
Tristan 38)
h/t: 2-0 **Att:** 75,000
Ref: M Gonzalez

SPAIN

During the spring, Valencia began to move up the table. Benitez's team had easily the best defensive record in the league with the impassable Argentinian pair of Pellegrino and Ayala playing in the middle at the back in front of Spain's first choice international goalkeeper Santiago Cañizares. Valencia also began to score from all over the pitch, especially from the midfield, which combined the talents of Pablo Aimar and Ruben Baraja. A 2-0 victory at Barcelona showed the team's unmistakable class under pressure. Real Madrid also scored freely – but outside the Champions League, where it looked unbeatable, its form was poor. The Spanish Cup Final saw Real go down to an ecstatic Deportivo at the Bernabeu, and defeats by struggling sides Rayo Vallecano and Real Sociedad took the team off the top of the table.

With two weekends to go, Valencia came from behind to win with ten men against Espanyol at the Mestalla. Raul Talmundo's 31st-minute penalty put Espanyol 1-0 up and then the home side's Carboni was sent off a minute later. But Ruben Baraja, the heart of Valencia's midfield, scored twice to take the points. As Real Madrid went down 3-0 to Real Sociedad, it left Valencia four points clear with two games to go. With a 2-0 win at Málaga the following week, Valencia took its first title in 31 years.

International Club Performances 2001–02

CLUB	COMPETITION	PROGRESS
Barcelona	Champions League	Semi-finals
RC Deportivo	Champions League	Quarter-finals
Real Madrid	Champions League	Winners
RCD Mallorca	Champions League	1st Group Phase
	UEFA Cup	3rd Round
RC Celta	UEFA Cup	2nd Round
Valencia CF	UEFA Cup	Quarter-finals
Real Zaragoza	UEFA Cup	2nd Round

Top Goalscorers 2001–02

PLAYER	CLUB	NATIONALITY	GOALS
Diego Tristan	RC Deportivo	Spanish	21
Patrick Kluivert	Barcelona	Dutch	18
Fernando Morientes	Real Madrid	Spanish	18
Catanha	RC Celta	Brazilian	17
Javier Saviola	Barcelona	Argentinian	17
Raul Tamudo	RCD Espanyol	Spanish	17

Real Sociedad's (right) crushing 3-0 win over Real Madrid left Valencia needing three points from its last two matches.

Left: *After 31 years of waiting, Valencia won La Liga with a final day victory over Málaga at home in the Mestalla. Major celebrations followed.*

Above: *The flying Ruben Baraja's goals from midfield were a major factor in Valencia's hugely successful season.*

Below: *Valencia's Pablo Aimar in action against Garcia and Carvalho of Espanyol. Down to ten men, Valencia came from behind to win 2-1 taking the team four points clear with two games to go. With most of the team's goals coming from mid-field, Valencia relied on Aimar and Baraja during the run-in, although both players missed much of the season.*

Association Football in Spain

1898: Athletic Bilbao formed. Spain's oldest football only club — **1895**

1901: First Catalan league championship

1902: First Spanish Cup Final — **1905**

⚽ **1904:** Affiliation to FIFA by regional associations across Spain

1913: Formation of FA: Real Federación Española de Fútbol — **1915**

1920: First international, v Denmark, won 1–0, venue: Brussels

1925

1929: National league established. Professionalism legalized

1936–37: Catalan and Valencian teams play in Mediterranean League, during Civil War — **1935**

1937–39: League and Cup abandoned during the Spanish Civil War

1940: Franco's government abolishes regional championships — **1945**

SPAIN

1953: Alfredo di Stefano chooses Real Madrid over Barcelona — **1955**

⚽ **1954:** Affiliation to UEFA

1963: Ban on foreign players introduced — **1965**

1973: Ban on foreign players lifted — **1975**

1990: Alcohol at games banned

1992: Fireworks at games banned

2000: Luis Figo transfers from Barcelona to Real Madrid for a then record transfer fee — **1995**

2001: Real Madrid break world transfer fee again for Zinedine Zidane from Juventus — **2005**

Real Madrid, *Spanish champions for the fourth consecutive year in 1964, included almost the entire Spanish national team: (back row left to right) Vicente, Isidro, Santamaria (from Uruguay), Casado, Muller (from France), Zoco; (front row) Amancio, Felo, di Stefano, Puskas (from Hungary) and Gento.*

Key

🏳️	International football	○	Competition winner
⚽	Affiliation to FIFA	△	Competition runner-up
⚽	Affiliation to UEFA		
🚗	War		

■ World Cup host
● World Cup winner
▲ World Cup runner-up
■ European Championships host
● European Championships winner
△ European Championships runner-up

Alav – CD Alavés
Atl B – Athletic Bilbao
Atl M – Atlético Madrid
Barca – Barcelona
Esp – RCD Español
RCD – RCD Mallorca
Real M – Real Madrid
Val – Valencia
Zara – Real Zaragoza

International Competitions

	European Cup	UEFA Cup	European Cup-Winners' Cup
1956:	○ Real M		
1957:	○ Real M		
1958:	○ Real M	○ Barca	
1959:	○ Real M		
1960:	○ Real M	○ Barca	
1961:	△ Barca		
1962:	△ Real M	○ Val	△ Barca
1963:		○ Val	△ Atl M
1964:	●● ■ △ Real M	○ Zara	△ Val	△ Atl M
1966:	○ Real M	○ Barca △ Zara	
1969:			△ Barca
1971:			△ Real M
1974:	△ Atl M		
1977:			△ Atl B
1979:		○ Barca	
1980:		○ Val	
1981:	△ Real M		
1982:	■	○ Barca	
1983:			△ Real M
1984:	▲		
1985:		○ Real M	
1986:	△ Barca	○ Real M	△ Atl M
1988:		△ Esp	
1989:			○ Barca
1991:			△ Barca
1992:	○ Barca		
1994:	△ Barca		
1995:		○ Zara	
1997:		○ Barca	
1998:	○ Real M		
1999:			△ RCD
2000:	○ Real M △ Val		
2001:	△ Val	△ Alav	
2002:	○ Real M		

The Royal House in Spain has played a big part in the nation's footballing history. Many of the big clubs bear the name 'Real' meaning 'royal', and the Copa del Rey (Cup of the King) is named after King Alfonso XIII (1886–1931).

★ **Athletic Bilbao** 1898

RC Deportivo 1904

Sporting Gijón 1905

La Coruña ●

Santiago
SD Compostela 1962

Pontevedra ● 1928

Celta Vigo 1923

Vigo ●

Merger of Fortuna and Sporting

Spain: The main clubs

Cadiz 1910 — Team name with year of formation

● Club formed before 1912
● Club formed 1912–25
● Club formed 1925–50
○ Club formed after 1950
★ Founder members of National League (1929)
👕 Winners Copa del Rey 1902–29
🏴 English origins
➕ Swiss origins
▦ Catalonian regional identity
🔗 Galician regional identity
🏴󠁥󠁳󠁰󠁶󠁿 Basque regional identity
Foreign student origins
Mining origins
🚲 Originated from a cycling club
Student origins
🚂 Railway workers
👑 Royal house

Spain

ORIGINS AND GROWTH OF FOOTBALL

SPAIN'S OLDEST FOOTBALL CLUB, Real Club Recreativo de Huelva, was founded in 1889 as an informal sports club with a football team based around the British presence of railway and copper-mine workers. Over the next decade clubs formed in Madrid, the Basque Country, Barcelona and Seville. British influences through sailors, miners and expatriate traders were significant in Seville, Barcelona and Bilbao.

Modern Spanish history is dominated by the political and cultural struggles between the centre (especially Madrid and Castille) and the regions of Spain. This was immediately reflected in the organization of Spanish football. Strong regional leagues were established in the first years of the 20th century, the first in Catalonia in 1901. These continued despite the establishment of a national professional league in 1929. The Spanish monarchy's concern with centralizing power extended to the establishment of the Copa del Rey in 1902 by King Alfonso XIII – a national championship among regional champions. The Royal House had also seen fit to bestow its patronage on clubs across the country.

The Spanish Civil War (1936–39) was a struggle between right and left but also between the centre and the regions. With the victory of Franco's centralizing nationalist forces, regional leagues were abolished, foreign influences in club origins played down and the Copa del Rey renamed the Copa del Generalisimo. Atlético Madrid was forced to change name – to Atlético Aviación – but received the crack Air Force football squad as part of the deal. Strict control of the press and most social and political institutions saw football clubs become an even more significant symbol of regional identities. With the death of Franco in 1975, Spain returned to democracy and a revived regionalism. Spanish club performances in European tournaments have been second only to Italy.

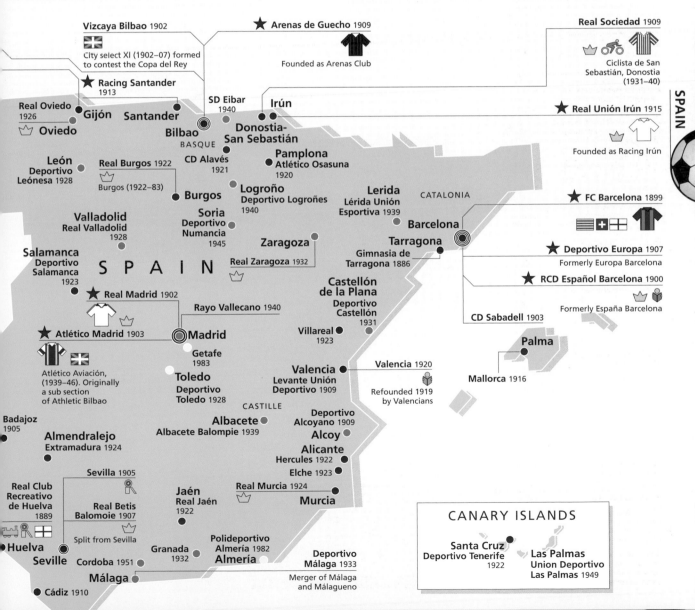

Vizcaya Bilbao 1902
City select XI (1902–07) formed to contest the Copa del Rey

★ **Arenas de Guecho** 1909
Founded as Arenas Club

Real Sociedad 1909
Ciclista de San Sebastián, Donostia (1931–40)

★ **Racing Santander** 1913

Real Oviedo 1926
Oviedo
Gijón   **Santander**

SD Eibar 1940
Bilbao
BASQUE

Irún
Donostia-San Sebastián

★ **Real Unión Irún** 1915
Founded as Racing Irún

León
Deportivo Leónesa 1928

Real Burgos 1922
Burgos (1922–83)
Burgos

CD Alavés 1921

Pamplona
Atlético Osasuna 1920

Logroño
Deportivo Logroñes 1940

Lerida
Lérida Unión Esportiva 1939

CATALONIA

★ **FC Barcelona** 1899

Valladolid
Real Valladolid 1928

Soria
Deportivo Numancia 1945

Zaragoza
Real Zaragoza 1932

Barcelona

Tarragona
Gimnasia de Tarragona 1886

★ **Deportivo Europa** 1907
Formerly Europa Barcelona

Salamanca
Deportivo Salamanca 1923

S P A I N

★ **RCD Español Barcelona** 1900
Formerly España Barcelona

★ **Real Madrid** 1902

Rayo Vallecano 1940

Castellón de la Plana
Deportivo Castellón 1931

CD Sabadell 1903

Palma

★ **Atlético Madrid** 1903
Atlético Aviación, (1939–46). Originally a sub section of Athletic Bilbao

Getafe 1983
◉ **Madrid**

Villareal 1923

Valencia 1920
Refounded 1919 by Valencians

Mallorca 1916

Toledo
Deportivo Toledo 1928

CASTILLE

Valencia
Levante Unión Deportivo 1909

Badajoz 1905

Almendralejo
Extremadura 1924

Albacete
Albacete Balompie 1939

Deportivo Alcoyano 1909
Alcoy

Alicante
Hercules 1922
Elche 1923

Sevilla 1905

Real Club Recreativo de Huelva 1889

Real Betis Balomoie 1907
Split from Sevilla

Jaén
Real Jaén 1922

Real Murcia 1924
Murcia

Huelva
Seville   **Cordoba** 1951

Granada 1932

Polideportivo Almería 1982
Almería

Deportivo Málaga 1933
Merger of Málaga and Málagueno

Málaga

Cádiz 1910

CANARY ISLANDS

Santa Cruz
Deportivo Tenerife 1922

Las Palmas
Union Deportivo Las Palmas 1949

SPAIN

Barcelona

FOOTBALL CITY

ALTHOUGH FC BARCELONA was one of the key institutions in the creation of Catalan nationalism in the 20th century, it was founded and initially run by a Swiss, Hans Gamper, and an Englishman, Arthur Witty, both expatriate businessmen attracted by the city's dynamic economic growth. The team's first game was played on Christmas Eve 1899 at the racetrack in Bonanova against FC Catala and, while the team's opponents were Catalan, Barcelona's team was overwhelmingly foreign. But the Catalan nationalism that was growing rapidly at the turn of the century could absorb foreign influences: Barcelona was coached by foreigners throughout the 1920s and 1930s and had regularly fielded foreign players. On top of that, Andalusian immigrants, attracted to the booming industrial estates of the city in the 1950s, swelled its support. The club's cosmopolitanism was matched by success and, by the early 1930s, the club had acquired a major stadium in Les Corts, a series of national and regional titles, a massive following and a fierce, politically-charged rivalry with Real Madrid.

Barça and Catalan nationalism

The weight of these nationalist identities was given a massive boost by the outcome of the Spanish Civil War (1936–39). Centralist and right-wing forces under General Franco brutally suppressed the regional, left-wing forces that included most of Barcelona, Catalonia and FC Barcelona. In the 1940s and 1950s, Madrid's political domination of Catalonia, interference in the running of the club, and repression of nearly all forms of political opposition, made the connection between supporting FC Barcelona and Catalan nationalism even clearer, a connection that has remained in the years since Franco's death and the subsequent democratization and devolution of Spain.

In the long shadow cast by Barça sits the city's second club, RCD Espanyol. The club was founded by a group of students with the Castilian name Español – an attempt to wind up the Catalan nationalists down the road – and it traditionally attracts state employees and those migrant workers from Andalusia with Castilian sentiments. But with only two cup wins and some near misses in the late 1980s and early 1990s to its name, its challenge has been symbolic rather than sporting. Time and tastes have forced even this bastion of Royalism and Centralism to take the Catalan spelling for its name. To make matters worse, the club was forced to clear an enormous debt by selling its Sarria stadium and moving into the large but unatmospheric Olympic stadium on Montjuïc.

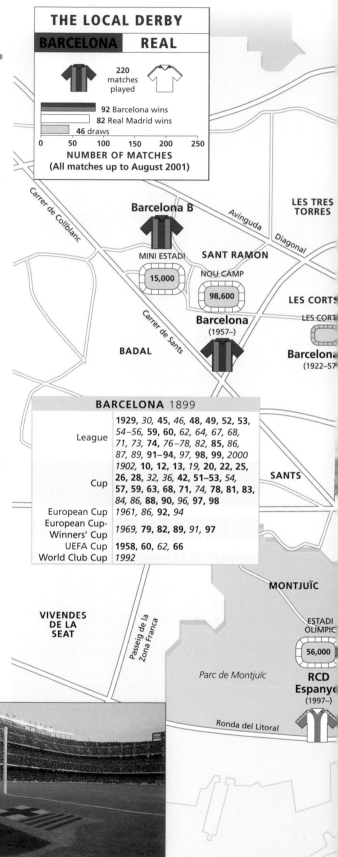

THE LOCAL DERBY

BARCELONA	REAL

220 matches played

92 Barcelona wins
82 Real Madrid wins
46 draws

NUMBER OF MATCHES
(All matches up to August 2001)

BARCELONA 1899

League	**1929, 30, 45, 46, 48, 49, 52, 53, 54–56, 59, 60,** 62, 64, 67, 68, 71, 73, **74,** 76–78, 82, **85, 86, 87, 89, 91–94,** 97, 98, 99, 2000
Cup	1902, 10, 12, 13, 19, 20, 22, 25, 26, 28, 32, 36, 42, 51–53, 54, **57,** 59, **63, 68, 71,** 74, 78, 81, 83, 84, 86, **88,** 90, 96, **97, 98**
European Cup	1961, 86, **92,** 94
European Cup-Winners' Cup	1969, 79, 82, 89, 91, 97
UEFA Cup	**1958, 60,** 62, 66
World Club Cup	1992

NOU CAMP

98,600	**Club:** Barcelona
	Built: 1957
	Original Capacity: 90,000
	Rebuilt: 1982
	Significant Matches: 1982 World Cup: five matches; 1992 Barcelona Olympics: opening ceremony, football Final; European Cup Final: 1989, 1999; European Cup-Winners' Cup Final: 1982

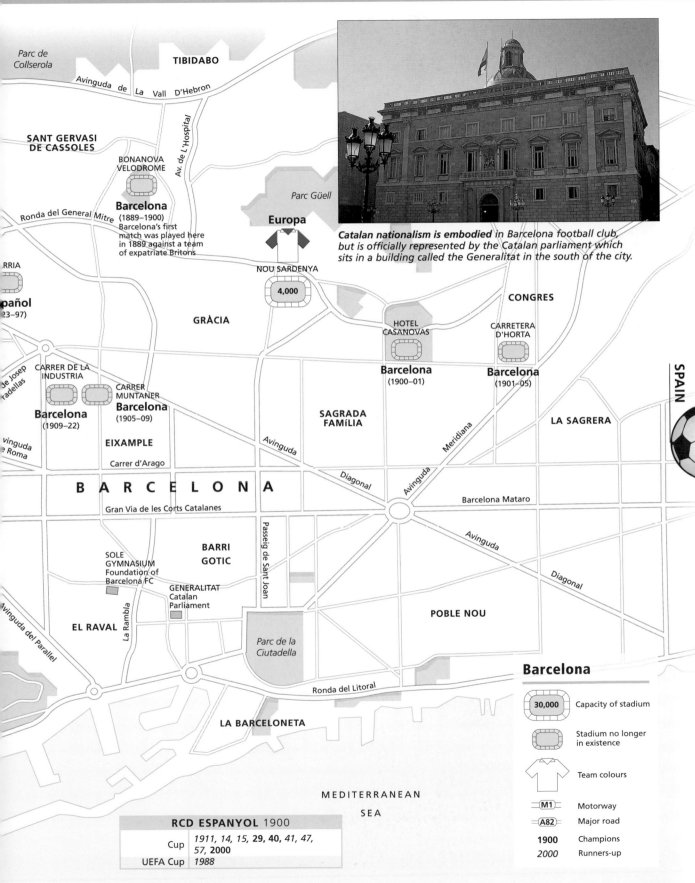

Parc de Collserola

TIBIDABO

Avinguda de La Vall D'Hebron

SANT GERVASI
DE CASSOLES

BONANOVA
VELODROME

Barcelona
(1889–1900)
Barcelona's first
match was played here
in 1889 against a team
of expatriate Britons

Ronda del General Mitre

Av. de L'Hospital

Parc Güell

Europa

NOU SARDENYA

4,000

RRIA

pañol
23–97)

GRÀCIA

CONGRES

HOTEL
CASANOVAS

CARRETERA
D'HORTA

Barcelona
(1900–01)

Barcelona
(1901–05)

SPAIN

de Josep
radellas

CARRER DE LA
INDUSTRIA

CARRER
MUNTANER

Barcelona
(1909–22)

Barcelona
(1905–09)

LA SAGRERA

vinguda
e Roma

EIXAMPLE

Carrer d'Arago

SAGRADA
FAMÍLIA

Avinguda

Meridiana

B A R C E L O N A

Gran Via de les Corts Catalanes

Diagonal

Avinguda

Barcelona Mataro

Avinguda

Passeig de Sant Joan

BARRI
GOTIC

Diagonal

SOLE
GYMNASIUM
Foundation of
Barcelona FC

GENERALITAT
Catalan
Parliament

POBLE NOU

La Rambla

Avinguda del Parallel

EL RAVAL

*Parc de la
Ciutadella*

Ronda del Litoral

LA BARCELONETA

MEDITERRANEAN
SEA

*Catalan nationalism is embodied in Barcelona football club,
but is officially represented by the Catalan parliament which
sits in a building called the Generalitat in the south of the city.*

Barcelona

30,000	Capacity of stadium
	Stadium no longer in existence
	Team colours
M1	Motorway
A82	Major road
1900	Champions
2000	Runners-up

RCD ESPANYOL 1900	
Cup	*1911, 14, 15,* **29,** *40, 41, 47, 57,* **2000**
UEFA Cup	*1988*

Madrid

FOOTBALL CITY

SPAIN

REAL MADRID GREW OUT OF AN ELITE CLUB called Football Sky, which was founded in 1895. A team split in 1900 saw Español de Madrid emerge, which transmuted into Madrid FC in 1902. When King Alfonso XIII accepted the offer of royal patronage in 1920, the team became known as Real. Although Real Madrid was successful in the national championships in the first decade of the 20th century, it did not acquire a permanent home until the construction of the Campo O'Donnell in 1912, and a proper stadium had to await the construction of Chamartín in 1924.

Located in the most exclusive financial and residential district of Madrid, Real was transformed by the arrival of Santiago Bernabéu as president and the Franco regime at the end of the Spanish Civil War. Although Franco was undoubtedly a Real fan, and his regime benefited hugely from the successful international exposure the great Real team of the 1950s brought, his real influence on the club is probably less than Bernabéu and the network of financiers and bankers he amassed. Constant access to funds has allowed Real to build one of the world's largest stadiums, fund record-breaking transfers, and return after two quiet decades to dominant ways, winning three European Cups (1998, 2000 and 2002). This has also allowed Real to accumulate the biggest debts in global football, only paid off by the sale of its training ground in 2001 for massive real estate development.

Hard-won success

Atlético was founded in 1903 by three Basques studying in Madrid as an offshoot of their home team, Athletic Bilbao. The team played in Athletic's blue and white stripes before switching to its current red and white stripes in 1911. The club performed poorly before the Civil War, only returning to the league afterwards because Oviedo's ground had been destroyed and they could no longer play in the league. It merged with the air force's brilliant side, Atlético Aviacion, which brought it two immediate titles. Although historically it is among the most successful teams in Spain, Atlético is better known for the fanaticism of its *ultras* (fans) and the erratic and financially dubious behaviour of the team's long term president, Jesus Gil. The club's recent poor fortunes have often left it behind the tiny Rayo Vallecano, which survives on a shoestring in the city's rough southern suburbs.

The Royal Palace in Madrid: the Spanish Royal House has played a big part in the history of Spanish football. Madrid FC became Real or 'Royal' Madrid in 1920, when King Alphonso XIII accepted the offer of royal patronage of the team. General Franco too was a Real fan, and with such supporters as this it is little wonder that Real has come to be associated with the elite elements of Spanish society.

VINCENTE CALDERÓN (Estadio Manzanares)

57,500

Club: Atlético Madrid
Built: 1966
Rebuilt: 1982
Significant Matches: 1982 World Cup: three group matches

SANTIAGO BERNABÉU

106,500

Club: Real Madrid
Built: 1947
Original Capacity: 75,000
Rebuilt: 1982, 1998
Significant Matches: 1964 European Championships: Final; 1982 World Cup: three group matches; European Cup Finals: 1957, 69, 80

PEÑA GRANDE

M40

TETUÁN

M30

CIUDAD LINEAL

CHAMARTÍN

CIUDAD DEPORTIVO
Real Madrid's old training ground

Real Madrid
(1948–)

Real Madrid
(1924–47)

SANTIAGO BERNABÉU

106,500

RACE COURSE
16 April 1905
First international game played in Spain:
Real Madrid v Gallia Sport, result: 1–1

REAL MADRID 1902	
League	*1929*, **32**, **33**, *34–36*, **42**, **45**, **54**, **55**, **57**, **58**, *59*, **60**, **61–65**, *66*, **67–69**, **72**, **75**, **76**, **78–80**, *81*, **83**, **84**, **86–90**, **92**, **93**, **95**, **97**, **99**, **2001**
Cup	*1903*, **05–08**, *16*, **17**, *18*, *24*, *29*, *30*, **33**, **34**, *36*, **40**, *43*, **46**, **47**, *58*, *60*, *61*, **62**, *68*, **70**, **74**, **75**, *79*, **80**, **82**, *83*, **89**, *90*, *92*, **93**, *2002*
European Cup	**1956–60**, *62*, **64**, *66*, *81*, **98**, **2000**, *02*
European Cup-Winners' Cup	*1971*, *83*
UEFA Cup	**1985**, **86**
World Club Cup	**1960**, *66*, **98**, *2000*

CIUDAD UNIVERSITARIA

METROPOLITANO

Atlético Madrid
(1923–66)

M30

A6

ARGÜELLES

M A D R I D

CHAMARTÍN

Offices of La Liga

SPAIN

Offices of *Marca*, Madrid's leading sports daily and significant supporters of Real

Río Manzanares

M30

Casa de Campo

CHAMBERÍ

SALAMANCA

CAMPO O'DONNELL

LA PLAZA DE CIBELES
Traditional site of victory celebrations

Real Madrid
(1912–24)

Atlético Madrid
(1913–24)

RETIRO

M30

ROYAL PALACE

A5

CENTRO

REAL FEDERACIÓN ESPAÑOLA DE FÚTBOL HEADQUARTERS

A3

PALACIO

ESTADIO VINCENTE CALDERÓN
(previously Estadio Manzanares)

57,500

Atlético Madrid
(1966–)

ARGANZUELA

PUENTE DE VALLECAS

NUEVO VALLECAS
MARÍA TERESA
RIVERO SÁNCHEZ

15,500

Rayo Vallecano

Madrid

57,500	Capacity of stadium
	Stadium no longer in existence
	Team colours
A5	Motorway
	Major road
1900	Champions
2000	Runners-up

USERA

ATLÉTICO MADRID 1903	
League	**1940**, **41**, *44*, **50**, **51**, *58*, **61**, *63*, *65*, **66**, **70**, **73**, *74*, **77**, **85**, **91**, **96**
Cup	*1921*, *26*, *56*, *60*, **61**, *64*, **65**, **72**, *75*, *76*, **85**, *87*, **91**, **92**, **96**, *99*, **2000**
European Cup	*1974*
European Cup-Winners' Cup	**1962**, *63*, **86**
World Club Cup	**1974**

Spain

FANS AND OWNERS

THERE IS A MIXED ECONOMY in the ownership of clubs in Spain; some are run as sporting and social clubs, others are private limited companies, some with a single dominant investor and others with multiple-share ownership. The two biggest clubs in the country, Real Madrid and Barcelona, are owned by their members, or *socios*, who select the paid officials that run the clubs in highly politicized and expensive elections. The biggest incomes and highest attendances of Spain's top teams are concentrated among the big five – Real, Barcelona, Valencia, Athletic Bilbao and RC Deportivo from La Coruña, although when Atlético Madrid is in the top flight, it joins that elite group.

The rising tide of debt

But despite huge TV income, other investments, and a lot of European success, Spanish clubs are heavily indebted. Real has recently escaped from a crippling debt of around $150 million by selling its city-centre training ground. In the last couple of seasons, smaller clubs with smaller assets have seen board resignations, unpaid creditors and a search for new investors (Las Palmas, for example, is over £30 million in debt). Worse still, the bankruptcy of Atlético Madrid in 2002 led to an investigation by the Spanish treasury which has revealed unpaid taxes among the top clubs for the years 1996–99 of £129 million. Clubs with debts of more than one third of their capital are technically bankrupt in Spain – and this would apply to about a third of the Primera Liga if the debts were immediately enforced.

Spanish fans were traditionally organized in *peñas* or supporters' clubs, often based around a particular bar, which arranged away trips and social events. With the passing of Franco's authoritarian regime and the development of a distinctive youth culture in Spain, it was inevitable that the

ultra model would be imported from Italy by a new generation of supporters. The first *ultra* groups emerged in Madrid in 1982 at both Real (*Ultras Sur*) and Atlético (*El Frente Atlético*) and they have more recently been joined by groups at Barcelona (*ICC – Inter City Cules*), Sevilla (*Peña Biri-Biri*) and Athletic Bilbao. Although there has been some violence between groups outside the stadiums, the phenomenon appears to have peaked since a Real Sociedad fan was stabbed outside Atlético Madrid's Vincente Calderón stadium in 1998. Barriers, fences and moats have become commonplace fixtures at Spanish stadiums.

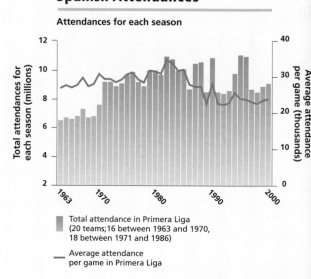

Spanish Attendances

Attendances for each season

- Total attendance in Primera Liga (20 teams;16 between 1963 and 1970, 18 between 1971 and 1986)
- Average attendance per game in Primera Liga

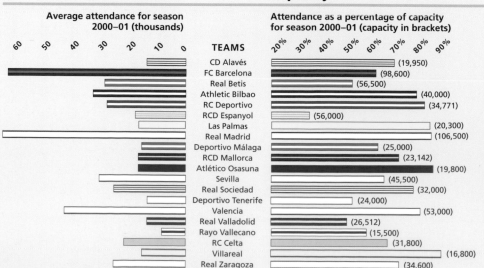

Average Attendance

Average attendance for season 2000–01 (thousands)

Capacity

Attendance as a percentage of capacity for season 2000–01 (capacity in brackets)

TEAMS	Capacity
CD Alavés	(19,950)
FC Barcelona	(98,600)
Real Betis	(56,500)
Athletic Bilbao	(40,000)
RC Deportivo	(34,771)
RCD Espanyol	(56,000)
Las Palmas	(20,300)
Real Madrid	(106,500)
Deportivo Málaga	(25,000)
RCD Mallorca	(23,142)
Atlético Osasuna	(19,800)
Sevilla	(45,500)
Real Sociedad	(32,000)
Deportivo Tenerife	(24,000)
Valencia	(53,000)
Real Valladolid	(26,512)
Rayo Vallecano	(15,500)
RC Celta	(31,800)
Villareal	(16,800)
Real Zaragoza	(34,600)

Jesus Gil, owner of Atlético Madrid, is being tried on charges of embezzling £16.4 million during his tenure as Mayor of Marbella.

Majority and Leading Shareholders

Team	● Madrid City of origin	Personal share	Many small shareholders	Owned by Socios	Retail company	Media company

Teams shown were members of La Liga 2001–02

RC Deportivo

Athletic Bilbao

Augusto César Lendoiro

José María Arrate

● La Coruña

RC Celta

Horacio Gómez Araujo

Vigo

CD Alavés

Gonzalo Antón Sanjuán 61%

Valladolid

Real Valladolid

Palco Blancos

Prisa Media Group

Real Betis

Manuel Ruiz de Lopera

Sevilla

José Maria Gonzalez de Caldas

Bilbao

Alavés

Donostia-San Sebastian

Atlético Osasuna

Pamplona

Real Sociedad

Real Zaragoza

Alfonso Solans Solans

Pikolin mattress company

Zaragoza

Barcelona

RCD Espanyol

FC Barcelona

Real Madrid

Rayo Vallecano

Madrid

José Ruis de Lopera

SPAIN

Villareal

Villareal

Valencia

Valencia

RCD Mallorca

Mallorca

Bartolome Beltran

Antennae 3 TV company

Seville

Málaga

Deportivo Málaga

Fernando Puche

SPAIN

CANARY ISLANDS

Unión Deportivo Las Palmas

Tenerife

Las Palmas

Deportivo Tenerife

Gaecia Navarro

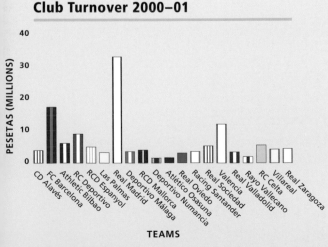

Club Turnover 2000–01

PESETAS (MILLIONS)

40 / 30 / 20 / 10 / 0

TEAMS

CD Alavés, FC Barcelona, Athletic Bilbao, RC Deportivo, RCD Espanyol, Las Palmas, Real Madrid, Deportivo Málaga, RCD Mallorca, Deportivo Numancia, Atlético Osasuna, Real Oviedo, Racing Santander, Real Sociedad, Valencia, Real Valladolid, Rayo Vallecano, RC Celta, Villareal, Real Zaragoza

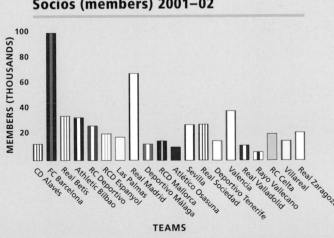

Socios (members) 2001–02

MEMBERS (THOUSANDS)

100 / 80 / 60 / 40 / 20 / 0

TEAMS

CD Alavés, FC Barcelona, Real Betis, Athletic Bilbao, RC Deportivo, RCD Espanyol, Las Palmas, Real Madrid, Deportivo Málaga, RCD Mallorca, Atlético Osasuna, Sevilla, Real Sociedad, Deportivo Tenerife, Valencia, Real Valladolid, Rayo Vallecano, RC Celta, Villareal, Real Zaragoza

Spain

PLAYERS AND MANAGERS

WHILE FITNESS IS ASSUMED among Spanish footballers, a certain professional craftiness is required to be regarded as a real player, and the possession of *calidad* ('quality of technique') is a Spanish footballer's most prized asset. This style is exemplified by the magisterial Raúl at today's Real Madrid. Of course, you also need a good nickname to get on. The leading goalscorer in Spanish football is known as 'Pichichi', named in honour of Rafael Moreno Aranzadi, the great Basque centre-forward who played for Athletic Bilbao in the 1920s. In his wake, Spain's great strikers have included Emilio Butragueño, nicknamed 'the Vulture' for his capacity to pick up and devour chances in the box, and Francisco Gento, 'El Supersonico', the only man to win six European Cup winner's medals.

Nationalism v cosmopolitanism

The roster of great Spanish players and managers expresses both the country's inward-looking nationalism and its outward-looking cosmopolitanism. On the playing side (and recently on the managerial side as well), Spanish football has drawn widely and deeply on the pool of foreign talent. In the postwar era, Franco's Spain was pleased to accept Alfredo di Stefano from Argentina and Ferenc Puskas from Hungary, and award Spanish citizenship to both. In the 1960s, nationalist paranoia saw a decade-long ban on foreign players until a new wave of talent arrived in the shape of Johan Cruyff at Barcelona in the 1970s and then Diego Maradona in the early 1980s. However, at Athletic Bilbao the strict Basque-only policy on players remains in place. In recent years, the enormous amount of money in the Spanish game has seen a steady rise in the number of overseas players, especially from Latin America, with Brazilians, Argentinians and Uruguayans flooding the top division.

Top 10 International Caps

PLAYER	CAPS	GOALS	FIRST MATCH	LAST MATCH
Andoni Zubizarreta	129	0	1985	1998
Fernando Ruiz Hierro*	83	27	1989	2001
José Antonio Camacho	81	0	1975	1988
Rafael Gordillo	75	3	1978	1988
Emilio Butragueño	69	26	1984	1992
Luis Miguel Arconada	68	0	1977	1985
Miguel González 'Michel'	66	21	1985	1992
Victor Muñoz	60	3	1981	1988
Luis Enrique*	57	12	1991	2001
Julio Salinas Fernández	56	22	1986	1996
Nadal	56	3	1991	2001
Carlos Alonso Santillana	56	15	1975	1985

Top 10 International Goalscorers

PLAYER	GOALS	CAPS	FIRST MATCH	LAST MATCH
Fernando Ruiz Hierro*	27	83	1989	2001
Emilio Butragueño	26	69	1984	1992
Alfredo di Stefano	23	31	1957	1961
Raúl González Blanco*	23	49	1996	2001
Julio Salinas Fernández	22	56	1986	1996
Miguel González 'Michel'	21	66	1985	1992
Telmo Zarraonandia 'Zarra'	20	20	1945	1951
Isidro Lángara	17	12	1932	1936
Luis Regueiro	16	25	1927	1936
José Martínez 'Pirri'	16	41	1966	1978

* Indicates players still playing at least at club level.
Nicknames are indicated between inverted commas.

Spanish International Managers

DATES	NAME	GAMES	WON	DRAWN	LOST
1955–56	Guillermo Eizaguirre	3	0	1	2
1957–59	Manuel Meana	12	7	3	2
1959–60	José Luis Costa, Ramón Gabilondo, José Luis Lasplazas	5	4	0	1
1961	Pedro Escartin	7	5	2	0
1962	Pablo Hernandez	3	1	0	2
1962–66	Jose Villalonga	22	9	5	8
1966–68	Domingo Balmanya	11	4	3	4
1968–69	Eduardo Toba	4	1	2	1
1969	Salvador Artigas, Luis Molowny, Miguel Munoz	4	2	1	1
1969–80	Ladislao Kubala	68	32	21	15
1980–82	José Santamaria	23	10	6	7
1982–88	Miguel Munoz	59	31	13	15
1988–91	Luis Suárez	27	15	4	8
1991–92	Vincente Miera	8	4	2	2
1992–98	Javier Clemente	62	36	19	7
1998–	José Antonio Camacho	36	24	6	6

All figures correct as of 14 November 2001.

Emilio Butragueño's 26 international goals included four in Spain's five-goal thrashing of Denmark in the second round of the 1986 World Cup Finals in Mexico.

SPAIN

Player of the Year

YEAR	PLAYER	CLUB
1976	Ángel	Real Madrid
1977	'Juanito'	Real Burgos
1978	'Migueli'	Barcelona
1979	'Quini'	Sporting Gijón
1980	Gordillo	Real Betis
1981	'Urruti'	RCD Español
1982	Tendillo	Valencia
1983	Señor	Real Zaragoza
1984	Cervantes	Real Murcia
1985	'Migueli'	Barcelona
1986	'Míchel'	Real Madrid
1987	Zubizarreta	Barcelona
1988	Larrañaga	Real Sociedad
1989	Fernando	Valencia
1990	Martín Vázquez	Real Madrid
1991	Goikoetxea	Barcelona
1992	Elduayen	Real Burgos
1993	'Fran'	RC Deportivo
1994	Guerrero	Athletic Bilbao
1995	Amavisca	Real Madrid
1996	Caminero	Atlético Madrid
1997	Raúl	Real Madrid
1998	Alfonso	Real Betis
1999	Raúl	Real Madrid
2000	Raúl	Real Madrid
2001	Marino	Alavés

Foreign Player of the Year

PLAYER	CLUB	NATIONALITY
Neeskens	Barcelona	Dutch
Cruyff	Barcelona	Dutch
Cruyff	Barcelona	Dutch
Stielike	Real Madrid	German
Stielike	Real Madrid	German
Stielike	Real Madrid	German
Stielike	Real Madrid	German
Barbas	Real Zaragoza	Argentinian
Barbas	Real Zaragoza	Argentinian
Schuster	Barcelona	German
Valdano	Real Madrid	Argentinian
Hugo Sánchez	Real Madrid	Mexican
Alemão	Atlético Madrid	Brazilian
Ruggeri	CD Logroñés	Argentinian
Hugo Sánchez	Real Madrid	Mexican
Schuster	Atlético Madrid	German
Laudrup	Barcelona	Danish
Dujkic	RC Deportivo	Yugoslavian
Stoichkov	Barcelona	Bulgarian
Zamorano	Real Madrid	Chilean
Mijatovic	Valencia	Yugoslavian
Ronaldo	Barcelona	Brazilian
Rivaldo	Barcelona	Brazilian
Figo	Barcelona	Portuguese
Figo	Barcelona	Portuguese
R. Carlos	Real Madrid	Brazilian

Manager of the Year

MANAGER	CLUB	NATIONALITY
Miljanic	Real Madrid	Yugoslavian
Aragonés	Atlético Madrid	Spanish
Molowny	Real Madrid	Spanish
Molowny	Real Madrid	Spanish
Molowny	Real Madrid	Spanish
Ormachea	Real Sociedad	Spanish
Ormachea	Real Sociedad	Spanish
Clemente	Athletic Bilbao	Spanish
Clemente	Athletic Bilbao	Spanish
Venables	Barcelona	English
Molowny	Real Madrid	Spanish
Clemente	RCD Español	Spanish
Beenhakker	Real Madrid	Dutch
Toshack	Real Sociedad	Welsh
Toshack	Real Madrid	Welsh
Cruyff	Barcelona	Dutch
Cruyff	Barcelona	Dutch
Inglesias	RC Deportivo	Spanish
Fernandez	Real Zaragoza	Spanish
Inglesias	RC Deportivo	Spanish
Antic	Atlético Madrid	Yugoslavian
Cantatore	Real Valladolid	Uruguayan
'Irureta'	RC Celta	Spanish
Cúper	RCD Mallorca	Argentinian
'Irureta'	RC Deportivo	Spanish
Mane	Alavés	Spanish

Awarded by *Don Ballon* magazine.

Top Goalscorers by Season 1975–2002

SEASON	PLAYER	CLUB	GOALS
1975–76	'Quini'	Real Sporting	18
1976–77	Kempes	Valencia	24
1977–78	Kempes	Valencia	28
1978–79	Krankl	Barcelona	26
1979–80	'Quini'	Real Sporting	24
1980–81	'Quini'	Barcelona	20
1981–82	'Quini'	Barcelona	26
1982–83	Rincón	Real Betis	20
1983–84	Da Silva	Real Valladolid	17
1983–84	'Juanito'	Real Madrid	17
1984–85	Sánchez	Atlético Madrid	19

SEASON	PLAYER	CLUB	GOALS
1985–86	H. Sánchez	Real Madrid	22
1986–87	H. Sánchez	Real Madrid	34
1987–88	H. Sánchez	Real Madrid	29
1988–89	Baltazar	Atlético Madrid	35
1989–90	H. Sánchez	Real Madrid	38
1990–91	Butragueño	Real Madrid	19
1991–92	Manolo	Atlético Madrid	27
1992–93	Bebeto	RC Deportivo	29
1993–94	Romario	Barcelona	30
1994–95	Zamorano	Real Madrid	28

SEASON	PLAYER	CLUB	GOALS
1995–96	Pizzi	Tenerife	31
1996–97	Ronaldo	Barcelona	34
1997–98	Vieri	Atlético Madrid	24
1998–99	Raúl	Real Madrid	25
1999–2000	Salva	Racing Santander	27
2000–01	Raúl	Real Madrid	24
2001–02	Tristan	RC Deportivo	21

Foreign Players in Spain (in top division squads)

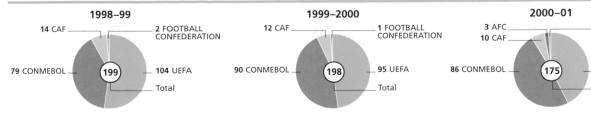

1998–99
14 CAF, 2 FOOTBALL CONFEDERATION, 79 CONMEBOL, 199 Total, 104 UEFA

1999–2000
12 CAF, 1 FOOTBALL CONFEDERATION, 90 CONMEBOL, 198 Total, 95 UEFA

2000–01
3 AFC, 10 CAF, 1 FOOTBALL CONFEDERATION, 86 CONMEBOL, 175 Total, 75 UEFA

SPAIN

Spain

PRIMERA LIGA 1981–2001

THE EARLY 1980s saw the Basque country rise to prominence in Spain, with titles for Real Sociedad and Athletic Bilbao. Both fielded Basque-only squads and in the relative freedom of the post-Franco years an intense Basque nationalism pervaded the mood of the crowds. At Bilbao, Javier Clemente built a tough, fiery team with Andoni Goikoetxea, the 'Butcher of Bilbao', leading a mean defensive line on Spain's wettest, slowest pitch. Although both teams have been permanent members of La Liga since then, neither has been able to sustain more than a season's serious challenge for the title. Most recently, Athletic, under Luis Fernandez, came second to Barcelona in 1998. Real Sociedad has abandoned its Basque-only policy and Athletic has been through a slew of foreign coaches including Howard Kendall, Guus Hiddink and Jupp Heynckes.

The 'Vulture Squad' v the 'Dream Team'

The Basque stranglehold on the title was broken by Barcelona in 1985 under English coach Terry Venables, only for the centre to reassert itself in the shape of Real Madrid and *La Quinta Del Buitre* – the 'Vulture Squad'. Despite an enormous turnover of managers and increasingly hysterical financial and administrative practices, Real had an inspired and disciplined spine in Emilio Butragueño (the 'Vulture'), Michel, Sanchis and Martín Vásquez. That was enough to take five straight titles in the 1980s.

At Barcelona, president José Luis Núñez lured ex-player and local hero Johan Cruyff back to the Bernabeu stadium as manager in 1988. Cruyff created a team made up of both homegrown players, like the young Pep Guardiola, and foreign internationals like Ronald Koeman, Hirsto Stoichkov and Michael Laudrup. The 'Dream Team', as it became known, took four titles in a row, though, rather ironically, two of them required lowly Tenerife to beat Real Madrid on the final day of the season to ensure the title went to Barça. The 1994 title came courtesy of Miroslav Djukic's last-minute penalty miss for the chasing RC Deportivo from La Coruña.

Despite the chaos and rising debts of Ramón Mendoza's Real Madrid, 1995 saw the club back at the top under Argentinian Jorge Valdano. Valdano was, of course, promptly fired, and in 1996 Atlético Madrid took its first title for over 20

years under its eccentric and improbable president Jesús Gil. Mayor of Marbella and inveterate dealer and fixer, Gil would eventually be convicted on a range of corruption charges in the late 1990s, and Atlético would plummet into the lower divisions, where it remained for several years. Over at Real, Mendoza was toppled by new president Lorenzo Sans. Sans brought in coach Fabio Capello, fresh from his success with Milan, and authorized a massive spend on the squad, bringing in Clarence Seedorf, Roberto Carlos and Davor Suker. It was enough to take the title in 1997 and the team went on to win the European Champions League the following season. However, a ridiculous turnover of managers once again saw the club unable to provide the consistency required to win the league title.

The arrival of the Dutchmen

That consistency was delivered by the new-look Barcelona who, having dispensed with both Bobby Robson and Ronaldo, brought in the architect of the new Ajax, Louis van Gaal. The core of the Dutch national squad, including the De Boers, Kluivert, Overmars, Cocu, Zenden and Reiziger, were purchased to play alongside Rivaldo and Luis Figo. Barcelona stormed the table in 1998 and 99. A triple was blocked by Deportivo La Coruña who finally made good on its promise throughout the 1990s and won in 2000. Real was back the following year, now augmented by Luis Figo, who'd been 'stolen' from Barcelona at the beginning of the season.

Competition in Spanish football has been fierce, with good sustainable sides built at RCD Mallorca under Hector Cuper in the mid-1990s, and Valencia (also led by Cuper) who contested two consecutive Champions League finals. The tiny Basque team CD Alavés, Galician RC Celta from Vigo and Real Zaragoza have also all proved tough regular competitors. The big southern clubs, Real Betis and Sevilla FC, have proved less successful, and both have tasted lower division football. However, despite the healthy competition, clubs in the lower reaches of the league are beset by debt, and recent demands from the Spanish treasury for unpaid taxes threaten to bankrupt half of the teams in La Liga.

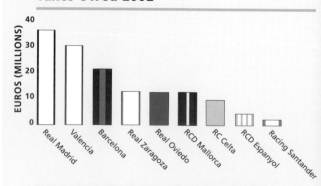

*The **Real Madrid v Barcelona** derby is at the heart of Spanish football. For the big two the season stands or falls on this result.*

Taxes Owed 2002

EUROS (MILLIONS)

Real Madrid, Valencia, Barcelona, Real Zaragoza, Real Oviedo, RCD Mallorca, RC Celta, RCD Espanyol, Racing Santander

Taxes owed to the Spanish government by Primera Liga clubs

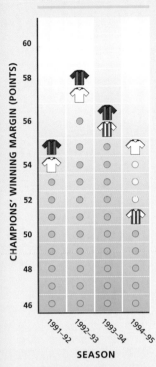

No one is bigger than Real Madrid. President Lorenzo Sanz saw his side win the Champions League in 2000 only to lose a snap election for the presidency to Florentine Pérez.

Champions' Winning Margin 1991–95

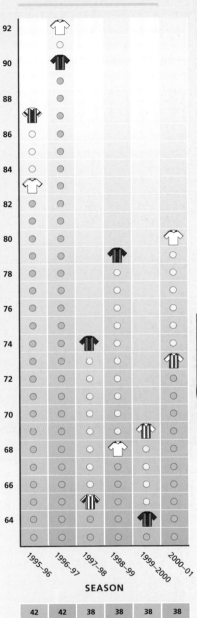

Total games played by each team (2 points awarded for a win)

Champions' Winning Margin 1995–2001

Total games played by each team (3 points awarded for a win)

 Atlético Madrid — Valencia
RC Deportivo — Athletic Bilbao
Barcelona — Real Madrid

Above: Johan Cruyff returned to Barcelona as coach, winning four consecutive league titles between 1991 and 94.

Right: José Núñez was elected president of Barcelona in 1978 after a bruising campaign. He ruled the club as something close to a fiefdom before his shock defeat to Joan Gaspart in the 2001 presidential elections.

SPAIN

Key to League Positions Table

- ▇ League champions
- ▇ Season of promotion to league
- ▇ Season of relegation from league
- ▇ Other teams playing in league
- 5 Final position in league

SPAIN

Real Betis broke the world transfer record to buy Brazilian Denilson of São Paulo. Relegation followed, but the team has clawed its way back into La Liga's top flight.

After six quiet years at Valencia, Gaizka Mendieta found his form under Hector Cuper and helped Valencia to two Champions League Finals, and himself to Lazio in 2001.

Spanish League Positions 1981–2001

TEAM	1981–82	1982–83	1983–84	1984–85	1985–86	1986–87	1987–88	1988–89	1989–90	1990–91	1991–92	1992–93	1993–94	1994–95	1995–96	1996–97	1997–98	1998–99	1999–2000	2000–01
CD Alavés																		16	6	10
Albacete Balompié											7	17	13	17	20					
Barcelona	2	4	3	1	2	2	6	2	3	1	1	1	1	4	3	2	1	1	2	4
Real Betis	6	11	5	14	8	9	16	18	20						3	8	4	8	11	18
Athletic Bilbao	4	1	1	3	3	13	4	7	12	12	14	8	5	8	15	6	2	8	11	12
Real Burgos										11	9	20								
Cádiz	16		16		15	18	12	15	15	18	18	19								
Deportivo Castellón	18								14	19										
RC Celta		17			18		7	8	19			11	15	13	11	16	6	5	7	6
SD Compostela													16	10	11	17				
RC Deportivo											17	3	2	2	9	3	12	6	1	2
Elche CF			17				20													
RCD Espanyol	13	9	10	8	11	3	15	17		16	16	18		6	4	12	10	7	14	9
CF Extremadura																19		17		
Sporting Gijón	14	8	13	4	6	4	9	13	13	5	8	12	14	18	18	15	20			
Hércules	17			15	17												21			
Unión Deportivo Las Palmas	15	16			13	14	20													11
Lérida Unión Esportiva													19							
Deportivo Logroñes								13	14	7	10	10	15	16	20		22			
Atlético Madrid	8	3	4	2	5	7	3	4	4	2	3	6	12	14	1	5	7	13	19	
Real Madrid	3	2	2	1	1	1	1	1	1	3	2	2	4	1	6	1	4	2	5	1
Deportivo Málaga		10	9	16			16	17											12	8
RCD Mallorca			17				6	18		10	15	20					5	3	10	3
CP Mérida																21		19		
Real Murcia					11	18		11	17	19										
CD Numancia																			17	20
Atlético Osasuna	10	14	15	6	14	16	5	10	8	4	15	10	20							15
Real Oviedo								12	11	6	11	16	9	9	14	17	18	14	16	18
CD Sabadell					15	19														
Deportivo Salamanca		13	18													22		15	20	
Racing Santander	12	18		11	12	17							8	12	17	13	14	15	15	19
Sevilla FC	7	5	8	12	9	12	10	9	6	8	12	7	6	5	12	20			20	
Real Sociedad	1	7	6	7	7	8	2	11	5	13	5	13	11	7	3	10	13	13		
Deportivo Tenerife									18	14	13	5	10	15	5	9	16	19		
Valencia	5	15	12	9	16		14	3	2	7	4	4	7	10	2	10	9	4	3	5
Real Valladolid	9	12	14	13	10	10	8	6	16	9	19		18	19	16	7	11	12	8	16
Rayo Vallecano									20			14	17			19	18		9	14
Villarreal																		18		7
Real Zaragoza	11	6	7	10	4	5	11		9	17	6	9	3	7	13	14	13	9	4	17

Primera Liga

Real Madrid	Team name
	League champions/ runners-up
1990, *92*	Champions in bold Runners-up in italics
	Other teams in the Primera Liga
● **Madrid**	City of origin

When RC Deportivo from La Coruña was promoted in 1991, club president Augusto César Lendorio announced 'Barcelona, Madrid, we are here'. With the 1999–2000 squad the team finally arrived, running away with the title under coach Javier Irureta.

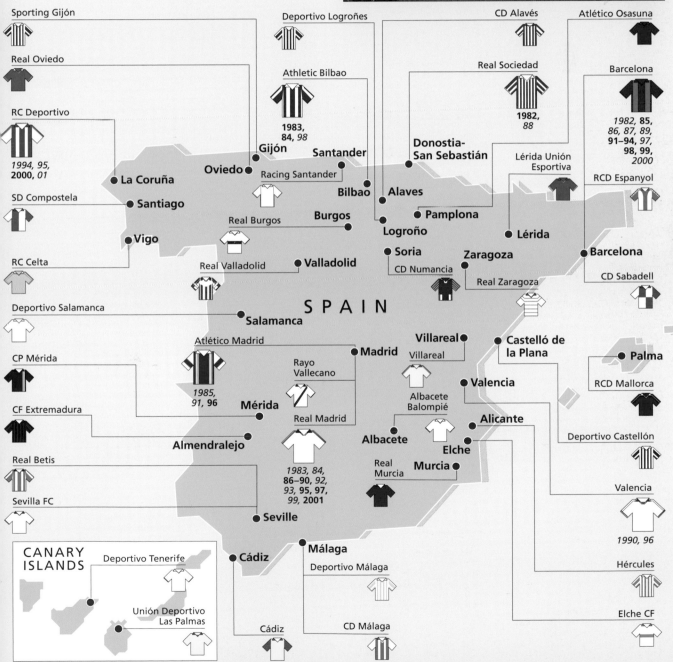

SPAIN

Sporting Gijón

Real Oviedo

RC Deportivo
1994, 95, **2000,** *01*

SD Compostela

RC Celta

Deportivo Salamanca

CP Mérida

CF Extremadura

Real Betis

Sevilla FC

Deportivo Logroñes

Athletic Bilbao
1983, *84,* **98**

Racing Santander

Real Burgos

Real Valladolid

Atlético Madrid
1985, *91,* **96**

Rayo Vallecano

Real Madrid
1983, *84,* **86–90,** *92,* **93,** *95,* **97,** *99,* **2001**

CD Alavés

Real Sociedad
1982, *88*

CD Numancia

Real Zaragoza

Lérida Unión Esportiva

Villareal

Albacete Balompié

Real Murcia

Atlético Osasuna

Barcelona
1982, **85,** *86,* **87,** *89,* **91–94,** *97,* **98,** *99,* **2000**

RCD Espanyol

CD Sabadell

Castelló de la Plana

RCD Mallorca

Deportivo Castellón

Valencia
1990, *96*

Hércules

Elche CF

● La Coruña
● Santiago
● Vigo
● Salamanca
● Oviedo
Gijón ● Santander
Bilbao ● Alaves ●
Burgos ●
● Valladolid
● Logroño
● Soria
Donostia- San Sebastián ●
Pamplona ●
● Lérida
● Zaragoza
● Barcelona
● Villareal
● Castelló de la Plana
● Palma
● Valencia
● Alicante
● Madrid
● Mérida
Almendralejo ●
● Albacete
Elche ●
Murcia ●
● Seville
● Cádiz
● Málaga

S P A I N

CANARY ISLANDS

Deportivo Tenerife

Unión Deportivo Las Palmas

Cádiz

Deportivo Málaga

CD Málaga

Spain

Real Federación Española de Fútbol
Founded: 1913
Joined FIFA: 1904
Joined UEFA: 1954

SPAIN

FROM ITS EARLIEST DAYS, SPANISH FOOTBALL had a strong regional character. A Catalonian league was up and running by 1901, and the first years of the 20th century saw the establishment of regional leagues all over the country. The first national league began in 1929 comprising ten clubs. It grew steadily to a peak of 22 clubs in the 1990s, but has now decreased in size to just 20.

The first national competition, the Copa del Rey, was created in 1902. Not surprisingly given its title, it was supported by the centralizing monarchy in the person of King Alfonso XIII. The name, if not the format, of the cup has shifted with Spain's constitution. In 1934 it became the short-lived Copa del Republica, but was halted by the civil war, and reinvented under Franco's regime as the Copa del Generalisimo. With the return of the monarchy after Franco's death, the name of the competition reverted to its original title, the Copa del Rey.

Spanish League Record 1929–2002

SEASON	CHAMPIONS	RUNNERS-UP
1929	Barcelona	Real Madrid
1930	Athletic Bilbao	Barcelona
1931	Athletic Bilbao	Racing Santander
1932	Real Madrid	Athletic Bilbao
1933	Real Madrid	Athletic Bilbao
1934	Athletic Bilbao	Real Madrid
1935	Real Betis	Real Madrid
1936	Athletic Bilbao	Real Madrid
1937–39	no championship	
1940	Atlético Aviación	Sevilla
1941	Atlético Aviación	Athletic Bilbao
1942	Valencia	Real Madrid
1943	Athletic Bilbao	Sevilla
1944	Valencia	Atlético Aviación
1945	Barcelona	Real Madrid
1946	Sevilla	Barcelona
1947	Valencia	Athletic Bilbao
1948	Barcelona	Valencia
1949	Barcelona	Valencia
1950	Atlético Madrid	RC Deportivo
1951	Atlético Madrid	Sevilla
1952	Barcelona	Athletic Bilbao
1953	Barcelona	Valencia
1954	Real Madrid	Barcelona
1955	Real Madrid	Barcelona
1956	Athletic Bilbao	Barcelona
1957	Real Madrid	Sevilla
1958	Real Madrid	Atlético Madrid
1959	Barcelona	Real Madrid
1960	Barcelona	Real Madrid
1961	Real Madrid	Atlético Madrid
1962	Real Madrid	Barcelona
1963	Real Madrid	Atlético Madrid
1964	Real Madrid	Barcelona
1965	Real Madrid	Atlético Madrid
1966	Atlético Madrid	Real Madrid
1967	Real Madrid	Barcelona
1968	Real Madrid	Barcelona
1969	Real Madrid	Las Palmas
1970	Atlético Madrid	Athletic Bilbao
1971	Valencia	Barcelona

Spanish League Record (*continued*)

SEASON	CHAMPIONS	RUNNERS-UP
1972	Real Madrid	Valencia
1973	Atlético Madrid	Barcelona
1974	Barcelona	Atlético Madrid
1975	Real Madrid	Real Zaragoza
1976	Real Madrid	Barcelona
1977	Atlético Madrid	Barcelona
1978	Real Madrid	Barcelona
1979	Real Madrid	Sporting Gijón
1980	Real Madrid	Real Sociedad
1981	Real Sociedad	Real Madrid
1982	Real Sociedad	Barcelona
1983	Athletic Bilbao	Real Madrid
1984	Athletic Bilbao	Real Madrid
1985	Barcelona	Atlético Madrid
1986	Real Madrid	Barcelona
1987	Real Madrid	Barcelona
1988	Real Madrid	Real Sociedad
1989	Real Madrid	Barcelona
1990	Real Madrid	Valencia
1991	Barcelona	Atlético Madrid
1992	Barcelona	Real Madrid
1993	Barcelona	Real Madrid
1994	Barcelona	RC Deportivo
1995	Real Madrid	RC Deportivo
1996	Atlético Madrid	Valencia
1997	Real Madrid	Barcelona
1998	Barcelona	Athletic Bilbao
1999	Barcelona	Real Madrid
2000	RC Deportivo	Barcelona
2001	Real Madrid	RC Deportivo
2002	Valencia	RC Deportivo

Spanish League Summary

TEAM	TOTALS	CHAMPIONS & RUNNERS-UP (BOLD) (*ITALICS*)
Real Madrid	28, 15	**1929**, *32, 33, 34–36, 42, 45, 54, 55, 57, 58, 59, 60, 61–65, 66, 67–69, 72, 75, 76, 78–80, 81, 83, 84, 86–90, 92, 93, 95, 97, 99, 2001*
Barcelona	16, 20	**1929**, *30, 45, 46, 48, 49, 52, 53, 54–56, 59, 60, 62, 64, 67, 68, 71, 73, 74, 76–78, 82, 85, 86, 87, 89, 91–94, 97, 98, 99, 2000*
Atlético Madrid (including Atlético Aviación)	9, 8	**1940, 41, 44, 50, 51, 58, 61, 63, 65, 66, 70, 73, 74, 77, 85, 91, 96**
Athletic Bilbao	8, 7	**1930, 31, 32, 33, 34, 36, 41, 43, 47, 52, 56, 70, 83, 84, 98**
Valencia	5, 6	**1942, 44, 47, 48, 49, 53, 71, 72, 90, 96, 2002**
Real Sociedad	2, 2	**1980, 81, 82, 88**
RC Deportivo	1, 5	*1950, 94, 95, 2000, 01, 02*
Sevilla	1, 4	*1940, 43, **46**, 51, 57*
Real Betis	1, 0	**1935**

This summary only features clubs that have won the Spanish League. For a full list of league champions and runners-up please see the League Record above.

Spanish Cup Record 1902–2002

YEAR	WINNERS	SCORE	RUNNERS-UP
1902	Vizcaya Bilbao	2-1	Barcelona
1903	Athletic Bilbao	3-2	Real Madrid
1904	Athletic Bilbao	w/o	
1905	Real Madrid	1-0	Athletic Bilbao
1906	Real Madrid	4-1	Athletic Bilbao
1907	Real Madrid	1-0	Vizcaya Bilbao
1908	Real Madrid	2-1	Vigo Sporting
1909	Ciclista San Sebastián	3-1	Español Madrid
1910	Athletic Bilbao	1-0*	Basconia
1910	Barcelona	3-2**	Español Madrid
1911	Athletic Bilbao	3-1	RCD Español
1912	Barcelona	2-0	Gimnastica Madrid
1913	Barcelona	2-2, (replay) 0-0, (replay) 2-1*	Real Sociedad
1913	Racing Irún	2-2, (replay) 1-0**	Athletic Bilbao
1914	Athletic Bilbao	2-1	España Barcelona
1915	Athletic Bilbao	5-0	RCD Español
1916	Athletic Bilbao	4-0	Real Madrid
1917	Real Madrid	0-0, (replay) 2-1	Arenas Guecho Bilbao
1918	Real Unión Irún	2-0	Real Madrid
1919	Arenas Guecho Bilbao	5-2 (aet)	Barcelona
1920	Barcelona	2-0	Athletic Bilbao
1921	Athletic Bilbao	4-1	Atlético Madrid
1922	Barcelona	5-1	Real Unión Irún
1923	Athletic Bilbao	1-0	Europa Barcelona
1924	Real Unión Irún	1-0	Real Madrid
1925	Barcelona	2-0	Arenas Guecho Bilbao
1926	Barcelona	3-2 (aet)	Atlético Madrid
1927	Real Unión Irún	1-0 (aet)	Arenas Guecho Bilbao
1928	Barcelona	1-1, (replay) 1-1, (replay) 3-1	Real Sociedad
1929	RCD Español	2-1	Real Madrid
1930	Athletic Bilbao	3-2 (aet)	Real Madrid
1931	Athletic Bilbao	3-1	Real Betis
1932	Athletic Bilbao	1-0	Barcelona
1933	Athletic Bilbao	2-1	Real Madrid
1934	Real Madrid	2-1	Valencia
1935	Sevilla	3-0	Sabadell
1936	Real Madrid	2-1	Barcelona
1937–38	*no competition*		
1939	Sevilla	6-2	Racing Ferrol
1940	RCD Español	3-2 (aet)	Real Madrid
1941	Valencia	3-1	RCD Español
1942	Barcelona	4-3 (aet)	Athletic Bilbao
1943	Athletic Bilbao	1-0 (aet)	Real Madrid
1944	Athletic Bilbao	2-0	Valencia
1945	Athletic Bilbao	3-2	Valencia
1946	Real Madrid	3-1	Valencia
1947	Real Madrid	2-0 (aet)	RCD Español
1948	Sevilla	4-1	RC Celta
1949	Valencia	1-0	Athletic Bilbao
1950	Athletic Bilbao	4-1 (aet)	Valladolid
1951	Barcelona	3-0	Real Sociedad
1952	Barcelona	4-2 (aet)	Valencia
1953	Barcelona	2-1	Athletic Bilbao
1954	Valencia	3-0	Barcelona
1955	Athletic Bilbao	1-0	Sevilla
1956	Athletic Bilbao	2-1	Atlético Madrid
1957	Barcelona	1-0	RCD Español
1958	Athletic Bilbao	2-0	Real Madrid
1959	Barcelona	4-1	Granada
1960	Atlético Madrid	3-1	Real Madrid
1961	Atlético Madrid	3-2	Real Madrid
1962	Real Madrid	2-1	Sevilla
1963	Barcelona	3-1	Real Zaragoza
1964	Real Zaragoza	2-1	Atlético Madrid
1965	Atlético Madrid	1-0	Real Zaragoza
1966	Real Zaragoza	2-0	Athletic Bilbao
1967	Valencia	2-1	Athletic Bilbao

Spanish Cup Record (*continued*)

YEAR	WINNERS	SCORE	RUNNERS-UP
1968	Barcelona	1-0	Real Madrid
1969	Athletic Bilbao	1-0	Elche
1970	Real Madrid	3-1	Valencia
1971	Barcelona	4-3	Valencia
1972	Atlético Madrid	2-1	Valencia
1973	Athletic Bilbao	2-0	Castellón
1974	Real Madrid	4-0	Barcelona
1975	Real Madrid	0-0 (aet)(4-3 pens)	Atlético Madrid
1976	Atlético Madrid	1-0	Real Zaragoza
1977	Real Betis	2-2 (aet)(8-7 pens)	Athletic Bilbao
1978	Barcelona	3-1	Las Palmas
1979	Valencia	2-0	Real Madrid
1980	Real Madrid	6-1	Castilla
1981	Barcelona	3-1	Sporting Gijón
1982	Real Madrid	2-1	Sporting Gijón
1983	Barcelona	2-1	Real Madrid
1984	Athletic Bilbao	1-0	Barcelona
1985	Atlético Madrid	2-1	Athletic Bilbao
1986	Real Zaragoza	1-0	Barcelona
1987	Real Sociedad	2-2 (aet)(4-2 pens)	Atlético Madrid
1988	Barcelona	1-0	Real Sociedad
1989	Real Madrid	1-0	Valladolid
1990	Barcelona	2-0	Real Madrid
1991	Atlético Madrid	1-0 (aet)	Mallorca
1992	Atlético Madrid	2-0	Real Madrid
1993	Real Madrid	2-0	Real Zaragoza
1994	Real Zaragoza	0-0 (aet)(5-4 pens)	RC Celta
1995	RC Deportivo	2-1†	Valencia
1996	Atlético Madrid	1-0 (aet)	Barcelona
1997	Barcelona	3-2 (aet)	Real Betis
1998	Barcelona	1-1 (aet)(5-4 pens)	Mallorca
1999	Valencia	3-0	Atlético Madrid
2000	RCD Espanyol	2-1	Atlético Madrid
2001	Real Zaragoza	3-1	RC Celta
2002	RC Deportivo	2-1	Real Madrid

w/o denotes walk over

* Copa de la Federación Española de Fútbol.

** Copa de la Unión Española de Clubs de Fútbol.

† Match was abandoned in the 80th minute due to torrential rain (at 1-1) and finished a few days later.

Spanish Cup Summary

TEAM	TOTALS	WINNERS & RUNNERS-UP (BOLD) (*ITALICS*)
Barcelona	24, 9	*1902,* **10, 12, 13,** *19,* **20,** *22,* **25, 26, 28,** *32, 36,* **42, 51–53,** *54, 57, 59, 63, 68, 71, 74, 78, 81, 83,* **84,** *86,* **88, 90, 96, 97, 98**
Athletic Bilbao	23, 11	**1903, 04,** *05, 06,* **10, 11,** *13,* **14–16,** *20, 21,* **23, 30–33,** *42,* **43–45,** *49, 50, 53, 55, 56, 58,* **66, 67, 69, 73,** *77,* **84,** *85*
Real Madrid	17, 18	*1903,* **05–08,** *16,* **17,** *18,* **24,** *29, 30, 33, 34, 36,* **40,** *43,* **46, 47,** *58,* **60,** *61, 62, 68,* **70, 74, 75,** *79,* **80, 82,** *83,* **89,** *90, 92, 93,* **2002**
Atlético Madrid	9, 8	*1921, 26, 56,* **60, 61, 64, 65,** *72,* **75, 76, 85,** *87,* **91, 92, 96,** *99, 2000*
Valencia	6, 9	*1934,* **41,** *44–46,* **49,** *52,* **54,** *67, 70–72,* **79,** *95,* **99**
Real Zaragoza	5, 4	*1963,* **64,** *65, 66, 76, 86,* **93, 94, 2001**
Real Unión Irún (includes Racing Irún)	4, 1	**1913, 18,** *22,* **24, 27**
RCD Espanyol (includes RCD Español, España Barcelona)	3, 6	*1911, 14, 15,* **29,** *40, 41, 47, 57,* **2000**
Sevilla	3, 2	**1935, 39, 48,** *55, 62*

This summary only features clubs that have won the Spanish Cup three or more times. For a full list of cup winners and runners-up please see the Cup Record above.

Italy

THE SEASON IN REVIEW 2001–02

THE FOOTBALL WAS OFTEN STERILE, the crowds were often low, but the drama of Serie A this season was unmatched. The Italian pre-season was particularly rich with continuing investigations into players with false Italian and European Community passports playing in the league and a spate of leading players testing positive for the banned substance Nandrolone (including Edgar Davids at Juventus and Jaap Stam at Lazio). The managerial merry-go-round reached new speeds: Internazionale acquired Argentinian Hector Cuper from Valencia; Faith Terim of Galatasaray arrived in Milan only to depart soon afterwards. Lazio swapped Dino Zoff for Zaccheroni, and Marcello Lippi returned to his old haunt at Juventus. Accusations of match-fixing, favouritism and corruption have maintained their usual fever pitch. Best of all, the struggle for the presidency of the Italian league provided a continuous scrap that remains unresolved.

Chievo storms the league

Juventus and Roma both showed good form early on. When Roma beat Juventus 2-0 in Turin, Capello's team looked like it might have what it takes to retain the *Scudetto*. But the real revelations of the first half of the season were Inter and Chievo. Inter seemed to finally acquire what millions of lire and innumerable managers could not: team play, solidity and consistency. Cuper's Inter was playing a tight defensive game with Toldo impressive in goal. Moreover, the second string strikers Kallon and Adriano were finding the net in the absence of the injured Ronaldo and Vieri. Chievo, a tiny team from a tiny suburb of Verona, had stormed Serie B last year and the team was unphased when it stepped up into the top flight. Disciplined, gritty and tireless, Luigi Del Neri's team drew on unknowns, old players from smaller clubs and a great deal of heart; enough heart to actually take them briefly to the top of the table before Christmas. By contrast, Lazio, Milan and Parma were all struggling and their coaches eventually paid the price.

Roberto Baggio had a great season for Brescia, which had Italian fans calling for his inclusion in the 2002 World Cup squad.

Above: Carlo Ancelotti was an early-season replacement for Milan coach Faith Terim. Ancelotti's Milan always played below expectations, going out in the UEFA Cup semi-final and slipping out of the top six in Serie A, only scraping into the last Champions League spot in the closing weeks of the season.

Above: Luigi Del Neri makes his point to the Chievo team and it must be a good one. In its first season in Serie A, Del Neri's team topped the league, finished fifth and had the pleasure of seeing city rival Hellas Verona relegated.

Serie A League Table 2001–02

CLUB	P	W	D	L	F	A	Pts	
Juventus	34	20	11	3	64	23	71	Champions League
Roma	34	19	13	2	58	24	70	Champions League
Internazionale	34	20	9	5	62	35	69	Champions League
Milan	34	14	13	7	47	33	55	Champions League
Chievo	34	14	12	8	57	52	54	UEFA Cup
Lazio	34	14	11	9	50	37	53	UEFA Cup
Bologna	34	15	7	12	40	40	52	
Perugia	34	13	7	14	38	46	46	
Atalanta	34	12	9	13	41	49	45	
Parma	34	12	8	14	43	47	44	UEFA Cup
Torino	34	10	13	11	37	39	43	
Piacenza	34	11	9	14	49	43	42	
Brescia	34	9	13	12	43	52	40	
Udinese	34	11	7	16	41	52	40	
Verona	34	11	6	17	41	53	39	Relegated
Lecce	34	6	10	18	36	56	28	Relegated
Fiorentina	34	5	7	22	28	63	22	Relegated
Venezia	34	3	9	22	30	61	18	Relegated

Promoted clubs: Como, Empoli, Modena, Reggina.

Italian Cup

2002 FINAL (2 legs)

April 25 – Stadio delle Alpi, Turin
Juventus 2-1 Parma
*(Amoruso 4 pen,   (Nakata 90)
Zalayeta 56)*
h/t: 1-0 **Att:** 35,874
Ref: P-L Collina

May 11 – Stadio Ennio Tardini, Parma
Parma 1-0 Juventus
(Junior 4)
h/t: 1-0 **Att:** 26,864
Ref: G Paparesta

Parma won on away goals

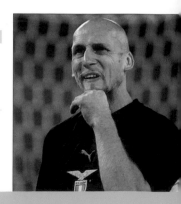

Champions and runners-up:
Juventus's Marc Iuliano clashes
with Roma's Gabriel Batistuta.

Left: Jaap Stam's controversial
early season transfer from
Manchester United to Lazio
was followed by a positive
test for banned drugs and
a long period of enforced
absence from the game.

ITALY

The new year began with Roma at the top of the table closely followed by Inter, Chievo, Juventus and Milan. Down at the bottom, Fiorentina and Venezia were already looking doomed. While Venezia is used to life at the bottom of Serie A, it was another matter for Fiorentina, until recently a regular contender for honours. But, as the business interests of club president Vittorio Cecchi Gori have plummeted, so has the club's finances. During the last couple of years Gori has sold off the club's key assets Batistuta, Rui Costa and goalkeeper Toldo. Worse still, he has already spent the club's season ticket income until 2006 and the TV income to 2004. Not surprisingly, players' wages are being paid late or not at all.

Throughout the spring, Italian clubs performed below expectation in European competition. Roma and Juventus failed to qualify from the second group stage of the Champions League. Milan and Inter negotiated tricky quarter-finals in the UEFA Cup (against Hapoel Tel Aviv and Valencia respectively) only to be beaten in the semi-finals by Borussia Dortmund and Feyenoord. Combined with a mounting realization among the clubs and the press that Italian football finances were looking more overstretched than ever, the *Gazzetta dello Sport* announced a 'Crisis in Calcio'. In addition to already struggling Fiorentina, the paper revealed that other clubs were late paying wages and transfer payments (including Lazio, Venezia and six clubs in Serie B). It also claimed that the league's overall operating loss had climbed to 1,710 million Euros a year and the actual extent of accumulated debt was colossal.

Right to the wire

In the closing weeks of the campaign Inter beat its nearest challenger Roma 3-1 at the San Siro, thanks mainly to a vintage performance from Uruguayan Alvaro Recoba. With Vieri and Ronaldo back in the team, it looked as if Inter's first *Scudetto* for 13 years might be in sight. But with Juventus mounting a last-minute charge, winning five out of five, and Roma holding firm, Inter dropped points in a disastrous home defeat against Atalanta and a draw at struggling Piacenza. With one game to go, Inter was a point ahead of Juventus and two ahead of Roma. The team controlled its own destiny with a final match at Lazio. With Ronaldo and Vieri fit, Inter took the lead twice in the first half only to be pegged back by Karel Poborsky equalizers. In the second half the team went to pieces and Lazio made it 4-2. Juventus made no mistakes, beating Perugia 2-0 and winning its 26th *Scudetto*.

The final action of the season saw Parma take home the Italian Cup. A 2-1 defeat at Juventus in the first leg of the Final was overturned by a 1-0 victory in the second, Parma winning on the away goals rule.

International Club Performances 2001–02

CLUB	COMPETITION	PROGRESS
Juventus	Champions League	2nd Group Phase
Lazio	Champions League	1st Group Phase
Roma	Champions League	2nd Group Phase
Parma	Champions League	3rd Qualifying Round
	UEFA Cup	4th Round
Fiorentina	UEFA Cup	3rd Round
Internazionale	UEFA Cup	Semi-finals
Milan	UEFA Cup	Semi-finals

Top Goalscorers 2001–02

PLAYER	CLUB	NATIONALITY	GOALS
Dario Hubner	Piacenza	Italian	24
David Trezuguet	Juventus	French	24
Christian Vieri	Inter	Italian	22
Marco Di Viao	Parma	Italian	20

Francesco Totti, Roma's playmaker, cuts the Lazio defence to ribbons as Roma score five.

Jubilant fans demand the tie of Marcello Lippi, Juventus' coach.

Above: A dismal league season and persistent financial problems were finally redeemed for Parma by a UEFA Cup spot and victory in the Italian Cup over Juventus.

Left: Ronaldo weeps as Inter implode at Lazio and the Scudetto slips away.

Below: Del Piero began to find his best form again as Juventus relentlessly chased the title in the closing weeks of the season.

Centre left: David Trezuguet, Serie A's top scorer, celebrates a goal in the final day defeat of Udinese.

Association Football in Italy

1887: Palestra Ginnastica Libertas, Italy's oldest club formed (later merged into Fiorentina)

1898: Formation of FA: Federazione Italiana Giuoco Calcio. First national championship

1905: Affiliation to FIFA

1910: First international, v France, won 6–2, venue: Milan

1916–19: League abandoned during war

1922: First Italian Cup Final
1929: Mussolini de-anglicizes name changes for Genoa and Inter who become Genova and Ambrosiana Inter

1930: National championship reorganized into national league; professionalism legalized

1944–45: League abandoned during war

1949: Torino, dominant team of the decade, killed in Mount Superga air crash

1954: Affiliation to UEFA
1964: Foreign players banned

1968: FICF, Federazione Italiana Calcio Femminile founded.

First women's international, v Czechoslovakia, won 2–0, venue: Viareggio

1970: Breakaway Women's FA formed – FFIGC

1972: Reunification of women's association to form the FIGCF, Federazione Italiana Giuoco Calcio Femminile

1980: Ban on foreign players lifted. FIGCF becomes associate member of FIGC (national FA)

1986: FIGCF fully incorporated into FIGC

1997: Clubs required to convert themselves into limited companies

1998: Lazio is first Italian club to float on the stock exchange

Timeline years: 1885, 1890, 1895, 1900, 1905, 1910, 1915, 1920, 1925, 1930, 1935, 1940, 1945, 1950, 1955, 1960, 1965, 1970, 1975, 1980, 1985, 1990, 1995, 2000, 2005

ITALY

Valentino Mazzola leads out Il Grande Torino; four-time consecutive champions (1946–49), backbone of the national team, tragically killed in the Mount Superga air crash.

Key

- International football
- Affiliation to FIFA
- Affiliation to UEFA
- Women's football
- War
- Disaster
- World Cup host
- World Cup winner
- World Cup runner-up
- European Championships host
- European Championships winner
- European Championships runner-up
- Competition winner
- Competition runner-up

Fiore – Fiorentina
Inter – Internazionale
Juve – Juventus
Nap – Napoli
AC – Milan
Samp – Sampdoria

International Competitions

1934: (World Cup winner, World Cup host)
1938: (World Cup winner)

	European Cup	UEFA Cup	European Cup-Winners' Cup
1957:	△ Fiore		
1958:	△ AC		
1961:		○ Roma	○ Fiore
1962:			△ Fiore
1963:	○ AC		
1964:	○ Inter		
1965:	○ Inter	△ Juve	
1967:	△ Inter		
1968:			○ AC
1969:	○ AC		
1970:		△ Juve	
1971:			
1972:	△ Inter		
1973:	△ Juve		○ AC
1974:			△ AC
1977:		○ Juve	
1980:			
1982:			
1983:	△ Juve		○ Juve
1984:	△ Roma		
1985:	○ Juve		
1989:	○ AC	○ Nap	
1990:	○ AC	○ Juve △ Fiore	△ Samp
1991:		○ Inter △ Roma	○ Samp
1992:	△ Samp	△ Torino	
1993:	△ AC	○ Juve	○ Parma
1994:	○ AC	○ Inter	
1995:	△ AC	○ Parma △ Juve	△ Parma
1996:	○ Juve		
1997:	△ Juve	○ Inter	
1998:	△ Juve	○ Inter △ Lazio	
1999:		○ Parma	○ Lazio
2000:			

Milan 1899
Milan Cricket and Football Club (1899–1905). Milan Football Club (1905–38)

Pro Vercelli 1892

Juventus 1897
Originated from the Massimo d'Azeglio Grammar School

Torino 1906
Merger FC Torinese and splinter group from Juventus (in 1901 FC Torinese founded 1887, merged with Internazionale Torino)

Casale 1909

Alessandria 1920
Merger of US Alessandria and Alessandria FC

Genoa 1893*
Genoa Football and Cricket Club (1893–99), Genoa FC (1899–1929) Genova (1893, 1929–45)

Sampierdarenese 1901
Merged with Andrea Doria to become Sampdoria in 1946

Map labels: Com / Cal, Var F, Gallaratese 1909, Novara Calcio 1908, Verce, Casal, Turin, Alessandria, Novese 1908, Geno, Vado 1908, **Parma** 1938 – Began in 191... as Verdi, ther... Parma. Bankr... in 1968 and re-established...

Italy: The main clubs

Cagliari 1920 — Team name with year of formation

- Club formed before 1912
- Club formed 1912–25
- Club formed 1925–50
- Club formed after 1950
- Winners of Amateur Championship (1899–1929)
- Runners-up in Amateur Championship
- English origins
- Swiss origins
- Originated from a cricket club
- Originated from a school or college
- 10 Scudettos†
- 20 Scudettos

* Shirts shown are in teams' original colours

†*Scudetto = Italian Championship*
1 star awarded & worn for 10 Scudettos
2 stars awarded & worn for 20 Scudettos

SARDIN...

Cagli... 1920

Italy

ORIGINS AND GROWTH OF FOOTBALL

UNLIKE MUCH OF CONTINENTAL EUROPE, Italy had its own traditions of folk football – the Florentine *Calcio* and the Roman *Harpastum* – to draw upon when association football first arrived in the late 19th century. British influences combined with domestic interests to produce a flourishing football scene in Northern Italy around Genoa, Turin and Milan. English expatriate cricket clubs started Genoa and AC Milan, while the first organized game of football is said to have been arranged by Edorado Bosio of Turin, a businessman with extensive connections in Britain.

The first leagues

The early organization of Italian football reflected the divided geographical loyalties of the nation and the weakness of national institutions. The national Football Association was set up in 1898; it changed location four times before settling in Rome in the 1920s. It also faced challenges to its authority from the clubs and rival organizations. Regional leagues and championships were early to form, and remained so strong that, despite the creation of a national championship as early as 1898, it was a rather low-key and disorganized affair. With the advent of professionalism the national league finally became the dominant competition in 1930. Football continued to be dominated by teams from the industrial cities of the north, with only Rome and Naples able to sustain teams of sufficient weight to challenge them.

The national game

The popularity of Italian football with the public, politicians and business exceeded that of almost any other nation in the first half of the 20th century. Industrialists, like Pirelli (tyres and AC Milan) and Agnelli (cars and Juventus), were very active participants in the game. Italy won two of its three World Cups in the 1930s. In the postwar era Italian domestic football's sophistication, politicization and wealth continued to develop and expand, delivering from the early 1960s onwards an extraordinary catalogue of European club success.

ITALY

Internazionale 1908
Splinter from Milan. Merged with US Milanese (1928). Renamed Ambrosiana Inter (1929–46)

Chievo 1929
Hellas Verona 1903
Vicenza 1902
Udinese 1896
Tristina 1918
Venezia 1907
Padova 1910
Citadella 1973
Merger of US Citadellese and AS Olympia
Bologna 1909*

Lecce Calcio 1908
ergamo talanta 907
Brescia 1918
onza 2
Brescia Calcio 1911
lan
Mantova 1911
enza
Parma
Legnano 1913
Modena 1912
Ferrara 1907
Ravenna 1913
Reggiana 1914
Lucchese-Libertas 1905
Cesena 1940
Pistoia **Pistoiese** 1921
Pisa 1909
Empoli 1921
Livorno
Siena 1904
Ancona 1905
Ascoli Calcio 1898
Livorno 1915
Perugia 1905
Terni **Ternana** 1925
Pescara 1936

Udine
Treviso 1909
Venice
Verona
Padua
Trieste

SAN MARINO (see inset)

Fiorentina 1926
Merger of Palestra Ginnastica Libertas, Sportive and CS Firenze

Florence

Roma 1927
Merger in 1927 of Fortitudo, Pro Roma, Roma FBC and Alba

Rome

ITALY

Lazio 1900
SP Lazio (1900–25)

Napoli 1926
Merger of Internaples and Naples

Naples

Savoia 1908 1908

Foggia 1920
Avellino 1912
Salerno **Salernitana** 1919
Bari 1928
Merger of FC Bari and US Ideale as US Bari (1928–45)
Lecce 1908

smos 1979
gore Falciano
2
Juvenes 1953
ertas 28
nne 6
Domagnano 1966
Calcio Faetano 1962
SAN MARINO
Tre Fiori 1949
rita 7

ermo 1899
Palermo (1892–1942)
rmo Juvem (1942–45)
Palermo (1945–87)

Cosenza 1914
Crotone 1923
Catanzaro 1929
Reggina Calcio 1914
Messina 1945

SICILY

Catania 1946
Merger of Virtus and US Cantanese

Vittorio Pozzo (1886–1968) was Italy's first great coach. He was active in the management of Torino over two decades and coach of the national side that won the World Cup in 1934 and 1938.

Turin

FOOTBALL CITY

MILAN MAY HAVE GLAMOUR AND STYLE, but when it comes to the hard grit of winning, Turin has no equal – between them the city's two clubs, Torino and Juventus, have won over 30 Scudetti. In 1887, Eduardo Bosio went back to Turin after a trip to England and took a football with him. Soon after, clubs began to form: Internazionale Torino and FC Torinese were up and running and competing in the fledgling national championships. They fused in 1906 as Torino. Juventus was founded by students in 1897, and took its first title in 1905. The teams settled in the south of the city, their stadiums separated by a single road. The amateur era was quiet for both sides, but with the coming of professionalism Turin's economic and demographic weight really began to count. Juventus has been tied to the Agnelli family and Fiat for over 50 years; its support is strong among southern Italian immigrants to the city and also has a national and international dimension. Torino, by contrast, has claimed deeper and wider roots in the city itself and in its people, not least among Fiat's workforce.

Success and tragedy

Juve, *la Vecchia Signora* (the 'Old Lady') as the club is known, has an extraordinary record. In every decade since the 1920s it has won the domestic championship; it has won every European competition going; and along with the glory, the club has earned the distaste and envy of every other team in the country. Torino, by contrast, has had only one truly great era, that of Il Grand Torino when the team won four successive *Scudetti* from 1946 to 1949. Under coach Vittorio Pozzo, Il Grand Torino was led by the charismatic striker Valentino Mazzola. In May 1949, following a friendly match, the entire squad was killed in the Superga air crash (see box). This tragedy saw the heart torn from Torino and two decades of mid-table football followed. Only in 1976 was the club able to lay a few ghosts to rest when it won the championship once more under the triumphant Gigi Radice. Since then, despite several new investors and endless waves of optimism, a cycle of relegation and promotion has been Torino's fate. Both clubs moved to the Stadio delle Alpi on the northern outskirts of town after the 1990 World Cup. Unloved and strangely sterile, the delle Alpi is barely ever half full, even for big games.

The scene after the aircrash on the mountain of Superga, on the outskirts of Turin, which killed all 31 passengers when a plane came down in mist and torrential rain on 4 May 1949.

THE SUPERGA AIRCRASH

On 4 May 1949, a Fiat G212 airliner left Lisbon with the Torino squad on board. They had been playing a friendly match against Benfica in honour of the great Portuguese player Franciso Ferriera. The plane carried 31 passengers, including 18 Torino squad members, two club directors, four other club staff and three journalists. In mist and torrential rain, the plane, heading for the Aeritalia airfield, was seen emerging from a bank of cloud and crashing into an embankment below the Superga Basilica, a church and monastic complex set on the hills rising to the east of the city. There were no survivors. Two days later, funerals were held at the Palazzo Madama. Half a million people lined the streets of the city centre to pay their last respects, led by the youth teams of Torino and Juventus in full kit.

Cars being tested on the roof of the Fiat factory in Turin in 1929. Despite its sponsorship of Juventus, the company's workforce is split in its support of the city's two big clubs.

STADIO DELLE ALPI

69,041

Clubs: Juventus, Torino
Built: 1990
Original Capacity: 71,000
Record Attendance: 71,010 Juventus v Internazionale, 28 Apr 1998
Significant Matches: 1990 World Cup: five matches including semi-final

STADIO COMMUNALE

Club: Currently Juventus' training ground. Torino is likely to play here in 2003
Built: 1933
Original Capacity: 25,000

ITALY

JUVENTUS 1897

League 1898–1929	*1903, 04, 05, 06,* **26**
League 1930–2002	**1931–35**, *38,* **46**, *47,* **50**, *52,* **53, 54**, *58,* **60, 61**, *63,* **67**, *72,* **73, 74, 75**, *76,* **77, 78**, *80,* **81, 82**, *83,* **84, 86**, *87,* **92**, *94,* **95**, *96,* **97, 98**, *2000, 01,* **02**
Cup	**1938**, *42,* **59, 60, 65**, *73,* **79, 83, 90**, *92,* **95**, *2002*
European Cup	*1973,* **83**, *85,* **96**, *97,* **98**
European Cup-Winners' Cup	**1984**
UEFA Cup	**1977**, *90,* **93**, *95*
Fairs Cup	*1965, 71*
World Club Cup	*1973,* **85**, *96*

TORINO 1906

League 1898–1929	*1907,* **27, 28**, *29*
League 1930–2002	*1939, 42,* **43**, *46–49,* **76, 77**, *85*
Cup	**1936**, *38,* **43**, *63,* **64**, *68,* **70**, *71,* **80–82, 88**, *93*
UEFA Cup	*1992*

Torrente Stura

Juventus   **Torino**

(1990–)   (1990–)
STADIO DELLE ALPI

69,041

Juventus has agreed to buy the stadium from Turin City Council in order to redevelop it. On completion Torino will move to Stadio Communale

Dora Riparia

A4

T U R I N

SS590

SS25

COLLEGNO

CORSO MARSIGLIA

BIRRERIA VOIGT
3 December 1906 Torino founded here

SS10

SUPERGA BASILICA
4 May 1949 A plane carrying the great Torino squad of the era crashed into the Superga Basilica in the mountains east of Turin. 31 passengers were killed

Juventus
(1923–33)

GRUGLIASCO

1 November 1897 Juventus founded by a group of D'Azeglio students kicking around on Corso Re Umberto

JUVENTUS OFFICES

PALAZZA MADAMA
6 May 1949 Site of the Superga funerals

Fiume Po

PIAZZA D'ARMI

Juventus (1900–23)

CORSO RE UMBERTO

TORINO OFFICES

Internazionale Torino

FC Torinese

LICEO MASSIMO D'AZEGLIO

Juventus (1933–90)
Torino (1960–90)

STADIO COMMUNALE

Torrente Sangone

FIAT CAR FACTORY

FILADELPHIA
Torino (1926–60)

MIRAFIORI
Mirafiori housing estate is home to the core of the Fiat workforce and is a hotbed of Torino support

SS23

A21

SS20

SS29

THE LOCAL DERBY
'Il derby della Mole'

JUVENTUS	TORINO

98 matches played

43 Juventus wins
28 Torino wins
27 draws

0	25	50	75	100	125

NUMBER OF MATCHES
(Serie A games up to July 2002)

Turin

69,000	Capacity of stadium
	Stadium no longer in use for top-flight football
	Team colours
	Team no longer in existence
A21	Motorway
SS20	Major road
1900	Champions
2000	Runners-up

Milan

FOOTBALL CITY

THE MILAN FOOTBALL AND CRICKET CLUB was founded in 1899 by a mixture of English and Swiss expatriate businessmen led by the Englishman Alfred Edwards. Milan FC achieved early success, winning three national championships before 1907. In 1908, disaffected members of the club, resenting its Anglo dominance, split to form a new club called Internazionale. Rivalry between the two clubs has consumed the city ever since, although the social meaning of the conflict has changed. At first Inter attracted the elite and middle class, and Milan the working class, though over time this relationship seems to have shifted.

Class divide

Milan moved to the San Siro in 1926, financed by the millions of tyre magnate Piero Pirelli. Internazionale played in the Arena in the centre of town. With the arrival of Fascism, Inter's cosmopolitan leanings looked suspect, and the club was forced to merge with US Milanese and change its name to Ambrosiana-Inter. Despite its name, the team proved brilliant, with a forward line led by the great Giuseppe Meazza. In 1946, it joined its city rival at the San Siro. Milan's English connections made the team even more suspicious to the Fascist authorities and it was only after the Second World War that the club really flourished: four *Scudetti* in the 1950s, followed by two in the 1960s as well as two great European Cup victories. Inter took the European Cup twice (1964 and 65) under the charismatic Helenio Herrera who brought the playing style of *catenaccio* (see page 471) and strict squad discipline to the city, and helped encourage the first organized fan clubs, or *tifosi*, who would travel to Inter's away games in Europe.

In the 1980s and 1990s it was Milan that prospered. Money flooded into the club from the Berlusconi fortune and, under Arrigo Sacchi and Fabio Capello, Milan became the dominant force in European football. Inter has countered with the oil-based fortunes of Massimo Moratti (whose father had owned the club in the 1950s). Inter's spending in the transfer market has been phenomenal (including the purchase of Christian Vieri and Ronaldo for almost £50 million), but so far only one UEFA Cup trophy sits in the cabinet under the Moratti regime.

ITALY

MILAN 1899	
League 1898–1929	**1901**, *02*, **06, 07**
League 1930–2002	*1948, 50,* **51, 52, 55, 56, 57, 59, 61, 62,** *65,* **68,** *71–73,* **79, 88,** *90,* **91,** *92–94,* **96,** *99*
Cup	*1942,* **67,** *68,* **71,** *72,* **73,** *75,* **77,** *85,* **90,** *98*
European Cup	*1958,* **63,** *69,* **89, 90,** *93,* **94,** *95*
European Cup-Winners' Cup	**1968,** *73, 74*
World Club Cup	*1963,* **69,** *89,* **90,** *93,* **94**

STADIO GIUSEPPE MEAZZA (SAN SIRO)

85,700

Clubs:	Internazionale, Milan
Built:	1926
Original Capacity:	35,000
Rebuilt:	1955, 1990
Significant Matches:	1934 World Cup: three matches; 1990 World Cup: five matches; European Cup Finals: 1965, 70, 2001

INTERNAZIONALE 1908	
League 1898–1929	**1910, 20**
League 1930–2002	**1930,** *33–35,* **38, 40, 41, 49, 51, 53, 54,** *62,* **63,** *64,* **65, 66,** *67,* **70, 71, 80, 89,** *93,* **98**
Cup	**1939,** *59,* **65,** *77,* **78, 82,** *2000*
European Cup	**1964, 65,** *67, 72*
UEFA Cup	**1991, 94,** *97,* **98**
World Club Cup	**1964, 65**

The Piazza del Duomo in the centre of the city is the traditional location of victory celebrations for fans of both Milan and Internazionale.

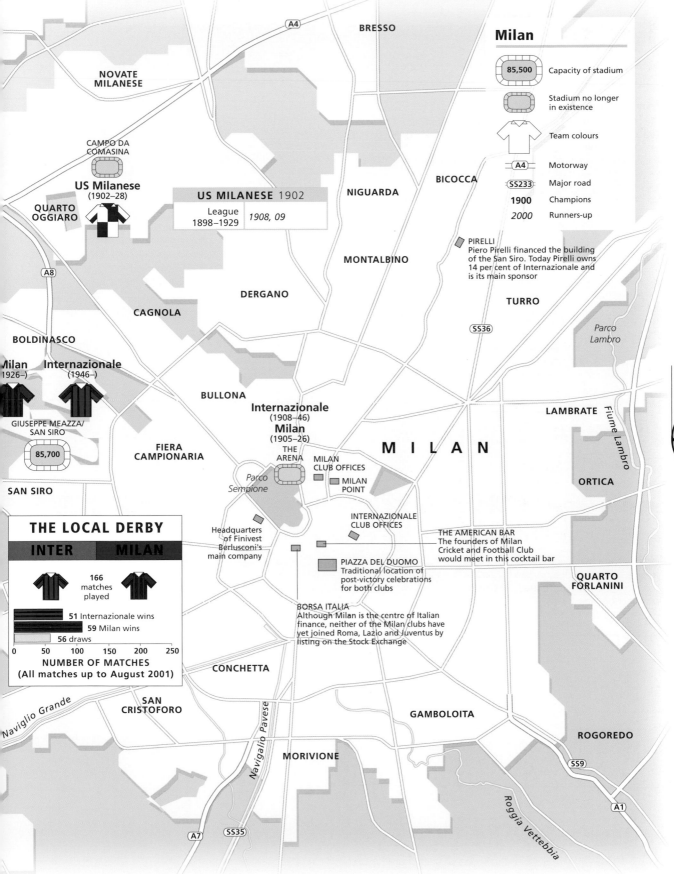

Milan

85,500	Capacity of stadium
	Stadium no longer in existence
	Team colours
A4	Motorway
SS233	Major road
1900	Champions
2000	Runners-up

BRESSO

A4

NOVATE MILANESE

CAMPO DA COMASINA

US Milanese
(1902–28)

QUARTO OGGIARO

A8

US MILANESE 1902

League 1898–1929	*1908, 09*

NIGUARDA

BICOCCA

MONTALBINO

PIRELLI
Piero Pirelli financed the building of the San Siro. Today Pirelli owns 14 per cent of Internazionale and is its main sponsor

DERGANO

TURRO

CAGNOLA

SS36

BOLDINASCO

Parco Lambro

Milan
1926–)

Internazionale
(1946–)

BULLONA

Internazionale
(1908–46)
Milan
(1905–26)

M I L A N

LAMBRATE

Fiume Lambro

GIUSEPPE MEAZZA/ SAN SIRO

85,700

FIERA CAMPIONARIA

THE ARENA

Parco Sempione

MILAN CLUB OFFICES

MILAN POINT

ORTICA

SAN SIRO

INTERNAZIONALE CLUB OFFICES

THE AMERICAN BAR
The founders of Milan Cricket and Football Club would meet in this cocktail bar

Headquarters of Finivest Berlusconi's main company

PIAZZA DEL DUOMO
Traditional location of post-victory celebrations for both clubs

QUARTO FORLANINI

BORSA ITALIA
Although Milan is the centre of Italian finance, neither of the Milan clubs have yet joined Roma, Lazio and Juventus by listing on the Stock Exchange

CONCHETTA

Naviglio Grande

SAN CRISTOFORO

Naviglio Pavese

GAMBOLOITA

ROGOREDO

MORIVIONE

Roggia Vettebbia

SS9

A7   SS35

A1

ITALY

THE LOCAL DERBY

INTER	MILAN

166 matches played

51 Internazionale wins

59 Milan wins

56 draws

0   50   100   150   200   250

NUMBER OF MATCHES
(All matches up to August 2001)

Rome

FOOTBALL CITY

LAZIO WAS FOUNDED IN 1900 by an Italian army officer, Luigi Bigarelli, and adopted Greek colours and secluded itself in the wealthy northern suburbs of the city. The team soon acquired the well-appointed Rondinella stadium to play in and Benito Mussolini as a fan. But Il Duce's plans for the capital of the new Roman Empire extended to its football stadium, and he moved Lazio to his monumental and bombastic Fascist Party stadium (the PNF) in the 1930s, and strutted around the city when Italy hosted and won the 1938 World Cup.

Lazio acquired a proper rival with the creation of Roma in 1927 from the fusion of four small clubs (Alba, Fortitudo, ProRoma and Roma FBC). Roma settled in the working-class streets of Testaccio, which still remains its spiritual heartland. Roma too was shipped out to the PNF until after the war, and both clubs moved again to the new Olympic stadium built across the Tiber in the north-east of the city in the early 1950s.

Investment pays off

Although prosperity and geographical mobility have fractured the old core areas of club support, Roma's fans are more working-class, left-wing and urban in origin, while Lazio has drawn on more middle-class support in the city along with fans from across the Lazio region. Recently it has attracted more vociferous, right-wing *ultras* from the city's southern housing projects. These new fans first made their presence felt when Lazio won its first *Scudetto* in 1974, with a rough, tough squad schooled in the Estudiantes sides of the 1960s and inspired by Argentinian coach Juan Carlos Lorenzo.

Since the late 1990s, Rome has at last become the country's footballing capital. Under the presidencies of Sensi and Cragnotti, Roma and Lazio became the first Italian clubs to float on the stock exchange, and both have spent hugely to create the city's most cosmopolitan and powerful squads. Lazio's double in 1999, and Roma's first *Scudetto* for almost 20 years in 2001, have been the pay-off. But how long the giants from the north can be held off remains to be seen.

This aerial shot of Rome was taken just before the 1960 Olympic Games and shows the Olimpico (centre left) and other smaller arenas which were also used for the Games.

ITALY

OLIMPICO

Club:	Lazio, Roma, Italy
Built:	1952
Original Capacity:	80,000
Rebuilt:	1989–90
Significant Matches:	1990 World Cup: six matches including Final; 1968 European Championships: Final and replay; 1980 European Championships: Final; European Cup Finals: 1977, 84, 96

82,566

LAZIO 1900

League 1898–1929	*1913, 14, 23*
League 1930–2002	*1937,* **74, 95,** *99,* **2000**
Cup	**1958,** *61,* **98, 2000**
European Cup- Winners' Cup	**1999**
UEFA Cup	*1998*

ROMA 1927

League 1930–2002	*1931, 36,* **42,** *81,* **83,** *84,* **86, 2001,** *02*
Cup	*1937, 41,* **64, 69, 80,** *81,* **84, 86, 91,** *93*
European Cup	*1984*
UEFA Cup	*1991*
Fairs Cup	**1961**

FLAMINIO

Club:	Lodigiani (major games; others are played at Tre Fontane in the southern suburbs). Roma and Lazio played here in 1989 during rebuilding of Olimpico
Built:	1953
Original Capacity:	55,000
Significant Matches:	1934 World Cup: Final (as PNF); 1960 Rome Olympics

24,500

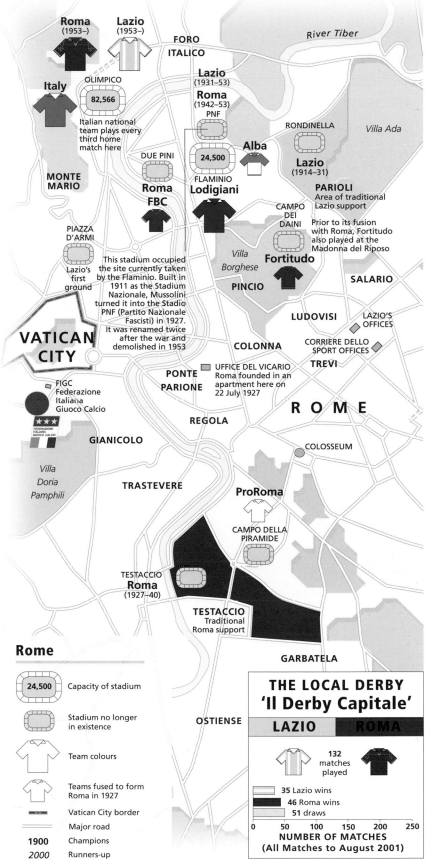

Roma (1953–)
Lazio (1953–)

FORO ITALICO

River Tiber

Italy

OLIMPICO
82,566
Italian national team plays every third home match here

Lazio (1931–53)
Roma (1942–53)
PNF
24,500
FLAMINIO

DUE PINI

Roma FBC

MONTE MARIO

PIAZZA D'ARMI
Lazio's first ground

Alba

Lodigiani

RONDINELLA

Villa Ada

Lazio (1914–31)

PARIOLI
Area of traditional Lazio support

CAMPO DEI DAINI
Prior to its fusion with Roma, Fortitudo also played at the Madonna del Riposo

Fortitudo

SALARIO

Villa Borghese

PINCIO

LUDOVISI

LAZIO'S OFFICES

This stadium occupied the site currently taken by the Flaminio. Built in 1911 as the Stadium Nazionale, Mussolini turned it into the Stadio PNF (Partito Nazionale Fascisti) in 1927. It was renamed twice after the war and demolished in 1953

VATICAN CITY

FIGC
Federazione Italiana Giuoco Calcio
FEDERAZIONE ITALIANA GIUOCO CALCIO ★★★

GIANICOLO

Villa Doria Pamphili

PONTE PARIONE

REGOLA

COLONNA

UFFICE DEL VICARIO
Roma founded in an apartment here on 22 July 1927

TREVI

CORRIERE DELLO SPORT OFFICES

R O M E

ITALY

COLOSSEUM

TRASTEVERE

ProRoma

CAMPO DELLA PIRAMIDE

TESTACCIO
Roma (1927–40)

TESTACCIO
Traditional Roma support

GARBATELA

OSTIENSE

Rome

24,500	Capacity of stadium
	Stadium no longer in existence
	Team colours
	Teams fused to form Roma in 1927
	Vatican City border
	Major road
1900	Champions
2000	Runners-up

THE LOCAL DERBY 'Il Derby Capitale'

LAZIO	ROMA

132 matches played

35 Lazio wins
46 Roma wins
51 draws

0   50   100   150   200   250
NUMBER OF MATCHES
(All Matches to August 2001)

Italy

FANS AND OWNERS

UNTIL RECENTLY, nearly every club in Italy was privately owned by a single dominant figure on the board and linked to a large company with which it had made its fortune. This is still the case at the Milan giants, Internazionale and Milan, and the clubs of the smaller northern cities. But in the last few years the enormous demand for capital that success in Italian football requires has led Roma, Lazio and Juventus to the stock market for partial flotation, although in each case, a majority shareholder remains in charge. Equally enormous wage bills have swallowed the astronomical income of Italian clubs. Attendances have stagnated or fallen, TV income is jeopardized by the pirating of satellite channels on a massive scale, and European performances have dipped. Not surprisingly, the debt of many clubs has risen substantially. The crisis in Italian football is biting hardest at the clubs that have failed to deliver on ambitious expenditures: Napoli, Sampdoria and Genoa have all changed hands as owners' finances and patience have run out, while Fiorentina has spent most of the 2002 season in bankruptcy courts, and has courted the Dutch construction firm, van den Herik, as investors.

Italy's lay religion

The huge, working-class crowds that gathered on a Sunday afternoon for Italian football always had an element of ritual and religion to them. In the 1970s, young Italian fans organized themselves into groups called *ultras* which specialized in the construction of vast banners, choreographed displays of colours, drumming, singing and chanting. The fierce localism of these groups means that no similar following for the national team exists. By 1983, symbolic contest turned to organized violence and the earlier left-wing bent of some *ultra* groups was replaced by the presence of the far right. In the 1990s, a new generation of *ultras* have emerged, older groups have fragmented, and increased policing has subdued the scene, though the 2000–01 season saw a renewed spate of violence outside grounds and attacks by fans on poorly performing players and coaches.

ITALY

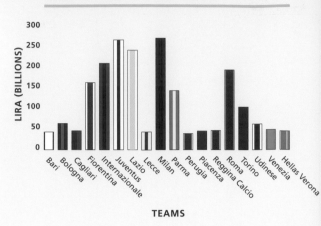

Club Turnover 1999–2000

(Bar chart. Y-axis: LIRA (BILLIONS), 0 to 300. X-axis: TEAMS — Bari, Bologna, Cagliari, Fiorentina, Internazionale, Juventus, Lazio, Lecce, Milan, Parma, Perugia, Piacenza, Reggina Calcio, Roma, Torino, Udinese, Venezia, Hellas Verona)

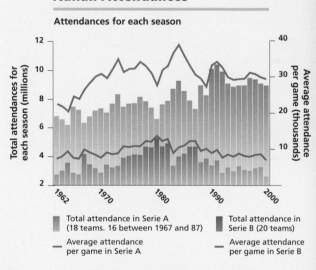

Italian Attendances

Attendances for each season

(Chart. Left Y-axis: Total attendances for each season (millions), 2 to 12. Right Y-axis: Average attendance per game (thousands), up to 40. X-axis: 1962, 1970, 1980, 1990, 2000)

- ▮ Total attendance in Serie A (18 teams. 16 between 1967 and 87)
- ▮ Total attendance in Serie B (20 teams)
- — Average attendance per game in Serie A
- — Average attendance per game in Serie B

Lazio fans claim to be the boss. Since the early 1980s, Lazio ultras – the Irriducibili *in particular – have acquired a notorious right-wing reputation.*

Average Attendance

Average attendance for season 2000–01 (thousands)

(scale: 60, 50, 40, 30, 20, 10, 0)

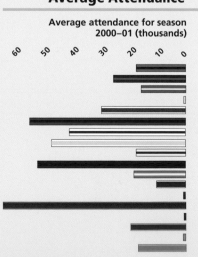

Capacity

Attendance as a percentage of capacity for season 2000–01 (capacity in brackets)

(scale: 30%, 40%, 50%, 60%, 70%, 80%)

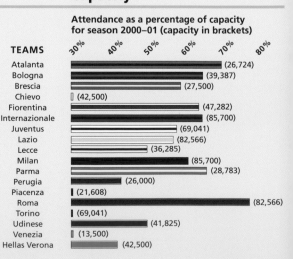

TEAMS	Capacity
Atalanta	(26,724)
Bologna	(39,387)
Brescia	(27,500)
Chievo	(42,500)
Fiorentina	(47,282)
Internazionale	(85,700)
Juventus	(69,041)
Lazio	(82,566)
Lecce	(36,285)
Milan	(85,700)
Parma	(28,783)
Perugia	(26,000)
Piacenza	(21,608)
Roma	(82,566)
Torino	(69,041)
Udinese	(41,825)
Venezia	(13,500)
Hellas Verona	(42,500)

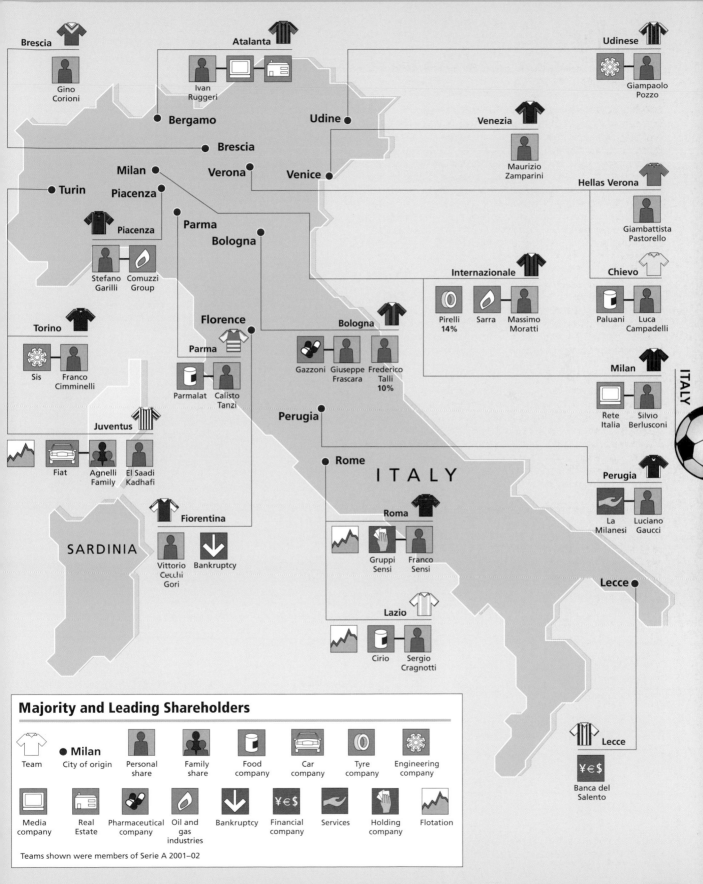

Brescia
Gino Corioni

Atalanta
Ivan Ruggeri

Udinese
Giampaolo Pozzo

Bergamo

Udine

Venezia
Maurizio Zamparini

Milan
Turin
Piacenza

Verona

Venice

Hellas Verona
Giambattista Pastorello

Piacenza
Stefano Garilli — Comuzzi Group

Parma
Bologna

Chievo
Paluani — Luca Campadelli

Florence

Internazionale
Pirelli 14% — Sarra — Massimo Moratti

Torino
Sis — Franco Cimminelli

Parma
Parmalat — Calisto Tanzi

Bologna
Gazzoni — Giuseppe Frascara — Frederico Talli 10%

Milan
Rete Italia — Silvio Berlusconi

Juventus
Fiat — Agnelli Family — El Saadi Kadhafi

Perugia

Perugia
La Milanesi — Luciano Gaucci

SARDINIA

Fiorentina
Vittorio Cecchi Gori — Bankruptcy

Rome

Roma
Gruppi Sensi — Franco Sensi

ITALY

ITALY

Lecce

Lazio
Cirio — Sergio Cragnotti

Lecce
Banca del Salento

Majority and Leading Shareholders

Team

● Milan
City of origin

Personal share

Family share

Food company

Car company

Tyre company

Engineering company

Media company

Real Estate

Pharmaceutical company

Oil and gas industries

Bankruptcy

Financial company

Services

Holding company

Flotation

Teams shown were members of Serie A 2001–02

Italy

PLAYERS AND MANAGERS

ITALIAN PLAYERS AND MANAGERS HAVE perhaps the most intensely pressurized and scrutinized footballing careers in the world. Italy's extraordinarily voracious and dedicated sporting press leaves no stone unturned in analyzing performance, rumour, gossip and behaviour. Of course, there are salaries and adulation to match, tied to an obsessive culture of training, discipline and, in many cases, the prescription of pre-match sex. In the 1990s, foreigners have come in increasing numbers into the Italian game, with many of the very best Germans, Dutch, Yugoslavs, Argentinians and Brazilians finding their way to Serie A. Similarly, foreign coaches have begun to find their way at the top of the Italian game. As a consequence, the capacity of Italian teams to absorb and deal with pressure and grind out results has been formidable.

The art of defence

What marks out Italian football culture from many others is that it is perhaps the only nation where defenders are not only regarded with a respect usually reserved for strikers, but that defending is considered an art form full of technical virtuosity and perfect timing that has no superior. Gianni Facchetti redefined the role of the modern sweeper and full-back at Internazionale in the 1960s, where man-marking left him free to build and join attacks and score freely. His modern descendents include Claudio Gentile, Gaetano Scirea, Franco Baresi, Giuseppe Bergomi, Paolo Maldini, and more recently Alessandro Nesta. Scirea in particular was noted for the grace rather than the viciousness of his tackling. That said, Italian strikers have proved their enduring worth in the guise of Giuseppe Meazza, Gianni Rivera, Paolo Rossi and Roberto Baggio. Nicknamed '*il condino divino*', or the divine ponytail, Baggio was the leading forward of his era, noted not only for his hair but also for his quiet Buddhism and ferocious goalscoring. Riots broke out in the streets of Florence when his transfer to Juventus was announced in 1990.

Marco Tardelli turns in triumph after scoring for Italy in the 1982 World Cup Final against West Germany. Tardelli is one of only a select few players to have won every major domestic European honour, as well as a World Cup winner's medal.

Top 20 International Caps

PLAYER	CAPS	GOALS	FIRST MATCH	LAST MATCH
Paolo Maldini*	120	7	1988	2002
Dino Zoff	112	0	1968	1983
Giacinto Facchetti	94	3	1963	1977
Franco Baresi	81	1	1982	1994
Giuseppe Bergomi	81	6	1982	1998
Marco Tardelli	81	6	1976	1985
Demitrio Albertini*	78	2	1991	2002
Gaetano Scirea	78	2	1975	1986
Giancarlo Antognoni	73	7	1974	1983
Antonio Cabrini	73	9	1978	1987
Claudio Gentile	71	1	1975	1984
Alessandro Mazzola	70	22	1963	1974
Tarcisio Burgnich	66	2	1963	1974
Francesco Graziani	64	23	1975	1983
Franco Causio	63	6	1972	1983
Roberto Donadoni	63	5	1986	1996
Alessandro Altobelli	61	25	1980	1988
Dino Baggio*	60	7	1991	1999
Gianni Rivera	60	14	1962	1974
Umberto Caligaris	59	0	1922	1934
Gianluca Vialli	59	16	1985	1992

Top 15 International Goalscorers

PLAYER	GOALS	CAPS	FIRST MATCH	LAST MATCH
Luigi Riva	35	42	1965	1974
Giuseppe Meazza	33	53	1930	1939
Silvio Piola	30	34	1935	1952
Roberto Baggio*	27	55	1988	1999
Adolfo Baloncieri	25	47	1920	1930
Alessandro Altobelli	25	61	1980	1988
Francesco Grazziani	23	64	1975	1983
Alessandro Mazzola	22	70	1963	1974
Paolo Rossi	20	48	1977	1986
Roberto Bettega	19	42	1975	1983
Fillipo Inzaghi*	16	36	1997	2002
Alessandro Del Piero*	16	46	1995	2002
Gianlucca Vialli	16	59	1985	1992
Julio Libonatti	15	17	1926	1931
Gino Colaussi	15	26	1935	1940

* Indicates players still playing at least at club level.

Italian International Managers

DATES	NAME	GAMES	WON	DRAWN	LOST
1960	Gipo Viani	3	1	1	1
1960–62	Giovanni Ferrari	16	7	5	4
1962–66	Edmondo Fabbri	29	18	6	5
1966–67	Helenio Herrera	4	3	1	0
1967–74	Ferruccio Valcareggi	58	31	21	6
1974–77	Fulvio Bemardini	22	12	4	6
1977–86	Enzo Bearzot	104	51	28	25
1986–92	Azeglio Vicini	54	32	15	7
1992–96	Arrigo Sacchi	53	34	11	8
1996–98	Cesare Maldini	20	10	8	2
1998–2000	Dino Zoff	23	11	7	5
2000–	Giovanni Trapattoni	13	9	3	1

All figures correct as of 14 February 2002.

Player of the Year

YEAR	PLAYER	CLUB
1976	Sala	Torino
1977	Sala	Torino
1978	Filippi	Vicenza
1979	Filippi	Napoli
1980	Castellini	Napoli
1981	Krol	Napoli
1982	Causio	Udinese
1983	Vierchowod	Roma
1984	Platini	Juventus
1985	Maradona	Napoli
1986	Renato	Torino
1987	Zenga	Internazionale
1988	Mancini	Sampdoria
1989	Brehme	Internazionale
1990	Baresi	Milan
1991	Mancini	Sampdoria
1992	Rijkaard	Milan
1993	Signori	Lazio
1994	Massaro	Milan
1995	Sousa	Juventus
1996	Chiesa	Sampdoria
1997	Pagliuca	Internazionale
1997	Peruzzi	Juventus
1997	Thuram	Parma
1998	Totti	Roma
1999	Almeyda	Lazio
2000	Frey	Verona
2001	R. Baggio	Brescia

Awarded by *Guiedo Sportivo* magazine.

Championship Winning Managers

YEAR	MANAGER	CLUB
1976	Radice	Torino
1977	Trappatoni	Juventus
1978	Trappatoni	Juventus
1979	Liedholm [Swe]	Milan
1980	Bersellini	Internazionale
1981	Trappatoni	Juventus
1982	Trappatoni	Juventus
1983	Liedholm [Swe]	Roma
1984	Trappatoni	Juventus
1985	Bagnoli	Verona
1986	Trappatoni	Juventus
1987	Bianchi	Napoli
1988	Sacchi	Milan
1989	Trappatoni	Internazionale
1990	Bigon	Napoli
1991	Boskov [Yugo]	Sampdoria
1992	Capello	Milan
1993	Capello	Milan
1994	Capello	Milan
1995	Lippi	Juventus
1996	Capello	Milan

Winning Managers (*continued*)

YEAR	MANAGER	CLUB
1997	Lippi	Juventus
1998	Lippi	Juventus
1999	Zaccheroni	Milan
2000	Ericksson [Swe]	Lazio
2001	Capello	Roma

Top Goalscorers 1929–2002

SEASON	PLAYER	CLUB	GOALS
1929–30	Meazza	Internazionale	31
1930–31	Volk	Roma	29
1931–32	Petrone	Fiorentina	25
1931–32	Schiavio	Bologna	25
1932–33	Borel II	Juventus	29
1933–34	Borel II	Juventus	32
1934–35	Guaita	Roma	28
1935–36	Meazza	Internazionale	25
1936–37	Piola	Lazio	21
1937–38	Meazza	Internazionale	20
1938–39	Boffi	Milan	19
1938–39	Puricelli	Bologna	19
1939–40	Boffi	Milan	24
1940–41	Puricelli	Bologna	22
1941–42	Boffi	Milan	22
1942–43	Piola	Lazio	21
1943–45	*no competition*		
1945–46	Castiglione	Torino	13
1946–47	V. Mazzola	Torino	29
1947–48	Boniperti	Juventus	27
1948–49	Nyers	Internazionale	26
1949–50	Nordahl	Milan	35
1950–51	Nordahl	Milan	34
1951–52	J. Hansen	Juventus	30
1952–53	Nordahl	Milan	26
1953–54	Nordahl	Milan	23
1954–55	Nordahl	Milan	27
1955–56	Pivatelli	Bologna	29
1956–57	Da Costa	Roma	22
1957–58	Charles	Juventus	28
1958–59	Angelillo	Internazionale	33
1959–60	Sivori	Juventus	27
1960–61	Brighenti	Sampdoria	27
1961–62	Altafini	Milan	22
1961–62	Milani	Fiorentina	22
1962–63	Manfredini	Roma	19
1962–63	Nielsen	Bologna	19
1963–64	Nielsen	Bologna	21
1964–65	A. Mazzola	Internazionale	17
1964–65	Orlando	Fiorentina	17
1965–66	Vinicio	Vicenza	25
1966–67	Riva	Cagliari	18
1967–68	Prati	Milan	15
1968–69	Riva	Cagliari	20

Top Goalscorers (*continued*)

SEASON	PLAYER	CLUB	GOALS
1969–70	Riva	Cagliari	21
1970–71	Boninsegna	Inter	24
1971–72	Boninsegna	Internazionale	22
1972–73	P. Pulici	Torino	17
1972–73	Rivera	Milan	17
1972–73	I. Savoldi	Bologna	17
1973–74	Chignaglia	Lazio	24
1974–75	P. Pulici	Torino	18
1975–76	P. Pulici	Torino	21
1976–77	Graziani	Torino	21
1977–78	P. Rossi	Vicenza	24
1978–79	Giordano	Lazio	19
1979–80	Bettega	Juventus	16
1980–81	Pruzzo	Roma	18
1981–82	Pruzzo	Roma	15
1982–83	Platini	Juventus	16
1983–84	Platini	Juventus	20
1984–85	Platini	Juventus	18
1985–86	Pruzzo	Roma	19
1986–87	Virdis	Milan	17
1987–88	Maradona	Napoli	15
1988–89	Serena	Internazionale	22
1989–90	van Basten	Milan	19
1990–91	Vialli	Sampdoria	17
1991–92	van Basten	Milan	25
1992–93	Signori	Lazio	26
1993–94	Signori	Lazio	23
1994–95	Batistuta	Fiorentina	26
1995–96	Signori	Lazio	24
1995–96	Protti	Bari	24
1996–97	Inzaghi	Atalanta	24
1997–98	Bierhoff	Udinese	27
1998–99	Amoroso	Udinese	22
1999–2000	Schevchenko	Milan	24
2000–01	Crespo	Lazio	26
2001–02	Hubner	Piacenza	24
2001–02	Trezuguet	Juventus	24

Five championships in Italy, and one in Spain with Real Madrid in 1997, have made Fabio Capello one of Europe's most sought-after managers.

ITALY

Foreign Players in Italy (in top division squads)

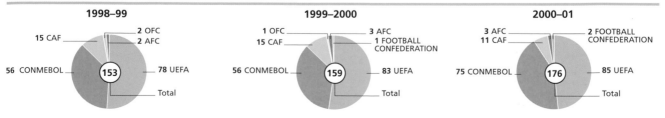

1998–99
15 CAF
2 OFC
2 AFC
56 CONMEBOL
78 UEFA
153
Total

1999–2000
1 OFC
3 AFC
15 CAF
1 FOOTBALL CONFEDERATION
56 CONMEBOL
83 UEFA
159
Total

2000–01
3 AFC
2 FOOTBALL CONFEDERATION
11 CAF
75 CONMEBOL
85 UEFA
176
Total

Italy

SERIE A 1981–2001

THE 1980s BEGAN IN Serie A as the 1970s had ended: with Juventus, under Giovanni Trapattoni, fielding the core of the Italian national squads for the 1978 and 1982 World Cups, playing with an iron defence and spring-loaded counterattacks, and winning the *Scudetto*. As foreigners were allowed back into the Italian game, Juventus scooped up Liam Brady and the sublime Michel Platini, winning the *Scudetto* again in 1984 and 86. But between these triumphs the title went to smaller, battling sides. Roma won in 1983 under Swede Nils Liedholm and the inspirational Brazilian Falcão. Hellas Verona, under Osvaldo Bagnoli, was promoted from Serie B in 1982 with a core of good Italian players. The team added foreigners Elkjaer and Briegel, pushed hard and took its first and only *Scudetto* in 1985. A burst of money and stars followed, only to see the club disappear from Serie A for most of the 1990s.

Off the field, the legal and economic framework of Italian football was beginning to change, and 1981 saw the introduction of contract freedom for players and the first bidding war for TV rights between the state-owned RAI and Silvio Berlusconi's private channels. RAI won the first round but the steady ratcheting up of the value of TV rights had begun: simultaneously, transfer and wages costs began their inexorable rise.

When Trapattoni and Platini left Juventus in 1986, a power vacuum opened in Serie A and the next five years saw four clubs take the title. First off the mark was Napoli. Under president Ferlaino Corrado, Napoli signed Diego Maradona from Barcelona for a record-breaking fee of £5 million. When the club couldn't find the cash to pay, an appeal for donations saw fans queuing up at the San Paolo stadium to contribute. Coming off his extraordinary performance at the 1986 World Cup, Maradona and coach Ottavio Bianchi took Napoli to its first *Scudetto* (the most southerly in the league's history) and a second three years later in 1990, although accusations of playacting in a crucial game at Atalanta have tarnished the triumph. Maradona's departure saw the side in steady decline until its relegation in 1998.

Berlusconi arrives

Milan had been a shadow of the team's former self, relegated in 1981 after accusations of match-fixing against its president Felice Colombo; the club bounced back only to be relegated again in 1983. In 1986, TV and property magnate Silvio Berlusconi bought the club and its debts, and began turning Milan into a serious business. Installing Arrigo Sacchi as manager, Milan combined a skilled but tough back four (Baresi, Maldini, Tassoti and Costacurta) with Saachi's aggressive pressing game in midfield. The team took the title in 1988 and, adding the star quality of Dutch imports Gullit, van Basten and Rijkaard, went on to take two European Cups. Titles also went to the old money at Internazionale in 1989, and the new money at Sampdoria in

After waiting 16 years and enduring city-rival Lazio winning the Scudetto in 2000, Roma took the title in 2001. Francesco Totti celebrates his goal against Parma on the last day of the season.

From cruise ship crooner to media mogul, from president of Milan to Italian prime minister, Silvio Berlusconi has been the single most significant operator in Italian football for almost 20 years.

ITALY

1990. Genoa's second team finally acquired some serious backing in the form of oil magnate Paolo Mantovani, who astutely built a team around Roberto Mancini and Gianluca Vialli.

The avalanche of TV money and increased attendances that followed the success of Italia '90 saw the old order reassert itself. At Milan, Sacchi had given way to his junior Fabio Capello and the Dutch masters to a new generation of foreign stars (Desailly, Weah, Boban and Savicevic). They duly delivered four out of the next five titles, including an amazing run of 58 unbeaten matches (1991–93) and an entire season 1991–92 undefeated in Serie A. Juventus ended almost a decade without titles, winning under Marcello Lippi in 1995 and again in 1997 and 98. Lippi's squad included Zidane, Davids and Del Piero.

Hysterical spending

Challenges to the big two came from Internazionale, whose hysterical spending in the transfer market, and its turnover of managers, has been second to none. Parma and Fiorentina have also spent big, but cup and European success have not been matched by success in the gruelling league battle. Atalanta, Udinese and Bologna have all established themselves as regular mid-table stayers. The presence of clubs from the south has steadily diminished and only Lecce and Bari have been able to sustain more than a season in the top flight.

The Milan-Juventus monopoly was finally broken by the capital's two big clubs, Lazio and Roma in 2000 and 2001. Their victories owe a lot to the steely nerves of their owners (being the first two Italian clubs to float on the stock exchange) and their managers (Sven-Göran Eriksson and Fabio Capello), after phenomenal transfer spending.

Italian League Income (in million lire)

SEASON	1997–98	1998–99	1999–2000	2000–01
Revenue	650	714	1059	1151
Costs	872	1049	1465	1861
Gross profit	-222	-335	-406	-710
Net profit	-38	-11	35	-133

Total for all Serie A clubs

La Vecchia Signora, the 'Old Lady': after a barren spell in the early 1990s, Juventus has come back and has finished in the top two in all but one season since 1994.

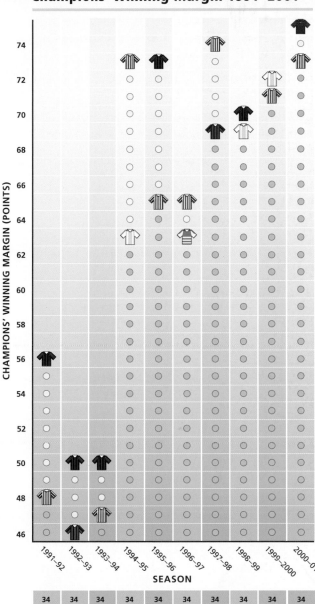

Champions' Winning Margin 1991–2001

CHAMPIONS' WINNING MARGIN (POINTS)

SEASON

34	34	34	34	34	34	34	34	34	34

**Total games played by each team
(2 points awarded for a win until 1995, when 3 points awarded)**

| ▦ Internazionale | ▦ Juventus | ⬦ Lazio |
| ▦ Milan | ▦ Parma | ■ Roma |

Sources of Income 2001

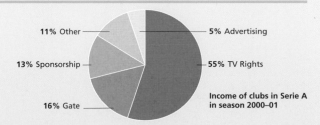

11% Other
5% Advertising
13% Sponsorship
55% TV Rights
16% Gate

Income of clubs in Serie A in season 2000–01

ITALY

Key to League Positions Table

- ■ League champions
- ■ Season of promotion to league
- ■ Season of relegation from league
- ■ Other teams playing in league
- | 5 | Final position in league

Gianluca Vialli helped Sampdoria *to the very top of Italian football in the early 1990s. A decade later Vialli was sacked by Watford and Sampdoria have slumped to Serie B.*

Fabio Capello, Scudetto *winner with both Milan and Roma, works on his worry lines.*

Italian League Positions 1981–2001

SEASON

TEAM	1981–82	1982–83	1983–84	1984–85	1985–86	1986–87	1987–88	1988–89	1989–90	1990–91	1991–92	1992–93	1993–94	1994–95	1995–96	1996–97	1997–98	1998–99	1999–2000	2000–01
Ancona											17									
Ascoli Calcio	6	13	10	14		12	12	12	18		18									
Atalanta			10	8	15		6	7	10	11	7	17		13	10	16				7
Avellino	8	9	11	13	12	8	15													
Bari				15				10	13	15			12	15		11	10	14	18	
Bologna	15					14		14	8	18						7	8	9	11	10
Brescia												14		18		15				8
Cagliari	12	14								14	13	6	12	9	10	15		12	17	
Catania			16																	
Catanzaro	7	16																		
Cesena	10	15					9	13	14	17										
Chievo																				
Como Calcio	16				11	9	9	11	18											
Cremonese			16		13			17			17		10	13	17					
Empoli						16											12	18		
Fiorentina	2	5	3	9	4	10	8	7	12	12	12	16		10	4	9	5	3	7	9
Foggia											9	11	9	16						
Genoa	13	12	14					11	4	14	13	11	14							
Internazionale	5	3	4	3	6	3	5	1	3	3	8	2	13	6	7	3	2	8	4	5
Juventus	1	2	1	6	1	2	6	4	4	7	2	4	2	1	2	1	1	6	2	2
Lazio		13	15					10	9	11	10	5	4	2	3	4	7	2	1	3
Lecce				16				9	13	15		18					17		13	13
Milan	14		8	5	7	5	1	3	2	2	1	1	1	4	1	11	10	1	3	6
Napoli	4	10	12	8	3	1	2	2	1	8	4	11	6	7	12	13	18			17
Padova													15	18						
Parma										6	7	3	5	3	6	2	6	4	5	4
Perugia																16		14	10	11
Pescara						14	16				18									
Piacenza													15		14	14	13	13	18	
Pisa		11	15		14		13	17		16										
Reggina Calcio												14	17		18				12	14
Roma	3	1	2	7	2	7	3	8	6	9	5	10	7	5	5	12	4	5	6	1
Salernitana Sport																		15		
Sampdoria		7	7	4	11	6	4	5	5	1	6	7	3	8	6	9	16			
Torino	9	8	5	2	5	11	7	15		5	3	9	8	11	16			15		
Udinese	11	6	9	12	13	16		15				14	16		11	5	3	7	8	12
Venezia																		11	16	
Hellas Verona		4	6	1	10	4	10	11	16		16					17			9	15
Vicenza															9	8	14	17		16

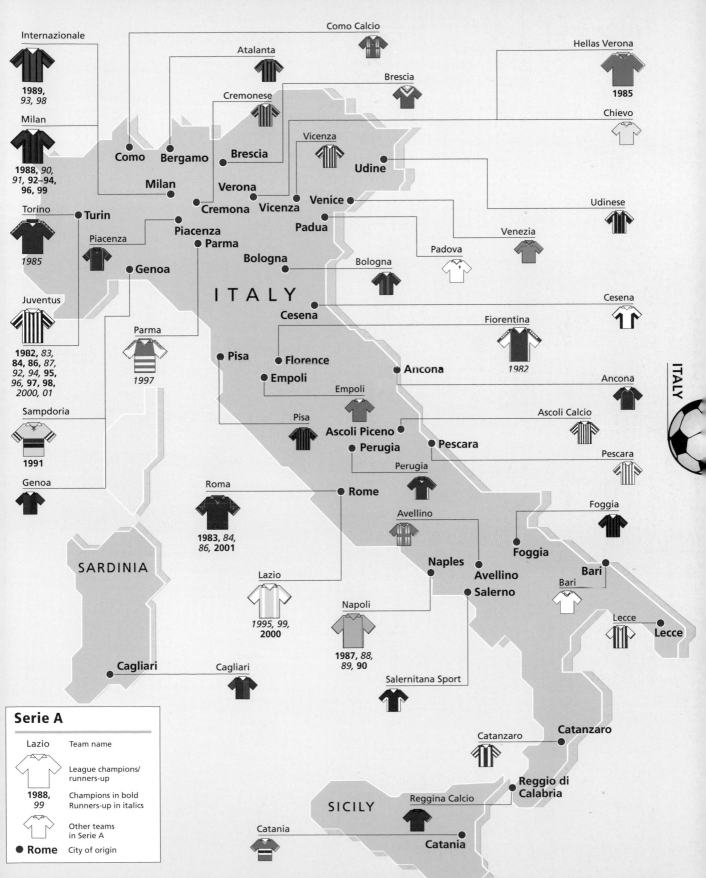

Como Calcio

Internazionale
1989, *93, 98*

Atalanta

Hellas Verona
1985

Brescia

Chievo

Milan
1988, *90,* **91,** *92–94,* **96, 99**

Cremonese

Vicenza

Como **Bergamo** **Brescia**

Udine

Torino
1985

Milan

Verona

Vicenza

Venice

Udinese

Turin

Cremona

Venezia

Piacenza

Piacenza

Padua

Parma

Padova

Juventus
1982, *83,* **84, 86, 87,** *92, 94,* **95,** *96,* **97, 98, 2000, 01**

Genoa

Bologna

Bologna

Cesena

Parma
1997

ITALY

Cesena

Fiorentina
1982

Cesena

Sampdoria
1991

Pisa

Florence

Ancona

Ancona

Genoa

Empoli

Empoli

Ancona

Pisa

Ascoli Calcio

Ascoli Piceno

Pescara

Perugia

Pescara

Perugia

Roma

Rome

Avellino

Foggia

Roma
1983, *84,* *86,* **2001**

Naples

Foggia

SARDINIA

Lazio

Avellino

Avellino

Bari

Bari

Napoli
1987, *88,* *89,* **90**

Salerno

Lazio
1995, *99,* **2000**

Lecce

Lecce

Cagliari

Cagliari

Salernitana Sport

Catanzaro

Catanzaro

Reggio di Calabria

SICILY

Reggina Calcio

Catania

Catania

Serie A

Lazio — Team name

1988, *99* — Champions in bold Runners-up in italics

— Other teams in Serie A

● **Rome** — City of origin

ITALY

225

Italy

Federazione Italiana Giuoco Calcio
Founded: 1898
Joined FIFA: 1905
Joined UEFA: 1954

REGULAR COMPETITIVE FOOTBALL LEAGUES had been established in Italy in the 1890s, and the national championship was created in 1898. However, like most things national in Italy, it was in reality rather fragmented and regional. Until 1910 the national component of the championship consisted of various play-off rounds between champions from the north, centre and south of the country and it was only in 1910, and for one season, that a single national league format was used. Indeed, the regional component grew so large that there were 18 separate regional leagues of wildly different standards.

With the advent of professionalism, a single national league was re-established in 1930, and this formed the basis of today's Serie A, the top national division. The title is known as *Lo Scudetto*, and refers to the tricolor shield that the previous year's champions are entitled to wear on their shirts. During the 1980s and 90s Serie A was regarded by many as the most exciting league in Europe.

The Copa Italia, a national cup competition, is a rather more low-key affair, played first in 1922 and again for a few years in the 1930s before being re-established in 1958 to provide an Italian entrant for the Cup-Winners' Cup. The bottom clubs in Serie A do not join until the second round, and the top eight join in the third round.

Football is a team game and one player does not always make a difference. However, Diego Maradona inspired Napoli to two Italian championships and UEFA Cup glory during his seven-year stay.

Italian Amateur League Record 1898–1929

SEASON	CHAMPIONS	RUNNERS-UP
1898	Genoa	Internazionale Torino
1899	Genoa	Internazionale Torino
1900	Genoa	FC Torinese
1901	Milan	Genoa
1902	Genoa	Milan
1903	Genoa	Juventus
1904	Genoa	Juventus
1905	Juventus	Genoa
1906	Milan	Juventus
1907	Milan	Torino
1908	Pro Vercelli	US Milanese
1909	Pro Vercelli	US Milanese
1910	Internazionale	Pro Vercelli
1911	Pro Vercelli	Vicenza
1912	Pro Vercelli	Vicenza
1913	Pro Vercelli	Lazio
1914	Casale	Lazio
1915	Genoa*	
1916–19	*no championship*	
1920	Internazionale	Livorno
1921	Pro Vercelli	Pisa
1922	Novese	Sampierdarenese
1922	Pro Vercelli**	Fortitudo
1923	Genoa	Lazio
1924	Genoa	Savoia
1925	Bologna	Alba
1926	Juventus	Alba
1927	Torino†	Bologna
1928	Torino	Genoa
1929	Bologna	Torino

* Genoa awarded title after league suspended at start of First World War.
** CCI organized championship.
† Torino's title was revoked because of alleged payments to a Juventus player before its match which Torino won 2-1.

Italian Professional League Record 1930–2002

SEASON	CHAMPIONS	RUNNERS-UP
1930	Ambrosiana Inter	Genoa
1931	Juventus	Roma
1932	Juventus	Bologna
1933	Juventus	Ambrosiana Inter
1934	Juventus	Ambrosiana Inter
1935	Juventus	Ambrosiana Inter
1936	Bologna	Roma
1937	Bologna	Lazio
1938	Ambrosiana Inter	Juventus
1939	Bologna	Torino
1940	Ambrosiana Inter	Bologna
1941	Bologna	Ambrosiana Inter
1942	Roma	Torino
1943	Torino	Livorno
1944–45	*no championship*	
1946	Torino	Juventus
1947	Torino	Juventus
1948	Torino	Milan
1949	Torino	Internazionale
1950	Juventus	Milan
1951	Milan	Internazionale
1952	Juventus	Milan
1953	Internazionale	Juventus
1954	Internazionale	Juventus
1955	Milan	Udinese
1956	Fiorentina	Milan

ITALY

Italian Professional League Record (*continued*)

SEASON	CHAMPIONS	RUNNERS-UP
1957	Milan	Fiorentina
1958	Juventus	Fiorentina
1959	Milan	Fiorentina
1960	Juventus	Fiorentina
1961	Juventus	Milan
1962	Milan	Internazionale
1963	Internazionale	Juventus
1964	Bologna	Internazionale
1965	Internazionale	Milan
1966	Internazionale	Bologna
1967	Juventus	Internazionale
1968	Milan	Napoli
1969	Fiorentina	Cagliari
1970	Cagliari	Internazionale
1971	Internazionale	Milan
1972	Juventus	Milan
1973	Juventus	Milan
1974	Lazio	Juventus
1975	Juventus	Napoli
1976	Torino	Juventus
1977	Juventus	Torino
1978	Juventus	Vicenza
1979	Milan	Perugia
1980	Internazionale	Juventus
1981	Juventus	Roma
1982	Juventus	Fiorentina
1983	Roma	Juventus
1984	Juventus	Roma
1985	Verona	Torino
1986	Juventus	Roma
1987	Napoli	Juventus
1988	Milan	Napoli
1989	Internazionale	Napoli
1990	Napoli	Milan
1991	Sampdoria	Milan
1992	Milan	Juventus
1993	Milan	Internazionale
1994	Milan	Juventus
1995	Juventus	Lazio
1996	Milan	Juventus
1997	Juventus	Parma
1998	Juventus	Internazionale
1999	Milan	Lazio
2000	Lazio	Juventus
2001	Roma	Juventus
2002	Juventus	Roma

Italian League Summary

TEAM	TOTALS	CHAMPIONS & RUNNERS-UP (BOLD) (*ITALICS*)
Juventus	26, 19	*1903, 04,* **05, 06, 26, 31–35,** *38, 46, 47, 50, 52, 53, 54,* **58, 60, 61,** *63,* **67,** *72,* **73,** *74,* **75, 76, 77, 78, 80, 81, 82,** *83,* **84, 86,** *87,* **92,** *94,* **95,** *96,* **97, 98,** *2000,* **01, 02**
Milan	16, 12	**1901,** *02,* **06, 07,** *48,* **50,** *51,* **52, 55, 56, 57,** *59,* **61, 62,** *65,* **68,** *71–73,* **79, 88, 90, 91, 92–94, 96, 99**
Internazionale (includes Ambrosiana Inter)	13, 12	**1910, 20, 30,** *33–35,* **38,** *40,* **41,** *49,* **51,** *53,* **54,** *62,* **63,** *64,* **65, 66, 67, 70, 71, 80, 89,** *93,* **98**
Genoa	9, 4	**1898–1900, 01,** *02–04,* **05,** *15,* **23, 24,** *28,* **30**
Torino	8, 6	*1907,* **27, 28,** *29,* **39,** *42,* **43,** *46–49,* **76,** *77,* **85**
Bologna	7, 4	**1925,** *27,* **29, 32, 36, 37,** *39,* **40, 41, 64, 66**

Italian League Summary (*continued*)

TEAM	TOTALS	CHAMPIONS & RUNNERS-UP (BOLD) (*ITALICS*)
Pro Vercelli	7, 1	**1908, 09,** *10,* **11–13, 21,** *22*
Roma	3, 6	*1931, 36,* **42,** *81,* **83,** *84, 86,* **2001,** *02*
Lazio	2, 6	*1913, 14, 23, 37,* **74,** *95, 99,* **2000**
Fiorentina	2, 5	**1956,** *57–60,* **69,** *82*
Napoli	2, 4	*1968, 75,* **87,** *88, 89,* **90**
Cagliari	1, 1	*1969,* **70**
Casale	1, 0	**1914**
Novese	1, 0	**1922**
Sampdoria	1, 0	**1991**
Verona	1, 0	**1985**
Vicenza	0, 3	*1911, 12, 78*
Alba	0, 2	*1925, 26*
Internazionale Torino	0, 2	*1898, 99*
Livorno	0, 2	*1920, 43*
US Milanese	0, 2	*1908, 09*
FC Torinese	0, 1	*1900*
Fortitudo	0, 1	*1922*
Parma	0, 1	*1997*
Perugia	0, 1	*1979*
Pisa	0, 1	*1921*
Sampierdarenese	0, 1	*1922*
Savoia	0, 1	*1924*
Udinese	0, 1	*1955*

Italian Cup Record 1922–2002

YEAR	WINNERS	SCORE	RUNNERS-UP
1922	Vado	1-0 (aet)	Udinese
1923–35		*no competition*	
1936	Torino	5-1	Alessandria
1937	Genoa	1-0	Roma
1938	Juventus	3-1, 2-1 (2 legs)	Torino
1939	Internazionale	2-1	Novara
1940	Fiorentina	1-0	Genoa
1941	Venezia	3-3 (aet), (replay) 1-0	Roma
1942	Juventus	1-1 (aet), (replay) 4-1	Milan
1943	Torino	4-0	Venezia
1944–57		*no competition*	
1958	Lazio	1-0	Fiorentina
1959	Juventus	4-1	Internazionale
1960	Juventus	3-2 (aet)	Fiorentina
1961	Fiorentina	2-0	Lazio
1962	Napoli	2-1	Spal
1963	Atalanta	3-1	Torino
1964	Roma	0-0 (aet), (replay) 1-0	Torino
1965	Juventus	1-0	Internazionale
1966	Fiorentina	2-1 (aet)	Catanzaro
1967	Milan	1-0	Padova
1968	Torino	(mini-league format)	Milan
1969	Roma	(mini-league format)	Cagliari
1970	Bologna	(mini-league format)	Torino
1971	Torino	(mini-league format)	Milan
1972	Milan	2-0	Napoli
1973	Milan	1-1 (5-2 pens)	Juventus
1974	Bologna	0-0 (5-4 pens)	Palermo
1975	Fiorentina	3-2	Milan
1976	Napoli	4-0	Verona
1977	Milan	2-0	Internazionale
1978	Internazionale	2-1	Napoli
1979	Juventus	2-1 (aet)	Palermo
1980	Roma	0-0 (3-2 pens)	Torino
1981	Roma	1-1, (replay) 1-1 (5-3 pens)	Torino

Italian Cup Record (continued)

YEAR	WINNERS	SCORE	RUNNERS-UP
1982	Internazionale	1-0, 1-1 (2 legs)	Torino
1983	Juventus	0-2, 3-0 (aet) (2 legs)	Verona
1984	Roma	1-1, 1-0 (2 legs)	Verona
1985	Sampdoria	1-0, 2-1 (2 legs)	Milan
1986	Roma	1-2, 2-0 (2 legs)	Sampdoria
1987	Napoli	3-0, 1-0 (2 legs)	Atalanta
1988	Sampdoria	2-0, 1-2 (aet) (2 legs)	Torino
1989	Sampdoria	0-1, 4-0 (2 legs)	Napoli
1990	Juventus	0-0, 1-0 (2 legs)	Milan
1991	Roma	3-1, 1-1 (2 legs)	Sampdoria
1992	Parma	0-1, 2-0 (2 legs)	Juventus
1993	Torino	3-0, 2-5 (2 legs)	Roma
1994	Sampdoria	0-0, 6-1 (2 legs)	Ancona
1995	Juventus	2-0, 1-0 (2 legs)	Parma
1996	Fiorentina	1-0, 2-0 (2 legs)	Atalanta
1997	Vicenza	0-1, 3-0 (aet) (2 legs)	Napoli
1998	Lazio	0-1, 3-1 (2 legs)	Milan
1999	Parma	1-1, 2-2 (2 legs)	Fiorentina
2000	Lazio	2-1, 0-0 (2 legs)	Internazionale
2001	Fiorentina	1-0, 1-1 (2 legs)	Parma
2002	Parma*	1-2, 1-0 (2 legs)	Juventus

* Denotes winners on away goals rule.

***The San Siro plays host** to one of the most hotly-contested derbies in Italian football: Milan v Internazionale. The fans of both sides greet the teams with a show with flags, scarves and flares.*

Italian Cup Summary

TEAM	TOTALS	WINNERS & RUNNERS-UP (BOLD) (ITALICS)
Juventus	9, 3	**1938, 42, 59, 60, 65,** *73,* **79, 83, 90,** *92,* **95,** *2002*
Roma	7, 3	*1937, 41,* **64, 69, 80, 81, 84, 86,** *91,* **93**
Fiorentina	6, 3	**1940,** *58,* **60, 61, 66,** *75,* **96,** *99,* **2001**
Torino	5, 8	**1936,** *38,* **43,** *63, 64,* **68,** *70, 71, 80–82, 88,* **93**
Milan	4, 7	*1942,* **67,** *68, 71,* **72, 73,** *75,* **77,** *85, 90,* **98**
Sampdoria	4, 2	**1985,** *86,* **88, 89,** *91,* **94**
Internazionale	3, 4	**1939,** *59,* **65,** *77, 78, 82,* **2000**
Napoli	3, 4	**1962,** *72, 76, 78,* **87,** *89, 97*
Parma	3, 2	**1992,** *95,* **99,** *2001,* **02**
Lazio	3, 1	**1958,** *61,* **98, 2000**
Bologna	2, 0	**1970, 74**
Atalanta	1, 2	**1963,** *87, 96*
Genoa	1, 1	**1937,** *40*
Venezia	1, 1	**1941,** *43*
Vado	1, 0	**1922**
Vicenza	1, 0	**1997**
Verona	0, 3	*1976, 83, 84*
Palermo	0, 2	*1974, 79*
Alessandria	0, 1	*1936*
Ancona	0, 1	*1994*
Cagliari	0, 1	*1969*
Catanzaro	0, 1	*1966*
Novara	0, 1	*1939*
Padova	0, 1	*1967*
Spal	0, 1	*1962*
Udinese	0, 1	*1922*

ITALY

Malta

Malta Football Association
Founded: 1900
Joined FIFA: 1959
Joined UEFA: 1960

THE MALTA FOOTBALL ASSOCIATION was formed in 1900, when the island was still under British rule. It was in turn affiliated to the FA in London, rather than FIFA, for the first half of the century. A league was first played in 1910, and in 1935 the Malta FA Trophy competition was inaugurated. Self-government of the country began in 1947, though membership of FIFA in 1959 (and UEFA in 1960) preceded Malta's full independence, gained in 1964. Despite this, the country played their first World Cup qualifying campaign in an African group in 1960.

League and cup competitions have been dominated by five teams – Floriana, Sliema Wanderers, Valletta, Hamrun Spartans and Hibernians. There are ten teams in the top flight playing each other three times a season (extended from twice in a season in 1996). All games are played in the Ta' Qali national stadium in Valletta. Promotion and relegation is a simple two up, two down system. In addition to the Maltese Trophy Cup (listed here) top teams also compete in the Löwenbrau Super Cup and the Löwenbrau Fives Cup.

Maltese League Record 1910–2002

SEASON	CHAMPIONS	SEASON	CHAMPIONS
1910	Floriana	1952	Floriana
1911	no championship	1953	Floriana
1912	Floriana	1954	Sliema Wanderers
1913	Floriana	1955	Floriana
1914	Hamrun Spartans	1956	Sliema Wanderers
1915	Valletta United	1957	Sliema Wanderers
1916	no championship	1958	Floriana
1917	St George's	1959	Valletta
1918	Hamrun Spartans	1960	Valletta
1919	KOMR Militia	1961	Hibernians
1920	Sliema Wanderers	1962	Floriana
1921	Floriana	1963	Valletta
1922	Floriana	1964	Sliema Wanderers
1923	Sliema Wanderers	1965	Sliema Wanderers
1924	Sliema Wanderers	1966	Sliema Wanderers
1925	Floriana	1967	Hibernians
1926	Sliema Wanderers	1968	Floriana
1927	Floriana	1969	Hibernians
1928	Floriana	1970	Floriana
1929	Floriana	1971	Sliema Wanderers
1930	Sliema Wanderers	1972	Sliema Wanderers
1931	Floriana	1973	Floriana
1932	Valletta United	1974	Valletta
1933	Sliema Wanderers	1975	Floriana
1934	Sliema Wanderers	1976	Sliema Wanderers
1935	Floriana	1977	Floriana
1936	Sliema Wanderers	1978	Valletta
1937	Floriana	1979	Hibernians
1938	Sliema Wanderers	1980	Valletta
1939	Sliema Wanderers	1981	Hibernians
1940	Sliema Wanderers	1982	Hibernians
1941–44	no championship	1983	Hamrun Spartans
1945	Valletta	1984	Valletta
1946	Valletta	1985	Rabat Ajax
1947	Hamrun Spartans	1986	Rabat Ajax
1948	Valletta	1987	Hamrun Spartans
1949	Sliema Wanderers	1988	Hamrun Spartans
1950	Floriana	1989	Sliema Wanderers
1951	Floriana	1990	Valletta

Maltese League Record (continued)

SEASON	CHAMPIONS	SEASON	CHAMPIONS
1991	Hamrun Spartans	1999	Valletta
1992	Valletta	2000	Birkirkara
1993	Floriana	2001	Valletta
1994	Hibernians	2002	Hibernians
1995	Hibernians		
1996	Sliema Wanderers		
1997	Valletta		
1998	Valletta		

Maltese Cup Record 1935–2002

YEAR	WINNERS	YEAR	WINNERS
1935	Sliema Wanderers	1972	Floriana
1936	Sliema Wanderers	1973	Gżira United
1937	Sliema Wanderers	1974	Sliema Wanderers
1938	Floriana	1975	Valletta
1939	Melita St Julians	1976	Floriana
1940	Sliema Wanderers	1977	Valletta
1941–44	no competition	1978	Valletta
1945	Floriana	1979	Sliema Wanderers
1946	Sliema Wanderers	1980	Hibernians
1947	Floriana	1981	Floriana
1948	Sliema Wanderers	1982	Hibernians
1949	Floriana	1983	Hamrun Spartans
1950	Floriana	1984	Hamrun Spartans
1951	Sliema Wanderers	1985	Żurrieq
1952	Sliema Wanderers	1986	Rabat Ajax
1953	Floriana	1987	Hamrun Spartans
1954	Floriana	1988	Hamrun Spartans
1955	Floriana	1989	Hamrun Spartans
1956	Sliema Wanderers	1990	Sliema Wanderers
1957	Floriana	1991	Valletta
1958	Floriana	1992	Hamrun Spartans
1959	Sliema Wanderers	1993	Floriana
1960	Valletta	1994	Floriana
1961	Floriana	1995	Valletta
1962	Hibernians	1996	Valletta
1963	Sliema Wanderers	1997	Valletta
1964	Valletta	1998	Hibernians
1965	Sliema Wanderers	1999	Valletta
1966	Floriana	2000	Sliema Wanderers
1967	Floriana	2001	Valletta
1968	Sliema Wanderers	2002	Birkirkara
1969	Sliema Wanderers		
1970	Hibernians		
1971	Hibernians		

San Marino

Federazione Sammarinese Giuoco Calcio
Founded: 1931
Joined FIFA: 1988
Joined UEFA: 1988

San Marino is a tiny independent enclave in northern Italy. Organized football dates back to the 1930s, but it was only in 1988 that they joined UEFA and began to play internationals. The league has 16 teams in two groups of eight with the top three in each progressing to an end of season play-off for the championship.

SEASON	LEAGUE CHAMPIONS
1998	Folgore
1999	Faetano
2000	Folgore
2001	Cosmos
2002	Domagnano

YEAR	CUP WINNERS
1997	Murata
1998	Faetano
1999	Cosmos
2000	Tre Penne
2001	Domagnano

MALTA, SAN MARINO

Austria

Österreichischer Fussball-Bund
Founded: 1904
Joined FIFA: 1905
Joined UEFA: 1954

IN AUSTRIA, EARLY COMPETITIVE FOOTBALL was firmly centred on the capital, Vienna. A local cup competition – Der Challenge Cup – ran from 1897 to 1911, and included teams invited from Hungary. It was superseded by a Vienna-based league. After the 1938 *Anschluss* with Germany, Austria's top clubs competed in a greater German league as well as their own, and indeed won that competition a number of times. After the Second World War the league was re-established on a national basis, the top flight consisting of ten teams playing each other four times a season.

The Austrian Cup was first played in 1919, and although it lapsed during the Second World War and for nearly a decade afterwards, it has been running annually again since 1959.

Austrian League Record 1911–2002

SEASON	CHAMPIONS	RUNNERS-UP
1911	SK Rapid Wien	Wiener Sport-Club
1912	SK Rapid Wien	Wiener Sport-Club
1913	SK Rapid Wien	Wiener Association FC
1914	Wiener Association FC	SK Rapid Wien
1915	Wiener AC	Wiener Association FC
1916	SK Rapid Wien	FAC Wien
1917	SK Rapid Wien	FAC Wien
1918	FAC Wien	SK Rapid Wien
1919	SK Rapid Wien	SC Rudolfshügel Wien
1920	SK Rapid Wien	SV Amateure Wien
1921	SK Rapid Wien	SV Amateure Wien
1922	Wiener Sport-Club	SC Hakoah Wien
1923	SK Rapid Wien	SV Amateure Wien
1924	SV Amateure Wien	First Vienna FC
1925	SC Hakoah Wien	SV Amateure Wien
1926	SV Amateure Wien	First Vienna FC
1927	Admira Wien	Brigittenauer AC Wien
1928	Admira Wien	SK Rapid Wien
1929	SK Rapid Wien	Admira Wien
1930	SK Rapid Wien	Admira Wien
1931	First Vienna FC	Admira Wien
1932	Admira Wien	First Vienna FC
1933	First Vienna FC	SK Rapid Wien
1934	Admira Wien	SK Rapid Wien
1935	SK Rapid Wien	Admira Wien
1936	Admira Wien	First Vienna FC
1937	Admira Wien	FK Austria Wien
1938	SK Rapid Wien	Wiener Sport-Club
1939	Admira Wien	SC Wacker Wien
1940	SK Rapid Wien	SC Wacker Wien
1941	SK Rapid Wien	SC Wacker Wien
1942	First Vienna FC	FC Wien
1943	First Vienna FC	Wiener AC
1944	First Vienna FC	FAC Wien
1945	SK Rapid Wien	SC Wacker Wien
1946	SK Rapid Wien	FK Austria Wien
1947	SC Wacker Wien	SK Rapid Wien
1948	SK Rapid Wien	SC Wacker Wien
1949	FK Austria Wien	SK Rapid Wien
1950	FK Austria Wien	SK Rapid Wien
1951	SK Rapid Wien	SC Wacker Wien
1952	SK Rapid Wien	FK Austria Wien
1953	FK Austria Wien	SC Wacker Wien
1954	SK Rapid Wien	FK Austria Wien
1955	First Vienna FC	Wiener Sport-Club
1956	SK Rapid Wien	SC Wacker Wien

Austrian League Record (*continued*)

SEASON	CHAMPIONS	RUNNERS-UP
1957	SK Rapid Wien	First Vienna FC
1958	Wiener Sport-Club	SK Rapid Wien
1959	Wiener Sport-Club	SK Rapid Wien
1960	SK Rapid Wien	Wiener Sport-Club
1961	FK Austria Wien	First Vienna FC
1962	FK Austria Wien	Linzer ASK
1963	FK Austria Wien	Admira Energie
1964	SK Rapid Wien	FK Austria Wien
1965	Linzer ASK	SK Rapid Wien
1966	Admira Energie	SK Rapid Wien
1967	SK Rapid Wien	Wacker Innsbruck
1968	SK Rapid Wien	Wacker Innsbruck
1969	FK Austria Wien	Wiener Sport-Club
1970	FK Austria Wien	Wiener Sport-Club
1971	Wacker Innsbruck	Austria Salzburg
1972	Wacker Innsbruck	FK Austria Wien
1973	Wacker Innsbruck	SK Rapid Wien
1974	VÖEST Linz	Wacker Innsbruck
1975	Wacker Innsbruck	VÖEST Linz
1976	FK Austria/WAC	Wacker Innsbruck
1977	Wacker Innsbruck	SK Rapid Wien
1978	FK Austria/WAC	SK Rapid Wien
1979	FK Austria Wien	Wiener Sport-Club
1980	FK Austria Wien	VÖEST Linz
1981	FK Austria Wien	SK Sturm Graz
1982	SK Rapid Wien	FK Austria Wien
1983	SK Rapid Wien	FK Austria Wien
1984	FK Austria Wien	SK Rapid Wien
1985	FK Austria Wien	SK Rapid Wien
1986	FK Austria Wien	SK Rapid Wien
1987	SK Rapid Wien	FK Austria Wien
1988	SK Rapid Wien	FK Austria Wien
1989	FCS Tirol Innsbruck	FC Admira Wacker
1990	FCS Tirol Innsbruck	FK Austria Wien
1991	FC Tirol Innsbruck	FK Austria Wien
1992	FK Austria Wien	SV Austria Salzburg
1993	FK Austria Wien	SV Austria Salzburg
1994	SV Austria Salzburg	FK Austria Wien
1995	SV Austria Salzburg	SK Sturm Graz
1996	SK Rapid Wien	SK Sturm Graz
1997	SV Austria Salzburg	SK Rapid Wien
1998	SK Sturm Graz	SK Rapid Wien
1999	SK Sturm Graz	FC Tirol Innsbruck
2000	FC Tirol Innsbruck	SK Sturm Graz
2001	FC Tirol Innsbruck	SK Rapid Wien
2002	FC Tirol Innsbruck	SK Sturm Graz

Liechtenstein

Liechtensteiner Fussballverband
Founded: 1934
Joined FIFA: 1974
Joined UEFA: 1992

L.F.V.

YEAR	CUP WINNERS
1998	FC Vaduz
1999	FC Vaduz
2000	FC Vaduz
2001	FC Vaduz
2002	FC Vaduz

It's hard to run a league with only 35,000 inhabitants, and the handful of registered club sides in the Fussballverband play in the lower reaches of the Swiss league. However, Liechtenstein's annual cup has been running since 1946, during which time the trophy has been won 30 times by FC Vaduz.

AUSTRIA, LIECHTENSTEIN

Austrian League Summary

TEAM	TOTALS	CHAMPIONS & RUNNERS-UP (BOLD) (ITALICS)
SK Rapid Wien	32, 21	1911–13, *14*, 16, *17*, *18*, 19–21, *23*, *28*, *29*, *30*, *33*, *34*, 35, *38*, *40*, *41*, *45*, *46*, *47*, *48*, *49*, *50*, 51, *52*, *54*, *56*, *57*, *58*, *59*, 60, 64, *65*, *66*, *67*, *68*, *73*, *77*, 78, *82*, 83, *84–86*, 87, *88*, 96, *97*, 98, 2001
FK Austria Wien (Includes SV Amateure Wien)	18, 17	1920, *21*, *23*, 24, 25, *26*, *37*, *46*, 49, 50, *52*, *53*, *54*, *61–63*, 64, *69*, 70, 72, 79–81, *82*, 83, 84–86, *87*, 88, *90*, *91*, 92, *93*, 94

This summary only features the top two clubs in the Austrian League. For a full list of league champions and runners-up please see the League Record opposite.

Austrian Cup Record 1919–2002

YEAR	WINNERS	SCORE	RUNNERS-UP
1919	SK Rapid Wien	3-0	Wiener Sport-Club
1920	SK Rapid Wien	5-2	SV Amateure Wien
1921	SV Amateure Wien	2-1	Wiener Sport-Club
1922	Wiener Association FC	2-1	SV Amateure Wien
1923	Wiener Sport-Club	3-1	SC Wacker Wien
1924	SV Amateure Wien	8-6 (aet)	SK Slovan Wien
1925	SV Amateure Wien	3-1	First Vienna FC
1926	SV Amateure Wien	4-3	First Vienna FC
1927	SK Rapid Wien	3-0	FK Austria Wien
1928	Admira Wien	2-1	Wiener AC
1929	First Vienna FC	3-2	SK Rapid Wien
1930	First Vienna FC	1-0	FK Austria Wien
1931	Wiener AC	16 pts-15 pts (league system)	FK Austria Wien
1932	Admira Wien	6-1	Wiener AC
1933	FK Austria Wien	1-0	Brigittenauer AC Wien
1934	Admira Wien	8-0	SK Rapid Wien
1935	FK Austria Wien	5-1	Wiener AC
1936	FK Austria Wien	3-0	First Vienna FC
1937	First Vienna FC	2-0	Wiener SC
1938	WAC Schwarz-Rot	1-0	Wiener SC
1939–45	no competition		
1946	SK Rapid Wien	2-1	First Vienna FC
1947	Wacker Wien	4-3	FK Austria Wien
1948	FK Austria Wien	2-0	SK Sturm Graz
1949	FK Austria Wien	5-2	Vorwärts Steyr
1950–58	no competition		
1959	Wiener AC	2-0	SK Rapid Wien
1960	FK Austria Wien	4-2	SK Rapid Wien
1961	SK Rapid Wien	3-1	First Vienna FC
1962	FK Austria Wien	4-1	Grazer AK
1963	FK Austria Wien	1-0	Linzer ASK
1964	Admira Energie	1-0	FK Austria Wien
1965	Linzer ASK	1-1, 1-0	Wiener Neustadt
1966	Admira Energie	1-0	SK Rapid Wien
1967	FK Austria Wien	1-2,1-0 (aet)(2 legs)	Linzer ASK
1968	SK Rapid Wien	2-0	Grazer AK
1969	SK Rapid Wien	2-1	Wiener Sport-Club

Austrian Cup Record (*continued*)

YEAR	WINNERS	SCORE	RUNNERS-UP
1970	Wacker Innsbruck	1-0	Linzer ASK
1971	FK Austria Wien	2-1 (aet)	SK Rapid Wien
1972	SK Rapid Wien	1-2, 3-1	Wiener Sport-Club
1973	Wacker Innsbruck*	1-0, 1-2	SK Rapid Wien
1974	FK Austria Wien	2-1, 1-1	Austria Salzburg
1975	Wacker Innsbruck	3-0, 0-2	Sturm Graz
1976	SK Rapid Wien*	1-0, 1-2	Wacker Innsbruck
1977	FK Austria Wien	1-0, 3-0	Wiener Sport-Club
1978	Wacker Innsbruck	1-1, 2-1	VÖEST Linz
1979	Wacker Innsbruck	1-0, 1-1	FC Admira/Wacker
1980	FK Austria Wien	0-1, 2-0	Austria Salzburg
1981	Grazer AK	0-1, 2-0 (aet)(2 legs)	Austria Salzburg
1982	FK Austria Wien	1-0, 3-1	Wacker Innsbruck
1983	SK Rapid Wien	3-0, 5-0	Wacker Innsbruck
1984	SK Rapid Wien*	1-3, 2-0	FK Austria Wien
1985	SK Rapid Wien	3-3 (aet) (4-3 pens)	FK Austria Wien
1986	FK Austria Wien	6-4 (aet)	SK Rapid Wien
1987	SK Rapid Wien	2-0, 2-2	FC Tirol Innsbruck
1988	Kremser SC*	2-0, 1-3	FC Tirol Innsbruck
1989	FC Tirol Innsbruck	0-2, 6-2	FC Admira/Wacker
1990	FK Austria Wien	3-1 (aet)	SK Rapid Wien
1991	SV Stockerau	2-1	SK Rapid Wien
1992	FK Austria Wien	1-0	FC Admira/Wacker
1993	Wacker Innsbruck	3-1	SK Rapid Wien
1994	FK Austria Wien	4-0	FC Linz
1995	SK Rapid Wien	1-0	DSV Leoben
1996	SK Sturm Graz	3-1	FC Admira/Wacker
1997	SK Sturm Graz	2-1	First Vienna FC
1998	SV Ried im Innkreis	3-1	SK Sturm Graz
1999	SK Sturm Graz	1-1 (aet) (4-2 pens)	Linzer ASK
2000	Grazer AK	2-2 (aet) (4-3 pens)	Austria Salzburg
2001	FC Kärnten	2-1 (aet)	FC Tirol Innsbruck
2002	Grazer AK	3-2	SK Sturm Graz

* Denotes winners on away goals rule.

Austrian Cup Summary

TEAM	TOTALS	WINNERS & RUNNERS-UP (BOLD) (ITALICS)
FK Austria Wien (includes SV Amateure Wien)	22, 9	1920, *21*, 22, 24–26, *27*, 30, 31, *33*, 35, 36, *47*, 48, 49, 60, 62, 63, 64, 67, 71, 74, 77, *80*, 82, *84*, *85*, 86, 90, 92, 94
SK Rapid Wien	14, 11	1919, *20*, 27, *29*, *34*, *46*, *59*, *60*, 61, *66*, 68, 69, *71*, 72, *73*, *76*, 83–85, *86*, 87, 90, 91, 93, 95

This summary only features the top two clubs in the Austrian Cup. For a full list of league champions and runners-up please see the Cup Record above.

Slovenia

Nogometna Zveza Slovenije
Founded: 1920
Joined FIFA: 1992
Joined UEFA: 1993

A separate national league and cup competition have been running in Slovenia since the country's independence in 1991.

SEASON	LEAGUE CHAMPIONS
1998	NK Maribor
1999	NK Maribor
2000	NK Maribor
2001	NK Maribor
2002	NK Maribor

YEAR	CUP WINNERS
1998	Rudar Velenje
1999	NK Maribor
2000	SCT Olimpija Ljubljana
2001	HIT Gorica
2002	HIT Gorica

Switzerland

Schweizerischer Fussballverband
Founded: 1895
Joined FIFA: 1904
Joined UEFA: 1954

A national championship began in Switzerland in 1898, contested by regional league winners. A national cup followed in 1926 and a national league in 1934.

SEASON	LEAGUE CHAMPIONS
1998	Grasshopper-Club
1999	Servette FC Genève
2000	FC St. Gallen
2001	Grasshopper-Club
2002	FC Basel

YEAR	CUP WINNERS
1998	Lausanne-Sports
1999	Lausanne-Sports
2000	FC Zurich
2001	Servette FC Genève
2002	FC Basel

Central Europe

THE SEASONS IN REVIEW 2001–02

ALTHOUGH SOME REGULARS WON championships in central Europe, this was a season for smaller clubs and outsiders. In Poland, Legia Warszawa took its first title for seven years on the penultimate weekend; a draw with Odra Wodzisław was enough to leave the team three points ahead (with a better head-to-head record) than chasing Wisła Kraków. Amica Wronki, in third place, achieved its best-ever position in the league. Second and third met in the Cup Final, with Wisła thrashing Amica 8-2 over two legs. In the Czech Republic, the Prague monopoly on the title was cracked by Slovan Liberec. Alongside its domestic duties, Slovan had a fantastic UEFA Cup run, beating Olympique Lyonnais before finally succumbing to Borussia Dortmund in the quarter-finals. At home, Slovan kept just ahead of the chasing Viktoria Žižkov and Sparta Praha, but needed Slavia Praha to beat Žižkov on the final day of the season to secure the title. In Slovakia, MSK Žilina recorded its first-ever championship title as all other contenders squandered their chances and opportunities. While in Hungary too, ZTE, a small club from Zalaegerszegi (a town in the south-west), won its first-ever title after Budapest giants MTK had led the table by 11 points at the halfway stage.

Enjoy it while you can. Champions Tirol Innsbruck celebrate, but the team's parlous financial condition has seen it forcibly relegated from the Austrian Bundesliga.

Lothar Matthäus says goodbye to Rapid Vienna after guiding the team to its worst-ever finish in the Austrian Bundesliga.

Austrian Bundesliga Table 2001–02

CLUB	P	W	D	L	F	A	Pts	
FC Tirol Innsbruck	36	23	6	7	63	20	75	*
SK Sturm Graz	36	18	11	7	68	42	65	Champions League
Grazer AK	36	17	12	7	69	39	63	Champions League
FK Austria Wien	36	14	11	11	53	38	53	UEFA Cup
FC Kämten	36	14	8	14	40	52	50	UEFA Cup
SV Salzburg	36	13	10	13	42	40	49	
SW Bregenz	36	12	9	15	51	70	45	
SK Rapid Wien	36	11	10	15	37	49	43	
SV Ried	36	9	9	18	36	54	36	
Vfb Admira Wacker Mödling	36	3	6	27	25	80	15	*

*FC Tirol was refused a playing licence by Austrian FC and was relegated to the third division and denied its Champions League place. Vfb Admira Wacker Mödling retain its place in the Bundesliga despite finishing in last place.

Austrian International Club Performances 2001–02

CLUB	COMPETITION	PROGRESS
FC Tirol Innsbruck	Champions League	3rd Qualifying Phase
	UEFA Cup	2nd Round
Grazer AK	UEFA Cup	1st Round
Kamten	UEFA Cup	1st Round
Rapid Wien	UEFA Cup	2nd Round

Austrian Top Goalscorers 2001–02

PLAYER	CLUB	NATIONALITY	GOALS
Ronald Brunmayr	Grazer AK	Austrian	27
Axel Lawaree	SW Bregenz	Belgian	20
Ivica Vastic	SK Sturm Graz	Austrian	16
Roman Wallner	Rapid Wien	Austrian	12

Austrian Cup

2002 FINAL

May 12 – Stadion Liebenau, Graz
SK Sturm Graz 2-3 Grazer AK
(Vastic 58, 92 pen)   *(Brunmayr 15 pen, 20, Kusi-Asare 35)*
h/t: 0-3 **Att:** 15,400
Ref: Brugger

CENTRAL EUROPE

Czech Republic League Table 2001–02

CLUB	P	W	D	L	F	A	Pts	
Slovan Liberec	30	19	7	4	55	26	64	Champions League
Sparta Praha	30	20	3	7	55	19	63	Champions League
Viktoria Žižkov	30	19	6	5	42	20	63	UEFA Cup
Bohemians Praha	30	14	6	10	40	35	48	
Slavia Praha	30	12	11	7	45	34	47	UEFA Cup (cup winners)
Banik Ostrava	30	12	8	10	43	36	44	
FK Teplice	30	12	5	13	37	41	41	
FK Jablonec 97	30	10	10	10	35	33	40	
FC Stavo Artikel Brno	30	10	10	10	34	42	40	
Sigma Olomouc	30	9	10	11	29	31	37	UEFA Cup (Fair play)
1. FC Synot	30	10	6	14	31	38	36	
SK Hradec Králové	30	9	8	13	28	42	35	
Marila Příbram	30	9	7	14	27	39	34	
Chmel Blšany	30	8	5	17	35	51	29	
FC Drnovice	30	7	5	18	31	45	26	Relegated
SFC Opava	30	5	3	22	23	58	18	Relegated

Promoted clubs: É. Budijovice, FC Zlin.

Czech Rep International Club Performances 2001–02

CLUB	COMPETITION	PROGRESS
Slavia Praha	Champions League	3rd Qualifying Phase
	UEFA Cup	1st Round
Sparta Praha	Champions League	2nd Group Phase
Slovan Liberec	UEFA Cup	Quarter-finals
Marila Příbram	UEFA Cup	2nd Round
Viktoria Žižkov	UEFA Cup	1st Round

Czech Republic Top Goalscorers 2001–02

PLAYER	CLUB	NATIONALITY	GOALS
Jiri Stajner	Slovan Liberec	Czech	15
Jan Nezmar	Slovan Liberec	Czech	14
Milan Pacanda	Stavo Artikel Brno	Czech	13
Milan Buros	Banik Ostrava	Czech	11

Czech Republic Cup

2002 FINAL

May 13 – Rosickeho, Prague
Sparta Praha **1-2** Slavia Praha
(Novotny 23) *(Dostek 2, 19)*
h/t: 1-2 **Ref:** Vidlak
Att: 8,820

Slovan Liberec celebrates in Prague city centre after its final league match against Bohemians, at the end of an extraordinary season.

***Tamas Elek** of MTK Hungária (in green) dispossesses Zoltan Balogh of Ferencváros during the local derby in February 2002. At one point, MTK had an 11-point lead in the league, but in the second half of the season the side crumbled and only finished in third spot.*

Hungarian Champions League Table 2001–02

CLUB	P	W	D	L	F	A	Pts	
Zalahús ZTE FC	5	3	1	1	76	47	71	Champions League
Ferencváros	5	3	1	1	66	39	69	UEFA Cup
MTK Hungária FC	5	1	0	4	62	47	67	
Dunaferr SE	5	2	0	3	71	47	59	
Videoton	5	3	0	2	56	53	55	
Újpesti FC	5	2	0	3	65	69	50	UEFA Cup (cup winners)

Hungarian Relegation League Table 2001–02

CLUB	P	W	D	L	F	A	Pts	
Kispest-Honvéd FC	5	2	3	0	51	70	47	
Matáv Sopron	5	0	4	1	54	60	44	
Debreceni VSC	5	2	2	1	47	53	44	
Győri ETO FC	5	0	4	1	48	64	42	
Haladás VFC	5	1	3	1	48	68	41	Relegated
Vasas DH	5	1	2	2	51	78	32	Relegated

Promoted clubs: Békéscsaba, Siófok.
The Hungarian season is divided into two. In the first half of the season 12 clubs play each other three times. The top six go into a final championship league taking the points with them and play each other once. The bottom six go into a similar relegation league.

Hungarian International Club Performances 2001–02

CLUB	COMPETITION	PROGRESS
Ferencváros	Champions League	2nd Qualifying Phase
Debreceni VSC	UEFA Cup	1st Round
Dunaferr SE	UEFA Cup	Qualifying Round

Hungarian Top Goalscorers 2001–02

PLAYER	CLUB	NATIONALITY	GOALS
Atilla Tököli	Dunaferr SE	Hungarian	26
Krisztián Kenesei	Zalahús ZTE FC	Hungarian	21
Bélla Illés	MTK Hungária FC	Hungarian	18
István Tóth	Matáv Sopron	Hungarian	16

Hungarian Cup

2002 FINAL

May 1 – Györi Stadium, Györ
Újpesti FC **2-1** Haladás-Milos
(Vagner 25, 119) *(Halmosi 75)*
(after golden goal extra time)
h/t: 1-0 **90 mins:** 1-1
Ref: Ábrahám **Att:** 12,000

Slovenia and Austria went more closely to form. Slovenia's Maribor Pivovarna began the season looking for its sixth consecutive championship and, though competition arrived, it was from an unexpected quarter. Primorje Ajdovščina chased the team all the way and when Maribor drew on the penultimate weekend of the season, the title fight went right down to the wire. On the last weekend, first and second in the league faced each other, but in the end it was easy as Maribor saw off the challenger 3-0. In Austria the title went to FC Tirol Innsbruck who ran away with the championship despite being mired in debts in excess of £10 million even after selling key players like Marc Ziegler and Marco Zwyssig. Things were sufficiently desperate for manager Joachim Loew to announce in March that he and the players had not been paid since Christmas and the board risked losing the squad – by law employees unpaid for three months are free to walk away from their contracts. A last-minute loan from a local bank averted the club's implosion, but the country's best club will not be allowed to compete in the top flight next season

Polish Champions League Table 2001–02

CLUB	P	W	D	L	F	A	Pts	
Legia Warszawa	14	7	7	0	19	10	42	Champions League
Wisła Kraków	14	8	3	3	22	14	41	UEFA Cup (cup winners)
Amica Wronki	14	7	3	4	21	11	36	UEFA Cup
Polonia Warszawa	14	5	4	5	16	18	32	UEFA Cup
Odra Wadzisław	14	2	5	7	12	19	27	
GKS Katowice	14	4	5	5	10	15	26	
Ruch Chorzów	14	3	4	7	14	18	23	
Pogoń Szczecin	14	2	5	7	8	17	23	

Polish Relegation League Table 2001–02

CLUB	P	W	D	L	F	A	Pts	
Górnik Zabrze	14	8	4	2	23	11	34	
Widzew Łódź	14	6	7	1	19	8	31	
Zagłębie Lublin	14	5	5	4	18	16	29	
Groclin Dysko-bolia Grodzisk	14	6	2	6	18	15	28	
KSZO Ostrowiec	14	4	5	5	14	19	25	
RKS Radomsko	14	3	6	5	13	18	23	Relegated
Slask Wrocław	14	2	4	8	14	22	19	Relegated
Stomil Olsztyn	14	2	7	5	11	21	18	Relegated

Promoted clubs: Garbarnia SJ, Lech Poznań, Orlen Płock.
The Polish season is divided into two. In the first half of the season two leagues of eight clubs play each other twice. The top four from each group go into a final championship league taking their points with them and play each other twice. The bottom four from each group go into a similar relegation league.

Polish International Club Performances 2001–02

CLUB	COMPETITION	PROGRESS
Wisła Kraków	Champions League UEFA Cup	3rd Qualifying Round 2nd Round
Pogoń Szczecin	UEFA Cup	Qualifying Round
Legia Warszawa	UEFA Cup	2nd Round
Polonia Warszawa	UEFA Cup	1st Round

Polish Top Goalscorers 2001–02

PLAYER	CLUB	NATIONALITY	GOALS
Maciej Zurawski	Wisła Kraków	Polish	21
Grzegorg Rasiak	G Dyskobolia G	Polish	14
Cezary Kucharski	Legia Warszawa	Polish	13
Lukasz Sosin	Odra Wodzisław	Polish	12

Polish Cup

2002 FINAL (2 legs)

May 7 – Amica Stadium, Wronki
Amica Wronki 2-4 Wisła Kraków
(Dawidowski 19, Zienczuk 64 pen)   *(Frankowski 55, Kosowski 70, 85, Zurawki 72)*
h/t: 1-0 **Att:** 3,000
Ref: G. Gilewski

May 10 – Wisla Stadium, Krakow
Wisła Kraków 4-0 Amica Wronki
(Frankowski 18, 85, Zurawski 27, Uche 90)
h/t: 2-0 **Att:** 8,000
Ref: J. Granat

Martin Durica of MSK Žilina (in yellow) blocks Trenčin's David Hlava to ensure a 1-0 win and a first title for the small provincial club from south-west Slovakia.

Slovakian Mars Superliga Table 2001–02

CLUB	P	W	D	L	F	A	Pts	
MSK Žilina	33	20	6	7	57	31	66	Champions League
Matador Púchov	33	16	8	9	43	29	56	UEFA CUP
SCP Ružomberok	33	15	8	10	47	35	53	
Inter Bratislava	33	14	8	11	48	37	50	
Slovan Bratislava	33	14	8	11	40	35	50	
Artmedia Petrzalka	33	11	13	9	50	39	46	
Ozeta Dukla Trenčin	33	12	9	12	39	42	45	
Tartan Prešov	33	7	7	19	31	59	28	
1. FC Košice	33	4	12	17	26	61	24	Relegated

Promoted club: Spartak Trnava.
FK VTJ KOBA Senek enter the UEFA Cup as cup winners.

Slovakian International Club Performances 2001–02

CLUB	COMPETITION	PROGRESS
Inter Bratislava	Champions League UEFA Cup	3rd Qualifying Phase 1st round
Slovan Bratislava	UEFA Cup	1st round
Matador Púchov	UEFA Cup	1st round
SCP Ružomberok	UEFA Cup	1st round

Slovakian Top Goalscorers 2001–02

PLAYER	CLUB	NATIONALITY	GOALS
Marek Mintal	MSK Žilina	Slovakian	21
Lubos Pernis	Matador Púchov	Slovakian	15
Robert Vittek	Slovan Bratislava	Slovakian	14
Henrick Bencik	Artmedia Petrzalka	Slovakian	11

Slovakian Cup

2002 FINAL

May 8 – SNP, Povaska Bystrica
Matador
Púchov 1-1 Koba Senec
(Breska 79)   *(Lukác 49)*
(after extra time)
h/t: 0-0 **90 mins:** 1-1
Att: 4,584 **Ref:** Stredak

Koba Senec won 4-2 on penalties

The Legia Warszawa team celebrates its Polish league triumph.

having been forcibly demoted by the Austrian FA. Tirol's misfortune is Admira's good fortune – after a truly appalling season Admira's relegation has been averted. Also leaving will be Lothar Matthäus. In his first season as a coach at Rapid Wien, he led the club to its worst-ever league finish.

There was only ever going to be one champion in Switzerland. After waiting 22 years for another title, Basel took the league at a canter. Christian Gross's side was head and shoulders above the rest of the league, powered by the goals of Argentinian striker

Christian Giminez. Basel completed the double, dispatching Grasshopper-Club 2-1 in the Swiss Cup Final. Outside Basel, Swiss football was beset by financial problems throughout the season, culminating in the Swiss Football Federation's announcement in April that six out of 12 of the teams in the top division (Servette, Lugano, Lausanne-Sports, Neuchâtel Xamax, Sion and Luzern) would not receive a playing license for next season given their dire accounts. Servette looked in even more trouble when backers Canal Plus decided to withdraw their support.

Slovenian Premier League Table 2001–02

CLUB	P	W	D	L	F	A	Pts	
NK Maribor	33	19	9	5	64	23	66	Champions League
Primorje Ajdovščina	33	18	6	9	57	26	60	UEFA Cup
NK Koper	33	15	11	7	45	26	56	
SCT Olimpija Ljubljana	33	14	9	10	38	40	51	
HIT Gorica	33	15	6	12	9	42	51	UEFA Cup (cup winners)
Mura Murska Sobota	33	14	7	12	36	34	49	
NK Publikum	33	14	6	13	50	39	48	
NK Rudar Velenje	33	11	9	13	46	52	42	
Esotec Smartno	33	9	13	11	41	40	40	
Korotan Prevalje	33	9	8	16	27	46	35	
NK Živila Triglav	33	9	5	19	34	60	32	Relegated
NK Domzale	33	3	7	23	26	75	16	Relegated

Promoted clubs: NK Dravograd, Ljubljana.

Slovenian International Club Performances 2001–02

CLUB	COMPETITION	PROGRESS
Nk Maribor	Champions League	2nd Qualifying Phase
HIT Gorica	UEFA Cup	1st Round
Olimpija Ljubljana	UEFA Cup	1st Round

Slovenian Top Goalscorers 2001–02

PLAYER	CLUB	NATIONALITY	GOALS
Romano Obilinovic	Primorje Ajdovščina	Slovenian	17
Samir Duro	NK Maribor	Bosnian	15
Damir Pekic	NK Maribor	Slovenian	14
Senag Tiganj	Olimpija Ljubljana	Slovenian	12

Slovakia's leading player Zlato Zlatovic took the national team to the World Cup but was sent home early for criticizing the coach in public.

Slovenian Cup

2002 FINAL (2 legs)

May 1 – Sportni Park, Nova Gorica
HIT Gorica 4-0 Aluminij
(Krsic 5, Kidricevo
Pus 26, 60,
Srebnic 88)
h/t: 2-0 Att: 700
Ref: Damir

May 8 – Kidricevo, Kidricevo
Aluminij 1-2 HIT Gorica
Kidricevo *(Ekmecic 61,*
(Ceh 54) *Kremenovic 90)*
h/t: 0-0 Att: 1,200
Ref: Drago

Swiss Championship Play-off Table 2001–02

CLUB	P	W	D	L	F	A	Pts	
FC Basel	14	11	0	3	36	16	55	Champions League
Grasshopper-Club	14	7	5	2	28	17	45	UEFA Cup (cup winners)
FC Lugano	14	7	2	5	33	19	42	UEFA Cup
Servette FC	14	6	3	5	25	23	38	UEFA Cup
FC Zurich	14	6	2	6	14	17	35	
FC St. Gallen	14	4	4	6	18	20	34	
BSC Young Boys Berne	14	4	3	7	18	25	31	
FC Sion	14	1	1	12	10	35	21	

The Swiss season is divided into two. The first half of the season is a regular 12-club league with each team playing each other twice. For the second half of the season, the top eight teams go into a final championship league (taking half their points with them) where they play each other twice. The bottom four teams join the top four from the second division in a promotion/relegation league.

Swiss International Club Performances 2001–02

CLUB	COMPETITION	PROGRESS
Grasshopper-Club	Champions League	3rd Qualifying Phase
	UEFA Cup	3rd Round
FC Lugano	Champions League	2nd Qualifying Phase
FC St. Gallen	UEFA Cup	2nd Round
Servette	UEFA Cup	4th Round

Swiss Top Goalscorers 2001–02

PLAYER	CLUB	NATIONALITY	GOALS
Richard Nuñez	Grasshopper-Club	Uruguayan	28
Christian Giminez	FC Basel	Argentinian	27
Julio Rossi	FC Lugano	Argentinian	21
Murat Yakin	FC Basel	Swiss	15

Swiss Cup

2002 FINAL

May 12 – St. Jakob-Park, Basel
FC Basel 2-1 Grasshopper-
(Tum 5, Club
Yakin 113 pen) *(Petric 38)*
(after extra time)
h/t: 1-1 Att: 30,000
Ref: SR Lemba

George Koumantarakis of Basel fires a header towards the Grasshopper-Club goal despite the close attentions of defender Boris Smiljanic. Basel won this league match 4-1 and went on to beat the same team in the Cup Final the following month.

Association Football in Central Europe

CENTRAL EUROPE

1890

1893: Czechoslovakia's oldest clubs, Sparta Praha and Slavia Praha, formed

1896: Prague-based Czech league established

1895

1900

1901: Formation of Czech FA, Českomoravský Fotbalový Svaz

1905

1906: Poland's oldest club, KS Cracovia, formed

1906: Czech affiliation to FIFA

1910

1915: Czech Stredocesky league established

1918: Polish independent republic formed

1919: Formation of Polish FA: Polski Związek Piłki Nóżnej

1915

1920: Czechoslovakia's first international, v Yugoslavia, won 7-0, venue: Antwerp

1920

1921: Poland's first international, v Hungary, lost 0-1, venue: Budapest. First national league

1922: Formation of Czechoslovak FA

1926: First Polish Cup Final

1925

1923: Polish affiliation to FIFA. Czechoslovakian affiliation to FIFA

1930

1925: National Czechoslovak league established and professionalism introduced

1935

1939–44: During war and occupation, Czechoslovak football divided into separate leagues and cups

1940

1939–45: No football in Poland during the war

1945–46: Polish borders radically redrawn, many Polish clubs transferred to Soviet leagues and some German clubs to the Polish league. Communist reorganization of clubs. League re-established

1946–48: Communist takeover and reorganization of Czechoslovak football

1945

1950

1949: League and Cup reorganized on a national basis

1955

1951: Polish Cup re-established

1954: Czechoslovakian affiliation to UEFA. Polish affiliation to UEFA

1960

1961: Czechoslovak Cup established

1965

1970

1993: Czechoslovakia separates into Czech Republic and Slovakia. Independent leagues, cups and FAs created. Separate affiliation to UEFA and FIFA. Legia Warszawa stripped of league title after match-fixing scandal

1975

1976: Czechoslovakia win European Championships

1980

1985

1990

1996: Czech Republic runners-up in European Championships. Widzew Łódź and Legia Warszawa have their grounds closed for a season after worst incidents of football violence in Poland

1995

2000

2005

Key

International football (Czech Republic)	
International football (Poland)	
Affiliation to FIFA	
Affiliation to UEFA	
War	

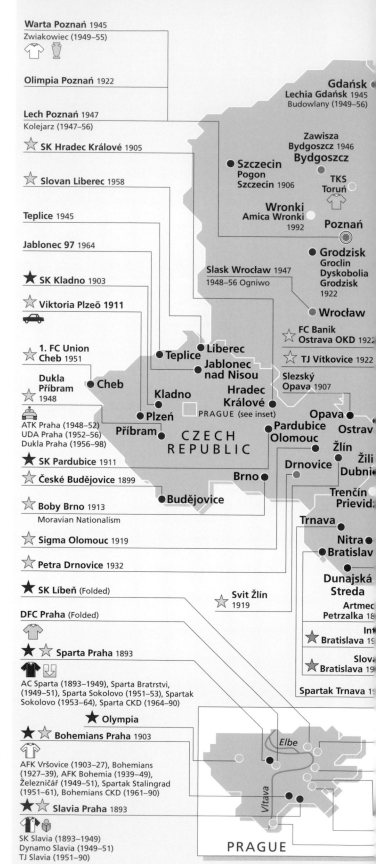

Warta Poznań 1945
Zwiakowiec (1949–55)

Olimpia Poznań 1922

Lech Poznań 1947
Kolejarz (1947–56)

SK Hradec Králové 1905

Slovan Liberec 1958

Teplice 1945

Jablonec 97 1964

SK Kladno 1903

Viktoria Plzeō 1911

1. FC Union Cheb 1951

Dukla Příbram 1948

ATK Praha (1948–52)
UDA Praha (1952–56)
Dukla Praha (1956–98)

SK Pardubice 1911

České Budějovice 1899

Boby Brno 1913
Moravian Nationalism

Sigma Olomouc 1919

Petra Drnovice 1932

SK Líbeň (Folded)

DFC Praha (Folded)

Sparta Praha 1893

AC Sparta (1893–1949), Sparta Bratrstvi, (1949–51), Sparta Sokolovo (1951–53), Spartak Sokolovo (1953–64), Sparta CKD (1964–90)

Olympia

Bohemians Praha 1903

AFK Vršovice (1903–27), Bohemians (1927–39), AFK Bohemia (1939–49), Železničář (1949–51), Spartak Stalingrad (1951–61), Bohemians CKD (1961–90)

Slavia Praha 1893

SK Slavia (1893–1949)
Dynamo Slavia (1949–51)
TJ Slavia (1951–90)

Gdańsk
Lechia Gdańsk 1945
Budowlany (1949–56)

Zawisza Bydgoszcz 1946
Bydgoszcz

Szczecin
Pogon Szczecin 1906

TKS Toruń

Wronki
Amica Wronki 1992

Poznań

Grodzisk
Groclin Dyskobolia Grodzisk 1922

Slask Wrocław 1947
1948–56 Ogniwo

Wrocław

FC Banik Ostrava OKD 1922

TJ Vítkovice 1922

Teplice
Liberec
Jablonec nad Nisou
Hradec Králové

Slezský Opava 1907

Cheb
Kladno
PRAGUE (see inset)

Opava

Plzeň
Příbram

Pardubice
Olomouc
Ostrav

CZECH REPUBLIC

Žlín

Drnovice

Žili
Dubni

Brno

Budějovice

Trenčín
Prievid.

Svit Žlín 1919

Trnava

Nitra
Bratislav

Dunajská Streda
Artmed
Petrzalka 18

In
Bratislava 19

Slov
Bratislava 19

Spartak Trnava 19

Elbe

Vltava

PRAGUE

Central Europe

ORIGINS AND GROWTH OF FOOTBALL

IN BOHEMIA, PRAGUE PRODUCED the first football clubs, Sparta and Slavia, in 1893. A Prague league was running by 1896, followed by the Charity Cup in 1906. With the collapse of the Austro-Hungarian Empire, Czech and Slovak football were brought together and with the coming of professionalism in 1925 a new fully national league was established. Under Communist rule Dukla Praha (now Dukla Příbram) broke the Slavia–Sparta stranglehold with support from the Czech army. Slovan Bratislava also rose to challenge the Prague duopoly. With the separation of the Czech Republic and Slovakia, football in the region divided once again into separate leagues and cup competitions.

Like Czechoslovakia, Poland's football organizations preceded independence. KS Cracovia was formed in 1906 and Wisław (who wore the white star of Polish independence) in 1908, and clubs formed in Warsaw and Katowice before the formation of modern Poland in 1919. The national league was dominated by these three cities until the Second World War. After the war, Polish football was given the usual Communist treatment with name changes, and clubs were allocated to, or taken over by, a variety of state institutions. Under this order Polish football had its golden era, qualifying for every World Cup between 1974 and 1986, reaching the semi-finals in 1974 and 1982.

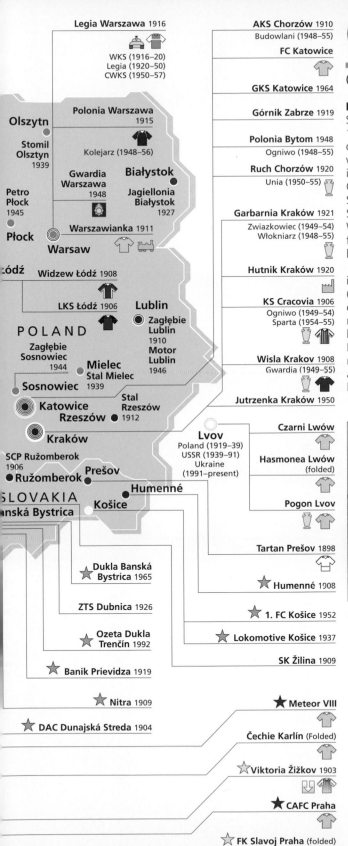

***Dukla Praha** is one of Central Europe's most successful teams. Here the team celebrates a goal against Real Madrid in the 1964 European Cup. However, Dukla lost the tie 6-2 on aggregate.*

Central Europe: The main clubs

Teplice 1945	Team name with year of formation	
●	Club formed before 1912	
●	Club formed 1912–25	
●	Club formed 1925–50	
	Club formed after 1950	
★	Founder members of Prague League 1912	
👕	Founder members of 1925/27 Czech/Polish League	
🏆	Polish champions 1921–39	
☆	Founder members of Czech League 1994	
☆	Founder members of Slovakian League 1994	
	Intellectuals/Universities	
🚗	Linked to Skoda car company	
	Originated from army	
	Railway workers	
	Steel workers	
	Warsaw police	
	Working class	
👕 ●	Colours and date unknown	

Map labels:

Legia Warszawa 1916
WKS (1916–20)
Legia (1920–50)
CWKS (1950–57)

Olsztyn
Stomil Olsztyn 1939

Polonia Warszawa 1915
Kolejarz (1948–56)

Gwardia Warszawa 1948

Petro Płock 1945

Płock

Warszawianka 1911
Warsaw

Białystok
Jagiellonia Białystok 1927

Łódź
Widzew Łódź 1908
LKS Łódź 1906

Lublin
Zagłębie Lublin 1910
Motor Lublin 1946

POLAND

Zagłębie Sosnowiec 1944

Mielec
Stal Mielec 1939

Sosnowiec

Katowice
Rzeszów
Stal Rzeszów 1912

Kraków

SCP Ružomberok 1906
Ružomberok

Prešov

SLOVAKIA
Banská Bystrica

Humenné
Košice

AKS Chorzów 1910
Budowlani (1948–55)
FC Katowice

GKS Katowice 1964

Górnik Zabrze 1919

Polonia Bytom 1948
Ogniwo (1948–55)

Ruch Chorzów 1920
Unia (1950–55)

Garbarnia Kraków 1921
Zwiazkowiec (1949–54)
Włokniarz (1948–55)

Hutnik Kraków 1920

KS Cracovia 1906
Ogniwo (1949–54)
Sparta (1954–55)

Wisla Krakov 1908
Gwardia (1949–55)

Jutrzenka Kraków 1950

Lvov
Poland (1919–39)
USSR (1939–91)
Ukraine (1991–present)

Czarni Lwów

Hasmonea Lwów (folded)

Pogon Lvov

Tartan Prešov 1898

Humenné 1908

Dukla Banská Bystrica 1965

ZTS Dubnica 1926

Ozeta Dukla Trenčín 1992

Banik Prievidza 1919

Nitra 1909

DAC Dunajská Streda 1904

1. FC Košice 1952

Lokomotive Košice 1937

SK Žilina 1909

Meteor VIII

Čechie Karlín (Folded)

Viktoria Žižkov 1903

CAFC Praha

FK Slavoj Praha (folded)

SOUTHEAST EUROPE

Association Football in Southeast Europe

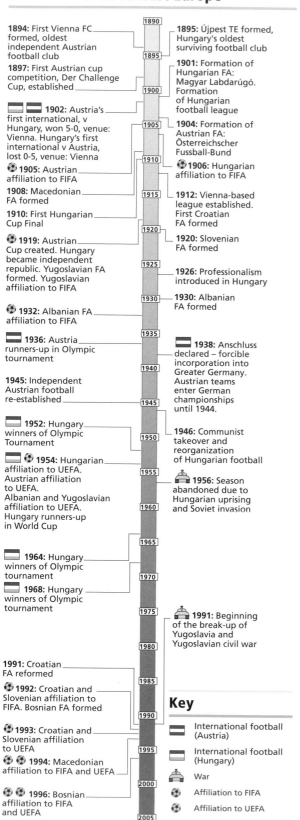

1894: First Vienna FC formed, oldest independent Austrian football club

1897: First Austrian cup competition, Der Challenge Cup, established

1902: Austria's first international, v Hungary, won 5-0, venue: Vienna. Hungary's first international v Austria, lost 0-5, venue: Vienna

1905: Austrian affiliation to FIFA

1908: Macedonian FA formed

1910: First Hungarian Cup Final

1919: Austrian Cup created. Hungary became independent republic. Yugoslavian FA formed. Yugoslavian affiliation to FIFA

1932: Albanian FA affiliation to FIFA

1936: Austria runners-up in Olympic tournament

1945: Independent Austrian football re-established

1952: Hungary winners of Olympic Tournament

1954: Hungarian affiliation to UEFA. Austrian affiliation to UEFA. Albanian and Yugoslavian affiliation to UEFA. Hungary runners-up in World Cup

1964: Hungary winners of Olympic tournament

1968: Hungary winners of Olympic tournament

1991: Croatian FA reformed

1992: Croatian and Slovenian affiliation to FIFA. Bosnian FA formed

1993: Croatian and Slovenian affiliation to UEFA

1994: Macedonian affiliation to FIFA and UEFA

1996: Bosnian affiliation to FIFA and UEFA

1895: Újpest TE formed, Hungary's oldest surviving football club

1901: Formation of Hungarian FA: Magyar Labdarúgó. Formation of Hungarian football league

1904: Formation of Austrian FA: Österreichscher Fussball-Bund

1906: Hungarian affiliation to FIFA

1912: Vienna-based league established. First Croatian FA formed

1920: Slovenian FA formed

1926: Professionalism introduced in Hungary

1930: Albanian FA formed

1938: Anschluss declared – forcible incorporation into Greater Germany. Austrian teams enter German championships until 1944.

1946: Communist takeover and reorganization of Hungarian football

1956: Season abandoned due to Hungarian uprising and Soviet invasion

1991: Beginning of the break-up of Yugoslavia and Yugoslavian civil war

Timeline: 1890, 1895, 1900, 1905, 1910, 1915, 1920, 1925, 1930, 1935, 1940, 1945, 1950, 1955, 1960, 1965, 1970, 1975, 1980, 1985, 1990, 1995, 2000, 2005

Key

- International football (Austria)
- International football (Hungary)
- War
- Affiliation to FIFA
- Affiliation to UEFA

First Vienna FC 1894

Wiener SC 1893

Cricket FV 1894

Wiener AC 1900

Wiener AF 1912

Rapid Wien 1898
Founded as Wiener Arbeiter-Fussballklub till 1899

Hat factory team
FC Wien 1918
Nicholson (1918–32)

FK Austria 1911
Amateure (1911–26), 1973 absorbed Wiener Athletik

Hertha 19
Rudolfshüg... 19
1. Simmering SC Wien 19
Hakoah 19

FC Admira Mödling 1971
Merger of Admira Wien 1905 and Wacker Wien, 1908. Moved from Florisdorf to Maria Enzendorf as FC Admira Wacker then merged with Vfb Mödling 1997

VIENNA

Kremser FC 1919
Vorwärts Steyr 1919
FC Stahl Linz 1949
Linzer ASK 1908
SV Ried 1912
Sturm Graz 1909

VIENN (see inse
Krems
Linz
Maria Enzersdorf
Vfb Mödling 1911
Ried Im Innkreis
Steyr
SV Gloggnitz 1922
Graz
Grazer AK 1902

SW Bregenz 1920
Bregenz
Lustenau
Austria Lustenau 1914

Innsbruck
FC Tirol 1914

Salzburg
Austria Salzberg 1933

AUSTRIA
SK Austria 1920
Klagenfurt

SLOVENIA (see inset)

NK Maribor 1958
Rudar Velenje 1948
SLOVENIA
Feroterm Pohorje 1956
Ruse
Nova Gorica
Celje
Publikum Celje 1946
Ljubljana
Primorje Ajdovščina 1924
Sct Olimpija Ljubljana 1911
Hit Gorica 1938

Varazdin
Zagreb
Istra Pula 1961
Rijeka 1946
Pula

Dinamo Zagreb 1945
Zagreb 1949
Varteks Varaždin 1931
Slaven Belupo Koprivnica 1912
Osijek 1946
Ciballia Vinkovci 1947
Marsonia Slavonski Brod 1909

Sibenik 1932
Split
Hajduk Split 1911

OFK Beograd 1911
Obilic Beograd 1924
Partizan Beograd 1945
Crvena Zvezda Beograd 1945
Cukaricki Beograd 1926
Rad Beograd 1958

Zeleznik Beograd 1930

BELGRADE

Danube

Buducnost Banovici
Rudar Kakanj
Boksit Milici
Zeljeznicar Sarajevo 1921
Sarajevo 1946
Lushnja 1927

Southeast Europe

ORIGINS AND GROWTH OF FOOTBALL

FOOTBALL ARRIVED EARLY in Central and Eastern Europe and rose in popularity quickly with stylish, innovative play. The first football association in Vienna was founded by M.D. Nicholson, a Thomas Cook travel agent, in 1904. In Hungary, clubs emerged in the 1880s and 90s, often from gym clubs. MTK was made up of liberal Jewish defectors from a pro-Hapsburg national gym club. A league was founded in 1901 and a cup competition in 1910.

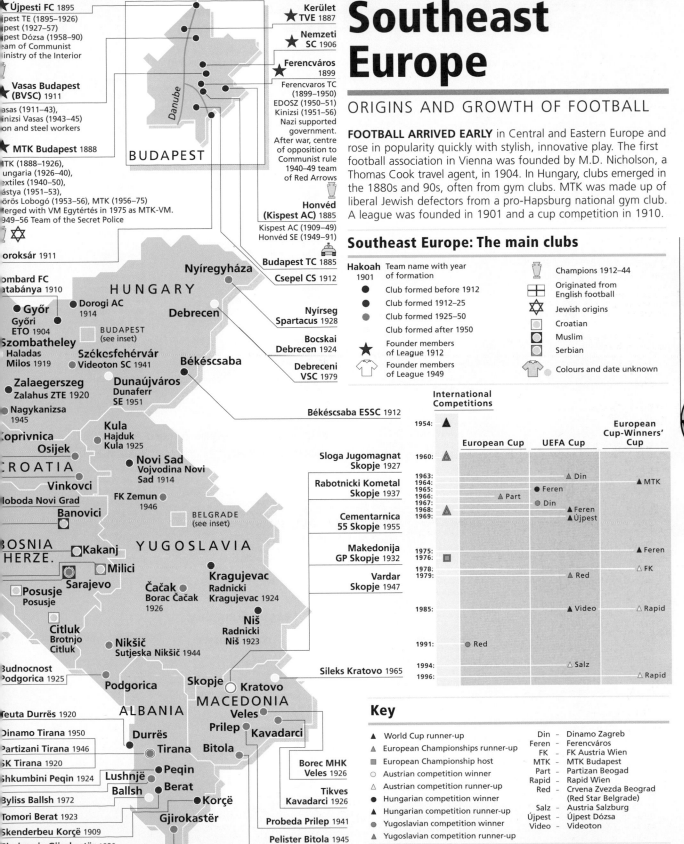

Southeast Europe: The main clubs

Hakoah 1901	Team name with year of formation		Champions 1912–44
●	Club formed before 1912		Originated from English football
●	Club formed 1912–25		Jewish origins
●	Club formed 1925–50		Croatian
●	Club formed after 1950		Muslim
★	Founder members of League 1912		Serbian
	Founder members of League 1949		Colours and date unknown

BUDAPEST

Újpesti FC 1895
Újpest TE (1895–1926)
Újpest (1927–57)
Újpest Dózsa (1958–90)
Team of Communist Ministry of the Interior

Vasas Budapest (BVSC) 1911
Vasas (1911–43),
Kinizsi Vasas (1943–45)
Iron and steel workers

MTK Budapest 1888
MTK (1888–1926),
Hungaria (1926–40),
Textiles (1940–50),
Bástya (1951–53),
Vörös Lobogó (1953–56), MTK (1956–75),
Merged with VM Egyértés in 1975 as MTK-VM.
1949–56 Team of the Secret Police

Soroksár 1911

★ Kerület TVE 1887

★ Nemzeti SC 1906

★ Ferencváros 1899
Ferencvaros TC (1899–1950)
EDOSZ (1950–51)
Kinizsi (1951–56)
Nazi supported government.
After war, centre of opposition to Communist rule 1940–49 team of Red Arrows

Honvéd (Kispest AC) 1885
Kispest AC (1909–49)
Honvéd SE (1949–91)

Budapest TC 1885

Csepel CS 1912

HUNGARY

Nyíregyháza

Lombard FC Tatabánya 1910

Győr
Győri ETO 1904

Dorogi AC 1914

Debrecen

Szombatheley
Haladas Milos 1919

Székesfehérvár
Videoton SC 1941

Békéscsaba

Zalaegerszeg
Zalahus ZTE 1920

Dunaújváros
Dunaferr SE 1951

Nagykanizsa 1945

Nyírség Spartacus 1928

Bocskai Debrecen 1924

Debreceni VSC 1979

Békéscsaba ESSC 1912

CROATIA

Koprivnica

Osijek

Kula
Hajduk Kula 1925

Novi Sad
Vojvodina Novi Sad 1914

Vinkovci

Sloboda Novi Grad

FK Zemun 1946

Banovici

BOSNIA HERZE.

Kakanj

Milici

Sarajevo

Posusje
Posusje

Citluk
Brotnjo Citluk

Budnocnost Podgorica 1925

BELGRADE (see inset)

YUGOSLAVIA

Čačak
Borac Čačak 1926

Kragujevac
Radnicki Kragujevac 1924

Niš
Radnicki Niš 1923

Nikšič
Sutjeska Nikšič 1944

Podgorica

Skopje

Kratovo

Sloga Jugomagnat Skopje 1927

Rabotnicki Kometal Skopje 1937

Cementarnica 55 Skopje 1955

Makedonija GP Skopje 1932

Vardar Skopje 1947

Sileks Kratovo 1965

MACEDONIA

Veles

Prilep

Kavadarci

ALBANIA

Teuta Durrës 1920

Dinamo Tirana 1950

Partizani Tirana 1946

SK Tirana 1920

Shkumbini Peqin 1924

Byliss Ballsh 1972

Tomori Berat 1923

Skenderbeu Korçë 1909

Shqiponja Gjirokastër 1930

Durrës

Tirana

Bitola

Peqin

Lushnjë

Ballsh

Berat

Korçë

Gjirokastër

Borec MHK Veles 1926

Tikves Kavadarci 1926

Probeda Prilep 1941

Pelister Bitola 1945

International Competitions

	European Cup	UEFA Cup	European Cup-Winners' Cup
1954:	▲		
1960:	▲		
1963:		△ Din	
1964:			▲ MTK
1965:		▲ Part	
1966:		● Feren	
1967:	▲	● Din	
1968:	▲	▲ Feren	
1969:		▲ Újpest	
1975:			▲ Feren
1976:	■		
1978:			△ FK
1979:		▲ Red	
1985:		▲ Video	△ Rapid
1991:	● Red		
1994:			△ Salz
1996:			△ Rapid

Key

- ▲ World Cup runner-up
- △ European Championships runner-up
- ■ European Championship host
- ○ Austrian competition winner
- △ Austrian competition runner-up
- ● Hungarian competition winner
- ▲ Hungarian competition runner-up
- ● Yugoslavian competition winner
- ▲ Yugoslavian competition runner-up

- Din – Dinamo Zagreb
- Feren – Ferencváros
- FK – FK Austria Wien
- MTK – MTK Budapest
- Part – Partizan Beograd
- Rapid – Rapid Wien
- Red – Crvena Zvezda Beograd (Red Star Belgrade)
- Salz – Austria Salzburg
- Újpest – Újpest Dózsa
- Video – Videoton

Czech Republic (including former Czechoslovakia)

Českomoravský Fotbalový Svaz
Founded: 1901
Joined FIFA: 1906
Joined UEFA: 1954

FOOTBALL PROSPERED EARLY in the 20th century in this Bohemian province of the Austro-Hungarian Empire; the Prague-based Středočeský League and Czech Charity Cup were up and running before the First World War. With the postwar creation of Czechoslovakia, Bohemian, Moravian and Slovakian football were fused to create a professional Czech league in 1925.

During the Second World War, Germany absorbed part of Czechoslovakia, and created a newly independent, but German, satellite: Slovakia. Separate Slovak and Czech leagues and cups were played during the war. The Czechoslovak league was recreated under the Communists in 1946 and remained until the separation of the Czech Republic and Slovakia in 1993, after which two separate national leagues have operated.

Separate cups for the two nations were established under the Communists with a play-off to decide the Czechoslovakian Cup.

Czech League Record 1925–93

SEASON	CHAMPIONS	RUNNERS-UP
1925	SK Slavia Praha	AC Sparta Praha
1926	AC Sparta Praha	SK Slavia Praha
1927	AC Sparta Praha	SK Slavia Praha
1928	Victoria Žižkov	SK Slavia Praha
1929	SK Slavia Praha	Victoria Žižkov
1930	SK Slavia Praha	AC Sparta Praha
1931	SK Slavia Praha	AC Sparta Praha
1932	AC Sparta Praha	SK Slavia Praha
1933	SK Slavia Praha	AC Sparta Praha
1934	SK Slavia Praha	AC Sparta Praha
1935	SK Slavia Praha	AC Sparta Praha
1936	AC Sparta Praha	SK Slavia Praha
1937	SK Slavia Praha	AC Sparta Praha
1938	AC Sparta Praha	SK Slavia Praha
1939	AC Sparta Praha	SK Slavia Praha
1940	SK Slavia Praha	AC Sparta Praha
1941	SK Slavia Praha	SK Plzeň
1942	SK Slavia Praha	SK Prostějov
1943	SK Slavia Praha	AC Sparta Praha
1944	AC Sparta Praha	SK Slavia Praha
1945	no championship	
1946	AC Sparta Praha	SK Slavia Praha
1947	SK Slavia Praha	AC Sparta Praha
1948	AC Sparta Praha	SK Slavia Praha
1948*	Dynamo Slavia Praha	Škoda Plzeň
1949	NV Bratislava	Bratrstvi Sparta Praha
1950	NV Bratislava	Bratrstvi Sparta Praha
1951	NV Bratislava	Sparta CKD Praha
1952	Sparta CKD Sokolovo	NV Bratislava
1953	ÚDA Praha	Spartak Sokolovo Praha
1954	Spartak Sokolovo Praha	Baník Ostrava
1955	Slovan Bratislava	ÚDA Praha
1956	Dukla Praha	Slovan Bratislava
1957*		
1958	Dukla Praha	Spartak Sokolovo Praha
1959	RH Bratislava	Dukla Praha
1960	Spartak Hradec Králové	Slovan Bratislava
1961	Dukla Praha	RH Bratislava
1962	Dukla Praha	Slovan Nitra
1963	Dukla Praha	Jednota Trenčín
1964	Dukla Praha	Slovan Bratislava
1965	Sparta Praha	Tatran Prešov
1966	Dukla Praha	Sparta Praha

Czech League Record (*continued*)

SEASON	CHAMPIONS	RUNNERS-UP
1967	Sparta Praha	Slovan Bratislava
1968	Spartak Trnava	Slovan Bratislava
1969	Spartak Trnava	Slovan Bratislava
1970	Slovan Bratislava	Spartak Trnava
1971	Spartak Trnava	VSS Košice
1972	Spartak Trnava	Slovan Bratislava
1973	Spartak Trnava	Tatran Prešov
1974	Slovan Bratislava	Dukla Praha
1975	Slovan Bratislava	Inter Bratislava
1976	Baník Ostrava	Slovan Bratislava
1977	Dukla Praha	Inter Bratislava
1978	ZJS Brno	Dukla Praha
1979	Dukla Praha	Baník Ostrava
1980	Baník Ostrava	ZJS Brno
1981	Baník Ostrava	Dukla Praha
1982	Dukla Praha	Baník Ostrava
1983	Bohemians Praha	Baník Ostrava
1984	Sparta Praha	Dukla Praha
1985	Sparta Praha	Bohemians Praha
1986	FC Vítkovice	Sparta Praha
1987	Sparta Praha	FC Vítkovice
1988	Sparta Praha	Dukla Praha
1989	Sparta Praha	Baník Ostrava
1990	Sparta Praha	Baník Ostrava
1991	Sparta Praha	Slovan Bratislava
1992	Slovan Bratislava	Sparta Praha
1993	Sparta Praha	Slavia Praha

* Between 1948 and 1956 the Czech League was played during the summer months. The 1957–58 season result is therefore given as 1958.

Czech Republic League Record 1994–2002

SEASON	CHAMPIONS	RUNNERS-UP
1994	Sparta Praha	Slavia Praha
1995	Sparta Praha	Slavia Praha
1996	Slavia Praha	Sigma Olomouc
1997	Sparta Praha	Slavia Praha
1998	Sparta Praha	Slavia Praha
1999	Sparta Praha	FK Teplice
2000	Sparta Praha	Slavia Praha
2001	Sparta Praha	Slavia Praha
2002	Slovan Liberec	Sparta Praha

Czech League Summary

TEAM	TOTALS	CHAMPIONS & RUNNERS-UP (BOLD) (*ITALICS*)
Sparta Praha (includes AC Sparta Praha, Bratrstvi Sparta Praha, Sparta CKD Praha, Sparta CKD Sokolovo and Spartak Sokolovo)	**28**, *19*	*1925*, **26**, **27**, **30**, **31**, **32**, **33–35**, **36**, **37**, **38**, **39**, *40*, *43*, **44**, **46**, *47*, **48**, *49–51*, **52**, *53*, **54**, *58*, **65**, *66*, **67**, **84**, **85**, *86*, **87–91**, *92*, **93–95**, **97–2001**, *02*
Slavia Praha (includes SK Slavia Praha and Dynamo Slavia Praha)	**15**, *17*	**1925**, *26–28*, **29–31**, *32*, **33–35**, *36*, **37**, *38*, **39**, **40–43**, *44*, **46**, *47*, *48*, **48***, *93–95*, **96**, *97*, *98*, *2000*, *01*
Marila Příbram (includes ÚDA Praha and Dukla Praha)	**11**, *7*	**1953**, *55*, **56**, **58**, **59**, **61–64**, *66*, **74**, *77*, **78**, **79**, **81**, **82**, *84*, **88**

This summary only features the top three clubs in the Czech League. For a full list of league champions and runners-up please see the League Records opposite.

CZECH REPUBLIC

Czech Cup Record 1918–93

YEAR	WINNERS	SCORE	RUNNERS-UP
1918	Sparta Praha	4-1	Slavia Praha
1919	Sparta Praha	2-0	Viktoria Žižkov
1920	Sparta Praha	5-1	Viktoria Žižkov
1921	Viktoria Žižkov	3-0	Sparta Praha
1922	Slavia Praha	3-2	Chechie Karlín
1923	Sparta Praha	3-1	Slavia Praha
1924	Sparta Praha	5-1	AFK Vršovice
1925	Sparta Praha	7-0	CAFC Vinohrady
1926	Slavia Praha	10-0	CAFC Vinohrady
1927	Slavia Praha	1-0	Sparta Praha
1928	Slavia Praha	1-1, (replay) 1-1, (replay) 3-2	Sparta Praha
1929	Viktoria Žižkov	3-1	SK Libeň
1930	Slavia Praha	4-2	SK Kladno
1931	Sparta Praha	3-1	Slavia Praha
1932	Slavia Praha	2-1	Sparta Praha
1933	Viktoria Žižkov	2-1	Sparta Praha
1934	Sparta Praha	6-0	SK Kladno
1935	Slavia Praha	4-1	Bohemians Praha
1936	Sparta Praha	1-1, (replay) 1-0	Slavia Praha
1937–39	no competition		
1940	Viktoria Žižkov	5-3	Sparta Praha
1940*	ASO Olomouc	3-1, 2-1 (2 legs)	SK Prostějov
1941	Slavia Praha	13-2	SS Plincner
1941*	Slavia Praha	2-3, 6-3 (2 legs)	Viktoria Plzeň
1942	Bohemians Praha	8-6	Sparta Praha
1942*	Slavia Praha	5-2, 5-5 (2 legs)	Bohemians Praha
1943*	Sparta Praha	3-1, 7-1 (2 legs)	Viktoria Plzeň
1944*	Sparta Praha	4-2, 4-3 (2 legs)	Viktoria Plzeň
1945	Slavia Praha	1-1, 5-2 (2 legs)	SK Rakovník
1946	Sparta Praha	6-0, 3-0 (2 legs)	Slezská Ostrava
1947–50	no competition		
1951	Kovosmalt Trnava	1-0	Armaturka Ústi
1952	ATK Praha	4-3	Sokol Hradec Králové
1953–54	no competition		
1955	Slovan Bratislava	2-0	ÚDA Praha
1956–59	no competition		
1960	RH Brno	3-1	Dynamo Praha
1961	Dukla Praha	3-0	Dynamo Žilina
1962	Slovan Bratislava	1-1, 4-1 (2 legs)	Dukla Praha
1963	Slovan Bratislava	0-0, 9-0 (2 legs)	Dynamo Praha
1964	Spartak Praha Solokovo	4-1	VSS Košice
1965	Dukla Praha	0-0 (aet)(5-3 pens)	Slovan Bratislava
1966	Dukla Praha	2-1, 4-0	Tatran Prešov
1967	Spartak Trnava	2-4, 2-0 (5-4 pens)	Sparta Praha
1968	Slovan Bratislava	0-1, 2-0	Dukla Praha
1969	Dukla Praha	1-1, 1-0	VCHZ Pardubice
1970	TJ Gottwaldov	3-3, 0-0 (4-3 pens)	Slovan Bratislava
1971	Spartak Trnava	2-1, 5-1	Škoda Plzeň
1972	Sparta Praha	0-1, 4-3 (aet)(4-3 pens)	Slovan Bratislava
1973	Baník Ostrava	1-2, 3-1	VSS Košice
1974	Slovan Bratislava	0-1, 1-0 (aet)(4-3 pens)	Slavia Praha
1975	Spartak Trnava	3-1, 1-0	Sparta Praha
1976	Sparta Praha	3-2, 1-0	Slovan Bratislava
1977	Lokomotíva Košice	2-1	Sklo Union Teplice
1978	Baník Ostrava	1-0	Jednota Trenčín
1979	Lokomotíva Košice	2-1	Baník Ostrava
1980	Sparta Praha	2-0	ZTS Košice
1981	Dukla Praha	4-1	Dukla Banská Bystrica
1982	Slovan Bratislava	0-0 (aet)(4-2 pens)	Bohemians Praha
1983	Dukla Praha	2-1	Slovan Bratislava
1984	Sparta Praha	4-2	Inter Bratislava
1985	Dukla Praha	3-2	Lokomotíva Košice
1986	Spartak Trnava	1-1 (aet)(4-3 pens)	Sparta Praha
1987	DAC Dunajská Streda	0-0 (aet)(3-2 pens)	Sparta Praha
1988	Sparta Praha	2-0	Inter Bratislava
1989	Sparta Praha	3-0	Slovan Bratislava
1990	Dukla Praha	1-1 (aet)(5-4 pens)	Inter Bratislava
1991	Baník Ostrava	6-1	Spartak Trnava

Czech Cup Record (*continued*)

YEAR	WINNERS	SCORE	RUNNERS-UP
1992	Sparta Praha	2-1	Tatran Prešov
1993	1. FC Košice	5-1	Sparta Praha

* Denotes results in the short-lived Cesky' Pohár (Czech Cup).

Czech Republic Cup Record 1994–2002

YEAR	WINNERS	SCORE	RUNNERS-UP
1994	Viktoria Žižkov	2-2 (aet)(6-5 pens)	Sparta Praha
1995	SK Hradec Králové	0-0 (aet)(3-1 pens)	Viktoria Žižkov
1996	Sparta Praha	4-0	FC Petra Drnovice
1997	Slavia Praha	1-0 (aet)	FK Dukla Praha
1998	FK Jablonec	2-1 (asdet)	FC Petra Drnovice
1999	Slavia Praha	1-0 (asdet)	FC Slovan Liberec
2000	FC Slovan Liberec	2-1	Baník Ratíškovice
2001	Viktoria Žižkov	2-1 (aet)	Sparta Praha
2002	Slavia Praha	2-1	Sparta Praha

Czech Cup Summary

TEAM	TOTALS	WINNERS & RUNNERS-UP (BOLD) (*ITALICS*)
Sparta Praha (includes Spartak Praha Sokolovo)	21, 16	**1918–20**, **21**, **23–25**, **27**, **28**, **31**, **32**, **33**, **34**, **36**, **40**, **41***, **42**, **43***, **44***, **46**, **64**, **67**, **72**, **75**, **76**, **80**, **84**, *86*, *87*, *88*, *89*, *92*, *93*, *94*, *96*, **2001**, *02*
Slavia Praha (includes Dynamo Praha)	14, 7	*1918*, **22**, **23**, **26–28**, **30**, *31*, **32**, **35**, **36**, **41**, **41***, *42**, **45**, *60*, *63*, **74**, *97*, *99*, **2002**
Marila Příbram (includes ÚDA Praha, and Dukla Praha)	8, 3	*1955*, **61**, *62*, **65**, **66**, *68*, **69**, **81**, **83**, **85**, **90**
Slovan Bratislava (includes Internacional Bratislava)	6, 9	**1955**, **62**, **63**, *65*, **68**, *70*, *72*, **74**, *76*, **82**, *83*, *84*, *88–90*
Viktoria Žižkov	6, 3	*1919*, *20*, **21**, **29**, **33**, **40**, **94**, *95*, **2001**
Spartak Trnava	4, 1	**1967**, **71**, **75**, **86**, *91*
Baník Ostrava	3, 1	**1973**, **78**, *79*, **91**
Lokomotíva Košice	2, 1	**1977**, *79*, *85*

This summary only features clubs that have won the Czech Cup two or more times. For a full list of league champions and runners-up please see the Cup Record left.

Slovakia

Slovensky Futbalovy Zvaz
Founded: 1938
Joined FIFA: 1994
Joined UEFA: 1993

SEASON	LEAGUE CHAMPIONS
1998	1. FC Košice
1999	Slovan Bratislava
2000	Internacional Bratislava
2001	Internacional Bratislava
2002	MSK Zilina

YEAR	CUP WINNERS
1998	Spartak Trnava
1999	Slovan Bratislava
2000	Internacional Bratislava
2001	Internacional Bratislava
2002	Koba Senec

Though football has been played in Slovakia since the late 19th century, it has mostly been part of Czechoslovakian football. When Slovakia gained political independence from Czechoslovakia in 1993, a national 'Superliga' was formed. A Slovakian Cup started in 1970.

CZECH REPUBLIC, SLOVAKIA

Hungary

Magyar Labdarúgó Szövetség
Founded: 1901
Joined FIFA: 1906
Joined UEFA: 1954

THE HUNGARIAN FOOTBALL ASSOCIATION and the league championship were both established in 1901, but drew on a decade's competitive football firmly centred on Budapest. Hungarian football was always quite separate from any other part of the Austro-Hungarian Empire, which disintegrated in 1918. The amateur years (1901–26) were dominated by the Budapest teams MTK Budapest and Ferencváros, and saw the establishment of a national cup competition in 1910. During the Second World War, the league carried on until 1944, with teams from outside Hungary. The 1944 champions, Nagyváradi AC, were from north-western Romania.

After the war, domestic football was treated to the usual Communist takeover and reorganization. Not surprisingly, the army-backed team Honvéd dominated the era. The 1956 uprising against both Soviet occupiers and homegrown Communists saw the league abandoned and the rapid departure of star players Puskas, Kocis and Czibor for Spain. The final decades of Communist rule saw Honvéd and Ujpesti in the forefront of the Hungarian league.

The post-Communist era has seen a return of MTK (now called MTK Hungária FC) and Ferencváros to prominence, though woeful finances, betting scandals and stadium violence have left all in the league struggling.

Hungarian Amateur League Record 1901–26

SEASON	CHAMPIONS	RUNNERS-UP
1901	BTC	MUE
1902	BTC	FTC
1903	FTC	BTC
1904	MTK	FTC
1905	FTC	Postas
1906	no championship	
1907	FTC	MAC
1908	MTK	FTC
1909	FTC	MAC
1910	FTC	MTK
1911	FTC	MTK
1912	FTC	MTK
1913	FTC	MTK
1914	MTK	FTC
1915–16	no championship	
1917	MTK	Törekvés
1918	MTK	FTC
1919	MTK	FTC
1920	MTK	KAC
1921	MTK	ÚTE
1922	MTK	FTC
1923	MTK	ÚTE
1924	MTK	FTC
1925	MTK	FTC
1926	FTC	MTK

Hungarian Professional League Record 1927–2002

SEASON	CHAMPIONS	RUNNERS-UP
1927	Ferencváros	Újpest
1928	Ferencváros	Hungária
1929	Hungária	Ferencváros
1930	Újpest	Ferencváros

Hungarian League Record (*continued*)

SEASON	CHAMPIONS	RUNNERS-UP
1931	Újpest	Hungária
1932	Ferencváros	Újpest
1933	Újpest	Hungária
1934	Ferencváros	Újpest
1935	Ujpest	Ferencváros
1936	Hungária	Újpest
1937	Hungária	Ferencváros
1938	Ferencváros	Újpest
1939	Újpest	Ferencváros
1940	Ferencváros	Hungária
1941	Ferencváros	Újpest
1942	Csepeli WMFC	Újpest
1943	Csepeli WMFC	Nagyváradi AC
1944	Nagyváradi AC	Ferencváros
1945	no championship	
1946	Újpest	Vasas
1947	Újpest	Kispest
1948	Csepel	Vasas
1949	Ferencváros	Hungária
1950	Honvéd	EDOSZ
1950*	Honvéd	Textiles
1951	Bástya	Honvéd
1952	Honvéd	Bástya
1953	Vörös Lobogó	Honvéd
1954	Honvéd	Vörös Lobogó
1955	Honvéd	Vörös Lobogó
1956	no championship**	
1957	Vasas SC	Hungária
1958	MTK	Honvéd
1959	Csepel	MTK
1960	Újpest Dozsa	Ferencváros
1961	Vasas SC	Újpest Dozsa
1962	Vasas SC	Újpest Dozsa
1963	Ferencváros	MTK
1963*	Győri V. ETO	Honvéd
1964	Ferencváros	Honvéd
1965	Vasas SC	Ferencváros
1966	Vasas SC	Ferencváros
1967	Ferencváros	Újpest Dozsa
1968	Ferencváros	Újpest Dozsa
1969	Újpest Dozsa	Honvéd
1970	Újpest Dozsa	Ferencváros
1971	Újpest Dozsa	Ferencváros
1972	Újpest Dozsa	Honvéd
1973	Újpest Dozsa	Ferencváros
1974	Újpest Dozsa	Ferencváros
1975	Újpest Dozsa	Honvéd
1976	Ferencváros	Videoton
1977	Vasas SC	Újpest Dozsa
1978	Újpest Dozsa	Honvéd
1979	Újpest Dozsa	Ferencváros
1980	Honvéd	Újpest Dozsa
1981	Ferencváros	Tatabánya
1982	Rába ETO Győr	Ferencváros
1983	Rába ETO Győr	Ferencváros
1984	Honvéd	Rába ETO Győr
1985	Honvéd	Rába ETO Győr
1986	Honvéd	PMSC
1987	MTK-VM	Újpest Dozsa
1988	Honvéd	Tatabánya
1989	Honvéd	Ferencváros
1990	Újpest Dozsa	MTK-VM
1991	Honvéd	Ferencváros
1992	Ferencváros	Vác FC Samsung
1993	Kispest-Honvéd	Vác FC Samsung
1994	Vác FC Samsung	Kispest HFC
1995	Ferencváros	ÚTE
1996	Ferencváros	BVSC

Hungarian League Record (*continued*)

SEASON	CHAMPIONS	RUNNERS-UP
1997	MTK	ÚTE
1998	Újpesti FC	Ferencváros
1999	MTK Hungária FC	Ferencváros
2000	Dunaferr FC	MTK Hungária FC
2001	Ferencváros	Dunaferr FC
2002	Zalahús Zte FC	Ferencváros

* Extra autumn leagues played during these years.
** League championship was abandoned following the Soviet invasion.

Hungarian League Summary

TEAM	TOTALS	CHAMPIONS & RUNNERS-UP (BOLD) (*ITALICS*)
Ferencváros (includes FTC and EDOSZ)	27, *31*	*1902*, **03**, *04*, **05**, *07*, *08*, **09–13**, *14*, *18*, *19*, *22*, *24*, *25*, **26–28**, *29*, *30*, **32**, **34**, *35*, *37*, **38**, *39*, **40**, **41**, *44*, **49**, *50*, *60*, **63**, **64**, *65*, *66*, **67**, **68**, *70*, *71*, *73*, *74*, **76**, *79*, **81**, *82*, *83*, *89*, *91*, **92**, **95**, **96**, *98*, *99*, **2001**, *02*
MTK Hungária FC (includes MTK, Hungária, Vörös Lobogó, Bástya, MTK-VM and Textiles)	21, *18*	**1904**, **08**, **10–13**, **14**, **17–25**, *26*, *28*, **29**, *31*, *33*, **36**, **37**, *40*, *49*, **50***, **51**, *52*, **53**, *54*, *55*, *57*, **58**, *59*, *63*, **87**, **90**, **97**, **99**, *2000*
Újpesti FC (includes ÚTE, Újpest and Újpest Dozsa)	19, *18*	*1921*, *23*, *27*, **30**, **31**, *32*, **33**, *34*, **35**, *36*, **38**, **39**, *41*, *42*, **46**, **47**, **60**, *61*, *62*, *67*, *68*, **69–75**, *77*, **78**, *79*, *80*, *87*, **90**, *95*, *97*, **98**
Kispest-Honvéd FC (includes Kispest, Kispest HFC and Honvéd)	13, *11*	*1947*, **50**, **50***, *51*, **52**, *53*, **54**, *55*, *58*, **63***, **64**, *69*, *72*, *75*, *78*, **80**, **84–86**, **88**, **89**, **91**, **93**, *94*

* Denotes honours in extra autumn leagues.
This summary only features the top four clubs in the Hungarian League. For a full list of league champions and runners-up please see the League Record above.

Hungarian Cup Record 1910–2002

YEAR	WINNERS	SCORE	RUNNERS-UP
1910	MTK	1-1, (replay) 3-1	BTC
1911	MTK	1-0	MAC
1912	MTK	w/o	FTC
1913	FTC	2-1	BAK
1914	MTK	4-0	MAC
1915–21		no competition	
1922	FTC	2-2, (replay) 1-0	ÚTE
1923	MTK	4-1	ÚTE
1924		no competition	
1925	MTK	4-0	ÚTE
1926	Kispest AC	1-1, (replay) 3-2 (aet)	Budapest EAC
1927	Ferencváros	3-0	Újpest
1928	Ferencváros	5-1	Attila Miskolc
1929		no competition	
1930	Bocskai Debrecen	5-1	Bástya Szeged
1931	Kerület TVE	4-1	Ferencváros
1932	Hungária	1-1, (replay) 4-3	Ferencváros
1933	Ferencváros	1-1	Újpest
1934	Soroksar	2-2, (replay) 1-1, (replay) 2-0	BSZKRT
1935	Ferencváros	2-1	Hungária
1936–40		no competition	
1941	Szolnoki MAV	3-0	Salgótarján BTC
1942	Ferencváros	6-2	DIMAVAG
1943	Ferencváros	3-0	Salgótarján BTC
1944	Ferencváros	2-2, (replay) 3-1	Kolozsvári AC

Hungarian Cup Record (*continued*)

YEAR	WINNERS	SCORE	RUNNERS-UP
1945–51		no competition	
1952	Bástya	3-2	Dorogi AC
1953–54		no competition	
1955	Vasas	3-2	Honvéd
1956	Ferencváros	2-1	Salgótarján BTC
1957–63		no competition	
1964	Honvéd	1-0	Győri V. ETO
1965	Győri V. ETO	4-0	Diósgyőri VTK
1966	Győri V. ETO	1-1, (replay) 3-2	Ferencváros
1967	Győri V. ETO	1-0	Salgótarján BTC
1968	MTK	2-1	Honvéd
1969	Újpest Dozsa	3-1	Honvéd
1970	Újpest Dozsa	3-2	Komio Bányász
1971		no competition	
1972	Ferencváros	2-1	Tatabánya Bányász
1973	Vasas	4-3	Honvéd
1974	Ferencváros	3-1	Komio Bányász
1975	Újpest Dozsa	3-2	Haladás VSE
1976	Ferencváros	1-0	MTK-VM
1977	Diósgyőri VTK	*	Ferencváros
1978	Ferencváros	4-2	Pécsi MSC
1979	Rába ETO Győr	1-0	Ferencváros
1980	Diósgyőri VTK	3-1	Vasas
1981	Vasas	1-0	Diósgyőri VTK
1982	Újpest Dozsa	2-0	Videoton
1983	Újpest Dozsa	3-2	Honvéd
1984	Siófoki Bányász	2-1	Rába ETO Győr
1985	Honvéd	5-0	Tatabánya Bányász
1986	Vasas	0-0 (5-4 pens)	Ferencváros
1987	Újpest Dozsa	3-2	Pécsi MSC
1988	Békéscsaba ESSC	3-2	Honvéd
1989	Honvéd	1-0	Ferencváros
1990	Pécsi MSC	2-0	Honvéd
1991	Ferencváros	1-0	Vác Izzo FC
1992	Újpest Dozsa	1-0	Vác FC Samsung
1993	Ferencváros	1-1, (replay) 1-1 (5-3 pens)	Szombathely Haladás VSE
1994	Ferencváros	3-0, 2-1 (2 legs)	Honvéd
1995	Ferencváros	2-0, 4-3 (2 legs)	Vác FC Samsung
1996	Honvéd	1-0, 2-0 (2 legs)	BVSC Dreher
1997	MTK Hungária FC	6-0, 2-0 (2 legs)	BVSC Budapest
1998	MTK Hungária FC	1-0	Újpesti FC
1999	Debreceni VSC	2-1	Lombard FC Tatabánya
2000	MTK Hungária FC	3-1	Vasas DH
2001	Debreceni VSC	5-2	Videoton
2002	Újpesti FC	2-1	Szombathely Haladás VSE

w/o denotes walk over
* A league format was used to determine the winner of the 1977 cup.

Hungarian Cup Summary

TEAM	TOTALS	WINNERS & RUNNERS-UP (BOLD) (*ITALICS*)
Ferencváros (includes FTC)	18, *8*	*1912*, **13**, **22**, **27**, **28**, *31*, *32*, **33**, **35**, **42–44**, **56**, *66*, **72**, **74**, **76**, *77*, *78*, *79*, *86*, **89**, **91**, **93–95**
MTK Hungária FC (includes MTK, Hungária, Bástya and MTK-VM)	12, *2*	**1910–12**, **14**, **23**, **25**, **32**, *35*, **52**, **68**, *76*, **97**, **98**, **2000**
Újpesti FC (includes ÚTE, Újpest and Újpest Dozsa)	8, *6*	*1922*, *23*, *25*, *27*, *33*, **69**, **70**, **75**, **82**, **83**, **87**, **92**, *98*, **2002**

This summary only features the top three clubs in the Hungarian Cup. For a full list of cup winners and runners-up please see the Cup Record above.

Poland

Polski Związek Piłki Nóżnej
Founded: 1919
Joined FIFA: 1923
Joined UEFA: 1954

FOOTBALL ARRIVED IN POLAND before it became a nation state. While the game took off in the cities of Łódź, Kraków and Warsaw in the early 20th century, the modern Polish state did not emerge until after the First World War. Carved out of parts of the German, Russian and Austrian empires, the new Poland quickly acquired a football association in 1919, and a national league followed two years later. However, Poland's borders have not stayed still since then, and the Polish league is littered with clubs who are now located in other states. Pogoń Lwów – who won four championships in the 1920s – comes from what was once the Soviet Union and is now the Ukraine. The city of Gdańsk (previously Danzig), home to several top teams, was once part of Germany as were Szczecin and Wrocław (previously Stettin and Breslau).

Cup football was slower in coming to Poland, with a single tournament held in 1926 and then nothing until the Communist-initiated Puchar Polski began in 1951. Alongside the new cup competition, Poland's new Communist rulers reorganized football at every level with extensive changes of clubs' names and control. The collapse of the Communist regime saw a further swathe of name changes and increasing problems of crowd violence. The latter culminated in October 1996, with a riot between fans of Widzew Łódź and Legia Warszawa, which resulted in each team's stadium being closed for the rest of the season.

The current league consists of an 18-club top flight and two 18-club second divisions, one based in the east of the country and one in the west. Four teams are relegated from the first division, replaced by promotions for the winners and runners-up from the regional leagues. There are currently plans to radically reduce the number of teams in the top flight.

Polish League Record 1921–2002

SEASON	CHAMPIONS	RUNNERS-UP
1921	Cracovia Kraków	Polonia Warszawa
1922	Pogoń Lwów	Warta Poznań
1923	Pogoń Lwów	Wisła Kraków
1924	*no championship*	
1925	Pogoń Lwów	Warta Poznań
1926	Pogoń Lwów	Polonia Warszawa
1927	Wisła Kraków	I.FC Katowice
1928	Wisła Kraków	Warta Poznań
1929	Warta Poznań	Garbarnia Kraków
1930	Cracovia Kraków	Wisła Kraków
1931	Garbarnia Kraków	Wisła Kraków
1932	Cracovia Kraków	Pogoń Lwów
1933	Ruch Chorzów	Pogoń Lwów
1934	Ruch Chorzów	Cracovia Kraków
1935	Ruch Chorzów	Pogoń Lwów
1936	Ruch Chorzów	Wisła Kraków
1937	Cracovia Kraków	AKS Chorzów
1938	Ruch Chorzów	Warta Poznań
1939–45	*no championship*	
1946	Polonia Warszawa	Warta Poznań
1947	Warta Poznań	Wisła Kraków
1948	Cracovia Kraków	Wisła Kraków
1949	Wisła Kraków	Ogniwo Kraków
1950	Wisła Kraków	Ruch Chorzów
1951	Ruch Chorzów*	

Polish League Record (*continued*)

SEASON	CHAMPIONS	RUNNERS-UP
1952	Ruch Chorzów	Ogniwo Kraków
1953	Ruch Chorzów	Wawel Kraków
1954	Polonia Bytom	LKS Łódź
1955	Legia Warszawa	Stal Sosnowiec
1956	Legia Warszawa	Ruch Chorzów
1957	Górnik Zabrze	Gwardia Warsawa
1958	LKS Łódź	Polonia Bytom
1959	Górnik Zabrze	Polonia Bytom
1960	Ruch Chorzów	Legia Warszawa
1961	Górnik Zabrze	Polonia Bytom
1962	Polonia Bytom	Górnik Zabrze
1963	Górnik Zabrze	Ruch Chorzów
1964	Górnik Zabrze	Zagłębie Sosnowiec
1965	Górnik Zabrze	Szombierkj Bytom
1966	Górnik Zabrze	Wisła Kraków
1967	Górnik Zabrze	Zagłębie Sosnowiec
1968	Ruch Chorzów	Legia Warszawa
1969	Legia Warszawa	Górnik Zabrze
1970	Legia Warszawa	Ruch Chorzów
1971	Górnik Zabrze	Legia Warszawa
1972	Górnik Zabrze	Zagłębie Sosnowiec
1973	Stal Mielec	Ruch Chorzów
1974	Ruch Chorzów	Górnik Zabrze
1975	Ruch Chorzów	Stal Mielec
1976	Stal Mielec	GKS Tychy
1977	Śląsk Wrocław	Widzew Łódź
1978	Wisła Kraków	Śląsk Wrocław
1979	Ruch Chorzów	Widzew Łódź
1980	Szombierkj Bytom	Widzew Łódź
1981	Widzew Łódź	Wisła Kraków
1982	Widzew Łódź	Śląsk Wrocław
1983	Lech Poznań	Widzew Łódź
1984	Lech Poznań	Widzew Łódź
1985	Górnik Zabrze	Legia Warszawa
1986	Górnik Zabrze	Legia Warszawa
1987	Górnik Zabrze	Pogoń Szczecin
1988	Górnik Zabrze	GKS Katowice
1989	Ruch Chorzów	GKS Katowice
1990	Lech Poznań	Zagłębie Lubin
1991	Zagłębie Lubin	Górnik Zabrze
1992	Lech Poznań	GKS Katowice
1993	Lech Poznań**	
1994	Legia Warszawa	GKS Katowice
1995	Legia Warszawa	Widzew Łódź
1996	Widzew Łódź	Legia Warszawa
1997	Widzew Łódź	Legia Warszawa
1998	LKS-PTAK Łódź	Polonia Warszawa
1999	Wisła Kraków	Widzew Łódź
2000	Polonia Warszawa	Wisła Kraków
2001	Wisła Kraków	Pogoń Szczecin
2002	Legia Warszawa	Wisła Kraków

* Ruch Chorzów finished sixth, but as the league programme was not completed it was awarded the title because of its cup win.

** Lech Poznań was awarded the title after Legia Warszawa and LKS Łódź (who finished first and second) were penalized for match-fixing allegations.

Polish League Summary

TEAM	TOTALS	CHAMPIONS & RUNNERS-UP (BOLD) (*ITALICS*)
Ruch Chorzów	**14**, *5*	**1933–36, 38**, *50*, **51–53, 56, 60**, *63*, *68*, *70*, **73, 74, 75, 79, 89**
Górnik Zabrze	**14**, *4*	**1957**, *59*, **61**, *62*, **63–67**, *69*, **71, 72**, *74*, **85–88**, *91*

Polish League Summary (*continued*)

TEAM	TOTALS	CHAMPIONS & RUNNERS-UP (BOLD) (*ITALICS*)
Wisła Kraków	7, 10	*1923,* **27, 28,** *30, 31, 36, 47, 48,* **49,** **50,** *66,* **78, 81, 99, 2000, 01,** *02*
Legia Warszawa	7, 7	**1955,** *56,* **60, 68, 69, 70,** *71,* **85,** *86,* **94, 95,** *96, 97,* **2002**
Cracovia Kraków	5, 1	**1921,** *30,* **32,** *34,* **37,** *48*
Lech Poznań	5, 0	**1983, 84, 90, 92, 93**
Widzew Łódź	4, 7	*1977, 79, 80,* **81, 82,** *83,* **84,** *95,* *96, 97, 99*
Pogoń Lwów	4, 3	**1922, 23, 25, 26,** *32,* **33,** *35*
Warta Poznań	2, 5	*1922,* **25,** *28,* **29,** *38, 46, 47*
Polonia Warszawa	2, 3	*1921,* **26,** *46, 98,* **2000**
LKS Łódź	2, 1	*1954,* **58, 98**
Stal Mielec	2, 1	**1973,** *75,* **76**
Polonia Bytom	2, 3	*1954,* **58,** *59,* **61,** *62*
Śląsk Wrocław	1, 2	**1977,** *78,* **82**
Garbarnia Kraków	1, 1	*1929,* **1931**
Szombierkj Bytom	1, 1	*1965,* **80**
Zagłębie Lubin	1, 1	**1990,** *91*
GKS Katowice	0, 4	*1988, 89, 92, 94*
Zagłębie Sosnowiec	0, 3	*1964, 67, 72*
Ogniwo Kraków	0, 2	*1949, 52*
AKS Chorzów	0, 1	*1937*
GKS Tychy	0, 1	*1976*
Gwardia Warszawa	0, 1	*1957*
I.FC Katowice	0, 1	*1927*
Pogoń Szczecin	0, 1	*1987*
Stal Sosnowiec	0, 1	*1955*
Wawel Kraków	0, 1	*1953*

Polish Cup Record 1926–2002

YEAR	WINNERS	SCORE	RUNNERS-UP
1926	Wisła Kraków	2-1	Sparta Lwów
1927–50	*no competition*		
1951	Ruch Chorzów	2-0	Wisła Kraków
1952	Polonia Warszawa	1-0	Legia Warszawa
1953	*no competition*		
1954	Gwardia Warszawa	0-0 (aet)(replay)3-1	Wisła Kraków
1955	Legia Warszawa	5-0	Lechia Gdańsk
1956	Legia Warszawa	3-0	Górnik Zabrze
1957	LKS Łódź	2-1	Górnik Zabrze
1958–61	*no competition*		
1962	Zagłębie Sosnowiec	2-1	Górnik Zabrze
1963	Zagłębie Sosnowiec	2-0	Ruch Chorzów
1964	Legia Warszawa	2-1 (aet)	Polonia Bytom
1965	Górnik Zabrze	4-0	Czarni Zagań
1966	Legia Warszawa	2-1 (aet)	Górnik Zabrze
1967	Wisła Kraków	2-0 (aet)	Raków Częstochowa
1968	Górnik Zabrze	3-0	Ruch Chorzów
1969	Górnik Zabrze	2-0	Legia Warszawa
1970	Górnik Zabrze	3-1	Ruch Chorzów
1971	Górnik Zabrze	3-1	Zagłębie Sosnowiec
1972	Górnik Zabrze	5-2	Legia Warszawa
1973	Legia Warszawa	0-0 (aet)(4-2 pens)	Polonia Bytom
1974	Ruch Chorzów	2-0	Gwardia Warszawa
1975	Stal Rzeszów	0-0 (aet)(3-2 pens)	ROW II Rybnik
1976	Śląsk Wrocław	2-0	Stal Mielec
1977	Zagłębie Sosnowiec	1-0	Polonia Bytom
1978	Zagłębie Sosnowiec	2-0	Piast Gliwice
1979	Arka Gdynia	2-1	Wisła Kraków
1980	Legia Warszawa	5-0	Lech Poznań
1981	Legia Warszawa	1-0 (aet)	Pogoń Szczecin
1982	Lech Poznań	1-0	Pogoń Szczecin
1983	Lechia Gdańsk	2-1	Piast Gliwice
1984	Lech Poznań	3-0	Wisła Kraków
1985	Widzew Łódź	0-0 (aet)(3-1 pens)	GKS Katowice
1986	GKS Katowice	4-1	Górnik Zabrze
1987	Śląsk Wrocław	0-0 (aet)(4-3 pens)	GKS Katowice
1988	Lech Poznań	1-1 (aet)(3-2 pens)	Legia Warszawa

Polish Cup Record (*continued*)

YEAR	WINNERS	SCORE	RUNNERS-UP
1989	Legia Warszawa	5-2	Jagiellonia Białystok
1990	Legia Warszawa	2-0	GKS Katowice
1991	GKS Katowice	1-0	Legia Warszawa
1992	Miedz Legnica	1-1 (aet)(4-3 pens)	Górnik Zabrze
1993	GKS Katowice	1-1 (aet)(5-4 pens)	Ruch Chorzów
1994	Legia Warszawa	2-0	LKS Łódź
1995	Legia Warszawa	2-0	GKS Katowice
1996	Ruch Chorzów	1-0	GKS Bełchatów
1997	Legia Warszawa	2-0	GKS Katowice
1998	Amica Wronki	5-3 (aet)	Aluminium Konin
1999	Amica Wronki	1-0	GKS Bełchatów
2000	Amica Wronki	2-2, 3-0 (2 legs)	Wisła Kraków
2001	Polonia Warszawa	2-1, 2-2 (2 legs)	Górnik Zabrze
2002	Wisła Kraków	4-2, 4-0 (2 legs)	Amica Wronki

Polish Cup Summary

TEAM	TOTALS	WINNERS & RUNNERS-UP (BOLD) (*ITALICS*)
Legia Warszawa	12, 5	*1952,* **55, 56, 64, 66,** *69, 72,* **73, 80, 81,** *88,* **89, 90, 91, 94, 95,** *97*
Górnik Zabrze	6, 7	*1956, 57, 62,* **65,** *66,* **68–72,** *86, 92,* **2001**
Zagłębie Sosnowiec	4, 1	**1962, 63,** *71,* **77,** *78*
GKS Katowice	3, 5	*1985,* **86,** *87,* **90,** *91,* **93,** *95,* **97**
Wisła Kraków	3, 5	**1926,** *51, 54,* **67,** *79, 84,* **2000,** *02*
Ruch Chorzów	3, 4	**1951,** *63, 68,* **70, 74,** *93,* **96**
Amica Wronki	3, 1	**1998–2000,** *02*
Lech Poznań	3, 1	*1980,* **82, 84, 88**
Polonia Warszawa	2, 0	**1952, 2001**
Śląsk Wrocław	2, 0	**1976, 87**
Gwardia Warszawa	1, 1	**1954,** *74*
Lechia Gdańsk	1, 1	*1955,* **83**
LKS Łódź	1, 1	**1957,** *94*
Arka Gdynia	1, 0	**1979**
Miedz Legnica	1, 0	**1992**
Stal Rzeszów	1, 0	**1975**
Widzew Łódź	1, 0	**1985**
Polonia Bytom	0, 3	*1964, 73, 77*
GKS Bełchatów	0, 2	*1996, 99*
Piast Gliwice	0, 2	*1978, 83*
Pogoń Szczecin	0, 2	*1981, 82*
Aluminium Konin	0, 1	*1998*
Czarni Zagań	0, 1	*1965*
Jagiellonia Białystok	0, 1	*1989*
Raków Częstochowa	0, 1	*1967*
ROW II Rybnik	0, 1	*1975*
Sparta Lwów	0, 1	*1926*
Stal Mielec	0, 1	*1976*

Zbigniew Boniek is widely regarded as the greatest ever Polish footballer. He made his name with Widzew Łódź, Polish League Champions in 1981 and 82, but it was his performances for the national team in the 1982 World Cup that persuaded Juventus of Italy to pay £1.1 million for him – then a record for a Polish player.

Belarus

Football Federation of the Republic of Belarus
Founded: 1989
Joined FIFA: 1992
Joined UEFA: 1993

Estonia

Eesti Jalgpalli Liit
Founded: 1921
Joined FIFA: 1923–43, 1992
Joined UEFA: 1992

BELARUS IS NOW AN INDEPENDENT NATION sandwiched between the western border of Russia and the eastern border of Poland. For nearly all of its history it has been a province of Imperial Russia or a republic of the Soviet Union. Speaking a variant of the Russian language, the Belarusians (or White Russians) imported football from Moscow and the Ukraine in the early years of the 20th century. The top Belarusian team – Dinamo Minsk – played in the top Soviet league while most clubs of the region languished in obscure regional leagues.

Independence was established in 1992, and the Belarusians set up their own independent FA and organized a national league and cup competition. Dinamo Minsk has continued to prosper, but other teams are now on the scene as a wave of new post-Communist clubs have emerged and old Soviet-era backers have receded. The top league has 16 teams playing home and away. The league, like many in the region, has switched from having a split season with a winter break to a single season starting in the spring.

Without doubt the best Belarusian player these days is Vasily Baranov. Captain of the national team, he plays his club football in Russia for Spartak Moskva.

FOOTBALL ARRIVED IN ESTONIA via English merchant seamen, having dockside kickabouts with the locals. The earliest converts appear to have been boys' gangs in the capital and port city of Riga. It rapidly spread to other Estonian cities before the First World War. In Narva, Russian textile workers adopted the game and played by the newly-imported Russian rules. In the university town of Tartu, German-speaking students and German rules predominated. In Tallinn itself, English coaches and English rules were followed.

Despite the chaos of the First World War and the arrival of formal independence from the Russian Empire in 1918, a national league was up and running (under a single set of rules) by 1920. A national cup competition was first played in 1938, just in time for all football to stop for the war. Like its neighbours the same fate befell Estonian society and football: German invasion, Soviet recapture, and absorption as a region into the Soviet Union; Estonia left FIFA in 1943. Independence, a national FA and a new national league and national cup competition were established in 1991. The season was played with a winter break in two phases, but has now switched to a single phase starting in the spring.

Estonian League Record 1921–2001

SEASON	CHAMPIONS		SEASON	CHAMPIONS
1921	Sport Tallinn		1940	Olümpia Tartu
1922	Sport Tallinn		1941–90	*no national championship*
1923	Kalev Tallinn			
1924	Sport Tallinn		1991	TVMK Tallinn
1925	Sport Tallinn		1992	FC Norma Tallinn
1926	TJK Tallinn		1993	FC Norma Tallinn
1927	Sport Tallinn		1994	FC Norma Tallinn
1928	TJK Tallinn		1995	FC Flora Tallinn
1929	Sport Tallinn		1996	FC Lantana Tallinn
1930	Kalev Tallinn		1997	FC Lantana Tallinn
1931	Sport Tallinn		1998	FC Flora Tallinn
1932	Sport Tallinn		1998*	FC Flora Tallinn
1933	Sport Tallinn		1999	FC Levadia Maardu
1934	Estonia Tallinn		2000	FC Levadia Maardu
1935	Estonia Tallinn		2001	FC Flora Tallinn
1936	Estonia Tallinn			
1937	*no championship*			
1938	Estonia Tallinn			
1939	Estonia Tallinn			

* Extra transitional autumn league – played in order to allow a season to start in spring and end in autumn.

Belarus League Record 1992–2001

SEASON	CHAMPIONS		SEASON	CHAMPIONS
1992	Dinamo Minsk		1999	FC BATE Borisov
1993	Dinamo Minsk		2000	Slavia Mazyr
1994	Dinamo Minsk		2001	Belshyna Babruisk
1995	Dinamo Minsk			
1995*	Dinamo Minsk			
1996	MPKC Mozyr			
1997	Dinamo Minsk			
1998	Dnepr-Transmash Mogilev			

* Extra transitional autumn league – played in order to allow a season to start in spring and end in autumn.

Belarus Cup Record 1992–2002

YEAR	CUP WINNERS		YEAR	CUP WINNERS
1992	Dinamo Minsk		1999	Belshyna Babruisk
1993	Neman-Belkard Grodno		2000	Slavia Mazyr
1994	Dinamo Minsk		2001	Belshyna Babruisk
1995	Dynamo '93		2002	FK Homel
1996	MPKC Mozyr			
1997	Belshyna Babruisk			
1998	Lokomotiv-96 Vitebsk			

Estonian Cup Record 1938–2002

YEAR	CUP WINNERS		YEAR	CUP WINNERS
1938	Sport Tallinn		1996	Tallinna Sadam
1939	TJK Tallinn		1997	Tallinna Sadam
1940	TJK Tallinn		1998	FC Flora Tallinn
1941–90	*no national competition*		1999	FC Levadia Maardu
			2000	FC Levadia Maardu
1991	TVMK Tallinn		2001	Trans Narva
1992	*no competition*		2002	FC Levadia Tallinn
1993	Nikol Tallinn			
1994	FC Norma Tallinn			
1995	FC Flora Tallinn			

BELARUS, ESTONIA

Latvia =

Football Association of Latvia
Founded: 1921
Joined FIFA: 1923–43, 1991
Joined UEFA: 1992

Lithuania

Lietuvos Futbolo Federacija
Founded: 1922
Joined FIFA: 1923–43, 1992
Joined UEFA: 1992

LATVIAN FOOTBALL HAS FOLLOWED a similar course to that of its Baltic neighbours: early stirrings before the First World War, a national FA arriving with political independence after the war, and national cup and league competitions beginning soon afterwards. As usual, everything stopped for the Second World War, which saw German invasion and occupation (1940–43) and then occupation by the Red Army. The Soviet Union absorbed Latvia, and Latvian football was reduced to a rather poor local league for 50 years.

Independence in 1991 brought a truly national league and cup competition and a whole swathe of new clubs that now occupy the top division. The new league was played in two phases to accommodate a winter break. In 1999 Latvia switched to a single phase season starting in the spring and ending before winter conditions become too harsh. Ten teams play in the top league, playing home and away twice during the course of the year. Whatever the format, contemporary Latvian football has been completely dominated by Skonto Riga.

LITHUANIA IS THE LARGEST and most southerly of the three Baltic States. Like the others, it has spent most of the modern era as part of either the Tsarist Russian Empire or the Communist Soviet Union. Independence came after the First World War in 1918, but it would take another four years of postwar chaos to achieve a national football association (affiliated to FIFA in 1923) and a national league competition. The league ran from 1922 to 1939, after which war intervened. Initially occupied by the Germans, Lithuania was recaptured by the Soviets and absorbed into the Soviet Union; a mere region now rather than a nation, Lithuania left FIFA in 1943.

As everywhere, the Communists reorganized Lithuanian football in their own image, and most of today's clubs can date their origins to the postwar decades. Although Lithuanian clubs could play in the top Soviet division, very few managed the transition, and a local regional league was played. Lithuania declared independence from the Soviet Union in 1990, which was formally settled in 1991. With independence came a new football association, league and cup competition. For all but one season this has been a standard 16-team league format, with the top eight and bottom eight forming mini-leagues in the second half of the season. In the 1996–97 season a two-phase league was tried, but the experiment was not successful.

Latvian League Record 1910–2001

SEASON	CHAMPIONS	SEASON	CHAMPIONS
1910	RV Union (Riga)*	1937	*no championship*
1911	Britannia FC (Riga)	1938	Olimpija Liepāja
1912	RV Union (Riga)	1939	Olimpija Liepāja
1913	SV Kaiserwood (Riga)	1940	RFK Riga
1914	Britannia FC (Riga)	1941–90	*no national championship*
1915	Britannia FC (Riga)		
1916–21	*no championship*	1991	Skonto Riga
1922	Kaiserwood Riga	1992	Skonto Riga
1923	Kaiserwood Riga	1993	Skonto Riga
1924	RFK Riga	1994	Skonto Riga
1925	RFK Riga	1995	Skonto Riga
1926	RFK Riga	1996	Skonto Riga
1927	Olimpija Liepāja	1997	Skonto Riga
1928	Olimpija Liepāja	1998	Skonto Riga
1929	Olimpija Liepāja	1999	Skonto Riga
1930	RFK Riga	2000	Skonto Riga
1931	RFK Riga	2001	Skonto Riga
1932	SKA Riga		
1933	Olimpija Riga		
1934	RFK Riga		
1935	RFK Riga		
1936	Olimpija Liepāja		

* Awarded to RV Union after disqualification of British FC (Riga) later renamed Britannia FC.

Latvian Cup Record 1937–2001

YEAR	CUP WINNERS	YEAR	CUP WINNERS
1937	RFK Riga	1996	RAF Jelgava
1938	Rigas Vilki Riga	1997	Skonto Riga
1939	RFK Riga	1998	Liepāja
1940–90	*no national competition*	1999	FK Riga
1991	Celtnieks Daugavpils	2000	Skonto Riga
1992	Skonto Riga	2001	Skonto Riga
1993	RAF Jelgava		
1994	Olimpija Riga		
1995	Skonto Riga		

Lithuanian League Record 1922–2001

SEASON	CHAMPIONS	SEASON	CHAMPIONS
1922	LFLS Kaunas	1940–90	*no national championship*
1923	LFLS Kaunas		
1924	Kovas Kaunas	1991	Zalgiris Vilnius
1925	Kovas Kaunas	1992	Zalgiris Vilnius
1926	Kovas Kaunas	1993	Ekranas Panevėžys
1927	LFLS Kaunas	1994	ROMAR Mažeikiai
1928	KSS Klaipėda	1995	Inkaras Kaunas
1929	KSS Klaipėda	1996	Inkaras Kaunas
1930	KSS Klaipėda	1997	Kareda Šiauliai
1931	KSS Klaipėda	1998	Kareda Šiauliai
1932	LFLS Kaunas	1999	Zalgiris Vilnius
1933	Kovas Kaunas	1999*	Zalgiris Kaunas
1934	MSK Kaunas	2000	FBK Kaunas
1935	Kovas Kaunas	2001	FBK Kaunas
1936	Kovas Kaunas		
1937	KSS Klaipėda		
1938	KSS Klaipėda		
1939	LGSF Kaunas		

* Extra transitional autumn league – played in order to allow a season to start in spring and end in autumn.

Lithuanian Cup Record 1991–2002

YEAR	CUP WINNERS	YEAR	CUP WINNERS
1992	Lietuvos Vilnius	1999	Kareda Šiauliai
1993	Zalgiris Vilnius	2000	Ekranas Panevėžys
1994	Zalgiris Vilnius	2001	Atlantas Klaipėda
1995	Inkaras Kaunas	2002	FBK Kaunas
1996	Kareda Šiauliai		
1997	Zalgiris Vilnius		
1998	Ekranas Panevėžys		

Greece

THE SEASON IN REVIEW 2001–02

IT WAS ALL CHANGE at the summit of Greek football over the summer of 2001, with AEK finally sold by Netmed, the Dutch pay TV giants, to the Antonopolous brothers, who immediately installed former Porto coach Fernando Santos. Panathinaikos paid a record Greek domestic transfer fee to bring in Cypriot striker Michalis Konstantinou, while Olympiakos splashed out on Christian Karembeu and Colombian defender Jorge Bermudez.

At the turn of the year, AEK led by five points from Olympiakos, with lowly Xanthi and PAOK also in contention. Through the winter and spring these four, as well as the rapidly improving Panathinaikos, kept it very close at the top. On the positive side, Pana's run to the quarter-finals of the Champions League showed the improving quality of Greek football. But while Greece enjoyed its most open and hotly contested title race for years, violence on and off the pitch continued to trouble it. Regular stadium bans for fans and scuffles inside and outside grounds were compounded by the extraordinary scenes at Panathiniakos' Apostolos Nikolaidis stadium in March. Panthinaikos led rivals Olympiakos 1-0, when, deep into injury time, a penalty was awarded to Olympiakos by referee Ioakim Efthymiadis. The visitors scored, and at the final whistle Pana boss Angelos Phillipides and coach Sergio Markarian led a charge towards the referee followed by a baying mass of players and supporters. Efthymiadis was escorted from the pitch by the police with serious head wounds. Accusations of match-fixing continue to circulate, while some clubs continue to appease the violent *ultras* with free tickets and subsidized transport.

The decisive league game was played in mid-April; Olympiakos beat AEK 4-3 and went top. A week later in the Greek Cup Final, AEK took revenge. In a frenetic game AEK won 2-1, punishing Olympiakos, who went down to ten men halfway through the second half with the game at 1-1. But the Piraeus giants had the last laugh, going into the league's final round level with AEK but leading on head-to-head records. Away to Aris in Thessaloniki, where home fans had been banned after violent incidents earlier in the season, Olympiakos showed no mercy, leaving with a 5-1 victory and taking its sixth consecutive championship. Just to emphasise the volatile nature of Greek football, 6,000 Olympiakos fans waiting at the airport in Athens to welcome the victorious team home were prevented from approaching the aeroplane by the police. A riot ensued and tear gas was used to disperse the crowd. Three policemen and dozens of fans were hurt.

Greek League Table 2001–02

CLUB	P	W	D	L	F	A	Pts	
Olympiakos	26	17	7	2	69	30	58	Champions League
AEK Athens	26	19	1	6	65	28	58	Champions League
Panathanikos	26	16	7	3	52	25	55	UEFA Cup
PAOK	26	14	6	6	54	45	48	UEFA Cup
Xanthi	26	12	6	8	34	26	42	UEFA Cup
Iraklis	26	9	9	8	32	35	36	UEFA Cup
Panionios	26	8	11	7	37	33	35	
OFI Crete	26	9	6	11	32	33	33	
Aris	26	7	8	11	25	34	29	
Aegaleo	26	7	5	14	26	45	26	
Akratitos	26	6	5	15	29	41	23	
Ionikos	26	5	7	14	21	47	22	
Panahaiki	26	3	9	14	26	55	18	
Ethnikos Asteras	26	4	5	17	19	44	17	Relegated

Promoted clubs: Giannina, Kallithea Athens, Proodeftiki Piraeus.

International Club Performances 2001–02

CLUB	COMPETITION	PROGRESS
Olympiakos	Champions League	1st Group Phase
Panathinaikos	Champions League	Quarter-finals
AEK Athens	UEFA Cup	4th Round
PAOK	UEFA Cup	3rd Round

Top Goalscorers 2001–02

PLAYER	CLUB	NATIONALITY	GOALS
Alekos Alexandris	Olympiakos	Greek	19
Demis Nikolaidis	AEK	Greek	16
Vassilis Tsartas	AEK	Greek	16
Giorgias Georgiadis	PAOK	Greek	15

Above: Michalis Konstantinou begins to pay back his record Greek transfer fee and celebrates a goal for Panathinaikos.

Right: AEK Athens President Filon Antonopoulos lifts the Greek Cup after his team's 2-1 victory over Olympiakos.

Greek Cup

2002 FINAL

April 27 – OAKA, Athens

AEK 2-1 Olympiakos

(Konstantinidis 52,   (Giovanni 70)
Ivic 83)

h/t: 0-0 **Att:** 60,000
Ref: A Mpriakos

Christian Karembeu helped Olympiakos to a sixth consecutive Greek title, but the team was disappointed in Europe.

Above: Xanthi v PAOK. For the first time in years, the Greek league was closely contested all season. Although they fell away, both Xanthi (from a small town in Greek Macedonia) and PAOK (from Thessaloniki) threatened the dominance of Athens' big three for much of the season.

Top left: Referee Ioakim Efthymiadis, bleeding from a head wound, struggles towards the dressing rooms with the help of armed police after being attacked by Panathinaikos fans, players and officials for awarding a last-minute penalty to Olympiakos, from which was scored the equalizing goal.

Top right: Panathinaikos coach Sergio Markarian leaves the chaos after leading the charge at referee Efthymiadis; he was subsequently fined and banned from the touchline.

Association Football in Greece

GREECE

1895

1900

1906: First Athens v Salonika match

1905

1910

1915

1920: First international, v Sweden, lost 0-9, venue: Antwerp **1920**

1926: Formation of FA **1925**

1927: Affiliation to FIFA

1928: National championship established **1930**

1932: First Greek Cup Final **1935**

1934: Enter World Cup

1940

1941–45: League abandoned during the war. Cup abandoned until 1947 **1945**

1950: League abandoned due to civil war **1950**

1952: League abandoned due to disagreement between top clubs **1955**

1954: Affiliation to UEFA

1960: Reorganization of National League **1960**

1962 and 1964: Cup Final abandoned due to violence between Olympiakos and Panathinaikos fans **1965**

1970

1971: Panathinaikos runners-up in European Cup **1975**

1979: Full-time professionalism introduced **1980**

1980: First appearance in European Championships Finals **1985**

1981: Karaiskakis Stadium disaster. 21 spectators crushed to death after Olympiakos beat AEK Athens 6-0 **1990**

1995

1994: First appearance in World Cup finals **2000**

2005

Despite football's enormous popularity in Greece, the national team has only managed a single qualification for the World Cup Finals, in the USA in 1994. However, losses against Argentina (above), Bulgaria and Nigeria meant that the team went out at the group stage.

The last time anyone other than Olympiakos or Panathinaikos, the two giants of Greek domestic football, won the Greek league was in 1994 when AEK from Athens finished seven points clear of Panathinaikos. However, Athens' rival Panathinaikos got its revenge by beating AEK 4-2 on penalties to claim the 1994 Greek Cup.

International Competitions

European Cup

1971: △ Pan

UEFA Cup

European Cup-Winners' Cup

Key

🏳️ International football
⚽ Affiliation to FIFA
⚽ Affiliation to UEFA
War
💥 Disaster
△ Competition runner-up
Pan – Panathinaikos

SALONIKA

Makedonikos Thessaloniki 1928
Thermaikos Thessaloniki 1925

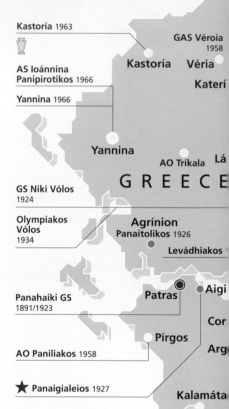

Kastoría 1963

GAS Véroia 1958

AS Ioánnina Panipirotikos 1966

Kastoría   Véria

Yannina 1966

Kateri

Yannina

AO Tríkala Lá

GREECE

GS Niki Vólos 1924

Olympiakos Vólos 1934

Agrínion
Panaitolikos 1926

Levádhiakos

Panahaiki GS 1891/1923

Patras   Aigi

Cor

Pírgos   Arg

AO Paniliakos 1958

★ Panaigialeios 1927

Kalamáta

Greece: The main clubs

Pierikos 1961 Team name with year of formation
● Club formed before 1912
● Club formed 1912–25
● Club formed 1925–50
Club formed after 1950
★ Founder members of National League 1960
League winners 1960–2002
Cup winners 1932–2002
English origins
Refugees
Elite
Working class
● Date unknown

Greece

ORIGINS AND GROWTH OF FOOTBALL

FOOTBALL ARRIVED IN GREECE via British sailors and traders who played quayside games in the big commercial ports in the late 19th century. The key point of entry was Salonika in the north, which was part of the Ottoman Empire until 1912. The early development of the game suffered from official disapproval; nonetheless it was popular enough for a match to be played between Salonika and Athens at the 1906 Intermediate Olympics – a match that ended in fighting between players and fans and set the tone for subsequent Greek football culture.

The growth of football and the birth of many clubs was shaped by the turbulent years before and after the First World War, during which the modern Greek nation state emerged. The Ottoman Empire gave up its hold on northern Greece and a massive wave of refugees arrived there from the Turkish mainland. AEK Athens and PAOK Salonica were founded by refugees from Istanbul, and Panionios by refugees from Izmir.

Organization arrives

It was only in 1926 that a national FA was finally formed and a championship was established in which the leading clubs from Athens and Salonika took part. A cup was added in 1932 and the national championship was expanded to include champions from other regions. In 1959, a single national league was created and full-time professionalism finally arrived in 1979.

Both competitions have been dominated by the big teams from Athens with rare successes for provincial teams. Despite enormous domestic support and a great deal of money, the international returns for clubs and the national team have been minimal. A single qualification for the World Cup, in 1994, and Panathinaikos' defeat in the 1971 European Cup Final to Ajax are the highlights. In the last decade progress at club level has been marred by crowd violence and what appears to be extensive corruption and tax dodging in the game.

GREECE

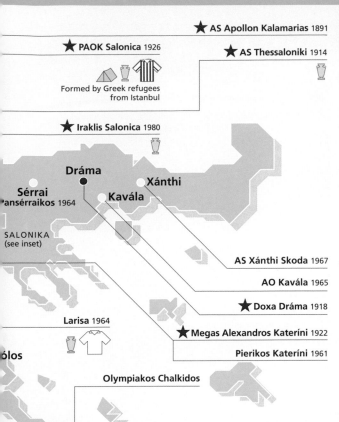

- ★ AS Apollon Kalamarias 1891
- ★ PAOK Salonica 1926
- ★ AS Thessaloniki 1914

Formed by Greek refugees from Istanbul

- ★ Iraklis Salonica 1980

Dráma
Xánthi
Sérrai
Pansérraikos 1964
Kavála

SALONIKA (see inset)

- AS Xánthi Skoda 1967
- AO Kavála 1965
- ★ Doxa Dráma 1918

Larisa 1964

- ★ Megas Alexandros Kateríni 1922
- Pierikos Kateríni 1961

ólos

- Olympiakos Chalkidos

Chalkida
dhia

- AO Chalkida 1931

Elefsina
Mégara

- AO Panelefsiniakos 1931

ATHENS/ PIRAEUS (see inset)

- Vyzas Mégaron 1928
- ★ Pankorinthiakos 1931
- PAE FC Korinthos 1963
- Panargiakos 1926
- AO Kalamáta 1967

Iráklion
OFI Crete 1925

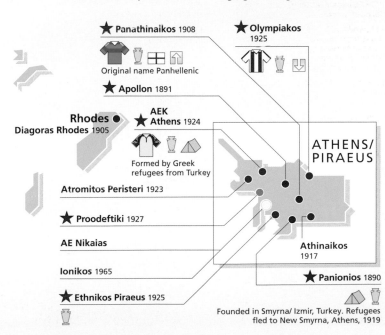

- ★ Panathinaikos 1908
- ★ Olympiakos 1925

Original name Panhellenic

- ★ Apollon 1891

Rhodes
Diagoras Rhodes 1905

- ★ AEK Athens 1924

Formed by Greek refugees from Turkey

ATHENS/ PIRAEUS

- Atromitos Peristeri 1923
- ★ Proodeftiki 1927
- AE Nikaias
- Ionikos 1965
- ★ Ethnikos Piraeus 1925

- Athinaikos 1917
- ★ Panionios 1890

Founded in Smyrna/ Izmir, Turkey. Refugees fled to New Smyrna, Athens, 1919

Athens

FOOTBALL CITY

ATHENS MAY BE THE SPIRITUAL HOME of the Olympics, but in the material world football is king. Although Athens is home to a dozen pro and semi-pro teams, the crown is really contested by the big three: Panathinaikos, AEK Athens and Olympiakos. Panathinaikos was originally founded by English bankers and merchants as Panhellenic, and only adopted its Greek name in 1908. Since then Pana has retained an elite following and demeanour. It rose in the 1960s, peaking in 1971 as defeated European Cup finalists (losing 2-0 to Ajax), and also contesting the World Club Cup (losing 3-2 on aggregate to Nacional from Uruguay). Pana is a club with tradition and its older fans gathered around the team's old city centre stadium, Apostolos Nikolaidis, abandoned when the team moved north to the Spiyros Louis. The club has since returned.

Pana acquired proper opposition with the foundation of Olympiakos in 1925, led by the five Andrianopoulos brothers. Lying at the heart of the working-class port district of Piraeus, the club converted the old Olympic velodrome into the Karaiskakis Stadium. Plans to redevelop the stadium after Olympiakos left for the OAKA stadium have been abandoned after protracted bureaucratic and political struggles and the club has announced it will be building a new stadium from scratch in 2003.

The city's third club, AEK Athens (Athlitiki Enosii Konstantinopolous), was founded in 1924 by Greek refugees who had fled from Turkish Constantinople (now Istanbul) and who built the team's original Nea Filadelphia stadium, now called Nikos Goumas. Panionios, to the south-east of the city centre, was actually founded by a community of Greek refugees in 1890 in what was Smyrna and is now Turkish Izmir.

GREECE

OAKA 'SPIYROS LOUIS'

74,443	**Club:** Olympiakos
	Built: 1982
	Original Capacity: 75,000
	Rebuilt: 2002–04
	Record Attendance: 73,537 Olympiakos v Ajax, 1983
	Significant Matches: European Cup Finals: 1983, 1994; European Cup-Winners' Cup Final: 1987

PERISTERI

E94

HAIDARI

Proodeftiki Aigaleo

Halkidona

KORIDALOS

DIMOTICO NEAPOLIS

PERISTERION

4,350

Ionikos Nikea

6,000

12,500

KORIDALOS

Atromitos

NIKEA

MOSCHATO

DRAPETSONA

YORGOS KARAISKAKIS

A reconstruction of the stadium is currently stalled by economic and political difficulties. Its completion date is uncertain

Olympiakos (1925–97)

Ethnikos Piraeus (1925–98)

PIRAEUS

SARONIC GULF

Like rivals Olympiakos, Panathinaikos has a fanatical following. Violence on the terraces has traditionally been a problem, particularly during local derbies, but with Panathinaikos regularly appearing in the Champions League, the problem seems likely to spread to other countries.

AEK ATHENS	1924
League	**1939, 40,** *46,* **58–60,** *63,* **65,** *67,* **68,** *70,* **71,** *75, 76,* **78, 79,** *81,* **88, 89, 90,** *92–94,* **96, 97,** *99, 2002*
Cup	**1932,** *39,* **48, 49, 50,** *53,* **56, 64, 66, 78, 79, 83,** *94,* **95, 96, 97, 2000, 02**

OLYMPIAKOS	1925
League	**1931, 33, 34, 36–38, 47, 48,** *49,* **51,** *53,* **54–59,** *61, 62,* **64,** *66,* **67, 68, 69,** *72,* **73–75,** *77, 79,* **80–83,** *84,* **87,** *89,* **91, 92,** *95,* **97–2002**
Cup	*1947,* **51–54,** *55,* **57–61, 63, 65,** *66,* **68, 69, 71, 73, 74, 75,** *76,* **81,** *86,* **88,** *90,* **92,** *93,* **99,** *2001,* **02**

E75

Olympiakos
(1997–2003)

AEK Athens

Panathinaikos
(1984–2000)

PEFKI

KAMATERO

NIKOS GOUMAS

22,014

IRAKLIO

STADIO OAKA
'SPIYROS LOUIS'
(NATIONAL STADIUM)

74,443

MAROUSI

GIPEDO RIZOUPOLIS

16,500

Greece

VRILISIA

N. LIOSIA

Apollon Athinon

FILOTHEI

PANATHINAIKOS	1908
League	**1930, 31, 32,** *36,* **49,** *53,* **54, 55,** *57,* **60–62,** *63,* **64, 65, 66, 69, 70,** *72,* **74, 77,** *82,* **84, 85, 86, 87, 90, 91,** *93,* **94, 95, 96,** *98,* **2000,** *01*
Cup	*1940,* **48, 49,** *55,* **60,** *65,* **67, 68, 69,** *72,* **75, 77,** *82,* **84,** *86,* **88, 89,** *91,* **93–95,** *97–99*
European Cup	*1971*
World Club Cup	*1971*

AGH. ANABIRI

Olympiakos

GALATSI

Olympiakos is sharing with
Apollon 2002–04 due to
stadium redevelopment

HALANDRI

ATHENS

Panathinaikos
(1922–84, 2000–)

NEO PSICHIKO

VERAN ZEROU STREET
AEK founded in a
sports shop here by
Emilios Ionas and
Kostas Dimoponlos

APOSTOLOS
NIKOLAIDIS

26,000

HOLARGOS

AMERIKIS SQUARE
Pana's first regular
playing field

PAPAGOS

ZOGRAFOU

Original location
of the University of
Athens, George Calafatis,
founder of Panathinaikos,
studied here in the 1890s

GREECE

Olympiakos

40,000

RENDI

ACROPOLIS

Olympiakos plan a new
stadium here should the
reconstruction of the
Karaiskakis fall through

KAISARIADIS

5,000

KESARIANI

TAVROS

ELLINKI
PODOSFEREKI
OMOSPONDIA
National Football
Association offices

VIRONAS

Ethnikos Astir

KALITHEA

DAFNI

VYRONAS

5,000

MITOS

NEA SMYRNIS

KESARANI

4,300

Athinaikos

12,000

Panionios

Ethnikos
Piraeus
(1998–)

ILIOUPOLI

PALEO
FALIRO

ALIMOS

YORGOS KARAISKAKIS	
31,032	**Club:** None at present
	Built: 1895
	Rebuilt: 1936, 1999–2002 (abandoned)
	Record Attendance: 42,415 Olympiakos v AEK, 7 Apr 1965
	Significant Matches: European Cup-Winners' Cup Final: 1971

PANIONIOS	1890
Cup	**1979, 98**

Athens

12,000	Capacity of stadium
40,000	Proposed site of new stadium
	Stadium no longer in use for top-flight football
	Team colours
E94	Motorway
	Major road
1900	Champions
2000	Runners-up

Greece

Hellenic Football Federation
Founded: 1926
Joined FIFA: 1927
Joined UEFA: 1954

GREEK FOOTBALL WAS ORGANIZED AND PLAYED at a regional level before the national level. Local leagues were operating in Athens and Salonika long before a national Greek FA was set up in 1926. In 1928 an Athens-Salonika league was set up, but the national championships were decided by play-offs with regional league champions. In 1960, a fully-fledged national league was created. It became full-time professional in 1979. There are 18 clubs in the top division with a standard three up, three down promotion and relegation system.

The Greek Cup was established in 1932 and now consists of four two-legged rounds followed by a Final. Over the years tournaments have either not been held due to war or have been cancelled due to extensive crowd trouble at Olympiakos v Panathinaikos derbies. In 1962 the Final between these two teams was abandoned by the referee as violence spilled over onto the pitch. In 1964, the two teams met in a semi-final and again the game could not be completed. The tournament was consequently abandoned and the cup was awarded to AEK Athens, winners of the other semi-final.

Greek League Record 1928–2002

SEASON	CHAMPIONS	RUNNERS-UP
1928	Aris Salonica	Ethnikos Piraeus
1929	*no championship*	
1930	Panathinaikos	Aris Salonica
1931	Olympiakos	Panathinaikos
1932	Aris Salonica	Panathinaikos
1933	Olympiakos	Aris Salonica
1934	Olympiakos	Iraklis Salonica
1935	*no championship*	
1936	Olympiakos	Panathinaikos
1937	Olympiakos	PAOK Salonica
1938	Olympiakos	Apollon Athens
1939	AEK Athens	Iraklis Salonica
1940	AEK Athens	PAOK Salonica
1941–45	*no championship*	
1946	Aris Salonica	AEK Athens
1947	Olympiakos	Iraklis Salonica
1948	Olympiakos	Apollon Athens
1949	Panathinaikos	Olympiakos
1950	*no championship*	
1951	Olympiakos	Panionios
1952	*no championship*	
1953	Panathinaikos	Olympiakos
1954	Olympiakos	Panathinaikos
1955	Olympiakos	Panathinaikos
1956	Olympiakos	Ethnikos Piraeus
1957	Olympiakos	Panathinaikos
1958	Olympiakos	AEK Athens
1959	Olympiakos	AEK Athens
1960	Panathinaikos	AEK Athens
1961	Panathinaikos	Olympiakos
1962	Panathinaikos	Olympiakos
1963	AEK Athens	Panathinaikos
1964	Panathinaikos	Olympiakos
1965	Panathinaikos	AEK Athens
1966	Olympiakos	Panathinaikos
1967	Olympiakos	AEK Athens
1968	AEK Athens	Olympiakos
1969	Panathinaikos	Olympiakos
1970	Panathinaikos	AEK Athens

Greek League Record (*continued*)

SEASON	CHAMPIONS	RUNNERS-UP
1971	AEK Athens	Panionios
1972	Panathinaikos	Olympiakos
1973	Olympiakos	PAOK Salonica
1974	Olympiakos	Panathinaikos
1975	Olympiakos	AEK Athens
1976	PAOK Salonica	AEK Athens
1977	Panathinaikos	Olympiakos
1978	AEK Athens	PAOK Salonica
1979	AEK Athens	Olympiakos
1980	Olympiakos	Aris Salonica
1981	Olympiakos	AEK Athens
1982	Olympiakos	Panathinaikos
1983	Olympiakos	Larisa
1984	Panathinaikos	Olympiakos
1985	PAOK Salonica	Panathinaikos
1986	Panathinaikos	OFI Crete
1987	Olympiakos	Panathinaikos
1988	Larisa	AEK Athens
1989	AEK Athens	Olympiakos
1990	Panathinaikos	AEK Athens
1991	Panathinaikos	Olympiakos
1992	AEK Athens	Olympiakos
1993	AEK Athens	Panathinaikos
1994	AEK Athens	Panathinaikos
1995	Panathinaikos	Olympiakos
1996	Panathinaikos	AEK Athens
1997	Olympiakos	AEK Athens
1998	Olympiakos	Panathinaikos
1999	Olympiakos	AEK Athens
2000	Olympiakos	Panathinaikos
2001	Olympiakos	Panathinaikos
2002	Olympiakos	AEK Athens

Greek League Summary

TEAM	TOTALS	CHAMPIONS & RUNNERS-UP (BOLD) (*ITALICS*)
Olympiakos	31, 15	**1931, 33, 34, 36–38, 47, 48, 49, 51, 53,** *54–59,* **61, 62, 64, 66, 67, 68, 69, 72, 73–75, 77, 79, 80–83, 84, 87,** *89, 91, 92, 95,* **97–2002**
Panathinaikos	18, 17	**1930,** *31, 32, 36,* **49,** *53, 54, 55, 57,* **60–62,** *63,* **64, 65,** *66,* **69, 70, 72, 74, 77, 82, 84, 85, 86, 87, 90, 91,** *93, 94, 95, 96,* **98, 2000, 01**
AEK Athens	11, 16	**1939, 40,** *46, 58–60,* **63,** *65, 67, 68, 70,* **71,** *75, 76,* **78, 79,** *81, 88,* **89,** *90,* **92–94,** *96, 97, 99,* **2002**
Aris Salonica	3, 3	**1928, 32,** *30, 33, 46, 80*
PAOK Salonica	2, 4	*1937, 40,* **73,** *76, 78,* **85**
Larisa	1, 1	*1983,* **88**
Iraklis Salonica	0, 3	*1934, 39, 47*
Apollon Athens	0, 2	*1938, 48*
Ethnikos Piraeus	0, 2	*1928, 56*
Panionios	0, 2	*1951, 71*
OFI Crete	0, 1	*1986*

GREECE

Greek Cup Record 1932–2002

YEAR	WINNERS	SCORE	RUNNERS-UP
1932	AEK Athens	5-3	Aris Salonica
1933	Ethnikos Piraeus	2-2, (replay) 2-1	Aris Salonica
1934–38		*no competition*	
1939	AEK Athens	2-1	PAOK Salonica
1940	Panathinaikos	3-1	Aris Salonica
1941–46		*no competition*	
1947	Olympiakos	5-0	Iraklis Salonica
1948	Panathinaikos	2-1	AEK Athens
1949	AEK Athens	0-0, (replay) 2-1 (aet)	Panathinaikos
1950	AEK Athens	4-0	Aris Salonica
1951	Olympiakos	4-0	PAOK Salonica
1952	Olympiakos	2-2, (replay) 2-0	Panionios
1953	Olympiakos	3-2	AEK Athens
1954	Olympiakos	2-0	Doxa Drama
1955	Panathinaikos	2-0	PAOK Salonica
1956	AEK Athens	2-1	Olympiakos
1957	Olympiakos	2-0	Iraklis Salonica
1958	Olympiakos	5-1	Doxa Drama
1959	Olympiakos	2-1	Doxa Drama
1960	Olympiakos	1-1, (replay) 3-0	Panathinaikos
1961	Olympiakos	3-0	Panionios
1962		*not awarded**	
1963	Olympiakos	3-0	Pierikos Katerini
1964	AEK Athens	**	
1965	Olympiakos	1-0	Panathinaikos
1966	AEK Athens	w/o	Olympiakos
1967	Panathinaikos	1-0	Panionios
1968	Olympiakos	1-0	Panathinaikos
1969	Panathinaikos	1-1†	Olympiakos
1970	Aris Salonica	1-0	PAOK Salonica
1971	Olympiakos	3-1	PAOK Salonica
1972	PAOK Salonica	2-1	Panathinaikos
1973	Olympiakos	1-0	PAOK Salonica
1974	PAOK Salonica	2-2 (4-3 pens)	Olympiakos
1975	Olympiakos	1-0	Panathinaikos
1976	Iraklis Salonica	4-4 (6-5 pens)	Olympiakos
1977	Panathinaikos	2-1	PAOK Salonica
1978	AEK Athens	2-0	PAOK Salonica
1979	Panionios	3-1	AEK Athens
1980	Kastoria	5-2	Iraklis Salonica
1981	Olympiakos	3-1	PAOK Salonica
1982	Panathinaikos	1-0	Larisa
1983	AEK Athens	2-0	PAOK Salonica
1984	Panathinaikos	2-0	Larisa
1985	Larisa	4-1	PAOK Salonica
1986	Panathinaikos	4-0	Olympiakos
1987	OFI Crete	1-1 (3-1 pens)	Iraklis Salonica
1988	Panathinaikos	2-2 (4-3 pens)	Olympiakos
1989	Panathinaikos	3-1	Panionios
1990	Olympiakos	4-2	OFI Crete
1991	Panathinaikos	3-0, 2-1 (2 legs)	Athinaikos
1992	Olympiakos	1-1, 2-0 (2 legs)	PAOK Salonica
1993	Panathinaikos	1-0	Olympiakos
1994	Panathinaikos	3-3 (aet)(4-2 pens)	AEK Athens
1995	Panathinaikos	1-0 (aet)	AEK Athens
1996	AEK Athens	7-1	Apollon
1997	AEK Athens	0-0 (5-3 pens)	Panathinaikos
1998	Panionios	1-0	Panathinaikos
1999	Olympiakos	2-0	Panathinaikos
2000	AEK Athens	2-0	Ionikos
2001	PAOK Salonica	4-2	Olympiakos
2002	AEK Athens	2-1	Olympiakos

w/o denotes walk over
* Final between Olympiakos and Panathinaikos abandoned at 0-0, cup not awarded.
** AEK Athens awarded cup by Greek FA.
† Panathinaikos won on toss of a coin.

Greek Cup Summary

TEAM	TOTALS	WINNERS & RUNNERS-UP (BOLD) (*ITALICS*)
Olympiakos	20, *10*	**1947, 51–54**, *55*, **57–61, 63, 65**, *66*, **68, 69, 71, 73, 74, 75, 76, 81, 86, 88, 90, 92**, *93, 99*, **2001, 02**
Panathinaikos	15, *9*	**1940**, *48, 49*, **55**, *60*, **65**, *67*, **68, 69**, *72, 75*, **77, 82, 84, 86, 88, 89, 91**, *93–95, 97–99*
AEK Athens	13, *5*	**1932**, *39*, **48, 49, 50**, *53*, **56**, *64, 66*, **78**, *79*, **83**, *94, 95*, **96, 97, 2000, 02**
PAOK Salonica	3, *12*	*1939, 51, 55, 70, 71*, **72**, *73*, **74**, *77, 78, 81, 83, 85, 92*, **2001**
Panionios	2, *4*	*1952*, **61**, *67*, **79**, *89*, **98**
Aris Salonica	1, *4*	**1932**, *33, 40, 50*, **70**
Iraklis Salonica	1, *4*	*1947*, **57**, *76, 80, 87*
Larisa	1, *2*	*1982, 84*, **85**
OFI Crete	1, *1*	**1987**, *90*
Ethnikos Piraeus	1, *0*	**1933**
Kastoria	1, *0*	**1980**
Doxa Drama	0, *3*	*1954, 58, 59*
Apollon	0, *1*	*1996*
Athinaikos	0, *1*	*1991*
Ionikos	0, *1*	*2000*
Pierikos Katerini	0, *1*	*1963*

***Olympiakos and Panathinaikos** (in green) have dominated Greek football since its early days. Their rivalry is geographical, social and sporting, and often boils over on derby day, resulting in violence and injury.*

Turkey

THE SEASON IN REVIEW 2001–02

THE USUAL ISTANBUL CONTENDERS, Galatasaray, Fenerbahçe and Beşiktaş, battled in the Turkish league this season against a backdrop of financial constraints, match-fixing scandals and fiercely fought presidential elections. Digiturk, one of the main purchasers of TV rights, has looked in trouble. Beşiktaş and Galatasaray's partial stock market flotations have been poorly received and, in March, the newspaper *Milliyet* released taped conversations with Ali Fevzi Bir (ex-chairman of Oz Fanrayi Creditspor) that hinted at match-fixing involving Göztepe, Gaziantepspor, Gençlerbirligi and Bursaspor. Bir has subsequently been arrested and has implicated the presidents of the big three, the TFF, and five top-flight referees.

Galatasaray and Istanbulspor made the early season running but Gala's European campaigns and Istanbulspor's lack of depth saw both slip. At the turn of the year, Beşiktaş and Galatasaray were level at the top with Fenerbahçe and Instanbulspor staying in touch. From there it was all downhill for Beşiktaş; beaten 1-0 by Galatasaray in a top-of-the-table clash in March, the team's form disintegrated. The team's poor season culminated in defeat in the Turkish Cup Final against Kocaelispor from Izmir. While Beşiktaş wasted its chances, Kocaelispor sat deep and broke on the counter. Already leading 1-0, the team from Izmir scored from the spot when Ibrahim Uzulmez deliberately handled the ball in the 58th minute. Beşiktaş was broken; the final score was 4-0. Intense celebrations followed for a victory that symbolized the city of Izmir's rebirth after the disastrous earthquakes of the previous year. In a display of unbelievable petulance, the Beşiktaş squad refused to come out of the dressing room for the presentation of the cup.

Though near the top throughout the season Fenerbahçe never pushed hard at leaders Galatasaray, and could only beat them 1-0 when the team was down to seven men. Galatasaray settled the title with a game to go, beating Kocaelispor away 2-1. Gala's victory was founded on the shrewd management of Romanian Mircea Lucescu. Despite losing Jardel, Tafferel, Popescu and five other leading squad members during the summer of 2001, facing an arduous Champions League schedule and a mounting injury list, Lucescu nurtured a team characterized by a phenomenal workrate and the capacity to score from every position. His reward has been the sack, as Galatasaray confirmed that ex-coach Faith Terim will be returning in 2002.

Turkish League Table 2001–02

CLUB	P	W	D	L	F	A	Pts	
Galatasaray SK	34	24	6	4	75	31	78	Champions League
Fenerbahçe SK	34	24	3	7	70	31	75	Champions League
Beşiktaş	34	18	8	8	69	39	62	UEFA Cup
MKE Ankaragücü	34	15	8	11	72	58	53	UEFA Cup
Denizlispor	34	12	12	10	65	52	48	UEFA Cup
Gaziantepspor	34	13	9	12	57	52	48	
Gençlerbirligi	34	11	12	11	47	51	45	
Göztepe SC	34	12	9	13	38	56	45	
Istanbulspor	34	12	8	14	33	38	44	
Bursaspor K	34	13	5	16	48	60	44	
Kocaelispor	34	12	7	15	45	60	43	UEFA Cup
Diyarbakirspor	34	10	10	14	41	50	40	
Trabzonspor K	34	11	7	16	49	60	40	
Malatyaspor	34	11	7	16	34	50	40	
Samsunspor	34	10	8	16	32	43	38	
Rizespor	34	9	10	15	43	51	37	Relegated
Antalyaspor	34	9	10	15	46	61	37	Relegated
Yozgatspor	34	6	9	19	46	67	27	Relegated

Promoted clubs: Altay, Adanaspor, Elazigspor.

International Club Performances 2001–02

CLUB	COMPETITION	PROGRESS
Fenerbahçe SK	Champions League	1st Group Phase
Galatasaray SK	Champions League	2nd Group Phase
Gaziantepspor	UEFA Cup	1st Round
Gençlerberlingi	UEFA Cup	1st Round

Top Goalscorers 2001–02

PLAYER	CLUB	NATIONALITY	GOALS
Arif Erdem	Galatasaray SK	Turkish	23
Ilhan Mansiz	Beşiktaş	Turkish	22
Agustine Ahinful	MKE Ankaragücü SK	Ghanaian	21

Turkish Cup

2002 FINAL

April 3 – Atatürk Stadium, Bursa
Kocaelispor 4-0 Beşiktaş
(Haspolatli 44,
Lazarov 59,
Dobra 82,
Topraktepe 83)
h/t: 1-0 **Att:** 19,700
Ref: Metin Tokat

Top right: Coach Mircea Lucescu celebrates after Galatasaray become league champions.

Right: The Emperor returns: after being fired by AC Milan early in the season, Faith Terim's return to Galatasaray was rumoured for months.

Bottom right: Out of the frying pan into the fire: Christoph Daum fled German football after a series of drug scandals but, despite good early form, Beşiktaş lost the Cup Final and abandoned its challenge for the league.

Below: Kocaelispor celebrates its first Turkish Cup triumph.

It was an empty-handed year for Istanbul's third and fourth teams; Istanbulspor's Yagcioglu presses Ilhan Mansiz of Beşiktaş.

Galatasaray lift the Turkish league trophy; Berkant Göktan, Ümit Karan and Sébastien Perez (left to right) look suitably pleased.

TURKEY

Association Football in Turkey

1895: First recorded football game played in Izmir · 1895

· 1900

1903: Beşiktaş, Turkey's oldest club, founded

1905: First Istanbul League started · 1905

· 1910

· 1915

 ⚽ **1923:** Formation of FA: Türkiye Futbol Federasyono. Affiliation to FIFA. First international, v Romania, drawn 2-2, venue: Istanbul · 1920 · 1925

1924: New Istanbul League established · 1930

· 1935

1937: National championship by play-off introduced · 1940

· 1945

· 1950

1951: Professionalism introduced

🇹🇷 **1954:** First appearance in World Cup · 1955

1959: National League established · 1960

⚽ **1962:** Affiliation to UEFA

1963: First Turkish Cup Final · 1965

· 1970

🌵 **1971:** Kayseri Stadium disaster, stand collapses at Kayserispor v Siwas, 44 killed · 1975

· 1980

· 1985

· 1990

· 1995

1996: First appearance in European Championships

2000: Galatasaray win UEFA Cup · 2000

· 2005

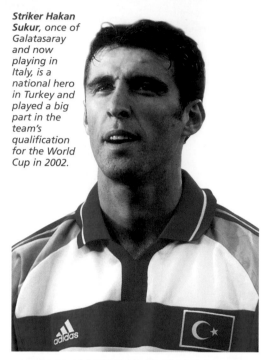

Striker Hakan Sukur, once of Galatasaray and now playing in Italy, is a national hero in Turkey and played a big part in the team's qualification for the World Cup in 2002.

Galatasaray's victory against Arsenal in the 2000 UEFA Cup Final was the first major triumph for a Turkish football club.

Key

🇹🇷	International football	🌵	Disaster
⚽	Affiliation to FIFA	○	Competition winner
⚽	Affiliation to UEFA	Galat -	Galatasaray

International Competitions

	European Cup	UEFA Cup	European Cup-Winners' Cup
2000:		○ Galat	

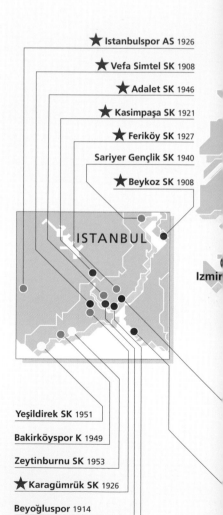

Turkey: The main clubs

Altay GK 1914 — Team name with year of formation

● Club formed before 1912
● Club formed 1912–25
● Club formed 1925–50
○ Club formed after 1950

★ Founder members of National League (1959)

👕 Champions (1959–2001)

🏆 Cup winners

⚱ Originated from a school or college

★ **Istanbulspor AS** 1926
★ **Vefa Simtel SK** 1908
★ **Adalet SK** 1946
★ **Kasimpaşa SK** 1921
★ **Feriköy SK** 1927
Sariyer Gençlik SK 1940
★ **Beykoz SK** 1908

ISTANBUL

Izmir

Yeşildirek SK 1951
Bakirköyspor K 1949
Zeytinburnu SK 1953
★ **Karagümrük SK** 1926
Beyoğluspor 1914
★ **Galatasaray SK** 1905

Turkey

ORIGINS AND GROWTH OF FOOTBALL

WHEN FOOTBALL FIRST APPEARED on the playing fields of Istanbul in the late 19th century, it was met with suspicion by the ruling authorities. The last Sultan of the Ottoman Empire, already in terminal decline and fearful of Western political and cultural influences, banned his subjects from playing. Not surprisingly, football was initially concentrated in the Jewish, Christian and Greek communities of Istanbul. But the game was unstoppable. Beşiktaş was established in 1903 with the support of Osman Pasha, a member of the Sultan's government, Turkish high school students formed Galatasaray in 1905, and Fenerbahçe – the last of Turkey's big three – grew out of St. Joseph's, a French college in the city, in 1907. An Istanbul Sunday amateur league was created in 1905, but the development of organized football was held back by the First World War, the subsequent

collapse of the Ottoman Empire and the creation of the Turkish Republic. The new republic, declared by Kemal Atatürk in 1923, was led by a diehard Fenerbahçe fan and the formation of a national FA and official regional and Istanbul leagues quickly followed. As transport improved and the quality of the provincial game rose, a national championship was created in 1937, with play-offs between top Istanbul clubs and regional champions.

The game's growing popularity saw professionalism introduced in 1951 and the creation of a fully-fledged national league in 1959. However, it is only in the 1990s that these factors have begun to generate international success with the national team performing well at the 1996 and 2000 European Championships, Galatasaray's victory in the UEFA Cup 2000 and the national team's amazing run to the semi-finals of the 2002 World Cup.

TURKEY

★ Karşiyaka SK 1912

★ Altinordu SK 1923

★ Izmirspor K 1923

★ Altay GK 1914

★ Göztepe SK 1925

ISTANBUL (see inset)

Zonguldak
Zonguldakspor K 1966

Samsun

Samsunspor K 1965

Trabzonspor K 1967

Caykur Rizespor 1968

Rizespor K 1953

Orduspor K 1967

Rize

Adapazari
Sakaryaspor K 1965

Izmit
Kocaelispor K 1966

rsa

Bursaspor K 1963

Karabük
DC Karabukspor 1969

Bolu
Boluspor K 1965

ANKARA (see inset)

Yozgat
Yimpas Yozgatspor 1959

Kirikkale
MKE Kirikkalespor K 1967

Ordu

Trabzon

Giresun
Giresunspor K 1967

Erzurum

Erzurumspor K 1968

T U R K E Y

ikesir
kesirspor 1966

Eskişehir
Eskişehirspor K 1965

Van
Vanspor K 1974

ydin
ydinspor K 1966

Denizli
Denizlispor K 1966

Antalya
Antalyaspor K 1966

Konya
Konyaspor K 1981

Mersin
Mersin Idmanyurdu SK 1925

Adana

Kayseri
Kayserispor K 1966

Kahramanmaraş
Kahramanmaraşspor K 1969

Gaziantep
Gaziantepspor K 1969

Diyarbakir

Siirt
Siirt Jet PA 1969

Diyarbakirspor K 1968

Adanaspor AS SK 1954

Adana Demirspor K 1940

★ Beşiktaş JK 1903

man Pasha, a member of Sultan's Court, was the club's first patron

★ Fenerbahçe SK 1907

★ Hacettepe SK 1945

★ Gençlerbirligi SK 1923

★ Sekerspor KD 1947

ANKARA

★ Ankara Dermispor 1932

★ MKE Ankaragücü SK 1910

PTT SK 1954

★ Seker Hilal SK Ankara 1958

Istanbul

FOOTBALL CITY

ISTANBUL, IN ITS FORMER LIFE as Constantinople, was the seat of the Byzantine and Ottoman Empires for more than 1,500 years. In 1923, when the Turkish Revolution swept the Ottoman sultanate away, political power migrated to Ankara, but footballing power and the national FA have always remained in Istanbul. It is a power that rests on the presence of Turkey's three leading clubs: Galatasaray and Beşiktaş in the old European centre of the city, and Fenerbahçe across the Bosporus in Asian Turkey. Between them, they have completely dominated Turkish football.

English merchants first played football in Istanbul in the late 19th century, and by 1904 had set up the first Istanbul league schedule. The Ottoman sultan, Abdülhamid III, banned this pernicious British game from Istanbul as contrary to Islamic law. However, non-Muslims were exempt from the ruling, and clubs began to form across the city, starting in foreign schools and Christian and Jewish areas.

The big three

The social and political allegiances of the big three are not entirely clear cut. Fenerbahçe considers itself the people's team, drawing on the populism of its greatest fan – the leader of the Turkish revolution himself – Kemal Ataturk. While Fenerbahçe is the best-supported club, Galatasaray is the richest, and has made the most of the recent boom in European football with success in the UEFA Cup (2000) and flotation on the Turkish stock exchange (2002). Beşiktaş, despite considerable domestic success, is stuck as the capital's 'third team'. All three can muster ferocious support at home, which has spilled into violence at both Fener-Gala derbies and at big European games. Visits by Manchester United (1993) and Leeds United (2000), whose teams have been greeted at Istanbul airport with signs reading 'Welcome to Hell', have seen violence and some have ended with fans' deaths.

Beyond the big three, other Istanbul teams have had a presence in the top Turkish division. In the south-west, Zeytinburnu has risen out of the concrete and neglect of one of Istanbul's poorest districts. In the far west of the city, Istanbulspor has won the city league and rose for a time on the money of Istanbul media magnate Cem Uzan. North of the city centre on the banks of the Bosporus, Sariyer GK held onto a mid-table position throughout the 1990s.

For more than 1,500 years the seat of the Ottoman and Byzantine Empires, Istanbul is also the home city of Turkish football. A mosque towers over Beşiktaş's İnönü stadium.

TURKEY

BJK İNÖNÜ

35,000	Club:	Beşiktaş JK
	Built:	1938
	Original Capacity:	39,000
	Record Attendance:	39,000 Beşiktaş v Malmö, 1994

IKITELLI
BAYRAMPASA STADI

11,000

Istanbulspor AS

E80

ISTANBULSPOR AS 1926

Istanbul League 1924–58	1932

VEFA SIMTEL SK 1908

Istanbul League 1924–58	1925, 47
League 1959–2002	1959

Istanbul

45,000	Capacity of stadium
	Minor clubs
	Team colours
	Minor clubs that are ground sharing
100	Motorway
	Major road
1900	Champions
2000	Runners-up

ISTANBUL AIRPORT

100

Yeşildirek SK

BAKIRKÖY

YEŞİLKÖY

ALI SAMI YEN

20,000

Club: Galatasaray SK
Built: 1953
Original Capacity: 30,000
Rebuilding planned: 2003–05 (provisional capacity of 41,000)

SÜKRÜ SARACOGLU

54,000

Club: Fenerbahçe SK
Built: 1948
Original Capacity: 25,000
Rebuilt: 1999–2001. Rebuilding planned: 2002–03 (provisional capacity of 63,000)

BOSPORUS CLUBS

Sariyer Gençlick SK	Beykoz SK
YUSUF ZIYA ÖNIS STADI	
12,000	

GALATASARAY SK 1905

Istanbul League 1924–58	*1924*, **25–27**, *29*, *30*, **31**, *35*, *36*, *42*, *49*, *51*, *52*, *54*, **55**, **56**, *57*, *58*
League 1959–2002	*1961*, *62*, *63*, *66*, *69*, **71–73**, *75*, *79*, *86*, **87**, **88**, *91*, **93**, **94**, **97–2000**, **01**, **02**
Cup	**1963–66**, *69*, **73**, **76**, *80*, **82**, **85**, **91**, **93**, **94**, **95**, **96**, **98**, **99**, **2000**
UEFA Cup	**2000**

Galatasaray SK

ALI SAMI YEN

20,000

BEŞIKTAŞ JK 1903

Istanbul League 1924–58	**1924**, *33*, **34**, *39–43*, *44*, **45**, **46**, *48*, *49*, **50–52**, *53*, **54**, *55*
League 1959–2002	**1960**, *63–65*, **66**, **67**, *68*, *74*, **82**, *85*, **86**, **87–89**, **90–92**, *93*, **95**, *97*, **99**, **2000**
Cup	*1966*, **75**, *77*, *84*, **89**, **90**, *93*, **94**, **98**, **99**, *2002*

TURKEY

I S T A N B U L

GAZIOSMANPAŞA

BALAT
Centre of Istanbul's Jewish community and enthusiastic footballers at the turn of the century

EYÜP

FERER
Centre of Istanbul's Greek community before the Greco-Turkish war (1920–23) and hotbed of football

Kasimpaşa SK

GALATASARAY HIGH SCHOOL
Galatasaray SK founded by students from the school

BJK İNÖNÜ

35,000

ORTAKÖY

(Bosporus)

GALATASARAY ISLAND
Owned by Galatasaray, the club has built a swimming pool and restaurant on the island

Beşiktaş JK

Karadeniz Boğazi

BEYOĞLU

BEYLERBEYI

Halic

BAYRAMPAŞA

FATIH

Kasimpaşa SK

ÜSKÜDAR

ÜMRANIYE

Vefa Simtel SK

EMINÖNÜ

SULTAN'S PALACE

Vefa Simtel SK

ZEYTINBURNU

10,000

ZEYTINBURNU

Zeytinburnu SK

MARMARA DENIZI (SEA OF MARMARA)

KADIKÖY

E80

...irköyspor K

SÜKRÜ SARACOGLU

54,000

Fenerbahçe SK

FENERBAHÇE

ERENKÖY

100

FENERBAHÇE SK 1907

Istanbul League 1924–58	*1926*, *27*, *29*, **30**, *31*, *33*, *34*, **35–37**, *38–41*, *43*, **44**, *45*, *46*, *47*, **48**, *50*, **53**, *56*, **57**, *58*
League 1959–2002	*1959*, *60*, **61**, *62*, *64*, **65**, *67*, **68**, **70**, *71*, *73*, **74**, **75**, **76**, *77*, **78**, *80*, **83**, *84*, **85**, **89**, *90*, *92*, *94*, **96**, *98*, **2001**, *02*
Cup	*1963*, *65*, **68**, *74*, *79*, **83**, *89*, *96*, *2001*

261

Turkey

Türkiye Futbol Federasyonu
Founded: 1923
Joined FIFA: 1923
Joined UEFA: 1962

TURKEY

THE ORIGINS OF ORGANIZED football in Turkey are very much centred on Istanbul with a regular Istanbul league created in 1905. However, a combination of disapproval by the ruling Ottoman authorities and the First World War led to two decades of decline. In the immediate aftermath of the Turkish Revolution, a national football association was created in 1923, and a new Istanbul league followed a year later.

Between 1937 and 1950 a national championship was contested in play-offs between the top Istanbul clubs and regional champions. Professionalism arrived in 1951, but it took until 1959 to create a single national league. A national cup competition was set up in 1963.

Turkish League Summary

TEAM	TOTALS	CHAMPIONS & RUNNERS-UP (BOLD) (*ITALICS*)
Galatasaray SK	15, 7	*1961*, **62, 63**, *66*, **69**, *71–73*, *75*, *79*, *86*, **87, 88**, *91*, **93, 94**, **97–2000**, *01*, **02**
Fenerbahçe SK	14, 14	**1959**, *60*, *61*, *62*, **64, 65**, *67*, **68, 70**, *71*, *73*, **74, 75**, *76*, *77*, **78**, *80*, **83**, *84*, **85**, *89*, *90*, *92*, *94*, **96**, *98*, **2001**, *02*
Beşiktaş JK	9, 13	**1960**, *63–65*, *66*, *67*, *68*, *74*, **82**, *85*, **86**, *87–89*, **90–92**, *93*, **95**, *97*, *99*, *2000*
Trabzonspor K	6, 5	**1976, 77, 78**, *79–81*, **82**, *83*, **84**, *95*, *96*
Eskişehirspor K	0, 3	*1969, 70, 72*
Adanaspor K	0, 1	*1981*
Vefa SK	0, 1	*1959*

Turkish League Record 1959–2002

SEASON	CHAMPIONS	RUNNERS-UP
1959	Fenerbahçe SK	Vefa SK
1960	Beşiktaş JK	Fenerbahçe SK
1961	Fenerbahçe SK	Galatasaray SK
1962	Galatasaray SK	Fenerbahçe SK
1963	Galatasaray SK	Beşiktaş JK
1964	Fenerbahçe SK	Beşiktaş JK
1965	Fenerbahçe SK	Beşiktaş JK
1966	Beşiktaş JK	Galatasaray SK
1967	Beşiktaş JK	Fenerbahçe SK
1968	Fenerbahçe SK	Beşiktaş JK
1969	Galatasaray SK	Eskişehirspor K
1970	Fenerbahçe SK	Eskişehirspor K
1971	Galatasaray SK	Fenerbahçe SK
1972	Galatasaray SK	Eskişehirspor K
1973	Galatasaray SK	Fenerbahçe SK
1974	Fenerbahçe SK	Beşiktaş JK
1975	Fenerbahçe SK	Galatasaray SK
1976	Trabzonspor K	Fenerbahçe SK
1977	Trabzonspor K	Fenerbahçe SK
1978	Fenerbahçe SK	Trabzonspor K
1979	Trabzonspor K	Galatasaray SK
1980	Trabzonspor K	Fenerbahçe SK
1981	Trabzonspor K	Adanaspor K
1982	Beşiktaş JK	Trabzonspor K
1983	Fenerbahçe SK	Trabzonspor K
1984	Trabzonspor K	Fenerbahçe SK
1985	Fenerbahçe SK	Beşiktaş JK
1986	Beşiktaş JK	Galatasaray SK
1987	Galatasaray SK	Beşiktaş JK
1988	Galatasaray SK	Beşiktaş JK
1989	Fenerbahçe SK	Beşiktaş JK
1990	Beşiktaş JK	Fenerbahçe SK
1991	Beşiktaş JK	Galatasaray SK
1992	Beşiktaş JK	Fenerbahçe SK
1993	Galatasaray SK	Beşiktaş JK
1994	Galatasaray SK	Fenerbahçe SK
1995	Beşiktaş JK	Trabzonspor K
1996	Fenerbahçe SK	Trabzonspor K
1997	Galatasaray SK	Beşiktaş JK
1998	Galatasaray SK	Fenerbahçe SK
1999	Galatasaray SK	Beşiktaş JK
2000	Galatasaray SK	Beşiktaş JK
2001	Fenerbahçe SK	Galatasaray SK
2002	Galatasaray SK	Fenerbahçe SK

Turkish Cup Record 1963–2002

YEAR	WINNERS	SCORE	RUNNERS-UP
1963	Galatasaray SK	2-1, 2-1 (2 legs)	Fenerbahçe SK
1964	Galatasaray SK	0-0, w/o (2 legs)	Altay GK
1965	Galatasaray SK	0-0, 1-0 (2 legs)	Fenerbahçe SK
1966	Galatasaray SK	1-0	Beşiktaş JK
1967	Altay GK	2-2*	Göztepe SK
1968	Fenerbahçe SK	2-0, 0-1 (2 legs)	Altay GK
1969	Göztepe SK	1-0, 1-1 (2 legs)	Galatasaray SK
1970	Göztepe SK	1-2, 3-1 (2 legs)	Eskişehirspor K
1971	Eskişehirspor K	0-1, 2-0 (2 legs)	Bursaspor K
1972	MKE Ankaragücü SK	0-0, 3-0 (2 legs)	Altay GK
1973	Galatasaray SK	3-1, 1-1 (2 legs)	MKE Ankaragücü SK
1974	Fenerbahçe SK	0-1, 3-0 (2 legs)	Bursaspor K
1975	Beşiktaş JK	0-1, 2-0 (2 legs)	Trabzonspor K
1976	Galatasaray SK	1-1, 1-1 (5-4 pens) (2 legs)	Trabzonspor K
1977	Trabzonspor K	1-0, 0-0 (2 legs)	Beşiktaş JK
1978	Trabzonspor K	3-0, 0-0 (2 legs)	Demirspor K
1979	Fenerbahçe SK	1-2, 2-0 (2 legs)	Altay GK
1980	Altay GK	1-0, 1-1 (2 legs)	Galatasaray SK
1981	MKE Ankaragücü SK	2-1, 0-0 (2 legs)	Boluspor K
1982	Galatasaray SK	3-0, 1-2 (2 legs)	MKE Ankaragücü SK
1983	Fenerbahçe SK	2-0, 2-1 (2 legs)	Mersin Idmanyurdu SK
1984	Trabzonspor K	2-0	Beşiktaş JK
1985	Galatasaray SK	2-1, 0-0 (2 legs)	Trabzonspor K
1986	Bursaspor K	2-0	Altay GK
1987	Gençlerbirligi SK	5-0, 1-2 (2 legs)	Eskişehirspor K
1988	Sakaryaspor K	2-0, 1-1 (2 legs)	Samsunspor K
1989	Beşiktaş JK	1-0, 2-1 (2 legs)	Fenerbahçe SK
1990	Beşiktaş JK	2-0	Trabzonspor K
1991	Galatasaray SK	3-1	MKE Ankaragücü SK
1992	Trabzonspor K	0-3, 5-1 (2 legs)	Bursaspor K
1993	Galatasaray SK	1-0, 2-2 (2 legs)	Beşiktaş JK
1994	Beşiktaş JK	3-2, 0-0 (2 legs)	Galatasaray SK
1995	Trabzonspor K	3-2, 1-0 (2 legs)	Galatasaray SK
1996	Galatasaray SK	1-0, 1-1 (2 legs)	Fenerbahçe SK
1997	Kocaelispor K	1-0, 1-1 (2 legs)	Trabzonspor K
1998	Beşiktaş JK	1-1, 1-1 (4-2 pens)	Galatasaray SK
1999	Galatasaray SK	0-0, 2-0 (2 legs)	Beşiktaş JK
2000	Galatasaray SK	5-3 (aet)	Antalyaspor
2001	Gençlerbirligi SK	2-2 (aet)(4-1 pens)	Fenerbahçe SK
2002	Kocaelispor	4-0	Beşiktaş JK

w/o denotes walk over

* Altay GK won on toss of a coin.

Turkish Cup Summary

TEAM	TOTALS	WINNERS & RUNNERS-UP (BOLD) (ITALICS)
Galatasaray SK	13, 5	**1963–66, 69, 73, 76, 80, 82, 85, 91, 93, 94, 95, 96, 98, 99, 2000**
Beşiktaş JK	5, 6	*1966,* **75, 77,** *84,* **89, 90, 93, 94,** *98, 99, 2002*
Trabzonspor K	5, 5	*1975, 76,* **77, 78, 84, 85, 90, 92, 95, 97**
Fenerbahçe SK	4, 5	*1963,* **65,** *68, 74, 79, 83, 89, 96, 2001*

This summary only features clubs that have won the Turkish Cup four or more times. For a full list of cup winners and runners-up please see the Cup Record left.

Armenia

Football Federation of Armenia

Founded: 1992
Joined FIFA: 1992
Joined UEFA: 1993

Independent domestic football only came with independence in 1991. Leading clubs Ararat Yerevan, Tsement Ararat and Shirak Gyumri dominate the Armenian game. However, only international matches generate much interest, with tiny crowds at most league games.

SEASON	LEAGUE CHAMPIONS
1997	Pyunik Yerevan
1997*	FK Yerevan
1998	Tsement Ararat
1999	Shirak Gyumri
2000	Araks Ararat
2001	Pyunik Yerevan

YEAR	CUP WINNERS
1998	Tsement Ararat
1999	Tsement Ararat
2000	MIKA Ashtarak
2001	MIKA Ashtarak
2002	Pyunik Yerevan

* Transitional season.

Azerbaijan

Association of Football Federations of Azerbaijan

Founded: 1992
Joined FIFA: 1994
Joined UEFA: 1994

The national championship was originally decided through mini-leagues. Today, a more conventional system is used. The country's best-known club is Neftçi Baku.

SEASON	LEAGUE CHAMPIONS
1998	Kapaz Gäncä
1999	Kapaz Gäncä
2000	Şämkir
2001	Şämkir
2002	Şämkir

YEAR	CUP WINNERS
1998	Kapaz Gäncä
1999	Neftçi Baku
2000	Kapaz Gäncä
2001	Şafa Baku
2002	*abandoned*

Bulgaria

Bŭlgarski Futbolen Sŭyuz
Founded: 1923
Joined FIFA: 1924
Joined UEFA: 1954

A national league started in 1937, but was reconstituted in 1946 by the Communists. The Bulgarian Cup, which began in 1938, was known as the Soviet Army Cup between 1946 and 1991.

SEASON	LEAGUE CHAMPIONS
1998	Lovech
1999	Lovech
2000	Levski Sofia
2001	Levski Sofia
2002	Levski Sofia

YEAR	CUP WINNERS
1998	Levski Sofia
1999	CSKA Sofia
2000	Levski Sofia
2001	Lovech
2002	Levski Sofia

Cyprus

Kipriaki Omospondia Podosferu

Founded: 1934
Joined FIFA: 1948
Joined UEFA: 1962

The division of the island in 1974 between Greek and Turkish areas also divided the league. Turkish Northern Cyprus has its own organization but is not recognized by FIFA.

SEASON	LEAGUE CHAMPIONS
1998	Anorthosis Famagusta
1999	Anorthosis Famagusta
2000	Anorthosis Famagusta
2001	Omonia Nicosia
2002	APOEL Nicosia

YEAR	CUP WINNERS
1998	Anorthosis Famagusta
1999	APOEL Nicosia
2000	Omonia Nicosia
2001	Apollon Limassol
2002	Anorthosis Famagusta

Georgia

Georgian Football Federation
Founded: 1990
Joined FIFA: 1992
Joined UEFA: 1992

Uniquely among ex-Soviet republics, Georgia managed to establish a separate national league and cup before formal political independence in 1991. Georgian football has been dominated by Dinamo Tbilisi.

SEASON	LEAGUE CHAMPIONS
1998	Dinamo Tbilisi
1999	Dinamo Tbilisi
2000	Torpedo Kutaisi
2001	Torpedo Kutaisi
2002	Torpedo Kutaisi

YEAR	CUP WINNERS
1998	Dinamo Batumi
1999	Torpedo Kutaisi
2000	Lokomotivi Tbilisi
2001	Torpedo Kutaisi
2002	Lokomotivi Tbilisi

Israel

Israel Football Association
Founded: 1928
Joined FIFA: 1929
Joined UEFA: 1992

An FA was affiliated to the Asian Football Confederation before the creation of Israel in 1948. Political upheavals have affected Israeli football since then, but membership of UEFA in 1992 has stabilized the situation.

SEASON	LEAGUE CHAMPIONS
1998	Beitar Jerusalem
1999	Hapoel Haifa
2000	Hapoel Tel-Aviv
2001	Maccabi Haifa
2002	Maccabi Haifa

YEAR	CUP WINNERS
1998	Maccabi Haifa
1999	Hapoel Tel-Aviv
2000	Hapoel Tel-Aviv
2001	Maccabi Tel-Aviv
2002	Maccabi Tel-Aviv

Moldova

Federaţia Moldoveneasca de Fotbal

Founded: 1990
Joined FIFA: 1994
Joined UEFA: 1992

Moldova was formed from the break up of the Soviet Union in 1991, with the formation of a national FA and national league and cup competitions preceding a formal state of independence.

SEASON	LEAGUE CHAMPIONS
1998	Zimbru Chişinău
1999	Zimbru Chişinău
2000	Zimbru Chişinău
2001	Serif Tiraspol
2002	Serif Tiraspol

YEAR	CUP WINNERS
1998	Zimbru Chişinău
1999	Serif Tiraspol
2000	Constructorul Chişinău
2001	Serif Tiraspol
2002	Serif Tiraspol

Romania

Federaţia Romăna de Fotbal
Founded: 1908
Joined FIFA: 1930
Joined UEFA: 1954

ROMANIANS took to football earlier and more enthusiastically than any other Balkan nation, and despite war, revolution and penury, football remains an enduring passion in the country. The national FA was set up in 1908, with the considerable support of Prince Carol, heir to the Romanian throne. The first national league was set up in 1910, with play-offs to contest the title until 1934. In 1935, a formal national league and cup competition were established.

The Communist re-creation of Romanian football after the Second World War involved considerable change. Cities were generally restricted to a single team; many clubs that had explicitly regional and ethnic connections (Hungarian, Jewish and German teams) were transformed or wound down. The league was cancelled in 1957 to allow the new season to start in the autumn of that year and finish in spring the following year.

Romanian League Record 1910–2002

SEASON	CHAMPIONS	RUNNERS-UP
1910	Olimpia Bucureşti	not known
1911	Olimpia Bucureşti	not known
1912	United FC Ploieşti	not known
1913	Colentina Bucureşti	not known
1914	Colentina Bucureşti	not known
1915	Romănia-Americana	not known
1916	Prahova Ploieşti	not known
1917–19	no championship	
1920	Venus Bucureşti	not known
1921	Venus Bucureşti	not known
1922	Chinezul Timişoara	Victoria Cluj
1923	Chinezul Timişoara	Victoria Cluj
1924	Chinezul Timişoara	CAO Oradea
1925	Chinezul Timişoara	UCAS Petroşani
1926	Chinezul Timişoara	Juventus Bucureşti
1927	Chinezul Timişoara	Coltea Braşov
1928	Coltea Braşov	Jiul Lupeni
1929	Venus Bucureşti	Romănia Cluj
1930	Juventus Bucureşti	Gloria CFR Arad
1931	UDR Reşiţa	SG Sibiu
1932	Venus Bucureşti	UDR Reşiţa
1933	Ripensia Timişoara	Universitatea Cluj
1934	Venus Bucureşti	Ripensia Timişoara
1935	Ripensia Timişoara	CAO Oradea
1936	Ripensia Timişoara	AMEFA Arad
1937	Venus Bucureşti	Rapid Bucureşti
1938	Ripensia Timişoara	Rapid Bucureşti
1939	Venus Bucureşti	Ripensia Timişoara
1940	Venus Bucureşti	Rapid Bucureşti
1941	Unirea Tricolor	Rapid Bucureşti
1942–46	no championship	
1947	IT Arad	Carmen Bucureşti
1948	IT Arad	CFR Timişoara
1949	ICO Oradea	CFR Bucureşti
1950	Flamura Roşie	Lokomotiva Buch
1951	CCA Bucureşti	Dinamo Bucureşti
1952	CCA Bucureşti	Dinamo Bucureşti
1953	CCA Bucureşti	Dinamo Bucureşti
1954	Flamura Roşie	CCA Bucureşti
1955	Dinamo Bucureşti	Flacără Ploieşti
1956	CCA Bucureşti	Dinamo Bucureşti
1957*		
1958	Petrolul Ploieşti	CCA Bucureşti

Romanian League Record (*continued*)

SEASON	CHAMPIONS	RUNNERS-UP
1960	CCA Bucureşti	Steagul Rosu Braşov
1961	CCA Bucureşti	Dinamo Bucureşti
1962	Dinamo Bucureşti	Petrolul Ploieşti
1963	Dinamo Bucureşti	Steaua Bucureşti
1964	Dinamo Bucureşti	Rapid Bucureşti
1965	Dinamo Bucureşti	Rapid Bucureşti
1966	Petrolul Ploieşti	Rapid Bucureşti
1967	Rapid Bucureşti	Dinamo Bucureşti
1968	Steaua Bucureşti	FC Argeş Piteşti
1969	UT Arad	Dinamo Bucureşti
1970	UT Arad	Rapid Bucureşti
1971	Dinamo Bucureşti	Rapid Bucureşti
1972	FC Argeş Piteşti	UT Arad
1973	Dinamo Bucureşti	Universitatea Craiova
1974	Universitatea Craiova	Dinamo Bucureşti
1975	Universitatea Craiova	ASA Tîrgu Mureş
1976	Steaua Bucureşti	Dinamo Bucureşti
1977	Dinamo Bucureşti	Steaua Bucureşti
1978	Steaua Bucureşti	FC Argeş Piteşti
1979	FC Argeş Piteşti	Dinamo Bucureşti
1980	Universitatea Craiova	Steaua Bucureşti
1981	Universitatea Craiova	Dinamo Bucureşti
1982	Dinamo Bucureşti	Universitatea Craiova
1983	Dinamo Bucureşti	Universitatea Craiova
1984	Dinamo Bucureşti	Steaua Bucureşti
1985	Steaua Bucureşti	Dinamo Bucureşti
1986	Steaua Bucureşti	Sportul Studentesc
1987	Steaua Bucureşti	Dinamo Bucureşti
1988	Steaua Bucureşti	Dinamo Bucureşti
1989	Steaua Bucureşti	Dinamo Bucureşti
1990	Dinamo Bucureşti	Steaua Bucureşti
1991	Universitatea Craiova	Steaua Bucureşti
1992	Dinamo Bucureşti	Steaua Bucureşti
1993	Steaua Bucureşti	Dinamo Bucureşti
1994	Steaua Bucureşti	Universitatea Craiova
1995	Steaua Bucureşti	Universitatea Craiova
1996	Steaua Bucureşti	National Bucureşti
1997	Steaua Bucureşti	National Bucureşti
1998	Steaua Bucureşti	Rapid Bucureşti
1999	Rapid Bucureşti	Dinamo Bucureşti
2000	Dinamo Bucureşti	Rapid Bucureşti
2001	Steaua Bucureşti	Dinamo Bucureşti
2002	Dinamo Bucureşti	National Bucureşti

* There were no recorded league champions for 1957 as Romania's football league changed from a winter-to-winter season to an autumn-to-spring season.

Romanian League Summary

TEAM	TOTALS	CHAMPIONS & RUNNERS-UP (BOLD) (*ITALICS*)
Steaua Bucureşti (includes CCA Bucureşti)	21, 9	**1951–53,** *54,* **56,** *58,* **60, 61,** *63,* **68, 76,** *77,* **78,** *80,* **84,** *85–89,* **90–92,** *93–98,* **2001**
Dinamo Bucureşti	15, 19	*1951–53,* **55,** *56,* **59,** *61,* **62–65,** *67,* **69,** *71,* **73,** *74,* **76,** *77,* **79,** *81,* **82–84,** *85, 87–89,* **90,** *92, 93, 99,* **2000,** *01, 02*
Venus Bucureşti	8, 0	**1920, 21, 29, 32, 34, 37, 39, 40**
Chinezul Timişoara	6, 0	**1922–27**
Universitatea Craiova	5, 5	*1973,* **74, 75, 80, 81,** *82, 83,* **91,** *94, 95*
Ripensia Timişoara	4, 2	**1933,** *34,* **35, 36, 38,** *39*
UT Arad (includes IT Arad)	4, 1	**1947, 48, 69, 70,** *72*
Petrolul Ploieşti	3, 1	**1958, 59,** *62,* **66**
Rapid Bucureşti	2, 11	*1937, 38, 40, 41, 64–66,* **67,** *70, 71, 98,* **99,** *2000*
FC Argeş Piteşti	2, 2	*1968,* **72,** *78,* **79**
Colentina Bucureşti	2, 0	**1913, 14**
Flamura Roşie	2, 0	**1950, 54**

Romanian League Summary

TEAM	TOTALS	CHAMPIONS & RUNNERS-UP (BOLD) (ITALICS)
Olimpia Bucureşti	2, 0	**1910, 11**
Coltea Braşov	1, 1	_1927,_ **28**
Juventus Bucureşti	1, 1	_1926,_ **30**
UDR Reşiţa	1, 1	**1931,** _32_
ICO Oradea	1, 0	**1949**
Prahova Ploieşti	1, 0	**1916**
România-Americana	1, 0	**1915**
Unirea Tricolor	1, 0	**1941**
United Ploieşti	1, 0	**1912**
National Bucureşti	0, 3	_1996, 97, 2002_
CAO Oradea	0, 2	_1924, 35_
Victoria Cluj	0, 2	_1922, 23_
AMEFA Arad	0, 1	_1936_
ASA Tîrgu Mureş	0, 1	_1975_
Carmen Bucureşti	0, 1	_1947_
CFR Bucureşti	0, 1	_1949_
CFR Timişoara	0, 1	_1948_
Flacără Ploieşti	0, 1	_1955_
Gloria CFR Arad	0, 1	_1930_
Jiul Lupeni	0, 1	_1928_
Lokomotiva Buch	0, 1	_1950_
România Cluj	0, 1	_1929_
SG Sibiu	0, 1	_1931_
Sportul Studentesc	0, 1	_1986_
Steagul Rosu Braşov	0, 1	_1960_
UCAS Petroşani	0, 1	_1925_
Universitatea Cluj	0, 1	_1933_

Romanian Cup Record 1934–2002

YEAR	WINNERS	SCORE	RUNNERS-UP
1934	Ripensia Timişoara	5-0	Universitatea Cluj
1935	CFR Bucureşti	6-5 (aet)	Ripensia Timişoara
1936	Ripensia Timişoara	5-1	Unirea Tricolor
1937	Rapid Bucureşti	5-1	Ripensia Timişoara
1938	Rapid Bucureşti	3-2	CAMT Timişoara
1939	Rapid Bucureşti	2-0	Sportul Studentesc
1940	Rapid Bucureşti	2-2 (aet), (replay) 4-4 (aet), (replay) 2-2 (aet), (replay) 2-1	Venus Bucureşti
1941	Rapid Bucureşti	4-3	Unirea Tricolor
1942	Rapid Bucureşti	7-1	Universitatea Cluj
1943	Tirnu Severin	4-0	Sportul Studentesc
1944–47		no competition	
1948	IT Arad	3-2	CFR Timişoara
1949	CSCA Bucureşti	2-1	CSU Cluj
1950	CCA Bucureşti	3-1	Flamura Roşie
1951	CCA Bucureşti	3-1 (aet)	Flacără Medias
1952	CCA Bucureşti	2-0	Flacără Ploieşti
1953	Flamura Roşie	1-0 (aet)	CCA Bucureşti
1954	Metalul Reşiţa	2-0	Dinamo Bucureşti
1955	CCA Bucureşti	6-3	Progresul Oradea
1956	Progresul Oradea	2-0	Metalul Turzil
1957		no competition	
1958	Ştiinţa Timişoara	1-0	Progresul Bucureşti
1959	Dinamo Bucureşti	4-0	Minerul Baia Mare
1960	Progresul Bucureşti	2-0	Dinamo Bucureşti
1961	Arieşul Turda	2-1	Rapid Bucureşti
1962	Steaua Bucureşti	5-1	Rapid Bucureşti
1963	Petrolul Ploieşti	6-1	Siderurgistul Galaţi
1964	Dinamo Bucureşti	5-3	Steaua Bucureşti
1965	Ştiinţa Cluj	2-1	Dinamo Piteşti
1966	Steaua Bucureşti	4-0	IT Arad
1967	Steaua Bucureşti	6-0	Foresta Fălticeni
1968	Dinamo Bucureşti	3-1 (aet)	Rapid Bucureşti
1969	Steaua Bucureşti	2-1	Dinamo Bucureşti
1970	Steaua Bucureşti	2-1	Dinamo Bucureşti
1971	Steaua Bucureşti	3-2	Dinamo Bucureşti

Romanian Cup Record (continued)

YEAR	WINNERS	SCORE	RUNNERS-UP
1972	Rapid Bucureşti	2-0	Jiul Petroşani
1973	Chimia Vîlcea	1-1 (aet), (replay) 3-0	Constructorul Galatizi
1974	Jiul Petroşani	4-2	Politehnica Timişoara
1975	Rapid Bucureşti	2-1 (aet)	Universitatea Craiova
1976	Steaua Bucureşti	1-0	CSU Galaţi
1977	Universitatea Craiova	2-1	Steaua Bucureşti
1978	Universitatea Craiova	3-1	Olimpia Satu Mare
1979	Steaua Bucureşti	3-0	Sportul Studentesc
1980	Politehnica Timişoara	2-1 (aet)	Steaua Bucureşti
1981	Universitatea Craiova	6-0	Politehnica Timişoara
1982	Dinamo Bucureşti	3-2	FC Baia Mare
1983	Universitatea Craiova	2-1	Politehnica Timişoara
1984	Dinamo Bucureşti	2-1	Steaua Bucureşti
1985	Steaua Bucureşti	2-1	Universitatea Craiova
1986	Dinamo Bucureşti	1-0	Steaua Bucureşti
1987	Steaua Bucureşti	1-0	Dinamo Bucureşti
1988	Steaua Bucureşti	2-1*	Dinamo Bucureşti
1989	Steaua Bucureşti	1-0	Dinamo Bucureşti
1990	Dinamo Bucureşti	6-4	Steaua Bucureşti
1991	Universitatea Craiova	2-1	FC Bacău
1992	Steaua Bucureşti	1-1 (aet)(3-2 pens)	Politehnica Timişoara
1993	Universitatea Craiova	2-0	Dacia Unirrea Brăila
1994	Gloria Bistraţi	1-0	Universitatea Craiova
1995	Petrolul Ploieşti	1-1 (aet)(5-3 pens)	Rapid Bucureşti
1996	Steaua Bucureşti	3-1	Gloria Bistraţi
1997	Steaua Bucureşti	4-2	National Bucureşti
1998	Rapid Bucureşti	1-0	Universitatea Craiova
1999	Steaua Bucureşti	2-2 (aet)(4-2 pens)	Rapid Bucureşti
2000	Dinamo Bucureşti	2-0	Universitatea Craiova
2001	Dinamo Bucureşti	4-2	Rocar Bucureşti
2002	Rapid Bucureşti	2-1	Dinamo Bucureşti

* Match abandoned at 1-1. However, Romanian FA awarded the match to Steaua as 2-1 victory.

Romanian Cup Summary

TEAM	TOTALS	WINNERS & RUNNERS-UP (BOLD) (ITALICS)
Steaua Bucureşti (includes CCA Bucureşti)	20, 7	**1950–52,** _53, 55,_ **62,** _64,_ **66, 67, 69–71, 76, 77, 79,** _80,_ **84, 85, 86, 87–89, 90, 92, 96, 97, 99**
Rapid Bucureşti	10, 5	**1937–42,** _61, 62,_ **68,** _72,_ **75,** _95, 98, 99,_ **2002**
Dinamo Bucureşti	9, 9	_1954, 59,_ **60, 64, 68,** _69–71,_ **82, 84, 86,** _87–89,_ **90, 2000, 01,** _02_
Universitatea Craiova	6, 5	_1975,_ **77, 78, 81, 83,** _85,_ **91, 93,** _94, 98,_ **2000**
Ripensia Timişoara	2, 2	**1934,** _35,_ **36,** _37_
Petrolul Ploieşti	2, 0	**1963, 95**
Politehnica Timişoara	1, 4	_1974,_ **80,** _81, 83, 92_
Flamura Roşie	1, 1	**1950,** _53_
Gloria Bistraţi	1, 1	**1994,** _96_
IT Arad	1, 1	**1948,** _66_
Jiul Petroşani	1, 1	**1972,** _74_
Progresul Bucureşti	1, 1	_1958,_ **60**
Progresul Oradea	1, 1	**1955,** _56_
Arieşul Turda	1, 0	**1961**
CFR Bucureşti	1, 0	**1935**
Chimia Vîlcea	1, 0	**1973**
CSCA Bucureşti	1, 0	**1949**
Metalul Reşiţa	1, 0	**1954**
Ştiinţa Cluj	1, 0	**1965**
Ştiinţa Timişoara	1, 0	**1958**
Tirnu Severin	1, 0	**1943**

This summary only features the clubs who have won the Romanian Cup. For a full list of runners-up please see the Cup Record above.

ROMANIA

Yugoslavia

Fudbalski Savez Jugoslavije
Founded: 1919
Joined FIFA: 1919
Joined UEFA: 1993

BEFORE THE FIRST WORLD WAR, clubs existed in Belgrade, Split, Zagreb and elsewhere. After the postwar dismemberment of the Ottoman and Austro-Hungarian Empires, the new state of Yugoslavia was formed. With it, in 1919, came a national FA. A national league was established in 1923 but, like Yugoslavia, it was fragmented by the Second World War. Croatia's alliance with Germany saw the creation of an independent Croatian league which lasted for the duration of the war.

With the end of the war and the triumph of General Tito's Communist partisans, Yugoslavian football was reorganized and a national league re-created. It has run continuously ever since, despite the raging civil war in the 1990s and the ensuing departure of Slovenian, Croatian, Bosnian and Macedonian states and clubs.

Yugoslavian League Record 1923–91

SEASON	CHAMPIONS	RUNNERS-UP
1923	Gradanski Zagreb	SASK Sarajevo
1924	Yugoslavia Beograd	Hajduk Split
1925	Yugoslavia Beograd	Gradanski Beograd
1926	Gradanski Zagreb	Yugoslav Beograd
1927	Hajduk Split	BSK Beograd
1928	Concordia Zagreb	Hajduk Split
1929	Hajduk Split	BSK Beograd
1930	Concordia Zagreb	Yugoslav Beograd
1931	BSK Beograd	Concordia Zagreb
1932	Concordia Zagreb	Hajduk Split
1933	BSK Beograd	Hajduk Split
1934	*no championship*	
1935	BSK Beograd	Yugoslav Beograd
1936	BSK Beograd	Slavia Sarajevo
1937	Gradanski Zagreb	Hajduk Split
1938	HASK Zagreb	BSK Beograd
1939	BSK Beograd	Gradanski Beograd
1940	Gradanski Zagreb	BSK Beograd
1941–46	*no championship*	
1947	Partizan Beograd	Dinamo Zagreb
1948	Dinamo Zagreb	Hajduk Split
1949	Partizan Beograd	Crvena Zvezda
1950	Hajduk Split	Crvena Zvezda
1951	Crvena Zvezda	Dinamo Zagreb
1952	Hajduk Split	Crvena Zvezda
1953	Crvena Zvezda	Hajduk Split
1954	Dinamo Zagreb	Partizan Beograd
1955	Hajduk Split	BSK Beograd
1956	Crvena Zvezda	Partizan Beograd
1957	Crvena Zvezda	Vojvodina Novi Sad
1958	Dinamo Zagreb	Partizan Beograd
1959	Crvena Zvezda	Partizan Beograd
1960	Crvena Zvezda	Dinamo Zagreb
1961	Partizan Beograd	Crvena Zvezda
1962	Partizan Beograd	Vojvodina Novi Sad
1963	Partizan Beograd	Dinamo Zagreb
1964	Crvena Zvezda	OFK Beograd
1965	Partizan Beograd	FK Sarajevo
1966	Vojvodina Novi Sad	Dinamo Zagreb
1967	FK Sarajevo	Dinamo Zagreb
1968	Crvena Zvezda	Dinamo Zagreb
1969	Crvena Zvezda	Dinamo Zagreb
1970	Crvena Zvezda	Partizan Beograd
1971	Hajduk Split	Željezničar Sarajevo
1972	Željezničar Sarajevo	Crvena Zvezda

Yugoslavian League Record (*continued*)

SEASON	CHAMPIONS	RUNNERS-UP
1973	Crvena Zvezda	Velez Mostar
1974	Hajduk Split	Velez Mostar
1975	Hajduk Split	Vojvodina Novi Sad
1976	Partizan Beograd	Hajduk Split
1977	Crvena Zvezda	Dinamo Zagreb
1978	Partizan Beograd	Crvena Zvezda
1979	Hajduk Split	Dinamo Zagreb
1980	Crvena Zvezda	FK Sarajevo
1981	Crvena Zvezda	Hajduk Split
1982	Dinamo Zagreb	Crvena Zvezda
1983	Partizan Beograd	Dinamo Zagreb
1984	Crvena Zvezda	Partizan Beograd
1985	FK Sarajevo	Hajduk Split
1986	Partizan Beograd	Crvena Zvezda
1987	Partizan Beograd	Velez Mostar
1988	Crvena Zvezda	Partizan Beograd
1989	Vojvodina Novi Sad	Crvena Zvezda
1990	Crvena Zvezda	Dinamo Zagreb
1991	Crvena Zvezda	Dinamo Zagreb

Yugoslavian League Record 1992–2002

SEASON	CHAMPIONS	RUNNERS-UP
1992	Crvena Zvezda	Partizan Beograd
1993	Partizan Beograd	Crvena Zvezda
1994	Partizan Beograd	Crvena Zvezda
1995	Vojvodina Novi Sad	Crvena Zvezda
1996	Partizan Beograd	Crvena Zvezda
1997	Partizan Beograd	Crvena Zvezda
1998	FK Obilić	Crvena Zvezda
1999	Partizan Beograd	FK Obilić
2000	Crvena Zvezda	Partizan Beograd
2001	Crvena Zvezda	Partizan Beograd
2002	Partizan Beograd	Crvena Zvezda

Yugoslavian League Summary

TEAM	TOTALS	CHAMPIONS & RUNNERS-UP (BOLD) (*ITALICS*)
Crvena Zvezda	**21**, *16*	*1949, 50*, **51**, *52, 53*, **56**, *57*, **59**, **60**, *61*, **64**, **68–70**, *72*, **73**, **77**, *78*, **80**, **81**, *82*, **84**, *86*, **88**, *89*, **90–92**, *93–98*, **2000**, **01**, *02*
Partizan Beograd	**17**, *10*	**1947**, *49*, **54**, *56*, *58*, *59*, **61–63**, **65**, *70*, **76**, *78*, **83**, *84*, **86**, **87**, *88*, **92**, **93**, **94**, **96**, **97**, **99**, *2000*, *01*, **02**
Hajduk Split	**9**, *10*	*1924*, **27**, *28*, *29*, *32*, *33*, *37*, *48*, **50**, **52**, *53*, **55**, **71**, **74**, **75**, *76*, **79**, *81*, *85*
BSK Beograd	**5**, *5*	*1927*, *29*, **31**, *33*, **35**, **36**, *38*, *39*, **40**, *55*

This summary only features the top four clubs in the Yugoslavian League. For a full list of league champions and runners-up please see the League Record above.

Yugoslavian Cup Record 1947–91

YEAR	WINNERS	SCORE	RUNNERS-UP
1947	Partizan Beograd	**2-0**	Naša Krila Zemun
1948	Crvena Zvezda	**3-0**	Partizan Beograd
1949	Crvena Zvezda	**3-2**	Naša Krila Zemun
1950	Crvena Zvezda	**1-1**, (replay) **3-0**	Dinamo Zagreb
1951	Dinamo Zagreb	**2-0, 2-0** (2 legs)	Vojvodina Novi Sad
1952	Partizan Beograd	**6-0**	Crvena Zvezda
1953	BSK Beograd	**2-0**	Hajduk Split
1954	Partizan Beograd	**4-1**	Crvena Zvezda
1955	BSK Beograd	**2-0**	Hajduk Split

YUGOSLAVIA

Yugoslavian Cup Record (*continued*)

YEAR	WINNERS	SCORE	RUNNERS-UP
1956		*no competition*	
1957	Partizan Beograd	5-3	Radnicki Beograd
1958	Crvena Zvezda	4-0	Velez Mostar
1959	Crvena Zvezda	3-1	Partizan Beograd
1960	Dinamo Zagreb	3-2	Partizan Beograd
1961	Vardar Skopje	2-1	Varteks Varaždin
1962	OFK Beograd	4-1	Spartak Subotica
1963	Dinamo Zagreb	4-1	Hajduk Split
1964	Crvena Zvezda	3-0	Dinamo Zagreb
1965	Dinamo Zagreb	2-1	Budučnost Titograd
1966	OFK Beograd	6-2 (aet)	Dinamo Zagreb
1967	Hajduk Split	2-1	FK Sarajevo
1968	Crvena Zvezda	7-0	FK Bor
1969	Dinamo Zagreb	3-3, (replay) 3-0	Hajduk Split
1970	Crvena Zvezda	2-2, (replay) 1-0 (aet)	Olimpia Ljubljana
1971	Crvena Zvezda	4-0	Sloboda Turzia
1972	Hajduk Split	2-1	Dinamo Zagreb
1973	Dinamo Zagreb	2-1	Crvena Zvezda
1974	Hajduk Split	1-1, (replay) 2-1	Crvena Zvezda
1975	Hajduk Split	1-0	Borac Banja Luka
1976	Hajduk Split	1-0 (aet)	Dinamo Zagreb
1977	Hajduk Split	2-0 (aet)	Budučnost Titograd
1978	NK Rijeka	1-0 (aet)	Trepca Mitrovica
1979	NK Rijeka	0-0, (replay) 2-1	Partizan Beograd
1980	Dinamo Zagreb	1-1, (replay) 1-0	Crvena Zvezda
1981	Velez Mostar	3-2	Željeznicar Sarajevo
1982	Crvena Zvezda	2-2, (replay) 4-2	Dinamo Zagreb
1983	Dinamo Zagreb	3-2	FK Sarajevo
1984	Hajduk Split	0-0, (replay) 2-1	Crvena Zvezda
1985	Crvena Zvezda	1-1, (replay) 2-1	Dinamo Zagreb
1986	Velez Mostar	3-1	Dinamo Zagreb
1987	Hajduk Split	1-1 (aet)(9-8 pens)	NK Rijeka
1988	Borac Banja Luka	1-0	Crvena Zvezda
1989	Partizan Beograd	6-1	Velez Mostar
1990	Crvena Zvezda	1-0	Hajduk Split
1991	Hajduk Split	1-0	Crvena Zvezda

Yugoslavian Cup Record 1992–2002

YEAR	WINNERS	SCORE	RUNNERS-UP
1992	Partizan Beograd	1-0, 2-2 (2 legs)	Crvena Zvezda
1993	Crvena Zvezda	0-1, 1-0 (5-4 pens)(2 legs)	Partizan Beograd
1994	Partizan Beograd	3-2, 6-1 (2 legs)	Spartak Subotica
1995	Crvena Zvezda	4-0, 0-0 (2 legs)	FK Obilić
1996	Crvena Zvezda	3-0, 3-1 (2 legs)	Partizan Beograd
1997	Crvena Zvezda	0-0, 1-0 (2 legs)	Vojvodina Novi Sad
1998	Partizan Beograd	0-0, 2-0 (2 legs)	FK Obilić
1999	Crvena Zvezda	4-2, 4-0 (2 legs)	Partizan Beograd
2000	Crvena Zvezda	4-0	Napradak Kruševac
2001	Partizan Beograd	1-0	Crvena Zvezda
2002	Crvena Zvezda	1-0	Sartid Smederovo

Yugoslavian Cup Summary

TEAM	TOTALS	WINNERS & RUNNERS-UP (BOLD) (*ITALICS*)
Crvena Zvezda	**19**, *10*	**1948–50**, *52, 54*, **58, 59, 64, 68, 70, 71**, *73, 74*, **80, 82**, *84*, **85**, *88*, **90**, *91*, **92**, *93*, **95–97**, *99*, **2000**, *01*, **02**
Partizan Beograd	**9**, *7*	**1947**, *48*, **52, 54, 57**, *59*, **60**, *79*, **89, 92**, *93*, **94**, *96*, **98**, *99*, **2001**
Hajduk Split	**9**, *5*	*1953, 55*, **63**, *67*, **69**, *72*, **74–77**, *84*, **87**, *90*, **91**
Dinamo Zagreb	**8**, *8*	*1950*, **51**, *60*, **63**, *64*, **65, 66, 69**, *72*, **73**, *76*, **80**, *82, 83, 85, 86*

This summary only features the top four clubs in the Yugoslavian Cup.
For a full list of cup winners and runners-up please see the Cup Record above.

Albania

Federata Shqiptarë e Futbollit
Founded: 1930
Joined FIFA: 1932
Joined UEFA: 1954

Albania's national league began in 1929 (prior to the formation of the national FA), and the cup competition in 1947. Both tournaments have been dominated by teams from the capital city, Tirana.

SEASON	LEAGUE CHAMPIONS
1998	Vllaznia Shkodër
1999	SK Tirana
2000	SK Tirana
2001	Vllaznia Shkodër
2002	Dinamo Tirana

YEAR	CUP WINNERS
1998	Apolonia Fier
1999	SK Tirana
2000	Teuta Durrës
2001	SK Tirana
2002	SK Tirana

Bosnia-Herzegovina

Nogometni Savez Bosne i Hercegovine
Founded: 1992
Joined FIFA: 1996
Joined UEFA: 1996

A Bosnian FA was established in 1992 and league football in separate Serbian, Muslim and Croat leagues in 1996. The top two teams from each league play for the national championship.

SEASON	LEAGUE CHAMPIONS
1998	Željeznicar Sarajevo
1999	*Play-offs cancelled*
2000	Brotnjo Citluk
2001	Željeznicar Sarajevo
2002	Željeznicar Sarajevo

YEAR	CUP WINNERS
1998	Sarajevo
1999	Sarajevo
2000	Željeznicar Sarajevo
2001	Željeznicar Sarajevo
2002	Sarajevo

Croatia

Croatian Football Federation
Founded: 1912, 1991
Joined FIFA: 1992
Joined UEFA: 1993

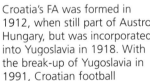

Croatia's FA was formed in 1912, when still part of Austro-Hungary, but was incorporated into Yugoslavia in 1918. With the break-up of Yugoslavia in 1991, Croatian football regained its independence.

SEASON	LEAGUE CHAMPIONS
1998	Dinamo Zagreb
1999	Dinamo Zagreb
2000	Dinamo Zagreb
2001	Hajduk Split
2002	NK Zagreb

YEAR	CUP WINNERS
1998	Dinamo Zagreb
1999	Osijek
2000	Hajduk Split
2001	Dinamo Zagreb
2002	Dinamo Zagreb

Macedonia

Macedonian Football Union
Founded: 1908
Joined FIFA: 1994
Joined UEFA: 1994

Contemporary Macedonia emerged from the break-up of the former Yugoslavia in 1991. National football competitions, cup and league, rapidly followed independence, starting in the 1992–93 season.

SEASON	LEAGUE CHAMPIONS
1998	Sileks Kratovo
1999	Sloga Jugomagnat Skopje
2000	Sloga Jugomagnat Skopje
2001	Sloga Jugomagnat Skopje
2002	Vardar Skopje

YEAR	CUP WINNERS
1998	Vardar Skopje
1999	Vardar Skopje
2000	Sloga Jugomagnat Skopje
2001	Pelister Bitola
2002	Pobeda Prilep

Russia

THE SEASON IN REVIEW 2001

OLEG ROMANTSEV'S SPARTAK Moskva maintained its winning streak, making a total of six-in-a-row and nine-out-of-ten championship titles in the post-Soviet Russian league. Though the winners were the same, there was at last serious competition for the title from both Lokomotiv Moskva and Zenit St. Peterburg. Spartak began the season poorly, having sold club captain Andrei Tikhonov to the footballing wastelands of Krylya Sovetov Samara after disagreements with coach Romantsev. Sovetov had a fantastic run of form in the first half of the season, topping the table at the halfway mark, only to fade in the second half. Yegor Titov, Russian Footballer of the Year, was Spartak's new captain, top goalscorer and midfield lynchpin, but he alone could not prevent a poor start to the season and a prolonged mid-season dip in form. Spartak was revived by the return of striker Vladimir Beschastnykh. After seven years at Werder Bremen and Racing Santander (a good deal of it on the bench), he scored in his first game at CSKA and Spartak never relinquished its lead.

Competition came from Lokomotiv Moscow and Zenit St. Peterburg. Lokomotiv, rarely for a Russian club, has carefully husbanded its resources, and with new sponsorship deals and a new stadium under construction the club has been steadily rebuilding. Coach Yuriy Syamin has carefully blended a youthful home-grown squad with successful foreign imports like Nigerian striker James Obiorah and South African winger Jacob Lekgetho. Zenit has had to survive without foreign reinforcements, but its fast, fit squad gave everyone trouble, most imperiously when it thrashed CSKA 6-1 and sent coach Pavel Sadyrin on his way. With two games to go, Spartak clinched the title, beating Zenit at home to take the team out of reach of chasing Lokomotiv.

Above: Russian Cup Final, June 2001. Lokomotiv (in red) may not have broken Spartak's grip on the league but is creating its own in the cup. In a thrilling see-saw match, Anzhi Makhachkala took the lead in the 89th minute, only to see Lokomotiv equalize in injury time and win 4-3 on penalties to take its fourth cup in six years.

Left: Vladimir Beschastnykh spent nearly two years on the bench at Racing Santander in Spain, his conflict with coach Benitez so bad that Russian newspapers reported him as saying he often supported the opposition, hoping the coach would be sacked. Santander was relegated and Beschastnykh brought his speed and work-rate up front back to his first club, Spartak, in 2001.

Russian League Table 2001 – First Level

CLUB	P	W	D	L	F	A	Pts	
Spartak Moskva	30	17	9	4	56	30	60	Champions
Lokomotiv Moskva	30	16	8	6	53	24	56	Champions League
Zenit Sankt-Peterburg	30	16	8	6	52	35	56	UEFA Cup
Torpedo Moskva	30	15	7	8	53	42	52	
Krylya Sovetov Samara	30	14	7	9	38	23	49	
Saturn Moscow Region	30	13	8	9	45	22	47	
CSKA Moskva	30	12	11	7	39	30	47	
Sokol Saratov	30	12	5	13	31	42	41	
Dinamo Moskva	30	10	8	12	43	51	38	
Rotor Volgograd	30	8	8	14	38	42	32	
Alania Vladikavkaz	30	8	8	14	31	47	32	
Rostselmash Rostov-na-Donu	30	8	8	14	29	43	32	
Anzhi Makhachkala	30	7	11	12	28	34	32	
Torpedo-ZIL Moskva	30	7	10	13	22	35	31	
Fakel Voronezh	30	8	4	18	30	53	28	Relegated
Chernomorets Novorossiysk	30	5	8	17	19	54	23	Relegated

Promoted clubs: Uralan Elista, Shinnik Yaroslavl.

Russian Cup

2001 FINAL

June 20 – Dinamo Stadium, Moscow

Locomotiv 1-1 Anzhi
Moskva   Makhachkala
(Janashia 90)   (N. Sirkhayev 89)
Att: 8,000
Ref: Valentin Ivanov

Lokomotiv Moskva won 4-3 on pens

International Club Performances 2001–02

CLUB	COMPETITION	PROGRESS
Lokomotiv Moskva	Champions League	1st Group Stage
	UEFA Cup	3rd Round
Spartak Moskva	Champions League	1st Group Stage
Dinamo Moskva	UEFA Cup	2nd Round
Torpedo Moskva	UEFA Cup	1st Round

Top Goalscorers 2001

PLAYER	CLUB	NATIONALITY	GOALS
Dmitriy Vyaz'mikin	Torpedo Moskva	Russian	18
Andrey Fed'kov	Sokol Saratov	Russian	14
James Obiorah	Lokomotiv Moskva	Nigerian	14
Serghei Rogaciov	Saturn Ramensko	Moldovan	14

RUSSIA

Brazilian striker Louis Robson, in action for Spartak, helped the club win its sixth league championship in a row.

Above: Ruslan Nigmatullin, Russia's leading goalkeeper, was the foundation of Lokomotiv Moskva's solid defence. He agreed to stay with the club until the end of the season, but a European transfer can't be far away.

Left: James Obiorah. While many imported players in the Russian league have found conditions hard going, Nigerian forward Obiorah was outstanding for Lokomotiv during the 2001 season.

Below: Rolan Gusev, former captain of Dinamo Moskva, lines up for CSKA. New owner, Yevgeni Giner, has finally found the money to begin rebuilding the old army team.

Ukraine

THE SEASON IN REVIEW 2001–02

THE OLD ORDER has finally passed. The last Ukrainian season was marked by the death of its greatest coach, Valeri Lobanovsky, who had coached Dynamo Kyiv and the Russian and Ukrainian national teams over the last four decades. Lobanovsky assembled the most sophisticated and dedicated coaching set-up in Soviet football, with the emphasis on strength, speed and the coordination of player's movement – a scientific model of football training and tactics that had come to dominate the Ukrainian game. With his death at 71, the torch passed to Dynamo's assistant coach; but his empire was under assault. For the first time in a decade a sustained and, in the end, unstoppable challenge was mounted to Dynamo Kyiv's domination of Ukrainian football.

In October 2001, Shakhtar president Rinat Akhmetov announced that the Italian Nevio Scala was to coach the club. Scala brought youth into the side and utterly rejected the Lobanovsky model of obsessional statistical post-match analysis as the center of his coaching strategy. His cavalier posture struck a resounding note. The team outperformed itself, creeping up and then overtaking leaders Dynamo Kyiv in the spring. Shakhtar's threat was made real in the Ukrainian Cup Final, where Dynamo equalized twice before Shakhtar took the cup in extra time. In the final weeks of the season, Shakhtar's resolve was unbroken and the team took its first – anyone but Dynamo's first – Ukrainian league title with a nervy 1-0 victory over Zakarpattya.

Above: 'I always get my man'. Shakhtar Donetsk president Rinat Akhmetov (left) unveils his secret weapon: Italian coach Nevio Scala.

Right: Valeri Lobanovsky coached not only Dynamo, but also the Ukrainian national team. His death in May 2002 was marked with a state funeral and his body lay in state in Dynamo's stadium, allowing over 100,000 people to pay their last respects.

Ukrainian Premier League Table 2001–02

CLUB	P	W	D	L	F	A	Pts	
Shakhtar Donetsk	26	20	6	0	49	10	66	Champions League
Dynamo Kyiv	26	20	5	1	62	9	65	Champions League
Metalurg Donetsk	26	12	6	8	38	28	42	UEFA Cup
Metalist Kharkov	26	11	7	8	35	36	40	UEFA Cup
Metalurg Zaporizhzhya	26	11	7	8	25	22	40	
Dnipro Dnipropetrovsk	26	11	7	8	30	20	40	
Tavriya Simferopol	26	8	6	12	27	36	30	
SKA Karpati Lvov	26	7	8	11	19	31	29	
Kyrvbas Kryvi-Rih	26	6	10	10	28	40	28	
Metalurg Mariupol	26	6	8	12	29	42	26	
Vorskla Poltava	26	6	7	13	19	33	25	
Arsenal Kyiv*	26	6	5	15	18	28	23	
Polihraftechnika Oleksandriya	26	5	8	13	21	39	23	
Zakarpattya Uzhgorod	26	5	6	15	23	49	21	Relegated

Promoted clubs: Obolon Kyiv, SC Volyn-1 Lutsk, Chernomorets Odesa.
*CSCA Kyiv was renamed Arsenal Kyiv during the winter break.

Top Goalscorers 2001–02

PLAYER	CLUB	NATIONALITY	GOALS
Serhiy Shyschenko	Metalurg Donetsk	Ukrainian	12
Vitaliy Pushkutsa	Metalist Kharkov	Ukrainian	10
Valentin Belkevich	Dynamo Kyiv	Belarussian	9
Andrei Vorobei	Shakhtar Donetsk	Ukrainian	9

Ukrainian Cup

2002 FINAL
May 26 – Olympic Stadium, Kyiv
Shakhtar 3-2 Dynamo
Donetsk   Kyiv
(Popov 10,   (Byalkevich 31,
Atelkin 82,   Shatskikh 50)
Vorobei 99)
(after extra time)
h-t: 1-1 **90 mins:** 2-2 **Att:** 80,000
Ref: Melnychuk

Right: Metalurg Donetsk (in blue) and Dynamo Kyiv battle during a league match. Metalurg finished third but was over 20 points behind Dynamo and Shakhtar.

International Club Performances 2001–02

CLUB	COMPETITION	PROGRESS
Dynamo Kyiv	Champions League	1st Group Stage
Shakhtar Donetsk	Champions League	3rd Qualifying Round
	UEFA Cup	1st Round
Arsenal Kyiv	UEFA Cup	2nd Round
Dnipro Dnipropetrovsk	UEFA Cup	1st Round

UKRAINE

Andrei Vorobei was Shakhtar's leading scorer in the team's first Ukrainian championship season.

Above: *Action from the league meeting between Dynamo (in blue) and Zakarpattya. Dynamo finished second in the league for the first time since 1991; Zakarpattya from Uzhgorod was relegated.*

*By beating **Dynamo** in the Ukrainian Cup Final, Shakhtar Donetsk has announced the end of the old order. Here Shakhtar's captain receives the magnificent trophy.*

RUSSIA

Association Football in Russia

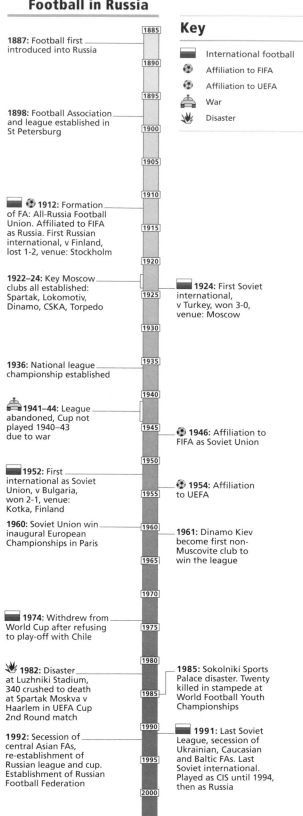

1887: Football first introduced into Russia | 1885

| 1890

1898: Football Association and league established in St Petersburg | 1895 / 1900

| 1905

1912: Formation of FA: All-Russia Football Union. Affiliated to FIFA as Russia. First Russian international, v Finland, lost 1-2, venue: Stockholm | 1910 / 1915 / 1920

1922–24: Key Moscow clubs all established: Spartak, Lokomotiv, Dinamo, CSKA, Torpedo | 1925

1924: First Soviet international, v Turkey, won 3-0, venue: Moscow | 1925

| 1930

1936: National league championship established | 1935

| 1940

1941–44: League abandoned, Cup not played 1940–43 due to war | 1945

1946: Affiliation to FIFA as Soviet Union | 1945 / 1950

1952: First international as Soviet Union, v Bulgaria, won 2-1, venue: Kotka, Finland | 1955

1954: Affiliation to UEFA | 1955

1960: Soviet Union win inaugural European Championships in Paris | 1960

1961: Dinamo Kiev become first non-Muscovite club to win the league | 1965

| 1970

1974: Withdrew from World Cup after refusing to play-off with Chile | 1975

| 1980

1982: Disaster at Luzhniki Stadium, 340 crushed to death at Spartak Moskva v Haarlem in UEFA Cup 2nd Round match | 1985

1985: Sokolniki Sports Palace disaster. Twenty killed in stampede at World Football Youth Championships | 1985

| 1990

1992: Secession of central Asian FAs, re-establishment of Russian league and cup. Establishment of Russian Football Federation | 1995

1991: Last Soviet League, secession of Ukrainian, Caucasian and Baltic FAs. Last Soviet international. Played as CIS until 1994, then as Russia | 1990 / 1995

| 2000

| 2005

Key

	International football
	Affiliation to FIFA
	Affiliation to UEFA
	War
	Disaster

Russia: The main clubs

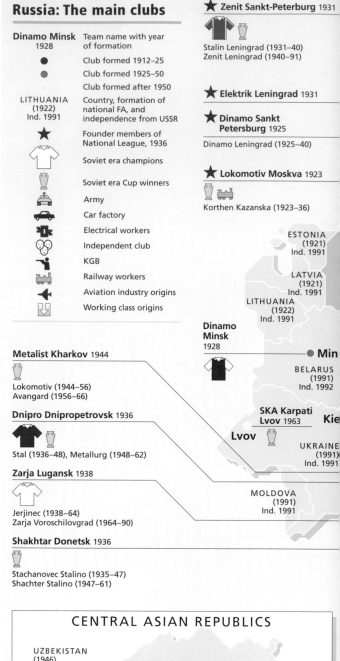

Dinamo Minsk 1928

● Team name with year of formation
● Club formed 1912–25
● Club formed 1925–50
○ Club formed after 1950

LITHUANIA (1922) Ind. 1991 Country, formation of national FA, and independence from USSR

★ Founder members of National League, 1936

Soviet era champions

Soviet era Cup winners

Army

Car factory

Electrical workers

Independent club

KGB

Railway workers

Aviation industry origins

Working class origins

★ **Zenit Sankt-Peterburg** 1931
Stalin Leningrad (1931–40)
Zenit Leningrad (1940–91)

★ **Elektrik Leningrad** 1931

★ **Dinamo Sankt Petersburg** 1925
Dinamo Leningrad (1925–40)

★ **Lokomotiv Moskva** 1923
Korthen Kazanska (1923–36)

Metalist Kharkov 1944
Lokomotiv (1944–56)
Avangard (1956–66)

Dnipro Dnipropetrovsk 1936
Stal (1936–48), Metallurg (1948–62)

Zarja Lugansk 1938
Jerjinec (1938–64)
Zarja Voroschilovgrad (1964–90)

Shakhtar Donetsk 1936
Stachanovec Stalino (1935–47)
Shachter Stalino (1947–61)

ESTONIA (1921) Ind. 1991
LATVIA (1921) Ind. 1991
LITHUANIA (1922) Ind. 1991
Dinamo Minsk 1928
● Min
BELARUS (1991) Ind. 1992
SKA Karpati Lvov 1963 Kie
Lvov
UKRAINE (1991) Ind. 1991
MOLDOVA (1991) Ind. 1991

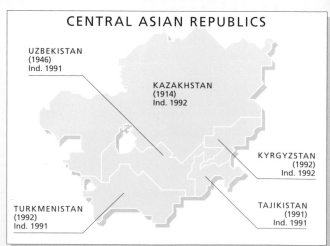

CENTRAL ASIAN REPUBLICS

UZBEKISTAN (1946) Ind. 1991
KAZAKHSTAN (1914) Ind. 1992
KYRGYZSTAN (1992) Ind. 1992
TAJIKISTAN (1991) Ind. 1991
TURKMENISTAN (1992) Ind. 1991

Russia (including the former Soviet Union)

ORIGINS AND GROWTH OF FOOTBALL

THE EARLIEST REPORTS OF FOOTBALL IN RUSSIA are of games played by British traders and bankers, gradually joined by Russian students, cadets and clerks. In 1894, Harry Charnock, general manager of the Morozov Mill, east of Moscow, introduced the game to his workers who played as Orekhovoclub Sport. In 1896, a set of rules was first translated into Russian and the following year, Sport, the first Russian club, was established in St. Petersburg. The popularity of football rose rapidly in the years before the First World War with leagues formed in St. Petersburg (1901), Moscow (1912), and finally an all-Russian FA in 1912.

In the chaotic years of revolution and civil war after 1917, the military initially took over all football clubs, and began a drive to bring the game to Central Asia. During the 1920s, however, under the New Economic Policy, competitive sport was officially frowned upon and the game remained disorganized. But under Stalin it was revived, new clubs were established, each explicitly linked to a state institution (the secret police, the army, railway unions, cooperatives etc.) and a seven-team league began in 1936. Moscow remained the centre of the Soviet game but new teams and powers emerged after the Second World War in Kiev, Tbilisi and Leningrad. Crowds remained huge in the 1950s and 60s, and though political interference was rife, football provided a peculiarly depoliticized space in Soviet life. With the break up of the Soviet Union football associations, leagues and cups have all fragmented. The economic decline of Russia has left the game in deep trouble.

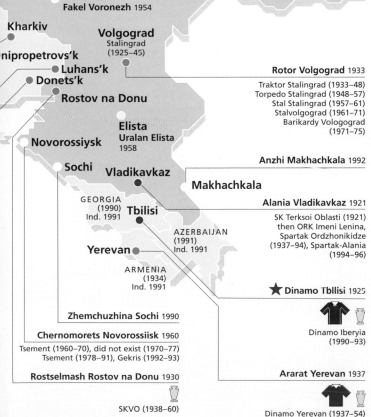

Key

- ● European Championships winner
- ▲ European Championships runner-up
- ○ Competition winner
- △ Competition runner-up

Kiev – Dinamo Kiev
Mos – Dinamo Moskva
Tbil – Dinamo Tbilisi

Moscow

FOOTBALL CITY

MOSCOW'S FOOTBALLING HISTORY began in 1894 when Harry Charnock, the English manager of the Morozov mill, arranged for a company football pitch to be created and a team established. Though Charnock failed to break the link between his Russian workers' leisure time and their consumption of vodka (as he had hoped), he certainly established football in the wider culture. Before the First World War, a Moscow league was up and running, and indigenous Russian teams began to outnumber the English and other foreign teams in the capital. However, the political upheavals of the time pretty much stopped football in its tracks. By the mid-1920s, the Bolsheviks had come to recognize the power and popularity of the game, and with their usual unpleasant thoroughness began its nationwide reorganization. All of Moscow's five main clubs date from this era, and all have been linked to one arm of the Soviet state or another.

The influence of state institutions

Dinamo Moskva, in the north-west of the city, had its roots in Charnock's Orekhovo Club, but when Felix Dzerzhinsky – future leader of the KGB – took charge in 1923, it became a team sponsored by the secret police. CSKA, further to the east, was the Red Army's side; Lokomotiv was tied to the railway workers' union; and Torpedo in the south was for many years part of the great Zil automobile empire. The collapse of Zil in the face of Mercedes and BMW has seen only a shadow outfit continue as Torpedo Zil, while the main team has tried to reinvent itself at the Luzhiniki stadium.

Spartak was notionally attached to a food producers' co-operative, and was the only team to achieve any kind of autonomy from state institutions. Led by Nikolai Starostin, who spent three years in prison camps for his temerity in challenging CSKA and Dinamo at the height of Stalin's rule, Spartak has not surprisingly been the people's choice. In post-Communist Moscow, Spartak is the only side to regularly attract significant crowds, and has utterly dominated the new Russian league.

RUSSIA

Felix Dzerzhinsky, leader of the Russian secret police, took charge of Dinamo Moskva in 1923. His statue, which stood in Red Square, was torn down during the political unrest of 1991.

MOSCOW STADIUM DISASTERS

Moscow is second only to Glasgow in the number of tragedies and disasters endured by the footballing public. In October 1982, Spartak Moskva was playing at the then Lenin (now Luzhniki) stadium, in a second-round UEFA Cup match against Haarlem of the Netherlands. With the score at 1-0, Spartak scored a late second goal to make the tie safe, sparking a surge in one very cramped section of open and icy terracing. How many were killed and injured in the ensuing crush is uncertain, as the Soviet authorities banned any domestic reporting. Initial reports suggested 70 dead and 100 injured but plausible claims of 340 dead have been made. In August 1985, at a World Youth Championship match between the Soviet Union and Canada at the Sokolniki Sports Palace, at least 20 people were killed in a panic-stricken stampede after the lights failed. In the late 1980s, persistent and regular rioting and fighting between CSKA and Spartak fans at the Luzhniki saw a number of deaths and injuries.

Since the events of 1991, Spartak has completely dominated Russian football and its success attracts the largest crowds in the city.

Nikolai Starostin, revered founder, star player and 'club leader' of Spartak Moskva, was associated with the club from its foundation in 1922 to his death in 1996. He was arrested by Stalin in 1942 and spent three years in the gulag prison camps for his association with the club.

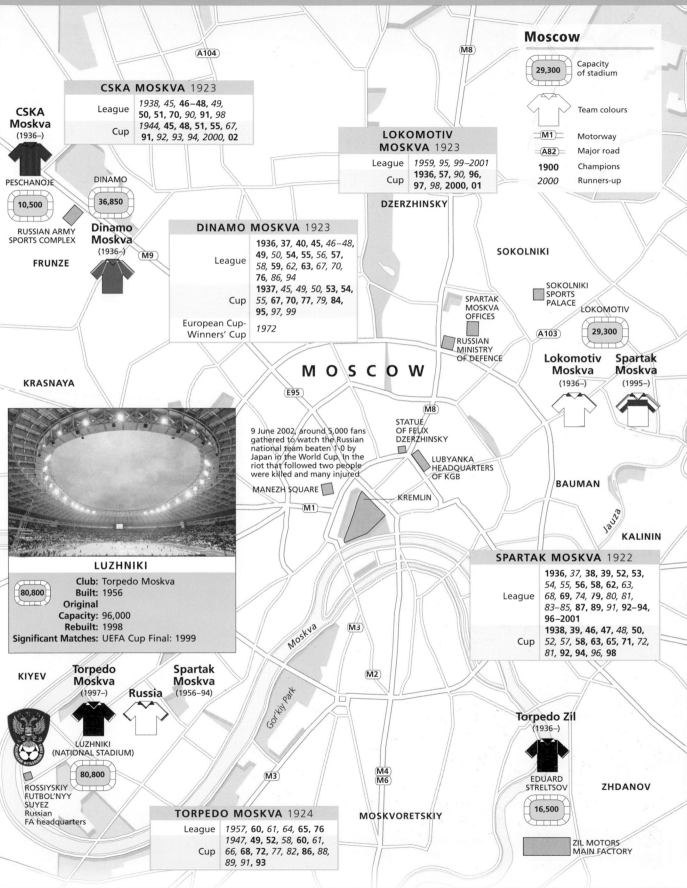

Moscow

29,300	Capacity of stadium
	Team colours
M1	Motorway
A82	Major road
1900	Champions
2000	Runners-up

CSKA MOSKVA 1923

League	*1938, 45,* **46–48,** *49,* **50, 51, 70, 90, 91,** *98*
Cup	*1944,* **45, 48, 51, 55, 67, 91,** *92, 93, 94,* **2000,** *02*

CSKA Moskva (1936–)

PESCHANOJE

10,500

RUSSIAN ARMY SPORTS COMPLEX

FRUNZE

DINAMO

36,850

Dinamo Moskva (1936–)

M9

LOKOMOTIV MOSKVA 1923

League	*1959, 95, 99–2001*
Cup	**1936, 57,** *90,* **96, 97, 98, 2000, 01**

DZERZHINSKY

SOKOLNIKI

DINAMO MOSKVA 1923

League	**1936, 37, 40, 45,** *46–48,* **49,** *50,* **54, 55,** *56,* **57,** *58,* **59,** *62, 63,* **67,** *70, 76, 86,* **94**
Cup	**1937, 45, 49, 50, 53, 54, 55, 67, 70, 77,** *79,* **84, 95, 97, 99**
European Cup-Winners' Cup	*1972*

SPARTAK MOSKVA OFFICES

RUSSIAN MINISTRY OF DEFENCE

SOKOLNIKI SPORTS PALACE

LOKOMOTIV

29,300

Lokomotiv Moskva (1936–)

Spartak Moskva (1995–)

A103

KRASNAYA

M O S C O W

E95

9 June 2002, around 5,000 fans gathered to watch the Russian national team beaten 1-0 by Japan in the World Cup. In the riot that followed two people were killed and many injured

STATUE OF FELIX DZERZHINSKY

M8

LUBYANKA HEADQUARTERS OF KGB

BAUMAN

MANEZH SQUARE

M1

KREMLIN

KALININ

Jauza

LUZHNIKI

80,800

Club: Torpedo Moskva
Built: 1956
Original Capacity: 96,000
Rebuilt: 1998
Significant Matches: UEFA Cup Final: 1999

SPARTAK MOSKVA 1922

League	**1936,** *37,* **38, 39,** *52, 53, 54, 55,* **56,** *58,* **62,** *63,* **68, 69,** *74,* **79,** *80,* **81,** *83–85,* **87, 89,** *91,* **92–94, 96–2001**
Cup	**1938,** *39,* **46, 47,** *48,* **50,** *52,* **57,** *58,* **63,** *65,* **71,** *72,* **81,** *92,* **94,** *96,* **98**

KIYEV

Torpedo Moskva (1997–)

Russia

Spartak Moskva (1956–94)

M2

LUZHNIKI (NATIONAL STADIUM)

80,800

Gor'kiy Park

Moskva

M3

M3

M4
M6

MOSKVORETSKIY

Torpedo Zil (1936–)

EDUARD STRELTSOV

16,500

ZHDANOV

ROSSIYSKIY FUTBOL'NYY SUYEZ Russian FA headquarters

TORPEDO MOSKVA 1924

League	*1957,* **60,** *61, 64,* **65,** *76*
Cup	*1947, 49,* **52,** *58,* **60, 61, 66,** *68,* **72, 77,** *82, 86,* **88,** *89, 91,* **93**

ZIL MOTORS MAIN FACTORY

Russia and Ukraine

THE VYSSHAYA LIGA AND THE VISCHCHA LIGA 1992–2001

RUSSIA AND UKRAINE

WITH THE BREAK-UP OF the Soviet Union in 1991, Soviet football also broke into separate national leagues. Out of the chaos emerged the Vysshaya Liga in Russia and the Vischcha Liga in the Ukraine. In the new Russia, teams dependent for funding and support on the old order – especially Dinamo and CSKA from Moscow – found the post-Communist going hard. Spartak Moskva, always the outsider, quickly aligned itself with sponsors Gazprom – the oil and gas giant spirited away from the wreckage of the Soviet state by ruthless carpetbaggers – and has comprehensively dominated the league under chain-smoking coach Oleg Romantsev, winning the league nine times in ten years. Challengers have arisen in the provinces, where ambitious local officials and politicians have backed Alania Vladikavkaz and Rotor Volgograd. In Moscow, Torpedo and Lokomotiv have nurtured local talent and crept their way into contention. Rotor has boasted Russia's finest striker of the era in Oleg Veretennikov, who has refused to move to a bigger club and who was the victim of an unprovoked acid attack in 1997.

Dominance of Dynamo

Post-Communist Ukraine has proved to be an even tighter footballing monopoly than that found in Russia, with every championship going to Dynamo Kyiv, many with barely a threat to the leaders during the whole season. Under Soviet-era boss Valeri Lobanovsky, Dynamo has proved fantastically connected to money and power in the new Ukraine, and has such resources that its reserves regularly win the Second Division championship but are barred from promotion.

By contrast, many smaller teams are in such terrible financial circumstances that they have refused promotion (like Torpedo Zaporizhya in 1999). CSKA Kyiv has left the army and been bought up by the city council. Renamed Arsenal Kyiv, it may challenge the champions, but so far only Shakhtar Donetsk, from the Ukraine's coal mining region, has really pushed Dynamo. The closest challenge came in the final game of the 2001 season; Dynamo needed a win to take the title, and went 1-0 down to Dnipro Dnipropetrovsk. However, two late goals saw the club take the title again.

Some things don't change. Communist or capitalist, Valeri Lobanovsky and assistant Anatoly Puzach cast their steely gaze over Dynamo Kyiv. Lobanovsky's death in 2002 has cast a giant shadow over Ukrainian football.

CSKA Moskva
1998

Dinamo Moskva
1994

Lokomotiv Moskva
1995, 99–2001

Spartak Moskva
1992–94, 96–2001

Dynamo Kyiv
1993 –2001

Shakhtar Donetsk
1994, 97–2001

Rotor Volgograd
1993, 97

Alania Vladikavkaz
1992, 95, 96

Chornomorets Odesa
1995, 96

Dnipro Dnipropetrovsk
1993

Moscow

R U S S I A

Kiev •

U K R A I N E

Volgograd •

Dnipropetrovsk •
Odesa

Donetsk •

Vladikavkaz •

Vysshaya Liga and Vischcha Liga

Dynamo Kyiv	Team name
	League champions/ runners-up
1982, *83*	Champions in bold Runners-up in italics
● **Moscow**	City of origin

Veteran Oleg Veretennikov celebrates another goal for Rotor Volgograd on his way to a record 141 goals in the Vysshaya Liga.

Key to League Positions Tables

- ■ League champions
- ■ Other teams playing in league
- ■ Season promoted to league
- ■ Season of relegation from league
- **5** Final position in league

Russian League Positions 1992–2001

TEAM	SEASON									
	1992	1993	1994	1995	1996	1997	1998	1999	2000	2001
Kamaz-Chally Nab. Chelny		10	6	9	14	18				
Baltika Kaliningrad					7	9	15			
Textilschik Kamyshin	10	4	7	10	17					
Kuban Krasnodar	18									
Lada Togliatti			16		18					
Anzhi Makhachkala									4	13
Asmaral Moskva	7	18								
CSKA Moskva	5	9	10	6	5	12	2	3	8	7
Dinamo Moskva	3	3	2	4	4	3	9	5	5	9
Lokomotiv Moskva	4	5	3	2	6	5	3	2	2	2
Spartak Moskva	1	1	1	3	1	1	1	1	1	1
Torpedo Moskva	11	4	11	5	12	11	11	4	3	4
Torpedo ZIL-Moskva										14
Okean Nakhodka	13	16								
Lokomotiv Nizhniy Novgorod	6	11	8	12	8	17		11	15	
Chernomorets Novorossiisk			11	13	6	10	14	6	16	
Rostselmash Rostov-Na-Donu	8	17		14	11	13	6	7	12	12
Zenit Sankt-Peterburg	16			10	8	5	8	7		3
Krylya Sovetov Samara	14	14	13	15	9	7	12	12	14	5
Sokol Saratov										8
Zhemchuzhina Sochi		13	9	13	15	14	13	15		
Dinamo Stravropol	15	12	15							
Saturn Ramonsko								10	9	6
Dinamo-Gazovik Tyumen	20		12	16						
FK Tyumen						15	16			
Uralan Elista						7	9	16		
Alania Vladikavkaz	2	6	5	1	2	10	8	6	10	11
Luch Vladivostok			15							
Rotor Volgograd	12	2	4	7	3	2	4	13	11	10
Fakel Voronezh	17					16			13	15
Shinnik Yaroslavl	19					4	14	16		
Uralmash Yekaterinburg	9	8	14	8	16					

Ukrainian League Positions 1992–2001

TEAM	SEASON								
	1992–93	1993–94	1994–95	1995–96	1996–97	1997–98	1998–99	1999–2000	2000–01
Stal' Alchevsk									13
Bukovyna Cherivtsi	12	17							
Dnipro Dnipropetrovsk	2	4	3	3	4	4	12	11	3
Metalurg Donetsk						6	14	7	5
Shakhtar Donetsk	4	2	4	10	2	2	2	2	2
Prikarpattya Ivano-Frankivsk			11	11	13	10	15	14	
Metalist Kharkov	5	18				6	5	9	
Kremin Kremenchuk	9	15	10	9	15				
Kryvbas Kryvi-Rih	8	6	6	14	12	8	3	3	11
CSCA Kyiv		4	11	13	7	10	6		
Dynamo Kyiv	1	1	1	1	1	1	1	1	1
Zirka Kyrovohrad				6	10	11	11	16	
Zarja Lugans'k	15	14	16	18					
Volun-1 Luts'k	11	11	15	17					
SKA Karpati Lvov	6	5	8	8	5	3	4	9	10
Metalurg Mariupol						12	5	8	4
SK Mykolajv		13	16			16			
Chornomorets Odesa	3	3	2	2	7	15		15	
Naftovyk Okhtyrka									
Polihraftechnika Oleksandriya									
Vorskla Poltava					3	5	10	4	12
Veres Rivne	16	12	18						
Temp Shepetivka		9	17						
Tavriya Simferopol	10	8	5	12	6	14	9	13	7
Nyva Ternopil		7	12	13	9	7	13	12	14
Zakarpattya Uzhgorod									
Nyva Vynnytsya	14	10	14	15	16				
Metalurg Zaporizhzhya	7	16	9	8	9	8	8	6	8
Torpedo Zaporizhzhya	13	13	7	7	14	16			

Russia (including the former Soviet Union)

Rossiyskiy Futbol'nyy Soyuz
Founded: 1912, 1991
Joined FIFA: 1912, 1992
Joined UEFA: 1954

ALTHOUGH FOOTBALL HAD arrived in Moscow by the turn of the 19th century, it was slow to spread beyond the major Russian cities. A national football association, founded in 1912, was unable to create a national league from the small-scale affairs in Moscow and St. Petersburg. The re-creation of a domestic football programme under the Communists was slow, as they found it hard to arrange and play national league football in a country so geographically huge, so bereft of functioning transportation and in a state of social upheaval. But, by 1936, the trains were reliable enough and the clubs settled enough for an all-Soviet league and cup to be established.

With a break for the war, these competitions continued until 1991, but the 1991–92 season saw both state and league fragment with the emergence of independent Baltic (Lithuania, Latvia, Estonia) and Caucasian (Georgia, Armenia, Azerbaijan) states, as well as the Ukraine, Moldova and Belarus (for details of these leagues see pages 246–47 and 263). The Central Asian republics of the former Soviet Union soon followed (Turkmenistan, Kazakhstan, Kyrgyzstan, Tajikistan and Uzbekistan). Details of these leagues can be found on pages 416–17.

Soviet Union League Record 1936–91

SEASON	CHAMPIONS	RUNNERS-UP
1936	Dinamo Moskva	Dinamo Kiev
1936*	Spartak Moskva	Dinamo Moskva
1937	Dinamo Moskva	Spartak Moskva
1938	Spartak Moskva	CDKA Moskva
1939	Spartak Moskva	Dinamo Tbilisi
1940	Dinamo Moskva	Dinamo Tbilisi
1941–44	no championship	
1945	Dinamo Moskva	CDKA Moskva
1946	CDKA Moskva	Dinamo Moskva
1947	CDKA Moskva	Dinamo Moskva
1948	CDKA Moskva	Dinamo Moskva
1949	Dinamo Moskva	CDKA Moskva
1950	CDKA Moskva	Dinamo Moskva
1951	CDKA Moskva	Dinamo Tbilisi
1952	Spartak Moskva	Dinamo Kiev
1953	Spartak Moskva	Dinamo Tbilisi
1954	Dinamo Moskva	Spartak Moskva
1955	Dinamo Moskva	Spartak Moskva
1956	Spartak Moskva	Dinamo Moskva
1957	Dinamo Moskva	Torpedo Moskva
1958	Spartak Moskva	Dinamo Moskva
1959	Dinamo Moskva	Lokomotiv Moskva
1960	Torpedo Moskva	Dinamo Kiev
1961	Dinamo Kiev	Torpedo Moskva
1962	Spartak Moskva	Dinamo Moskva
1963	Dinamo Moskva	Spartak Moskva
1964	Dinamo Tbilisi	Torpedo Moskva
1965	Torpedo Moskva	Dinamo Kiev
1966	Dinamo Kiev	SKA Rostov-na-Donu
1967	Dinamo Kiev	Dinamo Moskva
1968	Dinamo Kiev	Spartak Moskva
1969	Spartak Moskva	Dinamo Kiev
1970	CSKA Moskva	Dinamo Moskva
1971	Dinamo Kiev	Ararat Yerevan
1972	Zarja Vorosch'grad	Dinamo Kiev
1973	Ararat Yerevan	Dinamo Kiev
1974	Dinamo Kiev	Spartak Moskva

Soviet Union League Record (*continued*)

SEASON	CHAMPIONS	RUNNERS-UP
1975	Dinamo Kiev	Shakhtar Donetsk
1976	Dinamo Moskva	Ararat Yerevan
1976*	Torpedo Moskva	Dinamo Kiev
1977	Dinamo Kiev	Dinamo Tbilisi
1978	Dinamo Tbilisi	Dinamo Kiev
1979	Spartak Moskva	Shakhtar Donetsk
1980	Dinamo Kiev	Spartak Moskva
1981	Dinamo Kiev	Spartak Moskva
1982	Dinamo Minsk	Dinamo Kiev
1983	Dnipro Dnipropetrovsk	Spartak Moskva
1984	Zenit Leningrad	Spartak Moskva
1985	Dinamo Kiev	Spartak Moskva
1986	Dinamo Kiev	Dinamo Moskva
1987	Spartak Moskva	Dnipro Dnipropetrovsk
1988	Dnipro Dnipropetrovsk	Dinamo Kiev
1989	Spartak Moskva	Dnipro Dnipropetrovsk
1990	Dinamo Kiev	CSKA Moskva
1991	CSKA Moskva	Spartak Moskva

* Extra transitional autumn league – played in order to allow a season to start in spring and end in autumn.

Soviet Union League Summary

TEAM	TOTALS	CHAMPIONS & RUNNERS-UP (BOLD) (*ITALICS*)
Dinamo Kiev	13, 11	*1936, 52, 60,* **61,** *65,* **66–68,** *69,* **71,** *72, 73,* **74,** *75,* **76, 77,** *78,* **80, 81,** *82,* **85, 86,** *88,* **90**
Spartak Moskva	12, 12	**1936,** *37,* **38, 39,** *52, 53,* **54,** *55,* **56,** *58,* **62,** *63,* **68,** *69,* **74,** *79,* **80, 81,** *83–85,* **87,** *89,* **91**
Dinamo Moskva	11, 11	**1936,** *36,* **37,** *40,* **45,** *46–48,* **49,** *50,* **54, 55,** *56,* **57,** *58, 59,* **62,** *63,* **67,** *70,* **76,** *86*

This summary only features the top three clubs in the Soviet Union League. For a full list of league champions and runners-up please see the League Record above.

Soviet Union Cup Record 1936–92

YEAR	WINNERS	SCORE	RUNNERS-UP
1936	Lokomotiv Moskva	2-0	Dinamo Tbilisi
1937	Dinamo Moskva	5-2	Dinamo Tbilisi
1938	Spartak Moskva	3-2	Elektrik Leningrad
1939	Spartak Moskva	3-1	Stalinets Leningrad
1940–43	no competition		
1944	Zenit Leningrad	2-1	CDKA Moskva
1945	CDKA Moskva	2-1	Dinamo Moskva
1946	Spartak Moskva	3-2	Dinamo Tbilisi
1947	Spartak Moskva	2-0	Torpedo Moskva
1948	CDKA Moskva	3-0	Spartak Moskva
1949	Torpedo Moskva	2-1	Dinamo Moskva
1950	Spartak Moskva	3-0	Dinamo Moskva
1951	CDSA Moskva	2-1	Komanda Kalinin
1952	Torpedo Moskva	1-0	Spartak Moskva
1953	Dinamo Moskva	1-0	Kriliya Kuybyshev
1954	Dinamo Moskva	2-1	Spartak Yerevan
1955	CDSA Moskva	2-1	Dinamo Moskva
1956	no competition		
1957	Lokomotiv Moskva	1-0	Spartak Moskva
1958	Spartak Moskva	1-0	Torpedo Moskva

Soviet Union Cup Record (*continued*)

YEAR	WINNERS	SCORE	RUNNERS-UP
1959		*no competition*	
1960	Torpedo Moskva	4-3	Dinamo Tbilisi
1961	Shakhtar Donetsk	3-1	Torpedo Moskva
1962	Shakhtar Donetsk	2-0	Znarnia Truda O-Z
1963	Spartak Moskva	2-1	Shakhtar Donetsk
1964	Dinamo Kiev	1-0	Kriliya Kuybyshev
1965	Spartak Moskva	0-0, (replay) 2-1	Dinamo Minsk
1966	Dinamo Kiev	2-0	Torpedo Moskva
1967	Dinamo Moskva	3-0	CSKA Moskva
1968	Torpedo Moskva	1-0	Pakhtakor Tashkent
1969	SKA Karpati Lvov	2-1	SKA Rostov-na-Donu
1970	Dinamo Moskva	2-1	Dinamo Tbilisi
1971	Spartak Moskva	2-2, (replay) 1-0	SKA Rostov-na-Donu
1972	Torpedo Moskva	0-0, (replay) 1-1 (aet)(5-1 pens)	Spartak Moskva
1973	Ararat Yerevan	2-1	Dinamo Kiev
1974	Dinamo Kiev	3-0	Zarja Voroshilovgrad
1975	Ararat Yerevan	2-1	Zarja Voroshilovgrad
1976	Dinamo Tbilisi	3-0	Ararat Yerevan
1977	Dinamo Moskva	1-0	Torpedo Moskva
1978	Dinamo Kiev	2-1	Shakhtar Donetsk
1979	Dinamo Tbilisi	0-0 (aet)(5-4 pens)	Dinamo Moskva
1980	Shakhtar Donetsk	2-1	Dinamo Tbilisi
1981	SKA Rostov-na-Donu	1-0	Spartak Moskva
1982	Dinamo Kiev	1-0	Torpedo Moskva
1983	Shakhtar Donetsk	1-0	Metalist Kharkov
1984	Dinamo Moskva	2-0	Zenit Leningrad
1985	Dinamo Kiev	2-1	Shakhtar Donetsk
1986	Torpedo Moskva	1-0	Shakhtar Donetsk
1987	Dinamo Kiev	3-3 (aet)(4-2 pens)	Dinamo Minsk
1988	Metalist Kharkov	2-0	Torpedo Moskva
1989	Dnipro Dnipropctrovsk	1-0	Torpedo Moskva
1990	Dinamo Kiev	6-1	Lokomotiv Moskva
1991	CSKA Moskva	3-2	Torpedo Moskva
1992	Spartak Moskva	2-0	CSKA Moskva

Soviet Union Cup Summary

TEAM	TOTALS	WINNERS & RUNNERS-UP (BOLD) (*ITALICS*)
Spartak Moskva	**10**, *5*	**1938, 39, 46, 47,** *48,* **50,** *52, 57,* **58,** **63, 65, 71,** *72, 81,* **92**
Dinamo Kiev	**8**, *1*	**1964, 66,** *73,* **74, 78, 82, 85, 87, 90**
Dinamo Moskva	**7**, *5*	**1937,** *45, 49, 50,* **53, 54,** *55,* **67, 70,** **77,** *79,* **84**
Torpedo Moskva	**6**, *9*	*1947, 49, 52, 58,* **60,** *61,* **66,** *68,* **72,** *77, 82,* **86,** *88, 89, 91*
CSKA Moskva (includes CDKA Moskva, CDSA Moskva)	**5**, *3*	*1944,* **45, 48, 51, 55,** *67,* **91,** *92*

This summary only features the clubs that have won the Soviet Union Cup five times or more. For a full list of cup winners and runners-up please see the Cup Record above.

Russian League Record 1992–2001

SEASON	CHAMPIONS	RUNNERS-UP
1992	Spartak Moskva	Alania Vladikavkaz
1993	Spartak Moskva	Rotor Volgograd
1994	Spartak Moskva	Dinamo Moskva
1995	Alania Vladikavkaz	Lokomotiv Moskva
1996	Spartak Moskva	Alania Vladikavkaz
1997	Spartak Moskva	Rotor Volgograd
1998	Spartak Moskva	CSKA Moskva
1999	Spartak Moskva	Lokomotiv Moskva
2000	Spartak Moskva	Lokomotiv Moskva
2001	Spartak Moskva	Lokomotiv Moskva

Russian League Summary

TEAM	TOTALS	CHAMPIONS & RUNNERS-UP (BOLD) (*ITALICS*)
Spartak Moskva	9, 0	**1992–94, 96–2001**
Alania Vladikavkaz	1, 2	**1992,** *95, 96,*
Lokomotiv Moskva	0, 4	*1995, 99–2001*
Rotor Volgograd	0, 2	*1993, 97*
CSKA Moskva	0, 1	*1998*
Dinamo Moskva	0, 1	*1994*

Russian Cup Record 1993–2002

YEAR	WINNERS	SCORE	RUNNERS-UP
1993	Torpedo Moskva	1-1 (aet)(5-3 pens)	CSKA Moskva
1994	Spartak Moskva	2-2 (aet)(4-2 pens)	CSKA Moskva
1995	Dinamo Moskva	0-0 (aet)(8-7 pens)	Rotor Volgograd
1996	Lokomotiv Moskva	3-2	Spartak Moskva
1997	Lokomotiv Moskva	2-0	Dinamo Moskva
1998	Spartak Moskva	1-0	Lokomotiv Moskva
1999	Zenit Sankt-Peterburg	3-1	Dinamo Moskva
2000	Lokomotiv Moskva	3-2 (aet)	CSKA Moskva
2001	Lokomotiv Moskva	1-1 (aet)(4-3 pens)	Anzhi Makhachkala
2002	CSKA Moskva	2-0	Zenit Sankt-Peterburg

Russian Cup Summary

TEAM	TOTALS	WINNERS & RUNNERS-UP (BOLD) (*ITALICS*)
Lokomotiv Moskva	4, 1	**1996,** *97,* **98,** **2000, 01**
Spartak Moskva	2, 1	**1994,** *96,* **98**
CSKA Moskva	1, 3	*1993, 94,* **2000,** *02*
Dinamo Moskva	1, 2	**1995,** *97, 99*
Zenit Sankt-Peterburg	1, 1	**1999,** *2002*
Torpedo Moskva	1, 0	**1993**
Anzhi Makhachkala	0, 1	*2001*
Rotor Volgograd	0, 1	*1995*

Ukraine

Football Federation of Ukraine
Founded: 1991
Joined FIFA: 1992
Joined UEFA: 1992

SEASON	LEAGUE CHAMPIONS
1998	Dynamo Kyiv
1999	Dynamo Kyiv
2000	Dynamo Kyiv
2001	Dynamo Kyiv
2002	Shakhtar Donetsk

YEAR	CUP WINNERS
1998	Dynamo Kyiv
1999	Dynamo Kyiv
2000	Dynamo Kyiv
2001	Shakhtar Donetsk
2002	Shakhtar Donetsk

Ukrainian football has until recently been played in the shadow of the institutions and competitions of the Soviet Union. A separate national league and cup were established after independence was gained from the USSR in 1991. The league has since been dominated by Dynamo Kyiv.

The UEFA Cup

TOURNAMENT REVIEW 2001–02

WITH THREE QUALIFYING ROUNDS, six further rounds proper and the addition of Champions League losers in the third round, the UEFA Cup 2001–02 was a vast pan-European marathon in which the eastern and southern European contingents and small west European teams were gradually forced out. The quarter-finals saw Hector Cuper's Internazionale squeeze past his old club Valencia, an all-Dutch tie between PSV and Feyenoord going to penalties, Israel's Hapoel Tel Aviv lining up against Milan, and unheard of Slovan Liberec from the Czech Republic facing Borussia Dortmund. Hapoel, already the most successful Israeli team in European competition, had ridden a wave of national euphoria to beat Chelsea, Parma and Lokomotiv Moskva, while tiny Slovan had dispensed with Lyon. Both had been forced to play home games away, and both gave their monied opponents a serious fright before the natural economic order asserted itself.

In the semis, Borussia Dortmund smashed Milan 4-0 at the Westfalenstadion, while Feyenoord edged a 1-0 at the San Siro. In the second legs, both Milan teams turned on the quality but it was too late. So, as the smoke cleared at De Kuip, the Final was a Dutch-German affair. In his last match, defender Jurgen Kohler was caught for speed in bringing down Feyenoord's Tomasson in the box, leading to a red card and a penalty for the Dutch. Van Hooijdonk made no mistake with the spot kick and doubled the lead with a free kick seven minutes later. Borussia played with extraordinary heart and discipline and despite a third Feyenoord goal for Tomasson, the team clawed its way back into contention with two goals and relentless pressure. But it was too much to ask.

THIRD ROUND (2 legs)

PAOK **3-2** PSV
(Greece)   (Netherlands)
PSV **4-1** PAOK

PSV won 6-4 on aggregate

Fiorentina **0-1** Lille OSC
(Italy)   (France)
Lille OSC **2-0** Fiorentina

Lille OSC won 3-0 on aggregate

Valencia **1-0** Celtic
(Spain)   (Scotland)
Celtic **1-0** Valencia

Valencia won 5-4 on pens

Servette **0-0** Hertha Berlin
(Switzerland)   (Germany)
Hertha Berlin **0-3** Servette

Servette won 3-0 on aggregate

Ipswich Town **1-0** Internazionale
(England)   (Italy)
Internazionale **4-1** Ipswich Town

Internazionale won 4-2 on aggregate

Rangers **0-0** PSG
(Scotland)   (France)
PSG **0-0** Rangers

Rangers won 4-3 on pens

Feyenoord **1-0** SC Freiburg
(Netherlands)   (Germany)
SC Freiburg **2-2** Feyenoord

Feyenoord won 3-2 on aggregate

AEK **3-2** Litex Lovech
(Greece)   (Bulgaria)
Litex Lovech **1-1** AEK

AEK won 4-3 on aggregate

Grasshoppers **1-2** Leeds United
(Switzerland)   (England)
Leeds United **2-2** Grasshoppers

Leeds United won 4-3 on aggregate

Parma **1-1** Brøndby
(Italy)   (Denmark)
Brøndby **0-3** Parma

Parma won 4-1 on aggregate

Girondins de
Bordeaux **1-0** Roda JC
(France)   (Netherlands)
Girondins de
Roda JC **2-0** Bordeaux

Roda JC won 2-1 on aggregate

Slovan Liberec **3-1** RCD Mallorca
(Czech Rep.)   (Spain)
RCD Mallorca **1-2** Slovan Liberec

Slovan Liberec won 5-2 on aggregate

Hapoel   Lokomotiv
Tel Aviv **2-1** Moskva
(Israel)   (Russia)
Lokomotiv   Hapoel
Moskva **0-1** Tel Aviv

Hapoel Tel Aviv won 3-1 on aggregate

FC   Borussia
København **0-1** Dortmund
(Denmark)   (Germany)
Borussia   FC
Dortmund **1-0** København

Borussia Dortmund won 2-0
on aggregate

Milan **2-0** Sporting CP
(Italy)   (Spain)
Sporting CP **1-1** Milan

Milan won 3-1 on aggregate

Club   Olympique
Brugge **4-1** Lyonnais
(Belgium)   (France)
Olympique   Club
Lyonnais **3-0** Brugge

Olympique Lyonnais won
on away goals

FOURTH ROUND (2 legs)

Roda JC **0-1** Milan
Milan **0-1** Roda JC

Milan won 3-2 on pens

Borussia
Lille OSC **1-1** Dortmund
Borussia
Dortmund **0-0** Lille OSC

Borussia Dortmund won on away goals

Valencia **3-0** Servette
Servette **2-2** Valencia

Valencia won 5-2 on aggregate

PSV **0-0** Leeds United
Leeds United **0-1** PSV

PSV won 1-0 on aggregate

Olympique   Slovan
Lyonnais **1-1** Liberec
Slovan   Olympique
Liberec **4-1** Lyonnais

Slovan Liberec won 5-2 on aggregate

Hapoel
Tel Aviv **0-0** Parma
Hapoel
Parma **1-2** Tel Aviv

Hapoel Tel Aviv won 2-1 on aggregate

Internazionale **3-1** AEK
AEK **2-2** Internazionale

Internazionale won 5-3 on aggregate

Rangers **1-1** Feyenoord
Feyenoord **3-2** Rangers

Feyenoord won 4-3 on aggregate

Dortmund's Amoroso cuts through Slovan Liberec's defence. Slovan's amazing UEFA Cup run was finally halted at the Westfalenstadion.

Hapoel fans saw their team take a quarter-final first-leg lead to the San Siro. Though no longer funded by Israel's trade unions, the fans of Tel Aviv's smallest team retain their left-wing qualities.

QUARTER-FINALS (2 legs)

Hapoel Tel Aviv **1-0** Milan
Milan **2-0** Hapoel Tel Aviv

Milan won 2-1 on aggregate

Internazionale **1-1** Valencia
Valencia **0-1** Internazionale

Internazionale won 2-1 on aggregate

PSV **1-1** Feyenoord
Feyenoord **1-1** PSV

Feyenoord won 5-4 on pens

Slovan Borussia
Liberec **0-0** Dortmund
Borussia Slovan
Dortmund **4-0** Liberec

Borussia Dortmund won 4-0 on aggregate

SEMI-FINALS (2 legs)

April 4 – San Siro, Milan
Internazionale **0-1** Feyenoord
(Cordoba o.g. 51)

April 11 – De Kuip, Rotterdam
Feyenoord **2-2** Internazionale
(van Hooijdonk 17, (C. Zanetti 84,
Tomasson 34) Kallon 92 pen)

Feyenoord won 3-2 on aggregate

April 4 – Westfalenstadion, Dortmund
Borussia **4-0** Milan
Dortmund
(Amoroso 8 pen,
34, 39,
Heinrich 62)

April 11 – San Siro, Milan
Milan **3-1** Borussia
(F. Inzaghi 11, Dortmund
Contra 19, (Ricken 94)
Serginho 92 pen)

Borussia Dortmund won 5-3
on aggregate

2002 FINAL

May 8 – De Kuip, Rotterdam
Feyenoord **3-2** Borussia
(van Hooijdonk Dortmund
33 pen, 40, (Amorso 47 pen,
Tomasson 50) Koller 58)
h/t : 2-0 **Att:** 48,500
Ref: Melo Pereira (Portugal)

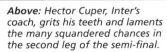

Above: Hector Cuper, Inter's coach, grits his teeth and laments the many squandered chances in the second leg of the semi-final.

Above Left: Ronaldo's return to form and fitness came too late for Inter, and a fierce 2-2 draw at De Kuip could not cancel out defeat by a single own goal at the San Siro. In 34 years and eight games, no Italian side has won in Rotterdam.

Left: Tomas Rosicky, Dortmund's Czech midfield playmaker, was a key force in unleashing the potential of the squad this season.

Below: Feyenoord – UEFA Cup winners 2002 – the club's first European success for 28 years. The last Dutch team to win a European title, Ajax in 1995, was immediately dismembered in the transfer market. Does the same fate await Feyenoord?

THE UEFA CUP

Pierre van Hooijdonk viciously curves the ball over the Dortmund wall for his and Feyenoord's second goal in a frantic, entertaining Final.

The UEFA Cup

TOURNAMENT OVERVIEW

IN 1950, THE SWISS VICE-PRESIDENT of FIFA, Ernst Thommen, proposed a competition between select XIs from European cities with industrial fairs. Bizarre as the concept may seem it was strongly supported by Sir Stanley Rous, president of FIFA. Representatives from 12 cities met in Basle to draw up rules for the competition with matches planned to coincide with the industrial fairs. As a consequence, the first edition of the Fairs Cup took nearly three years to complete (1955–58) and was won by Barcelona who beat a London XI over two legs.

Fixture congestion forced the tournament into a single season alongside the European Cup in 1960–61 and Barcelona found itself competing in both. The team went out in the quarter-finals leaving the way for Roma to take the trophy. The rest of the 1960s saw Spanish dominance, initially maintained by Valencia and Real Zaragoza, before giving way to four successive English victories (1968–71).

In 1971, UEFA finally took the competition over, renamed it the UEFA Cup, and awarded places systematically to the highest-placed league clubs not entering other competitions. In the mid-1990s, the disintegration of the Soviet Union saw the competition contested by over 100 clubs with additional places available via UEFA Fair Play awards and the Intertoto Cup.

The 1970s were dominated by English (five winners), German (two) and Dutch (two) teams. The 1980s saw clubs from smaller leagues doing well: RSC Anderlecht from Belgium won it once and IFK Göteborg from Sweden won it twice.

In the 1990s, however, it was the Italian sides who dominated. Between 1989 and 99, Italian clubs took the title eight times, including four all-Italian finals. However, new challengers have risen: 2000 saw Galatasaray win Turkey's first European victory and 2001 saw the return of Liverpool to winning ways.

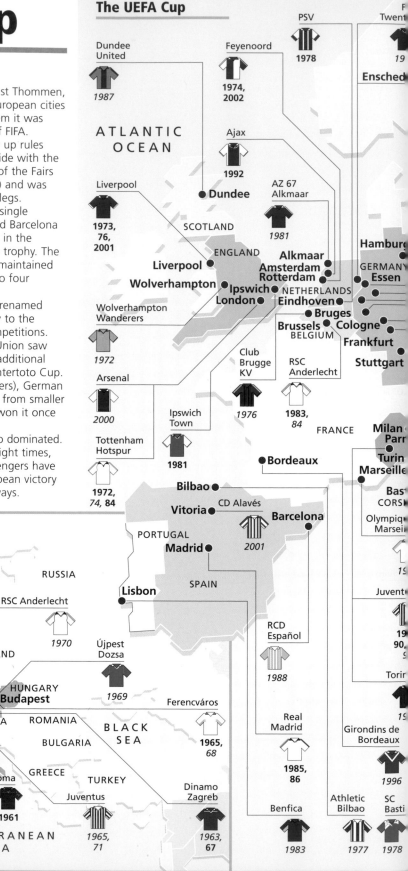

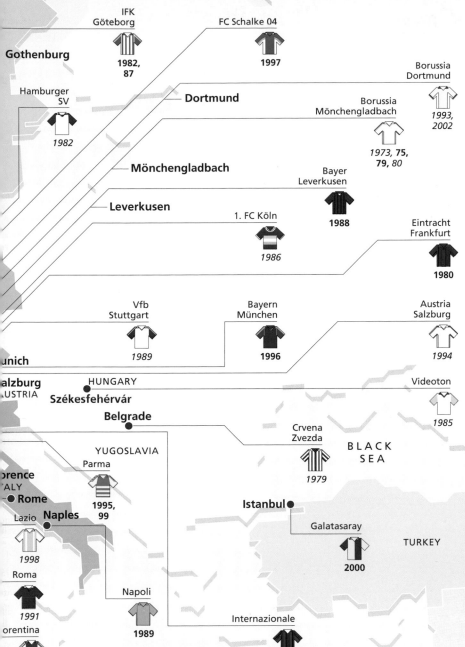

IFK Göteborg
1982, 87

Gothenburg

FC Schalke 04
1997

Hamburger SV
1982

Borussia Dortmund
1993, 2002

Dortmund

Borussia Mönchengladbach
1973, **75, 79,** *80*

Mönchengladbach

Bayer Leverkusen
1988

Leverkusen

1. FC Köln
1986

Eintracht Frankfurt
1980

Vfb Stuttgart
1989

Bayern München
1996

Austria Salzburg
1994

...unich

...alzburg
...USTRIA

HUNGARY
Székesfehérvár

Videoton
1985

Belgrade

YUGOSLAVIA

Crvena Zvezda
1979

BLACK SEA

Parma
1995, 99

...rence
...ALY
● Rome

Lazio
1998

Naples

Roma
1991

...orentina

1990

Napoli
1989

Istanbul ●

Galatasaray
2000

TURKEY

Internazionale
1991, 94, 97, 98

MEDITERRANEAN SEA

The Fairs Cup and the UEFA Cup

Number of wins (by country)

The Fairs Cup	The UEFA Cup
5+ times	9+ times
2–4 times	6–8 times
1 time	2–5 times
0 times	1 time
	0 times

Team details

HUNGARY — Country
● **Budapest** — City of origin
Ferencváros — Team name
— Team colours
1965, *68* — Winners in bold / Runners-up in italic

The UEFA Cup 1958–2002

COUNTRY	WINNERS	RUNNERS-UP
Italy	9	6
Germany	6	7
England	6	3
Netherlands	4	2
Spain	2	3
Sweden	2	0
Belgium	1	2
Turkey	1	0
France	0	3
Austria	0	1
Hungary	0	1
Portugal	0	1
Scotland	0	1
Yugoslavia	0	1

In one of the most extraordinary UEFA Cup Finals for many years, Liverpool beat CD Alavés of Spain 5-4 after extra time in 2001. In a cruel twist of fate, the winning strike was this own goal by Alavés's Delfi Geli.

Consecutive participation

NUMBER OF CONSECUTIVE YEARS

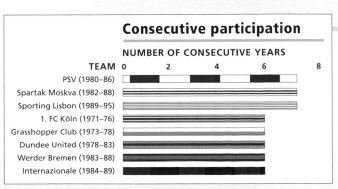

TEAM	0	2	4	6	8

PSV (1980–86)
Spartak Moskva (1982–88)
Sporting Lisbon (1989–95)
1. FC Köln (1971–76)
Grasshopper Club (1973–78)
Dundee United (1978–83)
Werder Bremen (1983–88)
Internazionale (1984–89)

The UEFA Cup

ERNST THOMMEN'S International Industrial Fairs Inter City Cup was open to teams from cities that had hosted international trade fairs. The first tournament, in 1956, had ten entrants from ten cities. Two-leg, home and away rounds were played over three years to produce the first winner of the (now abbreviated) Fairs Cup. The away goals rule was first introduced into the tournament in 1967, and, in 1971, penalties replaced the toss of a coin for drawn matches. In 1972 it became the UEFA Cup. In 1998 the two-leg final was replaced by a single match at a neutral venue.

From 1961 the tournament spread its net, with three places allocated to each UEFA nation. Places are now allocated on a nation's past performance in European competition, though national associations can allocate those places as they choose. With the merger of the Cup-Winners' Cup into an expanded UEFA Cup in 2000, national cup winners are generally awarded a place and preliminary rounds have been added. Defeated teams from the preliminary round of the Champions League now enter the first round, and third-place teams from the Champions League first-round mini-leagues enter the third round.

1955–58 FINAL (2 legs)
March 5 – Stamford Bridge, London
London 2-2 Barcelona
Select XI (Spain)
(England) (Tejada 7,
(Greaves 10, Martinez 35)
Langley 88 pen)

May 1 – Nou Camp, Barcelona
Barcelona 6-0 London
(Suarez 6, 8, **Select XI**
Evaristo 52, 75,
Martinez 43,
Verges 63)
Barcelona won 8-2 on aggregate

1958–60 FINAL (2 legs)
March 29 – St. Andrew's, Birmingham
Birmingham 0-0 Barcelona
City (Spain)
(England)

May 4 – Nou Camp, Barcelona
Barcelona 4-1 Birmingham
(Czibor 6, 48, **City**
Martinez 43, (Hooper 82)
Coll 78)
Barcelona won 4-1 on aggregate

1960–61 FINAL (2 legs)
September 27 – St. Andrew's, Birmingham
Birmingham 2-2 Roma
City (Italy)
(England) (Manfredini
(Hellawell 78, 30, 56)
Orritt 85)

October 11 – Stadio Olimpico, Rome
Roma 2-0 Birmingham
(Farmer o.g. 56, **City**
Pestrin 90)
Roma won 4-2 on aggregate

1961–62 FINAL (2 legs)
August 9 – Luis Casanova, Valencia
Valencia 6-2 Barcelona
(Spain) (Spain)
(Yosu 14, 42, (Kocsis 4, 20)
Guillot 35, 54, 67,
Nunez 74)

September 9 – Nou Camp, Barcelona
Barcelona 1-1 Valencia
(Kocsis 46) (Guillot 87)
Valencia won 7-3 on aggregate

1962–63 FINAL (2 legs)
June 12 – Dinamo Stadion, Zagreb
Dinamo Zagreb 1-2 Valencia
(Yugoslavia) (Spain)
(Zambata 13) (Waldo 64,
Urtiaga 67)

June 25 – Mestalla, Valencia
Valencia 2-0 Dinamo Zagreb
(Manio 68,
Nunez 78)
Valencia won 4-1 on aggregate

1963–64 FINAL
June 25 – Nou Camp, Barcelona
Real Zaragoza 2-1 Valencia
(Spain) (Spain)
(Villa 40, (Urtiaga 41)
Marcelino 83)

1964–65 FINAL
June 23 – Communale, Turin
Ferencváros 1-0 Juventus
(Hungary) (Italy)
(Fenyvesi 74)

1965–66 FINAL (2 legs)
September 14 – Nou Camp, Barcelona
Barcelona 0-1 Real Zaragoza
(Spain) (Spain)
(Canario 30)

September 21 – La Romareda, Zaragoza
Real Zaragoza 2-4 Barcelona
(Marcelino (Pujol 3, 86, 119,
24, 87) Zaballa 89)
(after extra time)
Barcelona won 4-3 on aggregate

1966–67 FINAL (2 legs)
August 30 – Dinamo Stadion, Zagreb
Dinamo Zagreb 2-0 Leeds United
(Yugoslavia) (England)
(Cercek 39, 59)

September 6 – Elland Road, Leeds
Leeds United 0-0 Dinamo Zagreb
Dinamo Zagreb won 2-0 on aggregate

1967–68 FINAL (2 legs)
September 7 – Elland Road, Leeds
Leeds United 1-0 Ferencváros
(England) (Hungary)
(Jones 41)

September 11 – Nep, Budapest
Ferencváros 0-0 Leeds United
Leeds United won 1-0 on aggregate

1968–69 FINAL (2 legs)
May 29 – St. James Park, Newcastle
Newcastle 3-0 Újpest Dozsa
United (Hungary)
(England)
(Moncur 63, 72,
Scott 83)

June 11 – Nep, Budapest
Újpest Dozsa 2-3 Newcastle
(Bene 31, **United**
Gorocs 44) (Moncur 46,
Arentoft 50,
Foggon 74)
Newcastle United won 6-2 on aggregate

1969–70 FINAL (2 legs)
April 22 – Parc Astrid, Brussels
RSC Anderlecht 3-1 Arsenal
(Belgium) (England)
(Devrindt 25, (Kennedy 82)
Mulder 30, 74)

April 28 – Highbury, London
Arsenal 3-0 RSC Anderlecht
(Kelly 25,
Radford 75,
Sammels 76)
Arsenal won 4-3 on aggregate

1970–71 FINAL (2 legs)
May 26 – Communale, Turin
Juventus 0-0 Leeds United
(Italy) (England)
Match abandoned after 51 mins
due to waterlogged pitch

REPLAY
May 28 – Communale, Turin
Juventus 2-2 Leeds United
(Bettega 27, (Madeley 48,
Capello 55) Bates 77)

June 3 – Communale, Turin
Leeds United 1-1 Juventus
(Clarke 12) (Anastasi 20)
Leeds United won on away goals rule

1971–72 FINAL (2 legs)
May 3 – Molineux, Wolverhampton
Wolverhampton 1-2 Tottenham
Wanderers Hotspur
(England) (England)
(McCalliog 72) (Chivers 57, 87)

May 17 – White Hart Lane, London
Tottenham 1-1 Wolverhampton
Hotspur Wanderers
(Mullery 30) (Wagstaffe 41)
Tottenham Hotspur won 3-2
on aggregate

1972–73 FINAL (2 legs)
May 9 – Anfield, Liverpool
Liverpool 0-0 Borussia
(England) **Mönchen-**
gladbach
(West Germany)
Match abandoned after 27 mins
due to waterlogged pitch

REPLAY
May 10 – Anfield, Liverpool
Liverpool 3-0 Borussia
(Keegan 21, 32, **Mönchen-**
Lloyd 61) **gladbach**

May 23 – Bokelberg, Mönchengladbach
Borussia 2-0 Liverpool
Mönchen-
gladbach
(Heynckes 29, 40)
Liverpool won 3-2 on aggregate

1973–74 FINAL (2 legs)
May 21 – White Hart Lane, London
Tottenham 2-2 Feyenoord
Hotspur (Netherlands)
(England) (Van Hanegem 43,
(England 39, De Jong 85)
Van Daele o.g. 64)

May 28 – Feyenoord, Rotterdam
Feyenoord 2-0 Tottenham
(Rijsbergen 43, **Hotspur**
Ressel 84)
Feyenoord won 4-2 on aggregate

1974–75 FINAL (2 legs)
May 7 – Rheinstadion, Düsseldorf
Borussia 0-0 FC Twente
Mönchen- (Netherlands)
gladbach
(West Germany)

September 11 – Arke, Enschede
FC Twente 1-5 Borussia
(Drost 76) **Mönchen-**
gladbach
(Simonsen 2, 86,
Heynckes
9, 50, 60)
Borussia Mönchengladbach won 5-1
on aggregate

1975–76 FINAL (2 legs)
April 28 – Anfield, Liverpool
Liverpool 3-2 Club Brugge KV
(England) (Belgium)
(Kennedy 59, (Lambert 5,
Case 61, Cools 15)
Keegan 65)

May 19 – Olympiastadion, Bruges
Club Brugge KV**1-1** Liverpool
(Lambert 11)   (Keegan 15)

Liverpool won 4-3 on aggregate

1976–77 FINAL (2 legs)
May 4 – Communale, Turin
Juventus **1-0** Athletic Bilbao
(Italy)   (Spain)
(Tardelli 15)

May 18 – San Mames, Bilbao
Athletic Bilbao **2-1** Juventus
(Churruca 11,   (Bettega 7)
Carlos 78)

Juventus won on away goals rule

1977–78 FINAL (2 legs)
April 26 – Furiani, Bastia
SC Bastia **0-0** PSV
(France)   (Netherlands)

May 9 – Philips, Eindhoven
PSV **3-0** SC Bastia
(W. Van der
Kerkhof 24,
Deijkers 67,
Van der Kuijlen 69)

PSV Eindhoven won 3-0 on aggregate

1978–79 FINAL (2 legs)
May 9 – Red Star, Belgrade
Crvena Zvezda **1-1** Borussia
(Yugoslavia)   Mönchen-
(Sestic 21)   gladbach
                 (West Germany)
                 (Jurisic o.g. 60)

May 23 – Rheinstadion, Düsseldorf
Borussia **1-0** Crvena Zvezda
Mönchen-
gladbach
(Simonsen 15)

Borussia Mönchengladbach won 2-1
on aggregate

1979–80 FINAL (2 legs)
May 7 – Bokelberg, Mönchengladbach
Borussia **3-2** Eintracht
Mönchen-   Frankfurt
gladbach   (West Germany)
(West Germany) (Karger 37,
(Kulik 44, 88, Hlzenbein 71)
Matthäus 76)

May 21 – Waldstadion, Frankfurt
Eintracht **1-0** Borussia
Frankfurt   Mönchen-
(Schaub 81)   gladbach

Eintracht Frankfurt won on away
goals rule

1980–81 FINAL (2 legs)
May 6 – Portman Road, Ipswich
Ipswich Town **3-0** AZ 67 Alkmaar
(England)   (Netherlands)
(Wark 28,
Thijssen 46,
Mariner 56)

May 20 – Alkmaarderhout, Alkmaar
AZ 67 Alkmaar **4-2** Ipswich Town
(Welzl 7,   (Thijssen 4,
Metgod 25,   Wark 32)
Tol 40, Jonker 74)

Ipswich Town won 5-4 on aggregate

1981–82 FINAL (2 legs)
May 5 – Nya Ullevi, Gothenburg
IFK Göteborg **1-0** Hamburger SV
(Sweden)   (West Germany)
(Tord Holmgren
87)

May 19 – Volksparkstadion, Hamburg
Hamburger SV **0-3** IFK Göteborg
(Nilsson 6,
Corneliusson 26,
Fredriksson 63)

IFK Göteborg won 4-0 on aggregate

1982–83 FINAL (2 legs)
May 4 – Heysel, Brussels
RSC Anderlecht **1-0** Benfica
(Belgium)   (Portugal)
(Brylle 29)

May 18 – Estadio da Luz, Lisbon
Benfica **1-1** RSC Anderlecht
(Sheu 36)   (Lozana 38)

RSC Anderlecht won 2-1 on aggregate

1983–84 FINAL (2 legs)
May 9 – Parc Astrid, Brussels
RSC Anderlecht **1-1** Tottenham
(Belgium)   Hotspur
(Olsen 85)   (England)
                 (Miller 57)

May 23 – White Hart Lane, London
Tottenham **1-1** RSC Anderlecht
Hotspur   (Czerniatynski 60)
(Roberts 84)
(after extra time)

Tottenham Hotspur won 4-3 on pens

1984–85 FINAL (2 legs)
May 8 – Sostol, Székesfehérvár
Videoton **0-3** Real Madrid
(Hungary)   (Spain)
                 (Michel 31,
                 Santillana 77,
                 Valdano 89)

May 22 – Santiago Bernabeu, Madrid
Real Madrid **0-1** Videoton
                 (Majer 86)

Real Madrid won 3-1 on aggregate

1985–86 FINAL (2 legs)
April 30 – Santiago Bernabeu, Madrid
Real Madrid **5-1** 1. FC Köln
(Spain)   (West Germany)
(Sanchez 38,   (Allofs 29)
Gordillo 42,
Valdano 51, 84,
Santillana 89)

May 6 – Olympiastadion, Berlin
1. FC Köln **2-0** Real Madrid
(Bein 22,
Geilenkirchen 72)

Real Madrid won 5-3 on aggregate

1986–87 FINAL (2 legs)
May 6 – Nya Ullevi, Gothenburg
IFK Göteborg **1-0** Dundee
(Sweden)   United
(Pettersson 38) (Scotland)

May 20 – Tannadice Park, Dundee
Dundee **1-1** IFK Göteborg
United   (Nilsson 22)
(Clark 60)

IFK Göteborg won 2-1 on aggregate

1987–88 FINAL (2 legs)
May 4 – Sarria, Barcelona
RCD Español **3-0** Bayer
(Spain)   Leverkusen
(Losada 45, 56, (West Germany)
Soler 49)

May 18 – Haberland Stadion, Leverkusen
Bayer **3-0** RCD Español
Leverkusen
(Tita 57,
Götz 63,
Cha Bumkun 81)
(after extra time)
Bayer Leverkusen won 3-2 on pens

1988–89 FINAL (2 legs)
May 3 – San Paolo, Naples
Napoli **2-1** Vfb Stuttgart
(Italy)   (West Germany)
(Maradona 68, (Gaudino 17)
Careca 87)

May 17 – Neckarstadion, Stuttgart
Vfb Stuttgart **3-3** Napoli
(Klinsmann 27,   (Alemo 18,
De Napoli o.g. 70, Ferrara 39,
Schmäler 89)   Careca 62)

Napoli won 5-4 on aggregate

1989–90 FINAL (2 legs)
May 2 – Stadio Communale, Turin
Juventus **3-1** Fiorentina
(Italy)   (Italy)
(Galia 3,   (Buso 10)
Casiraghi 59,
De Agostini 73)

May 16 – Partenio, Avellino
Fiorentina **0-0** Juventus

Juventus won 3-1 on aggregate

1990–91 FINAL (2 legs)
May 8 – Guiseppe Meazza, Milan
Internazionale **2-0** Roma
(Italy)   (Italy)
(Mätthaus 55,
Berti 67)

May 22 – Stadio Olimpico, Rome
Roma **1-0** Internazionale
(Rizzitelli 81)

Internazionale won 2-1 on aggregate

1991–92 FINAL (2 legs)
April 29 – Stadio Delle Alpi, Turin
Torino **2-2** Ajax
(Italy)   (Netherlands)
(Casagrande   (Jonk 17,
65, 82)   Pettersson 73)

May 13 – Olympisch Stadion, Amsterdam
Ajax **0-0** Torino

Ajax won on away goals rule

1992–93 FINAL (2 legs)
May 5 – Westfalenstadion, Dortmund
Borussia **1-3** Juventus
Dortmund   (Italy)
(Germany)   (D. Baggio 27,
(M. Rummenigge R. Baggio 31, 74)
2)

May 19 – Delle Alpi, Turin
Juventus **3-0** Borussia
(D. Baggio 5, 40, Dortmund
Möller 65)

Juventus won 6-1 on aggregate

1993–94 FINAL (2 legs)
April 26 – Ernst-Happel-Stadion, Vienna
Austria **0-1** Internazionale
Salzburg   (Italy)
(Austria)   (Berti 35)

May 11 – Giuseppe Meazza, Milan
Internazionale **1-0** Austria
(Jonk 63)   Salzburg

Internazionale won 2-0 on aggregate

1994–95 FINAL (2 legs)
May 3 – Tardini, Parma
Parma **1-0** Juventus
(Italy)   (Italy)
(D. Baggio 5)

May 17 – Giuseppe Meazza, Milan
Juventus **1-1** Parma
(Vialli 33)   (D. Baggio 54)

Parma won 2-1 on aggregate

1995–96 FINAL (2 legs)
May 1 – Olympia, Munich
Bayern **2-0** Girondins de
München   Bordeaux
(Germany)   (France)
(Helmer 35,
Scholl 60)

May 15 – Bordeaux
Girondins de **1-3** Bayern
Bordeaux   München
(Dutuel)   (Scholl 53,
                 Kostadinov 65,
                 Klinsmann 79)

Bayern München won 5-1 on aggregate

1996–97 FINAL (2 legs)
May 7 – Parkstadion, Gelsenkirchen
FC Schalke 04 **1-0** Internazionale
(Germany)   (Italy)
(Wilmots 70)

May 21 – Giuseppe Meazza, Milan
Internazionale **1-0** FC Schalke 04
(Zamorano 84)
(after extra time)

FC Schalke 04 won 4-1 on pens

1997–98 FINAL
May 6 – Parc des Princes, Paris
Lazio **0-3** Internazionale
(Italy)   (Italy)
               (Zamorano 5,
               Zanetti 60,
               Ronaldo 70)

1998–99 FINAL
May 12 – Luzhniki, Moscow
Parma **3-0** Olympique
(Italy)   Marseille
(Crespo 26,   (France)
Vanoli 36,
Chiesa 55)

1999–2000 FINAL
May 17 – Parken, Copenhagen
Galatasaray **0-0** Arsenal
(Turkey)   (England)
(after extra time)
Galatasaray won 4-1 on pens

2000–01 FINAL
May 16 – Westfalenstadion, Dortmund
Liverpool **5-4** CD Alavés
(England)   (Spain)
(Babbel 4,   (Alonzo 27,
Gerrard 16,   Moreno 48, 51,
McAllister 41 pen, Cruyff 89)
Fowler 73,
Geli o.g. 116)
(after extra time)

2001–02 FINAL
May 8 – De Kuip, Rotterdam
Feyenoord **3-2** Borussia
(Netherlands)   Dortmund
(van Hooijdonk   (Germany)
33 pen, 40,   (Amoroso 47 pen,
Tomasson 50)   Koller 58)

The European Cup-Winners' Cup

TOURNAMENT OVERVIEW

WITH THE SUCCESS OF THE EUROPEAN CUP clear to all, and entry to the Fairs Cup initially restricted to certain cities, pressure built up for a further European club competition. The European Cup-Winners' Cup was officially set up in February 1960 at a meeting in Vienna, and was originated by the organizing committee of the now tiring Mittel Europa Cup. Based on the same format as the European Cup, the tournament was open to the winners of national knockout competitions (or losing finalists, if the winners were going to compete in the European Cup). Of course, not all European nations possessed a domestic cup, but with the establishment of the tournament, they all soon acquired one. Only ten teams entered the first tournament, which was won by Fiorentina, beating Glasgow Rangers 4-1 on aggregate – Italy's first European club triumph. The tournament was taken over and expanded by UEFA for the 1961–62 competition and that final saw Atlético Madrid beat champions Fiorentina 3-0 in a replay. In 1963, Atlético Madrid lost 5-1 to Tottenham Hotspur in a single match Final in Rotterdam.

Over the next ten years British clubs won the cup four times, German clubs twice, with Slovan Bratislava's victory over Barcelona in 1969 the first win for an Eastern European club in the competition. The rest of the 1970s saw further Eastern European success (1. FC Magdeburg, Dinamo Kiev) and RSC Anderlecht's run of three consecutive finals 1976–78 (of which the team won the first and last).

The late 1980s and 90s saw a much wider spread of teams getting to the Final, with some smaller clubs securing victory: Belgium's KV Mechelen beat Ajax in 1988, with Sampdoria beating RSC Anderlecht in 1990. Barcelona, winners in 1997, chose to enter the newly expanded Champions League the following year. This was perhaps the death knell for the tournament, whose significance appeared to be slipping. The final tournament was held in 1999 and won by Lazio before the whole show was wrapped up into the newly-expanded UEFA Cup.

West Ham captain Bobby Moore shakes hands with TSV 1860 München's Rudi Brunnenmeier before the start of the 1965 European Cup-Winners' Cup Final at Wembley. West Ham won the cup with two goals in two minutes from Alan Sealey.

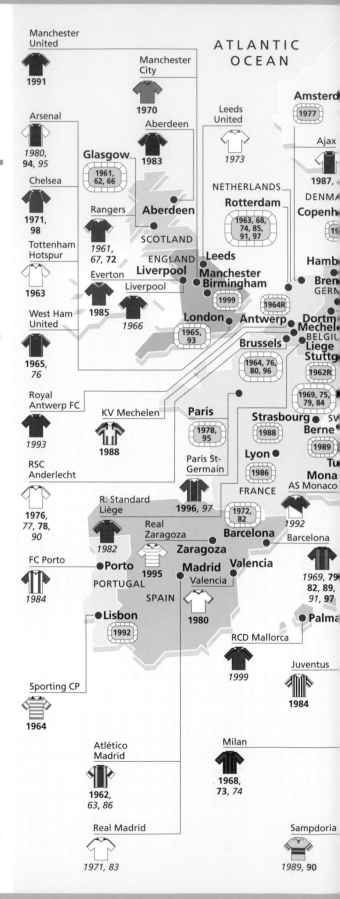

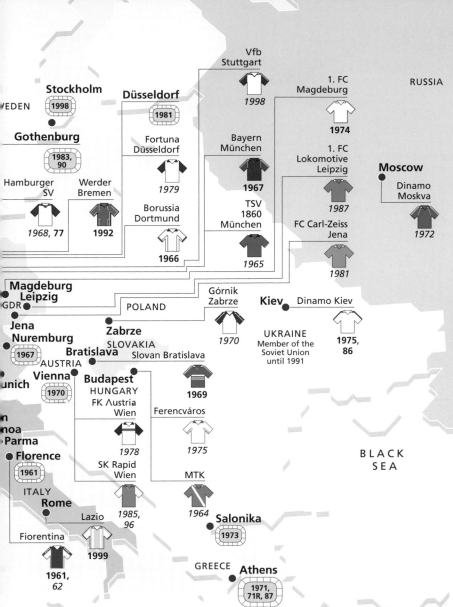

The European Cup-Winners' Cup

Number of wins in the European Cup-Winners' Cup (by country)

- 8+ times
- 5–7 times
- 2–4 times
- 1 time
- 0 times

Team details

ITALY — Country
● **Florence** — City of origin
Fiorentina — Team name
— Team colours
1961, *62* — Winners in bold / Runners-up in italic
● **Amsterdam**
1977R — Host city of Final and year, R means replay

Clubs that won without winning their domestic cup

YEAR	TEAM
1961	Fiorentina
1972	Rangers
1978	RSC Anderlecht
1981	Dinamo Tbilisi
1997	Barcelona

GEORGIA ● T'bilisi
Dinamo Tbilisi

1981

Pavel Nedved *of Lazio strikes home the winning goal against Mallorca in the 81st minute of the last-ever Cup-Winners' Cup Final at Villa Park in Birmingham, England, in May 1999.*

Consecutive participation

NUMBER OF CONSECUTIVE YEARS

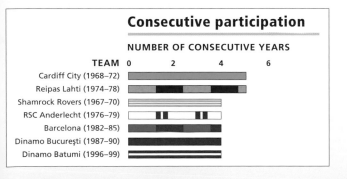

TEAM	
Cardiff City (1968–72)	
Reipas Lahti (1974–78)	
Shamrock Rovers (1967–70)	
RSC Anderlecht (1976–79)	
Barcelona (1982–85)	
Dinamo Bucureşti (1987–90)	
Dinamo Batumi (1996–99)	

The European Cup-Winners' Cup

THE CUP-WINNERS' CUP was the last of the major European tournaments to be established, and the first to be completely abandoned. It was first organized by UEFA in 1960–61, and ran for 39 years. The competition was open to the previous year's winners and the winners of national cup competitions. Throughout the whole of the tournament's history the same format was used: two-leg home and away rounds, with away goals counting double, and penalties to decide drawn matches. The final has always been a single match played at a neutral venue.

When the tournament was first created, many UEFA nations had no national cup competition, and if nothing else, the Cup-Winners' Cup ensured that knockout-format cup football would spread right across the continent. In its final years, preliminary rounds were introduced to produce 17 entrants from among the weaker footballing nations for a 32-club first round. Fourteen places were reserved for the strongest national leagues and one for the previous year's winner. The last Final was played in 1999. The cup has been effectively merged with the expanded UEFA cup, as national cup winners now enter that competition.

1960–61 FINAL (2 legs)
May 17 – Ibrox, Glasgow
Rangers 0-2 Fiorentina
(Scotland)　(Italy)
(Milani 12, 88)
h/t: 0-1 **Att:** 80,000
Ref: Steiner (Austria)

May 27 – Communale, Florence
Fiorentina 2-1 Rangers
(Milani 12,　(Scott 60)
Hamrin 88)
h/t: 1-0 **Att:** 50,000
Ref: Hernadi (Hungary)

Fiorentina won 4-1 on aggregate

1961–62 FINAL
May 10 – Hampden Park, Glasgow
Atlético 1-1 Fiorentina
Madrid　(Italy)
(Spain)　*(Hamrin 27)*
(Peiro 11)
h/t: 1-1 **Att:** 27,000
Ref: Wharton (Scotland)

REPLAY
September 5 –
Neckarstadion, Stuttgart
Atlético 3-0 Fiorentina
Madrid
(Jones 8,
Mendoca 27,
Peiro 59)
h/t: 2-0 **Att:** 38,000
Ref: Tschenscher (West Germany)

1962–63 FINAL
May 15 – De Kuip, Rotterdam
Tottenham 5-1 Atlético
Hotspur　**Madrid**
(England)　(Spain)
(Greaves 16, 80,　(Collar 47)
White 35,
Dyson 67, 85)
h/t: 2-0 **Att:** 49,000
Ref: Van Leuwen (Netherlands)

1963–64 FINAL
May 13 – Heysel, Brussels
Sporting CP 3-3 MTK
(Portugal)　(Hungary)
(Mascarenhas 40,　(Sandor 18, 75,
Figueiredo 45, 80)　Kuti 73)
(after extra time)
h/t: 2-1 **Att:** 30,000
Ref: Van Nuffel (Belgium)

REPLAY
May 15 – Bosuilstadion, Antwerp
Sporting CP 1-0 MTK
(Morais 19)
h/t: 1-0 **Att:** 19,000
Ref: Versyp (Belgium)

1964–65 FINAL
May 19 – Wembley, London
West Ham 2-0 TSV 1860
United　**München**
(England)　(West Germany)
(Sealey 70, 72)
h/t: 0-0 **Att:** 100,000
Ref: Zsolt (Hungary)

1965–66 FINAL
May 5 – Hampden Park, Glasgow
Borussia 2-1 Liverpool
Dortmund　(England)
(West Germany)　*(Hunt 68)*
(Held 62,
Libuda 109)
(after extra time)
h/t: 0-0 **90 mins:** 1-1
Att: 41,000 **Ref:** Schwinte (France)

1966–67 FINAL
May 31 – Frankenstadion, Nüremberg
Bayern 1-0 Rangers
München　(Scotland)
(West Germany)
(Roth 108)
(after extra time)
h/t: 0-0 **90 mins:** 0-0
Att: 69,000 **Ref:** Lo Bello (Italy)

1967–68 FINAL
May 23 – De Kuip, Rotterdam
Milan 2-0 Hamburger SV
(Italy)　(West Germany)
(Hamrin 3, 19)
h/t: 2-0 **Att:** 53,000
Ref: Ortiz (Spain)

1968–69 FINAL
May 21 – St Jakob, Basle
Slovan 3-2 Barcelona
Bratislava　(Spain)
(Czechoslovakia)　*(Zaldua 16,*
(Cvetler 2,　Rexach 52)
Hrivnak 30,
Jan Capkovic 42)
h/t: 3-1 **Att:** 19,000
Ref: Van Raven (Netherlands)

1969–70 FINAL
May 29 – Prater, Vienna
Manchester 2-1 Górnik
City　**Zabrze**
(England)　(Poland)
(Young 11,　(Oslizlo 70)
Lee 43)
h/t: 2-0 **Att:** 10,000
Ref: Schiller (Austria)

1970–71 FINAL
May 19 – Karaiskakis, Piraeus
Chelsea 1-1 Real Madrid
(England)　(Spain)
(Osgood 55)　(Zoco 30)
h/t: 0-0 **90 mins:** 1-1 **Att:** 42,000
Ref: Scheurer (Switzerland)

REPLAY
May 21 – Karaiskakis, Piraeus
Chelsea 2-1 Real Madrid
(Dempsey 31,　(Fleitas 75)
Osgood 39)
h/t: 2-0 **Att:** 19,917
Ref: Bucheli (Switzerland)

1971–72 FINAL
May 24 – Nou Camp, Barcelona
Rangers 3-2 Dinamo
(Scotland)　**Moskva**
(Stein 23,　(Russia)
Johnston 40, 49)　(Estrekov 60,
Makovikov 87)
h/t: 2-0 **Att:** 24,000
Ref: Ortiz (Spain)

1972–73 FINAL
May 16 – Kaftantzoglio, Salonica
Milan 1-0 Leeds United
(Italy)　(England)
(Chiarugi 5)
h/t: 1-0 **Att:** 45,000
Ref: Michas (Greece)

1973–74 FINAL
May 8 – De Kuip, Rotterdam
1. FC 2-0 Milan
Magdeburg　(Italy)
(East Germany)
(Lanzi o.g. 40,
Seguin 74)
h/t: 1-0 **Att:** 4,000
Ref: Van Gemert (Netherlands)

1974–75 FINAL
May 14 – St Jakob, Basle
Dinamo Kiev 3-0 Ferencváros
(Russia)　(Hungary)
(Onischenko
18, 39,
Blokhin 67)
h/t: 2-0 **Att:** 10,000
Ref: Davidson (Scotland)

1975–76 FINAL
May 5 – Heysel, Brussels
RSC Anderlecht 4-2 West Ham
(Belgium)　**United**
(Rensenbrink　(England)
42, 73,　(Holland 28,
Van der Elst　Robson 68)
48, 87)
h/t: 1-1 **Att:** 58,000
Ref: Wurtz (France)

1976–77 FINAL
May 11 – Olympisch, Amsterdam
Hamburger SV 2-0 RSC Anderlecht
(West Germany)　(Belgium)
(Volkert 78,
Magath 88)
h/t: 0-0 **Att:** 66,000
Ref: Partridge (England)

1977–78 FINAL
May 3 – Parc des Princes, Paris
RSC Anderlecht 4-0 FK Austria
(Belgium)　**Wien**
(Rensenbrink　(Austria)
13, 41,
Van Binst 45, 80)
h/t: 2-1 **Att:** 48,000
Ref: Alginder (West Germany)

1978–79 FINAL
May 16 – St Jakob, Basle
Barcelona 4-3 Fortuna
(Spain)　**Düsseldorf**
(Sanchez 5,　(West Germany)
Asensi 34,　(K. Allofs 8,
Rexach 104,　Seel 41, 114)
Krankl 111)
(after extra time)
h/t: 2-2 **90 mins:** 2-2
Att: 58,000 **Ref:** Palotai (Hungary)

1979–80 FINAL

May 15 – Heysel, Brussels
Valencia **0-0** Arsenal
(Spain)   (England)
(after extra time)
h/t: 0-0 **90 mins:** 0-0
Att: 36,000
Ref: Christov (Czechoslovakia)
Valencia won 5-4 on pens

1980–81 FINAL

May 13 – Rheinstadion, Düsseldorf
Dinamo **2-1** FC Carl-Zeiss
Tbilisi   Jena
(Georgia)   (East Germany)
(Gutsayev 67,   (Hoppe 63)
Daraselia 86)
h/t: 0-0 **Att:** 9,000
Ref: Lattanzi (Italy)

1981–82 FINAL

May 12 – Nou Camp, Barcelona
Barcelona **2-1** R Standard
(Spain)   Liège
(Simonsen 44,   (Belgium)
Quini 63)   (Vandersmissen 7)
h/t: 1-1 **Att:** 100,000
Ref: Eschweller (West Germany)

1982–83 FINAL

May 11 – Nya Ullevi, Gothenburg
Aberdeen **2-1** Real Madrid
(Scotland)   (Spain)
(Black 4,   (Juanito 15)
Hewitt 112)
(after extra time)
h/t: 1-1 **90 mins:** 1-1
Att: 17,000 **Ref:** Menegali (Italy)

1983–84 FINAL

May 16 – St Jakob, Basle
Juventus **2-1** FC Porto
(Italy)   (Portugal)
(Vignola 12,   (Sousa 29)
Boniek 41)
h/t: 2-1 **Att:** 60,000
Ref: Galler (Switzerland)

1984–85 FINAL

May 15 – De Kuip, Rotterdam
Everton **3-1** SK Rapid Wien
(England)   (Austria)
(Gray 57,   (Krankl 85)
Steven 72,
Sheedy 85)
h/t: 0-0 **Att:** 50,000
Ref: Casarin (Italy)

1985–86 FINAL

May 2 – Gerland, Lyon
Dinamo Kiev **3-0** Atlético
(Russia)   Madrid
(Zavarov 4,   (Spain)
Blokhin 85,
Yevlushenko 87)
h/t: 1-0 **Att:** 50,000
Ref: Wohrer (Austria)

1986–87 FINAL

May 13 – Olympic, Athens
Ajax **1-0** 1. FC
(Netherlands)   Lokomotive
(van Basten 21) Leipzig
(East Germany)
h/t: 1-0 **Att:** 35,000
Ref: Agnolin (Italy)

1987–88 FINAL

May 11 – Meinau, Strasbourg
KV Mechelen **1-0** Ajax
(Belgium)   (Netherlands)
(Den Boer 53)
h/t: 0-0 **Att:** 40,000
Ref: Pauly (West Germany)

1988–89 FINAL

May 10 – Wankdorf, Berne
Barcelona **2-0** Sampdoria
(Spain)   (Italy)
(Salinas 4,
Rekarte 79)
h/t: 1-0 **Att:** 45,000
Ref: Courtney (England)

1989–90 FINAL

May 9 – Nya Ullevi, Gothenburg
Sampdoria **2-0** RSC Anderlecht
(Italy)   (Belgium)
(Vialli 105, 107)
(after extra time)
h/t: 0-0 **90 mins:** 0-0
Att: 20,000 **Ref:** Galler (Switzerland)

1990–91 FINAL

May 15 – De Kuip, Rotterdam
Manchester **2-1** Barcelona
United   (Spain)
(England)   (Koeman 79)
(Bruce 67,
Hughes 74)
h/t: 0-0 **Att:** 48,000
Ref: Karlsson (Sweden)

1991–92 FINAL

May 6 – Estadio da Luz, Lisbon
Werder Bremen **2-0** AS Monaco
(Germany)   (France)
(K. Allofs 41,
Rufer 54)
h/t: 1-0 **Att:** 15,000
Ref: D'Elia (Italy)

1992–93 FINAL

May 12 – Wembley, London
Parma **3-1** Royal
(Italy)   Antwerp FC
(Minotti 9,   (Belgium)
Melli 30,   (Severeyns 11)
Cuoghi 83)
h/t: 2-1 **Att:** 37,000
Ref: Assenmacher (Germany)

1993–94 FINAL

May 4 – Park Stadion, Copenhagen
Arsenal **1-0** Parma
(England)   (Italy)
(Smith 19)
h/t: 1-0 **Att:** 33,765
Ref: Krondl (Czechoslovakia)

1994–95 FINAL

May 10 – Parc des Princes, Paris
Real Zaragoza **2-1** Arsenal
(Spain)   (England)
(Esnaider 68,   (Hartson 77)
Nayim 119)
(after extra time)
h/t: 0-0 **90 mins:** 1-1
Att: 42,424 **Ref:** Ceccarini (Italy)

1995–96 FINAL

May 8 – King Baudoui, Brussels
Paris Saint- **1-0** SK Rapid
Germain   Wien
(France)   (Austria)
(N'Gotty 28)
h/t: 1-0 **Att:** 37,500
Ref: Pairetto (Italy)

1996–97 FINAL

May 14 – De Kuip, Rotterdam
Barcelona **1-0** Paris Saint-
(Spain)   Germain
(Ronaldo 37 pen) (France)
h/t: 1-0 **Att:** 50,000
Ref: Merk (Germany)

1997–98 FINAL

May 13 – Rasunda, Stockholm
Chelsea **1-0** Vfb Stuttgart
(England)   (Germany)
(Zola 71)
h/t: 0-0 **Att:** 30,216
Ref: Braschi (Italy)

1998–99 FINAL

May 19 – Villa Park, Birmingham
Lazio **2-1** RCD Mallorca
(Italy)   (Spain)
(Vieri 7,   (Dani 11)
Nedved 81)
h/t: 1-1 **Att:** 33,000
Ref: Benko (Austria)

THE EUROPEAN CUP-WINNERS' CUP

***The 1982–83 European Cup-Winners' Cup** Final was played in Gothenburg, Sweden, in appalling weather conditions. Both Real Madrid and Aberdeen scored in the first 15 minutes, but the match was level after 90. In the 112th minute, Aberdeen's substitute John Hewitt dived forward to head the ball past the Real keeper and clinch the cup for the only time in the Scottish club's history.*

The European Champions League

TOURNAMENT REVIEW 2001–02

THE EUROPEAN CHAMPIONS LEAGUE

IN A YEAR IN WHICH European football was forced to consider the corrosive consequences of money on the game as well as the possibility that TV rights and TV coverage have peaked, and the game's administrators also realized that overkill was feasible, the European Champions League came under deeper scrutiny. Despite these murmurings, it was clear that among Europe's biggest clubs, the Champions League is steadily establishing itself as the major prize. For the challengers in every country, entry into the tournament – even into the qualifying rounds – is becoming financially essential. For the very biggest, no other prize will accommodate their levels of ambition and hunger for international coverage. In its centenary year, Real Madrid's hierarchy made it abundantly clear that, domestic competitions notwithstanding, the club must win its ninth European Cup. With the Final set for Hampden Park in Glasgow, there was also the irresistible possibility of Manchester United's manager Sir Alex Ferguson (who had announced his retirement at the end of the season) playing out his final game in his home town.

The group phases

The opening group phase went broadly to form. There were surprisingly strong performances from Nantes and Panathinaikos, paralleled with appallingly bad starts to their domestic seasons. Dortmund, Celtic and Lyon played well, winning tough matches, but they were all squeezed out of their difficult groups. The second group phase, strung out over the Christmas break, was a tight if not always compelling affair. Five clubs from outside the big five leagues made it this far: Sparta Praha, Galatasaray, Panathinaikos, Porto and Boavista, but the gap between the very biggest clubs and the others began to emerge more clearly.

Manchester United and Bayern München exchanged draws in a group they dominated. Real Madrid, playing its most consistent football of the season, romped home in its group. Panathinaikos made the quarter-finals amid delirious scenes. The Greek team's results included a home draw with Real, the only points dropped by the Spaniards during this stage. Leverkusen and Deportivo forced out Arsenal and Juventus, whose away form consistently let the team down. In the process, Juventus recorded its lowest ever attendance at a Champions League match – less than 8,000 saw its final game at home to Arsenal. Group B proved to be the most enthralling, with Barcelona and Liverpool just finding the edge over Roma and Galatasaray, whose game at the Olimpico descended into a brawl in the tunnel after a fantastically

GROUP PHASE 1

GROUP A

CLUB	P	W	D	L	F	A	Pts	
Real Madrid (Spain)	6	4	1	1	13	5	13	Group Phase 2
Roma (Italy)	6	2	3	1	6	5	9	Group Phase 2
Lokomotiv Moskva (Russia)	6	2	1	3	9	9	7	UEFA Cup
RSC Anderlecht (Belgium)	6	0	3	3	4	13	3	

GROUP B

CLUB	P	W	D	L	F	A	Pts	
Liverpool (England)	6	3	3	0	7	3	12	Group Phase 2
Boavista FC (Portugal)	6	2	2	2	8	7	8	Group Phase 2
Borussia Dortmund (Germany)	6	2	2	2	6	7	8	UEFA Cup
Dynamo Kyiv (Ukraine)	6	1	1	4	5	9	4	

GROUP C

CLUB	P	W	D	L	F	A	Pts	
Panathinaikos (Greece)	6	4	0	2	8	3	12	Group Phase 2
Arsenal (England)	6	3	0	3	9	9	9	Group Phase 2
RCD Mallorca (Spain)	6	3	0	3	4	9	9	UEFA Cup
Schalke 04 (Germany)	6	2	0	4	9	9	6	

GROUP D

CLUB	P	W	D	L	F	A	Pts	
FC Nantes (France)	6	3	2	1	8	3	11	Group Phase 2
Galatasaray (Turkey)	6	3	1	2	5	4	10	Group Phase 2
PSV (Netherlands)	6	2	1	3	6	9	7	UEFA Cup
Lazio (Italy)	6	2	0	4	4	7	6	

GROUP E

CLUB	P	W	D	L	F	A	Pts	
Juventus (Italy)	6	3	2	1	11	8	11	Group Phase 2
FC Porto (Portugal)	6	3	1	2	7	5	10	Group Phase 2
Celtic (Scotland)	6	3	0	3	8	11	9	UEFA Cup
Rosenborg (Norway)	6	1	1	4	4	6	4	

GROUP F

CLUB	P	W	D	L	F	A	Pts	
Barcelona (Spain)	6	5	0	1	12	5	15	Group Phase 2
Bayer Leverkusen (Germany)	6	4	0	2	10	9	12	Group Phase 2
Olympique Lyonnais (France)	6	3	0	3	10	9	9	UEFA Cup
Fenerbahçe (Turkey)	6	0	0	6	3	12	0	

GROUP G

CLUB	P	W	D	L	F	A	Pts	
RC Deportivo (Spain)	6	2	4	0	10	8	10	Group Phase 2
Manchester United (England)	6	3	1	2	10	6	10	Group Phase 2
Lille OSC (France)	6	1	3	2	7	7	6	UEFA Cup
Olympiakos (Greece)	6	1	2	3	6	12	5	

GROUP H

CLUB	P	W	D	L	F	A	Pts	
Bayern München (Germany)	6	4	2	0	14	5	14	Group Phase 2
Sparta Praha (Czech Rep.)	6	3	2	1	10	3	11	Group Phase 2
Feyenoord (Netherlands)	6	1	2	3	7	14	5	UEFA Cup
Spartak Moskva (Russia)	6	0	2	4	7	16	2	

Life in the big pond. Five consecutive Greek championships, but again Olympiakos went straight out at the first group stage.

GROUP PHASE 2

GROUP A

CLUB	P	W	D	L	F	A	Pts	
Manchester United	6	3	3	0	13	3	12	Quarter-Finals
Bayern München	6	3	3	0	5	2	12	Quarter-Finals
Boavista FC	6	1	2	3	2	8	5	
FC Nantes	6	0	2	4	4	11	2	

GROUP B

CLUB	P	W	D	L	F	A	Pts	
Barcelona	6	2	3	1	7	7	9	Quarter-Finals
Liverpool	6	1	4	1	4	4	7	Quarter-Finals
Roma	6	1	4	1	6	5	7	
Galatasaray	6	0	5	1	5	6	5	

GROUP C

CLUB	P	W	D	L	F	A	Pts	
Real Madrid	6	5	1	0	14	5	16	Quarter-Finals
Panathinaikos	6	2	2	2	7	8	8	Quarter-Finals
Sparta Praha	6	2	0	4	6	10	6	
FC Porto	6	1	1	4	3	7	4	

GROUP D

CLUB	P	W	D	L	F	A	Pts	
Bayer Leverkusen	6	3	1	2	11	11	10	Quarter-Finals
RC Deportivo	6	3	1	2	7	6	10	Quarter-Finals
Arsenal	6	2	1	3	8	8	7	
Juventus	6	2	1	3	7	8	7	

...other desolate night at ...e Stadio delle Alpi for a ...ventus Champions League ...tch – the club has ...cided to redevelop ...e unloved stadium ...the end of the season.

Nantes' disastrous domestic form was mirrored by brilliant early European form. Nestor Fabri scores against a miserable Lazio.

Above: Panathinaikos celebrates qualification for the knockout stage in the team's best performance in the competition for nearly 30 years.

Right: Rosenborg's Sigurd Rushfeldt and Celtic's Johan Mjallby battle for third spot in Group E. Rosenborg's regular Champions League paydays keep the club at the top of Norwegian football.

THE EUROPEAN CHAMPIONS LEAGUE

bad-tempered 1-1 draw. With the beginning of the knockout quarter-finals, again with no Italian representation, the quality and the tension of the games began to grow. Real Madrid met last year's champions Bayern München in a repeat of last year's semi-final. Real reversed the outcome this year after a bitter war of words and accusation in the press and two tough, hard-fought matches. Barcelona faced Panathinaikos, whose hopes soared on a fantastic 1-0 victory at home against the Catalans, but in the return at the Nou Camp, Barcelona made no mistake and demolished its Athenian opponents. Manchester United faced Deportivo, who had beaten the team home and away in the opening phase, but United played its best football of the tournament to earn a semi-final spot against rising Bayer Leverkusen. Under the charismatic Klaus Toppmöller, Leverkusen's inventive play saw the Germans narrowly beaten at Anfield before finishing the job by beating Liverpool 4-2 in the second leg at the BayArena.

In the event, Leverkusen faced a depleted United (no Beckham and a recovering Keane on the bench) and deservedly beat the team, albeit on away goals. The pairing of Real and Barça in the second semi saw all TV viewing records in Spain broken and an estimated TV audience of 500 million in 100 countries. Real rose to the occasion, silenced the Nou Camp with a 2-0 victory and celebrated with a 1-1 draw at home to take the team to its 12th European Cup Final and the possibility of *La Novena* – a ninth cup.

Below: You've really gone and done it now. Juan Sebastian Veron looks at Deportivo's Aldo Duscher after the tackle that broke David Beckham's metatarsal bone.

Bottom: Tempers flare at the Bayern v Real Madrid quarter-final first leg as Hierro explains to Effenberg why he is wrong.

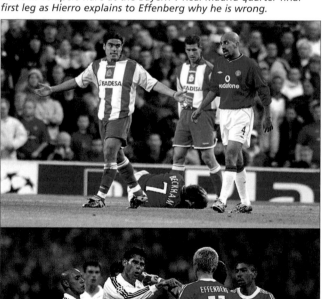

The final action

In Glasgow, both finalists had already lost their respective cup finals and abandoned or squandered their chance of a domestic league title. The pressure to finish the season with a victory was immense. In a Final truly deserving of the competition, Real took the lead early on with a soft goal, as Raúl pounced on a defensive error and snicked the ball home. Leverkusen, whose spirit was undaunted, equalized with a header from Brazilian defender Lucio. But on the stroke of half time it took a great player and a great moment to decide the match. An elegant, high lob from a racing Roberto Carlos on the wing hung in the air behind and to the left of Zidane on the edge of the area. With an extraordinary turn of speed and grace he swivelled, connected and sent the ball tearing into the goal. After that, despite concerted pressure, seven minutes of injury time and three goal-line clearances by Real in the dying minutes, there was no way back for Leverkusen.

QUARTER-FINALS (2 legs)

April 3 – Apostolos Nikolaidis, Athens
Panathinaikos 1-0 Barcelona
(Bassinas 78 pen)
Att: 15,000

April 9 – Nou Camp, Barcelona
Barcelona 3-1 Panathinaikos
(Saviola 61,   (Konstantinou 7)
L. Enrique 22, 49)
Att: 90,000

Barcelona won 3-2 on aggregate

April 2 – Olympic Stadium, Munich
Bayern   Real
München 2-1 Madrid
(Effenburg 81,   (Geremi 12)
Pizarro 87)
Att: 60,000

April 10 – Santiago Bernabeu, Madrid
Real   Bayern
Madrid 2-0 München
(Helguera 68,
Guti 84)
Att: 75,000

Real Madrid won 3-2 on aggregate

April 2 – Estadio La Riazor, La Coruña
RC Deportivo 0-2 Manchester
United
(Beckham 15,
van Nistelrooy 41)
Att: 32,351

April 10 – Old Trafford, Manchester
Manchester 3-2 RC Deportivo
United   (Blanc o.g. 44,
(Solskjaer 23, 56,   Djalminha 90)
Giggs 69)
Att: 65,875

Manchester United won 5-2
on aggregate

April 3 – Anfield, Liverpool
Liverpool 1-0 Bayer
(Hyypia 44)   **Leverkusen**
Att: 42,454

April 9 – BayArena, Leverkusen
Bayer 4-2 Liverpool
Leverkusen   (Xavier 42,
(Ballack 15, 63,   Litmanen 79)
Berbatov 68,
Lucio 84)
Att: 22,500

Bayer Leverkusen won 4-3 on aggregate

SEMI-FINALS (2 legs)

April 23 – Nou Camp, Barcelona
Barcelona 0-2 Real Madrid
(Zidane 55,
McManaman 90)
Att: 98,000

May 1 – Bernabeu, Madrid
Real Madrid 1-1 Barcelona
(Raúl 43)   (Helguera o.g. 48)
Att: 73,000

Real Madrid won 3-1 on aggregate

April 24 – Old Trafford, Manchester
Manchester   Bayer
United 2-2 Leverkusen
(Zivkovic o.g. 29,   (Ballack 62,
van Nistelrooy   Neuville 75)
67 pen)
Att: 66,534

April 30 – BayArena, Leverkusen
Bayer   Manchester
Leverkusen 1-1 United
(Neuville 45)   (Keane 28)
Att: 22,500

Bayer Leverkusen won on
away goals

2002 FINAL

May 15 – Hampden Park, Glasgow
Real Madrid 2-1 Bayer
(Raúl 9,   Leverkusen
Zidane 45)   (Lucio 14)
h/t: 2-1 **Att:** 52,000
Ref: Urs Meier (Switzerland)

Konstantinou of Panathinaikos scores at the Nou Camp, but Barça won the quarter-final 3-2.

Oliver Neuville grabs a late equalizer for Bayer Leverkusen at Old Trafford.

Steve McManaman lobs Barça's keeper Bonano to seal an imperious 2-0 semi-final victory for Real in the enemy's heartland.

What a relief! After losing the domestic league and cup, Real Madrid gets the trophy its centenary demanded.

Real's Zinedine Zidane swivels, volleys and watches the ball crash into the roof of the net to seal the team's victory in the Champions League Final. Bayer Leverkusen's Michael Ballack doesn't want to look.

The European Champions League

THE EUROPEAN CHAMPIONS LEAGUE

TOURNAMENT OVERVIEW

ORGANIZED EUROPEAN CLUB COMPETITIONS began in 1927 with the Mittel Europa Cup, contested by the leading teams in Austria, Hungary, Italy and Czechoslovakia. Although it was revived after the Second World War, Cold War divisions made the logistics difficult. Moreover, the power base of club football had shifted west and the Latin Cup was established in 1949 among the champions of France, Italy, Spain and Portugal. Based on this model of two aggregate legs and a single-match Final, Gabriel Hunot, editor of French sports paper *L'Equipe*, proposed the creation of a European Cup, contested by its national champions in 1955. Formally sanctioned by FIFA, the cup was first contested in 1956. But Chelsea, the English champions at the time, was not allowed to compete by the FA.

Real win five in a row

Thus the European Cup began as a small affair with no sponsors, and barely any television coverage. The first Final was won by Real Madrid beating Stade de Reims 4-3 in Paris. The following year, against the wishes of the English FA, Manchester United entered the tournament. On the flight home from a successful quarter-final second-leg match against Red Star Belgrade the core of the squad was killed in an air crash in Munich. Fatally weakened, United was put out in the semi-finals by Real Madrid who went on to win the Final against Fiorentina. Madrid won a further three consecutive titles, culminating in their extraordinary 7-3 demolition of Eintracht Frankfurt in the 1960 Final at Hampden Park in Glasgow, thought by many who saw it to have been the finest match ever seen.

With Real on the slide, the next five cups fell two apiece to Benfica and Internazionale, with a win for Milan in between, before a sixth Real victory in 1966. A shift of footballing power northward soon followed with British victories in 1967 and 1968 (Celtic and Manchester United). Four Dutch victories, three for Ajax, began the 1970s followed by three victories for Bayern München. Liverpool's triumph in 1977 began a series of six consecutive English victories. Liverpool's last Final, in 1985, was the occasion of the Heysel Stadium disaster after which English clubs were banned from European competition for six years. In their absence, the cup went east for the first time to Steaua Bucureşti of Romania.

Birth of the Champions League

Under considerable pressure from big clubs and TV companies the tournament was steadily expanded and reformatted during the late 1990s as the European Champions League, with winning teams playing at least 16 matches to get to the Final and more clubs from the bigger leagues getting into the tournament. The huge sums of TV and sponsorship money the Champions League generates has made it the biggest footballing event outside the World Cup.

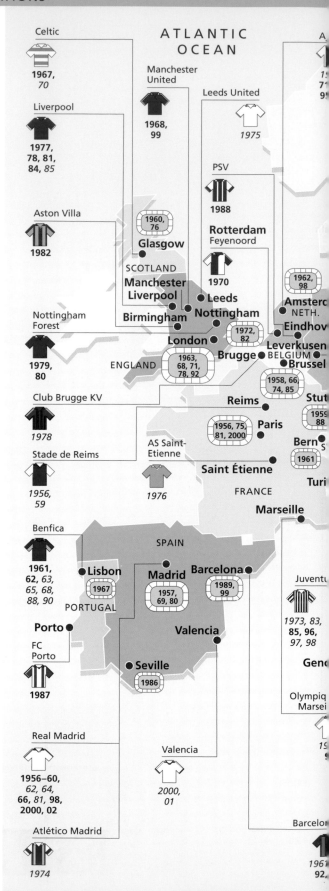

Malmö FC
1979

Eintracht Frankfurt
1960

Hamburger SV
1980,
83

Borussia Dortmund
1997

Bayern München
1974–76
82, 87,
99, **2001**

Bayer Leverkusen
2002

Borussia
Mönchengladbach
1977

Crvena Zvezda
1991

Partizan Beograd
1966

lmö

mburg

RMANY

rtmund

rankfurt

unich
1979,
93, 97

●**Vienna**
AUSTRIA
1964, 87,
90, 95

ilan
965, 70,
2001

Steaua Bucureşti
1986,
89

ROMANIA

●**Bucharest**
Belgrade ●
1973

**BLACK
SEA**

Fiorentina
1957

●**Florence**
ITALY

●**Rome**
1977,
84, 96

Bari
1991

YUGOSLAVIA

Internazionale
1964, 65,
67, 72

GREECE

Milan
1958, **63, 69,**
89, 90, 93,
94, 95

●**Athens**
1983,
94

Panathinaikos
1971

Roma
1984

**MEDITERRANEAN
SEA**

Sampdoria
1992

The European
Champions League

**Number of wins in the European
Champions League (by country)**

▨	8+ times
▨	5–7 times
▨	2–4 times
☐	1 time
☐	0 times

Team details

PORTUGAL	Country
● Lisbon	City of origin
Benfica	Team name
👕	Team colours
1961, 62 *63, 65, 68,* *88, 90*	Winners in bold Runners-up in italic
● Belgrade	
1973	Host city of Final and year

*Karlheinz Riedle (yellow shirt, second from left) heads
the ball past Juventus keeper Angelo Peruzzi to score
Borussia Dortmund's second goal in their 3-1 victory
in the 1997 Final in Munich.*

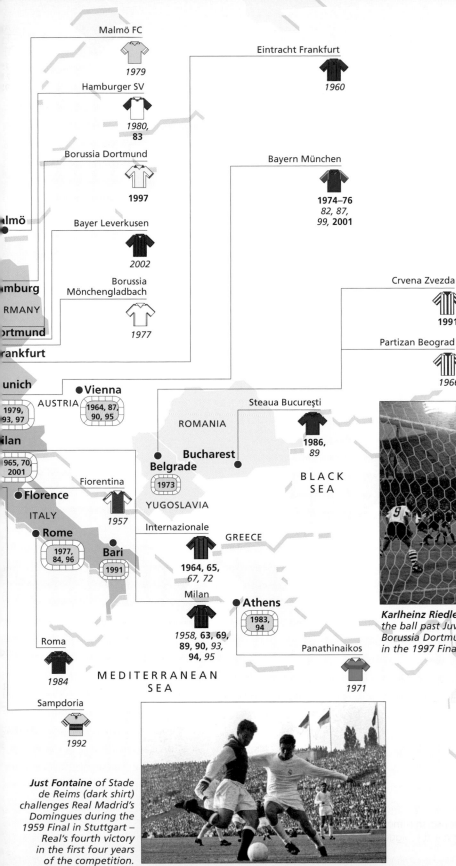

*Just Fontaine of Stade
de Reims (dark shirt)
challenges Real Madrid's
Domingues during the
1959 Final in Stuttgart –
Real's fourth victory
in the first four years
of the competition.*

The European Champions
League 1956–2002

COUNTRY	WINNERS	RUNNERS-UP
Spain	10	9
Italy	9	12
England	9	2
Germany	6	7
Netherlands	6	2
Portugal	3	5
France	1	4
Romania	1	1
Scotland	1	1
Yugoslavia	1	1
Belgium	0	1
Greece	0	1
Sweden	0	1

The European Champions League

THE EUROPEAN CUP was established in 1955 after a meeting called by Gabriel Hunot, then editor of the French sports newspaper *L'Equipe*. Although the initial tournament had an eclectic mix of national champions and other big clubs, it was soon codified and run by UEFA with entry restricted to national champions and the previous year's winner. Two-leg matches in each round were played with a single final match at a neutral venue. In 1992, mini-leagues were played to produce the finalists. In 1995, there was a shift back to two-leg quarter- and semi-finals, but the really big change in the competition's format came in 1996. Under pressure from the big clubs for more games and more money, UEFA created qualifying rounds for smaller countries and a first round of four mini-leagues of four to produce eight quarter-finalists.

In 2000 the tournament was expanded even further, with two places guaranteed to the strongest leagues in Europe and extra routes in for clubs via a longer qualifying round. The first round now consists of eight groups of four clubs with 16 progressing into the second round. Third-place teams qualify for the later rounds of the UEFA Cup, while teams defeated in the preliminary stages are entered for the first round of the UEFA Cup. The final 16 play in four groups of four to produce eight quarter-finalists. Two-legged matches determine the finalists, who still play a single match at a neutral venue. These days a team may need to play more than 20 matches to win the European Champions League.

1955–56 FINAL
June 13 – Parc des Princes, Paris
Real Madrid 4-3 Stade de Reims
(Spain)   (France)
(di Stefano 15,   (Leblond 6,
Rial 30, 79,   Templin 10,
Marquitos 71)   Hidalgo 62)
h/t: 2-2 **Att:** 38,239
Ref: Ellis (England)

1956–57 FINAL
May 30 – Santiago Bernabeu, Madrid
Real Madrid 2-0 Fiorentina
(Spain)   (Italy)
(di Stefano
70 pen,
Gento 76)
h/t: 0-0 **Att:** 120,000
Ref: Horn (Netherlands)

1957–58 FINAL
May 29 – Heysel, Brussels
Real Madrid 3-2 Milan
(Spain)   (Italy)
(di Stefano 74,   (Schiaffino 69,
Rial 79,   Grillo 78)
Gento 107)
(after extra time)
h/t: 0-0 **90 mins:** 2-2
Att: 70,000 **Ref:** Alsteen (Belgium)

1958–59 FINAL
June 3 – Neckar, Stuttgart
Real Madrid 2-0 Stade de Reims
(Spain)   (France)
(Mateos 2,
di Stefano 47)
h/t: 1-0 **Att:** 72,000
Ref: Dusch (France)

1959–60 FINAL
May 18 – Hampden Park, Glasgow
Real Madrid 7-3 Eintracht
(Spain)   Frankfurt
(di Stefano   (West Germany)
26, 29, 74,   (Kress 18,
Puskas 44, 56,   Stein 72, 76)
60 pen, 71)
h/t: 3-1 **Att:** 127,621
Ref: Mowat (Scotland)

1960–61 FINAL
May 31 – Wankdorf, Bern
Benfica 3-2 Barcelona
(Portugal)   (Spain)
(Aguas 30,   (Kocsis 20,
Ramallets o.g. 31,   Czibor 75)
Coluna 54)
h/t: 2-1 **Att:** 33,000
Ref: Dienst (Switzerland)

1961–62 FINAL
May 2 – Olympic, Amsterdam
Benfica 5-3 Real Madrid
(Portugal)   (Spain)
(Aguas 25,   (Puskas
Cavem 34,   17, 23, 38)
Coluna 61,
Eusebio
68 pen, 78)
h/t: 2-3 **Att:** 68,000
Ref: Horn (Netherlands)

1962–63 FINAL
May 22 – Wembley, London
Milan 2-1 Benfica
(Italy)   (Portugal)
(Altafini 58, 66)   (Eusebio 18)
h/t: 0-1 **Att:** 45,000
Ref: Netherlands (England)

1963–64 FINAL
May 27 – Prater, Vienna
Internazionale 3-1 Real Madrid
(Italy)   (Spain)
(Mazzola 43, 76,   (Felo 69)
Milani 62)
h/t: 1-0 **Att:** 72,000
Ref: Stoll (Austria)

1964–65 FINAL
May 27 – San Siro, Milan
Internazionale 1-0 Benfica
(Italy)   (Portugal)
(Jair 42)
h/t: 1-0 **Att:** 80,000
Ref: Dienst (Switzerland)

1965–66 FINAL
May 11 – Heysel, Brussels
Real Madrid 2-1 Partizan
(Italy)   Beograd
(Amancio 70,   (Yugoslavia)
Serena 76)   (Vasovic 55)
h/t: 0-0 **Att:** 55,000
Ref: Kreitlein (West Germany)

1966–67 FINAL
May 25 – Estadio da Luz, Lisbon
Celtic 2-1 Internazionale
(Scotland)   (Italy)
(Gemmell 62,   (Mazzola 6 pen)
Chalmers 83)
h/t: 0-1 **Att:** 55,000
Ref: Tschenscher (West Germany)

1967–68 FINAL
May 29 – Wembley, London
Manchester 4-1 Benfica
United   (Portugal)
(England)   *(Jaime Graca 78)*
(Charlton 54, 98,
Best 92,
Kidd 95)
(after extra time)
h/t: 0-0 **90 mins:** 1-1
Att: 100,000 **Ref:** Lo Bello (Italy)

1968–69 FINAL
May 28 – Santiago Bernabeu, Madrid
Milan 4-1 Ajax
(Italy)   (Netherlands)
(Prati 7, 39, 74,   (Vasovic 61 pen)
Sormani 66)
h/t: 2-0 **Att:** 50,000
Ref: Ortiz (Spain)

1969–70 FINAL
May 6 – San Siro, Milan
Feyenoord 2-1 Celtic
(Netherlands)   (Scotland)
(Israel 29,   (Gemmell 31)
Kindvall 116)
(after extra time)
h/t: 1-1 **90 mins:** 1-1
Att: 53,187 **Ref:** Lo Bello (Italy)

1970–71 FINAL
June 2 – Wembley, London
Ajax 2-0 Panathinaikos
(Netherlands)   (Greece)
(Van Dijk 5,
Haan 87)
h/t: 1-0 **Att:** 90,000
Ref: Taylor (England)

1971–72 FINAL
May 31 – De Kuip, Rotterdam
Ajax 2-0 Internazionale
(Netherlands)   (Italy)
(Cruyff 48, 77)
h/t: 0-0 **Att:** 61,000
Ref: Helies (France)

1972–73 FINAL
May 30 – Crvena Zvezda, Belgrade
Ajax 1-0 Juventus
(Netherlands)   (Italy)
(Rep 4)
h/t: 1-0 **Att:** 93,000
Ref: Gugulovic (Yugoslavia)

1973–74 FINAL
May 15 – Heysel, Brussels
Bayern 1-1 Atlético
München   Madrid
(West Germany)   (Spain)
(Schwarzenbeck   (Luis Aragones
120)   113)
(after extra time)
h/t: 0-0 **90 mins:** 0-0
Att: 65,000 **Ref:** Loraux (Belgium)

REPLAY
May 17 – Heysel, Brussels
Bayern 4-0 Atlético
München   Madrid
(Hoeness 28, 81,
Müller 57, 70)
h/t: 1-0 **Att:** 23,000
Ref: Delcourt (Belgium)

1974–75 FINAL
May 28 – Parc des Princes, Paris
Bayern 2-0 Leeds
München   United
(West Germany)   (England)
(Roth 71,
Müller 81)
h/t: 0-0 **Att:** 48,000
Ref: Kitabdjian (France)

1975–76 FINAL
May 12 – Hampden Park, Glasgow
Bayern 1-0 AS Saint-
München   Etienne
(West Germany)   (France)
(Roth 57)
h/t: 0-0 **Att:** 54,684
Ref: Palotai (Hungary)

1976–77 FINAL
May 25 – Olimpico, Rome
Liverpool 3-1 Borussia
(England)   Mönchen-
(McDermott 27,   gladbach
Smith 65,   (West Germany)
Neal 82 pen)   (Simonsen 51)
h/t: 1-0 **Att:** 57,000
Ref: Wurtz (France)

1977–78 FINAL
May 10 – Wembley, London
Liverpool 1-0 Club Brugge KV
(England)   (Belgium)
(Dalglish 64)
h/t: 0-0 **Att:** 92,000
Ref: Corver (Netherlands)

1978–79 FINAL
May 30 – Olympiastadion, Munich
Nottingham 1-0 Malmö FF
Forest   (Sweden)
(England)
(Francis 44)
h/t: 1-0 **Att:** 57,500
Ref: Linemayr (Austria)

1979–80 FINAL
May 28 – Santiago Bernabeu, Madrid
Nottingham 1-0 Hamburger SV
Forest   (West Germany)
(England)
(Robertson 19)
h/t: 1-0 **Att:** 51,000
Ref: Garrido (Portugal)

1980–81 FINAL
May 27 – Parc des Princes, Paris
Liverpool 1-0 Real Madrid
(England)   (Spain)
(A. Kennedy 82)
h/t: 0-0 **Att:** 48,360
Ref: Palotai (Hungary)

1981–82 FINAL
May 26 – De Kuip, Rotterdam
Aston Villa 1-0 Bayern
(England)   **München**
(Withe 67)   (West Germany)
h/t: 0-0 **Att:** 45,000
Ref: Konrath (France)

1982–83 FINAL
May 25 – Olympic, Athens
Hamburger SV 1-0 Juventus
(West Germany)   (Italy)
(Magath 9)
h/t: 1-0 **Att:** 73,500
Ref: Rainea (Romania)

1983–84 FINAL
May 30 – Olimpico, Rome
Liverpool 1-1 Roma
(England)   (Italy)
(Neal 15)   *(Pruzzo 38)*
(after extra tlme)
h/t: 1-1 **90 mins:** 1-1
Att: 69,693 **Ref:** Fredriksson (Sweden)
Liverpool won 4-2 on pens

1984–85 FINAL
May 29 – Heysel, Brussels
Juventus 1-0 Liverpool
(Italy)   (England)
(Platini 57 pen)
h/t: 0-0 **Att:** 60,000
Ref: Daina (Switzerland)

1985–86 FINAL
May 7 – Sanchez Pizjuan, Seville
Steaua 0-0 Barcelona
Bucureşti   (Spain)
(Romania)
(after extra time)
h/t: 0-0 **90 mins:** 0-0
Att: 75,000 **Ref:** Vautrot (France)
Steaua Bucureşti won 2-0 on pens

1986–87 FINAL
May 27 – Prater, Vienna
FC Porto 2-1 Bayern
(Portugal)   **München**
(Madjer 77,   (West Germany)
Juary 81)   *(Kogl 25)*
h/t: 0-1 **Att:** 62,000
Ref: Ponnet (Belgium)

1987–88 FINAL
May 25 – Neckar, Stuttgart
PSV 0-0 Benfica
(Netherlands)   (Portugal)
(after extra time)
h/t: 0-0 **90 mins:** 0-0
Att: 68,000 **Ref:** Agnolin (Italy)
PSV won 6-5 on pens

1988–89 FINAL
May 24 – Nou Camp, Barcelona
Milan 4-0 Steaua
(Italy)   **Bucureşti**
(Gullit 18, 38,   (Romania)
van Basten 27, 46)
h/t: 3-0 **Att:** 100,000
Ref: Tritschler (West Germany)

1989–90 FINAL
May 23 – Prater, Vienna
Milan 1-0 Benfica
(Italy)   (Portugal)
(Rijkaard 67)
h/t: 0-0 **Att:** 58,000
Ref: Kohl (Austria)

1990–91 FINAL
May 29 – San Nicola, Bari
Crvena Zvezda 0-0 Olympique
(Yugoslavia)   **Marseille**
(France)
(after extra time)
h/t: 0-0 **90 mins:** 0-0
Att: 58,000 **Ref:** Lanese (Italy)
Crvena Zvezda won 5-3 on pens

1991–92 FINAL
May 20 – Wembley, London
Barcelona 1-0 Sampdoria
(Spain)   (Italy)
(Koemann 111)
(after extra time)
h/t: 0-0 **90 mins:** 0-0 **Att:** 70,827
Ref: Schmidhuber (Germany)

1992–93 FINAL
May 26 – Olympiastadion, Munich
Olympique 1-0 Milan
Marseille   (Italy)
(France)
(Boli 43)
h/t: 1-0 **Att:** 64,400
Ref: Rothlisberger (Switzerland)

1993–94 FINAL
May 18 – Olympic, Athens
Milan 4-0 Barcelona
(Italy)   (Spain)
(Massaro 22, 45,
Savicevic 47,
Desailly 59)
h/t: 2-0 **Att:** 70,000
Ref: Don (England)

1994–95 FINAL
May 24 – Ernst-Happel Stadion, Vienna
Ajax 1-0 Milan
(Netherlands)   (Italy)
(Kluivert 83)
h/t: 0-0 **Att:** 49,500
Ref: Craciunescu (Romania)

1995–96 FINAL
May 22 – Olimpico, Rome
Juventus 1-1 Ajax
(Italy)   (Netherlands)
(Ravanelli 12)   *(Litmanen 40)*
(after extra time)
h/t: 1-1 **90 mins:** 1-1
Att: 70,000 **Ref:** Diaz Vega (Spain)
Juventus won 4-2 on pens

1996–97 FINAL
May 28 – Olympiastadion, Munich
Borussia 3-1 Juventus
Dortmund   (Italy)
(Germany)   *(Del Piero 64)*
(Riedle 29, 34,
Ricken 71)
h/t: 2-0 **Att:** 65,000
Ref: Puhl (Hungary)

1997–98 FINAL
May 20 – Arena, Amsterdam
Real Madrid 1-0 Juventus
(Spain)   (Italy)
(Mijatovic 66)
h/t: 0-0 **Att:** 50,000
Ref: Krug (Germany)

1998–99 FINAL
May 26 – Nou Camp, Barcelona
Manchester 2-1 Bayern
United   **München**
(England)   (Germany)
(Sheringham 89,   *(Basler 6)*
Solskjaer 90)
h/t: 0-1 **Att:** 90,000
Ref: Collina (Italy)

1999–2000 FINAL
May 24 – Stade St Denis, Paris
Real Madrid 3-0 Valencia
(Spain)   (Spain)
(Morientes 39,
McManaman 67,
Raúl 75)
h/t: 1-0 **Att:** 78,000
Ref: Braschi (Italy)

2000–01 FINAL
May 23 – San Siro, Milan
Bayern 1-1 Valencia
München   (Spain)
(Germany)   *(Mendieta 3 pen)*
(Effenberg
51 pen)
(after sudden death extra time)
h/t: 0-1 **90 mins:** 1-1 **Att:** 74,000
Ref: Jol (Netherlands)
Bayern München won 5-4 on pens

2001–02 FINAL
May 15 – Hampden Park, Glasgow
Real Madrid 2-1 Bayer
(Spain)   **Leverkusen**
(Raúl 8,   (Germany)
Zidane 45)   *(Lucio 14)*
h/t: 2-1 **Att:** 52,000
Ref: Meier (Switzerland)

Experts seldom agree on much, but many pundits concur that the 1959–60 European Cup Final between Real Madrid and Eintracht Frankfurt at Hampden Park was the finest match ever seen. Here, Ferenc Puskas makes it 5-1 from the penalty spot on the hour. Real went on to win 7-3.

THE EUROPEAN CHAMPIONS LEAGUE

The European Championships

TOURNAMENT OVERVIEW

HENRI DELAUNAY, head of the French FA, proposed the idea of a European nations tournament as early as 1927, but in the absence of a European football federation it failed to materialize. With the foundation of UEFA in 1954 Delaunay revived the idea. After much internal politics and the usual scepticism, UEFA announced that the first finals would be held in 1960. Though Delaunay died in 1955, he was honoured when the trophy was named the Henri Delaunay Cup. The format of the early tournaments was a series of two-leg qualifying rounds played home and away, producing four finalists who would contest semi-finals and a Final over a week in a single location.

The first finals, held in France, are best remembered for the controversial quarter-final between Spain and the USSR. Franco's love of football was more than matched by his hatred of Communism and he refused the Soviet team entry into Spain. UEFA awarded the tie to the Soviets. Under the inspirational Lev Yashin, the USSR won the Final beating Yugoslavia 2-1 in extra time. In 1964 and 68 the hosts, Spain and Italy, won the tournament. Spain, having allowed the Soviets in this time, beat them 2-1, and Italy beat Yugoslavia in a replayed Final.

Penalties and golden goals

In 1972, the Nations Cup was renamed the European Championships and West Germany thrashed the USSR 3-0 in a warm-up for their 1974 World Cup victory. But in Yugoslavia in 1976, Eastern Europe struck back when the Czechs beat the Germans in a tense penalty shootout. In 1980, the tournament was expanded to eight teams and in 1996 to 16, including group games to determine the finalists.

The 1980s saw two truly great teams take the trophy. In 1984, Platini's France swept to victory, while in 1988, the Dutch, with Gullit, van Basten and Rijkaard, triumphed. In 1992, Denmark, a late entrant in place of Yugoslavia (then embroiled in a civil war), made it to the Final and beat the favourites Germany 2-0. But the Germans were back four years later, defeating the English hosts in an excruciating penalty shootout before a rematch of the 1976 Final saw them beating the Czechs with a golden goal by Oliver Bierhoff – the first time an 'official' golden goal had decided the Final of a major competition. In 2000, France confirmed their status as the world's No.1 team by beating Italy 2-1, with a last-minute equalizer and a golden goal in extra time.

The European Championships (1960–2000)

YEAR	WINNERS	SCORE	RUNNERS-UP
1960	USSR	2-1	Yugoslavia
1964	Spain	2-1	USSR
1968	Italy	1-1, (replay) 2-0 (aet)	Yugoslavia
1972	West Germany	3-0	USSR
1976	Czechoslovakia	2-2 (5-3 pens)	West Germany
1980	West Germany	2-1	Belgium
1984	France	2-0	Spain
1988	Netherlands	2-0	USSR
1992	Denmark	2-0	Germany
1996	Germany	2-1 (golden goal)	Czech Republic
2000	France	2-1 (golden goal)	Italy

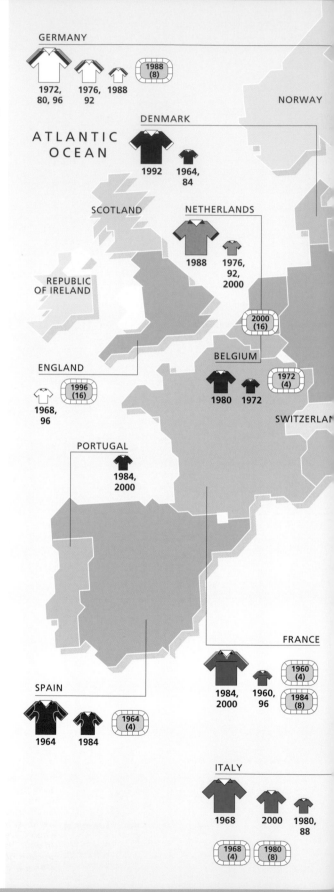

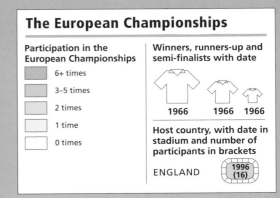

The European Championships

Participation in the European Championships

- 6+ times
- 3–5 times
- 2 times
- 1 time
- 0 times

Winners, runners-up and semi-finalists with date

| 1966 | 1966 | 1966 |

Host country, with date in stadium and number of participants in brackets

ENGLAND 1996 (16)

WEDEN
1992
1992 (8)

RUSSIA (includes USSR 1917–91)
1960   1964, 72, 88   1968

CZECH REPUBLIC
1976   1996   1960, 80

YUGOSLAVIA
1960, 68   1976   1976 (4)

HUNGARY
1964, 72

SLOVENIA

ROMANIA

CROATIA

BULGARIA

BLACK SEA

GREECE

TURKEY

MEDITERRANEAN SEA

Czechoslovakia's Antonin Panenka chips his penalty over Sepp Maier in the German goal to win the 1976 tournament in Belgrade, Yugoslavia.

Germany's revenge against the Czech Republic came at Wembley in 1996 when Oliver Bierhoff (in white) scored a precious golden goal winner in extra time.

The European Championships Top Goalscorers

YEAR	SCORER	NATIONALITY	GOALS
1960	Ivanov Jerkovic	Russian Yugoslavian	2
1964	Pereda Novak	Spanish Hungarian	2
1968	Drazij	Yugoslavian	2
1972	G. Müller	W. German	4
1976	D. Müller	W. German	4
1980	Allofs	W. German	3
1984	Platini	French	8
1988	van Basten	Dutch	5
1992	Bergkamp Brolin Larsen Riedle	Dutch Swedish Danish German	3
1996	Shearer	English	5
2000	Kluivert Milosevic	Dutch Yugoslavian	6

Euro 2000

TOURNAMENT REVIEW

EURO 2000 WAS QUITE SIMPLY the best competition in the history of the tournament. The technical quality of play was often spellbinding, the games were predominantly open, attacking and creative, and the best team won. Four cities in each of the host nations were chosen to stage the matches. In the Netherlands these were Amsterdam, Rotterdam, Arnhem and Eindhoven, and in Belgium they were Brussels, Bruges, Liège and Charleroi.

Football's success story

Euro 2000 earned lavish praise for the positive and creative football played by most of the competing teams and it set standards that future tournaments may have trouble matching. Latin sides in particular treated fans to a spectacle of open, attacking football, and high-quality, technical and tactical skill. These teams excelled at the expense of their European neighbours from Germany, England and Scandinavia. In the Final, France and Italy played a final befitting a major championship. The French victory, via a 'golden goal' in the dying moments of injury time, was consistent with the high drama and spirit of adventure that characterized the tournament.

Build-up to the tournament

France, the reigning World Champions, looked set to take the championship title right from the outset. The Netherlands, despite a series of poor results in pre-tournament friendly matches, had been tipped by the experts to do well. The all-Spanish Champions League Final in June between Real Madrid and Valencia suggested that Spain might have the confidence to win. England, Denmark, Slovenia and Turkey managed to squeeze in through the play-offs, and Germany, at their lowest ebb for decades, secured a place as European Champions. Slovenia and Norway made their debuts in the tournament, while for some players it was their last performance on the international stage. Dennis Bergkamp, Lothar Matthäus, Gheorghe Hagi, Laurent Blanc and Alan Shearer all made farewell appearances at Euro 2000.

Co-host the Netherlands was one of the favourites at the start of Euro 2000 despite a series of poor results in pre-tournament friendlies. However, the team was drawn in Group D – the Group of Death – with France, the Czech Republic and Denmark.

Domestic Clubs at Euro 2000

Clubs with the most players at Euro 2000

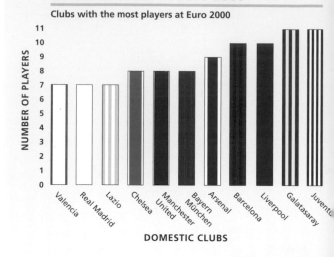

NUMBER OF PLAYERS

Valencia, Real Madrid, Lazio, Chelsea, Manchester United, Bayern München, Arsenal, Barcelona, Liverpool, Galatasaray, Juventus

DOMESTIC CLUBS

Euro 2000: The Venues

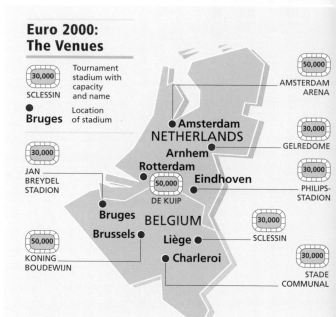

- 30,000 — Tournament stadium with capacity and name — SCLESSIN
- **Bruges** — Location of stadium

50,000 — AMSTERDAM ARENA
30,000 — GELREDOME
30,000 — PHILIPS-STADION
30,000 — SCLESSIN
30,000 — STADE COMMUNAL

30,000 — JAN BREYDEL STADION
50,000 — KONING BOUDEWIJN
50,000 — DE KUIP

Amsterdam
NETHERLANDS
Arnhem
Rotterdam
Eindhoven
Bruges
BELGIUM
Brussels
Liège
Charleroi

THE GROUP STAGES

Portugal won Group A convincingly, demonstrating its ever-increasing status on the world stage, and Romania took second place with a last-minute penalty against England, who performed disappointingly despite the 1-0 victory over the old enemy, Germany, who finished in an unaccustomed last spot in the group. Italy dominated Group B, winning all three of their games. Group C's qualifiers, Spain and Yugoslavia, provided the match of the tournament when Spain, which was a goal down, hit two group-winning goals in injury time.

In Group D, Denmark was brushed aside with ease, not scoring a point, and the Czech Republic was prised out of the competition by the Netherlands after a questionable late penalty, but the co-host deserved its head-of-group status with some stunning displays to confound the pre-tournament form indications.

Qualification Groups

GROUP 1	GROUP 2	GROUP 3	GROUP 4	GROUP 5	GROUP 6	GROUP 7	GROUP 8	GROUP 9
Italy	Norway	Germany	France	Sweden	Spain	Romania	Yugoslavia	Czech Republic
Denmark	Slovenia	Turkey	Ukraine	England	Israel	Portugal	Rep. of Ireland	Scotland
Switzerland	Latvia	Finland	Russia	Poland	Austria	Slovakia	Croatia	Estonia
Wales	Greece	N. Ireland	Iceland	Bulgaria	Cyprus	Hungary	Macedonia	Bosnia-
Belarus	Albania	Moldova	Armenia	Luxembourg	San Marino	Azerbaijan	Malta	Herzegovina
	Georgia		Andorra			Liechtenstein		Lithuania
								Faeroe Islands

THE EUROPEAN CHAMPIONSHIPS

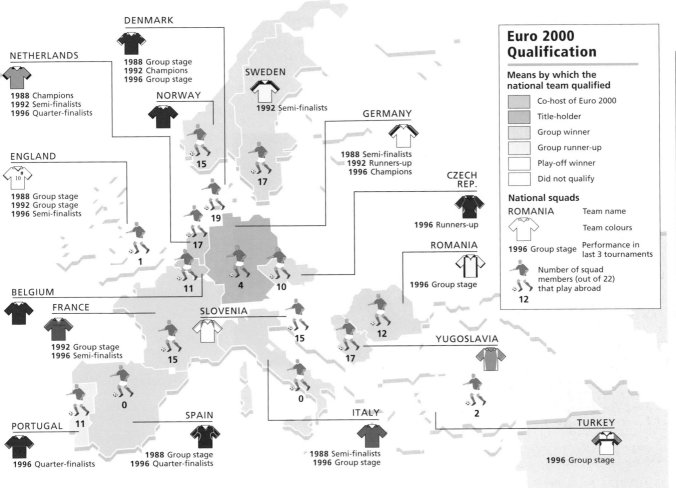

DENMARK
1988 Group stage
1992 Champions
1996 Group stage

NETHERLANDS
1988 Champions
1992 Semi-finalists
1996 Quarter-finalists

NORWAY

SWEDEN
1992 Semi-finalists

GERMANY
1988 Semi-finalists
1992 Runners-up
1996 Champions

ENGLAND
1988 Group stage
1992 Group stage
1996 Semi-finalists

CZECH REP.
1996 Runners-up

ROMANIA
1996 Group stage

BELGIUM

FRANCE
1992 Group stage
1996 Semi-finalists

SLOVENIA

YUGOSLAVIA

PORTUGAL
1996 Quarter-finalists

SPAIN
1988 Group stage
1996 Quarter-finalists

ITALY
1988 Semi-finalists
1996 Group stage

TURKEY
1996 Group stage

15, 17, 19, 17, 1, 11, 4, 10, 15, 15, 0, 12, 17, 0, 2, 11

Euro 2000 Qualification

Means by which the national team qualified
- Co-host of Euro 2000
- Title-holder
- Group winner
- Group runner-up
- Play-off winner
- Did not qualify

National squads

ROMANIA — Team name

— Team colours

1996 Group stage — Performance in last 3 tournaments

12 — Number of squad members (out of 22) that play abroad

GROUP A	
GERMANY	ROMANIA
ENGLAND	PORTUGAL

GROUP B	
BELGIUM	SWEDEN
TURKEY	ITALY

GROUP C	
SPAIN	NORWAY
YUGOSLAVIA	SLOVENIA

GROUP D	
FRANCE	DENMARK
NETHERLANDS	CZECH REP.

GROUP A

Germany **1-1** Romania
England **2-3** Portugal
Romania **0-1** Portugal
England **1-0** Germany
England **2-3** Romania
Portugal **3-0** Germany

	P	W	D	L	F	A	Pts
Portugal	3	3	0	0	7	2	9
Romania	3	1	1	1	4	4	4
England	3	1	0	2	5	6	3
Germany	3	0	1	2	1	5	1

GROUP B

Belgium **2-1** Sweden
Turkey **1-2** Italy
Italy **2-0** Belgium
Sweden **0-0** Turkey
Turkey **2-0** Belgium
Italy **2-1** Sweden

	P	W	D	L	F	A	Pts
Italy	3	3	0	0	6	2	9
Turkey	3	1	1	1	3	2	4
Belgium	3	1	0	2	2	5	3
Sweden	3	0	1	2	2	4	1

GROUP C

Spain **0-1** Norway
Yugoslavia **3-3** Slovenia
Slovenia **1-2** Spain
Norway **0-1** Yugoslavia
Slovenia **0-0** Norway
Yugoslavia **3-4** Spain

	P	W	D	L	F	A	Pts
Spain	3	2	0	1	6	5	6
Yugoslavia	3	1	1	1	7	7	4
Norway	3	1	1	1	1	1	4
Slovenia	3	0	2	1	4	5	2

GROUP D

France **3-0** Denmark
Netherlands **1-0** Czech Rep.
Czech Rep. **1-2** France
Denmark **0-3** Netherlands
Denmark **0-2** Czech Rep.
France **2-3** Netherlands

	P	W	D	L	F	A	Pts
Netherlands	3	3	0	0	7	2	9
France	3	2	0	1	7	4	6
Czech Rep.	3	1	0	2	3	3	3
Denmark	3	0	0	3	0	8	0

THE EUROPEAN CHAMPIONSHIPS

THE QUARTER-FINALS

With the exception of the Netherlands, the quarter-finals were dominated by Mediterranean teams. This pattern was replicated in UEFA's inventory of the top 50 players of the tournament – only two Scandinavians, one English, and one German player made the list. All four quarter-finals were decided in 90 minutes without recourse to penalty shootouts. Spain was knocked out by France, and Yugoslavia was thrashed by a rejuvenated Netherlands. Romania and Turkey were swiftly and cleanly despatched from the tournament by Italy and Portugal respectively.

June 24 – Amsterdam Arena
Attendance 30,000

PORTUGAL 2-0 TURKEY
h/t: 1-0

	Scorers	
Gomes 44, 56		
☐☐☐☐☐	Yellow cards	☐☐☐
	Red cards	■

June 24 – Koning Boudewijn, Brussels
Attendance 41,000

ROMANIA 0-2 ITALY
h/t: 0-2

	Scorers	Totti 33, Inzaghi 43
	Yellow cards	☐
■	Red cards	

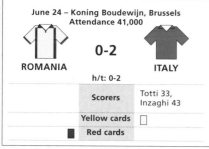

June 25 – De Kuip, Rotterdam
Attendance 50,000

NETHERLANDS 6-1 YUGOSLAVIA
h/t: 1-0

Kluivert 24, 38, 54, Govedarica 51 o.g., Overmars 78, 90	Scorers	Milosevic 90
☐	Yellow cards	
	Red cards	

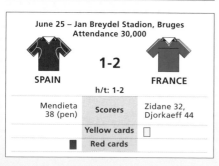

June 25 – Jan Breydel Stadion, Bruges
Attendance 30,000

SPAIN 1-2 FRANCE
h/t: 1-2

Mendieta 38 (pen)	Scorers	Zidane 32, Djorkaeff 44
	Yellow cards	☐
■	Red cards	

THE SEMI-FINALS

The drama began to intensify during the semi-finals. France secured victory over Portugal with a controversial penalty awarded in extra time. The aggrieved Portuguese players erupted around the referee, but the decision was not reversed. Italy's game against the Netherlands stretched to a penalty shootout. Playing against ten men, the Netherlands team pitted its best attacking play against a stoic, skilled and intelligent Italian defence. However, by full-time the Netherlands had already missed two penalties, and, inevitably, missed four more in the shootout.

Fabio Cannavaro (above) was a key player in Italy's defensive line. Italy's defensive strategy for most of Euro 2000 contrasted sharply with the attacking style displayed by the other national teams at the event.

June 28 – Amsterdam Arena, Amsterdam
Attendance 45,000

FRANCE 2-1 PORTUGAL
(France won on golden goal)
h/t: 0-1, f/t: 1-1

Henry 51, Zidane 117 (pen & golden goal)	Scorers	Gomes 19
☐	Yellow cards	
	Red cards	

June 29 – Stade Communal, Charleroi
Attendance 50,000

ITALY 0-0 NETHERLANDS
(Italy won 3-1 on pens)

	Scorers	
☐☐☐☐☐☐	Yellow cards	☐☐☐☐
■	Red cards	

THE FINAL

France and Italy battled ferociously for the boost of an early goal right from the start of the match, and the French almost grabbed a shock lead after five minutes. Italy, who had a near-miss two minutes later, eventually scored early in the second half. The French responded by attacking Italy's goal relentlessly and eventually scored an equalizer in the fourth minute of injury time. France had the majority of all the attacking attributes – shots, corners and goals – and dominated possession and territorial advantage throughout. However, it finally took a 'golden goal', scored in extra time by substitute David Trezeguet, for the reigning World title-holders to claim the European Championship.

The Golden Goal

1: Pires charges down the left and crosses to Trezeguet

The Starting Line-Up

July 2 – De Kuip, Rotterdam
Attendance 50,000

Maldini (C) 3 — Albertini 4 — Dugarry 21 — Thuram 15
Iuliano 15 — di Biaggio 14 — Deschamps (C) 7 — Desailly 8
Toldo 12 — Nesta 13 — Delvecchio 21 — Henry 12 — Zidane 10 — Barthez 16
Fiore 18 — Blanc 5
Cannavaro 5 — Vieira 4
Pessotto 11 — Totti 20 — Djorkaeff 6 — Lizarazu 3

ITALY	Referee	FRANCE
Formation: 5-4-1	A Frisk (Sweden)	Formation: 4-3-3
Manager Dino Zoff		**Manager** Roger Lemerre
Substitutes del Piero (10), Ambrosini (16), Montella (19)		**Substitutes** Pires (11), Wiltord (13), Trezeguet (20)

2: Trezeguet smashes the ball into the roof of the net

The French national squad became the first reigning World Champions to lift the Henri Delaunay trophy and is only the second team to win the European Championships more than once.

Highlights of the Game

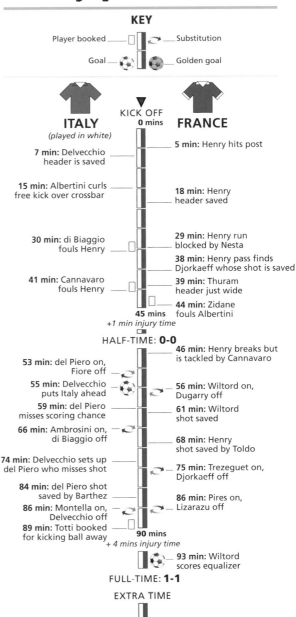

KEY
Player booked — Substitution
Goal — Golden goal

ITALY (played in white) — KICK OFF 0 mins — FRANCE

5 min: Henry hits post
7 min: Delvecchio header is saved
15 min: Albertini curls free kick over crossbar
18 min: Henry header saved
29 min: Henry run blocked by Nesta
30 min: di Biaggio fouls Henry
38 min: Henry pass finds Djorkaeff whose shot is saved
39 min: Thuram header just wide
41 min: Cannavaro fouls Henry
44 min: Zidane fouls Albertini
45 mins +1 min injury time

HALF-TIME: 0-0

46 min: Henry breaks but is tackled by Cannavaro
53 min: del Piero on, Fiore off
55 min: Delvecchio puts Italy ahead
56 min: Wiltord on, Dugarry off
59 min: del Piero misses scoring chance
61 min: Wiltord shot saved
66 min: Ambrosini on, di Biaggio off
68 min: Henry shot saved by Toldo
74 min: Delvecchio sets up del Piero who misses shot
75 min: Trezeguet on, Djorkaeff off
84 min: del Piero shot saved by Barthez
86 min: Montella on, Delvecchio off
86 min: Pires on, Lizarazu off
89 min: Totti booked for kicking ball away
90 mins + 4 mins injury time
93 min: Wiltord scores equalizer

FULL-TIME: 1-1

EXTRA TIME
103 min: Trezeguet scores the golden goal
103 mins

ITALY 1-2 FRANCE

Italy			Match Statistics	France		
First Half	Second Half	Extra Time		First Half	Second Half	Extra Time
45%	35%	20%	Possession	55%	65%	80%
4(3)	3(1)	0	Attempts (on target)	9(4)	7(4)	6(5)
18	16	6	Successful tackles	22	24	12
5	3	3	Fouls conceded	4	6	1
1	3	0	Corners won	6	5	2
3	1	0	Offside	2	3	1

The European Championships

THE EUROPEAN CHAMPIONSHIPS are the most prestigious European national competition. Established in 1957, the first competition was held in 1960, and since then the Henri Delaunay Cup has been contested every four years, as with the World Cup. The Championship is open to the senior national representative teams of all UEFA's member associations, and the qualifying competition and final round are staged over the two-year period following every FIFA World Cup. The first tournaments comprised only semi-finals and Finals. In 1976 quarter-finals were added, and in 1980 eight teams competed in two mini-leagues before the semi-finals. Expansion in 1996 saw 16 teams compete in four leagues to produce eight quarter-finalists.

1960 FRANCE

SEMI-FINALS

Yugoslavia **5-4** France
(Galic 11,   (Vincent 12,
Zanetic 55,   Heutte 43, 62,
Knez 75,   Wisnieski 52)
Jerkovic 77, 79)

Soviet Union **3-0** Czechoslovakia
(V. Ivanov 34, 56,
Ponedelnik 65)

THIRD PLACE PLAY-OFF

Czechoslovakia **2-0** France
(Bubernik 58,
Pavlovic 88)

FINAL

July 10 – Parc des Princes, Paris
Soviet Union **2-1** Yugoslavia
(Metreveli 49,   (Galic 41)
Ponedelnik 113)
(after extra time)
h/t: 0-1 **90 mins:** 1-1
Att: 17,966 **Ref:** Ellis (England)

1964 SPAIN

SEMI-FINALS

Spain **2-1** Hungary
(Pereda 35,   (Bene 85)
Amancio 115)
(after extra time)

Soviet Union **3-0** Denmark
(Voronin 19,
Ponedelnik 40,
V. Ivanov 87)

THIRD PLACE PLAY-OFF

Hungary **3-1** Denmark
(Bene 11,   (Bertelsen 81)
Novák
107 pen, 110)
(after extra time)

FINAL

June 21 – Santiago Bernabeu, Madrid
Spain **2-1** Soviet Union
(Pereda 6,   (Khusainov 8)
Marcelino 84)
h/t: 1-1 **Att:** 105,000
Ref: Holland (England)

1968 ITALY

SEMI-FINALS

Yugoslavia **1-0** England
(Dzajic 86)

Italy **0-0** Soviet Union
(after extra time)
Italy won on toss of coin

THIRD PLACE PLAY-OFF

England **2-0** Soviet Union
(R. Charlton 39,
Hurst 63)

FINAL

June 8 – Stadio Olimpico, Rome
Italy **1-1** Yugoslavia
(Domenghini 80)   (Dzajic 38)
(after extra time)
h/t: 0-1 **90 mins:** 1-1
Att: 85,000 **Ref:** Dienst (Switzerland)

REPLAY

June 10 – Stadio Olimpico, Rome
Italy **2-0** Yugoslavia
(Riva 11,
Anastasai 32)
h/t: 2-0 **Att:** 50,000
Ref: Ortiz (Spain)

1972 BELGIUM

SEMI-FINALS

Soviet Union **1-0** Hungary
(Konkov 53)

West Germany **2-1** Belgium
(G. Müller 24, 71)   (Polleunis 83)

THIRD PLACE PLAY-OFF

Belgium **2-1** Hungary
(Lambert 24,   (Kü 53 pen)
Van Himst 28)

FINAL

June 18 – Stade Heysel, Brussels
West Germany **3-0** Soviet Union
(G. Müller 27, 58,
Wimmer 52)
h/t: 1-0 **Att:** 50,000
Ref: Marschall (Austria)

1976 YUGOSLAVIA

SEMI-FINALS

Czechoslovakia **3-1** Netherlands
(Ondrus 20,   (Ondrus o.g. 74)
Nehoda 115,
F. Vesely 118)
(after extra time)

West Germany **4-2** Yugoslavia
(Flohe 65,   (Popivoda 20,
D. Müller 82,   Dzajic 30)
114, 119)
(after extra time)

THIRD PLACE PLAY-OFF

Netherlands **3-2** Yugoslavia
(Geels 27, 107,   (Katalinski 43,
Van de Kerkhof 39)   Dzajic 82)
(after extra time)

FINAL

June 20 – Red Star, Belgrade
Czechoslovakia **2-2** West Germany
(Svehlik 8,   (D. Müller 28,
Dobiás 25)   Hölzenbein 89)
(after extra time)
h/t: 2-1 **90 mins:** 2-2
Att: 33,000 **Ref:** Gonella (Italy)
Czechoslovakia won 5-3 on pens

1980 ITALY

GROUP 1

West Germany **1-0** Czechoslovakia
Netherlands **1-0** Greece
West Germany **3-2** Netherlands
Czechoslovakia **3-1** Greece
Czechoslovakia **1-1** Netherlands
West Germany **0-0** Greece

	P	W	D	L	F	A	Pts
West Germany	3	2	1	0	4	2	5
Czechoslovakia	3	1	1	1	4	3	3
Netherlands	3	1	1	1	4	4	3
Greece	3	0	1	2	1	4	1

GROUP 2

England **1-1** Belgium
Italy **0-0** Spain
Belgium **2-1** Spain
Italy **1-0** England
England **2-1** Spain
Italy **0-0** Belgium

	P	W	D	L	F	A	Pts
Belgium	3	1	2	0	3	2	4
Italy	3	1	2	0	1	0	4
England	3	1	1	1	3	3	3
Spain	3	0	1	2	2	4	1

THIRD PLACE PLAY-OFF

Czechoslovakia **1-1** Italy
(Jurkemik 48)   (Graziani 74)
(after extra time)
Czechoslovakia won 9-8 on pens

FINAL

June 22 – Stadio Olimpico, Rome
West Germany **2-1** Belgium
(Hrubesch 10, 88)   (Vandereycken
72 pen)
h/t: 1-0 **Att:** 48,000
Ref: Rainea (Romania)

1984 FRANCE

GROUP 1

France **1-0** Denmark
Belgium **2-0** Yugoslavia
France **5-0** Belgium
Denmark **5-0** Yugoslavia
France **3-2** Yugoslavia
Denmark **3-2** Belgium

	P	W	D	L	F	A	Pts
France	3	3	0	0	9	2	6
Denmark	3	2	0	1	8	3	4
Belgium	3	1	0	2	4	8	2
Yugoslavia	3	0	0	3	2	10	0

GROUP 2

West Germany **0-0** Portugal
Spain **1-1** Romania
West Germany **2-1** Romania
Portugal **1-1** Spain
Spain **1-0** West Germany
Portugal **1-0** Romania

	P	W	D	L	F	A	Pts
Spain	3	1	2	0	3	2	4
Portugal	3	1	2	0	2	1	4
West Germany	3	1	1	1	2	2	3
Romania	3	0	1	2	2	4	1

SEMI-FINALS

France **3-2** Portugal
(Domergue   (Jordão 73, 97)
24, 114,
Platini 119)
(after extra time)

Spain **1-1** Denmark
(Maceda 66)   (Lerby 6)
(after extra time)
Spain won 5-4 on pens

FINAL

June 27 – Parc des Princes, Paris
France **2-0** Spain
(Platini 56,
Bellone 90)
h/t: 0-0 **Att:** 47,000
Ref: Christov (Czechoslovakia)

1988 WEST GERMANY

GROUP 1

West Germany **1-1** Italy
Spain **3-2** Denmark
West Germany **2-0** Denmark
Italy **1-0** Spain
West Germany **2-0** Spain
Italy **2-0** Denmark

	P	W	D	L	F	A	Pts
West Germany	3	2	1	0	5	1	5
Italy	3	2	1	0	4	1	5
Spain	3	1	0	2	3	5	2
Denmark	3	0	0	3	2	7	0

GROUP 2

Rep. of Ireland **1-0** England
Soviet Union **1-0** Netherlands
Netherlands **3-1** England
Soviet Union **1-1** Rep. of Ireland
Soviet Union **3-1** England
Netherlands **1-0** Rep. of Ireland

	P	W	D	L	F	A	Pts
Soviet Union	3	2	1	0	5	2	5
Netherlands	3	2	0	1	4	2	4
Rep. of Ireland	3	1	1	1	2	2	3
England	3	0	0	3	2	7	0

European Championship Winners

Soviet Union 1960	Spain 1964	Italy 1968	West Germany 1972, 80	Czechoslovakia 1976	France 1984, 2000	Netherlands 1988	Denmark 1992	Germany 1996

SEMI-FINALS

Netherlands **2-1** West Germany
(R. Koeman 74 pen, van Basten 89) *(Matthäus 55 pen)*

Soviet Union **2-0** Italy
(Litovchenko 60, Protasov 62)

FINAL

June 25 – Olympiastadion, Munich
Netherlands **2-0** Soviet Union
(Gullit 33, van Basten 54)
h/t: 1-0 **Att:** 72,300
Ref: Vautrot (France)

1992 SWEDEN

GROUP A

Sweden **1-1** France
Denmark **0-0** England
France **0-0** England
Sweden **1-0** Denmark
Denmark **2-1** France
Sweden **2-1** England

	P	W	D	L	F	A	Pts
Sweden	3	2	1	0	4	2	5
Denmark	3	1	1	1	2	2	3
France	3	0	2	1	2	3	2
England	3	0	2	1	1	2	2

GROUP B

Netherlands **1-0** Scotland
Germany **1-1** CIS
Germany **2-0** Scotland
Netherlands **0-0** CIS
Netherlands **3-1** Germany
Scotland **3-0** CIS

	P	W	D	L	F	A	Pts
Netherlands	3	2	1	0	4	1	5
Germany	3	1	1	1	4	4	3
Scotland	3	1	0	2	3	3	2
CIS	3	0	2	1	1	4	2

SEMI-FINALS

Germany **3-2** Sweden
(Hässler 11, Riedle 59, 88) *(Brolin 64, Andersson 89)*

Denmark **2-2** Netherlands
(H. Larsen 5, 32) *(Bergkamp 23, Rijkaard 85)*
(after extra time)
Denmark won 5-4 on pens

FINAL

June 26 – Nya Ullevi, Gothenburg
Denmark **2-0** Germany
(Jensen 18, Vilfort 78)
h/t: 1-0 **Att:** 37,000
Ref: Galler (Switzerland)

1996 ENGLAND

GROUP A

England **1-1** Switzerland
Netherlands **0-0** Scotland
Netherlands **2-0** Switzerland
England **2-0** Scotland
Scotland **1-0** Switzerland
England **4-1** Netherlands

	P	W	D	L	F	A	Pts
England	3	2	1	0	7	2	7
Netherlands	3	1	1	1	3	4	4
Scotland	3	1	1	1	1	2	4
Switzerland	3	0	1	2	1	4	1

GROUP B

Spain **1-1** Bulgaria
France **1-0** Romania
Bulgaria **1-0** Romania
France **1-1** Spain
France **3-1** Bulgaria
Spain **2-1** Romania

	P	W	D	L	F	A	Pts
France	3	2	1	0	5	2	7
Spain	3	1	2	0	4	3	5
Bulgaria	3	1	1	1	3	4	4
Romania	3	0	0	3	1	4	0

GROUP C

Germany **2-0** Czech Rep.
Italy **2-1** Russia
Czech Rep. **2-1** Italy
Germany **3-0** Russia
Italy **0-0** Germany
Czech Rep. **3-3** Russia

	P	W	D	L	F	A	Pts
Germany	3	2	1	0	5	0	7
Czech Rep.	3	1	1	1	5	6	4
Italy	3	1	1	1	3	3	4
Russia	3	0	1	2	4	8	1

GROUP D

Denmark **1-1** Portugal
Croatia **1-0** Turkey
Portugal **1-0** Turkey
Croatia **3-0** Denmark
Portugal **3-0** Croatia
Denmark **3-0** Turkey

	P	W	D	L	F	A	Pts
Portugal	3	2	1	0	5	1	7
Croatia	3	2	0	1	4	3	6
Denmark	3	1	1	1	4	4	4
Turkey	3	0	0	3	0	5	0

QUARTER-FINALS

England **0-0** Spain
(after extra time)
England won 4-2 on pens

France **0-0** Netherlands
(after extra time)
France won 5-4 on pens

Germany **2-1** Croatia
(Klinsmann 21 pen, Sammer 59) *(Suker 51)*

Czech Rep. **1-0** Portugal
(Poborsky 53)

SEMI-FINALS

Czech Rep. **0-0** France
(after extra time)
Czech Rep. won 6-5 on pens

Germany **1-1** England
(Kuntz 16) *(Shearer 3)*
(after extra time)
Germany won 6-5 on pens

FINAL

June 30 – Wembley, London
Germany **2-1** Czech Rep.
(Bierhoff 73, 94) *(Berger 58 pen)*
h/t: 0-0 **90 mins:** 1-1
Att: 76,000 **Ref:** Pairetto (Italy)
Germany won on golden goal in extra time

2000 BELGIUM AND THE NETHERLANDS

GROUP A

Germany **1-1** Romania
Portugal **3-2** England
Portugal **1-0** Romania
England **1-0** Germany
Romania **3-2** England
Portugal **3-0** Germany

	P	W	D	L	F	A	Pts
Portugal	3	3	0	0	7	2	9
Romania	3	1	1	1	4	4	4
England	3	1	0	2	5	6	3
Germany	3	0	1	2	1	5	1

GROUP B

Belgium **2-1** Sweden
Italy **2-1** Turkey
Italy **2-0** Belgium
Sweden **0-0** Turkey
Turkey **2-0** Belgium
Italy **2-1** Sweden

	P	W	D	L	F	A	Pts
Italy	3	3	0	0	6	2	9
Turkey	3	1	1	1	3	2	4
Belgium	3	1	0	2	2	5	3
Sweden	3	0	1	2	2	4	1

GROUP C

Norway **1-0** Spain
Yugoslavia **3-3** Slovenia
Spain **2-1** Slovenia
Yugoslavia **1-0** Norway
Spain **4-3** Yugoslavia
Slovenia **0-0** Norway

	P	W	D	L	F	A	Pts
Spain	3	2	0	1	6	5	6
Yugoslavia	3	1	1	1	7	7	4
Norway	3	1	1	1	1	1	4
Slovenia	3	0	2	1	4	5	2

GROUP D

France **3-0** Denmark
Netherlands **1-0** Czech Rep.
France **2-1** Czech Rep.
Netherlands **3-0** Denmark
Netherlands **3-2** France
Czech Rep. **2-0** Denmark

	P	W	D	L	F	A	Pts
Netherlands	3	3	0	0	7	2	9
France	3	2	0	1	7	4	6
Czech Rep.	3	1	0	2	3	3	3
Denmark	3	0	0	3	0	8	0

QUARTER-FINALS

Portugal **2-0** Turkey
(Nuno Gomes 44, 56)

Italy **2-0** Romania
(Totti 33, Inzaghi 43)

Netherlands **6-1** Yugoslavia
(Kluivert 24, 38, 54, Govedarica o.g. 51, Overmars 78, 90) *(Milosevic 90)*

France **2-1** Spain
(Zidane 33, Djorkaeff 44) *(Mendieta 38 pen)*

SEMI-FINALS

France **2-1** Portugal
(Henry 51, Zidane 117 pen) *(Nuno Gomes 19)*
France won on golden goal in extra time

Italy **0-0** Netherlands
(after extra time)
Italy won 3-1 on pens

FINAL

July 2 – De Kuip, Rotterdam
France **2-1** Italy
(Wiltord 90, Trezeguet 103) *(Delvecchio 55)*
France won on golden goal in extra time
h/t: 0-0 **90 mins:** 1-1
Att: 55,000 **Ref:** Frisk (Sweden)

*Dutch striker **Marco van Basten** scores against England to give the Netherlands a 3-1 victory in the team's group game in the 1988 European Championships. The Dutch went on to win the tournament.*

THE CONMEBOL NATIONS

COLOMBIA
1924, 1938, 1971
Federación
Colombiana
de Fútbol
1940
(1936–50,
1954)

1975, **2001**

GUYANA
(affiliated to
CONCACAF)

VENEZUELA
1926
Federación
Venezolana
de Fútbol
1952 (1952)

SURINAM
(affiliated to
CONCACAF)

FRENCH
GUIANA
(affiliated to the
French FA)

ATLANTIC
OCEAN

ECUADOR
1925
Asociación
Ecuatoriana
de Fútbol
1930 (1926)

BRAZIL
1914
Confederação
Brasileira
de Futebol
1916 (1923)

1950, **58, 62,**
70, 94, *98*

1919, *21*, **22,**
37, **49**, *53*, *57*,
59, *83*, **89**, *91*,
95, **97**, *99*

PERU
1922
Federación
Peruana
de Fútbol
1926 (1924)

1939, 75

BOLIVIA
1925
Federación
Boliviana
de Fútbol
1926 (1926)

1963, *97*

PACIFIC
OCEAN

ASUNCIÓN
CONMEBOL
Headquarters

PARAGUAY
1906
Asociación
Paraguaya
de Fútbol
1921 (1921)

1922, 29, 47,
49, 53, 63, 79

CHILE
1895
Federación
de Fútbol de Chile
1916 (1912)

1955, *56*,
79, *87*

ARGENTINA
1893
Asociación
del Fútbol
Argentino
1916
(1912)

1930, **78,**
86, 90

1917, *20*, **21,**
23, *24*, **25**, *26*,
27, 29, 37, *42*,
47, 55, 57, 59,
67, **91, 93**

URUGUAY
1900
Asociación
Uruguaya
de Fútbol
1916 (1923)

1930, 50

1917, *19*, **20**,
23, **24, 26**, *27*,
39, *42*, **67**, *83*,
87, *89*, **95**, *99*

CONMEBOL

C.S.F.

South American
Tournaments
and Cup Competitions:
Copa América
Copa Libertadores
Copa Pan-Americana

The Development of South American Football

1910 First unoffical
Copa América

1960 Copa Libertadores
established

1910 ——— **1920** | **1950** ——— **1960**

1916
CONMEBOL
founded

1917 First offical
Copa América

1954 South
American Youth
Cup established

1968 Cop
Interaméricar
established

The CONMEBOL Nations

Key

Date of affiliation to CONMEBOL	Formation of National FA — **COUNTRY**
	1916
▨ Founder member	Name of Football Association
▨ 1917–29	Date of affiliation to CONMEBOL — **1916 (1912)** — Date of affiliation to FIFA
▨ 1930–49	Team colours
☐ 1950–present	World Cup — **1990** — Winners in bold
	Copa América — *2000* — Runners-up in italic
	(Official tournaments only)

The CONMEBOL Nations

CONMEBOL (CONFEDERACIÓN SUDAMERICANA DE FÚTBOL) was founded in 1916 and is the first and oldest of the world's regional football confederations. In July 1916, an informal international football tournament was held in Buenos Aires, Argentina, between the hosts, Chile, Uruguay and Brazil, part of a festival celebrating 100 years of independence from Spain. Recognizing the growing power and influence of the European-based and controlled FIFA (founded 1904), Héctor Gomez, a Uruguayan educationalist, took the opportunity to gather representatives of the four football associations and created CONMEBOL.

Since then CONMEBOL has grown to represent all of the South American nations minus Surinam and Guyana (members of CONCACAF) and French Guiana (which remains affiliated to the French FA). Its headquarters is in the Paraguayan capital, Asunción, from where it exerts considerable influence over FIFA as well as more local footballing matters. Its major international tournament, the Copa América, had been played on a varying but approximately biennial basis since 1916. Since then other international club tournaments have been established, including the prestigious Copa Libertadores in 1960, and a variety of other smaller competitions.

Ronaldo of Brazil tangles with Javier Zanetti of Argentina in the 1999 Copa América quarter-final, which Brazil won 2-1. Brazil went on to win the Final.

The Copa Mercosur (picture above shows San Lorenzo [in red] v Flamengo from Brazil in action in 2001 tournament) and the *Copa Merconorte* (picture below shows 2001 winners Millonarios of Colombia) were both set up in 1998 to generate TV income for South America's top clubs. In 2002 the two tournaments are being replaced by the Copa Pan-Americana.

Timeline

1971 Unofficial South American Footballer of the Year award established

1986 CONMEBOL South American Footballer of the Year Award established

1991 Teams from CONCACAF first invited to Copa América. South American Women's Championship established

1992 Copa CONMEBOL established

1993 Copa de Oro established

1996 Last Copa de Oro

1998 Copa Mercosur and Copa Merconorte established

2002 Copa Pan-Americana to replace Copa Mercosur and Merconorte

Calendar of Events	
Club Tournaments	Copa Libertadores 2002–03
	Copa Pan-Americana 2002
International Tournaments	Copa América 2003
	South American Under–17 Championship
	South American Under–20 Championship

Colombia

COLOMBIA

THE SEASON IN REVIEW 2001

THREE PLAYERS BROKE BONES on the opening day of the 2001 Colombian championship: Hugo Arias of Real Cartagena, Juan Carlos Jaramillo of Millonarios and Antonio Moreno of Tolima; an ominous sign of things to come. The opening championship, the Torneo Mustang I, saw the little known Tuluá take a midway lead onto which it held for the rest of the campaign. The Apertura ended in early July, a few weeks before Colombia was due to host the Copa América 2001. Soon afterwards there began a spate of bombings in Bogotá, Cali and Medellín, as part of Colombia's enduring civil war. For a few weeks the Copa was in doubt, but it eventually went ahead, ending in victory for the hosts who beat Mexico 1-0 in the Final amidst great local excitement.

Pipped at the post
In the second half of the championship, another outsider, Once Caldas, took the prize. But then the usual suspects lined up in the championship play-off tournament for the top eight teams: Deportivo Cali, América, Tolima, Millonarios, Independiente Santa Fé and Independiente Medellín, joined by Tuluá and Once Caldas. The title went to América, who decisively beat Independiente Medellín over two legs. Off the field, violence permeated most of the domestic season. Millonarios players received death threats, and Atlético Nacional was forced to train in secret after angry fans had attacked its training complex. Caldas players were injured when a bomb went off in their hotel in Cali before a match with América, while trouble brewed at all the Medellín derby fixtures.

Colombian League Table* 2001

CLUB	P	W	D	L	F	A	Pts	
Once Caldas	44	23	12	9	71	43	**81**	Qualified for Second Phase
Deportivo Cali	44	21	11	12	65	46	**74**	Qualified for Second Phase
América de Cali	44	20	8	16	68	62	**68**	Qualified for Second Phase
Deportes Tolima	44	19	11	14	62	52	**68**	Qualified for Second Phase
CD Millonarios	44	19	8	17	66	54	**65**	Qualified for Second Phase
Corporación Tuluá	44	17	14	13	53	47	**65**	Qualified for Second Phase
Independiente Santa Fé	44	18	9	17	57	52	**63**	Qualified for Second Phase
Independiente Medellín	44	17	12	15	64	48	**63**	Qualified for Second Phase
Atlético Nacional	44	17	12	15	48	46	**63**	
Envigado FC	44	16	13	15	63	66	**61**	
Atlético Júnior	44	14	14	16	49	52	**56**	
Deportivo Pasto	44	14	14	16	44	61	**56**	
Deportivo Pereira	44	15	8	21	45	65	**53**	
Real Cartagena	44	11	13	20	43	59	**46**	
Atlético Huila	44	11	9	24	48	76	**42**	
Atlético Bucaramanga	44	8	16	20	27	44	**40**	

Promoted clubs: Unión Magdelena, Deportes Quindio.
* Results of Apertura and Clausura combined.

Second Phase – Group A

CLUB	P	W	D	L	F	A	Pts	
América	6	2	4	0	8	5	**10**	Qualified for Final
Once Caldas	6	2	3	1	10	10	**9**	
Independiente Santa Fé	6	1	5	0	6	4	**8**	
CD Millonarios	6	0	2	4	3	8	**2**	

Second Phase – Group B

CLUB	P	W	D	L	F	A	Pts	
Independiente Medellín	6	3	2	1	9	5	**11**	Qualified for Final
Corporación Tuluá	6	3	1	2	5	5	**10**	
Deportivo Cali	6	2	2	2	5	5	**8**	
Deportes Tolima	6	1	1	4	5	9	**4**	

International Club Performances 2001

CLUB	COMPETITION	PROGRESS
América de Cali	Copa Libertadores Copa Merconorte	Quarter-finals Group Stage
Atlético Júnior	Copa Libertadores	2nd Round
Deportivo Cali	Copa Libertadores	Group Stage
Atlético Nacional	Copa Merconorte	Group Stage
CD Millonarios	Copa Merconorte	Winners

Top Goalscorers 2001

NAME	CLUB	GOALS
Carlos Alberto Castro	CD Millonarios	29
Jorge Horacio Serna	Ind Medellín	29
Sergio Alejandro Galván	Once Caldas	23
Julián Vásquez	América de Cali	22
Iván José Velásquez	Atlético Nacional	20

Left: Norberto Cadavid, ex-América and Colombian international player, became another footballing victim of Colombia's drug-fuelled civil war when he was shot dead in the centre of Medellín in 2001. A similar fate befell ex-Deportivo Cali player Aldemar Sanchez.

Below: Rene Higuita (left), Colombia's maverick, scorpion-kicking goalkeeper, finally bowed out of the game after being sacked by his club, Junior Barranquilla, for failing to turn up to a training session.

Above: Once Caldas and Corporación Tuluá (left) were the season's surprise sides, winning the Apertura and Clausura respectively – but once again the play-offs let the big teams back into the championship.

Left and below: Despite a chaotic season in Colombia, América de Cali (in red) reached the quarter-finals of the Copa Libertadores (left) and won the championship, beating Independiente Medellín in a two leg play-off (below).

Championship Play-off

2001 FINAL (2 legs)
December 16 – Atanasio Girardot, Medellín
Ind. Medellín 0-1 América de Cali
(Vásquez 66)
h/t: 0-0 **Att:** 52,000
Ref: Ruiz
December 19 – Pascual Guerrero, Cali
América de Cali 2-0 Ind. Medellín
(Mafla 34,
Vásquez 41)
h/t: 2-0 **Att:** 50,000
Ref: Ramírez
América de Cali won 3-0 on aggregate

Association Football in Colombia

Early 1880s: Football introduced to Colombia, mainly on Atlantic coast — 1880

1890

1900

1910

1924: First federation formed. Liga de Football del Atlántico started in Barranquilla — 1920

🌐 **1936:** Affiliation to FIFA

▬ **1938:** Formation of national FA: Associación Colombiana de Fútbol. First international, v Mexico, lost 1-3, venue: Mexico City — 1930

🌐 **1940:** Affiliation to CONMEBOL — 1940

1948: National professional league, the *DiMayor*, established — 1950

1948–53: *El Dorado.* National federation suspended from FIFA, massive import of foreign players — 1960

1968: League format shifts to Apertura and Clausura Championships with a mini-league for the top teams at the end of the year — 1970

1971: National FA reformed — 1980

1984: Colombia withdraws from hosting World Cup

1989: League season abandoned after the assassination of a referee — 1990

▬ **2001:** Colombia beat Mexico to win the Copa América — 2000

2010

COLOMBIA

Carlos Valderrama, *Colombia's finest player.*

Key

▬	International football
🌐	Affiliation to FIFA
🌐	Affiliation to CONMEBOL
■	Copa América host
●	Copa América winner
▲	Copa América runner-up
○	Competition winner
△	Competition runner-up

Amér	– América de Cali
Atl N	– Atlético Nacional
D Cali	– Deportivo Cali
Indep	– Independiente Santa Fé
Mill	– Millonarios

International Competitions

	Copa Libertadores	Copa CONMEBOL	Copa Merconorte
1975:	▲		
1978:	△D Cali		
1985:	△ Amér		
1986:	△ Amér		
1987:	△ Amér		
1989:	○ Atl N		
1995:	△ Atl N		
1996:	△ Amér	△ Indep	
1998:			○Atl N △D Cali
1999:	△ D Cali		○Amér △Indep
2000:			○Atl N △Mill
2001:	● ■		○Mill

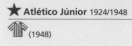
★ **Atlético Júnior** 1924/1948

 (1948)

Sporting Barranquilla 1950

★ **Deportivo Barranquilla** 1949

Deportivo 'Unicosta' 1995

★ **Once Caldas** 1948

👕 (1950) ⚽ 🧤

German Gómez García, club president, shot 1990. Guillermo Gómez Melgarejo, club vice-president, shot 1992

★ **Deportivo Caldas** 1947

Atlético Manizales 1954

Deportes Quindío 1947

👕 (1953)

Corporación Tuluá 1967

Escuela Sarimento Lora 1984

Barranquilla
Cartagena
Real Cartagena 🍁 1971

Medellín ◎
Envigado ●

Manizales ◎
Pereira ●
Armenia ●

Tuluá ○
Cali ◎
Ibagué ○
Deportes Tolima 1955

Neiva
Atlético Huila 1990

Pasto
● **Deportivo Pasto** 1949

Asociación 1962

Boca Júniors 1939

👕 (1951, 52)

★ **Deportivo Cali** 1928

👕 (1949)

★ **América de Cali** 1924

⚽ 🔗

Controlled by Miguel Rodríguez Orejuelas, Cali cartel

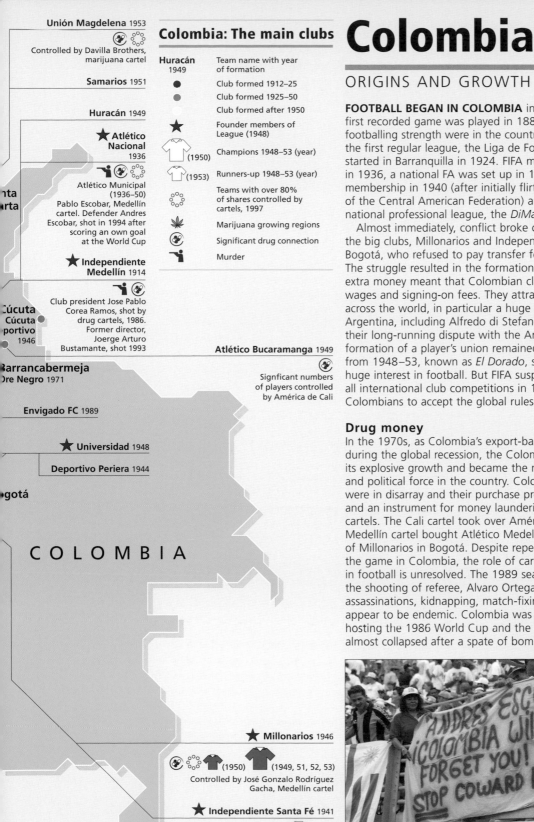

Colombia: The main clubs

Huracán 1949	Team name with year of formation
●	Club formed 1912–25
●	Club formed 1925–50
○	Club formed after 1950
★	Founder members of League (1948)
👕 (1950)	Champions 1948–53 (year)
👕 (1953)	Runners-up 1948–53 (year)
⚙	Teams with over 80% of shares controlled by cartels, 1997
🍁	Marijuana growing regions
⚗	Significant drug connection
🏃	Murder

Unión Magdelena 1953 — Controlled by Davila Brothers, marijuana cartel

Samarios 1951

Huracán 1949

★ Atlético Nacional 1936 — Atlético Municipal (1936–50) Pablo Escobar, Medellín cartel. Defender Andres Escobar, shot in 1994 after scoring an own goal at the World Cup

★ Independiente Medellín 1914 — Club president Jose Pablo Corea Ramos, shot by drug cartels, 1986. Former director, Joerge Arturo Bustamante, shot 1993

Cúcuta Cúcuta Deportivo 1946

Barrancabermeja Dre Negro 1971

Envigado FC 1989

★ Universidad 1948

Deportivo Periera 1944

Bogotá

COLOMBIA

Atlético Bucaramanga 1949 — Signficant numbers of players controlled by América de Cali

★ Millonarios 1946 — (1950) (1949, 51, 52, 53) Controlled by José Gonzalo Rodríguez Gacha, Medellín cartel

★ Independiente Santa Fé 1941 — (1948) Signficant numbers of players controlled by América de Cali

Colombia

ORIGINS AND GROWTH OF FOOTBALL

FOOTBALL BEGAN IN COLOMBIA in the early 1880s and the first recorded game was played in 1888. The early areas of footballing strength were in the country's northern ports and the first regular league, the Liga de Football del Atlántico, started in Barranquilla in 1924. FIFA membership followed in 1936, a national FA was set up in 1938, CONMEBOL membership in 1940 (after initially flirting with membership of the Central American Federation) and, in 1948, a new national professional league, the *DiMayor*, was established.

Almost immediately, conflict broke out between the FA and the big clubs, Millonarios and Independiente Santa Fé from Bogotá, who refused to pay transfer fees to foreign clubs. The struggle resulted in the formation of a rebel league. The extra money meant that Colombian clubs could offer massive wages and signing-on fees. They attracted star players from across the world, in particular a huge contingent from Argentina, including Alfredo di Stefano, who moved north as their long-running dispute with the Argentinian FA over the formation of a player's union remained deadlocked. The era from 1948–53, known as *El Dorado*, saw massive crowds and huge interest in football. But FIFA suspended Colombia from all international club competitions in 1949 and forced the Colombians to accept the global rules on transfers in 1954.

Drug money
In the 1970s, as Colombia's export-based industries collapsed during the global recession, the Colombian drug industry began its explosive growth and became the most powerful economic and political force in the country. Colombian clubs' finances were in disarray and their purchase provided both social status and an instrument for money laundering for the different drug cartels. The Cali cartel took over América, Pablo Escobar's Medellín cartel bought Atlético Medellín and took control of Millonarios in Bogotá. Despite repeated efforts to normalize the game in Colombia, the role of cartels and drug money in football is unresolved. The 1989 season was cancelled after the shooting of referee, Alvaro Ortega, on cartel orders, while assassinations, kidnapping, match-fixing and money laundering appear to be endemic. Colombia was forced to pull out of hosting the 1986 World Cup and the 2001 Copa América almost collapsed after a spate of bombings and shootings.

COLOMBIA

Colombian fans remember full-back Andres Escobar, who was shot dead in Medellín after returning from the 1994 World Cup. He had scored an own goal in a shock 2-1 defeat by the United States.

Colombia

APERTURA AND CLAUSURA 1992–2001

IN 1989, THREE PRESIDENTIAL CANDIDATES were assassinated in Colombia; Gonzalo Rodriguez-Gacha, a hit man for the Medellín drugs cartel and effective owner of Bogotá's Millonarios, was killed in a shootout with police; Miguel Rodriguez Orejuela, leader of the Cali drugs cartel and owner of América de Cali, was in prison; and the football season was cancelled at the play-off stage after referee Alvaro Ortega was shot in Medellín. Ortega, it was said, had failed to ensure the right result in the Medellín derby that season. In 1991, the Colombian FA appeared to be overhauling football's connections to what Colombians call *el narcotráfico*. Reform arrived in the shape of a new national league incorporating promotion and relegation, but the chaos continued. Pablo Escobar, leader of the Medellín cartel and owner of Atlético Nacional, was finally arrested by police in 1992. He escaped, only to be shot a year later. Juan José Bellini, former president of the Colombian FA and director of América, was imprisoned in 1997 on drug trafficking and corruption charges. A similar fate befell directors at Unión Magdalena and Millonarios.

Matters are no different today, and the last decade has seen Colombian football played under conditions of civil war and endemic violence. The country has been divided between the drug cartels, the left-wing paramilitaries FARC, an assortment of right-wing paramilitary groups, the military, the government and, most recently, the US government and army. Money laundering through football clubs continues, and the combination of drugs money, narcotics and gambling has ensured that players, club directors and referees are regularly threatened and even killed. Most recently, the Copa América 2001 was almost lost by Colombia after a spate of bombings and shootings in the big cities.

Not surprisingly, it is still the big clubs (those that were most closely connected to *el narcotráfico*) that have retained control over Colombian football. Since 1990, América de Cali has won five championships, three titles have gone to Atlético Nacional, and two each to Atlético Junior and Deportivo Cali. Introducing relegation and promotion has seen some provincial outfits get a chance but only Atlético Bucaramanga has made the play-offs.

Colombian League Positions Table 1992–2001

SEASON

TEAM	1992 A	1992 C	Play-Offs	1993 A	1993 C	Play-Offs	1994 A	1994 C	Play-Offs	1995	1995-96 A	1995-96 C	Play-Offs	1996-97 A	1996-97 C	Play-Offs	1998 A	1998 C	Play-Offs	1999 A	1999 C	Play-Offs	2000 A	2000 C	Play-Offs	2001 A	2001 C	Play-Offs
Atlético Júnior	5(A)	2	SF	1(B)	2	C	10	4	QF	C	3(B)	8		7	4(A)		7	7(A)		4	4		6	3	RU	8	12	
Atlético Nacional	2(A)	3	RU	2(B)	9	SF	1	1	C	3	1(B)	3	SF	2	4(B)		2	1(B)	QF	2	6	C	5	7		12	3	
Atlético Bucaramanga	3(B)	9	QF	3(B)	8	QF	14	15			6(A)	13		8	2(A)	RU	14	4(B)		9	9		15	10		15	16	
América de Cali	5(B)	1	C	6(A)	4	SF	2	10	SF	2	2(B)	2	SF	1	6(A)	C	8	5(B)	QF	1	10	RU	2	1	C	7	5	C
Deportivo Cali	1(A)	7	SF	5(A)	3	QF	6	6	QF	4	1(A)	1	C	3	1(B)		5	2(A)	C	7	5		1	15		2	4	QF
Real Cartagena	8(B)	16																					10	13		13	14	
Cúcuta Deportivo	6(A)	14		8(B)	11		7	9		16				16														
Deportivo 'Unicosta'											8(B)						8(B)											
Envigado FC	3(A)	10		5(B)	6		4	8	QF	12	6(B)	7		12	5(B)		13	4(A)		14	12		8	12		10	7	
Atlético Huila				2(A)	15		8	7		15	4(B)	16					8	7(B)		16	16		11	11		14	15	
Independiente Medellín	6(B)	15		4(B)	1	RU	9	3	SF	7	8(A)	12		5	8(A)		4	2(B)	QF	8	3		13	9		5	10	RU
Millonarios	4(A)	4	QF	3(A)	7	QF	5	5	RU	14	4(A)	6	RU	15	2(B)		9	5(A)	QF	11	1		4	4		9	2	QF
Once Caldas	4(B)	12		1(A)	5	QF	3	5	QF	8	5(A)			10	5(A)		1	1(A)	RU	3	7		12	6		3	1	QF
Deportivo Pasto																	12	8		14	8					16	6	
Deportivo Pereira	7(A)	5		4(A)	10		16	13		6	7(B)	11		14	7(B)											11	11	
Deportes Quindío	7(B)	11		7(B)	13		15	11		10	7(A)	14		12	1(A)		11	3(A)	QF	13	15		16	14				
Independiente Santa Fé	1(B)	6	QF	7(A)	14		12	14		5	5(B)	15		11	7(A)		3	8(A)	QF	10	13		9	2	SF	6	9	QF
Deportes Tolima	8(A)	13		8(A)	16		9	2(A)			4	3(A)		10	6(B)					5	11		3	5	SF	4	8	QF
Corporación Tuluá							13	16		11	8(B)	9		9	6(B)		12	3(B)		6	2		7	16		1	13	QF
Unión Magdalena	2(B)	8	QF	6(B)	12		11	12		13	3(A)	10		6	3(B)		15	6(A)		15	14							

(A) = Group A   (B) = Group B

Except for 1995, the season is divided into two leagues, Apertura and Clausura (marked A and C on the table).
Also called Torneo Mustang I and II. The winners play off to decide the championship

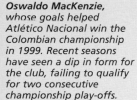

Oswaldo MacKenzie, *whose goals helped Atlético Nacional win the Colombian championship in 1999. Recent seasons have seen a dip in form for the club, failing to qualify for two consecutive championship play-offs.*

Atlético Júnior

1993, 95, *2000*

Deportivo 'Unicosta'

Pablo Escobar, *leader of the Medellín drug cartel and lifelong Atlético Nacional fan, combined ruthless violence in the narcotics trade with philanthropic housing and playing field programmes in the city, while extensively bankrolling his favourite team.*

COLOMBIA

Key to League Positions Table

	League champions
	Season of promotion to league
	Season of relegation from league
	Other teams playing in league
	Qualified for championship play-off
5	Final position in league

Barranquilla
Cartagena
Santa Marta

Real Cartagena

Unión Magdelena

Cúcuta Deportivo

Atlético Bucaramanga

1997

Medellín
Envigado FC

Manizales   Deportivo Pereira

Pereira

Armenia   Deportes Quindío

Once Caldas

Tuluá

1998

Cali   **Ibagué**

Bogotá

América de Cali

Neiva

Corporación Tuluá

1992, *95, 97, 99,* **2000, 01**

Deportivo Cali

1996, **98**

Pasto

Atlético Nacional

1992, **94, 99**

Independiente Medellín

1993, **2001**

Atlético Huila

Independiente Santa Fé

C O L O M B I A

Colombian League

América de Cali	Team name
	League champions/ runners-up
1992, *95*	Champions in bold Runners-up in italics
	Other teams in the league
● Cali	City of origin

Deportes Tolima

Millonarios

Deportivo Pasto

1994, 96

Colombia

Federación Colombiana de Fútbol
Founded: 1924, reformed 1938, 1971
Joined FIFA: 1936–1950, 1954
Joined CONMEBOL: 1940

FOOTBALL WAS A LATE DEVELOPER in Colombia, with the first regular competition only established in the city of Barranquilla in 1924, and a national organization only created in 1938. But it would take until 1948 for the first professional national league to be set up: the *DiMayor*. The league broke away from the Colombian FA in 1950, before rejoining it and FIFA (which it had been a member of between 1936 and 1950) in 1954. It retained a simple format until 1968 when it switched to a season consisting of Apertura (opening), Clausura (closing) and play-off championships. The 1989 national championship has no recorded victor as the season was abandoned following the assassination of a referee and widespread allegations of drug-money handling, illegal gambling and match fixing throughout the game. Colombia has no significant national cup competition.

Colombian League Record 1948–2001

SEASON	CHAMPIONS	RUNNERS-UP
1948	Independiente Santa Fé	Atlético Júnior
1949	Millonarios	Deportivo Cali
1950	Once Caldas	Millonarios
1951	Millonarios	Boca Júniors
1952	Millonarios	Boca Júniors
1953	Millonarios	Atlético Quindio
1954	Atlético Nacional	Atlético Quindio
1955	Independiente Medellín	Atlético Nacional
1956	Atlético Quindio	Millonarios
1957	Independiente Medellín	Deportes Tolima
1958	Independiente Santa Fé	Millonarios
1959	Millonarios	Independiente Medellín
1960	Independiente Santa Fé	América di Cali
1961	Millonarios	Independiente Medellín
1962	Millonarios	Deportivo Cali
1963	Millonarios	Independiente Santa Fé
1964	Millonarios	Cucuta Deportivo
1965	Deportivo Cali	Atlético Nacional
1966	Independiente Santa Fé	Independiente Medellín
1967	Deportivo Cali	Millonarios
1968	Unión Magdalena	Deportivo Cali
1969	Deportivo Cali	América di Cali
1970	Deportivo Cali	Atlético Júnior
1971	Independiente Santa Fé	Atlético Nacional
1972	Millonarios	Deportivo Cali
1973	Atlético Nacional	Millonarios
1974	Deportivo Cali	Atlético Nacional
1975	Independiente Santa Fé	Millonarios
1976	Atlético Nacional	Deportivo Cali
1977	Atlético Júnior	Deportivo Cali
1978	Millonarios	Deportivo Cali
1979	América di Cali	Independiente Santa Fé
1980	Atlético Júnior	Deportivo Cali
1981	Atlético Nacional	Deportes Tolima
1982	América di Cali	Deportes Tolima
1983	América di Cali	Atlético Júnior
1984	América di Cali	Millonarios
1985	América di Cali	Deportivo Cali
1986	América di Cali	Deportivo Cali
1987	Millonarios	América di Cali
1988	Millonarios	Atlético Nacional
1989	*not awarded**	
1990	América di Cali	Atlético Nacional

Colombian League Record (*continued*)

SEASON	CHAMPIONS	RUNNERS-UP
1991	Atlético Nacional	América di Cali
1992	América di Cali	Atlético Nacional
1993	Atlético Júnior	Independiente Medellín
1994	Atlético Nacional	Millonarios
1995	Atlético Júnior	América di Cali
1996	Deportivo Cali	Millonarios
1997	América di Cali	Atlético Bucaramanga
1998	Deportivo Cali	Once Caldas
1999	Atlético Nacional	América di Cali
2000	América di Cali	Atlético Júnior
2001	América di Cali	Independiente Medellín

* The 1989 season was abandoned due to alleged criminal activities and the killing of a referee.

Colombian League Summary

TEAM	TOTALS	CHAMPIONS & RUNNERS-UP (BOLD) (*ITALICS*)
Millonarios	**13**, *9*	**1949**, *50*, **51–53**, *56*, *58*, **59**, **61–64**, *67*, *72*, *73*, *75*, **78**, *84*, **87**, **88**, *94*, *96*
América di Cali	**11**, *6*	*1960*, *69*, *79*, **82–86**, *87*, **90**, *91*, *92*, **95**, **97**, *99*, **2000**, **01**
Deportivo Cali	**7**, *10*	*1949*, *62*, **65**, *67*, *68*, **69**, **70**, *72*, **74**, *76–78*, *80*, *85*, *86*, **96**, **98**
Atlético Nacional	**7**, *7*	**1954**, *55*, **65**, *71*, **73**, *74*, **76**, **81**, *88*, *90*, **91**, *92*, **94**, **99**
Independiente Santa Fé	**6**, *2*	**1948**, **58**, **60**, *63*, **66**, **71**, **75**, *79*
Atlético Júnior	**4**, *4*	*1948*, *70*, **77**, **80**, *83*, **93**, **95**, **2000**
Independiente Medellín	**2**, *5*	**1955**, *57*, **59**, *61*, *66*, *93*, **2001**
Atlético Quindio	**1**, *2*	*1953*, *54*, **56**
Once Caldas	**1**, *1*	**1950**, *98*
Unión Magdalena	**1**, *0*	**1968**
Deportes Tolima	**0**, *3*	*1957*, *81*, *82*
Boca Júniors	**0**, *2*	*1951*, *52*
Atlético Bucaramanga	**0**, *1*	*1997*
Cúcuta Deportivo	**0**, *1*	*1964*

Millonarios from Bogotá is the most successful club in Colombia. The team poses for the cameras after winning the 1952 league title.

Venezuela

Federación Venezolana de Fútbol
Founded: 1926
Joined FIFA: 1952
Joined CONMEBOL: 1952

AN ORGANIZED NATIONAL LEAGUE was set up in Caracas in 1921. However, the game has failed to take off, given the popularity of the national sport of baseball, and this has left Venezuela as the weakest of the ten footballing nations in South America. League teams turned professional in 1955 but have had very little success in the Copa Libertadores. The national team has also failed to make an impact in the Copa América.

Venezuelan Amateur League Record 1921–54

SEASON	CHAMPIONS	RUNNERS-UP
1921	América	Centro Atlético
1922	Centro Atlético	América
1923	América	Centro Atlético
1924	Centro Atlético	Vargas (La Guaira)
1925	Loyola SC	Venzóleo
1926	Centro Atlético	Venzóleo
1927	Venzóleo	Centro Atlético
1928	Deportivo Venezuela	Centro Atlético
1929	Deportivo Venezuela	Unión SC
1930	Centro Atlético	Unión SC
1931	Deportivo Venezuela	Centro Atlético
1932	Unión SC	Dos Caminos SC
1933	Deportivo Venezuela	Dos Caminos SC
1934	Unión SC	Dos Caminos SC
1935	Unión SC	Dos Caminos SC
1936	Dos Caminos SC	Centro Atlético
1937	Dos Caminos SC	Litoral SC
1938	Dos Caminos SC	Litoral SC
1939	Unión SC	Litoral SC
1940	Unión SC	Dos Caminos SC
1941	Litoral SC	Dos Caminos SC
1942	Dos Caminos SC	Loyola SC
1943	Loyola SC	Litoral SC
1944	Loyola SC	Dos Caminos SC
1945	Dos Caminos SC	Loyola SC
1946	Deportivo Español	Centro Atlético
1947	Unión SC	Universidad Central
1948	Loyola SC	Unión SC
1949	Dos Caminos SC	Universidad Central
1950	Unión SC	La Salle FC
1951	Universidad Central	Loyola SC
1952	La Salle FC	Loyola SC
1953	Universidad Central	La Salle FC
1954	Deportivo Vasco	Loyola SC

Venezuelan Professional League Record 1955–2002

SEASON	CHAMPIONS	RUNNERS-UP
1955	La Salle FC	Deportivo Español
1956	Banco Obrero	La Salle FC
1957	Universidad Central	La Salle FC
1958	Deportivo Portugués	Deportivo Español
1959	Deportivo Español	Deportivo Portugués
1960	Deportivo Portugués	Deportivo Español
1961	Deportivo Italia	Banco Agricola y Pecuario
1962	Deportivo Portugués	Universidad Central
1963	Deportivo Italia	Deportivo Portugués
1964	Deportivo Galicia	Tiquire Flores
1965	Lara FC	Deportivo Italia
1966	Deportivo Italia	Deportivo Galicia
1967	Deportivo Portugués	Deportivo Galicia
1968	Unión Deportivo Canarias	Deportivo Italia
1969	Deportivo Galicia	Valencia FC

Venezuelan League Record (*continued*)

SEASON	CHAMPIONS	RUNNERS-UP
1970	Deportivo Galicia	Deportivo Italia
1971	Valencia FC	Deportivo Italia
1972	Deportivo Italia	Deportivo Galicia
1973	Portuguesa FC	Valencia FC
1974	Deportivo Galicia	Portuguesa FC
1975	Portuguesa FC	Deportivo Galicia
1976	Portuguesa FC	Estudiantes de Mérida
1977	Portuguesa FC	Estudiantes de Mérida
1978	Portuguesa FC	Deportivo Galicia
1979	Deportivo Táchira	Deportivo Galicia
1980	Estudiantes de Mérida	Portuguesa FC
1981	Deportivo Táchira	Estudiantes de Mérida
1982	Atlético San Cristóbal	Deportivo Táchira
1983	Universidad de Los Andes	Portuguesa FC
1984	Deportivo Táchira	Deportivo Italia
1985	Estudiantes de Mérida	Deportivo Táchira
1986	Unión Atlético Táchira	Estudiantes de Mérida
1987	CS Maritimo	Unión Atlético Táchira
1988	CS Maritimo	Unión Atlético Táchira
1989	Mineros de Guayana	Pepeganga Margarita
1990	CS Maritimo	Unión Atlético Táchira
1991	Universidad de Los Andes	CS Maritimo
1992	Caracas FC	Minervén
1993	CS Maritimo	Minervén
1994	Caracas FC	Trujillanos
1995	Caracas FC	Minervén
1996	Minervén	Mineros de Guayana
1997	Caracas FC	Atlético Zulia
1998	Atlético Zulia	Estudiantes de Mérida
1999	ItalChacoa	Unión Atlético Táchira
2000	Deportivo Táchira	ItalChacao
2001	Caracas FC	Trujillanos
2002	Nacional Táchira	Estudiantes de Mérida

Venezuelan League Summary

TEAM	TOTALS	CHAMPIONS & RUNNERS-UP (BOLD) (*ITALICS*)
Unión SC	7, 3	*1929, 30,* **32, 34, 35,** *39,* **40, 47,** *48,* **50**
Dos Caminos SC	6, 7	*1932–35,* **36–38,** *40, 41,* **42,** *44,* **45,** *49*
Portuguesa FC	5, 3	**1973,** *74,* **75–78,** *80,* **83**
Caracas FC	5, 0	**1992, 94, 95, 97, 2001**
Centro Atlético	4, 7	*1921,* **22, 23,** *24,* **26,** *27, 28,* **30,** *31,* **36,** *46*
Deportivo Galicia	4, 6	**1964,** *66, 67,* **69, 70,** *72,* **74,** *75, 78, 79*
Deportivo Italia	4, 5	**1961, 63, 65,** *66, 68, 70, 71,* **72,** *84*
Loyola SC	4, 5	**1925,** *42,* **43, 44,** *45,* **48,** *51, 52, 54*
Deportivo Portugués	4, 2	**1958,** *59, 60,* **62,** *63,* **67**
Deportivo Táchira	4, 2	**1979,** *81,* **82, 84,** *85,* **2000**
CS Maritimo	4, 1	**1987, 88, 90,** *91,* **93**
Deportivo Venezuela	4, 0	**1928, 29, 31, 33**
Universidad Central	3, 3	*1947, 49,* **51,** *53,* **57,** *62*

This summary only features clubs that have won the Venezuelan League three or more times. For a full list of league champions and runners-up please see the League Records above.

VENEZUELA

Bolivia

Federación Boliviana de Fútbol
Founded: 1925
Joined FIFA: 1926
Joined CONMEBOL: 1926

BOLIVIAN FOOTBALL CAN BE TRACED back to the formation of the first team, Oruro Royal Club, in 1896. Its first matches were against the clubs Nimbles Sports and Northern, formed by workers on the La Paz to Antofagasta railway. Football spread to the major cities high in the Andes over the next decade. Local leagues were formed and early national competitions between local league champions ran from 1914 to 1925. An official national tournament was held in 1926 after the creation of a national football federation. Teams from the capital La Paz, like Bolivar, The Strongest and Littoral, dominated the early years of Bolivian football. They have been challenged more recently by the Cochabamba team, Jorge Wilstermann and the Santa Cruz teams, Oriente Petrolero and Blooming.

Professionalism arrived in 1951 and between 1954 and 1957 a *Torneo Integrado* was held between the champions of the three major leagues in La Paz, Cochabamba and Oruro. In 1958 a national league was finally established. In 1977 this structure was replaced with the one in use today.

The season is split into two with an Apertura (opening) championship played at the beginning of the year, and a Clausura (closing) championship played at the end. Both are in a league format. The top four from the Apertura compete in semi-finals and final play-offs. The finalists join the top four from the Clausura league in a final hexagonal tournament. The top two from this six-club mini-league then play off for the national championship.

A cup competition – La Copa Simón Bolívar – has also run intermittently in Bolivia. Between 1960 and 1976 the winners became the Bolivian entrant to the Copa Libertadores. It was revived in 1989 as a way of organizing promotion from the regional to the national leagues.

Bolivian League Record 1958–2001

SEASON	CHAMPIONS	SEASON	CHAMPIONS
1958	Jorge Wilstermann	1982	Bolívar
1959	Jorge Wilstermann	1983	Bolívar
1960	Jorge Wilstermann	1984	Blooming
1961	Deportivo Municipal	1985	Bolívar
1962	Chaco Petrolero	1986	The Strongest
1963	The Strongest/Aurora	1987	Bolívar
1964	The Strongest	1988	Bolívar
1965	Deportivo Municipal	1989	The Strongest
1966	Bolívar	1990	Oriente Petrolero
1967	Jorge Wilstermann	1991	Bolívar
1968	Bolívar	1992	Bolívar
1969	CD Universitario	1993	The Strongest
1970	CD Chaco Petrolero	1994	Bolívar
1971	Oriente Petrolero	1995	CS San José
1972	Jorge Wilstermann	1996	Bolívar
1973	Jorge Wilstermann	1997	Bolívar
1974	The Strongest	1998	Blooming
1975	Guabirá	1999	Blooming
1976	Bolívar	2000	Jorge Wilstermann
1977	The Strongest	2001	Oriente Petrolero
1978	Bolívar		
1979	Oriente Petrolero		
1980	Jorge Wilstermann		
1981	Jorge Wilstermann		

Bolivian Cup Record 1960–76

YEAR	WINNERS	YEAR	WINNERS
1960	Jorge Wilstermann	1969	CD Universitario
1961	Deportivo Municipal	1970	Chaco Petrolero
1962–63	*no competition*	1971	Oriente Petrolero
1964	The Strongest	1972	Jorge Wilstermann
1965	Deportivo Municipal	1973	Jorge Wilstermann
1966	Bolívar	1974	The Strongest
1967	Jorge Wilstermann	1975	Guabirá
1968	Bolívar	1976	Bolívar

Bolivian Cup Record 1989–2001

YEAR	WINNERS	YEAR	WINNERS
1989	Enrique Happ	1998	Unión Central
1990	Universidad	1999	Atlético Pompeya
1991	Enrique Happ	2000	Iberoamericano
1992	Enrique Happ	2001	San José
1993	Real Santa Cruz		
1994	Stormers		
1995	Municipal		
1996	Blooming		
1997	Real Potosí		

Ecuador

Asociación Ecuatoriana de Fútbol
Founded: 1925
Joined FIFA: 1926
Joined CONMEBOL: 1930

THE FIRST ECUADORIAN CLUB, CS Pastria, was formed in the port city of Guayaquil in 1908, around a decade after visiting sailors had first played football in Ecuador. Local tournaments were organized in Guayaquil before and after the First World War, culminating in a short-lived city league which existed between 1922 and 1929.

Football spread slowly to the interior of the country and it was only in 1957 that the national football federation was reconstituted and a national league established. The league has been dominated by teams from Guayaquil (Barcelona and Emelec) and Quito (Deportivo, El Nacional and Liga Deportivo Universitaria).

The league has an awesomely complex structure. In the top division, Primera A, 12 teams compete home and away for the Apertura championships: the winners qualifying for the Copa Libertadores. In the Clausura championships the teams are first divided into three groups of four playing home and away. The winners and runners-up of each group then go into a group of six and the third and fourth placed teams go into a second group of six. The winners of the first mini-league then play off against the winners of the Apertura to determine the overall national champions. The bottom two in the second mini-league are relegated. Note that teams carry over bonus points or penalty points from their performance in the Apertura to the second phase of the Clausura.

Ecuadorian League Record 1957–2001

SEASON	CHAMPIONS	SEASON	CHAMPIONS
1957	Emelec	1964	Deportivo
1958	*no championship*	1965	9 du Octubre
1959	*no championship*	1966	Barcelona
1960	Barcelona	1967	El Nacional
1961	Emelec	1968	Deportivo
1962	Everest	1969	LDU
1963	Barcelona	1970	Barcelona

BOLIVIA, ECUADOR

Ecuadorian League Record (*continued*)

SEASON	CHAMPIONS	SEASON	CHAMPIONS
1971	Barcelona	1989	Barcelona
1972	Emelec	1990	Barcelona
1973	El Nacional	1991	Valdez
1974	El Nacional	1992	El Nacional
1975	LDU	1993	Barcelona
1976	Deportivo	1994	Emelec
1977	El Nacional	1995	Barcelona
1978	El Nacional	1996	El Nacional
1979	Emelec	1997	Barcelona
1980	Barcelona	1998	LDU
1981	LDU	1999	LDU
1982	El Nacional	2000	Olmedo
1983	El Nacional	2001	Emelec
1984	El Nacional		
1985	Barcelona		
1986	El Nacional		
1987	Barcelona		
1988	Emelec		

Peru

Federación Peruana de Fútbol
Founded: 1922
Joined FIFA: 1924
Joined CONMEBOL: 1926

FOOTBALL WAS INTRODUCED TO PERU at the turn of the 19th century by British residents in the capital Lima. Many teams grew out of expatriate tennis and cricket clubs. A local league was formed in 1912, but it was only in 1922 that a national football federation was established.

A formalized Lima-based league was set up in 1926 and in 1931 Peruvian football went professional. In 1966 the league was expanded to encompass the strongest teams from the regional competitions. In 1972 the league changed again with a Lima-based metropolitan league and a network of regional leagues producing qualifiers for a national championship tournament. Lima teams have consistently led Peruvian football: Universitario de Deportes, Sporting Cristal, Alianza Lima, Sport Boys and Deportivo Municipal, all come from the capital.

In 1976 a single national league was established but with a fantastically complex structure. Again split into two leagues – Apertura and Clausura – the championship is decided via a play-off between the two champions, unless one club has won both. The winners claim a place in the Copa Libertadores. The six teams with the highest points total across the season (excluding the champions) then compete in an end-of-season play-off league to determine Peru's second spot in the competition. The two clubs with the overall lowest points total are relegated. The winners of the Lima regional league and the winners of the Copa Perú (a tournament between regional champions) are promoted to the top division.

Peruvian League Record 1926–2001

SEASON	CHAMPIONS	SEASON	CHAMPIONS
1926	Sport Progreso	1933	Alianza Lima
1927	Alianza Lima	1934	Universitario de Deportes
1928	Alianza Lima	1935	Sport Boys
1929	Universitario de Deportes	1936	no championship
1930	Atlético Chalaco	1937	Sport Boys
1931	Alianza Lima	1938	Deportivo Municipal
1932	Alianza Lima	1939	Universitario de Deportes

Peruvian League Record (*continued*)

SEASON	CHAMPIONS	SEASON	CHAMPIONS
1940	Deportivo Municipal	1973	Desensor Lima
1941	Universitario de Deportes	1974	Universitario de Deportes
1942	Sport Boys	1975	Alianza Lima
1943	Deportivo Municipal	1976	Unión Huaral
1944	FC Sucre	1977	Alianza Lima
1945	Universitario de Deportes	1978	Alianza Lima
1946	Universitario de Deportes	1979	Sporting Cristal
1947	Atlético Chalaco	1980	Sporting Cristal
1948	Alianza Lima	1981	Melgar FBC
1949	Universitario de Deportes	1982	Universitario de Deportes
1950	Deportivo Municipal	1983	Sporting Cristal
1951	Sport Boys	1984	Sport Boys
1952	Alianza Lima	1985	Universitario de Deportes
1953	FC Sucre	1986	Colegio San Agustín
1954	Alianza Lima	1987	Universitario de Deportes
1955	Alianza Lima	1988	Sporting Cristal
1956	Sporting Cristal	1989	Unión Huaral
1957	Centro Iqueño	1990	Universitario de Deportes
1958	Sport Boys	1991	Sporting Cristal
1959	Universitario de Deportes	1992	Universitario de Deportes
1960	Universitario de Deportes	1993	Universitario de Deportes
1961	Sporting Cristal	1994	Sporting Cristal
1962	Alianza Lima	1995	Sporting Cristal
1963	Alianza Lima	1996	Sporting Cristal
1964	Universitario de Deportes	1997	Alianza Lima
1965	Alianza Lima	1998	Universitario de Deportes
1966	Universitario de Deportes	1999	Universitario de Deportes
1967	Universitario de Deportes	2000	Universitario de Deportes
1968	Sporting Cristal	2001	Alianza Lima
1969	Universitario de Deportes		
1970	Sporting Cristal		
1971	Universitario de Deportes		
1972	Sporting Cristal		

PERU

Peruvian football club Union Minas, which plays at 4,380m in the Andes near the border with Bolivia, holds the record for the professional team which plays at the highest altitude in the world. Half-time refreshment for the players comes in the form of oxygen.

Brazil

BRAZIL

THE SEASON IN REVIEW 2001

WHEN OVERCROWDING in Vasco da Gama's stadium led to a stand collapsing, over 100 injuries and the abandonment of the second leg of the 2000 National Championship Final, the ramshackle state of Brazilian football was laid bare. In 2001, this tottering edifice looked shakier than ever. The domestic season was played out against a dreadful World Cup qualification campaign, unsuccessful international club campaigns, and the relentless investigations of two parliamentary inquiries into Brazilian football. Richard Teixeira, president of the CBF, spent most of the year trying to explain just how the millions of Nike and Globo dollars in Brazilian football have ended up in the campaign accounts of politicians and the coffers of the federal police association. Ex-national and now Corinthians coach, Wanderley Luxemburgo, had his numerous bank accounts explored in public.

The first half of the season was the inevitable scrum of chaotic fixtures – multi-layered State Championships, the Copa do Brasil, inter-state championships, as well as international competitions. In the Carioca (Rio League), Flamengo snatched the title from Vasco, scoring with two minutes to go to win 4-3. In the Paulista (São Paulo League), gimmickry included a spray-on 10-yard free kick marker and penalty shootouts after draws. Old-fashioned impatience saw Portuguesa, Palmeiras and Corinthians all change their managers. In Minas Gerias, the little-fancied América beat Atlético Mineiro to take the championship.

Brazilian National Championship 2001 – First Phase

CLUB	P	W	D	L	F	A	Pts	
São Cãetano	27	18	5	4	48	25	59	Qualified for Second Phase
Atlético Paranaense	27	15	6	6	58	40	51	Qualified for Second Phase
Fluminense	27	14	9	4	44	29	51	Qualified for Second Phase
Atlético Mineiro	27	15	4	8	50	34	49	Qualified for Second Phase
Grêmio	27	14	5	8	39	29	47	Qualified for Second Phase
Ponte Preta	27	13	8	6	53	48	47	Qualified for Second Phase
São Paulo	27	13	7	7	48	34	46	Qualified for Second Phase
Bahia	27	13	6	8	43	38	45	Qualified for Second Phase
Internacional	27	12	4	11	38	40	40	
Goiás	27	12	3	12	38	32	39	
Vasco da Gama	27	10	9	8	57	36	39	
Palmeiras	27	12	2	13	40	47	38	
Portuguesa	27	11	4	12	31	33	37	
Paraná	27	11	3	13	35	37	36	
Santos	27	9	9	9	37	32	36	
Vitória	27	9	9	9	33	37	36	
Coritiba	27	9	8	10	31	32	35	
Corinthians	27	9	7	11	46	45	34	
Guarani	27	9	6	12	29	45	33	
Gama	27	8	9	10	40	34	33	
Cruzeiro	27	9	5	13	36	43	32	
Juventude	27	6	12	9	29	37	30	
Botafogo-RJ	27	8	5	14	41	51	29	
Flamengo	27	8	5	14	25	39	29	
Santa Cruz	27	7	6	14	31	50	27	Relegated
América-MG	27	6	7	14	32	46	25	Relegated
Botafogo-SP	27	6	7	14	23	41	25	Relegated
SC Recife	27	5	4	18	24	46	19	Relegated

Promoted clubs: Paysandu, Figueirense

Brazilian State Championships 2001

STATE	CHAMPIONS
Bahia	Bahia
Rio de Janeiro	Flamengo
Goiás	Villa Nova
Paraná	Atlético Paranaense
Rio Grand Du Sol	Grêmio
São Paulo	Corinthians
Minas Gerias	América (Belo Horizonte)
Ceara	Fortaleza

The old wolf finally calls it a day. After an appalling National Championship, Flamengo manager Mario Zagallo resigned. Despite his attachment to the lucky number 13 shirt, Zagallo left after the team's 13th defeat of the season.

Richard Teixeira (left), president of the CBF, and Wanderley Luxemburgo, previously national team manager, face the press after the publication of the Althoff report. Teixeira tries to explain why the CBF has a $16 million debt at the same time that sponsorship and TV money has been flooding in. Luxemburgo tries to remember how he forgot to declare 3 million reals to the tax authorities.

Vasco da Gama might be in crisis – players wages unpaid and the directors accused of corruption – but Romario da Souza keeps on going. In impeccable style his rash of goals helped Vasco to the Final of the Carioca, though his 21 goals in the National Championship were not enough to keep Vasco in contention for the title.

Paranaense claims its first national title

The National Championship started with a gigantic 28 teams. A dismal, gruelling competition on the field was enlivened by the chaos and cruelty of the game off it. Nearly three-quarters of the coaches were sacked; Santos fans broke into the team's training camp, berating and attacking players; dressing room discord and late wages tore Vasco and Palmeiras apart. Almost every big club failed to make an impact, with only São Paulo, Grêmio and Atlético Mineiro securing a place in the quarter-finals; and only the latter progressed to the semi-final stage. Sailing above the mire, two small teams made it to the Final, the gritty São Cãetano and Atlético Paranaense, who are among the few solvent clubs in Brazilian football. Fired by Alex Mineiro's goalscoring (he scored a hat trick in the first leg), Atlético Paranaense finally took its first national title.

The year finished dramatically with the publication of Senator Geraldo Althoff's report on the game. While an earlier congressional report had been heavily doctored before publication, Althoff's report emerged relatively unscathed. The accounts and practices of the big state football authorities, major clubs and powerful agents all came under extended scrutiny. It has not been a pretty sight: salaries, expenses, foreign visits and perks have, needless to say, been lavish; taxes, wages and creditors have gone unpaid. Whether any of the 17 leading figures in Brazilian football against whom the report recommends criminal proceedings will actually go on trial remains an open question.

BRAZIL

Atlético Paranaense's Alex Mineiro (left) fights for the ball against Marcao of Fluminense during their semi-final in the Brazilian National Championship in Curitiba. Mineiro's goals were one of the main reasons that Atlético won the championship for the first time in its history.

Brazilian National Championship – Second Phase

QUARTER-FINALS

December 5

São Cãetano 0-0 Bahia
(after extra time)
São Cãetano qualified due to better First-Phase record

Atlético 2-1 São Paulo
Paranaense *(Gerlin 67 pen)*
(Kléber 28,
Mineiro 80)

Fluminense 3-2 Ponte Preta
(Decossau 17, *(Humberto 79,*
Alves 91, 112) *Macedo 98)*
(after extra time)

Atlético 3-0 Grêmio
Mineiro
(Guilherme
50 pen, 82,
Marques 62)

SEMI-FINALS

December 9

São Cãetano 2-1 Atlético
(Magrão 29, 78) **Mineiro**
(Valdo 18)

Atlético 3-2 Fluminense
Paranaense *(Alves 44, 74)*
(Mineiro 48,
69, 89)

FINAL (2 legs)

December 16 – Joaquim Américo Stadium, Curitiba

Atlético 4-2 São Cãetano
Paranaense *(Mancini 31,*
(Ilan 4, *Paulo 53)*
Mineiro 55,
79, 90 pen)
h/t: 1-1 **Att:** 31,740
Ref: Simon

December 23 – Anacletto Campanella Stadium, São Cãetano do Sul

São Cãetano 0-1 Atlético
Paranaense
(Mineiro 66)
h/t: 0-0 **Att:** 21,007
Ref: Simon

International Club Performances 2001

CLUB	COMPETITION	PROGRESS
Cruzeiro	Copa Libertadores	Quarter-finals
Palmeiras	Copa Libertadores	Semi-finals
São Cãetano	Copa Libertadores	Second Round
Vasco da Gama	Copa Libertadores	Quarter-finals
	Copa Mercosur	Group Stage
Corinthians	Copa Mercosur	Semi-finals
Flamengo	Copa Mercosur	Runners-up
Grêmio	Copa Mercosur	Semi-finals
São Paulo	Copa Mercosur	Group Stage

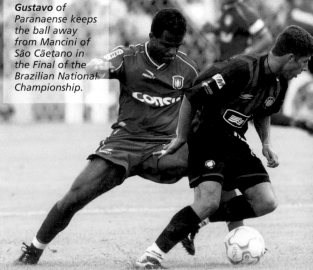

Gustavo of Paranaense keeps the ball away from Mancini of São Cãetano in the Final of the Brazilian National Championship.

The Grêmio team celebrates
winning the Copa do Brasil after
decisively beating Corinthians at
the Morumbi in São Paulo.

Copa do Brasil

2001 FINAL (2 legs)

June 10 – Estádio Olímpico, Porto Alegre
Grêmio 2-2 Corinthians
(Luís Mário 64, 69)   *(Marcelinho*
Carioca 28,
Müller 50)
h/t: 0-1   **Att:** 80,000
Ref: Rezende de Rfeitas

June 17 – Morumbi, Sâo Paulo
Corinthians 1-3 Grêmio
(Ewérthon 76)   *(Marinho 42,*
Zinho 47,
Marcelinho
Paraibo 87)
h/t: 0-1   **Att:** 70,000
Ref: Pereira da Silva

Atlético Paranaense *fans*
celebrate victory by waving
strips of newspaper.

Corinthians'
Marcelinho
Carioca (left)
and Grêmio's
Anderson Lima
battle for the
ball during the
Copa do Brasil
Final second leg
in São Paulo.

BRAZIL

Association Football in Brazil

1894: Charles Miller returns to Brazil from England with first imported football equipment. First recorded match, São Paulo

1898: First club, Associacao Atletica of Mackenzie College, São Paulo founded

1901: São Paulo League, Campeonata Paulista de Futebol, established

1905: Bahia State League (first provincial league) established

1906: Rio League established

 1914: CBD founded: Confederação Brasileira de Desportos. First international v Argentina, lost 3-0, venue: Buenos Aires

1916: Affiliation to CONMEBOL

1923: Affiliation to FIFA

1933: Professionalism legalized

1950: Rio-São Paulo Tournament established

1959: Brazilian Cup established

1967: Rio-São Paulo Tournament replaced by Taca de Prata

1968: Brazilian Cup discontinued

1971: Fully-fledged National League established, replaces Taca de Prata

1980: CBF (Confederação Brasileira de Futbol) replaces CBD

1982: First women's international, v Spain

1989: Brazilian Cup re-established

2000: Massive judicial investigation launched into the finances of Brazilian football. National championship replaced by one-off João Havelange Tournament

Timeline: 1890, 1895, 1900, 1905, 1910, 1915, 1920, 1925, 1930, 1935, 1940, 1945, 1950, 1955, 1960, 1965, 1970, 1975, 1980, 1985, 1990, 1995, 2000, 2005

International Competitions

1919:	● ■
1921:	▲
1922:	● ■
1925:	▲
1937:	▲
1945:	▲
1946:	▲
1949:	● ■
1950:	▲ ■ ■
1953:	▲
1957:	▲ ▲
1958:	● ▲
1959:	▲ ▲
1962:	●
1970:	●
1983:	▲ ■
1989:	● ■
1991:	▲
1994:	●
1995:	▲
1997:	●
1998:	▲
1999:	●

Complete with his 'Miss World Cup' sash, *Gylmar the Brazilian goalkeeper is held up in triumph after victory in the 1962 World Cup Final against Czechoslovakia in Chile.*

Key

 International football

⚽ Affiliation to FIFA

⚽ Affiliation to CONMEBOL

⚽ Women's football

■ World Cup host

● World Cup winner

▲ World Cup runner-up

■ Copa América host

● Copa América winner

▲ Copa América runner-up

○ Competition winner

△ Competition runner-up

Atl M	– Atlético Mineiro
Bota	– Botafogo
Cruz	– Cruzeiro
Flam	– Flamengo
Grêm	– Grêmio
Inter	– Internacional
Palm	– Palmeiras
São P	– São Paulo
Vasco	– Vasco da Gama

Copa Libertadores

Year	Winner/Runner-up
1961:	△ Palm
1962:	○ Santos
1963:	○ Santos
1968:	△ Palm
1974:	△ São P
1976:	○ Cruz
1977:	△ Cruz
1980:	△ Inter
1981:	○ Flam
1983:	○ Grêm
1984:	△ Grêm

Copa Libertadores / Copa CONMEBOL / Copa Mercosur

Year	Copa Libertadores	Copa CONMEBOL	Copa Mercosur
1992:	○ São P	○ Atl M	
1993:	○ São P	○ Bota	
1994:	△ São P	○ São P	
1995:	○ Grêm		△ Atl M
1997:	○ Cruz	○ Atl M	
1998:	○ Vasco	○ Santos	
1999:	○ Palm		○ Palm △ Cruz
2000:	△ Palm		○ Flam △ Palm
2001:			○ Vasco △ Palm △ Flam

Atlética Ponte Preta 1900

Guarani FC 1911

Coritiba 1909

Paraná Clube 1989
Merger of Colorado and Pinheiros

Atlético Paranaense 1924

Criciúma EC 1947

Comerciaro (1978)

RORAIM (1995)

AMAZONAS (1914)

ACRE (1989)

RONDÔNIA (1945)

Brazil: The main clubs

Santos 1912 — Team name with year of formation

● Club formed before 1912

● Club formed 1912–25

● Club formed 1925–50

Club formed after 1950

PARÁ (1913) — State (year of championship foundation)

Founded 1900–10

Founded 1910–20

Founded 1920–50

Founded 1950–80

Founded 1980–95

Team colours

English origins

German origins

Italian origins

Portuguese origins

Lower class

Upper class

Originated from a cricket club

Originated from a rowing club

Railway company origins

Brazil

ORIGINS AND GROWTH OF FOOTBALL

THE EARLIEST REPORTS OF FOOTBALL in Brazil are of British and Dutch sailors playing on the Rio dockside in the 1870s and of British and Brazilian railway workers in São Paulo in 1882. But the written record begins with Charles Miller. Brazilian-born of English coffee-merchant parentage, Miller was educated in England. With a game for Hampshire against the Corinthians under his belt, he returned to Brazil in 1894 with a collection of footballs and a raging enthusiasm. Collecting together Englishmen from the São Paulo Railway, the local gas company and the London and Brazilian bank, he organized the first 'official' football match in São Paulo in 1895. Within five years teams had sprung up in São Paulo and Rio, drawing on German colleges and gym clubs, Portuguese immigrants, English companies, as well as members of elite cricket and rowing clubs.

The race issue

São Paulo's Campeonata Paulista de Futebol was the first organized tournament which started in 1901, followed by leagues in Bahia (1904) and Rio de Janeiro (1905). A national association running all sports, the CBD, was set up in 1914 with a football section. The elite and predominantly white origins of Brazilian football soon came into conflict with the mass popularity of the game on the issue of race. Carlos Alberto, a mulatto of mixed race, played for Fluminense in 1916 with rice flour on his face to lighten his complexion. In 1921, President Pesoa called for an all-white team to represent Brazil in the Copa América.

But in 1923, Vasco da Gama won the Rio Championship with a team dominated by black and mixed-race players. Rio's big teams, flushed with fear for their sporting and social status, organized an alternative league and sought to exclude black players by making the signing of a team sheet a pre-condition of participation. But the sporting and economic logic was against exclusion, and as players of all races began moving to Italy and elsewhere, professionalism was introduced into the Rio Championships in 1933 and quickly spread.

Uniõn São João 1981

EC Vitória 1899
Club de Cricket Victoria (1899–1946)

EC Bahia 1931
Merger of Atlética de Bahia and Club Bahiano de Tenis

América FC 1915

SC Recife 1905

AMAPÁ (1944)

RIO GRANDE DO NORTE (1920)

Araras

PARÁ (1913)

MARANHÃO (1918)

CEARÁ (1920)

Natal

PIAUÍ (1918)

PARAIABA (1917)

Recife

PERNAMBUCO (1915)

B R A Z I L

ALAGOAS (1927)

TOCANTINS (1993)

SERGIPE (1918)

Salvador

MATO GROSSO (1974)

DISTRITO FEDERAL (1973)

BAHIA (1905)

Brasília
SE Gama 1975

Goiás EC 1943   Goiânia

MINAS GERAIS

GOAIS (1944)

ESPÍRITO SANTO (1940)

Atlético Bragantino 1928

Belo Horizonte

Campinas

Bragança Paulista

Rio de Janeiro

RIO DE JANEIRO (1906)

MATO GROSSO DO SUL (1979)

São Paulo

Atlético Mineiro 1908

SÃO PAULO (1902)

Curitiba

Santos 1912

Cruzeiro EC 1921

PARANÁ (1915)

SC Corinthians 1910

Palestra Italia (1921–42)

SANTA CATARINA (1927)

Criciúma

RIO GRANDE DO SUL (1919)

Botafogo SP 1918

Flamengo 1895

Caxias du Sul

Porto Alegre

Portuguesa de Desportos 1920

CR Vasco da Gama 1898

Atlética das Palmeiras 1914

EC Juventude 1913

Societa Palestra Italia (1914–42)

Fluminense 1902

São Paulo FC 1935

SC Internacional 1909   Grêmio 1903

Botafogo 1914

The 1970 World Cup-winning Brazilian team is regarded by many as the finest football team ever. The side that faced Italy in the Final included: (back row left to right) Carlos Alberto, Brito, Piazza, Felix, Clodoaldo, Everaldo, Gerson; (front row) Jairzinho, Rivelino, Tostão, Pele and Paulo Cesar.

São Paulo

FOOTBALL CITY

SÃO PAULO IS THE INDUSTRIAL and commercial heart of Brazil. After an English public school education, Charles Miller (son of a coffee merchant family) returned to São Paulo in 1894 with a football. In 1895, he organized a game among British workers at the São Paulo Railway Company, the London and Brazilian Bank and the Gas Company on the Varzea do Carmo. More games were organized between football sections formed by the British at São Paulo Athletic Club and Mackenzie College. The word spread and Germans from the city's gymnastic clubs created SC Germania. Together with another club, CA Paulistino, these teams formed the city's first league in 1901. Within a year, São Paulo had over 60 clubs and the game began to spread beyond its European elite circles.

The five big teams of the professional era emerged a decade or so after this initial explosion. In 1910, Corinthians was founded by railway workers in Bom Retiro, and named after the English amateurs who had recently toured the city. In 1912, the Rio team América relocated to the port area of the city. After considering various names, like 'Africa' and 'Concordia', it settled on the area's name, Santos, for its new club. In 1914, the city's Italian immigrant population created Club Sociedada Esportivo Palestra Italia. During the Second World War, anti-Italian sentiment saw the side change its name to Palmeiras. The Portuguese community followed with the creation of Portuguesa from the merger of five clubs (Lusiadas, Portugal Marinhense, 5 de Outobro, Luzitano and Marques de Pombal).

Professionalism and disaster

These four clubs were among those teams which were paying their players and pushing for the development of a professional game in the 1920s. The last of the big five, São Paulo, rose out of the ashes of an earlier team of the same name. São Paulo 'I' was formed in 1930, when CA Paulistino stopped playing football in protest over the adoption of professionalism, and the club's players joined AA de Palmeiras. The venture folded in 1935 and São Paulo 'II' drew on what was left of the team to start again. By then a professional city league had been created.

The decades that followed were a peak for São Paulo football – a rash of stadium building, including the city government's funding of the Pacaembu, and the arrival of Pele at Santos. The club's victories in the Copa Libertadores in the early 1960s at last allowed the city to eclipse Rio. Forty years on, Corinthians and Palmeiras are the city's leading clubs, but their financial situation is now dire; gate takings are low, and all the clubs are mired in significant debt.

São Paulo, *Brazil's industrial and commercial heartland, has witnessed decades of explosive economic and demographic growth that has created extremes of wealth (in the central business district featured here) and poverty in the sprawling shanty towns of the city's periphery: perfect conditions for the creation of massive fan bases.*

CÍCERO POMPEU DE TOLEDO – MORUMBI

Club:	São Paulo
Built:	1960
Original Capacity:	120, 000
Record Attendance:	138,032 Corinthians v Ponte Preta, 1977
Significant Matches:	2000 Club World Championship: six group matches

80,000

BRAZIL

SÃO PAULO
SEE ENLARGEMENT FOR MORE DETAIL

AA Portuguesa Santos

ULRICO MURSA
15,000

Santos

URBANO CALDEIRA 'VILA BELMIRO'
18,500

SANTOS

ATLANTIC OCEAN

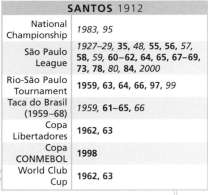

SANTOS 1912

National Championship	*1983, 95*
São Paulo League	*1927–29,* **35,** *48,* **55, 56, 57, 58,** *59,* **60–62, 64, 65, 67–69, 73, 78,** *80,* **84, 2000**
Rio-São Paulo Tournament	**1959, 63, 64, 66, 97,** *99*
Taca do Brasil (1959–68)	*1959,* **61–65,** *66*
Copa Libertadores	**1962, 63**
Copa CONMEBOL	**1998**
World Club Cup	**1962, 63**

CORINTHIANS 1910

National Championship	**1976,** *90,* **94, 98,** *99*
São Paulo League	**1914,** *18,* **22–24,** *25,* **28–30, 36,** *37–39,* **41,** *42, 43, 45–47,* **51, 52, 54, 55,** *62,* **66,** *68,* **74, 77,** *79,* **82, 83,** *84,* **87, 88,** *91,* **93, 95, 97, 98, 99, 2001, 02**
Rio-São Paulo Tournament	**1950, 53, 54,** *63,* **66,** *93*
Copa do Brasil (1989–2002)	**1995,** *2001,* **02**
FIFA Club World Championship	**2000**

LIMAO · CASA VERDE

Palmeiras

PALESTRA ITÁLIA 'PARQUE ANTÁRCTICA'
32,000

Rio Tiete

BOM RETIRO

VILA GUILHERME

OSWALDO TEIXEIRA DUARTE 'CANDIDÉ'
22,000

PARI

VILA MARIA

Via Presidente Dutra

ALFREDO SCHURING 'PARQUE SÃO JORGE'
15,000

LAPA

PERDIZES

'PACAEMBU' Paulo Machado de Carvalho. This municipal stadium is used for big games by all the city's leading clubs
40,000

SANTA CECILIA

Portuguesa

CONDO RODOLFO CRESPI
9,000

Corinthians

BRAZIL

VILA MADALENA

REPUBLICA

BRAS

Juventus

ALTO DA MOOCA

CONSOLACAO

BELA VISTA

S Ã O P A U L O

PINHEIROS

São Paulo AC

CAMBUCI

Avenida Reboucas

Avenida Brasil

São Paulo

JARDIM AMERICA

JARDIM PAULISTA

SC Germania

FEDERAÇÃO PAULISTA DE FUTEBOL STATE FA HEADQUARTERS

IPIRANGA

Avenida Paulista

BUTANTA

CÍCERO POMPEU DE TOLEDO 'MORUMBI'
80,000

Rio Tiete

BROOKLIN PAULISTANA Birth place of Rivellino

PORTUGUESA 1920

National Championship	*1996*
São Paulo League	**1935, 36,** *40, 60, 73,* **75, 85**
Rio-São Paulo Tournament	**1952, 55,** *65*

SÃO PAULO 1935

National Championship	*1971, 73,* **77,** *81,* **86,** *89, 90,* **91**
São Paulo League	*1930,* **31,** *32–34,* **38,** *41,* **43, 44, 45, 46,** *48,* **49,** *50,* **52, 53,** *56, 57, 58,* **63,** *67,* **70, 71, 72,** *75,* **78, 80, 81,** *82, 83,* **85, 87,** *89,* **91, 92,** *94, 96,* **97, 98, 2000**
Rio-São Paulo Tournament	*1965, 98,* **2001,** *02*
Copa do Brasil (1989–2002)	*2000*
Copa Libertadores	*1974,* **92, 93,** *94*
Copa CONMEBOL	**1994**
Supercopa	**1993,** *97*
World Club Cup	**1992, 93**

PALMEIRAS 1914

National Championship	**1972, 73,** *78,* **93, 94,** *97*
São Paulo League	**1920,** *21,–23,* **26, 27,** *31,* **32–34, 35,** *36, 37,* **39, 40,** *42,* **44,** *47,* **49, 50,** *51, 53, 54,* **59,** *61,* **63, 64, 65, 66,** *69–71,* **72, 74, 76,** *86,* **92, 93, 94,** *95, 96,* **99**
Rio-São Paulo Tournament	**1931,** *51,* **55,** *61, 62,* **65,** *93,* **2000**
Taca do Brasil (1959–68)	**1960, 67**
Copa do Brasil (1989–2002)	*1996,* **98**
Copa Libertadores	*1961, 68,* **99,** *2000*
Copa Mercosur	**1998,** *99,* **2000**
World Club Cup	*1999*

São Paulo

32,000 — Capacity of stadium

— Minor clubs

— Stadium no longer in use for top-flight football

— Team colours

— Early São Paulo teams

—— Major road

1900 — Champions

2000 — Runners-up

Rio de Janeiro

FOOTBALL CITY

UNCONFIRMED REPORTS TELL OF British sailors playing football in Rio's docks throughout the late 19th century. The expatriate British elite played cricket (in Paissandu and Rio Cricket Sud in Niteroi) and formed rowing clubs. After a match between São Paulo and Rio in 1901, a rash of football clubs were set up among the expatriates: Fluminense in 1902, América and Botafogo in 1904. Fluminense attracted the pinnacle of society, students from the Alfredo Gomez College formed Botafogo, and Bangu were in effect the works' team of the British managers at a textile firm in the suburbs. In 1906 a local tournament, the Carioca, was established. In 1911, defectors from Fluminense joined Flamengo rowing club to create a Flamengo football section.

The literacy test

At first, elite control of Rio football was more absolute than in São Paulo, and the white expatriates, professionals and students of these clubs dominated the game. But in 1923, Vasco da Gama, a team formed by Portuguese immigrants, came into the top division, fielding four black players among poor white players. The key difference was that they were professionals, and the team was unstoppable. The big elite clubs left the league and formed their own (LMDT), which ran the following year without Vasco. But the crowds went to Vasco, and the club – along with two others – was eventually asked to join the LMDT. However, pre-match paperwork in the league required literacy of all players, and Vasco's advantage was eradicated until the literacy test was abolished in 1929. By the early 1930s, all the clubs were paying players in an intense competitive struggle, and inevitably a professional league was established in 1933.

Although Vasco is a perennial challenger, and often the victor, the Flamengo-Fluminense rivalry is the key to football in Rio. In a single game, this local derby condenses the divisions of class and race in the city; Fluminense (the aristocracy) versus Flamengo (the people). It is this intensity for football, reflected citywide, that saw the creation of the world's largest football stadium – the Maracana – and the national disaster of defeat in the 1950 World Cup. Today, the clubs share power in Rio with the Confederação Brasileira de Futebol, who chose to locate here rather than in the capital Brasília, and the nation's gigantic TV company – Globo. The rising tide of accusations of corruption, match fixing and interference are now lapping at the doors of the presidents of the major Rio clubs and the Rio FA.

BRAZIL

MARIO FILHO – MARACANA	
95,095	**Clubs:** Botafogo, Flamengo, Fluminense
	Built: 1950
	Original Capacity: 180,000
	Rebuilt: 1993–98
	Record Attendance: 183,341 1969 Brazil v Paraguay, World Cup
	Significant Matches: 1950 World Cup: seven matches including final pool match; Copa América: 1989 final pool matches

Football in Rio reflects the divisions of class and race in the city. This is embodied in the Fla-Flu derby which pits the people (in the shape of Flamengo) against the aristocracy (in the shape of Fluminense).

BANGU 1904	
National Championship	*1985*
Rio League	*1916*, **33**, *51*, *59*, *64*, *65*, **66**, *67*, *85*

MENDHANHA
(465)
MOCA BONITA 15,000
Bangu
ÍTALO DEL CIMA
25,000
Campo Grande
CAMPO GRANDE
BANGU

(116)
DUQUE DE CAXIAS Birthplace of Jairzinho
ANICETO MOSCOSO
MADUREIRA 10,000
Madureira
RIO DE JANEIRO
JACAREPAGUA

Olaria AC
(040)
RUA BARIRI
18,000
RAMOS
(210)
PILARES
EDSON PASSOS
15,000
América

Baia de Gunabara
(101)
CENTRO
SEE CENTRAL RIO FOR MORE DETAIL

NITEROI Birthplace of Gerson
(108)
COPACABANA

AMÉRICA 1904	
Rio League	*1911*, *13*, *14*, **16**, *17*, *21*, **22**, *28*, *29*, *31*, *35*, *50*, *54*, *55*, *60*

(101)
(071)
ATLANTIC OCEAN

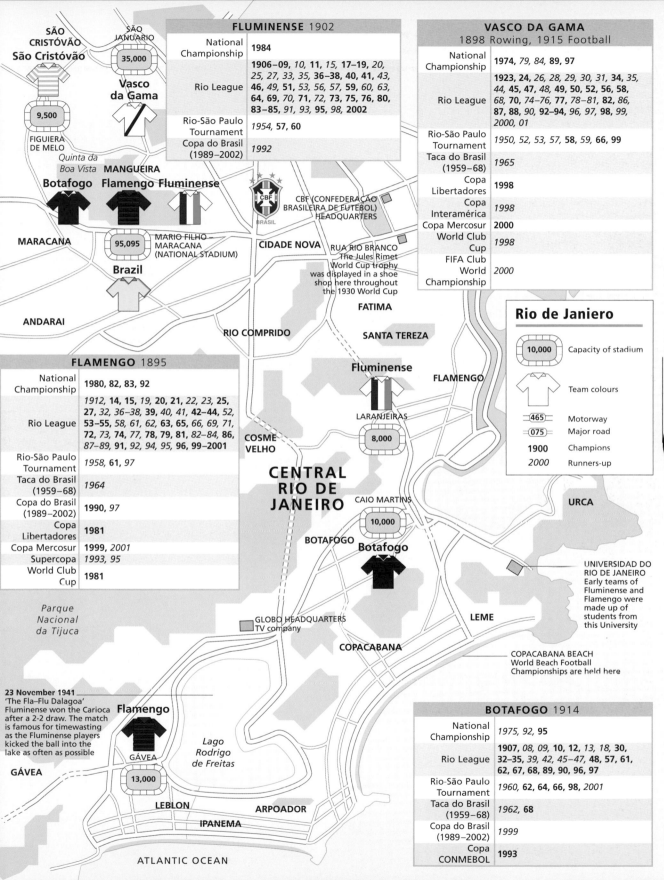

SÃO CRISTÓVÃO
São Cristóvão

SÃO JANUARIO
35,000

Vasco da Gama

9,500

FIGUIERA DE MELO

Quinta da Boa Vista MANGUEIRA

Botafogo Flamengo Fluminense

MARACANA

95,095 MARIO FILHO – MARACANA (NATIONAL STADIUM)

Brazil

ANDARAI

CBF (CONFEDERAÇÃO BRASILEIRA DE FUTEBOL) HEADQUARTERS

CIDADE NOVA

RUA RIO BRANCO
The Jules Rimet World Cup trophy was displayed in a shoe shop here throughout the 1930 World Cup

FATIMA

RIO COMPRIDO

SANTA TEREZA

Fluminense

LARANJEIRAS
8,000

FLAMENGO

COSME VELHO

CENTRAL RIO DE JANEIRO

CAIO MARTINS
10,000

BOTAFOGO
Botafogo

URCA

UNIVERSIDAD DO RIO DE JANEIRO
Early teams of Fluminense and Flamengo were made up of students from this University

LEME

Parque Nacional da Tijuca

GLOBO HEADQUARTERS
TV company

COPACABANA

COPACABANA BEACH
World Beach Football Championships are held here

23 November 1941
'The Fla–Flu Dalagoa' Fluminense won the Carioca after a 2-2 draw. The match is famous for timewasting as the Fluminense players kicked the ball into the lake as often as possible

Flamengo

GÁVEA

Lago Rodrigo de Freitas

GÁVEA
13,000

LEBLON ARPOADOR

IPANEMA

ATLANTIC OCEAN

BRAZIL

FLUMINENSE 1902

National Championship	**1984**
Rio League	*1906–09, 10, 11, 15, 17–19, 20,* 25, 27, 33, 35, **36–38**, 40, 41, 43, 46, 49, 51, 53, 56, 57, 59, 60, 63, 64, 69, 70, 71, 72, 73, 75, 76, 80, 83–85, 91, 93, 95, 98, **2002**
Rio-São Paulo Tournament	*1954,* **57, 60**
Copa do Brasil (1989–2002)	*1992*

VASCO DA GAMA
1898 Rowing, 1915 Football

National Championship	**1974,** *79, 84,* **89,** *97*
Rio League	**1923,** *24, 26,* **28, 29, 30, 31,** *34, 35,* **44, 45, 47, 48,** *49, 50, 52,* **56,** *58, 68, 70,* **74–76,** *77,* **78–81,** *82, 86, 87, 88, 90,* **92–94, 96,** *97,* **98,** *99,* **2000,** *01*
Rio-São Paulo Tournament	*1950, 52, 53,* **57,** *58, 59, 66,* **99**
Taca do Brasil (1959–68)	*1965*
Copa Libertadores	**1998**
Copa Interamérica	*1998*
Copa Mercosur	**2000**
World Club Cup	*1998*
FIFA Club World Championship	*2000*

FLAMENGO 1895

National Championship	**1980, 82, 83, 92**
Rio League	*1912,* **14, 15,** *19, 20, 21, 22, 23,* **25,** *27, 32,* **36–38,** *39, 40, 41,* **42–44,** *52,* **53–55,** *58, 61, 62,* **63,** *65, 66, 69, 71, 72, 73, 74,* **77, 78, 79,** *81, 82–84, 86, 87–89,* **91, 92, 94, 95, 96,** *99–2001*
Rio-São Paulo Tournament	*1958,* **61,** *97*
Taca do Brasil (1959–68)	*1964*
Copa do Brasil (1989–2002)	**1990,** *97*
Copa Libertadores	**1981**
Copa Mercosur	**1999, 2001**
Supercopa	*1993, 95*
World Club Cup	**1981**

BOTAFOGO 1914

National Championship	*1975, 92,* **95**
Rio League	**1907,** *08, 09,* **10,** *12, 13,* **18, 30,** *32–35,* **39,** *42,* **45–47,** *48, 57, 61,* **62,** *67, 68,* **89,** *90,* **96, 97**
Rio-São Paulo Tournament	*1960,* **62, 64, 66,** *98,* **2001**
Taca do Brasil (1959–68)	*1962,* **68**
Copa do Brasil (1989–2002)	*1999*
Copa CONMEBOL	**1993**

Rio de Janiero

10,000	Capacity of stadium
	Team colours
465	Motorway
075	Major road
1900	Champions
2000	Runners-up

Brazil

BRAZIL

FANS AND OWNERS

FOR MOST OF THEIR EXISTENCE Brazilian football clubs have operated in the legal twilight zone. As they have grown and their income has risen, they have become the perfect vehicles for those seeking influence, prestige and money. The chaotic, corrupt and opaque character of these clubs was supposed to be resolved by the Pele Law, passed in 1998 by the then Minister of Sport. The new law stated that Brazilian clubs were to become either civil or commercial companies regulated by law or, alternatively, they could spin off their professional arms as separate entities and outside investors could buy into them, bringing in modern management and much needed investment. The Pele Law also sought to modernize the archaic and inequitable player-club contracts and was therefore fiercely opposed by the leading teams or the Clube dos Treze, as they are better known. The 'Club of 13' was formed in 1997 to squeeze a better TV deal out of Globo, which they did. However, this being Brazil, the 13 are really 17.

Financial partners

Since the Pele Law came into force only a few clubs have explored the possibility of recruiting financial partners, and many of the schemes have ended in disaster. The American bank Hicks Muse, Tate and First (HMTF), operating as Pan-American Sports Teams, bought into Cruzeiro and Corinthians, while ISL, FIFA's marketing agents until their spectacular bankruptcy in mid-2001, bought into Grêmio and Flamengo. Nations Bank investment in Vasco da Gama has already been dissolved, while Parmalat has pulled out of its long-standing relationship with Palmeiras. But investors have rightly been cautious, as the Dias-Althoff report into Brazilian football revealed that corruption and waste are endemic and numerous leading figures in the clubs, state football authorities and the CBF have been recommended for criminal prosecution.

Violence on and off the pitch

The anarchy and viciousness of Brazil's clubs is paralleled by many of their fans. The big clubs have all acquired organized and often violent supporters' groups called *Torcida Organizada*. Equipped with firecrackers, noise bombs and, increasingly, with guns, these groups have ensured that violence inside and outside the grounds has been on the rise. In 2000, Vagner Jose Lima was killed when armed São Paulo fans attacked a small group of Corinthians supporters in the Bexiga district. São Paulo fans standing by their broken-down bus were shot at by a passing bus full of Santos fans. In 2001, Santos fans broke into the squad's training camp, attacking and berating the players for their poor performances. Four shootings were reported at the Bahia v Vitória derby in Salvador and shootings at Flamengo matches are common. Television coverage of, and judicial intervention in the violence is minimal as Globo seeks to protect its investments. But, whatever they show, the viciousness of the contemporary Brazilian game, dominated by fouling and diving, is mirrored in the stands. The concentration of power and money in the leading clubs is paralleled by the level of support for the big clubs. As the *Placar* survey shows, Flamengo, Corinthians, São Paulo, Vasco and Palmeiras are way out in front, with fans not only in their home towns but in other major cities.

Top left: Eurico Miranda, Brazilian senator and President of Vasco da Gama, is alleged to have embezzled £6 million from the club, despite the club's enormous debts, not to mention the obstruction of justice and electoral fraud.

Top right: The emperor has no clothes. Teixeira stands accused of innumerable charges of corruption. Although the CBF cannot by law pay salaries, Teixeira received £150,000 in 2000 alone.

Above: Wanderley Luxemburgo arrives for a good grilling at the Dias-Althoff inquiry. He was accused of tax evasion and taking bungs for player tranfers.

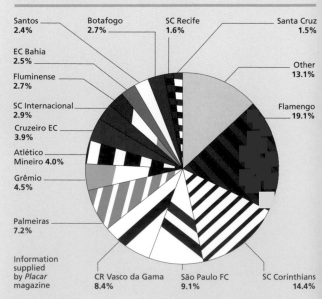

Club Support in Brazil 2001

Santos 2.4%
Botafogo 2.7%
SC Recife 1.6%
Santa Cruz 1.5%
EC Bahia 2.5%
Fluminense 2.7%
Other 13.1%
SC Internacional 2.9%
Flamengo 19.1%
Cruzeiro EC 3.9%
Atlético Mineiro 4.0%
Grêmio 4.5%
Palmeiras 7.2%
Information supplied by *Placar* magazine
CR Vasco da Gama 8.4%
São Paulo FC 9.1%
SC Corinthians 14.4%

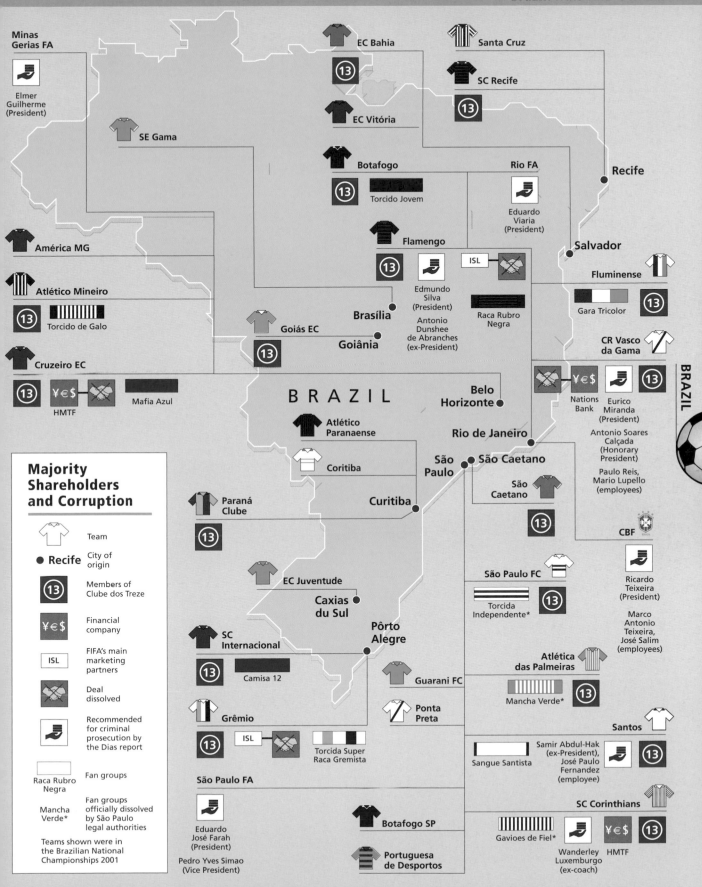

Minas Gerias FA
Elmer Guilherme (President)

EC Bahia

Santa Cruz

SC Recife

EC Vitória

SE Gama

Botafogo
Torcido Jovem

Rio FA
Eduardo Viaria (President)

Recife

Flamengo
Edmundo Silva (President)
Antonio Dunshee de Abranches (ex-President)

ISL

Raca Rubro Negra

Salvador

América MG

Fluminense
Gara Tricolor

Atlético Mineiro
Torcido de Galo

Brasília

Goiás EC
Goiânia

CR Vasco da Gama

Cruzeiro EC
HMTF
Mafia Azul

BRAZIL

Belo Horizonte

Nations Bank
Eurico Miranda (President)
Antonio Soares Calçada (Honorary President)
Paulo Reis, Mario Lupello (employees)

BRAZIL

Atlético Paranaense

Coritiba

Rio de Janeiro

São Paulo

São Caetano

São Caetano

CBF

Majority Shareholders and Corruption

Team

● **Recife** City of origin

13 Members of Clube dos Treze

¥€$ Financial company

ISL FIFA's main marketing partners

Deal dissolved

Recommended for criminal prosecution by the Dias report

Fan groups

Raca Rubro Negra

Mancha Verde* Fan groups officially dissolved by São Paulo legal authorities

Teams shown were in the Brazilian National Championships 2001

Paraná Clube

EC Juventude
Caxias du Sul

Pôrto Alegre

SC Internacional
Camisa 12

Grêmio
ISL
Torcida Super Raca Gremista

São Paulo FA
Eduardo José Farah (President)
Pedro Yves Simao (Vice President)

Guarani FC

Ponta Preta

Botafogo SP

Portuguesa de Desportos

São Paulo FC
Torcida Independente*

Ricardo Teixeira (President)

Marco Antonio Teixeira, José Salim (employees)

Atlética das Palmeiras
Mancha Verde*

Santos
Sangue Santista
Samir Abdul-Hak (ex-President), José Paulo Fernandez (employee)

SC Corinthians
Gavioes de Fiel*
Wanderley Luxemburgo (ex-coach)
HMTF

Brazil

PLAYERS AND MANAGERS

FOOTBALL BEGAN IN BRAZIL as a game of the rich, white elite; black and mixed-race players were dissuaded, banned or disguised with make-up by the leading clubs until the rise of the predominantly black and very successful Vasco da Gama from Rio de Janeiro in the 1930s. Since the advent of professionalism, black players have dominated the game and the popular archetype on which their style of play is based is described as the *Malandro*: the wide boy from the *favellas*, who waltzes through life on a stream of trickery and cunning, guile and style, and who moves with the grace of the *capoeira* master (a black Brazilian version of *t'ai chi*). From the heady mix of black Brazilian urban culture sprang two generations of extraordinarily gifted, stylish players: Garrincha, Gerson, Pele, Jairzhino, Rivelino and Carlos Alberto, and with them came the 'Beautiful Game' as well as three World Cups.

Exodus
The great Brazilian teams of this golden era played their club football almost exclusively in Brazil, but with the steady decline of the Brazilian economy, an exodus of talent to Europe and Japan has become a tidal wave (see South American Exodus, pages 476–477). Today's leading Brazilian players (Cafu, Ronaldo, Roberto Carlos and Rivaldo) all play their football in Spain and Italy.

It is not only the Brazilian economy that has been in decline. The World Cup of 1970 represented the high point of Brazilian football. Despite a flickering renaissance in the early 1980s around players like Zico, Socrates and old-style manager Tele Santana, there has been a steady erosion of the *Malandro* as international and club managers have insisted on aggression, defence, persistent fouling and winning at any cost, exemplified by the dour, mechanical Brazilian team under Phil Scolari who only just scraped into the 2002 World Cup Finals – winning the tournament will have brought a welcome check to this despondent outlook. Brazilian managers have also been caught in the web of corruption that has engulfed Brazilian football, including ex-national coach Wanderley Luxemburgo, who was sacked in 2000 and is currently under investigation by the police.

Mario Zagallo brought a semblance of order to the Brazilian manager's job between 1995 and 1998. He is the longest-lasting manager of a national team that has had 125 managers since it first played an international match.

Top 10 International Caps

PLAYER	CAPS	GOALS	FIRST MATCH	LAST MATCH
Marcos Evangelista de Moeis **'Cafu'***	101	5	1990	2002
Claudio **Taffarel**	101	0	1987	1998
Djalma **do Santos**	98	3	1952	1968
Gylmar dos Santos Neves **'Gilmar'**	94	0	1953	1969
Carlos Caetano Beldorn Verri **'Dunga'**	91	6	1982	1998
Edson Arantes do Nascimento **'Pele'**	91	77	1957	1971
Roberto **Rivelino**	91	25	1965	1978
Nascimento dos Santos **Aldair***	82	3	1989	2001
Roberto Carlos da Silva*	82	6	1992	2002
Jair Ventura Filho **'Jairzinho'**	81	34	1963	1982

Top 10 International Goalscorers

PLAYER	GOALS	CAPS	FIRST MATCH	LAST MATCH
Edson Arantes do Nascimento **'Pele'**	77	91	1957	1971
Romario da Souza Faria*	54	68	1987	2001
Artur Antunes Coimbra **'Zico'**	48	71	1971	1989
Jose Roberto Gama de Oliveira **'Bebeto'**	38	75	1985	1998
Ronaldo Luis Nazario da Lima*	36	54	1994	1999
Jair Ventura Filho **'Jairzinho'**	34	81	1963	1982
Ademir Marques de Menezes	31	39	1945	1953
Eduardo Goncalves de Andrade **'Tostao'**	30	53	1966	1972
Thomaz Soaras da Silva **'Zizihno'**	30	55	1942	1957
Antonio de Oliveira Filho **'Careca'**	29	60	1982	1993

* Indicates players still playing at least at club level.
Bold indicates players recognized by either their first name, last name or nickname. Nicknames are indicated between inverted commas.

Brazilian International Managers*

DATES	NAME	GAMES	WON	DRAWN	LOST
1979–80	Jaime Valente	12	7	2	3
1980–82	Tele Santana and	38	29	6	3
	Carlos Alberto Parreira	6	3	3	0
1983	Gilson Nunes,	3	2	0	1
	Carlos Alberto Parreira	7	1	4	2
	and Cleber Camerino	9	7	2	0
1984	Edu Antunes	3	1	1	1
	and Cleber Camerino	6	4	1	1
1985	Evaristo de Macedo	6	3	0	3
1985–86	Tele Santana	17	11	3	3
1986	Jair Pereira	4	2	2	0
1987–88	Carlos Alberto Silva	45	29	11	5
1989–90	Sebastiao Lazaroni	35	21	7	7
1990–91	Falcão	17	6	7	4
1991–92	Ernesto Paulo	8	4	1	3
1992–94	Carlos Alberto Parreira	45	26	14	4
1994–95	Mario Zagallo	3	3	0	0
1995	Pupo Giminez	5	3	2	0
1995–98	Mario Zagallo	90	65	17	8
1998–2000	Wanderley Luxemburgo	34	22	7	5
2000–01	Emerson Leao	10	3	4	3
2001–	Luis Filipe Scolari	12	7	0	5

* Only includes managers who have been in charge on a regular basis.
All figures correct as of 14 February 2002.

BRAZIL

Player of the Year

YEAR	PLAYER	CLUB
1973	Ancheta	Grêmio
1973	Cejas	Santos
1974	Zico	Flamengo
1975	Waldir Peres	São Paulo
1976	Elias Figueroa	Internacional
1977	Toninho Cerezo	Atlético Mineiro
1978	Falcão	Internacional
1979	Falcão	Internacional
1980	Toninho Cerezo	Atlético Mineiro
1981	Jesus	Grêmio
1982	Zico	Flamengo
1983	Costa	Atlético Paranaense
1984	Costa	Vasco da Gama
1985	Mahrino	Bangu Atlético
1986	Careca	São Paulo
1987	Renato Gaucho	Flamengo
1988	Taffarel	Internacional
1989	Rocha	São Paulo
1990	Sampaio	Santos
1991	Mauro da Silva	Bragantino
1992	Junior	Flamengo
1993	Sampaio	Palmeiras
1994	Marcio Amoroso	Guarani
1995	Giovanni	Santos
1996	Djalminha	Palmeiras
1997	Edmundo	Vasco da Gama
1998	Edilson	Corinthians
1999	Marcelinho	Corinthians
2000	Romario	Vasco da Gama
2001	Alex Mineiro	Atlético Paranaense

Awarded by *Placar* magazine as the Bola de Ouro.

Jairzinho was the first player ever to have scored in every round of the World Cup Finals on the way to victory. Here he celebrates the last goal of his record-breaking feat in the Final of the 1970 tournament against Italy in Mexico City.

Championship-Winning Managers

YEAR	MANAGER	CLUB
1971	Santana	Atlético Mineiro
1972	Brandao	Palmeiras
1973	Brandao	Palmeiras
1974	Travaglini	Vasco da Gama
1975	Minelli	Internacional
1976	Minelli	Internacional
1977	Minelli	São Paulo
1978	Silva	Guarani
1979	Andrade	Internacional
1980	Coutinho	Flamengo
1981	Andrade	Grêmio
1982	Torres	Flamengo
1983	Parriera	Flamengo
1984	Andrade	Coritiba
1985	Pepe	São Paulo
1986	Carlinhos	Flamengo
1987	Picerni	Sport Club Recife
1988	Macedo	Bahia
1989	Rosa	Vasco da Gama
1990	Batista	Corinthians
1991	Santana	São Paulo
1992	Carlinhos	Flamengo
1993	Luxemburgo	Palmeiras
1994	Luxemburgo	Palmeiras
1995	Autuori	Botafogo
1996	Scolari	Grêmio
1997	Lopes	Vasco da Gama
1998	Luxemburgo	Corinthians
1999	Oliveira	Corinthians
2000	Santana	Vasco da Gama
2001	Geninho	Atlético Paranaense

BRAZIL

Top Goalscorers 1971–2001

SEASON	PLAYER	CLUB	GOALS
1971	Dario	Atlético Mineiro	15
1972	Dario	Atlético Mineiro	17
1972	Pedro Rocha	São Paulo	17
1973	Ramon	Santa Cruz	21
1974	Roberto Dinamite	Vasco da Gama	16
1975	Flávio	Internacional	16
1976	Dario	Internacional	16
1977	Reinaldo	Atlético Mineiro	28
1978	Paulinho	Vasco da Gama	19
1979	Roberto Cesar	Cruzeiro	12
1980	Zico	Flamengo	21
1981	Nunes	Flamengo	16
1982	Zico	Flamengo	20
1983	Serginho	Santos	22
1984	Roberto Dinamite	Vasco da Gama	16
1985	Edmar	Guarani	20
1986	Careca	São Paulo	25
1987	Muller	São Paulo	10
1988	Nilson	Internacional	15
1989	Túlio	Goiás	11
1990	Charles	Bahia	11

SEASON	PLAYER	CLUB	GOALS
1991	Paulinho	Santos	15
1992	Bebeto	Vasco da Gama	18
1993	Guga	Santos	15
1994	Túlio	Botafogo	19
1994	Amoroso	Guarani	19
1995	Túlio	Botafogo	23
1996	Nunes	Grêmio	16
1997	Edmundo	Vasco da Gama	29
1998	Viola	Santos	21
1999	Guilherme	Atlético Mineiro	28
2000	Adhemar	São Cãetano	22
2001	Alex Mineiro	Atlético Paranaense	21

Romario da Souza Faria has been one of Brazil's leading goalscorers since the late 1980s. He began his career with Vasco da Gama, moved to Europe to play for PSV and Barcelona, before returning home to Vasco via Flamengo. His continued success was underlined when he was voted Brazilian Player of the Year in 2000.

Brazil

THE CAMPEONATO BRASILEIRO 1971–2001

BRAZIL WAS THE LAST major footballing nation to organize a national club tournament – the enormous size of the country, poor transport links and the huge inequalities in wealth and footballing prowess were major obstacles to overcome. However, in 1967, the Torneio Rio-São Paulo (between the leading clubs of the leading football cities) was expanded to include other state champions and renamed the Taça Roberto Gomes Pedrosa. In line with the then military dictatorship's desire for all things national, the Campeonato Brasileiro was first organized by the CBD in 1971. It began as a 20-team league with the top clubs going into a play-off round. Since then its format has changed every single year for almost three decades. Numbers of divisions, methods of qualification and classification, relegation and promotion have wildly fluctuated. Ticket sales were included in the classifications system in 1974, and in 1975 an extra point was awarded for winning matches by more than two goals. A struggle over TV money in 1987 saw two national tournaments – the big clubs' Copa União and the CBF's yellow module – played side-by-side.

In 1996, leading Rio club Fluminense was relegated but managed to maintain its position in the top flight by having the following year's league expanded by four clubs. However, this just delayed the inevitable as big clubs kept playing badly, so a two-season averaging system for relegation was introduced to try and bypass any awkward seasons. Nevertheless, Botafogo still managed to be relegated in 1999. The club went straight to the football authorities and won back two points from a game earlier in the season against São Paulo who had fielded an ineligible player. That meant that the small club Gama had to take the drop. Gama headed for the courts and was reinstated only to see FIFA ban the club from CBF leagues for having the temerity to resort to national courts rather than FIFA itself.

The deadlock was broken by the big clubs who organized a national championship – the monstrously complex 116-team Copa João Havelange – that began in 2000 with Gama and Botafogo both playing in the top division. Emblematic of the state of Brazilian football, a dreary, poorly attended championship culminated in a chaotic Final between Vasco and São Cáetano. Massive overcrowding in Vasco's stadium for the second leg led to a huge terrace crush, the game was abandoned and hundreds were injured.

While the emergency services attempted to deal with chaos at Vasco's São Januário stadium in the final play-off of the 2000 Brazilian championships, Eurico Miranda, Vasco president, tried to order ambulances and helicopters away, and demanded that the match be concluded. In a display of unabashed cynicism, he claimed the trophy as Vasco was leading when play was abandoned.

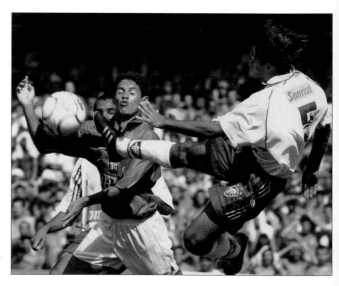

For all the fervour of Rio's big derby, neither Flamengo nor Fluminense have made a serious challenge on the Brazilian national championship for almost a decade, and both teams continue to disappoint their massive fan base.

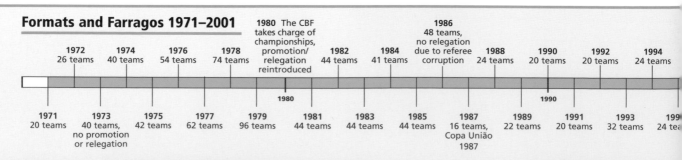

Formats and Farragos 1971–2001

1971 20 teams

1972 26 teams

1973 40 teams, no promotion or relegation

1974 40 teams

1975 42 teams

1976 54 teams

1977 62 teams

1978 74 teams

1979 96 teams

1980 The CBF takes charge of championships, promotion/ relegation reintroduced

1981 44 teams

1982 44 teams

1983 44 teams

1984 41 teams

1985 44 teams

1986 48 teams, no relegation due to referee corruption

1987 16 teams, Copa União 1987

1988 24 teams

1989 22 teams

1990 20 teams

1991 20 teams

1992 20 teams

1993 32 teams

1994 24 teams

1996 24 tea

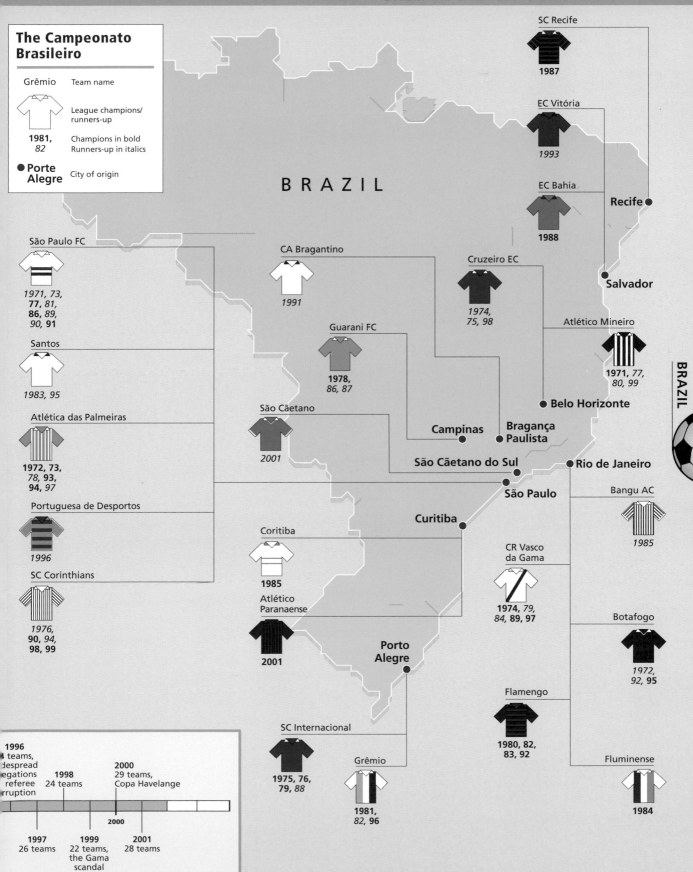

The Campeonato Brasileiro

Grêmio — Team name

League champions/runners-up

1981, 82 — Champions in bold / Runners-up in italics

● Porte Alegre — City of origin

B R A Z I L

SC Recife
1987

EC Vitória
1993

EC Bahia
1988

Recife ●

CA Bragantino
1991

Cruzeiro EC
1974, 75, 98

Salvador

São Paulo FC
1971, 73, **77,** *81,* **86,** *89, 90,* **91**

Guarani FC
1978, *86, 87*

Atlético Mineiro
1971, *77,* **80, 99**

Santos
1983, 95

São Cãetano
2001

Campinas ●

Belo Horizonte ●

Bragança Paulista ●

Atlética das Palmeiras
1972, 73, 78, 93, 94, *97*

São Cãetano do Sul

Rio de Janeiro ●

Portuguesa de Desportos
1996

São Paulo ●

Bangu AC
1985

SC Corinthians
1976, **90,** *94,* **98, 99**

Coritiba
1985

Atlético Paranaense
2001

Curitiba ●

CR Vasco da Gama
1974, *79,* **84, 89,** *97*

Botafogo
1972, **92,** *95*

Porto Alegre ●

Flamengo
1980, 82, 83, *92*

Fluminense
1984

SC Internacional
1975, 76, 79, *88*

Grêmio
1981, *82,* **96**

1996 4 teams, widespread allegations referee corruption
1997 26 teams
1998 24 teams
1999 22 teams, the Gama scandal
2000 29 teams, Copa Havelange
2001 28 teams

BRAZIL

Brazil

BRASIL

Confederação Brasileira de Futebol
Founded: 1914
Joined FIFA: 1923
Joined CONMEBOL: 1916

THE ORGANIZATION OF Brazilian football parallels the uneven geography of this enormous nation. League football began at state rather than national level. The Campeonata Paulista de Futebol began in São Paulo in 1901. Rio's league, the Liga Metropolitan de Football, followed in 1905. For the first half of the 20th century Brazilian football was dominated by these two leagues, and a series of inter-city cups established the effective national champions. Simultaneously, state leagues were established all over the country, with significant areas of footballing strength developing beyond Rio and São Paulo.

With the creation of the Copa Libertadores de América, the Taca do Brasil was established as a national cup competition to determine Brazil's entrants. It was discontinued in 1968, replaced first by the Taca de Prata (or Roberto Gomes Pedrosa Cup) and then by a fully-fledged national league in 1971. The formats of the latter have changed in a complex and Byzantine fashion to ensure, irrespective of performance, regular pay days for the biggest clubs. In 1989 a new national cup competition, the Copa do Brasil, was established with equally shifting formats and the winners also enter the Copa Libertadores alongside the national champions.

State leagues continue to run in the early part of the season ensuring an unrelenting schedule of football all year round.

São Paulo League Record 1902–2002

SEASON	CHAMPIONS	SEASON	CHAMPIONS
1902	São Paulo Athletic	1935	Santos/Portuguesa
1903	São Paulo Athletic	1936	Palestra Itália/Portuguesa
1904	São Paulo Athletic	1937	Corinthians
1905	Atlético Paulistano	1938	Corinthians
1906	Germania	1939	Corinthians
1907	Internacional	1940	Palestra Itália
1908	Atlético Paulistano	1941	Corinthians
1909	Atlética das Palmeiras	1942	Palmeiras
1910	Atlética das Palmeiras	1943	São Paulo
1911	São Paulo Athletic	1944	Palmeiras
1912	Americano	1945	São Paulo
1913	Americano/Atlético Paulista	1946	São Paulo
1914	Corinthians/Atlético São Bento	1947	Palmeiras
1915	Germania/Atlética das Palmeiras	1948	São Paulo
1916	Corinthians/Atlético Paulista	1949	São Paulo
1917	Atlético Paulistano	1950	Palmeiras
1918	Atlético Paulistano	1951	Corinthians
1919	Atlético Paulistano	1952	Corinthians
1920	Palestra Itália	1953	São Paulo
1921	Atlético Paulistano	1954	Corinthians
1922	Corinthians	1955	Santos
1923	Corinthians	1956	Santos
1924	Corinthians	1957	São Paulo
1925	Atlética São Bento	1958	Santos
1926	Palestra Itália/Atlético Paulista	1959	Palmeiras
1927	Palestra Itália/Atlético Paulista	1960	Santos
1928	Corinthians/Internacional	1961	Santos
1929	Corinthians/Atlético Paulista	1962	Santos
1930	Corinthians	1963	Palmeiras
1931	São Paulo	1964	Santos
1932	Palestra Itália	1965	Santos
1933	Palestra Itália	1966	Palmeiras
1934	Palestra Itália	1967	Santos

São Paulo League Record (*continued*)

SEASON	CHAMPIONS	SEASON	CHAMPIONS
1968	Santos	1987	São Paulo
1969	Santos	1988	Corinthians
1970	São Paulo	1989	São Paulo
1971	São Paulo	1990	Atlético Bragantino
1972	Palmeiras	1991	São Paulo
1973	Santos/Portuguesa	1992	São Paulo
1974	Palmeiras	1993	Palmeiras
1975	São Paulo	1994	Palmeiras
1976	Palmeiras	1995	Corinthians
1977	Corinthians	1996	Palmeiras
1978	Santos	1997	Corinthians
1979	Corinthians	1998	São Paulo
1980	São Paulo	1999	Corinthians
1981	São Paulo	2000	São Paulo
1982	Corinthians	2001	Corinthians
1983	Corinthians	2002	Ituano
1984	Santos		
1985	São Paulo		
1986	Atlética Internacional		

Rio League Record 1906–2002

SEASON	CHAMPIONS	SEASON	CHAMPIONS
1906	Fluminense	1950	Vasco da Gama
1907	Fluminense/Botafogo	1951	Fluminense
1908	Fluminense	1952	Vasco da Gama
1909	Fluminense	1953	Flamengo
1910	Botafogo	1954	Flamengo
1911	Fluminense	1955	Flamengo
1912	Botafogo/Paissandu	1956	Vasco da Gama
1913	América	1957	Botafogo
1914	Flamengo	1958	Vasco da Gama
1915	Flamengo	1959	Fluminense
1916	América	1960	América
1917	Fluminense	1961	Botafogo
1918	Fluminense	1962	Botafogo
1919	Fluminense	1963	Flamengo
1920	Flamengo	1964	Fluminense
1921	Flamengo	1965	Flamengo
1922	América	1966	Bangu Atlético
1923	Vasco da Gama	1967	Botafogo
1924	Vasco da Gama	1968	Botafogo
1925	Flamengo	1969	Fluminense
1926	São Cristovoa	1970	Vasco da Gama
1927	Flamengo	1971	Fluminense
1928	América	1972	Flamengo
1929	Vasco da Gama	1973	Fluminense
1930	Botafogo	1974	Flamengo
1931	América	1975	Fluminense
1932	Botafogo	1976	Fluminense
1933	Botafogo/Bangu Atlético	1977	Vasco da Gama
1934	Botafogo/Vasco da Gama	1978	Flamengo
1935	Botafogo/America	1979	Flamengo
1936	Fluminense	1979*	Flamengo
1937	Fluminense	1980	Fluminense
1938	Fluminense	1981	Flamengo
1939	Flamengo	1982	Vasco da Gama
1940	Fluminense	1983	Fluminense
1941	Fluminense	1984	Fluminense
1942	Flamengo	1985	Fluminense
1943	Flamengo	1986	Flamengo
1944	Flamengo	1987	Vasco da Gama
1945	Vasco da Gama	1988	Vasco da Gama
1946	Fluminense	1989	Botafogo
1947	Vasco da Gama	1990	Botafogo
1948	Botafogo	1991	Flamengo
1949	Vasco da Gama	1992	Vasco da Gama

BRAZIL

Rio League Record (*continued*)

SEASON	CHAMPIONS
1993	Vasco da Gama
1994	Vasco da Gama
1995	Fluminense
1996	Flamengo
1996*	Botafogo
1997	Botafogo
1998	Vasco da Gama

SEASON	CHAMPIONS
1999	Flamengo
2000	Flamengo
2001	Flamengo
2002	Fluminense

* Extra tournament.

Rio-São Paulo Tournament Record 1931–2002

SEASON	CHAMPIONS	RUNNERS-UP
1931	Palestra Itália	
1932–49	*no competition*	
1950	Corinthians	Vasco da Gama
1951	Palmeiras	Corinthians
1952	Portuguesa	Vasco da Gama
1953	Corinthians	Vasco da Gama
1954	Corinthians	Fluminense
1955	Portuguesa	Palmeiras
1956	*no competition*	
1957	Fluminense	Vasco da Gama
1958	Vasco da Gama	Flamengo
1959	Santos	Vasco da Gama
1960	Fluminense	Botafogo
1961	Flamengo	Palmeiras
1962	Botafogo	Palmeiras
1963	Santos	Corinthians
1964	Santos/Botafogo	
1965	Palmeiras	Portuguesa/São Paulo
1966	Corinthians/Santos/ Vasco da Gama/Botafogo	
1967–92	*no competition*	
1993	Palmeiras	Corinthians
1994–96	*no competition*	
1997	Santos	Flamengo
1998	Botafogo	São Paulo
1999	Vasco da Gama	Santos
2000	Palmeiras	Atlético Mineiro
2001	São Paulo	Botafogo
2002	Corinthians	São Paulo

Brazilian National Championship Record 1971–2001

SEASON	CHAMPIONS	RUNNERS-UP
1971	Atlético Mineiro	São Paulo
1972	Palmeiras	Botafogo
1973	Palmeiras	São Paulo
1974	Vasco da Gama	Cruzeiro
1975	Internacional	Cruzeiro
1976	Internacional	Corinthians
1977	São Paulo	Atlético Mineiro
1978	Guarani	Palmeiras
1979	Internacional	Vasco da Gama
1980	Flamengo	Atlético Mineiro
1981	Grêmio	São Paulo
1982	Flamengo	Grêmio
1983	Flamengo	Santos
1984	Fluminense	Vasco da Gama
1985	Coritiba	Bangu Atlético
1986	São Paulo	Guarani
1987	Sport Club Recife	Guarani
1988	Bahia	Internacional
1989	Vasco da Gama	São Paulo
1990	Corinthians	São Paulo
1991	São Paulo	Atlético Bragantino
1992	Flamengo	Botafogo
1993	Palmeiras	Vitória
1994	Palmeiras	Corinthians
1995	Botafogo	Santos

Brazilian National Championship Record (*continued*)

SEASON	CHAMPIONS	RUNNERS-UP
1996	Grêmio	Portuguesa
1997	Vasco da Gama	Palmeiras
1998	Corinthians	Cruzeiro
1999	Corinthians	Atlético Mineiro
2000	*no official championship*	
2001	Atlético Paranaense	São Cáetano

Brazilian National Championship Summary

TEAM	TOTALS	CHAMPIONS & RUNNERS-UP (BOLD) (*ITALICS*)
Palmeiras	**4**, *2*	**1972, 73,** *78,* **93, 94,** *97*
Flamengo	**4**, *0*	**1980, 82, 83, 92**
São Paulo	**3**, *5*	*1971, 73,* **77,** *81, 86, 89, 90,* **91**
Corinthians	**3**, *2*	*1976,* **90, 94, 98, 99**
Vasco da Gama	**3**, *2*	**1974,** *79, 84,* **89,** *97*
Internacional	**3**, *1*	**1975, 76, 79,** *88*
Grêmio	**2**, *1*	**1981,** *82,* **96**
Atlético Mineiro	**1**, *3*	**1971,** *77, 80, 99*
Botafogo	**1**, *2*	*1972,* **92,** *95*
Guarani	**1**, *2*	**1978,** *86, 87*
Atlético Paranaense	**1**, *0*	**2001**
Bahia	**1**, *0*	**1988**
Coritiba	**1**, *0*	**1985**
Fluminense	**1**, *0*	**1984**
Sport Club Recife	**1**, *0*	**1987**

This summary only features clubs that have won the Brazilian National Championship. For a full list of league champions and runners-up please see the League Record above.

Copa do Brasil Record 1989–2002

YEAR	WINNERS	SCORE	RUNNERS-UP
1989	Grêmio	**0-0, 2-1** (2 legs)	Sport Club Recife
1990	Flamengo	**1-0, 0-0** (2 legs)	Goias
1991	Criciuma	**1-1, 0-0** (2 legs)	Grêmio
1992	Internacional	**1-2, 1-0** (2 legs)	Fluminense
1993	Cruzeiro	**0-0, 2-1** (2 legs)	Grêmio
1994	Grêmio	**0-0, 1-0** (2 legs)	Ceara
1995	Corinthians	**2-1, 1-0** (2 legs)	Grêmio
1996	Cruzeiro	**1-1, 2-1** (2 legs)	Palmeiras
1997	Grêmio	**0-0, 2-2** (2 legs)	Flamengo
1998	Palmeiras	**0-1, 2-0** (2 legs)	Cruzeiro
1999	Juventude	**2-1, 0-0** (2 legs)	Botafogo
2000	Cruzeiro	**0-0, 2-1** (2 legs)	São Paulo
2001	Grêmio	**2-2, 3-1** (2 legs)	Corinthians
2002	Corinthians	**2-1, 1-1** (2 legs)	Brasiliense

Copa do Brasil Summary

TEAM	TOTALS	WINNERS & RUNNERS-UP (BOLD) (*ITALICS*)
Grêmio	**4**, *3*	**1989,** *91,* **93, 94, 95,** *97,* **2001**
Cruzeiro	**3**, *1*	**1993,** *96,* **98, 2000**
Corinthians	**2**, *1*	**1995,** *2001,* **02**
Flamengo	**1**, *1*	**1990,** *97*
Palmeiras	**1**, *1*	*1996,* **98**
Criciuma	**1**, *0*	**1991**
Internacional	**1**, *0*	**1992**
Juventude	**1**, *0*	**1999**
Botafogo	**0**, *1*	*1999*
Brasiliense	**0**, *1*	*2002*
Ceara	**0**, *1*	*1994*
Fluminense	**0**, *1*	*1992*
Goias	**0**, *1*	*1990*
São Paulo	**0**, *1*	*2000*
Sport Club Recife	**0**, *1*	*1989*

BRAZIL

Argentina

THE SEASON IN REVIEW 2001–02

TO THE OUTSIDE WORLD, Argentinian football looked in a healthy state. The national team qualified for the 2002 World Cup in imperious style, head and shoulders above the rest of the Latin American qualifying group. In international club competitions, San Lorenzo won the last edition of the made-for-TV Copa Mercosur, while Boca Juniors made it two Copa Libertadores in a row. But domestically the game is in the grip of a financial crisis that has been deepened and exposed by the cataclysmic state of the wider Argentinian economy. The season began with the serious threat of a players' strike over massive levels of unpaid wages, only narrowly averted in a deal brokered by the Argentinian FA.

With every single Argentinian first division club (except Colón from Santa Fé) in serious debt, it was fitting that the biggest debtors of them all, Racing Club, a club technically bankrupt for the last two years, should win the Apertura. With debts of over £43 million, the courts held Racing in limbo until Fernando Marin, owner of legal firm Blanquiceleste, stepped in, took over the debts and began clearing out the stables. With a hard-working team that cost virtually nothing to put together, Racing took an early lead that it never relinquished. As the Apertura reached its climax, Argentina officially defaulted on all its foreign loans, and the value of the peso (previously tied to the dollar) plummeted. Football clubs' debts, many denominated in

Apertura League Table 2001–02

CLUB	P	W	D	L	F	A	Pts
Racing Club	19	12	6	1	34	17	42
River Plate	19	12	5	2	51	16	41
Boca Juniors	19	9	6	4	41	27	33
Colón	19	8	8	3	24	16	32
San Lorenzo	19	8	7	4	28	22	31
Estudiantes	19	7	6	6	27	28	27
Gimnasia LP	19	7	6	6	30	35	27
Chacarita Juniors	19	6	8	5	24	22	26
Belgrano	19	6	8	5	17	18	26
Independiente	19	7	5	7	26	28	26
Argentinos Juniors	19	7	4	8	22	27	25
Lanús	19	7	4	8	21	28	25
Nueva Chicago	19	7	3	9	26	33	24
Newell's Old Boys	19	6	5	8	29	28	23
Vélez Sarsfield	19	5	7	7	27	30	22
Rosario Central	19	5	5	9	18	26	20
Unión	19	3	9	7	23	25	18
Banfield	19	4	6	9	16	25	18
Huracán	19	3	5	11	22	39	14
Talleres	19	4	1	14	18	37	13

Apertura Top Goalscorers

PLAYER	CLUB	GOALS
Martin Cardetti	River Plate	17
Diego Forlán	Independiente	11
Facundo Sava	Gimnasia LP	11
Ernesto Farías	Estudiantes LP	10
Estaban Cambiasso	River Plate	9

Right: The 35-year wait. The Racing Club players celebrate their goal, away to Vélez Sarsfield, which gave them the final point needed to take the club's first national championship in 35 years.

Right, bottom corner: Martin Cardetti, top scorer in the Apertura, but not enough to take the title.

Right: River's 6-1 final day victory against Rosario Central in the Apertura was imposing but ultimately fruitless.

The tear gas from January's economic riots clears long enough for Avellaneda, home of Racing Club, to celebrate.

ARGENTINA

dollars, instantly rose. As the savings and incomes of the Argentinian middle-classes evaporated, rioting and protest broke out on the streets of Buenos Aires and other provincial cities. The government fell and over 20 people were killed. It looked for a moment as if the football season could not be concluded, but the decisive games of the final day of the Apertura were brought forward: Racing at Vélez Sarsfield and River Plate at Rosario Central. River hammered Rosario 6-1, atoning for the team's lax and inconsistent form earlier on in the season. Racing grabbed the point it needed in front of 50,000 ecstatic fans at Vélez and 40,000 more watching screens at its own ground. The club's first title in 35 years saw an eruption of street parties and celebrations in the streets of Avellaneda.

The Clausura did eventually begin on time, but neither financial problems nor violence abated. All the clubs laboured under massive financial constraints, made worse by the diminishing sponsorship and advertising revenue available in a rapidly declining economy. San Lorenzo's plight was so bad that the entire squad was put up for sale and the courts filled with players demanding unpaid wages. Boca-River derbies continued to be unnerving and unpredictable encounters. In January, at a friendly played at the José Maria Minella Stadium in La Plata, River supporters burst into the Boca end intent on stealing their opponents' flags; in minutes a pitched battle was raging, seats were flying and the game was abandoned. A number of cases of knife wounds were reported afterwards and the police dispersed the 50,000 crowd with volleys of tear gas. In February, at the Avellaneda derby between Racing and Independiente, one fan was shot and one stabbed as opposing groups conducted running battles in the street. Inside the ground, play was delayed after a smoke bomb was thrown at Racing's keeper. When Racing met Boca, the game was abandoned with one minute to go, with Racing leading 2-1 and suddenly awarded a penalty. A hail of missiles exploded from the Boca fans and the game was stopped.

On the pitch, River Plate seemed to find new reserves of energy and led from the front, with decisive derby victories against Racing and Boca. Following a late slip to lowly Lanús, Fernando Cavenaghi (top scorer in the Clausura) hit a hat-trick as River destroyed Argentinos Juniors 5-1 to take the Clausura with a game to spare. It was River's coach Ramon Diaz's seventh title with the club. How many of the squad will remain to contest another with him next year remains to be seen.

International Club Performances 2001–02

CLUB	COMPETITION	PROGRESS
Boca Juniors	Copa Libertadores 2001	Champions
	Copa Mercosur 2001	Group Stage
River Plate	Copa Libertadores 2001	Quarter-finals
	Copa Mercosur 2001	Group Stage
Rosario Central	Copa Libertadores 2001	Semi-finals
San Lorenzo	Copa Libertadores 2001	Group Stage
	Copa Mercosur 2001	Champions
Vélez Sarsfield	Copa Libertadores 2001	Group Stage
	Copa Mercosur 2001	Group Stage
Independiente	Copa Mercosur 2001	Quarter-finals

Clausura League Table 2001–02

CLUB	P	W	D	L	F	A	Pts
River Plate	18	12	4	2	36	11	40
Gimnasia LP	18	11	3	4	31	21	36
Boca Juniors	18	9	5	4	25	17	32
Huracán	18	9	2	7	25	22	29
Racing Club	18	8	5	5	19	17	29
Newell's Old Boys	18	8	4	6	26	24	28
Banfield	18	7	6	5	19	18	27
San Lorenzo	18	6	8	4	23	19	26
Estudiantes LP	18	6	6	6	30	26	24
Vélez Sarsfield	18	6	5	7	26	20	23
Colón	18	6	5	7	24	23	23
Lanús	18	5	8	5	18	18	23
Nueva Chicago	18	5	6	7	14	20	21
Rosario Central	18	5	5	8	18	23	20
Unión	18	5	5	8	20	27	20
Argentinos Juniors	18	5	5	8	20	30	20
Chacarita Juniors	18	4	8	6	21	22	20
Belgrano	18	5	3	10	15	22	18
Talleres	18	5	1	12	12	29	16
Independiente	18	3	6	9	13	26	15

Relegated teams: Argentinos Juniors, Belgrano.
Promoted teams: Arsenal, Olimpia.

Clausura Top Goalscorers

PLAYER	CLUB	GOALS
Fernando Cavenaghi	River Plate	15
Facunda Sava	Independiente	12
Ernesto Farías	Estudiantes LP	11
Josemir Lujambio	Banfield	11
Daniel Montenegro	Huracán	11

Right: Massera of Gimnasia La Plata tries to get past Colotto of Unión from Santa Fé. Second spot in the Clausura was Gimnasia's best performance for some time.

Right: Ariel Ortega atop a hillock of River Plate players, celebrating the team's awesome victory in the Clausura over Boca Juniors at Boca's seemingly impregnable Bombonera.

Top left: *Fabricio Fuentes of Vélez Sarsfield (right) and Alberto Acosta of San Lorenzo fight for the ball. It was a miserable season for Vélez. The big Buenos Aries club had mid-table finishes, suffered an early exit from the Copa Libertadores and admitted mounting unpaid bills.*

Top right: *A hail of missiles, coins and who knows what strike players and officials alike in the Boca v Racing game. The referee bends down to examine the offending projectiles.*

Above: *Juan Riquelme knows that Boca's season and his World Cup chances are diminishing as an ankle injury takes its toll.*

Left: *Claudio Graf of Colón from Santa Fé steps over Muñoz of Talleres – prudence does pay, as Colón, the only financially solvent club in Argentina, finished fourth in the Apertura – a fantastic performance.*

ARGENTINA

Association Football in Argentina

1860s: British sailors bring football to Buenos Aires — 1860

1865: Buenos Aires Football Club (now defunct) founded — 1865

1870

1875

1880

1887: Quilmes and Gimnasia y Esgrima (La Plata) (oldest surviving clubs) founded — 1885

1890

1891: First championship played in Buenos Aires

1893: Argentine Association Football League first played — 1895

1900

1901: First international, v Uruguay, won 3-2, venue: Montevideo — 1905

1906: First provincial league formed: Liga Santiaguena de Futbol — 1910

1912: Rival Federacion Argentina de Football League set up — 1915
Affiliation to FIFA

1920

1914: Federacion Argentina de Football League disbanded — 1925

1916: Affiliation to CONMEBOL — 1930

1919: Associacion Amateurs founded as separate league in Buenos Aires — 1935

1926: Last season of Associacion Amateurs — 1940

1931: Professionalism introduced and professional league established — 1945

1950

1948: Players' strike: mass exodus of professionals to Colombia — 1955

1960

1967: National and Metropolitan (Buenos Aires) championships run in same season — 1965 / 1970

1975

1978: Argentina win World Cup in Buenos Aires — 1980

1985

1986: Single national championship established — 1990

1992: National championship shifts to Apertura and Clausura format — 1995

2000

2005

Argentina celebrates as Mario Kempes scores to give Argentina the lead during extra time in the 1978 World Cup Final in Buenos Aires.

International Competitions

Year	International Competitions	Copa Libertadores	Copa CONMEBOL	Copa Mercosur
1910:	● ■			
1916:	▲ ■			
1917:	▲			
1920:	▲			
1921:	● ■			
1923:	▲			
1924:	▲			
1925:	● ■			
1926:	●			
1927:	●			
1929:	● ■			
1930:	▲			
1935:	▲			
1937:	● ■			
1941:	●			
1942:	▲			
1945:	●			
1946:	● ■			
1947:	● ■			
1955:	●			
1957:	●			
1959*:	● ▲ ■			
1963:		△ Boca		
1964:		○ Indep		
1965:		○ Indep		
1966:		△ River		
1967:	▲	○ Racing		
1968:		○ Estud		
1969:		○ Estud		
1970:		○ Estud		
1971:		△ Estud		
1972:		○ Indep		
1973:		○ Indep		
1974:		○ Indep		
1975:		○ Indep		
1976:		△ River		
1977:		○ Boca		
1978:	● ■	○ Boca		
1979:		△ Boca		
1984:		○ Indep		
1985:		○ Argen		
1986:	●	○ River		
1987:	■			
1988:		△ Newell		
1990:	▲			
1991:	●	△ Newell		
1992:				
1993:	●			
1994:		○ Vélez		
1995:		○ River	○ Rosario	
1996:			○ Lanús	
1997:			△ Lanús	
1998:			△ Rosario	
2000:		○ Boca		
2001:		○ Boca		

Key

- 📷 International football
- ⚽ Affiliation to FIFA
- ⚽ Affiliation to CONMEBOL
- ■ World Cup host
- ● World Cup winner
- ▲ World Cup runner-up
- ■ Copa América host
- ● Copa América winner
- ▲ Copa América runner-up
- ○ Competition winner
- △ Competition runner-up
- * An extra unofficial tournament was held in 1959. See pages 370–71

- Argen – Argentinos Juniors
- Boca – CA Boca Juniors
- Estud – CA Estudiantes
- Indep – CA Independiente
- Newell – CA Newell's Old Boys
- River – CA River Plate
- Rosario – CA Rosario Central
- Racing – Racing Club
- Vélez – Vélez Sarsfield
- Lanús – CA Lanús

Gimnasia y Esgrima 1930

JUJUY (1975)

San Salvador de JuJuy

SALTA (1921)

Salta

CATAMARCA

TUCUMÁN (1919)

San Miguel de Tucumán

SANTIAGO DEL ESTERO (1906)

Rafaela Atlético Rafaela 1907

SANT... FÉ

LA RIOJA (1919)

CÓRDOBA (1913)

SAN JUAN (1922)

San Juan San Martín 1907

Córdoba

Rosario

Pergamino Douglas Haig 1918

MENDOZA (1922)

Godoy Cruz Godoy Cruz Antonio Tomba 1921

Florencio Varela Defensa y Justicia

Lomas de Zam... CA Los Andes 191...

LA PAMPA (1926)

Junín

Olavarría

Bahia Blanca Olimpo 1910

NEUQUÉN

Cipolletti Club Cipolletti 1926

RÍO NEGRO (1985)

CHUBUT

ARGENTINA

★ CA Estudiantes 1905

Split from Gimnasia y Esgrima

★ Vélez Sarsfield 1910

CA All Boys 1913

SANTA CRUZ

CA Español 1956

★ Racing Club 1903

Argentina

ORIGINS AND GROWTH OF FOOTBALL

IN THE LAST QUARTER of the 19th century, Buenos Aires had a vibrant British community of around 40,000 people, with their own network of banks, schools and social events. It was in this outpost of Britain's informal empire that Buenos Aires Football Club was founded in 1867. Around 1880, Alexander Watson Hutton arrived to teach at St Andrew's Scottish School. In 1884, he founded his own English high school, hired a games master and started football both there and at other schools in the city. A championship was first played between these teams in 1891. In 1893, under Hutton's leadership, five clubs founded the Argentine Association Football League, a championship which has continued unbroken to the present day.

The growth of the sport was rapid. By 1901, the AAFL were organizing four divisions in Buenos Aires alone. Outside the capital the first club was Lobos Athletic (1892), while Newell's Old Boys (1903) and Rosario Central (1905) established football in Rosario, Argentina's second city. Regular internationals with Uruguay across the River Plate began in 1901. In the first decade of the 20th century football became progressively less British and more Argentinian. The biggest clubs (Racing, Boca and River Plate) emerged from immigrant and indigenous groups. The AFA began to publish rules in Spanish. The transition of power and influence became clear when the annual match between Argentinos and Británicos saw Británicos lose 5-1, a defeat from which it never recovered.

The national organization of football was bedevilled by successive splits (1912–14, 1919–27) and the formation of alternative national organizations and rival leagues. Matters were settled due to pressure from the onset of professionalism, the need to stop the best players going to play in Italy, and the need to rationalize impossibly large leagues and uneven competition between clubs. In 1931, a national professional league of 18 big clubs was established.

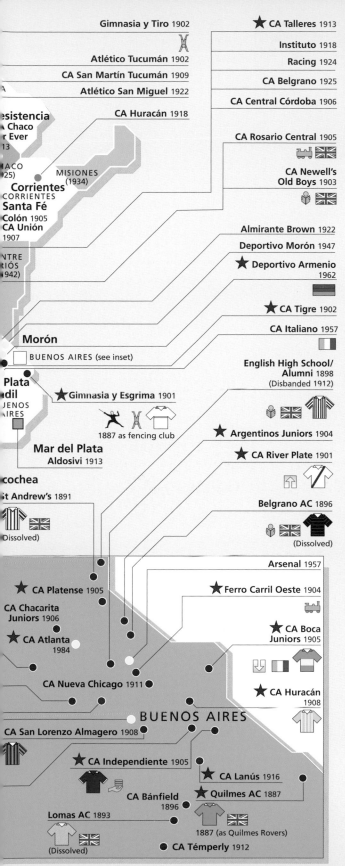

Argentina: The main clubs

Colón 1905	Team name with year of formation		Pre-professional champions
●	Club formed before 1912		Armenian origins
●	Club formed 1912–25		British origins
●	Club formed 1925–50		French origins
○	Club formed after 1950		Italian origins
JUJUY (1975)	State (year of Championship foundation)		Spanish origins
			Railway workers
	Founded 1900–10		Originated from a fencing club
	Founded 1901–20		Originated from a gymnastics club
	Founded 1920–50		Originated from a school
	Founded 1950–80		Shop workers
	Founded 1980–95		Elite
	No championship		Working class
□	City with regional league (colour coded as above)		Colours unknown
★	Founder members of pre-professional league		

Buenos Aires

FOOTBALL CITY

SOME OF THE HISTORY OF BUENOS AIRES can be seen in the pattern and density of the football clubs that stud this enormous city of over 11 million people. In the 1860s, Buenos Aires had a population of just 170,000, of whom maybe 40,000 were Britons organizing and servicing a massive wave of British investment in Argentina. Schools, colleges, social and athletics clubs sprung up. As early as 1867, a British Buenos Aires Football Club had been set up, only to switch to rugby in 1887. The arrival of Alexander Watson Hutton at St. Andrews Scottish School in 1882, and at the English High School in 1884, was a catalyst. Teams at his schools began to play old boys clubs, and in 1891 a local championship was held. It was repeated in 1893 and has been played ever since.

The decline of British influence

In the following decade, dozens of British clubs appeared all over the city, some beginning to attract spectators. But in 1901, an Argentinian fencing and gymnastic club in La Plata – Argentina's new administrative centre to the south of Buenos Aires – formed a football section. Although the league was still dominated by British teams like Alumni, Lomas Athletic and Belgrano, the shift to Spanish-speaking players and Argentinian teams gathered pace quickly. The city's biggest clubs were founded in a few short years: River Plate in 1901, Racing Club in 1903, Boca Juniors and Independiente in 1905. By 1912, the AFA was using Spanish, and Alumni, for one, had disbanded.

Simultaneously, Buenos Aires grew explosively. By 1914, it had grown almost ten-fold with 1.5 million inhabitants, and it has barely stopped since. Its regular, grid-like structure created a series of neighbourhoods with clear boundaries, which have often been populated with specific immigrant groups or social classes, and every neighbourhood has acquired its own football team. The names speak for themselves: Deportivo Italiano, Deportivo Armenio, Deportivo Español, the list goes on. Everything about Buenos Aires' development was accelerated. British teams, including Southampton, Nottingham Forest, Tottenham and Everton, were regularly touring the city before the First World War. International matches with Uruguay were played regularly, and the first informal South American championship was held in the city in 1910.

The big city teams

The 1920s were consumed by the struggle over payments and professionalism until, in 1931, a professional league was established and the biggest teams in the city came to define and dominate the game. River Plate and Boca Juniors were both founded in Boca, the poor docks area in the city centre. River, which was formed from the merger of Santa Rosa and Rosales, migrated north and settled in the Retiro district of the city, acquiring a mass following with a distinctly elite tone. Boca, founded by an Irishman and a group of Italian students, has stayed close to its roots in the district. Alternately the two strongest teams through this era, their derby matches remain the highpoint of the city's season. Further south in the industrial zone of Avellaneda, Racing Club and Independiente play the city's other major derby. Independiente was founded by employees of the City of London department store.

The Avenida 9 Julio is Buenos Aires' main thoroughfare. The spiritual home of Argentinian football since the 1860s, the city houses some 30 professional football teams.

Buenos Aires

30,000	Capacity of stadium
	Team colours
M1	Motorway
A82	Major road
1900	Champions
2000	Runners-up

CIUDAD DE
VINCENTE LÓPEZ

31,000

Platense

MUNRO

CIUDAD DE
CASEROS

18,500

...udiantes

BUENOS
AIRES

SEE CENTRAL BUENOS AIRES
FOR MORE DETAIL

Buenos Aires, *together with Montevideo across the mouth of the River Plate, is the cradle of football in South America. It was in these two great cities that the first South American international matches took place in the early years of the 20th century.*

ARGENTINA

RIO DE LA
PLATA

DON BOSCO

QUILMES

CENTENÁRIO

32,000

Quilmes

BERAZATEGUI

CA Banfield

FLORENCIO
SOLÁ

16,500

Talleres

30,000

TALLERES

EDUARDO
GALLARDÓN

FRAGATA
SARMIENTO

35,000

10,000

MONTE
GRANDE

Los Andes

CD Italiano

**Almirante
Brown**

JOSÉ
MARÍA EZEIZA

LONGCHAMPS

GLEW

...RISTÁN
...JÁREZ

GIMNASIA Y ESGRIMA 1901

Amateur League (1891–1930)	**1929**
FAF League (1912–14)	*1913*
AAF League (1919–26)	*1924*
Apertura League (1992–2002)	*1999*
Clausura League (1992–2002)	*1995, 96, 2002*

ESTUDIANTES LA PLATA 1905

Amateur League (1891–1930)	*1919, 30*
FAF League (1912–14)	**1913**, *14*
Metropolitan League (1967–85)	**1967**, *68*, **82**
National League (1967–85)	*1967, 75*, **83**
Copa Libertadores	**1968–70**, *71*
Copa Interamerica	**1969**
World Club Cup	**1968**, *69, 70*

**Gimnasia y
Esgrima**

11

JUAN CARLOS
ZERILLO

20,401

ENSENADA

VILLA
ELISA

**Estudiantes
La Plata**

LUIS JORGE
HIRSCHI

26,000

LA PLATA

QUILMES 1887

Amateur League (1891–1930)	*1895*, **1912**
Metropolitan League (1967–85)	**1978**
National League (1967–85)	*1982*

Racing, who took the name of a Parisian team of the time, was founded by French immigrants and attracted a well-heeled fan base that included the Peron family, a connection that took them all the way to the top, winning three championships in a row between 1949 and 1951.

Corruption rears its head

Argentina's long economic decline saw the city's leading clubs accumulate significant debts. In 1967, the government baled them out, but at the price of reorganizing the season and introducing provincial clubs from Rosario and Sante Fé into the competition. Under the Military Junta (1976–83), the city's clubs became more closely enmeshed with political factions in the government. On the bright side, a major clean up and stadium renovation programme was carried out in the run up to the 1978 World Cup. However, the economy has continued to falter, and the problem of massive corruption continues to plague the city's teams, while the spread of poverty fuels the criminal gangs that now run the clubs' *ultra* fan groups.

La Boca, once a poor area around the city's docks and the original home of both Boca Juniors and River Plate, is now an attractive and bohemian artists' quarter which attracts tourists by the thousand.

ESTADIO DR CAMILO CICHERO, LA BOMBONERA

58,750

Club: Boca Juniors
Built: 1940
Original Capacity: 60,000
Rebuilt: 1949–53, 1995

ESTADIO ANTONIO VESPUCIO LIBERTI DE NUNEZ, 'MONUMENTAL'

76,689

Clubs: River Plate, Argentina
Built: 1938
Original Capacity: 100,000, Argentina v Brazil, Copa América, 4 April 1959
Rebuilt: 1973
Significant Matches: Copa América: 1959, 87; 1978 World Cup

CENTRAL BUENOS AIRES

Chacarita Juniors

GUTIERREZ

23,000

Parque Sarmiento

DEFENSOR DE BELGRANO

8,500

Belgrano

Avenida Cabildo

Avenida Crisólogo Larralde

Avenida Forest

CHACARITA JUNIORS 1906	
Metropolitan League (1967–85)	1969

ARGENTINOS JUNIORS 1904	
Amateur League (1891–1930)	1926
Metropolitan League (1967–85)	1980, 84
National League (1967–85)	1985
Copa Libertadores	1985
Copa Interamerica	1986
World Club Cup	1985

HUMBOL

12,000

Atlan

BOYACA

Vélez Sarsfield

JOSE AMALFITANI 'EL FORTIN'

49,806

Constructed on a lagoon filled with the rubble of the railway industry

CA All Boys

12,000

ISLAS MALVINAS

Neuva Chicago

NUEVA CHICAGO

28,500

In the early 20th century, this area was home to Argentina's meat-packing industry, which rivalled that of Chicago. The area was quickly populated by immigrants

Avenida Bo

Avenida Nazca

Av. San Pedrito

Avenida Rivadavia

Autopista Perito Moreno

Avenida Eva Peron

Autopista Luis J. Dellepiane

NUEVA ESPAÑA

32,500

CD Espa

Parque Almirante Guillerm Brown

VÉLEZ SARSFIELD 1910	
AAF League (1919–26)	1919
Argentine League (1931–66, 86–91)	1953
Metropolitan League (1967–85)	1971, 79
National League (1967–85)	**1968**, 85
Apertura League (1992–2002)	1994, 96
Clausura League (1992–2002)	1992, 93, 96, 98
Copa Libertadores	**1994**
Copa Interamerica	**1996**
Supercopa	**1996**
World Club Cup	**1994**

SAN LORENZO 1908	
Amateur League (1891–1930)	**1927**
AAF League (1919–26)	**1923, 24, 25, 26**
Argentine League (1931–66, 86–91)	*1931, 33, 36, 41, 42,* **46, 57, 59, 61, 88**
Metropolitan League (1967–85)	**1968,** 72, 83
National League (1967–85)	*1971,* 72, 74
Apertura League (1992–2002)	*1995*
Clausura League (1992–2002)	**1995, 2001**

ARGENTINA

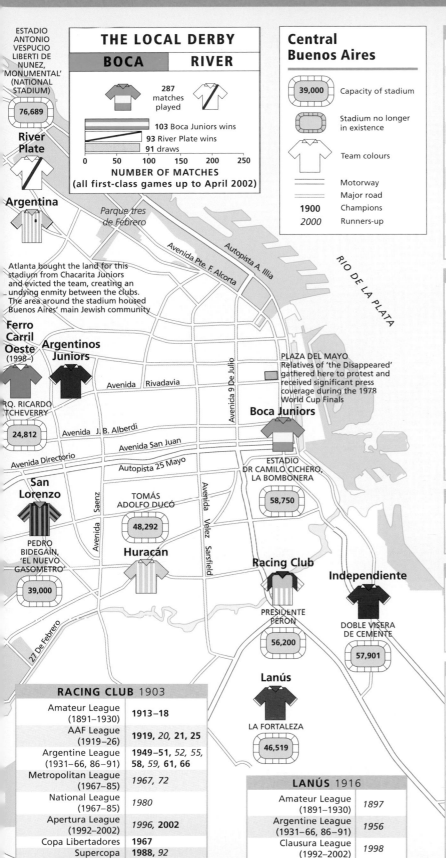

THE LOCAL DERBY

| BOCA | RIVER |

287 matches played

103 Boca Juniors wins
93 River Plate wins
91 draws

NUMBER OF MATCHES
(all first-class games up to April 2002)

0 50 100 150 200 250

Central Buenos Aires

39,000 — Capacity of stadium

Stadium no longer in existence

Team colours

Motorway

Major road

1900 Champions

2000 Runners-up

ESTADIO ANTONIO VESPUCIO LIBERTI DE NUNEZ, 'MONUMENTAL' (NATIONAL STADIUM)

76,689

River Plate

Argentina

Parque tres de Febrero

Atlanta bought the land for this stadium from Chacarita Juniors and evicted the team, creating an undying enmity between the clubs. The area around the stadium housed Buenos Aires' main Jewish community

Ferro Carril Oeste (1998–)

Argentinos Juniors

RQ. RICARDO TCHEVERRY

24,812

Avenida Pte. F. Alcorta
Autopista A. Illia
RIO DE LA PLATA

Avenida Rivadavia
Avenida J. B. Alberdi
Avenida San Juan
Avenida Directorio
Autopista 25 Mayo

Avenida 9 De Julio
Avenida Saenz
Avenida Velez Sarsfield

San Lorenzo

PEDRO BIDEGAIN, 'EL NUEVO GASOMETRO'

39,000

TOMÁS ADOLFO DUCÓ

48,292

Huracán

27 De Febrero

Boca Juniors

ESTADIO DR CAMILO CICHERO, LA BOMBONERA

58,750

PLAZA DEL MAYO
Relatives of 'the Disappeared' gathered here to protest and received significant press coverage during the 1978 World Cup Finals

Racing Club

PRESIDENTE PÉRON

56,200

Independiente

DOBLE VISERA DE CEMENTE

57,901

Lanús

LA FORTALEZA

46,519

ARGENTINA

RIVER PLATE 1901

Amateur League (1891–1930)	*1909, 17, 18*
AAF League (1919–26)	**1920,** *21, 22*
Argentine League (1931–66, 86–91)	**1932, 36, 37,** *38, 39,* **41, 42,** *43,* **44, 45, 47, 48, 49, 52, 53, 55–57,** *60,* **62, 63,** *65,* **66,** *86,* **90**
Metropolitan League (1967–85)	**1969, 70, 75, 77, 79, 80**
National League (1967–85)	*1968,* **69,** *72, 73,* **75, 76,** *78,* **79, 81, 84**
Apertura League (1992–2002)	**1992,** *93,* **94, 95, 97, 98, 2000,** *01, 02*
Clausura League (1992–2002)	**1997,** *99,* **2000,** *01, 02*
Copa Libertadores	*1966, 76,* **86, 96**
Copa Interamerica	**1987**
Supercopa	*1991,* **97**
World Club Cup	**1986,** *96*

BOCA JUNIORS 1905

Amateur League (1891–1930)	**1919, 20, 23, 24, 26,** *27–29,* **30**
Argentine League (1931–66, 86–91)	**1931,** *33,* **34, 35, 40, 43, 44,** *45–47,* **50, 54, 58,** *62,* **64, 65,** *89,* **91**
Metropolitan League (1967–85)	*1973, 76, 78,* **81**
National League (1967–85)	**1969, 70, 76**
Apertura League (1992–2002)	*1992, 93,* **98, 99, 2001**
Clausura League (1992–2002)	**1999**
Copa Libertadores	*1963,* **77, 78,** *79,* **2000,** *01*
Copa Interamerica	*1978*
Supercopa	**1989,** *94*
World Club Cup	**1977, 2000,** *01*

FERRO CARRIL OESTE 1904

Metropolitan League (1967–85)	*1981, 84*
National League (1967–85)	*1981,* **82, 84**

HURACÁN 1908

Amateur League (1891–1930)	**1921, 22,** *23, 25,* **28**
Metropolitan League (1967–85)	**1973,** *75, 76*
Clausura League (1992–2002)	*1994*

INDEPENDIENTE 1905

FAF League (1912–14)	*1912*
AAF League (1919–26)	**1922,** *23,* **26**
Argentine League (1931–66, 86–91)	*1932, 34, 35, 37,* **38, 39, 40, 48,** *54,* **60, 63, 64,** *89,* **90**
Metropolitan League (1967–85)	**1970, 71,** *77, 82, 83*
National League (1967–85)	**1967,** *77, 78, 83*
Apertura League (1992–2002)	*1997*
Clausura League (1992–2002)	*1993,* **94,** *2000*
Copa Libertadores	**1964, 65, 72–75, 84**
Copa Interamerica	**1973, 74, 76**
Supercopa	**1989,** *94,* **95**
World Club Cup	**1964, 65, 72,** *73, 74,* **84**

RACING CLUB 1903

Amateur League (1891–1930)	**1913–18**
AAF League (1919–26)	**1919,** *20, 21,* **25**
Argentine League (1931–66, 86–91)	**1949–51,** *52, 55,* **58, 59,** *61,* **66**
Metropolitan League (1967–85)	*1967, 72*
National League (1967–85)	*1980*
Apertura League (1992–2002)	*1996,* **2002**
Copa Libertadores	**1967**
Supercopa	**1988,** *92*
World Club Cup	**1967**

LANÚS 1916

Amateur League (1891–1930)	*1897*
Argentine League (1931–66, 86–91)	*1956*
Clausura League (1992–2002)	*1998*
Copa CONMEBOL	**1996,** *97*

Argentina

FANS AND OWNERS

ARGENTINA'S CLUBS ARE IN CRISIS. With the exception of Colón from Santa Fé, every single club in the Argentinian first division (2001–02) is in debt. With the massive devaluation of the Peso and the emergency changes to banking in Argentina, these debts have become larger, though exactly how large nobody knows. Players and creditors go regularly unpaid, and at both national and club level players' strikes and lawsuits have been endemic. Yet money has still been flooding into the clubs. Player sales, overwhelmingly to Europe, have earned the clubs over half a billion dollars since 1975 ($360 million of which has been made in the last five years), television deals have improved massively, and although attendances have passed their peak, they are still significant.

So where has the money gone? Mostly it has been spent on massive, ludicrously paid squads, and been lost to corruption and skimming on all the transfers by club officials and agents. Racing Club was the first to collapse under the weight of debt, declaring bankruptcy in 2000, and allowed by government fiat to keep playing and trading until a private buyer could be found. Although still in debt, Racing, now owned by Fernando Marin and his company Blanquiceleste, is on an upward financial and footballing curve, while San Lorenzo, Boca and River Plate are all over $30 million in debt. These big clubs remain in the hands of small cliques of members and are constantly prey to internal feuding and struggles over elected officials. Some, like Boca, continue to count wealthy patrons among their boards, but most are administratively and financially crippled. The absence of transparent financial accounts from these murky institutions means that the data available on levels of debt is likely to underestimate the difficulties of Argentinian clubs.

The *barra bravas*

Another place that the money has gone is to the *barra bravas* – the organized supporters clubs attached to every team. The *barras* emerged in the 1950s as a combination of local street gangs and die-hard fans. Their fearsome and noisy displays at the stadiums and their small-scale criminal organization made them perfect vehicles for manipulation by club officials. An understanding between the two saw the *barras* at each club's disposal when it required its own players and coaches controlled, and when votes were required in the fierce politicking during elections for club boards. In return, the *barras* received match tickets (often resold) and cash. As a consequence, a lot of the data available on attendances needs to be scrutinized carefully. Free tickets are not recorded in the data, and indeed some of the sales of cheaper seats go unrecorded.

The older leadership of the *barras* began to disappear in the 1990s, when firearms, flares, noise bombs and drugs became standard equipment. *Barra* groups now have less to do with football and have become a network of career professionals, providing income for poor urban men with an interest in organized crime. The gangs regularly hijack buses to go to games, fleecing fans and food-sellers on the way, and shootings near grounds have become a regular feature of the weekend's fixtures. The clubs, police and judiciary have been slow to act and, while CCTV in the top division is bringing some change, the violence seems to be migrating to the lower divisions.

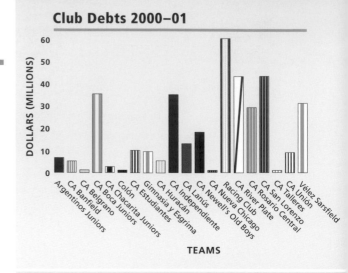

Club Debts 2000–01

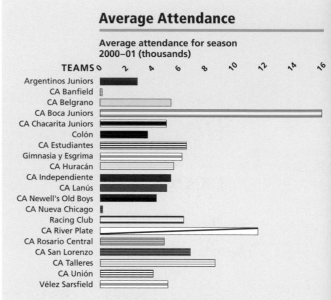

Average Attendance

Average attendance for season 2000–01 (thousands)

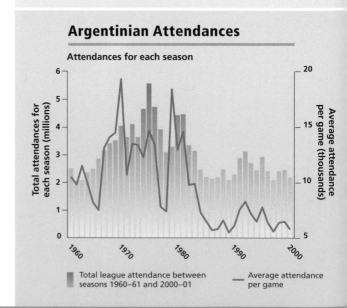

Argentinian Attendances

Attendances for each season

Total league attendance between seasons 1960–61 and 2000–01

Average attendance per game

Colón

La Banda de Rulo,
La Barra del Tablon,
La Banda del Santa Rosa

CA Unión

La Barra
de la Bombas

CA Talleres

Las Violetas, La Fiel,
Los Bulldogs,
La Barra de Juan

Santa Fé

CA Belgrano

Cordoba

Los Piratas,
La Banda del 2004,
La Banda del Jeton,
La Banda del Mosquito

Rosario

CA Newell's Old Boys

Cacho, Pimpi,
El Preso,
El Sapo, La lata,
Los Anticannals,
La San Roque

Rosario Central

La Banda del Chapero,
La Banda de los Pillines

BUENOS AIRES
(see inset)

La Plata

Gimnasia y Esgrima

La 22

ARGENTINA

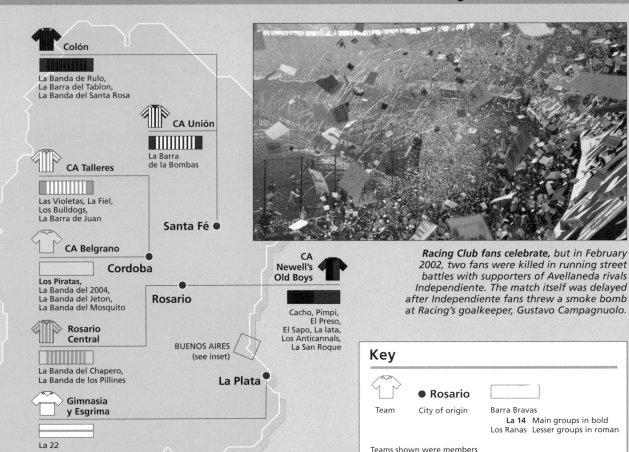

Racing Club fans celebrate, but in February 2002, two fans were killed in running street battles with supporters of Avellaneda rivals Independiente. The match itself was delayed after Independiente fans threw a smoke bomb at Racing's goalkeeper, Gustavo Campagnuolo.

Key

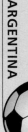

Team   ● City of origin   Rosario

Barra Bravas

La 14   Main groups in bold
Los Ranas   Lesser groups in roman

Teams shown were members
of the Primera Division 2001–02

Argentinos Juniors

La Banda
de la Paternal

CA Estudiantes

CA Chacarita Juniors

Los Mismos
de Siempre

Vélez Sarsfield

La Pandilla
de liniers

CA San Lorenzo Almagero

La Butteler

CA River Plate

Los Borrachos
del Tablon

BUENOS
AIRES

CA Boca Juniors

La 12

CA Independiente

Los Narigones

CA Banfield

CA Nueva Chicago

Los Perales,
La Pirelli

CA Huracán

La Jose C.Paz

Racing Club

La Guardia Imperial,
Racing Stones, La 95,
Los Acedmicos

CA Lanús

La 14,
La de la Pena,
Los Ranas

Fernando Marin, owner of legal firm Blanquiceleste and now Racing Club, may be the first of a new generation of private owners of Argentinian clubs.

Argentina

PLAYERS AND MANAGERS

PLAYERS AND MANAGERS in Argentina appear to come from one of two schools of football: open, silky and stylish on the one hand; defensive, caustic and rough on the other. In the person of Maradona the two can be seen in an individual. These two sides of Argentinian football style are best expressed in the contrasting styles of the two managers that led Argentina to World Cup victories: César Menotti in 1978 and Carlos Bilardo in 1986. Menotti came from the city of Rosario and inherited its traditions of stylish football and radical politics. Although to some onlookers he was compromised by winning the 1978 cup for the Junta he despised, his claim that his team played in the old style of a lost Argentina was read as a coded condemnation of the generals. Bilardo, by contrast, built an altogether rougher, tougher team in the mould of the spiky and aggressive Estudiantes team of the 1960s in which he played and for whom gamesmanship and trickery were the essence of the game.

From a trickle to a flood

Although football's popularity in Argentina has never wavered, the smooth running of both football and the economy certainly have. Not surprisingly, Argentinian football is marked by waves of emigration and unrest among its players. In the late 1940s, a prolonged players' strike saw a mass exodus of stars to the newly reinvigorated Colombian professional league and subsequently many left for Spain and Italy, claiming citizenship there on the basis of their grandparents' origins. Alfredo di Stefano, the leading player of his age, played only a handful of games for Argentina before decamping to Real Madrid and the Spanish national team. By the 1990s, the steady flow had turned into a rush as almost the entire national squad earned their wages around the Mediterranean, while at the end of 2001 their compatriots at home were on strike again, chasing unpaid wages from bankrupt clubs.

Top 20 International Caps

PLAYER	CAPS	GOALS	FIRST MATCH	LAST MATCH
Diego Simeone*	104	11	1988	2002
Oscar Ruggeri	97	7	1983	1994
Diego Maradona	91	34	1977	1994
Ariel Ortega*	76	17	1993	2001
Gabriel Batistuta*	75	55	1991	2001
Roberto Ayala*	74	3	1994	2002
America Gallego	73	3	1975	1982
Daniel Passarella	70	22	1976	1986
Javier Zanetti*	64	3	1994	2002
Alberto Tarantini	61	1	1974	1982
Jorge Olguin	60	0	1976	1982
Roberto Sensini*	60	0	1987	2000
Jorge Burruchaga	59	13	1983	1990
Ubaldo Fillol	58	0	1974	1985
Rene Houseman	55	13	1973	1979
Osvaldo Ardiles	53	8	1975	1982
Ricardo Giusti	53	0	1983	1990
Claudio Caniggia*	49	16	1987	2002
Claudio Javier Lopez*	47	10	1995	2001
Miguel Brindisi	46	17	1969	1974
Juan Sebastian Veron*	46	7	1996	2002

Top 10 International Goalscorers

PLAYER	GOALS	CAPS	FIRST MATCH	LAST MATCH
Gabriel Batistuta*	55	75	1991	2001
Diego Maradona	34	91	1977	1994
Luis Artime	24	16	1961	1967
Leopoldo Luque	22	45	1975	1981
Daniel Passarella	22	70	1976	1986
Hermino Masantonio	21	19	1935	1942
Jose Sanfillipo	21	30	1956	1962
Mario Kempes	20	43	1973	1982
Rene Jenjaudro Pontoni	19	29	1942	1947
Norberto Mendez	19	31	1945	1956
Jose Moreno	19	34	1936	1950

* Indicates players still playing at least at club level.

Argentinian International Managers

DATES	NAME	GAMES	WON	DRAWN	LOST
1940–58	Guillermo Stábile	110	74	18	18
1959	Victorio Luis Spinetto	6	5	1	0
1959	José Manuel Moreno	5	2	1	2
1960	Guillermo Stábile	10	6	1	3
1960–61	Victorio Luis Spinetto	10	5	3	2
1961	José D'Amico	2	1	0	1
1962	Juan Carlos Lorenzo*	5	2	2	1
1962	Jim López	2	1	1	0
1963	Horacio Amable Torres	8	4	1	3
1963	José D'Amico	2	1	0	1
1964–65	José Maria Minella*	15	9	5	1
1966	Juan Carlos Lorenzo	6	2	2	2
1967	Jim López	5	4	0	1
1967	Carmelo Faraone	2	0	0	2
1967–68	Renato Cesarini	5	1	1	3
1968	José Maria Minella	8	2	3	3
1969	Humberto Maschio	4	1	3	0
1969	Adolfo Alfredo Pedernera	4	1	1	2
1970–72	Juan José Pizzuti	23	10	8	5
1972–73	Omar Enrique Sivori	13	8	2	3
1974	Vladislao Wenceslao Cap	10	4	3	3
1974–82	César Luls Menotti	84	51	17	16
1983–90	Carlos Salvador Bilardo	70	36	23	11
1990–94	Alfio Oscar Basile	43	23	14	6
1994–98	Daniel Alberto Passarella	56	35	11	10
1999–	Marcelo Alberto Bielsa	36	22	9	5

* One match under different manager.
All figures correct as of 14 February 2002.

César Menotti's Argentina played some of the best football ever in the finals of its victorious 1978 World Cup campaign.

Carlos Bilardo led an aggressive and tricky Argentina, complete with Diego Maradona, to World Cup glory in Mexico in 1986.

Player of the Year

YEAR	PLAYER	CLUB
1970	Yazalde	Independiente
1971	Pastoriza	Independiente
1972	Bargas	Chacarita Juniors
1973	Brindisi	Huracán
1974	Raimondo	Independiente
1975	Scotta	San Lorenzo
1976	Passarella	River Plate
1977	Fillol	River Plate
1978	Kempes	Valencia [Sp]
1979	Maradona	Argentinos Juniors
1980	Maradona	Argentinos Juniors
1981	Maradona	Boca Juniors
1982	Gatti	Boca Juniors
1983	Bochini	Independiente
1984	Marcico	Ferro Carril Oeste
1985	Francescoli	River Plate
1986	Maradona	Napoli [Ita]
1987	Fabbri	Racing Club
1988	Paz	Racing Club
1989	Moreno	Independiente
1990	Goycochea	Racing Club/Millonarios
1991	Ruggeri	Vélez Sarsfield
1992	Islas	Independiente
1993	Bello	River Plate
1994	Montoya	Boca Juniors
1995	Francescoli	River Plate
1996	Chilavert	Vélez Sarsfield
1997	Salas	River Plate
1998	Batistuta	Fiorentina [Ita]
1999	Saviola	River Plate
2000	Riquelme	Boca Juniors
2001	Riquelme	Boca Juniors

Awarded by the Argentinian Association of Sports Journalists.

Top Goalscorers 1931–2002

SEASON	PLAYER	CLUB	GOALS
1930–31	Zozaya	Estudiantes	33
1931–32	Ferreyra	River Plate	43
1932–33	Varallo	Boca Juniors	34
1933–34	Barrera	Racing Club	34
1934–35	Cosso	Vélez Sarsfield	33
1935–36	Barrera	Racing Club	32
1936–37	Erico	Independiente	47
1937–38	Erico	Independiente	43
1938–39	Erico	Independiente	40
1939–40	Langara	San Lorenzo	33
1939–40	Benitez Caceres	Racing Club	33
1940–41	Canteli	Newell's Old Boys	30
1941–42	Martino	San Lorenzo	25
1942–43	Arrieta	Lanús	23
1942–43	Labruna	River Plate	23
1942–43	Frutos	Platense	23
1943–44	Mellone	Huracán	26
1944–45	Labruna	River Plate	25
1945–46	Boye	Boca Juniors	24
1946–47	di Stefano	River Plate	27
1947–48	Santos	Rosario Central	21
1948–49	Simes	Racing Club	26
1948–49	Pizzuti	Banfield	26
1949–50	Papa	San Lorenzo	24
1950–51	Vernazza	River Plate	22
1951–52	Ricagni	Huracán	28
1952–53	Pizzuti	Racing Club	22
1952–53	Benavidez	San Lorenzo	22

Top Goalscorers (*continued*)

SEASON	PLAYER	CLUB	GOALS
1953–54	Berni	San Lorenzo	19
1953–54	Conde	Vélez Sarsfield	19
1953–54	Borello	Boca Juniors	19
1954–55	Massei	Rosario Central	21
1955–56	Castro	Rosario Central	17
1955–56	Grillo	Independiente	17
1956–57	Zarate	River Plate	22
1957–58	Sanfilippo	San Lorenzo	28
1958–59	Sanfilippo	San Lorenzo	31
1959–60	Sanfilippo	San Lorenzo	34
1960–61	Sanfilippo	San Lorenzo	26
1961–62	Artime	River Plate	25
1962–63	Artime	River Plate	25
1963–64	Veira	San Lorenzo	17
1964–65	Carone	Vélez Sarsfield	19
1965–66	Artime	Independiente	23
1967 M	Acosta	Lanús	18
1967 N	Artime	Independiente	11
1968 M	Obberti	Los Andes	13
1968 N	Wehbe	Vélez Sarsfield	13
1969 M	Machado da Silva	Racing Club	14
1969 N	Fischer	San Lorenzo	14
1969 N	Bulla	Platense	14
1970 M	Mas	River Plate	16
1970 N	Bianchi	Vélez Sarsfield	18
1971 M	Bianchi	Vélez Sarsfield	36
1971 N	Obberti	Newell's Old Boys	10
1971 N	Luniz	Juventud Antoniana	10
1972 M	Brindisi	Huracán	21
1972 M	Morete	River Plate	14
1973 M	Mas	River Plate	17
1973 M	Curioni	Boca Juniors	17
1973 M	Pena	Estudiantes	17
1973 N	Gomez Voglino	Atlanta	18
1974 M	Morete	River Plate	18
1974 N	Kempes	Rosario Central	25
1975 M	Scotta	San Lorenzo	32
1975 N	Scotta	San Lorenzo	28
1976 M	Kempes	Rosario Central	21
1976 N	Eresuma	San Lorenzo	12
1976 N	Luduena	Talleres	12
1976 N	Marchetti	Unión	12
1977 M	Alvarez	Argentinos Juniors	27
1977 N	Letanu	Estudiantes	13
1978 M	Andreuchi	Quilmes	22
1978 M	Maradona	Argentinos Juniors	22
1978 N	Reinaldi	Talleres	18
1979 M	Fortunato	Estudiantes	14
1979 M	Maradona	Argentinos Juniors	14
1979 N	Maradona	Argentinos Juniors	12
1980 M	Maradona	Argentinos Juniors	25
1980 N	Maradona	Argentinos Juniors	17
1981 M	Chaparro	Instituto	20
1981 N	Bianchi	Vélez Sarsfield	15
1982 N	Juarez	FC Oeste	22
1982 M	Morete	Independiente	20
1983 N	Husillos	Loma Negra	11
1983 M	Ramos	Newell's Old Boys	30

Top Goalscorers (*continued*)

SEASON	PLAYER	CLUB	GOALS
1984 N	Pasculli	Argentinos Juniors	9
1984 M	Francescoli	River Plate	24
1985 N	Comas	Vélez Sarsfield	12
1986†	Francescoli	River Plate	25
1986–87	Palma	Rosario Central	20
1987–88	Rodriguez	Deportivo Español	18
1988–89	Gorosito	San Lorenzo	20
1988–89	Dertycia	Argentinos Juniors	20
1989–90	Cozzoni	Newell's Old Boys	23
1990–91	Gonzalez	Vélez Sarsfield	18
1991–92 A	Diaz	River Plate	14
1991–92 C	Latorre	Boca Juniors	9
1992–93 A	Acosta AF	San Lorenzo	12
1992–93 C	Da Silva	River Plate	13
1993–94 A	Martinez	Boca Juniors	12
1993–94 C	Crespo	River Plate	11
1993–94 C	Espina	Platense	11
1994–95 A	Francescoli	River Plate	12
1994–95 C	Flores	Vélez Sarsfield	14
1995–96 A	Calderon	Estudiantes	13
1995–96 C	Lopez	Lanús	12
1996–97 A	Reggi	FC Oeste	11
1996–97 C	Martinez	Boca Juniors	15
1997–98 A	Da Silva	Rosario Central	15
1997–98 C	Sosa	Gimnasia	17
1998–99 A	Palermo	Boca Juniors	20
1998–99 C	Calderon	Independiente	17
1999–2000 A	Saviola	River Plate	15
1999–2000 C	Fuentes	Colón	17
2000–01 A	Angel	River Plate	13
2000–01 C	Romeo	San Lorenzo	15
2001–02 A	Cardetti	River Plate	17
2001–02 C	Cavenaghi	River Plate	15

M Metropolitan League   **N** National League
† Reverted to a single league   **C** Clausura League
A Apertura League

ARGENTINA

Claudio Caniggia has remained playing at the top level for more than 15 years. His clubs have included River Plate, Boca Juniors, Verona and SL Benfica, and he currently plays for Rangers in Scotland.

Argentina

PRIMERA DIVISION 1985–2001

THE MID-1980s BEGAN with a reform of the old league system in which two separate tournaments – a Torneo Nacional and a Torneo Metropolitano – were played side-by-side. In 1985, a single national league kicked off. The increased representation of provincial sides (outside Buenos Aires) was confirmed with a series of titles for the two big Rosario teams, Rosario Central in 1987 and Newell's Old Boys in 1988 and 91. Newell's Old Boys built the club's success on an extensive scouting network and intensive youth policy, which produced strikers like Ariel Cozzoni. However, the big Buenos Aires clubs continued to win championships with one each for River Plate, Independiente and Boca Juniors, as well as victories for these teams plus Racing Club and San Lorenzo in the Liguilla – the qualifying tournament for the lucrative Copa Libertadores.

The financial screw

In 1992, another reorganization took place, with the national league being split into two separate 17-game leagues: the Apertura and Clausura. Competition has been open with championships going to River Plate, Boca Juniors, Independiente, San Lorenzo and Vélez Sarsfield. Although the financial screw has been on most clubs for the last decade, the big Buenos Aires clubs have pulled ahead of the others with bigger squads, more players imported from other Latin American countries and more lucrative sales of stars to top European clubs. During the 1990s, River Plate fielded Hernan Crespo, Oscar Ruggeri, Marcello Salas and Enzo Francescoli. Vélez Sarsfield, under coach Carlos Bianchi, starred Paraguayan goalkeeper José Luis Chilavert and striker José Flores and took back-to-back championships and a Copa Libertadores.

Most recently, Boca Juniors, also under Bianchi, has built a series of inspiring squads. Whenever the team has won a competition, however, the squad has been dismantled to pay the bills. Occasional challengers have included Gimnasia from La Plata, Racing Club and Lanús. Teams from Santa Fé and Córdoba have also reached the top flight and managed to hang in there. Nearly all clubs in Argentina are now in deep financial crisis, and almost every stadium is blighted by violence on match days.

Boca Juniors, 1997: another squad, another sales pitch. Boca Juniors' conveyor belt of talent keeps being sold on to Europe. The club has earnt over $100 million from transfers in the last 15 years.

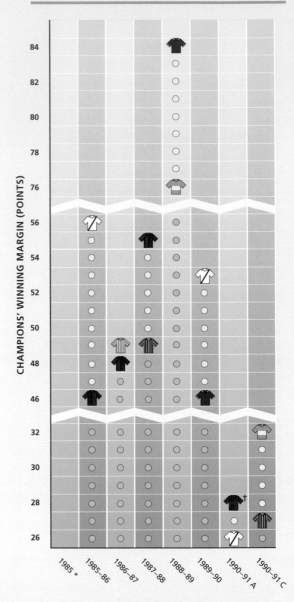

Champions' Winning Margin 1985–91

CHAMPIONS' WINNING MARGIN (POINTS)

SEASON

36	36	38	38	38	38	19	19

**Total games played by each team
(2 points awarded for a win except in 1989–90,
when 3 points were awarded for a win and
2 points for a win on penalties)**

* Championship decided by play-off
† Newell's Old Boys won national title by play-off for 1991

 Boca Juniors   River Plate   Independiente

 Newell's Old Boys   San Lorenzo    Rosario Central

Argentinian Players Transferred Abroad 1985–2001

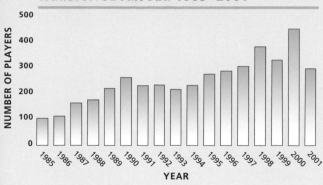

NUMBER OF PLAYERS / YEAR (1985–2001)

Income from Foreign Transfers 1985–2001

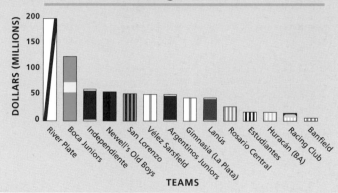

DOLLARS (MILLIONS)

TEAMS: River Plate, Boca Juniors, Independiente, Newell's Old Boys, San Lorenzo, Vélez Sarsfield, Argentinos Juniors, Gimnasia (La Plata), Lanús, Rosario Central, Estudiantes, Huracán (BA), Racing Club, Banfield

Argentinian League Positions 1985–1991

Key to League Positions Table

- ▦ League champions
- ▢ Season of promotion to league
- ▢ Season of relegation from league
- ▢ Other teams playing in league
- ▢ Qualified for championship play-off
- **5** Final position in league

*In the 1990–91 season the winners of the Apertura, Newell's Old Boys, and the winners of the Clausura, Boca Juniors, played-off for the national title. Newell's Old Boys won the title after a penalty shootout.

Newell's Old Boys — 1986, 87, 88, 91 A, 91*

Rosario Central — 1987

Argentinos Juniors

Boca Juniors — 1989, 91 C, 91* / 1986, 90

Independiente — 1989, 90 / 1987

Racing Club — 1988

River Plate — 1986, 90, 91 A / 1989

San Lorenzo — 1988, 91 C / 1991

ARGENTINA — Rosario — Buenos Aires

Primera Division 1986–91

Symbol	Meaning
Independiente	Team name
Team shirt	League champions/runners-up
1989, 90	Champions in bold / Runners-up in italics
Shirt (Copa)	Winners of Copa Libertadores Liguilla
● **Buenos Aires**	City of origin

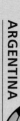

ARGENTINA

TEAM	1985	1985–86	1986–87	1987–88	1988–89	1989–90	1990–91 A	1990–91 C
Argentinos Juniors	1	4	17	7	7	9	4	18
Deportivo Armenio			13	19				
Banfield				18				
CA Belgrano								
Boca Juniors	5	4	12	2	3	8		1
CA Chacarita Juniors	19							
CA Chaco For Ever				17	14	19		
Deportivo Español	2	14	7	3	19	18	17	
Estudiantes	16	12	16	7	16	7	9	
Ferro Carril Oeste	6	5	14	18	6	4	16	
Gimnasia y Esgrima (La Plata)	9	12	5	10	6	4	14	
Huracán (Buenos Aires)	13						8	6
Independiente	9	3	11	1	2	10	5	
Instituto	11	8	14	20	20			
CA Italiano		20						
Lanús						20	12	
Deportivo Mandiyú				12	10	17	3	
Newell's Old Boys	2	2	1	12	10	1*	8	
Quilmes								
CA Platense	16	18	10	15	10	14	9	
Racing	18	15	17	15	17			
Racing Club		5	3	9	6	13	3	
River Plate	1	10	4	4	1	2	9	
Rosario Central		1	7	12	3	4	15	
San Lorenzo	6	5	2	5	15	10	2	
CA San Martín					17			
Unión Santa Fé	14	16	18		10	18	12	
Talleres	8	11	20	6	10	10	20	
CA Témperley	15	18						
Vélez Sarsfield	2	12	8	6	11	5	3	6

SEASON

River Plate and the club's fans remain the most powerful force in Argentinian soccer. However, despite big crowds and big transfers, the club remains mired in an ever deepening pit of debt.

Key to League Positions Table

- League champions
- Season of promotion to league
- Season of relegation from league
- Other teams playing in league
- **5** Final position in league
- **A** Apertura
- **C** Clausura

ARGENTINA

Carlos Bianchi finally returned Boca Juniors to winning ways in the late 1990s after a lean era. Since his appointment, the club has won three championships and two Copa Libertadores.

The flamboyant José Luis Chilavert has helped San Lorenzo take two championships and the Copa Libertadores in the last few years.

Argentinian League Positions 1991–2001

TEAM	1991-92 A	1991-92 C	1992-93 A	1992-93 C	1993-94 A	1993-94 C	1994-95 A	1994-95 C	1995-96 A	1995-96 C	1996-97 A	1996-97 C	1997-98 A	1997-98 C	1998-99 A	1998-99 C	1999-2000 A	1999-2000 C	2000-01 A	2000-01 C
Almagro																			18	10
Argentinos Juniors	9	15	18	10	11	13	5	20	16	20			8	8	6	11	12	16	17	4
Banfield				9	7	8	13	19	18	20	19									
CA Belgrano	15	10	7	13	16	9	6	15	20	13					19	9	18	14	16	16
Boca Juniors	2	4	1	6	4	7	13	4	2	5	10	9	2	6	1	1	3	7	1	3
CA Chacarita Juniors																	8	15	9	6
Colón									13	9	8	2	14	16	5	12	16	3	10	13
Deportivo Español	13	2	11	4	18	14	18	4	17	11	18	16	17	19						
Estudiantes	17	16	7	13	20	15			9	3	10	16	10	11	11	15	10	17	7	9
Ferro Carril Oeste	9	10	4	16	10	15	14	13	17	9	14	10	12	11	17	19	19	20		
Gimnasia y Esgrima (Jujuy)					17	12	8	14	10	20	14	4	19	19	19					
Gimnasia y Esgrima (La Plata)	4	8	16	10	10	15	8	2	13	2	6	13	4	3	2	8	3	9	3	18
Gimnasia y Tiro			16	19									19	17						
Huracán (Buenos Aires)	9	9	4	6	11	2	14	19	5	7	18	14	19	18	16	20			8	7
CA Huracán (Corrientes)											17	15								
Independiente	9	12	15	2	4	1	11	9	13	12	2	4	7	10	14	5	8	2	14	17
Instituto																	16	11		
Lanús			7	15	4	9	6	9	2	3	2	10	11	2	4	16	10	11	15	14
CA Los Andes																		19	19	
Deportivo Mandiyú	6	16	12	10	13	20	19	18												
Newell's Old Boys	18	1	20	17	13	9	4	15	11	17	8	2	18	8	6	7	12	5	13	12
CA Nueva Chicago																				
Quilmes	20	20																		
CA Platense	6	6	18	18	13	5	14	7	11	14	15	8	9	14	20	18				
Racing Club	13	7	16	6	2	9	11	6	2	7	4	7	13	15	3	13	6	18	20	5
River Plate	1	5	2	3	1	5	1	9	7	14	1	1	1	6	14	2	1	1	2	2
Rosario Central	15	12	12	6	18	3	8	7	10	6	5	18	3	13	6	4	2	13	12	20
San Lorenzo	3	19	2	4	7	3	2	1	5	19	6	6	4	5	6	3	4	3	5	1
CA San Martín			12	19																
Unión Santa Fé	19	16									16	10	14	19	6	5	12	8	11	15
Talleres	6	12	7	20		20	15								11	16	5	10	4	11
Vélez Sarsfield	4	2	6	1	2	18	3	3	1	1	13	5	4	1	11	13	7	5	6	8

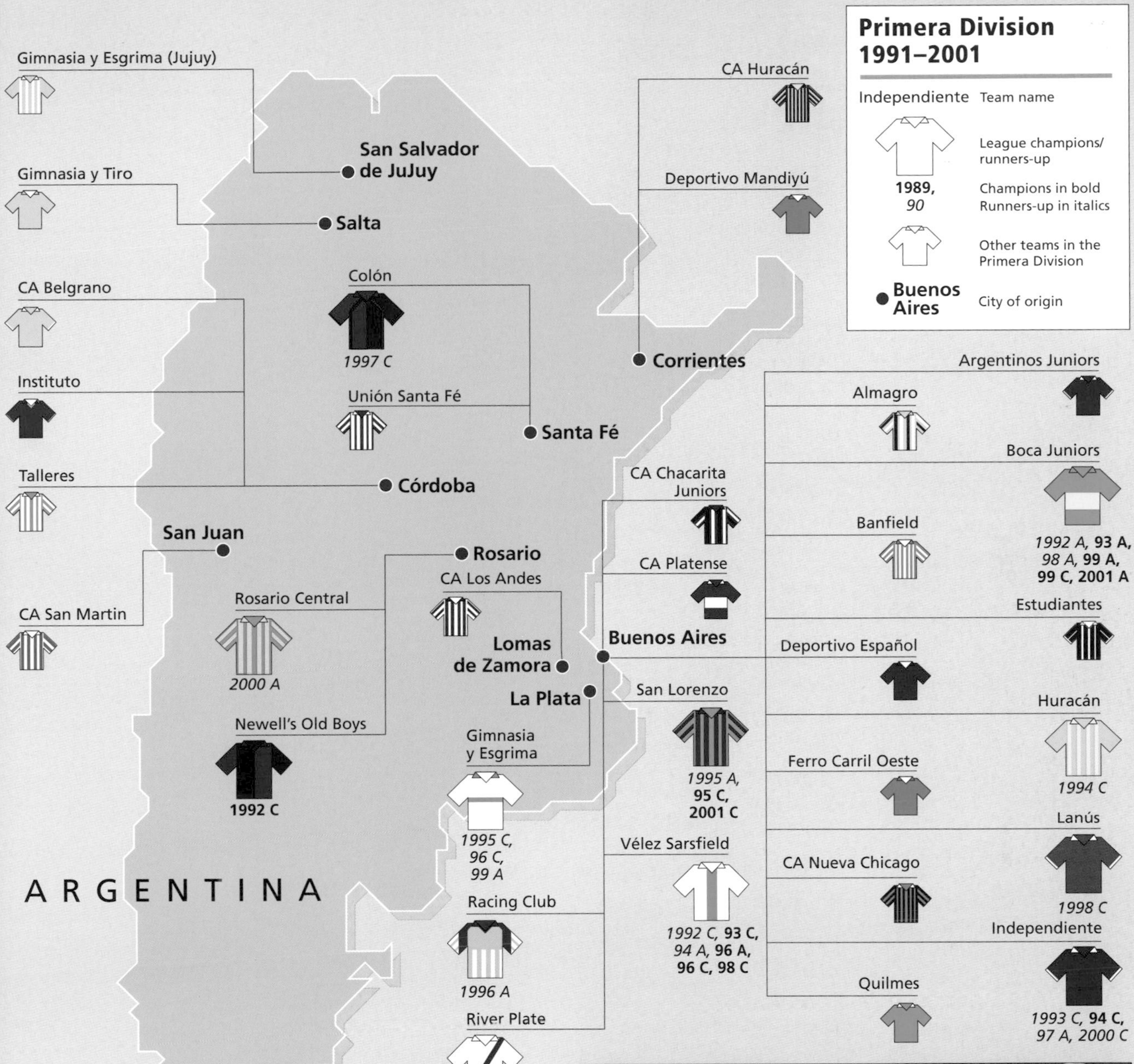

Primera Division 1991–2001

Independiente	Team name
(shirt)	League champions/ runners-up
1989, *90*	Champions in bold Runners-up in italics
(shirt)	Other teams in the Primera Division
● **Buenos Aires**	City of origin

Gimnasia y Esgrima (Jujuy)

Gimnasia y Tiro

San Salvador de JuJuy
●

Salta
●

CA Belgrano

Colón
1997 C

Instituto

Unión Santa Fé

Talleres

Córdoba
●

Santa Fé
●

CA Huracán

Deportivo Mandiyú

Corrientes
●

San Juan
●

CA San Martin

Rosario Central
2000 A

Rosario
●

Newell's Old Boys
1992 C

CA Los Andes

Lomas de Zamora
●

La Plata
●

Buenos Aires
●

CA Chacarita Juniors

CA Platense

Gimnasia y Esgrima
1995 C, 96 C, 99 A

San Lorenzo
1995 A, **95 C, 2001 C**

Racing Club
1996 A

Vélez Sarsfield
1992 C, 93 C, 94 A, 96 A, 96 C, 98 C

River Plate
1992 A, *93 A,* **94 A,** *95 A,* **97 A, 97 C, 98 A,** *99 C,* **2000 A,** *00 C,* **01 A,** *01 C*

Almagro

Deportivo Español

Ferro Carril Oeste

CA Nueva Chicago

Quilmes

Argentinos Juniors

Banfield

Boca Juniors
1992 A, 93 A, 98 A, 99 A, **99 C, 2001 A**

Estudiantes

Huracán
1994 C

Lanús
1998 C

Independiente
1993 C, **94 C,** *97 A,* **2000 C**

A R G E N T I N A

ARGENTINA

The 'Super Classico' 1998: Boca Juniors v River Plate is one of the few games for which attendances have not fallen in recent years.

Argentina

Asociación del Fútbol Argentino
Founded: 1893
Joined FIFA: 1912
Joined CONMEBOL: 1916

THE ARGENTINE LEAGUE championship is, outside of the UK, the world's oldest league. It was established in 1891 by expatriate Briton Alexander Hutton under the auspices of the Argentine Association Football League (AAFL). English teams and colleges (Alumni, Lomas Athletic and English High School) dominated the early years of the league until Racing Club's victory in 1913 signalled a shift of power to Argentinian clubs. This division in Argentine football was reflected in two splits that created parallel football associations and league championships in the years 1912–14 and 1919–26.

Professionalism and a professional league were established in 1931. For the next four decades, Argentine football was dominated by the big five from Buenos Aires (Boca Juniors, Independiente, Racing Club, River Plate and San Lorenzo). From 1967 to 1985 the championship was divided into two consecutive leagues, the Metropolitan and National. A single league was re-established in the mid-1980s and an extra tournament for the top teams was created – the Pre-Libertadores Liguilla – with a place in the lucrative Copa Libertadores at stake. Both tournaments were replaced in the early 1990s by the division of the season into two short leagues – the Apertura (opening) and Clausura (closing) championships.

Cup football has never proved popular in Argentina and, despite cups being donated by government ministers and Swedish ambassadors, no tournament has ever lasted very long.

Argentine Amateur League Record 1891–1930

SEASON	CHAMPIONS
1891	St Andrew's
1892	no championship
1893	Lomas Athletic
1894	Lomas Athletic
1895	Lomas Athletic
1896	Lomas Athletic
1897	Lomas Athletic
1898	Lomas Athletic
1899	Belgrano Athletic
1900	English High School
1901	Alumni
1902	Alumni
1903	Alumni
1904	Belgrano Athletic
1905	Alumni
1906	Alumni
1907	Alumni
1908	Belgrano
1909	Alumni
1910	Alumni
1911	Alumni
1912	Quilmes
1913	Racing Club
1914	Racing Club
1915	Racing Club
1916	Racing Club
1917	Racing Club
1918	Racing Club
1919	Boca Juniors
1920	Boca Juniors
1921	Huracán

SEASON	CHAMPIONS
1922	Huracán
1923	Boca Juniors
1924	Boca Juniors
1925	Huracán
1926	Boca Juniors
1927	San Lorenzo
1928	Huracán
1929	Gimnasia Y Esgrima
1930	Boca Juniors

FAF League Record 1912–14

SEASON	CHAMPIONS
1912	Estudianil Porteno
1913	Estudiantes LP
1914	Estudianil Porteno

AAF League Record 1919–26

SEASON	CHAMPIONS
1919	Racing Club
1920	River Plate
1921	Racing Club
1922	Independiente
1923	San Lorenzo
1924	San Lorenzo
1925	Racing Club
1926	Independiente

Argentine Professional League Record 1931–66

SEASON	CHAMPIONS	RUNNERS-UP
1931	Boca Juniors	San Lorenzo
1932	River Plate	Independiente
1933	San Lorenzo	Boca Juniors
1934	Boca Juniors	Independiente
1935	Boca Juniors	Independiente
1936	River Plate	San Lorenzo
1937	River Plate	Independiente
1938	Independiente	River Plate
1939	Independiente	River Plate
1940	Boca Juniors	Independiente
1941	River Plate	San Lorenzo
1942	River Plate	San Lorenzo
1943	Boca Juniors	River Plate
1944	Boca Juniors	River Plate
1945	River Plate	Boca Juniors
1946	San Lorenzo	Boca Juniors
1947	River Plate	Boca Juniors
1948	Independiente	River Plate
1949	Racing Club	River Plate
1950	Racing Club	Boca Juniors
1951	Racing Club	Banfield
1952	River Plate	Racing Club
1953	River Plate	Vélez Sarsfield
1954	Boca Juniors	Independiente
1955	River Plate	Racing Club
1956	River Plate	Lanús
1957	River Plate	San Lorenzo
1958	Racing Club	Boca Juniors
1959	San Lorenzo	Racing Club
1960	Independiente	River Plate
1961	Racing Club	San Lorenzo
1962	Boca Juniors	River Plate
1963	Independiente	River Plate
1964	Boca Juniors	Independiente
1965	Boca Juniors	River Plate
1966	Racing Club	River Plate

Metropolitan League Record 1967–85

SEASON	CHAMPIONS	RUNNERS-UP
1967	Estudiantes	Racing Club
1968	San Lorenzo	Estudiantes
1969	Chacarita Juniors	River Plate
1970	Independiente	River Plate
1971	Independiente	Vélez Sarsfield
1972	San Lorenzo	Racing Club
1973	Huracán	Boca Juniors
1974	Newell's Old Boys	Rosario Central
1975	River Plate	Huracán
1976	Boca Juniors	Huracán
1977	River Plate	Independiente
1978	Quilmes	Boca Juniors
1979	River Plate	Vélez Sarsfield
1980	River Plate	Argentinos Juniors
1981	Boca Juniors	Ferro Carril Oeste
1982	Estudiantes	Independiente
1983	Independiente	San Lorenzo
1984	Argentinos Juniors	Ferro Carril Oeste
1985	no championship	

ARGENTINA

National League Record 1967–85

SEASON	CHAMPIONS	RUNNERS-UP
1967	Independiente	Estudiantes
1968	Vélez Sarsfield	River Plate
1969	Boca Juniors	River Plate
1970	Boca Juniors	Rosario Central
1971	Rosario Central	San Lorenzo
1972	San Lorenzo	River Plate
1973	Rosario Central	River Plate
1974	San Lorenzo	Rosario Central
1975	River Plate	Estudiantes
1976	Boca Juniors	River Plate
1977	Independiente	Talleres
1978	Independiente	River Plate
1979	River Plate	Unión Santa Fé
1980	Rosario Central	Racing Club
1981	River Plate	Ferro Carril Oeste
1982	Ferro Carril Oeste	Quilmes
1983	Estudiantes	Independiente
1984	Ferro Carril Oeste	River Plate
1985	Argentinos Juniors	Vélez Sarsfield

Argentine League Record 1986–91

SEASON	CHAMPIONS	RUNNERS-UP
1986	River Plate	Newell's Old Boys
1987	Rosario Central	Newell's Old Boys
1988	Newell's Old Boys	San Lorenzo
1989	Independiente	Boca Juniors
1990	River Plate	Independiente
1991*	Newell's Old Boys	Boca Juniors

Apertura League Record 1992–2002

SEASON	CHAMPIONS	RUNNERS-UP
1992	River Plate	Boca Juniors
1993	Boca Juniors	River Plate
1994	River Plate	Vélez Sarsfield
1995	River Plate	San Lorenzo
1996	Vélez Sarsfield	Racing Club
1997	River Plate	Independiente
1998	River Plate	Boca Juniors
1999	Boca Juniors	Gimnasia y Esgrima LP
2000	River Plate	Rosario Central
2001	Boca Juniors	River Plate
2002	Racing Club	River Plate

Clausura League Record 1992–2002

SEASON	CHAMPIONS	RUNNERS-UP
1992	Newell's Old Boys	Vélez Sarsfield
1993	Vélez Sarsfield	Independiente
1994	Independiente	Huracán
1995	San Lorenzo	Gimnasia y Esgrima LP
1996	Vélez Sarsfield	Gimnasia y Esgrima LP
1997	River Plate	Colón
1998	Vélez Sarsfield	Lanús
1999	Boca Juniors	River Plate
2000	River Plate	Independiente
2001	San Lorenzo	River Plate
2002	River Plate	Gimnasia y Esgrima LP

* In the 1990–91 season the winners of the Apertura, Newell's Old Boys, and the winners of the Clausura, Boca Juniors, played-off for the national title. Newell's Old Boys won the title after a penalty shoot-out.

Argentine League Summary 1931–2002

TEAM	TOTALS	CHAMPIONS & RUNNERS-UP (BOLD) (*ITALICS*)
River Plate	30, 25	**1932, 36, 37,** *38, 39,* **41, 42,** *43, 44, 45, 47, 48, 49,* **52, 53, 55–57,** *60, 62, 63, 65, 66,* **68†,** *69†,* **69*,** *70*,* **72†,** *73†,* **75*,** *75†, 76†,* **77*,** *78†, 79†,* **79*, 80*, 81†,** *84†,* **86, 90, 92§,** *93§,* **94§,** *95§,* **97#,** *97§, 98§,* **99#, 2000§,** *2000#,* **01§,** *01#,* **02§,** *02#*
Boca Juniors	19, 12	*1931,* **33,** *34, 35,* **40,** *43,* **44,** *45–47,* **50, 54,** *58,* **62,** *64, 65,* **69†,** *70†, 73*,* **76*,** *76†,* **78*,** *81†,* **89,** *91,* **92§,** *93§,* **98§,** *99§,* **99#, 2001§**
Independiente	13, 14	*1932,* **34,** *35,* **37,** *38,* **39,** *40, 48,* **54,** *60,* **63,** *64,* **67†,** *70*,* **71*,** *77*,* **77†,** *78†,* **82*,** *83*, 83†,* **89, 90,** *93#,* **94#,** *97§,* **2000#**
San Lorenzo	9, 10	**1931,** *33,* **36,** *41,* **42, 46,** *57,* **59,** *61,* **68*,** *71†,* **72*,** *72†,* **74†,** *83*, 88,* **95#,** *95§,* **2001#**
Racing Club	7, 7	**1949–51,** *52,* **55,** *58,* **59,** *61,* **66, 67*,** *72*, 80†,* **96§, 2002§**
Vélez Sarsfield	5, 6	*1953,* **68†,** *71*, 79*, 85†,* **92#,** *93#,* **94§,** *96§,* **96#,** *98#*
Rosario Central	4, 4	**1970†,** *71†,* **73†,** *74†,* **74*, 80†,** *87,* **2000§**
Newell's Old Boys	4, 2	**1974*,** *86,* **87, 88, 91,** *92#*
Estudiantes	3, 3	**1967*,** *67†,* **68*,** *75†, 82*,* **83†**
Ferro Carril Oeste	2, 3	**1981*, 81†,** *82†,* **84***
Argentinos Juniors	2, 1	*1980*,* **84*, 85†**
Huracán	1, 3	**1973*,** *75*, 76*, 94#*
Quilmes	1, 1	**1978*,** *82†*
Chacarita Juniors	1, 0	**1969***
Gimnasia y Esgrima (La Plata)	0, 4	*1995#, 96#, 99§, 2002#*
Lanús	0, 2	*1956, 98#*
Banfield	0, 1	*1951*
Colón	0, 1	*1997#*
Talleres	0, 1	*1977†*
Unión Santa Fé	0, 1	*1979†*

* denotes winners/runners-up of Metropolitan League
† denotes winners/runners-up of National League
§ denotes winners/runners-up of Apertura League
# denotes winners/runners-up of Clausura League

Pre-Libertadores Liguilla Record 1986–91

SEASON	CHAMPIONS
1986	Boca Juniors
1987	Independiente
1988	Racing Club
1989	River Plate
1990	Boca Juniors
1991	San Lorenzo

Pre-Libertadores Liguilla Summary

TEAM	TOTAL	WINNERS
Boca Juniors	2	1986, 90
River Plate	1	1989
Independiente	1	1987
Racing Club	1	1988
San Lorenzo	1	1991

ARGENTINA

Uruguay

THE SEASON IN REVIEW 2001

URUGUAY'S FOOTBALL SEASON KICKED OFF with the resignation of the national coach Daniel Passarella in February after an appalling World Cup qualification campaign and an extraordinarily complicated new format for the season. The qualification campaign was saved at the last possible moment when Uruguay beat Australia in Montevideo to win in a two-legged play-off for the last place available at the World Cup in 2002. The new format for the season was designed to maintain interest in the competition throughout the year and give teams from the interior (outside Montevideo) more places in the competition. There were also restrictions on the number of teams from the interior that could be relegated.

Nacional come from behind

In the Torneo Clasificatorio, Peñarol was the form team and Nacional looked for a while like it might not qualify at all. But, as things got serious in both the Apertura and Clausura, Peñarol began to fade. Danubio, revitalized at its refurbished stadium, took the Apertura, beating Fénix 1-0 in the final game with a goal from veteran striker Da Silva – who had last played for the club when it won the National Championship in 1988. Nacional took the Clausura on the last day with a 2-0 victory over Peñarol, avenging a defeat earlier in the season through goals by Sebastian Abreu and Richard Morales. Morales, who had missed most of the previous season due to imprisonment, also missed a month of the 2001 season; he was arrested again after an incident in a Montevideo nightclub. In the National Championship Final, Nacional squeezed past Danubio, coming from behind in both legs to claim victory.

Copa Libertadores qualification

Uruguay has three places in the newly expanded Copa Libertadores. One is reserved for the winner of the Torneo Clasificatorio; one place is reserved for the winner of the National Championship. A composite league table is then created of the entire season and the four best teams that have not already qualified for the Copa Libertadores qualify for a three game mini-league or Libertadores Liguilla. The winner of this competition takes the third spot.

Nacional players celebrate after their last Clausura game in the Centenario Stadium in Montevideo. Nacional beat Peñarol 2-0 to become champions of the Clausura tournament.

Apertura Torneo – Final Table

CLUB	P	W	D	L	F	A	Pts	
Danubio	9	7	1	1	17	4	**22**	Apertura Winners
Peñarol	9	6	3	0	18	7	**21**	
Nacional	9	6	0	3	15	9	**18**	
Montevideo Wanderers	9	5	2	2	14	11	**17**	
Defensor Sporting	9	3	4	2	20	15	**13**	
Fénix	9	4	1	4	16	13	**13**	
Deportivo Tacuarembó	9	2	2	5	9	14	**8**	
Bella Vista (Montevideo)	9	2	0	7	12	20	**6**	
Bella Vista (Paysandú)	9	1	2	6	5	19	**5**	
Juventud	9	1	1	7	10	24	**4**	

Clausura Torneo – Final Table

CLUB	P	W	D	L	F	A	Pts	
Nacional	9	6	3	0	19	7	**21**	Clausura Winners
Danubio	9	6	0	3	19	13	**18**	
Peñarol	9	5	1	3	11	10	**16**	
Defensor Sporting	9	4	1	4	15	18	**13**	
Montevideo Wanderers	9	3	3	3	12	10	**12**	
Juventud	9	3	4	2	12	11	**10***	
Deportivo Tacuarembó	9	3	1	5	9	9	**10**	
Fénix	9	2	4	3	10	12	**10**	
Bella Vista (Paysandú)	9	2	3	4	13	18	**9**	
Bella Vista (Montevideo)	9	1	0	8	8	20	**3**	

* Juventud had three points deducted for fielding an ineligible player.

Relegated clubs: Renistas, Huracán.
Promoted clubs: Progresso, Villa Española.

National Championship

2001 FINAL (2 legs)

December 2 – Centenario, Montevideo
Nacional 2-2 Danubio
(Abreu 32,   (Cardozo o.g. 11,
Vanzini 36)   Da Silva 15)
h/t: 0-2   **Att:** 80,000
Ref: Larrionda

December 5 – Estadio Burgueño, Maldonado
Danubio 1-2 Nacional
(Olivera 3)   (Abreu 18,
     Varela 60)
h/t: 1-1   **Att:** 30,000
Ref: Feldinan
Nacional won 4-3 on aggregate

The structure of the season
The Uruguayan season acquired a new structure for 2001. It now opens with an 18-team first division, with teams playing each other once (17 games), but organized into three groups of six. This is collectively known as the Torneo Clasificatorio. The top two from each group together with the four next best teams go into a ten-team championship competition; the bottom eight go into a relegation competition. The championship competition involves two nine-game leagues: the Apertura and the Clausura. The winners of these two leagues play-off in a two-leg National Championship Final. The bottom eight play-off to avoid two relegation places.

International Club Performances 2001

CLUB	COMPETITION	PROGRESS
Nacional	Copa Libertadores	Second Round
	Copa Mercosur	Group Stage
Peñarol	Copa Libertadores	Group Stage
	Copa Mercosur	Group Stage
Defensor Sporting	Copa Libertadores	Group Stage

Copa Libertadores Qualifiers 2002

TEAM AND QUALIFICATION
Nacional as champions
Peñarol as winners of Torneo Clasificatorio
Montevideo Wanderers as winners of Liguilla

URUGUAY

Nacional players Gustavo Varela (left) and Limberg Gutierrez (right) tussle with Eber Moas of Danubio for the ball during the second leg of the Championship Final at the Burgueño stadium, Maldonado. Nacional won 4-3 on aggregate to become 2001 Uruguayan champions.

Sebastian Abreu of Nacional celebrates his goal against Peñarol during the last match of the Clausura.

Joe Bizera (left) of Nacional battles with Pablo Bengoechea of Peñarol on the final day of the Clausura.

Martin Aviola of Fénix shields the ball from Danubio's Omar Pouso during an Apertura match. A 1-0 victory for Danubio saw the team win a place in the Final against the Clausura winners.

Montevideo

FOOTBALL CITY

AT THE HEART OF MONTEVIDEO'S football landscape is the Centenario stadium, built for the first World Cup in 1930. Described by Jules Rimet as a 'temple of football', it is shared by the city's two biggest clubs: Peñarol and Nacional (who retain smaller grounds as well). It sits in the centre of a city that saw some of the earliest club championships and international matches in Latin America, and which hosts almost every team in the Uruguayan top division (and almost half the population of the country). Together with Buenos Aires, across the mouth of the River Plate, Montevideo is the cradle of football in Latin America.

The substantial expatriate British community, mostly involved in shipping and banking, was playing football informally in the 1880s and setting up schools and sports clubs across the city. Albion Cricket Club, formed in 1891, created a football section in 1893. British railway engineers set up CURCC (Central Uruguayan Railways Cricket Club) in 1891 and took to football soon after. The team first split from the company and then transformed itself into Peñarol in 1913. Peñarol is one half of the most successful double act in world football. Together with its rival, Nacional, they have won over 80 per cent of the Uruguayan championships ever played.

Nacional v Peñarol

Nacional was set up in 1899 by local students in self-conscious opposition to the foreigners running CURCC. Since this time, the team's social and political affiliations have always remained with the nationalist elite. In 1903, the Uruguayan FA put the Nacional squad in the national colours in a representative match against Argentinian Buenos Aires. Nacional still celebrates the occasion annually. Peñarol continues to be associated with the poorest, immigrant strands of Montevideo society. The annual derby matches are keenly contested. A similar derby is played out in a smaller way in the western suburb of Cerro, which has been absorbed into the city in the last few decades. Older, more middle-class residents have remained true to the area's original team, Rampla Juniors, while the new working-class immigrants tend to favour the recently-arrived Cerro.

Beyond the big two, Montevideo spawned an enormous number of clubs encouraged by the opening of Grand Central Park in 1900 by a tramway company who wanted people to use the park for football. Although over a hundred years of footballing history have passed, British influences linger on in many of the clubs' names – Liverpool, Racing, Wanderers and River Plate.

Montevideo docks: River Plate was originally founded in the Customs House in the docks area of the city at the beginning of the 20th century.

URUGUAY

BELLA VISTA	1920	
Amateur League (1900–1931)	*1924*
National League (1932–2001)	1990

CERRO	1922	
National League (1932–2001)	*1960*

RAMPLA JUNIORS	1914	
Amateur League (1900–1931)	*1923*, **27, 28**
National League (1932–2001)	*1932, 40, 64*

PROGRESO	1917	
National League (1932–2001)	**1989**

THE LOCAL DERBY

NACIONAL	PEÑAROL

466 matches played

147 Nacional wins
171 Peñarol wins
148 draws

0   50   100   150   200   250

NUMBER OF MATCHES
(all matches up to December 2001)

Montevideo

73,600	Capacity of stadium
16,000	Club's second stadium
	Team colours
	Second teams
M1	Motorway
A82	Major road
1900	Champions
2000	Runners-up

MANGA
Rentistas
PARQUE RENTISTAS
10,000
CASAVALLE

PIEDRAS BLANCAS
Danubio
JARDINES DEL HIPODROMO
16,000
PUNTA DE RIELES

Banado de Carrasco

WANDERERS 1902

Amateur League (1900–1931)	**1906**, *07*, **09**, *11*, *22*, *26*, **31**
National League (1932–2001)	*1980, 85*

Sud América   ITUZAINGO
CERRITO
VILLA ESPAÑOLA
CARLOS ANGEL FOSSA
6,000
AHUALPA
ELLA STA
UNION

DANUBIO 1932

National League (1932–2001)	*1954, 83,* **88**, *2001*

Villa Española
PLAY AT VARIETY OF STADIUMS

El Tanque Sisley
VICTOR DELLA VALLE
6,000

PASO CARRASCO

Miramar Misiones
MENDEZ PIANA
4,000

M O N T E V I D E O

Nacional   Uruguay
PARQUE CENTRAL
16,000
REDUCTO
iver
ate
LA BLANQUEADA

Nacional   Peñarol
CENTENARIO (NATIONAL STADIUM)
73,609

MAROÑAS   **Basáñez**
LA BOMBONERA
6,000
MALVIN NORTE

CARRASCO

Huracán
MALVIN NUEVO
PARQUE HURACÁN
8,000
PUNTA GORDA

ARQUE DERICO AROLDI
RETIRO
TRES CRUCES
PARQUE PALERMO
6,500
12,000

Central Español
LAS ACASIAS
PARQUE BATLLE
12,000
ATLANTIC OCEAN

ENTRO CORDON
ASOCIACIÓN URUGUAYA DE FÚTBOL HEADQUARTERS
AUF

Peñarol
LUIS FRANZINI
PUNTA CARRETAS
18,000

Defensor Sporting

CENTENARIO

73,609

Clubs:	Nacional, Peñarol, Uruguay
Built:	1930
Original Capacity:	80,000
Significant Matches:	1930 World Cup: nine matches, including semi-final and Final; Copa América: 1942, 56, 67, and Finals 83, 95

DEFENSOR SPORTING 1913

National League (1932–2001)	**1976**, *82*, **87**, *91*, *93*, *97*

CENTRAL ESPAÑOL 1905

National League (1932–2001)	**1984**

NACIONAL 1899

Amateur League (1900–1931)	*1901*, **02, 03**, *05, 06, 08*, **12, 13,** *15–17*, **18**, *19, 20, 21,* **22–24**, *29*, **31**
National League (1932–2001)	**1933, 34**, *35–38*, **39–43, 44, 45, 46, 47**, *49*, **50, 51, 52, 53, 55–57**, *58, 59*, **61, 62**, *63*, **65, 66, 67, 68, 69–72**, *73–75*, **77**, *78, 79, 80, 81*, **83, 86**, *87*, **89–91, 92**, *94–96*, **98**, *99*, **2000, 01**
Copa Libertadores	*1964, 67, 69,* **71, 80, 88**
Copa Interamérica	**1972**, *81*, **89**
Supercopa	*1990*
World Club Cup	**1971, 80, 88**

PEÑAROL 1899

Amateur League (1900–1931)	**1900, 01**, *02, 03*, **05**, *07*, **09, 10, 11**, *12*, **14–17**, *18*, **20, 21, 26**, *27*, **28, 29**
National League (1932–2001)	**1932, 33, 34**, *35–38*, **39**, *41–43*, **44, 45, 46, 47, 49, 50, 51, 52**, *53, 54*, **55–57, 58–62**, *63*, **64, 65, 66, 67, 68, 69–72**, *73–75*, **76, 77**, *78, 79*, **81, 82**, *84*, **85**, *86*, **88, 93–97**, *98*, **99**, *2000*
Copa Libertadores	**1960, 61**, *62*, **65, 66**, *70*, **82**, *83*, **87**
Copa CONMEBOL	*1993, 94*
World Club Cup	**1960, 61, 66, 82**, *87*

URUGUAY

Uruguay

PRIMERA DIVISIÓN PROFESIONAL 1982–2000

THE 1980s BEGAN chaotically in Uruguay, with a brutal military government presiding over economic decline and urban disorder. With very strict controls and limits placed on conventional politics, many leading political figures migrated into the administration of football, including Julio Maria Sanguinetti, future Uruguayan president and then-president of Peñarol. Similarly, Tabaré Vázquez, future leader of the leftist Encuentro Progresista party, was president of Progresso. The *junta*, recognizing the popular appeal of the sport, were prepared to bale out clubs as the economic squeeze destroyed their balance sheets.

Military rule ended and democratic elections were held in 1984, and for a time it seemed that the old order of Peñarol and Nacional championship victories had been swept aside. That year the title went unexpectedly to the tiny Montevideo club Central Español, led by the top-scoring striker José Villareal. Indeed, the country's lesser lights won a whole string of championships in the late 1980s. Defensor took two, aided by the free-scoring Gerardo Miranda, followed by Danubio and Bella Vista.

The 1990s saw Peñarol and Nacional take back their stranglehold on the league, though Defensor amalgamated with a popular basketball club to become Defensor Sporting and won the Clausura in 1997. The club has maintained its challenge to the big two by shrewd spending, an active youth policy and lucrative forays into the Copa Libertadores. However, nearly all other clubs, big and small, struggled financially throughout the 1990s, and only the sale of players overseas (some 400 in the late 1990s) and the sale of bonds to long-suffering fans kept clubs afloat. In 1998, Frontera Riviera became the first side from outside Montevideo to be promoted to the top flight. The growing strength of provincial football was recognized by changes in the structure of the Uruguayan league. Places were guaranteed to clubs from outside Montevideo, and relegation systems changed to ensure a Montevideo-provincial balance.

Primera División Profesional

Peñarol — Team name

League champions/runners-up

1985, 88 — Champions in bold / Runners-up in italics

Other teams in the Primera División Profesional

● Rocha — City of origin

Deportivo Tacuarembó

Tacuarembó

Frontera Riviera

Bella Vista

● Paysandú

URUGUAY

Las Piedras

Rocha

Maldonado

MONTEVIDEO (see inset)

Rocha

Frontera Riviera

Deportivo Maldonado

Juventude

Racing Club

Bella Vista — 1990

Villa Española — Play at variety of stadiums

Rentistas

Danubio — 1983, 88

Liverpool FC

Cerro

Wanderers — 1985

Sud América

Miramar Misiones

El Tanque Sisley

MONTEVIDEO

Fénix

Central Español — 1984

Basáñez

Peñarol — 1982, 84, 85, 86, 88, 93–97, 98, 99, 2000

Progresso — 1989

Defensor Sporting — 1982, 87, 91, 93, 94

River Plate — 1992

Rampla Juniors

Huracán

Nacional — 1983, 86, 87, 89–91, 92, 95–97, 98, 99, 2000

URUGUAY

__Nacional v Peñarol 2001:__ Most of Uruguay's social divisions continue to be played out in this derby – Colorados v Blancos, Italians v Spanish, working-class v middle-class. Although the match still attracts immense crowds and may even determine the Uruguayan championships, the big two have failed to make their mark recently in the big continental competitions, and both are perilously in debt.

Key to League Positions Table

- League champions
- Season of promotion to league
- Season of relegation from league
- Other teams playing in league
- **5** Final position in league

URUGUAY

Uruguayan League Positions 1982–2000

TEAM	1982	1983	1984	1985	1986	1987	1988	1989	1990	1991	1992	1993	1994 A	1994 C	1995 A	1995 C	1996 A	1996 C	1997 A	1997 C	1998 A	1998 C	1999 A	1999 C	2000 A	2000 C
Basáñez												3	12	13	8											
Bella Vista (Montevideo)	4	4	5	13	5	3	11	5	1	9	5	11	13	11							2	6	4	8	7	9
Bella Vista (Paysandú)																							13	11	15	12
Central Español			1	8	3	10	9	12	4	6	13		12	5	5	12	12	7								
Cerro	10	8	12	4	10	9	8	4	12	7	11	6	4	3	7	11	10	11	11	5			6	10	5	7
Danubio	7	2	4	11	9	6	1	7	6	5	3	3	11	10	10	5	4	5	9	12	11	5	3	3	2	4
Defensor Sporting	2	3	8	12	8	1	3	6	8	1	6	2	1	6	4	6	2	4	4	1	4	7	2	4	3	2
El Tanque Sisley										14																
Fénix					12																					
Frontera Riviera																							11	9	16	15
Huracán	14	11	9	10	7	12	4	10	14	11		12					5	3	8	7	10	9	8	5	18	13
Juventude																									12	11
Liverpool FC	11					5	11	7	8	10	9	9	7	2	7	9	10	5	4	12	8	15	6	14	17	
Deportivo Maldonado																							9	13	9	14
Miramar Misiones	12	10	13		11	12																				
Nacional	3	1	3	5	1	2	7	2	2	1	4	6	2	3	1	3	1	6	1	6	1	1*	1	2	1	3*
Peñarol	1	7	2	1	2	8	2	3	3	4	1	2	1*	1	2*	1	6*	3	2*	3	4	5	1*	4		1
Progresso	8	6	10	6	6	7	13	1	11	12	9	5	8	13	11	10										
Racing Club									5	10	8	13							12	10					11	8
Rampla Juniors	9	12	7	7	11	13							8	10	9	12	3	6	2	6	11	7	10	14	12	
Rentistas								9	9	13	12								10	8	8	2	7	15	6	10
River Plate	13	13		3	13	4	10	13	13		2	10	7	8	9	4	7	8	2	3	5	3	10	7	10	6
Rocha																									13	16
Sud América	6	9	11	9												8	13	11	12							
Deportivo Tacuarembó																							12	14	8	5
Villa Española																			9	11					17	
Wanderers	5	5	6	2	4	5	6	8	10	3	7	7	5	4	6	9	8	9	7	9	6	12				

*Denotes championship play-off winners.

Since 1993 the season has been divided into two leagues, Apertura and Clausura (marked A and C on the table), the winners of which play off to decide the championship.

In 1997 Nacional (winners of the Apertura) and Peñarol (the team with the most points overall) played off for the championship.

Uruguay

Asociación Uruguaya de Fútbol
Founded: 1900
Joined FIFA: 1923
Joined CONMEBOL: 1916

THE FIRST RECORDED FOOTBALL MATCHES IN URUGUAY

took place in autumn 1878 in Montevideo between teams made up of British residents and visiting British sailors. The first club, Albion FC, was set up in 1886 by an Englishman, William Pool. A national football association was founded in 1900 and an amateur league soon followed, although it was initially restricted to only four clubs from Montevideo – Albion FC, Central Uruguayan Railways Cricket Club (later to become Peñarol), Uruguay Athletic Club and Deutsche Fussball Klub. Club numbers steadily expanded and though again restricted to the capital city the first three decades of the 20th century were a golden era for Uruguayan football. Enormous domestic interest was sustained and enhanced by amazing international successes: victory at the 1924 and 1928 Olympic Games – both held in Europe – and hosting and winning the 1930 World Cup. On the back of this wave of economic and sporting success, professionalism and a reconstituted national league were established in 1932.

Since then Uruguayan football has been dominated by two teams – Nacional and Peñarol, both from the capital Montevideo – more completely than any other significant footballing nation. Between them they have won the national championship over 80 times, ceding the title to only eight other clubs in over a century. In fact, all the country's major clubs are based in Montevideo and concern has often been aired about its metropolitan bias. To counter the effect of this bias a regional league system run by the Organization del Futbol del Interior has been established to ensure continued interest in the sport outside the capital.

The league is currently split into two halves – the Apertura (opening) and Clausura (closing) Championship. A play-off between the two champions for the national title is held at the end of the season, unless the same team wins both championships. The four teams with the best overall record (over the two halves of the season) play-off in an end-of-season mini-league to determine the second Uruguayan entrant to the Copa Libertadores. The league format has recently changed again to ensure provincial representation in the top flight.

Uruguayan League Record 1900–2001

SEASON	CHAMPIONS	SEASON	CHAMPIONS
1900	Peñarol	1917	Nacional
1901	Peñarol	1918	Peñarol
1902	Nacional	1919	Nacional
1903	Nacional	1920	Nacional
1904	no championship	1921	Peñarol
1905	Peñarol	1922	Nacional
1906	Wanderers	1923	Nacional
1907	Peñarol	1924	Nacional
1908	River Plate	1925	no championship
1909	Wanderers	1926	Peñarol
1910	River Plate	1927	Rampla Juniors
1911	Peñarol	1928	Peñarol
1912	Nacional	1929	Peñarol
1913	River Plate	1930	no championship
1914	River Plate	1931	Wanderers
1915	Nacional	1932	Peñarol
1916	Nacional	1933	Nacional

Uruguayan League Record (continued)

SEASON	CHAMPIONS	SEASON	CHAMPIONS
1934	Nacional	1970	Nacional
1935	Nacional	1971	Nacional
1936	Peñarol	1972	Nacional
1937	Peñarol	1973	Peñarol
1938	Peñarol	1974	Peñarol
1939	Nacional	1975	Peñarol
1940	Nacional	1976	Defensor
1941	Nacional	1977	Nacional
1942	Nacional	1978	Peñarol
1943	Nacional	1979	Peñarol
1944	Peñarol	1980	Nacional
1945	Peñarol	1981	Peñarol
1946	Nacional	1982	Peñarol
1947	Nacional	1983	Nacional
1948	no championship	1984	Central Español
1949	Peñarol	1985	Peñarol
1950	Peñarol	1986	Nacional
1951	Peñarol	1987	Defensor
1952	Nacional	1988	Danubio
1953	Peñarol	1989	Progreso
1954	Peñarol	1990	Bella Vista
1955	Nacional	1991	Defensor
1956	Nacional	1992	Nacional
1957	Nacional	1993	Peñarol
1958	Peñarol	1994	Peñarol
1959	Peñarol	1995	Peñarol
1960	Peñarol	1996	Peñarol
1961	Peñarol	1997	Peñarol
1962	Peñarol	1998	Nacional
1963	Nacional	1999	Peñarol
1964	Peñarol	2000	Nacional
1965	Peñarol	2001	Nacional
1966	Nacional		
1967	Peñarol		
1968	Peñarol		
1969	Nacional		

Chile

Federación de Fútbol de Chile
Founded: 1895
Joined FIFA: 1912
Joined CONMEBOL: 1916

FOOTBALL ARRIVED IN CHILE in the late 19th century via visiting British sailors in the coastal ports of Valparaíso and Viña del Mar. The first clubs were formed in the early 1890s, the earliest being Santiago Wanderers formed in Valparaíso in 1892. It was soon joined by others, especially in the capital Santiago, and in 1895 a national FA was founded.

The geography of Chile – very long, very thin – militated against the formation of a regular national tournament and regional leagues quickly developed instead.

At the prompting of the most successful clubs, a national league was established in 1933 and professionalism legalized. However, it was not until the 1950s that teams from outside Santiago entered the league, and not until 1971 that Unión San Felipe won the title for a provincial city.

The national league ran as a conventional single league until 1997 when the season was split into two championships – Apertura and Clausura. In 1998, the league reverted to a single championship format, with the top four behind the champions playing-off for Chile's second slot in the Copa Libertadores. It was not until 1991 that a Chilean club, Colo Colo, won the Copa Libertadores. A national cup competition – the Copa Chile – was established in 1958 (but was not played between 1962–73).

Paraguay

Asociación Paraguaya de Fútbol
Founded: 1906
Joined FIFA: 1921
Joined CONMEBOL: 1921

THE TOP DIVISION IN PARAGUAY has 13 clubs playing an Apertura and a Clausura championship each year. Both championships are split into two. The first half consists of a straight league with each team playing the others once. Draws are not allowed and penalty shootouts take place if the score is level at the end of 90 minutes (victory by this method is only worth two points as against three for a normal-time win). Out of this league, the top eight teams form two mini-leagues, which produce the contestants for knockout semi-finals and Finals. The national champions are decided by a two-leg play-off between Apertura and Clausura champions.

Chilean League Record 1933–2001

SEASON	CHAMPIONS	SEASON	CHAMPIONS
1933	Magallanes	1970	Colo Colo
1934	Magallanes	1971	Unión San Felipe
1935	Magallanes	1972	Colo Colo
1936	Audax Italiano	1973	Unión Española
1937	Colo Colo	1974	Huachipato
1938	Magallanes	1975	Unión Española
1939	Colo Colo	1976	Everton
1940	Universidad de Chile	1977	Unión Española
1941	Colo Colo	1978	Palestino
1942	Santiago Morning	1979	Colo Colo
1943	Unión Española	1980	Cobreloa
1944	Colo Colo	1981	Colo Colo
1945	Green Cross	1982	Cobreloa
1946	Audax italiano	1983	Colo Colo
1947	Colo Colo	1984	Universidad Católica
1948	Audax italiano	1985	Cobreloa
1949	Universidad Católica	1986	Colo Colo
1950	Everton	1987	Universidad Católica
1951	Unión Española	1988	Cobreloa
1952	Everton	1989	Colo Colo
1953	Colo Colo	1990	Colo Colo
1954	Universidad Católica	1991	Colo Colo
1955	Palestino	1992	Cobreloa
1956	Colo Colo	1993	Colo Colo
1957	Audax italiano	1994	Universidad de Chile
1958	Santiago Wanderers	1995	Universidad de Chile
1959	Universidad de Chile	1996	Colo Colo
1960	Colo Colo	1997	Universidad Católica
1961	Universidad Católica	1998	Colo Colo
1962	Universidad de Chile	1999	Universidad de Chile
1963	Colo Colo	2000	Universidad de Chile
1964	Universidad de Chile	2001	Santiago Wanderers
1965	Universidad de Chile		
1966	Universidad Católica		
1967	Universidad de Chile		
1968	Santiago Wanderers		
1969	Universidad de Chile		

Chilean Cup Record 1958–2002

YEAR	WINNERS	YEAR	WINNERS
1958	Colo Colo	1988	Colo Colo
1959	Santiago Wanderers	1989	Colo Colo
1960	*no competition*	1990	Colo Colo
1961	Santiago Wanderers	1991	Universidad Católica
1962–73	*no competition*	1992	Unión Española
1974	Colo Colo	1993	Unión Española
1975	Palestino	1994	Colo Colo
1976	*no competition*	1995	Universidad Católica
1977	Palestino	1996	Colo Colo
1978	*no competition*	1997	*no competition*
1979	Universidad de Chile	1998	Universidad de Chile
1980	Deportes Iquique	1999	*no competition*
1981	Colo Colo	2000	Universidad de Chile
1982	Colo Colo	2001	Universidad de Chile
1983	Universidad Católica	2002	*not known*
1984	Everton		
1985	Colo Colo		
1986	Cobreloa		
1987	Cobresal		

Paraguayan League Record 1906–2001

SEASON	CHAMPIONS	SEASON	CHAMPIONS
1906	Guaraní	1957	Olimpia
1907	Guaraní	1958	Olimpia
1908	*no championship*	1959	Olimpia
1909	Nacional	1960	Olimpia
1910	Libertad	1961	Cerro Porteño
1911	Nacional	1962	Olimpia
1912	Olimpia	1963	Cerro Porteño
1913	Cerro Porteño	1964	Guaraní
1914	Olimpia	1965	Olimpia
1915	Cerro Porteño	1966	Cerro Porteño
1916	Olimpia	1967	Guaraní
1917	Libertad	1968	Olimpia
1918	Cerro Porteño	1969	Guaraní
1919	Cerro Porteño	1970	Cerro Porteño
1920	Libertad	1971	Olimpia
1921	Guaraní	1972	Cerro Porteño
1922	*no championship*	1973	Cerro Porteño
1923	Guaraní	1974	Cerro Porteño
1924	Nacional	1975	Olimpia
1925	Olimpia	1976	Libertad
1926	Nacional	1977	Cerro Porteño
1927	Olimpia	1978	Olimpia
1928	Olimpia	1979	Olimpia
1929	Olimpia	1980	Olimpia
1930	Libertad	1981	Olimpia
1931	Olimpia	1982	Olimpia
1932–34	*no championship*	1983	Olimpia
1935	Cerro Porteño	1984	Guaraní
1936	Olimpia	1985	Olimpia
1937	Olimpia	1986	Sol de América
1938	Olimpia	1987	Cerro Porteño
1939	Cerro Porteño	1988	Olimpia
1940	Cerro Porteño	1989	Olimpia
1941	Cerro Porteño	1990	Cerro Porteño
1942	Nacional	1991	Sol de América
1943	Libertad	1992	Cerro Porteño
1944	Cerro Porteño	1993	Olimpia
1945	Libertad	1994	Cerro Porteño
1946	Nacional	1995	Olimpia
1947	Olimpia	1996	Cerro Porteño
1948	Olimpia	1997	Olimpia
1949	Guaraní	1998	Olimpia
1950	Cerro Porteño	1999	Olimpia
1951	Sportivo Luqueño	2000	Olimpia
1952	Presidente Hayes	2001	Cerro Porteño
1953	Sportivo Luqueño		
1954	Cerro Porteño		
1955	Cerro Porteño		
1956	Olimpia		

Copa Libertadores 2001

TOURNAMENT REVIEW

THE COPA LIBERTADORES 2001 was relaunched with a new format, a new TV deal and new sponsors. Where previously a gruelling group stage had only dropped five teams from 21, the expanded entry in 2001 of 32 teams lost 16 of them after the group stage, encouraging attacking football from the off.

There were a few surprises in the opening stages. The second round saw the smaller teams eliminated, while big names such as River Plate, Vasco da Gama, América and Cruzeiro were all put out in the quarter-finals. Boca Juniors faced Palmeiras in the first semi-final – a rematch of the previous year's Final. With the teams closely matched, both ties ended 2-2 with Boca winning on penalties. In the other semi-final, Cruz Azul faced Rosario Central. Rosario had played its strongest teams in the Libertadores all season and was consequently looking at bottom spot in the Argentinian Clausura. But it was to no avail; a 2-0 defeat at the Azteca could not be redeemed in a furious 3-3 draw at home.

The annual Boca cull

The Final proved to be a more cautious affair, Boca stealing the first leg 1-0 at the Azteca, and Cruz winning by the same margin in Buenos Aires. However, Boca won 3-1 on penalties. For Boca coach Carlos Bianchi this was his third victory in the Copa Libertadores, equalling the total set by Osvaldo Zubeldia as manager of Estudiantes (1968–70). But there is no peace for the wicked. After winning the cup in 2000, Bianchi lost five core members of his squad. In the aftermath of this last victory, and with Boca Juniors' balance sheet looking very unhealthy, the squad looks set for yet another cull.

COPA LIBERTADORES

Santiago of Defensor Sporting (in blue) is tackled by Fabrinho of São Cãetano during one of their Group 7 matches.

Cruz Azul fans before the first leg of the Final, at the Azteca, Mexico City.

GROUP STAGES

GROUP 1

CLUB	P	W	D	L	F	A	Pts	
Rosario Central (Argentina)	6	4	1	1	13	4	**13**	Second Round
Atlético Junior (Colombia)	6	3	1	2	10	6	**10**	Second Round
Vélez Sarsfield (Argentina)	6	3	0	3	5	8	**9**	
Universitario (Peru)	6	0	2	4	3	13	**2**	

GROUP 2

CLUB	P	W	D	L	F	A	Pts	
Palmeiras (Brazil)	6	5	1	0	16	5	**16**	Second Round
Cerro Porteño (Paraguay)	6	4	1	1	17	6	**13**	Second Round
Universidad de Chile	6	1	1	4	5	13	**4**	
Sport Boys (Peru)	6	0	1	5	3	17	**1**	

GROUP 3

CLUB	P	W	D	L	F	A	Pts	
Nacional (Uruguay)	6	4	2	0	9	2	**14**	Second Round
Deportivo Concepción (Chile)	6	2	1	3	8	8	**7**	Second Round
San Lorenzo (Argentina)	6	2	1	3	9	10	**7**	
Jorge Wilsterman (Bolivia)	6	2	0	4	7	13	**6**	

GROUP 4

CLUB	P	W	D	L	F	A	Pts	
Cruzeiro (Brazil)	6	5	1	1	15	4	**16**	Second Round
Emelec (Ecuador)	6	2	3	3	7	6	**9**	Second Round
Olimpia (Paraguay)	6	1	2	2	10	13	**5**	
Sporting Cristal (Peru)	6	1	0	0	4	13	**3**	

GROUP 5

CLUB	P	W	D	L	F	A	Pts	
River Plate (Argentina)	6	4	0	2	13	6	**12**	Second Round
El Nacional (Ecuador)	6	3	0	3	8	9	**9**	Second Round
Guaraní (Paraguay)	6	2	1	3	9	11	**7**	
The Strongest (Bolivia)	6	2	1	3	10	14	**7**	

GROUP 6

CLUB	P	W	D	L	F	A	Pts	
Vasco da Gama (Brazil)	6	6	0	0	16	5	**18**	Second Round
América de Cali (Colombia)	6	4	0	2	10	9	**12**	Second Round
Peñarol (Uruguay)	6	1	1	4	7	10	**4**	
Deportivo Tachira (Venezuela)	6	0	1	5	3	12	**1**	

GROUP 7

CLUB	P	W	D	L	F	A	Pts	
Cruz Azul (Mexico)	6	4	1	1	12	7	**13**	Second Round
São Cãetano (Brazil)	6	2	2	2	6	4	**8**	Second Round
Defensor Sporting (Uruguay)	6	2	1	3	8	11	**7**	
Olmedo (Ecuador)	6	2	0	4	11	15	**6**	

GROUP 8

CLUB	P	W	D	L	F	A	Pts	
Boca Juniors (Argentina)	6	5	0	1	7	5	**15**	Second Round
Cobreloa (Chile)	6	3	1	2	8	7	**10**	Second Round
Deportivo Cali (Colombia)	6	3	0	3	13	8	**9**	
Oriente (Bolivia)	6	0	1	5	6	14	**1**	

SECOND ROUND (2 legs)

Cobreloa **2-3** Rosario Central
Rosario Central **1-1** Cobreloa

Rosario Central won 4-3 on aggregate

El Nacional **1-2** Cruzeiro
Cruzeiro **4-1** El Nacional

Cruzeiro won 6-2 on aggregate

América de Cali **2-0** Nacional
Nacional **1-3** América de Cali

América won 5-1 on aggregate

Deportes **1-3** Vasco
Concepción   da Gama
Vasco **1-0** Deportes
da Gama   Concepción

Vasco da Gama won 4-1 on aggregate

Emelec **2-0** River Plate
River Plate **5-0** Emelec

River Plate won 5-2 on aggregate

São Cãetano **1-0** Palmeiras
Palmeiras **1-0** São Cãetano

Palmeiras won 5-3 on pens

Atlético Junior **2-3** Boca Juniors
Boca Juniors **1-1** Atlético Junior

Boca Juniors won 4-3 on aggregate

Cerro Porteño **2-1** Cruz Azul
Cruz Azul **3-1** Cerro Porteño

Cruz Azul won 4-3 on aggregate

QUARTER-FINALS (2 legs)

Rosario Central **1-0** América de Cali
América de Cali **3-2** Rosario Central

Rosario Central won 4-3 on pens

Palmeiras **3-3** Cruzeiro
Cruzeiro **2-2** Palmeiras

Palmeiras won 3-2 on pens

River Plate **0-0** Cruz Azul
Cruz Azul **3-0** River Plate

Cruz Azul won 3-0 on aggregate

Vasco da Gama **0-1** Boca Juniors
Boca Juniors **3-0** Vasco da Gama

Boca Juniors won 4-0 on aggregate

Boca's keeper Córdoba makes
a save in the penalty shootout
at the end of the second leg.
Boca won 3-1 on penalties.

SEMI-FINALS (2 legs)

Boca Juniors **2-2** Palmeiras
Palmeiras **2-2** Boca Juniors

Boca Juniors won 3-2 on pens

Cruz Azul **2-0** Rosario Central
Rosario Central **3-3** Cruz Azul

Cruz Azul won 5-3 on aggregate

2001 FINAL (2 legs)

June 20 – Azteca Stadium, Mexico City
Cruz Azul 0-1 Boca Juniors
(Delgado 79)
h/t: 0-0   **Att:** 115,000
Ref: Rezende (Brazil)

June 28 – La Bombonera, Buenos Aires
Boca Juniors 0-1 Cruz Azul
(Palencia 45)
h/t: 0-1   **Att:** 60,000
Ref: Hidalgo (Peru)

Boca Juniors won 3-1 on pens

Boca's Delgado celebrates
after scoring the winner
in the first leg of the Final.

In the second leg of the Final, played
at La Bombonera in Buenos Aires,
Cruz Azul snatched a 1-0 lead through
Palencia and held on to take the game
to penalties. But Boca held its nerve in
the shootout; Cruz missed three
and Córdoba saved one for Boca.

Copa Libertadores

TOURNAMENT OVERVIEW

SOUTH AMERICA'S first international club competition was held in 1948 in Chile, staged by Santiago's leading club Colo Colo. The winners were Brazil's Vasco da Gama, but the event proved a financial disaster and was not repeated. But by the late 1950s the success of UEFA's European Cup and the offer of a World Club Cup between European and South American champions spurred clubs and federations into action. The Copa Libertadores was launched at a meeting in Montevideo in 1960.

The opening match was played in April 1960 between San Lorenzo and Bahia ending in a 3-0 win for the home side. San Lorenzo went on to meet the eventual winners, Peñarol, of Montevideo. The format was so popular with the Uruguayan crowds that San Lorenzo played both legs of the tie in Montevideo. Peñarol beat Olimpia of Paraguay to take the title and then beat Palmeiras to win again in 1961. Peñarol were the Real Madrid of the Copa Libertadores – the team that recognized and reaped the massive commercial potential of the new tournament.

Shifting power base

But when Peñarol's reign was terminated in 1962 by Pele's Santos, the tournament suddenly acquired glamour. In the Final, Santos had won 2-1 at Peñarol. But just after half-time in the return leg, Peñarol led 3-2. A stone thrown from the crowd knocked the referee unconscious and the game was suspended for an hour. At the restart what appeared to be a Santos equalizer was ruled out when the linesman was also knocked unconscious. The game finally finished after almost three and a half hours, and after much wrangling the score was left 3-2 to Peñarol. In a play-off at the Monumental in Buenos Aires Santos won 3-0.

The shifting power base of South American club football can be traced through the Copa Libertadores results. Following Santos' second win (1963), the cup stayed with Uruguayan and Argentinian teams until Cruzeiro's victory in 1976. Argentinian teams dominated the 1980s, but in the 1990s Brazilian clubs regained their prowess. However, Boca Juniors' double in 2000 and 2001 has broken the pattern once again.

Racing Club of Argentina won its only Copa Libertadores in 1967, beating Nacional of Uruguay in the Final. Its line-up featured Raffo (front row, far right) whose 14 goals made him the tournament's leading scorer that year.

Copa Libertadores
Top Goalscorers (1960–2001)

YEAR	SCORER	TEAM	COUNTRY	GOALS
1960	Spencer	Peñarol	Uruguay	7
1961	Panzutto	Independiente Santa Fé	Colombia	4
1962	Spencer	Peñarol	Uruguay	6
	Coutinho	Santos	Brazil	
	Raymondi	Emelec	Ecuador	
1963	Sanfillipo	Boca Juniors	Argentina	7
1964	Rodríguez	Independiente	Argentina	6
1965	Pelé	Santos	Brazil	8
1966	Onega	River Plate	Argentina	17
1967	Raffo	Racing Club	Argentina	14
1968	Tupãzinho	Palmeiras	Brazil	11
1969	Ferrero	Santiago Wanderers	Chile	8
1970	Bertocchi	Liga Universitaria Quito	Ecuador	9
	Mas	River Plate	Argentina	
1971	Castronovo	Peñarol	Uruguay	10
	Artime	Nacional	Uruguay	
1972	Toninho	São Paulo	Brazil	6
	Cubillas	Alianza Lima	Peru	
	Rojas	Alianza Lima	Peru	
	Ramírez	Universitario de Deportes	Peru	
1973	Caszely	Colo Colo	Chile	9
1974	Morena	Peñarol	Uruguay	7
	Terto	São Paulo	Brazil	
	Rocha	São Paulo	Brazil	
1975	Morena	Peñarol	Uruguay	8
	Ramírez	Universitario de Deportes	Peru	
1976	Palhinha*	Cruzeiro	Brazil	13
1977	Scotta	Deportivo Cali	Colombia	5
	Silva	Portuguesa FC	Venezuela	
1978	Scotta	Deportivo Cali	Colombia	8
	La Rosa	Alianza Lima	Peru	
1979	Miltão	Guaraní	Brazil	6
	Oré	Universitario de Deportes	Peru	
1980	Victorino	Nacional	Uruguay	6
1981	Zico	Flamengo	Brazil	11
1982	Morena	Peñarol	Uruguay	7
1983	Luzardo	Nacional	Uruguay	8
1984	Tita	Flamengo	Brazil	8
1985	Sánchez	Blooming	Bolivia	11
1986	De Lima	Deportivo	Ecuador	9
1987	Gareca	América de Cali	Colombia	7
1988	Iguarán	Millonarios	Colombia	5
1989	Aguillera	Peñarol	Uruguay	10
	Amarilla	Olimpia	Paraguay	
1990	Samaniego	Olimpia	Paraguay	7
1991	Gaúcho	Flamengo	Brazil	8
1992	Palhinha**	São Paulo	Brazil	7
1993	Almada	Universidad Católica	Chile	9
1994	Rivas	Minervén	Venezuela	7
1995	Jardel	Grêmio	Brazil	12
1996	De Ávila	América de Cali	Colombia	11
1997	Acosta	Universidad Católica	Chile	11
1998	Sergio João	Bolívar	Bolivia	10
1999	Bonilla	Deportivo Cali	Colombia	6
	Baiano	Corinthians	Brazil	
	Gauchinho	Cerro Porteño	Paraguay	
	Morán	Estudiantes de Mérida	Venezuela	
	Sosa	Nacional	Uruguay	
	Zapata	Deportivo Cali	Colombia	
2000	Luizão	Corinthians	Brazil	14
2001	Lopes	Palmeiras	Brazil	9

* Wanderlei Eustáquio de Oliveira
** Jorge Ferreira da Silva

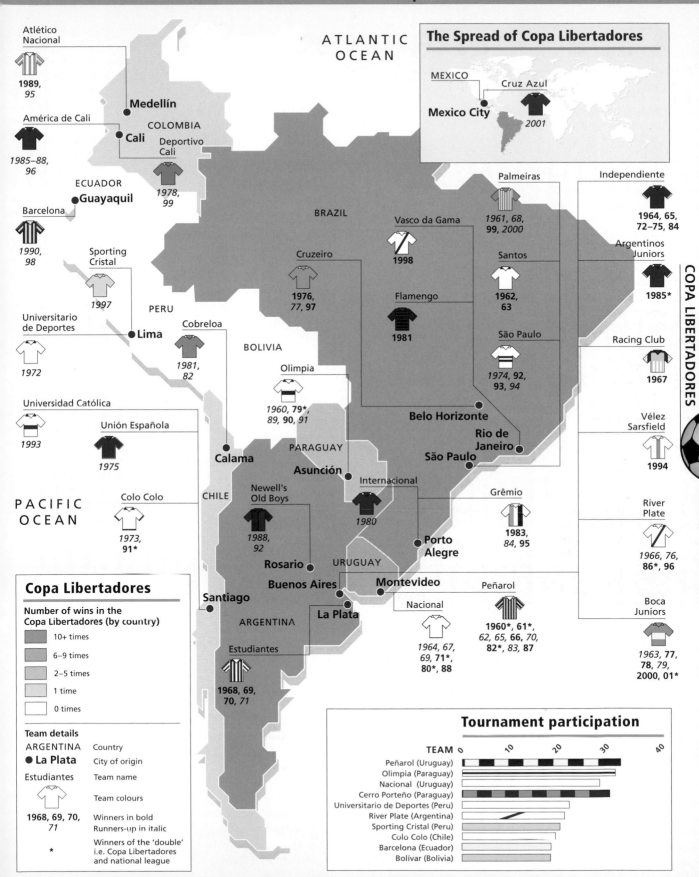

Atlético Nacional
1989, *95*

Medellín

COLOMBIA

América de Cali
1985–88, *96*

Cali

Deportivo Cali
1978, *99*

ECUADOR
Guayaquil

Barcelona
1990, *98*

Sporting Cristal
1997

Universitario de Deportes
1972

PERU
Lima

Cobreloa
1981, *82*

BOLIVIA

Universidad Católica
1993

Unión Española
1975

Calama

PACIFIC OCEAN

Colo Colo
1973, **91***

CHILE

Newell's Old Boys
1988, *92*

Rosario

Santiago

ARGENTINA

Estudiantes
1968, 69, 70, 71

La Plata

Olimpia
1960, **79***, *89*, **90, 91**

PARAGUAY

Asunción

Buenos Aires

Internacional
1980

URUGUAY

Montevideo

Porto Alegre

Nacional
1964, 67, 69, **71***, **80***, **88**

Peñarol
1960*, **61***, *62*, **65, 66**, *70*, **82***, **83, 87**

BRAZIL

Vasco da Gama
1998

Cruzeiro
1976, 77, 97

Flamengo
1981

Palmeiras
1961, **68**, *99*, **2000**

Santos
1962, 63

São Paulo
1974, *92, 93*, **94**

Belo Horizonte

Rio de Janeiro

São Paulo

Grêmio
1983, *84*, **95**

ATLANTIC OCEAN

Independiente
1964, 65, 72–75, 84

Argentinos Juniors
1985*

Racing Club
1967

Vélez Sarsfield
1994

River Plate
1966, **76**, *86***, **96**

Boca Juniors
1963, 77, *78, 79*, **2000, 01***

COPA LIBERTADORES

The Spread of Copa Libertadores

MEXICO
Cruz Azul

Mexico City
2001

Copa Libertadores

Number of wins in the Copa Libertadores (by country)

- 10+ times
- 6–9 times
- 2–5 times
- 1 time
- 0 times

Team details

ARGENTINA — Country
● **La Plata** — City of origin
Estudiantes — Team name
— Team colours
1968, 69, 70, 71 — Winners in bold / Runners-up in italic
* — Winners of the 'double' i.e. Copa Libertadores and national league

Tournament participation

TEAM	0	10	20	30	40
Peñarol (Uruguay)					
Olimpia (Paraguay)					
Nacional (Uruguay)					
Cerro Porteño (Paraguay)					
Universitario de Deportes (Peru)					
River Plate (Argentina)					
Sporting Cristal (Peru)					
Colo Colo (Chile)					
Barcelona (Ecuador)					
Bolívar (Bolivia)					

Copa Libertadores

THE COPA LIBERTADORES is the oldest and most prestigious South American international club championship. When first played, in 1960, it was contested by national champions in a knockout competition with matches played over two legs. From 1962, it consisted of three mini-leagues of three to decide three semi-finalists to meet the previous year's champions. In 1968, it expanded to 20 teams with two places allocated to each member of CONMEBOL. Five leagues of four produced eight quarter-finalists who met the previous year's champion in three further mini-leagues of three. In 1988, the format switched to two-leg knockouts for the quarter-finals, semi-finals and Final. The Final is now determined by aggregate scores, but had, until 1988, been determined by aggregate points over the final matches. Extra time and penalties are used to decide tied fixtures.

Each nation chooses its own method of filling its two places in the competition; for example, in Uruguay, the top six clubs play an end-of-season mini-league, while in Chile one place goes to the national champion and a second to the winner of a play-off among the next four teams in the league.

1960 FINAL (2 legs)
June 12 – Centenario, Montevideo
Peñarol 1-0 Olimpia
(Uruguay)　　(Paraguay)
(Spencer 79)

June 19 – Sajonia, Asunción
Olimpia 1-1 Peñarol
(Recalde 28)　(Cubilla 83)
Peñarol won on points aggregate

1961 FINAL (2 legs)
June 9 – Centenario, Montevideo
Peñarol 1-0 Palmeiras
(Uruguay)　　(Brazil)
(Spencer 89)

June 11 – Pacaembú, São Paulo
Palmeiras 1-1 Peñarol
(Nardo 77)　(Sasia 2)
Peñarol won on points aggregate

1962 FINAL (2 legs)
July 28 – Centenario, Montevideo
Peñarol 1-2 Santos
(Uruguay)　　(Brazil)
(Spencer 18)　(Coutinho 29, 70)

Aug 2 – Villa Belmiro, Santos
Santos 2-3 Peñarol
(Dorval 27,　(Spencer 73,
Mengalvio 50)　Sasia 18, 48)

PLAY-OFF
Aug 30 – Monumental, Buenos Aires
Santos 3-0 Peñarol
(Coutinho 11
Pele 48, 89)

1963 FINAL (2 legs)
September 3 – Maracaná, Rio de Janeiro
Santos 3-2 Boca Juniors
(Brazil)　　(Argentina)
(Coutinho 2, 21,　(Sanfilippo
Lima 28)　43, 89)

September 11 – La Bombonera, Buenos Aires
Boca Juniors 1-2 Santos
(Sanfilippo 46)　(Coutinho 50,
Pele 82)
Santos won on points aggregate

1964 FINAL (2 legs)
Aug 6 – Centenario, Montevideo
Nacional 0-0 Independiente
(Uruguay)　　(Argentina)

Aug 12 – La Doble Visera, Avellaneda
Independiente 1-0 Nacional
(Rodriguez 35)
Independiente won on points aggregate

1965 FINAL (2 legs)
April 9 – La Doble Visera, Avellaneda
Independiente 1-0 Peñarol
(Argentina)　　(Uruguay)
(Bernao 83)

April 12 – Centenario, Montevideo
Peñarol 3-1 Independiente
(Goncalves 14,　(De la Mata 88)
Reznik 43,
Rocha 46)

PLAY-OFF
April 15 – Estadio Nacional, Santiago
Independiente 4-1 Peñarol
(Acevedo 10,　(De la Mata 88)
Bernao 27,
Avallay 33,
Mura 82)

1966 FINAL (2 legs)
May 12 – Centenario, Montevideo
Peñarol 2-0 River Plate
(Uruguay)　　(Argentina)
(Abaddie 75,
Joya 85)

May 18 – Monumental, Buenos Aires
River Plate 3-2 Peñarol
(D. Onega 38,　(Rocha 32,
Sarnari 52,　Spencer 50)
E. Onega 73)

PLAY-OFF
May 20 – Estadio Nacional, Santiago
Peñarol 4-2 River Plate
(Spencer 57, 101,　(D. Onega 37,
Abbadie 72,　Solari 42)
Rocha 109)
(after extra time)

1967 FINAL (2 legs)
August 15 – Mozart Y Cuyo, Avellaneda
Racing Club 0-0 Nacional
(Argentina)　　(Uruguay)

August 25 – Centenario, Montevideo
Nacional 0-0 Racing Club

PLAY-OFF
August 29 – Estadio Nacional, Santiago
Racing Club 2-1 Nacional
(Cardozo 14,　(Esparrago 79)
Raffo 43)

1968 FINAL (2 legs)
May 2 – La Plata, La Plata
Estudiantes 2-1 Palmeiras
(Argentina)　　(Brazil)
(Veron 83,　(Servillio 50)
Flores 87)

May 7 – Pacaembú, São Paulo
Palmeiras 3-1 Estudiantes
(Tupazinho 10, 68,　(Veron 72)
Reinaldo 54)

PLAY-OFF
May 15 – Centenario, Montevideo
Estudiantes 2-0 Palmeiras
(Ribaudo 13,
Veron 82)

1969 FINAL (2 legs)
May 15 – Centenario, Montevideo
Nacional 0-1 Estudiantes
(Uruguay)　　(Argentina)
(Flores 66)

May 22 – La Plata, La Plata
Estudiantes 2-0 Nacional
(Flores 31,　(Veron 72),
Conigliaro 37)
Estudiantes won on points aggregate

1970 FINAL (2 legs)
May 21 – La Plata, La Plata
Estudiantes 1-0 Peñarol
(Uruguay)　　(Argentina)
(Togneri 87)

June 2 – Centenario, Montevideo
Peñarol 0-0 Estudiantes
Estudiantes won on points aggregate

1971 FINAL (2 legs)
May 26 – La Plata, La Plata
Estudiantes 1-0 Nacional
(Uruguay)　　(Argentina)
(Romeo 60)

June 2 – Centenario, Montevideo
Nacional 1-0 Estudiantes
(Masnik 17)

PLAY-OFF
June 9 – Estadio Nacional, Lima
Nacional 2-0 Estudiantes
(Esparrago 22,
Artime 65)

1972 FINAL (2 legs)
May 17 – Estadio Nacional, Lima
Universitario 0-0 Independiente
de Deportes　　(Argentina)
(Peru)

May 24 – Cordero, Avellaneda
Independiente 2-1 Universitario
(Maglioni 6, 60)　de Deportes
(Rojas 79)
Independiente won on points aggregate

1973 FINAL (2 legs)
May 22 – Cordero, Avellaneda
Independiente 1-1 Colo Colo
(Argentina)　　(Chile)
(Mendoza 75)　(Caszely 71)

May 29 – Estadio Nacional, Santiago
Colo Colo 0-0 Independiente

PLAY-OFF
June 6 – Centenario, Montevideo
Independiente 2-1 Colo Colo
(Mendoza 25,　(Caszely 39)
Giachello 107)

1974 FINAL (2 legs)
October 12 – Pacaembú, São Paulo
São Paulo 2-1 Independiente
(Brazil)　　(Argentina)
(Rocha 48,　(Saggioratto 28)
Mirandinha 50)

October 16 – Cordero, Avellaneda
Independiente 2-0 São Paulo
(Bochini 34,
Balbuena 48)

PLAY-OFF
October 19 – Estadio Nacional, Santiago
Independiente 1-0 São Paulo
(Pavoni 37)

1975 FINAL (2 legs)
June 18 – Estadio Nacional, Santiago
Unión Española 1-0 Independiente
(Chile)　　(Argentina)
(Ahumada 87)

June 25 – Cordero, Avellaneda
Independiente 3-1 Unión Española
(Rojas 1,　(Las Heras 56)
Pavoni 58,
Bertoni 83)

PLAY-OFF
June 29 – Defensores del Chaco, Asunción
Independiente 2-0 Unión Española
(Ruiz Moreno 29,
Bertoni 65)

1976 FINAL (2 legs)
July 21 – Mineirão, Belo Horizonte
Cruzeiro 4-1 River Plate
(Brazil)　　(Argentina)
(Nelinho 22,　(Mas 62)
Palinha 29, 40,
Waldo 80)

July 28 – Monumental, Buenos Aires
River Plate 2-1 Cruzeiro
(J.J. Lopez 10,　(Palinha 48)
Gonzalez 76)

PLAY-OFF
July 30 – Estadio Nacional, Santiago
Cruzeiro 3-2 River Plate
(Nelinho 24,　(Mas 59,
Ronaldo 55,　Urquiza 64)
Joazinho 88)

1977 FINAL (2 legs)

September 6 – La Bombonera, Buenos Aires
Boca Juniors 1-0 Cruzeiro
(Argentina)   (Brazil)
(Veglio 3)

September 11 – Mineirão, Belo Horizonte
Cruzeiro 1-0 Boca Juniors
(Nelinho 76)

PLAY-OFF

September 14 – Centenario, Montevideo
Cruzeiro 0-0 Boca Juniors
Boca Juniors won 5-4 on pens

1978 FINAL (2 legs)

November 23 – Pascual Guerrero, Cali
Deportivo Cali 0-0 Boca Juniors
(Colombia)   (Argentina)

November 28 – La Bombonera, Buenos Aires
Boca Juniors 4-0 Deportivo Cali
(Perotti 15, 85
Mastrangelo 60
Salinas 71)
Boca Juniors won on points aggregate

1979 FINAL (2 legs)

July 22 – Defensores del Chaco, Asunción
Olimpia 2-0 Boca Juniors
(Paraguay)   (Argentina)
(Aquino 3
Piazza 27)

July 27 – La Bombonera, Buenos Aires
Boca Juniors 0-0 Olimpia
Olimpia won on points aggregate

1980 FINAL (2 legs)

July 30 – Biera Rio, Porto Alegre
Internacional 0-0 Nacional
(Brazil)   (Uruguay)

August 6 – Centenario, Montevideo
Nacional 1-0 Internacional
(Victorino 35)
Nacional won on points aggregate

1981 FINAL (2 legs)

November 13 – Maracanã, Rio de Janeiro
Flamengo 2-1 Cobreloa
(Brazil)   (Chile)
(Zico 12, 30)   *(Merello 65)*

November 20 – Estadio Nacional, Santiago
Cobreloa 1-0 Flamengo
(Merello 79)

PLAY-OFF

November 23 – Centenario, Montevideo
Flamengo 2-0 Cobreloa
(Zico 18, 79)

1982 FINAL (2 legs)

November 26 – Centenario, Montevideo
Peñarol 0-0 Cobreloa
(Uruguay)   (Chile)

November 30 – Estadio Nacional, Santiago
Cobreloa 0-1 Peñarol
(Morena 89)
Peñarol won on points aggregate

1983 FINAL (2 legs)

July 22 – Centenario, Montevideo
Peñarol 1-1 Grêmio
(Uruguay)   (Brazil)
(Morena 35)   *(Tita 12)*

July 28 – Olimpico, Porto Alegre
Grêmio 2-1 Peñarol
(Caio 9,   *(Morena 70)*
Cesar 87)
Grêmio won on points aggregate

1984 FINAL (2 legs)

July 24 – Olimpico, Porto Alegre
Grêmio 0-1 Independiente
(Brazil)   (Argentina)
(Burruchaga 24)

July 27 – Cordero, Avellaneda
Independiente 0-0 Grêmio
Independiente won on points aggregate

1985 FINAL (2 legs)

October 17 – La Bombonera, Buenos Aires
Argentinos 1-0 América de Cali
Juniors   (Colombia)
(Argentina)
(Comisso 40)

October 22 – Pascual Guerrero, Cali
América de Cali 1-0 Argentinos
(Ortiz 3)   Juniors

PLAY-OFF

October 24 – Defensores del Chaco, Asunción
Argentinos 1-1 América de Cali
Juniors   *(Gareca 42)*
(Comisso 37)
Argentinos Juniors won 5-4 on pens

1986 FINAL (2 legs)

October 22 – Pascual Guerrero, Cali
América de Cali 1-2 River Plate
(Colombia)   (Argentina)
(Cabanas 47)   *(Funes 22,*
Alonso 25)

October 29 – Monumental, Buenos Aires
River Plate 1-0 América de Cali
(Funes 70)
River Plate won on points aggregate

1987 FINAL (2 legs)

October 21 – Pascual Guerrero, Cali
América de Cali 2-0 Peñarol
(Colombia)   (Uruguay)
(Battaglia 21,
Cabanas 35)

October 28 – Centenario, Montevideo
Peñarol 2-1 América de Cali
(Aguirre 58,   *(Cabanas 19)*
Villar 86)

PLAY-OFF

October 31 – Estadio Nacional, Santiago
Peñarol 1-0 América de Cali
(Aguirre 119)

1988 FINAL (2 legs)

October 19 – Parque de la Independencia, Rosario
Newell's 1-0 Nacional
Old Boys   (Uruguay)
(Argentina)
(Gabrich 60)

October 26 – Centenario, Montevideo
Nacional 3-0 Newell's
(Vargas 10,   Old Boys
Ostolaza 30,
De Leon 81)
Nacional won 3-1 on aggregate

1989 FINAL (2 legs)

May 24 – El Bosque, Asunción
Olimpia 2-0 Atlético
(Paraguay)   Nacional
(Bobadilla 56,   (Colombia)
Sanabria 60)

May 31 – El Campin, Bogotá
Atlético 2-0 Olimpia
Nacional
(Amarilla 46,
Usurriaga 64)
Atlético Nacional won 5-4 on pens

1990 FINAL (2 legs)

October 3 – El Bosque, Asunción
Olimpia 2-0 Barcelona
(Paraguay)   (Ecuador)
(Amarilla 47,
Samaniego 65)

October 10 – Modelo, Guayaquil
Barcelona 1-1 Olimpia
(Trobbiani 61)   *(Amarilla 80)*
Olimpia won 3-1 on aggregate

1991 FINAL (2 legs)

May 29 – Defensores del Chaco, Asunción
Olimpia 0-0 Colo Colo
(Paraguay)   (Chile)

June 5 – Estadio Nacional, Santiago
Colo Colo 3-0 Olimpia
(Perez 13, 18,
Herrera 85)
Colo Colo won 3-0 on aggregate

1992 FINAL (2 legs)

June 10 – Parque de la Independencia, Rosario
Newell's 1-0 São Paulo
Old Boys   (Brazil)
(Argentina)
(Berizzo 38)

June 17 – Pacaembú, São Paulo
São Paulo 1-0 Newell's
(Rai 65)   Old Boys
São Paulo won 3-2 on pens

1993 FINAL (2 legs)

May 19 – Pacaembú, São Paulo
São Paulo 5-1 Universidad
(Brazil)   Católica
(Lopez o.g. 31,   (Chile)
Dinho 41,   *(Almada 85 pen)*
Gilmar 55,
Rai 61,
Muller 65)

May 26 – San Carlos de Aponquindo, Santiago
Universidad 2-0 São Paulo
Católica
(Lunari 9,
Almada 16 pen)
São Paulo won 5-3 on aggregate

1994 FINAL (2 legs)

August 24 – José Amalfitani, Buenos Aires
Vélez Sarsfield 1-0 São Paulo
(Argentina)   (Brazil)
(Asad 35)

August 31 – Pacaembú, São Paulo
São Paulo 1-0 Vélez Sarsfield
(Muller 32 pen)
Vélez Sarsfield won 5-3 on pens

1995 FINAL (2 legs)

August 24 – Olimpico, Porto Alegre
Grêmio 3-1 Atlético
(Brazil)   Nacional
(Marulanda o.g.   (Colombia)
36, Jardel 40,   *(Angel 71)*
Paulo Nunes 56)

August 30 – Atanasio Girardot, Medellín
Atlético 1-1 Grêmio
Nacional   *(Dinho 85)*
(Aristizabal 13)
Grêmio won 4-2 on aggregate

1996 FINAL (2 legs)

June 19 – Pascual Guerrero, Cali
América de Cali 1-0 River Plate
(Colombia)   (Argentina)
(De Avila 72)

June 26 – Monumental, Buenos Aires
River Plate 2-0 América de Cali
(Crespo 7, 14)
River Plate won 2-1 on aggregate

1997 FINAL (2 legs)

August 6 – San Martin de Porres, Lima
Sporting Cristal 0-0 Cruzeiro
(Peru)   (Brazil)

August 13 – Mineirão, Belo Horizonte
Cruzeiro 1-0 Sporting Cristal
(Elivelton 75)
Cruzeiro won 1-0 on aggregate

1998 FINAL (2 legs)

August 12 – São Januario, Rio de Janeiro
Vasco da Gama 2-0 Barcelona
(Brazil)   (Ecuador)
(Donizete 7,
Luizao 33)

August 26 – Monumental Isidro Romero, Guayquil
Barcelona 1-2 Vasco da Gama
(De Avila 79)   *(Luizao 24,*
Donizete 45)
Vasco da Gama won 4-1 on aggregate

1999 FINAL (2 legs)

June 2 – Pascual Guerrero, Cali
Deportivo Cali 1-0 Palmeiras
(Colombia)   (Brazil)
(Bonilla 42)

June 16 – Morumbi, São Paulo
Palmeiras 2-0 Deportivo Cali
(Evair 63 pen,   *(Zapata 69 pen)*
Oseas 75)
Palmeiras won 2-1 on aggregate

2000 FINAL (2 legs)

June 14 – La Bombonera, Buenos Aires
Boca Juniors 2-2 Palmeiras
(Argentina)   (Brazil)
(Arruabarrena   *(Pena 43,*
22, 61)   *Euller 63)*

June 21 – Parque Antarctica, São Paulo
Palmeiras 0-0 Boca Juniors
Boca Juniors won 4-2 on pens

2001 FINAL (2 legs)

June 20   Azteca, Mexico City
Cruz Azul 0-1 Boca Juniors
(Mexico)   (Argentina)
(Delgado 79)

June 28 – La Bombonera, Buenos Aires
Boca Juniors 0-1 Cruz Azul
(Palencia 45)
Boca Juniors won 3-1 on pens

***Boca Juniors** of Argentina claimed the 2001 Copa with victory over Cruz Azul of Mexico.*

Copa América

TOURNAMENT OVERVIEW

COPA AMÉRICA

INTERNATIONAL FOOTBALL started early in South America with Argentina and Uruguay contesting the Lipton Cup (donated by Sir Thomas Lipton, the English tea merchant) beginning in 1905, and the Newton Cup from 1906. With regular international football across the River Plate and the opening of a rail link to Chile, the Argentine FA invited Uruguay, Chile and Brazil to Buenos Aires for a four-way tournament in 1910 (this is now thought of as the first 'unofficial' Copa América, as CONMEBOL was not formed until 1916). The Brazilians decided not to show, but the tournament went ahead with victories for Uruguay and Argentina over Chile. For the deciding match, 40,000 fans gathered at Gimnasia's stadium – and promptly burnt down a stand. The game was abandoned. The next day, a heavily policed rematch at Racing Club's ground saw Argentina win 4-1.

The second tournament was held in 1916 to celebrate the centenary of Argentinian independence. This time the Brazilians did show, but Uruguay won the title. In 1917, the holders hosted and won the first official championships in Montevideo. Two years later it was the turn of Brazil, and Rio aristocrats Fluminense built a new stadium to stage the matches. In a final play-off with Uruguay, Freidenriech, the Brazilian striker, ended the match with a goal after 43 minutes of extra time. Brazil won again in 1922, but the 1920s really belonged to Uruguay and Argentina. After a six-year gap (1929–35), while domestic struggles over professionalism were worked out, the tournament resumed appropriately with Uruguayan (1935) and Argentinian (1937) victories.

Argentina and Brazil dominant

A protracted players' strike in Argentina saw the team withdraw from both the 1949 and 1953 tournaments, but over the era as a whole it was the dominant side. Peru's victory in 1939, and Bolivia's in 1963, gave the continent's minnows a look-in. By the early 1960s the popularity of the tournament was declining as the Copa Libertadores took off and club versus country disputes over player availability sharpened. With Argentina and Brazil fielding consistently weak teams, the tournament took an eight-year break (1967–75) before recommencing as a finals-only event.

The tournament was relaunched in 1987 with all matches held in a single host country during the European close season to maximize player availability and TV and sponsorship money. The perennial problem of creating a tournament format with ten teams was solved in 1993 by inviting two outside nations – Mexico and the USA. This format has been replicated since with appearances for South Korea, Costa Rica and Japan as well. In the modern era, Argentina and Brazil have won when they have fielded their strongest sides, but their weaker teams have let the Uruguayans and the Colombians in.

Unofficial tournaments

YEAR	WINNERS	RUNNERS-UP	THIRD PLACE
1910	Argentina	Uruguay	Chile
1916	Uruguay	Argentina	Brazil
1935	Uruguay	Argentina	Brazil
1941	Argentina	Uruguay	Chile
1945	Argentina	Brazil	Chile
1946	Argentina	Brazil	Paraguay
1956	Uruguay	Chile	Argentina
1959	Uruguay	Argentina	Brazil

Copa América: winners and runners-up

TEAM COLOURS	COUNTRY	TOTAL WINS, YEARS	TOTAL RUNNERS-UP, YEARS
15	Argentina	**15:** 1910*, 21, 25, 27, 29, 37, 41*, 45*, 46*, 47, 55, 57, 59, 91, 93	**10:** 1916*, 17, 20, 23, 24, 26, 35*, 42, 59*, 67
14	Uruguay	**14:** 1916*, 17, 20, 23, 24, 26, 35*, 42, 56*, 59*, 67, 83, 87, 95	**7:** 1910*, 19, 27, 39, 41*, 89, 99
6	Brazil	**6:** 1919, 22, 49, 89, 97, 99	**11:** 1921, 25, 37, 45*, 46*, 53, 57, 59, 83, 91, 95
	Paraguay	**2:** 1953, 79	**5:** 1922, 29, 47, 49, 63
	Peru	**2:** 1939, 75	0
1	Bolivia	**1:** 1963	**1:** 1997
1	Colombia	**1:** 2001	**1:** 1975
0	Chile	0	**4:** 1955, 56*, 79, 87
0	Mexico	0	**2:** 1993, 2001

* honours in unofficial tournaments

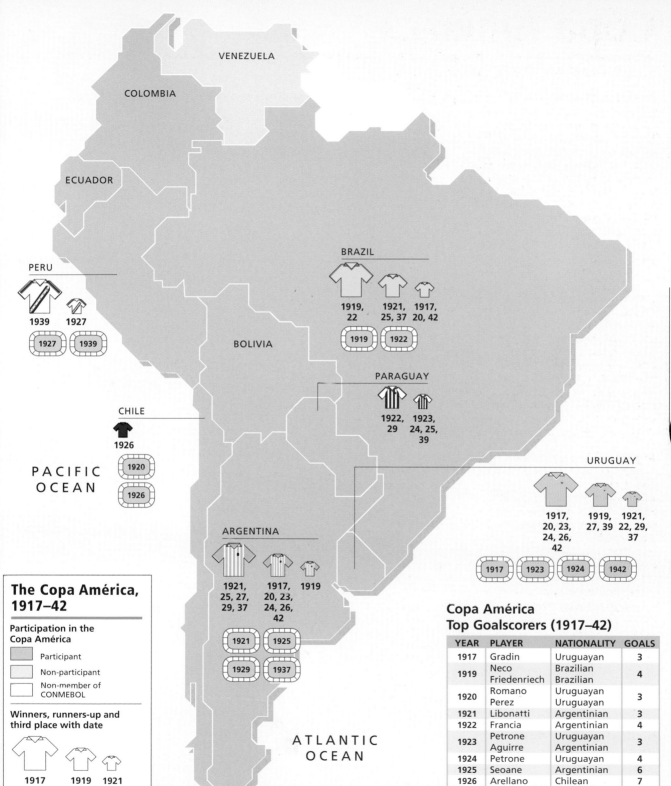

VENEZUELA

COLOMBIA

ECUADOR

PERU

1939 1927

1927 1939

BOLIVIA

BRAZIL

1919, 22   1921, 25, 37   1917, 20, 42

1919   1922

PARAGUAY

1922, 29   1923, 24, 25, 39

CHILE

1926

1920

1926

PACIFIC OCEAN

URUGUAY

1917, 20, 23, 24, 26, 42   1919, 27, 39   1921, 22, 29, 37

1917   1923   1924   1942

ARGENTINA

1921, 25, 27, 29, 37   1917, 20, 23, 24, 26, 42   1919

1921   1925

1929   1937

ATLANTIC OCEAN

COPA AMÉRICA

The Copa América, 1917–42

Participation in the Copa América

Participant

Non-participant

Non-member of CONMEBOL

Winners, runners-up and third place with date

1917   1919   1921

Host country, with date in stadium

URUGUAY   1917

Copa América Top Goalscorers (1917–42)

YEAR	PLAYER	NATIONALITY	GOALS
1917	Gradin	Uruguayan	3
1919	Neco	Brazilian	4
	Friedenriech	Brazilian	
1920	Romano	Uruguayan	3
	Perez	Uruguayan	
1921	Libonatti	Argentinian	3
1922	Francia	Argentinian	4
1923	Petrone	Uruguayan	3
	Aguirre	Argentinian	
1924	Petrone	Uruguayan	4
1925	Seoane	Argentinian	6
1926	Arellano	Chilean	7
1927	Figueroa	Uruguayan	4
1929	Gonzalez	Paraguayan	5
1937	Toro	Chilean	7
1939	Fernandez	Peruvian	7
1942	Masantonio	Argentinian	7
	Marino	Argentinian	

COPA AMÉRICA

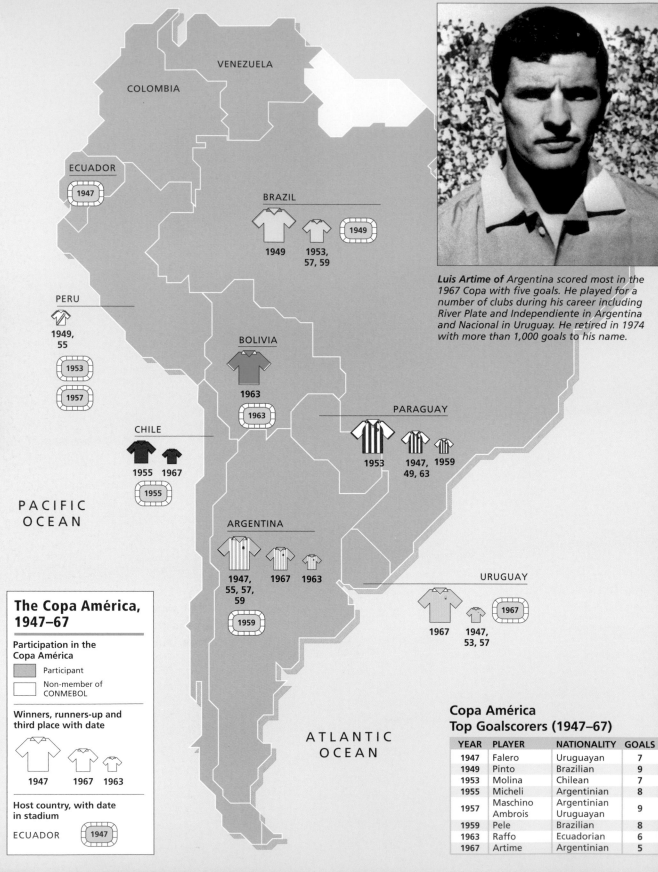

VENEZUELA

COLOMBIA

ECUADOR
1947

BRAZIL
1949   1953,   1949
        57, 59

PERU
1949,
55
1953
1957

BOLIVIA
1963
1963

PARAGUAY
1953   1947,   1959
        49, 63

CHILE
1955   1967
1955

ARGENTINA
1947,   1967   1963
55, 57,
59
1959

URUGUAY
1967   1947,   1967
        53, 57

PACIFIC
OCEAN

ATLANTIC
OCEAN

*Luis Artime of Argentina scored most in the
1967 Copa with five goals. He played for a
number of clubs during his career including
River Plate and Independiente in Argentina
and Nacional in Uruguay. He retired in 1974
with more than 1,000 goals to his name.*

The Copa América, 1947–67

Participation in the Copa América

Participant

Non-member of CONMEBOL

Winners, runners-up and third place with date

1947   1967   1963

Host country, with date in stadium

ECUADOR   1947

Copa América Top Goalscorers (1947–67)

YEAR	PLAYER	NATIONALITY	GOALS
1947	Falero	Uruguayan	7
1949	Pinto	Brazilian	9
1953	Molina	Chilean	7
1955	Micheli	Argentinian	8
1957	Maschino	Argentinian	9
	Ambrois	Uruguayan	
1959	Pele	Brazilian	8
1963	Raffo	Ecuadorian	6
1967	Artime	Argentinian	5

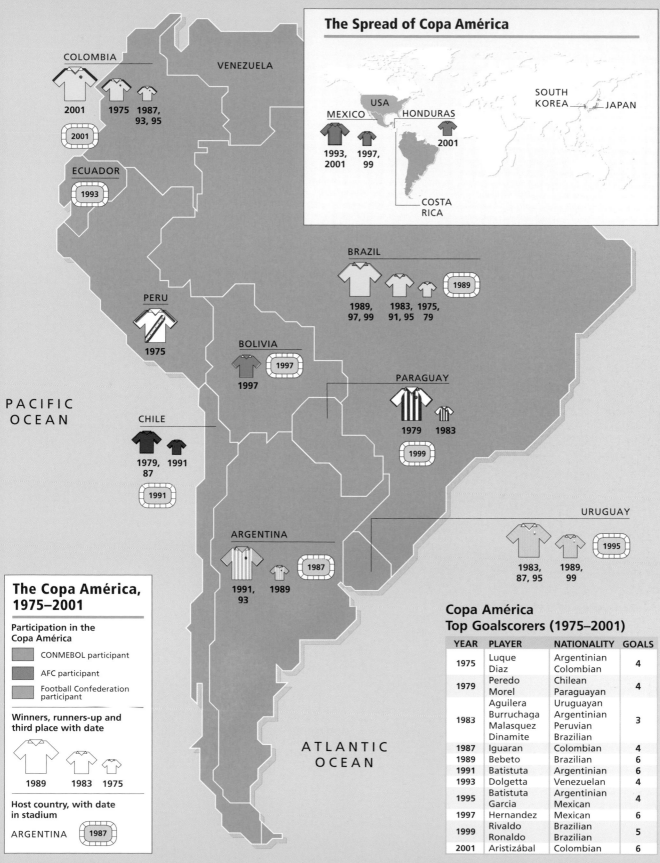

The Spread of Copa América

COLOMBIA
2001 1975 1987, 93, 95
2001

VENEZUELA

MEXICO USA
1993, 1997, 2001 99

HONDURAS
2001

COSTA RICA

SOUTH KOREA → JAPAN

ECUADOR
1993

BRAZIL
1989, 97, 99 1983, 91, 95 1975, 79
1989

PERU
1975

BOLIVIA
1997 1997

PARAGUAY
1979 1983
1999

PACIFIC OCEAN

CHILE
1979, 87 1991
1991

URUGUAY
1983, 87, 95 1989, 99
1995

ARGENTINA
1991, 93 1989 1987

ATLANTIC OCEAN

COPA AMÉRICA

The Copa América, 1975–2001

Participation in the Copa América

- CONMEBOL participant
- AFC participant
- Football Confederation participant

Winners, runners-up and third place with date

1989 1983 1975

Host country, with date in stadium

ARGENTINA 1987

Copa América Top Goalscorers (1975–2001)

YEAR	PLAYER	NATIONALITY	GOALS
1975	Luque	Argentinian	4
	Diaz	Colombian	
1979	Peredo	Chilean	4
	Morel	Paraguayan	
	Aguilera	Uruguayan	
1983	Burruchaga	Argentinian	3
	Malasquez	Peruvian	
	Dinamite	Brazilian	
1987	Iguaran	Colombian	4
1989	Bebeto	Brazilian	6
1991	Batistuta	Argentinian	6
1993	Dolgetta	Venezuelan	4
1995	Batistuta	Argentinian	4
	Garcia	Mexican	
1997	Hernandez	Mexican	6
1999	Rivaldo	Brazilian	5
	Ronaldo	Brazilian	
2001	Aristizábal	Colombian	6

Copa América 2001

TOURNAMENT REVIEW

COLOMBIA LOST THE right to host the 1986 World Cup because of fears of disruption and chaos created by the endemic violence born of a massive narcotics industry. It went on to almost lose the 2001 Copa América to a wave of bombings and shootings that heralded yet another breakdown of the country's fragile peace process. Throughout May and early June, the civil war between the government, left-wing paramilitaries FARC and right-wing paramilitaries erupted with bombings in Bogotá, Cali and Medellín. Twelve people were killed and over 200 injured in the cities due to host two groups and the Final. However, the CSF (South American Football Confederation) repeatedly confirmed Colombia as hosts as president Andrés Pastrana promised massive troop deployments during the tournament.

In late June, Hernán Mejía Campuzano, vice-president of the Colombian Football Federation, was kidnapped by FARC paramilitaries. The CSF, panicked, announced that the Copa would now take place with an alternative host. Campuzano was promptly released, and headed straight for a meeting of the CSF executive in Buenos Aires. There, on 30 June, the Copa was returned to Colombia, but was to be played in 2002. Finally, on 5 July, under pressure from both Colombian president Andrés Pastrana and Brazilian TV company Traffic, the CSF announced that the Copa would go ahead as planned in Colombia, kicking off just six days later. Pastrana had gone on national TV declaring that the cup was essential to the maintenance of national pride and solidarity. Traffic threatened lawsuits resulting from loss of return on the $7 million it had invested in the TV rights.

COPA AMÉRICA

COLOMBIA
1995 Third place
1997 Quarter-finalists
1999 Quarter-finalists
Deportivo Cali **4**

VENEZUELA
1995 Group stage
1997 Group stage
1999 Group stage
Caracas FC **5**
7

ECUADOR
1995 Group stage
1997 Quarter-finalists
1999 Group stage
El Nacional **7**
3

PERU
1995 Group stage
1997 Semi-finalists
1999 Quarter-finalists
Alizino Lima **4**
Sporting Cristal **4**
3

BOLIVIA
1995 Quarter-finalists
1997 Runners-up
1999 Group stage
Oriente Petrolo **5**
3

CHILE
1995 Group stage
1997 Group stage
1999 Semi-finalists
Santiago Wanderers **4**
7

URUGUAY
1995 Champions
1997 Group stage
1999 Runners-up
Defensor Sporting **4**
Danubio **4**
Wanderers **4**
1

BRAZIL
1995 Runners-up
1997 Champions
1999 Champions
Barcelona **2**
Cruziero **2**
Milan **2**
Palmerias **2**
9

ARGENTINA
1995 Quarter-finalists
1997 Quarter-finalists
1999 Quarter-finalists

PARAGUAY
1995 Quarter-finalists
1997 Quarter-finalists
1999 Quarter-finalists
Sportivo Luqueño **6**
3

Copa América 2001 Qualification

Means by which the national team qualified
- Host
- Participant
- Withdrew
- Did not enter

National squads

COLOMBIA — Team name
— Team shirt
1995 Third place — Performance in last 3 tournaments
Oriente Petrolo **5** — Number of players from club team in national squad
12 — Number of squad members (out of 22) that play abroad

Foreign participants in Copa América 2001

- Participant
- Withdrew
- Late replacement

CANADA

MEXICO
1995 Quarter-finalists
1997 Third place
1999 Third place
3

COSTA RICA
1997 Group stage
5

HONDURAS
2

Not everyone was convinced by the CSF and by Pastrana's assurances. Argentina and Canada, who were due to play group games in Medellín, thought better of it and withdrew. Costa Rica and Honduras agreed to make up the numbers.

If the political prospects for the tournament looked poor, the sporting prospects were not that much better. The long South American World Cup qualification tournament had already stolen much of the Copa's thunder. Argentina, the strongest of the South American sides, was not present, Uruguay sent a reserve squad, and no settled Brazilian squad existed to be sent. Barranquilla, a humid port on the coast, and Bogotá, high up in the Andes, both presented serious problems of acclimatization for the players.

A massive police presence was promised by President Pastrana in order to persuade the CSF to allow Colombia to host the tournament.

Copa América 2001: The Venues

Cali Location of stadium

Scene of bomb attacks

Tournament stadium with capacity and name:
45,600 PASCUAL GUERRERO

Barranquilla — 50,220 METROPOLITANO

52,800 ATANASIO GIRARDOT

Medellín

34,000 HERNÁN RAMÍREZ VILLEGAS

Manizales

Pereira

Arménia

29,000 CENTENARIO

Bogotá — EL CAMPÍN

Cali

COLOMBIA

45,600 PASCUAL GUERRERO

35,000 PALOGRANDE

The Development of Copa América 2001

May Bombs In Medellín and Bogotá kill 12 and injure hundreds

25 June Hernán Campuzano, vice-president of the FCF, kidnapped by FARC guerrillas

28 June CONMEBOL announces tournament to be held elsewhere; Colombia threatens to withdraw unless it is played in Colombia

5 July CONMEBOL announce tournament to take place on original dates

9 July Costa Rica agrees to participate

11 July Tournament begins

May

June

July

4 May Car bomb in Cali injures dozens including Colombian players and coaches

26 June CONMEBOL ratifies Colombia as hosts for Copa América

27 June CONMEBOL suspends decision, Campuzano released

30 June Colombia reinstated as hosts, but tournament postponed to 2002

6 July Argentina withdraws

7 July Canada withdraws

10 July Honduras agrees to participate

THE GROUP STAGES

In Group A, Colombia and Chile outclassed Ecuador and Venezuela. Colombia, under Francisco Maturana, fielded a young team with an experienced defence, including Mario Yepes and Ivan Córdoba. In Group B, the poor form of Brazil continued, beaten by Mexico and threatened for much of the game by an experimental Paraguayan side. In Group C, late arrivals Costa Rica and Honduras hit form and qualified along with Uruguay.

COLOMBIA — A — CHILE
ECUADOR — VENEZUELA

BRAZIL — B — MEXICO
PERU — PARAGUAY

COSTA RICA — C — HONDURAS
URUGUAY — BOLIVIA

GROUP A

Chile 4-1 Ecuador
Colombia 2-0 Venezuela
Chile 1-0 Venezuela
Colombia 1-0 Ecuador
Ecuador 4-0 Venezuela
Colombia 2-0 Chile

	P	W	D	L	F	A	Pts
Colombia	3	3	0	0	5	0	9
Chile	3	2	0	1	5	3	6
Ecuador	3	1	0	2	5	5	3
Venezuela	3	0	0	3	0	7	0

GROUP B

Peru 3-3 Paraguay
Mexico 1-0 Brazil
Brazil 2-0 Peru
Paraguay 0-0 Mexico
Peru 1-0 Mexico
Brazil 3-1 Paraguay

	P	W	D	L	F	A	Pts
Brazil	3	2	0	1	5	2	6
Mexico	3	1	1	1	1	1	4
Peru	3	1	1	1	4	5	4
Paraguay	3	0	2	1	4	6	2

GROUP C

Uruguay 1-0 Bolivia
Costa Rica 1-0 Honduras
Uruguay 1-1 Costa Rica
Honduras 2-0 Bolivia
Costa Rica 4-0 Bolivia
Honduras 1-0 Uruguay

	P	W	D	L	F	A	Pts
Costa Rica	3	2	1	0	6	1	7
Honduras	3	2	0	1	3	1	6
Uruguay	3	1	1	1	2	2	4
Bolivia	3	0	0	3	0	7	0

COPA AMÉRICA

THE QUARTER-FINALS

Chile and Peru gave Mexico and Colombia easy quarter-final victories, though the Peruvians held out against a rampant Colombian attack for the first 50 minutes. It required an inspired shot from Aristizábal to break the deadlock and a header ten minutes later to seal it. Costa Rica and Uruguay met again after drawing 1-1 in the group stage – Uruguay went through to the last four winning 2-1. The big upset came in the Brazil v Honduras tie. The Hondurans were expected to play for a draw and penalties, but their passing and movement were too much for a lethargic, leaden Brazil, and they triumphed 2-0.

22 July – Pereira
Attendance 20,000

Chile	0-2	Mexico
	h/t: 0-1	
	Scorers	Arellano 17, Osorno 78
□□	Yellow cards	□□□
	Red cards	

22 July – Arménia
Attendance 29,000

Costa Rica	1-2	Uruguay
	h/t: 0-0	
Wanchope 52	Scorers	Lemos 60 (pen) Lima 87
□□□□	Yellow cards	□□□
	Red cards	

23 July – Arménia
Attendance 30,000

Colombia	3-0	Peru
	h/t: 0-0	
Aristizábal 50, 69 Hernández 66	Scorers	
□	Yellow cards	□□
	Red cards	

23 July – Manizales
Attendance 30,000

Brazil	0-2	Honduras
	h/t: 0-0	
	Scorers	Belletti 57 o.g. Martínez S. 88
□□	Yellow cards	□□
■	Red cards	■

THE SEMI-FINALS

Colombia proved too strong for Honduras with the team's stars Freddy Grisales and Victor Hugo Aristizábal combining to put the hosts 2-0 ahead and so progress to the Final. Throughout the tournament Grisales gave Colombia's midfield energy and purpose while Aristizábal scored six goals – the biggest tally in a Copa América since Pele in 1959. Mexico was compact and composed in the victory over Uruguay, but picked up injuries and suspensions to key players, late red cards for García Aspe and Vidrio proving costly in the Final.

25 July – Pereira
Attendance 20,000

Mexico	2-1	Uruguay
	h/t: 1-1	
Borgetti 14 García Aspe 67 (pen)	Scorers	Morales R. 32
□□□□	Yellow cards	□□□□
■■	Red cards	■■

26 July - Manizales
Attendance 40,000

Colombia	2-0	Honduras
	h/t: 1-0	
Bedoya 6 Aristizábal 63	Scorers	
□□	Yellow cards	□□□□
	Red cards	

THIRD PLACE PLAY-OFF

Honduras continued to show great form in the third-fourth play-off match, and the team's teenage winger, Fabian Estoyanoff, ran the Uruguayan right-wing ragged. But Uruguay dug in and found equalizers to both the Honduran strikes. However, when it came to penalties, the Honduran players held their nerve.

July 29 - Bogotá
Attendance 47,000

Uruguay	2-2 (after extra time) Honduras won 5-4 on pens	Honduras
	h/t: 2-2 f/t: 2-2	
Bizera 21 Martínez 44	Scorers	Martínez S. 14 Izaguirre 41
□□□□	Yellow cards	□□
	Red cards	

THE FINAL

Without captain Aspe and centre-backs Vidrio and Márquez, Mexico barely troubled Colombia in the Final. Cue a short burst of national celebration that the tournament had been peaceful and well supported and had ended in a home victory. It is a shame but no surprise that since the tournament Colombian politics and peace negotiations have shown no sign of following a similar path.

The Colombian squad celebrates its victory by holding up the Copa América trophy in a shower of red, yellow and blue ticker tape. A peaceful tournament and a home victory more than justified the decision to award the Copa to Colombia.

The Winning Goal

With 64 minutes on the clock, Colombia was awarded a free kick on the right-hand side of the pitch. Ivan López curled in a cross and Colombian captain Ivan Córdoba leapt over the Mexican defence to head powerfully into the net past keeper Oscar Pérez.

The Starting Line-Up

July 29 - El Campín, Bogotá
Attendance 46,310

MEXICO	Referee	COLOMBIA
Formation: 3-5-2	● Ubaldo Aquino (Paraguay)	Formation: 4-4-2
Manager		**Manager**
Javier Aguirre		Francisco Maturana

Substitutes

MEXICO			COLOMBIA
Sánchez	1	8	Ferriera
Victorino	10	11	Arriaga
Osorno	11	12	Calero
Reyes	16	16	González
Hierro	17	18	Castillo
Zepeda	19	21	Diaz
Martinez	22	23	Molina

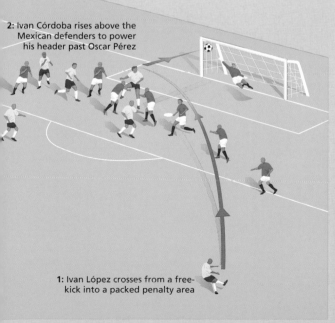

2: Ivan Córdoba rises above the Mexican defenders to power his header past Oscar Pérez

1: Ivan López crosses from a free-kick into a packed penalty area

Highlights of the Game

KEY

Player booked	▯	⇄ Substitution
Player sent off	▮	⚽ Goal

MEXICO ▼ KICK OFF 0 mins **COLOMBIA**

1 min: Play interrupted briefly as a parachutist drifted onto the pitch crashing into the sideline advertising placards

5 min: Victor Aristizábal hits the post

20 min: Bedoya

28 min: Vargas

31 min: Castillo on, Aristizábal off after a collision with goalie Oscar Pérez almost draws a penalty

35 min: Coach Javier Aguirre refused to leave the bench after being sent off for stepping out of coach's area

45 mins

HALF-TIME: 0-0

54 min: Victorino on, Arellano off

65 min: Ivan Córdoba puts Colombia ahead

67 min: Osorno on, Johan Rodríguez off

70 min: Ramón Carlos Morales

74 min: Zepeda on, Alberto Rodríguez off

79 min: Juan Rodríguez sent off for a violent tackle

87 min: Molina on, Hernández off

90 min: Gerardo Torrado sent off for violent conduct

90 mins
+ 3 mins injury time

93 min: Molina

FULL-TIME: 0-1

Colombian full-back *Ivan Córdoba rises to meet Ivan López's free kick and heads the only goal of the Final of Copa América 2001.*

Copa América

THE COPA AMÉRICA is the oldest continental football tournament. Unofficial tournaments were played as far back as 1910 and 1916, with the first official tournament held in 1917. The small number of South American nations and the vast differences in the strength of teams across the continent have produced an ever-changing range of tournament formats.

Most of the early tournaments were based on a mini-league format with play-offs in the event of ties. In 1975 CONMEBOL radically changed the format by playing the first rounds of the competition all over South America. Three groups of three played for three semi-final places, the fourth slot going to the reigning champions. Public interest, already at a low level, dipped even further with this bizarre elongated format, and in 1987 the tournament was re-established in a single host nation over two or three weeks.

In 1989 and 1991 two leagues of five were played to produce four semi-finalists, and from 1993 the tournament was enlarged, with two places being given to teams invited from the rest of the Americas and Asia: the USA, Costa Rica, Mexico and Japan have all participated. Twelve teams allow for a model based on three groups of four with winner, runners-up and the two best-placed third teams going on to knockout quarter-finals.

1910 ARGENTINA*
1 Argentina
2 Uruguay
3 Chile

1916 ARGENTINA*
1 Uruguay
2 Argentina
3 Brazil

1917 URUGUAY
1 Uruguay
2 Argentina
3 Brazil

1919 BRAZIL
1 Brazil (after play-off)
2 Uruguay
3 Argentina

PLAY-OFF
May 29 – das Laranjeiras, Rio de Janeiro
Brazil 1-0 Uruguay
(Friedenreich 122)
(after extra time)
h/t: 0-0 **90 mins:** 0-0
Att: 28,000 **Ref:** Barbera (Argentina)

1920 CHILE
1 Uruguay
2 Argentina
3 Brazil

1921 ARGENTINA
1 Argentina
2 Brazil
3 Uruguay

1922 BRAZIL
1 Brazil (after play-off)
2 Paraguay
3 Uruguay

PLAY-OFF
October 22 – das Laranjeiras, Rio de Janeiro
Brazil 3-1 Paraguay
(Neco 11,   (G. Rivas 60)
Formiga 48, 89)
h/t: 1-0 **Att:** 20,000
Ref: Guevara (Chile)

1923 URUGUAY
1 Uruguay
2 Argentina
3 Paraguay

1924 URUGUAY
1 Uruguay
2 Argentina
3 Paraguay

1925 ARGENTINA
1 Argentina
2 Brazil
3 Paraguay

1926 CHILE
1 Uruguay
2 Argentina
3 Chile

1927 PERU
1 Argentina
2 Uruguay
3 Peru

1929 ARGENTINA
1 Argentina
2 Paraguay
3 Uruguay

1935 PERU*
1 Uruguay
2 Argentina
3 Peru

1937 ARGENTINA
1 Argentina (after play-off)
2 Brazil
3 Uruguay

PLAY-OFF
February 1 – Gasómetro, Buenos Aires
Argentina 2-0 Brazil
(De la Mata 109,
122)
(after extra time)
h/t: 0-0 **90 mins:** 0-0
Att: 80,000 **Ref:** Macias (Argentina)

1939 PERU
1 Peru
2 Uruguay
3 Paraguay

1941 CHILE*
1 Argentina
2 Uruguay
3 Chile

1942 URUGUAY
1 Uruguay
2 Argentina
3 Brazil

1945 CHILE*
1 Argentina
2 Brazil
3 Chile

1946 ARGENTINA*
1 Argentina
2 Brazil
3 Paraguay

1947 ECUADOR
1 Argentina
2 Paraguay
3 Uruguay

1949 BRAZIL
1 Brazil (after play-off)
2 Paraguay
3 Peru

PLAY-OFF
May 11 – São Januario, Rio de Janeiro
Brazil 7-0 Paraguay
(Ademir 17,
27, 48,
Tesourinha 43, 70,
Jair 72, 89)
h/t: 3-0 **Att:** 55,000
Ref: Berrick (England)

1953 PERU
1 Paraguay (after play-off)
2 Brazil
3 Uruguay

PLAY-OFF
April 1 – Nacional, Lima
Paraguay 3-2 Brazil
(A. Lopez 14,   (Baltazar 56, 65)
Gavilan 17,
R. Fernández 41)
h/t: 3-0 **Att:** 35,000
Ref: Dean (England)

1955 CHILE
1 Argentina
2 Chile
3 Peru

1956 URUGUAY*
1 Uruguay
2 Chile
3 Argentina

1957 PERU
1 Argentina
2 Brazil
3 Uruguay

1959 ARGENTINA
1 Argentina
2 Brazil
3 Paraguay

1959 ECUADOR*
1 Uruguay
2 Argentina
3 Brazil

1963 BOLIVIA
1 Bolivia
2 Paraguay
3 Argentina

1967 URUGUAY
1 Uruguay
2 Argentina
3 Chile

1975 FINAL** (2 legs)
October 16 – El Campín, Bogotá
Colombia 1-0 Peru
(P. Castro)
Att: 50,000 **Ref:** Comesaña (Argentina)

October 22 – Nacional, Lima
Peru 2-0 Colombia
(Zárate,
Ramírez)
Att: 50,000 **Ref:** Silvagno (Chile)

PLAY-OFF
October 28 – Olímpico, Caracas
Peru 1-0 Colombia
(Sotil 25)
h/t: 1-0 **Att:** 30,000
Ref: Barreto (Uruguay)

Copa América Winners

Argentina
1910, 21, 25, 27, 29,
37, 41*, 45*, 46* 47,
55, 57, 59, 91, 93

Uruguay
1916*, 17, 20, 23, 24,
26, 35*, 42, 56*, 59*,
67, 83, 87, 95

Brazil
1919, 22, 49,
89, 97, 99

Peru
1939, 75

Paraguay
1953, 79

Bolivia
1963

Colombia
2001

1979 FINAL** (2 legs)
November 28 – Defensores del Chaco,
Asunción
Paraguay 3-0 Chile
*(C. Romero 12, 65,
M. Morel 36)*
h/t: 2-0 **Att:** 40,000
Ref: Da Rosa (Uruguay)

December 5 – Nacional, Santiago
Chile 1-0 Paraguay
(Rivas 10)
h/t: 1-0 **Att:** 55,000
Ref: Barreto (Uruguay)

PLAY-OFF
December 11 – José Amalfitani, Buenos Aires
Paraguay 0-0 Chile
h/t: 0-0 **Att:** 6,000
Ref: Coelho (Brazil)
Paraguay won on goal difference

1983 FINAL** (2 legs)
October 27 – Centenario, Montevideo
Uruguay 2-0 Brazil
*(Francescoli
41 pen, Diogo 80)*
h/t: 1-0 **Att:** 65,000
Ref: Ortiz (Paraguay)

November 4 – Fonte Nova, Salvador
Brazil 1-1 Uruguay
(Jorginho 23)   (Aguilera 77)
h/t: 1-0 **Att:** 95,000
Ref: Perez (Peru)
Uruguay won 3-1 on aggregate

1987 ARGENTINA
THIRD PLACE PLAY-OFF
July 11 – Monumental, Buenos Aires
Colombia 2-1 Argentina
*(G. Gomez 8,   (Caniggia 86)
Galeano 27)*
h/t: 2-0 **Att:** 15,000
Ref: Corujo (Venezuela)

FINAL
July 12 – Monumental, Buenos Aires
Uruguay 1-0 Chile
(Bengochea 56)
h/t: 0-0 **Att:** 35,000
Ref: Romualdo Arppi (Brazil)

1989 BRAZIL
1 Brazil
2 Uruguay
3 Argentina

1991 CHILE
1 Argentina
2 Brazil
3 Chile

1993 ECUADOR
THIRD PLACE PLAY-OFF
July 3 – Reales Tamarindos, Portoviejo
Colombia 1-0 Ecuador
(Valencia 84)
h/t: 0-0 **Att:** 18,000
Ref: Arbolda (Venezuela)

FINAL
July 4 – Monumental, Guayaquil
Argentina 2-1 Mexico
(Batistuta 65, 84)   (Galindo 76 pen)
h/t: 0-0 **Att:** 40,000
Ref: Marcio Rezende (Brazil)

1995 URUGUAY
THIRD PLACE PLAY-OFF
July 22 – Campus Municipal, Maldonado
Colombia 4-1 United States
*(Quinonez 31,   (Moore 53 pen)
Valderrama 38,
Asprilla 50,
Rincon 76)*
h/t: 2-0 **Att:** 2,500
Ref: Imperatore (Chile)

FINAL
July 23 – Centenario, Montevideo
Uruguay 1-1 Brazil
(Bengoechea 48)   (Tulio 30)
(after extra time)
90 mins: 0-0 **Att:** 58,000
Ref: Brizio Carter (Mexico)
Uruguay won 5-3 on pens

1997 BOLIVIA
THIRD PLACE PLAY-OFF
June 28 – Jesús Bermúdez, Oruro
Mexico 1-0 Peru
(Hernández 82)
Ref: Borgesano (Venezuela)

FINAL
June 29 – Hernando Siles, La Paz
Brazil 3-1 Bolivia
*(Edmundo 40,   (E. Sanchez 44)
Ronaldo 79,
Ze Roberto 90)*
h/t: 1-1 **Att:** 50,000
Ref: Nieves (Uruguay)

1999 PARAGUAY
THIRD PLACE PLAY-OFF
July 17 – Defensores del Chaco, Asunción
Mexico 2-1 Chile
*(Palencia 26,   (Palacios 81)
Zepeda 86)*
Att: 4,000 **Ref:** Elizondo (Argentina)

* Unofficial.
** No fixed venues for these tournaments; matches were played home and away.

FINAL
July 18 – Defensores del Chaco, Asunción
Brazil 3-0 Uruguay
*(Rivaldo 20, 27,
Ronaldo 46)*
h/t: 2-0 **Att:** 40,000
Ref: Ruiz (Colombia)

2001 COLOMBIA
THIRD PLACE PLAY-OFF
28 July – El Campín, Bogotá
Honduras 2-2 Uruguay
*(Martínez 14, 45)   (Bizera 22,
Izaguirre 42)*
h/t: 2-2 **Att:** 47,000
Ref: Hidalgo (Peru)
Honduras won 5-4 on pens

FINAL
29 July – El Campín, Bogotá
Colombia 1-0 Mexico
(I. Cordoba 65)
h/t: 0-0 **Att:** 47,000
Ref: Aquino (Paraguay)

The 1999 Copa América Final between Brazil and Uruguay took place in the Defensores del Chaco stadium in Asunción, Paraguay. Brazil won 3-0 with two goals from Rivaldo and one from Ronaldo. Mexico beat Chile 2-1 in the same stadium to claim third place.

COPA AMÉRICA

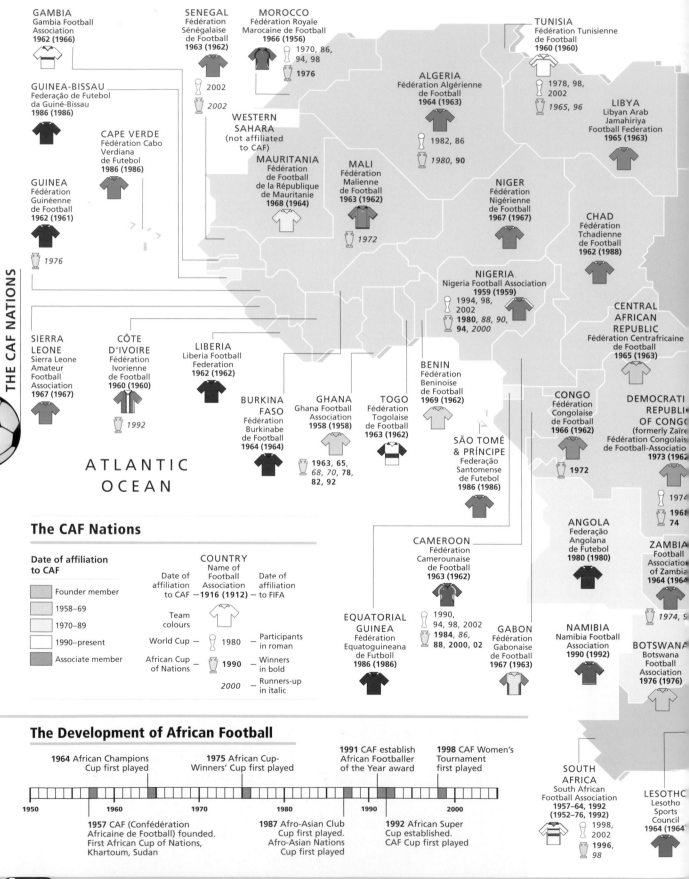

THE CAF NATIONS

GAMBIA
Gambia Football Association
1962 (1966)

GUINEA-BISSAU
Federação de Futebol da Guiné-Bissau
1986 (1986)

CAPE VERDE
Fédération Cabo Verdiana de Futebol
1986 (1986)

GUINEA
Fédération Guinéenne de Football
1962 (1961)
1976

SENEGAL
Fédération Sénégalaise de Football
1963 (1962)
2002
2002

MOROCCO
Fédération Royale Marocaine de Football
1966 (1956)
1970, 86, 94, 98
1976

WESTERN SAHARA
(not affiliated to CAF)

MAURITANIA
Fédération de Football de la République de Mauritanie
1968 (1964)

MALI
Fédération Malienne de Football
1963 (1962)
1972

ALGERIA
Fédération Algérienne de Football
1964 (1963)
1982, 86
1980, 90

NIGER
Fédération Nigérienne de Football
1967 (1967)

TUNISIA
Fédération Tunisienne de Football
1960 (1960)
1978, 98, 2002
1965, 96

LIBYA
Libyan Arab Jamahiriya Football Federation
1965 (1963)

CHAD
Fédération Tchadienne de Football
1962 (1988)

CENTRAL AFRICAN REPUBLIC
Fédération Centrafricaine de Football
1965 (1963)

SIERRA LEONE
Sierra Leone Amateur Football Association
1967 (1967)

CÔTE D'IVOIRE
Fédération Ivoirienne de Football
1960 (1960)
1992

LIBERIA
Liberia Football Federation
1962 (1962)

BURKINA FASO
Fédération Burkinabe de Football
1964 (1964)

GHANA
Ghana Football Association
1958 (1958)
1963, 65, *68, 70*, 78, 82, 92

TOGO
Fédération Togolaise de Football
1963 (1962)

BENIN
Fédération Beninoise de Football
1969 (1962)

NIGERIA
Nigeria Football Association
1959 (1959)
1994, 98, 2002
1980, *88*, **90**, *94, 2000*

SÃO TOMÉ & PRÍNCIPE
Federação Santomense de Futebol
1986 (1986)

CONGO
Fédération Congolaise de Football
1966 (1962)
1972

DEMOCRATIC REPUBLIC OF CONGO
(formerly Zaïre)
Fédération Congolaise de Football-Association
1973 (1962)
1974
1968, 74

ATLANTIC OCEAN

CAMEROON
Fédération Camerounaise de Football
1963 (1962)
1990, 94, 98, 2002
1984, *86*, **88, 2000**, *02*

EQUATORIAL GUINEA
Fédération Equatoguineana de Futboll
1986 (1986)

GABON
Fédération Gabonaise de Football
1967 (1963)

ANGOLA
Federação Angolana de Futebol
1980 (1980)

NAMIBIA
Namibia Football Association
1990 (1992)

ZAMBIA
Football Association of Zambia
1964 (1964)
1974, 9

BOTSWANA
Botswana Football Association
1976 (1976)

SOUTH AFRICA
South African Football Association
1957–64, 1992
(1952–76, 1992)
1998, 2002
1996, *98*

LESOTHO
Lesotho Sports Council
1964 (1964)

The CAF Nations

Date of affiliation to CAF

- Founder member
- 1958–69
- 1970–89
- 1990–present
- Associate member

COUNTRY
Name of Football Association
Date of affiliation to CAF — **1916 (1912)** — Date of affiliation to FIFA

Team colours

World Cup — 1980 — Participants in roman

African Cup of Nations — **1990** — Winners in bold

2000 — Runners-up in italic

The Development of African Football

1964 African Champions Cup first played

1975 African Cup-Winners' Cup first played

1991 CAF establish African Footballer of the Year award

1998 CAF Women's Tournament first played

1950 — 1960 — 1970 — 1980 — 1990 — 2000

1957 CAF (Confédération Africaine de Football) founded. First African Cup of Nations, Khartoum, Sudan

1987 Afro-Asian Club Cup first played. Afro-Asian Nations Cup first played

1992 African Super Cup established. CAF Cup first played

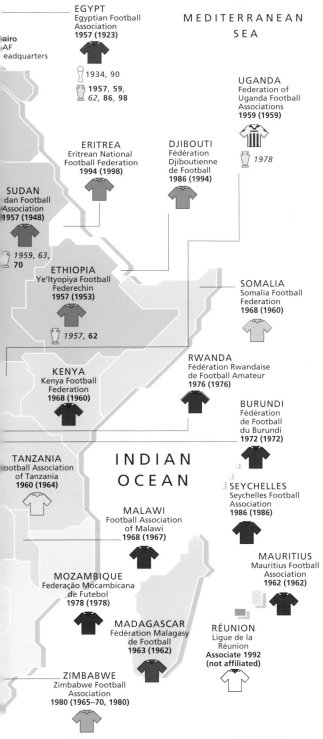

EGYPT
Egyptian Football
Association
1957 (1923)

MEDITERRANEAN
SEA

🏆 1934, 90

🏆 1957, 59,
62, 86, 98

Cairo
CAF
Headquarters

UGANDA
Federation of
Uganda Football
Associations
1959 (1959)

ERITREA
Eritrean National
Football Federation
1994 (1998)

DJIBOUTI
Fédération
Djiboutienne
de Football
1986 (1994)

🏆 *1978*

SUDAN
Sudan Football
Association
1957 (1948)

🏆 *1959, 63,
70*

ETHIOPIA
Ye'Ityopiya Football
Federechin
1957 (1953)

SOMALIA
Somalia Football
Federation
1968 (1960)

🏆 *1957*, 62

KENYA
Kenya Football
Federation
1968 (1960)

RWANDA
Fédération Rwandaise
de Football Amateur
1976 (1976)

BURUNDI
Fédération
de Football
du Burundi
1972 (1972)

TANZANIA
Football Association
of Tanzania
1960 (1964)

INDIAN
OCEAN

SEYCHELLES
Seychelles Football
Association
1986 (1986)

MALAWI
Football Association
of Malawi
1968 (1967)

MAURITIUS
Mauritius Football
Association
1962 (1962)

MOZAMBIQUE
Federação Moçambicana
de Futebol
1978 (1978)

MADAGASCAR
Fédération Malagasy
de Football
1963 (1962)

RÉUNION
Ligue de la
Réunion
**Associate 1992
(not affiliated)**

ZIMBABWE
Zimbabwe Football
Association
1980 (1965–70, 1980)

SWAZILAND
National Football
Association of
Swaziland
1976 (1976)

CAF

**African Tournaments
and Cup Competitions:**
African Cup of Nations
CAF Cup
African Champions League
African Cup-Winners' Cup
CAF Super Cup

The CAF Nations

CAF (CONFEDERATION AFRICAINE DE FOOTBALL) was first proposed in 1956 by representatives of the only independent nations then in Africa: Egypt, Ethiopia, Sudan and South Africa. With FIFA support the organization was inaugurated in Khartoum in 1957 and then based in Cairo, Egypt. Politics intervened in CAF's development immediately when the South Africans proposed sending either an all-black or all-white team to the first African Cup of Nations in Sudan. South Africa was then suspended and remained outside the CAF until 1994.

With only three members CAF's global and continental influence was small but the wave of decolonization that swept Africa from the late 1950s rapidly increased its membership, while the quality and popularity of African football has steadily enhanced CAF's status and power at the FIFA table. CAF votes and influence were central to the success of João Havelange in winning the FIFA presidency in 1974 and African representation at the World Cup has climbed to five places.

Despite the size of the continent, the expense of travel and the often-shaky finances of local football associations, CAF has now established three international club tournaments and the biennial African Nations Cup. Within CAF there are also five regional federations: the Arab Football Union, Confederation of East and Central African Football Associations, Confederation of Southern African Football Federations, Union of Football Associations of Central Africa and West African Football Union, each of which organizes its own cup competition.

Chaotic scenes like this one, as people jostle for a good view before a league match between Hearts of Oak and Asante Kotoko in Accra Stadium in Ghana, are commonplace at African football matches.

Calendar of Events	
Club Tournaments	Africans Champions League 2003 African Cup-Winners' Cup 2003 CAF Cup 2003 CAF Super Cup 2003
International Tournaments	African Cup of Nations 2004, Qualifying Tournament

THE CAF NATIONS

Africa

THE SEASONS IN REVIEW 2000–01, 2001–02

ALTHOUGH THERE WERE sporadic problems at football matches this season, including a death in Senegal after police released tear gas at a league match between Stade Mbour and Jeanne d'Arc, African football put the truly disastrous stadium tragedies of early 2001 behind it. The African Cup of Nations, held in Mali (see pages 408–409), was a success despite the limitations of the Malian infrastructure; five African sides – the most ever – headed for the World Cup in Japan and South Korea; and with Isaac Hayatou's bid for the FIFA presidency Africa appeared to be rising to the very top of the global football power structure.

The African Champions League saw South Africa's Mamelodi Sundowns meet Egyptian side Al Ahly. In the opening leg in Pretoria, all of Sundowns' pressure could only gain a 1-1 draw. The Zambian Kampamba scored a superb solo goal for the Sundowns, taking the ball from the centre circle all the way to the box before registering. But in the second half Al Ahly caught them on the counter, and snatched an equalizer. But the team from Cairo needn't have worried; back on home ground in the second leg it was 3-0 to Al Ahly with Khaled Bebo scoring a hat-trick to take Al Ahly's third African Champions Cup.

In the Cup-Winners' Cup, South African side Kaizer Chiefs, who despite over 30 domestic trophies has never progressed beyond the second round of an African cup competition, won its first. The team was up against the Angolan side Inter Clube, the Luanda police team which had been a second division no-hoper until recently. The Chiefs always looked a cut above Inter, drawing 1-1 in Angola and winning 1-0 at home.

JS Kabylie retained the CAF Cup in a controversial Final. Opponents, Tunisian side Étoile du Sahel, had just fired coach Khaled Ben Sassi five days before the first leg but had managed to take a 2-1 lead at home in Sousse. In the return match it proved too slender a margin, as an intimidating home crowd of over 80,000 roared the Algerians on. A brutal, foul-ridden game ensued, descending at one point into an attack on the referee. Kabylie levelled the tie when Brahim Zafour knocked the Étoile goalkeeper over and headed the loose ball home, and the Algerians won the cup on away goals.

Top 15 African Leagues

COUNTRY	CHAMPIONS	RUNNERS-UP	CUP WINNERS
Algeria†	CR Belouizdad	USM Alger	USM Alger
Angola	Petro Atlético	Atlético Sport Aviacao	†Deportivo Sonangol
Cameroon	Cotonsport	Tonnerre Yaoundé	†Fovu
Côte d'Ivoire	ASEC	Satellite FC	†Alliance Bouaké
DRC†	AS Vita Club	DC Motema Pembe	TP Mazembe
Egypt	Ismaily	Al Ahly	Zamalek
Ghana	Hearts of Oak	Asante Kotoko	†Asante Kotoko
Kenya	Oserian Fastac	Mathare United	AFC Leopards
Morocco	Hassania US d'Agadir	WAC Casablanca	FAR Rabat*
Nigeria†	Enyimba	MPA	Dolphin FC
Senegal	Jeanne d'Arc	SONACOS	AS Douanes
South Africa	Santos	Supersport Utd	†Santos
Tanzania†	Simba FC	Mtibwa Sugar	Police
Tunisia	Espérance Sportive	Étoile du Sahel	CS Hammam-Lif
Zambia†	Nkana FC	Zanaco	Power Dynamos

† data for season 2000–01, the rest correct to summer 2002.
* 1999 winner – played March 2001.

Champions League

2001 FINAL (2 legs)

Dec 8 – Pretoria
Mamelodi 1-1 Al Ahly
Sundowns (Egypt)
(South Africa) *(Abdelhafiz 58)*
(Kampamba 26)
h/t: 1-0 Att : 5,000
Ref: Codja (Benin)

Dec 21 – Cairo
Al Ahly 3-0 Mamelodi
(Bebo 37 pen, **Sundowns**
44, 89)
h/t: 2-0 Att: 80,000
Ref: El Arjoun (Morocco)

Al Ahly won 4-1 on aggregate

Cup-Winners' Cup

2001 FINAL (2 legs)

Nov 17 – Luanda
Inter Clube 1-1 Kaizer Chiefs
(Angola) (South Africa)
(Esengo 27) *(Jukelile 20)*
h/t: 1-1 Att: 15,000
Ref: Abdulkadir (Tanzania)

Dec 1 – Johannesburg
Kaizer Chiefs 1-0 Inter Clube
(Mabedi 89 pen)
h/t: 0-0 Att: 50,000
Ref: Al-Ghandour (Egypt)

Kaizer Chiefs won 2-1 on aggregate

CAF Cup

2001 FINAL (2 legs)

Nov 10 – Sousse
Étoile du Sahel 2-1 JS Kabylie
(Tunisia) (Algeria)
(Keita 14, 74) *(Boubrit 42)*
h/t: 1-1 Att: 19,000
Ref: Hellemalik (Ethiopia)

Nov 23 – Algiers
JS Kabylie 1-0 Étoile du Sahel
(Zafour 28)
h/t: 1-0 Att: 80,000
Ref: Hidalgo (Peru)

JS Kabylie won on away goals rule

Super Cup

2002 FINAL

March 15 – Cairo
Al Ahly 4-1 Kaizer Chiefs
(Egypt) (South Africa)
(Bebo 7, *(Nzama 20)*
Ghaly 30,
Al-Hadary 65,
Abdelhafiz 69)
h/t : 2-1 Att: 60,000
Ref: Shelmani (Libya)

Inter Clube, one of Luanda's smaller teams, lost out in the domestic league to oil-funded giants Petro Atlético but won the 2002 Angolan Cup and made the Final of the Cup-Winners' Cup, where the team lost to South Africa's Kaizer Chiefs over two legs.

AFRICA

Below: JS Kabilye's Brahim Zafour knocks the ball out of the keeper's hands to score the only goal in the second leg of the CAF Cup Final...

Below, centre: ... and the players celebrate with the trophy. The club lost the Algerian league after political upheaval in the team's Berber-dominated province forced them to forfeit two home games.

Mamelodi Sundowns of South Africa (in yellow) relinquished its domestic crown this season and lost the Final of the Champions League to Egypt's Al Ahly.

Issa Hayatou, president of CAF, challenged Sepp Blatter for the FIFA presidency in 2002, but lost to the master of football geopolitics by 139 votes to 56.

Al Ahly, CAF's African Team of the 20th Century, celebrates another successful season by winning the 2002 Super Cup, beating South Africa's Kaizer Chiefs in the Final.

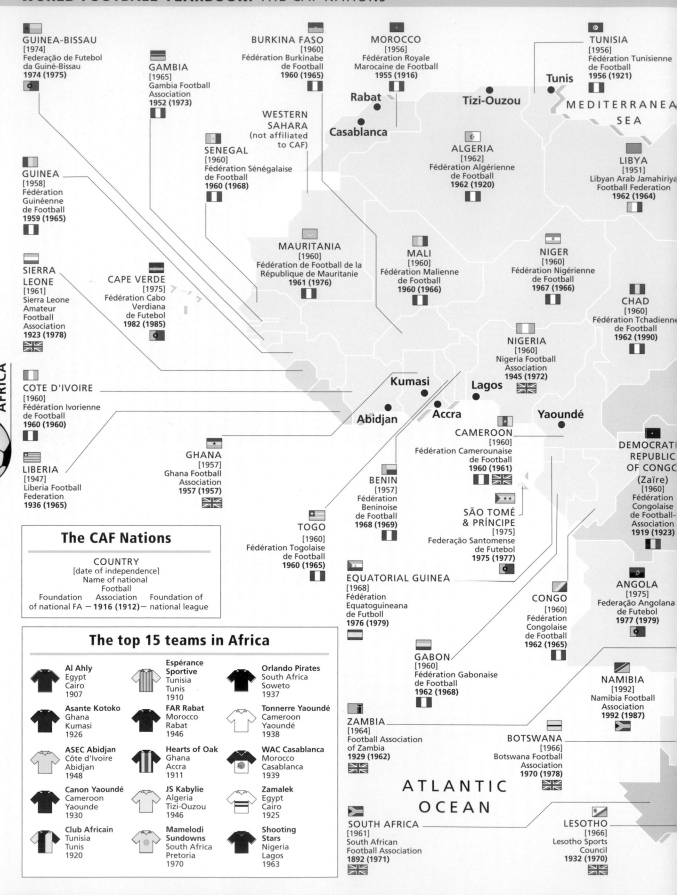

AFRICA

GUINEA-BISSAU
[1974]
Federação de Futebol
da Guiné-Bissau
1974 (1975)

GAMBIA
[1965]
Gambia Football
Association
1952 (1973)

BURKINA FASO
[1960]
Fédération Burkinabe
de Football
1960 (1965)

MOROCCO
[1956]
Fédération Royale
Marocaine de Football
1955 (1916)

TUNISIA
[1956]
Fédération Tunisienne
de Football
1956 (1921)

Tunis

Rabat

Tizi-Ouzou

Casablanca

MEDITERRANEAN
SEA

**WESTERN
SAHARA**
(not affiliated
to CAF)

SENEGAL
[1960]
Fédération Sénégalaise
de Football
1960 (1968)

ALGERIA
[1962]
Fédération Algérienne
de Football
1962 (1920)

LIBYA
[1951]
Libyan Arab Jamahiriya
Football Federation
1962 (1964)

GUINEA
[1958]
Fédération
Guinéenne
de Football
1959 (1965)

**SIERRA
LEONE**
[1961]
Sierra Leone
Amateur
Football
Association
1923 (1978)

CAPE VERDE
[1975]
Fédération Cabo
Verdiana
de Futebol
1982 (1985)

MAURITANIA
[1960]
Fédération de Football de la
République de Mauritanie
1961 (1976)

MALI
[1960]
Fédération Malienne
de Football
1960 (1966)

NIGER
[1960]
Fédération Nigérienne
de Football
1967 (1966)

CHAD
[1960]
Fédération Tchadienne
de Football
1962 (1990)

NIGERIA
[1960]
Nigeria Football
Association
1945 (1972)

Kumasi

Lagos

COTE D'IVOIRE
[1960]
Fédération Ivoirienne
de Football
1960 (1960)

Abidjan

Accra

Yaoundé

CAMEROON
[1960]
Fédération Camerounaise
de Football
1960 (1961)

**DEMOCRAT
REPUBLIC
OF CONGO**
(Zaïre)
[1960]
Fédération
Congolaise
de Football-
Association
1919 (1923)

LIBERIA
[1947]
Liberia Football
Federation
1936 (1965)

GHANA
[1957]
Ghana Football
Association
1957 (1957)

BENIN
[1957]
Fédération
Beninoise
de Football
1968 (1969)

**SÃO TOMÉ
& PRÍNCIPE**
[1975]
Federação Santomense
de Futebol
1975 (1977)

TOGO
[1960]
Fédération Togolaise
de Football
1960 (1965)

EQUATORIAL GUINEA
[1968]
Fédération
Equatoguineana
de Futboll
1976 (1979)

CONGO
[1960]
Fédération
Congolaise
de Football
1962 (1965)

ANGOLA
[1975]
Federação Angolana
de Futebol
1977 (1979)

GABON
[1960]
Fédération Gabonaise
de Football
1962 (1968)

NAMIBIA
[1992]
Namibia Football
Association
1992 (1987)

ZAMBIA
[1964]
Football Association
of Zambia
1929 (1962)

BOTSWANA
[1966]
Botswana Football
Association
1970 (1978)

ATLANTIC
OCEAN

SOUTH AFRICA
[1961]
South African
Football Association
1892 (1971)

LESOTHO
[1966]
Lesotho Sports
Council
1932 (1970)

The top 15 teams in Africa

Al Ahly
Egypt
Cairo
1907

Asante Kotoko
Ghana
Kumasi
1926

ASEC Abidjan
Côte d'Ivoire
Abidjan
1948

Canon Yaoundé
Cameroon
Yaounde
1930

Club Africain
Tunisia
Tunis
1920

**Espérance
Sportive**
Tunisia
Tunis
1910

FAR Rabat
Morocco
Rabat
1946

Hearts of Oak
Ghana
Accra
1911

JS Kabylie
Algeria
Tizi-Ouzou
1946

**Mamelodi
Sundowns**
South Africa
Pretoria
1970

Orlando Pirates
South Africa
Soweto
1937

Tonnerre Yaoundé
Cameroon
Yaoundé
1938

WAC Casablanca
Morocco
Casablanca
1939

Zamalek
Egypt
Cairo
1925

**Shooting
Stars**
Nigeria
Lagos
1963

CENTRAL
AFRICAN
REPUBLIC
[1960]
Fédération
Centrafricaine
de Football
1937 (1973)

ERITREA
[1993]
Eritrean National
Football Federation
1992 (1993)

African Origins

**Date of formation
of national
Football Association**

By 1899
1900–39
1940–79
After 1980

Colonizing countries

Belgium
Britain
France
Germany
Italy
Portugal
South Africa
Spain

RWANDA
[1962]
Fédération
Rwandaise
de Football
Amateur
1972 (1981)

Cairo

EGYPT
[1954]
Egyptian Football
Association
1921 (1949)

SUDAN
[1956]
Sudan Football
Association
1936 (1959)

DJIBOUTI
[1977]
Fédération
Djiboutienne
de Football
1977 (1987)

ETHIOPIA
[1941]
Ye'Ityopiya Football
Federechin
1943 (1943)

SOMALIA
[1960]
Somalia Football
Federation
1951 (1967)

KENYA
[1963]
Kenya Football
Federation
1932 (1963)

UGANDA
[1962]
Federation of Uganda
Football Associations
1924 (1966)

INDIAN
OCEAN

BURUNDI
[1962]
Fédération
de Football
du Burundi
1948 (1972)

TANZANIA
[1964]
Football Association
of Tanzania
1930 (1965)

SEYCHELLES
[1976]
Seychelles
Football
Association
1976 (1979)

MAURITIUS
[1968]
Mauritius Football
Association
1952 (1970)

MADAGASCAR
[1960]
Fédération Malagasy
de Football
1961 (1968)

RÉUNION
[French overseas
region]
Ligue de la
Réunion
1975 (1976)

Pretoria

Soweto

ZIMBABWE
[1965 Rhodesia UDI
1980 Zimbabwe]
Zimbabwe Football
Association
1950 (1963)

MOZAMBIQUE
[1975]
Federação
Mocambicana
de Futebol
1975 (1976)

SWAZILAND
[1968]
National Football
Association of Swaziland
1964 (1980)

MALAWI
[1964]
Football Association
of Malawi
1966 (1986)

Africa

ORIGINS AND GROWTH OF FOOTBALL

FOOTBALL ARRIVED IN AFRICA via the usual routes – British sailors, missionaries, traders and administrators – but it was, of course, filtered through the various colonial establishments that ran the continent at the turn of 19th century. French, Belgian and Portuguese colonialists also imported football into the continent in the early years of the 20th century. As a consequence, organized football remained in schools and colleges for the most part, and independent national football associations and teams did not exist in most of the continent. The exception was the creation of the South African FA in 1892.

During the inter-war years, football began to gain a substantial following among Africans. By the 1920s, leagues had developed across North Africa (Egypt, Tunisia, Algeria and Morocco) and matches were played between French colonies. Egypt, the strongest footballing nation, played at both Olympic and World Cup tournaments as early as 1920. In the 1930s, Nigerian football acquired organized leagues and inter-colony matches were played in British West Africa. Belgian Congo (later Zaïre, or Democratic Republic of Congo) and Ghana also acquired formal football leagues in this era, but in these countries it was the European colonists that retained administrative control.

Not surprisingly, the development of African football in the postwar years is intimately connected to the process of decolonization and the establishment of new states. CAF, formed from the only independent African nations in 1957 (Egypt, Ethiopia, Sudan and South Africa), held its first tournament that year to celebrate Sudanese independence, and almost immediately expelled South Africa for its continuing racial segregation of football teams and players.

The enormous popularity and domestic political significance of football in Africa since independence can be seen from politicians' desire to be associated with the game (the Zambian national team was known as the 'Kenneth Kaunda XI'), the political reorganization of clubs and leagues (in Algeria, all teams were allocated to nationalized industrial groupings in the1970s) and political battles over the control of national FAs. Football has continued to be strong in North Africa, but has more recently been challenged by the rise of Nigeria, Ghana, DR Congo, Cameroon and South Africa as significant footballing nations.

AFRICA

Hugely successful domestically, Al Ahly from Cairo was voted CAF Club of the Century in 2000, having attained three victories in the African Champions League and four in the African Cup-Winners' Cup.

Egypt

Egyptian Football Asscoiation
Founded: 1921
Joined FIFA: 1923
Joined CAF: 1957

FOOTBALL ARRIVED IN Egypt during the British armed occupation at the turn of the 19th century. No British clubs from the era survive, but the dominant force in Egyptian football, the Cairo-based Al Ahly, was founded in 1907. The club has come to represent the republican strand of Egyptian nationalist politics, a fact confirmed when Nasser was made honorary president of the club in 1954. The team's eternal rival – Zamalek – was founded in 1911 as Kaser-el-nil, becoming Al Mukhtalat in 1925. Its allegiance became clear when the football fanatic King Farouk lent his support and name to the club in 1940. When Farouk was deposed in 1952, the club became Zamalek.

The prescience of Egyptian football can be seen from the early formation of the Egyptian FA (1921), preceding national independence by a year. A cup was donated that year by the king to create the first national competition. In 1920, Egypt played at the Olympic Games in Antwerp, the first African nation ever to do so. In 1924 in Amsterdam, Egypt made it to the quarter-finals, and in 1928, the semi-finals. Egypt was the first African side to play in the World Cup Finals (1934) and supplied the first African referee to the World Cup in 1966.

During the Second World War, Egyptian and Allied military teams played extensively, and in 1949, a national league was created alongside the cup. Politics has never been far from Egyptian football and in 1958 the army took over the national FA and professionalized the game through the back door. With the outbreak of the Arab-Israeli Six-Day War in 1967, Egyptian domestic football was regularly disrupted until after the Yom Kippur War in the 1970s. Enormous and fanatical support has tragically been accompanied by a series of disasters including a riot at the 1966 Cairo derby between Zamalek and Al Ahly that saw over 300 injured when the military took control of the stadium. In 1974, a wall collapsed at Zamalek during a friendly match against Dukla Praha killing 49 people.

Egyptian League Record 1949–2002

SEASON	CHAMPIONS	SEASON	CHAMPIONS
1949	Al Ahly	1974	no championship
1950	Al Ahly	1975	Al Ahly
1951	Al Ahly	1976	Al Ahly
1952	no championship	1977	Al Ahly
1953	Al Ahly	1978	Zamalek
1954	Al Ahly	1979	Al Ahly
1955	no championship	1980	Al Ahly
1956	Al Ahly	1981	Al Ahly
1957	Al Ahly	1982	Al Ahly
1958	Al Ahly	1983	Al Mokaoulom
1959	Al Ahly	1984	Zamalek
1960	Zamalek	1985	Al Ahly
1961	Al Ahly	1986	Al Ahly
1962	Al Ahly	1987	Al Ahly
1963	Al Tersana	1988	Zamalek
1964	Zamalek	1989	Al Ahly
1965	Zamalek	1990	no championship
1966	Olympia	1991	Al Ismaily
1967	Al Ismaily	1992	Zamalek
1968–72	no championship	1993	Zamalek
1973	Mahala	1994	Al Ahly

Egyptian League Record (continued)

SEASON	CHAMPIONS	SEASON	CHAMPIONS
1995	Al Ahly	2001	Zamalek
1996	Al Ahly	2002	Al Ismaily
1997	Al Ahly		
1998	Al Ahly		
1999	Al Ahly		
2000	Al Ahly		

Cup of Egypt 1949–2002

YEAR	WINNERS	YEAR	WINNERS
1949	Al Ahly	1980	no competition
1950	Al Ahly	1981	Al Ahly
1951	Al Ahly	1982	no competition
1952	Zamalek	1983	Al Ahly
1953	Al Ahly	1984	Al Ahly
1954	Al Tersana	1985	Al Ahly
1955	Zamalek	1986	Al Tersana
1956	Al Ahly	1987	no competition
1957	Zamalek	1988	Zamalek
1958	Zamalek and Al Ahly*	1989	Al Ahly
1959	Zamalek	1990	Al Mokaoulom
1960	Zamalek	1991	Al Ahly
1961	Al Ahly	1992	Al Ahly
1962	Zamalek	1993	Al Ahly
1963	Al Ittihad	1994	no competition
1964	Quanah	1995	Al Mokaoulom
1965	Al Tersana	1996	Al Ahly
1966	Al Ahly	1997	Al Ismaily
1967	Al Tersana	1998	Al Masry
1968–72	no competition	1999	Zamalek
1973	Al Ittihad	2000	Al Ismaily
1974	no competition	2001	Al Ahly
1975	Zamalek	2002	Zamalek
1976	Al Ittihad		
1977	Zamalek		
1978	Al Ahly		
1979	Zamalek		

* Cup shared.

Zamalek from Cairo is the second best supported team in Egypt. The club enjoyed the support of King Farouk during the 1940s. It remains the most dangerous rival of neighbours Al Ahly.

EGYPT

Football in Egypt

League champions
3 times or more
1966

League champions
1–2 times
1966

Other teams

Cup of Egypt
winners
1966

● **Cairo** City of origin

○ African Champions
League

◐ African Cup-Winners' Cup

◉ CAF Cup

1973 Winners in bold

1973 Runners-up in italics

* Title shared

Al Ahly

(See box
bottom right)

Al Mokaoulom
(Arab Contractors)

1983 **1990,
95** **1982,
83, 96**

Al Tersana
(Arsenal)

1963 **1954,
65, 67, 86**

Zamalek

(See box
above top right)

Tanta

Mahala

1974
1973

Al
Mansurah

ZAMALEK SPORTING CLUB

40,000 | **City:** Cairo
Founded: 1925
Stadium: Hassan Helmi

ZAMALEK	
League	*1951, 53, 54, 56–59,* **60,** *61–63,* **64, 65, 66, 73, 77, 78,** *79–83,* **84,** *85–87,* **88, 89, 92, 93,** *95–99,* **2001**
Cup of Egypt	*1949,* **52, 53,** *55,* **57,** *58*,* **59, 60, 62,** *63,* **75, 77,** *78,* **79, 88, 92, 99, 2002**
Farouk Cup	**1932, 35, 38, 41,** *43*,* **44,** *48*
African Champions League	**1984,** *86,* **93,** *94,* **96**
African Cup-Winners' Cup	**2000**
African Super Cup	**1993,** *96, 2000*

Alexandria

El
Mahalla
el Kubra

Port
Said

El
Mansûra *Suez
Canal*

Tanta

Ismailiya

Cairo

Olympia

1966

Al Ittihad
(Union Recreation)

**1963,
73, 76**

Al Masry

1998

Quanah

1964

Al Ismaily

2000 **1969** **1997,
2000** **1967,
91, 2002**

EGYPT

Nile

*Jubilant Al Ismaily
players celebrate after
their 4-0 victory over
Al Mokaoulom in the
2000 Cup of Egypt
Final. Four goals in
13 minutes of the
second half sealed
their triumph.*

*Lake
Nasser*

AL AHLY NATIONAL SPORTING CLUB

20,000 | **City:** Cairo
Founded: 1907
Stadium: Mokhtar el Tetch

AL AHLY	
League	**1949–51, 53, 54, 56–59, 61, 62, 67, 75–77, 78,** *79–82,* **84,** *85–87,* **88, 89, 91, 93, 94–2000, 01, 02**
Cup of Egypt	**1949–51,** *52,* **53, 56,** *58*,* **59, 61, 66,** *73,* **76, 78, 81, 83–85, 89, 91–93, 96, 97, 2001**
Farouk Cup	**1924, 25,** *26,* **27, 28, 30, 31, 37, 40, 41, 42,** *43*,* **44, 45–47**
African Champions League	**1982,** *83,* **87, 2001**
African Cup-Winners' Cup	**1984–86, 93**
African Super Cup	*1993,* **2001**

North Africa

APART FROM EGYPT (see pages 386–87) football arrived in North Africa at the turn of the 19th century via the colonial administration of French North Africa. Within a quarter of a century, leagues were up and running in Algeria (1920s), Morocco (1916) and Tunisia (1921). In the ex-Italian colony of Libya a league was finally established in 1964. Under French control a North African Club Championship was established (1919–49), and before independence internationals were played in the North African Cup (1919–30). In Algeria, separate regional leagues were played until independence (in Algiers, Constantine and Oran).

Successive club name changes indicate the degree of political involvement in football in Algeria; JS Kabylie was formally known as JE Tizi-Ouzou in an attempt to suppress the club's identification with regionalist sentiments. In Morocco royal and military patronage is evident in the leading clubs' names.

Algeria

Fédération Algérienne de Football
Founded: 1962
Joined FIFA: 1963
Joined CAF: 1964

Algerian League Record 1963–2001

SEASON	CHAMPIONS	SEASON	CHAMPIONS
1963	USM Algiers	1985	JE Tizi-Ouzou
1964	USM Annaba	1986	JE Tizi-Ouzou
1965	CR Belcourt	1987	Entente Sétif
1966	CR Belcourt	1988	Mouloudia d'Oran
1967	NA Hussein-Dey	1989	JE Tizi-Ouzou
1968	Entente Sétif	1990	KS Kabylie
1969	CR Belcourt	1991	MO Constantine
1970	CR Belcourt	1992	Mouloudia d'Oran
1971	Mouloudia d'Oran	1993	Mouloudia d'Oran
1972	Mouloudia d'Algiers	1994	US Chaouia
1973	JS Kabylie	1995	JS Kabylie
1974	JS Kabylie	1996	USM Alger
1975	Mouloudia d'Algiers	1997	CS Constantine
1976	Mouloudia d'Algiers	1998	USM El Harrach
1977	JS Kawkabi	1999	MC Alger
1978	Mouloudia d'Algiers	2000	CR Belouizdad
1979	Mouloudia d'Algiers	2001	CR Belouizdad
1980	JE Tizi-Ouzou		
1981	RS Kouba		
1982	JE Tizi-Ouzou		
1983	JE Tizi-Ouzou		
1984	GCR Mascara		

Algerian Cup Record 1963–2001

YEAR	WINNERS	YEAR	WINNERS
1963	Entente Sétif	1972	Hamra-Annaba
1964	Entente Sétif	1973	Mouloudia d'Algiers
1965	MC Saida	1974	USM Maison Carrée
1966	CR Belcourt	1975	Mouloudia d'Oran
1967	Entente Sétif	1976	Mouloudia d'Algiers
1968	Entente Sétif	1977	JS Kawkabi
1969	CR Belcourt	1978	CM Belcourt
1970	CR Belcourt	1979	MS Hussein-Dey
1971	Mouloudia d'Algiers	1980	Entente Sétif

Algerian Cup Record (*continued*)

YEAR	WINNERS	YEAR	WINNERS
1981	USK Algiers	1994	JS Kabylie
1982	DNC Algiers	1995	CR Belouizdad
1983	Mouloudia d'Algiers	1996	USM Alger
1984	Mouloudia d'Oran	1997	USM Alger
1985	Mouloudia d'Oran	1998	WA Tlemoen
1986	JE Tizi-Ouzou	1999	USM Alger
1987	USM El-Harrach	2000	MC Ouargla
1988	USK Algiers	2001	USM Alger
1989	*no competition*		
1990	Entente Sétif		
1991	USM Bel Abbés		
1992	JS Kabylie		
1993	*no competition*		

Morocco

Fédération Royale Marocaine de Football
Founded: 1955
Joined FIFA: 1956
Joined CAF: 1966

Moroccan League Record 1916–2002

SEASON	CHAMPIONS	SEASON	CHAMPIONS
1916	CA Casablanca	1963	FAR Rabat
1917	US Marocaine	1964	FAR Rabat
1918	US Marocaine	1965	MAS Fès
1919	US Marocaine	1966	WAC Casablanca
1920	Olympique Marocaine	1967	FAR Rabat
1921	Olympique Marocaine	1968	FAR Rabat
1922	Olympique Marocaine	1969	WAC Casablanca
1923	US Fès	1970	FAR Rabat
1924	Olympique Marocaine	1971	RS Settat
1925	US Fès	1972	ADM Casablanca
1926	US Athletique	1973	KAC Kenitra
1927	Stade Marocaine	1974	RBM Beni Mellal
1928	*no championship*	1975	MC Oujda
1929	US Athletique	1976	WAC Casablanca
1930	Stade Marocaine	1977	WAC Casablanca
1931	US Marocaine	1978	WAC Casablanca
1932	US Marocaine	1979	MAS Fès
1933	US Marocaine	1980	Chebab Mohammedia
1934	US Marocaine	1981	KAC Kenitra
1935	US Marocaine	1982	KAC Kenitra
1936	Olympique Marocaine	1983	MAS Fès
1937	Olympique Marocaine	1984	FAR Rabat
1938	US Marocaine	1985	MAS Fès
1939	US Marocaine	1986	WAC Casablanca
1940	US Marocaine	1987	FAR Rabat
1941	US Marocaine	1988	Raja Casablanca
1942	US Marocaine	1989	FAR Rabat
1943	US Marocaine	1990	WAC Casablanca
1944	Stade Marocaine	1991	WAC Casablanca
1945	Racing Avant-Garde	1992	KAC Marrakech
1946	US Marocaine	1993	WAC Casablanca
1947	US Athletique	1994	Olympic Casablanca
1948	WAC Casablanca	1995	COD Meknes
1949	WAC Casablanca	1996	Raja Casablanca
1950	WAC Casablanca	1997	Raja Casablanca
1951	WAC Casablanca	1998	Raja Casablanca
1952–56	*no championship*	1999	Raja Casablanca
1957	WAC Casablanca	2000	Raja Casablanca
1958	KAC Marrakech	2001	Raja Casablanca
1959	EJS Casablanca	2002	Hassania US d'Agadir
1960	KAC Kenitra		
1961	FAR Rabat		
1962	FAR Rabat		

NORTH AFRICA

Moroccan Cup Record 1957–2000

YEAR	WINNERS	YEAR	WINNERS
1957	MC Oujda	1981	WAC Casablanca
1958	MC Oujda	1982	Raja Casablanca
1959	FAR Rabat	1983	CLAS Casablanca
1960	MC Oujda	1984	FAR Rabat
1961	KAC Kenitra	1985	FAR Rabat
1962	MC Oujda	1986	FAR Rabat
1963	KAC Marrakech	1987	KAC Marrakech
1964	KAC Marrakech	1988	*no competition*
1965	KAC Marrakech	1989	WAC Casablanca
1966	COD Meknes	1990–91	*no competition*
1967	FUS Rabat	1992	Olympic Casablanca
1968	Raja Casablanca	1993	KAC Marrakech
1969	RS Settat	1994	WAC Casablanca
1970	WAC Casablanca	1995	FAR Rabat
1971	FAR Rabat	1996	Raja Casablanca
1972	Chabab Mohammedia	1997	WAC Casablanca
1973	FUS Rabat	1998	WAC Casablanca
1974	Raja Casablanca	1999	FAR Rabat
1975	Chabab Mohammedia	2000	*not known*
1976	FUS Rabat		
1977	Raja Casablanca		
1978	WAC Casablanca		
1979	WAC Casablanca		
1980	MAS Fès		

Tunisia

Fédération Tunisienne de Football
Founded: 1956
Joined FIFA: 1960
Joined CAF: 1960

Tunisian League Record 1921–2002

SEASON	CHAMPIONS	SEASON	CHAMPIONS
1921	Racing Club	1956	CS Hammam-Lif
1922	Stade Gauloise	1957	Stade Tunisien
1923	Stade Gauloise	1958	Étoile du Sahel
1924	Racing Club	1959	Espérance Sportive
1925	Sporting Club	1960	Espérance Sportive
1926	Stade Gauloise	1961	Stade Tunisien
1927	Sporting Club	1962	Stade Tunisien
1928	Avant Garde	1963	Étoile du Sahel
1929	US Tunisienne	1964	Club Africain
1930	US Tunisienne	1965	Stade Tunisien
1931	Italia de Tunis	1966	Étoile du Sahel
1932	US Tunisienne	1967	Club Africain
1933	Sfax Railway	1968	Sfax Railway
1934	Italia de Tunis	1969	CS Sfax
1935	Italia de Tunis	1970	Espérance Sportive
1936	Italia de Tunis	1971	CS Sfax
1937	Savoia de la Goulette	1972	Étoile du Sahel
1938	CS Gabesien	1973	Club Africain
1939–40	*no championship*	1974	Club Africain
1941	Espérance Sportive	1975	Espérance Sportive
1942–43	*no championship*	1976	Espérance Sportive
1944	CA Bizerte	1977	JS Kairouan
1945	CA Bizerte	1978	CS Sfax
1946	Club Africain	1979	Club Africain
1947	Club Africain	1980	Club Africain
1948	CA Bizerte	1981	CS Sfax
1949	Étoile du Sahel	1982	Espérance Sportive
1950	CS Hammam-Lif	1983	CS Sfax
1951–55	*no championship*	1984	CA Bizerte

Tunisian League Record (*continued*)

SEASON	CHAMPIONS	SEASON	CHAMPIONS
1985	Espérance Sportive	1996	Club Africain
1986	Étoile du Sahel	1997	Espérance Sportive
1987	Étoile du Sahel	1998	Espérance Sportive
1988	Espérance Sportive	1999	Espérance Sportive
1989	Espérance Sportive	2000	Espérance Sportive
1990	Club Africain	2001	Espérance Sportive
1991	Espérance Sportive	2002	Espérance Sportive
1992	Club Africain		
1993	Espérance Sportive		
1994	Espérance Sportive		
1995	CS Sfax		

Tunisian Cup Record 1922–2001

YEAR	WINNERS	YEAR	WINNERS
1922	Avant Garde	1968	Club Africain
1923	Racing Club	1969	Club Africain
1924	Stade Gauloise	1970	Club Africain
1925	Sporting Club	1971	CS Sfax
1926	Stade Gauloise	1972	Club Africain
1927-28	*no competition*	1973	Club Africain
1929	US Tunisienne	1974	Étoile du Sahel
1930	US Tunisienne	1975	Étoile du Sahel
1931	Racing Club	1976	Club Africain
1932	US Tunisienne	1977	AS Marsa
1933	US Tunisienne	1978	*no competition*
1934	US Tunisienne	1979	Espérance Sportive
1935	Italia de Tunis	1980	Espérance Sportive
1936	Stade Gauloise	1981	Étoile du Sahel
1937	Sporting Club	1982	CA Bizerte
1938	Espérance Sportive	1983	Étoile du Sahel
1939–40	*no competition*	1984	AS Marsa
1941	US Ferryville	1985	CS Hammam-Lif
1942–43	*no competition*	1986	Espérance Sportive
1944	Olympique Tunis	1987	CA Bizerte
1945	Patrie FC Bizerte	1988	COT Tunis
1946	CS Hammam-Lif	1989	Club Africain
1947	CS Hammam-Lif	1990	AS Marsa
1948	CS Hammam-Lif	1991	Étoile du Sahel
1949	CS Hammam-Lif	1992	Club Africain
1950	CS Hammam-Lif	1993	Olympique Beja
1951–55	*no competition*	1994	AS Marsa
1956	Stade Tunisien	1995	CS Sfaxien
1957	Étoile de Tunis	1996	Étoile du Sahel
1958	Stade Tunisien	1997	Espérance Sportive
1959	Étoile du Sahel	1998	Club Africain
1960	Stade Tunisien	1999	Espérance Sportive
1961	AS Marsa	2000	Club Africain
1962	Stade Tunisien	2001	CS Hammam-Lif
1963	Étoile du Sahel		
1964	Espérance Sportive		
1965	Club Africain		
1966	Stade Tunisien		
1967	Club Africain		

Libya

Libyan Arab Jamahiriya Football Federation
Founded: 1962
Joined FIFA: 1963
Joined CAF: 1965

SEASON	LEAGUE CHAMPIONS
1998	Al Mahalah
1999	Al Mahalah
2000	Al Ahly
2001	Al Medina
2002	Al Ittihad

West Africa

WHILE NORTH AFRICA WAS SLIGHTLY earlier in its adoption of football and both Central and Southern Africa have significant league and cup competitions, African football has been most enduringly strong in West Africa. At the head of the pack have been Nigeria (see pages 392–93), Guinea, Côte d'Ivoire, Ghana and Senegal. In Ghana and Nigeria football arrived with British imperial administrations in the early 20th century. Ghana's oldest and most successful team, Hearts of Oak, was founded in 1911. City-based and regional tournaments began in the 1920s and, post-independence, a national league was established in 1957 and a cup in 1958.

In French West Africa (including what are now Guinea, Senegal and Côte d'Ivoire) many football clubs were established in the 1930s. Côte d'Ivoire's leading clubs, Africa Sports, Stella Abidjan and Stade Abidjan, were all founded in 1936. In Côte d'Ivoire and Senegal national league and cup competitions followed independence in 1960.

The Senegalese are coming

But while Côte d'Ivoire's clubs have won both the African Champions League and the CAF Cup, Senegalese teams have yet to take an African championship. The national team did, however, reach the Final of the 2002 African Nations Cup in Mali beating Nigeria in the semi-final. In the Final it lost to Cameroon on penalties. The team started the tournament in confident mood having qualified in sensational style for the 2002 World Cup Finals where many pundits rightly tipped it to perform well, and it certainly didn't disappoint, with a stunning overall performance. The 5-0 thrashing of Namibia in the last game of the qualifying tournament saw the team through to the Finals and hopes of a bright future.

Guinea's national league began in 1965 and is dominated by Hafia Conrakry, three times winners of the African Champions League during the 1970s, but its fortunes have been on the wane in recent years.

Founded in 1911 Hearts of Oak, from Accra, is the most successful club in Ghana. Its greatest international success came in 2000 when it won the African Champions League, beating Espérance Sportive of Tunisia in the Final.

Ghana

Ghana Football Association
Founded: 1957
Joined FIFA: 1958
Joined CAF: 1958

Ghanaian League Record 1957–2001

SEASON	CHAMPIONS	SEASON	CHAMPIONS
1957	Hearts of Oak	1982	Asante Kotoko
1958	Hearts of Oak	1983	Asante Kotoko
1959	Asante Kotoko	1984	Hearts of Oak
1960	Eleven Wise FC	1985	Hearts of Oak
1961	Real Republicans	1986	Asante Kotoko
1962	Real Republicans	1987	Asante Kotoko
1963	Asante Kotoko	1988	Asante Kotoko
1964	Asante Kotoko	1989	Hearts of Oak
1965	Asante Kotoko	1990	Hearts of Oak
1966	BA United	1991	Asante Kotoko
1967	Asante Kotoko	1992	Asante Kotoko
1968	Asante Kotoko	1993	Asante Kotoko
1969	Asante Kotoko	1994	Goldfields
1970	Great Olympics	1995	Goldfields
1971	Hearts of Oak	1996	Goldfields
1972	Asante Kotoko	1997	Hearts of Oak
1973	Hearts of Oak	1998	Hearts of Oak
1974	Great Olympics	1999	Hearts of Oak
1975	Asante Kotoko	2000	Hearts of Oak
1976	Hearts of Oak	2001	Hearts of Oak
1977	Sekondi Hasaacas		
1978	Hearts of Oak		
1979	Hearts of Oak		
1980	Asante Kotoko		
1981	Asante Kotoko		

Ghanaian Cup Record 1958–2001

YEAR	CUP WINNERS	YEAR	CUP WINNERS
1958	Asante Kotoko	1984	Asante Kotoko
1959	Cornerstones	1985	Sekondi Hasaacas
1960	Asante Kotoko	1986	Okwahu United
1961	*no competition*	1987	Hearts of Oak
1962	Real Republicans	1988	Hearts of Oak
1963	Real Republicans	1989	Hearts of Oak
1964	Real Republicans	1990	Asante Kotoko
1965	Real Republicans	1991	Asante Kotoko
1966–68	*no competition*	1992	Voradep
1969	Cape Coast Dwarfs	1993	Goldfields
1970–72	*no competition*	1994	Hearts of Oak
1973	Hearts of Oak	1995	Hearts of Oak
1974	Hearts of Oak	1996	Hearts of Oak
1975	Great Olympics	1997	Ghaphoa
1976	Asante Kotoko	1998	Asante Kotoko
1977	*no competition*	1999	Hearts of Oak
1978	Asante Kotoko	2000	Hearts of Oak
1979	Hearts of Oak	2001	Asante Kotoko
1980	Sekondi Hasaacas		
1981	Hearts of Oak		
1982	Eleven Wise FC		
1983	Great Olympics		

Benin

Fédération Beninoise de Football
Founded: 1968
Joined FIFA: 1962
Joined CAF: 1969

SEASON	LEAGUE CHAMPIONS
1997	Mogas 90
1998	Dragons de l'Ouémé
1999	Dragons de l'Ouémé
2000	*no official championship*
2001	*no official championship*

WEST AFRICA

Benin *(continued)*

YEAR	CUP WINNERS
1997	Energie Sport
1998	Mogas 90
1999	Mogas 90
2000	Mogas 90
2001	Buffles de Borgou

Burkina Faso

Fédération Burkinabe de Football
Founded: 1960
Joined FIFA: 1964
Joined CAF: 1964

SEASON	LEAGUE CHAMPIONS
1997	ASFAY
1998	Racing Bobo-Dioulasso
1999	ASFAY
2000	USFA
2001	Etoile Filante

YEAR	CUP WINNERS
1997	AS Fonctionnaires
1998	AS Fonctionnaires
1999	Etoile Filante
2000	Etoile Filante
2001	Etoile Filante

Cape Verde

Fédération Cabo Verdiana de Futebol
Founded: 1982
Joined FIFA: 1986
Joined CAF: 1986

SEASON	LEAGUE CHAMPIONS
1997	Sporting Clube
1998	CS Mindelense
1999	Amarante
2000	Derby FC
2001	Onze Unidos

Côte d'Ivoire

Fédération Ivorienne de Football
Founded: 1960
Joined FIFA: 1960
Joined CAF: 1960

SEASON	LEAGUE CHAMPIONS
1997	ASEC Abidjan
1998	ASEC Abidjan
1999	Africa Sports
2000	ASEC Abidjan
2001	ASEC Abidjan

Côte d'Ivoire *(continued)*

YEAR	CUP WINNERS
1997	ASEC Abidjan
1998	Africa Sports
1999	ASEC Abidjan
2000	Stade Abidjan
2001	Alliance Bouaké

Gambia

Gambia Football Association
Founded: 1952
Joined FIFA: 1966
Joined CAF: 1962

SEASON	LEAGUE CHAMPIONS
1997	Real Banjul
1998	Real Banjul
1999	Ports Authority
2000	Real Banjul
2001	Wallidan

Guinea

Fédération Guinéenne de Football
Founded: 1959
Joined FIFA: 1961
Joined CAF: 1962

SEASON	LEAGUE CHAMPIONS
1997	*cancelled*
1998	AS Kaloum Stars
1999	*not held*
2000	Horoya AC
2001	Horoya AC

YEAR	CUP WINNERS
1997	AS Kaloum Stars
1998	AS Kaloum Stars
1999	Horoya AC
2000	Fello Stars Labé
2001	*not known*

Guinea-Bissau

Federação de Futebol da Guiné-Bissau
Founded: 1974
Joined FIFA: 1986
Joined CAF: 1986

SEASON	LEAGUE CHAMPIONS
1997	Sporting Clube de Bissau
1998	Sporting Clube de Bissau
1999	*no championship*
2000	Sporting Clube de Bissau
2001	*no championship*

Liberia

Liberia Football Federation
Founded: 1936
Joined FIFA: 1962
Joined CAF: 1962

SEASON	LEAGUE CHAMPIONS
1997	Invincible XI
1998	Invincible XI
1999	LPRC Oilers
2000	Mighty Barolle
2001	Mighty Barolle

Mali

Fédération Malienne de Football
Founded: 1960
Joined FIFA: 1962
Joined CAF: 1963

SEASON	LEAGUE CHAMPIONS
1997	Djoliba AC
1998	Djoliba AC
1999	Djoliba AC
2000	Stade Malien
2001	Stade Malien

YEAR	CUP WINNERS
1997	Stade Malien
1998	Djoliba AC
1999	Stade Malien
2000	Cercle Olympique
2001	Stade Malien

Mauritania

Fédération de Football de la République de Mauritanie
Founded: 1961
Joined FIFA: 1964
Joined CAF: 1968

SEASON	LEAGUE CHAMPIONS
1997	*no championship*
1998	*no championship*
1999	SDPA Rosso
2000	Mauritel
2001	*not known*

Niger

Fédération Nigérienne de Football
Founded: 1967
Joined FIFA: 1967
Joined CAF: 1967

Niger *(continued)*

SEASON	LEAGUE CHAMPIONS
1997	Sahel SC
1998	*no championship*
1999	Olympic FC
2000	JS Ténéré
2001	JS Ténéré

Senegal

Fédération Sénégalaise de Football
Founded: 1960
Joined FIFA: 1962
Joined CAF: 1963

SEASON	LEAGUE CHAMPIONS
1998	ASEC Ndiambour
1999	ASC Jeanne D'Arc
2000	ASC Diaraf
2001	ASC Jeanne D'Arc
2002	ASC Jeanne D'Arc

YEAR	CUP WINNERS
1998	ASC Yeggo
1999	ASEC Ndiambour
2000	Porte Autonome
2001	SONACOS
2002	AS Douanes

Sierra Leone

Sierra Leone Amateur Football Association
Founded: 1923
Joined FIFA: 1967
Joined CAF: 1967

SEASON	LEAGUE CHAMPIONS
1997	*not completed*
1998	*not completed*
1999	East End Lions
2000	Mighty Blackpool
2001	Mighty Blackpool

Togo

Fédération Togolaise de Football
Founded: 1960
Joined FIFA: 1962
Joined CAF: 1963

SEASON	LEAGUE CHAMPIONS
1997	Dynamic Togolais
1998	*no competition*
1999	Semassi
2000	*not completed*
2001	Dynamic Togolais

WEST AFRICA

Nigeria

Nigeria Football Association
Founded: 1945
Joined FIFA: 1959
Joined CAF: 1959

NIGERIA

THE FIRST RECORDED FOOTBALL IN NIGERIA dates from 1914 when matches between European players and King's College school were held in Lagos. Initially, teams were made up of white colonial administrators and soldiers, but by 1919 mixed European and African teams, such as Diamonds FC from Lagos, were competing for the War Memorial Cup. In 1931, the Lagos and District Amateur FA was created, followed by a national Nigerian football association and a national FA Cup in 1945.

The organization of Nigerian football was dominated almost exclusively by white Europeans, but on the field the best players were all Nigerian. In 1949, a Nigerian Select XI toured Britain and the first official Nigerian international match was played later that year against Sierra Leone. Membership of CAF and FIFA came in 1959, preceding independence from Britain by a year. For the first post-independence international, the national strip was changed and the Red Devils became the Green Eagles.

Biafran secession
Like everything else in Nigerian life, football was disrupted for the four years of the civil war (1967–70) and the secession of the state of Biafra. It was only in 1972 that a formal national league was created, won in its first year by the Mighty Jets from Jos. At the same time, from the ashes of Biafran independence, Enugu Rangers was founded, and politically and sportingly it has been the region's torchbearer. From its inception, Nigerian football has relied on public and private corporations to run football clubs; among the leading teams have been Lagos Railways, Bendel Insurance and Stationery Stores (all now defunct). Other once-powerful sides, such as Leventis United and Abiola Babes, have disappeared since their rich benefactors pulled out.

Nigerian football has proved increasingly successful on the international stage, with regular appearances at the World Cup, victories in the African Cup of Nations and a number of African club triumphs. However, problems with corruption, financial insecurity, the drain of talent to Europe and phenomenally dangerous stadiums have beset the game in recent years.

Stationery Stores from Lagos won the Nigerian Cup four times and the league title in 1992 before the company that sponsored it went out of business and the team folded.

Nigerian League Record 1972–2001

SEASON	CHAMPIONS	SEASON	CHAMPIONS
1972	Mighty Jets	1989	Iwuanyanwu Owerri
1973	Bendel Insurance	1990	Iwuanyanwu Owerri
1974	Rangers International	1991	Julius Berger
1975	Rangers International	1992	Stationery Stores
1976	Shooting Stars	1993	Iwuanyanwu Owerri
1977	Rangers International	1994	BCC Lions
1978	Racca Rovers	1995	Shooting Stars
1979	Bendel Insurance	1996	Udoji United
1980	Shooting Stars	1997	Eagle Cement
1981	Rangers International	1998	Shooting Stars
1982	Rangers International	1999	Lobi Stars
1983	Shooting Stars	2000	Julius Berger
1984	Rangers International	2001	Enyimba
1985	New Nigeria Bank		
1986	Leventis United		
1987	Iwuanyanwu Owerri		
1988	Iwuanyanwu Owerri		

Nigerian FA Challenge Cup 1945–2001

YEAR	WINNERS	YEAR	WINNERS
1945	Marine	1976	Rangers International
1946	Lagos Railways	1977	Shooting Stars
1947	Marine	1978	Bendel Insurance
1948	Lagos Railways	1979	Shooting Stars
1949	Lagos Railways	1980	Bendel Insurance
1950	GO Union	1981	Rangers International
1951	Lagos Railways	1982	Stationery Stores
1952	Lagos PAN Bank	1983	Rangers International
1953	Kano Pillars	1984	Leventis United
1954	Calabar Rovers	1985	Abiola Babes
1955	Port Harcourt	1986	Leventis United
1956	Lagos Railways	1987	Abiola Babes
1957	Lagos Railways	1988	Iwuanyanwu Owerri
1958	Port Harcourt	1989	BCC Lions
1959	Ibadan Lions	1990	Stationery Stores
1960	Lagos EDN	1991	El Kanemi Warriors
1961	Ibadan Lions	1992	El Kanemi Warriors
1962	Police	1993	BCC Lions
1963	Port Harcourt	1994	BCC Lions
1964	Lagos Railways	1995	Shooting Stars
1965	Lagos EDN	1996	Julius Berger
1966	Ibadan Lions	1997	BCC Lions
1967	Stationery Stores	1998	Wikki Tourists
1968	Stationery Stores	1999	Plateau United
1969	Ibadan Lions	2000	Niger Tornadoes
1970	Lagos EDN	2001	Dolphin FC
1971	Shooting Stars		
1972	Bendel Insurance		
1973	*no winner*		
1974	Rangers International		
1975	Rangers International		

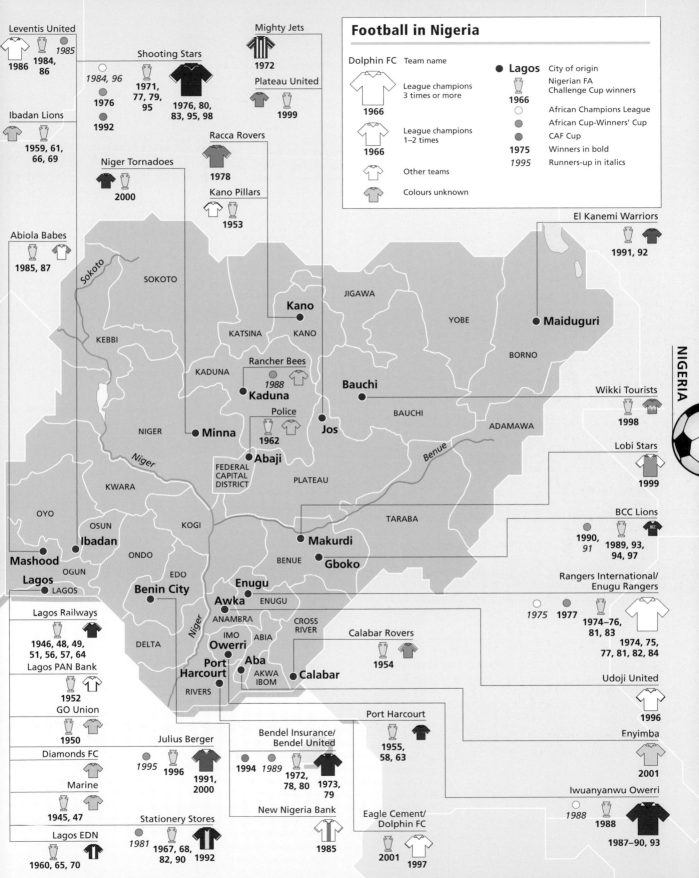

NIGERIA

Football in Nigeria

Dolphin FC — Team name

League champions 3 times or more
1966

League champions 1–2 times
1966

Other teams

Colours unknown

● Lagos — City of origin

Nigerian FA Challenge Cup winners
1966

○ African Champions League

● African Cup-Winners' Cup

● CAF Cup

1975 Winners in bold

1995 Runners-up in italics

Leventis United
1986   1984, 86   *1985*

Shooting Stars
1984, 96   1976   1992   1971, 77, 79, 95   1976, 80, 83, 95, 98

Mighty Jets
1972

Plateau United
1999

Ibadan Lions
1959, 61, 66, 69

Niger Tornadoes
2000

Racca Rovers
1978

Kano Pillars
1953

Abiola Babes
1985, 87

El Kanemi Warriors
1991, 92

SOKOTO
Sokoto
KEBBI
KATSINA
KADUNA
● **Kano**   KANO
JIGAWA
YOBE
BORNO
● **Maiduguri**

Rancher Bees
1988
● **Kaduna**

Bauchi
BAUCHI
ADAMAWA

Wikki Tourists
1998

Police
1962
● **Abaji**

● **Jos**

Lobi Stars
1999

NIGER
Niger
FEDERAL CAPITAL DISTRICT
PLATEAU
● **Minna**

BCC Lions
1990, *91*   1989, 93, 94, 97

KWARA
OYO
OSUN
KOGI
TARABA
Benue

Mashood
Lagos
LAGOS
● **Ibadan**
ONDO
EDO
BENUE
● **Makurdi**
● **Gboko**

Rangers International/ Enugu Rangers
1975   1977   1974–76, 81, 83   1974, 75, 77, 81, 82, 84

Lagos Railways
1946, 48, 49, 51, 56, 57, 64

Lagos PAN Bank
1952

GO Union
1950

Diamonds FC
1995   1996   1991, 2000

Marine
1945, 47

Lagos EDN
1981   1960, 65, 70   1967, 68, 82, 90   1992

Stationery Stores

● **Benin City**
Niger
DELTA
● **Enugu**
● **Awka**
ANAMBRA
ENUGU
IMO
● **Owerri**
● **Aba**
ABIA
AKWA IBOM
RIVERS
Port Harcourt
CROSS RIVER
● **Calabar**

Calabar Rovers
1954

Julius Berger

Bendel Insurance/ Bendel United
1994   *1989*   1972, 78, 80   1973, 79

New Nigeria Bank
1985

Port Harcourt
1955, 58, 63

Eagle Cement/ Dolphin FC
2001   1997

Udoji United
1996

Enyimba
2001

Iwuanyanwu Owerri
1988   1988   1987–90, 93

Cameroon

Fédération Camerounaise de Football
Founded: 1960
Joined FIFA: 1962
Joined CAF: 1963

CAMEROON WAS ORIGINALLY created and colonized by the Germans, from 1884 onwards. However, football did not follow until the expulsion of the Germans in 1916 by the British and French, who then received successive League of Nations and UN mandates to run the country. In the 1920s football developed among Africans in the colonial education system, and in the 1930s and 40s clubs and local competitions were established.

Political, sporting and social life in Cameroon is dictated by a series of linguistic and cultural divisions. Around a quarter of the population lives in the former British zone in the north-west – anglophone Cameroon. Its team is unquestionably PWD (Public Works Department) from Bamenda. The club's president in the late 1980s and early 90s was Ni John Frundi, founder and leader of the main opposition party, the SDF, and challenger in the bitter 1992 presidential elections. Rumours and accusations of corruption and match-fixing against the club abound among the politically and demographically dominant French-speaking parts of Cameroon.

Province and ethnicity

The rest of the country is formally francophone but is itself divided by province and ethnicity. The Bamileke from western Cameroon are allied with Racing Club Bafoussam at home and with Union Sportive and Diamant Yaoundé as migrants in the big cities. The Bassa and Douala from the Littoral province are tied to Dynamo Douala and the Beti from Centre province are concentrated in and around Yaoundé, supporting Canon and Tonnerre. In 1967, legislation was passed to disband ethnically-orientated organizations of all kinds, but football was exempted after huge public protest. Despite this, the national team is a multi-ethnic affair and a significant source of national unity, but, as ever, only when things are going well. The fantastic performance of the Cameroon national team at the 1990 World Cup, the best performance by an African team up to that time, was certainly used by President Biya in his bitter but successful campaign to retain the presidency in 1992.

Cameroon League 1961–2001

SEASON	CHAMPIONS	SEASON	CHAMPIONS
1961	Oryx Douala	1984	Tonnerre Yaoundé
1962	Caiman Douala	1985	Canon Yaoundé
1963	Oryx Douala	1986	Canon Yaoundé
1964	Oryx Douala	1987	Tonnerre Yaoundé
1965	Oryx Douala	1988	Tonnerre Yaoundé
1966	Diamant Yaoundé	1989	Racing Club Bafoussam
1967	Oryx Douala	1990	Union Sportive
1968	Caiman Douala	1991	Canon Yaoundé
1969	Union Sportive	1992	Racing Club Bafoussam
1970	Canon Yaoundé	1993	Racing Club Bafoussam
1971	Aigle Royale Nkongsamba	1994	Aigle Royale Nkongsamba
1972	Léopards Douala	1995	Racing Club Bafoussam
1973	Léopards Douala	1996	Unisport
1974	Canon Yaoundé	1997	Cotonsport
1975	Caiman Douala	1998	Cotonsport
1976	Union Sportive	1999	Sable Batié
1977	Canon Yaoundé	2000	Fovu Baham
1978	Union Sportive	2001	Cotonsport
1979	Canon Yaoundé		
1980	Canon Yaoundé		
1981	Tonnerre Yaoundé		
1982	Canon Yaoundé		
1983	Tonnerre Yaoundé		

Cameroon Cup 1956–2001

YEAR	WINNERS	YEAR	WINNERS
1956	Oryx Douala	1981	Dynamo Douala
1957	Canon Yaoundé	1982	Dragon Douala
1958	Tonnerre Yaoundé	1983	Canon Yaoundé
1959	Caiman Douala	1984	Dihep Nkam
1960	Lion Yaoundé	1985	Union Sportive
1961	Union Sportive	1986	Canon Yaoundé
1962	Lion Yaoundé	1987	Tonnerre Yaoundé
1963	Oryx Douala	1988	Panthère Sportive
1964	Diamant Yaoundé	1989	Tonnerre Yaoundé
1965	Lion Yaoundé	1990	Prévoyance Yaoundé
1966	Lion Yaoundé	1991	Tonnerre Yaoundé
1967	Canon Yaoundé	1992	Olympique Mvoylé
1968	Oryx Douala	1993	Canon Yaoundé
1969	Union Sportive	1994	Olympique Mvoylé
1970	Oryx Douala	1995	Canon Yaoundé
1971	Diamant Yaoundé	1996	Racing Club Bafoussam
1972	Diamant Yaoundé	1997	Union Sportive
1973	Canon Yaoundé	1998	Dynamo Douala
1974	Tonnerre Yaoundé	1999	Canon Yaoundé
1975	Canon Yaoundé	2000	Kumbo Strikers
1976	Canon Yaoundé	2001	Fovu Baham
1977	Canon Yaoundé		
1978	Canon Yaoundé		
1979	Dynamo Douala		
1980	Union Sportive		

After its strong showing at Italia '90, Cameroon, shown here in 1992, has established itself as the strongest national team in Africa. The World Cup in 2002 gives the team a chance to further enhance its reputation as a force in world football.

CAMEROON

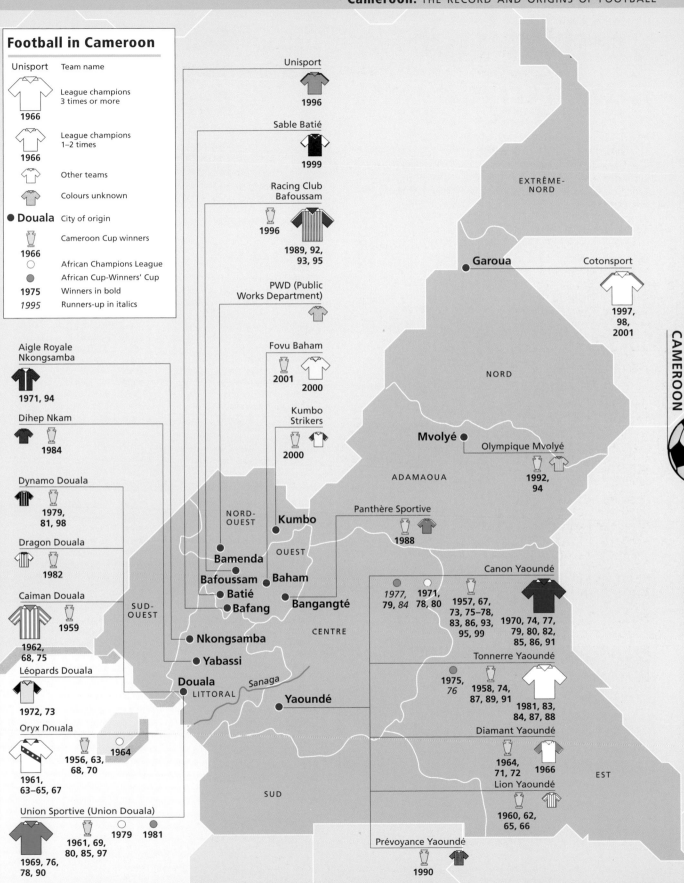

Football in Cameroon

Unisport	Team name
1966	League champions 3 times or more
1966	League champions 1–2 times
	Other teams
	Colours unknown
● Douala	City of origin
1966	Cameroon Cup winners
○	African Champions League
●	African Cup-Winners' Cup
1975	Winners in bold
1995	Runners-up in italics

Unisport
1996

Sable Batié
1999

Racing Club Bafoussam
1996
1989, 92, 93, 95

PWD (Public Works Department)

Fovu Baham
2001
2000

Kumbo Strikers
2000

Aigle Royale Nkongsamba
1971, 94

Dihep Nkam
1984

Dynamo Douala
1979, 81, 98

Dragon Douala
1982

Caiman Douala
1959
1962, 68, 75

Léopards Douala
1972, 73

Oryx Douala
1964
1956, 63, 68, 70
1961, 63–65, 67

Union Sportive (Union Douala)
1961, 69, 80, 85, 97
1979   1981
1969, 76, 78, 90

EXTRÊME-NORD

NORD

Garoua   Cotonsport
1997, 98, 2001

ADAMAOUA

Mvolyé ●   Olympique Mvolyé
1992, 94

Panthère Sportive
1988

NORD-OUEST

Kumbo

OUEST

Bamenda
Bafoussam   **Baham**
Batié
Bafang   **Bangangté**

SUD-OUEST

CENTRE

Canon Yaoundé
1977, 79, 84   1971, 78, 80   1957, 67, 73, 75–78, 83, 86, 93, 95, 99   **1970, 74, 77, 79, 80, 82, 85, 86, 91**

Nkongsamba

Yabassi

Douala ●   Sanaga
LITTORAL

Tonnerre Yaoundé
1975, 76   1958, 74, 87, 89, 91   **1981, 83, 84, 87, 88**

Yaoundé ●

Diamant Yaoundé
1964, 71, 72   1966

Lion Yaoundé
1960, 62, 65, 66

EST

SUD

Prévoyance Yaoundé
1990

CAMEROON

Central and East Africa

CENTRAL AND EAST AFRICA

ALTHOUGH EAST AND CENTRAL AFRICA are considered a single region by CAF, they are, in footballing terms, worlds apart. Central Africa has produced African club and national champions as well as World Cup qualifying national teams. East Africa's trophy cabinet is, by contrast, rather bare.

Central Africa's three key footballing nations are Cameroon (see pages 394–95), the Democratic Republic of Congo (or DRC, formerly known as Zaïre and the Belgian Congo) and Congo (formally known as Congo-Brazzaville and the French Congo). In the Belgian Congo, as it was then known, Africa's second oldest football association was established in the capital Léopoldville (now Kinshasa) in 1919, although a city league had been up and running since 1916. Zaïrian football's golden age lasted from independence in 1960 to the mid-1970s. The country's leading club, TP Englebert, won two and then lost two consecutive African Champions League Finals between 1967 and 1970, while the national side was the first sub-Saharan team to make it to the World Cup (1974). International matches were played between French and Belgian Congo between 1923 and 1950 in the Stanley Pool Championship (Stanley Pool is a lake that separates the capital cities of the two states).

Football first arrived in East Africa via British workers and colonists in Kenya, Uganda, Tanzania and Zanzibar. Kenya's oldest club, Mombassa FC, dates from 1906. The Gossage Cup, an international tournament between the four countries, was held between 1927 and 1972. Post-independence, national leagues were created. Kenya's Gor Mahia won the region's only African club championship – the Cup-Winners' Cup – in 1987, while two Ugandan teams have made it to the Final of the Champions League (Simba FC in 1972, and SC Villa in 1991). But otherwise, both at club and international level, the region's footballing record is weak. In Sudan, the 1930s saw the formation of leading Khartoum clubs Al Hilal and El Mourada. In Ethiopia a mixture of English and Italian influences introduced football during the 1930s, and a national league and football association accompanied independence in 1943.

SC Villa from Kampala (seen here in white) is one of Uganda's leading teams. Formerly known as Nakivubo Villa, the team has ten Ugandan league championships to its name.

Democratic Republic of Congo (formerly Zaïre)

Fédération Congolaise de Football-Association
Founded: 1919
Joined FIFA: 1962
Joined CAF: 1973

Democratic Republic of Congo League Record 1964–2001

SEASON	CHAMPIONS	SEASON	CHAMPIONS
1964	CS Imana	1985	US Tshinkunku
1965	Dragons	1986	FC Lupopo
1966	TP Englebert	1987	DC Motema Pembe
1967	TP Englebert	1988	AS Vita Club
1968	FC St. Eloi	1989	DC Motema Pembe
1969	TP Englebert	1990	FC Lupopo
1970	AS Vita Club	1991	Mikishi
1971	AS Vita Club	1992	US Bilombe
1972	AS Vita Club	1993	AS Vita Club
1973	AS Vita Club	1994	DC Motema Pembe
1974	CS Imana	1995	AS Bantous
1975	AS Vita Club	1996	*not known*
1976	TP Mazembe	1997	AS Vita Club
1977	AS Vita Club	1998	DC Motema Pembe
1978	CS Imana	1999	DC Motema Pembe
1979	AS Bilima	2000	TP Mazembe
1980	AS Vita Club	2001	TP Mazembe
1981	FC Lupopo		
1982	AS Bilima		
1983	Sanga Balende		
1984	AS Bilima		

Democratic Republic of Congo Cup Record 1964–2001

YEAR	WINNERS	YEAR	WINNERS
1964	DC Motema Pembe	1986	Kalamu
1965	AS Bilima	1987	Kalamu
1966	TP Mazembe	1988	Kalamu
1967	TP Mazembe	1989	Kalamu
1968	FC Lupopo	1990	DC Motema Pembe
1969–70	*no competition*	1991	DC Motema Pembe
1971	AS Vita Club	1992	US Bilombe
1972	AS Vita Club	1993	DC Motema Pembe
1973	AS Vita Club	1994	DC Motema Pembe
1974	DC Motema Pembe	1995	AC Sodigraf
1975	AS Vita Club	1996	AS Dragons
1976	TP Mazembe	1997	AS Dragons
1977	AS Vita Club	1998	AS Dragons
1978	DC Motema Pembe	1999	AS Dragons
1979	TP Mazembe	2000	TP Mazembe
1980	Lubumbashi Sport	2001	AS Vita Club
1981	AS Vita Club		
1982	AS Vita Club		
1983	AS Vita Club		
1984	DC Motema Pembe		
1985	DC Motema Pembe		

Burundi

Fédération de Football du Burundi
Founded: 1948
Joined FIFA: 1972
Joined CAF: 1972

SEASON	LEAGUE CHAMPIONS
1997	Maniema
1998	Vital'O FC
1999	Vital'O FC
2000	Vital'O FC
2001	Prince Louis FC

Central African Republic

Fédération Centrafricaine de Football
Founded: 1937
Joined FIFA: 1963
Joined CAF: 1965

SEASON	LEAGUE CHAMPIONS
1997	AS Tempete Mocaf
1998	*cancelled*
1999	*cancelled*
2000	Réal Olympique Castel
2001	*abandoned*

Chad

Fédération Tchadienne de Football
Founded: 1962
Joined FIFA: 1988
Joined CAF: 1962

SEASON	LEAGUE CHAMPIONS
1997	FC Tourbillon
1998	AS Coton Chad
1999	Renaissance
2000	FC Tourbillon
2001	*not known*

Congo

Fédération Congolaise de Football
Founded: 1962
Joined FIFA: 1962
Joined CAF: 1966

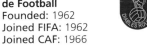

SEASON	LEAGUE CHAMPIONS
1997	Munisport
1998	Vita Club Mokanda
1999	Vita Club Mokanda
2000	Etoile du Congo
2001	Etoile du Congo

YEAR	CUP WINNERS
1997	EPB
1998	Etoile du Congo
1999	TP Mystère
2000	Etoile du Congo
2001	AS Police

Djibouti

Fédération Djiboutienne de Football
Founded: 1977
Joined FIFA: 1994
Joined CAF: 1986

Djibouti *(continued)*

SEASON	LEAGUE CHAMPIONS
1997	*not known*
1998	*not known*
1999	Force Nationale de Police
2000	CDE
2001	Force Nationale de Police

Equatorial Guinea

Fédération Equatoguineana de Futboll
Founded: 1976
Joined FIFA: 1986
Joined CAF: 1986

SEASON	LEAGUE CHAMPIONS
1997	Deportivo Mongomo
1998	*not known*
1999	Cafe Band Sportif
2000	CD Ela Nguema
2001	Akonangui FC

Ethiopia

Ye'Ityopiya Football Federechin
Founded: 1943
Joined FIFA: 1953
Joined CAF: 1957

SEASON	LEAGUE CHAMPIONS
1998	Mebrat Hail
1999	St. George
2000	St. George
2001	Mebrat Hail
2002	St. George

Gabon

Fédération Gabonaise de Football
Founded: 1962
Joined FIFA: 1963
Joined CAF: 1967

SEASON	LEAGUE CHAMPIONS
1997	FC 105
1998	FC 105
1999	Petrosport Port Gentil
2000	Mangasport
2001	FC 105

Kenya

Kenya Football Federation
Founded: 1932
Joined FIFA: 1960
Joined CAF: 1968

Kenya *(continued)*

SEASON	LEAGUE CHAMPIONS
1997	Utalii
1998	AFC Leopards
1999	Tusker FC
2000	Tusker FC
2001	Oserian Fastac

YEAR	CUP WINNERS
1997	Mathare United
1998	Mumias Sugar
1999	Mumias Sugar
2000	Mathare United
2001	AFC Leopards

Madagascar

Fédération Malagasy de Football
Founded: 1961
Joined FIFA: 1962
Joined CAF: 1963

SEASON	LEAGUE CHAMPIONS
1997	DAS Antanarivo
1998	DAS Antanarivo
1999	AS Fortior
2000	AS Fortior
2001	Stade Olympique de l'Emyrne

Rwanda

Fédération Rwandaise de Football Amateur
Founded: 1972
Joined FIFA: 1976
Joined CAF: 1976

SEASON	LEAGUE CHAMPIONS
1997	Rayon Sports
1998	Rayon Sports
1999	FC APR
2000	FC APR
2001	FC APR

São Tomé and Principe

Federação Santomense de Futebol
Founded: 1975
Joined FIFA: 1986
Joined CAF: 1986

SEASON	LEAGUE CHAMPIONS
1997	Sporting Praia Cruz
1998	GD Os Operários
1999	Sporting Praia Cruz
2000	Inter Bom-Bom
2001	Bairros Unidos FC

Somalia

Somalia Football Federation
Founded: 1951
Joined FIFA: 1960
Joined CAF: 1968

SEASON	LEAGUE CHAMPIONS
1997	Alba
1998	Ports Authority
1999	Horsed
2000	Elman FC
2001	*not known*

Sudan

Sudan Football Association
Founded: 1936
Joined FIFA: 1948
Joined CAF: 1957

SEASON	LEAGUE CHAMPIONS
1997	Al Merreikh
1998	Al Hilal
1999	Al Hilal
2000	Al Merreikh
2001	Al Merreikh

Tanzania

Football Association of Tanzania
Founded: 1930
Joined FIFA: 1964
Joined CAF: 1960

SEASON	LEAGUE CHAMPIONS
1997	Young Africans
1998	Maji Maji
1999	Prisons
2000	Young Africans
2001	Simba SC

Uganda

Federation of Uganda Football Associations
Founded: 1924
Joined FIFA: 1959
Joined CAF: 1959

SEASON	LEAGUE CHAMPIONS
1997	City Council SC
1998	SC Villa
1999	SC Villa
2000	SC Villa
2001	SC Villa

Southern Africa

IN ECONOMICS, POLITICS and in football, South Africa (see pages 400–401) is the giant of Southern Africa and the rest of the region has long lived in its shadow. The apartheid regime led to South Africa's exclusion from FIFA, CAF and global football in general until 1994, but throughout those years of exclusion, football retained a strong foothold in the country. So much so that the constant drain of players to their rich neighbour has limited the development of football in nearby Lesotho and Swaziland, while civil war has disrupted the game in Zimbabwe, Angola and Mozambique.

Railway workers

The most stable footballing nation in the region, Zambia, acquired a colonial FA in 1929 in the Northern Rhodesian FA. A national league and cup competition was set up following independence in 1962. In 1991, Zambian giants Power Dynamos won the Cup-Winners' Cup, the nation's only African championship victory. Like Zambia, football reached Zimbabwe with the arrival of British railway workers in the late 19th century, and a national league and cup were operating by the early 1960s. A Rhodesian FA was set up by Ian Smith's government in the wake of the declaration of independence in 1965, but was suspended by FIFA in 1970. The achievement of black majority rule in 1980 saw Zimbabwe's re-admission to FIFA, and a professional national league began in 1992.

Race politics also shamed football in Malawi. Before independence in 1966, a Nyasaland African FA (for black teams) and a Nyasaland FA (for white teams) ensured racially segregated football was played throughout the country.

Portuguese influence brought football to both Angola and Mozambique and in the shape of Mozambique's Eusebio created Africa's first global footballing star during the 1960s. But a chaotic process of Portuguese decolonization during 1975, as well as civil war, has left the region's societies and footballing cultures alike weak and disorganized.

Zimbabwean champions Dynamos, from Harare, took on ASEC Abidjan from Côte d'Ivoire in the 1998 African Champions League Final but lost 4-2 in the second leg after a 0-0 draw in the first leg.

Zimbabwe

Zimbabwe Football Association
Founded: 1950
Joined FIFA: 1965–70, 1980
Joined CAF: 1980

Zimbabwean League Record 1962–2001

SEASON	CHAMPIONS	SEASON	CHAMPIONS
1962	Bulawayo Rovers	1984	Black Rhinos
1963	Dynamos	1985	Dynamos
1964	St. Pauls	1986	Dynamos
1965	Dynamos	1987	Black Rhinos
1966	St. Pauls	1988	Zimbabwe Saints
1967	Tornados	1989	Dynamos
1968	Sables	1990	Highlanders
1969	Sables	1991	Dynamos
1970	Dynamos	1992	Black Aces
1971	Arcadia United	1993	Zimbabwe Highlanders
1972	Sables	1994	Dynamos
1973	Metal Box	1995	Dynamos
1974	Sables	1996	CAPS United
1975	Chibuku	1997	Dynamos
1976	Dynamos	1998	no championship
1977	Zimbabwe Saints	1999	Zimbabwe Highlanders
1978	Dynamos	2000	Zimbabwe Highlanders
1979	CAPS United	2001	Zimbabwe Highlanders
1980	Dynamos		
1981	Dynamos		
1982	Dynamos		
1983	Dynamos		

Zimbabwean Cup Record 1962–2001

YEAR	WINNERS	YEAR	WINNERS
1962	Bulawayo Rovers	1984	Black Rhinos
1963	Salisbury Callies	1985	Dynamos
1964	no competition	1986	Highlanders
1965	Salisbury City Wanderers	1987	Zimbabwe Saints
		1988	Dynamos
1966	Mangula	1989	Dynamos
1967	Salisbury Callies	1990	Highlanders
1968	Arcadia United	1991	Wankie FC
1969	Arcadia United	1992	CAPS United
1970	Wankie	1993	Tanganda
1971	Chibuku	1994	Blackpool
1972	Mangula	1995	Chapungu
1973	Wankie	1996	Dynamos
1974	Chibuku	1997	CAPS United
1975	Salisbury Callies	1998	CAPS United
1976	Dynamos	1999	not known
1977	Zimbabwe Saints	2000	Dynamos
1978	Zisco Steel	2001	Zimbabwe Highlanders
1979	Zimbabwe Saints		
1980	CAPS United		
1981	CAPS United		
1982	CAPS United		
1983	CAPS United		

Angola

Federação Angolana de Futebol
Founded: 1977
Joined FIFA: 1980
Joined CAF: 1980

SEASON	LEAGUE CHAMPIONS
1997	Petro Atlético
1998	Primeiro de Agosto
1999	Primeiro de Agosto
2000	Petro Atlético
2001	Petro Atlético

SOUTHERN AFRICA

Angola *(continued)*

YEAR	CUP WINNERS
1997	Petro Atlético
1998	Petro Atlético
1999	Sagrada Esperança
2000	Petro Atlético
2001	Sonangol

Botswana

Botswana Football Association
Founded: 1970
Joined FIFA: 1976
Joined CAF: 1976

SEASON	LEAGUE CHAMPIONS
1998	Notwane PG
1999	Mogoditshane Fighters
2000	Mogoditshane Fighters
2001	Mogoditshane Fighters
2002	Botswana Defence Force

YEAR	CUP WINNERS
1997	Notwane PG
1998	Botswana Defence Force
1999	Mogoditshane Fighters
2000	Mogoditshane Fighters
2001	TASC

Lesotho

Lesotho Sports Council
Founded: 1932
Joined FIFA: 1964
Joined CAF: 1964

SEASON	LEAGUE CHAMPIONS
1997	RL Defence Force
1998	RL Defence Force
1999	RL Defence Force
2000	Lesotho Prison Service
2001	RL Defence Force

YEAR	CUP WINNERS
1997	*not known*
1998	Arsenal
1999	*not known*
2000	RL Defence Force
2001	*not known*

Malawi

Football Association of Malawi
Founded: 1966
Joined FIFA: 1967
Joined CAF: 1968

Malawi *(continued)*

SEASON	LEAGUE CHAMPIONS
1997	Telecom Wanderers
1998	Telecom Wanderers
1999	Bata Bullets
2000	Bata Bullets
2001	Total Big Bullets

Mauritius

Mauritius Football Association
Founded: 1952
Joined FIFA: 1962
Joined CAF: 1962

SEASON	LEAGUE CHAMPIONS
1997	Sunrise Flacq United
1998	Hindu Scouts Club
1999	Fire Brigade FC
2000	*no championship*
2001	Olympique de Moka

YEAR	CUP WINNERS
1997	Sunrise Flacq United
1998	Fire Brigade FC
1999	*abandoned*
2000	*abandoned*
2001	USBBRH

Mozambique

Federação Mocambicana de Futebol
Founded: 1975
Joined FIFA: 1978
Joined CAF: 1978

SEASON	LEAGUE CHAMPIONS
1997	Ferroviário
1998	*no official championship*
1999	Ferroviário
2000	Costa do Sol
2001	Costa do Sol

YEAR	CUP WINNERS
1997	Maxaquene
1998	Costa do Sol
1999	Costa do Sol
2000	Costa do Sol
2001	Maxaquene

Namibia

Namibia Football Association
Founded: 1992
Joined FIFA: 1992
Joined CAF: 1990

The Zambian team which beat Mauritius 3-0 in Port Louis in a Nations Cup match on 25 April 1993. Two days later, en route to Senegal for a World Cup qualifier, the whole team was killed when their plane crashed off the coast of Gabon.

Namibia *(continued)*

SEASON	LEAGUE CHAMPIONS
1998	Black Africans Nashua
1999	Black Africans Nashua
2000	Blue Waters
2001	*no competition*
2002	Liverpool

YEAR	CUP WINNERS
1997	Black Africans Nashua
1998	Chief Santos
1999	Chief Santos
2000	Chief Santos
2001	*no competition*

Swaziland

National Football Association of Swaziland
Founded: 1964
Joined FIFA: 1976
Joined CAF: 1976

SEASON	LEAGUE CHAMPIONS
1998	Mbabane Highlanders
1999	Manzini Wanderers
2000	Mbabane Highlanders
2001	Mbabane Highlanders
2002	Manzini Wanderers

Swaziland *(continued)*

YEAR	CUP WINNERS
1997	Mbabane Highlanders
1998	Denver Sundowns
1999	*no official competition*
2000	*no official competition*
2001	*not known*

Zambia

Football Association of Zambia
Founded: 1929
Joined FIFA: 1964
Joined CAF: 1964

SEASON	LEAGUE CHAMPIONS
1997	Power Dynamos
1998	Nchanga Rangers
1999	Nkana FC
2000	Power Dynamos
2001	Nkana FC

YEAR	CUP WINNERS
1997	Power Dynamos
1998	Konkola Blades
1999	Zamsure
2000	Nkana FC
2001	Power Dynamos

Red Arrows from Lusaka (in red and black) was a fine cup team in the 1980s, winning the Zambian Cup in 1983 and 89. Today it is struggling in the Zambian Second Division.

South Africa

SOUTH AFRICAN
FOOTBALL ASSOCIATION

South African Football Association
Founded: 1892, 1991
Joined FIFA: 1952–76, 1992
Joined CAF: 1957–64, 1992

THE HISTORY OF FOOTBALL in South Africa is inevitably tied to the politics of race in the country. The first recorded game in South Africa took place in Natal in 1866 and the province also produced the first club – the white Pietermaritzburg Country – founded in 1879. Three further white clubs were quickly formed – Natal Wasps, Durban Alphas and Umgeni Stars – and in 1882 they formed the Natal FA. In 1891, a Cape Town FA was formed by four British military clubs, and a national organization, FASA (Football Association of South Africa), was formed in 1892. Western province joined in 1896 and Transvaal in 1899.

For all these organizational changes football was always secondary to rugby in the affections of white South Africans, but among the black population, football was always the dominant sport. In 1898, the first black club – Orange Free State Bantu FC – was founded, and an Orange Free State FA was set up in 1930 in Bloemfontein, the centre of African national politics; a Natal Bantu FA followed in 1931. All of these associations provided a crucial training ground for black administrators and politicians, including the ANC leader Albert Luthili. However, the sporting heart of black football was

Johannesburg and the mining towns of the Rand where the Transvaal Pirates, Swallows and Evergreen Mighty Greens flourished. Subsequently, the region has provided the other dominant forces in South African football – the Orlando Pirates, Mamelodi Sundowns and Kaizer Chiefs.

With the imposition of strict apartheid in 1948, the racial and political divide in football solidified. The SASF was formed in 1952 representing African and coloured football and it formally declared itself a non-racial organization in 1963. The older FASA remained resolutely white and was eventually expelled from CAF and FIFA for refusing to field mixed-race international sides. Domestically, a whites-only national professional league (the NPFL) ran from 1959, while the black NPSL was formed in 1971. The two effectively merged in 1978, the economics of township crowds weighing more heavily than the politics of racial separation. During the state of emergency in the 1980s, football matches and grounds provided a location for political rallies of all kinds and the ANC celebrated the release of political prisoners in 1989 and 1990 at the FNB Stadium in Johannesburg. In 1992, South Africa was readmitted to FIFA and CAF.

The Kaizer Chiefs from Johannesburg (in white) and the Mamelodi Sundowns from Pretoria are among the top teams in a strong South African football league.

South African League and Cup Winners 1971–2002

YEAR	LEAGUE CHAMPIONS (NPSL till 1984 then NSL)	CUP WINNERS	TOP EIGHT CUP WINNERS (NPSL till 1984 then NSL)
1971	Orlando Pirates	Kaizer Chiefs	
1972	Amazulu	Kaizer Chiefs	Orlando Pirates
1973	Orlando Pirates	Orlando Pirates	Orlando Pirates
1974	Kaizer Chiefs	Orlando Pirates	Kaizer Chiefs
1975	Orlando Pirates	Orlando Pirates	Moroka Swallows
1976	Orlando Pirates	Kaizer Chiefs	Kaizer Chiefs
1977	Kaizer Chiefs	Orlando Pirates	Kaizer Chiefs
1978	Lusitano Club	Wits University	Orlando Pirates
1979	Kaizer Chiefs	Kaizer Chiefs	Moroka Swallows
1980	Highlands Park	Orlando Pirates	Witbank Black Aces
1981	Kaizer Chiefs	Kaizer Chiefs	Kaizer Chiefs
1982	Durban City	Kaizer Chiefs	Kaizer Chiefs
1983	Durban City	Moroka Swallows	Orlando Pirates
1984	Kaizer Chiefs	Kaizer Chiefs	Wits University
1985	Bush Bucks	Bloemfontein Celtic	Kaizer Chiefs
1986	Rangers FC	Mamelodi United	Arcadia
1987	Jomo Cosmos	Kaizer Chiefs	Kaizer Chiefs
1988	Mamelodi United	Orlando Pirates	Mamelodi United
1989	Kaizer Chiefs	Moroka Swallows	Kaizer Chiefs
1990	Mamelodi United	Jomo Cosmos	Mamelodi United
1991	Kaizer Chiefs	Moroka Swallows	Kaizer Chiefs
1992	Kaizer Chiefs	Kaizer Chiefs	Kaizer Chiefs
1993	Mamelodi United	Witbank Aces	Orlando Pirates
1994	Orlando Pirates	Vaal Professionals	Kaizer Chiefs
1995	Cape Town Spurs	Cape Town Spurs	Wits University
1996	Kaizer Chiefs	Orlando Pirates	Orlando Pirates
1997	Manning Rangers	*no competition*	*no competition*
1998	Mamelodi Sundowns	Mamelodi Sundowns	*no competition*
1999	Mamelodi Sundowns	Supersport United	*no competition*
2000	Mamelodi Sundowns	Kaizer Chiefs	Orlando Pirates
2001	Orlando Pirates	Santos	Kaizer Chiefs
2002	Santos		

SOUTH AFRICA

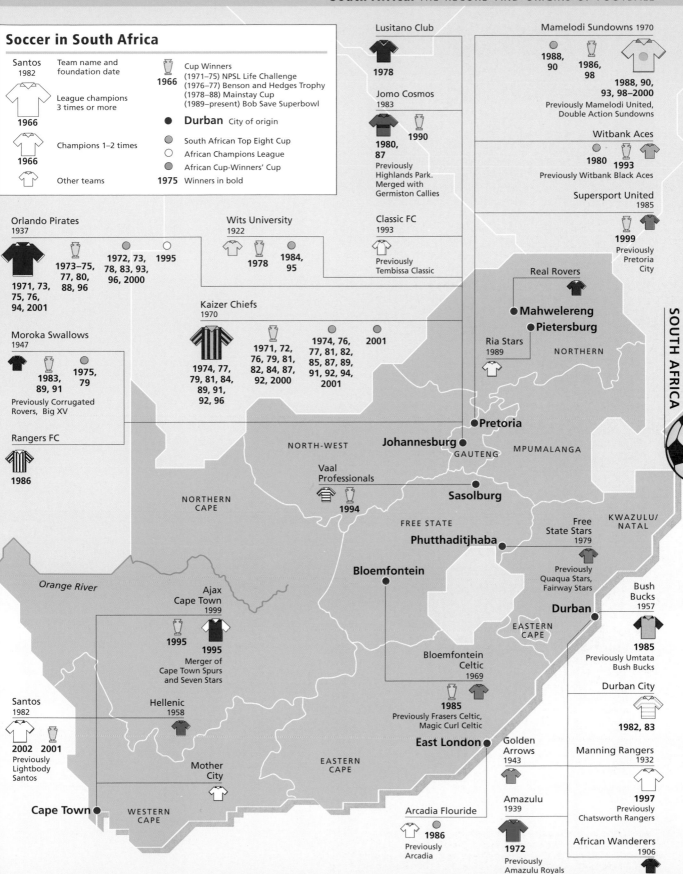

Soccer in South Africa

Santos
1982
Team name and foundation date

League champions 3 times or more
1966

Champions 1–2 times
1966

Other teams

1966
Cup Winners
(1971–75) NPSL Life Challenge
(1976–77) Benson and Hedges Trophy
(1978–88) Mainstay Cup
(1989–present) Bob Save Superbowl

● **Durban** City of origin

○ South African Top Eight Cup
○ African Champions League
○ African Cup-Winners' Cup

1975 Winners in bold

Lusitano Club
1978

Jomo Cosmos
1983
1980, 87   1990
Previously Highlands Park. Merged with Germiston Callies

Mamelodi Sundowns 1970
1988, 90   1986, 98
1988, 90, 93, 98–2000
Previously Mamelodi United, Double Action Sundowns

Witbank Aces
1980   **1993**
Previously Witbank Black Aces

Supersport United
1985
1999
Previously Pretoria City

Orlando Pirates
1937
1973–75, 77, 80, 88, 96   **1972, 73, 78, 83, 93, 96, 2000**   1995
1971, 73, 75, 76, 94, 2001

Wits University
1922
1978   **1984, 95**

Classic FC
1993
Previously Tembissa Classic

Real Rovers
● **Mahwelereng**
● **Pietersburg**

Ria Stars
1989

NORTHERN

Moroka Swallows
1947
1983, 89, 91   1975, 79
Previously Corrugated Rovers, Big XV

Kaizer Chiefs
1970
1974, 77, 79, 81, 84, 89, 91, 92, 96   **1971, 72, 76, 79, 81, 82, 84, 87, 92, 2000**   **1974, 76, 77, 81, 82, 85, 87, 89, 91, 92, 94, 2001**   2001

Rangers FC
1986

Pretoria ●
Johannesburg ●
GAUTENG
NORTH-WEST
MPUMALANGA

Vaal Professionals
1994

Sasolburg ●

NORTHERN CAPE

FREE STATE

KWAZULU/ NATAL

Free State Stars
1979
Previously Quaqua Stars, Fairway Stars

Phutthaditjhaba ●

Bush Bucks
1957
1985
Previously Umtata Bush Bucks

Orange River

Ajax Cape Town
1999
1995   **1995**
Merger of Cape Town Spurs and Seven Stars

Hellenic
1958

Mother City

Bloemfontein

Bloemfontein Celtic
1969
1985
Previously Frasers Celtic, Magic Curl Celtic

EASTERN CAPE

EASTERN CAPE

● **Durban**

Durban City
1982, 83

Manning Rangers
1932

Santos
1982
2002   2001
Previously Lightbody Santos

East London ●

Golden Arrows
1943

Amazulu
1939

1997
Previously Chatsworth Rangers

Cape Town ●
WESTERN CAPE

Arcadia Flouride
1986
Previously Arcadia

1972
Previously Amazulu Royals

African Wanderers
1906

SOUTH AFRICA

The African Champions League

TOURNAMENT OVERVIEW

IN A REVERSE OF EUROPEAN FOOTBALL'S development, where continental club competitions preceded international tournaments, the African Champions Cup (as it was first known) followed the African Cup of Nations by seven years. It was first played in 1964, with the strongest support coming from Ghana, who donated the tournament's Kwame Nkrumah trophy. Fourteen clubs played for the right to attend a finals tournament in Accra. The Ghanaian side, Real Republicans, (closely associated with President Nkrumah and dissolved two years later after his fall) performed poorly, and the first champions were the Cameroonian side Oryx Douala. No tournament was played in 1965, and in 1966 it was played as a straight knockout over two legs.

For the first decade the cup belonged to Central and West African clubs. The Zaïrians Tout Puissant Englebert, Asante Kotoko of Ghana and Hafia Conakry from Guinea all won the title at least once during those early years, interspersed by Cameroonian and Congolese triumphs. TP Englebert's first victory came after two drawn legs against Asante Kotoko, who then refused a further play-off to decide the Final. After this incident, aggregate scores and then penalties were introduced to decide tied matches.

In the 1980s and 90s, the power base of African club football shifted north of the Sahara. Egyptian, Moroccan, Algerian and Tunisian teams have taken the title 16 times since 1981. Orlando Pirates' victory in 1995, after many years of South African exclusion, suggested the balance of power might tip again, but the recent victories of Hearts of Oak and Raja Casablanca suggests not. Following European developments, the tournament became the African Champions League in 1997 and acquired a mini-league format at the quarter-finals stage.

Asante Kotoko of Kumasi, Ghana, appeared in seven African Champions League finals between 1967 and 1993, winning the trophy in 1970 and 1983. The team is pictured here before the 1993 Final against the Egyptian side Zamalek.

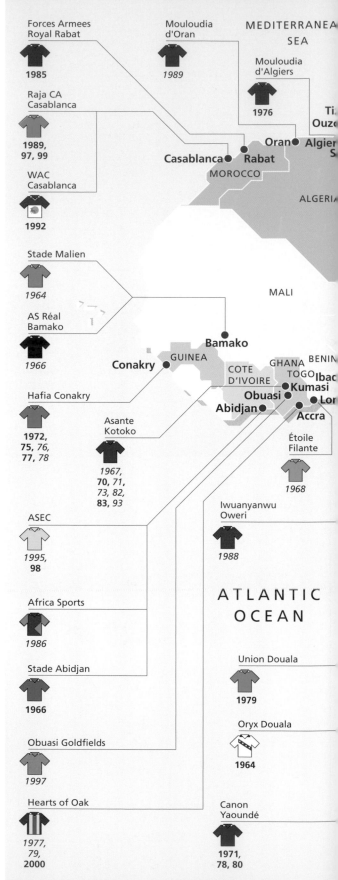

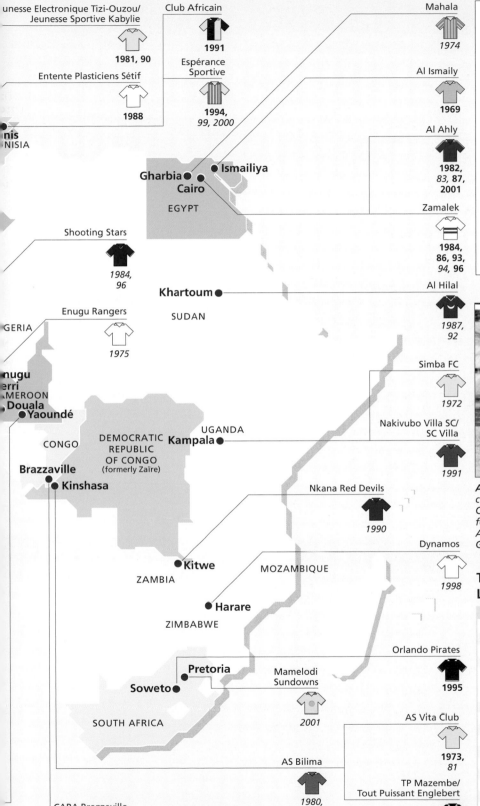

unesse Electronique Tizi-Ouzou/
Jeunesse Sportive Kabylie
1981, 90

Entente Plasticiens Sétif
1988

nis
NISIA

Club Africain
1991

Espérance Sportive
1994, *99, 2000*

Mahala
1974

Al Ismaily
1969

Al Ahly
1982, *83,* **87,** **2001**

Gharbia ● ● Ismailiya
● **Cairo**
EGYPT

Zamalek
1984, **86, 93,** **94, 96**

Shooting Stars
1984, **96**

Khartoum ●
SUDAN

Al Hilal
1987, *92*

Enugu Rangers
1975

GERIA

nugu
erri
MEROON
● Douala
● Yaoundé

Simba FC
1972

Nakivubo Villa SC/
SC Villa
1991

CONGO
DEMOCRATIC
REPUBLIC
OF CONGO
(formerly Zaïre)

UGANDA
Kampala ●

● Brazzaville
● Kinshasa

Nkana Red Devils
1990

Dynamos
1998

● Kitwe
ZAMBIA

MOZAMBIQUE

● Harare
ZIMBABWE

Orlando Pirates
1995

● Pretoria
Soweto ●
SOUTH AFRICA

Mamelodi Sundowns
2001

AS Vita Club
1973, *81*

AS Bilima
1980, *85*

CARA Brazzaville
1974

TP Mazembe/
Tout Puissant Englebert
1967, 68, **69, 70**

INDIAN
OCEAN

The African Champions League

Number of wins in the African Champions League (by country)

- 4+ times
- 3 times
- 2 times
- 1 time
- 0 times

Team details

EGYPT	Country
● Cairo	City of origin
Al Ahly	Team name
	Team colours
1982, *83,* **87, 2001**	Winners in bold / Runners-up in italic

Although naturally dominated by the continent's biggest clubs, the African Champions League is also a big stage for the little clubs. Here, ASEC from Adibjan (in yellow) take on FC 105 from Gabon in a qualifying match in 1999.

The African Champions League 1964–2001

COUNTRY	WINNERS	RUNNERS-UP
Egypt	8	3
Cameroon	5	0
Morocco	5	0
Algeria	4	1
Democratic Republic of Congo	3	5
Guinea	3	2
Ghana	3	8
Côte D'Ivoire	2	2
Tunisia	2	2
South Africa	1	1
Congo	1	0
Nigeria	0	4
Mali	0	2
Sudan	0	2
Uganda	0	2
Togo	0	1
Zambia	0	1
Zimbabwe	0	1

The African Champions League

THE OLDEST INTERNATIONAL African club competition is the African Champions League with its Sékou Touré Trophy. The competition was first played in 1964 with 14 participating clubs. The final four played in a three-day Final in Accra, Ghana. With a wave of decolonisation and state formation sweeping Africa in the 1960s, the tournament steadily expanded with all matches from the preliminary rounds being played over two legs. Aggregate points gave way to aggregate scores as a method of deciding draws. Replays were played for tied Finals, but in 1976 penalties were introduced. Since 1997, the quarter-finals have been played as two leagues of four teams, all playing each other home and away. The group winners progress to a two-leg Final.

The African Cup-Winners' Cup was started in 1975 for African domestic cup winners. If the cup winner is also in the African Champions League, the place goes to the defeated cup finalists. All matches are played over two legs; tied matches are decided on aggregate goals, away goals and, finally, penalties. Winners are awarded the Nelson Mandela Trophy. In 1992, a third African competition was created – the CAF Cup – for national league runners-up (or third- and fourth-placed teams, if clubs above them are involved in other international competitions). As with the Cup-Winners' Cup, all matches are played over two legs, and tied matches are decided on aggregate goals, away goals and, finally, penalties. The winners receive the Moshood Abiola Cup.

1964 FINAL
February 7 – Accra, Ghana
Oryx Douala **2-1** Stade Malien
(Cameroon)   (Mali)

1965 FINAL
no tournament

1966 FINAL (2 legs)
December 11 – Bamako, Mali
Réal Bamako **3-1** Stade Abidjan
(Mali)   (Côte d'Ivoire)

December 25 – Abidjan, Côte d'Ivoire
Stade Abidjan **4-1** Réal Bamako

Stade Abidjan won 5-4 on aggregate

1967 FINAL (2 legs)
November 19 – Kumasi, Ghana
Asante Kotoko **1-1** TP Englebert
(Ghana)   (Zaïre*)

November 26 – Kinshasa, Zaïre*
TP Englebert **2-2** Asante Kotoko

TP Englebert won after Asante Kotoko refused a play-off

1968 FINAL (2 legs)
March 16 – Kinshasa, Zaïre*
TP Englebert **5-0** Étoile Filante
(Zaïre*)   (Togo)

March 30 – Lomé, Togo
Étoile Filante **4-1** TP Englebert

TP Englebert won 6-4 on aggregate

1969 FINAL (2 legs)
December 22 – Kinshasa, Zaïre*
TP Englebert **2-2** Al Ismaily
(Zaïre*)   (Egypt)

January 9 – Cairo, Egypt
Al Ismaily **3-1** TP Englebert

Al Ismaily won 5-3 on aggregate

1970 FINAL (2 legs)
January 10 – Kumasi, Ghana
Asante Kotoko **1-1** TP Englebert
(Ghana)   (Zaïre*)

January 24 – Kinshasa, Zaïre*
TP Englebert **1-2** Asante Kotoko

Asante Kotoko won 3-2 on aggregate

1971 FINAL (2 legs)
December 5 – Kumasi, Ghana
Asante Kotoko **3-0** Canon Yaoundé
(Ghana)   (Cameroon)

December 19 – Yaoundé, Cameroon
Canon Yaoundé **2-0** Asante Kotoko
Result to be decided on points, not goal, aggregate so went to play-off

December 21 – Yaoundé, Cameroon
Canon Yaoundé **1-0** Asante Kotoko
Match abandoned at 1-0, result stood, Canon Yaoundé winners

1972 FINAL (2 legs)
December 10 – Conakry, Guinea
Hafia Conakry **4-2** Simba FC
(Guinea)   (Uganda)

December 22 – Kampala, Uganda
Simba FC **2-3** Hafia Conakry

Hafia Conakry won 7-4 on aggregate

1973 FINAL (2 legs)
November 25 – Kumasi, Ghana
Asante Kotoko **4-2** AS Vita Club
(Ghana)   (Zaïre*)

December 16 – Kinshasa, Zaïre*
AS Vita Club **3-0** Asante Kotoko

AS Vita Club won 5-4 on aggregate

1974 FINAL (2 legs)
November 29 – Brazzaville, Congo
CARA **4-2** Mahala
Brazzaville   (Egypt)
(Congo)

December 13 – Mahalla, Egypt
Mahala **1-2** CARA
Brazzaville

CARA Brazzaville won 6-3 on aggregate

1975 FINAL (2 legs)
December 7 – Conakry, Guinea
Hafia Conakry **2-1** Enugu Rangers
(Guinea)   (Nigeria)

December 20 – Lagos, Nigeria
Enugu Rangers **1-2** Hafia Conakry

Hafia Conakry won 4-1 on pens

1976 FINAL (2 legs)
December 5 – Conakry, Guinea
Hafia Conakry **3-0** Mouloudia
(Guinea)   d'Algiers
(Algeria)

December 12 – Algiers, Algeria
Mouloudia **3-0** Hafia Conakry
d'Algiers

Mouloudia d'Algiers won 4-1 on pens

1977 FINAL (2 legs)
December 4 – Accra, Ghana
Hearts of Oak **0-1** Hafia Conakry
(Ghana)   (Guinea)

December 18 – Conakry, Guinea
Hafia Conakry **3-2** Hearts of Oak

Hafia Conakry won 4-2 on aggregate

1978 FINAL (2 legs)
December 3 – Conakry, Guinea
Hafia Conakry **0-0** Canon Yaoundé
(Guinea)   (Cameroon)

December 17 – Yaoundé, Cameroon
Canon Yaoundé **2-0** Hafia Conakry

Canon Yaoundé won 2-0 on aggregate

1979 FINAL (2 legs)
December 2 – Accra, Ghana
Hearts of Oak **1-0** Union Douala
(Ghana)   (Cameroon)

December 16 – Yaoundé, Cameroon
Union Douala **1-0** Hearts of Oak

Union Douala won 5-3 on pens

1980 FINAL (2 legs)
November 30 – Yaoundé, Cameroon
Canon Yaoundé **2-2** AS Bilima
(Cameroon)   (Zaïre*)

December 14 – Kinshasa, Zaïre*
AS Bilima **0-3** Canon Yaoundé

Canon Yaoundé won 5-2 on aggregate

1981 FINAL (2 legs)
November 27 – Tizi-Ouzou, Algeria
JE Tizi-Ouzou **4-0** AS Vita Club
(Algeria)   (Zaïre*)

December 13 – Kinshasa, Zaïre*
AS Vita Club **0-1** JE Tizi-Ouzou

JE Tizi-Ouzou won 5-0 on aggregate

1982 FINAL (2 legs)
November 28 – Cairo, Egypt
Al Ahly **3-0** Asante Kotoko
(Egypt)   (Ghana)

December 12 – Kumasi, Ghana
Asante Kotoko **1-1** Al Ahly

Al Ahly won 4-1 on aggregate

1983 FINAL (2 legs)
November 27 – Cairo, Egypt
Al Ahly **0-0** Asante Kotoko
(Egypt)   (Ghana)

December 11 – Kumasi, Ghana
Asante Kotoko **1-0** Al Ahly

Asante Kotoko won 1-0 on aggregate

1984 FINAL (2 legs)
November 23 – Cairo, Egypt
Zamalek **2-0** Shooting Stars
(Egypt)   (Nigeria)

December 8 – Lagos, Nigeria
Shooting Stars **0-0** Zamalek

Zamalek won 2-0 on aggregate

1985 FINAL (2 legs)
November 30 – Rabat, Morocco
FAR Rabat **5-2** AS Bilima
(Morocco)   (Zaïre*)

December 22 – Lubumbashi, Zaïre*
AS Bilima **1-1** FAR Rabat

FAR Rabat won 6-3 on aggregate

1986 FINAL (2 legs)
November 28 – Cairo, Egypt
Zamalek **2-0** Africa Sports
(Egypt)   (Côte d'Ivoire)

December 21 – Abidjan, Côte d'Ivoire
Africa Sports **2-0** Zamalek

Zamalek won 4-2 on pens

1987 FINAL (2 legs)
November 29 – Khartoum, Sudan
Al Hilal **0-0** Al Ahly
(Sudan)   (Egypt)

December 18 – Cairo, Egypt
Al Ahly **2-0** Al Hilal

Al Ahly won 2-0 on aggregate

1988 FINAL (2 legs)
November 26 – Ibadan, Nigeria
Iwuanyanwu **1-0** Entente
Owerri　Sétif
(Nigeria)　(Algeria)

December 9 – Constantine, Algeria
Entente **4-0** Iwuanyanwu
Sétif　Owerri

Entente Sétif won 4-1 on aggregate

1989 FINAL (2 legs)
December 3 – Casablanca, Morocco
Raja **2-0** Mouloudia
Casablanca　d'Oran
(Morocco)　(Algeria)

December 15 – Oran, Algeria
Mouloudia **1-0** Raja
d'Oran　Casablanca

Raja Casablanca won 4-2 on pens

1990 FINAL (2 legs)
November 30 – Algiers, Algeria
JS Kabylie **1-0** Nkana Red
(Algeria)　Devils
　　　(Zaïre*)

December 22 – Lusaka, Zambia
Nkana Red **1-0** JS Kabylie
Devils

JS Kabylie won 5-3 on pens

1991 FINAL (2 legs)
November 23 – Tunis, Tunisia
Club Africain **5-1** Nakivubo Villa
(Algeria)　(Zaïre*)

December 14 – Kampala, Uganda
Nakivubo Villa **1-1** Club Africain

Club Africain won 6-2 on aggregate

1992 FINAL (2 legs)
November 29 – Casablanca, Morocco
WAC **2-0** Al Hilal
Casablanca　(Sudan)
(Morocco)

December 13 – Khartoum, Sudan
Al Hilal **0-0** WAC
　　　Casablanca

WAC Casablanca won 2-0 on aggregate

1993 FINAL (2 legs)
November 26 – Kumasi, Ghana
Asante Kotoko **0-0** Zamalek
(Ghana)　(Egypt)

December 10 – Cairo, Egypt
Zamalek **0-0** Asante Kotoko

Zamalek won 7-6 on pens

1994 FINAL (2 legs)
December 4 – Cairo, Egypt
Zamalek **0-0** Espérance
(Egypt)　Sportive
　　　(Tunisia)

December 17 – Tunis, Tunisia
Espérance **3-1** Zamalek
Sportive

Espérance Sportive won 3-1 on aggregate

1995 FINAL (2 legs)
Johannesburg, South Africa
Orlando Pirates **2-2** ASEC Abidjan
(South Africa)　(Côte d'Ivoire)

Abidjan, Côte d'Ivoire
ASEC Abidjan **0-1** Orlando Pirates

Orlando Pirates won 3-2 on aggregate

1996 FINAL (2 legs)
Lagos, Nigeria
Shooting Stars **2-1** Zamalek
(Nigeria)　(Egypt)

Cairo, Egypt
Zamalek **2-1** Shooting Stars

Zamalek won 5-4 on pens

1997 FINAL (2 legs)
November 30 – Obuasi, Ghana
Goldfields **1-0** Raja
(Ghana)　Casablanca
　　　(Morocco)

December 14 – Casablanca, Morocco
Raja **1-0** Goldfields
Casablanca

Raja Casablanca won 5-4 on pens

1998 FINAL (2 legs)
November 28 – Harare, Zimbabwe
Dynamos **0-0** ASEC Abidjan
(Zimbabwe)　(Côte d'Ivoire)

December 12 – Abidjan, Côte d'Ivoire
ASEC Abidjan **4-2** Dynamos

ASEC Abidjan won 4-2
on aggregate

1999 FINAL (2 legs)
November 27 – Casablanca, Morocco
Raja **0-0** Espérance
Casablanca　Sportive
(Morocco)　(Tunisia)

December 12 – Tunis, Tunisia
Espérance **0-0** Raja
Sportive　Casablanca

Raja Casablanca won 4-3 on pens

2000 FINAL (2 legs)
December 2 – Tunis, Tunisia
Espérance **1-2** Hearts of Oak
Sportive　(Ghana)
(Tunisia)

December 17 – Accra, Ghana
Hearts of Oak **3-1** Espérance
　　　Sportive

Hearts of Oak won 5-2 on aggregate

2001 FINAL (2 legs)
December 8 – Pretoria, South Africa
Mamelodi **1-1** Al Ahly
Sundowns　(Egypt)
(South Africa)

December 21 – Cairo, Egypt
Al Ahly **3-0** Mamelodi
　　　Sundowns

Al Ahly won 4-1 on aggregate

Walid Salheddine holds aloft the 2001 Champions League trophy for Al Ahly. Khaled Bebo scored a hat trick in the second leg.

The African Cup-Winners' Cup and CAF Cup

The African Cup-Winners' Cup 1975–2001

YEAR	WINNERS	RUNNERS-UP
1975	Tonnerre Yaoundé (Cameroon)	Stella Club (Côte d'Ivoire)
1976	Shooting Stars (Nigeria)	Tonnerre Yaoundé (Cameroon)
1977	Enugu Rangers (Nigeria)	Canon Yaoundé (Cameroon)
1978	Horoya AC (Guinea)	Milaha Athletic (Algeria)
1979	Canon Yaoundé (Cameroon)	Gor Mahia (Kenya)
1980	TP Mazembe (Zaïre*)	Africa Sports (Côte d'Ivoire)
1981	Union Douala (Cameroon)	Stationery Stores (Nigeria)
1982	Al Mokaoulom (Egypt)	Power Dynamos (Zambia)
1983	Al Mokaoulom (Egypt)	Agaza Lomé (Togo)
1984	Al Ahly (Egypt)	Canon Yaoundé (Cameroon)
1985	Al Ahly (Egypt)	Leventis United (Nigeria)
1986	Al Ahly (Egypt)	AS Sogara (Gabon)
1987	Gor Mahia (Kenya)	Espérance Sportive (Tunisia)
1988	CA Bizerte (Tunisia)	Rancher Bees (Nigeria)
1989	Al Merreikh (Sudan)	Bendel United (Nigeria)
1990	BCC Lions (Nigeria)	Club Africain (Tunisia)
1991	Power Dynamos (Zambia)	BCC Lions (Nigeria)
1992	Africa Sports (Côte d'Ivoire)	Vital'O FC (Burundi)
1993	Al Ahly (Egypt)	Africa Sports (Côte d'Ivoire)
1994	DC Motema Pembe (Zaïre*)	Kenya Breweries (Kenya)
1995	JS Kabylie (Algeria)	Julius Berger (Nigeria)
1996	Arab Contractors (Egypt)	AC Sodigraf (Zaïre*)
1997	Étoile du Sahel (Tunisia)	FAR Rabat (Morocco)
1998	Espérance Sportive (Tunisia)	Primeiro de Agosto (Angola)
1999	Africa Sports (Côte d'Ivoire)	Club Africain (Tunisia)

The African Cup-Winners' Cup (*continued*)

YEAR	WINNERS	RUNNERS-UP
2000	Zamalek (Egypt)	Canon Yaoundé (Cameroon)
2001	Kaizer Chiefs (South Africa)	Inter Clube (Angola)

The CAF Cup 1992–2001

YEAR	WINNERS	RUNNERS-UP
1992	Shooting Stars (Nigeria)	Nakivubo Villa (Uganda)
1993	Stella Club (Côte d'Ivoire)	Simba FC (Tanzania)
1994	Bendel Insurance (Nigeria)	Primeiro de Maio (Angola)
1995	Étoile du Sahel (Tunisia)	AS Kaloum Stars (Guinea)
1996	KAC Marrakech (Morocco)	Étoile du Sahel (Tunisia)
1997	Espérance Sportive (Tunisia)	Petro Atlético (Angola)
1998	CS Sfax (Tunisia)	ASC Jeanne d'Arc (Senegal)
1999	Étoile du Sahel (Tunisia)	WAC Casablanca (Morocco)
2000	JS Kabylie (Algeria)	Al Ismaili (Egypt)
2001	JS Kabylie (Algeria)	Étoile du Sahel (Tunisia)

* Zaïre is now known as the Democratic Republic of Congo

The African Cup of Nations

THE AFRICAN CUP OF NATIONS

TOURNAMENT OVERVIEW

THE COURSE OF THE AFRICAN CUP OF NATIONS inevitably parallels many aspects of Africa's postwar history. Prior to the massive wave of decolonization that swept the continent in the 1960s, only four nations were entered in the first tournament, in Sudan in 1957: Ethiopia, Egypt, South Africa and Sudan. South Africa was forced to withdraw by CAF because it refused to send a mixed-race team, and Egypt won the trophy easily, beating Ethiopia 4-0 in the Final.

In 1963 and 1965, Ghana, the first new nation to achieve independence in this era, announced West Africa's footballing prowess by winning both Finals against North African opposition. From Ghana, the baton passed to Central Africa, with the two Congos winning three of the next four tournaments.

In 1965, CAF ruled that each squad could only play two overseas-based players and the rule remained in force until 1982. By then, the rapidly increasing African presence in European leagues left the tournament without many of the leading stars of African football. The tournament further accommodated the power of European football by switching the finals to January, taking advantage of player availability during European football's mid-season break. Across this period, the growing strength of African football saw the tournament acquire a qualifying round and expand from four to eight participants in the finals. In 1992, it expanded again to 12 teams and in 1996 to 16.

With access to European-based players, the championships have been dominated by West Africa since the 1980s, with Ghana, Nigeria and Cameroon all taking the prize with an occasional look in for North African states and a resurgent post-apartheid South African victory in 1996.

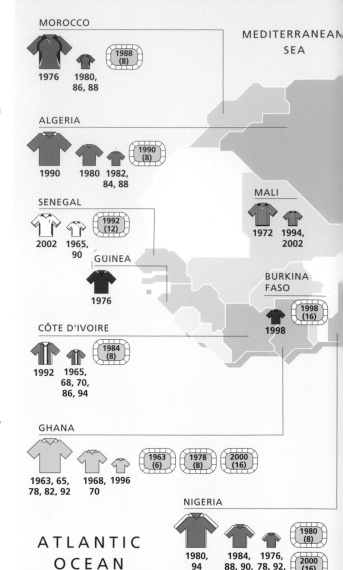

The African Cup of Nations (1956–2002)

YEAR	WINNERS	SCORE	RUNNERS-UP
1957	Egypt	4-0	Ethiopia
1959	Egypt	*final tournament*	Sudan
1962	Ethiopia	4-2	Egypt
1963	Ghana	3-0	Sudan
1965	Ghana	3-2	Tunisia
1968	Congo-Kinshasa	1-0	Ghana
1970	Sudan	1-0	Ghana
1972	Congo	3-2	Mali
1974	Zaïre	2-2, replay 2-0	Zambia
1976	Morocco	*final tournament*	Guinea
1978	Ghana	2-0	Uganda
1980	Nigeria	3-0	Algeria
1982	Ghana	1-1 (7-6 pens)	Libya
1984	Cameroon	3-1	Nigeria
1986	Egypt	0-0 (5-4 pens)	Cameroon
1988	Cameroon	1-0	Nigeria
1990	Algeria	1-0	Nigeria
1992	Ghana	0-0 (11-10 pens)	Côte d'Ivoire
1994	Nigeria	2-1	Zambia
1996	South Africa	2-0	Tunisia
1998	Egypt	2-0	South Africa
2000	Cameroon	2-2 (4-3 pens)	Nigeria
2002	Cameroon	0-0 (3-2 pens)	Senegal

The African Cup of Nations has been contested since 1957, but in recent years its colourful spectacle and top quality football has raised the tournament's profile.

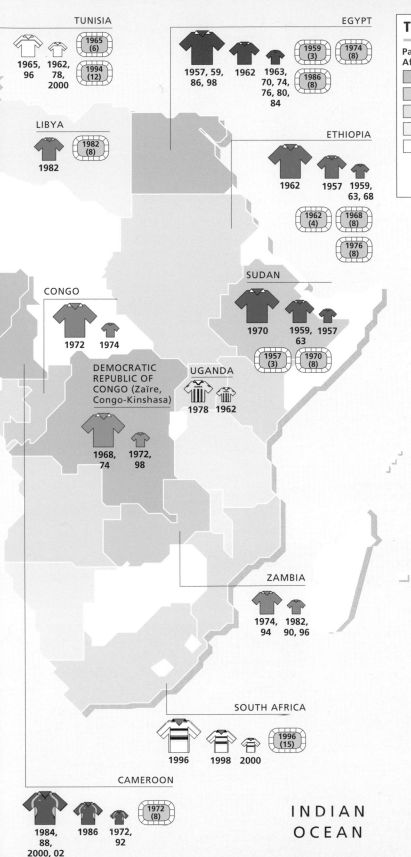

The African Cup of Nations

Participation in the African Nations Cup
- 10+ times
- 6–9 times
- 2–5 times
- 1 time
- 0 times

Winners, runners-up and semi-finalists with date

1966   1966   1966

Host country, with date of tournament and number of participants in brackets

CAMEROON   1976 (4)

TUNISIA — 1965 (6), 1994 (12) — 1965, 96 — 1962, 78, 2000

EGYPT — 1959 (3), 1974 (8), 1986 (8) — 1957, 59, 86, 98 — 1962 — 1963, 70, 74, 76, 80, 84

LIBYA — 1982 (8) — 1982

ETHIOPIA — 1962 (4), 1968 (8), 1976 (8) — 1962 — 1957 — 1959, 63, 68

SUDAN — 1957 (3), 1970 (8) — 1970 — 1959, 63 — 1957

CONGO — 1972 — 1974

DEMOCRATIC REPUBLIC OF CONGO (Zaïre, Congo-Kinshasa) — 1968, 74 — 1972, 98

UGANDA — 1978 — 1962

ZAMBIA — 1974, 94 — 1982, 90, 96

SOUTH AFRICA — 1996 (15) — 1996 — 1998 — 2000

CAMEROON — 1972 (8) — 1984, 88, 2000, 02 — 1986 — 1972, 92

INDIAN OCEAN

The African Cup of Nations Top Goalscorers

YEAR	SCORER	NATIONALITY	GOALS
1957	El Attar	Egyptian	5
1959	Al-Gohari	Egyptian	3
1962	Badawi	Egyptian	3
	Worku	Ethiopian	
1963	Chazli	Egyptian	6
1965	Acheampong	Ghanaian	3
	Kofi	Ghanaian	
	Mangle	Côte d'Ivoire	
1968	Pokou	Côte d'Ivoire	6
1970	Pokou	Côte d'Ivoire	8
1972	Keita	Malian	5
1974	Ndaye	from Zaire	9
1976	Mamadou	from Guinea	4
1978	Omondi	Ugandan	4
1980	Labied	Moroccan	3
	Odegbami	Nigerian	
1982	Alhassan	Ghanaian	4
1984	Zeid	Egyptian	4
1986	Milla	Cameroon	4
1988	Abdelhamid	Egyptian	2
	Belloumi	Algerian	
	Milla	Cameroon	
	Traore	Côte d'Ivoire	
1990	Menad	Algerian	4
1992	Yekini	Nigerian	4
1994	Yekini	Nigerian	5
1996	Bwalya	Zambian	5
1998	Hassan	Egyptian	7
	McCarthy	South African	
2000	Bartlett	South African	5
2002	Aghahowa	Nigerian	3
	Mboma	Cameroon	
	Olembe	Cameroon	

The African Cup of Nations 2002

TOURNAMENT REVIEW

THE AFRICAN CUP OF NATIONS

CAF'S COMMITMENT TO smaller and poorer African nations paid off in Mali, who managed to host a 16-nation, six-stadium tournament effectively. However, despite a great run by the home team, good attendances and balanced, competitive matches, the tournament will be remembered for a single act of violence. Before the Mali v Cameroon semi-final, local police attacked Cameroon's goalkeeping coach Thomas Nkono in full view of the crowd. Claims by CAF that he was the aggressor and by the Malian authorities that he had an incorrect ID card simply do not wash.

The group phase of the tournament was marred by rock hard pitches, imprecise finishing and very few goals. Qualification generally went with form, with Cameroon, Nigeria, Senegal and South Africa all winning their groups. Tunisia and Morocco played well below their best and went out, while home nation

Mali raised its game to qualify for the second phase. Liberia's exit saw the end of George Weah's legendary international career.

The quarter-finals were brought alive by Mali's 2-0 victory over South Africa, while Cameroon, Nigeria and Senegal's victories made the semi-finals all West African. Senegal and Cameroon proved worthy finalists, but both victories were overshadowed. Senegal v Nigeria descended into an orgy of red cards in an ill-tempered 30 minutes of extra time. Cameroon, taking revenge for mistreatment by the Malian authorities, convincingly dispatched the hosts 3-0. The Final was tense, with Cameroon having the best of the play. There were missed chances for Cameroon's N'Diefi and a disallowed goal for Eto'o. The match came down to penalties, and Senegal's captain Aliou Cissé saw his spot kick saved by Cameroon's Boukar Alioum; 3-2 to Cameroon.

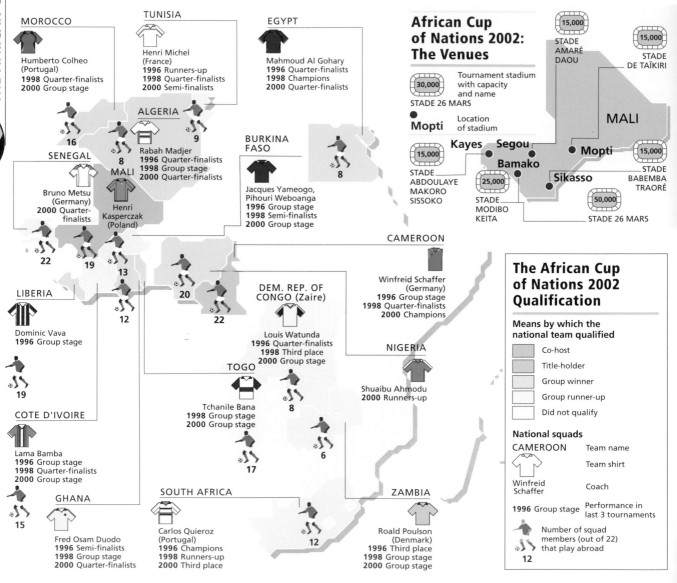

MOROCCO
Humberto Colheo (Portugal)
1998 Quarter-finalists
2000 Group stage

TUNISIA
Henri Michel (France)
1996 Runners-up
1998 Quarter-finalists
2000 Semi-finalists

EGYPT
Mahmoud Al Gohary
1996 Quarter-finalists
1998 Champions
2000 Quarter-finalists

ALGERIA
16
9
8
Rabah Madjer
1996 Quarter-finalists
1998 Group stage
2000 Quarter-finalists

BURKINA FASO
8
Jacques Yameogo, Pihouri Weboanga
1996 Group stage
1998 Semi-finalists
2000 Group stage

SENEGAL
Bruno Metsu (Germany)
2000 Quarter-finalists

MALI
Henri Kasperczak (Poland)
22
19
13
20
22
12

LIBERIA
Dominic Vava
1996 Group stage
19

CAMEROON
Winfreid Schaffer (Germany)
1996 Group stage
1998 Quarter-finalists
2000 Champions

DEM. REP. OF CONGO (Zaire)
Louis Watunda
1996 Quarter-finalists
1998 Third place
2000 Group stage

NIGERIA
Shuaibu Ahmodu
2000 Runners-up
8

TOGO
Tchanile Bana
1998 Group stage
2000 Group stage
17
6

COTE D'IVOIRE
Lama Bamba
1996 Group stage
1998 Quarter-finalists
2000 Group stage

GHANA
15
Fred Osam Duodo
1996 Semi-finalists
1998 Group stage
2000 Quarter-finalists

SOUTH AFRICA
Carlos Quieroz (Portugal)
1996 Champions
1998 Runners-up
2000 Third place

ZAMBIA
Roald Poulson (Denmark)
1996 Third place
1998 Group stage
2000 Group stage
12

African Cup of Nations 2002: The Venues

30,000 Tournament stadium with capacity and name
STADE 26 MARS
● Mopti Location of stadium

15,000 STADE AMARÉ DAOU
15,000 STADE DE TAÏKIRI

MALI

Kayes ● Segou ● Mopti
Bamako ●
Sikasso ●

STADE ABDOULAYE MAKORO SISSOKO
STADE MODIBO KEITA 25,000
STADE 26 MARS 50,000
STADE BABEMBA TRAORE 15,000

The African Cup of Nations 2002 Qualification

Means by which the national team qualified

Co-host
Title-holder
Group winner
Group runner-up
Did not qualify

National squads
CAMEROON — Team name
— Team shirt
Winfreid Schaffer — Coach
1996 Group stage — Performance in last 3 tournaments
— Number of squad members (out of 22) that play abroad
12

THE GROUP STAGES

GROUP A		
Mali **1-1** Liberia		
Nigeria **1-0** Algeria		
Mali **0-0** Nigeria		
Liberia **2-2** Algeria		
Mali **2-0** Algeria		
Nigeria **1-0** Liberia		

	P	W	D	L	F	A	Pts
Nigeria	3	2	1	0	2	0	7
Mali	3	1	2	0	3	1	5
Liberia	3	0	2	1	3	4	2
Algeria	3	0	1	2	2	5	1

GROUP B		
South Africa **0-0** Burkina Faso		
Morocco **0-0** Ghana		
South Africa **0-0** Ghana		
Morocco **2-1** Burkina Faso		
South Africa **3-1** Morocco		
Ghana **2-1** Burkina Faso		

	P	W	D	L	F	A	Pts
South Africa	3	1	2	0	3	1	5
Ghana	3	1	2	0	2	1	5
Morocco	3	1	1	1	3	4	4
Burkina Faso	3	0	1	2	2	4	1

GROUP C		
Cameroon **1-0** DR Congo		
Togo **0-0** Côte d'Ivoire		
Cameroon **1-0** Côte d'Ivoire		
DR Congo **0-0** Togo		
Cameroon **3-0** Togo		
DR Congo **3-1** Côte d'Ivoire		

	P	W	D	L	F	A	Pts
Cameroon	3	3	0	0	5	0	9
DR Congo	3	1	1	1	3	2	4
Togo	3	0	2	1	0	3	2
Côte d'Ivoire	3	0	1	2	1	4	1

GROUP D		
Senegal **1-0** Egypt		
Zambia **0-0** Tunisia		
Egypt **1-0** Tunisia		
Senegal **1-0** Zambia		
Egypt **2-1** Zambia		
Senegal **0-0** Tunisia		

	P	W	D	L	F	A	Pts
Senegal	3	2	1	0	2	0	7
Egypt	3	2	0	1	3	2	6
Tunisia	3	0	2	2	0	1	2
Zambia	3	0	1	2	1	3	1

THE QUARTER-FINALS

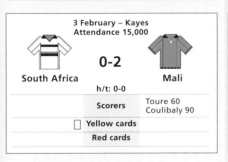

3 February – Kayes
Attendance 15,000

0-2

South Africa — Mali

h/t: 0-0

Scorers	Toure 60 Coulibaly 90
☐ Yellow cards	
Red cards	

3 February – Bamako
Attendance 25,000

1-0

Nigeria — Ghana

h/t: 0-0

Lawal 80	Scorers	
☐☐ Yellow cards		
Red cards		

4 February – Sikasso
Attendance 15,000

1-0

Cameroon — Egypt

h/t: 0-0

Mboma 62	Scorers	
☐☐ Yellow cards	☐	
Red cards		

4 February – Bamako
Attendance 25,000

2-0

Senegal — DR Congo

h/t: 1-0

Diao 30 Diouf 86	Scorers	
☐☐☐ Yellow cards	☐☐☐☐☐	
Red cards	■	

THE SEMI-FINALS

7 February – Bamako
Attendance 20,000

1-2
(after extra time)

Nigeria — Senegal

h/t: 0-1 f/t: 1-1

Aghahowa 88	Scorers	Diop 54 Diao 97
☐☐☐☐ Yellow cards		☐☐
■ ■ Red cards		■

7 February – Bamako
Attendance 50,000

0-3

Mali — Cameroon

h/t: 0-2

Scorers	Olembe 39, 45 Foe 84
☐ Yellow cards	
Red cards	

***Cameroon celebrates** after deservedly retaining the African Cup of Nations in Mali in 2002 after a tense Final against Senegal that ended in a penalty shootout.*

THIRD PLACE PLAY-OFF

February 9 - Mopti
Attendance 15,000

0-1

Mali — Nigeria

h/t: 0-1

Scorers	Aiyegbeni 29
☐☐☐☐ Yellow cards	
Red cards	

THE FINAL

10 February – Bamako
Attendance 50,000

0-0

Cameroon (Cameroon won 3-2 on pens) Senegal

h/t: 0-0

Scorers	
☐☐☐ Yellow cards	☐☐☐
Red cards	

The African Cup of Nations

ESTABLISHED ALONGSIDE the Confederation Africanne de Football (CAF) in 1957, the African Cup of Nations is the continent's main international tournament. Its timing has varied but has now been set for January to ensure that the increasingly large number of Africans who play in European leagues can attend during what is for many nations a midwinter break.

The early tournaments were small affairs with no qualifying rounds. Indeed, given the refusal of the CAF to accept an exclusively black or exclusively white South African team in 1957, the first tournament consisted of only two games. As the wave of decolonization crossed Africa in the late 1950s and 1960s the number of rounds, games and entrants steadily rose. Qualifying rounds were first introduced for the sixth tournament in 1968. By the early 1990s the final tournament had 12 entrants and this has now grown to 16.

1957 SUDAN

SEMI-FINALS
Ethiopia w/o South Africa
South Africa disqualified because of aparthied
Egypt 2-1 Sudan

FINAL
February 16 – Khartoum
Egypt 4-0 Ethiopia
(El Diba 4)
Att: 15,000 **Ref:** Youssef (Sudan)

1959 EGYPT

FINAL TOURNAMENT
May 22 – Cairo
Egypt 4-0 Ethiopia
(Gohri 29, 42, 73,
Cherbini 64)

May 22 – Cairo
Sudan 1-0 Ethiopia
(Drissa 40)

May 29   Cairo
Egypt 2-1 Sudan
(Issam 12, 89)   (Manzual 65)

1 Egypt
2 Sudan
3 Ethiopia

1962 ETHIOPIA

SEMI-FINALS
Ethiopia 4-2 Tunisia
Egypt 2-1 Uganda

THIRD PLACE PLAY-OFF
January 20 – Addis Ababa
Tunisia 3-0 Uganda
(Djedidi,
Moncef Chérif,
Meddeb)

FINAL
January 21 – Addis Ababa
Ethiopia 4-2 Egypt
(Girma 74,   (Badawi 35, 75)
Menguitsou
84, 117,
Italo 101)
(after extra time)
h/t: 0-1 **90 mins:** 2-2
Att: 20,000 **Ref:** Brooks (Uganda)

1963 GHANA

THIRD PLACE PLAY-OFF
November 30 – Accra
Egypt 3-0 Ethiopia
(Raidh,
Taha,
Chazli)

FINAL
December 1 – Accra
Ghana 3-0 Sudan
(Aggrey-Fynn
62 pen,
Mfum 72, 82)
h/t: 0-0 **Att:** 50,000
Ref: Abdelkader (Tunisia)

1965 TUNISIA

THIRD PLACE PLAY-OFF
November 21 – Zouiten, Tunis
Côte d'Ivoire 1-0 Senegal
(Yobone 35)

FINAL
November 21 – Zouiten, Tunis
Ghana 3-2 Tunisia
(Odoi 37, 96,   (Chetali 47,
O. Kofi 79)   Chaibi 67)
(after extra time)
h/t: 1-0 **Att:** 30,000
Ref: Chekaimi (Algeria)

1968 ETHIOPIA

SEMI-FINALS
Congo- 3-2 Ethiopia
Kinshasa*
(after extra time)
Ghana 4-3 Côte d'Ivoire

THIRD PLACE PLAY-OFF
January 21 – Addis Ababa
Côte d'Ivoire 1-0 Ethiopia
(Pokou 28)

FINAL
January 21 – Addis Ababa
Congo- 1-0 Ghana
Kinshasa*
(Kalala 66)
h/t: 0-0 **Att:** 12,000
Ref: Al Diba (Egypt)

1970 SUDAN

SEMI-FINALS
Ghana 2-1 Côte d'Ivoire
(after extra time)
Sudan 2-1 Egypt
(after extra time)

THIRD PLACE PLAY-OFF
February 16 – Khartoum
Egypt 3-1 Côte d'Ivoire
(Chazli 3, 14, 15)   (Losseni 72)

FINAL
February 16 – Khartoum
Sudan 1-0 Ghana
(El Issed 12)
h/t: 1-0 **Att:** 35,000
Ref: Tesfaye (Ethiopia)

1972 CAMEROON

SEMI-FINALS
Congo 1-0 Cameroon
Mali 4-3 Zaïre
(after extra time)

THIRD PLACE PLAY-OFF
March 4 – Yaoundé
Cameroon 5-2 Zaïre
(Akono 4 pen,   (Kakoko 13,
Ndongo 31,   Majanga 17)
Owona 32,
Mouthé 34,
Ndoga 42)

FINAL
March 5 – Yaoundé
Congo 3-2 Mali
(M'bono 57, 59,   (Diakhité 42,
M'Pelé 63)   M. Traoré 75)
h/t: 0-1 **Att:** 5,000
Ref: Aoussi (Algeria)

1974 EGYPT

SEMI-FINALS
Zaïre 3-2 Egypt
Zambia 4-2 Congo
(after extra time)

THIRD PLACE PLAY-OFF
March 11 – Cairo
Egypt 4-0 Congo
(M. Abdou 5,
Chehata 18, 80,
Abngreisha 62)

FINAL
March 12 – Cairo
Zaïre 2-2 Zambia
(Ndaye 65, 117)   (Kaushi 40,
                   Sinyangwe 120)
(after extra time)
h/t: 0-1 **90 mins:** 1-1
Att: 5,000 **Ref:** Gamar (Libya)

REPLAY
March 14 – Cairo
Zaïre 2-0 Zambia
(Ndaye 30, 76)
h/t: 1-0 **Att:** 1,000
Ref: Gamar (Libya)

1976 ETHIOPIA

FINAL PHASE
March 9 – Addis Ababa
Guinea 1-1 Nigeria
(P. Camara 88)   (Lawal 52)

March 9 – Addis Ababa
Morocco 2-1 Egypt
(Faras 23,   (A. Rehab 34)
Zahraoui 88)

March 11 – Addis Ababa
Morocco 2-1 Nigeria
(Faras 82,   (B. Otu 50)
Guezzar 87)

March 11 – Addis Ababa
Guinea 4-2 Egypt
(Léa 24, 65,   (Abdou 33,
Ghanem o.g. 53,   Siaguy 86)
Morciré 62)

March 14 – Addis Ababa
Nigeria 3-2 Egypt
(Ilerika 35, 62,   (Al-Khatib 7,
Lawal 82)   Ussama 41)

March 14 – Addis Ababa
Morocco 1-1 Guinea
(Baba 86)   (Chérif 33)

1 Morocco
2 Guinea
3 Nigeria

1978 GHANA

SEMI-FINALS
Ghana 1-0 Tunisia
Uganda 2-1 Nigeria

THIRD PLACE PLAY-OFF
March 16 – Accra
Nigeria w/o Tunisia
Tunisia withdrew at 1-1 after 30 mins.
Match awarded 2-0 to Nigeria

FINAL
March 18 – Accra
Ghana 2-0 Uganda
(Afriye 38, 64)
h/t: 1-0 **Att:** 40,000
Ref: El Ghoul (Libya)

1980 NIGERIA

SEMI-FINALS
Nigeria 1-0 Morocco
Egypt 2-2 Algeria
(after extra time)
Algeria won 4-2 on pens

THIRD PLACE PLAY-OFF
March 21 – Lagos
Morocco 2-0 Egypt
(Labied 9, 78)

FINAL
March 22 – Lagos
Nigeria 3-0 Algeria
(Odegbami 2, 42,
Lawal 50)
h/t: 2-0 **Att:** 80,000
Ref: Tesfaye (Ethiopia)

The African Cup of Nations Winners

Egypt
1957, 59, 86, 98

Ethiopia
1962

Ghana
1963, 65, 78, 82, 92

Congo
1972

Sudan
1970

Dem. Rep. of Congo (Zaïre)
1968, 74

Morocco
1976

Nigeria
1980, 94

Cameroon
1984, 88, 2000, 02

Algeria
1990

South Africa
1996

1982 LIBYA
SEMI-FINALS
Ghana 3-2 Algeria
(after extra time)
Libya 2-1 Zambia
THIRD PLACE PLAY-OFF
March 18 – Tripoli
Zambia 2-0 Algeria
(Kamba 2,
Munshya 25)

FINAL
March 19 – Tripoli
Ghana 1-1 Libya
(Al Hassan 35)   (Beshari 70)
(after extra time)
h/t: 0-1 90 mins: 1-1 Att: 50,000
Ref: Sohan Ramlochun (Mauritania)
Ghana won 7-6 on pens

1984 CÔTE D'IVOIRE
SEMI-FINALS
Nigeria 2-2 Egypt
(after extra time)
Nigeria won 8-7 on pens
Cameroon 0-0 Algeria
(after extra time)
Cameroon won 5-4 on pens

THIRD PLACE PLAY-OFF
March 17 – Abidjan
Algeria 3-1 Egypt
(Madjer 67,   (Abdelghani
Belloumi 70,   74 pen))
Yahi 88)

FINAL
March 17 – Abidjan
Cameroon 3-1 Nigeria
(Ndjeya 32,   (Lawal 10))
Abega 79,
Ebongue 84)
h/t: 1-1 Att: 50,000
Ref: Bennaceur (Tunisia)

1986 EGYPT
SEMI-FINALS
Egypt 1-0 Morocco
Cameroon 1-0 Côte d'Ivoire
(after extra time)

THIRD PLACE PLAY-OFF
March 20 – Cairo
Côte d'Ivoire 3-2 Morocco
(Salah 8,   (Ghiati 44,
Kaondio   Sahil 85)
38 pen, 68)

FINAL
March 21 – Cairo
Egypt 0-0 Cameroon
(after extra time)
h/t: 0-0 90 mins: 0-0
Att: 100,000 Ref: Bennaceur (Tunisia)
Egypt won 5-4 on pens

1988 MOROCCO
SEMI-FINALS
Cameroon 1-0 Morocco
Nigeria 1-1 Algeria
(after extra time)
Nigeria won 9-8 on pens

THIRD PLACE PLAY-OFF
March 26 – Casablanca
Algeria 1-1 Morocco
(Belloumi 87)   (Nader 67)
(after extra time)
Algeria won 4-3 on pens

FINAL
March 27 – Casablanca
Cameroon 1-0 Nigeria
(Kunde 55)
h/t: 1-0 Att: 50,000
Ref: Idrissa (Senegal)

1990 ALGERIA
SEMI-FINALS
Algeria 2-1 Senegal
Nigeria 2-0 Zambia

THIRD PLACE PLAY-OFF
March 15 – Algiers
Zambia 1-0 Senegal
(Chikabala 73)

FINAL
March 16 – Algiers
Algeria 1-0 Nigeria
(Oudjani 38)
h/t: 1-0 Att: 80,000
Ref: not known

1992 SENEGAL
SEMI-FINALS
Côte d'Ivoire 0-0 Cameroon
(after extra time)
Côte d'Ivoire won 3-1 on pens
Ghana 2-1 Nigeria

THIRD PLACE PLAY-OFF
January 21 – Dakar
Nigeria 2-1 Cameroon
(Ekpo 75,   (Maboang 85)
Yekini 88)
h/t: 2-1 Att: 2,000
Ref: Zeli (Côte d'Ivoire)

FINAL
January 26 – Dakar
Ghana 0-0 Côte d'Ivoire
(after extra time)
h/t: 0-0 90 mins: 0-0
Att: 60,000 Ref: Sene (Ghana)
Ghana won 11-10 on pens

1994 TUNISIA
SEMI-FINALS
Nigeria 2-2 Côte d'Ivoire
(after extra time)
Nigeria won 4-2 on pens
Zambia 4-0 Mali

THIRD PLACE PLAY-OFF
April 10 – Tunis
Côte d'Ivoire 3-1 Mali
(Koné 2,   (Diallo 46)
Ouattara 68,
Sié 70)

FINAL
April 10 – Tunis
Nigeria 2-1 Zambia
(Amunike 5, 46)   (Litana 3)
h/t: 1-1 Att: 25,000
Ref: Lim Kee Chong (Mauritania)

1996 SOUTH AFRICA
SEMI-FINALS
Tunisia 4-2 Zambia
South Africa 3-0 Ghana

THIRD PLACE PLAY-OFF
Zambia 1-0 Ghana

FINAL
Feb 3 – Johannesburg
South Africa 2-0 Tunisia
(Williams 73, 74)
h/t: 0-0 Att: 80,000
Ref: Massembe (Uganda)

1998 BURKINA FASO
SEMI-FINALS
South Africa 2-1 Congo-Kinshasa*
(after extra time)
Egypt 2-0 Burkina Faso

THIRD PLACE PLAY-OFF
March 27 – Municipal, Ouagadougou
Congo- 4-4 Burkina Faso
Kinshasa*
Congo-Kinshasa won 4-1 on pens

FINAL
February 28 – 4 Août, Ouagadougou
Egypt 2-0 South Africa
(A. Hassan 5,
T. Mostafa 13)
h/t: 2-0 Att: 40,000
Ref: Belgola (Morocco)

2000 GHANA/NIGERIA
SEMI-FINALS
Nigeria 2-0 South Africa
Cameroon 3-0 Tunisia

THIRD PLACE PLAY-OFF
February 12 – Accra
South Africa 2-2 Tunisia
(Bartlett 11,   (Zitouni 28, 90)
Novente 62)
South Africa won 4-3 on pens

FINAL
February 13 – Lagos
Cameroon 2-2 Nigeria
(Eto'o 26,   (Chukwu 44,
Mboma 31)   Okocha 47)
h/t: 1-2 90 mins: 2-2
Att: 40,000 Ref: Daami (Tunisia)
Cameroon won 4-3 on pens

2002 MALI
SEMI-FINALS
Senegal 2-1 Nigeria
Mali 0-3 Cameroon

THIRD PLACE PLAY-OFF
February 9 – Mopti
Mali 0-1 Nigeria
(Aiyegbeni 29)

FINAL
February 10 – Bamako
Cameroon 0-0 Senegal
h/t: 0-0 90 mins: 0-0
Att: 60,000 Ref: Al Ghandour (Egypt)
Cameroon won 3-2 on pens

* Another name for Democratic Republic of Congo/Zaïre

Cameroon's Rigobert Song holds up the African Cup of Nations after its victory in 2000.

THE AFC NATIONS

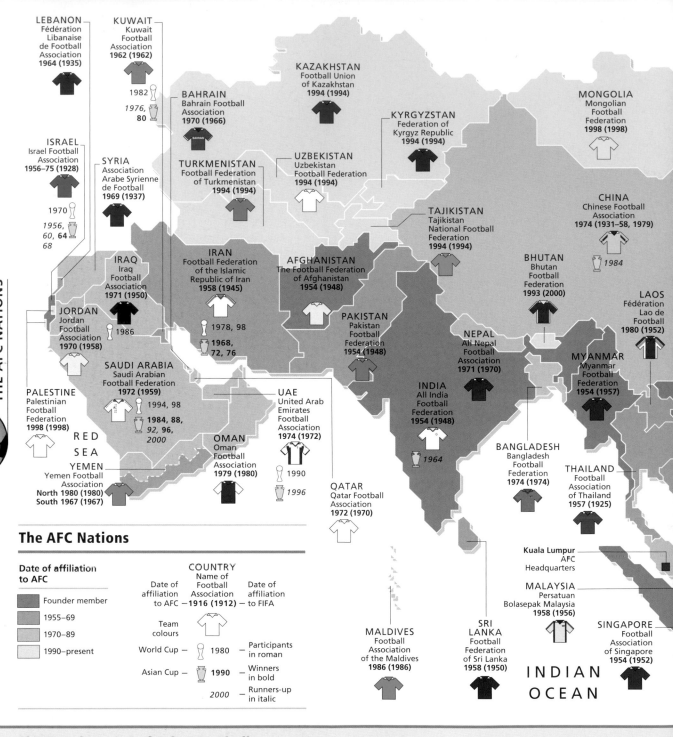

LEBANON
Fédération
Libanaise
de Football
Association
1964 (1935)

KUWAIT
Kuwait
Football
Association
1962 (1962)

1982
1976,
80

BAHRAIN
Bahrain Football
Association
1970 (1966)

KAZAKHSTAN
Football Union
of Kazakhstan
1994 (1994)

KYRGYZSTAN
Federation of
Kyrgyz Republic
1994 (1994)

MONGOLIA
Mongolian
Football
Federation
1998 (1998)

ISRAEL
Israel Football
Association
1956–75 (1928)

1970
1956,
60, **64**
68

SYRIA
Association
Arabe Syrienne
de Football
1969 (1937)

TURKMENISTAN
Football Federation
of Turkmenistan
1994 (1994)

UZBEKISTAN
Uzbekistan
Football Federation
1994 (1994)

TAJIKISTAN
Tajikistan
National Football
Federation
1994 (1994)

CHINA
Chinese Football
Association
1974 (1931–58, 1979)

1984

IRAQ
Iraq
Football
Association
1971 (1950)

1986

IRAN
Football Federation
of the Islamic
Republic of Iran
1958 (1945)

1978, 98
**1968,
72, 76**

AFGHANISTAN
The Football Federation
of Afghanistan
1954 (1948)

BHUTAN
Bhutan
Football
Federation
1993 (2000)

LAOS
Fédération
Lao de
Football
1980 (1952)

JORDAN
Jordan
Football
Association
1970 (1958)

PAKISTAN
Pakistan
Football
Federation
1954 (1948)

NEPAL
All Nepal
Football
Association
1971 (1970)

MYANMAR
Myanmar
Football
Federation
1954 (1957)

SAUDI ARABIA
Saudi Arabian
Football Federation
1972 (1959)

1994, 98
**1984, 88,
92, 96,**
2000

UAE
United Arab
Emirates
Football
Association
1974 (1972)

INDIA
All India
Football
Federation
1954 (1948)

1964

PALESTINE
Palestinian
Football
Federation
1998 (1998)

OMAN
Oman
Football
Association
1979 (1980)

1990

1996

BANGLADESH
Bangladesh
Football
Federation
1974 (1974)

THAILAND
Football
Association
of Thailand
1957 (1925)

R E D
S E A

YEMEN
Yemen Football
Association
North 1980 (1980)
South 1967 (1967)

QATAR
Qatar Football
Association
1972 (1970)

Kuala Lumpur
AFC
Headquarters

MALAYSIA
Persatuan
Bolasepak Malaysia
1958 (1956)

SINGAPORE
Football
Association
of Singapore
1954 (1952)

MALDIVES
Football
Association
of the Maldives
1986 (1986)

**SRI
LANKA**
Football
Federation
of Sri Lanka
1958 (1950)

I N D I A N
O C E A N

The AFC Nations

**Date of affiliation
to AFC**

▪	Founder member
▪	1955–69
▪	1970–89
▪	1990–present

COUNTRY
Name of
Football
Date of   Association   Date of
affiliation   **1916** (1912)   affiliation
to AFC   to FIFA

Team
colours

World Cup —   1980   — Participants
             in roman

Asian Cup —   **1990**   — Winners
             in bold

     2000   — Runners-up
             in italic

The Development of Asian Football

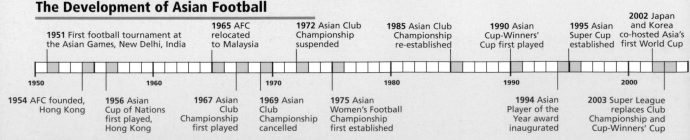

1951 First football tournament at
the Asian Games, New Delhi, India

1965 AFC
relocated
to Malaysia

1972 Asian Club
Championship
suspended

1985 Asian Club
Championship
re-established

1990 Asian
Cup-Winners'
Cup first played

1995 Asian
Super Cup
established

2002 Japan
and Korea
co-hosted Asia's
first World Cup

1950   1960   1970   1980   1990   2000

1954 AFC founded,
Hong Kong

1956 Asian
Cup of Nations
first played,
Hong Kong

1967 Asian
Club
Championship
first played

1969 Asian
Club
Championship
cancelled

1975 Asian
Women's Football
Championship
first established

1994 Asian
Player of the
Year award
inaugurated

2003 Super League
replaces Club
Championship and
Cup-Winners' Cup

The AFC Nations

SOUTH KOREA
Korea Football
Association
1954 (1948)

🏆 1954 (as Korea),
86, 90, 94, 98
🏆 **1956, 60,**
72, 80, 88

NORTH KOREA
Football Association
of the Democratic
People's Republic
of Korea
1974 (1958)

🏆 1966

ACAO
acau Football
sociation
76 (1976)

JAPAN
Japan Football
Association
1954 (1929–46, 1950)

🏆 1998
🏆 **1992,**
2000

**HONG
KONG**
Hong Kong
Football
Association
1954 (1954)

TAIWAN
Chinese Taipei
Football
Association
1954–75, 1990 (1954)

PACIFIC
OCEAN

VIETNAM
Vietnam
Football
Federation
1954 (1964)

PHILIPPINES
Philippines
Football
Federation
1954 (1928)

GUAM
Guam Soccer
Association
1996 (1996)

CAMBODIA
Cambodia
Football
Federation
1957 (1953)

BRUNEI
Football
Association of
Brunei Darussalam
1970 (1969)

INDONESIA
Persatuan
Sepakbola
Seluruh Indonesia
1954 (1952)

AFC

AFC
Asian Football Confederation

**Asian Tournaments
and Cup Competitions:**
Asian Cup
Asian Games
Asian Super League
Asian Women's Championship

THE AFC (ASIAN FOOTBALL CONFEDERATION) is the ruling FIFA affiliated body for Asian football. Prior to the AFC's formation international football was played at the 1951 and 1954 Asian Games. The Manila Games of 1954 provided the opportunity for representatives of Asian football to form the AFC, based in Hong Kong until relocating to Malaysia in 1965. The AFC's Asian Cup, open to professionals and amateurs, has superseded the Asian Games as the continent's premier international tournament.

The enormous size and diversity of Asia has presented organizational dilemmas. International tournaments involve vast travelling distances for often poor clubs and leagues, and most competitions have used regionally-based qualifying rounds. Travel aside, the AFC (which included Israel and Taiwan among its members) has been beset by international politics. Indonesia refused travel visas for both nations' teams at the 1962 Asian Games and pressure continued over the next decade for both nations to be expelled. China protested Taiwan's presence and Middle Eastern nations objected to Israel. At the 1974 Asian Games North Korea and Iran refused to play Israel and the next year Israel and Taiwan were expelled. In the 1990s AFC has been busy with the modernization and commercialization of Asian football and the promotion of its international club tournaments.

Lee Dong-gook of South Korea was the leading scorer in the 2000 Asian Cup despite his team losing to Saudi Arabia in the semi-finals. His efforts in the competition were rewarded with a loan spell at Werder Bremen in Germany, but he later returned to his regular club in South Korea, the Pohang Steelers.

Calendar of Events

Club Tournaments	AFC Super League 2003
	Arab Cup 2003
	Arab Cup-Winners' Cup 2003
International Tournaments	Asian Games 2002

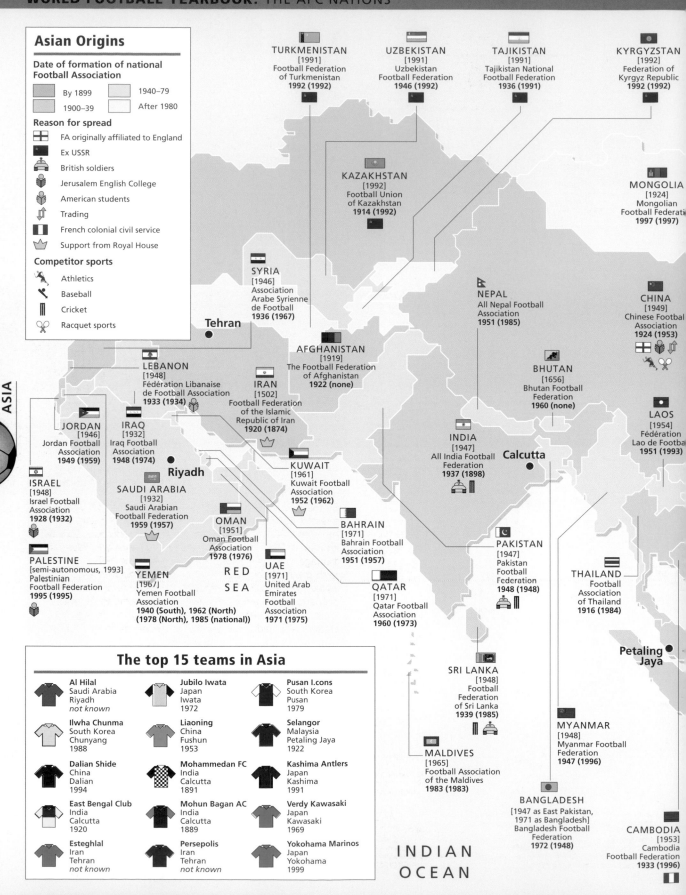

Asian Origins

Date of formation of national Football Association

- By 1899
- 1900–39
- 1940–79
- After 1980

Reason for spread

- FA originally affiliated to England
- Ex USSR
- British soldiers
- Jerusalem English College
- American students
- Trading
- French colonial civil service
- Support from Royal House

Competitor sports

- Athletics
- Baseball
- Cricket
- Racquet sports

ASIA

TURKMENISTAN
[1991]
Football Federation
of Turkmenistan
1992 (1992)

UZBEKISTAN
[1991]
Uzbekistan
Football Federation
1946 (1992)

TAJIKISTAN
[1991]
Tajikistan National
Football Federation
1936 (1991)

KYRGYZSTAN
[1992]
Federation of
Kyrgyz Republic
1992 (1992)

KAZAKHSTAN
[1992]
Football Union
of Kazakhstan
1914 (1992)

MONGOLIA
[1924]
Mongolian
Football Federation
1997 (1997)

SYRIA
[1946]
Association
Arabe Syrienne
de Football
1936 (1967)

NEPAL
All Nepal Football
Association
1951 (1985)

CHINA
[1949]
Chinese Football
Association
1924 (1953)

Tehran

AFGHANISTAN
[1919]
The Football Federation
of Afghanistan
1922 (none)

BHUTAN
[1656]
Bhutan Football
Federation
1960 (none)

LEBANON
[1948]
Fédération Libanaise
de Football Association
1933 (1934)

IRAN
[1502]
Football Federation
of the Islamic
Republic of Iran
1920 (1874)

LAOS
[1954]
Fédération
Lao de Football
1951 (1993)

JORDAN
[1946]
Jordan Football
Association
1949 (1959)

IRAQ
[1932]
Iraq Football
Association
1948 (1974)

INDIA
[1947]
All India Football
Federation
1937 (1898)

Calcutta

ISRAEL
[1948]
Israel Football
Association
1928 (1932)

SAUDI ARABIA
[1932]
Saudi Arabian
Football Federation
1959 (1957)

Riyadh

KUWAIT
[1961]
Kuwait Football
Association
1952 (1962)

PALESTINE
[semi-autonomous, 1993]
Palestinian
Football Federation
1995 (1995)

OMAN
[1951]
Oman Football
Association
1978 (1976)

BAHRAIN
[1971]
Bahrain Football
Association
1951 (1957)

PAKISTAN
[1947]
Pakistan
Football
Federation
1948 (1948)

YEMEN
[1967]
Yemen Football
Association
**1940 (South), 1962 (North)
(1978 (North), 1985 (national))**

UAE
[1971]
United Arab
Emirates
Football
Association
1971 (1975)

RED
SEA

QATAR
[1971]
Qatar Football
Association
1960 (1973)

THAILAND
Football
Association
of Thailand
1916 (1984)

Petaling
Jaya

SRI LANKA
[1948]
Football
Federation
of Sri Lanka
1939 (1985)

MYANMAR
[1948]
Myanmar Football
Federation
1947 (1996)

MALDIVES
[1965]
Football Association
of the Maldives
1983 (1983)

BANGLADESH
[1947 as East Pakistan,
1971 as Bangladesh]
Bangladesh Football
Federation
1972 (1948)

CAMBODIA
[1953]
Cambodia
Football Federation
1933 (1996)

INDIAN
OCEAN

The top 15 teams in Asia

Al Hilal
Saudi Arabia
Riyadh
not known

Jubilo Iwata
Japan
Iwata
1972

Pusan I.cons
South Korea
Pusan
1979

Ilwha Chunma
South Korea
Chunyang
1988

Liaoning
China
Fushun
1953

Selangor
Malaysia
Petaling Jaya
1922

Dalian Shide
China
Dalian
1994

Mohammedan FC
India
Calcutta
1891

Kashima Antlers
Japan
Kashima
1991

East Bengal Club
India
Calcutta
1920

Mohun Bagan AC
India
Calcutta
1889

Verdy Kawasaki
Japan
Kawasaki
1969

Esteghlal
Iran
Tehran
not known

Persepolis
Iran
Tehran
not known

Yokohama Marinos
Japan
Yokohama
1999

The AFC Nations

COUNTRY
[date of independence]
Name of national
Football
Foundation   Association   Foundation of
of national FA — **1916 (1912)**— national league

NORTH KOREA
[1945]
Football Association
of the Democratic
People's Republic
of Korea
1945 (1985)

SOUTH KOREA
[1945]
Korea Football
Association
1928 (1983)

JAPAN
Japan Football
Association
1921 (1965)

Dalian ●

Chunyang ●

Busan ●

● Kashima
● Kawasaki
Yokohama
Iwata

MACAO
[to China 2000]
Macau Football
Association
1939 (1973)

PACIFIC
OCEAN

hun

TAIWAN
[1949]
Chinese Taipei
Football Association
1936 (1994)

HONG KONG
[to China 1997]
Chinese Taipei
Football Association
1914 (1946)

GUAM
[Unincorporated
territory of the USA]
Guam Soccer
Association
1975 (1994)

ETNAM
954]
etnam Football
deration
62 (1981)

PHILIPPINES
[1946]
Philippines Football
Federation
1907 (1967)

BRUNEI
[1984]
Football Association
of Brunei Darussalam
1959 (none)

SINGAPORE
[1949]
Football Association
of Singapore
1892 (1981)

INDONESIA
[1949]
Persatuan Sepakbola
Seluruh Indonesia
1930 (1981)

MALAYSIA
[1957]
Persatuan
Bolasepak Malaysia
1933 (1921)

Asia

ORIGINS AND GROWTH OF FOOTBALL

FOOTBALL ARRIVED IN ASIA through the tentacles of the formal and informal British Empire as the nation's sailors, missionaries and teachers played football in the late 19th century in Japan and Korea. But these limited expatriate communities could not sustain formal clubs and leagues. The story in China and India, however, was different.

In Calcutta, clerks in Indian public service and teams from the British Army were playing regularly in the first decade of the 20th century and were soon joined by the locals, some of whom formed India's first indigenous club, Mohan Bagan, in 1889. The team was soon contesting the Indian Football Association Shield. British traders in Shanghai are on record as playing football as early as 1879, and in 1887 Shanghai Football Club was formed from the Shanghai Athletic Club. A Briton, John Prentice, set up another club – Engineers – and donated a cup contested by the various émigré teams in the city. Further south, Hong Kong FC was founded by Britons in 1886, and in 1896 the Hong Kong Shield was first contested in a tournament between civilian and military teams. Football was also played in Singapore in this era and by the early 20th century Shanghai had acquired its own FA (affiliated to London) and the Chinese themselves were beginning to play and form teams. Chinese football was represented in this era by the South China Athletic Association founded in 1904, which went on to represent China at the inaugural Far East Asian Olympic Games in 1913. Chinese resentment against European control of football culminated in 1931 when the nationalist Kuomintang government ordered all Chinese clubs to leave foreign leagues.

By the Second World War football had spread through the rest of Southeast Asia, though its popularity was limited. A more enthusiastic response came from Southwest Asia where both Iran and Iraq took up the game with royal and government patronage, a process that was repeated in the 1970s when oil wealth made the active promotion of football in the Gulf States possible. French colonists brought the game to Syria, while the British and Jewish emigrants brought the game to Palestine. In Central Asia, football primarily arrived via the Soviet occupiers who had taken control of the region in the 1930s.

The British Army was playing football regularly in India during the first decade of the 20th century. This picture shows action from an inter-regimental tournament played at Simla in 1907.

Southwest Asia

FOOTBALL BECAME POPULAR IN IRAN and Iraq well before the Second World War, with active royal support from the Shahs of Iran. Under the last Shah a programme of modernization and the importation of foreign coaches gave the game a huge boost. A national league was established in 1960, and became semi-professional in 1974. But football's development in Iran was stopped in its tracks by the Islamic revolution in 1978. The league only recommenced at the end of the Iran-Iraq War in 1988, and women were banned from matches until 1994. Nonetheless the depth of Iranian football saw them qualify for the 1998 World Cup. To their north, the states of Central Asia acquired football after their inclusion in the Soviet Union and all established independent FAs and national leagues in the wake of the break-up of the Soviet Union in 1991.

Football arrived in the Near East with French and British protectorate status and colonial administrations after the First World War. National leagues were established in Lebanon in 1934, Jordan in 1959 and Syria in 1981. The Gulf states, by contrast, have proved to be late starters and quick developers. With oil money to hand and active royal and state promotion, national leagues were established in Bahrain in 1957, Kuwait in 1962, Qatar in 1973, UAE in 1975 and Saudi Arabia in 1979, although the national King's Cup tournament has been running there since 1957. It is virtually impossible to get information about football in Afghanistan in recent years, although it is apparently still widely played. The Taleban discouraged competitiveness, so winners and losers alike are not recorded.

Although Saudi Arabia's Al Hilal has played second fiddle to Al Ittihad in the league in recent seasons, the Riyadh side has claimed two Asian Super Cups, two Asian Club Championships and has also won the Asian Cup-Winners' Cup twice.

Afghanistan

The Football Federation of Afghanistan
Founded: 1922
Joined FIFA: 1948
Joined AFC: 1954

SEASON	LEAGUE CHAMPIONS
1997	*not known*
1998	*not known*
1999	*not known*
2000	*not known*
2001	*not known*

Bahrain

Bahrain Football Association
Founded: 1951
Joined FIFA: 1966
Joined AFC: 1970

SEASON	LEAGUE CHAMPIONS
1998	West Riffa
1999	Muharraq
2000	West Riffa
2001	Muharraq
2002	Muharraq

YEAR	CUP WINNERS
1998	West Riffa
1999	East Riffa
2000	East Riffa
2001	Al Ahli
2002	Muharraq

Iran

Football Federation of the Islamic Republic of Iran
Founded: 1920
Joined FIFA: 1945
Joined AFC: 1958

SEASON	LEAGUE CHAMPIONS
1998	Esteghlal
1999	Piroozi
2000	Piroozi
2001	Esteghlal
2002	Piroozi

YEAR	CUP WINNERS
1997	Bargh
1998	*no competition*
1999	Piroozi
2000	Esteghlal
2001	Fajr Sepasi

Iraq

Iraq Football Association
Founded: 1948
Joined FIFA: 1950
Joined AFC: 1971

SEASON	LEAGUE CHAMPIONS
1998	Al Shorta
1999	Al Shorta
2000	Al Zawra
2001	Al Zawra
2002	Al Talaba

YEAR	CUP WINNERS
1998	Al Zawra
1999	Al Zawra
2000	Al Zawra
2001	*no competition*
2002	Al Talaba

Jordan

Jordan Football Association
Founded: 1949
Joined FIFA: 1958
Joined AFC: 1970

SEASON	LEAGUE CHAMPIONS
1997	Al Wihdat
1998	*abandoned*
1999	Al Faysali
2000	Al Faysali
2001	Al Faysali

YEAR	CUP WINNERS
1997	Al Wihdat
1998	Al Wihdat
1999	Al Faysali
2000	Al Wihdat
2001	Al Faysali

Kazakhstan

Football Union of Kazakhstan
Founded: 1914
Joined FIFA: 1994
Joined AFC: 1994

SEASON	LEAGUE CHAMPIONS
1997	Irtysh Bastan Pavlodar
1998	Yelimay Semipalatinsk
1999	Irtysh Bastan Pavlodar
2000	Zhenis Astana
2001	Zhenis Astana

Kuwait

Kuwait Football Association
Founded: 1952
Joined FIFA: 1962
Joined AFC: 1962

SEASON	LEAGUE CHAMPIONS
1998	Al Salmiya
1999	Al Qadisiya
2000	Al Salmiya
2001	Al Kuwait
2002	Al Arabi

YEAR	CUP WINNERS
1997	Kazmah
1998	Kazmah
1999	Al Arabi
2000	Al Arabi
2001	Al Salmiya

Kyrgyzstan

Federation of Kyrgyz Republic
Founded: 1992
Joined FIFA: 1994
Joined AFC: 1994

SEASON	LEAGUE CHAMPIONS
1997	Dinamo Bishkek
1998	Dinamo Bishkek
1999	Dinamo Bishkek
2000	SKA-PVO Bishkek
2001	SKA-PVO Bishkek

YEAR	CUP WINNERS
1997	Alga PVO Bishkek
1998	SKA-PVO Bishkek
1999	SKA-PVO Bishkek
2000	SKA-PVO Bishkek
2001	SKA-PVO Bishkek

Lebanon

Fédération Libanaise de Football Association
Founded: 1933
Joined FIFA: 1935
Joined AFC: 1964

SEASON	LEAGUE CHAMPIONS
1998	Al Ansar
1999	Al Ansar
2000	Al Nejmeh
2001	*abandoned*
2002	Al Nejmeh

Oman

Oman Football Association
Founded: 1978
Joined FIFA: 1980
Joined AFC: 1979

SEASON	LEAGUE CHAMPIONS
1998	Al Nasr
1999	Dhofar
2000	Al Arouba
2001	Dhofar
2002	Al Arouba

Palestine

Palestinian Football Federation
Founded: 1995
Joined FIFA: 1998
Joined AFC: 1998

SEASON	LEAGUE CHAMPIONS
1998	*not known*
1999	*not known*
2000	Khadamat Rafah
2001	*abandoned*
2002	*no championship*

Qatar

Qatar Football Association
Founded: 1960
Joined FIFA: 1970
Joined AFC: 1972

SEASON	LEAGUE CHAMPIONS
1998	Al Etehad
1999	Al Wakra
2000	Al Sadd
2001	Al Wakra
2002	Al Etehad

Saudi Arabia

Saudi Arabian Football Federation
Founded: 1959
Joined FIFA: 1959
Joined AFC: 1972

SEASON	LEAGUE CHAMPIONS
1998	Al Ahly
1999	Al Ittihad
2000	Al Ittihad
2001	Al Ittihad
2002	Al Hilal

Saudi Arabia *(continued)*

YEAR	CUP WINNERS
1998	Al Hilal
1999	Al Shabab
2000	Al Hilal
2001	Al Ittihad
2002	Al Ahly

Syria

Association Arabe Syrienne de Football
Founded: 1936
Joined FIFA: 1937
Joined AFC: 1969

SEASON	LEAGUE CHAMPIONS
1998	Al Jaish
1999	Al Jaish
2000	Jabla
2001	Al Jaish
2002	Al Jaish

YEAR	CUP WINNERS
1997	Al Jaish
1998	Al Jaish
1999	Jabla
2000	Al Jaish
2001	Hottin

Tajikistan

National Football Federation Tajikistan
Founded: 1936
Joined FIFA: 1994
Joined AFC: 1994

SEASON	LEAGUE CHAMPIONS
1997	Vakhsh Kurgan-Tyube
1998	Varzob Dushanbe
1999	Varzob Dushanbe
2000	Varzob Dushanbe
2001	Regar-TadAZ Tursunzade

Turkmenistan

Football Federation of Turkmenistan
Founded: 1992
Joined FIFA: 1994
Joined AFC: 1994

SEASON	LEAGUE CHAMPIONS
1997	*abandoned*
1998	Kopétdag Ashkhabad
1999	Nisa Ashkhabad
2000	Kopétdag Ashkhabad
2001	Nisa Ashkhabad

United Arab Emirates

United Arab Emirates Football Association
Founded: 1971
Joined FIFA: 1972
Joined AFC: 1974

SEASON	LEAGUE CHAMPIONS
1998	Al Ain
1999	Al Wahda
2000	Al Ain
2001	Al Wahda
2002	Al Ain

YEAR	CUP WINNERS
1997	Al Shabab
1998	Al Sharjah
1999	Al Ain
2000	Al Wahda
2001	Al Ain

Uzbekistan

Uzbekistan Football Federation
Founded: 1946
Joined FIFA: 1994
Joined AFC: 1994

SEASON	LEAGUE CHAMPIONS
1997	MHSK Tashkent
1998	Pachtakor Tashkent
1999	Dustlik Tashkent
2000	Dustlik Tashkent
2001	Neftchi Ferghana

YEAR	CUP WINNERS
1997	Pachtakor Tashkent
1998	Navbakhor Namangan
1999	*no competition*
2000	Dustlik Tashkent
2001	Pachtakor Tashkent

Yemen

Yemen Football Association
Founded: 1940 (South), 1962 (North). 1990
Joined FIFA: 1967 (South), 1980 (North). 1990
Joined AFC: 1967 (South), 1980 (North). 1990

SEASON	LEAGUE CHAMPIONS
1997	Al Wahda
1998	Al Wahda
1999	Al Ahli
2000	Al Ahli
2001	Al Ahli

South and East Asia

SOUTH AND EAST ASIA

FOOTBALL'S DEEPEST ROOTS in Asia are in India, where the game was extensively played by the British Army and the imperial administration. Calcutta is the home of Indian football and its local league championship has been running since 1898. More recently the spread of the game across the nation has seen the creation of the Santosh Trophy in 1971 (contested by state teams and the Indian Army) and the Federation Cup – a nationwide competition for clubs – in 1977. The National Football League was created in 1996. After the partition of British India in 1947, national FAs and leagues were established in what was West Pakistan (now Pakistan) and East Pakistan (now Bangladesh). In the case of Bangladesh the league was originally confined to Dhaka but went national in 2000.

Football in China began among English expatriates in Shanghai and Hong Kong at the turn of the 20th century. A separate national Chinese FA was founded in Beijing in 1924 and affiliated to FIFA in 1931. The Chinese FA left FIFA from 1958 to 1979 in protest at FIFA's recognition of Taiwan. A national league was founded in 1926 and disrupted by 30 years of invasion, civil war and revolution. Re-established in 1953, abandoned during the Cultural Revolution (1966–72), the league went professional in 1993. In contrast, Hong Kong's professional league dates from 1945 and is the oldest pro-league in Asia.

Football came to the Philippines via Spanish sailors in the late 19th century and an FA was set up in 1907. British soldiers brought football to Malaysia and, with Singaporean teams included, league and cup competitions have run since 1921. Thailand's league dates from 1916 and a pro-league from 1995. The Dutch brought football to Indonesia, and in 1930 seven regional associations and leagues were established which proved a basis strong enough for the country to appear as the Dutch East Indies in the 1938 World Cup Finals. A national league was created in 1979 and went professional in 1994. The French brought football to Vietnam, Cambodia and Laos. Cambodia's league dates from the 1950s, Vietnam's from 1981, after the conclusion of its wars of independence, and in Laos a national league was set up in 1997.

Mohun Bagan from Calcutta. The city rivalry with East Bengal is the most intense in Asian football. Mohun represents the indigenous West Bengalies of the city, and East Bengal Bangladesh's migrants.

Bangladesh

Bangladesh Football Federation
Founded: 1972
Joined FIFA: 1974
Joined AFC: 1974

SEASON	LEAGUE CHAMPIONS
1997	*no championship*
1998	Muktijoddha SKC
1999	Mohammedan SC
2000	Muktijoddha SKC
2001	Abahani Ltd

Bhutan

Bhutan Football Federation
Founded: 1960
Joined FIFA: 2000
Joined AFC: 1993

SEASON	LEAGUE CHAMPIONS
1997	Royal Bhutan Police
1998	Royal Bhutan Police
1999	Kamglung
2000	Phuentsholing FC
2001	Druk Star FC

Brunei

Football Association of Brunei Darussalam
Founded: 1959
Joined FIFA: 1969
Joined AFC: 1970

BRUNEI HAS NO unified national championship – there are four district leagues. However, a Brunei team has played with some success in the Malaysian M-League.

Cambodia

Cambodia Football Federation
Founded: 1933
Joined FIFA: 1953
Joined AFC: 1957

SEASON	LEAGUE CHAMPIONS
1997	Body Guards Club
1998	Royal Dolphins
1999	*no championship*
2000	National Police
2001	*not known*

China

Chinese Football Association
Founded: 1924
Joined FIFA: 1931–58, 1979
Joined AFC: 1974

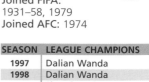

SEASON	LEAGUE CHAMPIONS
1997	Dalian Wanda
1998	Dalian Wanda
1999	Shandong Luneng Taishin
2000	Dalian Shide
2001	Dalian Shide

YEAR	CUP WINNERS
1997	Beijing Guoan
1998	Shanghai Shenhua
1999	Shangdong Luneng Taishan
2000	Chongqing Lifan
2001	Dalian Shide

Guam

Guam Soccer Association
Founded: 1975
Joined FIFA: 1996
Joined AFC: 1996

SEASON	LEAGUE CHAMPIONS
1997	Tumon Soccer Club
1998	Anderson Soccer Club
1999	Coors Light Silver Bullets
2000	Coors Light Silver Bullets
2001	Staywell Zoom S. Bullets

Hong Kong

Hong Kong Football Association
Founded: 1914
Joined FIFA: 1954
Joined AFC: 1954

SEASON	LEAGUE CHAMPIONS
1998	Instant-Dict
1999	Happy Valley
2000	South China
2001	Happy Valley
2002	Happy Valley

YEAR	CUP WINNERS
1998	Instant-Dict
1999	South China
2000	Happy Valley
2001	Instant-Dict
2002	South China

India

All India Football Federation
Founded: 1937
Joined FIFA: 1948
Joined AFC: 1954

SEASON	LEAGUE CHAMPIONS
1998	Mohun Bagan AC
1999	Salgoacar SC
2000	Mohun Bagan AC
2001	East Bengal Club
2002	Mohun Bagan AC

YEAR	CUP WINNERS
1997	Salgoacar
1998	Mohun Bagan AC
1999	*no competition*
2000	*no competition*
2001	Mohun Bagan AC

Malaysia

Persatuan Bolasepak Malaysia
Founded: 1933
Joined FIFA: 1956
Joined AFC: 1958

SEASON	LEAGUE CHAMPIONS
1997	Sarawak
1998	Penang
1999	Pahang
2000	Selangor
2001	Penang

YEAR	CUP WINNERS
1997	Selangor
1998	Perak
1999	Brunei
2000	Perak
2001	Terengganu

Myanmar

Myanmar Football Federation
Founded: 1947
Joined FIFA: 1957
Joined AFC: 1954

MYANMAR (FORMERLY BURMA) has no national championship but has a 12-team Premier League which is based in the city of Yangon (formerly Rangoon).

Singapore

Football Association of Singapore
Founded: 1892
Joined FIFA: 1952
Joined AFC: 1954

SEASON	LEAGUE CHAMPIONS
1997	Singapore Armed Forces
1998	Singapore Armed Forces
1999	Home United
2000	Singapore Armed Forces
2001	Geyland United

Indonesia

Persatuan Sepakbola Seluruh Indonesia
Founded: 1930
Joined FIFA: 1952
Joined AFC: 1954

SEASON	LEAGUE CHAMPIONS
1997	Persebaya Surabaya
1998	*season not finished*
1999	PSIS Semarang
2000	PSM Makassar
2001	Persija Jakarta

YEAR	CUP WINNERS
1997	Bandung Raya
1998	*abandoned*
1999	Persebaya Surabaya
2000	Pupuk Kaldim
2001	PSM Makassar

Maldives

Football Association of the Maldives
Founded: 1983
Joined FIFA: 1986
Joined AFC: 1986

SEASON	LEAGUE CHAMPIONS
1997	New Radiant
1998	Club Valencia
1999	Club Valencia
2000	Victory SC
2001	Victory SC

YEAR	CUP WINNERS
1998	New Radiant
1999	Club Valencia
2000	Victory SC
2001	New Radiant
2002	IFC

Nepal

All Nepal Football Association
Founded: 1951
Joined FIFA: 1970
Joined AFC: 1971

YEAR	CUP WINNERS
1997	Tribhuvan Army Club
1998	Mahendra Police
1999	Mahendra Police
2000	*no competition*
2001	Eastern Region

Pakistan

Pakistan Football Federation
Founded: 1948
Joined FIFA: 1948
Joined AFC: 1954

SEASON	LEAGUE CHAMPIONS
1997	Allied Bank Limited
1998	Pakistan International Airlines
1999	Allied Bank Limited
2000	Allied Bank Limited
2001	WAPDA

Taiwan

Chinese Taipei Football Association
Founded: 1936
Joined FIFA: 1954
Joined AFC: 1954–75, 1990

SEASON	LEAGUE CHAMPIONS
1997	Tai-power
1998	Tai-power
1999	Tai-power
2000	Tai-power
2001	Tai-power

Thailand

Football Association of Thailand
Founded: 1916
Joined FIFA: 1925
Joined AFC: 1957

SEASON	LEAGUE CHAMPIONS
1997	Sinthana
1998	Sinthana
1999	Royal Thai Air Force
2000	BEC Tero Sasana
2001	BEC Tero Sasana

Laos

Fédération Lao de Football
Founded: 1951
Joined FIFA: 1952
Joined AFC: 1980

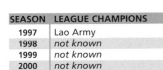

SEASON	LEAGUE CHAMPIONS
1997	Lao Army
1998	*not known*
1999	*not known*
2000	*not known*
2001	*not known*

Mongolia

Mongolian Football Federation
Founded: 1997
Joined FIFA: 1998
Joined AFC: 1998

SEASON	LEAGUE CHAMPIONS
1997	Delger
1998	Erchim
1999	ITI Bank Bars
2000	Erchim
2001	*not known*

Philippines

Philippines Football Federation
Founded: 1907
Joined FIFA: 1928
Joined AFC: 1954

YEAR	CUP WINNERS
1997	Air Force Hawks
1998	NCR South
1999	NCR B
2000	Navy
2001	*no competition*

Vietnam

Vietnam Football Federation
Founded: 1962
Joined FIFA: 1964
Joined AFC: 1954

SEASON	LEAGUE CHAMPIONS
1998	Hanoi Cong
1999	*no championship*
2000	Song Lam Nghe An
2001	Song Lam Nghe An
2002	Cang Saigon

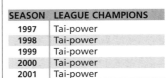

SOUTH AND EAST ASIA

South Korea

THE SEASON IN REVIEW 2001

WITH THE PROSPECT OF co-hosting the World Cup in 2002 looming over Korean football, 2001 was a season in which the K-League came into line with conventional practice in much of the rest of the world, abandoning golden goals and penalty shootouts and allowing drawn league matches. In addition, the end-of-season play-offs among the top four were abandoned and the championship was awarded to the team in the top spot at the end of the regular season.

The season began with the Adidas K-Cup. Pusan I.cons looked the form club but the team was beaten in the Final by Suwon Samsung Bluewings. In international club competition, Suwon played Japan's Jubilo Iwata in the Final of the Asian Champions Cup. Suwon had been beaten 3-0 by Iwata in the group stage quarter-final of the competition and went into the game as the underdogs. Fifteen minutes into the first half Suwon's Brazilian striker and the K-league's top scorer, Sandro Cardoso dos Santos, drove the ball inside Jubilo's right-hand post; Jubilo rose to the challenge but the team's few chances were squandered and Suwon won 1-0. Suwon went on to win the Asian Super Cup beating Saudi Arabia's Al Shabab, winners of the Asian Cup-Winners' Cup, 4-3 on aggregate over two legs. Suwon's Seo Jung-won scored twice in the second leg.

A close-run race

Suwon and Pusan were among the challengers in the most tightly contested K-League for some time. But once Suwon had relinquished its early lead in August, neither could catch eventual champions Songnam Ilhwa Chunma, though last year's champions, Anyang LG Cheetahs, were this year's runners-up and the team did its best to catch the leaders. Songnam's ace was its new Yugoslavian signing, Sasa Drakulic, who scored goals in the closing stages, and their Korean/Brazilian midfield line of Shin Tae-yong and Irine. The Korean FA Cup Final moved from its usual venue on sub-tropical Cheju Island to the new Seoul World Cup Stadium. In biting cold a crowd of over 40,000 saw one of the league's small clubs, Taejon Citizen, beat Pohang Steelers 1-0 to take its first-ever trophy.

Songnam Ilhwa Chunma players (from left) Sasa Drakulic, Shin Tae-yong and Kim Hum-soo celebrate winning the 2001 K-League championship, finishing two points clear of Anyang LG Cheetahs.

Korean FA Cup

2001 FINAL
November 25 – Seoul World Cup Stadium
Taejon Citizen 1-0 Pohang
(Kim Eun-Jung 54) Steelers
h/t: 0-0   **Att:** 40,000
Ref: Kwon Jong-Chul

Adidas K-Cup

2001 FINAL (2 legs)
May 9 – Suwon World Cup Stadium
Suwon 2-0 Pusan I.cons
Samsung
Bluewings
May 13 – Gudeok Stadium
Pusan I.cons 1-1 Suwon
Samsung
Bluewings
Suwon Samsung Bluewings won 3-1 on aggregate

South Korean K-League Table 2001

CLUB	P	W	D	L	F	A	Pts	
Songnam Ilhwa Chunma	27	11	12	4	35	20	**45**	Asian Club Championship
Anyang LG Cheetahs	27	11	10	6	30	23	**43**	Asian Club Championship
Suwon Samsung Bluewings	27	12	5	10	40	35	**41**	Asian Club Championship
Pusan I.cons (Busan)	27	10	11	6	38	33	**41**	
Pohang Steelers	27	10	8	9	28	29	**38**	
Ulsan Hyundai Horang-I	27	10	6	11	34	39	**36**	
Bucheon SK	27	7	14	6	29	29	**35**	
Chunnam Dragons	27	6	10	11	28	33	**28**	
Chonbuk Hyundai Motors	27	5	10	12	23	33	**25**	
Taejon Citizen (Daejon)	27	5	10	12	25	36	**25**	

Top Goalscorers 2001

PLAYER	CLUB	NATIONALITY	GOALS
Sandro Cardoso dos Santos	Suwon Samson Bluewings	Brazilian	13
Seo Jung-won	Suwon Samson Blue wings	Korean	11
Marco Paulo Paulini 'Paulinho'	Ulsan Hyundai	Brazilian	11
Woo Seong-yong	Pusan I.cons	Korean	11
Sasa Drakulic	Songnam Ilhwa Chunma	Yugoslavian	10

International Club Performances 2001

CLUB	COMPETITION	PROGRESS
Suwon Samsung Bluewings	Asian Super Cup	Winners
Songnam Ilhwa Chunma	Asian Cup-Winners' Cup	Second Round
Suwon Samsung Bluewings	Asian Club Championship	Winners

Action from the FA Cup Final – Taejon Citizen (in red) beat Pohang Steelers 1-0 to claim the club's first-ever trophy.

Choi Won-kwon of Anyang LG Cheetahs in action against Suwon Samsung Bluewings.

Seo Jung-won of Suwon Samsung Bluewings holding the Asian Super Cup.

Hong Myong-bo returned to South Korea after the 2001 season, joining Pohang Steelers after four years playing in the J.League.

South Korea

KFA

Korea Football Association
Founded: 1928
Joined FIFA: 1948
Joined AFC: 1954

SOUTH KOREA

FOR MOST OF the first half of the 20th century the whole Korean peninsula was occupied and colonized by the Japanese but a national FA was established in Seoul in 1928 and amateur football flourished in the cities. After the Second World War, the peninsula was divided into North and South (Soviet and US occupation zones, respectively), a division solidified by the stalemate of the Korean War (1949–53). The Korea Football Association joined FIFA in 1948 and was a founder member of the AFC (Asian Football Confederation) in 1954. Football struggled as baseball was the dominant spectator sport. However, in the early 1980s, with the financial support of Chaebol (a number of large Korean companies), a professional league was established. Chaebol have not been the only investors in Korean clubs. The religious foundation of the Moonies own Songnam Ilhwa Chunma. Alongside the league a number of cup competitions have been held, some sporadically. A Korean FA Cup began in 1996 to ensure Korean representation in the AFC's Asian Cup-Winners' Cup. The league has ten clubs, with the top six going into a championship play-off at the end of the season.

Honours have been spread around the country since the inception of the professional league and South Korean clubs have proved very successful in international club competitions, with four victories in the Asian Club Championship – including an all-South Korean Final in 1997 when the reigning champions Ilhwa Chunma were beaten by the Pohang Steelers. Two South Korean teams also contested the 2002 Final: Suwon Samsung Bluewings and Anyang LG Cheetahs. The Bluewings won 4-2 on penalties.

South Korean K-League Record 1983–2001

SEASON	CHAMPIONS	RUNNERS-UP
1983	Hallelujah	Daewoo
1984	Daewoo Royals	Yukong Elephants
1985	LG Hwangso	POSCO Atoms
1986	POSCO Atoms	LG Hwangso
1987	Daewoo Royals	Yukong Elephants
1988	POSCO Atoms	Hyundai Horang-i
1989	Yukong Elephants	LG Hwangso
1990	LG Hwangso	Daewoo Royals
1991	Daewoo Royals	Hyundai Horang-i
1992	POSCO Atoms	Ilhwa Chunma
1993	Ilhwa Chunma	LG Cheetahs
1994	Ilhwa Chunma	Yukong Elephants
1995	Ilhwa Chunma	Pohang Atoms
1996	Ulsan Hyundai Horang-i	Suwon Samsung Bluewings
1997	Pusan Daewoo Royals	Chunnam Dragons
1998	Suwon Samsung Bluewings	Ulsan Hyundai Horang-i
1999	Suwon Samsung Bluewings	Pusan Daewoo Royals
2000	Anyang LG Cheetahs	Puchon SK
2001	Songnam Ilhwa Chunma	Anyang LG Cheetahs

South Korean FA Cup Record 1996–2001

YEAR	WINNERS	SCORE	RUNNERS-UP
1996	Pohang Atoms	0-0 (7-6 pens)	Suwon Samsung Bluewings
1997	Chunnam Dragons	1-0	Chonan Ilhwa Chunma
1998	Anyang LG Cheetahs	2-1	Ulsan Hyundai Horang-i
1999	Chonan Ilhwa Chunma	3-0	Chonbuk Hyundai Dinos
2000	Chonbuk Hyundai Motors	2-0	Songnam Ilhwa Chunma
2001	Taejon Citizen	1-0	Pohang Steelers

Adidas K-Cup Record 1992–2001

YEAR	WINNERS	YEAR	WINNERS
1992	Ilhwa Chunma	2000	Suwon Samsung Bluewings
1993	POSCO Atoms		
1994	Yukong Elephants	2001	Suwon Samsung Bluewings
1995	Hyundai Horang-i		
1996	Puchon Yukong		
1997	Pusan Daewoo Royals		
1998	no competition		
1999	Suwon Samsung Bluewings		

Top Goalscorers 1983–2001

YEAR	SCORER	TEAM	NATIONALITY	GOALS
1983	Park Yun-gi	Yukong Elephants	Korean	9
1984	Baek Jong-cheol	Hyundai Horang-i	Korean	16
1985	Piyapong Pue-on	LG Hwangso	Korean	12
	Kim Yong-se	Yukong Elephants	Korean	
1986	Jeong Hae-won	Daewoo Royals	Korean	10
1987	Choi Sang-guk	POSCO Atoms	Korean	15
1988	Lee Gi-geun	POSCO Atoms	Korean	12
1989	Cho Gueng-yeon	POSCO Atoms	Korean	20
1990	Yun Sang-cheol	LG Cheetahs	Korean	12
1991	Lee Gi-geun	POSCO Atoms	Korean	16
1992	Im Geun-jae	LG Cheetahs	Korean	10
1993	Caha Sang-hae	POSCO Atoms	Korean	10
1994	Yun Sang-cheol	LG Cheetahs	Korean	21
1995	Roh Sang-rae	Chunnam Dragons	Korean	15
1996	Shin Tae-yong	Chonan Ilhwa Chunma	Korean	18
1997	Kim Hyun-seok	Ulsan Hyundai Horang-i	Korean	9
1998	Yoo Sang-chul	Ulsan Hyundai Horang-i	Korean	14
1999	Sasa Drakulic	Suwon Samsung Bluewings	Yugoslavian	14
2000	Kim Do-hoon	Chonbuk Hyundai Motors	Korean	12
2001	Sandro Dos Santos	Suwon Samsung Bluewings	Brazilian	13

Ulsan's Kim Hyun-seok celebrates after scoring his record breaking 102nd K-League goal in a match against Taejon in October 2001.

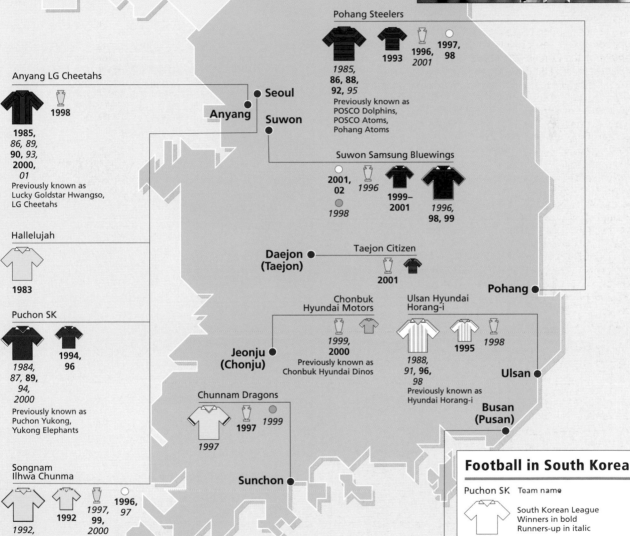

NORTH KOREA

SOUTH KOREA

Pohang Steelers

1993

1996, *2001*

1997, 98

1985, 86, 88, 92, 95

Previously known as POSCO Dolphins, POSCO Atoms, Pohang Atoms

Anyang LG Cheetahs

1998

1985, *86, 89,* **90, 93,** **2000,** *01*

Previously known as Lucky Goldstar Hwangso, LG Cheetahs

• Seoul

Anyang

Suwon

Suwon Samsung Bluewings

2001, 02

1996

1998

1999– 2001

1996, 98, 99

Hallelujah

1983

Daejon (Taejon) •

Taejon Citizen

2001

Pohang •

Ulsan Hyundai Horang-i

Puchon SK

1994, 96

1984, 87, 89, 94, 2000

Previously known as Puchon Yukong, Yukong Elephants

Chonbuk Hyundai Motors

1999, **2000**

Previously known as Chonbuk Hyundai Dinos

Jeonju (Chonju) •

1995

1998

1988, 91, 96, 98

Previously known as Hyundai Horang-i

Ulsan •

Chunnam Dragons

1997

1999

1997

Busan (Pusan) •

Songnam Ilhwa Chunma

1992

1997, 99, 2000

1996, 97

1992, 93–95, **2001**

Previously known as Chonan Ilhwa Chumna, Ilhwa Chunma

Sunchon •

Pusan I.cons

1983, 84, 87, 90, 91, 97, 99

Previously known as Pusan Daewoo Royals, Daewoo Royals, Daewoo

1997

1986

CHEJU-DO

Football in South Korea

Puchon SK	Team name
1966	South Korean League Winners in bold Runners-up in italic
1966	Winners of Adidas K-Cup
1966	South Korean FA Cup Winners in bold Runners-up in italic
● **Ulsan**	City of origin
○	Asian Club Championship
●	Asian Cup-Winners' Cup
1975	Winners in bold
1995	Runners-up in italic

Japan

THE SEASON IN REVIEW 2001

IN A SEASON WHERE headlines were often more concerned with Japanese players in Europe and the looming World Cup than domestic matters, the J.League showed contained, mature and exciting play. The First Stage was all Jubilo Iwata. Revitalized under new coach and ex-defender Mazakazu Suzuki, Jubilo opened the campaign with eight straight wins before Shimizu S-Pulse inflicted its only defeat in front of a record crowd (52,959) at the new World Cup stadium in Shizuoka. Undaunted, Jubilo's fast passing and aggressive high defensive line saw the team win by nine clear points from a pack of inconsistent rivals. Toshiya Fujita and Hiroshi Nanami were outstanding in midfield but Jubilo's season never truly recovered from the fact that the World Club Championship would not be taking place. A dispirited and injury-ridden side was soon afterwards beaten by the Bluewings 1-0 in the Final of the Asian Club Championship.

In the Second Stage, Kashima Antlers – winners of an unprecedented treble in 2000 – rose from its early season torpor and, despite being beaten twice by Jubilo, won the competition by a single point. In the two-leg Championship Play-off between the two stage winners a 2-2 draw at Jubilo was followed by an amazingly tense return match at Kashmira. The deadlock was finally broken by Mitsuo Ogasawara's golden goal from a direct free kick in the 100th minute. The Emperor's Cup was also won by a golden goal, scored by Marcelo Baron, to put Shimizu S-Pulse in the Asian Cup-Winners' Cup for the third year in succession. As defending champions, they had made it to the semi-finals in 2001, where the team was knocked out by China's Dalian Shide.

JAPAN

Edmundo's presence at Tokyo Verdy did not prevent the club finishing bottom of the First Stage of the J.League. However, six home wins in the Second Stage ensured a mid-table finish.

J.League Division 1 Table 2001

FIRST STAGE								
CLUB	P	W/OT*	D	L/OT*	F	A	Pts	
Jubilo Iwata	15	9/4	1	0/1	32	12	36	
JEF United	15	7/3	0	3/2	35	26	27	
Nagoya Grampus Eight	15	5/5	2	3/0	29	20	27	
Shimizu S-Pulse	15	6/4	0	3/2	28	18	26	
Gamba Osaka	15	7/2	0	3/3	29	22	25	
Kashiwa Reysol	15	6/2	0	5/2	29	23	22	
Urawa Red Diamonds	15	6/1	1	6/1	24	22	21	
Consadole Sapporo	15	6/0	3	4/2	20	21	21	
FC Tokyo	15	5/3	0	7/0	18	19	21	
Vissel Kobe	15	5/1	2	4/3	16	20	19	
Kashima Antlers	15	5/1	1	5/3	21	23	18	
Avispa Fukuoka	15	4/1	0	8/2	13	25	14	
Sanfrecce Hiroshima	15	3/2	0	8/2	25	33	13	
Cerezo Osaka	15	3/0	2	8/2	22	31	11	
Yokohama F. Marinos	15	3/0	2	7/3	13	24	11	
Tokyo Verdy	15	2/2	0	8/3	16	31	10	

SECOND STAGE								
CLUB	P	W/OT*	D	L/OT*	F	A	Pts	
Kashima Antlers	15	10/3	0	2/0	36	19	36	Asian Club Championship
Jubilo Iwata	15	9/4	0	2/0	31	14	35	
Sanfrecce Hiroshima	15	8/0	0	7/0	36	27	24	
Shimizu S-Pulse	15	5/4	0	5/1	34	27	23	Asian Cup-Winners' Cup
JEF United	15	7/0	2	6/0	25	28	23	
Nagoya Grampus Eight	15	7/0	1	6/1	27	25	22	
Kashiwa Reysol	15	6/0	3	6/0	29	23	21	
FC Tokyo	15	5/0	5	4/1	29	28	20	
Tokyo Verdy	15	6/0	2	5/2	22	26	20	
Yokohama F. Marinos	15	4/2	3	3/3	19	20	19	
Gamba Osaka	15	5/0	2	7/1	21	26	17	
Urawa Red Diamonds	15	4/0	3	5/3	20	24	15	
Vissel Kobe	15	3/0	5	6/1	25	32	14	
Consadole Sapporo	15	3/1	2	7/2	23	29	13	
Avispa Fukuoka	15	3/1	2	6/3	22	31	13	Relegated
Cerezo Osaka	15	2/3	0	10/0	19	39	12	Relegated

* 3 points for a win in 90 minutes;
2 points for a win in overtime.

Promoted clubs: Vegalta Sendai, Kyoto Purple Sanga.

Above: J.League Player of the Year, Toshiya Fujita, the playmaker at the heart of Jubilo Iwata's midfield.

Above right: Kashima Antlers celebrated the team's 10th anniversary by staging a series of fan weddings at its stadium at which some of the players gave celebratory readings.

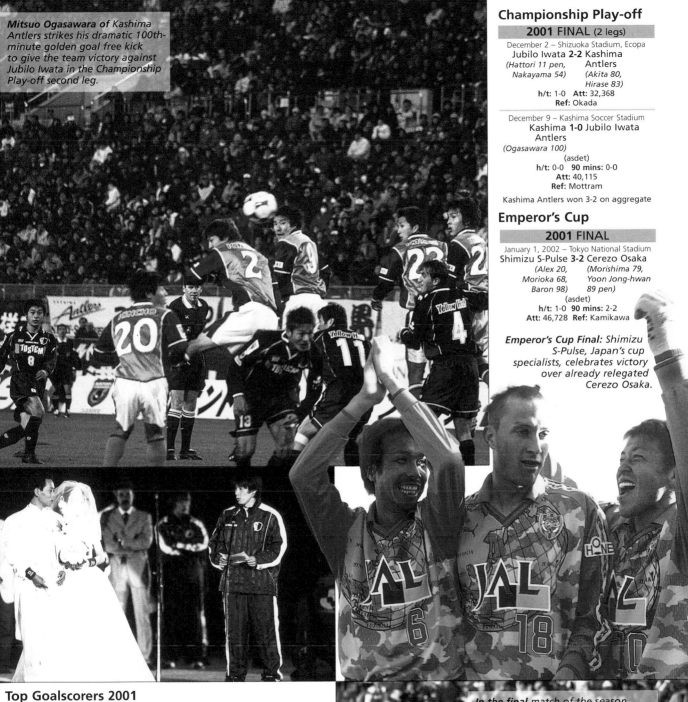

Mitsuo Ogasawara of *Kashima Antlers* strikes his dramatic 100th-minute golden goal free kick to give the team victory against *Jubilo Iwata* in the Championship Play-off second leg.

Championship Play-off

2001 FINAL (2 legs)

December 2 – Shizuoka Stadium, Ecopa
Jubilo Iwata 2-2 Kashima
(Hattori 11 pen,   **Antlers**
Nakayama 54)   (Akita 80,
                 Hirase 83)
h/t: 1-0   **Att:** 32,368
Ref: Okada

December 9 – Kashima Soccer Stadium
Kashima 1-0 Jubilo Iwata
Antlers
(Ogasawara 100)
(asdet)
h/t: 0-0   **90 mins:** 0-0
Att: 40,115
Ref: Mottram

Kashima Antlers won 3-2 on aggregate

Emperor's Cup

2001 FINAL

January 1, 2002 – Tokyo National Stadium
Shimizu S-Pulse 3-2 Cerezo Osaka
(Alex 20,   (Morishima 79,
Morioka 68,   Yoon Jong-hwan
Baron 98)   89 pen)
(asdet)
h/t: 1-0   **90 mins:** 2-2
Att: 46,728 **Ref:** Kamikawa

Emperor's Cup Final: Shimizu S-Pulse, Japan's cup specialists, celebrates victory over already relegated Cerezo Osaka.

Top Goalscorers 2001

PLAYER	CLUB	NATIONALITY	GOALS
Robson Luis Pereira	Consadole Sapporo	Brazilian	24
Raimundo da Silva Uéslei	Nagoya Grampus Eight	Brazilian	21
Choi Yong-soo	JEF United	South Korean	21

International Club Performances 2001

CLUB	COMPETITION	PROGRESS
Jubilo Iwata	Asian Club Championship	Runners-up
Nagoya Grampus Eight	Asian Cup-Winners' Cup	Quarter-finals
Shimizu S-Pulse	Asian Cup-Winners' Cup	Semi-finals

In the final match of the season, Avispa Fukuoka (in white) lost 3-2 to Gamba Osaka and was relegated.

Japan

THE J.LEAGUE 1992–2001

A NATIONAL FOOTBALL LEAGUE had been played in Japan since 1965, but the JSL was always a corporate amateur affair. Until the late 1980s there were no official professional contracts and teams were all sponsored by Japan's industrial giants as a combination of company welfare, advertising and philanthropy. With international club success in the 1980s coming to Japan (Furukawa Electric won the Asian Club Championship in 1987), the Japanese FA decided to organize a professional league.

The J.League was launched in 1993, with a capital injection of around $20 million. The top teams of the old JSL were revamped, corporate names were banned and hometown affiliations emphasized in clubs names and outlook. Riding the end of Japan's massive consumer binge of the early 1990s, the J.League proved enormously popular. Massive TV coverage, marketing and a slew of foreign players saw gate takings and income rise for four years. Brazilians, Italians and Eastern Europeans all made their way there towards the end of their careers, and more recently African players have followed in their footsteps.

Early years of the J.League

The early years of the J.League belonged to the leading teams of the JSL era: Yomiuri Club became Verdy Kawasaki and won the championship in 1993 and 94, and Nissan Motors became Yokohama Marinos and beat Verdy in the 1995 championship play-off. The late 90s saw a shift of power with titles alternating between two clubs with no pre-J.League pedigree, Kashima Antlers and Jubilo Iwata, before Kashima moved up a gear to take a treble of domestic trophies in 2000. Gamba Osaka, JEF United Ichihara, Nagoya Grampus Eight and Sanfrecce Hiroshima have proved the leagues underachievers.

Despite a dip in the late 1990s, as consumer indifference and economic stagnation set in, the quality of play and the size of crowds have risen again with the World Cup going to Japan in 2002. Distinctive fan cultures and solid gates have emerged at Shimizu S-Pulse, Uruwa Red Diamonds and Consadole Sapporo. Perhaps most importantly, a football gambling system – the Toto – was introduced in 2000 and has proved to be a massive commercial success.

JAPAN

The J.League: leading investors

Gamba Osaka — Team name in J.League

(Matsushita Electric) — Team name in JSL

 League champions/runners-up

1983, *84* — Champions in bold / Runners-up in italics

 Other teams in the J.League

● **Osaka** — City of origin

 Local consortium

 Railway company

 Car company

 Heavy industry

 Media company

Photographic industry

Gas industry

Airline industry

Electric company

 Electronics

 Local Government

Uruwa Red Diamonds
(Mitsubishi)

Mitsubishi — Satima Prefecture, Satima City

FC Tokyo

Tokyo Electric — Tokyo Gas

JEF United Ichihara
(JR East Furukuwa)

East Japan Railways — Furukawa Electric Company

Tokyo Verdy

Nippon Television

Nagoya Grampus Eight
(Toyota)

1996

Kashiwa Reysol
(Hitachi)

Hitachi — Kashiwa City

Kyoto Purple Sanga

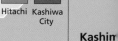

Kyoto City

J A P A N

Kashim

Kashiwa

Kawasaki
Yokohama
Hiratsuka
Nagoya
Shimizu
Iwata

Tok

Kobe **Kyoto**
Osaka

Hiroshima

Senda

Yokohama F Marinos
(Yokohama Flugels merged with Yokohama Marinos in 1999 (previously All Nippon Airways))

1995
2000

Nissan

Avispa Fukuoka
(Fukuoka Bluk)

Fukuoka

Sanfrecce Hiroshima
(Mazda)

1994 — Hiroshima City

Vissel Kobe

Kawasaki Steel

Jubilo Iwata

1997,
98, 99,
2001

Yamaha

Cerezo Osaka
(Yanmar Diesel)

Osaka City

Gamba Osaka
(Matsushita Electric)

Matsushita

Shimizu S-Pulse
(Shimizu)

1999

Bellmare Hiratsuka
(Fujita)

Hiratsuka City

All Nippo
Airways

Sapporo

Uruwa Red Diamond fans have created the most distinctive fan culture in the J.League, and the one most at odds with key elements of Japanese culture. Early fan groups were the first to boo their own players for poor performances and create an intimidating atmosphere for visiting teams.

Alessandro dos Santos, Brazilian-born midfield playmaker at Shimizu S-Pulse, has recently acquired Japanese citizenship and played for the national team.

Consadole Sapporo
(Toshiba)

Vegalta Sendai

Miyagi Prefecture, Sendai City

Kashima Antlers
(Sumitomo Honda)

Sumitomo Metals — *1993, 96, 97, 98, 2000, 01*

Verdy Kawasaki
(Yomiuri Club)

Nippon Television — *1993, 94, 95*

Kawasaki Frontale

Fujitsu

Key to League Positions Table

- ▮ League champions
- ▮ Season of promotion to league
- ▮ Season of relegation from league
- ▮ Other teams playing in league
- 5 Final position in league

JAPAN

Japanese League Positions 1992–2001

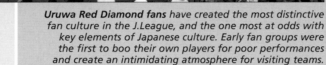

TEAM	1992–93	1992–93	1993–94	1993–94	1994–95	1994–95	1995–96	1996–97	1996–97	1997–98†	1997–98†	1998–99	1998–99	1999–2000	1999–2000	2000–01	2000–01
Avispa Fukuoka							15	17	15	18	15	11	15	14	6	12	15
Bellmare Hiratsuka			7	2	7	14	11	4	9	12	12	16	16				
Sanfrecce Hiroshima	6	5	1	4	10	12	14	10	13	13	9	6	8	10	11	13	3
JEF United Ichihara	5	9	6	9	6	7	9	15	14	11	18	15	11	11	16	2	5
Jubilo Iwata			11	7	5	9	4	6	1*	1	2	1	12*	5	3	1	2
Kashima Antlers	1	4	3	5	8	6	1	1	4	5	1*	9	6	8	1*	11	1*
Kashiwa Reysol					14	5	5	3	10	10	8	4	4	4	2	6	7
Kawasaki Frontale														15	15		
Verdy Kawasaki	2	1*	4	1*	2	1	7	16	12	6	17	2	10	9	10		
Vissel Kobe								14	17	17	14	12	7	7	14	10	13
Kyoto Purple Sanga									16	13	16	15	11	14	9	16	12
Nagoya Grampus Eight	9	8	8	12	4	2	2	12	5	3	6	8	2	12	7	3	6
Cerezo Osaka					9	10	13	11	8	9	13	5	5	2	9	14	16
Gamba Osaka	8	6	10	10	11	13	12	8	2	14	16	10	13	13	4	5	11
Consadole Sapporo												16	10			8	14
Vegalta Sendai																	
Shimizu S-Pulse	4	2	2	6	12	4	10	7	6	2	5	3	1	3	13	4	4
Tokyo Verdy																16	9
FC Tokyo														6	8	9	8
Uruwa Red Diamonds	10	10	12	11	3	8	6	9	7	7	3	13	14			7	12
Yokohama Flugels	7	7	5	8	13	11	3	2	11	8	7						
Yokohama F Marinos	3	3	9	8	1	3*	8	5	3	4	4	7	3	1	5	15	10

*Denotes championship play-off winners.
Except 1995–96, season is divided into two stages with a play-off to decide the championship.

†First year of promotion and relegation.

Japan

Japan Football Association
Founded: 1921
Joined FIFA: 1929–46, 1950
Joined AFC: 1954

A RUDIMENTARY VERSION of football has been played in Japan for over 1,500 years. The rapid modernization of Japan on Western lines after the Meiji restoration (1868) saw modern football established in schools and universities in the early years of the 20th century. In 1921, the first national cup competition was established, modelled on the English FA Cup. Breaking for the war, it was replaced in 1946 by the Emperor's Cup. An additional cup competition, the Japan Soccer League Cup, was launched in 1976 and renamed the J.League Cup in 1992. Winners of this competition enter the Asian Cup-Winners' Cup.

National league football started in 1965, based on teams supported by industrial groups (Toyota, Hitachi, Nissan etc.). Although popular, the league was always second to baseball in Japan. In 1993, with enormous new commercial backing, the old structures were abandoned and Japanese league football was relaunched as the J.League in a ten-team premier league, later expanded to 16. A second division was added in 1999. Teams score three points for a win, two points for a win in extra time (drawn games always go to extra time) and one for a draw. Until 1998, drawn games after extra time were decided by a penalty shootout. The season was then divided into opening and closing championships with play-offs to decide the winners.

Japanese League Record 1965–2001

SEASON	CHAMPIONS	RUNNERS-UP
1965	Toyo Industrial	Yahata Steel
1966	Toyo Industrial	Yahata Steel
1967	Toyo Industrial	Furukawa Electric
1968	Toyo Industrial	Yanmar Diesel
1969	Mitsubishi Heavy Industrial	Toyo Industrial
1970	Toyo Industrial	Mitsubishi Heavy Industrial
1971	Yanmar Diesel	Mitsubishi Heavy Industrial
1972	Hitachi	Yanmar Diesel
1973	Mitsubishi Heavy Industrial	Hitachi
1974	Yanmar Diesel	Mitsubishi Heavy Industrial
1975	Yanmar Diesel	Mitsubishi Heavy Industrial
1976*		
1977	Furukawa Electric	Mitsubishi Heavy Industrial
1978	Fujita Industrial	Mitsubishi Heavy Industrial
1978†	Mitsubishi Heavy Industrial	Yanmar Diesel
1979	Fujita Industrial	Yomiuri Club
1980	Yanmar Diesel	Fujita Industrial
1981	Fujita Industrial	Yomiuri Club
1982	Mitsubishi Heavy Industrial	Yanmar Diesel
1983	Yomiuri Club	Nissan Motors
1984	Yomiuri Club	Nissan Motors
1985*		
1986	Furukawa Electric	Nippon Kokan
1987	Yomiuri Club	Nippon Kokan
1988	Yamaha Motors	Nippon Kokan
1989	Nissan Motors	All Nippon Airways
1990	Nissan Motors	Yomiuri Club
1991	Yomiuri Club	Nissan Motors
1992	Yomiuri Club	Nissan Motors
1993	Verdy Kawasaki	Kashima Antlers
1994	Verdy Kawasaki	Sanfrecce Hiroshima
1995	Yokohama Marinos	Verdy Kawasaki
1996	Kashima Antlers	Nagoya Grampus Eight
1997	Jubilo Iwata	Kashima Antlers
1998	Kashima Antlers	Jubilo Iwata

Japanese League Record (*continued*)

SEASON	CHAMPIONS	RUNNERS-UP
1999	Jubilo Iwata	Shimizu S-Pulse
2000	Kashima Antlers	Yokohama Marinos
2001	Kashima Antlers	Jubilo Iwata

* There is no result as the season changed its start and finish date.

† Two seasons were played in this year.

Japanese League Summary

TEAM	TOTALS	CHAMPIONS & RUNNERS-UP (BOLD) (*ITALICS*)
Verdy Kawasaki (includes Yomiuri Club)	7, 4	*1979, 81,* **83, 84, 87,** *90,* **91–94,** *95*
Sanfrecce Hiroshima (includes Toyo Industrial)	5, 2	**1965–68,** *69,* **70,** *94*
Mitsubishi Heavy Industrial	4, 6	**1969,** *70, 71,* **73,** *74, 75, 77, 78,* **78†,** *82*
Yanmar Diesel	4, 4	*1968,* **71, 72,** *74, 75,* **78,** *80,* **82**
Jubilo Iwata (includes Yamaha Motors)	3, 2	**88,** *97,* **98,** *99,* **2001**
Kashima Antlers	4, 2	**1993,** *96,* **97,** *98,* **2000, 01**
Yokohama Marinos (includes Nissan Motors)	3, 5	**1983,** *84,* **89,** *90, 91, 92,* **95,** *2000*
Fujita Industrial	3, 1	**1978, 79,** *80,* **81**
Furukawa Electric	2, 1	*1967,* **77,** *86*
Hitachi	1, 1	**1972,** *73*
Nippon Kokan	0, 3	*1986–88*
Yahata Steel	0, 2	*1965, 66*
All Nippon Airways	0, 1	*1989*
Nagoya Grampus Eight	0, 1	*1996*
Shimizu S-Pulse	0, 1	*1999*

Japanese Cup Record 1921–2001

YEAR	WINNERS	SCORE	RUNNERS-UP
1921	Tokyo Shukyu-dan	1-0	Mikage Shukyu-dan
1922	Nagoya Shukyu-dan	1-0	Hiroshima Koto-shihan
1923	Astra Club	2-1	Nagoya Shukyu-dan
1924	Rijo FC	4-1	All Mikage Shihan Club
1925	Rijo FC	3-0	Tokyo University
1926		no competition	
1927	Kobe-Ichi Jr. Highschool Club	2-0	Rijo FC
1928	Waseda University WMW	6-1	Kyoto University
1929	Kwangaku Club	3-0	Housei University
1930	Kwangaku Club	3-0	Keio University BRB
1931	Tokyo University LB	5-1	Kobun Jr. Highschool
1932	Keio Club	5-1	Yoshino Club
1933	Tokyo University LB	4-1	Sendai Football Club
1934		no competition	
1935	All Keio Club	6-1	Tokyo Bunri University
1936	Keio University BRB	3-2	Fusei Senmon
1937	Keio University BRB	*	Kobe Commercial University
1938	Waseda University WMW	4-1	Keio University BRB
1939	Keio University BRB	3-2	Waseda University WMW
1940	Keio University BRB	1-0	Waseda University WMW

JAPAN

Japanese Cup Record (*continued*)

YEAR	WINNERS	SCORE	RUNNERS-UP
1941–45		no competition	
1946	Tokyo University LB	6-2	Kobe Keizai-dai Club
1947–48		no competition	
1949	Tokyo University LB	5-2	Kwangaku Club
1950	All Kwangaku	6-1	Keio University BRB
1951	Keio University BRB	3-2	Osaka Club
1952	All Keio University	6-2	Osaka Club
1953	All Kwangaku	5-4	Osaka Club
1954	Keio University BRB	5-3 (aet)	Toyo Industrial
1955	All Kwangaku	4-3	Chudai Club
1956	Keio University BRB	4-2	Yahata Steel
1957	Chuo University	2-1	Toyo Industrial
1958	Kwangaku Club	2-1	Yahata Steel
1959	Kwangaku Club	1-0	Chuo University
1960	Furukawa Electric	4-0	Keio University BRB
1961	Furukawa Electric	3-2	Chuo University
1962	Chuo University	2-1	Furukawa Electric
1963	Waseda University WMW	3-0	Hitachi
1964†	Yahata Steel	0-0 (aet)	Furukawa Electric
1965	Toyo Industrial	3-2	Yahata Steel
1966	Waseda University WMW	3-2 (aet)	Toyo Industrial
1967	Toyo Industrial	1-0	Mitsubishi Heavy Industrial
1968	Yanmar Diesel	1-0	Mitsubishi Heavy Industrial
1969	Toyo Industrial	4-1	Rikkyo University
1970	Yanmar Diesel	2-1 (aet)	Toyo Industrial
1971	Mitsubishi Heavy Industrial	3-1	Yanmar Diesel
1972	Hitachi	2-1	Yanmar Diesel
1973	Mitsubishi Heavy Industrial	2-1	Hitachi
1974	Yanmar Diesel	2-1	Eidai Industrial
1975	Hitachi	2-0	Fujita Industrial
1976	Furukawa Electric	4-1	Yanmar Diesel
1977	Fujita Industrial	4-1	Yanmar Diesel
1978	Mitsubishi Heavy Industrial	1-0	Toyo Industrial
1979	Fujita Industrial	2-1	Mitsubishi Heavy Industrial
1980	Mitsubishi Heavy Industrial	1-0	Tanabe Medecine
1981	NKK	2-0	Yomiuri Club
1982	Yamaha Motors	1-0 (aet)	Fujita Industrial
1983	Nissan Motors	2-0	Yanmar Diesel
1984	Yomiuri Club	2-0	Furukawa Electric
1985	Nissan Motors	2-0	Fujita Industrial
1986	Yomiuri Club	2-1	NKK
1987	Yomiuri Club	2-0	Mazda
1988	Nissan Motors	3-1 (aet)	Fujita Industrial
1989	Nissan Motors	3-2	Yamaha Motors
1990	Matsushita	0-0 (aet) (4-3 pens)	Nissan Motors
1991	Nissan Motors	4-1 (aet)	Yomiuri Club
1992	Yokohama Marinos	2-1 (aet)	Verdy Kawasaki
1993	Yokohama Flugels	6-2 (aet)	Kashima Antlers
1994	Bellmare Hiratsuka	2-0	Cerezo Osaka
1995	Nagoya Grampus Eight	3-0	Sanfrecce Hiroshima
1996	Verdy Kawasaki	3-0	Sanfrecce Hiroshima
1997	Kashima Antlers	3-0	Yokohama Flugels
1998	Yokohama Flugels	2-1	Shimizu S-Pulse
1999	Nagoya Grampus Eight	2-0	Sanfrecce Hiroshima
2000	Kashima Antlers	3-2 (asdet)	Shimizu S-Pulse
2001	Shimizu S-Pulse	3-2	Cerezo Osaka

* Final score unknown.
† This year the title was tied, as extra time did not produce a champion.

Japanese Cup Summary

TEAM	TOTALS	WINNERS & RUNNERS-UP (BOLD) (*ITALICS*)
Keio University BRB (includes Tokyo Bunri)	7, 5	*1930, 35*, **36, 37, 38, 39, 40, 50, 51, 54, 56**, *60*
Yokohama Marinos (includes Nissan Motors)	6, 1	**1983, 85, 88, 89**, *90*, **91, 92**
Mitsubishi Heavy Industrial	4, 3	*1967, 68*, **71**, *73*, **78**, *79*, **80**
Verdy Kawasaki (Includes Yomiuri Club)	4, 3	*1981*, **84**, *86, 87*, **91, 92, 96**
Furukawa Electric	4, 2	**1960, 61**, *62*, **64†**, *76*, **84**
Waseda University WMW	4, 2	*1928*, **38**, *39, 40*, **63, 66**
Kwangaku Club	4, 1	**1929, 30, 49, 58, 59**
Tokyo University LB	4, 1	*1925*, **31, 33**, *46*, **49**
Sanfrecce Hiroshima (includes Toyo Industrial and Mazda)	3, 8	*1954, 57*, **65**, *66*, **67**, *69, 70, 78, 87, 95, 96, 99*
Cerezo Osaka (includes Yanmar Diesel)	3, 7	**1968**, *70, 71, 72*, **74**, *76, 77, 83, 94, 2001*
Bellmare Hiratsuka (includes Fujita Industrial)	3, 4	*1975*, **77**, *79, 82, 85, 88*, **94**
All Kwangaku	3, 0	**1950, 53, 55**
Chuo University	2, 2	**1957**, *59, 61*, **62**
Hitachi	2, 2	*1963*, **72, 73**, *75*
Kashima Antlers	2, 1	*1993*, **97, 2000**
Rijo FC	2, 1	**1924**, *25*, **27**
Yokohama Flugels	2, 1	*1993*, **97, 98**
Nagoya Grampus Eight	2, 0	**1995, 99**
Yahata Steel	1, 3	*1956, 58*, **64†**, *65*
Shimizu S-Pulse	1, 2	*1998, 2000*, **01**
Nagoya Shukyu-dan	1, 1	**1922**, *23*
NKK	1, 1	**1981**, *86*
Yamaha Motors	1, 1	**1982**, *89*
All Keio Club	1, 0	**1935**
All Keio University	1, 0	**1952**
Astra Club	1, 0	**1923**
Keio Club	1, 0	**1932**
Kobe-Ichi Jr. Highschool Club	1, 0	**1927**
Matsushita	1, 0	**1990**
Tokyo Shukyu-dan	1, 0	**1921**
Osaka Club	0, 3	*1951–53*
All Mikage Shihan Club	0, 1	*1924*
Chudai Club	0, 1	*1955*
Eidai Industrial	0, 1	*1974*
Fusei Senmon	0, 1	*1936*
Hiroshima Koto-shihan	0, 1	*1922*
Housei University	0, 1	*1929*
Kobe Commercial University	0, 1	*1937*
Kobe Keizai-dai Club	0, 1	*1946*
Kobun Jr Highschool	0, 1	*1931*
Kyoto University	0, 1	*1928*
Mikage Shukyu-dan	0, 1	*1921*
Rikkyo University	0, 1	*1969*
Sendai Football Club	0, 1	*1933*
Tanabe Medecine	0, 1	*1980*
Yoshino Club	0, 1	*1932*

The Asian Cup & Asian Games

TOURNAMENT OVERVIEW

ALONE AMONG THE FOOTBALL REGIONS, Asia has two significant international competitions: the soccer tournament of the multi-sport, amateur-only Asian Games, first held in 1951, and the AFC-controlled Asian Cup, first held in 1956. The Asian Games have provided space for some of the older but perhaps weaker footballing nations to shine with early victories going to India, Burma (now Myanmar) and Taiwan, as well as the traditionally stronger countries of Israel and South Korea. Opportunities for the underdogs remain, with Uzbekistan winning the 1994 Games in Hiroshima. At the Tehran Games held in 1974, the host Iran beat Israel in its last appearance in Asian tournaments, as it was expelled from AFC the following year.

Shifting patterns

As football has become progressively richer and steadily more professionalized in Asia, the Asian Cup, open to professionals, has come to assume greater prestige in the region. Initially the final tournaments were held as mini-leagues, with the South Koreans and Israelis again dominating the early tournaments. Politics continued to haunt the tournament, with Pakistan and Afghanistan refusing to play Israel in the inaugural finals. From the 1970s, the football balance of power has steadily shifted, with victories going west – to Iran and Saudi Arabia (three-time winners in 1984, 88 and 96) and the UAE. More recently, the reinvigoration of Japanese football and the creation of the J.League has seen two Japanese victories (1992 and 2000).

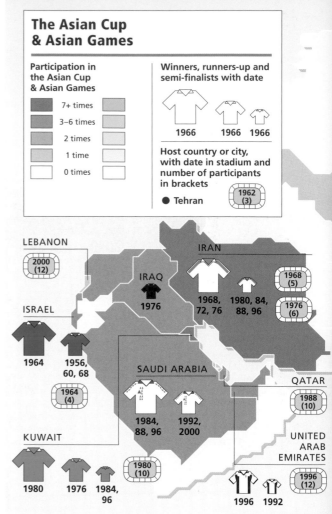

The Asian Cup & Asian Games

Participation in the Asian Cup & Asian Games
- 7+ times
- 3–6 times
- 2 times
- 1 time
- 0 times

Winners, runners-up and semi-finalists with date
1966 1966 1966

Host country or city, with date in stadium and number of participants in brackets
● Tehran
1962 (3)

LEBANON 2000 (12)

IRAN 1968, 72, 76 / 1980, 84, 88, 96 / 1968 (5) / 1976 (6)

IRAQ 1976

ISRAEL 1964 / 1956, 60, 68 / 1964 (4)

SAUDI ARABIA 1984, 88, 96 / 1992, 2000

QATAR 1988 (10)

KUWAIT 1980 / 1976 / 1984, 96 / 1980 (10)

UNITED ARAB EMIRATES 1996, 1992 / 1996 (12)

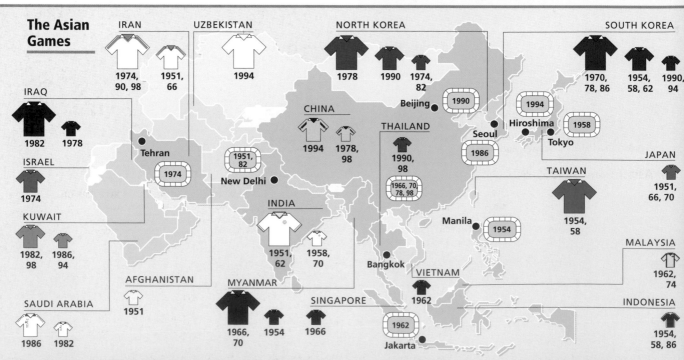

The Asian Games

IRAN 1974, 90, 98 / 1951, 66

UZBEKISTAN 1994

NORTH KOREA 1978 / 1990 / 1974, 82 / Beijing 1990

SOUTH KOREA 1970, 78, 86 / 1954, 58, 62 / 1990, 94 / Hiroshima 1994 / 1958

IRAQ 1982 / 1978

ISRAEL 1974

KUWAIT 1982, 98 / 1986, 94

SAUDI ARABIA 1986 / 1982

AFGHANISTAN 1951

Tehran ● / 1974

CHINA 1994 / 1978, 98

THAILAND 1990, 98 / 1966, 70, 78, 98

New Delhi ● / 1951, 82

INDIA 1951, 62 / 1958, 70

MYANMAR 1966, 70 / 1954 / 1966

SINGAPORE 1962 / Jakarta ●

Seoul ● 1986 / Tokyo / 1994

Manila ● / 1954

TAIWAN 1954, 58

VIETNAM 1962

Bangkok ●

JAPAN 1951, 66, 70

MALAYSIA 1962, 74

INDONESIA 1954, 58, 86

The Asian Cup

JAPAN
1992 (8)
1992, 2000

NORTH KOREA
1980

TAIWAN
1960, 68

SOUTH KOREA
1960 (4)
1956, 60   1972, 80, 88   1964, 2000

CHINA
1984   1976, 88, 92, 2000

INDIA
1964

MYANMAR
1968

HONG KONG
1956 (4)
1956, 64

THAILAND
1972 (6)
1972

CAMBODIA
1972

VIETNAM
1956, 60

SINGAPORE
1984 (10)

The Saudi Arabian players celebrate victory over the UAE in a penalty shootout to win the Asian Cup in 1996. It was the team's third victory in four tournaments.

Sergey Lebedev scored one of Uzbekistan's goals in the 4-2 win over China in the 1994 Asian Games Football Final.

The Asian Games (1951–98)

YEAR	WINNERS	SCORE	RUNNERS-UP
1951	India	1-0	Iran
1954	Taiwan	5-2	South Korea
1958	Taiwan	3-2	South Korea
1962	India	2-1	South Korea
1966	Myanmar	1-0	Iran
1970	Myanmar	0-0 (title shared)	South Korea
1974	Iran	1-0	Israel
1978	South Korea	0-0 (title shared)	North Korea
1982	Iraq	1-0	Kuwait
1986	South Korea	2-0	Saudi Arabia
1990	Iran	0-0 (4-1 pens)	North Korea
1994	Uzbekistan	4-2	China
1998	Iran	2-0	Kuwait

The Asian Cup (1956–2000)

YEAR	WINNERS	SCORE	RUNNERS-UP
1956	South Korea	*	Israel
1960	South Korea	*	Israel
1964	Israel	*	India
1968	Iran	*	Israel
1972	Iran	2-1	South Korea
1976	Iran	1-0	Kuwait
1980	Kuwait	3-0	South Korea
1984	Saudi Arabia	2-0	China
1988	Saudi Arabia	0-0 (4-3 pens)	South Korea
1992	Japan	1-0	Saudi Arabia
1996	Saudi Arabia	0-0 (asdet) (4-2 pens)	United Arab Emirates
2000	Japan	1-0	Saudi Arabia

* Tournament decided on league basis, no final match.

The Asian Club Championship

THE ASIAN CLUB CHAMPIONSHIP

TOURNAMENT OVERVIEW

THE ENORMOUS GEOGRAPHICAL SIZE OF ASIA and the relative weakness and unevenness of club football made the establishment of a regular international club tournament difficult. The AFC first decided to create a tournament modelled on the European Cup in 1962, but it took five years to set up. In the event, only six clubs took part in a finals tournament held in Bangkok, Thailand, in 1967. Eventual champions, Hapoel Tel Aviv, only played a single match – the Final – after a series of byes, beating the Malaysian side Selangor 2-1. Ten teams competed in 1969, again in Bangkok, with Maccabi Tel Aviv beating the Korean side Yangzee 1-0 to claim the title.

Hapoel appeared in the Final again in 1970, but lost 2-1 to the Iranian army team, Taj Club. The following year Maccabi got to the Final and was set to meet Al Shurta from Iraq, but the Iraqis refused to play the match for political reasons and Maccabi was awarded the trophy. Israeli dominance of the competition ended in 1975 when the country's teams were expelled from AFC because of the war in the Middle East. Continuing political problems meant that the competition was abandoned until 1985, but then it was revamped with a proper geographically based series of qualifying rounds and a six-team final tournament held that year in Jeddah in Saudi Arabia.

Since then the Asian football landscape has been transformed. The competition has been dominated since 1985 by teams from Japan (three victories) and South Korea (six victories). But there has also been success for the rapidly strengthening teams from the Gulf, like Al Saad from Qatar in 1989, Al Hilal and Al Nassr from Saudi Arabia in the 1990s; for the revamped clubs of post-revolutionary Iran, like Esteghlal and Pas Club; for the back-to-back winners Thai Farmers Bank (in 1994 and 95); and for the Chinese, for whom Liaoning from Shenyang took the title in 1990.

Thai Farmers Bank, from Bangkok, won the Asian Club Championship in 1994 and 95 only for the club to be disbanded when the bank went out of business in 2000.

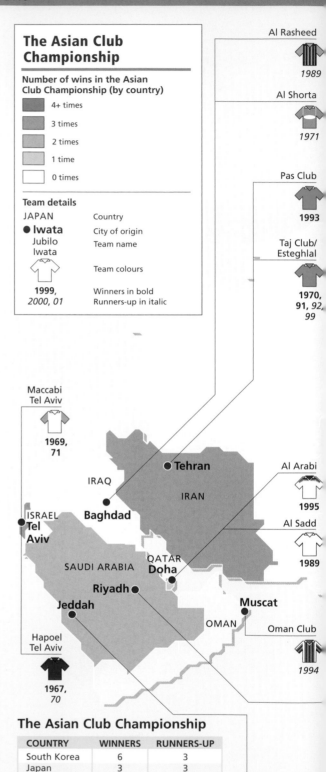

The Asian Club Championship

Number of wins in the Asian Club Championship (by country)

- 4+ times
- 3 times
- 2 times
- 1 time
- 0 times

Team details

JAPAN	Country
● Iwata	City of origin
Jubilo Iwata	Team name
	Team colours
1999, 2000, 01	Winners in bold / Runners-up in italic

The Asian Club Championship

COUNTRY	WINNERS	RUNNERS-UP
South Korea	6	3
Japan	3	3
Iran	3	2
Israel	3	1
Saudi Arabia	2	5
Thailand	2	0
China	1	2
Qatar	1	1
Iraq	0	2
Malaysia	0	1
Oman	0	1

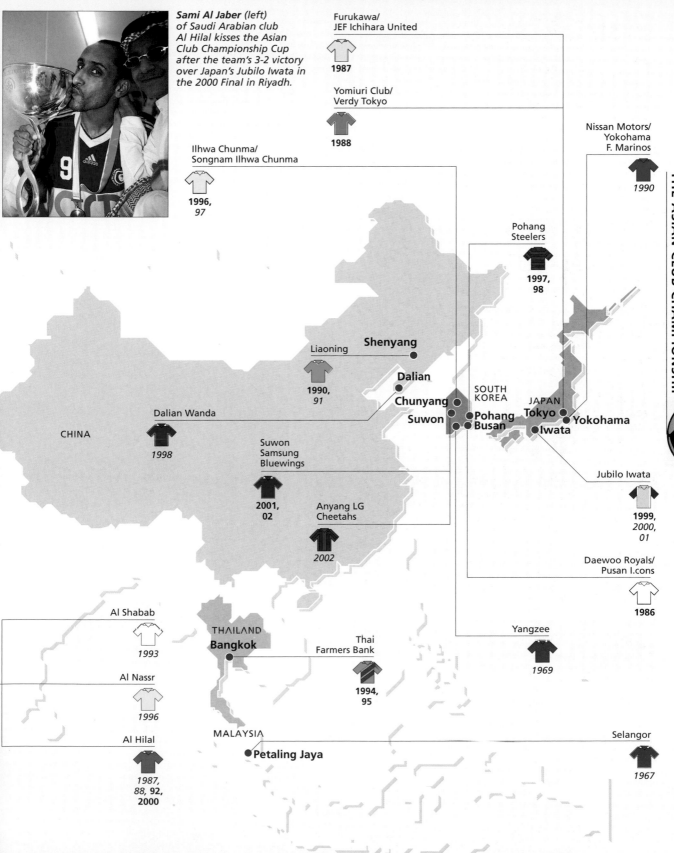

Sami Al Jaber (left) of Saudi Arabian club Al Hilal kisses the Asian Club Championship Cup after the team's 3-2 victory over Japan's Jubilo Iwata in the 2000 Final in Riyadh.

Furukawa/ JEF Ichihara United
1987

Yomiuri Club/ Verdy Tokyo
1988

Ilhwa Chunma/ Songnam Ilhwa Chunma
1996, 97

Nissan Motors/ Yokohama F. Marinos
1990

Pohang Steelers
1997, 98

Liaoning   **Shenyang**
1990, 91

Dalian Chunyang

Dalian

SOUTH KOREA

Suwon   **Pohang**
Busan

JAPAN
Tokyo   **Yokohama**
Iwata

Dalian Wanda
1998

CHINA

Suwon Samsung Bluewings
2001, 02

Anyang LG Cheetahs
2002

Jubilo Iwata
1999, 2000, 01

Daewoo Royals/ Pusan I.cons
1986

Al Shabab
1993

THAILAND
Bangkok

Thai Farmers Bank
1994, 95

Yangzee
1969

Al Nassr
1996

MALAYSIA
● **Petaling Jaya**

Selangor
1967

Al Hilal
1987, 88, 92, 2000

THE ASIAN CLUB CHAMPIONSHIP

The Asian Cup

The Asian Cup Winners

South Korea	Israel	Iran	Kuwait	Saudia Arabia	Japan
1956, 60	1964	1968, 72, 76	1980	1984, 88, 96	1992, 2000

ASIA HAS TWO MAJOR international football competitions. The Asian Cup is the competition run by the FIFA affiliate AFC (Asian Football Confederation) while the other football tournament is played at the Asian Games, which is a multi-sports competition. The Asian Games were first held in 1951 and have continued every four years, without qualifying tournaments and a group/knockout stage format. The Asian Cup began in 1956 and is also played on a four-year cycle, but from 1960 it has had a pre-tournament qualifying round based on geographical zones. It has become the pre-eminent Asian football competition.

Decolonization and international politics have continued to influence the entrants and outcome of the tournaments. Taiwan's place in Asian football has been contested by China, and vice-versa, with both claiming to be the sole Chinese representative. Israel's place in Asian football has been equally problematic. Israel achieved a bye into the 1956 Asian Nations Cup as neither Pakistan or Afghanistan would play them. Again Israel reached the 1974 Asian Games Final in Tehran without touching a ball, after North Korea and Kuwait refused to play them. In the end both Taiwan and Israel were expelled from the AFC in 1975. Israel now plays within UEFA.

1956 HONG KONG*
1 South Korea
2 Israel
3 Hong Kong

1960 SOUTH KOREA*
1 South Korea
2 Israel
3 Taiwan

1964 ISRAEL*
1 Israel
2 India
3 South Korea

1968 IRAN*
1 Iran
2 Israel
3 Myanmar

1972 THAILAND**
SEMI-FINALS
Iran **2-1** Cambodia
South Korea **1-1** Thailand
South Korea won 2-1 on pens

THIRD PLACE PLAY-OFF
Thailand **2-2** Cambodia
Thailand won 5-3 on pens

FINAL
May 19 – Bangkok
Iran **2-1** South Korea
(Jabary 48,   (Lee Whae-taek 65)
Khalani 107)
(after extra time)
h/t: 0-0 90 mins: 1-1
Att: 8,000

1976 IRAN
SEMI-FINALS
Iran **2-0** China
Kuwait **3-2** Iraq

THIRD PLACE PLAY-OFF
China **1-0** Iraq

FINAL
June 13 – Tehran
Iran **1-0** Kuwait
Att: 40,000

1980 KUWAIT
SEMI-FINALS
Kuwait **2-1** Iran
South Korea **2-1** North Korea

THIRD PLACE PLAY-OFF
Iran **3-0** North Korea

FINAL
September 28 – Kuwait City
Kuwait **3-0** South Korea
Att: 35,000

1984 SINGAPORE
SEMI-FINALS
Saudi Arabia **1-1** Iran
Saudi Arabia won 5-4 on pens
China **1-0** Kuwait

THIRD PLACE PLAY-OFF
Kuwait **1-1** Iran
Kuwait won 5-3 on pens

FINAL
December 16 – Singapore
Saudi Arabia **2-0** China
(Shaye Nafisah 10,
Majed
Abdullah 47)
h/t: 1-0 Att: 40,000

1988 QATAR
SEMI-FINALS
Saudi Arabia **1-0** Iran
South Korea **2-1** China
(after extra time)

THIRD PLACE PLAY-OFF
Iran **0-0** China
Iran won 3-0 on pens

FINAL
December 19 – Doha
Saudi Arabia **0-0** South Korea
(after extra time)
h/t: 0-0 90 mins: 0-0
Att: 25,000
Saudi Arabia won 4-3 on pens

1992 JAPAN
SEMI-FINALS
Japan **3-2** China
Saudi Arabia **2-0** UAE

THIRD PLACE PLAY-OFF
China **1-1** UAE
China won 4-3 on pens

FINAL
November 8 – Hiroshima
Japan **1-0** Saudi Arabia
(Takagi 6)
h/t: 1-0 Att: 40,000
Ref: Al Sharif (Syria)

1996 UNITED ARAB EMIRATES
SEMI-FINALS
Iran **0-0** Saudi Arabia
Saudi Arabia won 4-3 on pens
UAE **1-0** Kuwait

THIRD PLACE PLAY-OFF
Iran **1-1** Kuwait
Iran won 3-2 on pens

FINAL
December 21 – Abu Dhabi
UAE **0-0** Saudi Arabia
(after extra time)
h/t: 0-0 90 mins: 0-0 Att: 60,000
Ref: Mohammed Nazri Abdullah
(Malaysia)
Saudi Arabia won 4-2 on pens

2000 LEBANON
SEMI-FINALS
Saudi Arabia **2-1** South Korea
Japan **3-2** China

THIRD PLACE PLAY-OFF
South Korea **1-0** China

FINAL
October 28 – Beirut
Japan **1-0** Saudi Arabia
(Mochizuki 29)
h/t: 1-0 Att: 57,600
Ref: Ali Bujsaim (UAE)

* League format.
** Finals tournament.

Ryuzo Morioka, the Japanese captain, celebrates victory in the 2000 Asian Nations Cup Final after Japan defeated Saudi Arabia 1-0 in Beirut.

THE ASIAN CUP

The Asian Club Championship

THE ASIAN CLUB CHAMPIONSHIP, sometimes known as the Asian Champions Cup, is the leading international club competition in Asia. Originally conceived by the Asian Football Confederation in 1962, it took five years to launch the competition, which began as a six-team tournament played out in Bangkok. Geography has always dogged the competition, with Asia's enormous size making schedules difficult to arrange, and the inclusion of Israel in the AFC created significant conflicts with other members. In 1971, the Iraqi club Al Shorta, or Police Club, refused to play Maccabi Tel Aviv in the Final. The competition was only played again in 1985 by which time Israel had left the AFC.

The competition is open to national champions in all members of AFC. The early rounds are played on a geographical basis, dividing into East and West Asia. Semi-finals and a Final tournament are then staged in a single nation.

The other international club tournament in Asia is the Asian Cup-Winners' Cup which is open to cup winners of all AFC member states, or losing finalists if the cup winner is entered for the Asian Club Championship. Early rounds are played over two legs with a small finals tournament (semi-finals, Final, third place play-off) in a single host city. The competition began in 1990 with 18 entrants, though only 13 competed. By the mid-90s it was attracting more prize money and more teams. The Finals had been played over two legs, but in 1994 the format switched to the current finals tournament model. The last seven Finals have been won by either Japanese or South Korean teams, except for the Saudi Arabians' Al Hilal in 2000.

1967 FINAL
December 19 – Bangkok, Thailand
Hapoel Tel Aviv 2-1 Selangor
(Israel)   (Malaysia)

1968–69 FINAL
January 30 – Bangkok, Thailand
Maccabi Tel Aviv 1-0 Yangzee
(Israel)   (South Korea)

1970 FINAL
April 10 – Tehran, Iran
Taj Club 2-1 Hapoel Tel Aviv
(Iran)   (Israel)

1971 FINAL
April 2 – Bangkok, Thailand
Maccabi w/o Al Shorta
Tel Aviv   (Iraq)
(Israel)
Al Shorta withdrew from this match, awarded to Maccabi

1972 FINAL
tournament cancelled

1985–86 FINAL
January 24, 1986 – Jeddah, Saudi Arabia
Daewoo 3-1 Al Ahly
Royals   (Saudi Arabia)
(South Korea)

1986–87 TOURNAMENT
December, 1986 – Riyadh, Saudi Arabia
Al Talaba 2-2 Liaoning
Furukawa 4-3 Al Hilal
Furukawa 2-0 Al Talaba
Al Hilal 1-0 Liaoning
Furukawa 1-0 Liaoning
Al Hilal 2-1 Al Talaba

		P	W	D	L	F	A	Pts
1	Furukawa	3	3	0	0	7	3	6
2	Al Hilal	3	2	0	1	6	5	4
3	Liaoning	3	0	1	2	2	4	1
4	Al Talaba	3	0	1	2	3	6	1

1987–88 FINAL
Yomiuri Club w/o Al Hilal
(Japan)   (Saudi Arabia)
Al Hilal withdrew before 1st leg

1988–89 FINAL (2 legs)
March 31
Al Rasheed 3-2 Al Sadd
(Iraq)   (Qatar)

April 6
Al Sadd 1-0 Al Rasheed
Al Sadd won on away goals rule

1989–90 FINAL (2 legs)
April 22
Liaoning 2-1 Nissan Motors
(China)   (Japan)

April 29
Nissan Motors 1-1 Liaoning

1990–91 FINAL
July 29 – Dhaka, Bangladesh
Esteghlal 2-1 Liaoning
(Iran)   (China)

1991–92 FINAL
December 22, 1991 – Doha, Qatar
Al Hilal 1-1 Esteghlal
(Saudi Arabia)   (Iran)
(Hussein   (Amir Abbas 58)
Al Habashi 73)
(after extra time)
Al Hilal won 4-3 on pens

1992–93 FINAL
January 22 – Bahrain
Pas Club 1-0 Al Shabab
(Iran)   (Saudi Arabia)

1993–94 FINAL
February 7 – Bangkok, Thailand
Thai Farmers 2-1 Oman Club
Bank   (Oman)
(Thailand)   (Zahir Salim 44)
(Thawan
Thamniyai 4,
Sing Totavee 18)

1994–95 FINAL
January 29 – Bangkok, Thailand
Thai Farmers 1-0 Al Arabi
Bank   (Qatar)
(Thailand)
(Natipong
Sritong-in 82)

1995–96 FINAL
December 29 – Riyadh, Saudi Arabia
Ilhwa 1-0 Al Nassr
Chunma   (Saudi Arabia)
(South Korea)
(Lee Tae
Hong 110)
(after extra time)

1996–97 FINAL
March 9 – Kuala Lumpur, Malaysia
Pohang 2-1 Ilhwa
Steelers   Chunma
(South Korea)   (South Korea)
(Park Tae-ha 77,   (Park Ji-ho 79)
Hong Jong-kyong
118 pen)

1997–98 FINAL
April 5 – Hong Kong
Pohang 0-0 Dalian Wanda
Steelers   (China)
(South Korea)
Pohang Steelers won 6-5 on pens

1998–99 FINAL
April 30 – Tehran, Iran
Jubilo Iwata 2-1 Esteghlal
(Japan)   (Iran)
(Suzuki 36,   (Dinmohammadi
Nakayama 45)   66)

1999–2000 FINAL
April 22 – Riyadh, Saudi Arabia
Al Hilal 3-2 Jubilo Iwata
(Saudi Arabia)   (Japan)
(Ricardo   (Nakayama 18,
3, 89, 102)   Takahara 19)

2000–01 FINAL
May 26 – Suwon, South Korea
Suwon Samsung 1-0 Jubilo Iwata
Bluewings   (Japan)
(South Korea)
(Sandro dos
Santos 15)

2001–02 FINAL
April 5 – Tehran, Iran
Suwon Samsung 0-0 Anyang LG
Bluewings   Cheetahs
(South Korea)   (South Korea)
Suwon Samsung won 4-2 on pens

Masashi Nakayama's goals played a big part in getting Japan's Jubilo Iwata to the Asian Club Championship Finals in 1999, 2000 and 2001.

THE OFC NATIONS

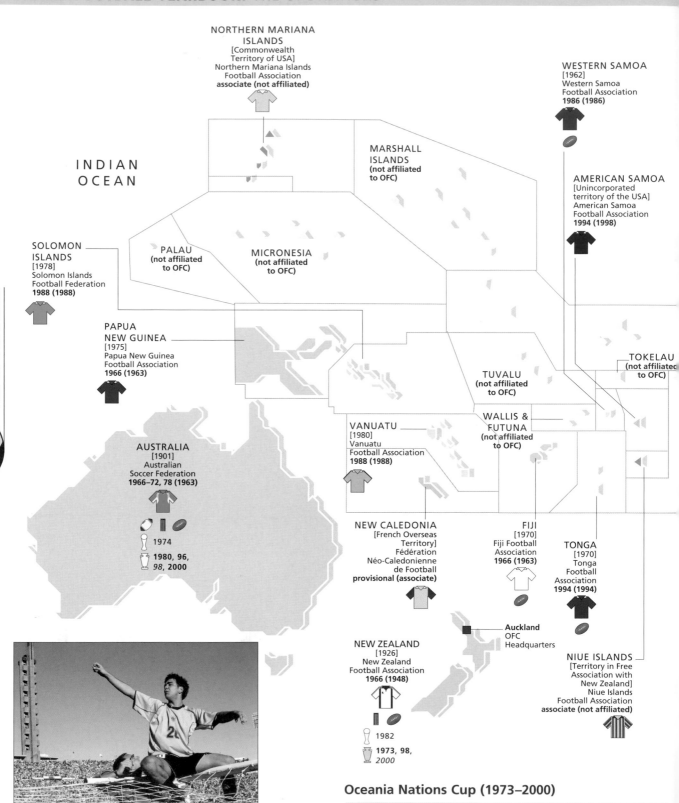

NORTHERN MARIANA ISLANDS
[Commonwealth Territory of USA]
Northern Mariana Islands Football Association
associate (not affiliated)

WESTERN SAMOA
[1962]
Western Samoa Football Association
1986 (1986)

INDIAN OCEAN

**MARSHALL ISLANDS
(not affiliated to OFC)**

AMERICAN SAMOA
[Unincorporated territory of the USA]
American Samoa Football Association
1994 (1998)

SOLOMON ISLANDS
[1978]
Solomon Islands Football Federation
1988 (1988)

**PALAU
(not affiliated to OFC)**

**MICRONESIA
(not affiliated to OFC)**

PAPUA NEW GUINEA
[1975]
Papua New Guinea Football Association
1966 (1963)

**TUVALU
(not affiliated to OFC)**

**TOKELAU
(not affiliated to OFC)**

AUSTRALIA
[1901]
Australian Soccer Federation
1966–72, 78 (1963)

1974

1980, 96, 98, 2000

VANUATU
[1980]
Vanuatu Football Association
1988 (1988)

**WALLIS & FUTUNA
(not affiliated to OFC)**

NEW CALEDONIA
[French Overseas Territory]
Fédération Néo-Caledonienne de Football
provisional (associate)

FIJI
[1970]
Fiji Football Association
1966 (1963)

TONGA
[1970]
Tonga Football Association
1994 (1994)

Auckland
OFC Headquarters

NEW ZEALAND
[1926]
New Zealand Football Association
1966 (1948)

1982

1973, 98, 2000

NIUE ISLANDS
[Territory in Free Association with New Zealand]
Niue Islands Football Association
associate (not affiliated)

Australia's attempt at reaching the 2002 World Cup Finals ended in disaster when it lost 3-0 in the second leg of a play-off against Uruguay having gone into the match with a 1-0 lead.

Oceania Nations Cup (1973–2000)

YEAR	WINNERS	SCORE	RUNNERS-UP
1973	New Zealand	2-0	Tahiti
1980	Australia	4-2	Tahiti
1996	Australia	6-0, 5-0 (2 legs)	Tahiti
1998	New Zealand	1-0	Australia
2000	Australia	2-0	New Zealand

The OFC Nations

The OFC Nations

Date of affiliation to OFC

	Founder member
	1967–89
	1990–present
	Associate member
	Provisional member

Competitor sports

- Australian Rules
- Cricket
- Rugby

COUNTRY
[Dependency]
Name of Football Association
Date of affiliation to OFC —**1967 (1980)** — Date of affiliation to FIFA

Team colours

World Cup — 1980 — Participants in roman

Oceania Cup — **1990** — Winners in bold

2000 — Runners-up in italic

Team colours unknown

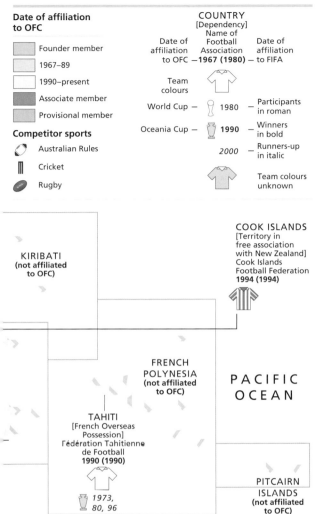

KIRIBATI
(not affiliated to OFC)

COOK ISLANDS
[Territory in free association with New Zealand]
Cook Islands Football Federation
1994 (1994)

FRENCH POLYNESIA
(not affiliated to OFC)

PACIFIC OCEAN

TAHITI
[French Overseas Possession]
Fédération Tahitienne de Football
1990 (1990)

1973, 80, 96

PITCAIRN ISLANDS
(not affiliated to OFC)

OFC

Oceania Tournaments and Cup Competitions:
Oceania Nations Cup
OFC Club Championship
Oceania Women's Tournament

The Development of Oceanian Football

1973 First Oceania Cup

1980 Second Oceania Cup

2000 Oceania Club Championship established

1960   1970   1980   1990   2000

1966 OFC, Oceania Football Confederation founded

1988 Oceania Footballer of the Year Award established

1996 Oceania Cup established as biennial tournament

1998 Oceania Women's Tournament established

The OFC Nations

THE OFC (OCEANIA FOOTBALL CONFEDERATION) was the last of the world's football confederations to be formed. Hardly surprising given that in the major countries of the region rugby (union and league), Australian Rules and cricket have provided very stiff competition for football, as indeed they have in Fiji and the smaller Pacific societies. Prior to OFC's formation in 1966 Australia and others had played in Asian World Cup qualifiers.

OFC consists of Australia, New Zealand, Papua New Guinea and the island states, statelets, archipelagoes and dependencies of the vast Pacific Ocean. Football's organization and strengths in the region are very asymmetrical. The Oceania Games, the Oceania qualifying rounds of the World Cup, has been dominated by Australia, where postwar immigrant communities from Europe have given the game a huge boost. The relative weakness of the region's other clubs and leagues mean that no international club tournament is held. Australia sought to rejoin Asia in the 1970s given the paucity of local competition, but was refused. Since then Oceania's World Cup qualifiers have led to play-offs with UEFA and CONMEBOL sides.

Harry Kewell of Leeds United is without doubt the jewel in Australia's footballing crown.

Calendar of Events	
Club Tournaments	OFC Club Championship 2002
International Tournaments	OFC Futsal Cup 2003

Oceania

FOOTBALL HAS ALWAYS STRUGGLED in Oceania, competing, especially in the most populated areas, with Australian Rules football and both rugby codes. Although a national FA was set up in Australia in 1882, football was only played at an amateur regional level. But its popularity was sustained and expanded by the new wave of European immigration to Australia in the mid-20th century – Italians, Hungarians, Croats and Greeks prominent among the soccer migrants and the names of the top clubs in the 1970s and 80s. In recent years the Australian Soccer Federation has encouraged more ethnically-neutral names in pursuit of the mainstream Australian sports dollar. A national league and a national cup competition were created in 1977. However, no team from Tasmania has ever been part of the league and it was nearly 23 years after starting that a team from Western Australia took part.

New Zealand's national league competition (although a split between leagues on each of the North and South Islands with a play-off between the winners for the national championship) dates from 1970s, and the main cup competition, the Chatham Cup (with a trophy donated by the Royal Navy ship HMS *Chatham*), has been played since 1923.

Australia

Australia Soccer Federation
Founded: 1961
Joined FIFA: 1963
Joined OFC: 1966–72, 1978

Australian League Record 1977–2001

SEASON	CHAMPIONS	RUNNERS-UP
1977	Sydney City	Marconi Fairfield
1978	West Adelaide	Sydney City
1979	Marconi Fairfield	Heidelberg United
1980	Sydney City	Heidelberg United
1981	Sydney City	South Melbourne
1982	Sydney City	Saint George
1983	Saint George	Sydney City
1984	South Melbourne	Sydney Olympic
1985	Brunswick	Sydney City
1986	Adelaide City	Sydney Olympic
1987	APIA Leichhardt	Preston
1988	Marconi Fairfield	Sydney Croatia
1989	Marconi Fairfield	Sydney Olympic
1990	Sydney Olympic	Marconi Fairfield
1991	South Melbourne	Melbourne Croatia
1992	Adelaide City	Melbourne Croatia
1993	Marconi Fairfield	Adelaide City
1994	Adelaide City	Melbourne Knights
1995	Melbourne Knights	Adelaide City
1996	Melbourne Knights	Marconi Fairfield
1997	Brisbane Strikers	Sydney United
1998	South Melbourne	Carlton
1999	South Melbourne	Sydney United
2000	Wollongong Wolves	Perth Glory
2001	Wollongong Wolves	South Melbourne

Australian League Summary

TEAM	TOTALS	CHAMPIONS & RUNNERS-UP (BOLD) (ITALICS)
Marconi Fairfield	4, 3	*1977,* **79, 88, 89,** *90, 93, 96*
Sydney City	4, 3	**1977,** *78,* **80–82,** *83, 85*
South Melbourne	4, 2	*1982,* **84, 91, 98, 99, 2001**
Adelaide City	3, 2	**1986,** *92,* **93, 94,** *95*
Melbourne Nights	2, 1	*1994,* **95, 96**
Wollongong Wolves	2, 0	**2000, 01**
Sydney Olympic	1, 3	**1984,** *86, 89,* **90**
Saint George	1, 1	**1982,** *83*
APIA Leichhardt	1, 0	**1987**
Brisbane Strikers	1, 0	**1997**
Brunswick	1, 0	**1985**
West Adelaide	1, 0	**1978**
Heidelberg United	0, 2	*1979, 80*
Melbourne Croatia	0, 2	*1991, 92*
Sydney United	0, 2	*1997, 99*
Carlton	0, 1	*1998*
Perth Glory	0, 1	*2000*
Preston	0, 1	*1987*
Sydney Croatia	0, 1	*1988*

Australian Cup Record 1977–2001

YEAR	WINNERS	SCORE	RUNNERS-UP
1977	Brisbane City	1-1 (aet)(5-3 pens)	Marconi Fairfield
1978	Brisbane City	2-1	Adelaide City
1979	Adelaide City	3-2	Saint George
1980	Marconi Fairfield	0-0, 3-0 (2 legs)	Heidelberg United
1981	Brisbane Lions	3-1	West Adelaide
1982	APIA Leichhardt	2-1	Heidelberg United
1983	Sydney Olympic	1-0, 1-0 (2 legs)	Heidelberg United
1984	Newcastle Rosebud	1-0	Melbourne Croatia
1985	Sydney Olympic	2-1	Preston
1986	Sydney City	3-2	West Adelaide
1987	Sydney Croatia	1-0, 1-0	South Melbourne
1988	APIA Leichhardt	0-0 (aet)(5-3 pens)	Brunswick
1989	Adelaide City	2-0	Sydney Olympic
1990	South Melbourne	4-1	Sydney Olympic
1991	Parramatta Eagles	1-0	Preston Macedonia
1992	Adelaide City	2-1	Marconi Fairfield
1993	Heidelberg United	2-1	Parramatta Eagles
1994	Parramatta Eagles	2-0	Sydney United
1995	Melbourne Knights	6-0	Heidelberg United
1996	South Melbourne	3-1	Newcastle Breakers
1997	Collingwood Warriors	1-0	Marconi Fairfield
1998–2001	*no competition*		

Australian Cup Summary

TEAM	TOTALS	WINNERS & RUNNERS-UP (BOLD) (ITALICS)
Adelaide City	3, 1	*1978,* **79, 89, 92**
Sydney Olympic	2, 2	**1983, 85,** *89, 90*
Parramatta Eagles	2, 1	**1991,** *93,* **94**
South Melbourne	2, 1	*1987,* **90, 96**
APIA Leichhardt	2, 0	**1982, 88**
Brisbane City	2, 0	**1977, 78**
Heidelberg United	1, 4	*1980, 82, 83,* **93,** *95*
Marconi Fairfield	1, 3	**1977,** *80, 92, 97*
Brisbane Lions	1, 0	**1981**
Collingwood Warriors	1, 0	**1997**

Australian Cup Summary (*continued*)

TEAM	TOTALS	WINNERS & RUNNERS-UP
		(BOLD) (*ITALICS*)
Melbourne Nights	**1, 0**	**1995**
Newcastle Rosebud	**1, 0**	**1984**
Sydney City	**1, 0**	**1986**
Sydney Croatia	**1, 0**	**1987**
West Adelaide	0, 2	*1981, 86*
Brunswick	0, 1	*1988*
Melbourne Croatia	0, 1	*1984*
Newcastle Breakers	0, 1	*1996*
Preston	0, 1	*1985*
Preston Macedonia	0, 1	*1991*
Saint George	0, 1	*1979*
Sydney United	0, 1	*1994*

American Samoa

American Samoa Football Association
Founded: 1971
Joined FIFA: 1998
Joined OFC: 1994

SEASON	LEAGUE CHAMPIONS
1998	*unknown*
1999	Konika Machine FC
2000	PanSa Soccer Club
2001	*unknown*
2002	Leone Lions

Cook Islands

Cook Islands Football Federation
Founded: 1971
Joined FIFA: 1994
Joined OFC: 1994

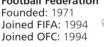

SEASON	LEAGUE CHAMPIONS
1998	*no championship*
1999	Tupapa FC
2000	Avatiu FC
2001	Sokattack Nikao
2002	Tupapa FC

YEAR	CUP WINNERS
1998	Teau-o-Tonga
1999	Tupapa FC
2000	Tupapa FC
2001	Avatiu FC
2002	Tupapa FC

Fiji

Fiji Football Asociation
Founded: 1938
Joined FIFA: 1963
Joined OFC: 1966

Fiji (*continued*)

SEASON	LEAGUE CHAMPIONS
1997	Ba
1998	Raymonds
1999	Kiwi Sports Labasa
2000	Foodtown Warriors Labasa
2001	*unknown*

YEAR	CUP WINNERS
1997	Labasa/Ba (*shared*)
1998	Ba
1999	Labasa
2000	Lautoka
2001	Nadroga

New Caledonia

Fédération Néo-Caledonienne de Football
Founded: 1960
Joined FIFA: 1966
Provisional member only

SEASON	LEAGUE CHAMPIONS
1997	JS Baco
1998	AS Poum
1999	ΓC Gaitcha
2000	JS Baco
2001	JS Baco

YEAR	CUP WINNERS
1997	CA Saint-Louis
1998	JS Traput
1999	JS Traput
2000	AS Magenta
2001	AS Magenta

New Zealand

New Zealand Football Association
Founded: 1938
Joined FIFA: 1948
Joined OFC: 1966

New Zealand (*continued*)

SEASON	LEAGUE CHAMPIONS
1997	Waitakere City
1998	Napier City Rovers
1999	Central United
2000	Napier City Rovers
2001	Central United

YEAR	CUP WINNERS
1997	Central United
1998	Central United
1999	Dunedin Technical
2000	Napier City Rovers
2001	Uni-Mount Wellington

Papua New Guinea

Papua New Guinea Football Asociation
Founded: 1962
Joined FIFA: 1963
Joined OFC: 1966

SEASON	LEAGUE CHAMPIONS
1997	ICF University
1998	ICF University
1999	Guria
2000	Unitech
2001	Sobou Lae

Solomon Islands

Solomon Islands Football Federation
Founded: 1988
Joined FIFA: 1988
Joined OFC: 1988

SEASON	LEAGUE CHAMPIONS
1997	*unknown*
1998	*unknown*
1999	*unknown*
2000	Lauga United
2001	*unknown*

Tahiti

Fédération Tahitienne de Football
Founded: 1938
Joined FIFA: 1990
Joined OFC: 1990

SEASON	LEAGUE CHAMPIONS
1997	AS Vénus
1998	AS Vénus
1999	AS Vénus
2000	AS Vénus
2001	AS Pirae

Tahiti (*continued*)

YEAR	CUP WINNERS
1997	AS Dragons
1998	AS Vénus
1999	AS Vénus
2000	AS Pirae
2001	AS Dragon

Tonga

Tonga Football Association
Founded: 1965
Joined FIFA: 1994
Joined OFC: 1994

SEASON	LEAGUE CHAMPIONS
1997	*unknown*
1998	SC Lotoha'apai
1999	SC Lotoha'apai
2000	*unknown*
2001	*unknown*

Vanuatu

Vanuatu Football Association
Founded: 1934
Joined FIFA: 1988
Joined OFC: 1988

SEASON	LEAGUE CHAMPIONS
1997	Tafea FC
1998	Tafea FC
1999	Tafea FC
2000	Tafea FC
2001	*unknown*

Western Samoa

Western Samoa Football Association
Founded: 1968
Joined FIFA: 1986
Joined OFC: 1986

SEASON	LEAGUE CHAMPIONS
1997	Kiwi FC
1998	Vaivase-tai
1999	Moata'a
2000	Titavi FC
2001	Gold Star

YEAR	CUP WINNERS
1997	Kiwi FC
1998	Togafuafua
1999	Moaula
2000	Sogi
2001	*unknown*

OCEANIA

The Football Confederation

Date of affiliation to the Football Confederation

- Founder member
- 1962–69
- 1970–89
- 1990–present

COUNTRY
Name of
Football
Association

Date of affiliation to the Football Confederation — **1916 (1912)** — Date of affiliation to FIFA

Team colours

World Cup — 1980 — Participants in roman

Gold Cup 1991– present (CONCACAF Championship 1963–89, CCCF Championship 1941–61) — **1990** — Winners in bold

2000 — Runners-up in italic

CANADA
The Canadian Soccer Association
1978 (1912–28, 1946)
1986
1985, 2000

BERMUDA
Bermuda Football Association
1966 (1962)

New York Football Confederation Headquarters

DOMINICAN REPUBLIC
Federación Dominicana de Fútbol
1964 (1958)

UNITED STATES OF AMERICA
United States Soccer Federation
1961 (1913)
1994, 98
1989, 91, 93, 98, **2002**

BELIZE
Belize National Football Association
1986 (1986)

BAHAMAS
The Bahamas Football Association
1981 (1968)

TURKS AND CAICOS ISLANDS
Football Association of Turks and Caicos
1998 (1998)

GULF OF MEXICO

CUBA
Associación de Fútbol de Cuba
1961 (1933)
1938

MEXICO
Federación Mexicana de Fútbol Asociación AC
1961 (1929)
1930, 50, 54, 58, 62, 66, 70, 78, 86, 94, 98
1965, 67, 71, 77, 93, 96, 98

EL SALVADOR
Federación Salvadoreña de Fútbol
1962 (1938)
1970, 83
1941, **43,** *63, 81*

CAYMAN ISLANDS
Cayman Islands Football Association
1992 (1992)

JAMAICA
Jamaica Football Association
1961 (1962)
1998

GUATEMALA
Federación Nacional de Fútbol de Guatemala
1961 (1933)
1943, 46, 48, 65, 67, 69

PACIFIC OCEAN

HAITI
Fédération Haïtienne de Football
1961 (1933)
1974
1957, *61, 71, 73, 77*

CARIBBEAN SEA

HONDURAS
Federación Nacional Autónoma de Fútbol de Honduras
1961 (1951)
1953, **81, 85, 91**

NICARAGUA
Federación Nicaraguense de Fútbol
1968 (1950)

COSTA RICA
Federación Constarricense de Fútbol
1962 (1921)
1990
1941, 46, 48, *51,* **53, 55, 60, 61, 63, 69, 89,** *2002*

PANAMA
Federación Nacional de Fútbol de Panama
1961 (1938)
1951

The Development of Football in America

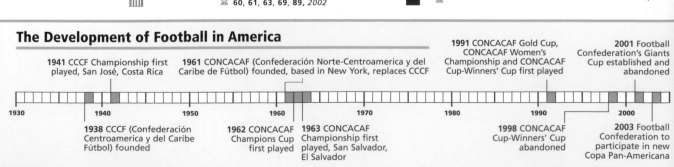

1941 CCCF Championship first played, San José, Costa Rica

1938 CCCF (Confederación Centroamerica y del Caribe Fútbol) founded

1961 CONCACAF (Confederación Norte-Centroamerica y del Caribe de Fútbol) founded, based in New York, replaces CCCF

1962 CONCACAF Champions Cup first played

1963 CONCACAF Championship first played, San Salvador, El Salvador

1991 CONCACAF Gold Cup, CONCACAF Women's Championship and CONCACAF Cup-Winners' Cup first played

1998 CONCACAF Cup-Winners' Cup abandoned

2001 Football Confederation's Giants Cup established and abandoned

2003 Football Confederation to participate in new Copa Pan-Americana

1930   1940   1950   1960   1970   1980   1990   2000

The Football Confederation

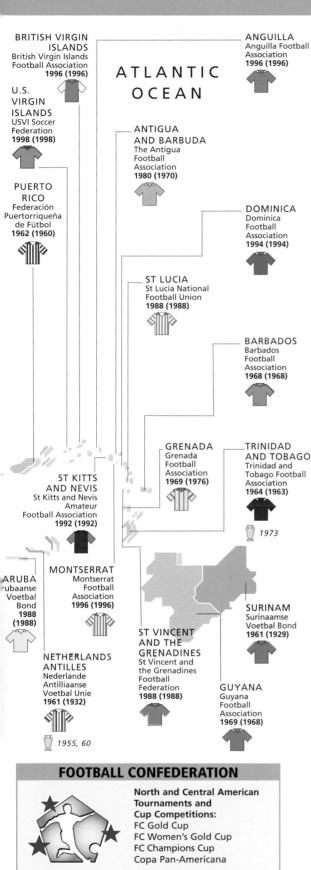

BRITISH VIRGIN ISLANDS
British Virgin Islands Football Association
1996 (1996)

ATLANTIC OCEAN

ANGUILLA
Anguilla Football Association
1996 (1996)

U.S. VIRGIN ISLANDS
USVI Soccer Federation
1998 (1998)

ANTIGUA AND BARBUDA
The Antigua Football Association
1980 (1970)

PUERTO RICO
Federación Puertorriqueña de Fútbol
1962 (1960)

DOMINICA
Dominica Football Association
1994 (1994)

ST LUCIA
St Lucia National Football Union
1988 (1988)

BARBADOS
Barbados Football Association
1968 (1968)

GRENADA
Grenada Football Association
1969 (1976)

TRINIDAD AND TOBAGO
Trinidad and Tobago Football Association
1964 (1963)

1973

ST KITTS AND NEVIS
St Kitts and Nevis Amateur Football Association
1992 (1992)

ARUBA
Arubaanse Voetbal Bond
1988 (1988)

MONTSERRAT
Montserrat Football Association
1996 (1996)

SURINAM
Surinaamse Voetbal Bond
1961 (1929)

NETHERLANDS ANTILLES
Nederlande Antilliaanse Voetbal Unie
1961 (1932)

1955, 60

ST VINCENT AND THE GRENADINES
St Vincent and the Grenadines Football Federation
1988 (1988)

GUYANA
Guyana Football Association
1969 (1968)

FOOTBALL CONFEDERATION

North and Central American Tournaments and Cup Competitions:
FC Gold Cup
FC Women's Gold Cup
FC Champions Cup
Copa Pan-Americana

THE ORGANIZATION OF FOOTBALL in North and Central America reflects the basic divisions and conflicts of the region. North America (USA and Canada) is on a different sporting and economic plane from the rest of the region. Mexico remains the singular dominant footballing power in the area, unsure whether to remain a big fish in a small pool or take a chance by joining the stronger footballing nations of South America.

Before the Second World War these divisions were reflected in the formation of both CCCF (Confederación Centroamerica y del Caribe de Fútbol) in 1938, made up of Central American and Caribbean nations, and NAFC (North American Football Confederation) in 1939, made up of Mexico, USA and Cuba. The NAFC held only two tournaments and its influence as a governing body dwindled. CCCF, without either Mexico or the USA, remained marginal.

In 1961 CONCACAF (Confederación Norte-Centroamerica y del Caribe de Fútbol) was created out of these former federations and was initially based in Guatemala City.

Over the last few decades one of CONCACAF's central missions has been to raise the profile of football in the USA in the hope of providing competition for Mexico and a steady flow of interest and money into the region's rather weak and one-sided international club competitions. As such CONCACAF has been transformed into the more Anglo-sounding Football Confederation, its headquarters have moved to New York and its regional tournament has been renamed the Gold Cup.

While the US has now both a stable professional league and held the 1994 World Cup, Mexican clubs have migrated south to CONMEBOL's Copa Libertadores. In response, the Football Confederation has abandoned some of its tournaments and joined with CONMEBOL to create the Copa Pan-Americana.

A member of the CONCACAF executive since 1990, Chuck Blazer, now General Secretary of the Football Confederation, has been the power behind the non-stop merry-go-round of ever-changing tournament formats.

Calendar of Events

Club Tournaments	Copa Pan-Americana 2002 FC Champions Cup 2003
International Tournaments	FC Gold Cup 2003

THE FOOTBALL CONFEDERATION

NORTH & CENTRAL AMERICA AND THE CARIBBEAN

Soccer is not new to North America having been played there since the 1870s. It thrived during the 1920s, especially in New England, with teams such as the Fall River Marksmen (in stripes) and Bethlehem Steel drawing big crowds and generating widespread interest in the game.

CANADA
[1867]
The Canadian
Soccer Association
1912 (1961)

**UNITED STATES
OF AMERICA**
[1776]
United States
Soccer Federation
1913 (1967/8)

Washington DC ●

**DOMINICAN
REPUBLIC**
[1865]
Federación
Dominicana
de Fútbol
1953 (1991)

BAHAMAS
[1973]
The Bahamas
Football Association
1967 (n/a)

**CAYMAN
ISLANDS**
[British dependent
territory]
Cayman Islands
Football Association
1966 (1996)

CUBA
[1901]
Associación de
Fútbol de Cuba
1924 (1912)

GULF OF
MEXICO

PACIFIC
OCEAN

MEXICO
[1836]
Federación Mexicana
de Fútbol Asociación AC
1927 (1941)

JAMAICA
[1962]
Jamaica Football
Association
1910 (1974)

Kingston

CARIBBEAN
SEA

**TURKS AND
CAICOS ISLANDS**
[British Crown Colony]
Football Association
of Turks and Caicos
1996 (1999)

Guadalajara ●

Mexico
City ●

Guatemala
City ●

Tegucigalpa ●

San
Salvador ●

Alajuela ●

● San
José

BELIZE
[1981]
Belize National
Football Association
1980 (1991)

GUATEMALA
[1838]
Federación Nacional de
Fútbol de Guatemala
1919 (1926)

HONDURAS
[1838]
Federación Nacional
Autónoma de
Fútbol de Honduras
1951 (1965)

EL SALVADOR
[1841]
Federación
Salvadoreña
de Fútbol
1935 (1972)

NICARAGUA
[1838]
Federación
Nicaraguense
de Fútbol
1931 (1963)

COSTA RICA
[1838]
Federación
Constarricense
de Fútbol
1921 (1921)

The top 15 teams in North & Central America and the Caribbean

Alajuelense Costa Rica Alajuela 1919	**DC United** USA Washington DC 1996	**Joe Public FC** Trinidad Port of Spain 1996
Alianza FC El Salvador San Salvador 1959	**Cruz Azul** Mexico Mexico City 1927	**Necaxa** Mexico Mexico City 1923
América Mexico Mexico City 1916	**Comunicaciones** Guatemala Guatemala City 1939	**Robin Hood** Surinam Paramaribo *not known*
Atlante Mexico Mexico City 1916	**CSD Municipal** Guatemala Guatemala City 1936	**Santos** Jamaica Kingston *not known*
Olimpia Honduras Tegucigalpa 1926	**Guadalajara** Mexico Guadalajara 1906	**Saprissa** Costa Rica San José 1935

North & Central America and the Caribbean

ORIGINS AND GROWTH OF FOOTBALL

IN NORTH AMERICA and the Caribbean the question remains: why has football developed in such a limited way? It was played in the USA through colleges and universities, in particular in the 1870s, but it soon fell behind in popularity to American football and baseball. The main areas of football strength were the New England industrial towns, New York, Los Angeles and St Louis.

However, for the most part football remained a game played by recent immigrants (Hispanic and European). Even when it did prosper (a professional national league ran through the 1920s and the USA made the semi-finals of the 1930 World Cup) the game was plagued by conflicts between professionals and amateurs, splits among the various leagues and, with the depression of the 1930s, the economic decimation of its main areas of support. The relative failure of men's football left open space in which American women's football could prosper in the 1970s. In Canada, Scottish immigrants led to the establishment of football in the 1880s, but again with little success.

The success of baseball within the USA was repeated all over the region. US military forces brought the game to Cuba, Nicaragua, Panama, Puerto Rico and the Dominican Republic. In Venezuela, baseball arrived with the US oil industry, which practically ran the country in the early years of the 20th century. In the Caribbean, cricket's popularity always restricted the growth of football (as the popularity of basketball does today). Only in Mexico (and later in Guatemala, Costa Rica and Honduras) has football truly prospered, introduced in the late 19th century by both British and Spanish expatriates.

The Football Confederation Nations

COUNTRY
[date of independence]
Name of national
Football
Foundation   Association   Foundation of
of national FA — **1916 (1912)**— national league

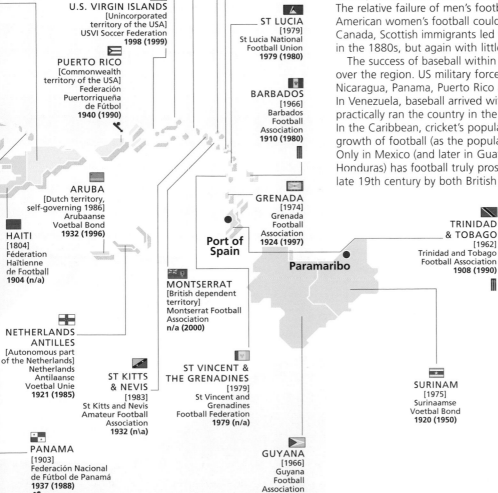

ATLANTIC OCEAN

BERMUDA
[Self-governing British Crown colony]
Bermuda Football Association
1928 (1996)

BRITISH VIRGIN ISLANDS
[British dependent territory]
British Virgin Islands Football Association
1974 (1996)

ANGUILLA
[British dependent territory]
Anguilla Football Association
1990 (1996)

ANTIGUA & BARBUDA
[1981]
The Antigua Football Association
1928 (1968)

DOMINICA
[1978]
Dominica Football Association
1970 (1990)

U.S. VIRGIN ISLANDS
[Unincorporated territory of the USA]
USVI Soccer Federation
1998 (1999)

ST LUCIA
[1979]
St Lucia National Football Union
1979 (1980)

PUERTO RICO
[Commonwealth territory of the USA]
Federación Puertorriqueña de Fútbol
1940 (1990)

BARBADOS
[1966]
Barbados Football Association
1910 (1980)

ARUBA
[Dutch territory, self-governing 1986]
Arubaanse Voetbal Bond
1932 (1996)

GRENADA
[1974]
Grenada Football Association
1924 (1997)

HAITI
[1804]
Féderation Haïtienne de Football
1904 (n/a)

Port of Spain

Paramaribo

TRINIDAD & TOBAGO
[1962]
Trinidad and Tobago Football Association
1908 (1990)

MONTSERRAT
[British dependent territory]
Montserrat Football Association
n/a (2000)

NETHERLANDS ANTILLES
[Autonomous part of the Netherlands]
Netherlands Antilaanse Voetbal Unie
1921 (1985)

ST KITTS & NEVIS
[1983]
St Kitts and Nevis Amateur Football Association
1932 (n\a)

ST VINCENT & THE GRENADINES
[1979]
St Vincent and Grenadines Football Federation
1979 (n/a)

SURINAM
[1975]
Surinaamse Voetbal Bond
1920 (1950)

PANAMA
[1903]
Federación Nacional de Fútbol de Panamá
1937 (1988)

GUYANA
[1966]
Guyana Football Association
1902 (1990)

North & Central America and the Caribbean Origins

Date of formation of national Football Association

	By 1899
	1900–39
	1940–79
	After 1980

Competitor sports

American football

Baseball

Basketball

Cricket

Ice hockey

The USA

United States Soccer Federation
Founded: 1913
Joined FIFA: 1913
Joined CONCACAF: 1961

IT IS CLAIMED THAT the Pilgrim Fathers saw native Americans playing a rudimentary form of football, Passuckquakkohowog, in Massachusetts in 1620, and there was some kind of football played at American colleges as early as the 1820s. However, when the game split between handling and kicking codes, it was the handling game that prevailed and went on to dominate college and then professional sports. In competition with American football, baseball, basketball and ice hockey, soccer has always had a marginal place in American culture.

A series of amateur cups were created at the turn of the 19th century and a single season of professional league football was played in 1894. The first sustainable professional league was created in 1921, and lasted until the early 1930s. The majority of the teams in the league came from the East Coast and attracted newly arrived immigrant populations. With the ASL's demise, a national professional game had to wait for the 1968 merger of the United Soccer Association and the National Professional Soccer League for the formation of the NASL. The NASL survived until 1984 and indeed thrived in the mid-70s as a steady stream of exotic foreign players (at the end of their careers) took up the increasingly attractive financial rewards of US soccer.

The decline of audiences and sponsorship money in the early 1980s left the USA without a national professional league. However, football continued to grow, especially among women. By hosting the World Cup in 1994, the USA was committed to re-establishing a professional league, and MLS – Major League Soccer – was created in 1996, while pre-existing smaller leagues merged to create unified Second and Third Divisions.

The ASL Record 1922–32

SEASON	CHAMPIONS	RUNNERS-UP
1922	Philadelphia Field Club	New York Field Club
1923	J & P Coats	Bethlehem Steel
1924	Fall River Marksmen	Bethlehem Steel
1925	Fall River Marksmen	Bethlehem Steel
1926	Fall River Marksmen	New Bedford Whalers
1927	Bethlehem Steel	Boston Wonder Workers
1928	Boston Wonder Workers	New Bedford Whalers
1929	Fall River Marksmen*	
1929†	Fall River Marksmen	Providence Gold Bugs
1930	Fall River Marksmen	New Bedford Whalers
1930†	Fall River Marksmen	New Bedford Whalers
1931	New York Giants	New Bedford Whalers
1932	*incomplete*	

* No play-off.
† Autumn league played.

The NASL Record 1967–84

YEAR	WINNERS	PLAY-OFF	RUNNERS-UP
1967*	Los Angeles Wolves	5-4	Washington Whips
1967**	Oakland Clippers	0-1, 4-1	Baltimore Bays
1968†	Atlanta Chiefs	0-0, 3-0	San Diego Toros
1969††	Kansas City Spurs		Tampa Bay Rowdies
1970	Rochester Lancers	3-0, 3-1	Washington Darts
1971	Dallas Tornado	1-2, 4-1, 2-0	Atlanta Chiefs
1972	New York Cosmos	2-1	St. Louis Stars
1973	Philadelphia Atoms	2-0	Dallas Tornado
1974	Los Angeles Aztecs	4-3	Dallas Tornado
1975	Tampa Bay Rowdies	2-0	Portland Timbers
1976	Toronto Metros-Croatia	3-0	Minnesota Kicks
1977	New York Cosmos	2-1	Seattle Sounders
1978	New York Cosmos	3-1	Tampa Bay Rowdies
1979	Vancouver Whitecaps	2-1	Tampa Bay Rowdies
1980	New York Cosmos	3-0	Fort Lauderdale Strikers
1981	Chicago Sting	1-0	New York Cosmos
1982	New York Cosmos	1-0	Seattle Sounders
1983	Tulsa Roughnecks	2-0	Toronto Blizzard
1984	Chicago Sting	2-0	Toronto Blizzard

* USA　　** NPSL　　† NASL　　†† No play-off

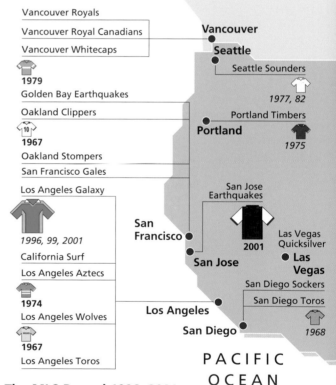

Vancouver Royals
Vancouver Royal Canadians
Vancouver Whitecaps
Vancouver

Seattle
Seattle Sounders
1977, 82

1979
Golden Bay Earthquakes

Oakland Clippers
1967

Portland Timbers
Portland
1975

Oakland Stompers
San Francisco Gales

Los Angeles Galaxy
1996, 99, 2001

San Jose Earthquakes
San Francisco
San Jose
2001

California Surf
Los Angeles Aztecs
1974
Los Angeles Wolves

Las Vegas Quicksilver
Las Vegas

San Diego Sockers
San Diego Toros

1967
Los Angeles Toros
Los Angeles
San Diego
1968

PACIFIC OCEAN

The MLS Record 1996–2001

YEAR	WINNERS	PLAY-OFF	RUNNERS-UP
1996	DC United	3-2	Los Angeles Galaxy
1997	DC United	2-1	Colorado Rapids
1998	Chicago Fire	2-0	DC United
1999	DC United	2-0	Los Angeles Galaxy
2000	Kansas City Wizards	1-0	Chicago Fire
2001	San Jose Earthquakes	2-1 (aet)	Los Angeles Galaxy

THE USA

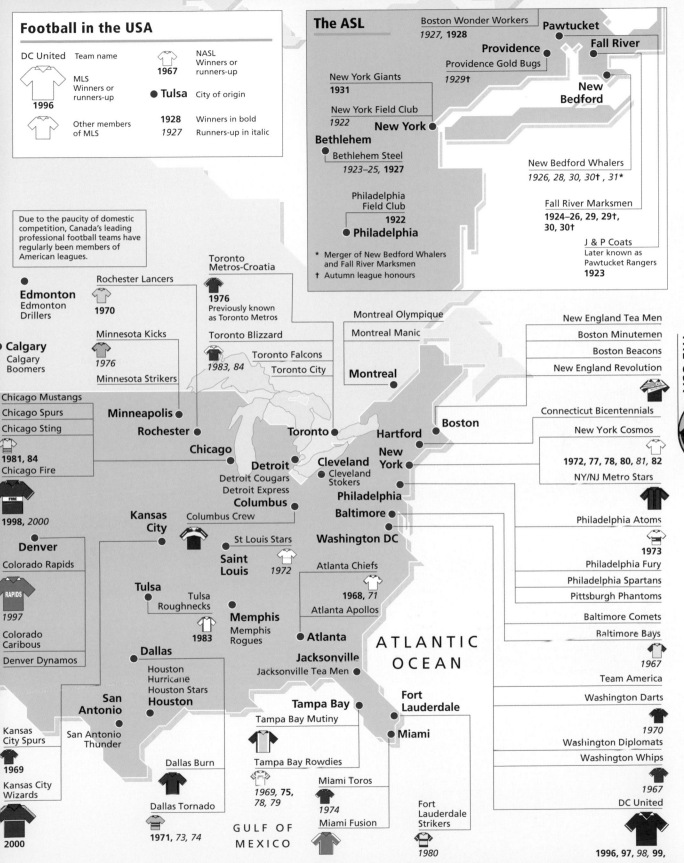

Football in the USA

DC United   Team name

MLS Winners or runners-up
1996

Other members of MLS

1967   NASL Winners or runners-up

● **Tulsa**   City of origin

1928   Winners in bold
1927   Runners-up in italic

The ASL

Boston Wonder Workers
1927, **1928**

Pawtucket

Providence

Fall River

Providence Gold Bugs
1929†

New Bedford

New York Giants
1931

New York Field Club
1922

● **New York**

Bethlehem
Bethlehem Steel
1923–25, **1927**

New Bedford Whalers
*1926, 28, 30, 30†, 31**

Philadelphia Field Club
1922

● **Philadelphia**

Fall River Marksmen
1924–26, *29, 29†,*
30, *30†*

J & P Coats
Later known as
Pawtucket Rangers
1923

* Merger of New Bedford Whalers
and Fall River Marksmen
† Autumn league honours

Due to the paucity of domestic competition, Canada's leading professional football teams have regularly been members of American leagues.

● **Edmonton**
Edmonton Drillers

Rochester Lancers
1970

Toronto Metros-Croatia
1976
Previously known as Toronto Metros

Montreal Olympique
Montreal Manic

New England Tea Men
Boston Minutemen
Boston Beacons
New England Revolution

● **Calgary**
Calgary Boomers

Minnesota Kicks
1976

Toronto Blizzard

Toronto Falcons
1983, 84
Toronto City

● **Montreal**

Connecticut Bicentennials

Chicago Mustangs
Chicago Spurs
Chicago Sting
1981, 84
Chicago Fire
1998, *2000*

Minnesota Strikers

Minneapolis ●

Rochester ●

Chicago ●

Toronto ●

Hartford ●

Boston ●

New York Cosmos
1972, 77, **78**, *80*, **81**, *82*
NY/NJ Metro Stars

● **Denver**
Colorado Rapids
1997
Colorado Caribous
Denver Dynamos

FIRE

RAPIDS

Detroit ●
Detroit Cougars
Detroit Express

Columbus ●
Columbus Crew

Cleveland ●
Cleveland Stokers

New York ●

Philadelphia ●
Philadelphia Atoms
1973
Philadelphia Fury
Philadelphia Spartans
Pittsburgh Phantoms

Kansas City
St Louis Stars

Saint Louis
1972

Baltimore ●
Washington DC ●

Baltimore Comets
Baltimore Bays
1967

Tulsa ●
Tulsa Roughnecks
1983

Atlanta Chiefs
1968, **71**
Atlanta Apollos

Team America

Washington Darts
1970

Memphis ●
Memphis Rogues

Dallas ●

● **Atlanta**

ATLANTIC OCEAN

Washington Diplomats
Washington Whips
1967

Kansas City Spurs
1969
Kansas City Wizards
2000

San Antonio ●
San Antonio Thunder

Houston Hurricane
Houston Stars
Houston ●

Dallas Burn

Dallas Tornado
1971, *73, 74*

Jacksonville ●
Jacksonville Tea Men

Tampa Bay ●
Tampa Bay Mutiny

Tampa Bay Rowdies
1969, **75**, *78, 79*

Miami Toros
1974

Miami Fusion

Fort Lauderdale

● **Miami**

Fort Lauderdale Strikers
1980

DC United
1996, 97, *98*, **99,**

GULF OF MEXICO

THE USA

445

Mexico

THE SEASON IN REVIEW 2001–02

INTERNATIONAL COMMITMENTS had a big impact on domestic Mexican football last season. Pachuca coach Javier Aguirre was summoned to rescue a hitherto disastrous World Cup qualifying campaign; Cruz Azul went all the way to the Final of the Copa Libertadores, while Necaxa and Guadalajara were often distracted by the Copa Merconorte, not to mention teams playing in CONCACAF tournaments as well.

The disruption caused to the domestic season was amplified by having 19 teams, with one team sitting out a fixture every week, and a raft of coaching changes. In the Winter Championship the early pacesetters were slumbering giants Guadalajara. Argentinian coach Oscar Ruggeri was brought in to sort out the mess and the club gave its best and fiercest performance in years. Pachuca, Aguirre's old club, also showed good form as it qualified for the Play-offs and then dispatched Guadalajara and Toluca to meet Tigres in the Final. Pachuca took the first leg confidently 2-0. In the second leg, an early Tigres goal saw them chasing an aggregate equalizer but Pachuca held on to take the title.

The Summer Championship began with the announcement that Necaxa from Mexico City would be relocating to Aguascalientes in 2003, while Irapuato was relocated and renamed Veracruz. A very open competition saw a surprise appearance in the Play-offs for La Piedad, but wealth and power reasserted itself when Televisa's two biggest teams, Necaxa and América, met in the two-leg Final. América triumphed 3-2 on aggregate after losing the first leg 2-0.

Winter Championship 2000–01 Play-offs

QUARTER-FINALS (2 legs)

Santos Laguna **1-1** Tigres
Guadalajara **1-1** Toluca
Atlante **1-2** Pachuca
Necaxa **2-0** Cruz Azul

Toluca **2-0** Guadalajara
Tigres **3-0** Santos Laguna
Cruz Azul **4-0** Necaxa
Pachuca **0-1** Atlante

SEMI-FINALS (2 legs)

Cruz Azul **1-0** Tigres
Pachuca **1-1** Toluca

Toluca **2-4** Pachuca
Tigres **1-0** Cruz Azul

FINAL (2 legs)

December 12 – Hidalgo, Pachuca
Pachuca **2-0** Tigres
(Silvani 23,
Santana 28)
Att: 24,000 **Ref:** not known

December 15 – Universitario, Tigres
Tigres **1-1** Pachuca
(Olalde 19)   *(Silvani 61)*
Att: 43,000 **Ref:** not known
Pachuca won 3-1 on aggregate

Above: Coach Javier Aguirre turned Pachuca around but left the domestic game to help Mexico qualify for the 2002 World Cup.

Below: Carlos Hermosillo (left), Mexico's leading striker, bowed out of the game this year. The event was marked with a friendly game v Cruz Azul (right) which featured a portly Maradona.

Winter Championship 2001–02 Tables

GROUP 1								
CLUB	P	W	D	L	F	A	Pts	
Cruz Azul	18	8	6	4	33	24	**30**	Qualified for Play-offs
Guadalajara	18	6	8	4	20	20	**26**	Qualified for Play-offs
Atlas	18	6	3	9	25	29	**21**	
Monterrey	18	4	8	6	23	31	**20**	
Celaya	18	5	4	9	27	33	**19**	

GROUP 2								
CLUB	P	W	D	L	F	A	Pts	
Toluca	18	8	8	2	33	22	**32**	Qualified for Play-offs
Santos Laguna	18	7	3	8	36	34	**24**	Qualified for Play-offs
Morelia	18	5	5	8	24	30	**20**	
Irapuato	18	4	7	7	27	26	**19**	
La Piedad	18	4	7	7	28	40	**19**	

GROUP 3								
CLUB	P	W	D	L	F	A	Pts	
Necaxa	18	6	9	3	21	20	**27**	Qualified for Play-offs
Atlante	18	6	8	4	24	22	**26**	Qualified for Play-offs
América	18	6	6	6	21	21	**24**	
UAG	18	4	7	7	21	23	**19**	
León	18	4	7	7	25	31	**19**	

GROUP 4								
CLUB	P	W	D	L	F	A	Pts	
Tigres	18	11	3	4	26	12	**36**	Qualified for Play-offs
Pachuca	18	9	5	4	29	24	**32**	Qualified for Play-offs
Puebla	18	5	8	5	22	22	**23**	
Pumas	18	3	8	7	21	22	**17**	

Top Goalscorers Winter 2001–02

PLAYER	CLUB	NATIONALITY	GOALS
Martin Rodriguez	Irapuato	Uruguayan	12
Alex Fernandez	Morelia	Brazilian	11
José Manuel Abundis	Atlante	Mexican	10

Pachuca's Caballero challenges for the ball with Olalde of Tigres in the Winter Championship Play-off Final.

Summer Championship 2001–02 Tables

GROUP 1								
CLUB	P	W	D	L	F	A	Pts	
Atlas	18	8	6	4	30	28	**30**	Qualified for Play-offs
Cruz Azul	18	7	6	5	32	29	**27**	Play-off for quarter-finals
Guadalajara	18	5	7	6	22	21	22	
Monterrey	18	5	5	8	21	28	20	
Celaya	18	5	5	8	19	29	20	

GROUP 2								
CLUB	P	W	D	L	F	A	Pts	
La Piedad	18	12	1	5	35	17	**37**	Qualified for Play-offs
Toluca	18	10	5	3	35	17	**35**	Qualified for Play-offs
Santos Laguna	18	9	4	5	42	31	**31**	Play-off for quarter-finals
Morelia	18	8	5	5	34	25	**29**	Play-off for quarter-finals
Veracruz	18	7	3	8	22	30	24	

GROUP 3								
CLUB	P	W	D	L	F	A	Pts	
Necaxa	18	7	6	5	34	23	**27**	Qualified for Play-offs
América	18	7	6	5	27	23	**27**	Qualified for Play-offs
Atlante	18	5	5	8	23	29	20	
Tecos UAG	18	2	8	8	25	34	14	
León	18	2	4	12	17	36	10	

GROUP 4								
CLUB	P	W	D	L	F	A	Pts	
Pumas	18	9	5	4	30	22	**32**	Qualified for Play-offs
Tigres	18	7	6	5	25	23	**27**	Play-off for quarter-finals
Pachuca	18	6	4	8	26	33	22	
Puebla	18	2	5	11	24	45	11	

Top Goalscorers Summer 2001–02

PLAYER	CLUB	NATIONALITY	GOALS
Sebastián Abreu	Cruz Azul	Uruguayan	19
Jared Borgetti	Santos	Mexican	14
José Cardozo	Toluca	Paraguayan	14
Claudio da Silva	La Piedad	Brazilian	13

International Performances 2001–02

CLUB	COMPETITION	PROGRESS
Cruz Azul	Copa Libertadores	Runners-up
Santos Laguna	FC Champions Cup	Tournament abandoned
Moriela	FC Champions Cup	Tournament abandoned
América	FC Giants Cup	Runners-up
Atlante	FC Giants Cup	Preliminary Round
Guadalajara	FC Giants Cup	Quarter-finals

Summer Championship 2001–02 Play-offs

QUARTER-FINALS (2 legs)

Necaxa **1-0** Toluca
América **3-1** La Piedad
Morelia **1-3** Pumas
Atlas **2-1** Santos Laguna

Toluca **0-2** Necaxa
La Piedad **1-3** América
Pumas **1-0** Morelia
Santos Laguna **2-1** Atlas

SEMI-FINALS (2 legs)

América **0-0** Pumas
Necaxa **1-0** Santos Laguna

Pumas **1-2** América
Santos Laguna **0-0** Necaxa

FINAL (2 legs)

May 23 – Azteca, Mexico City
América **0-2** Necaxa
(Ruiz 12, Alves 42)
Att: 90,000   **Ref:** Rodriguez

May 26 – Azteca, Mexico City
Necaxa **0-3** América
*(Patiño 58,
Zamorano 62,
Castillo 99)*
(after extra time)
Att: 90,000   **Ref:** Archundia

América won 3-2 on aggregate

Televisa v Televisa. Sosa of Necaxa (red and white stripes) climbs above Davino of América in the Summer Championship Play-off Final.

América's coach Manuel La Puente celebrates with his players after beating Necaxa in the Summer Championship Play-off Final.

Garcia of Toluca (left) and Ramirez of Guadalajara tussle for possession.

Association Football in Mexico

MEXICO

1900: First club, Pachuca founded — 1900

1903: First Mexico City League played — 1905

1908: Copa Tower first played — 1910

— 1915

1919: Copa Eliminatoria first played, replaced Copa Tower — 1920

 1923: First International, v Guatemala, won 3-2, venue: Guatemala City — 1925

1927: FMF founded Federación Mexicana de Fútbol — 1930

 1929: Affiliation to FIFA

1932: Last Copa Eliminatoria played. Copa Mexico first played — 1935

— 1940

1944: Primera Fuerza, national professional league established — 1945

1950: Second Division created — 1950

— 1955

 1961: Affiliation to CONCACAF — 1960

— 1965

1970: League shifts format to small leagues and play-offs — 1970

— 1975

 **1985:** Azteca disaster. Ten killed and 29 injured in crowd crush at UNAM v América, Mexican Cup Final — 1980

1990: Banned from the World Cup for fielding under- and over-age players in youth tournaments — 1985 / 1990

1993: Mexico first invited to Copa América

1996: League shifts format to Apertura and Clausura Championships with play-offs — 1995

1999: Mexican clubs first invited to Copa Libertadores — 2000

— 2005

The Azteca Stadium (capacity 110,000) in Mexico City is home to several clubs including the country's most popular team, América, and has hosted two World Cup Finals, in 1970 and 1986.

Key

International football	▲ Copa América runner-up
Affiliation to CONCACAF	○ Competition winner
Affiliation to FIFA	△ Competition runner-up
Disaster	CD Guad – CD Guadalajara
■ World Cup host	CD Tol – CD Toluca
● CONCACAF Championship/ Gold Cup winner	Cruz – Cruz Azul
	Monte – Monterrey
▲ CONCACAF Championship/ Gold Cup runner-up	Necaxa* – Necaxa (as Atlético Español)
	UAG – UAG 'Los Tecos'
	Univers – Universidad de Guadelajara

International Competitions

CONCACAF Champions' Cup

Year		Champions' Cup	Cup-Winners' Cup
1962:		○ CD Guad	
1963:		△ CD Guad	
1965:	●		
1967:	▲		
1968:		○ CD Tol	
1969:		○ Cruz	
1970:	■	○ Cruz	
1971:		○ Cruz	
1975:		○ Necaxa*	
1977:	●	○ América	
1978:		○ Univers	
1980:		○ UNAM	
1982:		○ UNAM	
1983:		○ Atlante	
1986:	■		
1987:		○ América	
1989:		○ UNAM	
1990:		○ América	
1991:		○ Puebla	
1992:		○ América	
1993:	▲●	△ León	○ Monte
1994:		△ Atlante	○ Necaxa
1995:			○ UAG
1996:	●	○ Cruz	
1997:		○ Cruz	
1998:	●	△ CD Tol	
2001:	▲		

CONCACAF Cup-Winners' Cup

CD Guadalajara 1906

Union FC (1906–08)

CD Atlas Guadalajara 1916

UAG, 'Los Tecos' 1971

Universidad de Guadalajara 1974

Purchased franchise from Torreón 1974. Withdrew from league football 1994

Mexico: The main clubs

CF Puebla Team name with year
1943   of formation

●	Club formed before 1912
●	Club formed 1912–25
●	Club formed 1925–50
○	Club formed after 1950
★	Founder members Mexico City League 1902
	Founder members Professional League 1943
	Amateur champions
	English origins
	Spanish origins
	Scottish origins
	Belgian founder
	Franchise purchase
	Originated from a school or college
	Working class

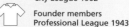 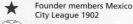  Colours and date unknown

Mexico

ORIGINS AND GROWTH OF FOOTBALL

FOOTBALL FIRST ARRIVED IN MEXICO CITY in the late 19th century via the expatriate British population and the French and Spanish immigrant communities. British mining engineers from the Compañía Real del Monte set up Pachuca Athletic Club, Mexico's first, in 1900. They contested the first championship with clubs of similar origins – Athletic, British Club, Reforma, Rovers, Mexico City Cricket Club and the Scottish-dominated champions Orizaba, all based in or near Mexico City.

Most of the British expatriate population left Mexico during the First World War and the game became dominated by Spanish speakers. A wave of Spanish clubs were formed at this time: Asturias, Real España, Cataluña and Aurora. Indigenous Mexican clubs were not far behind: Guadalajara was founded as Union FC in 1906, while América was formed as a merger of two clubs (Record FC and Colón FC) in 1916. At the same time, its eternal rival, Atlante, was founded as Sinaloa, changing its name to Lusitania and U-53, before settling on the current name in 1920. A national football association was founded in 1927 and affiliated to FIFA in 1929.

Cup and league established

The rapid growth of football in Mexico can be seen from the early development of national cup tournaments (the Copa Tower 1908–19, the Copa Eliminatoria 1920–32, and the Copa Mexico 1932–43) and the early arrival of professionalism in 1933. League football remained based on local and regional leagues until a single national league was established in 1944.

Mexico has been unable to translate these early strengths into enduring international success. It is easily the most powerful footballing nation in the CONCACAF region, but because of North American indifference and Central American and Caribbean weakness, neither its club teams nor its national team have been properly tested. Hosting two World Cups and regularly qualifying for others has not yielded a serious challenge for the trophy. The recent entry of Mexican clubs in the hitherto South American Copa Libertadores is the latest effort to break out from being a big fish in a small pond.

Torreón
Sold franchise to Universidad de Guadalajara, 1974

Santos Laguna 1979
Purchased Club Angles franchise in 1988

Ciudad Juárez 1988
Purchase of Cobra's franchise

Mexico's Cuauhtemoc Blanco brought joy to millions with his 'rabbit' jump during the World Cup in France 1998.

CF Monterrey 1945
UANL, 'Los Tigres' 1967

Tampico FC
Merged in 1982 with Ciudad Madero and purchase of Atlas Campesinos franchise

Asturias (Folded)
RC España (Folded)
British Club 1901 (Folded)
UNAM, 'Los Pumas' 1954

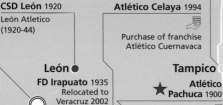

CSD León 1920
León Atlético (1920-44)

Atlético Celaya 1994
Purchase of franchise Atlético Cuernavaca

León
FD Irapuato 1935
Relocated to Veracruz 2002

Guadalajara
Atlético Morelia 1947
Previously known as Oro

Celaya

Tampico
Atlético Pachuca 1900
Reformed 1950, 1960

Mexico City
CD Toluca 1917

CD Cruz Azul 1927
Founded as Cruz Azul Jasso. Moved to Mexico City 1971

Nezahualcóyotl
Jasso
Orizaba

Cuernavaca
CD Zacatepec

CF Puebla 1943

Veracruz
CD Veracruz 1943
Folded 1983. Reformed in 1989 after purchasing Potros de Neza franchise

Rayos del Necaxa 1923
Merger of Luz y Fuerza and El Tranvias 1971, renamed Atlético Español. Renamed Necaxa in 1982

CD 'Toros Neza' 1981
Orignally known as Universidad Autónoma de Neza

Moctezuma (Folded)

Orizaba Charleston (Folded)

Marte FC (Folded)

CF América 1916
Merger of Record FC and Colón FC

Mexico CC 1901 (Folded)

Reforma AC 1901 (Folded)

CD Atlante 1916
Founded as Sinaloa. Changed to Lusitania in 1917 and U-53 in 1918, before CD Atlante in 1920

Mexico City

FOOTBALL CITY

MEXICO

AT THE TURN OF THE CENTURY, Mexico City was host to a considerable mercantile and financial British community. Football clubs, like Reforma and Mexico Cricket Club, sprang up across the city and a city league began in 1902. The First World War and the Mexican Revolution saw most of the British drift away along with their teams, to be replaced by a mixture of Spanish immigrant and indigenous Mexican teams. It is only the latter that have survived the coming of professionalism.

The centralization of political power and the sharp social divisions of Mexican society are reflected in the city's football. The capital's clubs, particularly Cruz Azul, América and Necaxa – teams with national followings outside of Mexico City – all represent a specific strand of Mexican society. Cruz Azul, the solidly working-class team, was founded in Jasso in 1927, before being bought by a cement company and transferred to the south of Mexico City. UNAM, or Los Pumas as the team is more often known, sprang from the National Autonomous University of Mexico. The university no longer runs the team but it continues to field student players and is most widely known for giving youth its chance on the pitch. The club's supporters lean towards the younger, more intellectual, left-wing strands of Mexican life. América, by contrast, is the team of the ruling order and support for the club is often interpreted as an act of social climbing and aspiration. Atlante, originally from the poorest part of the inner city, is the people's team, representing the most marginalized members of Mexican society, while the ever-expanding suburbs have their team in Toros Neza to the west of the city.

The influence of Televisa

The concentration of power in Mexican football can be seen from the three clubs that have played at the Azteca Stadium. Televisa, the nation's biggest media company with business in every part of the Americas, owns the stadium and all the clubs. In 1961, the company bought the long-faded América, spent more money, (including the purchase of the first major wave of foreign players in Mexico) and, through relentless promotion, created a national following for the club. Televisa has since strengthened its grip on Mexican football by buying the Azteca itself, Necaxa in 1983 (which it is now thinking of moving out of the city to the richer demographic fields of Aguascalientes) and Atlante in 1996. It has seen off all rivals to its pre-eminent position in TV coverage of Mexican football, helped gain host status for Mexico in two World Cups (1970 and 1986), and kept very close to the PRI – the political party that ruled Mexico uninterrupted from 1929 to 2000.

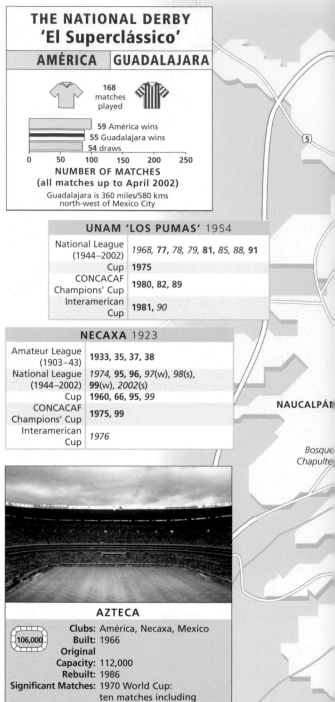

THE NATIONAL DERBY
'El Superclássico'

AMÉRICA	GUADALAJARA

168 matches played

59 América wins
55 Guadalajara wins
54 draws

0	50	100	150	200	250

NUMBER OF MATCHES
(all matches up to April 2002)

Guadalajara is 360 miles/580 kms
north-west of Mexico City

UNAM 'LOS PUMAS' 1954	
National League (1944–2002)	*1968*, **77, 78, 79**, *81*, **85, 88**, *91*
Cup	**1975**
CONCACAF Champions' Cup	**1980, 82, 89**
Interamerican Cup	**1981**, *90*

NECAXA 1923	
Amateur League (1903–43)	**1933, 35, 37, 38**
National League (1944–2002)	*1974*, **95, 96**, *97*(w), *98*(s), **99**(w), *2002*(s)
Cup	**1960, 66, 95**, *99*
CONCACAF Champions' Cup	**1975, 99**
Interamerican Cup	*1976*

AZTECA	
106,000	
Clubs:	América, Necaxa, Mexico
Built:	1966
Original Capacity:	112,000
Rebuilt:	1986
Significant Matches:	1970 World Cup: ten matches including semi-final, 3rd place play-off, Final; 1986 World Cup: nine matches including semi-final and Final; 1993 Gold Cup

Televisa, Mexico's leading TV company, is based in Mexico City, from where it runs its footballing empire. It owns most of the city's big clubs, including América, Necaxa and Atlante, as well as the Azteca Stadium.

5

NAUCALPÁN

Bosque
Chapulte

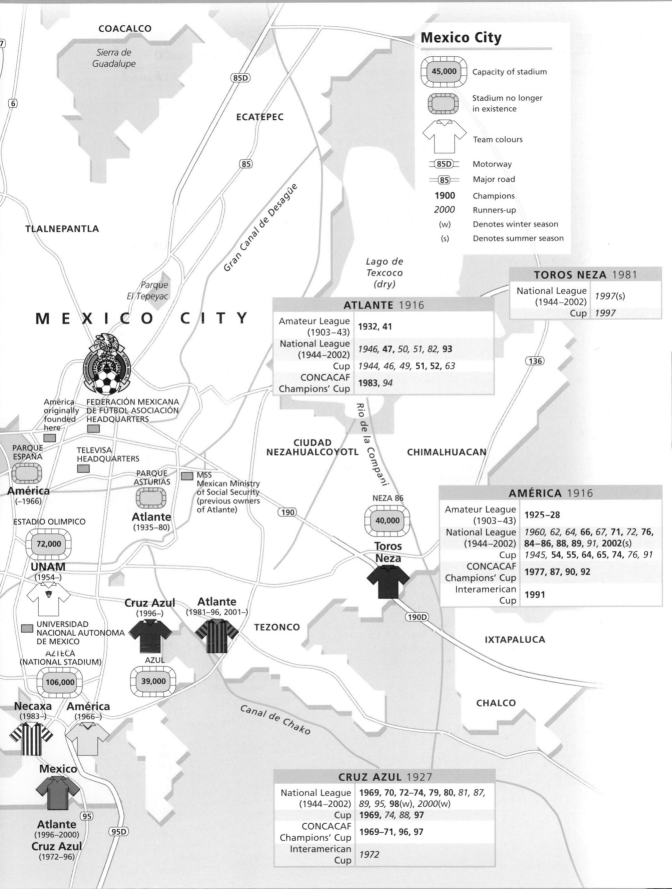

COACALCO

Sierra de Guadalupe

ECATEPEC

TLALNEPANTLA

Gran Canal de Desagüe

Parque El Tepeyac

M E X I C O   C I T Y

América originally founded here

FEDERACIÓN MEXICANA DE FÚTBOL ASOCIACIÓN HEADQUARTERS

PARQUE ESPAÑA

TELEVISA HEADQUARTERS

PARQUE ASTURIAS

América (–1966)

ESTADIO OLIMPICO

72,000

UNAM (1954–)

UNIVERSIDAD NACIONAL AUTONOMA DE MEXICO

Atlante (1935–80)

MSS Mexican Ministry of Social Security (previous owners of Atlante)

Cruz Azul (1996–)

Atlante (1981–96, 2001–)

AZUL

39,000

AZTECA (NATIONAL STADIUM)

106,000

Necaxa (1983–)

América (1966–)

Mexico

Atlante (1996–2000)

Cruz Azul (1972–96)

TEZONCO

Canal de Chako

Lago de Texcoco (dry)

Rio de la Compani

CIUDAD NEZAHUALCOYOTL

CHIMALHUACAN

NEZA 86

40,000

Toros Neza

IXTAPALUCA

CHALCO

Mexico City

45,000	Capacity of stadium
	Stadium no longer in existence
	Team colours
85D	Motorway
85	Major road
1900	Champions
2000	Runners-up
(w)	Denotes winter season
(s)	Denotes summer season

MEXICO

TOROS NEZA 1981

National League (1944–2002)	*1997*(s)
Cup	*1997*

ATLANTE 1916

Amateur League (1903–43)	**1932, 41**
National League (1944–2002)	*1946,* **47,** *50, 51, 82,* **93**
Cup	*1944, 46, 49,* **51, 52,** *63*
CONCACAF Champions' Cup	**1983,** *94*

AMÉRICA 1916

Amateur League (1903–43)	**1925–28**
National League (1944–2002)	*1960, 62, 64,* **66,** *67,* **71,** *72,* **76,** **84–86, 88, 89,** *91,* **2002**(s)
Cup	*1945,* **54, 55,** *64, 65,* **74,** *76,* **91**
CONCACAF Champions' Cup	**1977, 87, 90, 92**
Interamerican Cup	**1991**

CRUZ AZUL 1927

National League (1944–2002)	**1969, 70, 72–74, 79, 80,** *81,* **87,** *89, 95,* **98**(w), *2000*(w)
Cup	**1969,** *74, 88,* **97**
CONCACAF Champions' Cup	**1969–71, 96, 97**
Interamerican Cup	*1972*

Mexico

PRIMERA DIVISIÓN 1981–2001

THE 1980s BEGAN with media giants Televisa determined to make CF América – its key footballing property – the best team in Mexico. A change of strip and an open chequebook did the trick and in 1984, under Carlos Reynos, América took the title, pipping long-standing rival CD Guadalajara to the post. Four out of the next six titles followed, CF Monterrey winning in 1986 and Guadalajara getting one back the following year.

The Mexican league has been through a variety of changes. It has always concluded with the top eight or ten teams playing off (over two legs) to determine the title, but leagues, mini-leagues and groups have all been used to determine the top teams, while relegation is decided on a Byzantine, multiple-season averaging system. In 1996, the league was split into two separate halves – a winter and a summer championship. But whatever system has been used, league football in Mexico has proved a very attractive business proposition. Since the 1980s

In recent years, smaller provincial teams like Atlético Morelia (in hoops), seen here in action against UAG (in checks), have risen to challenge the traditional giants of Mexican football. Morelia's finest moment came in 2001 when the team beat another small club, Toluca, to take the Winter Championship.

Televisa has been joined by rival TV Azteca as multiple club proprietors, while cement, loan, brewing and petrochemical companies have all bought into Mexican clubs. Franchises (or membership of the league) can and have been bought and sold, enabling rich but relegated teams to buy their way back up.

América has continued to be a perennial contender but the title has yet to return to the Mexico City-based club. Instead honours have been shared between outsiders CD Atlante and CSD Léon, who both took surprise titles in the early 1990s; Televisa's other key team, Necaxa, who won three titles in the 1990s; and Cruz Azul, who finally delivered on its promise, winning in 1998. In the late 1990s, the real surprises came from the smaller provincial teams: Toluca, Pachuca, Atlético Morelia and Santos Laguna.

Key to League Positions Table

- ◼ League champions
- ◼ Other teams playing in league
- ◼ Season of promotion to league
- ◼ Qualified for championship play-off
- ◼ Season of relegation from league
- **5** Final position in league

Mexican League Positions 1981–2001

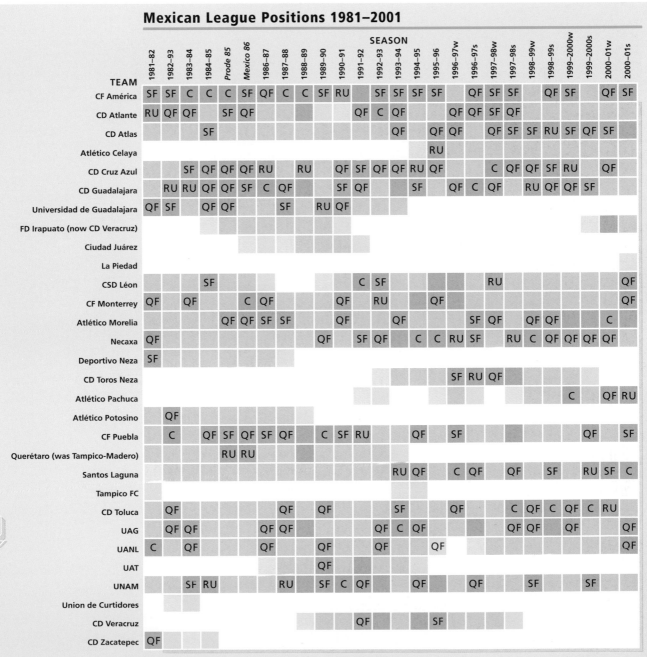

TEAM	1981–82	1982–83	1983–84	1984–85	Prode 85	Mexico 86	1986–87	1987–88	1988–89	1989–90	1990–91	1991–92	1992–93	1993–94	1994–95	1995–96	1996–97w	1996–97s	1997–98w	1997–98s	1998–99w	1998–99s	1999–2000w	1999–2000s	2000–01w	2000–01s
CF América	SF	SF	C	C	C	SF	QF	C	C	SF	RU		SF	SF	SF	SF		QF	SF	SF		QF	SF		QF	SF
CD Atlante	RU	QF	QF		SF	QF						QF	C	QF			QF	QF	SF	QF						
CD Atlas				SF										QF			QF	QF		QF	SF	SF	RU	SF	QF	SF
Atlético Celaya																RU										
CD Cruz Azul			SF	QF	QF	QF	RU		RU		QF	SF	QF	QF	RU	QF			C	QF	QF	SF	RU		QF	
CD Guadalajara		RU	RU	QF	QF	SF	C	QF			SF	QF			SF		QF	C	QF		RU	QF	QF	SF		
Universidad de Guadalajara	QF	SF		QF	QF			SF		RU	QF															
FD Irapuato (now CD Veracruz)																										
Ciudad Juárez																										
La Piedad																										
CSD Léon				SF								C	SF					RU								QF
CF Monterrey	QF		QF			C	QF			QF			RU		QF				SF	QF		QF	QF		C	QF
Atlético Morelia				QF	QF	SF	SF			QF		QF				SF	QF		QF	QF			C			
Necaxa	QF							QF		SF	QF		C	C	RU	SF		RU	C	QF	QF	QF	QF			
Deportivo Neza	SF																									
CD Toros Neza															SF	RU	QF									
Atlético Pachuca																					C			QF	RU	
Atlético Potosino		QF																								
CF Puebla		C		QF	SF	QF	SF	QF		C	SF	RU		QF		SF						QF			SF	
Querétaro (was Tampico-Madero)				RU	RU																					
Santos Laguna														RU	QF		C	QF		QF		SF		RU	SF	C
Tampico FC																										
CD Toluca		QF					QF		QF				SF			QF		C	QF	C	QF	C	RU			
UAG		QF	QF			QF	QF					QF	C	QF			QF	QF		QF						QF
UANL	C		QF				QF			QF			QF		QF											QF
UAT									QF																	
UNAM			SF	RU				RU		SF	C	QF			QF		QF			SF			SF			
Union de Curtidores																										
CD Veracruz										QF		SF														
CD Zacatepec	QF																									

In Mexico, the championship is decided by play-offs, involving eight or ten teams.

In 1986, two shorter championships called Prode 85 and Mexico 86 were held before and after the World Cup. They are counted as official championships.

Since 1996–97 the season has been divided into two, with winter and summer championships.

MEXICO

Mexico

Federación Mexicana de Fútbol Asociación AC
Founded: 1927
Joined FIFA: 1929
Joined CONCACAF*: 1961

MEXICO DOMINATES FOOTBALL in the Central American region. The national team has qualified for the finals of ten of the 15 World Cup tournaments, including Italia '90, when they were barred from the qualifying tournament by FIFA for having breached age regulations in a youth tournament. The country's unrivalled position has meant that the development of football has been hindered through lack of decent opposition.

Domestic competitions, however, have been hotly contested for a century. The first amateur league was established in 1903 by five clubs in Mexico City. The Primera Fuzera, based in Mexico City, ran alongside two provincial amateur leagues: Liga de Occidente and Liga Veracruzana. In 1943 the three competitions were fused to form a professional league and a second division was added in 1950. In 1970, the league format was changed to two then four groups, with a series of multi-leg play-off rounds to decide the championship.

Meanwhile, the Mexican Cup went through three incarnations during its amateur phase. These were the Copa Tower, which existed between 1908 and 1919; the Copa Eliminatoria between 1920 and 1932 (this tournament only accepted clubs that played in the Primera Fuerza); and the Copa Mexico between 1932 and 1943, a tournament that accepted clubs from all over the country. The Cup finally turned professional in 1944.

* In 1999 CONCACAF was renamed the Football Confederation.

Mexican League Record 1944–2002

SEASON	CHAMPIONS	RUNNERS-UP
1944	Asturias	España
1945	España	Puebla
1946	Veracruz	Atlante
1947	Atlante	León
1948	León	Oro
1949	León	Atlas
1950	Veracruz	Atlante
1951	Atlas	Atlante
1952	León	Guadalajara
1953	Tampico	Zacatepec
1954	Marte	Oro
1955	Zacatepec	Guadalajara
1956	León	Oro
1957	Guadalajara	Toluca
1958	Zacatepec	Toluca
1959	Guadalajara	León
1960	Guadalajara	América
1961	Guadalajara	Oro
1962	Guadalajara	América
1963	Oro	Guadalajara
1964	Guadalajara	América
1965	Guadalajara	Oro
1966	América	Atlas
1967	Toluca	América
1968	Toluca	UNAM
1969	Cruz Azul	Guadalajara
1970	Guadalajara	Cruz Azul
1970*	Cruz Azul	Guadalajara
1971	América	Toluca
1972	Cruz Azul	América
1973	Cruz Azul	León
1974	Cruz Azul	Atlético Español

Mexican League Record (*continued*)

SEASON	CHAMPIONS	RUNNERS-UP
1975	Toluca	León
1976	América	Unión de Guadalajara
1977	UNAM	Unión de Guadalajara
1878	UANL	UNAM
1979	Cruz Azul	UNAM
1980	Cruz Azul	UANL
1981	UNAM	Cruz Azul
1982	UANL	Atlante
1983	Puebla	Guadalajara
1984	América	Guadalajara
1985	América	UNAM
1986†	América	Tampico-Madero
1986†	Monterrey	Tampico-Madero
1987	Guadalajara	Cruz Azul
1988	América	UNAM
1989	América	Cruz Azul
1990	Puebla	Unión de Guadalajara
1991	UNAM	América
1992	León	Puebla
1993	Atlante	Monterrey
1994	UAG	Santos Laguna
1995	Necaxa	Cruz Azul
1996	Necaxa	Atlético Celaya
1997 (w)§	Santos Laguna	Necaxa
1997 (s)	Guadalajara	Toros Neza
1998 (w)	Cruz Azul	León
1998 (s)	Toluca	Necaxa
1999 (w)	Necaxa	Guadalajara
1999 (s)	Toluca	Atlas
2000 (w)	Pachuca	Cruz Azul
2000 (s)	Toluca	Santos Laguna
2001 (w)	Morelia	Toluca
2001 (s)	Santos Laguna	Pachuca
2002 (w)	Pachuca	Tigres
2002 (s)	América	Necaxa

* A short tournament was played before or after the 1970 World Cup in Mexico. It is counted as a championship.
† Due to the 1986 World Cup in Mexico, the 1985–86 season was cancelled and replaced by two short tournaments.
§ From 1997 a championship was played in both winter (**w**) and summer (**s**).

Mexican League Summary

TEAM	TOTALS	CHAMPIONS & RUNNERS-UP (BOLD) (*ITALICS*)
Guadalajara	10, 8	*1952*, **55**, **57**, *59–62*, **63**, **64**, **65**, **69**, **70**, *70*, **83**, **84**, **87**, 97 (s), *99* (w)
América	9, 6	*1960*, *62*, **64**, *66*, **67**, **71**, *72*, **76**, **84–86†**, **88**, **89**, **91**, **2002 (s)**
Cruz Azul	8, 6	**1969**, **70**, *70*, **72–74**, **79**, **80**, *81*, *87*, *89*, *95*, **98 (w)**, *2000 (w)*
León	5, 5	*1947*, **48**, **49**, **52**, **56**, *59*, **73**, *75*, **92**, **98 (w)**
Toluca	6, 4	*1957*, *58*, **67**, **68**, *71*, **75**, **98 (s)**, *99 (s)*, **2000 (s)**, **01 (w)**
Necaxa (includes Atlético Español)	3, 4	*1974*, **95**, **96**, **97 (w)**, *98 (s)*, *99* (w), *2002* (s)
UNAM	3, 5	*1968*, **77**, *78*, *79*, **81**, *85*, **88**, *91*
Atlante	2, 4	*1946*, **47**, *50*, *51*, *82*, **93**
Puebla	2, 2	*1945*, **83**, **90**, *92*
Santos Laguna	2, 2	*1994*, **97 (w)**, *2000 (s)*, **01 (s)**
Pachuca	2, 1	**2000 (w)**, *01 (s)*, **02 (w)**

MEXICO

Mexican League Summary (*continued*)

TEAM	TOTALS	CHAMPIONS & RUNNERS-UP (BOLD) (*ITALICS*)
UANL	**2, 1**	**1978,** *80,* **82**
Zacatepec	**2, 1**	**1953,** *55,* **58**
Veracruz	**2, 0**	**1946, 50**
Oro	**1, 5**	*1948, 54, 56, 61, 63, 65*
Atlas	**1, 3**	*1949, 51, 66,* **99 (s)**
Tampico-Madero (includes Tampico)	**1, 2**	**1953,** *86†,* **86†**
España	**1, 1**	*1944,* **45**
Monterrey	**1, 1**	**1986†,** *93*
Asturias	**1, 0**	**1944**
Marte	**1, 0**	**1954**
Morelia	**1, 0**	**2001 (w)**
UAG	**1, 0**	**1994**
Unión de Guadalajara	**0, 3**	*1976, 77, 90*
Atlético Celaya	**0, 1**	*1996*
Tigres	**0, 1**	*2002 (w)*
Toros Neza	**0, 1**	*1997 (s)*

(w) denotes winter season

(s) denotes summer season

† Due to the 1986 World Cup in Mexico, the league was replaced with two short tournaments. They both counted as championships.

Mexican Cup Record 1944–2002

YEAR	WINNERS	SCORE	RUNNERS-UP
1944	España	6-2	Atlante
1945	Puebla	6-4	América
1946	Atlas	5-4 (aet)	Atlante
1947	Moctezuma	4-3	Oro
1948	Veracruz	3-1	Guadalajara
1949	León	3-0	Atlante
1950	Atlas	3-1 (aet)	Veracruz
1951	Atlante	1-0	Guadalajara
1952	Atlante	2-0	Puebla
1953	Puebla	4-1	León
1954	América	1-1 (aet)(3-2 pens)	Guadalajara
1955	América	1-0	Guadalajara
1956	Toluca	2-1	Irapuato
1957	Zacatepec	2-1	León
1958	León	5-2 (aet)	Zacatepec
1959	Zacatepec	2-1	León
1960	Atlético Español	2-2 (aet)(10-9 pens)	Tampico
1961	Tampico	1-0	Toluca
1962	Atlas	3-3, (replay) 1-0	Tampico
1963	Guadalajara	2-1	Atlante
1964	América	1-1 (aet)(5-4 pens)	Monterrey
1965	América	4-0	Morelia
1966	Atlético Español	3-3, (replay) 1-0	León
1967	León	2-1	Guadalajara
1968	Atlas	2-1	Veracruz
1969	Cruz Azul	2-1 (aet)	Monterrey
1970	Guadalajara	3-2, 2-1 (2 legs)	Torreón
1971	León	0-0 (aet) (10-9 pens)	Zacatepec
1972	León	Final Group	Puebla
1973		no competition	
1974	América	2-1, 1-1 (2 legs)	Cruz Azul
1975	UNAM	Final Group	Unión de Guadalajara
1976	UANL	2-0, 1-2 (2 legs) won on away goals	América
1977–87		no competition	
1988	Puebla	0-0, 1-1 (2 legs)	Cruz Azul
1989	Toluca	2-1, 1-1 (2 legs)	Unión de Guadalajara
1990	Puebla	4-1, 0-2 (2 legs)	UANL
1991	Unión de Guadalajara	1-0, 0-0 (2 legs)	América

Mexican Cup Record (*continued*)

YEAR	WINNERS	SCORE	RUNNERS-UP
1992	Monterrey	4-2	Ciudad Juarez
1993–94		no competition	
1995	Necaxa	2-0	Veracruz
1996	UANL	1-1, 1-0 (2 legs)	Atlas
1997	Cruz Azul	2-0	Toros Neza
1998		no competition	
1999	Tigres	2-0	Necaxa
2000–02		no competition	

Mexican Cup Summary

TEAM	TOTALS	WINNERS & RUNNERS-UP (BOLD) (*ITALICS*)
León	**5, 4**	**1949,** *53, 57,* **58,** *59, 66,* **67,** *71, 72*
América	**5, 3**	*1945,* **54, 55,** *64,* **65,** *74,* **76,** *91*
Puebla	**4, 2**	**1945,** *52,* **53,** *72,* **88,** *90*
Atlas	**4, 1**	**1946, 50, 62, 68,** *96*
Necaxa (includes Atlético Español)	**3, 1**	**1960, 66, 95,** *99*
Guadalajara	**2, 5**	*1948, 51, 54, 55,* **63,** *67,* **70**
Atlante	**2, 4**	*1944, 46, 49,* **51, 52,** *63*
Cruz Azul	**2, 2**	**1969,** *74,* **88,** *97*
Zacatepec	**2, 2**	**1957,** *58,* **59,** *71*
Toluca	**2, 1**	**1956,** *61,* **89**
UANL	**2, 1**	**1976,** *90,* **96**
Veracruz	**1, 3**	**1948,** *50, 68, 95*
Monterrey	**1, 2**	*1964, 69,* **92**
Tampico	**1, 2**	*1960,* **61,** *62*
Unión de Guadalajara	**1, 2**	*1975,* **89,** *91*
España	**1, 0**	**1944**
Moctezuma	**1, 0**	**1947**
Tigres	**1, 0**	**1999**
UNAM	**1, 0**	**1975**
Ciudad Juarez	**0, 1**	*1992*
Irapuato	**0, 1**	*1956*
Morelia	**0, 1**	*1965*
Oro	**0, 1**	*1947*
Toros Neza	**0, 1**	*1997*
Torreón	**0, 1**	*1970*

Necaxa 1999–2000: *four times Mexican champions, the team was founded in Mexico City in 1923. Bought by Spanish businessmen in 1971, it played as Atlético Español until TV giant, Televisa, bought it in 1982 and renamed it Necaxa. It is currently planning to relocate outside Mexico City.*

MEXICO

Canada

The Canadian Soccer Association
Founded: 1912
Joined FIFA: 1912–28, 1946
Joined CONCACAF*: 1978

DESPITE FOOTBALL'S EARLY ARRIVAL, Canada proved stony ground for the development of the game. Clubs were forming in the last quarter of the 19th century and national cup and league competitions were established in 1912 and 1922 respectively, but the transition to a regular national professional league has proved elusive.

The game's lacklustre progression may be attributed to three factors. Firstly, the country's vast size makes the administration of a single, national competition difficult. Secondly, football faces fierce competition from the major North American sports of ice hockey, gridiron, baseball and basketball. Thirdly, as the names of leading clubs suggest, football has been a game for recent, non-Anglo immigrants: Toronto Scots and Ulsters, Eintracht Vancouver, Vancouver Croatia and Scarborough Azzurri, and has yet to really enter the mainstream.

The first attempt to create a modern professional league was the Eastern Canada Professional Soccer League. It lasted only five years, 1961–65, forcing top Canadian teams to play in various US leagues in the 1970s and 80s. A further attempt to professionalize and commercialize the game came with the Canadian Soccer League in 1987. It was disbanded in 1992. Again leading clubs have been forced into American pro leagues. The semi-professional Canadian Professional Soccer League was re-established in Ontario in 1998 and has so far survived and expanded into Quebec. Currently, plans exist for the amalgamation of the CPSL and the top professional clubs playing in America to form a national league.

* In 1999 CONCACAF was renamed the Football Confederation.

In 2000 Canada (in white) won the Gold Cup, beating Colombia 2-0 in the Final in Los Angeles. This was a major achievement for a team whose players almost all play outside their native country.

Canadian Soccer League Record 1987–1992

SEASON	CHAMPIONS	SEASON	CHAMPIONS
1987	Calgary Kickers	1990	Vancouver 86ers
1988	Vancouver 86ers	1991	Vancouver 86ers
1989	Vancouver 86ers	1992	Winnipeg Fury

Canadian Professional Soccer League Record 1998–2001

SEASON	CHAMPIONS	SEASON	CHAMPIONS
1998	St. Catharine's		
1999	Toronto Olympians		
2000	Toronto Croatia		
2001	St. Catharine's		

Canadian Challenge Cup Record 1913–2001

YEAR	WINNERS	YEAR	WINNERS
1913	Norwood Wanderers	1965	Vancouver Firefighters
1914	Norwood Wanderers	1966	British Columbia
1915	Winnipeg Scots	1967	Toronto
1916–18	*no competition*	1968	Toronto Royals
1919	Montreal Grand	1969	Columbus Vancouver
1920	Westinghouse Ontario	1970	*no competition*
1921	Toronto Scots	1971	Eintracht Vancouver
1922	Hillhurst Calgary	1972	New Westminster Blues
1923	Naniamo Wanderers	1973	Vancouver Firefighters
1924	Weston University	1974	Calgary Springer Kickers
1925	Toronto Ulsters		
1926	Weston University	1975	London Boxing Club Victoria
1927	Naniamo Wanderers		
1928	New Westminster Royals	1976	Victoria West SC
1929	CNR Montreal	1977	Columbus Vancouver
1930	New Westminster Royals	1978	Columbus Vancouver
1931	New Westminster Royals	1979	Victoria West SC
1932	Toronto Scots	1980	St. John Drydock
1933	Toronto Scots	1981	Toronto Ciociaro
1934	Verduns Montreal	1982	Victoria West SC
1935	Aldreds Montreal	1983	Vancouver Firefighters
1936	New Westminster Royals	1984	Victoria West SC
1937	Johnston Nationals	1985	Vancouver Croatia
1938	North Shore Vancouver	1986	Hamilton Steelers
1939	Radials Vancouver	1987	Lucania SC
1940–45	*no competition*	1988	Holy Cross
1946	Toronto Ulster United	1989	Scarborough Azzurri
1947	St. Andrews Vancouver	1990	Vancouver Firefighters
1948	Carsteel Montreal	1991	Norvan SC
1949	North Shore Vancouver	1992	Norvan SC
1950	Vancouver City	1993	West Side Rino
1951	Ulster United Toronto	1994	Edmonton Ital-Canadians
1952	Steelco Montreal		
1953	New Westminster Royals	1995	Mistral-Estrie
1954	Scottish Winnipeg	1996	Westside CIBC
1955	New Westminster Royals	1997	Edmonton Ital-Canadians
1956	Halecos Vancouver		
1957	Ukrainia SC Montreal	1998	RDP Condores
1958	New Westminster Royals	1999	Calgary CSFC
1959	Alouettes Montreal	2000	Luciana Winnipeg
1960	New Westminster Royals	2001	Halifax King of Donair
1961	Concordia Montreal		
1962	Scottish Winnipeg		
1963	*no competition*		
1964	Columbus Vancouver		

Central America

FOOTBALL IN CENTRAL AMERICA has had to compete with American sports, primarily baseball, for the affections and interest of fans and patrons. Where American influence (especially military influence) and occupation has been strongest, baseball has proved the winner, and football has been a minority sport in both Nicaragua and Panama. The region's strongest leagues have been traditionally in Costa Rica, Guatemala, Honduras and El Salvador. Football took off in the 1920s with leagues and clubs established in all of them. The Costa Rican league dates from 1921, the Salvadorian from 1926, and Guatemala began in 1919. Honduras has had formal tournaments since the 1920s but a properly constituted national league did not take off until 1965. All of these countries operate a complex national league system in which an opening championship (the Apertura) is followed by a closing (Clausura) championship. These are sometimes followed by a knockout competitions between the top six or eight teams in the league or with a final play-off between the winners of the two phases.

The centrality of football to popular culture and national identity in the region can be seen from an infamous event – the Futbal War. In 1969, El Salvador beat Honduras 3-2 in a World Cup qualifying match in Mexico City, following an unresolved two-leg play-off between the sides. This acted as the final trigger in a long-running border dispute between the states, and El Salvador invaded Honduras. Although little was resolved, over 2,000 people perished in the conflict.

Founded in 1935, Saprissa is one of the major teams in Costa Rica. Based in the capital, San José, it has won the Costa Rican League title over 20 times during its history.

* In 1999 CONCACAF was renamed the Football Confederation.

El Salvador

Federación Salvadoreña de Fútbol
Founded: 1935
Joined FIFA: 1938
Joined CONCACAF*: 1962

SEASON	LEAGUE CHAMPIONS
1997	Alianza FC
1998	Luis Angel Firpo
1999	Luis Angel Firpo
2000	Luis Angel Firpo
2001	CD Águila

Guatemala

Federación Nacional de Fútbol de Guatemala
Founded: 1919
Joined FIFA: 1933
Joined CONCACAF*: 1961

SEASON	LEAGUE CHAMPIONS
1998	Comunicaciones
1999	Comunicaciones
2000	(Apertura) Comunicaciones
2000	(Clausura) Municipal
2001	(Apertura) Municipal
2001	(Clausura) Comunicaciones
2002	(Apertura) Municipal
2002	(Clausura) Municipal

YEAR	CUP WINNERS
1998	Suchitepéquez
1999	Municipal
2000	*not known*
2001	*not known*
2002	Jalapa

Guyana

Guyana Football Association
Founded: 1902
Joined FIFA: 1968
Joined CONCACAF*: 1969

SEASON	LEAGUE CHAMPIONS
1997	Topp XX
1998	Santos FC
1999	*not known*
2000	*no championship*
2001	Fruta Conquerors

YEAR	CUP WINNERS
1998	Milerock
1999	Doc's Khelwalnas
2000	Topp XX
2001	Topp XX
2002	Victoria Kings

Honduras

Federación Nacional Autónoma de Fútbol de Honduras
Founded: 1951
Joined FIFA: 1951
Joined CONCACAF*: 1961

SEASON	LEAGUE CHAMPIONS
1998	Motagua
1999	Olimpia
2000	(Apertura) Motagua
2000	(Clausura) Motagua
2001	(Apertura) Olimpia
2001	(Clausura) Platense
2002	(Apertura) Motagua

Nicaragua

Federación Nicaraguense de Fútbol
Founded: 1931
Joined FIFA: 1950
Joined CONCACAF*: 1968

SEASON	LEAGUE CHAMPIONS
1998	Deportivo Walter Ferreti
1999	FC Real Estelí
2000	FC Diriangén
2001	Deportivo Walter Ferreti
2002	Jalapa

Panama

Federación Nacional de Fútbol de Panamá
Founded: 1937
Joined FIFA: 1938
Joined CONCACAF*: 1961

SEASON	LEAGUE CHAMPIONS
1997	Tauro FC
1998	Tauro FC
1999	Deportivo Árabe Unido
2000	Tauro FC
2001	Panamá Viejo FC

Surinam

Surinaamse Voetbal Bond
Founded: 1920
Joined FIFA: 1929
Joined CONCACAF*: 1961

SEASON	LEAGUE CHAMPIONS
1998	Transvaal
1999	SNL
2000	Transvaal
2001	Voorwaarts
2002	Voorwaarts

Belize

Belize National Football Association
Founded: 1980
Joined FIFA: 1986
Joined CONCACAF*: 1986

SEASON	LEAGUE CHAMPIONS
1997	Juventus
1998	Juventus
1999	Juventus
2000	Sagitún
2001	Kulture Yabra

Costa Rica

Federación Costarricense de Fútbol
Founded: 1921
Joined FIFA: 1921
Joined CONCACAF*: 1962

SEASON	LEAGUE CHAMPIONS
1998	Saprissa
1999	Saprissa
2000	Alajuelense
2001	Alajuelense
2002	Alajuelense

The Caribbean

THE CARIBBEAN

FOOTBALL IN THE CARIBBEAN has always been in fierce competition for players, fans and money with cricket, baseball and, increasingly, with basketball. Small populations and generally low incomes have made the competition fiercer and squeezed the space for football in the region. The strongest footballing traditions and leagues have been in Haiti, Cuba, Jamaica and Trinidad and Tobago.

Cuban football dates from the first decade of the 20th century, when it was played among Spaniards and Cubans educated in Britain. A league was established in the 1920s, and the first floodlit stadium in the region was built in Havana in 1928 – a subsequent wave of interest culminated in Cuba's appearance in the quarter-finals of the 1938 World Cup.

Football in Haiti dates from the same era with a national FA created in 1904, which became FIFA's first Caribbean member in 1933. Its most successful clubs, Violette Athlétique Club and Racing Club Haïtien, were founded in 1918 and 1923. Haiti was the first Caribbean nation to qualify for the World Cup Finals in 1974.

Jamaica's national FA was first established in 1910, joining FIFA after independence in 1962. Drawing on the increasingly large and dispersed global Jamaican diaspora, the national team qualified for the World Cup in 1998.

Trinidad and Tobago's national FA is even older (founded in 1908), though international success has eluded them both at club and national level.

Anguilla

Anguilla Football Association
Founded: 1990
Joined FIFA: 1996
Joined CONCACAF*: 1996

SEASON	LEAGUE CHAMPIONS
1997	*not known*
1998	Coca Cola Spartans Int.
1999	Attackers
2000	*no competition*
2001	Roaring Lions

Antigua and Barbuda

The Antigua Football Association
Founded: 1928
Joined FIFA: 1970
Joined CONCACAF*: 1980

SEASON	LEAGUE CHAMPIONS
1998	Empire
1999	Empire
2000	Empire
2001	Empire
2002	Parham FC

Aruba
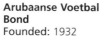

Arubaanse Voetbal Bond
Founded: 1932
Joined FIFA: 1988
Joined CONCACAF*: 1988

SEASON	LEAGUE CHAMPIONS
1997	SV River Plate Modiki
1998	SV Estrella
1999	SV Estrella
2000	Deportivo Nacional
2001	Deportivo Nacional

Bahamas

The Bahamas Football Association
Founded: 1967
Joined FIFA: 1968
Joined CONCACAF*: 1981

SEASON	LEAGUE CHAMPIONS
1997	Cavalier FC
1998	Cavalier FC
1999	Cavalier FC
2000	Abacom United FC
2001	Cavalier FC

Barbados

Barbados Football Association
Founded: 1910
Joined FIFA: 1968
Joined CONCACAF*: 1968

SEASON	LEAGUE CHAMPIONS
1997	Notre Dame SC
1998	Notre Dame SC
1999	Notre Dame SC
2000	Notre Dame SC
2001	Paradise

Bermuda

Bermuda Football Association
Founded: 1928
Joined FIFA: 1962
Joined CONCACAF*: 1966

SEASON	LEAGUE CHAMPIONS
1998	Vasco da Gama FC
1999	Vasco da Gama FC
2000	PHC Zebras
2001	Dandy Town Hornets SC
2002	North Village

British Virgin Islands

British Virgin Islands Football Association
Founded: 1974
Joined FIFA: 1996
Joined CONCACAF*: 1996

SEASON	LEAGUE CHAMPIONS
1998	BDO Binder Stingers (Black Lions)
1999	Veterans
2000	HBA Panthers
2001	HBA Panthers
2002	Future Stars United

YEAR	CUP WINNERS
1997	Beverley Kickers
1998	United Kickers
1999	*not known*
2000	Rangers
2001	*not known*

Cayman Islands

Cayman Islands Football Association
Founded: 1966
Joined FIFA: 1992
Joined CONCACAF*: 1992

SEASON	LEAGUE CHAMPIONS
1998	Scholars International
1999	Georgetown SC
2000	Western Union FC
2001	Scholars International
2002	Georgetown SC

Cuba

Associación de Fútbol de Cuba
Founded: 1924
Joined FIFA: 1933
Joined CONCACAF*: 1961

SEASON	LEAGUE CHAMPIONS
1998	Ciudad de la Habana
1999	*not known*
2000	FC Pinar del Río
2001	Ciudad de la Habana
2002	Ciego de Ávila

Dominica

Dominica Football Association
Founded: 1970
Joined FIFA: 1994
Joined CONCACAF*: 1994

SEASON	LEAGUE CHAMPIONS
1998	ACS Zebians
1999	Harlem Bombers
2000	Harlem Bombers
2001	Harlem Bombers
2002	Saint Joseph

Dominican Republic

Federación Dominicana de Fútbol
Founded: 1953
Joined FIFA: 1958
Joined CONCACAF*: 1964

SEASON	LEAGUE CHAMPIONS
1998	*no championship*
1999	FC Don Bosco
2000	*not known*
2001	CD Pantoja
2002	Baninter

Grenada

Grenada Football Association
Founded: 1924
Joined FIFA: 1976
Joined CONCACAF*: 1969

SEASON	LEAGUE CHAMPIONS
1997	Seven Seas Rock City
1998	Fontenoy United
1999	St. Andrews Football League Grenville
2000	DML Mutual Life Grenada Boys Secondary School St. George's
2001	Grenada Boys Secondary School St. George's

Haiti

Féderation Haïtienne de Football
Founded: 1904
Joined FIFA: 1933
Joined CONCACAF*: 1961

SEASON	LEAGUE CHAMPIONS
1997	AS Capoise
1998	FICA
1999	Violette Athlétique Club
2000	Racing Club Haïtien
2001	FICA

Jamaica

Jamaica Football Association
Founded: 1910
Joined FIFA: 1962
Joined CONCACAF*: 1961

SEASON	LEAGUE CHAMPIONS
1998	Waterhouse
1999	Tivoli Gardens
2000	Harbour View
2001	Arnett Gardens FC
2002	Arnett Gardens FC

Montserrat

Montserrat Football Association
Founded: not known
Joined FIFA: 1996
Joined CONCACAF*: 1996

Montserrat (continued)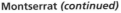

SEASON	LEAGUE CHAMPIONS
1997	abandoned
1998	abandoned
1999	abandoned
2000	Royal Montserrat Police Force
2001	Royal Montserrat Police Force

Netherlands Antilles

Nederlande Antilliaanse Voetbal Unie
Founded: 1921
Joined FIFA: 1932
Joined CONCACAF*: 1961

SEASON	LEAGUE CHAMPIONS
1997	UD Banda Bou
1998	Jong Colombia Boca Sami
1999	Jong Holland Willemstad
2000	Jong Colombia Boca Sami
2001	not known

Puerto Rico

Federación Puertorriqueña de Fútbol
Founded: 1940
Joined FIFA: 1960
Joined CONCACAF*: 1962

SEASON	LEAGUE CHAMPIONS
1998	Académicos de Quintana
1999	CF Nacional
2000	Académicos de Quintana
2001	Académicos de Quintana
2002	Académicos de Quintana

St Kitts and Nevis

St Kitts and Nevis Amateur Football Association
Founded: 1932
Joined FIFA: 1992
Joined CONCACAF*: 1992

SEASON	LEAGUE CHAMPIONS
1997	Newtown United
1998	Newtown United
1999	St. Paul's United
2000	no championship
2001	Garden Hotspurs FC

St Lucia

St Lucia National Football Union
Founded: 1979
Joined FIFA: 1988
Joined CONCACAF*: 1988

SEASON	LEAGUE CHAMPIONS
1997	Pioneers FC
1998	Mabouya Valley Rovers
1999	Roots Alley Ballers
2000	Roots Alley Ballers
2001	VSADC

St Vincent and the Grenadines

St Vincent and Grenadines Football Federation
Founded: 1979
Joined FIFA: 1988
Joined CONCACAF*: 1988

SEASON	LEAGUE CHAMPIONS
1997	ASC Le Geldar
1998	AS Jahouvey Mana
1999	AJ Saint-Georges
2000	AJ Saint-Georges
2001	Conquering Lions

Trinidad and Tobago

Trinidad and Tobago Football Association
Founded: 1908
Joined FIFA: 1963
Joined CONCACAF*: 1964

Trinidad and Tobago (continued)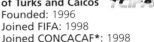

SEASON	LEAGUE CHAMPIONS
1997	Defence Force
1998	Joe Public FC
1999	Defence Force
2000	William's Connection FC
2001	William's Connection FC

Turks and Caicos Islands

Football Association of Turks and Caicos
Founded: 1996
Joined FIFA: 1998
Joined CONCACAF*: 1998

SEASON	LEAGUE CHAMPIONS
1999	Tropic All-Stars
2000	Masters
2001	SWA Sharks

U.S. Virgin Islands

USVI Soccer Federation
Founded: 1998
Joined FIFA: 1998
Joined CONCACAF*: 1998

SEASON	LEAGUE CHAMPIONS
2000	UWS Upsetters
2001	UWS Upsetters

* In 1999 CONCACAF was renamed Football Confederation.

Joe Public FC, based in Port of Spain, was runner-up in the Trinidad and Tobago League Championship in 1997, but the following year it took the title, and since then has remained one of the main teams on the island.

The CONCACAF and Gold Cups

TOURNAMENT OVERVIEW

THE FIRST INTERNATIONAL football tournament in the region was held as part of a local Olympic tournament in Havana in 1930. The organizing committee held two further games in 1935 and 1938 from which came the idea of an independent football tournament and organization. CCCF (Confederacion Centroamericano y del Caribe de Futbol) was set up in 1938 and held its first tournament in Costa Rica in 1941. The tournament's profile remained low for the next 30 years: the cost of participation was too high for most of the Caribbean teams, making it an exclusively Central American affair. The region's main football power, Mexico, did not participate, throwing its lot in with the US and Cuba in the North American Football Confederation.

This division was finally overcome with the formation of CONCACAF in 1963, which embraced the whole of the Americas outside CONMEBOL, and the first CONCACAF championship was held the same year. Low participation rates led to the 1973, 1977, 1981, 1985 and 1989 tournaments serving as qualifiers for the World Cups, but to no avail. With the accession of Trinidadian Chuck Blazer to the presidency of CONCACAF in 1991, the tournament was relaunched and rebranded as the Gold Cup. The name, designed to be more recognizable in the American market, was accompanied by increased sponsorship, invitations to Asian and South American teams and the promise of more tournaments hosted by the US.

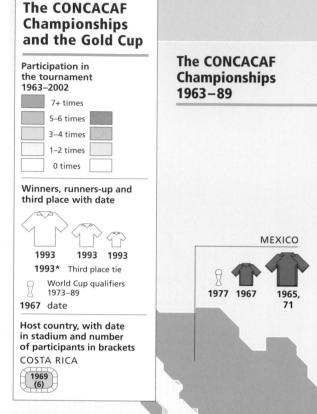

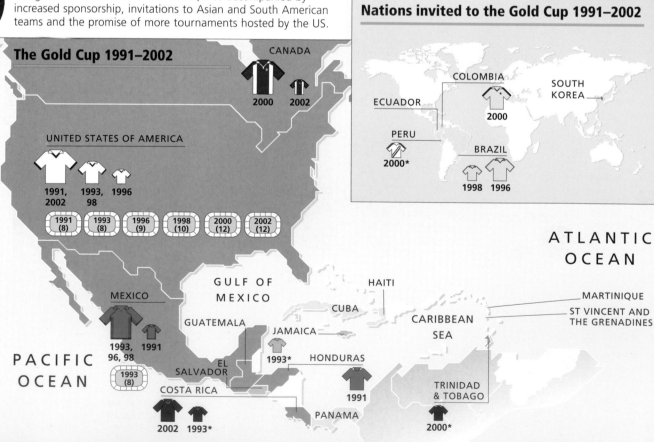

CANADA
1985

UNITED STATES
OF AMERICA

ATLANTIC
OCEAN

Cobi Jones (left) and Frankie Hejduk of the US men's national soccer team hold up the 2002 Gold Cup trophy after the 2-0 victory in the Final against Costa Rica at the Rose Bowl, Pasadena, California.

GUATEMALA

1967   1965,
        69

1965
(6)

GULF OF
MEXICO

CUBA

JAMAICA

HAITI

1971   1973

NETHERLANDS
ANTILLES

1963,
69

1971
(6)

TRINIDAD
& TOBAGO

HONDURAS

1981   1967

1967,
81 (6)

CARIBBEAN
SEA

SURINAM

NICARAGUA

PANAMA

EL SALVADOR

1963
(9)

1963

COSTA RICA

1963,   1965,   1989
69   71

1969
(6)

Mexico's three Gold Cup victories came in consecutive tournaments in the 1990s. In 1996, the Mexicans beat favourites Brazil, 2-0. Here, Villa and Davino combine to stop Caio's progress through midfield.

The Gold Cup 1991–2002

YEAR	WINNERS	SCORE	RUNNERS-UP
1991	USA	0-0 (4-3 pens)	Honduras
1993	Mexico	4-0	USA
1996	Mexico	2-0	Brazil
1998	Mexico	1-0	USA
2000	Canada	2-0	Colombia
2002	USA	2-0	Costa Rica

THE CONCACAF AND GOLD CUPS

461

The Globalization of Football

NATIONS, CLUBS AND FANS

THE GLOBALIZATION OF football takes many forms. In the first place it is simply the world's most popular sport and the membership of FIFA parallels the steady increase in the number of nations on the planet, as empires have crumbled and new states emerged. FIFA now has more members than the United Nations. FIFA was established by eight Western European nations in 1904, and by 1920 it had temporarily acquired the four British football associations, and its first North and South American members. In the 1920s, it expanded to take in more Europeans and Latin Americans, but the European empires in Asia and Africa gave little scope for new recruits. With the end of the Second World War a long wave of decolonization began which saw FIFA triple its membership by the mid-1980s as African, Caribbean and Asian states flooded in. With the break-up of the Soviet empire and Yugoslavia in the 1990s, a further expansion has taken place, supplemented by the inclusion of many small islands and dependent territories. The entry of Palestine into FIFA in 1998 is indicative of the importance of national football institutions in the creation of modern nations.

Club ownership

The ownership of clubs has nearly always been local, but a change is coming. Colonel Gadaffi's son has bought into Juventus and ENIC, a sports management company, has snapped up a portfolio of clubs in England, Greece and the Czech Republic. Even more common is the establishment of cross-border feeder clubs by some of Europe's biggest sides. The big clubs gain access to talent and scouting networks and a place to send their reserves for first-team action, while the small clubs get fees, and better access to big clubs' transfer budgets. In Spain and Germany, the phenomenon has been limited because the big clubs play their reserve sides in the lower leagues, so player loans are less necessary. But in England, the Netherlands and Italy, this option is not available and controls exist on multiple-club ownership. The Dutch have been the leading force in creating international feeder clubs. Ajax, in particular, has bought directly into and transformed Ajax Cape Town (formed after two former Cape Town clubs were bought and merged) and Obuasi Goldfields. Feyenoord and PSV have followed suit, as have leading English, Scottish and Italian clubs.

Today, the global reach of some football clubs is greater than ever. Clubs like Manchester United and Real Madrid have become global footballing brands, riding their waves of TV-transmitted glory. United in particular has capitalized on its fame, establishing massive support (and income streams) in South-East Asia and Scandinavia. Other clubs have similar ambitions. Football shirts of the world's leading clubs will soon be more commonly seen than advertisements for soft drinks in the world's more out-of-the-way places.

FIFA Membership

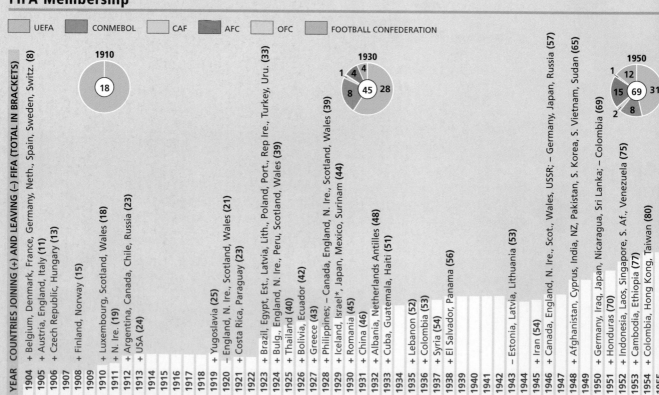

Legend: UEFA · CONMEBOL · CAF · AFC · OFC · FOOTBALL CONFEDERATION

1910: 18

1930: 45, 28, 8, 1, 4, 4

1950: 69, 31, 15, 2, 8, 1, 12

YEAR	COUNTRIES JOINING (+) AND LEAVING (−) FIFA (TOTAL IN BRACKETS)
1904	+ Belgium, Denmark, France, Germany, Neth., Spain, Sweden, Switz. (8)
1905	+ Austria, England, Italy (11)
1906	+ Czech Republic, Hungary (13)
1907	
1908	+ Finland, Norway (15)
1909	
1910	+ Luxembourg, Scotland, Wales (18)
1911	+ N. Ire. (19)
1912	+ Argentina, Canada, Chile, Russia (23)
1913	+ USA (24)
1914	
1915	
1916	
1917	
1918	
1919	+ Yugoslavia (25)
1920	− England, N. Ire., Scotland, Wales (21)
1921	+ Costa Rica, Paraguay (23)
1922	
1923	+ Brazil, Egypt, Est., Latvia, Lith., Poland, Port., Rep Ire., Turkey, Uru. (33)
1924	+ Bulg., England, N. Ire., Peru, Scotland, Wales (39)
1925	+ Thailand (40)
1926	+ Bolivia, Ecuador (42)
1927	+ Greece (43)
1928	+ Philippines; − Canada, England, N. Ire., Scotland, Wales (39)
1929	+ Iceland, Israel*, Japan, Mexico, Surinam (44)
1930	+ Romania (45)
1931	+ China (46)
1932	+ Albania, Netherlands Antilles (48)
1933	+ Cuba, Guatemala, Haiti (51)
1934	
1935	+ Lebanon (52)
1936	+ Colombia (53)
1937	+ Syria (54)
1938	+ El Salvador, Panama (56)
1939	
1940	
1941	
1942	
1943	− Estonia, Latvia, Lithuania (53)
1944	
1945	+ Iran (54)
1946	+ Canada, England, N. Ire., Scot., Wales, USSR; − Germany, Japan, Russia (57)
1947	
1948	+ Afghanistan, Cyprus, India, NZ, Pakistan, S. Korea, S. Vietnam, Sudan (65)
1949	
1950	+ Germany, Iraq, Japan, Nicaragua, Sri Lanka; − Colombia (69)
1951	+ Honduras (70)
1952	+ Indonesia, Laos, Singapore, S. Af., Venezuela (75)
1953	+ Cambodia, Ethiopia (77)
1954	+ Colombia, Hong Kong, Taiwan (80)
1955	

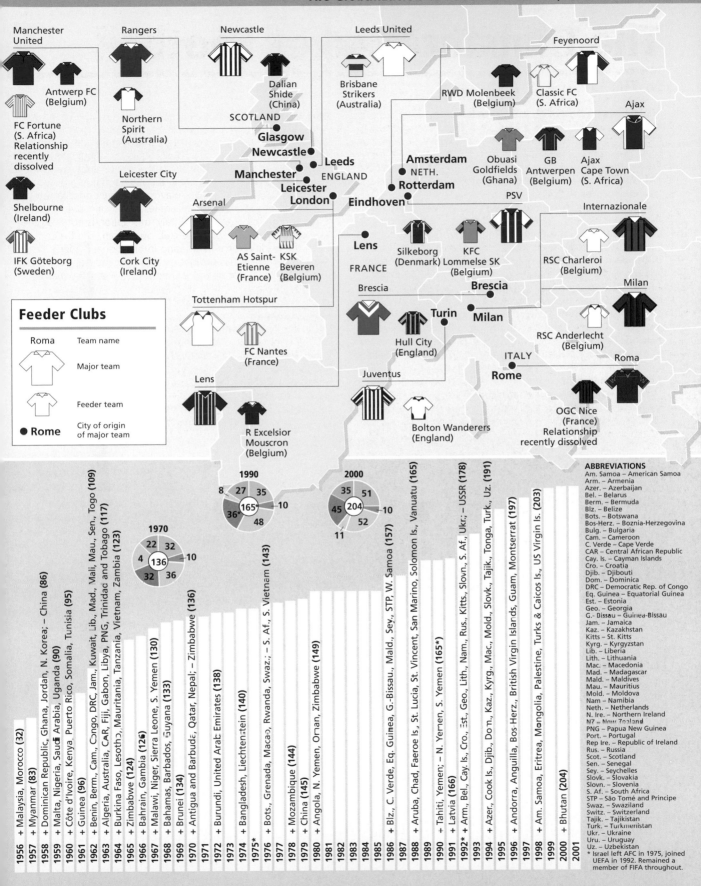

The Transfer Market

BUYERS, SELLERS AND RECORD-BREAKERS

THE TRANSFER MARKET

THE EXISTENCE OF THE TRANSFER MARKET arose from the introduction of player registration. Beginning in England with the establishment of professionalism, anyone who wanted to play professional football was required to register with the FA. However, the registration was held by the club, not by the player. If the player wanted to move to another club, that club would have to buy his registration; but selling clubs were under no obligation to release a player. Registration created a potential income stream for clubs and gave them enormous control over their players.

Transfer fees were regularly paid for players in England and Scotland in the early years of the 20th century. But the first escalation in the importance of transfers came in 1925 when Torino bought Julio Libonatti from Newell's Old Boys in Argentina. At the end of the Second World War, it was clear that the biggest resources lay with Italian clubs who steadily increased the world record transfer fee to £500,000 when Juventus bought Pietro Anastasi from Varese in 1968. As more money has come into the global game, the fees have risen further and faster. Diego Maradona's transfers in the early 1980s were another step up, and the arrival of pay-per-view TV and contemporary commercialism has sent the record through the roof – and seen the mantle of biggest spending clubs shift from Italy to Spain.

The Bosman breakthrough

All through the 20th century, players' unions in Britain, Italy and Latin America have sought to challenge this system of contracts. There has been some shift in the balance of power between players and clubs, but it was only in 1995 that the almost medieval system of control was decisively broken. The European court ruled, in the case of Belgian player Jean-Marc Bosman, that a selling club could not demand a fee from the buyer if a player's contract has finished. In effect, this meant that contracted players were assets of declining value, as they became free agents when their contracts ended. The peculiarities of the football labour market and transfer system clearly became apparent to the European Union; in 1999, they embarked on negotiations with UEFA, the international players' union FIFpro and FIFA, to bring them into line with European labour law. The new contract system, hammered out in 2001, will have global scope, allowing some payments for transfers of under-23 players when a club has nurtured and developed them, but otherwise transfer fees for out-of-contract players will become a thing of the past.

However, the fact remains that if a club wants a player badly enough, and it has the financial resources, it will buy him. It seems only a matter of time before the £50 million transfer fee becomes a reality.

Top Sales

Parma	Team name
	Team shirt
5	Number of sales in top 40 transfers
● Parma	City of origin

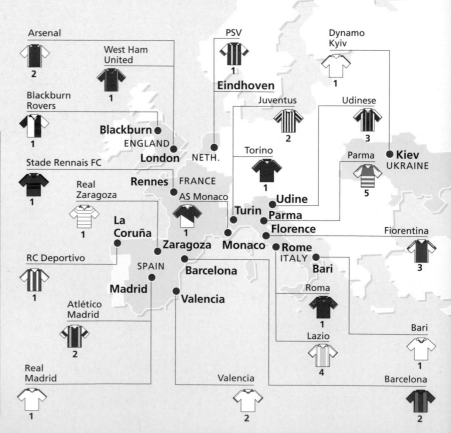

Top 40 Transfers*

FEE (millions)	NAME	FROM	TO	YEAR
£45.8	Zidane	Juventus	Real Madrid	2001
£37.5	Figo	Barcelona	Real Madrid	2000
£36	Crespo	Parma	Lazio	2000
£32.6	Buffon	Parma	Juventus	2001
£32	Vieri	Lazio	Internazionale	1999
£28	Rui Costa	Fiorentina	Milan	2001
£28	Veron	Lazio	Manchester United	2001
£27	Mendieta	Valencia	Lazio	2001
£25.5	Nedved	Lazio	Juventus	2001
£22	Annelka	Arsenal	PSG	2000
£22	Batistuta	Fiorentina	Roma	2000
£22	Denilson	São Paulo	Real Betis	1998
£22	Thuram	Parma	Juventus	2001
£20	Lõpez	Valencia	Lazio	2000
£20	Overmars	Arsenal	Barcelona	2000
£20	Saviola	River Plate	Barcelona	2001
£19.1	Nakata	Roma	Parma	2001
£19	Cassano	Bari	Roma	2001
£19	van Nistelrooy	PSV	Manchester United	2001
£19	Vieri	Atlético Madrid	Lazio	1998
£18	Amoroso	Udinese	Parma	1999
£18	Ferdinand	West Ham United	Leeds United	2001
£18	Ronaldo	Barcelona	Internazionale	1997
£18	Toldo	Fiorentina	Internazionale	2001
£18	Veron	Parma	Lazio	1999
£17	Inzhagi	Juventus	Milan	2001
£16.2	Shevchenko	Dynamo Kyiv	Milan	1999
£16	Milosevic	Real Zaragoza	Parma	2000
£16	Rivaldo	RC Deportivo	Barcelona	1997
£15.8	Amoroso	Parma	Borussia Dortmund	2001
£15	Hasselbaink	Atlético Madrid	Chelsea	2000
£15	Shearer	Blackburn Rovers	Newcastle United	1995
£14.9	Fiore	Udinese	Lazio	2001
£14.6	Almeyda	Lazio	Parma	2000
£14.6	Giannichedda	Udinese	Lazio	2001
£14	Trezeguet	Monaco	Juventrus	2000
£13.5	Nonda	Stade Rennais	Monaco	2000
£13.5	Seedorf	Real Madrid	Internazionale	1999
£13	Lentini	Torino	Milan	1992
£13	Samuel	Boca Juniors	Roma	2000

* Data correct up to May 2002

Inter president Massimo Moratti has spent more and more wildly over the past decade – more than any other club president in Europe – and still no Scudetto.

Parma, UEFA Cup winners 1998: With little footballing tradition and a tiny support base Parma has survived in the top flight with the money from Parmalat. Funds have been used to buy and sell players like Lillian Thuram (back row, third from left) for significant profit.

Record-breaking transfers

POUNDS STERLING (MILLIONS)

TRANSFERRED FROM		TRANSFERRED TO
2001 Zinedine Zidane (Juventus)		(Real Madrid)
2000 Luis Figo (Barcelona)		(Real Madrid)
1999 Christian Vieri (Lazio)		(Internazionale)
1998 Denilson (São Paulo)		(Real Betis)
1997 Ronaldo (Barcelona)		(Internazionale)
1995 Alan Shearer (Blackburn Rovers)		(Newcastle United)
1992 Gianluigi Lentini (Torino)		(Milan)

Top Buys

Lazio — Team name

Team shirt

7 — Number of buys in top 40 transfers

● Rome — City of origin

Financial Affairs

THE WORLD'S RICHEST CLUBS

IN THE LAST 15 YEARS, since the arrival of satellite and pay-per-view television, money has flooded into European football – so much so that not a single Latin American club is represented in the top 30 richest clubs. Within Europe, the biggest leagues financially (in descending order) are in England, Italy, Spain, Germany and France. Italy and England have 14 of the top 20 clubs between them. Manchester United remains the richest club on the planet, but Real Madrid, Bayern München and the Italian giants are all chasing hard. Lower down the list, the bigger French and German clubs get a look in as well as the two big Glasgow clubs, Ajax of Amsterdam and the leading Turkish club, Galatasaray.

The financial and commercial pressures at the apex of European football have seen a transformation in the form of ownership and regulation of big clubs. In Italy, Scotland and England, leading clubs have been floated on the stock market (as well as partial flotations at Ajax, Galatasaray and Borussia Dortmund). The leading Portuguese and Danish clubs have followed suit, but without much hope of reaching even the lower end of the rich list. However, the very poor performance of most football stocks has dampened the enthusiasm of investors and clubs like Internazionale, Milan, Schalke 04 and Hertha Berlin have all abandoned proposed IPOSs. In Spain, *socios* (fan-owner groups) continue to control the giants Barcelona and Real Madrid. In France, Germany and Turkey, clubs are changing their legal status to create commercial arms that can receive external investment and pay dividends. French clubs remain disadvantaged by the much higher employment and social security costs of star players.

The enormous amount of money at stake among the leading clubs saw the formation of the G-14 in 1988. This pressure group, made up of the leading European clubs, has lobbied hard for its member's interests with UEFA, FIFA and the European commission: limiting international call-ups for expensive players, mooting the formation of a European

Super League, pushing for the expansion of the Champions League and the redistribution of income. The lower reaches of professional football are bogged down in actual or impending bankruptcy all across Europe. It is clear that the value of TV rights has peaked, and the collapse of a number of TV companies and deals looks set to make problems worse. Though most of the elite clubs will be relatively unscathed, no team is invulnerable, as the fate of Fiorentina illustrates. A top 20 club in 2001, it spent most of 2002 in and out of insolvency courts.

Shirts of the biggest football clubs are now a common sight around the world. These Manchester United fans are hoping for good luck by meeting at a shrine in Tokyo dedicated to the Japanese God Daibutsu prior to the Toyota Cup Final in 1999 between United and Palmeiras.

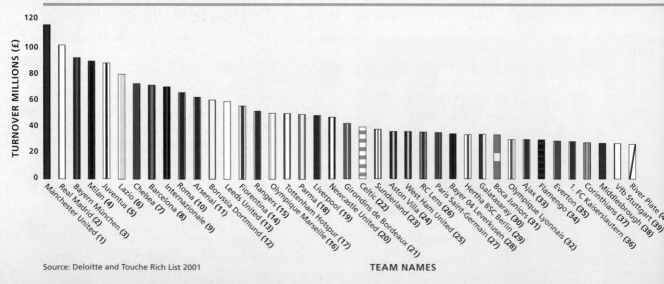

The World's Richest Clubs 2000

TURNOVER MILLIONS (£)

Manchester United (1), Real Madrid (2), Bayern München (3), Milan (4), Juventus (5), Lazio (6), Chelsea (7), Barcelona (8), Internazionale (9), Roma (10), Arsenal (11), Borussia Dortmund (12), Leeds United (13), Fiorentina (14), Rangers (15), Olympique Marseille (16), Tottenham Hotspur (17), Parma (18), Liverpool (19), Newcastle United (20), Girondins de Bordeaux (21), Celtic (22), Sunderland (23), Aston Villa (24), West Ham United (25), RC Lens (26), Paris Saint-Germain (27), Bayer 04 Leverkusen (28), Hertha BSC Berlin (29), Galatasaray (30), Boca Juniors (31), Olympique Lyonnais (32), Ajax (33), Flamengo (34), Everton (35), 1. FC Kaiserslautern (36), Middlesbrough (37), Corinthians (38), VfB Stuttgart (39), River Plate (40)

TEAM NAMES

Source: Deloitte and Touche Rich List 2001

FINANCIAL AFFAIRS

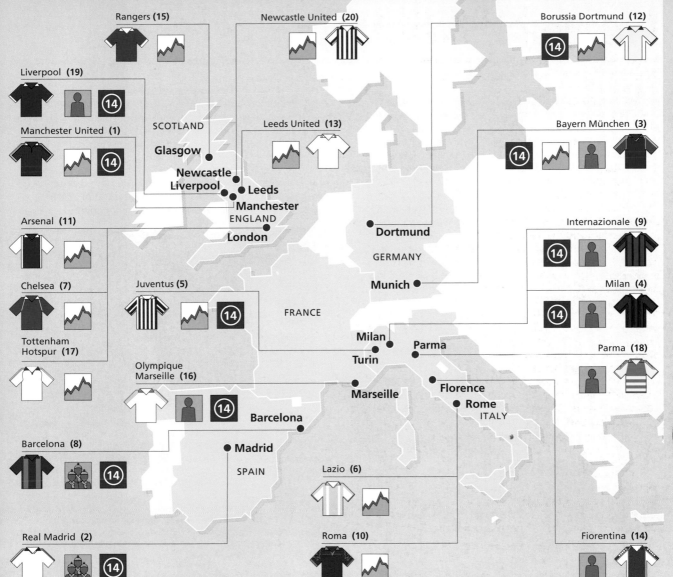

Rangers (15)

Newcastle United (20)

Borussia Dortmund (12)

Liverpool (19)

Bayern München (3)

Manchester United (1)

Leeds United (13)

SCOTLAND

Glasgow

Newcastle
Liverpool   Leeds

Manchester

ENGLAND

London

Internazionale (9)

Arsenal (11)

Dortmund

GERMANY

Milan (4)

Munich

Chelsea (7)

Juventus (5)

FRANCE

Milan   Parma

Turin

Parma (18)

Tottenham
Hotspur (17)

Olympique
Marseille (16)

Florence

Rome
ITALY

Marseille

Barcelona

Madrid

SPAIN

Barcelona (8)

Lazio (6)

Real Madrid (2)

Roma (10)

Fiorentina (14)

467

Europe's Richest Clubs 2000

Team Shirt	Manchester United (1) — Team name (and wealth ranking)

 Privately Owned

Socios

Flotation

 Group of 14

Ajax, Porto, PSG and PSV are also members of the Group of 14

Salary Comparison in Deutschmarks (Thousands)

	ENGLAND	ITALY	SPAIN	GERMANY	FRANCE
Player's net income (e.g.)	75	75	75	75	75
Player's taxes and social security	48	62.4	65.5	74	100.5
Club's social security	14.7	2.5	1.5	1.6	52.8
Gross cost to club	**137.7**	**139.9**	**142**	**150.6**	**228.3**

TV Rights Income for the Top European Leagues 2001–02

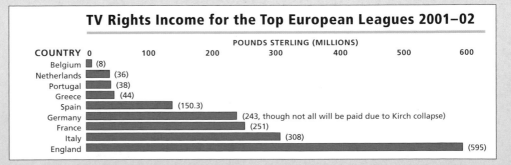

POUNDS STERLING (MILLIONS)

COUNTRY	0	100	200	300	400	500	600

Belgium (8)
Netherlands (36)
Portugal (38)
Greece (44)
Spain (150.3)
Germany (243, though not all will be paid due to Kirch collapse)
France (251)
Italy (308)
England (595)

Football Stadiums

THE LARGEST GROUNDS AND STADIUM DISASTERS

THE GREAT FOOTBALL STADIUMS OF THE WORLD are truly some of the most extraordinary structures of the 20th century. Enormous national stadiums have been built by governments hoping to benefit from the nationalism and grandeur generated by the international game. Modernist cathedrals have been created by the great clubs in pursuit of money and vanity. Yet although many stadiums are architectural triumphs, others are prime examples of appalling town planning.

While money has always been available for constructing stadiums to grand designs, the money and time necessary to make them safe has not. England and Scotland, the first countries to host truly enormous football crowds, have among the poorest stadium safety records of the Western nations. Outside of Europe, the precarious state of football's infrastructure compared to the size of crowds is most stark in Africa, where in 2000 alone four separate stadium disasters saw over 100 people killed. In Latin America persistent crowd trouble and undisciplined policing has added to this dangerous cocktail, making repeated disaster, death and injury at major football matches almost inevitable.

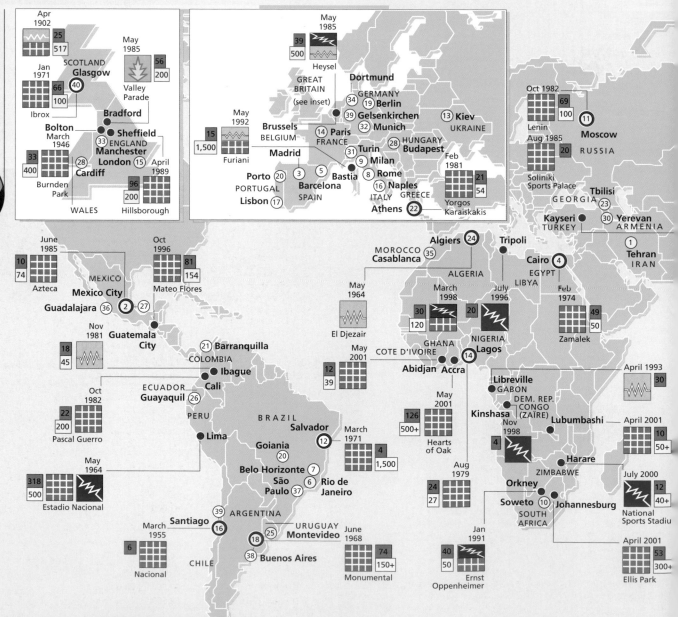

The Mario Filho stadium in Rio de Janeiro was opened in 1950 with 140,000 seats plus standing room for 40,000. Better known as the Maracana, it is the biggest stadium the world has ever seen, but a renovation in 1965 reduced its capacity to 95,095.

Key

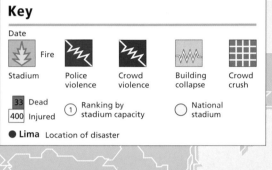

A fire at Bradford City's Valley Parade ground, England, in 1985 claimed the lives of 56 supporters and injured hundreds of others. This disaster led to new legislation governing the safety of British sports grounds.

Top 40 Stadiums (by capacity)

RANK	STADIUM	CAPACITY	TEAMS
1	Azadi, Iran	120,000	Piroozi, Esteghlal, Pas Club, Saypa, Bank Melli
1	Saltlake, India	120,000	Mohammedan FC, Mohun Bagan AC, East Bengal Club
2	Azteca, Mexico	109,815	Atlante, América, Necaxa
3	Santiago Bernabeu, Spain	106,500	Real Madrid
4	Nasser International Stadium, Egypt	100,000	Al Ahly, Zamalek
5	Nou Camp, Spain	98,600	Barcelona
6	Maracana, Brazil	95,095	Flamengo, Fluminense
7	Magalhaes Pinto, Brazil	90,464	Cruzeiro, Atlético Mineiro
8	Olimpico, Italy	86,517	Roma, Lazio
9	Giuseppe Meazza, Italy	85,700	Milan, Internazionale
10	FNB, South Africa	85,000	Orlando Pirates
11	Luzhniki, Russia	84,745	Spartak Moskva, Torpedo Moskva
12	Octavio Mangabeira, Brazil	82,500	Bahia
13	Olimpiyskiy, Ukraine	82,000	Dynamo Kyiv
14	Shahalam, Malaysia	80,000	Selangor
14	Shanghai, China	80,000	Shanghai Shenhua
14	Stade de France, France	80,000	
14	Surelere St, Nigeria	80,000	
15	Wembley, England	79,045	
16	Nacional, Chile	78,000	Universidad De Chile
16	San Paolo, Italy	78,000	Napoli
17	Estadio Da Luz, Portugal	77,844	SL Benfica
18	A.V.Liberti, Argentina	76,689	River Plate
19	Olympiastadion, Germany	76,243	Hertha BSC Berlin
20	Das Antas, Portugal	76,000	FC Porto
20	Serra Dourada, Brazil	76,000	Goias
21	Metroplitano, Colombia	75,000	Atlético Júnior
22	Spyros Louis, Greece	74,770	Panathinaikos, Olympiakos
23	Boris Paichadze, Georgia	74,380	Dinamo Tbilisi, FC Tbilisi
24	El Djezair, Algeria	74,000	
25	Centenario, Uruguay	73,609	Nacional, Peñarol
26	Isidoro Romero Cabro, Ecuador	73,000	Barcelona
27	Olimpico Universitario, Mexico	72,400	UNAM
28	Millennium, Wales	72,000	
28	Nepstadion, Hungary	72,000	
29	Worker's, China	70,000	Beijing Guoan
29	Yokohama International, Japan	70,000	Yokohama Marinos
30	Hrazdan, Armenia	69,500	Kilikia Yerevan, FK Yerevan
31	Delle Alpi, Italy	69,041	Juventus, Torino
32	Olimpiastadion, Germany	69,000	Bayern München, TSV 1860 München
33	Old Trafford, England	68,936	Manchester United
34	Westfalenstadion, Germany	68,600	Borussia Dortmund
35	Mohammed V, Morocco	67,000	WAC Casablanca, Raja Casablanca
36	Estadio Jalisco, Mexico	66,000	Atlas
37	Cicero Pompeu De Toldedo, Brazil	65,000	São Paulo
38	Presidente Perón, Argentina	64,161	Racing Club
39	David Arellano, Chile	62,500	Colo Colo
39	Park Stadion, Germany	62,500	FC Schalke 04
40	Celtic Park, Scotland	60,953	Celtic

Playing Styles

THE EARLIEST STYLES OF FOOTBALL were overwhelmingly attack oriented, with the emphasis on individuals dribbling with the ball while protected by their teammates. The introduction of the offside rule in 1867 limited this system and also prevented the problem of long balls and 'goal hanging'. Early innovations in England and Scotland shifted the emphasis from dribbling and hoofing the ball to quick, short passes and the increased use of space and movement on the pitch. Early pioneers of this style included the Royal Engineers and the 12 clubs who founded the English FA, as well as Scottish professionals and coaches in England and throughout Europe.

Key to Abbreviations

(GK) - Goalkeeper
(FB) - Full-back
(LB) - Left-back
(RB) - Right-back
(3/4B) - 3/4-back
(CB) - Centre-back
(LCB) - Left centre-back

(RCB) - Right centre-back
(HB) - Half-back
(WH) - Wing-half
(M) - Midfielder
(F) - Forward

(IF) - Inside-forward
(CF) - Centre-forward
(C) - Centre
(W) - Winger
(LW) - Left-winger
(RW) - Right-winger
opp. - Opposition

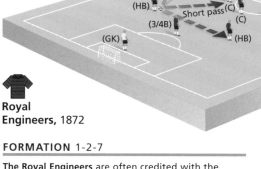

Royal Engineers, 1872

FORMATION 1-2-7

The Royal Engineers are often credited with the development of the first innovative football formations and tactics. The standard 1-2-7 formation was subtly adapted with the seven forwards split into four wingers and three centre-forwards, and the long ball and charge supplemented with short passes.

FORMATION 2-3-5

With the advent of short passing, two forwards were brought back to protect the defence, exemplified by Preston North End's league winning 2-3-5 formation. Defenders covered attacking forwards, the half-backs patrolled the wings and the centre-back in midfield was free to move from defence to attack as required.

Preston North End, 1888

Arsenal, 1926

FORMATION M-W

M-W, perfected by Herbert Chapman's Arsenal team in the 1920s, was a response to the change in the offside rule. Strict man-marking in the back three and withdrawn inside-forwards were complemented by passing through the midfield to the centre-forward, inside-forwards and wingers.

FORMATION M-U

The great Hungarian side retained the old M formation at the back but innovated at the front. A deep-lying centre-forward pulled the opposition markers out of position leaving space for the inside-forwards to raid the opposition box, helped by the fact that they were not required to track back in defence.

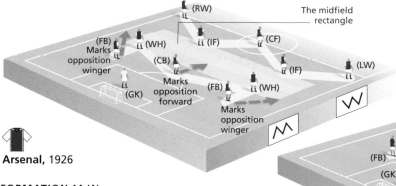

Hungary, 1953

The Development of Formations

| 1860 | 1870 | 1880 | 1890 | 1920 | 1930 | 1940 |

Pre-1867 Pre-eminence of dribbling

1867 Offside rule first introduced

1870s First formations emerge – attributed to the Royal Engineers playing 1-2-7

1880s Passing game and wing play, developed particularly in Scotland, begin to transform the game and push more players into midfield

1888–90 Preston North End (the Invincibles), win the first professional league with settled 2-3-5 formation

1925 Change in the offside rule

1934 Karl Rappan introduces the sweeper into the Swiss game

A new 2-3-5 formation was the mainstay of professional football at the start of the 20th century. However, its limits were soon discovered, and the offside rule gave ample opportunity for quick full-backs to exploit it. In response, play was often confined to a narrow strip near the halfway line. Revisions to the offside rule were capitalized on by Herbert Chapman's M-W formation, which became the standard formation for the next 30 years.

Outside Britain, tactical innovation continued in the inter-war era. Karl Rappan in Switzerland began to develop an early version of *catenaccio*, while the technical virtuosity of central Europeans encouraged a greater emphasis on midfield play and accurate passing. The rise of the European game was confirmed by Hungary's historic 6-3 victory over England at Wembley in 1953.

In the 1960s and 1970s the flat back four was introduced. *Catenaccio* was perfected by Helenio Herrera's Internazionale, and the sweeper role was given an attacking edge by Franz Beckenbauer's Bayern München. Most exciting of all, Ajax and then Holland played total football, in which all players were required to take up whatever position and role the play of the game dictated. In the 1990s, the 4-4-2 system has come to dominate the global game, with only the occasional side braving the reintroduction of wing-backs in flexible 3-5-2/5-3-2 systems.

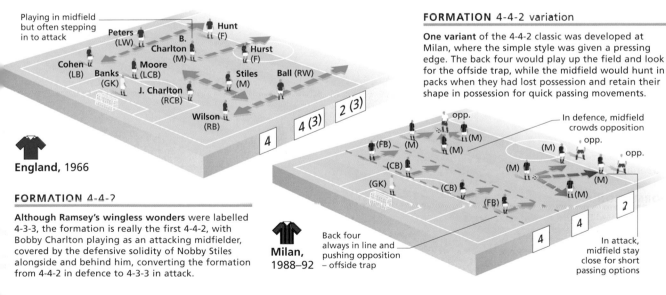

Brazil, 1958

FORMATION 4-2-4

The flat back four was invented in part to counter the innovations of the Hungarians. Centre-backs zonally marked the inside-forwards, while attacking full-backs supported the two-man midfield. Brazil's outstanding 1958 team combined this with the necessary midfield genius of a playmaker like Garrincha.

England, 1966

FORMATION 4-4-2

Although Ramsey's wingless wonders were labelled 4-3-3, the formation is really the first 4-4-2, with Bobby Charlton playing as an attacking midfielder, covered by the defensive solidity of Nobby Stiles alongside and behind him, converting the formation from 4-4-2 in defence to 4-3-3 in attack.

FORMATION 1-4-3-2

Catenaccio, meaning 'bolt' in Italian, combines a flat back four with a sweeper playing behind them. The back four man-mark and pressure the opposition, any spaces being filled by the patrolling sweeper. Very tight defence needed to be combined with speedy counter-attacks and rapid passes out of defence.

Internazionale, 1963

FORMATION 4-4-2 variation

One variant of the 4-4-2 classic was developed at Milan, where the simple style was given a pressing edge. The back four would play up the field and look for the offside trap, while the midfield would hunt in packs when they had lost possession and retain their shape in possession for quick passing movements.

Milan, 1988–92

PLAYING STYLES

THE SHIFTING BALANCE

The Football Confederation

CONFEDERATION RANKING	WORLD RANKING	COUNTRY
1	7	Mexico
2	13	USA
3	26	Honduras
4	29	Costa Rica
5	35	Trinidad & Tobago

Data correct for May 2002

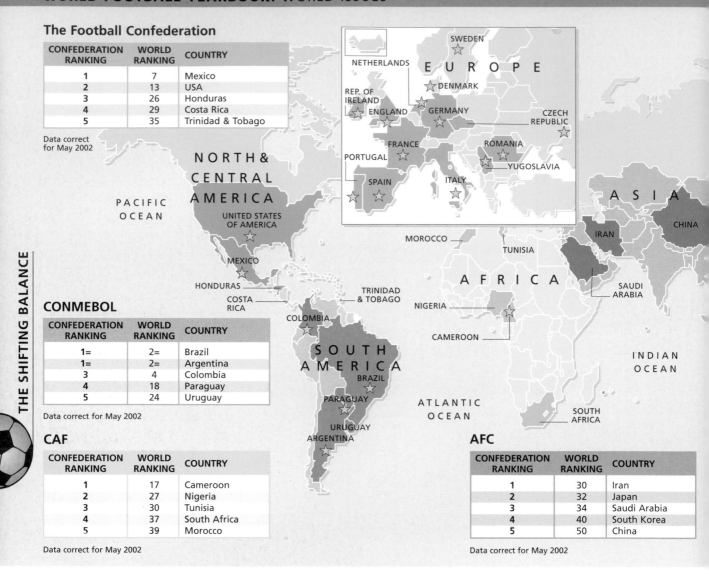

CONMEBOL

CONFEDERATION RANKING	WORLD RANKING	COUNTRY
1=	2=	Brazil
1=	2=	Argentina
3	4	Colombia
4	18	Paraguay
5	24	Uruguay

Data correct for May 2002

CAF

CONFEDERATION RANKING	WORLD RANKING	COUNTRY
1	17	Cameroon
2	27	Nigeria
3	30	Tunisia
4	37	South Africa
5	39	Morocco

Data correct for May 2002

AFC

CONFEDERATION RANKING	WORLD RANKING	COUNTRY
1	30	Iran
2	32	Japan
3	34	Saudi Arabia
4	40	South Korea
5	50	China

Data correct for May 2002

The Shifting Balance

POWER IN WORLD FOOTBALL

Just who is the best team in the world? Which nations are on the up and which are on the way down? Where is football's centre of gravity? A simple way of addressing this question is to look at World Cup results. Latin America and Europe are the only regional contenders, as no team from another continent had ever even made the semi-finals until the South Koreans' extraordinary progress in 2002. Given that South America has a fifth of the membership of UEFA, its performance at the World Cup is extraordinary, and almost wholly dependent on three nations: Argentina, Uruguay and Brazil. At club level, there are too few points of real comparison (apart from the World Club Cup), though on a financial level it is clear that Europe, and Western Europe in particular, stands head and shoulders above everyone.

But World Cup results tell just one strand, albeit an important one, of football's shifting balance of power. At a political and institutional level the make-up of FIFA, where every nation has one vote, is instructive. For the first 40 years of its existence, FIFA had a European majority and a major Latin American lobby group. Since the 1960s, the growth of African and Asian membership has made them the majority. Looking at results over time, FIFA's ranking system, first calculated in 1993, provides a rolling measure of national and continental strengths. Ratings are calculated by looking at results over the previous six years, factoring in the strength of the opposition and the importance of tournaments and competitive matches. At the turn of the century, Europe continues to dominate the top 20, Latin America takes three or four spots and occasional visitors include Mexico, Nigeria and Japan. However, FIFA's rankings give undue emphasis to a team's best performances, and allows many of its poor performances to be discounted. It also looks at the game over a very long period, and is often out of kilter with more contemporary form.

FIFA's Top 20 Ranked Nations

RANK	1993	1997	2001
1	Germany	Brazil	France
2	Italy	Germany	Argentina
3	Brazil	Czech Republic	Brazil
4	Norway	England	Portugal
5	Spain	Mexico	Colombia
6	Denmark	France	Italy
7	Netherlands	Romania	Spain
8	Argentina	Denmark	Netherlands
9	Sweden	Italy	Mexico
10	Rep. of Ireland	Colombia	England
11	England	Spain	Germany
12	Switzerland	Russia	Yugoslavia
13	Romania	Norway	Czech Republic
14	Russia	Japan	Paraguay
15	France	Morocco	Romania
16	Mexico	Chile	Sweden
17	Uruguay	Argentina	Denmark
18	Nigeria	Sweden	Rep. of Ireland
19	Czech Republic	Croatia	Croatia
20	Portugal	Yugoslavia	Belgium

UEFA

CONFEDERATION RANKING	WORLD RANKING	COUNTRY
1	1	France
2	5	Portugal
3	6	Italy
4	8	Spain
5	9	Netherlands
6	10	Yugoslavia
7	11	Germany
8	12	England
9	14	Romania
10=	15=	Rep. of Ireland
10=	15=	Czech Republic

Data correct for May 2002

OFC

CONFEDERATION RANKING	WORLD RANKING	COUNTRY
1	48	Australia
2	85	New Zealand
3	125	Fiji
4	128	Tahiti
5	137	Solomon Islands

Data correct for May 2002

World Cup performance

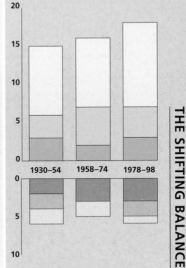

Back where they belong: Rivaldo (left) and Ronaldo celebrate Brazil's fifth World Cup triumph in Yokohama, Japan, in June 2002 – a victory that is sure to see them return to the top of the FIFA rankings.

Key to Confederation Rankings

UEFA, CONMEBOL, CAF, AFC, OFC, FOOTBALL CONFEDERATION

Top 5 (Europe Top 10)
Members
Associate members
Non-members
☆ Current top 20 World Rankings (as of May 2002)

Make up of FIFA by Confederation

UEFA, CONMEBOL, CAF, AFC, OFC, THE FOOTBALL CONFEDERATION

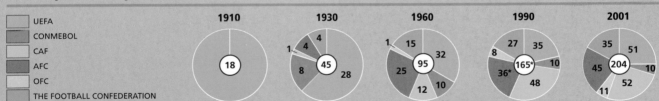

1910: 18
1930: 45 (4, 1, 4, 8, 28)
1960: 95 (1, 15, 32, 10, 12, 25)
1990: 165* (27, 35, 10, 48, 36*, 8)
2001: 204 (35, 51, 10, 52, 11, 45)

* See page 462-463 for details on Israel

African Exodus

PLAYERS ON THE MOVE

THE EXTRAORDINARY RISE AND ENDURING PROBLEMS of African football are reflected in the migration of Africa's top players. Since Eusebio left Mozambique for Lisbon's SL Benfica in the early 1960s, Africans have been making their mark in European club football. However, as the locations of the African Player of the Year awards indicate, it is only since the 1980s that the northward migration of players has really begun.

The enormous pool of talent in African football, combined with desperate economic conditions at home and ever richer, more open European leagues, has seen a massive flow of talent to Europe. Nigeria, Cameroon, South Africa and the DRC are all key exporters of players. Their destinations remain concentrated in the richest leagues (Spain, Germany and Italy) and in countries with African imperial pasts (Portugal, Belgium, France and Britain), but such are the wage differentials between the continents that there are now Africans playing in almost every European league from the Caucasus to the Low Countries.

Indeed, many Africans are taking European citizenship and playing for European national teams as well as clubs. However, as is usual in the scramble for riches, there are plenty of casualties. Unscrupulous scouts and agents have shipped promising youngsters north only to leave them high and dry when clubs don't pick them up. And if they do eventually make it to the playing field, they must often endure the predictable and grotesque racism of certain elements of the European footballing public.

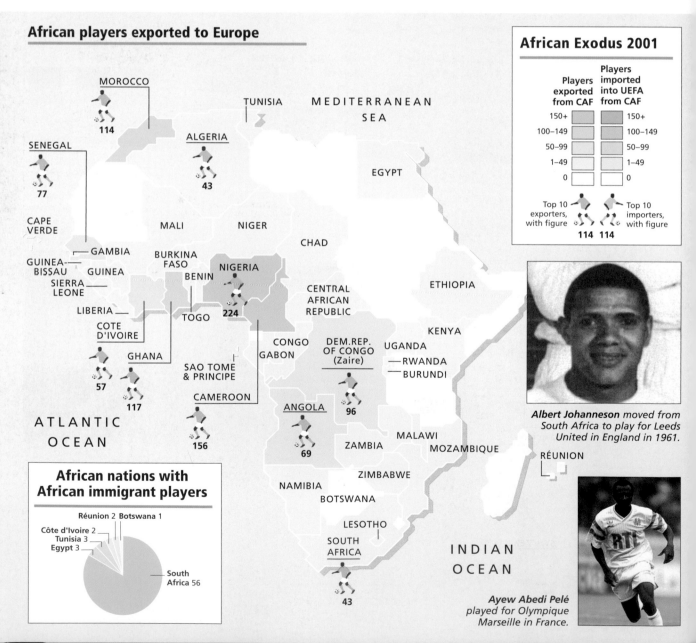

African players exported to Europe

African Exodus 2001

	Players exported from CAF	Players imported into UEFA from CAF
150+		150+
100–149		100–149
50–99		50–99
1–49		1–49
0		0

Top 10 exporters, with figure — 114

Top 10 importers, with figure — 114

MOROCCO 114
SENEGAL 77
ALGERIA 43
TUNISIA
MEDITERRANEAN SEA
EGYPT
CAPE VERDE
MALI
NIGER
CHAD
GAMBIA
GUINEA-BISSAU
GUINEA
BURKINA FASO
BENIN
NIGERIA 224
ETHIOPIA
SIERRA LEONE
LIBERIA
TOGO
CENTRAL AFRICAN REPUBLIC
KENYA
COTE D'IVOIRE
GHANA 57
SAO TOME & PRINCIPE
CONGO
GABON
DEM.REP. OF CONGO (Zaire) 96
UGANDA
RWANDA
BURUNDI
CAMEROON 117
ANGOLA 69
MALAWI
MOZAMBIQUE
ATLANTIC OCEAN
156
ZAMBIA
ZIMBABWE
NAMIBIA
BOTSWANA
RÉUNION
LESOTHO
SOUTH AFRICA 43
INDIAN OCEAN

African nations with African immigrant players

Réunion 2 Botswana 1
Côte d'Ivoire 2
Tunisia 3
Egypt 3
South Africa 56

Albert Johanneson moved from South Africa to play for Leeds United in England in 1961.

Ayew Abedi Pelé played for Olympique Marseille in France.

France Football: African Player of the Year

YEAR	PLAYER	NATIONALITY	CLUB	COUNTRY
1970	Keita	Malian	AS Saint-Etienne	France
1971	Sunday	Ghanaian	Asante Kotoko	Ghana
1972	Souleymane	Guinean	Hafia Conakry	Guinea
1973	Bwanga	Congolese	TP Mazembe	Zaire
1974	Moukila	Congolese	CARA Brazzaville	Congo
1975	Faras	Moroccan	Chebab Mohammedia	Morocco
1976	Milla	Cameroonian	Canon Yaoundé	Cameroon
1977	Dhiab	Tunisian	Espérance Sportive	Tunisia
1978	Razak	Ghanaian	Asante Kotoko	Ghana
1979	N'Kono	Cameroonian	Canon Yaoundé	Cameroon
1980	Manga-Onguene	Cameroonian	Canon Yaoundé	Cameroon
1981	Belloumi	Algerian	GCR Mascara	Algeria
1982	N'Kono	Cameroonian	RCD Español	Spain
1983	Al-Khatib	Egyptian	Al Ahly	Egypt
1984	Abega	Cameroonian	Toulouse FC	France
1985	Tomoumi	Moroccan	FAR Rabat	Morocco
1986	Zaki	Moroccan	Mallorca	Spain
1987	Madjer	Algerian	FC Porto	Portugal
1988	Bwalya	Zambian	Club Brugge KV	Belgium
1989	Weah	Liberian	AS Monaco	France
1990	Milla	Cameroonian	Saint Denis	Réunion
1991	Abedi Pelé	Ghanaian	Olympique Marseille	France
1992	Abedi Pelé	Ghanaian	Olympique Marseille	France
1993	Abedi Pelé	Ghanaian	Olympique Marseille	France
1994	Weah	Liberian	Paris Saint-Germain	France
1995	Weah	Liberian	Milan	Italy
1996	Kanu	Nigerian	Internazionale	Italy

CAF African Player of the Year

YEAR	PLAYER	NATIONALITY	CLUB	COUNTRY
1992	Abedi Pelé	Ghanaian	Olympique Marseille	France
1993	Yekini	Nigerian	Vitória Setúbal	Portugal
1994	Amunike	Nigerian	Sporting CP	Portugal
1995	Weah	Liberian	Milan	Italy
1996	Kanu	Nigerian	Internazionale	Italy
1997	Ikpeba	Nigerian	AS Monaco	France
1998	Hadji	Moroccan	RC Deportivo	Spain
1999	Kanu	Nigerian	Arsenal	England
2000	Mboma	Cameroonian	Parma	Italy
2001	Diouf	Senegalese	RC Lens	France

Where African Players play 2001

UEFA
979

FOOTBALL CONFEDERATION
12

OFC
4

AFC
102

CAF
64

CONMEBOL
3

African players in Europe 2001

ATLANTIC OCEAN

FINLAND

NORWAY SWEDEN

ENGLAND
59

DENMARK

SCOTLAND

NETHERLANDS
56

GERMANY
123

BELARUS

RUSSIA

POLAND

BELGIUM

UKRAINE

CZECH. REP

FRANCE
145

AUSTRIA
SLOVENIA

188

MOLDOVA

ITALY
34

BLACK SEA

BULGARIA

TURKEY
39

PORTUGAL
111

SPAIN
28

SWITZERLAND
44

GREECE

CYPRUS

MALTA

MEDITERRANEAN SEA

ISRAEL

Patrick Mboma:
CAF Player of the Year 2000.

South American Exodus

PLAYERS ON THE MOVE

FOR MOST OF THE 19th AND 20th CENTURIES, South America has been a destination of European migration. But in the world of football the traffic has been in the opposite direction since the end of the First World War. Records show that some Argentinians were playing in Italy before 1914, but the earliest recorded transfer across the South Atlantic is probably Julio Libonatti from Newell's Old Boys to Torino in 1925.

The Olympic tournaments showcased American talent to the rich clubs of Europe. Leading striker Raimondo Orsi left Argentina for Juventus and as an *oriundi* (a descendant of Italian migrants) played for Italy in the 1934 World Cup. In 1931 Vasco da Gama's tour of Spain ended with their stars Fausto and Jaguare staying on in Barcelona. Only the coming of professionalism in Latin America slowed the flow to European

clubs, though the exodus resumed after the Second World War especially during the players' strikes in Argentina and Uruguay in the late 1940s. The great Argentinian forward line of the 1950s – Sivori, Machio, Angellilio – all transferred to Italian clubs.

In a fit of footballing autarchy Spain, Portugal and Italy banned the further signing of foreigners in the 1970s and numbers dropped. With the removal of the ban in the 1980s and the steady disintegration of many Latin American economies, the flow increased, aided and abetted by the extensive use of false passports suggesting players have European grandparents. Today, some 400 Latin Americans play in Europe and not merely in their old Latin strongholds, but in every major and many minor leagues as well. More significantly, the leading players from recent World Cup squads almost all play their football in Europe.

South American players exported to Europe and Japan

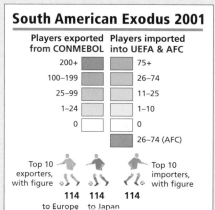

South American Exodus 2001

Players exported from CONMEBOL		Players imported into UEFA & AFC	
200+		75+	
100–199		26–74	
25–99		11–25	
1–24		1–10	
0		0	
		26–74 (AFC)	

Top 10 exporters, with figure
114 to Europe **114** to Japan

Top 10 importers, with figure
114

Julio Libonatti left Newell's Old Boys of Rosario, Argentina, in 1925 to join Torino in Italy – the earliest recorded major football tranfer across the South Atlantic.

South American players in Europe and Japan 2001

ICELAND

ATLANTIC OCEAN

ENGLAND
9

SCOTLAND

NETHERLANDS
9

DENMARK

FINLAND

SWEDEN

RUSSIA

GERMANY
15

POLAND

CZECH. REP

SLOVAKIA

MOLDOVA

BELGIUM

FRANCE
12

AUSTRIA
SLOVENIA
SAN MARINO
19

HUNGARY

ROMANIA

CROATIA

BLACK SEA

ITALY

MACEDONIA
ALBANIA

TURKEY
11

PORTUGAL
81

SPAIN
91

SWITZERLAND
30

50

GREECE
29

CYPRUS

MALTA

MEDITERRANEAN SEA

ISRAEL

JAPAN
26

Juan Sebastian Veron played for several clubs in Italy before moving to Manchester United of England in 2001, a move thrown into doubt over the validity of his passport.

SOUTH AMERICAN EXODUS

Argentinian World Cup Squad 2002

NAME	CLUB	COUNTRY
Burgos	Atlético Madrid	Spain
Ayala	Valencia	Spain
Sorin	Cruzeiro	Brazil
Pochettino	PSG	France
Almeyda	Parma	Italy
Samuel	Roma	Italy
Lopez	Lazio	Italy
Zanetti	Internazionale	Italy
Batistuta	Roma	Italy
Ortega	River Plate	Argentina
Veron	Manchester United	England
Cavallero	RC Celta	Spain
Placente	Bayer Leverkusen	Germany
Simeone	Lazio	Italy
Husain	River Plate	Argentina
Aimar	Valencia	Spain
Lopez	RC Celta	Spain
Gonzalez	Valencia	Spain
Crespo	Lazio	Italy
Gallardo	AS Monaco	France
Caniggia	Rangers	Scotland
Chamot	Milan	Italy
Bonano	Barcelona	Spain

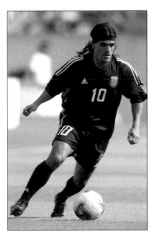

Ariel Ortega took the usual path in summer 2002 moving from River Plate to Galatasaray in Turkey.

Brazilian World Cup Squad 2002

NAME	CLUB	COUNTRY
Marcos	Palmeiras	Brazil
Cafu	Roma	Italy
Lucio	Bayer Leverkusen	Germany
Roque Junior	Milan	Italy
Edmilson	Olympique Lyonnais	France
Roberto Carlos	Real Madrid	Spain
Richardinho	Corinthians	Brazil
Gilberto Silva	Atlético Mineiro	Brazil
Ronaldo	Internazionale	Italy
Rivaldo	Barcelona	Spain
Ronaldinho	PSG	France
Dida	Corinthians	Brazil
Belletti	São Paulo	Brazil
Anderson Polga	Grêmio	Brazil
Kleberson	Atlético Paranaense	Brazil
Junior	Parma	Italy
Denilson	Real Betis	Spain
Vempeta	Corinthians	Brazil
Juninho	Flamengo	Brazil
Edilson	Cruzeiro	Brazil
Luizao	Grêmio	Brazil
Rogerio Ceni	São Paulo	Brazil
Kaka	São Paulo	Brazil

Top 20 Players

TOP 20 PLAYERS

THE 20 GREATEST FOOTBALL PLAYERS – it's a list asking for trouble, inviting argument and fierce criticism. However, no book on the beautiful game would be complete without one. One category of players is automatic and uncontested – everyone's favourites: Pele, Maradona, Beckenbauer, Cruyff, Eusebio, di Stefano, van Basten, Puskas, Best, Yashin and Platini. But then it becomes more difficult. To simplify matters, this selection does not include any players from the amateur era. It was only in the early 1930s that all the major footballing nations ran professional leagues, so this list starts there. From the pre-war era comes Giuseppe Meazza; dominant at club level, he also won two World Cup winner's medals. Stanley Matthew's career spanned many eras, and he gets the nod for his longevity, his integrity and his popularity. From the postwar years come players from a spread of nations and eras. From Brazil comes Garrincha for speed and guile; from England, Bobby Moore fills out the defenders on the list; from Germany, the unstoppable goalscorer Gerd Müller; from Italy, the only football culture in which defenders are revered in the same way as strikers, the archetype Franco Baresi; and from Scotland comes Kenny Dalglish, the most successful player in British football. For a second goalkeeper it is Schmeichel over Banks and Zoff, and from the game now it has to be Zidane. Apologies to Nilton Santos, Daniel Passarella, Denis Law, Ruud Gullit and Raymond Kopa, who should all have been included, among others...

Marco van Basten

Born: October 31,1964
Country: Netherlands
Position: Striker
Caps: 58
Goals: 24
Teams: Ajax
  ▲1987
  ●1982–84
  Milan
  ●1989, 90
  ●1988, 92, 93
Honours: World Footballer of the Year (WS): 1988, 92
World Player of the Year (FIFA): 1992
European Footballer of the Year (FF): 1988, 89, 92

Marco van Basten was the consummate modern goalscorer. He made his professional debut with Ajax in 1983, filling in for his mentor Johan Cruyff. He scored, and went on scoring, 128 goals in 133 games for Ajax in five years, including the winning goals in the 1987 European Cup-Winners' Cup Final. He won the European Golden Boot (top domestic scorer) in 1986. He moved to Milan in 1987 where the goals continued to come and alongside Milan's domestic and international trophies he won the European Footballer of the Year award three times. His international career began in 1983 and saw him score the amazing volley that won the Netherlands the 1988 European Championships Final against the Soviet Union. Persistent ankle injuries saw him retire from the game in 1993 after the European Cup Final against Marseille.

Franco Baresi

Born: May 8, 1960
Country: Italy
Position: Defender
Caps: 81
Goals: 1
Teams: Milan
  ●1989, 90
  ●1988, 92, 93, 94

Franco Baresi played his entire footballing career with a single club, Milan. He joined them as a teenager in 1977 (his elder brother Giuseppe joined rivals Internazionale). Baresi came to dominate and redefine the role of the modern sweeper through the 1980s and 90s. Always calm under pressure, his brilliant reading of the game, sharp intelligence and effortlessly timed tackling provided the defensive base onto which Milan could graft the attacking power of Dutchmen Ruud Gullit and Marco van Basten. But he was always more than a stopper; launching attacks for others and making powerful runs to give his side an extra attacking option. In the late 1980s, Baresi captained Milan and took them to two European Cup successes and four Serie A championships (suspension would deprive him of the chance to captain Milan in a third successful European Cup Final against Barcelona in 1994). Baresi's international career began in 1982 and culminated in his captaincy of the national team at the 1994 World Cup. The lynchpin of the team, he underwent knee surgery during the tournament, but returned to lead them in the Final against Brazil. A brilliant match and tournament was tragically capped when Baresi shot over the bar in the penalty shootout that decided the tournament in Brazil's favour.

Franz Beckenbauer

Born: September 11, 1945
Country: West Germany
  ■1974
  ■1967
Position: Defender
Caps: 103
Goals: 13

Teams: TSV 1860 München
  Bayern München
  ●1974–76
  ▲1967
  ●1969, 73, 74
  New York Cosmos
  Hamburger SV
Honours: European Footballer of the Year: 1972, 76

Franz Beckenbauer is a rarity – a footballer of intelligence and grace; a successful player and coach; and, as Germany's victory in the race to secure the World Cup in 2006 shows, a sharp political operator and administrator. Little wonder that his nickname is 'Der Kaiser'. He began his career with TSV 1860 München, but was quickly snapped up by big city rivals Bayern where he remained until 1976. He made his debut in 1964 and was chosen for the national squad a year later, a place he retained until 1977. He remains West Germany's most capped player. At Bayern, he matured from midfielder to an attacking sweeper, adept in defence, ruthless coming forward, always passing into space. After winning three European Cups with Bayern he played for New York Cosmos and Hamburger SV before retiring. He returned to the game as national team coach in 1984.

Key ■ World Cup   ▲ World Club Cup   ■ European Championships   ● European Cup/Champions League   ◆ UEFA Cup

George **Best**

Born: May 22, 1946
Country: Northern Ireland
Position: Striker
Caps: 37
Goals: 9
Teams: Manchester United
● 1968
● 1965, 67
Dunstable
Stockport County
Los Angeles Aztecs
Cork Celtic
Fulham
Fort Lauderdale
Strikers
Motherwell
Hibernian
San José Earthquakes
Honours: European Footballer
of the Year (FF): 1968

George Best arrived in Manchester from Belfast in 1963 to play for United at the age of 17. Ten years at Old Trafford yielded two league titles, the European Cup and the European Footballer of the Year award in 1968. More importantly, they saw some of the finest football ever seen in England. Best had speed, ferocity and extraordinary balance and grace on the ball. He played 361 league games for United, scoring 137 goals. Best was the first footballer to rise to the dizzy heights of global fame usually reserved for film and pop stars. Nicknamed 'El Beatle' in Spain, he lived a very public life of glamour, celebrity and heavy drinking. By 1973 he had begun to fall out with United and quit. A series of comebacks began at Stockport County, and while the grace remained, the speed and power were lost forever.

Kenny **Dalglish**

Born: March 4, 1951
Country: Scotland
Position: Striker
Caps: 102
Goals: 30
Teams: Celtic
(player) ● 1972–74, 77
Liverpool
● 1979, 80, 82, 83,
84
● 1978, 81, 84
(player/ Liverpool
manager) ● 1986, 88, 90

Kenny Dalglish is the most successful footballer Scotland has ever produced. He began his career at Celtic in 1967 where he played 204 league goals, scoring a total of 112 goals. He was sold in 1977 for a transfer fee of £440,000 (then a UK record) to Liverpool, where he played 354 league games, scoring 118 goals. He progressed to player/manager of the team at Anfield in 1985 and in his first season became the first player/manager to win an English league and cup double. He retired suddenly from the game in 1991, only to return six months later as manager of Blackburn Rovers. Success again followed, with promotion to the top flight, followed in 1995 by the league title, Blackburn's first major trophy for 81 years. As a player he possessed pace, authority and clarity, and was the idol of the fans. In total, as a player and a manager he has won 26 major trophies, collected 102 caps and scored 30 international goals – a record he holds with Denis Law.

Johan **Cruyff**

Born: April 25, 1947
Country: Netherlands
Position: Striker
Caps: 48
Goals: 33
Teams: Ajax (twice)
● 1971–73
● 1966–68, 70, 72,
73, 83
Barcelona
● 1974
Los Angeles Aztecs
Washington Diplomats
Levante
Feyenoord
● 1984
Honours: European Footballer
of the Year (FF);
1971, 73, 74

Christened 'Pythagoras in boots', Johan Cruyff's brilliance lay in an ability to understand instantly the disposition of force on a football field, to see where space was available and to find the move, the pass, the feint that put the ball with the man who had the space – and all on 40 cigarettes a day. He was the pivot around which Ajax and manager Rinus Michels played total football – a style which the Dutch national squad would embrace in the 1970s. He also shook up the cosy patrician world of Dutch football, revolutionizing the treatment of players. After domestic and international success Cruyff moved on to Barcelona where he inspired the Catalans to win the championship in his first season. After quitting the game and the fags, he went on to coach Ajax and Barcelona, steering the latter to four consecutive league championships and the European Cup in 1992.

Alfredo **di Stefano**

Born: July 4, 1926
Country: Argentina, Spain
Position: Striker
Caps: 8 (Argentina),
31 (Spain)
Goals: 6 (Argentina),
23 (Spain)
Teams: Los Cardales
(youth team)
River Plate (twice)
● 1947
Huracán
Millonarios
● 1951, 52
Barcelona
Real Madrid
● 1956–60
● 1954, 55, 57, 58,

Alfredo di Stefano was born in a Barracas, a working-class suburb of Buenos Aires. His father played for River Plate and both sons went on to play professional football. Alfredo began with River Plate in 1944, developed on loan at Huracán, and returned to River in 1947 as the finished article. An explosive centre-forward, he combined individual skills with team-organizing abilities. He first came to international notice in the Argentinian team, victors of the 1947 Copa América. When Argentina's players went on strike over pay in 1949, he was bought by Millonarios, the leading team in the non-FIFA Colombian league. On a tour with Millonarios in Spain in 1952 he was spotted by both Barcelona and Real Madrid. Barcelona tried to buy him from River Plate, Real from Millonarios. The Spanish state intervened saying he should play a season with each, but indifferent form at Barcelona saw him transfer to Real. Under di Stefano, Real won two Spanish championships and the first five consecutive European Cups.

▲ European Cup-Winners' Cup ■ Copa América ● Copa Libertadores ○ National League

TOP 20 PLAYERS

Eusebio da Silva Ferreira

Born: January 25, 1942
Country: Portugal
Position: Striker
Caps: 64
Goals: 41
Teams: Gruppo Desportico de Maputo
SL Benfica
● 1961, 62
● 1963–65, 67–69, 71–73
Boston Minutemen
Toronto Metros
Croatia
Las Vegas Quicksilver
Monterrey
Honours: European Footballer of the Year (FF): 1965

Eusebio da Silva Ferreira was born in Mozambique, then a Portuguese colony, in 1942. He first travelled to Portugal in 1961 for a trial with Sporting CP. However, it is said that he was snatched off the aeroplane by officials of city rivals SL Benfica for whom he was to play for most of his career. In 13 seasons at SL Benfica, he won eight league championships, the European Cup (1962) and the European Golden Boot twice (1968 and 73). Prior to Mozambiquan independence Eusebio's international career lay with Portugal and he made his debut in 1961, scoring in a defeat against Luxembourg. He was the top scorer at the 1966 World Cup with nine goals, including four against the North Koreans in an amazing comeback – Portugal, 3-0 down after 22 minutes, won the match 5-3 and went on to take fourth place. Not always adequately rewarded for his play, Eusebio played out the twilight of his career in North America.

Diego **Maradona**

Born: October 30, 1960
Country: Argentina
■ 1986
Position: Striker
Caps: 90
Goals: 34
Teams: Argentinos Juniors
Boca Juniors (twice)
● 1981
Barcelona
Napoli
◆ 1989
● 1987, 1990
Sevilla
Newell's Old Boys
Quilmes
Honours: World Footballer of the Year (WS): 1986
South America,
El Mundo:
1979, 80, 86, 89, 90, 92

A teenage sensation in Argentina in the late 1970s and early 1980s, Diego Maradona was transferred for record-breaking fees to Barcelona (1983) and Napoli (1987). Short and stocky, Maradona possessed an explosive burst of pace, the most exquisite ball control under pressure of any footballer ever. He has also provided the game with some of its finest melodrama. He was sent off for dangerous play at the 1982 World Cup Final, almost single-handedly won the 1986 World Cup for Argentina, and scraped them into the 1990 finals before his ignominious dismissal and ban in 1994. He has been on the comeback trail ever since.

Garrincha (Manoel Francisco dos Santos)

Born: October 28, 1933
Died: January 20, 1983
Country: Brazil
■ 1958, 62
Position: Winger
Caps: 50
Goals: 12
Teams: Pao Grande
Botafogo
Corinthians
Athlético Junior
Flamengo
Red Star Paris

In the pantheon of Brazilian football Garrincha stands just below the hallowed figure of Pele. He was born Manoel Francisco dos Santos (his nickname means 'little bird'). As a child he required repeated corrective surgery on both legs, which were so twisted that it was thought likely that he would never walk. Despite this he proved to be an irresistibly fast, infectious and incisive right winger, making and scoring goals at the very highest levels. His club career was a little chaotic, with spells at many clubs in Brazil, Colombia and France, but at international level he was pivotal in Brazil's 1958 and 1962 World Cup victories. His reputation as a difficult character threatened his place in the 1958 World Cup squad and only a players' deputation led by Nilton Santos persuaded coach Vincente Feola to include him. On the day, he delivered both crosses for Brazil's goals in the 1958 Final, and after Pele's injury in Chile in 1962 he became the driving force of the side. Top scorer in the tournament, he scored twice in both the quarter- and semi-final victories. Injury eventually caught up with him and persistent knee problems forced him to quit the game. He tragically died of alcohol poisoning in 1983.

Stanley **Matthews**

Born: February 1, 1915
Died: February 23, 2000
Country: England
Position: Winger
Caps: 54
Teams: Stoke City
Blackpool
● 1953
Honours: European Footballer of the Year (FF): 1956

Stanley Matthews never won a league championship, in a career as a professional footballer that spanned 33 years. Nor can he claim a single international honour from his 54 caps. Two second division titles with Stoke City and a single FA Cup triumph with Blackpool are his lot, yet it is unquestionable that he should be included in this company. Although he had a spell with Blackpool in mid-career, Matthews played most of his football at Stoke, making his professional debut in March 1932 and playing his final game in February 1965. His international career was similarly long; he played his last England game at the age of 42. He quickly acquired the nickname 'The Wizard of the Dribble' and was the leading English player of his era. Playing outside-right, his speed, ball control, capacity for moves, feints and changes of pace, opened up the tightest of defences. But Stoke simply could not mount a challenge on the league. His moment came with Blackpool in 1953 in what has since become known as the Matthews Final. Blackpool were 3-1 down to Bolton Wanderers until a blizzard of extraordinary wing play from Matthews successively carved the Bolton defence open – and Blackpool won it 4-3. Matthews was never booked and never sent off in his entire career.

Key ■ World Cup ▲ World Club Cup ■ European Championships ● European Cup/Champions League ◆ UEFA Cup

Giuseppe **Meazza**

Born: August 23, 1910
Died: August 21, 1979
Country: Italy
    ■1934, 38
Position: Striker
Caps: 53
Goals: 33
Teams: Internazionale
    ●1930, 38
    Milan
    Juventus
    Varese
    Atalanta

Giuseppe Meazza was the leading striker of the first decade of Italian professional football and one of only two players who played in both of Italy's World Cup victories in 1934 and 1938 (the other was Giovanni Ferrari). Born in Milan, Meazza made his debut with Internazionale at the age of 17 and in his first full season with the club (1928–29) he was the top scorer with 33 goals. In his debut match with the national squad he scored twice as Italy beat Switzerland 4-2, the first of ten goals in his first year of international football and of the 33 goals in total he scored for Italy. During the late 1930s, Meazza found himself at odds with the hierarchy at Internazionale, which was by then run by Fascist Party representative Ferdinando Pozzani. After a decade with the club he crossed the city to rivals Milan where he stayed for four seasons before playing out the end of his career at Juventus, Varese and Atalanta. He was joint coach of the Italian national squad for couple of years in the 1950s. As one of the few players to have played for both Milanese giants, the San Siro was renamed in his honour after his death in 1979.

Gerd **Müller**

Born: November 3, 1945
Country: Germany
    ■1970
    ■1972
Position: Striker
Caps: 62
Goals: 68
Teams: TSV Nordlingen
    Bayern München
    ●1974–76
    ▲1967
    ●1969, 72–74
Honours: European Footballer
    of the Year: 1970

Gerd Müller joined Bayern München in 1964. Coach Zlatko Cajkovski is reputed to have said 'I'm not putting that little elephant in among my string of thoroughbreds.' But his short, stocky centre-forward proved to be the most prolific goalscorer in German football history. Nicknamed 'Der Bomber', Müller was the most ruthless goal poacher in the penalty area, and especially the six-yard area, ever; Helmut Schon called him 'my little goalscorer'. With prods, pokes, balls stolen, flicked and dug out of the ground, Müller took every half chance that came his way. In his club career he racked up 365 goals and helped take Bayern from the regional leagues to three successive European Cup victories. At international level, a mere 62 caps yielded him an incredible 68 goals. Some have scored more international goals, but no one comes close to Muller's goals to games ratio. More than that, he could find goals for the very biggest occasion: ten at the 1970 Mexico World Cup, four more for the victorious West German team in 1974, including the winner in the Final against the Netherlands.

Bobby **Moore**

Born: April 21, 1941
Died: February 24, 1993
Country: England
    ■1966
Position: Defender
Caps: 108
Goals: 2
Teams: West Ham United
    ▲1965
    Fulham
    Herning
    San Antonio Thunder
    Seattle Sounders
    Team America

Born in Barking in Essex, Bobby Moore joined east London's leading club, West Ham United, as an amateur, turning professional in 1958. He stayed at Upton Park for 16 years, playing 544 league matches before moving to Fulham. A long and distinguished club career only brought one FA Cup triumph in 1964 and a European Cup-Winners' Cup medal in 1965, both with West Ham. But it was in his international performances that Moore truly shone. He made his international debut against Peru just before the 1962 World Cup, the first of 108 caps, and missed only ten England games in the following ten years. In 1966, he led England to their greatest international triumph, winning the World Cup on home soil. Prior to the 1970 World Cup, while the England squad was training in Colombia, Moore was falsely accused of stealing jewellery from a shop in Bogotá; diplomatic intervention secured his release from custody. He displayed a characteristic icy calm and composure in the face of what was evidently a false charge. Moore went on to play in a similar fashion in Mexico, where he was acknowledged by no less an authority than Pele as the 'world's greatest defender'.

Pele (Edson Arantes do Nascimento)

Born: October 23, 1940
Country: Brazil
    ■1958, 62, 70
    ■1962, 63
Position: Striker
Caps: 92
Goals: 77
Teams: Bauru (youth team)
    Santos
    ●1963, 64
    ●1959, 63, 64
    New York Cosmos
    ●1977

Pele is credited with 1,282 goals in 1,365 matches for his two clubs and the national Brazilian team. He was a member of three World Cup winning squads 1958, 1962 and 1970. His club career was mainly spent with the São Paulo team Santos, who he inspired to two victories in the Copa Libertadores and the World Club Cup. Yet none of this captures the indelible impression he has left on the game. Born Edson Arantes do Nascimento, he was teased at school with the moniker Pele and fought it, but it stuck. He joined Santos at the age of 15, was in the national squad at 16 and in the World Cup squad at 17. He was capable of scoring and making goals from any position in the final third of the field. His armoury included dipping free kicks, powerful twisting runs and dribbles, languid and deadly flicks and touches and unstoppable headers. Respected and honoured in every corner of the globe, Pele's three years in the US saw football reach its most popular point. In retirement, he has been drawn into the dangerous maw of Brazilian politics. His attempts to reform the cesspool of Brazilian football finances as Minister of Sport have barely scratched the surface of tax evasion and corruption that are eating away at the Brazilian game.

▲ European Cup-Winners' Cup   ■ Copa América   ● Copa Libertadores   ● National League

TOP 20 PLAYERS

TOP 20 PLAYERS

Michel **Platini**

Born: June 21, 1955
Country: France
■ 1984
Position: Striker
Caps: 72
Goals: 41
Teams: AS Nancy
AS Saint-Etienne
Juventus
● 1985
▲ 1984
● 1984, 86
Honours: World Footballer of
the Year (WS):
1984, 85
European Footballer
of the Year: 1983

Michel Platini played much of his career in France with Nancy and St-Etienne, but his greatest years were spent at Juventus (1983–87). Considered by the club to be its greatest player ever, he was top scorer in Italy for three seasons and helped Juventus to two Serie A titles, the European Cup and the European Cup-Winners' Cup. Internationally his influence on the previously weak French national squad was immense, inspiring fantastic performances at the 1982 and 86 World Cups (France made it to the semi-finals in both) as well as victory at the 1984 European Championships in which he was top scorer. After retiring from playing he coached the French national team (but stood down after the 1992 European Championships). He has proved more adept in the intensely political world of football administration, was the director and chief organizer of the 1998 World Cup in France and is set to succeed to the presidency of UEFA.

Peter **Schmeichel**

Born: November 18, 1963
Country: Denmark
■ 1992
Position: Goalkeeper
Teams: Hvidovre BK
Brøndby IF
● 1985, 87, 88, 90, 91
Manchester United
● 1999
● 1993, 94, 96, 97, 99
Sporting CP
● 2000
Aston Villa
Manchester City

Peter Schmeichel is the most accomplished and influential goalkeeper of his generation. In Sweden, 1991, he came to the attention of Manchester United, who bought him from Brøndby IF for a mere £750,000. During the next eight seasons he helped the club to win five English league championships, three FA Cups and a European Cup. Schmeichel marshals his defence with an uncommon ferocity and seems able to inspire his teams to victory. His shot-stopping has been brilliant, his capacity to make himself huge in a striker's eyes legendary and his power and bravery in the air without match. He also scores goals – most famously in a 1995 UEFA Cup tie for Manchester United against Rotor Volgograd. Schmeichel's charismatic power was also evident in inspiring the Danish team to victory in the 1992 European Championships and in his first seasons at Sporting CP in Lisbon, when the sleeping giants of Portuguese football finally regained its crown.

Ferenc **Puskas**

Born: April 2, 1927
Country: Hungary, Spain
Position: Striker
Caps: 84 (Hungary),
4 (Spain)
Goals: 83 (Hungary)
Teams: Kispest
Honvéd
● 1950, 52, 54, 55
Real Madrid
▲ 1999
● 1959, 60, 66
● 1961–65

Ferenc Puskas remains the best remembered of the Magical Magyars – the revolutionary and scintillating Hungarian team of the early 1950s. Born into a footballing family, he joined Budapest club Kispest at the age of 16 and was a member of the international squad at 18. Puskas began as an immensely quick and agile inside-left, and then became the attacking edge of Hungary's innovative forward play – a deep-lying centre-forward. With Puskas, Hungary won the 1952 Olympics and thrashed England on home soil for the first time in the immortal 6-3 win at Wembley in 1953, only to lose to West Germany in the 1954 World Cup Final. In 1956, Honvéd were on tour in Western Europe when the Hungarian Uprising broke out. Puskas decided to stay in Western Europe and was welcomed at Real Madrid. Paired with di Stefano, Puskas' career blossomed; four-time top scorer in the Spanish league, and three-time European Cup winner, he eventually received Spanish citizenship and a place in the national squad at the 1962 World Cup. He retired in 1966 and took up coaching, peaking when he took unfancied Panathinaikos to the 1971 European Cup Final.

Lev **Yashin**

Born: October 22, 1929
Died: March 20, 1990
Country: Soviet Union
■ 1960
Position: Goalkeeper
Caps: 75
Teams: Dynamo Moskva
● 1954, 55, 57, 59, 63
Honours: European Footballer
of the Year (FF): 1963

Lev Yashin remains the only goalkeeper to receive the prestigious European Footballer of the Year award and is considered to be the greatest goalkeeper of the modern era. During his career he is reputed to have kept a clean sheet in 270 games and to have saved over 150 penalties. His sporting life began without a commitment to football; Yashin split his time between playing ice hockey and playing football for Dynamo Moskva, only choosing football as a full-time career in 1953 when Dynamo's first-team goalkeeper fell injured. A year later he made his international debut, and in 1956 he played in the Soviet side that won the Olympics tournament. Known as the 'Black Panther' because of his favoured black strip, he was renowned for his agility and the stunning speed of his reactions. A career of 22 seasons spent entirely with Dynamo Moskva brought five Soviet championship titles and appearances at three World Cup tournaments. In retirement, Yashin ran the Soviet Ministry of Sport's football department and was awarded the Order of Lenin by his country.

Key ■ World Cup ▲ World Club Cup ■ European Championships ● European Cup/Champions League ◆ UEFA Cup

Zinedine **Zidane**

Born: June 23, 1972
Country: France
■ 1998
■ 2000
Position: Midfielder
Teams: Bordeaux
Juventus
● 1997, 98
Real Madrid
● 2002
Honours: World Footballer of the
Year (WS): 1998
World Footballer of the
Year (FIFA): 1998, 2000
European Footballer
of the Year: 1998

Zinedine Zidane was the midfield controller at the heart of France's fantastically successful team of the late 1990s and is probably the most technically accomplished player of his generation. Born of Algerian parents in Marseille, he began his career with Cannes before joining Bordeaux in 1992. In 1996, he was snapped up by Italian giants Juventus. Two Italian league championships followed before his decisive play in both the 1998 World Cup and Euro 2000. In 1998, he missed a game after receiving a red card in a match against Saudi Arabia. Returning for the quarter-finals, his playmaking was decisive in beating Italy and Croatia. Against Brazil in the Final, two headed goals won the cup for France. At Euro 2000, a dozen moments of the sublimest skill, flicks, pace and vision gave France the edge against increasingly tough opponents. In the summer of 2001, he transferred to Real Madrid for the world record sum of £43.5 million and helped them to success in the 2002 Champions League Final by scoring the winning goal.

Top 10 Managers

COMPILING A LIST of the ten greatest managers is an impossible task and, inevitably, omissions are many. For example, Brian Clough won two European Cups with a tiny budget at Nottingham Forest, Mario Zagallo has had a hand in multiple World Cup victories for Brazil, while Ottmar Hitzfeld's reign at Borussia Dortmund and Bayern München are reaping rewards that must place him close to the top. In the end, this list draws on a number of different reasons for its inclusions.

Several of them have delivered the goods in some of the toughest leagues in the world. Bela Guttman alone has won premier club tournaments in the two major footballing continents (Europe and Latin America). Herbert Chapman and Vittorio Pozzo invented the role of the modern football manager, while Herrera and Michels can all claim significant roles in the invention of new tactics and modes of play; and for sheer personality Bill Shankly is the unquestionable champion.

Herbert **Chapman**

Born: January 19, 1878
Died: January 6, 1934
Nationality: British (England)
Teams: Northampton Town
Notts County
Tottenham Hotspur
Leeds City
Huddersfield Town
● 1924, 25
Arsenal
● 1930, 31

Herbert Chapman was the first great football manager, the man who shaped and defined the role for a generation. A long playing career began at the turn of the 19th century. He turned professional in 1901 with Northampton Town before moving to Notts County and Tottenham. In 1907, he went into management with Northampton then moved north in 1912 to become club secretary at the now defunct Leeds City. Under Chapman, the team recorded its best-ever league performances. In 1919, the club was expelled from the Football League for making illegal wartime payments to players and Chapman was temporarily banned. He returned to management in 1921 with Huddersfield and stormed to two league titles. In 1925, he arrived at Arsenal where he fashioned the greatest English team of the inter-war era. On the field he innovated the game, creating the W-M formation of play, calling for floodlit games, white balls and numbered shirts. Off the field he took charge of coaching, tactics and local politics in a way no manager had combined before. He even persuaded the local council to rename the nearest tube stop Arsenal. He died mid-season in 1934 as Arsenal set course for a third league title under him.

Sir Alex **Ferguson**

Born: December 31, 1941
Nationality: British (Scotland)
Teams: Scotland
East Stirlingshire
St Mirren
Aberdeen
▲ 1983
● 1980, 84, 85
Manchester United
▲ 1999
● 1999
▲ 1991
● 1992, 94, 96,
97, 99–2001

Sir Alex Ferguson comes from the extraordinary seam of Scottish working class culture that has yielded teams, players and managers of authority, grit and canniness. His playing career led to spells as player-manager with both East Stirlingshire and St Mirren. But it was at Aberdeen that he made his mark. With minimal resources the Dons broke the hegemony of the Old Firm in Scottish football winning three league titles, three Scottish cups and the European Cup-Winners' Cup between 1980 and 1985. An unsuccessful stint as Scotland manager at the 1986 World Cup was followed by his appointment at Manchester United. After a slow start, Ferguson began to fashion the most comprehensive domination of the English league that any club has achieved — seven out of nine Premiership titles, including two doubles and a treble in 1999 with victory in the European Cup. Ferguson's teams have acquired an enormous psychological resilience and the capacity to win games from behind, while he is also the most successful British manager to elevate the manipulation of the sporting media to an art form.

▲ European Cup-Winners' Cup　　■ Copa América　　● Copa Libertadores　　● National League

TOP 10 MANAGERS

Bela **Guttman**

Born: 1900
Died: 1981
Nationality: Hungarian
Teams: Enschede
Újpest
⬤1939
Dynamo Bucharest
Vasa Budapest
Honvéd
Padova
Triestina Milan
⬤1955
FC Porto
⬤1959
SL Benfica
⬤1961, 62
⬤1960, 61, 63
Peñarol
▲1961
⬤1961
⬤1962, 64
Servette
Panathinaikos
FK Austria

Bela Guttman is the only manager to have won the top club trophy in both Europe and Latin America. He played as an amateur for MTK in Budapest and Hakoah in Vienna, as well as for the Hungarian Olympic team of 1924. Managerial posts and trophies followed at Enschede in Holland, Újpest Dosza in Hungary, Dinamo Bucharest in Romania and Honvéd in Hungary. His greatest successes include SL Benfica winning the 1961 European Cup, a Serie A title with Milan, and Peñarol, Uruguay, winning the national league and the Copa Libertadores.

Rinus **Michels**

Born: February 2, 1928
Nationality: Dutch
Teams: Netherlands
■1988
Ajax
⬤1971
⬤1966, 67, 68, 70
Barcelona
⬤1974
Los Angeles Aztecs
1. FC Köln
Bayer Leverkusen

Rinus Michels began his career in the amateur era of Dutch football, playing as striker for the Netherlands national team. In 1965, he took control at Ajax, then struggling against relegation and turned the team around. 'Iron Rinus' was legendary for his insistence on discipline, rigour and constant improvement. He is known to have stood guard by hotel lifts to prevent late-night drinking by his players and his mind games in training could be cruel, but invariably effective. In the next six years Ajax won four Dutch league titles and three Dutch Cups, culminating in the first of Ajax's three European Cup victories in 1971. But his legacy is far greater than that. Under his lead, the career of Johan Cruyff was nurtured and developed and with it the notion of total football was elaborated at Ajax and intertwined with it. Michels proved himself equally adept at international level, taking the national team to the World Cup Final in 1974 and winning the 1988 European Championships. He has had the rare talents required to mould coherent fluid teams from the potentially explosive, unstable mix of talent, petulance and individualism that characterizes Dutch football.

Helenio **Herrera**

Born: April 17, 1917
Died: November 9, 1997
Nationality: Argentinian
Teams: Italy
Spain
Putuex
Red Star 93
Atlético Madrid
⬤1950, 51
Malaga
Valladolid
Sevilla
Barcelona
◆1960
⬤1959
Internazionale
▲1964, 65
⬤1964, 65
⬤1963, 65, 66
Roma

Helenio Herrera is among the most travelled and most successful of football coaches. Born in Argentina and raised in Morocco, he began a playing career in France. In the late 1940s, he coached a succession of top French teams before moving to Spain where four spells with both Atlético Madrid and Barcelona yielded league championships. Herrera's Spanish sides were aggressive and attacking but this style proved ineffective when he arrived at Internazionale in the early 1960s. Here, he reinvented and perfected the *catenaccio* (meaning a bolt or a padlock in Italian) system of defence – using a sweeper and man-to-man marking among the back four – combined with lethal counterattacking. Il Grande Inter won two European Cups and two World Club Cups under him as well as three league titles.

Bob **Paisley**

Born: January 21, 1919
Died: February 14, 1996
Nationality: British (England)
Teams: Liverpool
⬤1970, 78, 81
◆1976
⬤1976, 77,
79, 80, 82, 83

Bob Paisley's football career was almost entirely spent with Liverpool. A player with the club in the late 1940s, he joined the coaching team in 1954 and was a key member of Shankly's staff before taking over as manager in 1974. Under him, Liverpool played their greatest football and achieved the greatest triumphs: six English league titles and three European Cup wins. In contrast to his predecessor, Paisley appeared uncommunicative and unexcitable, and always cultivated an image of working-class understatement and simplicity. But as Graeme Souness, no shrinking violet himself, said of his time at Liverpool, '...let me tell you, he ruled Anfield with a rod of iron. He was a commanding man and there were few who dared mess around with him.' Anecdotal tales of his love of carpet slippers and a morning routine of tea at the local garage and picking horses from the paper have hidden the workings of the keenest of footballing brains. On the pitch he insisted that the short, swift passing game, the search for space and the application of intelligence were the route to victory. Off the pitch Paisley's attention to detail, accumulation of information and astonishingly accurate diagnosis of player injuries helped mould and sustain the club during its most successful period.

Key ■ World Cup   ▲ World Club Cup   ■ European Championships   ⬤ European Cup/Champions League   ◆ UEFA Cup

Vittorio **Pozzo**

Born: March 2, 1886
Died: December 21, 1968
Nationality: Italian
Teams: Torino
Italy
■ 1934, 38

Vittorio Pozzo brought the art of football management to Italy, defining the role for a generation. He learned his football in England where he had come to study before the First World War, though it seems he studied Manchester United more than anything else. On his return to Italy, he played a major part in the split between Juventus and a new club Torino. He became a regular part of the Torino set-up, as well as coaching the Italian team in the 1912 Olympic Games. But it was in the professional era of Italian football and at international level that Pozzo made his biggest mark. Appointed full-time national team coach in 1929, he took Italy to two successive World Cup victories in 1934 on home soil and in France in 1938. 'Il Vecchio Maestro', as he became known, was welcomed on his return to Turin with the victorious team as a national hero. To top this off, the Azzurri had also won the Olympic gold medal at the 1936 Olympics in Berlin with a team of students, and Pozzo was the coach. He remains the only European manager to win two World Cups and his record of 63 victories in 95 matches in 19 years makes him the most successful Italian international manager ever. He retired in 1948 to become a journalist on *La Stampa* for whom he reported on many Italian international matches.

Jock **Stein**

Born: October 5, 1903
Died: November 10, 1985
Nationality: British (Scotland)
Teams: Scotland
Dunfermline Athletic
▲ 1961
Hibernian
Celtic
● 1967
● 1966–74, 77
Leeds United

Jock Stein began his football career with Scottish club Albion Rovers in the late 1940s. He soon transferred to Celtic, became captain, and led the team to a league and cup double in 1954, after which injury forced his early retirement from the game. He became Celtic's assistant coach and then moved to Dunfermline Athletic as manager in 1960, leading them to a surprise victory in the 1961 Scottish FA Cup. A short period at Hibernian followed, before his return to Celtic as manager in 1964. Stein's Celtic team won an extraordinary nine league championship titles between 1966 and 74, not to mention nine Scottish FA Cups and six League Cups. Moreover, he led Celtic to their greatest moment of all – victory in the 1967 European Cup Final against Internazionale in Lisbon. A brief and unhappy spell as manager of Leeds United was followed by his appointment as manager of the Scottish national squad, steering them successfully to both the 1982 and 1986 World Cup finals tournaments. He died in 1985, struck down by a heart attack in the closing minutes of the Scotland v Wales World Cup qualifying match.

Bill **Shankly**

Born: September 2, 1913
Died: September 29, 1981
Nationality: British (Scotland)
Teams: Carlisle United
Grimsby Town
Workington
Huddersfield Town
Liverpool
◆ 1973
● 1964, 66, 73

Bill Shankly's playing career took him to Carlisle, Preston and five Scottish caps before beginning a long march through the lower echelons of English football league management. Spells with Grimsby, Workington and Huddersfield brought him to Liverpool in 1959 – a great club languishing in the Second Division. Shankly remained at Liverpool until 1974, winning three league titles, two FA Cups and the UEFA Cup. However, his legendary status derives from his extraordinary charisma, his dry wit, and the establishment of Liverpool FC as an institution that would reach the very heights of global football in the late 1970s and early 1980s. Shankly's powers of motivation drew on all these things – legend has him demanding the team throw their shirts on the floor before the match and ordering them to take a bath as they wouldn't be needed... 'I'll throw these shirts out on the field and the shirts will beat Ipswich themselves'; opponents were derided as having 'hearts as big as a caraway seed'; and his own team members were deliberately given the wrong meal before a match to put them in a suitably angry mood for the occasion. Shankly is honoured at Anfield, having the main gates named after him that bear the legend 'You'll never walk alone'.

Giovanni **Trapattoni**

Born: March 17, 1939
Nationality: Italian
Teams: Italy, Milan
Juventus
▲ 1985
● 1985
◆ 1977, 93
▲ 1984
● 1977, 78, 81, 82, 84, 86
Internazionale
◆ 1991
● 1989
Bayern München
● 1997
Cagliari
Fiorentina

Trapattoni's football career began in the late 1950s as wing-half for Milan, winning two European Cup winner's medals (1963 and 69). After retiring from playing, he became Milan's youth coach and for a time was the caretaker manager of their first team, winning the 1973 Cup-Winners' Cup. In 1976, he moved to Juventus where a decade in charge brought six Italian championships, one each of the three European club competitions, the European Super Cup and the World Club Cup. Like all of his teams the mighty Juventus of this era was characterized by unhurried, solid defence and lethal counter-attacking potential. His squad provided the steely backbone of the Italian World Cup winning side in 1982. In the excruciating hothouse pressure of Italian football, Trapattoni serenely reigns as the most successful coach. A spell at Internazionale in the 1980s saw another Serie A title as well as the UEFA Cup before a period at Bayern München in the mid-90s saw him become the first foreign coach to win a Bundesliga title. He coached Italy at the 2002 World Cup.

▲ European Cup-Winners' Cup ■ Copa América ● Copa Libertadores ● National League

World Players of the Year

THE SEASON IN REVIEW 2001

THERE WAS A REAL DIFFERENCE of opinion among the judges of the major player awards in 2001. The FIFA World Footballer of the Year, based on a poll of 130 national team coaches, went to Luis Figo, just ahead of David Beckham. The Ballon d'Or of *France Football*, for the European Player of the Year, is based on a poll of the paper's European correspondents and they went for Michael Owen ahead of Raúl of Real Madrid. In a poll of readers, *World Soccer* magazine also made Owen Footballer of the Year. The choice of Figo is odd given his quiet season with Real and the fact that his peak performances were at Euro 2000. Owen, by contrast, helped take Liverpool to a cup triple (English League Cup, FA Cup and UEFA Cup) showing electric pace and vision throughout the season. In South America, the Footballer of the Year award went to Juan Román Riquelme, the midfield lynchpin of Boca Juniors, who took a second consecutive Copa Libertadores in 2001.

World Footballer of the Year (FIFA)

YEAR	PLAYER	CLUB	NATIONALITY
1991	Lothar Matthäus	Internazionale	German
1992	Marco van Basten	Milan	Dutch
1993	Roberto Baggio	Juventus	Italian
1994	Romario	Barcelona	Brazilian
1995	George Weah	Milan	Liberian
1996	Ronaldo	PSV/Barcelona	Brazilian
1997	Ronaldo	Barcelona/Inter	Brazilian
1998	Zinedine Zidane	Juventus	French
1999	Rivaldo	Barcelona	Brazilian
2000	Zinedine Zidane	Juventus	French
2001	Luis Figo	Real Madrid	Portuguese

Elected by FIFA.

European Player of the Year

YEAR	PLAYER	CLUB	NATIONALITY
1956	Stanley Matthews	Stoke City	English
1957	Alfredo di Stefano	Real Madrid	Spanish
1958	Raymond Kopa	Real Madrid	French
1959	Alfredo di Stefano	Real Madrid	Spanish
1960	Luis Suárez	Barcelona	Spanish
1961	Omar Sivori	Juventus	Italian
1962	Josef Masopust	Dukla Praha	Czech
1963	Lev Yashin	Dinamo Moskva	Soviet
1964	Denis Law	Manchester United	Scottish
1965	Eusébio	SL Benfica	Portuguese
1966	Bobby Charlton	Manchester United	English
1967	Florian Albert	Ferencváros	Hungarian
1968	George Best	Manchester United	Irish
1969	Gianni Rivera	Milan	Italian
1970	Gerd Müller	Bayern München	German
1971	Johan Cruyff	Ajax	Dutch
1972	Franz Beckenbauer	Bayern München	German
1973	Johan Cruyff	Ajax	Dutch
1974	Johan Cruyff	Ajax	Dutch
1975	Oleg Blokhin	Dynamo Kyiv	Soviet
1976	Franz Beckenbauer	Bayern München	German
1977	Allan Simonsen	Borussia Mönchengladbach	Danish
1978	Kevin Keegan	Hamburger SV	English
1979	Kevin Keegan	Hamburger SV	English
1980	Karl-Heinz Rummenigge	Bayern München	German

European Player of the Year (*continued*)

YEAR	PLAYER	CLUB	NATIONALITY
1981	Karl-Heinz Rummenigge	Bayern München	German
1982	Paolo Rossi	Juventus	Italian
1983	Michel Platini	Juventus	French
1984	Michel Platini	Juventus	French
1985	Michel Platini	Juventus	French
1986	Igor Belanov	Dynamo Kyiv	Soviet
1987	Ruud Gullit	Milan	Dutch
1988	Marco van Basten	Milan	Dutch
1989	Marco van Basten	Milan	Dutch
1990	Lothar Matthäus	Internazionale	German
1991	Jean-Pierre Papin	Olympique Marseille	French
1992	Marco van Basten	Milan	Dutch
1993	Roberto Baggio	Juventus	Italian
1994	Hristo Stoichkov	Barcelona	Bulgarian
1995	George Weah	Milan	Liberian
1996	Matthias Sammer	Borussia Dortmund	German
1997	Ronaldo	Barcelona	Brazilian
1998	Zinedine Zidane	Juventus	French
1999	Rivaldo	Barcelona	Brazilian
2000	Luis Figo	Barcelona	Portuguese
2001	Michael Owen	Liverpool	English

Elected by *France Football* magazine.

South American Footballer of the Year

YEAR	PLAYER	CLUB	NATIONALITY
1971	Tostão*	Cruzeiro	Brazilian
1972	Teofilio Cubillas*	Alianza Lima	Peruvian
1973	Pele*	Santos	Brazilian
1974	Elias Figueroa*	Internacional	Chilean
1975	Elias Figueroa*	Internacional	Chilean
1976	Elias Figueroa*	Internacional	Chilean
1977	Zico*	Flamengo	Brazilian
1978	Mario Kempes*	Valencia	Argentinian
1979	Diego Maradona*	Argentinos Juniors	Argentinian
1980	Diego Maradona*	Boca Juniors	Argentinian
1981	Zico*	Flamengo	Brazilian
1982	Zico*	Flamengo	Brazilian
1983	Socrates*	Corinthians	Brazilian
1984	Enzo Francescoli*	River Plate	Uruguayan
1985	Romero*	Fluminense	Paraguayan
1986	Ruben Paz*	Racing Club	Uruguayan
1986	Antonio Alzamendi*	River Plate	Uruguayan
1987	Diego Maradona*	Napoli	Argentinian
1987	Carlos Valderrama	Deportivo Cali	Colombian
1988	Diego Maradona*	Napoli	Argentinian
1988	Ruben Paz	Racing Club	Uruguayan
1989	Bebeto*	Vasco da Gama	Brazilian
1989	Gabriel Batistuta	Boca Juniors/ Fiorentina	Argentinian
1990	Diego Maradona*	Sevilla	Argentinian
1990	Raul Amarilla	Olimpia	Paraguayan
1991	Oscar Ruggeri	Vélez Sarsfield	Argentinian
1992	Rai	São Paulo	Brazilian
1993	Carlos Valderrama	Atlético Junior	Colombian
1994	Cafu	São Paulo	Brazilian
1995	Enzo Francescoli	River Plate	Uruguayan
1996	Jose Luis Chilavert	Vélez Sarsfield	Paraguayan
1997	Marcelo Salas	River Plate	Chilean
1998	Martin Palermo	Boca Juniors	Argentinian
1999	Javier Saviola	River Plate	Argentinian
2000	Romario	Vasco da Gama	Brazilian
2001	Juan Román Riquelme	Boca Juniors	Argentinian

* Elected by *El Mundo*, Caracas; all others elected by *El Pais*, Montevideo.

WORLD PLAYERS OF THE YEAR

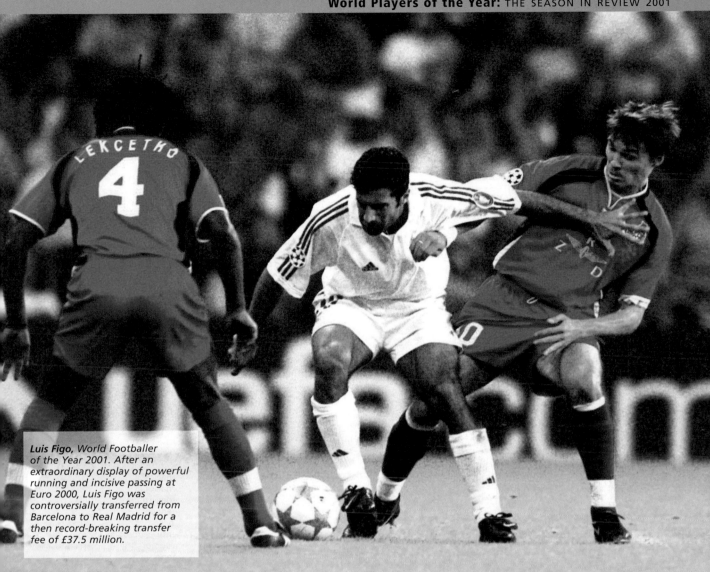

Luis Figo, *World Footballer of the Year 2001. After an extraordinary display of powerful running and incisive passing at Euro 2000, Luis Figo was controversially transferred from Barcelona to Real Madrid for a then record-breaking transfer fee of £37.5 million.*

Michael Owen, *European Player of the Year 2001. Is there anyone sharper in the box? Here he scores England's third and his second goal in England's thrilling 5-1 victory against Germany in the 2002 World Cup qualifier.*

Juan Román Riquelme *of Boca Juniors was South American Footballer of the Year 2001.*

Index

INDEX

Index compiled by Indexing Specialists UK Limited, Hove, Sussex

INDEX

ACKNOWLEDGEMENTS

THANKS TO:
Sarah Bond for love, support and telling me to make it happen.
Andy Jones for inspiration.
Johnny Acton, Barbara Wyllie and Sophie Woodward for research and Johnny for endless conversation and discussion.
Bob Bickerton for truly the most extraordinary knowledge of football colours one could imagine.
Eric Weil for invaluable assistance with Latin America.
Soccer Investor for letting me wander through their library and illuminating me every Wednesday.
Historians, press officers, information officers, librarians, statisticians, archivists at national and regional FAs, leagues and clubs,
as well as hundreds and hundreds of fans' websites of so many clubs that I don't even know where to start.
Thanks also for help with pictures and facts to Tanya Belonovskaya, Agustín Beltrame, George Chilvers, Patricia Quijano Dark, David Litterer,
Jen Little, Tim Maitland, Emmanuel Maradas, Tim Miller, Pavel Petrov, Luca Ponchiroli, Olexi Scherbak, Sergey Ukladov and Sunil Warrier.

BIBLIOGRAPHY

WEBSITES
www.fifa.com
www.onefootball.com
www.rsssf.com
www.transfermarkets.co.uk
www.uefa.com
www.worldstadiums.com

YEARBOOKS AND ENCYCLOPEDIAS
Football Asia, Kuala Lumpur, Asian Football Confederation, annual.
Ballard J. and Suff P., **The Dictionary of Football**, Boxtree, Basingstoke, 1999.
Creswell P. and Evans S., **European Football: A Fan's Handbook**, Rough Guide, London, 1998.
Deloitte and Touche Annual Review of Football Finance, Manchester, annual.
Il Calcio Italiano Analisi Economico, Deloitte and Touche, Milan, annual.
Hammond M. (ed.), **The European Football Yearbook**, Sports Projects, Birmingham, annual.
Jelinek R. and Tomes J., **Prvni Fotbalovy Atlas Sveta**, Inforkart, Prague, 2000.
Oliver G., **The Guinness Book of World Soccer**, 2nd Edition, Guinness, Enfield, 1995.
Presti S. (ed.), **Annuario del Calcio Mondiale**, SET, Torino, annual.
Radnedge K., **The Complete Encyclopedia of Football**, Carlton Books, London, 1999.
Ricci F. (ed.), **Pro-Sports African Football Yearbook**, Fillipo Maria Ricci, Rome, annual.
Rollin J., **The Rothmans Football Yearbook**, Headline Books, London, annual.
FA Premier League National Fan Survey, Sir Norman Chester Centre for Football Research, Leicester, annual survey.
Van Hoof S., Parr M., Yamenetti C., **The North and Latin American Football Guide**, Heart Books, Rijmenam, annual.

MAGAZINES AND NEWSPAPERS
African Football, AS, A Bola, Calcio 2000, Don Balon, L'Equipe, Football Asia, France Football, Gazetta dello Sport, Guido Sportivo, Kicker, Lance, Marca, Placar, Soccer Analyst, Soccer Investor, Voetbal International, When Saturday Comes, World Soccer. The Daily Telegraph, The Financial Times, The Independent.

OVERVIEWS, GLOBAL HISTORIES, COLLECTIONS
Armstrong G. and Giullianoti R. (eds.), **Entering the Field: New Perspectives on World Football**, Berg, Oxford, 1997.
Armstrong G. and Giullianoti R. (eds.), **Football Cultures and Indentities**, Macmillan, Basingstoke, 1998.
Armstrong G. and Giullianoti R. (eds.), **Fear and Loathing in World Football**, Berg, Oxford, 2001.
Finn G. and Giullianoti R. (eds.), **Football Cultures: Local Contest, Global Visions**, Cass, London, 2000.
Giulianotti R., **Football: A Sociology of the Global Game**, Polity Press, Cambridge, 1999.
Glanville B., **The Story of the World Cup**, Faber, London, 2001.
Inglis S., **The Football Grounds of England and Wales**, Willow, London, 1983.
Inglis S., **Sightlines: A Stadium Odyssey**, Yellow Jersey, London, 2000.
Kuper S., **Football Against the Enemy**, Orion, London, 1994.
Murray B., **The World's Game: A History of Soccer**, University of Illinois Press, Urbana, 1994.
Sugden J. and Tomlinson A., **Who Rules the People's Game? FIFA and the contest for World Football**, Polity Press, Cambridge, 1998.
Sugden J. and Tomlinson A., **Hosts and Champions: Soccer Cultures, National Identities and the USA World Cup**, Arena, Aldershot, 1994.
Walvin J., **The People's Game: The History of Football Revisited**, Mainstream, London, 1994.

BRAZIL
Bellos A., **Futbol: The Brazillian Way of Life**, Bloomsbury, London, 2002.
Lever J., **Soccer Madness**, University of Chicago Press, Chicago, 1983.

FRANCE
Ruhn C. (ed.), **Le Foot: The Legends of French Football**, Abacus, London, 2000.
Holt R., **Sport and Society in Modern France**, Macmillan, Basingstoke, 1981.

ITALY
Manna A. and Gibbs M., **The Day Italian Football Died**, Breedon Books, Derby, 2000.
Parks T., **A Season with Verona**, Secker and Warburg, London, 2002.

JAPAN
Birchall J., **Ultra Nippon: How Japan Reinvented Football**, Headline, London, 2000.
Moffet S., **Japanese Rules: Why Japan Needed Football and How it Got it**, Yellow Jersey, London, 2002.

LATIN AMERICA
Mason T., **Passion of the People? Football in South America**, Verso, London, 1995.
Taylor C., **The Beautiful Game: A Journey Through Latin American Football**, Phoenix, London, 1998.

NETHERLANDS
Winner D., **Brilliant Orange: The Neurotic Genius of Dutch Football**, Bloomsbury, London, 2000.

SPAIN
Burns J., **Barça, A People's Passion**, Bloomsbury, London, 1999.
Hall P., **Morbo: The Story of Spanish Football**, When Saturday Comes, London, 2001.

USSR
Edleman R., **Serious Fun: A History of Spectator Sports in the Soviet Union**, Oxford University Press, Oxford, 1993.

PICTURE CREDITS

(t=top, b=bottom, l=left, c=centre, m=middle, r=right)

All pictures supplied by **EMPICS**, except the following:
Action Images 23b, 47, 55, 71t, 86, 97m, 226, 305, 449, 469b, 478t, 480br; **AFP** 271br; **African Soccer Magazine** 381, 382, 383tl, m & bl, 385, 386, 387, 390, 392, 394, 396, 398, 399 (both), 400, 402, 403, 405; **Agence Shot**, Tokyo 424t, 425 (all); **Allsport** 269r, 302-3b; **AML/Stanley Chou** 421bl; **Ancient Art & Architecture Collection Ltd** 12bl; **Associated Press** 48bl, 54t, 143, 164, 307t & bl, 318l, 320 & 321 (all), 356, 357 (all pics), 364, 365tr & b, 446t; **Gavin Barker** 383tr & 385br; **Bridgeman Art Library** 12t;

Clarín, Buenos Aires 319, 336, 337, 338, 339, 347 (both), 365tl & b, 476; **Digital Sports Archive** (John Todd) 461t; **Edifice** (photo by Doroto Boisot) 193; **EPA** 147; **Mary Evans Picture Library** 13t; **FIFA Football Museum** 12br, 13m, bl, bc & br; **Football Federation** 441; **Getty Images – Hulton Archive** 14, 15, 22tl, tc, tr, mr, bl & bc, 23tl & tc, 34, 45l, 73, 122, 140, 144b, 160, 178, 181, 190r, 194l, 212t & bl, 214b, 480tl, 481br, 485tl; **ITAR-TASS Photo Agency** 268t, 269tl, 270t, 271tl, tr & bl; **Vikas Khot** 418; **Korotaev**, Russia 269bl; **Manchester Evening News** 79m; **Tony Matthews** 71b; **National Army Museum**, London 415; **National Soccer Hall of Fame** 442 (courtesy Colin Jose and David Litterer); **Offside** 317; **Pics United**, Eindhoven 113t, 117b, 119t, 125b,

128, 129, 131; **Pitch Photos** 420, 421t, 423; **Danilo Pizarro**, *El Tiempo*, Bogotá 308t, 309 (all); **Press Association** 233b, 235r, 318r; 328tr & b; **Reuters** 11, 158m & b, 159t, 177br, 187t, 188b, 189 (both), 232 (both), 233t, 308b, 328tl; 332, 333, 361, 375, 376, 377, 446ml & mr, 447 (all pics), 452; **Rex Features** 72, 125t, 142b, 274t, 313, 450l; **South American Pictures** 324l, 326 (both), 342, 343, 344t, 358; **Sporting Pictures (UK) Ltd** 172, 198; **Derek Stewart** 102; **TASR**, Slovakia 243r; **Topham Picturepoint** 372; **WSG Asia Ltd** 413, 421bm, 421br, 432, 433. Picture on page 120 taken from *Brilliant Orange*, David Winner, Bloomsbury, 2000. Pictures on pages 210 and 211 taken from *The Day Italian Football Died*, Alexandra Manna & Mike Gibbs, Breedon Books, 2000.